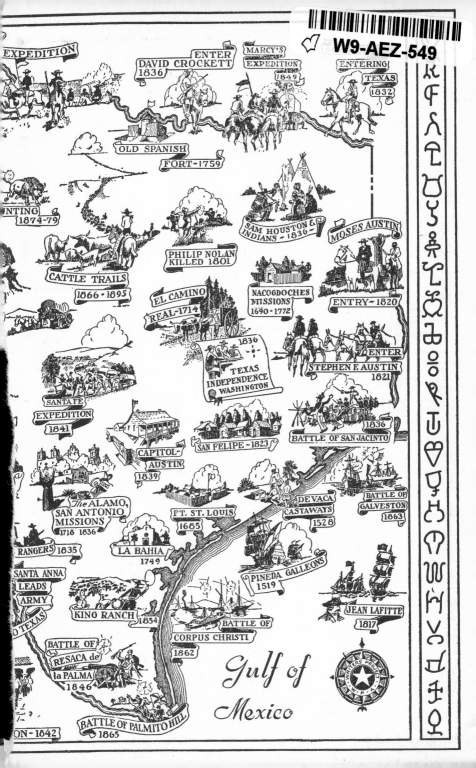

TEXAS

A Guide to the Lone Star State

TEXAS

A Guide to the Lone Star State

NEW REVISED EDITION
HARRY HANSEN, *Editor*

Writers Program. Texas.

Originally Compiled by the Federal Writers' Program
of the Work Projects Administration
in the State of Texas

AMERICAN GUIDE SERIES

ILLUSTRATED

HASTINGS HOUSE · *Publishers* · New York

This book was originally sponsored by the
Texas State Highway Commission

First Edition, 1940
New Revised Edition, 1969

SBN: 8038–7055–8
Library of Congress Catalog Card Number: 68–31690
Copyright 1940, by Texas State Highway Commission
Copyright © 1969, by Hastings House, Publishers, Inc.
Printed in the U. S. A.

A Note About the New Edition

Texas, on the eve of the 1970 decade, is a State more populous, more productive, and wealthier per capita than it was when the original edition of *Texas, A Guide to the Lone Star State,* was published. Its tremendous energy, applied to vast natural resources, has brought it new highways, expanding industries, prosperous foreign and domestic markets, crowded ports, an upsurge of higher education and culture, and airplanes and spacecraft preempting the sky. There were many indications that an updating of the *Guide* was needed.

The *Guide* appeared in 1940, when the AMERICAN GUIDE SERIES was a product of the Federal Government's efforts to provide work for the unemployed in fields in which they were most capable. Henry G. Alsberg became director and outlined many of the patterns followed by the series. The book was sponsored by the Texas State Highway Commission. Sponsor of the Texas Writers' Program was the Bureau of Research in the Social Sciences of the University of Texas, Warner E. Gettys, Ph.D., director. The State Supervisor was J. Frank Dobie. Scores of authorities helped compile this compendium of Texas life and lore, while a small regiment of researchers swarmed through the cities and towns and established the Tours.

The fine historical material essential for an understanding of the past in Texas has been retained, but matters of contemporary importance have been thoroughly revised. The appeal of the *Guide* to visitors and tourists has been enhanced, and many new pages are devoted to parks and recreation grounds, hunting and fishing areas, opportunities for enjoying the seashore, the new inland lakes, and the unspoiled wilderness. The publisher hopes that the *Guide* continues to be, what it was intended originally, an honest and accurate mirror of Texas life.

Contents

Part I. Texas: Yesterday and Today

Part II.   Fifteen Texas Cities

Part III.   Along the State's Highways

Page

Part IV. Appendices

Illustrations

Maps

xix

General Information

Highway Information for Tourists: More than 66,000 miles of highways are available, giving the motorist access to every part of Texas. There are three classifications for roads: the U. S. Interstate System of 3,025 miles, which connects with continental roads; the primary roads, consisting of the U. S. numbered roads and their alternate routes and the State Highways, and the secondary roads, Farm-to-Market and Ranch-to-Market. Loop and spur roads also are indicated. All these are to be found on the Official Texas Highway Travel Map, published annually, which may be had free from the Highway Department. It shows two kinds of distances, the miles between towns and the miles between junctions. Small inset maps show the access roads to the major cities. The Department has its headquarters in Austin, seven highway tourist bureaus, and 25 district offices. Information by mail may be obtained by addressing its Travel and Information Division at Austin, 78701. Tourist bureaus are located in the rotunda of the State Capitol, Austin, and at Anthony, Denison, Gainesville, Orange, Texarkana, Waskom and Wichita Falls. There are district offices in 25 of the major cities. Consult also the Chambers of Commerce, hotels and motels.

Governor John Connally in January, 1968, made public the Texas Travel Trails, by means of which visitors can choose routes that will carry them through areas of the State most interesting to them. Included are the Forest Trail, which passes through four national forests in its 780 miles from East Texas to Kilgore; the Pecos Trail, 626 miles, which takes in the legendary Southwest; Independence Trail, 585 miles, touching many historic places where the Republic was forged; the Plains Trail, 584 miles, where Amarillo and Lubbock are the largest cities; the Lakes Trail, 697 miles, providing a survey of vast reservoir developments; the Brazos Trail, with reminiscences of the great cattle drives; the Tropical Trail, the Hill Country Trail, the Forts Trail, and the Mountain Trail. Brochures, with maps, may be had from the Travel and Information Division of the Texas Highway Department. A vast amount of specific and general information can be provided by the Texas Tourist Development Agency, Capitol Station, Austin.

Motor Vehicle Regulations: Maximum speed on highways, 70 mph during the day, 65 mph at night for motor cars; house trailers under 32 ft. and 4,500 lbs., may be towed 60 mph by day, 55 mph by night, otherwise 45 mph; trucks and trailers, 60 mph and 55 mph; buses, 70 mph and 65 mph. Town and city speeds are usually 20 mph, school zones, 10 mph. Non-resident motorists 18 and over with driver's license from home state may drive in Texas without a Texas license. A motorist who takes up residence in Texas must register his car with the Texas Highway Department and carry a stamp certifying annual inspection. College students and military personnel are exempt from registration. Consult Drivers License Division, Texas Department of Public Safety, San Antonio.

Mobile homes (trailers), need no permit if within 13 ft., 6 in. tall, 35 ft. long for single units. Combination units may be 55 ft. long, 8 ft. tall, 8 ft. wide. Permit is needed for when a combination unit exceeds those dimensions, with a maximum of 75 ft. long, 10 ft. wide. Oversize units may not move after dark on Saturdays, Sundays and holidays. A permit is good for a continuous movement of 10 days, cost $5.

The State gasoline tax is 5¢ a gallon; one-fourth of the revenue is given to the public schools, one-half to the State highways, and one-fourth to debt service and farm-to-market road maintenance. Of the vehicle fees 70 percent goes to the general highway fund and 30 percent to counties for local road maintenance.

Principal Highways for Entering Texas. From Arkansas: US 59 and 71, after a junction with US 70 from Hot Springs and Little Rock, enter at Texarkana, as does US 67, also from Little Rock, and US 82. To bypass Texarkana leave 59, 70 and 71 at DeQueen, Ark., drive south on State 41.

From Louisiana: US 71 runs south from Texarkana in Arkansas and Louisiana, 70 *m.,* to Shreveport, La. US 79 and 80 from Vicksburg and Monroe move through Shreveport into Texas. US 171 moves south in Louisiana parallel with the Texas border, connecting with Texas via US 84 and 190 and several State roads.

From Oklahoma: US 70, from Hot Springs, Little Rock and Oklahoma points runs parallel to the Red River and the Texas northern border as far west as Wichita Falls and enters Texas 36 *m.* beyond. It has junctions with the following routes crossing the Red River into Texas: US 259, 271 and 69 jointly, 75, 77, 81, 277 and 281 jointly, 183. One other road, 283, not connected with 70, enters Texas from the north. West from Oklahoma into Texas go 62, 66, 60. South into the Panhandle go 83, 54, 287, and 385.

From New Mexico: West into Texas: US 87, from Denver, Colorado Springs; 54, 66, from Santa Fe; 60 and 84 jointly, separating at border, 60 for Amarillo, 84 for Lubbock; 380, 82, 62 and 180 jointly. North into Texas: State 18, US 285, 62 and 180 jointly from Carlsbad through the Guadalupe Mountains to El Paso; 80, 85, 54 to El Paso.

From Mexico: Crossings of the Rio Grande. Juarez to El Paso. Ojinaga to Presidio. Ciudad Acuna to Del Rio. Piedras Negras to Eagle Pass. Nuevo Laredo to Laredo. Nuevo Guerrero to Falcon. Miguel Aleman to Roma. Camargo to Rio Grande City. Reynosa to Hidalgo. Rio Bravo to Progreso. Matamoros to Brownsville.

To Texas by Rail and Air: Ten principal railroad systems enter Texas and connect with all important cities and towns. The ten, in the order of mileage, are the Santa Fe, Southern Pacific and affiliate, the Cotton Belt; Missouri Pacific and affiliate, the Texas & Pacific; Missouri-Kansas-Texas, Burlington, Rock Island, Kansas City Southern and Frisco. They control 31 other lines, while 15 are independent, making a total of 46 rail organizations serving Texas. Cooperatively used depots are frequently found.

Airlines reaching Texas include American Airlines, Braniff, Central, Continental, Delta, Eastern, Frontier, National, Pan American, Trans World, and Trans-Texas. Also KLM and Mexicana.

State Fish and Game Regulations: Laws governing hunting and fishing are quite detailed and should be studied by all sportsmen. The time and season for taking game is specifically stated for all parts of the State in the *Texas Hunting Guide*, published annually by the Parks and Wildlife Department, Austin. There also are special supplements dealing with archery, migratory game birds, and mourning and white-winged doves. These publications can be had from game wardens, county clerks and license dealers. For more detailed information about areas consult the local game warden or county attorney. There are rules governing guns, hours, bag limits, tags, inspection, and locations. It is illegal to hunt game animals at night, to use deer calls, to hunt in any State or Federal park, or in a Wildlife Management Area, unless a number of permits to hunt surplus wildlife are allowed by the authorities.

Licenses: Texas citizens (six-months' residence necessary to qualify) pay $3.15, except for certain exemptions. Non-residents, $25; five-day migratory bird license, $5. Migratory waterfowl license, $10. Resort hunting license, $3.15. Manager of shooting preserve, $5; of shooting resort, $10. Fur license, resident trapper, $1, non-resident, $200. Retail fur buyer, $5; wholesale, $25.

The Golden Passport is the entrance permit to all Federal parks and recreation areas. It costs $7 and is good for one year. It admits the holder and all occupants of his motor car. For those not wishing annual permits there is a charge of $1 for one day's stay, also including all occupants of the automobile. Those entering by other than a private noncommercial vehicle the charge is 50¢ a day. Proceeds go to the Land and Water Conservation Fund.

Fishing is one of the most rewarding sports in Texas. The Federal Government estimates that about 20,000,000 lbs. of fish are taken out of coastal and inland waters annually by 750,000 sportsmen. The State and the Federal Bureau of Sport Fisheries & Wildlife cooperate to stock streams. Texas maintains 13 pondfish hatcheries and annually supplies more than 15,000,000 warm-water fish. Some of the best fishing spots in Central Texas are below the dams that impound the Highland lakes.

There are 230 kinds of fish in waters of the State, including large-mouthed bass, spotted bass, crappie, calico bass, bluegill, sunfish (several varieties), goggle eye, rock bass, yellow bass, white bass, catfish (including large channel cat), pickerel, gar, drum. Salt water fish include Spanish mackerel, kingfish, gulf pike, sheepshead, pompano, redfish, southern flounder, spade fish, red snapper, sea trout, jewfish, tarpon, mullet and menhaden. Fishing for flounder with lights at night is possible along the beaches. Small outboards are used to troll for king and Spanish mackerel. At Coast ports larger boats are available for groups fishing for pompano, sailfish, red snapper, grouper, and black and red drum. Trout is plentiful in the upper Rio Grande region.

A fishing license costs $2.15 for residents and nonresidents and expires August 31. Regulations regarding size, bag, and season vary in the counties; consult local authorities. Fishing equipment can be rented at resorts.

Accommodations: Tourist lodges and auto camps are available generally. Dude ranches are popular in the southwestern and western sections. Accommodations in the Big Bend National Park should be reserved; address the Park, Texas 79834. At the height of the season along the coast, advance reservations should be made at resort hotels and lodges. During hunting season, hunters should arrange for guides and lodging.

Poisonous Plants, Reptiles, Insects: Rattlesnakes are common throughout the State. Suction kits for first aid are available at most drug stores, but in case of snakebite, consult a physician at once. Copperheads and cotton mouth water mocassins are usually found along streams. The most dangerous of Texas' four poisonous reptiles, the coral snake, is encountered less often but occurs over a wide area. Red, yellow and black rings extend completely around the body of the coral snake. The State's only poisonous spider is the black widow, small, black, with a bright red spot on its body; it is found chiefly in the southwestern area (*the bite of this spider usually requires immediate medical attention*). Centipedes, scorpions, tarantulas, vinegaroons, and several other venomous insects exist in Texas; their bites are less dangerous than painful. Jellyfish, sting rays, and Portuguese men-of-war are often in the Gulf or bay waters of the coast; their stings are painful but not dangerous. Poison ivy is common; the berries of sumac are poisonous.

Apparel and Equipment: During the summer light clothing should be worn; in winter an overcoat or heavy jacket is necessary during the sudden northers. Along the coast beach wearing apparel is ideal for summer, but persons subject to sunburn should exercise caution. Boots, with trousers and jackets of heavy materials, are most suitable for jaunts through the chaparrel and mountainous regions. In the trans-Pecos section travelers should carry water for drinking and for radiators off main traveled highways. Tourists in the eastern part of the State should have mosquito bars and lotions when camping. Avoid dry canyons and creek beds at all seasons. Floods come suddenly and fill these ravines without warning. It is extremely dangerous to camp in any ravine, canyon or creek bed at any time.

Alcoholic Beverages: Local option determines whether an area is "wet" or "dry." Alcoholic beverages are strictly controlled. Visitors entering the State may not possess more than one gallon of alcoholic beverages for personal use, and military personnel may not have more than one quart. Such beverages (distilled spirits, beer) may not be sold from 10 P.M. to 9 A.M. daily, nor all day on Sunday, whereas such beverages may not be consumed in a public place from 12:15 A.M. to 7 A.M., and on Sunday from 12:15 A.M. to 1 P.M.

Other Regulations: It is unlawful to dig in archaeological sites west of the Pecos without the written consent of the owner of the land. In other regions the laws of trespass apply. It is unlawful to pick wildflowers, cacti, bluebonnets or ornamental plants on private property without the owner's consent, or in public parks, or along the roadside. Fires may not be kindled on private property, in parks, or forest preserves.

Recreation Guides: Texas, by the extent and variety of its domain, offers more opportunities for recreation than any other state. Every form of outdoor activity can be fully exercized in Texas. All areas open to public enjoyment are carefully patrolled. The extent of the facilities can be understood by an enumeration of the areas available. The Federal Government controls one national park, Big Bend; and is developing another, Guadalupe Mountains; it has one historic monument, Fort Davis, and one seashore, Padre Island; 21 so-called recreation areas around Federal reservoirs, four national forests, and six wildlife areas. The four national forests alone have 22 areas of special usefulness to campers, fishermen, hikers, swimmers, and occupants of motor trailers. In addition the State provides lavishly for all interested in the great outdoors. A mere list of areas that have been developed does not indicate the opulence of natural phenomena. There are 40 State Parks, so designated, which appeal to those who enjoy tramping over the landscape, or penetrating thick vegetation, or searching for Indian artifacts, in the Sandhills near Monahans; or becoming spelunkers in the caves of Edwards Plateau. In addition there are seven local parks, and 22 historic monuments, many of which are also called State Parks, although visits there are usually limited to weekends. Then the State makes another special category called Recreation Areas, and these number about 44 at last count. Therefore it behooves the visitor to inquire carefully what sort of outdoor life he prefers.

One Federal aim is to place recreation areas within easy reach of the large urban populations, so that the outdoors may be enjoyed without traveling long distances. On May 4, 1966 President Lyndon B. Johnson established the President's Council on Recreation and National Beauty, as well as a Citizens' Advisory Commission, to work with the Bureau of Outdoor Recreation to expand Federal areas. The State of Texas cooperates with numerous other agencies to support conservation, reclaim blighted areas, overcome waste of resources, and fight air and water pollution.

The Texas Highway Department publishes its map of roads and the *Travel Handbook*. The *Texas Almanac for 1968–1969* publishes maps of all counties showing access roads, and lists many recreational areas. The U. S. Department of the Interior publishes a complete list in its *Natural Resources of Texas*. For other Texas information address The Superintendent of Documents, U. S. Government Printing Office, Washington, D. C., 20402.

Trips to Mexico from Texas: Passports are not required of U.S. citizens entering Mexico as tourists. However, Americans should carry some proof of citizenship, such as birth certificate, voter's registration card, etc., to avoid unnecessary delays. Naturalized citizens should carry naturalization papers or U. S. passport. All persons 15 years of age and over who plan to visit the interior of Mexico (instead of just border towns) must have a tourist card good for 180 days. Cost is $3; a 30-day visa is free. Every American should carry his vaccination certificate (good for 3 years), for this is required for re-entry into the United States.

Motor car permits must be obtained from the Mexican customs office at port of entry. They are good for 180 days and issued free. Trailers also need permits. Proof of ownership, such as a driver's license, should be carried. If car has an owner other than the driver, the latter must have a notarized permit from the owner.

Tourists are advised to carry full coverage for accidents and liability. Most U. S. insurance policies are valid only along the border. Authorities recommend the purchase of Mexican motor car insurance before spending a night in Mexico or traveling in the interior. Short-term insurance may be obtained from travel agencies on the Texan side of the border.

Tourists may carry cameras and films. No guns may be taken into Mexico without a permit; consult the Mexican consulates about fish and game regulations. Fish caught in Mexican waters may be taken back without restrictions; game, however, needs a permit (free) from the Texas Parks and Wildlife Department.

Military personnel and U. S. Government employees and their immediate families with identification (ID cards) may enter Mexico free for 29 days. Allied officers must have a visa and tourist card. Military may not wear uniforms in Mexico unless on official business.

Return to the United States: On leaving Mexico visitors must report to the Mexican customs for cancellation of their entry cards. Americans may bring back merchandise duty free up to $100 per person per month, if they have been in Mexico 12 days, provided the articles are for personal use or gifts and not for resale. Each adult may bring back one quart of alcoholic beverages every 31 days, paying the State liquor tax. Cigarets are limited to two packs duty free. Military personnel stationed in Texas are considered Texas citizens under this rule. The United States does not permit the entry of most fruits, plants, vegetables, and pets, unless requirements of the Public Health Service and the Department of Agriculture are met. No parrots, parakeets, or love birds may be brought in. Some perfumes are not duty free; consult the Customs.

Climate: The vast terrain of Texas has wide variations in climate and weather conditions, but many areas have sunshine three-fourths of the year. With about 800 miles from the top of the Panhandle to the southernmost point, and elevations ranging from mountains 8,500 ft. tall in the southwest to rice lands under sea level at the Gulf Coast, Texas has no average weather. The Weather Bureau describes the State as generally warm temperate, but there can be 100° and more in the dry Southwest in summer, and 24° and less in the winter Panhandle. Heavy snow falls in the Northwest and North Central Texas, where Austin had 6 in. in 1966, are to be expected, but precipitation has been below normal there in recent years, although flash floods in the spring have flooded the Sulphur, Sabine, Trinity, and Brazos River basins. In 1966 Dallas had an unusual amount of rain, 15.40 in., and 14 persons in the County were drowned by a flood on April 28. The Meteorological Table gives the extremes in temperature for certain cities as follows: Abilene, days above 90°, 103; days 32° and lower, 54; Amarillo, 73 and 106; Austin, 112 and 25; Brownsville, 114 and 2; Corpus Christi, 97 and 9; Dallas, 98 and 40; El Paso, 108 and 63; Fort Worth, 92 and 48; Galveston, 12 and 4; Houston, 91 and 7; Midland-Odessa, 106 and 73; Port Arthur-Beaumont, 95 and 20; San Angelo, 126 and 56; San Antonio, 118 and 20; Waco, 105 and 38; Wichita Falls, 107 and 67.

Calendar of Annual Events

All around the year there are fairs, livestock exhibits, rodeos, fiestas and competitive sports in Texas. A calendar is published semi-annually by the Travel & Information Division of the Texas Highway Department. This and other travel material may be obtained free from the Tourist Bureaus or by writing the Information Division, P. O. Box 5064, Austin, Texas, 78703. The following list places events in the approximate weeks in which they take place.

JANUARY

First Week—New Year's Day Swim, Corpus Christi; Sun Carnival, El Paso; Hereford and Quarter Horse Show, Odessa; Horse Races, El Paso; Greyhound Races, Juarez; New Year's Day Cotton Bowl Classic, Dallas.

Second Week—Auto Show, Fort Worth; Fat Livestock Show, Coleman; Junior Livestock, Borger; Area Livestock, Sweetwater; Youth Fair, Brownwood; Domino Tournament, Hallettsville; Junior Livestock, Kerrville.

Third Week—South Texas Lamb & Sheep Expo., Donna; Shuffleboard Tournament, Harlingen; Dimmit Co. Livestock, Carrizo Springs; Junior Livestock, San Saba, Polled Hereford Bull Sale, Lamesa; Fat Stock, Amarillo; Citrus Fiesta, Mission.

Fourth Week—Golden Gloves, Corpus Christi; 4-H and FFA Livestock, Lyford; Lions Club Show, Carthage; Junior Livestock, San Antonio; Junior Livestock, Pecos; Southwestern Expo., Fort Worth; Youth Show, Junction; Livestock, Jourdanton; Junior Livestock, Dalhart; Life Begins at 40 Golf, Harlingen; All-Valley Shuffleboard, Weslaco; National Boat, Travel, Sports Show, Houston.

FEBRUARY

First Week—Auto Show, Brownwood; Texas Open Golf, San Antonio; Charro Days, Brownsville; Horse Races, El Paso; Junior Livestock, Pearsall; Three State Singers, Marshall; Livestock, Rodeo, El Paso; Polled Hereford, Brownwood.

Second Week—Hobby Show, Weslaco; Livestock, San Antonio; Texas Trail Ride, Hallettsville to San Antonio; Indoor Track, Dallas; Junior Livestock, Littlefield; Spindletop Bridge Tournament, Beaumont.

Third Week—Salt Grass Trail, Brenham; George Washington Fiesta, Eagle Pass and Laredo; Livestock, Rodeo, Houston; Junior Livestock, Jacksboro; Country Fair, Los Fresnos.

Fourth Week—Boat Show, Corpus Christi; Eastern Panhandle Livestock, Shamrock; Southwestern Livestock, El Paso; Heart of Texas Band Festival, Brody.

MARCH

First Week—Spring Fiesta, McAllen; Band Festival, Lamesa; Auto-Rama, Corpus Christi; Horse Races, El Paso; Boat and Ski Club Show, Borger; Mother-in-law Day, Amarillo; Fine Arts Show, Wichita Falls.

Second Week—Top o' Texas Junior Livestock, Pampa; Birthday Celebration, Borger; Stock Show, Rodeo, San Angelo; Junior Boys' Livestock, Lamesa; Border Olympics, Laredo; County Fair, Gatesville; Jaycee Stock Show, Victoria; Hub City Relays, Alice; Boat, Sports & Vacation Show, Amarillo; Burnet County Bowmen, Marble Falls; Invitational Painting Show, Longview; Rio Grande Valley Livestock, Mercedes; Fayette County Junior Livestock, La Grange; West Texas Relays, Odessa.

Third Week—Southwestern Exposition, Fort Worth; Gems and Minerals, San Antonio; Junior Livestock, Stephenville; South Plains Junior Livestock, Lubbock; A. B. C. Rodeo, Lubbock; American Kennel Club, Longview; Junior Fat Stock, Littlefield; South Texas Traditional Art Show, Corpus Christi; Easter Fires Pageant, Fredericksburg; Easter Pageant, Junction; Livestock Judging, Sweetwater.

Fourth Week—Hobby Show, San Antonio; Rio Grande Valley Music Festival, Harlingen; Fat Stock, Plainview; San Angelo Relays, San Angelo; Junior Livestock, and 4-H, FFA Achievement Day, Conroe; Dogwood Trails, Palestine; Rattlesnake Roundup, Big Spring; Southwestern Ballet Festival, Wichita Falls; International Fair, Laredo; Texas Relays, Austin; Southwest Texas All-College Radio, San Marcos; Arts & Crafts Festival, Killeen; Azalea Trail, Tyler.

APRIL

First Week—Rose Relays, Tyler; Quarter Horse Meet, Goliad; Flower Show, Tyler; Gems and Minerals, Wichita Falls; Horse Races, Saturday and Sunday into May, El Paso; Livestock, Austin; Indian Reservation, Livingston Fiesta Gardens, weekends through May, Austin; Spacecraft Center Tours, Sundays, Clear Lake; Gardens, Sam Houston Memorial, Huntsville; Home Show, Fort Worth; Wildflower Trail, Fort Yoakum; Festival of Arts, Temple; Fine Arts Competition, Lubbock; Garden Clubs at Sam Houston Shrine, Huntsville; National Indoor AAU, Dallas; Intercollegiate Rodeo, Huntsville; Queen Coronation, Yorktown; Quarter Horse Show, Gatesville.

Second Week—Onion Fiesta, Raymondville; Western Days Fiddlers, Yorktown; Appaloosa Horse Show, Gatesville; Relays, Paris; Quarter Horse Show, Sulphur Springs and Del Rio; Rodeo, Yorktown; All-Star Rodeo, Dallas; Historical Pilgrimage, Bastrop; Pan-American Days, Edinburg; Bluebonnet Trails, Brenham; Astrodome Season opens, Houston; Southwest Sports Show, Dallas; Garden Club Flower Show, La Marque; Pan American Days, McAllen; Charity Horse Show, San Antonio; Sports Car Competition, Richland Hills; Flower Show, Uvalde; FFA Rodeo, Hillsboro; U. of Texas Roundup, Austin; Sheriff's Posse Rodeo, Orange; Strawberry Festival, Poteet; American Hot Rod Assn., Odessa.

Third Week—Flower Shows, Mabank, Austin, Port Arthur; Duchess Contest, Mission; Quarter Horse Show, Lubbock and Nederland; Singing Convention, Huntsville; and Stephenville; Outdoor Art, Buchanan Dam; Bluebonnet Trail Festival, Buchanan Dam; Fiesta, San Antonio; Historical Trek, Montgomery; Cotton Festival, McKinney; River Oaks Tennis, Houston; Open PGA, Dallas; Neches River Festival, Beaumont; Surfing Contest, Galveston; State College Rodeo, Nacogdoches; San Jacinto Observance, Houston; Junior College Rodeo, Wharton; Flower Show, Teague; Polka Festival, Ennis; Art Festival,

Breckenridge; Pilgrimage of Homes, Waco; Possum Kingdom Pageant, Mineral Wells; Quarter Horse Show, Colorado City; Bloodless Bullfights, Dallas; Bluebonnet Trails, Ennis; Boat Races, Fort Worth.

Fourth Week—Rattlesnake Derby, McCamey; Iris Show, Brownwood; Shrimp Festival, Galveston; Tennis Tournament, Dallas; Buccaneer Days, Corpus Christi; Flower Show, Wichita Falls; Arabian Horse Show, Nacogdoches; Jamboree, Smithville; Dairy Days, Cleveland; Texas Open Golf, San Antonio; Choral Contest, Brownsville; Highland Lakes Tennis, Marble Falls; Rodeo, Dilley; Jazz Festival, Austin; Historic Pilgrimage, Jefferson; Pageant, Grad Prairie; Pageant, Big Spring; Art Show, Stephenville; Six Flags Over Texas opens, Arlington; Boat Races, Austin; Race Meet, Sonora; Blessing of the Shrimp Fleet, Galveston; House Tours, Port Arthur.

MAY

First Week—Three-day tour of historical homes, Jefferson; Fish Day, Lake Kemp, Seymour; Art Foundations, Corpus Christi; Indian Reservation, Livingston; Bow Fishing, Marble Falls; Mounted Patrol Rodeo, Lufkin; Charity Horse Show, Beaumont; NIRA Rodeo, Alpine; Rodeo, Killeen; Cinco de Mayo Festivals at Dallas, Corpus Christi, Laredo, San Antonio; Zaragoza Anniversary, Goliad; All-Boy Rodeo, Carthage; Junior Rodeo, Marble Falls; Gems and Minerals, Waco; Rodeo, Mesquite; Horse Races, El Paso; Open Golf, Midland; Cotton Festival, Waxahatchie; Antique Show, Smithville; Appaloosa Horse Show, Bovina; Water Skiing, Austin; Iris Show, Lubbock; Spacecraft Center Tours, Sundays, Clear Lake; Women's Golf, Victoria.

Second Week—Dairy Festival, Sulphur Springs; Japanese Flower Show, Nassau Bay; Lions Club Rodeo, Jasper; Amateur Rodeo, Breckenridge; Sheriff's Posse Rodeo, Giddings; Rodeo, Mineral Wells; Oil-O-Rama, Freer; Fish Fry, Mathis; Quarter Horse Races, Uvalde; Maifest, Brenham; Boat Races, Fort Worth; Tackle Drop, Denison.

Third Week—Colonial National Golf, Fort Worth; Jaycee Rodeo, Orange; Charity Horse Show, Dallas; Pioneer Days Rodeo, Fort Worth; Square Dance Festival, Houston; FFA Rodeo, Mason; Water Festival, Orange; Fine Arts, Austin; Art Fair, Paris; Art Show, Columbus; Fiesta at Laguna Gloria Museum, Austin; Magnolia Homes, Columbus; Marine Opening, Galveston.

Fourth Week—Lipton Sailing Regatta, Galveston; Rose Show, Lubbock; Home Show, Dallas; Junior Rodeo, Marta; Golf Tournament, Carrizo Springs; Quarter Horse Show, Ozona and Sonora; Old Fiddlers, Athens; Golf, Borger; Drag Boat Races, Austin; Bartering Days, Canton; Boat Races, Denison; Splash Day, Ennis; Red River Rodeo, Wichita Falls.

JUNE

First Week—Fiesta Noche del Rio, Tuesday, Thursday, Friday, Saturday, June to September, San Antonio; Sheriff's Posse Rodeo, Jacksboro; Rodeos also at Rusk, Van Horn, Llano, Sulphur Springs, Galveston, Mesquite, Lockhart; Golf, Brady; Lake Meredith Festival, Borger; Bow Fishing, Marble Falls; Fiesta Gardens, Austin; Horse Show, Richland Hills; Golf, Lampasas; Model Airplane Meet, Longview; Pioneer Village opens, Corsicana; Tour of Homes, San Augustine; Boat Races, Fort Worth; Women's Golf, Lubbock; Charity Horse Show, Bellaire.

Second Week—Charity Horse Show, Bellaire; Oilmen's Golf, Longview; Y. M. Business League Rodeo, Beaumont; Oilmen's Golf, McAllen; Roundup Rodeo, Vernon; Youth Rodeo, Alice; Dogie Days, Dumas; Tom Tom Rodeo,

Yoakum; Jaycee Rodeo, Mexia and Gatesville; Rodeo, Mabank; Pageant, Carthage; Fiddlers' Festival, Crockett; Rendezvous, Clear Lake Area; Rendezvous Art Festival, Kemah; Sailboat Regatta, Clear Lake; Canoe Race, Kemah-League City; Air Show, League City; Water Skiing, Nassau Bay; Junior Olympics, Webster; Tennis, Paris; Queen's Coronation, Clear Lake; Pageant, Longview; Fishing Rodeo, Mathis; Sand Bass Festival, Denison; Roundup Rodeo, Gladewater; High School Rodeo, Hallettsville.

Third Week—Watermelon Jubilee, Stockdale; Rodeos at San Saba; Archer City, Lamesa, Uvalde; Fort Griffin Fandangle, Albany; Golf, Paris; Frontier Days, Killeen; Texas Tour, Waco; Naval Relief Show, Corpus Christi; Cypress City Celebration, Sabinal; Boat Races, San Marcos; Community Barge Dance, Clear Lake; Power Boat Races, Clear Lake; Lefthanded Golfers, Seguin; Cowboy Reunion, Big Spring.

Fourth Week—Rodeos at Seagraves, Plainview, Sulphur Springs; Vegetable Festival, Munday; Alley Arts & Crafts, Hillsboro; Hunter-Jumper Show, Junction, Quarter Horse Show, Carthage; Air Show, Crockett; Art Festival, Refugio; Pageant, Pecos; Watermelon Thump, Luling; Miss Wool of America Pageant, San Angelo.

JULY

First Week—Many places observe Independence Day with pageants, parades, fireworks and band concerts, adding them to established programs. Water Skiing, Paris; Fort Richardson Frontier Fair, Jacksboro; Fishing Fiesta, Freeport; Golf, Paris; Rodeo, Pecos and Belton; Will Rogers Range Riders, Amarillo; Cowboy Reunion, Stamford; Ceramic Arts, Dallas; Jaycee Fishing, Carthage; Horse Races, through July, Fredericksburg; Jubilee, Brady; American Legion Rodeo, Alvin; Fireworks Spectacular, Dallas; Pageant, Seguin; Soaring Championship Contest, Marfa-Alpine; Boat Races, Denison; Redfish Fishing, Raymondville and Port Mansfield; Water Skiing, Buffalo Lakes, Lubbock; Small Fry Fishing, Nocona; FFA Rodeo, Shamrock; Three-mile Swim, Carthage; Pageant, Mexia; Old Fiddlers, Winnsboro; Sports Car Races, Galveston; Rodeos at Hillsboro, Crockett, Wharton; Frontier Days, Timpson; Boat Races, Fort Worth.

Second Week—Music Festival, Austin; Peach Festival, Pittsburg; Horseman's Club, Cuero; Rodeos, usually three days each, at Coleman, Cuero, Nederland, Pittsburg, Mineola.

Third Week—Rolling Pin Throwing Tournament, Pittsburg; Jazz Festival, Corpus Christi; Funtier Nights, Wednesdays through August, San Antonio; Water Carnival, Fort Stockton; Old Settlers' Reunion, Big Spring; Horse Show, Rusk; Rodeos at Livingston, Sonora, Freer, Seymour, Austin, Marble Falls, Wills Point, Mason.

Fourth Week—Night in Old Fredericksburg; Quarter Horse Show, Giddings and Coleman; Miss Texas Pageant, Fort Worth; Home Show, Corpus Christi; Highland Lakes Regatta on Lake LBJ, Kingsland; 250-mile Enduro Speedboat Races, Austin; Canoe Race, Canton; Rodeos at Bonham, Weatherford, Pampa, Yoakum, Ozone, Hereford, Brownfield, Brownwood.

AUGUST

First Week—Funtier Nights (one a week), San Antonio; Water Sports, Mercedes; Peach and Melon Festival, De Leon; Phillips Free Fair, Borger; Texas League All-Star Game, Dallas-Fort Worth; Horse Show, Nacogdoches; Homecoming, Bastrop; Livestock, Kaufman; XIT Rodeo, Dalhart; Rodeo, Saturdays to Sept., Mesquite; Outdoor Art, Buchanan Dam; Highland Lakes Canoe Races, Austin; Old Fiddlers, Burnet; Tip of Texas Horse Show, Mercedes; Aqua Festival, includes Auto Show, Drag Boat Races, Austin; Golf, Kerrville; Tri-State Senior Golf, Borger.

Second Week—Bronco Baseball Series, Kingsville; Race Meet & Billy Sale, Junction; 4-H Horse Show, Odessa; Governor's Cup Regatta, Lake Travis, Austin; Boat Races, Fort Worth; Rodeos at Paris, Port Lavaca, Big Spring, Robstown, Graham.

Third Week—Bull Town Days, Bovina; Championship Water Skiing, Austin; Oil Bowl Football, Wichita Falls; Chicken Fry, San Juan; Quarter Horse Show, Sulphur Springs; Old Settlers, Camp Wood.

Fourth Week—Red River Valley Exposition, Paris; Tennis Assn. Open, Dallas; County Fair, Fredericksburg; Rodeos at Canton, Breckenridge.

SEPTEMBER

First Week—Miss Tan America, Dallas; Performance Class Horse Show, Hillsboro; Fiesta Noche del Rio ends, San Antonio; Fishing Festival, Port Lavaca; Hot Rod Assn. Contest, Richland Hills; Final week of *Texas,* drama in Palo Duro canyon State Park; Labor Day Golf, Del Rio, Orange, Hondo, Pampa; Motorcycle Races, Laredo; Boat Races, Denison, Palacios; Jaycee Jubilee, Garland; Watermelon Feast, Shamrock; Fiesta Gardens, open weekends, Austin; Bargain Days, Galveston; Oil Exposition, Borger; Horse Races, Sequin; Art Festival, Lubbock; Firemen's Quarter Horse Show, Jacksboro.

Second Week—Appaloosa Horse Show, Texarkana; West Texas Fair, Abilene; PGA Tournament, Galveston; North Texas State Fair, Denton; Pioneer Reunion, Henrietta; County Fair, La Grange; Cotton Carnival, Brownsville.

Third Week—Mexican Independence Day Celebrations at Dallas, Corpus Christi, Laredo, San Antonio; Pioneer Reunion, Fair, Henrietta; County Fair, La Grange; Cotton Carnival, Brownsville; Quarter Horse Show, Texarkana; Dahlia Show, Lubbock; Boat Races, Fort Worth; Livestock Show, Longview; County Fairs at Clarksville, Lamesa, Brenham; Bass Tournament, Marble Falls; Autumn Trails Festival, Winnsboro; Jamboree, Moulton; Peanut Bowl Football, Eastland; Burnet County Bowmen, Marble Falls.

Fourth Week—East Texas Fair, Tyler; Junior Amateur Radio, Winnsboro Inter-State Fair, Dalhart; County Fair, Dumas; Sunland Park Races open, El Paso; Texoma Fish Bowl Contest, Denison; Panhandle-South Plains Fair, Lubbock; County Fair, Rosenberg.

OCTOBER

First Week—River Art Show, San Antonio; Southwestern Public Service Golf, Borger; Rockhound Show, Denison; Arts Festival, Houston; Luxury Travel Show, Dallas; Watercolor Show, Lubbock; Texas Prison Rodeo, Sundays, Huntsville; Art Exhibition, Tyler; Dog Show, Lubbock; Heart o' Texas Fair, Waco; Art Across America Exhibit, Houston; Fall Festival, Pecos; Home Improvement Show, Bellaire; Southwest Fly-in, Amateur aircraft, Georgetown; County Fairs at Palestine, Angleton, Center, Refugio, Snyder.

Second Week—Zonta Art Show, San Antonio; Poultry Festival, Nacodoches; Birdie Tournament, Carrizo Springs; Coin Club Show, Sweetwater; Rose Show, Lubbock; Saengerfest, Fredericksburg; Pan American Livestock, Dallas; State Fair of Texas, Dallas; Autumn Arts Fiesta, Amarillo; Free Air Show, Quanah; Sidewalk Art, Raymondville; Sandhill Crane Hunt, Muleshoe Wildlife Refuge, Miss Teen Age Pageant, Fort Worth; Rotary Golf, Houston; Columbus Day

Fiesta, Eagle Pass; Mr. Amigo Celebration, Brownsville; Skeet Contest, Dallas; Texas Rose Festival, Tyler; Elks Trail Ride, Hallettsville to Ottine; Antique Fair, Sweetwater; Art of Living Exhibit, Houston.

Third Week—South Texas State Fair, Beaumont; Quarter Horse Futurity, Laredo; Chrysanthemum Pilgrimage, Lubbock; Nieman-Marcus Fortnight, Dallas; Permian Basin Oil Show, Odessa; Baylor Homecoming, Waco; East Texas Jamboree, Gilmer; Cotton Festival, Plainview; Peanut Festival, Floresville; Confederate Air Force Art Show, Harlingen; Fiesta de Amistad, Del Rio; Princess Anna Contest, Mission Fairs at Bonham, Edna, Nacogdoches.

Fourth Week—Bird Show, Gatesville; County Fair, Alice; Cav-oil-cade, Port Arthur; Santa Getrudis Sale, Alice; Homecoming & Livestock Show, Bartlett Gulf Coast Fiddlers, Sinton; South Texas Beefmasters Sale, Alice.

NOVEMBER

First Week—Senior-Junior Forum Bazaar, Wichita Falls; Antiques Fair, Bellaire; Fair, Livestock, All-Girl Rodeo, Sweetwater; Fly-in Golf Tournament, McAllen; Horse Races, two days each week this month, El Paso; Chisholm Trail Roundup, Cuero; Garden Council Flower Show, Lampasas; Sun Island Festival, Galveston; Gregg Aviation Appreciation Day, Longview.

Second Week—Wurstfest, New Braunfels; Coin Show, Odessa; Veterans Day, Laredo; Fine Arts Festival, U. of Texas, Austin; Steer Roping, San Angelo; Scottish Clans Festival, Salado; Spanish Social Circle Festival, Houston.

Third Week—Tourists' Jamboree, Raymondville; Houston Champions Golf, Houston; Pecan Show, Junction; Holiday Balloon Parade, Dallas; South Texas Vegetables, San Antonio.

Fourth Week—Bronco Days, Edinburg; Christmas Parade, Lufkin; also Longview; Parade and Marching Band Competition, Sweetwater.

DECEMBER

First Week—Christmas Tree Festival, Muleshoe; Feliz Navidad, Raymondville; Santa Day Parade, Pampa; Christmas Parade, Carthage; Fall Flower Show, Lubbock; Hot Rod & Custom Show, Houston; Horse Races, El Paso; Christmas Parades, Copperas Cove and Denison; North Texas-Oklahoma Pecan Show, Nocona; Christmas in the Pines, Dickinson; Specialty Club Rabbit Show, Gatesville; Livestock, Georgetown; Fine Arts, Wichita Falls; Christmas Parade, Pearsall; Lions Club Christmas Parade, Alice.

Second Week—All Valley Vegetables, Pharr; Basketball Tournament, Odessa; Christmas Parade, Pittsburg; Poinsetta Show, Mission; Christmas Home Pilgrimage, Victoria; Candlelight Tours, Historic Homes, Houston.

Third Week—Christmas Pasados, Laredo; Bluebonnet Bowl, Rice Stadium, Houston; Santa Claus Visit, Eagle Pass; Sun Bowl Football, El Paso.

Fourth Week—Cowboys Christmas Ball, Gilmer; Sun Carnival, El Paso; Basketball Tournaments, San Angelo and Edinburg.

PART I

Texas: Yesterday and Today

Southwestern Empire

TEXAS, twenty-eighth State to be admitted to the Union (1845) and the only one which, as an independent nation, came in by treaty, derives its name from *tejas,* a word meaning "friend," "friendly," or "allies," which was used by several confederated Indian tribes as a greeting, and by early Spanish explorers as a general designation of all Indians in present-day East Texas. It is known as the Lone Star State, from the single star upon the red, white, and blue banner which waved over the Texas Republic and still is the State flag.

Only by comparisons can one grasp how much territory is embraced in Texas. Its area is equal to the combined areas of all New England, New York, New Jersey, Pennsylvania, Ohio and Illinois, or one-twelfth of the total area of continental United States. Texas is one of the three American states that added 1,000,000 persons to their population in the half decade, 1960–1965, according to the U. S. Bureau of the Census. The other states were California and New York. In 1960 the Bureau counted 9,579,677 people in Texas; in 1965 the Bureau estimated that the population had risen to 10,591,000, an increase of 10.6 percent. Of that number 169,000 were members of the Armed Forces, stationed in Texas. The sources of changes in population were vital statistics and migration. Thus the Bureau estimated an excess of births over deaths of 863,000, and a net civilian increase (entering and leaving the State permanently) of 154,000.

Texas is unique among the American states not only because it entered the Union by a treaty made as an independent republic, but also by reason of a clause in that treaty whereby "new states of convenient size, not exceeding four in number, in addition to said State of Texas, and having sufficient population, may hereafter, by the consent of said State, be formed out of the territory thereof, which shall be entitled to admission under the provisions of the Federal Constitution." The question, occasionally discussed, as to whether or not, if Texas insisted, the National Government would be obliged to admit the additional states, is academic; no desire has ever been seriously evinced on the part of Texans to split up the "southwestern empire" of which they are so proud, even though by doing so they might have ten United States Senators, instead of two.

Until only lately one of the last American frontiers, Texas even now is but sparsely inhabited in many areas. Once a province of Spain and then a part of the Mexican Empire and Republic, it still, along its southern border and for many miles northward, has a large Latin-American population. But yesterday an almost limitless open range, it today has more cattle than human beings and many a ranch whose area is better expressed in square miles than in acres.

Its history covers four centuries and has been enacted under six national flags. Well-preserved or restored Franciscan missions that were already aged before the American Revolution are among its landmarks. Its shrine is the chapel of the San Antonio de Valero mission-fortress called the Alamo, in which a century ago every defender met death but won undying fame. Where the San Jacinto River meets Buffalo Bayou is the battlefield upon which Sam Houston's little army defeated a greatly superior force and won Texas independence from Mexico.

The official motto of the State, derived from its name's earliest meaning, is "Friendship." The bluebonnet, which in spring carpets great areas, is the State flower. The official State song is "Texas, Our Texas," although in practice the University of Texas song, "The Eyes of Texas," is more commonly heard on official occasions. The State tree is the pecan; the State bird, the mockingbird.

Its culture derives from several races and many States.

Its crops—with cotton as king—include wheat in the temperate north and grapefruit and oranges in the subtropical south.

Its mineral wealth is enormous. Oil and gas underlie much of the State's surface, and reach far out under the Tidelands.

Houston, with its 50-mile ship channel to the Gulf, its Manned Spacecraft Center trying for the moon, and its railroads, is a commercial and shipping metropolis. The sky line of Dallas spreads above an ever-increasing industrial activity, and the initiative and public spirit of its people were exhibited to the world in its 1936 Centennial Exposition. San Antonio is a city of picturesque contrasts, with ancient Mission bells still ringing in its environs, its sparkling HemisFair of 1968 attesting to the vitality of its Latin American associations.

Fort Worth is the center of meat packing and of an immense airplane traffic. The great dome of the capitol at Austin dominates a magnificent collection of educational buildings, the property of a State university which—from its ownership of oil lands—gives promise of becoming the wealthiest in the world. El Paso, in the far west, has American energy and Mexican color. Galveston, on the Gulf, is picturesque, busy with shipping, and outside of its mighty sea wall possesses one of the most beautiful beaches in America.

In the Golden Triangle of Beaumont, Port Arthur and Orange the crude underground treasure flows into refineries that produce the greatest output of petrochemicals in the world.

The West of ranch and rodeo, big hats and handsome riding boots remains, but it is not violently "wild and woolly" as of old. Yet the standards and customs of the frontier have not wholly vanished, even in the large cities. The cattleman, cowboy, sheriff, and Texas Ranger ride more miles today behind a steering-wheel than astride a horse, but the six-shooter still arbitrates many a dispute, urban as well as rural, and juries are likely to be lenient as regards the resulting homicides if womenfolk are involved, or if a self-defense plea seems to have justification.

The visitor who expects any definite Texas accent or dialect to be general will be disappointed, for immigration has brought into the State some of the speech and idiom of every section of the country. On city streets Middle Western phrases and accents are as often heard as those of the eastern South. One can seldom be sure, without knowing the speaker's background, whether "evening" means afternoon as in the South, or after dark as in the North. Many provincial Texans use "ain't" in the same all-embracing way as many provincial New Englanders—for "am not," "is not," and "are not"—and some, whose infusion of Yankee blood, if any, is so far in the past as to have been forgotten, give "ow" the same nasal drawl as a native of northern Vermont—"the color is braown."

More Southern than Western is the State's approach to most political and social questions; more Western than Southern are the manners of most of its people. By tradition and practice the native Texan is expansive, friendly and hospitable. Within such limitations as are demanded by reasonable business acumen and social caution, the not discourteous stranger is usually accepted at approximately his own valuation until he gives evidence to the contrary.

Few men have seen all of Texas, and no visitor can hope to do so. But such part of it as may be selected for a tour can be seen very easily, for a huge network of concrete and blacktop roads crosses the State in every direction, international and regional airlines use the skies, and bus lines supplement rail travel between cities and ranch lands.

Regardless of what section the tourist desires to visit, enjoyment of his trip will be enhanced if he first gathers, from the general chapters which here follow, a comprehensive mental picture of the State as a whole and of the more notable achievements of its past and present.

Natural Setting

THE boundaries of Texas reach from the semi-tropical regions of the Rio Grande, a land of oranges and palms, past the wind-swept *Llano Estacado* to the northern boundary more than 800 miles distant, where there are broad, treeless plains, and where winter comes suddenly. On the eastern limits tall pine forests shade the slumbering bayous, while along the southwestern border stand the pink and purple canyons of the Big Bend, and the deserts of the trans-Pecos shimmer beneath a bright blue sky. The greatest distance from east to west is approximately 775 miles; from northwest to southeast, 801 miles.

Texas occupies a position midway between the Atlantic and the Pacific and, with the exception of Florida, is the most southerly State in the Union. Approximately equidistant from the Equator and the Arctic Circle, it covers more than 13 degrees of longitude and more than 10.5 degrees of latitude.

Four states, one foreign nation, and a gulf border Texas: Arkansas, Oklahoma, and New Mexico on the north; Louisiana, Arkansas, and Oklahoma on the east; Mexico and the Gulf of Mexico on the south; New Mexico and Mexico on the west.

Along the 800 miles of boundary between Texas and the Mexican Republic flows the stream named by the Spaniards *Rio Bravo del Norte*— Bold River of the North—but which in the United States is called the Rio Grande. Between the Sabine River on the east, which separates Texas from Louisiana, and the Rio Grande, seven rivers run southeasterly to the

Gulf, the principal ones being the Trinity, the Brazos, and the Colorado. Something like two-fifths of the State lies east of the Colorado, and in that area are many of the more important cities and a large proportion of the State's inhabitants.

According to the Census of 1960 Texas had a land area of 262,840 sq. mi., and an inland water area of 4,499 sq. mi. The Act of Congress verifying Texas' ownership of the coastal waters of the Gulf increased the water area by 3,825 sq. mi., making the total area under the jurisdiction of the State 271,214 sq. mi. Since 1960 the preservation of waters in new reservoirs has enlarged the inland water surface. In 1966 the General Land Office placed the total area of Texas at 276,600 sq. mi.

Primarily an inland empire, Texas nevertheless has the third longest coast line of the States, 370 miles. It stands midway between Latin America and the remainder of North America, and is thus the meeting place of many important land and sea routes.

Texas consists essentially of three gently sloping plains separated by abrupt steps or escarpments. These plains are really parts of the three broad continental divisions: the Coastal Plain, the Central Plains, and the Western High Plains. The trans-Pecos region in the extreme southwest, however, is characterized by rugged mountains, elevated basins, and deep canyons.

The Coastal Plain, from low shores and bluffs along the Gulf of Mexico, extends 150 to 300 miles to its inland margin at the great geological fault known as the Balcones Escarpment; the line of this escarpment runs from Denison, near the Red River, southward through Dallas, Waco, Austin, and San Antonio, then westward through Uvalde to Del Rio at the Rio Grande. Altitudes range from 600 to 1,000 feet.

The Central Plains are an extension of the lower part of the Western Plains below the Red River to the Pecos River, and from the Balcones Escarpment northwestward to the "Cap Rock." Altitudes range from 800 feet on the east to 3,000 feet at the western margins. There are four major divisions of this central plain: (1) north of the Colorado River and immediately west of the Balcones Escarpment, a region of low hills and broad valleys, called the Grand Prairie; (2) south of the Colorado River and bounded on the east and south by the Balcones Escarpment, a deeply eroded country of low hills and very narrow stream valleys fed by limestone springs, called the Edwards Plateau; (3) the broad plain west of the Grand Prairie; and (4) the uplift of the Central Mineral Region, a smaller area surrounded by the other three subregions and consisting of rugged hill country along the Colorado and its tributary, the Llano River.

The Western High Plains, bounded on the east by the "Cap Rock"— an abrupt escarpment with a zone of broken country below called "the breaks"—extend west to the New Mexico Line, and southward from the northernmost limit of the Panhandle to the Pecos Valley. Altitudes along the southern margin are 3,000 feet and at the northwest corner of the Panhandle reach 4,700 feet. These high plains are in two parts, locally called the Panhandle High Plains, which occupy all the Texas Panhandle except the extreme eastern tier of its counties, and the South Plains, below the Palo Duro Canyon and other draws tributary to the Red River.

In the Panhandle the High Plains are crossed by the deep valley of the Canadian River. Elsewhere they are a smooth, gently sloping treeless region, with more or less frequent depressions or sinks locally called "lakes" —which in fact they are after heavy rains. Except for the Canadian Valley and arroyos such as the Palo Duro and a few lesser narrow draws leading to the Cimarron on the north and to the Red, Brazos, and Colorado Rivers on the east, the region drains only to the local depressions. This Panhandle High Plains region, once thought to be a desert, was called the *Llano Estacado,* or Staked Plain.

Texas is a State of sharp natural contrasts, of regions having distinct features abruptly juxtaposed to other features; and, within the broad divisions, certain natural regions are clearly defined:

The Coastal Prairie, extending inland from 30 to 50 miles, is a highly productive region which was the scene of early settlement. It contains such port cities as Galveston, Houston, Texas City, Corpus Christi, Beaumont, and Port Arthur.

The Timber Belt, bounded on the north by the Coastal Prairie and extending from the middle part of the State almost to the Red River, has an area equal to that of Ohio. In this region grow the commercially important longleaf, shortleaf and loblolly pines, as well as numerous hardwoods.

The Rio Grande Plain, which includes the Rio Grande Delta and the richly fertile Lower Rio Grande Valley, is known chiefly for its winter gardens and citrus fruit.

The Blacklands, the richest agricultural land in the State and one of the great cotton producing areas, extends along the inner border of the Coastal Plain from the Red River southward. Five principal cities lie within this section: Fort Worth, Dallas, Waco, Austin, and San Antonio.

The Granite Mountain section of the Central Hilly Region, is composed largely of igneous formations and limestone and offers a great variety of minerals. The granite fields cover 2,500 square miles.

The Central Plains or *Central Basin,* contain, in McCullough County, the exact geographical center of Texas. Ranching occupies the drier region to the west; and most of the agricultural land lies along the course of the Colorado River and its tributaries.

The Western High Plains, part of them the early-discovered *Llano Estacado,* form a great tableland from 3,000 to 4,700 feet in elevation, the southern part of which lately has become a prolific cotton producing section. Wheat and grain fields occupy most of the northern part in a region formerly devoted to ranching.

The Edwards Plateau rises abruptly from the Coastal Plain on the south and occupies the south central portion of the State, with altitudes from 1,000 to 3,000 feet. The Guadalupe, Comal, San Marcos, Blanco, Pedernales, Llano, Medina, Frio, Nueces, Concho, San Saba, and Devil's Rivers, fed by innumerable creeks and springs, wind through green valleys and picturesque canyons in the limestone hills of this region, which is devoted to ranching and is filled with recreational resorts.

Trans-Pecos Texas, a triangular area as large as West Virginia, lying west of the Pecos River, north and east of the Rio Grande, and below the south line of New Mexico, is an elevated region of broad valleys or undrained basins, interspersed with several mountain groups, with peaks from 6,000 to nearly 9,000 feet. The basin valleys are at an altitude of 3,500 to 5,000 feet.

The mountain ranges in this most barren and yet most scenically attractive section of Texas, are part of the southern extension of the Rockies. Guadalupe Peak, the highest point in the State, has an altitude of 8,751 feet. Near it El Capitan rises 8,078 feet. Other tall peaks are Shumard, 8,628 ft., Bush, 8,676 ft., Pine Top, 8,676 ft., and Bartlett, 8,513, in the Culbertson County part of the new Guadalupe Mountains National Park, authorized 1966–1967. Also in this region is the impressive Big Bend National Park, with Mount Emory in the Chisos Mountains reaching 7,835 ft. The Davis Mountains have altitudes from 4,000 to 5,000 ft. near Alpine and Fort Davis.

To these natural regions may be added the Valley Lowlands along the Canadian River in the north, and the Rio Grande in the south.

CLIMATE

Texas climate is remarkable for its salubrity. Along the south coastal regions freezing temperatures are so rare that semitropical citrus fruits are grown in the Rio Grande Delta, while on the plateaus and tablelands of the northwest winters are as cold as in central Illinois. Some of the southern cities, especially San Antonio, are popular winter resorts, and the southwestern part of the State is noted for its high proportion of sunshiny days. In this section there are many winter days when the mercury readings are from 70° F. to 80° F. and spring and late autumn resemble the northern Indian summer.

The normal mean temperature for August, as recorded at eight points which cover every area, is from 75° to 86°; the normal mean temperature for January is from 33° to 60°. The highest temperature ever recorded officially in the State was 120° at Seymour, Baylor County, August 12, 1936; the lowest was 23° below zero, registered at Tulia, Swisher

County, February 11, 1899, and at Seminole, in Gaines County, February 8, 1933.

Along the Sabine River on the east the climate is humid; the annual rainfall is 55 inches. Westward the humidity and rainfall decrease gradually, until the extreme corner at El Paso has only nine inches of rainfall and a semidesert climate. Rainfall for the State as a whole is least during the winter months, gradually increasing from February through May and decreasing on the average through the summer months, with a heavier normal precipitation in September than in the other autumn months. Snowfall is light and infrequent for most of the State, as much because of the dryness of the winter months as their relative warmth. Infrequently, snow falls in south central Texas. Although the average annual snowfall in the Panhandle is said to be 10 inches, there are records of much heavier snowfalls; for instance, in February, 1964, the snow reached 18 to 26 inches there. Exceptional was the snowfall at Hale Center, in the Western High Plains, where 33 in. fell in one storm, Feb. 2–5, 1956.

Native Texans have a saying: "Only fools and strangers predict weather in Texas." Yet save in one respect—and in that respect only in degree—Texas weather is no more uncertain than in many another American section. The exception is the Texas "norther," which from autumn to late spring may be experienced in any part of the State.

A norther is a cold, sharp wind which sweeps down across the plains. Sometimes black clouds appear in the north, and the storm breaks swiftly with rain or sleet; sometimes there are few or no clouds, and the first warning on a warm sunny day is a sudden puff of north wind which quickly rises to a half gale. The mercury responds by dropping 10° or more in as many minutes, and then continues to fall less rapidly for hours. There are extreme records in south Texas of a drop of more than 50° in 36 hours. Ordinarily the norther reaches its coldest point on the second day, and by the fourth day the temperature is likely to have returned to normal.

Periodic storms, often of hurricane intensity, visit the Gulf Coast. Sea walls and breakwaters have been built for the protection of property. Tropical hurricanes usually occur in the equinoctial season. The great storm of Galveston, Sept. 8–9, 1900, in which more than 6,000 died, never has been surpassed. The people of the Gulf Coast and the Lower Rio Grande Valley have sharp memories of excessive damages inflicted by high winds and floods of recent date. The area around Brownsville had 90 per cent of its citrus destroyed in 1933 and again in 1966; in between numerous tornadoes ravaged the Coast. The international bridge at Laredo was washed out in 1954 and floods carried out a bridge 50 ft. above the Pecos River. In a hurricane of 1961 34 died, 465 were injured.

GEOLOGY AND PALEONTOLOGY

Long geologic ages ago, Texas was a mass of volcanic rock, pounded by a mighty ocean and overhung with mists. Through millions of years the land of the present State was subject to fairly frequent plunges beneath the primal seas.

In the Paleozoic age, only islands stood where the State now is. Near the end of this "old era" the mainland came slowly up from the bottom of the ocean. Toward the east it was low and swampy, and here grew immense forests destined to produce the coal of the Central Plains. The strange teeming invertebrate and air-breathing vertebrate life of that period was to furnish great resources of petroleum and natural gas. Hot, barren plains were formed to the west, with underlying deposits of salt, potash, gypsum and sulphur. Thus two of the State's natural divisions— the Central Hilly or Mineral Region, and the Central Plains—were completed during the Paleozoic period.

The land mass was elevated, eroded, and submerged again beneath the sea in the Mesozoic or middle life period. Millions of shell-bearing animals lived in these waters, and their shells in time made limey deposits which today are the basis of the fertility of the Blacklands. The soils of the Edwards Plateau are also derived from this period. This, the age of reptiles, left fossil remains of reptile-like birds and other strange forms of life.

As the Mesozoic era closed, the mountains of western Texas emerged from the floor of the sea. This mighty movement of the earth was accompanied by disturbances so great that volcanic activity left an indelible mark on the west Texas area, and the terrestrial contortions left great faults or breaks which extend from the vicinity of Del Rio to the Red River. Through these cracks issued volcanic materials which are visible south of the Edwards Plateau. At the conclusion of the Mesozoic period Texas contained three new regions—the black land prairies, the Edwards Plateau, and the western mountains.

Heavily forested swamps now skirted the land mass, and abundant vegetable and animal life provided for later deposits of petroleum, natural gas, and lignite. This geological belt extends across the center of the State from northeast Texas to the Rio Grande.

In the Cenozoic or recent life period the formation of the present-day Texas was completed by the elevation of the remainder of the Coastal Plain. This is the newest part of the North American Continent. During this, the age of mammals, vegetation assumed an aspect now familiar, and even the cold of the Pleistocene or ice age did not alter the land mass appreciably.

The High Plains were once the site of a vast inland lake. The deposits of silt laid down in it from the mountains to the west, provided the basis for its present agricultural development.

During each of the half dozen or more submergences of the State, deposits were laid down—sands, clays, gravels, limy muds, sulphur, salt, and gypsum. Naturally, many changes have taken place in these ancient deposits. The oldest sediments have hardened into schist or slate; limy muds formed coarse marbles. Younger rocks have changed also; calcareous ooze has become limestone, sands have turned into sandstone, and gravels into conglomerate. These changes have created vast mineral wealth.

Along the coast line many interesting examples of past and present geological changes can be seen. Raised beaches are not uncommon a short distance from shore. A beach of this kind, 30 feet high, runs through the city of Corpus Christi.

As the Rocky Mountain system rose, bringing the mountains of western Texas with it, the crust of the earth was tremendously faulted. This fault zone in Texas is easily identifiable along US 90 from Del Rio to San Antonio; here it is visible along a 150-mile course, in the Balcones Escarpment. Volcanic action followed the faulting, and molten materials oozed up through the rocks, and cinder cones and other formations resulted. One product of this upheaval is the trap rock or basalt hills occurring near Austin and Uvalde.

Ground water came from the zone faulting, and originated the springs which supply such rivers as the San Antonio, the San Marcos, the Comal, and the Guadalupe. The old rivers of the State are the Canadian, the Red, the Trinity, the Brazos, the Colorado, and the Rio Grande with its principal tributary, the Pecos. The Red River cut the Palo Duro Canyon, while the Rio Grande ate its way through mountains to form the Grand Canyon of the Santa Elena. Ground water made caverns and stored supplies for future artesian wells. The great forests that fell into the muddy ooze of remote geologic years occupied almost every sandy part of the State, conserving rainfall and preventing erosion.

More than any other agency, marine life of ancient seas furnished Texas its fertile soils. The shell life of the various geologic ages is distributed liberally through the entire series of unaltered sedimentary formations. In the Pennsylvania formations, or "coal measures"—found in an area northwest and southwest of Fort Worth—are traces of a fossil flora differing entirely from that of the present.

Geological formations in Texas range from those of the Archeozoic (first life) age through those of Cenozoic periods, and divide the State into large geologic units. Formations of the Coastal Plain dip toward the Gulf and are of the Cretaceous (age of reptiles and dinosaurs) and Cenozoic ages. Since Cretaceous time the Gulf of Mexico has been receiving sediments. The thickness of deposits ranges from 20,000 to 30,000 feet. Underlying much of this region at great depth are salt beds which have formed salt domes. Oil occurs in these, and also sulphur, salt, and gypsum.

The Central Hilly or Mineral Region still forms a pivot about which the rest of the State is built. Formations dip down from it and spread out like ripples. One of the seven granite shields in the United States, the Granite Mountain area presents an imposing appearance, with vast blocks or boulders of granite, sparkling with mica, piled one upon the other or in solid masses forming entire hills. Many of the hard rock minerals occur in this region, such as lead, some gold and copper, graphite, and many of the rare earth minerals.

North of the Central Hilly Region and extending to the Red River is another distinct geological division called the Wichita Plain. Underlying formations, chiefly Pennsylvanian (age of amphibians) and Permian (a Carboniferous period), consist chiefly of sandstone, shale and limestone. These formations have extensive petroleum reserves.

The northern and western parts of the Great Plains contain nonmarine recent formations; while the Edwards Plateau consists of Cretaceous formations lying on top of those of the Paleozoic age.

Perhaps the most interesting region of the State geologically is that of the trans-Pecos. In the vicinity of Marathon and in the Solitario Uplift north of Terlingua are mountains made during the Paleozoic era.

Great plateau areas of lava flows are found in the Davis Mountains, in the region between Alpine and Marfa and west of Mount Ord and the Santiago Mountains and the Sierra del Carmen on the Rio Grande. The country within the Big Bend is a great trough or syncline of Comanchean (Lower Cretaceous) and Upper Cretaceous rocks partly covered by lava flow and intruded by igneous rocks.

The oldest exposed rocks in the State are of pre-Cambrian age (all of geologic time prior to the Paleozoic). Their fossils, with rare exceptions, have been obliterated. These rocks are found in the Llano Uplift of the Central Hilly Region, the Van Horn district, and in the Franklin Mountains near El Paso. Paleozoic rocks are extensively exposed, chiefly in central, north, and west Texas. The three Mesozoic systems are found; Triassic deposits underlie the Great Plains as far south as the Pecos River; Jurassic rocks are confined to the Malone Mountains; and marine Cretaceous deposits, abounding with fossils, are widespread. Nonmarine Cenozoic deposits occur extensively in the western part of the State, although the principal belt of Cenozoic formations is that of east and south Texas bordering the Gulf Coast.

Earth movements in Texas continue to be erratic. A good example of this is found along the coastal area, where some parts of the mainland are slowly sinking and some rising as time works its changes.

Resources and their Conservation

FIRST among the natural resources of Texas is land, the amount and extent of which has since earliest times given rise to the word "empire" in connection with the State. In 1777 Padre Morfi wrote, "A proof of the astonishing fertility of the country is the multitude of nations which inhabit it." And to protect this great wealth of land modern conservation methods are being employed.

Soils of Texas range from loose, deep sands to heavy, dark clays, from yellow to black, from soils made by ancient geological formations to the alluvial deposits of modern times. The bleak alkali soils of the western deserts are at the opposite extreme from the rich rolling fields of the Blacklands.

Many different types of soil have been analyzed by scientists, and the principal ones have been classified as follows:

The loose sandy loams or clays of the Coastal Plain.

The East Texas Timber area soils.

Eastern Cross Timbers soils, and

Western Cross Timbers soils, both generally based on ancient unconsolidated marine animals and sandy.

The largely calcareous soils of the Rio Grande Plain.

The heavy, black soils of the Blacklands.

Limestone soils in central and western Texas, including the Edwards Plateau.

The none-calcareous soils of the North Central Plains, often called "the red prairies" because of color derived from weathering of ancient clays, sandstones, and shales.

Soils of the High Plains, where the surface is sometimes underlaid with "caliche," a calcareous deposit, and where soils vary from brown to red, with some clay loams.

Soils of the trans-Pecos area, largely composed of the wash from mountains, and often contain minerals that discourage plant life, although there is some alluvial land along the Rio Grande and in the eastern section.

Residual soils of the Central Hilly or Mineral Region, with types derived from weathering of sandstone, granites and other minerals.

The Soil Conservation Service is concerned chiefly with the control of rainfall water, to minimize erosion of farm and pasture lands, conserve the water where it falls and thus minimize flood hazards. The service makes studies of erosion problems, makes maps for the use of owners, lays off contour lines and terraces, constructs check dams and other preventive measures, lends farmers equipment to make outlet ditches, and provides landowners with facilities for reforestation work, in return for which landowners follow an approved method of cropping and keep a simple record of the erosion experiments.

Dust storms ravaged the plains of Texas in only a smaller degree than those of the other Great Plains states. The Great Plains Conservation Program became a Federal law only in 1956, with $150,000,000 available in 1957. The Secretary of Agriculture uses this in sharing the costs of conservation practices on farms and ranches. Any farmer or rancher who owns or rents land may qualify for the program, which includes range seeding, land conversion, terrace building, establishment of waterways, and brush control.

Soil and water conservation is so valuable to the people that they hold meetings and dinners to discuss it. Essays on the subject are promoted in the high schools; ministers preach sermons of soil stewardship; Boy Scouts add conservation of land to their studies while camping; FFA and 4-H leaders study proper grasses for pasturage, and conservation of wild life is made a part of regulations governing hunting in season.

WATER

In Texas the demand for water is so huge that continuous efforts are necessary to provide new sources for irrigation, industrial use and the municipal services. Ground water has been plentiful, but when 10,000,-000 acre-ft. of water are pumped from underground sources for irrigation in one year, depletion is near. The Texas Water Commission reported that 83 percent of the 7,700,000 acres under irrigation in 1965 received ground water. The steady rise in population, in the petrochemical industries and in the opening of new acreage to irrigation, have forced intensive efforts to build new dams and reservoirs, to protect existing resources from pollution, to remove brine from brackish areas, and even to accelerate the conversion of seawater to fresh.

The Federal Government's report on the water situation in Texas in a typical year, 1965—prepared by the U. S. Bureau of Mines and the Bureau of Economic Geology of the University of Texas—gives an indication of the vast expansion in the activity in which the Federal Government, the State and local bodies take part. It said that out of 130 major projects for conservation and flood control, seven completed that year added 7,352,000 acre-ft. of water to storage; 10 others under construction would add 10,556,000 acre-ft. (an acre-foot of water covers one acre one foot deep). The total conservation capacity on completion of these tasks by the Bureau of Reclamation and the Corps of Engineers of the U. S. Army, would rise to 26,830,000 acre-ft. from 13,792,000 acre-ft., and flood control storage would rise from 12,823,000 acre-ft. to 17,793,000 acre-ft.

The battle against water pollution is being waged by the Texas Water Pollution Board in cooperation with the U. S. Public Health Service and the Texas Water Commission, the Parks and Wildlife Commission, and the Railroad Commission. Waters are polluted by sewage, oil and gas operations, chemicals—including household detergents, waste from ships and boats, and agricultural pesticides. Such poisons kill fish and wildlife and damage recreation areas. The situation involves interstate practices and thus needs Federal help. The Public Health Service has given grants to more than 260 communities to build or enlarge sewage treatment works. It gives grants to colleges for research and training in water supply control.

So much good soil was washed away by floods or carried away in dust storms in the 1920–1935 period that in 1936 the United States Government enacted its first Flood Control Act. An amendment of 1944 gave Texas an opportunity to combat upstream floods, but it was 1949 before the first watershed with this aim was completed on Howard Creek near Jacksboro. In 1953 the Pilot Watershed Program provided Federal money for further conservation and gave Texas means of building four essential watersheds: at Cow Bayou Creek near Waco, Green Creek near Dublin, Calaveras Creek near San Antonio, and Escondido Creek near Kenedy. In 1954 Congress voted to give Federal aid to local watershed programs conserving up to 250,000 acres, and the Texas State Soil and Conservation Board took charge of the State's responsibility.

Watersheds must be regulated, so that water can be put to constructive use. Conservation of water means "conserving the raindrop where it falls," and "stopping the floods before they start." Today, throughout Texas the socalled small watershed program is proving most beneficial in holding soil, providing a measured supply of water for city use, irrigation and recreation, and stopping the ravages of floods. Millions of acres have been recovered for use. Soil and Water Conservation Districts have found multiple uses for their programs and have increased the economic welfare of their areas. These districts have found it profitable to form regional associations to promote their objects. Training for district supervisors has been instituted by the State Board, with the help of experienced workers in conservation. The policies of a district are determined by the farmers and ranchers who own the land and are either helped or hurt by a program. The district organization studies its local needs and adapts the program to them.

The Rio Grande Federal Irrigation Project was constructed by the United States Bureau of Reclamation under contract with the Elephant Butte Irrigation District (New Mexico) and El Paso County. For the irrigation of 67,000 acres, below El Paso, 650 miles of canals and laterals were constructed. The total area subject to irrigation is 155,000 acres.

The drainage area of the Rio Grande totals 48,475 sq. m., including 24,900 sq. m. drained by the tributary Pecos. Its flow is erratic, varying from slight flow to floods in excess of 600,000 cubic feet a second. Consequently great benefits are expected to accrue to both Texas and Mexico from the huge Falcon and Amistad dam and reservoir projects, in which Mexico has a part. When the Amistad is completed the two will irrigate approximately 1,000,000 additional acres of Texas soil.

What has been described as the largest municipal and industrial water development ever carried out by the Bureau of Reclamation is the Canadian River Project, which is geared to supply eleven cities in the Panhandle. The project includes Lake Meredith, 10 *m.* northwest of Borger in Hutchinson County, impounded by Sanford Dam. This lake covers 21,630 acres and its top capacity will be 1,408,000 acre-ft. of water. The distribution system calls for 322 miles of pipeline. The National Park Service was designated to administer the Sanford Recreation Area in cooperation with the Bureau of Sports Fisheries and Wildlife and the Bureau of Reclamation. This area is near the Alibates Flint Quarries and prehistoric pueblo ruins set aside by Congress as a national monument. So welcome were the opportunities for outdoor sports in this area that the authorities believe more than 1,000,000 people will choose it for annual outings in the next decade.

The Trinity basin extends for more than 450 miles, and along its course is the largest industrial development bordering any Texas stream. The Brazos, with a flow of more than 5,000,000 acre-ft. a year, presented one of the most difficult flood control problems, but the Brazos River Conservation and Reclamation District mastered the situation with a number of reservoirs that cover a huge area.

The Colorado River has dams that harness the flow and periodic floods. The largest of these is Buchanan Dam (formerly Hamilton Dam) in Burnet and Llano Counties. Marshall Ford Dam a few miles above Austin has a power plant with a capacity of 67,500 kilowatts. The largest hydroelectric power plant is at Denison on the Red River, 71,000 kilowatts, but the total for the State, 390,000 kilowatts, is small in comparison with the 12.5 million kilowatts raised by steam plants.

In the Edwards Plateau many streams originate from a vast underground water supply. Also derived from this source are Barton Springs, San Marcos Springs, Comal Springs, the San Antonio River and San Pedro Springs, and others. Seven Hundred Springs, on the South Llano River, are spectacular (*see Tour 16d*).

The largest river of the spring-fed group is the Guadalupe, which because of its steady flow has led in the creation of power. Twenty-five privately owned dams and power plants exist on the Guadalupe, and its tributary, the San Marcos. The Medina Dam near San Antonio, on the Medina River, pioneer storage project of magnitude, was built for irrigation, and Olmos Dam in San Antonio is one of the outstanding flood control measures. Two power dams have been built on Devil's River. On the Pecos River is Red Bluff Reservoir, of 285,000 acre-ft. capacity.

Lake Corpus Christi is the largest reservoir on the lower Nueces River, where Wesley E. Seale Dam impounds 185,900 acre-ft. of water, covering 15,300 acres. Located 4 *m.* southwest of Mathis, it spreads in Live Oak, San Patricio, and Jim Wells Counties.

In Texas, as elsewhere, the hope of obtaining an abundant supply of fresh water in the future is associated with desalination of seawater. The demonstration plant of the Office of Saline Water at Freeport is the oldest of the nation's experiments. It has a capacity of 1,000,000 gallons of fresh water per day, which it supplies to Freeport and to one of the city's industries.

MINERALS

Since 1901, when the tremendous oil gusher of Spindletop, at Beaumont, started Texas on the road to produce 1 billion barrels (of 42 gallons each) of crude oil a year, Texas has led the nation in the production of petroleum, natural gas, natural gas liquids, and many petrochemical derivatives, which, with other minerals, reached a value of more than $5 billion in 1966.

The continued expansion of the industry, and the enlargement of the markets for Texas' products, many of them in the State itself, have placed a premium on exploration for new fields. While some wells slipped in production, new ones more than made up the deficiency. An industry that completes more than 12,000 new wells in one year more than holds its place in competition. The increase in the use of jet fuel has brought it to fourth place among the major refined products; the expansion of manufacturing and electric-power plants accounts for the great use of residual fuel oil; more gasoline is needed to supply America's motor cars, and distillate fuel is in larger demand because it feeds diesel engines.

In 1953 the State of Texas extended its authority over an additional 3,676 sq. mi. of area when President Eisenhower signed the quitclaim of the United States to the submerged tidelands off the Texas Gulf Coast. This was the final act in a controversy of long standing. The presence of oil under the waters of the Gulf made the Tidelands extremely valuable. Texas contended that these had belonged to the Republic of Texas when it entered the Union, but the U. S. Supreme Court, by a vote of 4 to 3 (2 not voting) decided on June 5, 1950, that Texas lost title when it entered the Union. Congress passed two acts of quitclaim, granting the Texas claim to three leagues (10.35 miles) of the Tidelands, but President Truman vetoed both and Congress did not override the veto.

This led to a concerted effort of Texas political leaders to obtain title to the lands. In the national campaign of 1952 Eisenhower favored the Texan position and Adlai E. Stevenson supported that of the United States. Price Daniel, who, as attorney general, had argued the case for Texas, ran for the Senate on this issue and was supported by both Democrats and Republicans and elected. He then worked for a new quitclaim, which was passed by Congress and signed by President Eisenhower. The act gave some counties larger jurisdiction than others, based on their shorelines. Galveston County won the largest slice, 609 sq. mi. Most of the coastline from Louisiana to Galveston belonged to Jefferson County, so that Chambers County, with only a small coastline, won only 12 sq. mi., against Jefferson's 388. Kenedy County won 471 sq. mi. In all 12 counties along the Coast could now prospect for oil more than 10 miles beyond the shore line.

In the 1960s Texas enterprise redoubled its efforts to draw on the huge reservoir of oil under its coastal waters. Drilling rigs are multiplying and soon will contribute spectacularly to the State's wealth in oil.

Second only to crude oil as a resource is natural gas, of which Texas supplies 40 percent of what the nation uses. With 33,436 wells producing in 1965, Texas was able to market more than 6,636.6 billion cubic ft., of which more than 3,698.6 billion cu. ft. was used by Texas industries, principally in the petrochemical plants of the Gulf Coast, which need it for such products as ethylene, polyethylene, and butadene. Natural gas was utilized in the past for carbon black, which is used in paint, printer's ink and rubber, but more recently petroleum liquids have been replacing it. Many of the natural gases contain gasoline, butane and propane, and when these have been extracted the residue is returned under pressure to natural gas reservoirs, where it forces out the unrefined gas.

New ways of using helium have given added importance to this lightweight gas, which is refined chiefly in the Amarillo area. Texas' production of 1 billion cu. ft. a year places it second to Kansas. Helium is used in making nuclear energy equipment, quality control devices, sensitive electronic gear and in spacecraft research; at Dyess AFB it is used to force liquid fuels into the engines of Atlas missiles. Besides being produced by the two plants of the Bureau of Mines at Amarillo and Excell, helium is extracted from natural gas at the Phillips plants at Dumas and Grover.

Sulphur, the second greatest mineral resource, is found in honeycomb limestone formations, often occurring in salt domes on the Gulf Coastal Plain. Mines extend along the coast, beginning at Freeport. It is forced to the surface by superheated steam, which melts the underground deposits. It is also produced from "sour" natural gas. Texas produces approximately 75 per cent of the national supply.

While *conquistadores* sought in vain the mythical gold of Texas, humble peons of the Rio Grande plains were hauling salt through the wilderness to Spanish ships which lay off Padre Island. Later the great salt lakes north of Van Horn were the basis of the Salt War (*see Tour 19f*). Salt domes are found on the Coastal Plain and surface deposits on the western plains. Up to 94 percent of salt is recovered from brine, but evaporated and rock salt command higher values. There are salt domes in Duval County, and deposits at Grand Saline in Van Zandt County and in the vicinity of Palestine.

Lignite and coal, although largely undeveloped, are two of the State's greatest mineral resources. The coal beds have an estimated store of 7.5 billion tons and extend over north central and middle west Texas. Production has ceased because of the abundance of cheaper oil and gas. Lignite beds cover approximately 60,000 square miles, from Laredo to Texarkana. Lignite is used by the electrical industries and is mined from open pits in Harrison and Milam Counties. Important iron deposits exist in northeast Texas.

With the exception of oil, the greatest variety of minerals is found in the Central Hilly or Mineral Region and in the trans-Pecos area. Nonferrous metal reserves in the State are limited largely to silver and quicksilver. Extensive quicksilver deposits have been mined near Terlingua in the Big Bend.

Silver is found principally near Shafter, where a large mine in the Chinati Mountains has produced for more than half a century. Copper is found in the western and central mountains, also in the Permian basin of the north central area, but not in large quantities. Gold, also in small amounts, is found in western and central mountains. Undeveloped deposits of lead, manganese, zinc, tin, and other metals occur.

Large deposits of marble, limestone, graphite, granite, asphalt, gypsum, fuller's earth, and clay exist. There are whole mountains of granite (*see Tour 9b*). Limestones form a broad belt from the Red River to the

Rio Grande, and across the north central area. Gypsum deposits of the central plains and the trans-Pecos section are extensively developed. Sand, gravel, and silica are abundant. The largest asphaltic rock deposits are near Uvalde.

From the Panhandle southward into the Pecos region commercial deposits of potash occur in a great underlying bed of rock salt, which is the largest in the world. Titanium, tungsten, and uranium are found in southwestern Texas. Mineral waters are widely distributed. A dozen or more other minerals exist in unimportant quantities. A few of the semiprecious stones are found, and fresh-water pearls.

PLANTS

Variety in plant life is naturally an outstanding characteristic of a State having so many changes in climate, soil, topography, and rainfall. From the twisted salt cedars of the Gulf Coast to the lonely desert reaches of ocotillo and sotol of the west, through the great zone of wild flowers which annually carpet hundreds of square miles, Texas is a vast botanical exposition. About 4,000 different wild flowers grow in the State, and there are more than 12,000,000 acres of commercial forests, 550 kinds of grasses, and exactly 100 varieties of cactus.

From March until the end of October, with the exception of July, the State, except in rare years of exceeding drought, is covered with blooms. Texas in the wild-flower months means landscapes done in brilliant colors: bluebonnets spreading widely like deep cerulean pools, mountain pinks flaming on the hillsides, sunflowers lining country roads, daisies lying like spots of melting snow on the prairies.

In 1824 Dr. Luis Berlandier, a French botanist, made the first large botanical collection from the State and sent it to Paris. The strange Texas plants interested Thomas Drummond, an Englishman, who explored the region near Galveston in 1833–34. He was followed in 1836 by Ferdinand J. Lindheimer, a German and the first great Texas botanist.

Although there are definite plant zones in Texas, modern agencies, such as irrigation, have widely distributed the plants of each section beyond their original boundaries.

The region of the tall forests, or the humid division of the lower Sonoran Zone, is in east Texas, where the longleaf, shortleaf, and loblolly pines grow. The low forest area (including the Eastern and Western Cross Timbers) is west of the tall forests, and embraces all the central part of the State and the south section of the Gulf Coast, as well as parts of west and southwest Texas. This area, known as the lower Sonoran Zone of the Austral or Southern plant belt, is a region of postoak and blackjack oak, of mesquite, and of semitropical flora, with tall grasses prevailing. The upper Sonoran Zone of the Austral covers the Central Plains, one arm extending south into Kerr County. It includes the cedar brakes of the Edwards Plateau, and is generally a treeless section of short grass. The Transition Zone, found in the mountains which reach or exceed 6,000 feet, is characterized by vegetation typical of the Rocky Mountains. The Canadian plant zone is found in the Davis and Guadalupe Mountains. The Pecos River Valley and the Rio Grande Valley south to about Eagle Pass are known as the extreme arid region of the lower Sonoran Zone. Here about 50 per cent of the soil is barren, and such plants as the creosote bush and yucca predominate. The semi-arid region of the State is largely composed of plains covered by mesquite, overgrown in spots with thorny types of bush such as catclaw, which, usually combined with cacti, is known by the Mexican name of *chaparral* (thick brush). Chaparral early necessitated the wearing by cowboys of leather *chaparreras,* commonly called "chaps." The arid and semi-arid regions have perhaps the most sharply defined vegetation, although the prairies are the home of the wild flowers, and the southern extremities of the State have tropical flora.

The rain lily, retama, desert willow, and cenizo invariably bloom after rains. In some years bluebonnets appear in February, yet if rains are unseasonal they may scarcely bloom at all.

The best bluebonnet month is March, and the largest bluebonnet fields are in the vicinity of San Antonio, Austin and the counties between San Antonio and Houston, between San Antonio and Corpus Christi, and between Cuero and the coast. The bluebonnet was first called buffalo clover, wolfflower, and *el conejo* (the rabbit) because of the white tip's resemblance to a rabbit's tail; but when women from other parts of the United States began to live in Texas, its similarity in shape to a sunbonnet gained it the new name. In many localities laws protect the plant; in others it is conserved by annual gathering of the seeds. These and other native Texas wild flower seeds can be bought at the Witte Memorial Museum in San Antonio and elsewhere. The bluebonnet was adopted as the State flower in 1901.

One of the greatest natural resources of the State is its forests, the east Texas timber belt alone covering 11,000,000 acres. Trees representative of both the Atlantic and the Pacific slopes are found in Texas, including, in the Guadalupe, Chisos, and Davis Mountains, varieties of Pacific coast oak, pine, fir, and juniper. There are in the State approximately 26,500,-000 acres in forests, including pine and hardwoods, postoak, and cedar brakes. The pine-hardwood area of east Texas produces the most commercially valuable timber.

A major part of the plant conservation program of Texas is reforestation and the creation and maintenance of large State and national forest reserves and parks. Four national forests, with a total area of approximately 1,714,000 acres, are in the heart of the east Texas timber belt:

Sam Houston National Forest, Davy Crockett National Forest, the Angelina National Forest, and the Sabine National Forest. They are administered by the Forest Service, United States Department of Agriculture, and each unit is directly under the care of a forest ranger. Five State forests contain a total of 6,423 acres, where members of the Forest Service demonstrate methods of overcoming pests, developing the best stocks, and fighting fires. The worst enemy is the southern pine bark beetle. Under a law of 1963 the Forest Service has authority to apply remedies wherever the pest is found, even on private property. The Texas Forest Service protects about 11,250,000 acres of pine forests, and maintains an effective fire-fighting force. Demonstrations of conservation and anti-erosion methods are conducted in all State and national forests.

The pine is the most important tree, commercially, in Texas. The oak, second in importance, is found in more than 50 varieties, and the live oak is the monarch of the Texas low forests. The cypress of the eastern river courses, growing to heights of 150 feet or more, is the patriarch of native trees, going back to the time of the dinosaur. The mesquite, most common tree in southwest and central Texas, is valuable because in some localities it provides the only shade and the only fuel.

Texas grasses include about half of the 1,100 or 1,200 kinds found in the United States. As a commercial crop they have little value, but as an aid against erosion and the basis of the cattle industry, their value is incalculable.

Although cactus reaches its greatest development in arid and semi-arid regions of the State, it is found from tidewater to the highest peak. From central Texas to the trans-Pecos cactus is most abundant and diversified. Big Bend National Park has a great display of dagger yucca in bloom. Here rare varieties include the peyote or "dry whiskey," still sought by certain Indians for their ceremonials; and the lechugilla and sotol, which served in prehistoric times as the chief weaving material of the cave dwellers, are still used in making twine and other products.

The maguey, also called the American aloe or century plant, which blooms about every 20 years, is widely distributed. Yuccas are the showiest of the semi-arid plants, growing throughout south and southwest Texas. The guayule, or rubber plant, is found in the western part of the State, and the candelilla, or wax plant, in the Big Bend.

A brilliant wild flower is the verbena, which often covers wide areas with blooms. Phlox grows abundantly, as do primroses of many colors and sizes. Indian paintbrush and Indian blanket are known in other localities as Indian pink or paintcup. The daisy family is well represented, as are a large number of the composites. The milkweed with its white flowers, used by Mexicans to cure ringworm and rattlesnake bite, is perhaps the best known Texas weed, although the *loco* (crazy) weed is widely distributed.

Water plants include the lotus, or waterlily, and the water hyacinth. The latter grows so profusely in many streams and bayous of east Texas that it is considered a nuisance.

Wild fruits and berries cover a wide variety, from the blackberry and dewberry to the huckleberry of east Texas. Wild grapes are used for the making of wines and jellies, the mustang, common to most sections, being the largest producer.

Conservation of native plants is conducted by the Forest Service, the Soil and Water Conservation Board, and the Parks and Wildlife Commission. The State park system (1968) consists of 40 parks; there are also 22 historic monuments, some of which qualify as State parks (Jeff Davis State Park, Jim Hogg State Park, Fannin Battlefield State Park, etc.) In addition Texas has a group of local parks, recreation areas and semi-public places, and forests and recreation areas maintained by the Federal Government.

Among the regions of especial botanical interest are the Big Thicket in east Texas, a tangle of vines, plants, and shrubs, and Palmetto State Park in Gonzales County, a conservation area which presents a subtropical scene in a semi-arid setting. The Davis Mountain State Park near Fort Davis and Big Bend National Park are huge conservation areas of natural arid and semi-arid growth, which will be joined by the Guadalupe Mountains National Park.

ANIMALS

Once a factor in the business of empire building in Texas, the wildlife of the State still flourishes wherever civilization permits. An astonishing number of game animals exists, either in protected preserves or in the less populated regions, and the smaller mammals continue abundant. Arid sections hold in their rocks and sands more reptiles than can be found in almost any other part of the Nation. Furthermore, Texas lies directly in the path of the migratory birds from the eastern and western States, Canada, and Alaska. Millions of insects furnish food for the birds and variety for the naturalist. From the streams and bays of the State ninety million pounds of fish have been sold in the last quarter-century.

Texas was belated in enacting game laws. However, because of almost totally uninhabited sections in the State, with ideal climatic conditions, and with natural food plentiful, wildlife in Texas is still as varied as the area it covers.

There are several large natural regions where game abounds. The east Texas timber belt, especially in the national forests, is a natural game preserve, where are found deer, bobcats, and many of the smaller animals, also a wide variety of birds. On the Edwards Plateau, where the country is broken, well-watered, and sparsely inhabited, deer and wild turkeys abound, and wolves, panthers, small animals, and birds are plentiful. The coastal region has sheltered bays and inlets which are natural wildfowl preserves, and some of the islands, notably those between the mainland and St. Joseph's and Padre Islands, are the breeding and nesting grounds of waterfowl. The trans-Pecos region with its huge State and proposed national parks is one of the largest natural game preserves in the United States, with several million acres under the protection of Federal and State game wardens. The Guadalupe Mountains furnish another ideal wildlife region, and elk have been reintroduced there in protected areas. The Palo Pinto Mountain section is another region where game thrives.

Many of the wild creatures of early times have vanished or are almost extinct. The great buffalo herds, once estimated at 60,000,000 head in Texas, have dwindled to a few animals, principally the small herd on the Goodnight Ranch in the Panhandle. Texas bighorns, the mountain sheep which throve in the trans-Pecos, are a handful fostered by the game wardens of the Guadalupe Mountains. Pronghorn antelopes, depleted to not more than 2,000 head, are sometimes seen on the game preserves of western and south central Texas.

However, many of the wild animals that the pioneers hunted remain. Texas white-tailed deer have a wide range in south and central parts of the State. Mexican mule or black-tailed deer are found in the Pecos River and Big Bend areas. The small Sonora deer are in the Chisos Mountains On the northern edge of the Panhandle is the Plains white-tailed kind, and a variety believed to be another branch of the true white-tailed deer exists in extreme eastern Texas.

Black bears still live in the mountains of western Texas and in the thickets of the southeast. Wild turkeys are plentiful in certain sections, chiefly in the hilly region of Kimble, Kendall, Kerr, and Gillespie Counties and in central north Texas.

Mountain lions, or cougars, the great enemy of stockmen who annually lose cattle, sheep, goats, and horses to these wary killers, are found in the western mountains and hills. These cats, called panthers in the East, grow to great size in Texas, sometimes measuring seven or eight feet. The jaguarundi, a cat with a long body and tail and short legs, stalks in the underbrush along the Rio Grande. The small Texas bobcat is found in eastern and southern Texas and the plateau bobcat on the Central Plains and western mountains. The ocelot, also called the tiger-cat, is found in the brush of the Rio Grande. The muskhog or collared peccary, a vicious wild hog locally called javelina, is numerous from the Edwards Plateau to the Rio Grande, and also in the Big Bend.

The coyote is still found in almost every part of the State. Often he ventures upon the streets of small towns at night. This animal, the most numerous and pestiferous of the wolf family in Texas, is found in six varieties. Coyotes are so destructive to livestock that they are hunted by clubs of ranchmen and farmers (*see Tour 13a*). The United States Biological Survey helps to exterminate this and other animal pests, including rodents. The gray wolf, or lobo, once a menace on the plains, is extinct.

Texas fur-bearing animals include the red fox, the Florida gray fox, the Swift or Kit fox, the Arizona gray fox, the opossum (three varieties), the raccoon (two varieties), the Mexican badger, the skunk (eight varieties), the large brown mink, one kind of muskrat, two varieties of beavers, and a scant number of east Texas otters. Fox hunting is an east Texas sport.

Texas contains three kinds of jack rabbits, five varieties of small cottontail rabbits, a large mountain cottontail rabbit, and two kinds of marsh rabbits. Prairie dogs have interesting "towns" on the western plains. One of the curious native animals, found over a large part of the State, especially in the hilly regions, is the armadillo, an odd shell-covered creature the size of a large opossum, the ridged shell or armor of which is often used for making baskets. One of the armadillo's peculiarities is that all the young in each litter are of the same sex.

Notable in the rodent family is the Texas cotton rat of the eastern part of the State and the Rhoads cotton mouse of east Texas, which destroy cotton plants, and the rice rats, with which rice growers are said to "raise rice on shares."

Animals that live in trees include eight varieties of squirrels. Of especial interest is the east Texas flying squirrel, a timid creature which spreads its "wings," lateral folds of skin extending from its forelegs to its hindlegs, and sails from branch to branch remarkably like a bird. This animal is found from the Guadalupe River east to the Louisiana border.

Within its boundaries the State has three distinct types of bird life, besides the birds that cross the Rio Grande from Mexico and are in no other area of the United States. Nearly 700 different varieties of birds have been found in Texas. Migratory birds cross the State each year, and many spend the winter. Ducks and geese enter with the first cold weather, and many remain. Texas is the winter home of 22 varieties of ducks, eight of which breed here—the black-bellied tree duck, mottled duck, Mallard, blue-winged and cinnamon teal, shoveller, wood duck, and ruddy duck. Six varieties of geese, including brant, are among the visitors.

The Texas bobwhite, the blue or Arizona scaled quail, Gambel's quail, and Mearns' quail are found in western and southwestern Texas. Doves are numerous and widely distributed. There are two varieties of grouse or prairie chicken, one in west Texas and the Panhandle, and the Attwater variety (found nowhere else in the United States) in southeast Texas. The chachalaca, often called the Mexican pheasant, found in no other part of the United States, lives in the chaparral thickets along the Rio Grande.

The road runner or ground cuckoo, also locally called the chaparral bird, "Texas bird of paradise," and *paisano,* found over the entire middle and western parts of the State, is the clown of the highways. With plumage comically ruffled, this large long-legged bird runs swiftly along the ground instead of flying, and tries to race ahead of automobiles.

The State bird, the sweet-singing mockingbird, is found in two varieties. It is unlawful to kill or capture one.

Texas has all four of the deadly snakes found in the United States. Of the seven varieties of rattlesnakes, the best known is the western diamondback, which sometimes attains a length of nine feet. Along the rivers and lakes are found moccasins or "cottonmouths," and in eastern and central Texas, copperheads. The coral snake is widely distributed. Texas has about one-third of all the harmless varieties of snakes found in the United States.

The best-known Texas lizard is the horned toad, with a scaly body and tail and small horns. A symbol of the West, this little creature is often mounted and sold to tourists.

Alligators are found in the swamps and rivers of east Texas, and often attain great size.

In Texas streams and coastal waters are found 230 kinds of fish, 120 of which are fresh-water varieties. Streams of the Coastal Plain offer the greatest variety of fresh-water fish, of which the favorite is the large-mouthed black bass.

The State of Texas maintains 16 sanctuaries and preserves for the protection of wildlife. The largest is the Boykin-McGee Bend Area of 21,000 acres on the new Sam Rayburn Reservoir in East Texas. The others are Alabama Creek, Bannister Lake, Black Gap, Gus Engeling, Green Island in Laguna Madre, Lake Corpus Christi, Lydia Ann Island, Moore Plantation, Rockport, Second Chain of Islands, South Bird Island in Laguna Madre, Swan Island, Vingt et Un Islands, White Rock Creek, and Wichita County.

In 1963 the U. S. Bureau of Sports Fisheries and Wildlife established its seventh Texas wildlife refuge at Anahuac on the Gulf Coast. This is a wintering spot for Canada and snow geese. The Federal Government maintains the most publicized of the sanctuaries, the Aransas Refuge for the last of the whooping cranes, which travel 2,500 miles to avoid the Canadian winter, and of which fewer than 45 are known. The Laguna Atascosa Refuge on the south Texas coast shelters redheads, pintails and other water fowl. The Santa Ana Refuge of 1,980 acres is considered especially valuable for protecting bird life because of its heavy jungle; the 255 different kinds of birds seen there include the black-bellied treeduck, the chachalaca, the red-bellied pigeon and the green jay.

The U. S. Bureau of Sports Fisheries produces about 3,500,000 fish

History

MONUMENT AT SAM HOUSTON'S GRAVE, HUNTSVILLE.
IT BEARS ANDREW JACKSON'S WORDS: "THE WORLD WILL TAKE
CARE OF HOUSTON'S FAME." POMPEO COPPINI, SCULPTOR

Texas Parade

STEPHEN F. AUSTIN

Senate Chamber, State Capitol

SAM HOUSTON

Senate Chamber, State Capitol

THE ALAMO, SAN ANTONIO

Southern Pacific Railway

SAN JACINTO MEMORIAL, SAN JACINTO BATTLEFIELD
STATE PARK

Texas Parade

OLD AND RESTORED QUARTERS, FORT DAVIS NATIONAL
HISTORIC SITE

National Park Service

HISTORIC LOCOMOTIVE, C. P. HUNTINGTON,
OF SOUTHERN PACIFIC

Southern Pacific Railway

THE ANTE-BELLUM EXCELSIOR HOUSE IN JEFFERSON,
WITH CONTRASTS IN VEHICLES

Texas Tourist Development Agency

AT THE FREEDMAN PLANTATION IN JEFFERSON,
WHERE THE PAST IS RELIVED ON PILGRIMAGE DAYS

Texas Tourist Development Agency

CATTLE BRANDS, PANHANDLE-PLAINS MUSEUM, CANYON

Rothstein photo, Farm Security Administration

annually at five warm-water fish hatcheries in Texas, also supplying streams in adjacent states. It provides information on fish and shellfish, especially shrimp, and works to mitigate the harmful effects of pollution and dredging in the estuaries and bays where they breed.

First Americans

THE earliest definite trace of human life in Texas is associated with a period—perhaps 15,000 years ago—when the North American Continent was cold and a great sheet of ice covered the northern part of what is now the United States. A hunter killed a musk ox near the site of the present town of Colorado. Artifacts associated with the bones of that early kill are described in *Evidence of Early Man in North America,* by Edgar B. Howard.

The earliest known type of Texan has been classed by certain modern scientists as the Folsom man, but he remains a very dim figure in the haze of mystery that envelopes human advent and development here. Not only are his forbears a mystery, but equally so his descendants for thousands of years thereafter.

Some hundreds or possibly thousands of years ago a group called West Texas Cave Dwellers, who were possibly akin to the Basket Makers of New Mexico and Arizona, left behind articles of daily use, in burying places and in layer after layer of debris in dry cave shelters, and these remains are the foundation of all modern knowledge of their existence and habits. The members of this prehistoric group were longheaded (dolichocephalic), short of stature, slightly built, and had dark brown to black hair. The exact age of the relics of these people in the caves of the Big Bend area has not been determined, but by some archeologists is believed to be ancient.

That the West Texas Cave Dweller had developed a fairly high degree of culture is evident from the artifacts discovered in his cave shelters. Some of his net bags are of the same appearance and style as those produced commercially today, and virtually all his textiles and articles made of cordage are of unusual workmanship. Pipes, made of sections of reeds, indicate that he may have been one of the world's first smokers.

So far as is known, the West Texas Cave Dwellers had no written language, but many pictographs—a picture or series of pictures representing an idea—in various states of preservation, are found on the walls of caves and rock shelters. These also exist throughout southwest Texas; they vary in size, from tiny paintings no more than two inches in length and height, to others eight feet in height, with one group 17 feet long.

Petroglyphs, etched into rock walls, while not as numerous as pictographs, are found in the same vicinities. At one point near Shumla an expanse of limestone covering an area of approximately an acre is entirely covered with deep rock carvings.

There is some evidence that one group of the people of the late Basket Maker culture, or of the Cave Dwellers, migrated into central Texas. The prehistoric man of this part of the State left an abundance of bone, shell, and flint implements, but the heavy rainfall of that territory and the open and exposed condition of the mounds made the preservation of perishable objects, such as matting, skins, and wood, virtually impossible, and thus destroyed whatever proof there might have been of his kinship to the trans-Pecos people. It is certain, however, that he was highly skilled in the working of flint.

When the first Europeans reached the wilderness that was later named Texas, they found numerous aboriginal groups. From the north and west had come a type reminiscent of Pueblo culture—perhaps a southern culture of the sort found in the Playas regions of northern Chihuahua and southern New Mexico—whose habits were in strong contrast with those of the non-Pueblo people. They irrigated and cultivated the soil, and lived in adobe houses. Their center of culture was along the Rio Grande in the vicinity of El Paso.

One of the agricultural tribes settled on the banks of the Canadian River, in the Texas Panhandle, where the settlement seems to have flourished for a considerable period, and where stone slabs placed on edge were used for wall foundations. Driven out by the Apaches, they left behind the ruins of their villages and a wealth of artifacts of many kinds. Inquisitive cowboys and later amateur collectors carried away the greater part of these remains.

The Caddoes, whose culture was similar to that of the Mound Builders of the Mississippi Valley, invaded the eastern and northeastern parts of Texas. Although their mounds do not compare in size with those found in Wisconsin or Ohio, they possibly represent the southwestern frontier of the mound builder empire.

They lived over a vast area, extending from the piney woods to the Gulf and westward to middle west Texas. The Caddoes might be called the original "Texans" (see *Southwestern Empire*). They were a friendly people, living in semipermanent villages. It was among these Indians that the Franciscans established their missions in east Texas. The Caddoes included 12 different tribes; they fled Texas in the 1850's, and there are left today on reservations few of the once-powerful Caddoan stock.

Another of the larger groups included the Apaches, a ferocious people. The Lipan group of this tribe made murderous raids, from which they retreated as swiftly as they had come, into their fastnesses in the Edwards Plateau. Not only was there conflict between the Apaches and the whites, but also between the Apaches and the Comanches, until, pressed on the north by both whites and Comanches, the Apaches gradually retired westward and southward, many retreating below the Rio Grande.

But it was the Comanches who caused the settlers the most trouble. They were nomadic people, excellent horsemen, and their specialty was sweeping raids upon defenseless settlers, then a ride back to the limitless plains where they could not be tracked. They continued their depredations until 1875 when they were confined to reservations.

On the Texas coast were the Karankawas and the Attacapas, fish eaters. The Karankawas left numerous kitchen middens in which hacked human bones are found, indicating that they were cannibals. However, Cabeza de Vaca, who lived among them in the early sixteenth century, pictured them as tender-hearted folk, who, seeing the terrible plight of the wanderers "sat among the white men howling like brutes over our misfortunes." If, at that time, they were a kindly tribe, they later gave the Spaniards great trouble and still later were hostile toward the colonists. After a raid on a settlement on the Guadalupe River in 1844 they fled; some of them went to Mexico, and the remainder sought refuge on Padre Island.

Below San Antonio and extending south and east across the Rio Grande were the Coahuiltecans, a people weak in warfare, and among whom the Franciscans made their first converts.

Living in central Texas were the Tonkawas. They were hostile toward other tribes, though friendly to the white settlers. In 1855 the Tonkawas were moved to a reservation, and two years later a large number were killed by other Indians.

The greater part of the trans-Pecos region was occupied by the Mescalero Apaches, perhaps the most consistently warlike and savage of the Texas Indians.

As settlement pushed in from the Atlantic coast, more tribes, driven from their original habitats, retreated to Texas. Chief among these were Cherokees, Alabamas, Seminoles, Kickapoos, and Cooshattis.

A group of the Cherokees as early as 1822 tried to get title from the

Mexican government to land on which they had settled in east Texas. During the Texas Revolution, the temporary government granted them lands between the Sabine and Angelina Rivers. Afterward, Texas refused to ratify the treaty, and this brought on the Cherokee War. Sam Houston, who was an adopted member of the tribe, bitterly denounced the repudiation of the treaty and the explusion of the Cherokees.

After the departure of these Indians in 1839 the Texans had the Plains Indians, notably the Comanches, with whom to deal.

In 1840, it was agreed to hold a council in San Antonio between Texas leaders and Indian chiefs, and the Council House Fight ensued in which the warriors were killed (*see San Antonio*). This episode so inflamed the Comanches that, in August of that year, they made the greatest single raid ever conducted in Texas by Indians. A band of 1,000 warriors swept the valley of the Guadalupe, killing and ravaging. On their retreat the Indians were overtaken and decisively defeated in the Battle of Plum Creek (*see Tour 23b*). After this battle, and with a growing white population, rapid progress was made in pushing the frontier westward despite continued Indian raids.

After the annexation of Texas by the United States, a line of army posts was established along the Rio Grande and northward across the western part of the State to the Red River. These stations would have put an end to Indian troubles had it not been for the disorganization occasioned by the Civil War and the Reconstruction period. Particularly during 1865 and 1866 was the frontier terrorized by Indians.

These raids continued until the late 1870's though many of the Indians had been placed on reservations north of the Red River, and Sherman and Sheridan had marched into Texas and conducted investigations of Indian depredations that resulted in the trials of Chiefs Satank, Satanta, and Big Tree (*see Tour 9a*). Meanwhile General R. S. Mackenzie had been commissioned to round up the Indians and take them back to reservations. His campaign marked the close of Indian warfare.

The great Indian population has vanished, but the survivors have been multiplying in recent decades. In 1920 Texas had 2,109; in 1940, 1,103; in 1950, 2,736. The Census of 1960 found 5,750, of whom 4,101 were urban and 1,649 rural. The only Indian settlement remaining is that of the Alabamas and Cooshattis in the Big Thicket, Polk County.

No clear picture survives today of the Texas Indian as he was in those remote days of buffalo herds, populous villages, and savage power. The true archeology of the State lies in "The tales that dead men tell." Their tales are told by the things they made, used, and left behind hundreds of years ago; and the language in which they speak is comparable with that of the fossils of the lithosphere.

Texas is rich in artifacts. Reminders of the centuries when the Indians occupied the land are found in the mounds of oyster shells they discarded, in the kitchen middens that yield up bones and rocks shaped as utensils. Within recent decades much progress has been made in archaeological research, and numerous collections have become available for study of the prehistoric Southwest. Any inquiry into the living conditions of the pioneers must include the Indians who so often affected the survival of the pioneers.

The best of today's Indian collections are at the universities and colleges. One is the Museum of Anthropology in Pearce Hall at the University of Texas in Austin. Another is the Texas Memorial Museum at the University. Baylor University at Waco has two outstanding collections: the Strecker Museum, and the Texas History Collection. Anthropology enters into the extensive collections of the Witte Museum in San Antonio. The Hall of State in Fair Park, Dallas, has the collection of the Dallas Historical Society. The Big Bend Historical Museum on the grounds of Sul Ross College, Alpine, has an important collection. The West Texas Museum belongs to Texas Technological College at Lubbock. Similarly there is a museum at Southwest Texas State College in San Marcos. The El Paso Centennial Museum is at the University of Texas at El Paso. There are a number of collections associated with former forts, which were outposts on the Indian frontier, among them Fort Belknap, Fort Concho in San Angelo, and the Fort Bliss Museum in El Paso.

Many sites associated with Indian activities are marked and may be visited, although some are off the highways. Remains of cave dwellings are found in Big Bend National Park, and near Shumla, in Eagle Nest Canyon near Langtry, and in Seminole Canyon. Sudan, on US 84 in Lamb County, is near the long ridges of yellow sand where the winds are always uncovering prehistoric remains. The Caddoes and their successors left enough debris in their settlements to keep archaeologists busy many years digging in the Burned Rock Mounds of Bowie County. Near Paint Rock on US 83 in Concho County 1,500 Indian pictographs have been counted. There are pictographs, sites of primitive dwellings, and artifacts innumerable in the Hueco Mountains, just off US 62 out of El Paso. Indeed, there are few areas in Texas that do not have reminders of human occupancy over the centuries, though many of them still lie below the surface of the land.

History

ALONSO ALVAREZ DE PINEDA, searching in 1519 for a direct western water route to India and Cathay, explored the Gulf of Mexico from Florida to Yucatan, mapped the coast line, and sailed into the mouth of the *Rio de las Palmas* (the Rio Grande) to claim part of the lands of the Aztecs for the governor of Jamaica. The Pineda expedition not only made the first map of the Texas coast, but also accomplished the first civilized penetration into the region. As a result, the lower Rio Grande region can claim the distinction of being the second place to be visited by Europeans within the present limits of the United States; Ponce de Leon discovered Florida in 1513.

Rivalry prompted the next two *entradas* (entrances) into Texas. Francisco Garay, former companion of Christopher Columbus, was the rival of Cortés, conqueror of Mexico. Garay in 1520 sent, and in 1523 brought galleons loaded with cavaliers and with soldiers armed with crossbows to the Rio Grande; but Cortés defeated all his plans and his cities were never built. In 1527 the cruel Nuño de Guzmán conducted a slave trade among the natives of the Panuco region, whose kinsmen in the wilderness along the Rio Grande so effectively resisted the Spaniards that exploration of the interior of present-day Texas was halted. The advantages of the new land, all the more enticing because it was unexplored, brought the first strangers to Texas.

In 1528 a few half-dead Spaniards were hurled ashore by the sea somewhere on or near Galveston Island. They were the remnant of the

Narváez expedition to Florida which had met disaster, and were trying, in rude barges, and using their tattered shirts for sails and the manes and tails of their horses for rigging, to reach the Rio de las Palmas. Cabeza de Vaca, of a noble family, told the story.

Savage Karankawas soon surrounded the shipwrecked Spaniards. Cabeza, though held virtually a captive, impressed the Indians with his healing power and became respected and feared among them as a medicine man. In 1535, he and three companions escaped and made their way westward afoot, from tribe to tribe, until they had crossed the continent and had reached a port in the Gulf of California occupied by their countrymen. De Vaca's *Relación,* published in Spain in 1542, was the first descriptive story of the interior of this land claimed by the Spaniards—a hypothetical claim, all the interior being still in the hands of the Indians.

Now, however, began a long and colorful procession of white men into the region called New Spain. There were 92 expeditions from the time of Pineda to the year 1731. In 1541 the *conquistadores* of Coronado marched in, plumed and in coats of mail, fruitlessly seeking the fabulous Gran Quivira which, like the fabled Seven Cities of Cibola, was only an Indian myth. Survivors of the expedition of Don Hernando de Soto wandered, lost, below the lonely banks of the Red River (*see Wichita Falls*). Great though the dangers of hardship were, men seeking gold, land, slaves, or the salvation of human souls continued to cross the Rio Grande. They called the new country by various names—Amichel, the New Philippines, and finally *Tejas,* which in time became Texas.

In February, 1685, the little *Amiable* of the fleet of Robert Cavelier, Sieur de La Salle was wrecked in Matagorda Bay with supplies for a French colony aboard. The Frenchmen founded Fort St. Louis on Garcitas Creek, six small huts clustered about a fort in a rude stockade. This French threat spurred the Spanish settlement of Texas. When the order of Franciscan monks proposed a spiritual conquest of Texas through the establishment of missions, their plan was eagerly adopted. The easternmost Spanish outpost was established on May 25, 1690: the Mission San Francisco de los Tejas, northwest of the present community of Weches near the Neches River (*see Tour 5c*).

By 1731, a dozen missions had been established. Civilizations centered about their heavily buttressed walls, and the presidios or forts built to protect them.

Spanish settlers were persistent hunters, and buffaloes, wild horses, and small game were sources of food and profit. Cattle raising, Indian trading, and the business of smuggling contraband goods through both the Spanish and French frontiers may be said to have been the leading industries. Towns were small and primitive, but the style of life in many of the flat-roofed adobe houses was patterned after the grand manner of European society or the viceregal court in Mexico City. Colonial officials and their ladies had brought jewels and laces to the frontier. They gave lavish entertainments and drank good wine. Members of the lower classes, peons, attempted to copy the grandees. The result was an impermanent, artificial society which left, after more than a hundred years of Spanish occupation (1820), a population of less than 3,000 people, whose actual wealth was very small and whose efforts to develop the region had been confined largely to card tables and ballrooms.

Not so in the missions. There, life was patterned by brown-robed, sandaled monks and arranged to fall into an ordered routine, marked by the ringing of the bells in the chapel towers.

As a Spanish province Texas was ruled by a commandant general, with local councils or *ayuntamientos* presided over by *alcaldes* (civil magistrates with duties resembling those of mayors).

The center of the province, the seat of its civil government and its largest settlement, was San Antonio de Bexar, founded in 1718 (*see San Antonio*). Southeastward 80 miles stood the presidio of Nuestra Señora de Loreto de la Bahia del Espíritu Santo (the present Goliad) and its mission, the former erected on the San Antonio River in 1749. These two, San Antonio and Goliad, were the military strongholds. Nacogdoches, where a mission had been established in 1716, was the eastern outpost.

ERA OF FILIBUSTERERS

Anglo-Americans had long been interested in Texas, to which the absence of a natural barrier between Texas and Louisiana, other than the Sabine River, permitted easy access. Adventure, the desire to escape justice or debt, the lure of wealth waiting to be taken, called to men in the United States whose forefathers had for generations been pushing the frontier forward. It was thus inevitable that filibusterers should enter Texas.

Philip Nolan in 1800 led a party into the province, ostensibly to look for wild horses. Spanish soldiers overtook his force on March 21, 1801, and Nolan was killed.

After the United States acquired Louisiana, in 1803, a writer in New Orleans declared that "the Americans were already spreading out like oil upon a cloth."

For a time the dividing line between Texas and the United States was in dispute and therefore vague. Following the Louisiana Purchase, representatives of the two countries in 1806 set aside a long narrow strip of land between the holdings of their respective governments as the Neutral Ground, thus hoping to avert difficulties over the ownership of the eastern fringe of Texas. Yet shortly afterwards the expedition of Zebulon M. Pike, who was sent into the Southwest by General Wilkinson, served to center the attention of Anglo-American home seekers and adventurers once more upon Texas, a land reported to be rich and desirable. By the Treaty of 1819 between the United States and Spain, all claims to Texas were formally relinquished by the United States.

Meantime, the filibusterers continued their activities. In 1812–13 Bernardo Gutierrez de Lara and Augustus W. Magee invaded Texas, and in 1813 the invaders took San Antonio. During this episode the first Texas newspaper was published in Nacogdoches. The remnant of the expedition met a Spanish force under Joaquin Arredondo near the Medina River in August and was slaughtered, few escaping (*see Tour 9c*). Dr. James Long of Natchez, Mississippi, led two expeditions into Texas in 1819–1821, and proclaimed the independence of the province. His attempt and those of others proved unsuccessful.

Mexico won its independence from Spain in 1821, and Texas, with Coahuila, became a state of the Mexican Republic.

TEXAS UNDER MEXICO

Moses Austin, middle-aged St. Louis banker who had lost his fortune in the panic of 1819, secured in 1820 authority from the Spanish government to settle 300 families in Texas, but soon afterward he died. His son, Stephen, 28, assumed the colonizing task in 1821, and by 1831, had brought in 5,600 Anglo-Americans. The metropolis of the Austin colony was San Felipe de Austin, founded by Stephen Austin in 1823. This colonial town stood on the banks of the *Rio de los Brazos de Dios* (River of the Arms of God).

The life was rigorous, conditions primitive. Here women in drab calico (which sold for 50 cents a yard) stirred "hog and hominy" with home-made wooden spoons, and learned the use of the long rifle. They lived in bare, sometimes windowless, log cabins. Flour was $25 a barrel. Noah Smithwick credited a Texas housewife with the expression, "Texas is a heaven for men and dogs but hell for women and oxen."

Austin required every colonist to present evidence that his character was "perfectly unblemished, that he is a moral and industrious man, and absolutely free from the vice of intoxication." In 1829 he wrote, "You will be astonished to see all our houses with no other fastening than a wooden pin or door latch."

But as immigration increased many arrived who had urgent reasons for so doing. The letters, "G.T.T." were applied in connection with those who had "Gone to Texas" to escape justice. As in any frontier society, the two elements, moral and undesirable, were mingled.

The opening of Texas to colonization came at an opportune time to attract settlers from the United States. The westward movement of immigration in their own country had brought them to the door of Texas. A recent panic had wrecked fortunes, and the promise of economic recovery in a new land was a powerful incentive. Slave owners saw in Texas an opportunity to increase their profits and to hold, without opposition, their human chattels. Thus, the glowing accounts of the early travelers fell upon fertile ground. "A most delicious country," wrote a United States Senator who had visited Texas in 1829. ". . . (A) most delightful champaign (sic) country; dry, pure, elastic air, springs of sweet waters . . ."

Cotton farming was the chief commercial occupation of the settlers, although some of the farmers had formerly been doctors, lawyers, and clerks. They had inherited the instincts of the men who had hewn the Wilderness Road, for in many instances their fathers had helped hew it. Their lives showed the democratic simplicity Thomas Jefferson preached. This type of immigrant, independent, undeviating, individualistic, had come to live in a land claimed and governed by the Latin-American, so temperamentally different—sensitive, circumspect, respectful of tradition, and accustomed to blind obedience to authority.

It was thus inevitable that the question of civil rights should enter the Texas-Mexican relationship. Mexico had obtained its freedom after 300 years of subjection to Spain, and was untrained in self-government. In 1824 it adopted what has been called the most complex form of government ever devised by man. The Federal constitution of that year gave, Mexican authorities believed, the rights of free men to their colonists. But the Anglo-American colonist based his conception of personal rights upon those obtaining in the United States. He particularly resented denial of the right of a trial by jury and—the Roman Catholic faith being compulsory—the absence of religious freedom.

When Austin led the way, the other *empresarios* (colonizers) followed, and in 1829 there were contracts for nearly 7,000 families. Stephen Austin, representing the typical slaveholding, conservative element, was loyal to the Mexican government and strove to reduce the first symptoms of conflict.

A governor of Durango had written that the United States was "not dangerous as a conqueror, but as a greedy, aggressive knave."

Henry Clay attempted to prevent ratification of the Treaty of 1819 whereby the United States relinquished claims to Texas, and this did not lessen Mexico's suspicion and alarm. John Quincy Adams believed that by the terms of the Louisiana Purchase, Texas belonged to the United States. In 1825 he appointed Clay Secretary of State, and together they attempted to persuade Mexico to cede to the United States the territory east of the Rio Grande for one million dollars.

Hayden Edwards, an Anglo-American *empresario,* in 1826 proclaimed the Republic of Fredonia and organized a rebellion, after Mexican authorities had declared his colonization contract void (*see Tour*

22a). This abortive attempt at independence on the part of foreign colonizers was received in Mexico as a danger signal.

On April 6, 1830, a Mexican decree was passed checking further immigration from the United States. The object of the law was to colonize Texas with Mexicans and to distribute Mexican troops throughout the province.

Ill feeling grew. In June, 1832, battles occurred at Anahuac and Velasco between Texas farmers and the Mexican soldiers stationed there to enforce the laws.

THE TEXAS REVOLUTION

As Texas grew it desired a government separate from that of Coahuila, to which it was joined politically in a union which gave Mexicans control of its affairs. A convention was held in San Felipe in October, 1832, at which greater liberties under Mexican law were sought. Another convention was called in San Felipe in 1833, by which a proposed state constitution was adopted to be sent to Mexico for approval, and Austin went to Mexico to present this document and plead for civil rights. He was imprisoned and held for almost two years, three months of which he spent in a former dungeon of the Inquisition. This naturally aggravated the strained relations between the province and the national government.

Meantime, Sam Houston had come to Texas. Houston was a veteran of Andrew Jackson's Indian wars and had been Governor of Tennessee. As a United States Congressman he had won national attention, partly for his brilliance, and partly for the gaudy Indian blankets he wore, he in youth having been adopted by the Cherokees, who had named him *Co-lonneh* (the Raven). Following a disastrous marriage and another sojourn among the Cherokees, Houston at the age of 39 had chosen Nacogdoches as his home, and was quietly practicing law or attending colonial meetings where men spoke strongly of Mexican oppression. Born in Virginia, Houston was nevertheless essentially a product of the stormy Tennessee frontier. He was a natural leader of the aggressive, adventurous, land-hungry pioneers of the type that settled the West.

There were now, in Texas, men who dared to drink a new toast in the taverns of the wilderness: "Liberty and Texas."

A young South Carolina lawyer, William Barret Travis, was earning a reputation as a firebrand. Ladies called him "the gallant captain." Another fire-eater was James Bowie, mighty fighter and hunter whose deeds were already epic along the moving frontier, and whose name had been given to a type of knife which some said his brother Rezin had designed, and which he wielded with deadly skill.

Throughout Texas men like these were holding meetings. In Mexico a broker's son, Antonio Lopez de Santa Anna, who had risen to power, planned the swift subjection of the Texas rebels. Santa Anna became dictator under the title of *El Presidente*. In 1835, he dissolved the legislature of Coahuila and Texas.

The Mexican dictator sent troops northward. Travis went to Anahuac in June, 1835, and drove the Mexican garrison out.

At the psychological moment Austin came home. He had been released from prison, but his health was broken. The founder of the first Anglo-American colony spoke, and this is what he said: "Texas needs peace and local government. Its inhabitants are farmers, they need a calm and quiet life. But how can anyone remain indifferent when our rights, our all, appear to be in jeopardy?"

A Committee of Safety organized at Bastrop on the Colorado, May 17, 1835. Other committees organized.

The first clash of the Texas struggle occurred Octoger 2, 1835, when an assortment of farmers at Gonzales (*see Tour 23b*) defeated a Mexican force sent to take the town's cannon. A volunteer army gathered; they had squirrel guns, hunting knives, butcher knives. Smithwick, a soldier there, wrote, "I cannot remember that there was any distinct understanding as to the position we were to assume toward Mexico. Some were for independence, some for the Constitution of 1824 and some for anything, just so it was a row. But we were all ready to fight."

On October 9 a force of about 50 Texas volunteers captured the important fort at Goliad and seized $10,000 worth of military supplies. Stephen F. Austin was appointed commander in chief of the Texas army on October 10, and on October 12 Austin's army marched toward San Antonio. They numbered about 700, and not even the eloquence of Sam Houston, who believed the war was premature, could turn them from their purpose.

San Antonio was besieged by the Texans. On October 28 about 90 men led by James Bowie and James W. Fannin, Jr., defeated about 400 Mexicans who had surrounded them at the old mission of Concepcion, near Bexar. The engagement lasted less than half an hour.

Meantime, a "consultation" met at San Felipe on November 3, 1835, and issued a declaration of causes of war. A provisional government was adopted.

In the United States, young men were reading with interest a poster sent out by Sam Houston: "Volunteers from the United States will . . . receive liberal bounties of land. . . . Come with a good rifle, and come soon. . . . Liberty or death! Down with the usurper!"

Cincinnati, New Orleans, and Louisville became recruiting stations for volunteers.

There was a great frontiersman in the ragged Texas army, who heard the soldiers murmuring at an order to lift the siege of San Antonio. Ben Milam's voice suddenly rang out, "Who'll go with old Ben Milam into San Antonio?"

The answer they gave him is a Texas classic. They went, most of them with "old Ben Milam" (who was only 44) into Bexar, and on December 9, 1835, they took the city. Milam had been killed.

When the defeated Mexican army withdrew, the Texans thought the war was over.

But in Saltillo Santa Anna was assembling a large force. He burned candles to the Virgin of Guadalupe and robbed the church to hire soldiers. He flew into a frenzy and shouted, "If the Americans do not beware I shall march through their own country and plant the Mexican flag in Washington."

Travis had been ordered to the Alamo, the old mission at Bexar which had become a fort. On February 23, 1836, Santa Anna and his legions arrived at San Antonio.

During this period, bitter political controversies prevented the orderly supervision of military affairs in Texas, and the soldiers in San Antonio under Travis and Bowie, their leaders convinced that the Alamo must be held in order that Santa Anna's march into the interior might be blocked, had been left upon their own resources. Among the defenders was David Crockett, noted frontiersman and statesman of Tennessee. James Butler Bonham, another of the ragged little garrison, a lifelong friend of Travis, had borrowed the money to come to Texas that he might fight for its freedom. There were between 185 and 200 fighting men in the Alamo, most of them volunteers.

Before the Texans shut themselves inside the walls of the fort, some 20 or 30 noncombatants sought refuge there. Mrs. Susanna Dickerson (often inaccurately called Dickenson), wife of the artillery captain, and her infant daughter Angelina, were among the refugees. A blood red flag, the flag of no quarter, was hoisted by Santa Anna. This, and his demand for an unconditional surrender, were answered by the Texans with a cannon shot.

Travis' appeals for aid went unanswered except by 32 brave men of Gonzales, who marched in even after the doom of the fort seemed certain. Thirty-seven years later a story was published, as having been told soon after the battle by one who claimed to have escaped following the incident, that Travis, when hope of further aid had been abandoned, drew a line with his sword and asked all who would stay and die with him to cross it. For a number of reasons, most historians regard this, as, at best, a legend —and the heroism of the men of the Alamo needs no garnishing. They were there of their own choice. They remained, when they could have fled. They died.

For at daybreak of March 6, while the exhausted Texans slept (the

Mexican bombardment, which had been almost continuous, had temporarily ceased, thus offering a brief respite), nearly 3,000 of Santa Anna's more than 5,000 troops were unleashed against the Alamo, as the dreadful notes of the *deguello,* the no-quarter bugle call of Spain, sounded from the battery where the Mexican general waited.

Still a little dazed from sleep, the Texans sprang to their posts, and in the terrific fighting that followed, the Mexicans were twice repulsed as the long rifles of the frontiersmen, the farmers, the "Tennessee boys" under Crockett, took a dreadful toll. The steady fire of small arms and cannon resembled "a constant thunder." Travis fell as the third attack of the Mexicans succeeded in gaining a breach in the walls. The Mexicans now penetrated into the interior of the fortress, as the defenders fought them "muzzle to muzzle, hand to hand, musket and rifle, bayonet and bowie knife." A Mexican soldier wrote, "The Texians defended desperately every inch of the fort."

At last, however, overwhelming numbers prevailed. Most authorities agree that Crockett died beside the post he had been assigned to defend, although there is a story that he was one of several prisoners who, after the battle, were ordered shot by Santa Anna. Bowie, who had shared the command with Travis at first, only to fall ill after the siege had begun, was killed on his cot—fighting. There were 187 known victims among the Texans; no male defender survived. Santa Anna ordered the bodies burned. The 15 or more who were spared were women and children, slaves and servants.

Mexican losses are estimated at between 600 and 800. The battle, according to Santa Anna's official report, lasted more than an hour and a half. Because of the sacrifice made by the Texans and its subsequent results, the Alamo has become known as the shrine of Texas liberty (*see San Antonio*).

On March 2, 1836, the Texas Declaration of Independence was adopted by a convention of colonists at Washington on the Brazos River, a constitution was framed and adopted on March 17, and an ad interim government named.

Santa Anna moved swiftly to complete the conquest of Texas. The entire command (275 men) of Colonel James W. Fannin, Jr., surrendered of necessity on March 20 at the Coleto, to Mexicans under General Urrea. They were taken to Goliad, and about 330 men, including Fannin, were shot at Santa Anna's bidding (March 27). Colonel Ward's force, captured at Victoria March 24, was also massacred with Fannin's command (*see Tour 25b*).

The Mexican dictator took the field and the "Runaway Scrape"—the flight of Texas families—began. Women and children toiled across muddy prairies toward the Sabine as General Houston, in command of the Texas army, Fabianly retreated eastward. Historic San Felipe was burned by the Texans. Forty days passed while Houston played a game with Santa Anna, always maneuvering out of his reach. At last they were both in the bayou country near the present city of Houston. "Old Sam" addressed his men, and gave them in 16 words the slogan which won what has been listed among the decisive battles of the world: "Victory is certain! Trust in God and fear not! And remember the Alamo! Remember the Alamo!"

They took up the battle cry, "Remember the Alamo!" Someone added, "Remember Goliad!" and with these vengeful words in their mouths they marched to meet the Mexican army.

At the junction of Buffalo Bayou and the San Jacinto River the two forces met. The first day, April 20, was spent in skirmishing; the next day, too, seemed likely to pass without a serious clash. But at 3:30 in the afternoon, when many Mexican officers and men were enjoying a siesta, Houston suddenly gave a command to fall in. The Texans, weaving their way unseen through the long grass, were within point-blank range of the Mexican lines when Houston waved his old campaign hat. It was a signal, and the Texans, shouting, "Remember the Alamo! Remember Goliad!" stormed through the Mexican barricade. The Mexicans awakened in the wildest confusion to stand a moment before an irresistible force of hate and vengeance, and then either to flee or to fall. The battle became a rout, a shambles; and on the next day, Santa Anna, his army dead or prisoners, was brought in disguised as a peon. Houston, wounded, received him (*see Tour 6a*).

Houston reported that nearly 1,400 Mexicans opposed him. The Texans had nearly 1,000. Houston said the battle lasted only 18 minutes; 630 Mexicans were killed, and 730 taken prisoner. The Texans lost 9 dead and 34 wounded.

THE REPUBLIC

For ten years Texas was an independent nation—from March 2, 1836, the date of the declaration, to February 16, 1846, when it became the twenty-eighth State in the Union.

At its first national election, Sam Houston was chosen President of the Republic of Texas, and it was voted to seek annexation to the United States. Houston was inaugurated October 22, 1836.

Grave problems faced the Republic. The country was ravaged by war, the treasury was empty, the government was "land poor," with few sources of revenue other than quantities of cheap public land. The first Congress of the Republic in October, 1836, organized national and local government along typically United States lines.

In 1839 the homestead law was passed, providing that a man's home and implements could not be taken to satisfy a judgment. But the inducement of cheap land was sufficient to cause rapid settlement. By 1846 the frontier had moved west of the present cities of Fort Worth, Waco, Austin, and San Antonio. Land scrip entitled the holder to a section of land at 50 cents an acre. Frauds and land schemes led to confusion and even to bloodshed, which the General Land Office, established in 1837, failed to control. Financial expedients of the Republic included paper money. Yet the nation, beset by raiding Indians and threatened constantly by Mexico, continued unaided on its way. Public education was provided for in 1839–40 (*see Education*). The United States acknowledged the independence of Texas in 1837, France in 1839, and England and Holland in 1840.

The Texas Rangers, a body of fighting men organized in 1835, which, one writer said, "could ride like Mexicans, shoot like Tennesseeans, and fight like the very devil," protected the frontier. They were arrayed against the Indians, raiding Mexicans, and bands of outlaws.

In 1841 Texas attempted to extend jurisdiction over New Mexico, but the Santa Fé expedition ended in disaster. An invading Mexican army in 1842 took San Antonio, but following the Battle of the Salado, September 18, the Mexican force withdrew.

The Mier expedition marched on Mexico in November, 1842. Forced to surrender, the Texans were ordered to draw beans from a pot, and a tenth of the force—all who had drawn black beans—were shot.

ANNEXATION

Texas was becoming a blend of the South and the West, hardly a fusion of the two, yet having sections populated by men and women newly arrived from the other American frontiers, or from the slave-holding sections. Opponents of slavery in the United States, therefore, bitterly contested the annexation of Texas, while the South sought the entrance of another slave State.

The increasing economic development of the Republic and the threat that England, desiring a new source of cotton supply, would acquire Texas, influenced United States sentiment in favor of annexation. White population in the Republic increased from about 30,000 in 1836 to 102,-961 in 1846, and small farms were appearing in isolated sections. The first Texas railroad was projected in 1836, although it failed to materialize; wagon trains were rutting the prairies, bringing the elements of wealth with them.

After the prolonged national controversy during which a treaty of annexation was defeated in the United States Senate and the question became a Presidential campaign issue, Texas was offered annexation upon these terms: (1) it was to be annexed not as a territory, but as a State; (2) public lands of the State were to be retained and never to be surrendered to the Federal government, as in the case of other States; (3)

Texas was to pay its public debts; (4) if desired later, Texas might divide itself into as many as five States. This proposal was adopted by a joint resolution of both Houses of Congress of the United States, March 1, 1845.

July 4, 1845, a convention met in Austin and approved the annexation resolution, and thus Texas virtually became a State in the Union on that date. The people ratified the State constitution on October 13, 1845, and the Congress of the United States, by joint resolution (approved December 29, 1845), voted admittance into the Union. The first session of the legislature of the new State opened in Austin on February 16, 1846, and J. P. Henderson was inaugurated the first Governor. On that date the flag of the Republic with its single star was lowered, and the Stars and Stripes unfurled as Anson Jones, the last President of Texas, declaimed: "The Republic of Texas is no more."

STATEHOOD

Mexico had threatened that it would regard the annexation of Texas as a declaration of war by the United States. It now prepared to settle the question of Texas once more on the battlefield.

General Zachary Taylor marched his army toward the Rio Grande in March, 1846. The first battle of the Mexican War was fought on Texas soil at Palo Alto, about eight miles from Brownsville, on May 8.

When the Treaty of Guadalupe Hidalgo was signed on February 2, 1848, a major controversy arose over the State's boundaries. Mexico recognized the independence of Texas and accepted the Rio Grande as the boundary, and the United States acquired from Mexico a vast region from the Gila River to the forty-second parallel, and from the Pacific to the Rio Grande. Texas laid claims to a large part of this region—all the territory east of the Rio Grande.

In March, 1848, the State legislature passed a statute creating the County of Santa Fé, which included the region between the Pecos River and the Rio Grande and extending north to the forty-second parallel in what is now the State of Wyoming. Territory thus claimed by Texas embraced some 100,000 square miles, including parts of the present States of New Mexico, Oklahoma, Kansas, Wyoming, and Colorado.

Texas was a slave State, yet parts of the area involved, notably in the region of Santa Fé, New Mexico, opposed slavery, so that this and other conditions made Santa Fé County a national issue. In 1850 a compromise was effected, ending threats on the part of Texas that it would enforce its claims with arms. The State was paid $10,000,000 to surrender the disputed territory. New boundaries, virtually those of today, were fixed.

Because of its boundaries on three rivers, all of which are subject to violent floods and changes of course, Texas has had more boundary litigation than any other State. Even the compromise of 1850 did not settle the question. The Rio Grande especially refused to stay in a fixed channel (*see El Paso*).

Red River controversies, also caused largely by floods and the changing course of the river, have been notable for bitterness and bloodshed. One of them, the Greer County case, based upon the disputed location of the river's main fork, resulted in the loss from Texas to what is now Oklahoma of 1,511,576 acres of land.

Following the award of $10,000,000 in the 1850 boundary issue, Texas was able to clear its credit. The State emerged upon a period of internal development. A new constitution had been written in 1845, conformable to statehood. It provided for free public schools, one-tenth of the general revenues of the State being set apart for school purposes. By 1850, the population of the State had become 212,592.

The Federal government garrisoned at least 19 forts in the State for the protection of the people against Indians. Clashes between Texans and Mexicans continued, culminating in the capture of Brownsville in 1859 by Juan Cortinas, a Mexican border outlaw (*see Tour 9c*).

In 1848 the public domain was estimated at about 181,965,332 acres. The State used this wealth of land to obtain schools, railroads, and public institutions. Colonizers, offered rich land grants, brought foreign settlers to Texas, including the French socialists of Considerant's colony near Dallas, and Castro's colony in Castroville, also French. The Germans settled many communities, notably New Braunfels and Fredericksburg. It was necessary to create 89 new counties in the 1850's.

Before 1860 the population was almost entirely rural. Since the South had embraced the cause of annexation, politics in the State leaned heavily in that direction: "We are all Democrats in Texas," wrote Guy M. Bryan in 1845. The Know-Nothing Party had gained strength by 1855. The northeastern part of the State was developing rapidly, with most of the Mexicans, Germans, and scattered ranchers in west Texas. East of Waco and Fort Worth the tide of newcomers was tremendous. The first overland mail coach left San Antonio for San Diego on August 9, 1857.

THE CIVIL WAR AND RECONSTRUCTION

In February, 1861, the people of Texas, by popular vote, ratified an ordinance of secession. Sam Houston, who had become Governor in 1859, opposed secession and refused to subscribe to an oath supporting the constitution of the Confederacy. His office was declared vacant and he was deposed. A lonely and impoverished old man, he lived to see his star rise once more, feebly, when friends solicited him to run for the governorship in 1863; but he declined, and on July 26 of that year he died. The struggle between Houston and Austin had led to strange ends: Austin lost to

Houston in 1835 when Texas broke with Mexico, but before he died Houston had lost to the element which Austin typified.

Protected from the war by geography, Texas saw few major Civil War engagements. The Battle of Galveston in 1863 (*see Galveston*), and the Battle of Sabine Pass (*see Tour 5c*), served to prevent invasion by way of the coast. Sentiment in some sections was divided, and about 2,000 Texans enlisted in the Union army. Texas furnished the Confederacy huge amounts of supplies obtained from Europe through Mexico, besides those from its own resources. Crops were good.

The last land engagement of the war was fought on Palmito Hill, May 12–13, 1865.

On June 19, 1865, General Gordon Granger landed at Galveston and, in the name of the Federal government, proclaimed all slaves free and all laws enacted since 1861 null and void.

The "Radicals," or those of Northern sympathy, rose to power in State politics, and the Freedmen's Bureau and Union Leagues were created. Race riots flared, the Ku Klux Klan rode, and lawlessness gripped the State as thousands of freed Negroes, cast adrift, congregated in towns and near military camps, existing by begging or by occasionally doing odd jobs. In 1860, the assessed valuation of slaves in Texas was $64,000,000. Most of these Negroes fondly believed that the government would give them "forty acres and a mule."

From 1865 to 1869 Texas was under military government. In the latter year a constitution was framed by a convention called under the Reconstruction Acts of 1868. It created equal suffrage for whites and Negroes and made elaborate provisions for a free school system.

Largely through the effort of the Freedmen's Bureau, most of the freed Negroes had gone to work by 1866.

The legislature, in 1870, ratified the Thirteenth, Fourteenth and Fifteeth Amendments to the Constitution of the United States. Six weeks later, on March 30, the United States Congress readmitted Texas as a State of the Union.

The opposition of conservative citizens to the radical regime of Governor E. J. Davis led. to the "capture" of the legislative hall by Democrats, in 1874, and the inauguration of a conservative regime under Governor Richard Coke. Davis' appeal to President Grant for Federal troops to reinstate his government failed, and with the retirement of the radical leader Reconstruction ended in Texas (January 17, 1874). In spite of turmoil the State had prospered, and by 1870 population had gained 35 per cent over a ten-year period (from 604,215 in 1860 to 818,579 in 1870).

THE TRAIL DRIVERS AND THE CONQUEST
OF THE FRONTIER

The broad prairies of south, east and southwest Texas were being slowly settled by ranchmen before the Civil War. Texas found itself impoverished at the conclusion of the war, but with more than three million head of cattle on its ranges. Then the bold plan to drive cattle to distant markets was conceived (*see Agriculture and Livestock*). Cattlemen became acquainted with the unpopulated plains region as the business of the trails grew into a hundred million dollar enterprise. The Indians, who had retarded settlement westward, were subdued in 1875, and settlement of the Panhandle and the western plains began. The Rio Grande at last actually became the frontier.

Barbed wire was successfully introduced into Texas in 1876. The free range that had fostered the great herds of early days was doomed by this invention, also by the coming of the homesteaders. Cattle barons, enraged at the encroachment of sheep ranchers or farming "nesters" upon their former pastures, started the Fence-cutting War. Cattle thieves or "rustlers" also learned to cut fences. As the ranchers adopted barbed wire it became apparent that protection was necessary. They organized the Stock Raisers Association of Northwestern Texas, which later became the Texas and Southwestern Cattle Raisers Association. Texas Rangers attempted to curb the bitterness and bloodshed of the Fence-cutting War, but fence riders continued to patrol the barbed wire boundaries of big ranches until a law against fence cutting was passed in 1884.

To meet the needs of a period of great growth and expansion, a new constitution was framed in 1876. The registration of voters was abolished, and the supremacy of the people was assured in various provisions of the constitution, which remains in effect today.

A rapid and large influx of people and of capital swept into Texas in the seventies and eighties. Railroads outranked all other public enterprises. There was no system of regulation, and scandals developed.

The fight made by James Stephen Hogg (later Governor) upon the railroads was prompted by the farmers of Texas, who were known then in State politics through an organization called the Patrons of Husbandry, or the "Grangers." Agrarian leaders found another medium in the Populist or People's Party, the membership of which they controlled. Populist strength was greatest in 1896, but declined after 1900. The agrarian movement in Texas was cemented by this party. During its heyday, socialistic camp meetings were held by its members. Another effect of the railroad reform movement was the development of the Progressives, as Governor Hogg's political faction was called.

The railroads, more than any other single influence of their period, helped conquer the last State frontiers. Settlers followed the course of the new roads west.

Governor Hogg led the list of governors of this period who secured vigorous reforms. Notable among the measures passed were the anti-trust laws. Texas was the second State to pass such a law, in 1889, and the next year the Federal government passed a similar measure, the Sherman Anti-Trust Act.

Meantime, the period between the close of the Civil War and the mid-nineties was productive of "bad men" of all descriptions. The cattle trails, border disturbances and, chiefly, Reconstruction, all contributed their quota of gentlemen with notches on their guns. John Wesley Hardin and Sam Bass were probably the most notorious of the lot.

The Rough Riders, Theodore Roosevelt's famous volunteers, were trained in San Antonio, but other than a generous contribution of man-power, the Spanish-American War affected Texas but little.

THE TWENTIETH CENTURY

Since 1900 the development of Texas has been largely industrial and agricultural. The increase of railroad mileage, the construction of good roads, the development of irrigation and of farming generally in sections formerly devoted to the livestock industry or not used at all, caused the remarkable growth of the State and established its modern character. Texas grew up in the years from 1900 to 1920.

With a population in 1900 of 3,048,710, 82 per cent of which was rural, the State had recovered from the depression caused by the Civil War and the money panics of 1873 and 1893. Farms in the State were worth four times more than in 1880, and manufactures in 1899 totaled more than $90,000,000.

On September 8, 1900, a hurricane and tidal wave took about 6,000 lives in the city of Galveston. As a $20,000,000 loss was counted, the need of extraordinary measures to cope with the emergency was recognized. A local committee was given full authority to rehabilitate the city. They performed their duties so successfully that in 1901 Galveston applied for a new charter which would permit five commissioners to conduct the local government. The commission form of city government grew out of this experiment.

Pioneers at the opening of the century were cotton and wheat farmers, pushing the agricultural frontier into west Texas and northwestward into the Panhandle. At the time of the Civil War the cotton belt in Texas ended at the outskirts of Fort Worth and San Antonio. By 1900 cotton was being produced on the South Plains. Irrigation was a later develop-ment, notably of the Lower Rio Grande Valley.

Texas population has been greatly urbanized since 1900. By 1920 the number of urban communities had almost doubled, and in the next ten years this type of population grew from 32.4 per cent to 41 per cent. Texas lost its frontier character in the march of people to the cities. Consumer industries multiplied in consequence. With the exploitation of petroleum in the 20th century entirely new categories of workers appeared.

James E. Ferguson became Governor in 1915 as the champion of small farmers and aid for rural schools, and was reelected for a second term. His leniency toward criminals by frequent paroles stirred opposition, and this and other policies led to his impeachment in August, 1917. He was tried by the Senate, found guilty and removed from office. The lieutenant governor, William P. Hobby, succeeded him and was elected Governor for the next term, defeating Ferguson in the primaries. What became known as Fergusonism remained a live issue. Mrs. Miriam A. Ferguson, the former Governor's wife, entered the primary contest in 1924 and was elected, largely on opposition to the militant Ku Klux Klan. Women had voted in Texas since 1918. Mrs. Ferguson was defeated for reelection, but ran successfully again in 1932. During her term the prohibition law was changed to permit of 3.2 per cent alcohol in beer and wine. She reentered the primaries in 1940 but was outvoted, and the political controversy over "Pa and Ma" Ferguson ended.

Prohibition of alcoholic beverages became a political issue in 1886 and disturbed the State for decades, especially during national prohibition. Smuggling operations on the Coast and the Mexican border led to raids and murders. The 18th Amendment of 1933 disposed of the smuggling, but many communities in Texas voted for local option. Beer and distilled spirits may not be sold in 119 counties; in 16 counties only 4% beer is legal. In 122 counties distilled spirits may be served.

From 1912 on revolutions in Mexico created disturbances on the border. Mobilization of National Guard regiments converted the Texas side of the Rio Grande into a huge armed camp. By 1914 60,000 troops were quartered at Fort Bliss; it became the largest cavalry post, base of the First U. S. Cavalry Division. The raid of Francisco (Pancho) Villa on Columbus, New Mexico, in March, 1916, led to Pershing's punitive expedition into Mexico.

To the mild winter climate of Texas was due the erection of cantonments in and near most of the larger cities during World War I, and the State teemed with military activities. Nearly 210,000 Texans served. The two Texas divisions, the Thirty-sixth and the Ninetieth, participated in the fighting at St. Mihiel and in the Argonne Forest. Texas troops were in the Forty-second Division, which participated in the final battles.

During World War II the capacities of Texas as a great training camp were fully realized. About 1,250,000 troops trained at 15 posts and camps; 542,000 Texans served in the United States Army, and 750,000 in all services, including the Air Force, the Naval Air Force, the U. S.

Marines, and the U. S. Navy. The Army reported 15,764 Texans dead or missing; 8,403 were killed in action, 1,166 died of wounds. The Marines and Coast Guard had 3,023 killed in action.

Texas claimed a liberal quota of the top brass, starting with General Eisenhower, incontestably a native son, although taken to Kansas during the first year of his life. Admiral Chester W. Nimitz came from Fredericksburg and eleven other admirals called Texas their home state. A distinguished record was chalked up by Colonel Oveta Culp Hobby of Houston as organizer and first director of the Women's Army Auxiliary Corps, later the Women's Army Corps, and afterward first Secretary of the Department of Health, Education & Welfare, 1953–1955.

Since World War II the military installations have multiplied. Most of the active Army matters in Texas, Arkansas, Louisiana, Oklahoma and New Mexico are controlled by Fourth U. S. Army headquarters, Fort Sam Houston, San Antonio. Fort Bliss, El Paso, has an Air Defense Center where missile men are trained. In 1945 the German missile scientists led by Werner von Braun arrived there. The Third U. S. Army Corps and several Armored Divisions are at Fort Hood, near Killeen. Helicopter aviators are trained at Fort Wolters, near Mineral Wells. There are 16 Air Force bases in Texas, where every form of defense is represented. The most modern installation is the U. S. Manned Spacecraft Research Center in Harris County near Houston.

Government

THAT rugged spirit which built the first Anglo-American town in the wilderness was the heritage of Texas lawmakers, and the government of the State still wears the brand of the freedom-loving, expansively energetic men of the frontier.

First as a Spanish province, then as a Mexican state, and as an American republic, Texas' early government was adjusted to suit the character of the ruling element.

The Constitution of the State of Texas declares that "all political power is inherent in the people, and all free governments are founded on their authority, and instituted for their benefit. The faith of the people of Texas stands pledged to the preservation of a republican form of government, and, subject to this limitation only, they have at all times the inalienable right to alter, reform or abolish their government in such manner as they think expedient."

This is the fourth constitution of Texas. When Texas declared its independence at Washington on the Brazos March 2, 1836, the leaders drafted their first constitution and adopted it March 17. Another constitution was written before the Republic joined the United States and adopted in an election in 1845. The present constitution was adopted by vote of the people February 15, 1876. The Bill of Rights provides safeguards similar to those in the Constitution of the United States and "is excepted out of the general powers of government, and shall forever remain inviolate, and all laws contrary thereto . . . shall be void."

In Texas the people vote regularly on amendments to the State Constitution, which are submitted after the Legislature has voted to do so. Thus a great body of legislation that in other states is enacted under the powers given representatives is passed on directly by the people; there have been elections when as many as a dozen amendments have been submitted.

In 1905 political abuses led to the adoption of the Terrell Election Law. This abolished the old convention system of selecting party nominees, and created instead the primary election. Under this system candidates are named in primary elections held in July of even-numbered years. Failing a majority vote, the two highest candidates enter a second or "runoff" primary, held in August. In November the general election is held. Public interest, however, centers on the primaries, which are the real test.

The State Government of Texas is based on a constitution adopted in 1876 and amended many times since. Its administrative branch consists of the Governor, elected for two years in January of odd years and paid $25,000 annually; the Lieutenant Governor, the Attorney General, the Comptroller of Public Accounts, the Treasurer, the Commissioner of the General Land Office, the Commissioner of Agriculture, the Railroad Commission (three members), and the State Board of Education (21 members elected by 21 districts). The Governor appoints boards and commissions with special powers.

The Legislature has a Senate, with 31 members who serve four years and are paid $4,800, plus $12 per day for 120 days and 30 days of special sessions, and 10c a mile for travel; and a House of Representatives of 150 who receive the same pay. The Legislature convenes for a two-year session on the second Tuesday in January on odd years.

The judiciary of Texas comprises the State Supreme Court of the Chief Justice and eight Associate Justices elected for six-year terms; the Court of Criminal Appeals of five justices elected for six years. The Court appoints two judges to two-year terms as a Commission to Assist the Court. Both courts meet in Austin. There are thirteen Courts of Civil Appeals, each of three justices elected for four years and meeting in their respective districts. Justices of the Supreme Court and of the Criminal Appeals Court receive $20,000 annually; justices of the Civil Appeals courts earn $16,000: judges of the District Courts earn $12,000. There are more than 100 district courts. There also are county courts, justices of the peace, and police courts.

Texas is represented in the Congress of the United States by two senators and 23 Representatives, one of whom is elected at large. The Federal Government collects more than $4.2 billion in taxes in Texas and expends more than $4.5 billion annually, more than $1.2 billion of it in military contracts.

The State is divided into 254 counties which are the principal administrative units. Each county has a commissioners court consisting of four commissioners elected from individual precincts and an elective county judge. Cities of 5,000 or more population may govern themselves under a home-rule charter; smaller places are under the general laws of the State. The form of city government varies. The independence of local government in Texas often leads to wide discrepancies in such matters as taxes. Where one county may assess its property at 50 per cent of its true value, an adjoining county may use a 25 per cent basis. In 1965 175 cities had adopted home-rule charters and 130 had appointed city managers.

The Texas Legislature controls taxes and expenditures of the State. A provision in the constitution prohibits deficit financing and the appropriation of more funds than anticipated revenue. Representatives from rural areas, who occupy many seats in the Legislature, are generally conservative in their attitude toward appropriations and taxes. Texas does not have a corporate or personal income tax. It has a corporation franchise tax imposed on the invested capital, surplus, and long-term debt of a corporation to the extent that it does business in Texas. In 1961 the Legislature adopted a limited sales, excise and use tax of 2 per cent, with exemptions.

It takes more than $2.5 billion to run the State Government. This is wholly apart from expenditures by other political divisions—counties, towns, cities, school districts. The State balances its books by receipts of nearly a similar amount. In round numbers, the State appropriates about $500,000,000 for free school and vocational education, $450,000,000 for highways, $115,000,000 for higher education, $73,000,000 for eleemosynary and correctional institutions, $250,000,000 for public welfare and pays about $18,000,000 on the public debt.

It is illuminating to see where the tax receipts of about $1 billion (exclusive of license and registration fees) come from. The largest income, more than $200,000,000 comes from the tax on distributors of motor fuel gasoline. Almost as large is the return from the sales tax. The tax on oil production brings in around $125,000,000, and the natural and casinghead gas tax returns $66,000,000. The consumption of cigarettes aids the State by around $90,000,000 whereas liquor, wine, beer and ale return only $40,000,000. The motor vehicle tax brings in around $40,000,000.

Texas adopted a poll tax as a condition for voting by an amendment to the constitution in 1902, ordering that a receipt for a tax of $1.50 must be produced when voting. In 1964 the 24th amendment to the United States Constitution outlawed a poll tax in national elections. This did not affect the poll tax in state elections. Federal court action eventually abolished the poll tax for all elections. The Legislature then enacted a law requiring free annual registration for voting. Registration is made between October 1 and January 31 through the registrar of voters, who is the county tax assessor-collector. The registrar designates deputies and may approve a ballot by mail. The State reimburses the county for registration costs by paying 25¢ per registration. In 1967 2,982,862 voters were registered, Harris County leading with 529,690, Dallas County second with 341,623.

In Texas the penalties for crime are assessed by the juries which bring in verdicts, unless the defendant waives the jury and pleads guilty. In all cases in which the death penalty can be exacted, a jury must be impaneled to assess the penalty. There are a greater number of legal justifications for homicide than in some other States, many of them dating from frontier days when men, if they were to survive, often needed to "pack their own law in a holster." In explanation of a not uncommon attitude toward some of those responsible for violent deaths, a highly respected Texas jurist—not stating what the procedure ought to be but what it was—once said: "In Texas the first question to be decided by a jury in any homicide case is, 'Should the deceased have departed?' "

Texas normally votes Democratic in national elections. It voted heavily for Grover Cleveland in 1884, 1888, and 1892, and similarly supported William Jennings Bryan in 1896, 1900, and 1908. The Peoples (Populist) Party, with its demands for lifting the farmer's burdens, had a large following in Texas at the turn of the century, when it also nominated Bryan. In 1912 Texas voted for Woodrow Wilson; it remained faithful to the Democratic party until 1928, when it approved Herbert Hoover over Alfred E. Smith. After that it added heavily to the Roosevelt landslide, for the Depression had made deep inroads into Texas prosperity. It backed Truman, but when Dwight D. Eisenhower ran it switched to the Republican column and rolled up more than 1,000,000 votes for him. Subsequently the State voted majorities for John F. Kennedy, Lyndon B. Johnson and Hubert Humphrey.

Industry, Commerce, and Labor

IN THE 1960 decade Texas held its own as one of the most prosperous states in the Union, with practically everybody who could hold or wanted a job at work, and the percentage of unemployment lower than that of the whole country. This situation developed in spite of mechanization that substantially lowered the number of jobs available, especially on farms. The shortage of labor, if any, was in the cities, where business and the professions had more openings than the available manpower could fill.

On the Gulf Coast, the petrochemical industry was expanding in numerous fields, with practically no sizable additions to its manpower. Automation had done its work so well that the industry as a whole used only workers with scientific training, able to control the complicated machines. The quality of labor had increased; the numbers in the chemical field, third largest manufacturer, were proportionately fewer than in 1957.

On the farms the owners had adjusted themselves to a difficult situation when the Braceros, or Mexican migrants, were prohibited from returning to do seasonal work. This supply of cheap labor dried up when the Federal law permitting the entry of migrants ended December 31, 1964. It is still possible to employ foreign labor, but the employer must guarantee a job of one year's duration before the U. S. Immigration and Naturalization Service will grant a visa. Consequently the farmers had to employ Texas manpower—at better wages—or increase harvesting by machines. Up to then Texas annually had sent seasonal labor to other states; now farm jobs opened up at home. Farm owners, however, rushed to mechanize. Cotton picking is now 85 per cent mechanized. The effect can be seen in the shift of seasonal labor from fall to summer. Tomatoes are 40 per cent mechanized. Potatoes, beets, beans and spinach, all crops that produce big income, are partially mechanized. The man with the hoe, who used to put in many burdensome hours weeding garden truck, now sits on a vehicle and spreads herbicide. His numbers are fewer, and many of his former associates have had to learn new skills.

With such shrinkage of jobs in certain industries, whence comes the increase? By expansion elsewhere. This can be understood when it is seen that the index of business activity compiled by the Bureau of Business Research of the University of Texas averaged 174.3 (1957–1959 = 100) in the first eight months of 1966, compared with 159.3 in the same period of 1965. What this meant to the labor force is summarized by the Texas Employment Commission, which has as one of its aims assisting in the full utilization of manpower resources to promote maximum employment. It reported that the State's 1966 fiscal year opened with 4,014,900 in the labor force, increased by 60,900 to 4,075,800 by fiscal 1967. Employment rose from 3,807,000 to 3,942,200, an increase of 135,200. Since there were more jobs open than there were workers to fill them, unemployment declined by 24 per cent. And the labor situation for skilled and experienced workers was "tight."

The big gains at this time were in the manufacture of durable goods and in trade, services and government. This meant that money was being poured into industries with substantial payrolls, and that much of it was being used by consumers to buy goods and services. With 636,000 employed in manufacturing, durable goods accounted for 65.5 per cent of the gain of 35,100 jobs. The increase was chiefly in electrical machinery (electronic components) and the aircraft industry. The demand for helicopters and other aircraft, often governmental, was accelerating. Nondurable goods were expanding also—in food products, apparel, printing and publishing. Numerous technical periodicals, many dealing with the oil industry, are published in Texas.

In such an economic upturn the consumer played his part. Rising prices had not yet limited his demands. New shopping centers were reported from the major cities, and from rural areas that once were crossroads hamlets. The automobile, which clogged urban streets, was a welcome device for taking housewives to markets where they could park and shop in comfort. The State's wellbeing (average hourly wages in factories had reached a high of $2.57) was reflected in the rush to be better educated. In middle-class families college training of the young became almost compulsory, not to achieve status but to be ready for work that required a high degree of scientific and professional skills. Probably never before has

Industry and Commerce

OIL DRILLING SHIP, CUSS I, OPERATING OFF GULF COAST

Humble Oil Company

OCEAN-GOING TANKERS AT TEXACO PORT ARTHUR TERMINAL

Texaco, Inc.

PORT ARTHUR REFINERY, GULF OIL CORPORATION

Gulf Oil Corporation

APPAREL MART IN DALLAS MARKET CENTER
Squire Haskins photo Dallas Chamber of Commerce

LOADING FLOUR FOR EXPORT, GALVESTON HARBOR
Galveston Convention and Tourist Bureau

STORAGE TANKS AND HARBOR FACILITIES, CORPUS CHRISTI
Corpus Christi Chamber of Commerce

TURNING BASIN, PORT OF HOUSTON
Greater Houston Convention & Visitors' Council

MERCHANT VESSELS ALONG HOUSTON SHIP CHANNEL
Greater Houston Convention & Visitors' Council

HARBOR INSPECTION YACHT *SAM HOUSTON*
Greater Houston Convention & Visitors' Council

GAS UNIT IN DEEP GAS AREA, PECOS COUNTY

Gulf Oil Corporation

DRILLING RIG CREW CHANGING OIL DRILLING BIT

Humble Oil Co.

the rush to get a college education been based so strongly on the need to hold a useful place in a swiftly changing world.

After the Civil War packing plants located at Rockport and Fulton. Three were in operation at one time in Corpus Christi; others were at the mouth of the Rio Grande, serving markets in Mexico. On Matagorda Bay, "Shanghai" Pierce operated his own plant, as did King and Kenedy on their vast ranch holdings south of the Nueces. In this period before the introduction of commercial refrigeration, hides and tallow were the chief products. In some instances the hindquarters were salted down, and in others beef was pickled and packed in barrels. At one time a bone mill on Aransas Bay was making fertilizer from the refuse. In the late 1870's the hide and tallow industry was brought to an end. Buffaloes were being cleared from the plains, and for a decade and more millions of Texas cattle in great herds were driven north.

Then the railroads came, and with the growth of commercial centers and the extension of transportation facilities westward, packing houses were established in the larger places. Frank Hastings, in his *A Ranchman's Recollections,* said there was a packing house in Denison in 1874 or 1875. Also according to Hastings "the first application of ice to the packing industry in the United States seems to have been at Denison, Texas." In the 1870's, Fort Worth acquired a small packing plant. In 1966 there were 198 plants in Texas employing 10,294, shipping $499,432,000 worth.

One of the earlier handicraft industries—the making of cowboy boots —has persisted down to the present. Modern tanning plants have been developed, such as those at Sherman, Nocona, New Braunfels, Yoakum and Fredericksburg. There is a modern boot and shoe manufacturing plant in Fort Worth, and other towns have smaller factories. It is a striking fact that a good share of these Texas-made products are sold outside the State, while Texans depend largely on St. Louis and Boston for their shoes.

Lumbering became an important industry from the start. Before the railroads came, lumber was hauled long distances from the pine forests of east Texas into central Texas; and with the coming of railroads a wide market was rapidly established as the timberless prairies and plains were settled. The forests of the Austin colony whined with the activities of scattered sawmills in the 1830's, but by 1890 the lumber industry of the United States migrated southward and to the northwest. Production was heaviest in 1907, 1909, and 1913. The State's remaining virgin and second growth of pine timber is being cut at the rate of about a billion and a half feet of lumber a year. Plants of the pulp and paper industry have been established in Texas, and wood products other than lumber have been developed in several communities—such as the manufacture of furniture, the making of cross ties, telegraph and telephone poles, piling materials, and similar products. In connection with the production of ties, poles, and piling, the creosoting of this material has created a steadily growing industry, particularly in Houston and Beaumont.

Still another wood-products industry in Texas centers about the extensive cedar woodlands that cover the broken country of the State. For years these cedar brakes have supplied vast numbers of fence posts, and in places the production of charcoal has been of local importance. More recently the manufacture of cedar oil has attracted attention. As Texas has one of the largest reserves of cedar timber in the United States, the future of this industry seems assured. There were in 1940 a total of 535 sawmills, and 104 other wood-using industrial plants. But in 1967 the *Texas Almanac* reported approximately 200 sawmills and more than 926 wood-using plants, employing 34,000 with a payroll of more than $138,000,000.

At the turn of the century most commercial centers of the cotton-growing regions had one or more cottonseed oil mills. Especially was this true of the premier cotton-growing country of the rich Blacklands. In more recent years, with the increasing popularity of cottonseed oil products for cooking purposes, a number of modern vegetable oil refining plants of substantial size and output developed in Dallas, Houston, Sherman, San Antonio and elsewhere. In two decades, 1937–1957, cottonseed mills decreased from 144 to 64, but 56 others were processing edible fats and oils, marine fats and lard substitutes.

Oil-bearing crops (cottonseed, soybeans, peanuts, etc.) produce an annual income of more than $100,000,000.

Although the number of plants producing creamery butter, cheese, and ice cream decreased in the 1954–1964 decade, production was bigger in all categories. Dairying in Texas annually represents an income of more than $145,000,000.

Another group of manufacturing plants processing raw materials from Texas farms are the cotton textile mills at New Braunfels, Dallas, Mexia, Houston, Denison, Hillsboro, and other communities. Texas, first in the production of raw cotton, ranks low in the volume turned out by its cotton mills for 69 per cent of the crop is exported. Manufacture is confined largely to the production of coarser goods, such as duck, sheeting, ginghams, and denims.

The manufacture of flour to supply the home market has been a Texas industry for three-quarters of a century and more. In 1859 Carl Hilmer Guenther established the Pioneer Flour Mills of San Antonio. In recent years, particularly with the growth of the dairying and poultry industry, the manufacture of feedstuffs has become an important milling enterprise. Plants in the major cities have been materially affected by the shift of hard winter wheat production into the Panhandle.

An industry of ancient origin is that of the preparation of Mexican foods for home and outside markets. San Antonio and Austin have large canning plants for this purpose. Among other industries processing Texas agricultural materials are peanut products plants, poultry dressing and egg products plants, broom factories, and rice mills. Texas agriculture normally produces about $600,000,000 in new wealth annually.

All industries are dwarfed by the fabulous expansion of minerals, chiefly petroleum, natural gas, and natural gas liquids. Out of a total value of $5,074,764,000 for all mineral production reported for 1966 by the Bureau of Mines of the U. S. Dept. of Agriculture, crude petroleum accounted for $3,191,859,000. The petrochemical industry, located chiefly on the Gulf Coast, spread its prosperity to other industries by its needs for durable goods and transport, although it employed fewer laborers than many less profitable plants. In November, 1967, crude petroleum and natural gas industries employed 99,900; petroleum refining and related industries employed 36,300. A separate category was alloted to chemicals and allied products, employing 55,700. In contrast, transportation equipment employed 88,000, machinery (including electrical) 107,500.

Workers in the petrochemical industries had the highest weekly earnings in mid-1967, averaging $167.26 per week of 42 hours, or $3.26 an hour. Sulphur workers in the Gulf area averaged $152.15 a week, or $3.40 an hour.

Mining for metals is limited in Texas. Iron ore is produced in Cass, Cherokee, and Morris Counties, but iron ore pellets from Missouri and Canada have replaced locally mined ores as blast furnace feed. Improved magnesium markets have kept two Dow plants at Freeport busy. Mining and milling of uranium near Falls City is dependent on outside orders instead of Federal purchases. There is activity in extracting and fabricating of metals. More than 300 facilities process State-produced metals into semi-finished and finished products.

Texas sulphur mines yielded $74,955,000 worth of minerals in 1965. Salt production was valued at $30,771,000. Nonmetallic minerals, including the enormous production of gypsum, limestone, clays, and the like, yield a large annual income in both raw materials and pay rolls.

There were 580 factories making all kinds of apparel in 1963, employing more than 40,000.

Commercial fishing and fish processing is a most profitable industry in Texas, concentrated on the Gulf Coast. Shrimp is the leading crop and its consumption is increasing. In 1965 Texas fish products reached 154,220,-700 lbs., worth $35,561,165; of this total shrimp represented a value of more than $31,000,000. Both the State of Texas and the Federal Government recognize the importance of the shrimp industry to the welfare of the population. The U. S. Bureau of Commercial Fisheries has a major part in keeping the shellfish industry supplied with information about locations and crops, and finding ways to protect the waters from industrial pollution. The Bureau publishes a daily report in the *Market News* on the amount and character of the shrimp landed at ports. A comprehensive monthly report on all kinds of fish is published jointly by the Bureau and the Texas Parks and Wildlife Commission. The Bureau also provides funds for building and repairing fishing vessels and publicizes seafood in the State in order to increase consumption.

Changing trends in employment reflect the prosperity of the Texan economy. The Texas Employment Commission, making allowances for seasonal adjustments, could report in December, 1967, that in mid-November the labor force totaled 4,160,300, of which number 3,874,400 were nonagricultural workers. The growing population and the buoyant economy had added 105,700 workers to the civilian labor force during 1967, 132,000 of them in nonfarm jobs. There were 119,000 unemployed, 2.9 per cent of the civilian total.

Significant changes are the gradual decrease in farm employment and the rather rapid expansion of nonfarm employment. The largest gains in the first half of 1967 were in wholesale and retail trade. Department stores, food stores, eating and drinking places, furniture and specialty retail houses were employing more hands. Nonmanufacturing establishments provided 8 out of every 10 additional jobs filled in mid-summer. Expanding medical and health services helped increase the total for services to 500,000 workers.

Toward the end of 1967 strong gains in government, services, and trade boosted nonmanufacturing employment. State and local government units employed about 30,700 more workers than a year before, mainly because of the growth of educational facilities and other public services.

Manufacturing, especially of durable goods, added 21,000 employees during the year. Aircraft and electronics were the big gainers, with defense requirements contributing to the rise. Ordnance helped the durable goods record, with the needs of campaigning in Vietnam the big factor.

Houston has the largest number of nonagricultural employees—734,100 in November, 1967; with 15,900 unemployed, or 2.1 per cent. No other city comes near Houston in the numbers employed; Fort Worth, the nearest, has a labor force of 277,300; San Antonio is third with 261,-300.

Austin, Dallas, Fort Worth and Houston had an unemployment rate of under 3 per cent. Almost as low were employment rates in the Golden Triangle—Beaumont-Port Arthur-Orange—Corpus Christi, El Paso and San Antonio. Small areas in the southern part of the State were reported to have unemployment rates exceeding 6 per cent.

The July, 1967, insured unemployment rate for Texans was 0.9 per cent. The rate in July, 1966, was 1 per cent of the more than 2,230,000 workers covered under the Texas Unemployment Compensation Act, which is administered by TEC. The national insured jobless rate in July, was 2.8 per cent. The dollar volume of benefits paid to jobless Texans under the State program was $33,400,000 in fiscal, 1966, a 35 per cent drop from the $51,300,000 paid in 1965. The number of employers subject to the unemployment tax rose from 80,912, to 84,440, while tax collections remained fairly stable and reached $55,900,000. With the decline in benefits paid the balance in the Texas Unemployment Compensation Fund in August, 1966, was $283,390,634.

The State of Texas collects an unemployment tax from employers of four or more individuals. It has a right-to-work law that prohibits the closed shop, and the union shop. It makes mass picketing, secondary strikes, and boycotts illegal, and permits no checkoff of dues without the written consent of the employee.

One of the tasks prescribed for the Texas Employment Commission is to place handicapped persons in jobs. In 1966 TEC found jobs for 32,124, of whom 13,259 were disabled veterans. It cooperated with a number of other Texas agencies that are engaged in looking after the handicapped— the Governor's Committee; the Vocational Rehabilitation Division of the Texas Education Agency; the Texas Commission for the Blind; the Veterans Administration, and numerous municipal and private bodies. It is estimated that more than 1,400,000 veterans in Texas are in the labor force. In fiscal, 1966, TEC placed 96,386 veterans in nonagricultural jobs. This service was augmented when the Veterans' Readjustment Benefits Act became a law on March 3, 1966. Veterans who served in the Armed Forces after January 31, 1955, are entitled to counseling and jobs on the same basis as other veterans, with disabled men favored. About 200,000 veterans in Texas come under the provisions of this law.

Transportation

WHEN the ships of the first Anglo-Americans nosed into the silt-filled bays and rivers of the Texas coast, *El Camino Real* (The King's Highway), route of the explorers, and road of barefoot monks, which was not a road in fact but only a vague direction, alone connected the far-flung settlements which told the tale of three centuries of Spanish rule.

Moreover, 500 miles of unoccupied territory separated Texas from the frontier outposts of New Orleans, Natchez, Memphis, and St. Louis. The settlers had to cross this Indian-infested wild or dare the dangers of Gulf and river navigation. Nor were their difficulties lessened when they reached their destination.

The map shows Texas with 400 miles of seacoast and innumerable large rivers which would seem to make for easy communication and transportation, but in fact, that long indented sea line of bays and inlets protected by slivers of islands and attenuated peninsulas has no natural harbors or passes through which a ship can safely sail. The flow of the rivers is too irregular and the deposits of silt are too heavy to allow navigation except for short distances near the mouths. So here was a vast region, remote, trackless, with waterways that afforded but small natural assistance in penetration and whose harbors were so treacherous that they caused frequent disasters in wrecked shipping.

Nevertheless, the waterways were all the pioneers had. The vessels were small at best. Galveston Bay and Buffalo Bayou furnished water connection between Houston and Galveston. Produce from the northeast came down Cypress Bayou, across Lake Caddo to the Red River and thence to New Orleans. Sabine Lake, though treacherously shallow, and the Brazos, the Neches, the Sabine, and other rivers, furnished a modicum of transportation facilities.

The Texas Republic struggled valiantly to build roads and improve the waterways. As early as 1839 the Treasurer paid $520 from the nearly empty coffers of the Republic to have the Gulf harbors surveyed. Assisted by subscriptions from the benefited areas, the State had spent $272,000 in improving harbors and rivers by 1858. At the beginning of the Civil War, river navigation had reached its height.

But this did not touch the inland regions. Part of the Central National Road of the Republic of Texas, which was to extend from the Elm Fork of the Trinity to the Red River, was built through a grant of public land, which financed it. The contract called for a road 30 feet wide in which the stumps were not to be more than 12 inches high. But the Republic's efforts at road making did little to relieve the intolerable conditions of travel over trails indicated only by marked trees. Cumbersome oxcarts, with solid wheels sawed from the trunks of cottonwood trees and innocent of springs, bumped over the rutted prairies. Vehicles with spoked wheels sank hopelessly in the mud. Unbridged rivers with treacherous fords, quicksands, and impenetrable thickets obstructed travel. Horses and mules bogged with their riders in the river bottoms, and travelers frequently had to walk and lead their animals.

As the population increased, the counties gradually opened roads, and stage lines were established between principal towns. From four to six horses or mules drew the coach at the dizzy rate of five to eight miles an hour. When rains poured and roads became quagmires, passengers had to walk and pry mud from the wheels. The usual cost was ten cents a mile, each passenger being allowed a small amount of hand baggage.

The *Texas Almanac* of 1860 shows 31 stage lines. Traversing the southern part of the State, the San Antonio-San Diego line crossed 1,476 miles of desert and mountains. The Southern Overland Mail from St. Louis—popularly called the Butterfield Stage Line—swung across the interminable plains in a southwesterly direction from Preston on the Red River to El Paso, thence to San Francisco, 2,796 miles. The intrepid drivers, passengers, and armed guards of these coaches braved the dangers of hunger and thirst in desert stretches, bad weather in dangerous mountain passes, robbery by desperadoes, and death from Indians.

While the trip to California by stage took 25 to 30 days, the transportation of freight over these general routes was much slower. Drivers of oxwagons traveled in caravans for mutual protection. The cost of transportation was almost prohibitive, one dollar a hundred pounds for a hundred miles, which explains why the Blacklands and Grand Prairie, though marvelously fertile, remained long unsettled·while the population fringed the bays and rivers of the south and east.

The most fantastic contribution to the history of transportation in Texas was made in the spring of 1856, when a cargo of camels was brought from Tunis, Smyrna, and Constantinople by order of Jefferson Davis, then Secretary of War, to furnish transportation for soldiers in the Southwest.

A *khan* (camel station) with Arab and Egyptian attendants was set up at Camp Verde, but little use was made of the animals except to help lay a road across the desert to California in 1857 (*see Tour 17a*).

Before the Civil War, Texas had thrown itself furiously into agitation for railroads. The beginning of actual railway construction was in 1851, although a number of companies had been chartered earlier. The Buffalo Bayou, Brazos & Colorado Railway was the first road to be built in Texas. By 1860, it had been built between Harrisburg and Alleyton.

Meanwhile, construction had begun on other railroads, but it was a period of "loud profession and little deed" in which the legislature by special act incorporated more than 50 railroad companies and authorized the construction of many thousands of miles of line.

The result of many grandiose plans was the actual building of 492 miles of track operated by 11 weak companies, the construction financed largely by loans from the State school fund and grants of State land. Most of the roads were attempts to reach deep water at Sabine Pass and to connect the southwestern trade territory with Indianola and Port Lavaca. The immense inland area of the State was as yet untouched.

The Civil War put an end to further construction and so weakened what had already been done that the railroads, with the exception of the Houston and Texas Central, fell into a condition of bankruptcy, in which they remained until Texas was readmitted to the Union in 1870.

The Reconstruction period saw the cattle drives go north, as cattle could be made to transport themselves to market (*see History, also Agriculture and Livestock*).

But there was much to transport besides cattle. The frontier again was being pushed back, and the State was agitating for railroads into its farthermost parts. Building had begun again and with the wreckage salvaged from the war there were 500 miles in operation by 1870, confined to the coastal region. In 1872, the Missouri, Kansas and Texas entered the State from the north at Denison.

The thrill of that epochal railroad race when the Central Pacific met the Union Pacific in Utah in 1869, thus uniting the Atlantic and Pacific by rail, penetrated to Texas, and the race for the second transcontinental line shifted to the Southwest. All eyes were upon El Paso, "the Pass of the North," where the coast-to-coast rails would cross the Rocky Mountains. The Southern Pacific, building eastward from the Colorado River, raced with Jay Gould's Texas and Pacific Railway, to see which line would reach El Paso first. It was a railroad war in which the contending forces were armies of workers, chiefly Chinese, with weapons of picks and shovels, wheelbarrows and black powder. The Southern Pacific reached El Paso May 19, 1881. The Texas and Pacific, loser in the fight, was forced to enter into an agreement with the Southern Pacific for the use of the latter's trackage between Sierra Blanca and El Paso.

Meanwhile, west Texas had thrown itself into a fever of mass meetings, subscriptions, bonuses, and gifts to entice the railroads. The International and Great Northern was building north and south from the Red River to the Rio Grande, and the Texas and Pacific was completing its westward march along the 32d parallel. The fact that Texas had retained dominion over its public lands when it was admitted to the Union in 1845 gave the State a public asset, apparently limitless. But at first, grants of public lands were not sufficiently enticing to stimulate building in such a sparsely settled region. The railroads had to have money, so loans were made to them out of the permanent school fund.

This plan met with public disapproval, and the railroads directed their efforts toward securing aid through State bonds. By 1882 the State had made provisions for granting about four times as much vacant land as it had, other than that set aside as school land, and had actually issued certificates for nearly eight million acres more than it possessed. An act was passed on April 22, 1882, repealing all laws granting lands to persons for constructing railroads, but furious construction went on. By 1890, 8,700 miles of railroads had been built and the transportation system had taken on the shape it has since retained.

The railroads had received a total of 24,453,000 acres, more than 38,000 square miles, an area larger than the State of Indiana. The distribution of this vast tract of land among the 41 companies entitled to it, the recording and plotting of the field notes, the issuing of patents, the prevention of fraudulent locations, and the adjustment of conflicting claims between the companies and the immigrants who were constantly settling upon the lands, involved an administrative problem without parallel in any State of the Union, and equaled only by the problems of the Land Office of the Federal government.

Public protest over conditions believed to be unfair and in some cases irregular brought about the submission by the legislature for popular approval of an amendment to the State constitution authorizing the establishment of a railroad commission. James Stephen Hogg was then attorney general. He won great prominence by breaking up a railroad pool and forcing the railroads to surrender large tracts of public land which they held wrongfully.

In 1891 the legislature passed a law creating a railroad commission of three men, appointed by the governor, to adopt necessary rates, to correct abuses, and to enforce the same by penalties, the proper courts having jurisdiction. The body has functioned to this day, though the commissioners are now elected instead of appointed, and a few of its powers have in recent years been taken over by the Interstate Commerce Commission.

The railroads united the producing counties of Texas with their market and expedited movement of grain and livestock to the mills and packing plants of the Middle West. They also carried grain to the Gulf Coast for shipping to foreign ports. For three decades of the twentieth century they dominated transportation, finding little competition from the bus lines that were spreading across the map, nor from the commmercial air lines that were still not fully developed. The peak years for the railroads were 1943, 1944, and 1945, when troop movements and armament shipments proved the extreme usefulness of the railroads in wartime. In 1944 Texas railroads moved 25,948,032 passengers and had a top revenue of $80,971,647. But when the war ended the two rising competitors, bus and airplane, took a big spurt. By 1946 rail passenger traffic was down to 13,077,243, and there followed a gradual annual drop until it reached a low of 1,703,723 in 1965. In 1944 the passenger revenue per mile was $4,933.33; in 1965 it had dropped to $605.40. On the other hand freight revenue showed a considerable increase; the freight tonnage rose in 1965 to 181,553,163 from 173,074,704 in 1964, and the net revenue from railway operations was $121,779,405 as against $95,949,982. The Railroad Commission of Texas reported that the income of $18,781,936 in 1964 rose to $47,545,856 in 1965. When the United States Post Office withdrew its mail subsidy from the Santa Fe in 1967 the road announced a serious curtailment of its passenger services, which ran at a loss.

Yet the railroad situation in Texas is healthier today than in many other states where passengers prefer airplanes and short-haul freight is carried profitably in trucks. The long-haul services provided by the railroads for heavy freight have enabled them to compete with truck carriers. The multiplication of industries has helped keep up volume. The railroads have shown enterprise in promoting speedier deliveries, container and pick-a-back devices. Manufacturers are induced to locate in areas set aside for factories and offering direct access to railroads.

Railroads have been economizing by reducing superfluous trackage, but Texas still has more than any other state. The ten big systems that control 31 out of 46 railroads have 14,308 miles of mainline track in use, and about 6,000 additional miles in subsidiary facilities such as switching. The largest are the Santa Fe, with 3,539 miles; Southern Pacific, with 3,329: Missouri Pacific, with 2,018; M-K-T with 1,135, and Burlington, with 1,116. The other railroads are the Rock Island, the Kansas City Southern, and the Frisco; also the Cotton Belt, an affiliate of the Southern Pacific, and the Texas & Pacific, an affiliate of the Missouri Pacific. Fif-

teen lines are independent. All furnish connections, frequently in coopera-
tively-used passenger depots.

The importance of rail traffic is seen in the huge amounts of durable
goods and commodities carried. The railroads are not only needed to move
the products of agriculture, but also for hauling iron and steel, lumber
and petroleum products. In a typical year, 1963, the railroads carried
248,761 carloads of vegetables, 207,937 of corn, oats and other grains,
143,849 of wheat. They carried 35,614 carloads of cattle and calves;
230,860 of petroleum products, 209,486 of iron and steel. Nothing that
was mined, or cut from forests, or produced on farms and in factories
failed to find its way to the freight cars and fill nearly 4,000,000 carloads.

Within recent years railroad enterprise has been directed to improve-
ing loading and delivery of heavy freight. The systems have been cooperating with real estate boards and chambers of commerce to locate industrial
parks at easily accessible sites along the rights of way. Every railroad now
has a staff of engineers that works with manufacturers and real estate
bodies to provide suitable locations with shipping advantages.

Until 1900 Texas had inadequate facilities for shipping by water.
Since only small vessels could enter the State's best port at Galveston, the
State faced the need of large appropriations for developing the coastal
ports. By 1896, after seven years of labor and the expenditure of $3,000,-
000, a jetty system of immense boulders from Texas' granite hills extended from Galveston five miles into the Gulf of Mexico.

Blowing into prominence in 1901 with a tremendous oil gusher, Beaumont clamored for deep water. Through 50 miles from the sea, Houston
devised a means for bringing the Gulf of Mexico to its doors. By forming
public navigation corporations, voting bonds and proposing to the Federal
Government to pay half the cost of the project, Houston secured deep
water in 1915, and Beaumont in 1916.

This plan has since been followed in all deep water projects, development having gone on steadily. Orange, Sabine, and Port Neches were
added to the group of ports along the Sabine-Neches Canal, which also
serves Port Arthur and Beaumont with an average channel depth of 32
feet to the Gulf through Sabine Pass. Grouped about Galveston Bay and
Buffalo Bayou are the ports of Galveston, Houston, Texas City, and Port
Bolivar. Freeport became a deepwater port.

After the hurricanes of 1875 and 1886 had wiped out the old port of
Indianola, the trade of Matagorda Bay shifted to Corpus Christi Bay.
But deep water was not secured until 1926, when Corpus Christi dug
itself out 21 miles to the sea. Port Aransas and Ingleside are grouped
along this deep water channel.

Port Isabel and Brownsville became deepwater ports in 1935 and
1936. In 1962 an 18-ft. channel from Port Mansfield to the Gulf was

completed through Laguna Madre and Padre Island. In 1965 Victoria, in the center of Victoria County, reached deep water by building a barge canal 35 miles long.

Barge traffic between Texas ports has been greatly increased by the construction of the Gulf Intracoastal Waterway, 423 miles long, on which the principal tonnage carried is crude petroleum, fuel and lubricating oils, gasoline, and products used and produced by the petrochemical industry.

Motor trucks carry a large proportion of the freight formerly allotted to the railroads. There are more than 1,000,000 trucks using the roads, not counting farm trucks. The net income of the carriers is almost equal to that of the railroads. Motor buses have been decreasing slightly in cities, while statewide and intrastate bus lines, favored by tourists, are prospering, without a marked increase in numbers.

The growth of bus transportation is closely associated with the building of sound roads, which now cover more than 66,000 miles in Texas. The original support for road improvement came with the initiation of rural free delivery and was necessary to get the postman out of the mud. The Federal Government approved road aid in 1916 and turned its application over to state supervision. This led to the formation of the Texas Highway Department in 1917. Today the highways are administered by the State Highway Commission of three members, each appointed for six years. Executive management is vested in a State Highway Engineer, who is head of the large body devoted to construction and maintenance, located in Austin and with 25 district offices.

United States Highways and Texas State Highways already were serving the needs of the State when the Federal Government voted the law of 1944 that established the vast Interstate Highway System. Since then Interstate roads in Texas have greatly expanded facilities by enlarging major roads between cities, in most cases following the routes of the United States Highways. A total of 3,025 miles of Interstate roads has been allotted to Texas. Farm-to-market and ranch-to-market roads have been developed to meet local needs, financed by the State.

The State Highway Department disburses more than $4,500,000,000 annually including $7,500,000 for the Highway Patrol. Its fund is acquired by nearly 20 per cent of license fees, 32.26 per cent of the motor fuels tax (5¢ per gallon), and by several minor imposts, as well as reimbursement of about 46.28 per cent on construction from Federal and other funds. The State has issued no bonds for highways. About 6,000,000 vehicles of all kinds are registered annually in Texas. Passenger motor cars, about 4,200,000, exceed all other types, and the traffic congestion in city streets is largely due to them. Harris County (Houston) had 791,745 vehicles of all types in 1964; Dallas County (Dallas) had 666,519; Tarrant (Forth Worth) had 354,038 and Bexar County (San Antonio) had 341,898.

Texas early came into prominence in aviation on account of the excellent flying conditions, the general smoothness of the air, and the wide, level flying fields everywhere available. Before these conditions became definitely known and before the Wright brothers made their epochal flight, two mechanics of Beaumont, Johnson and Siefert, worked (1899) on an elaborate plan for a "genuine airship," which, however, never left the ground.

In September, 1909, Harold D. Hahl of Houston devised a plane of scraps of junk, pieces of a blimp he had tried to build, and an Eagle motor, using pictures of the Wright brothers' planes as a model. In this contrivance, he made a successful flight of three and a half miles. The next March, Lieutenant Benjamin D. Foulois, a student of the Wright brothers, made three successful flights at Fort Sam Houston, San Antonio. His experiments with his once-cracked-up Wright plane resulted in improvements adopted by the army, including landing wheels. He was the first flyer to use them.

Though flying circuses gave exhibitions over the State, it was not until the World War made the country flying conscious that schools of aviation were established. Eddie, Katherine, and Marjorie Stinson, assisted by their mother, part dreamer, part automobile mechanic, opened the Stinson School of Flying in San Antonio in 1915.

The three youngsters were experienced aviators by then, and soon had a group of young students about them. Fourteen Canadians received their preliminary training at the Stinson Flying School before going into the British Air Forces. Katherine became an exhibition flyer and made a tour of China and Japan, giving the first exhibition flights ever seen there. Eddie Stinson became a flying instructor at Kelly Field after the United States entered the war.

The big swing to air travel has taken place since World War II. Even with turbo-prop engines air travel to Chicago, Washington and New York was two-thirds faster than by rail. Air travel proved most useful for journeys inside the State. Then came jet engines, and Texans found the great oceans bridged overnight. Planes needed longer runways and Texas cities scrapped their original airports and began extensive rebuilding for the new age. Private planes appealed to executives and corporations and soon Texas had more than any other field in the country. Helicopters became useful in the construction of big dams, and were employed in such enterprises as the King Ranch, since they could be set down at any point on the vast grazing lands. By 1967 Texas was served by 11 American-flag airlines, two foreign lines, and one American freight carrier. In addition, large numbers of military planes, based at Fort Sam Houston, Kelly

Field, Lackland AFB, Randolph Field, Killeen AFB and elsewhere, crossed the skies, leaving behind long trails of white vapor.

Typical of the popularity of air travel are the totals for 1965: 5,635,-139 passengers enplaned at Texas airports an increase of more than 1,000,000 over 1964; 233,692 planes departed for domestic destinations, while 122,510 passengers were booked for foreign flights. Trans-Texas Airlines, with headquarters in Houston, served many of the smaller cities not reached by transcontinental services. Houston led in executive planes but was second in general aviation; Dallas, with 71,295 flights handled 2,279,251 passengers in one year, while Houston, with 37,024 flights, counted 1,273,302 passengers. In air mail and cargo tonnage Dallas likewise far outdistanced all other airports. The wide use of air mail services, more than 18,000,000 tons, explained the decline of railroad mail; Texans could not wait days to communicate with their correspondents on the Atlantic and Pacific seaboards.

Agriculture and Livestock

GREAT changes have taken place in production, processing, and marketing of Texas farm products since the end of World War II. Although Texas continues to hold third place in the United States for cash received for livestock and crops, it has seen the tillers of the soil, mainstay of its prosperity in the nineteenth century, become a minority in the State's population of more than 10,500,000 people. Yet the products of the farms have given employment to a much larger number of processors and distributors, possibly five times the number of those who actually farm. By means of soil improvement through irrigation and fertilization; by mechanization of cultivation and harvesting, and by quick transport to the markets, the value of farm products has gone up, and the incomes of owners and workers have risen.

Statistics depend a great deal on the manner in which they are collected. The Statistical Reporting Service of the U. S. Department of Agriculture relies on personal interviews with farmers and is able to give a dependable count, even though it may not be able to visit every farm. It reported that on January 1, 1967, there were 10,757,000 head of livestock on Texas farms, compared with 9,776,000 in 1966. Milk cows numbered 419,000, an increase from 392,000 of a year before; sheep and lambs numbered 4,802,000, as against 4,342,000, while hogs and pigs totaled 718,-000, compared with 621,000 in 1966.

Texas had 10 per cent of the livestock of the United States; held first place in the production of cotton lint, cottonseed, rice and grain sorghums; second place in carrots, cabbage, grapefruit and spinach; third place in turkeys and peanuts; fourth place in pecans; fifth in sheep, and sixth in chickens. Another authority estimated that the cash receipts of Texas farm marketing in 1966 were $1,323,200,000 for crops, and $1,352,400,000 for livestock, a total of $2,675,000,000.

With the great diversity of natural conditions, agriculture and ranching early claimed the sections of the State best adapted to their needs. Thus in the river valleys of eastern Texas the Caddoes had cultivated plots around their villages, and on the northern plains the Comanches early had horses. So sharp was the cleavage between farming and ranching in Texas that only since the beginning of the present century have cattle-men shown any decided tendency to plant feed crops for their stock, or farmers a desire to increase their cattle to an extent beyond domestic needs. And even with the number of stock farms in the State today, there are localities in which, because of geographic or climatic circumstances, farming or ranching is practiced exclusively.

In Texas the history and the story of agriculture and ranching become separate topics.

FARMING

Because of its area and great regional variation in soil and climate, there are few important crops which cannot be grown successfully in Texas, from wheat in the temperate north to citrus fruits in the subtropical south. Since the entrance into Texas in the 1820's of immigrants from the southern United States who brought their slaves and settled largely along the rivers and creeks in what is now the eastern, southeastern and central parts of the State, cotton raising has been the major agricultural industry.

Jared Groce first planted cotton on a commercial basis in Texas and hence has been called the Father of Texas Agriculture. As early as 1825 he had built a cotton gin, and slave labor cultivated his plantation on the banks of the Brazos (famous in history as the spot from which 11 years later, Sam Houston started the forced march which ended with the defeat and capture of Santa Anna). In 1823 the shipment of cotton by water to New Orleans was established, and 5,000 bales exported.

Earlier, several large tribes and confederations of Indians had planted fields of maize and squash which supported populous villages; and the monks had brought agricultural equipment to mission outposts. In their carefully guarded fields the missionaries "planted the soil, watered the crops . . . and gathered in the grain. . . . The women and children carded the cotton and spun it on *malacates,* the primitive Indian spindles, and men who had learned the art wove this into cloth. The natives worked so slowly and carefully, however, that it was necessary to have a

Spanish overseer constantly on hand, and even so, four native laborers were not equal to one European. Each mission raised corn and beans sufficient for its needs."

The primary motive for immigration into Texas was free or cheap land and the opportunities it offered. Although immigration was not confined to the agricultural class, the isolation from sources of supply made some farm operation necessary for most of the settlers. An excerpt from an old letter shows one of their handicaps: "I hired a young man . . . to live with me. . . . We would take our guns with us to the field to plough, and we would leave one gun at one end of the rows and one at the other; then we ploughed so that he would be at one end and I at the other, so that they" (the Indians) "could not cut us off from both our guns."

Yet by 1833 Stephen F. Austin reported to the Mexican government that there were 30 cotton gins in the municipalities of San Felipe de Austin and Brazoria, and that the Texas cotton crop of that year would amount to about 7,500 bales. During the days of the Texas Republic its fast-increasing importance as a cotton growing country is credited with having been a major factor in the friendliness of England and in the change of United States sentiment toward Texas annexation.

With the abolition of slavery and the chaotic conditions that followed the Civil War, cotton production decreased by 50 per cent. Then the overflow of immigrants, particularly to the Blacklands, brought cotton back to its old place of importance. As the population increased, landowners split vast tracts into smaller ones and rented them. Cotton was the "money crop" and it was also a labor crop, as no successful mechanical picker had been invented. The poor white and Negro farmers put their families in the fields. Soon there were white as well as Negro tenants, and Negro as well as white farmers.

The number of farms in Texas increased 185 per cent during the 1870's. By 1880 the rural population was 1,455,967, as compared with a total population of 1,591,749. In 1890 the rural population of the State was 84.4 per cent of the whole. Cotton remained the big crop.

It was not until 1900 that the real advance of the farmers upon the Plains began. The distance had been incredibly great, the Indians hostile, and the land unfriendly. Into this "treeless, desolate waste" the farmers followed the railroads, digging wells and erecting windmills to combat scarcity of rainfall and prolonged droughts. It was not until then that extensive development of grain crops in Texas started, although corn had been a staple food and feed crop of the early settlers. World War I so stimulated the demand for wheat that, in the five years following, the number of farms in the Plains region increased 48 per cent. Wind erosion set in after native buffalo grass had been plowed up, and State and Federal forestry services and the Civilian Conservation Corps of the 1930s fought it. Notwithstanding the continuing dust storms, the wheat production increased from 11,500,000 bushels in 1935 to 41,690,000 bushels in 1937. The 1960 crop was more than 50,000,000 bu.; in 1965, more than 75,000,000 bu. The earnings of wheat growers rose steadily; in 1963 farmers earned $76,522,000; two years later income passed $100,000,000. The returns in dollars, however, are not a true index; today, with fewer acres harvested, inflationary pressures also have affected prices.

Although diversification of crops has been increasing, cotton is still the mainstay of the State's agricultural and economic life. Texas easily leads the cotton growing States.

About 90 per cent of Texas cotton farmers participated in voluntary control programs of the Federal cotton acreage adjustment plan. Texas cotton acreage declined from an average of 15,598,000 acres in the 1928–32 period, to an average of 11,057,000 acres during the next four years of adjustment programs. Thus cotton acreage in the State was reduced 29 per cent, and production declined 28 per cent, but in conjunction with other influences, such as dollar devaluation and general recovery, total cotton income increased 38 per cent. A low point in cotton production was reached in 1946, when acreage dropped to 6,000,000 and only 1,669,000 bales were recorded. Then production moved up again. In 1964, 4,125,000 bales, valued at $595,990,000, were raised on less acreage —5,675,000. However, in 1965 the crop was 4,694,000 bales. State-wide yield per harvested acre averaged 402 pounds, a new record compared with the previous record of 383 pounds per acre in 1958. Participation in the Federal cotton program in 1966 reduced the planted cotton acreage to the lowest since 1890. Cotton in the Lower Rio Grande Valley was extremely late and totaled only 253,000 bales compared with 392,000 in 1965. However, the Dallas Cotton Exchange emphasized that with cotton the main crop on 90,000 Texas farms, it was worth $114 an acre in 1964–1965, as against $40 an acre for grain sorghum, wheat and corn.

Many farmers with reduced cotton planting have turned to grain sorghums. Texas produces more than any other state. In 1966 more than 5,500,000 acres were planted with grain sorghums, yielding a value of $314,813,000. In 1963 the income had been $228,925,000.

Rice is another product in which Texas leads the country. Up to 500,-000 acres are planted to rice in the Gulf Coast counties. In 1964 it had a value of $97,193,000.

Grapefruit leads citrus production, especially in the counties of Hidalgo, Cameron, Willacy, and Starr of the Lower Rio Grande Valley. The production curve, however, has turned down since the big years of 1937–1948, in part because severe frost hit the Valley in the winters of 1948–1949, 1951–1952 and 1962–1963. Production, which had been steadily increasing, reached a peak of 25,500,000 boxes of grapefruit valued at $21,675,000, in 1947, whereas oranges had a peak of 5,200,000 boxes, valued at $7,800,000, in 1948. After many trees were lost there was some replanting, and in 1961 production was back to 6,800,000 boxes of grapefruit, but the loss by freezing was so great that only 70,000 boxes were reported in 1963.

The wider distribution of farms raising vegetables and garden truck has kept crop averages high, although they, too, are affected by the freeze. Tomatoes, with four crops a year, average $12,000,000 income annually, but shipments vary (2,345 carload lots in 1962, 623 in 1964). Potatoes and spinach reach a value of $4,000,000, sweet potatoes up to $7,000,000. Other commercial crops that bring prosperity to the Texas farmer are onions, cabbage, lettuce, and bell peppers.

Watermelons bring in more than $4,500,000; cantalopes, more than $6,000,000, while lettuce, in all its varieties, is worth more than $5,000,-000 a year. Of interest is the income from green peppers, $1,500,000, more than three times that of beets.

Orchards have moderate yields in Texas, with peaches leading all fruit crops when not damaged by frost. In its 1964 summation the U. S. Department of Agriculture reported 465,353 bu. of peaches, as compared with 21,426 bu. of apples, 34,077 bu. of pears, and 71,757 bu. of plums. However, the comparison with the harvests of 1959, five years before, showed large discrepancies. While the quantity of apples showed little change, there had been 106,813 more bushels of peaches harvested in 1959. A similar result was recorded for grapes: 267,403 lbs. in 1959, dropping to 161, 922 in 1964. Figs, grown in the Lower Rio Grande Valley were not affected: 1,001,211 lbs. in 1964, substantially the same quantity as five years before.

Pecans provide the best paying nuts in Texas. The trees are native, and were found in the San Antonio area by the Spanish padres more than 300 years ago. The Government classified the 1964 crop in three categories, as follows: improved and wild and seedling pecans, 11,510,406 lbs.; improved pecans, 4,637,075 lbs.; wild and seedling pecans, 6,860,951 lbs. Tung nuts are cultivated in southeastern Texas for their oil, which is used in varnish and laquer.

In almost every locality, farming and livestock production are found together. The farmer uses his surplus land for stock, and the ranchman utilizes tillable land to raise feed for cattle. Stock farming has increased tremendously since ranchmen discovered that the growing of hay and small grains, in areas where other farming would be impracticable, releases them from the necessity of dependence upon grass. Beef cattle production was until recent years almost entirely confined to the large ranches, but the adoption of diversification as a farm policy has spread the breeding of beef cattle to the smallest farms of central Texas and other thickly populated areas where marketing conditions are encouraging.

New methods are being applied in the production and marketing of milk. The tendency is to have fewer milk cows and larger herds. In 1966 there were 402,000 milk cows. Milk production is around 3 billion pounds sometimes more, other times less. In 1959 more than 1,000,000 pounds of butter-fat cream were sold by farms; in 1964 the amount was down to 460,965 pounds. The principal dairying counties are Erath, Harris, Hopkins, Johnson and Wise. Jerseys are the favored stock; Holstein also are plentiful, and Guernseys come next.

Horses are as closely linked with the history of Texas as gold with that of the Pacific coast. Without horses the cattle industry would not have developed. Without horses it would be impossible to conduct the huge fenced ranches. The first settlers found herds of wild horses, mustangs, and horses used by the Indians. These mustangs were the first mounts of the Texans.

One of the earliest industries was the business of hunting and trapping wild horses. Using the mustangs as foundation stock, breeders have developed several types of mounts notable for their agility and stamina. The Steeldust was developed by fusing the mustang and the thoroughbred, for use as a cow pony; and polo ponies with mustang blood have won national recognition.

The first edition of this *Guide,* published in 1940, reported that the State had 679,000 head of horses on January 1, 1939. By 1964 this number had shrunk to 263,000, and in 1960 horses and mules were counted together and reached only 218,000. Most of the work horses have been replaced by machines, but saddle horses are still needed and account for a large proportion of the production.

Horses with unusual markings always have interested horsemen and two, the Palomino and the Appaloosa, have been popular for their coats. Both have made frequent appearances in circuses. Colonel William F. Cody, Buffalo Bill, liked to ride a spotted Appaloosa in his Wild West Show, and when in Paris in 1889 was painted astride this horse by Rosa Bonheur. Dr. Francis Haines, historian of the Appaloose Horse Club, wrote the text for a book about this breed in *Appaloose; the Spotted Horse in Art and History,* which was published for the Amon Carter Museum of Western Art of Fort Worth by the University of Texas Press. The director of the Museum, Mitchell A. Wilder, became interested in the phenomenon of the spotted horse when the horse club was staging its national show at the Will Rogers Coliseum.

Dr. Haines discovered that the spotted horse was already well-known in ancient times, and believes it came to the South American continent from Spain. He does not credit the tradition that the wild horses of western Texas were descended from stock left on the Plains by Coronado or De Soto's men. "These few lost horses, according to some imaginative people," he writes, "are supposed to have filled the Great Plains with their descendants in the course of a hundred years or so. The wild bands, started by these strays, are said to have supplied all the Indians of the buffalo country with horses through natural increase . . . Research has proved that there were no horses, wild or tame, in the buffalo country of Texas ninety years after Coronado passed that way. The first authentic account of the use of horses by western Indians is dated 1659, and the first positive evidence of wild horses anywhere on the Great Plains does not come until 1705."

An important adjunct to agriculture in many sections of Texas is the raising of hogs. The Austin colonists found large numbers of wild swine in the east Texas forests, and the razorback variety was an important item in the colonial diet. In more recent years swine production has decreased steadily. It is only necessary to consult the summary of hog production by decades to see the shrinkage. In 1910 Texas had more than 3,000,000 hogs on farms; by 1920 this was down to 2,580,000; in 1930 there were 1,673,000. A rise took place by 1940, when the total reached 2,293,000. But the slide went on; in 1965 Texas had 602,000 on farms, worth $11,739,000. Then production rose; in 1967 Texas had 718,000 hogs, worth $20,176,000.

Under the stimulus of modern poultry plants, the industry is increasing. Two large poultry shows are held annually in Dallas, and others are held in producing centers. These, and the increasing demand of farmers for better breeding stock have led to the development of fine fowls, principally Leghorns, Barred Plymouth Rocks, and Rhode Island Reds. The U. S. Dept. of Agriculture estimated that in 1966 Texas raised 17,258,-000 chickens; produced 152,918,000 broilers.

Texas is the leading turkey producing State. Many fine birds sold for breeding purposes are shipped to northern farmers. In 1964 sales brought a gross income to producers of $19,664,000.

The flora of Texas is particularly well adapted to beekeeping, and honey production is a leading industry in several sections. Five districts, determined by flora, produce large amounts of honey: the Rio Grande, the arid belt, the cotton belt, the east Texas region, and the Pecos country. The major honey bee plants are horsemint, cotton, mesquite, huajillo, and catclaw. Next to California, Texas has the largest number of commercial beekeepers. The shipping of bees to the north in combless packages has also become an important special industry. Many devote their time to the raising of queen bees to be shipped to northern beekeepers. The annual average honey production is in excess of 12,000,000 pounds, worth nearly $2,000,000. There were 239,000 colonies of bees in 1966 (*Texas Almanac*).

Nursery products have a useful place in the economy of Texas. Roses are cultivated with great success and Tyler, in Smith County, is justifiably called the Rose Capital of the Southwest. Cut flowers, potted plants, florist greens, and bedding plants bring in between $6,500,000 and $7,000,000 a year. More than 4,000,000 square feet are devoted to growing flowers under glass. Mushrooms and bulbs also are grown under glass or other protection, and these, together with seeds of vegetables and plants, account for a $1,000,000 return.

Agricultural education has been strongly supported by the State for nearly 100 years. Texas Agricultural and Mechanical University, the head of a system, began as a college in 1876, seven years before the opening of the University of Texas. It has two affiliated colleges—Prairie View A. and M. and Tarleton State; until 1968 it also had Arlington State College, which has been transferred to the University of Texas system. It has opened the James Connally Technical Institute (vocational) at Waco.

Through its Extension Service, the University carries out local farm programs, usually in its substations, also through agents and free literature. Field experiment stations, where practical research is conducted for the benefit of local farmers, have solved many problems and developed many new crops. The results of these agricultural experiments are printed and distributed widely. Bulletins are also distributed by the State Department of Agriculture, which co-operates with Agricultural and Mechanical University in educational activities. Boys and Girls Four-H Clubs are sponsored by the college, which awards prizes, and aids in conducting annual field meets and exhibits. The training of youth on the farm is a major project. County fairs are encouraged, and exert widespread influence in promoting the production of better farm products. There was even a laboratory under the supervision of the college for the study of honey production, situated in the heart of the beekeeping region. The pink bollworm, the flea hopper, and other Texas farm pests are combated by corps of workers in the agricultural substations.

Another important factor in the agricultural life of the State is the Luling Foundation. Here practical demonstration of all farm problems in an unusual farm institution has proved of steadily increasing value. Both livestock industry and agriculture are benefited by the research, experimentation, and demonstration work of the various educational agencies.

The Home Demonstration plan was first introduced in 1903 by S. A. Knapp, who obtained the help of the Dept. of Agriculture and the Fort Worth & Denver Railroad to eradicate the boll weevil, and tackled other farm problems until Texas A. and M. took up farm extension in 1912.

Agrarian movements began early in Texas (*see History*). The Grange was the first permanent organization, and the Farmers' Alliance had its origin in the State. The Farmers' Union early became a factor in Texas agriculture. County units have been sponsored by the Texas Farm Bureau, which is active in marketing, crop rotation, and similar activities. Both have their headquarters in Waco.

LIVESTOCK

Breeding of livestock has become a fine art in Texas, where much professional study and experiment have been devoted to improving the herds. Beef cattle are carefully selected for breeding or fattening at the spring roundup; calves may be sold by eight months; heavier cattle may be placed in feed lots and sold when between 12 and 18 months old. The principal breeds are the Aberdeen Angus, heavy black; the white-faced Hereford, with brownish body; the Shorthorn, brown body color; the Brahman, originally from India, which, when bred with the Shorthorn, produced the reddish-brown Santa Getrudis for the King Ranch. Also bred here are the Brangus, a combination of Braham and Angus; the Charolais, from France; the Charbray, bred from the Brahman and the Charolais, and the hefty Beefmaster, bred from Brahman, Hereford and Shorthorn.

Organizations that foster purebred livestock are scattered through the ranch country of Texas. Active ones, with location of headquarters, are the following: Texas Angus Assn. (Fort Worth); Texas Appaloosa Horse Club (Refugio); Texas Brahman Assn. (Placedo); American Brahman Breeders Assn. (Houston); American Charbray Breeders Assn. (Houston); American International Charolais Assn. (Houston); Lone Star Cutting Horse Assn. (Paris); Texas Hereford Assn. (Fort Worth); Holstein-Friesian Assn. of Texas (Sulphur Springs); Texas Jersey Cattle Club (Grapevine); American Paint Stock Horse Assn. (Fort Worth); Palomino Horse Breeders Assn. of America (Mineral Wells); Quarter Horse Assn. of America (Amarillo); American Rambouillet Sheep Breeders Assn. (San Angelo); Premier Santa Getrudis Assn. (Bryan); Santa Getrudis Breeders International (Kingsville); Texas Sheep and Goat Raisers Assn. (San Angelo); Purebred Sheep Breeders Assn. of Texas (Olney); American Angora Goat Breeders Assn. (Rockspring); Texas Angora Goat Raisers Assn. (Uvalde); Beefmaster Breeders Universal (San Antonio).

More, perhaps, than any other single symbol, the longhorn steer represents Texas. The cattle industry played a leading part in the development of the State, for it gave the State its first great businesss, and grew until Texas attained first place in beef production. On the dusty trails of the seventies and eighties the cattle industry of this country was born, and those trails started in Texas.

In Texas, as in other regions, the livestock industry has changed. Cattle kings no longer "take cold if they're not wearing a six-shooter." The cattle in early days were "tough to eat and tougher to handle," with horns that often had a spread of five or six feet. Today they are not longhorns but, largely, Shorthorns and Herefords, crossed with Brahmas. Where once the only pedigree needed was a brand, now ancestry is all-important. Only a few real longhorns remain, survivors of the early herds that built the State's first fortunes.

Development of the cattle industry can be divided into four periods. First, that of the introduction of Spanish cattle and the development of the wild native Texas longhorn; second, the east Texas period in which the modern ranch appeared; third, the era of the trail drives, when the modern cattle industry began; and fourth, the development of the western part of the State as a ranching stronghold.

The first cattle known to have entered Texas were 500 cows brought by Coronado in 1541. Many of the explorers, fearing a food shortage in an unknown land, brought livestock. Some of these cattle escaped and wandered through the wilderness, to become the nucleus of vast wild herds.

The Spanish colonists found a natural *pasto,* or pasture, covering southwest Texas. Reynosa, in 1757, with a population of 269, had 18,000 head of cattle. De Mezieres (1779) reported that a fat cow was worth only four *pesos,* yet the ranches flourished. Herds were driven to market in Louisiana by Spanish ranchers in defiance of customs laws. Thus, probably the first smuggling in the State was that of cattle. Owners marked their stock when possible, but most of the cattle were unbranded. The wild herds were not molested by the Indians, who preferred the meat of the buffalo.

It was in east Texas that modern ranching began. James Taylor White, the first real Anglo-American cattleman, established the first ranch of the modern type near Turtle Bayou in Chambers County (*see Tour 23a*). Other ranchers followed White to east Texas. They drove their herds to New Orleans to market, using the Old Beef Trail and others. Hides and tallow still had more value than beef.

The most important event to pioneer Texas cattlemen was the introduction of Brahma or Zebu cattle from India, a variety scientifically designated as *Bos Indicus* and differing radically from the European variety of *Bos Taurus.* It was not until after the Civil War that Brahmas were secured in large numbers. The first record of a successful crossing of these cattle with native stock was in 1874 when Captain Mifflin Kenedy experimented with his herds (*see Tour 9c*). Fever ticks had been a barrier to the introduction of Hereford, Shorthorn and other beef breeds in the coastal and southern area. The Brahmas and cattle produced by crossing them with other breeds proved to be immune from tick fever, and were also better beef cattle. As ticks have never been eradicated from some sections, Brahma blood is still essential to the State's livestock industry.

By 1860 there were more than three million head of cattle in Texas. The Union blockade prevented the shipment of large herds to supply the Confederate army, and at the close of the Civil War the State was overrun with cattle, many of them wild.

Longhorns were almost worthless in 1866. Range animals sold for $3 and $4 a head, although in the North butchers were paying from $30 to $40 a head for beeves. Everyone had cattle and nobody had wealth.

And in Texas, especially in the brush country, wild native stock had flourished. Here the Texas cowboy had emerged. There also were *vaqueros* (cowpunchers, from *vaca,* meaning cow), who were Mexicans. Both of these classes of cowboys had learned to pursue "strays" through the densest thickets. The term "maverick" had come into being as a synonym for unbranded cattle (*see Tour 22b*), and there were countless herds of longhorns, too valueless to be branded. Obviously, the thing to do was to drive the herds to shipping points. Yet the nearest railroads were in Kansas and Missouri, 1,000 to 1,500 miles distant.

A few adventurous spirits led the way across those untried miles to the railheads, in the late sixties. Trails, some of them bearing the names of the men who blazed them, came into being, such as the Chisholm Trail. Abilene, Kansas, became a roaring cowtown, followed by Dodge City and other shipping points that sprang up in the wake of the mighty movement of cattle. No other industry in the Southwest had such economic significance or such picturesque aspects. The driving of herds caused towns, customs, and a distinct type of people to grow up beside the trails (*see Tour 11a*). About five million Texas cattle were driven to market during the 15 years of trail driving, yet when the railroads reached Texas and the drives were no longer necessary, there were more cattle in the State than when the drives began.

As a result of the drives, ranchmen forged forward in undeveloped regions, establishing ranches not only in uninhabited parts of Texas but on the plains of the Middle West, in the Northwest and in the Indian Territory, now Oklahoma. With the cattle drives the Texas cowboy became a national figure, with his ten-gallon hat, high-cantled saddle, his wiry little pony (usually a native Texas mustang), and his peculiar vernacular.

Indians, buffalos, and lack of water had barred cattlemen from the Plains. The Indians were finally placed on reservations and the buffaloes were slaughtered. A few bold men drove their herds into the Panhandle in the 1870's. Others followed and thus began a new epoch in the industry. Colonel Charles Goodnight established the first large ranch in the Panhandle in 1876. He later experimented with crossbreeding buffaloes and Shorthorns, calling the product cattaloes, but the animal thus produced was not satisfactory. A few cattaloes are still seen on Panhandle ranches, but they are kept chiefly as curiosities.

Water had always been a problem on the Plains. Windmills solved this difficulty.

In the early days grass was free and the only property ranchers owned was horses and cattle. Each rancher claimed grazing rights for as much land as he could use. Although they had no title to their so-called holdings, ranchmen were willing to enforce their claims with six-shooters.

The period from the early seventies to about 1885 was the heyday of the Texas cattleman. All he needed to start a thriving business was a few cows. In 1882 there began a rush to the range; men flocked to Texas from all parts of the world to buy ranches, lured by tales of big, quick profits. English earls became cattle barons (*see Tour 16a*).

Naturally, such conditions could not last. The bubble burst in 1885. A drought on badly overstocked land had tragic consequences. One rancher left 15,000 head of cattle dead on the parched range. There was a rush to dispose of cattle, prices tumbled, many ranchers were bankrupt. Those who survived saw that a new day had dawned in the cattle business. The range had to be conserved, and to be conserved it had to be fenced. To be fenced it had to be owned. Following the invention of barbed wire in 1874, sample fences were built in many parts of the State. Range animals soon learned to stop at barbed wire fences, and the new invention was rapidly adopted by Texas cattlemen. In 1884 the XIT Ranch enclosed 3,050,000 acres.

When the large ranches were fenced, complications arose. Many had enclosed State school lands or lands belonging to the railroads, for surveys had not been the order of the day. There was a continuation of the strife caused earlier by the "nesters"—the ranchman's name for the farmers—when they fenced their small holdings. The Fence-cutting War was a stormy interlude in the cattle industry (*see History*).

Ranchers who had fences needed less help to handle their herds; the great tracts were divided into pastures, and grass was conserved by range rotation. The herds were separated into breeding groups and better stock was produced. Thus the longhorn steer was doomed, making way for a better animal. Within a few years longhorns were so scarce that zoos collected them. One of the few remaining small herds is that in Brackenridge Park, San Antonio.

As the farmers advanced westward across Texas, ranchmen suddenly found their land valuable and sold it, or they found themselves crowded, and moved. The trans-Pecos region and the extreme western plains became the cowman's stronghold. Here the industry still thrives. In 1906 the peak of production was reached with 9,500,000 head of cattle. By 1919 the number had decreased to 5,318,000. In subsequent years there was a steady increase; by 1965 there were more than 10,000,000 cattle, and beef cattle were well over 9,500,000. Whereas, in the days of the open range, all cattle were range-fed, the introduction of barbed wire necessitated the increasing practice of forage feeding, and with limited range facilities in large areas, many ranchmen have turned to raising their own forage crops. The practice of placing cattle in feed lots has helped to increase weight.

The cattleman still wears the ten-gallon hat and high-heeled boots, but he is a businessman, and his acreage, though smaller than in the early days, pays larger dividends because one Hereford steer brings on the market more than the price of three longhorns.

The cowboy also has changed. He oils windmills and keeps fences in repair. He rides in an automobile, often with his horse in a trailer; even the duties of the fence rider (ranch hand who examines and repairs fences) are often performed in this manner. But the Texas cowboy, like the rancher, is still the same at heart. The range is still his home.

Texas ranks first in the United States in the production of wool. Sheep raising began with the Spanish missions, but not until after the cattlemen had become firmly entrenched did sheep ranching develop. The war between sheep rancher and cattleman was bitter and long, but by 1940 there were 10,000,000 head of sheep on Texas ranges, and wool production reached 79,900,000 lbs., valued at $23,171,000. This record was not maintained. In the next twenty years the number of head slipped down to between 5,000,000 and 6,000,000.

Favorite breeds are the Rambouillet, a large animal of the Merino variety, and in the hill country, the Delaine, a smaller animal with long fine wool. Many ranchers use Hampshire rams for crossing with the fine wool breeds for the production of lambs for market. Texas wool is of good quality, comparing favorably with that of Australia and South America. Most of it is used in the United States. San Angelo and Kerrville are the big wool markets.

On the other hand, the number of Angora goats and the production of mohair have increased. Texas had 4,000,000 goats in 1965. In 1964 3,978,000 goats were valued at $29,835,000, and produced 28,872,000 lbs. of mohair, valued at $27,428,000. The Angora goat within a few years changed what was considered a waste land into valuable pastures. The first Angoras were introduced into Texas in 1858. Ranchers rushed to import breeding stock; and the Sultan of Turkey, who had inadvertently caused the importation to this country, placed an embargo on Angoras, too late. They already were being obtained from South Africa and South America.

Large numbers of goats are sold for slaughter, yet, strangely enough, markets do not offer goat meat and goat chops appear on no menu. One of the difficulties with popularizing this meat is that, unless the goat is rather young the flesh is likely to be somewhat strong and tough; tender young goat meat compares favorably with lamb. In the goat country, this meat is a staple item of diet. It is relished especially by Mexicans, the kids, called *cabritos,* being considered a great delicacy. Goat raisers a few years ago attempted to popularize the meat and adopted the name "chevon" to distinguish it from mutton. But the campaign failed, and *cabrito* is still a sectional dish, as well known to the remainder of Texas as the tamale, yet as seldom eaten by the average citizen. Vast changes in livestock raising have taken place in recent years. The *Texas Almanac 1966–1967,* enumerates some of them: "Marketing has decentralized to many local sales yards and packing plants, while transportation has partly shifted from rails to trucks. Irrigation pushed cotton and grains to the High Plains, Trans-Pecos, Southwest Texas, and Lower Rio Grande Valley, among other sections, breaking up many formerly large ranches. After the depression and droughts of the 1930s, and the institution of Federal acreage controls for such major crops as cotton, cattle raising made a strong comeback in eastern and central Texas, while the number of farms and acreage in row crops decreased . . . Much of Texas' cattle population is on rangeland, or grassfed animals coming from small grain pastures. However, there has been a marked increase in finishing of cattle in Texas feedlots."

Racial Elements

PEOPLE of Texas derive from many stocks. There have been immigrants for four centuries; at least 35 nations have contributed to the present citizenship, of which approximately one-half has been added since 1900.

The Census of 1960 counted 9,579,677 people in Texas, of whom 1,204,846 were nonwhite. The nonwhite total included 1,187,125 Negroes, 5,750 Indians, 4,172 Chinese and 4,053 Japanese. The foreign-born in Texas numbered 298,791, of whom 202,315 were born in Mexico, 19,506 in Germany, 12,176 in the British Isles, 7,960 in Canada, 5,054 in Czechoslovakia, 3,725 in Poland, and 2,228 in Ireland.

Naturally, the State's population is predominantly Anglo-American; Texas' history, culture, character and progress have been shaped primarily by this group. In west central and northwest Texas the people are almost entirely native-born white. After the establishment of the Austin colony in the 1820's, settlers from the United States came in steadily increasing numbers, at first primarily to secure cheap land and greater opportunity. Of the States that have contributed to the population, Tennessee leads, with Alabama, Arkansas and Mississippi following. Since 1920 the migration from the United States has been largely from the North.

Of Indians, first of the racial elements in Texas, only a remnant of the Alabama and Cooshatti tribes remains, with a few Piros and Tiguas near El Paso, and at Fort Clark a small group whose ancestors were Seminole and Negro.

The Spanish monks and *conquistadores* left a lasting imprint upon architecture, art, and music, and certain areas retain authentic Spanish tendencies. In San Antonio, for example, are descendants of Canary Island settlers of 1731. Among the older so-called Mexican families from San Antonio south to the Rio Grande, Spanish blood often predominates.

The State's largest single division of foreign white stock is that of Mexican origin. While Mexicans continue to enter the United States to become citizens, many native-born Texans are descended from Spanish and Mexican stock resident in the State for generations.

There are three principal classes of Texas Mexicans. In the older cities and localities, a relatively small group possesses strong traditions of family and culture, usually of Spanish origin. A widespread new middle class, recruited from both the upper and lower strata, has homes, standards of living, and businesses equal to those of any element. From this group have developed organizations designed to improve conditions generally among Texas citizens who came from Mexico and to foster ideals of American citizenship and amicable relations between the two peoples.

The third social stratum is that of the peon. The Mexicans crowd city slums or live as tenants or hands on farms and ranches. In the cities, this class is often used as the balance of power in machine politics, and unwittingly is a powerful factor in government. Although there are many Texas-Mexican landowners along the Rio Grande, the vast majority of Mexicans south of the Nueces River are still laborers.

In handicrafts, such as pottery, the Texas Mexicans excel, and their influence has been great in music, art, and architecture. Cheap Mexican labor is an important economic factor in agriculture and piece-work occupations, but migratory labor has been curtailed by Federal law.

During the 1820's and 1830's the Irish promoters, Power and Hewetson, McMullen and McGloin, brought colonists to an isolated and Indian-infested region between the Lavaca and Nueces Rivers, near the coast. Here, almost as soon as the settlements had been made, the storm of the Texas Revolution broke in the heart of the Irish holdings, and active was the participation of the colony in that and every military expedition and war in the State's history. It was not until 1900 that the predominately Irish counties of San Patricio, Refugio, Aransas, Bee, and Goliad began a period of rapid economic growth. Soldiers, politicians, and writers have come from the Irish in Texas, but immigration today is negligible.

Political disturbances in the 1840's drove many Germans to seek new lands where, possibly, an ideal German state might be established. Persecuted by the Diet of the German Confederation, members of the *Burschenschaften* or student's organization began to come to Texas. Soon the lure of economic betterment had attracted the German masses. Immigration societies were formed for the assistance of these voluntary exiles, and among them was the Society for the Protection of German Immigrants in

Texas, which fostered several colonies in the State (*see Tours 24b and 8c*). In the German communities of south central and southwestern Texas the customs and culture of the founders survive, their greatest contribution being in music, painting, literature, and quaint colonial architecture. The Germans early had schools, singing societies, and social organizations, a literary society in the 1850's, and they pioneered in agriculture and labor organizations. Many of their descendents still observe customs of German origin in Fredericksburg, New Braunfels, and other communities where their forebears settled.

Economic and political pressure prompted the coming of Alsatians. Settling first in isolated Castroville (1844), they remained a negative element in general development, contributing chiefly a graceful mode of colonial architecture. The French of La Reunion (*see Dallas*) were a more active factor in the development of their locality. Due to the proximity of Louisiana, there have been French in Texas since very early days, and the 1930 census showed 10,185 of this nationality.

In many communities of south central Texas, the Czechs are rapidly replacing other racial elements. They migrated in the 1840's and 1850's from political hardships in Europe. Essentially farmers, they soon acquired land and educated their children. The Czechs have repeatedly impressed themselves upon the public consciousness; they have held high public offices and have been especially active in the field of education. Czech settlements include Praha, Fayetteville, Dubina, Cameron, El Campo, Shiner, Flatonia, Rosenberg, and Jourdanton.

The Wends and Poles came in search of religious and political freedom. Serbin (*see Tour 24a*) is the mother colony of the Wends, and Panna Maria that of the Poles. Norwegians are found principally in Bosque County, and there is a college supported by them at Clifton. The Swedes in Texas have been prominent in educational and religious activities.

Negroes have been increasing their percentage of the total population, especially in the cities. Many have been displaced by farm machinery. The first black to arrive—Estevanico, a Moor—accompanied Cabeza de Vaca on his wanderings (1528–36). Luis Aury sold Negroes for $1 a pound in a slave market on Galveston Island in 1816; he was followed by Jean Lafitte, who preyed on ships carrying slaves that were being smuggled by dealers into the United States.

Austin's colonists were given permission to import slaves. These Negroes lived principally along the Brazos, Trinity, Neches, Sabine, and Colorado River bottoms, where cotton was first grown on a large scale. From that period until the present time the Negroes have been concentrated largely in the cotton-producing section in the eastern half of the State, where in five counties the Negro population exceeds the white. Some counties in the western part of the State have almost no Negroes. Urban centers of Negro population are Houston, Dallas, Fort Worth, San Antonio, Beaumont, and Waco. Thirty-eight per cent of the Negro population in 1930 was urban, 62 per cent rural, but this proportion no longer exists, because of the shift to cities in later decades. Many Negroes, however, own farms and trade in truck products. A survey made in 1936 showed Texas Negroes to be operating 1,736 retail stores, which were doing an annual business of more than $6,000,000.

Texas has lifted the ban against Negroes in educational institutions. Two institutions of higher learning originally for Negroes are State-supported—Texas Southern University at Houston and Prairie View Agricultural and Mechanical College at Prairie View. Other privately endowed colleges attended chiefly by Negroes are Hutson-Tillotson at Austin, Jarvis Christian at Hawkins, Bishop at Dallas, Wiley at Marshall, Paul Quinn at Waco, Mary Allen at Crockett, and Butler and Texas Colleges at Tyler. *See article on Education.*

Many other nationalities have contributed to the State's development, including the Italians, who are firmly established in business in the cities; the Japanese, who raise rice in eastern Texas; the Chinese, notable for their business houses in San Antonio and El Paso; the Belgians, who are chiefly truck farmers; and the Greeks, who often are fruit dealers and restaurant operators. The influx of English, Scotch, Austrian, Russian, and other foreign white groups has been large. Most of these nationalities, however, have contributed more to the State through individual members than as groups.

Folklore and Folkways

FOLK institutions of Texas have a range that corresponds to the size of the State and the wide diversity of racial influences. Ancient tribal dances, the inherited *fiestas* of the Mexicans, tall tales of the pioneers, and the colorful yarns and customs of cowboys are only part of the State's wealth of folk inheritances. The ghost of Jean Lafitte, the pirate, hardy Texas Rangers, and Br'er Rabbit, share honors in lore handed down from father to son.

In an area that reflects so many racial elements, and cherishes the long-established traditions of the Old South along with the more boisterous practices of the western frontier, there is a variety of influences which, taken collectively, represent a rich American culture still in the making. Approximately one-half of the State's inhabitants live on the soil—the cradle of most folkways. A large percentage of those residing in the cities are only one generation removed from the country. Hence one may be welcomed to play-parties in the metropolitan city of Dallas, hear the songs of the southern Negro on the docks of Houston, and find the genial old German custom of *Kaffeeklatsch* (afternoon coffee) in San Antonio.

Texas connotes the cowboy and his customs to a great majority of people. Representing (with few exceptions) the Anglo-American element, the cowboy bears the same relation of the folkways and folklore of Texas that the Indian does to those of Oklahoma. The feeling of the earth and sky while tending the herds, the rodeos, the round-ups, and the hardships accepted half humorously, half resignedly, have been factors in the development of cowpuncher lore which is surviving even the passing of the great ranches.

It is rather natural that a mythical super-cowboy should have been evolved around the chuck wagon and the bunkhouses. Pecos Bill, "the great-granddaddy of all cowboys," experienced such tremendous adventures that he even altered the topography of the State. There are various accounts of Pecos Bill's birth, but any puncher will declare, with a great deal of pride, that the hero was born in Texas. While his family was moving farther west, Bill dropped out of the wagon. Since there were 17 or 18 other children in the wagon, "Bill's ma and pa didn't miss him for two or three whole days; then it was too late to turn back and hunt for him."

But Bill was not one to starve. The coyotes—so goes the legend—"took him up and raised him." As he grew, he became so terrific that whenever the rattlesnakes heard him coming they hid in the cactus because his bite might poison them. He used mountain lions for saddle horses. Feeling that he needed a few pets around his shack, he invented centipedes and tarantulas.

Taking up a bet, Pecos Bill mounted an Oklahoma cyclone and traveled across three States. Mountains were leveled and forests uprooted. From this little jaunt there emerged the almost treeless Texas Panhandle. Bill would never have been "throwed" had not the cyclone, in desperation, "rained out from under him."

The great tragedy of Bill's life was his romance with Slue-Foot Sue. Bill always had an eye for the ladies, but Sue seems to have won his heart over all other women. On the morning of their wedding, Sue insisted on riding Bill's famous horse, "Widow Maker," since no other bronco had ever "throwed" her. When the bride mounted "Widow Maker," he pitched so high that Sue "had to duck her head, in order to keep from havin' it bumped by the moon." She was wearing the latest style of steel-spring bustle, so that each landing on the ground bounced her as high as before. For four days and nights the girl rebounded between heaven and earth. In the end, Bill had to shoot her rather than have her starve to death.

The preponderance of this type of folklore in Texas is accounted for by the fact that it is still being created, for the real Texas cowboy has not vanished; on the King Ranch alone there usually are about 700 of them. The cowboy's tendency to scoff at hardship or to extol virtue by exaggeration, a trait inherited from a frontier where living was difficult, continues to this day. By way of illustration is the story of the two cowboys who "get fired."

These cowboys were sent out to build a fence, and on the way they found a den of between five and ten thousand rattlesnakes, all the way from six to 14 feet long, lying stretched out, "froze stiff by a norther."

They "throwed a rope around a bundle of 'em" and began using them as fence posts, one cowboy hammering while the other held "the pointed end" into the ground. Speedily they finished the work, and the boss appreciated the saving in time and labor very much—so much that he rode right out to see the fence. Then they lost their jobs. And this was the explanation:

"When the sun commenced shining them blamed rattlesnakes thawed out an' carried off two miles of good barbed wire."

But cowboy lore is not all exaggerated, if colorful, myth. Two of the most popular range ballads, typical of much of the folklore, are "The Dying Cowboy" and "The Cowboy's Dream," dealing with the theme of death. Today, the residents of Archer City show one lone grave that is supposed to be the final resting place of the young cowpuncher who was buried far from home, "on the lone prairie." The second ballad reveals a profound religious instinct expressed in the familiar imagery of the cowboy:

> The trail to green pastures, though narrow,
> Leads straight to the home in the sky,
> To the headquarters ranch of the Father
> In the land of the sweet by and by.

The Texas Ranger is inseparable from the cowboy in the folk tradition of Texas. One of these early Rangers, "Mustang" Gray, is the subject of a popular Texas ballad, a romantic novel, and many tales.

With typical hospitality, Texas accords the same place in its folk tradition to violators of the law that it does to those who uphold authority. The people have never condoned lawbreaking as such, but they respect bravery in any individual. Even such recent outlaws as Clyde Barrow and Bonnie Parker are represented by two distinct ballads. Generally, all such desperadoes are portrayed in folk legends as modern Robin Hoods who took from the rich and gave to the poor. Thus the celebrated bandit, Sam Bass, is pictured as "a good boy who got into bad company."

Deep in the piney woods of east Texas there exists a predominantly Anglo-Saxon group whose folkways change little from year to year. These people retain a firm belief in the efficacy of conjure balls to dry up wells and of kerosene oil to cure most illnesses. "Hants" and fabulous monsters abound in the woods and thickets of this section. The ghost of one woman haunts a tree and protests to passersby about having been buried beside her husband's relatives. Whoever touches the tree is bound to die before sunset. "Old Coffin-head," a giant rattlesnake, roams the thickets (*see Tour 2*).

The mountaineers of the Austin hills are closely akin racially to the piney woods folk. These people are a remnant of the early mountain stock found in the Cumberlands and Ozarks. Elizabethan idioms persist in the vernacular, and here old English ballads, including "Barbara Allen," are heard.

Texas folk cultures are generally expressing themselves in new forms instead of dying. The oil field workers, for example, have borrowed the lumberjack hero, Paul Bunyan, and are now converting him into a gigantic figure of the derricks. A typical story is that of Paul's great post hole deal. Once while he was drilling for oil at Breckenridge, he struck a dry hole. Furious, he smashed the derrick with one blow of his fist. Then he saw an advertisement for 10,000 post holes wanted by a rancher in the Panhandle where "the wind blows prairie dog holes inside out." So Paul hitched a chain to a dry hole, pulled it up and, realizing that the hole was too long to handle in entirety, he cut it into proper lengths, shipped the pieces to the Panhandle and made a fortune. Another time, he built a pipe line from his Texas ranch to the Chicago stockyards and pumped his cattle through it, but the pipe was so big that half-grown yearlings would get lost in the threads and starve to death before they could get out.

The State's oldest racial observances are those of the Tiguas and Piros of the El Paso area, whose tribal dances, performed annually at Mission Nuestra Señora del Carmen at Ysleta, are of ancient origin (*see Tour 19f*). However, probably because of the small number of Indians remaining in the State, their influence in folklore is very slight except in nature lore and myths. One story of the bluebonnet is that a little girl burned her favorite doll in order that a long drought might be broken, and when she awoke next morning, the ground was covered with blue flowers the shade of the doll's headdress.

Innumerable feast days are observed by the Mexicans, with all the colorful pageantry that is part of the racial tradition. During the Christmas season, there are numerous performances of Los Pastores, a traditional Spanish miracle play whose actors are simple farmers and workers, and whose stage may be a back yard, a church, or a vacant storeroom. The play is generally opened with singing by a shepherd choir, and the choir thereafter interprets the drama. Angels next appear singing the glad tidings of Christ's birth, while Lucifer attempts to dissuade the shepherds from going to Bethehem. The men, nevertheless, desert their flocks, taking with them an old hermit who has waited all his life for this night. A lazy shepherd named Bartolo furnishes the comedy for the play, which is none the less reverent in its treatment. Arriving at the manger, the shepherds present the Christ Child with gifts of food. The observance of this play begins nine days before Christmas and lasts until January 6. Costumes are home-made and the actors for the most part must save pennies all year in order to adorn their shepherds' crooks and to secure the tinsel and finery necessary.

The *Posadas,* or Rests, held in memory of the journey to Bethlehem, are also celebrated by the Mexicans before Christmas. Small lanterns over doorways or swaying from treetops indicate places where this ceremony is to be held. Groups of nine families take part. The first family to participate stops at a house, singing Christmas carols. Admittance is refused them; they then ask for *posada,* or rest. The second family joins the first as they move on to a third house, and so on, the group singers increasing at each *posada.* Refreshments are served at the last house and prayers are recited by the assembled company before the manger or an improvised altar. The last *posada,* held on Christmas Eve, becomes an all-night watch, when the participants, after attending midnight Mass at the nearest church, return to celebrate until morning.

The *Dia de Inocentes* is celebrated December 28 in memory of the children who died under the edict of Herod in his search for the Christ Child. It is customary on this day to play tricks on one's friends in a manner similar to the occurrences on April Fool's Day. *Inocente* means foolish as well as innocent, hence the cry of "Inocente" after each discomfiture of a victim.

Originating in the remote provinces of Spain, the Blessing of the Animals (January 17), celebrates the feast of St. Anthony the Abbot, their protector. The event is marked by a procession of pets, from the canary to the family cow or horse, which are gayly decorated and taken in a parade to any parish church for the invocation of a blessing to provide them strength to serve their masters.

It is quite natural that the celebration of St. John's Day (June 24) should be associated with water and, accordingly, the ritual requires that all go to the nearest pond, river, or lake for an early morning dip. The custom also permits, if no body of water is available, a plain tub bath. Two other customs prevail on this day. One is haircutting. If a woman wishes to have luxuriant hair, she dampens the ends of her tresses and places them on the doorsill, where they are chopped off with a hatchet. The second is *Las Mañanitas,* traditional folk song. Any home in which a member of the family bears a name derived from John, is sure to be awakened on this day with a *serenata* by a group of singers. If the *Mañanitas* is agreeable to Juan or Juanita, the musicians are served refreshments.

The *matachines* are symbolic dances in which the rattling of a hollow nut imported from Mexico, and the soft patter of leather sandals, furnishes much of the rhythm. Performed at various places, they can be seen regularly on December 12. The word *matachin* means a dance performed by grotesque figures. Dating back further than the Spanish conquest, they were part of the Aztec ritual when Cortés entered Mexico. The Franciscans incorporated them into Christian festivals, in order to interpret religious symbolism. The first *matachines* were simple, with no pattern or significance apart from the obvious one of worship. Additions and interpolations were combined with special costumes and the ceremonial has become highly complicated. The ritual is passed from father to son and is closely guarded. Those who take part wear colorful clothing ornamented with feathers, reeds and beads.

One of the most interesting phases of Mexican folkways is the *remedio* —folk curing, the use of plants, herbs, charms, and incantations to cure disease or bewitchment. This lore is handed down from mother to daughter, usually, and there are remedies for everything, even for *susto*—fright. (The cure for this is cenizo leaves, boiled.) The cure for boils is to kill, cook, and eat a road runner or chaparral cock. Mexicans often touch a child they admire, otherwise it will become a victim of "the evil eye." Among the actual *remedios* on record is one which caused the ailing man to walk two miles in shoes in each of which a can of tomatoes had been emptied.

The Mexican tradition is historically connected with many of the legends of buried treasure to be found in Texas folklore. Cabeza de Vaca, Coronado (*see History*), and other Spanish explorers spun great tales of gold in Texas, or searched for it. James Bowie, hero of the Alamo, was supposed to have located the lost San Saba mine, legendary with the Spaniards. Countless men have expended money and energy in an attempt to find these lost mines or buried treasures. So far, the searches have revealed only a few old coins. But some Texans are still, as J. Frank Dobie describes them, Coronado's children. Let a Mexican cowpuncher or an old settler produce an ancient chart, and immediately somebody goes out to dig for hidden gold.

Among rural Negroes nature myths and proverbs are common, similar in general to those of Negroes of other States. They have, also, the same belief in the efficacy of charms and good-luck pieces to ward off bad luck or disease, and, in isolated communities, certain forms of "conjure" are prevalent. This folk culture is retreating before such influences as increased educational and economic development for the Negro masses and the urban Negro knows little of it.

The annual celebration by Negroes of June 19—the day when emancipation from slavery became effective in the State has been quite general; few Texas Negroes would consider working on "Juneteenth" if it can be avoided. The holiday is generally observed by a picnic at which everyone eats, dances and sings to his heart's content. During this celebration, the racial gift of melody asserts itself. Every Negro who can play a fiddle or guitar brings his instrument, while the others break spontaneously into the "blues," work songs, or spirituals.

A Texas contribution to Negro folkways is the barbecue stand, with its outgrowth of customs. Business deals are often closed and social engagements made at a barbecue stand, where meats cooked in open pits by Texas Negroes have a flavor which they claim is distinctive.

Perhaps the Texas Negro's largest contribution to folk material is in music, in the indigenous spirituals, work songs and other melodies that originate in the cotton field, over washtubs and at church.

In San Antonio and in the hill country north and west of that city, the Germans have preserved an authentic folk culture. A group of Germans of San Antonio still observe traditional customs. Folk dances are a cherished feature of parties in Gillespie County (*see Tour 24b*).

Other foreign groups of the state, including the Poles, the Swedes, the Wends, the Czechs, the Italians and other European groups, cling to their national customs. As comparative newcomers in Texas, they have not had time to develop an indigenous folklore, and their folkways remain those of the homeland. The community of Swedona is an example of the manner in which one of these racial units has preserved its old customs (*see Tour 16b*).

The Texas Folklore Society collects and preserves folk material, and has been a valuable agency in gathering obscure data from isolated communities. Its headquarters are at the University of Texas in Austin.

Education

EDUCATION is a major industry in Texas. The tremendous growth in educational facilities throughout the country since World War II has produced spectacular results in the State. The principal reasons are:

The upswing in population created needs that had to be met by school districts. The application of scientific methods to farming called for an understanding of machines. The electrical, electronic and defense industries called for skilled hands. Research in the professions, notably in medicine, became so productive that many new opportunities were opened. Municipalities saw that vocational training helped men fill jobs and therefore established two-year colleges, easy to enter. The multiplication of faculties increased the demand for educators with a doctor's degree. The GI bill of rights gave thousands of young men a chance to improve their training. The prosperity of the State expressed itself in the proliferation of foundations, which supported institutions of learning, and in the ability of middle-class families to send their young people to college. Universities discovered that the affluence of their alumni could be put to good use.

Finally the cornucopia of the Federal Government poured funds into educational programs and facilities. In 1966 the United States gave Texas a total of $115,438,000 for education. Elementary and secondary public schools received $39,757,000; higher educational programs received $1,932,000, and higher educational facilities $6,063,000. Then there was Federal support for vocational programs for those of lower than college grade. All Texas vocational programs in 1965 received $23,147,100; of this amount $639,000 was expended for training in agriculture, $581,000 for trade and industry, $398,000 for home economics, and $619,000 for technical education.

Even this enumeration does not conclude the channels of income for schools. The State contributed its part; in 1965–1966 fiscal year it provided $174,150,376 for higher education at specific colleges, $658,284,141 for the support of free school and vocational education, and contributed $59,183,770 toward teacher retirement. The State also appropriated funds for its schools for the cerebral palsied, blind, deaf and otherwise incapacitated.

In the fall of 1966 the public elementary and secondary schools enrolled 1,886,000 pupils, and the ratio of pupils to teacher was 24.2 to 1. The nonpublic schools enrolled 166,500. The public high schools graduated 121,795, with the sexes practically equal in numbers. Texas had 97 institutions of higher learning and in 1965 288,615 students enrolled, 79,815 of them for the first time.

As early as 1503 Spain ordered schools for the children of savages, and the Franciscans taught what might be called the first vocational training in Texas. But the first real public school was active in the Villa of San Fernando de Bexar (San Antonio) in 1746. After 1813 a school for 70 pupils was built in San Antonio, and after Mexico took over every new town set aside a block for school purposes. In 1828 free textbooks were provided for a school in San Antonio, probably the first instance of this kind.

Colonists from the United States who came early had scant means of bringing textbooks. They used whatever was available. One student would bring to class a copy of *Robinson Crusoe;* another, Goldsmith's *Natural History.* Even the best equipped frontier stores carried only "Murray's Grammars, Walker's Dictionaries, slate pencils and lead pencils." A housewife donated her pasteboard hat box to a teacher who used it in lieu of a blackboard. James N. Smith wrote, "The neighbors soon cut logs and built a comfortable school house." But in many instances even log buildings were not available, and classes were conducted in the open air under trees, or in the homes of settlers.

One of the greatest causes of friction between Texas and Mexico was the matter of schools. To mollify the colonists, the Mexican government at one time donated 17,712 acres of public lands for a school in Nacogdoches; it liberalized its school laws, and added "geography and good manners" to the curriculum. But such gestures ended in failures. The evidence is that Mexico also deplored the lack of schools. Juan N. Almonte wrote in 1834, "What is to be the fate of those unhappy Mexicans who dwell in the midst of savages without hope of civilization?"

Reasons for the failure of schools under Mexican rule were many: the impoverished condition of the national treasury, the difficulty of obtaining good teachers and textbooks, and the fact that Roman Catholic training, with which most of the immigrants from the United States were not in sympathy, was stressed. Among the pioneers were some who valued education and obtained private teachers for their children or sent them to the United States to school. Others cared little for schools, for they had come to earn their fortunes in a land which must first be subdued. Thus, unlike the eastern States, Texas did not establish the church and the school along with the home.

Many private schools opened in Texas during the period 1823–36. They were called "old field" or "cornfield" schools. Teachers moved from one plantation or log cabin to another, taking as pay whatever they could get. A Captain Beach told of hiring a team to haul his "salary"—a load of corn—100 miles to the nearest market. The average charge was $2 a month for tuition. As the younger folk usually helped their parents in the fields, school terms were as uncertain as the weather.

Nothing was accomplished toward the establishment of a regular public school system until Mirabeau B. Lamar, President of the Republic of Texas, in December, 1838, made an impassioned plea for free public schools. Addressing the Congress of the Republic, he said:

> If we desire to establish a Republican Government upon a broad and permanent basis, it will become our duty to adopt a comprehensive and well-regulated system of mental and moral culture. . . . A suitable appropriation of lands to the purpose of general education can be made at this time without inconvenience to the Government or the people; but defer it until the public domain shall have passed from our hands, and the uneducated youths of Texas will constitute the living monuments of our neglect and remissness.

In reply to Lamar's challenge the public school system of Texas was built. In 1839–40, through legislation and the efforts of Andrew J. Yates, educational leader, each county was allocated four leagues of public lands (17,712 acres) to be used for school purposes, and 50 leagues were set aside for the establishment of two colleges or universities—the present source of wealth of the University of Texas.

The indifference of many settlers toward public schools and the cheapness of the State's school lands long delayed the benefits Lamar had planned. Nevertheless, during the 1840's many private institutions were chartered. Rutesville, the first college actually to materialize, opened near La Grange in 1840. Two years later the University of San Augustine was opened, the first Texas educational institution to require laboratory work in science. Baylor University (*see Waco*) was chartered in 1845 and is the oldest college in the State. Other schools were launched by pioneer educators who, in 1845, formed the Texas Literary Institute to foster the cause of education in Texas.

Following annexation, provisions were made for two kinds of schools, "public" and "free." For the latter, one-tenth of the State's revenue was set aside; these schools were for orphaned and indigent children. Now began the factionalism which for 55 years was to retard educational progress in Texas. One group looked upon education as a purely private matter; another faction favored free schools for all children. Still others held that education was a charity for the indigent, or that it should be regulated by religious leaders. In 1846 Galveston voted taxes for the establishment and support of "free public schools." San Antonio had four free public schools in 1853, in a program described by Dr. Frederick Eby, author and educator, as "the first genuinely free school system to be opened in Texas."

The act establishing a uniform State school system was passed on January 31, 1854, but defects in the law and the popularity of private schools limited its benefits. The school system, like the State, was land-poor and the per capita allowance was only 62 cents.

German settlers led the way in the establishment of free schools supported by local taxes, and formed associations to organize and control them. The Masonic Order greatly aided the cause of education, in some instances even supplying school buildings. Churches founded 45 institutions in the State between 1846 and 1873.

The Civil War interrupted educational progress in Texas for almost 20 years. State school funds had virtually been wiped out, and in 1870 the National Bureau of Education reported that Texas was "the darkest field educationally in the United States." Public schools were reinstated in the constitution of 1869, which provided for the first time "a uniform system of public free schools for the gratuitous instruction of all the inhabitants between the ages of six and eighteen."

Co-education began in Texas in 1865 under the guidance of the Reverend Rufus C. Burleson, one of the founders of Waco University (now Baylor University). The designation of degrees for women graduates puzzled the more liberal educators who opened the doors to the fair sex. Keachi College (now nonexistent) offered the Maid of Arts and the Mistress of English Literature. Waco University had a Mistress of Arts degree. Andrew Female College (now nonexistent) at first conferred the degree of Graduate of the College upon women, but changed it to Mistress of Polite Literature.

During Reconstruction a drastic school system was established along military lines. Bitter opposition to this system crippled the educational program; reactionary reforms were noteworthy for extravagance.

Brenham established Texas' first municipal high school in 1875.

The State constitution of 1876 set aside "not more than one-fourth of the general revenue," for school purposes, and allocated one-half of the public domain, about 52 million acres, for school support. For a State university, one million acres of public land were reserved, and it was specified that the institution was to be laúnched as soon as possible "for the promotion of literature, and the arts and sciences." A State Board of Education was organized, but its members, all State officials, had little time to devote to educational matters. Separate schools were provided for white and Negro children.

Through a Federal land grant, the Agricultural and Mechanical College of Texas came into existence in 1876 (*see Tour 20b*). Its grant specified that it be a scientific and vocational college, but at first its courses were purely literary, a condition that led to criticism.

Governor O. M. Roberts played the most prominent role in the establishment of the modern school system. In 1879 he undertook the re-establishment of the Agricultural and Mechanical College along the lines provided in its grant, and by his influence helped establish Sam Houston State Teachers' College in Huntsville. In 1882 he assumed the leadership in organizing the University of Texas, which had been authorized by an act of the legislature in 1881. Governor Roberts changed public sentiment from hostility to enthusiasm for free public schools. An amendment authorizing the district school system and the right of districts to vote local taxes for school purposes, was passed in 1883. The school law of 1884, providing for greater support from the State, became the basis for all future educational progress. In 1915 the Compulsory Attendance Law was passed. Under this law all children between the ages of eight and 14, unless properly excused, are compelled to attend school. In 1918 a constitutional amendment authorized free textbooks.

As public school education developed in Texas, local school districts made provision for nonwhite pupils. Separate schools were established for whites and Negroes, and in some instances for Latin Americans. Higher education was made available to Negroes in schools established by religious groups. An effort by a Negro to attend the University of Texas was carried through the courts in 1950, before the Federal Government had enacted any Civil Rights legislation, and the appeal to the United States Supreme Court resulted in an order to the University to admit the applicant to Law School. This precedent levelled racial barriers. In May, 1954, the Supreme Court declared that a Negro should not be separated, or placed apart, since this generated a feeling of inferiority; "in public education the doctrine of separate but equal has no place." Texas school districts prepared to integrate. This was not always accomplished to the satisfaction of all citizens, but there were no violent incidents such as took place in the Deep South. When threats of disorder appeared in Mansfield, where a Federal court opened the high school to Negro students, Governor Shivers sent State Rangers to keep order and no violence resulted. Similarly, attempts of nonstudents to interfere with the attendance of Negroes at Lamar College in Beaumont were stopped. But there was strong opposition to integration in many school districts and the State Legislature reflected this by supporting movements for local option. In 1957 the Legislature passed a law making it illegal for a public school board to abolish segregation of white and Negro children without approval of the voters in an election. It also ordered closing of any school at which State or Federal Troops were needed. Desegration proceeded slowly, with some court actions, and was established more easily in western counties, where Negroes were relatively few. During the 1960s a large proportion of public schools was integrated. An influential factor in the change was the provision in the Civil Rights Act that schools would have to be integrated in order to obtain Federal funds. In some large cities, such as Houston, the charge that some schools were inferior to others did not apply, for the boards of education had taken care that all facilities should be of equal merit, whether for white or nonwhite students. For this reason the demands for taking children out of their neighborhood schools by buses did not meet local approval.

The leading institutions originally founded to provide higher education for Negro students are Prairie View Agricultural and Mechanical College at Prairie View, Texas Southern University at Houston, Huston-Tillotson at Austin, Jarvis Christian at Hawkins, Bishop at Dallas, Wiley at Marshall, Paul Quinn at Waco, Mary Allen at Crockett, Butler at Tyler, and Texas at Tyler.

Before the establishment of Texas State College for Women (now the Women's University) at Denton domestic science and practical arts were hardly recognized in education. This college led the way, in 1903, and within ten years all the leading schools had practical arts courses. Vocational education is now widespread in Texas. It began in 1917–18 when 39 public schools offered courses in vocational agriculture or home economics. The State Board of Vocational Education, the membership of which is identical with the State Board of Education, administers the public school vocational educational program. Federal funds are available to the State for vocational education.

The most important privately endowed university is Rice University in Houston. The Texas Arts and Industries University in Kingsville, Texas Technological College in Lubbock, and seven large State Colleges in Alpine, Canyon, Commerce, Denton, Huntsville, Nacogdoches, and San Marcos, are leading institutions. Among the major denominational schools are Baylor University in Waco, Baptist; Southwestern University in Georgetown, Methodist; Texas Christian University in Fort Worth, Christian; Southern Methodist University in Dallas, one of the largest educational institutions in the State; St. Mary's University, Our Lady of the Lake College, the Incarnate Word College, in San Antonio and St. Edwards University in Austin, Roman Catholic.

A helpful development in extending education has been the multiplying of junior colleges, of which Texas has more than thirty. They offer two years of college work to students who may not be able to attend a university, yet prepared them to continue in a senior college. Some of the courses are vocational and practical, thus cultivating aptitudes for certain occupations. An example of the value placed on a junior college by a community is the inauguration of a junior college with three campuses at once by the supervisors of Tarrant County in the city of Houston, with the avowed object of "supplying an increasing demand for semi-professional and technically trained employees without duplicating training already available. Adult educational courses and vocational training also will be available." Opportunities for adult education are being opened by many municipalities, which realize the need for mature workers who are familiar with electronic and computer skills.

One of the tools of education that reaches beyond the confines of the college campus is the public library. Thirty years ago a Texas city would be erecting a fine example of formal architecture to be called *the* public library; today the library has acquired additions and auxiliaries—Houston, Dallas and other cities have branches in all outlying parts and are adding more. In decades past an eyeless bust of Homer and a bearded portrait of Shakespeare were the symbols of a public library; today the symbol most expressive of its functions is the bookmobile, carrying essential works to readers at remote places. Circulation figures—the number of books drawn—used to be the principal measure of a library's usefulness; today its functions are greatly expanded. Periodicals from all over the world enlarge the reader's horizon; microfilm gives access to unique material in other collections; the union catalogue offers the resources of a group of libraries; reference services are keyed to community needs; films and records open new areas of communication, and books are available to the blind, the deaf and the shut-ins. In Texas many of the smaller libraries have county support; it is worth noting that in large cities the number of volumes often equals or exceeds the figures for population.

Religion

RELIGION came to Texas with the explorers and remains today a potent influence for spiritual and social welfare throughout the State. The Spaniards made a path with their guns and left the padres behind to convert the Indians. Fray Juan de Padilla is said to have marched in with Coronado in 1541. In the next century the padres gained a footing in East Texas, only to meet with the opposition of the French colonizers. They found a better field for substantial growth in the area around San Antonio, where the natives were friendly. Here Fray Antonio de Olivares founded the Mission of San Antonio de Valero in May, 1718. In subsequent decades the Franciscan padres directed the Indians to build the substantial mission establishments that still stand near San Antonio as monuments of the tenacity and energy of the founders.

Thus the Roman Catholic Church was the first to extend its authority in Texas, but the approximately 2,000,000 communicants that it has there today stem in large numbers from the Mexican immigrations. Church authority was curtailed when Mexico secularized the missions, and Texas was left almost without church influence. Protestantism was barred by the Imperial Colonization Law of 1823, which said that the Mexican government would protect "the liberty, property and civil rights of all foreigners who profess the Catholic religion (Roman Catholic Apostolic), the established religion of the empire." Sam Houston was among the settlers to be baptized in formal obedience to Mexican law.

Yet there were few priests in colonial Texas. Padre Muldoon, according to Noah Smithwick, was "the only authorized agent of Cupid east of San Antonio." He often charged $25 for a marriage service, for distances were great in those days. Under Mexican law no marriage outside the church was legal, and colonists already married were re-wed, while those wishing to marry signed a legal bond, set up housekeeping, and waited for their wedding until the padre came. John J. Linn wrote, "Not one in ten of the colonists introduced into Texas were Catholics; and to my knowledge no efforts were made to secure forcible subscription to the tenets of that church." While this was true, colonists were compelled to protect the property rights of their children. Thus, news of the coming of a priest was the signal for all to hasten to the house nearest his route, where mammoth wedding and baptismal ceremonies were held. These occasions were "the most pleasurably exciting events in the lives of the colonists." The first Republic of Texas Congress passed a law that all persons who had been married by bond but not by religious rite should have their unions solemnized by a "regular ordained minister of the gospel" or the judge of some civil court, and the children of those so married were by the same act made legitimate.

During the period of colonization in Texas, Dr. Lyman Beecher predicted that the American frontier was in danger of relapsing into barbarism. Yet as early as 1817 William Stevenson, Methodist missionary, was preaching to settlers in the Red River region. In the Austin colony, where there were 11 Baptist and several Methodist families, Thomas J. Pilgrim, Henry Stephenson and others held services in the 1820's. Occasional ministers conducted Protestant services for the colonists, though Mexico prohibited their activities. In the spring of 1832 Needham J. Alford, Methodist preacher, and Sumner Bacon, a Presbyterian, held a meeting in Sabine County near the present town of Milam. The matter was reported to Colonel Piedras, Mexican commandant at Nacogdoches.

"Are they stealing horses?" the commandant inquired. "No, Señor Commandant." "Are they killing anybody?" "No, Señor Commandant." "Are they doing anything bad?" "No, Señor Commandant." "Then leave them alone," the commandant ordered.

There are numerous examples of the ingenuity of the colonists in providing what might be called emergency religion. A Fourth of July barbecue was delayed until the fiddler could hold funeral services for a deceased stranger. A suspected murderer in the Austin colony was the only carpenter available; he made his victim's coffin before the neighbors gathered to conduct the funeral, "a large one for these parts." A frontier character known as "the Ring-Tailed Panther" forced a missionary at the point of a pistol to hold services for his dead dog.

In the pressing business of establishing homes and freedom in an isolated land it was perhaps inevitable that early settlers, wrestling so wholeheartedly with the material, should neglect the spiritual. After Texas became a Republic and the doors were opened to men of any faith, ministers found stony ground awaiting their sowing. The Reverend Oscar M. Addison, a Methodist, wrote in 1843: "I have gone ¾ of the way around my circuit and find nothing cheering, or encouraging, many of the members have backslidden, and are spiritually dead—some have been going to dancing school, and some have joined the Baptists."

Roman Catholic influence declined following the overthrow of Mexican authority, although many later settlers were of this faith. In 1838 the Reverend John Timon was sent to investigate conditions in Texas. He reported finding only two priests. In 1840 the Reverend J. M. Odin (later Bishop of Galveston) was given charge of the Roman Catholic church in Texas, and through his efforts that religion regained strength in the State.

On receiving news of the Battle of San Jacinto, the Methodist General Conference of 1836 sent the Reverend Martin Ruter to supervise a Texas mission. With him came two associates, Robert Alexander and Littleton Fowler.

In 1839 a system of circuit riding was inaugurated by the Methodists. Thereby the early Texas churchmen hoped to give even the remote communities religious services every six weeks. The circuit rider's visit was eagerly awaited. Missionaries still had need of courage. Their time was spent largely on horseback. The State was infested with Indians and travel was dangerous in the extreme. Every man went armed, the ministers no less than others. The diary (1839) of the Reverend Joseph P. Sneed gives some idea of the frontier preacher's routine:

> After dark Thursday 10 Oct, rode over to the Navadat (sic) passed no house for 30 miles . . . Friday, went down 6 miles to Texanna . . . Monday 14th Oct . . . Left Texanna rode 45 miles to Dr. Sullivans on Colorado . . . (On the) 15 rode about 48 miles . . . Rough fare Sunday 20, traveled this day contrary to my feelings and custom about 42 miles . . . Then northwest up the brassos (sic) camped in the bottom that night we kept guard all night to prevent bein supprized (sic) by the Indians the wolves howled around us and I slept very sound . . .

Baptist ministers likewise were early in the State. The Reverend Joseph L. Bays started preaching in private homes about 1820, and was later arrested for his activities in the Austin colony. The Reverend Mr. Pilgrim organized the first Sunday school in the Austin colony—perhaps the first in the State—but was compelled to abandon it because of opposition from the Mexican authorities. Texas' first Baptist church was established in Illinois in 1833, and a year later was transferred below the Red River. It was called the Pilgrim Church of Predestinarian Regular Baptists. All of the branches of this church were so-called "Hardshell."

The first Presbyterian church is believed to have been established in the Red River country in 1833. German immigrants were probably the first Lutherans in Texas. The first Texas minister of this faith was German, the Reverend Louis C. Ervenberg, who came in 1839. The Reverend Caleb S. Ives was the first Protestant Episcopal missionary; he settled in Matagorda in 1838. There were people of Jewish faith in the Austin colony, although the first known synagogue in Texas was not established until 1854. Disciples of Christ and Churches of Christ organized, it is believed, about 1842. Christian Scientists organized in Texas in 1886. Most of the other denominations came to the State later.

Camp meetings and revivals conducted in the open or under brush arbors were an important frontier institution. The Reverend Jesse Hord, a Methodist minister, described a meeting held in January, 1839:

> The scene was novel, solemn, imposing. A cloth tent, quite a log heap on fire, surrounded by men and women axiously inquiring 'the way of life,' and that in the midst of the almost undisturbed jungle of Old Caney bottom. . . . I read to them the Word of God, sung, prayed, exhorted them to 'flee the wrath to come,' and invited mourners, though we had no mourner's bench nor altar. . . . Many, if not every sinner of the assembled company, bowed and cried aloud for mercy. (From *A Brief History of Methodism in Texas,* by Homer S. Thrall.)

Even the fervor of a people thirsty for religion could not offset the damage done by irregularity of services. Contemporary writers complained of the lack of consistent moral training. The *Morning Star,* a Houston newspaper, said on June 18, 1839:

> It is a source of much astonishment and of considerable severe comment upon the religious character of our city, that while we have a theatre, a courthouse, a jail and even a capitol in Houston, we have not a single church. Efforts we know have been made by some persons, who feel interested in matters of this kind, to collect the necessary funds for the erection of a house of worship but of late we have not heard a word spoken about it.

Of all who earned reputations on the Texas frontier none came by his more honestly than Andrew Jackson Potter, "the fightin' parson." He was known from the Panhandle to the Gulf, a fire-eating preacher reclaimed from the profession of gambling and bartending. One incident of his career will tell the story of "Jack" Potter. On entering a small town in west Texas, Potter learned that the only available building for church services was the saloon. He obtained an "announcer" who stood in front of the building and cried:

> Oyez, oyez, there's goin' to be some hellfired racket here this mornin' gents, by Fightin' Parson Potter, a reformed gambler, gents, but now a shore-nuff gospel shark. It's a-goin' to begin in fifteen minutes, gents; all ye old whiskey soaks an' card sharpers better come on over an' learn to mend yer ways or the devil's gonna git ye quicker'n hell kin scorch a feather.

A crowd gathered, naturally, and so enthused were the hard-bitten listeners that the "congregation" insisted on "setting 'em up" for the parson after the services, but Potter refused a drink, so instead they "took up a mighty handsome collection."

The Roman Catholic Church and the Baptists have reported the largest number of members in recent decades. An inquiry by the Texas Council of Churches, 1960–1964, showed that the Roman Catholics had 669 churches and 1,978,925 members in eight large cities, while three Baptist organizations had 4,587 churches and 1,794,953 members in the State. The next largest denomination, the Methodist Church, had 2,051 churches and 682,640 members. Other denominations whose membership runs into six figures are the Protestant Episcopal, the United Presbyterian Church in the U. S. A., the Church of Christ, and the Disciples of Christ. The conservative, orthodox and reform Jewish congregations totaled 64. Many other denominations are represented in Texas. They include the Church of the Nazarene, the Pentecostal Churches, the Reorganized Church of the Latter-Day Saints, the Seventh Day Adventists, the Church of Jesus Christ, and the Brethren. The Church of Christ, Scientist, listed 109 churches but did not publish its membership. The Unitarian Church had 32 churches and 3,462 members and the Foursquare Gospel had 57 churches and 3,621 members. Two bodies of Friends counted 13 meeting houses and 843 members.

The churches play an important part in the cultural and educational development of Texas. They have actively supported and manned hospitals, and even today, when government funds are devoted to medical centers without religious ties, the denominations often play a major part, of which the Southwest Texas Methodist Hospital in the new Medical Center at San Antonio is a prime example. Many major colleges began under church auspices, among them Austin, Baylor, Bishop, Concordia, Dallas Christian, Fort Worth Christian, Houston Baptist, Howard Payne, Huston-Tillotson, Jacksonville, Jarvis Christian, Lon Morris, Lubbock, Mary Allen, Our Lady of the Lake, Port Arthur, St. Edwards, St. Mary's, San Marcos, Schreiner, Southwestern Christian, Southwestern University, Texas Christian, Tyler, Trinity, Wayland and Westminster. Numerous colleges stress Christian principles as fundamental in their communities. The number of colleges with a Baptist foundation exceeds all others, but the Methodist, Presbyterian and Christian denominations also have made education their chief concern.

The emphasis on religious principles has not meant that students and faculty must conform to specific creeds. Southern Methodist University of Dallas was established by The Methodist Church and is "devoted to the ideals of Christianity," but like many others it opens its doors to all. It explains: "Although the university is nonsectarian in its teaching, its relationship with The Methodist Church insures a high standard of moral and religious principles on campus. The faculty is composed of scholars from various churches, and in an average enrollment most of the religious faiths of America are represented. The student body is usually less than 50 per cent Methodist." A similar policy prevails in many of the colleges established on a religious foundation.

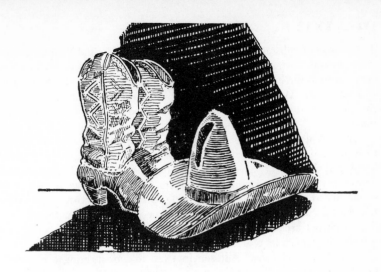

Social Life

I N ITS social life Texas is neither a typically Southern nor a typically Western State, although both influences are felt, and in sections one or the other predominates. In its tendency to preserve the social customs and traditions of the past, Texas partakes of the Old South; in its rodeos and barbecues it is as Western as the society built upon the cattle industry of the broad prairies.

As in the South, Texas—although more democratic in its acceptance of newcomers—builds its social strata largely upon names old in the State, and its social life upon time-honored customs and observances. In some sections, however, the State is new, and here social equations are based upon the usual standards of wealth, prominence, and merit. Perhaps the last quality has more power in Texas to unlock the doors of society and to admit the stranger to the circles of the elect than in any section of the United States other than the real West. Throughout the State certain early characteristics hold true—the noted hospitality of the old-time Texan prevails, and simplicity is the rule except in social strata based upon sudden wealth.

"The dust of the plains on the shoes and a big hat are still badges of old-established social position, hinting at kinship with cattle kings," one writer has said. And, "Remembering the Alamo is still a popular social pastime."

The background of social life in Texas is as colorful as its history. It began with the Spanish period of stately grand balls, of *fandangos*—public dances—on the plazas. The manners of the grandees and their ladies and the numerous fiestas of the lower classes made a colorful pattern embroidered against the background of the green wilderness and the red Indians (*see History*). With the arrival of the Anglo-American the social order changed, except that Mexican citizens preserved their own traditional customs.

In early-day Texas, the dependence of one man upon the other served to weld sections together and encourage greater social activity. The fellowship of the pioneers developed into a brand of hospitality which became known through the accounts of travelers. "Tall tales" were told of the sociability of the Texans, one even going so far as to picture a member of the Austin colony forcing a stranger at the point of a gun to visit him. The coffeepot became a symbol—it was "kept a-boiling," and any person who might happen by was expected to "light a spell" and visit.

The Reverend Oscar Addison in 1846 told of meeting a plantation owner who, though "not religious . . . thought well of it," and invited the circuit rider and his companion to dinner:

> After entering he said his old friend Parson Steele . . . generally took a gulp of brandy with him and would be happy for us to join him, of course, we declined. . . . (This) will serve to give you an idea of some of the kind of folks in this country. . . . We set down to a table groaning under the weight of the good things of life, wine was by us refused.

It was natural that the simplicity and affability of the pioneers should remove class barriers. A man's past mattered not in early Texas. What he was *did* matter. Yet strangely enough, descendants of these same Texans now value the past of any name, particularly if that name symbolizes something of Texas.

Pioneer Texans had home-talent dramatic clubs, dancing classes, home concerts and musicals, horse racing, and, most important of all, the celebrations attendant upon anniversaries such as the Fourth of July.

Mrs. Dilue Harris, speaking of a celebration held at Stafford's Point on September 1, 1836, wrote: "The barbecue, ball and election were at Mr. Dyer's near our house. . . . The ladies spent the day quilting. The young people began dancing at three o'clock and kept it up till next morning."

Following publication of an advertisement of a "Barbacue & Ice" at Beauchamp's Springs, at which congressional candidates were to speak, the editor of the *Houston Morning Star,* of July 4, 1839, said:

> (It will) not be an unfavorable opportunity for these gentlemen to express their true politics . . . provided . . . the liquors do not prove too powerful.

Settlers were invariably ready to hold an outdoor celebration. Weddings were observed with as much gayety as Independence Day. Guests rode horseback or came in wagons, and some traveled real distances—up to 100 miles. Noah Smithwick described a wedding of 1828: "When young folks danced in those days, they danced . . . they 'shuffled' and 'double-shuffled,' 'wired' and 'cut the pigeon's wing,' making the splinters fly. . . . The fiddle being rather too weak to make itself heard above the din of clattering feet, we had in another fellow with a clevis and pin to strengthen the orchestra, and we had a most enjoyable time."

The *Telegraph and Texas Register's* notice of a "splendid ball" (1839), said:

> The ball will be opened precisely at 1-2 past 8 o'clock P.M. Gentlemen will obtain Tickets of admission at the bar.

An advertisement in the *Morning Star* of August 16, 1839, announced:

> Mr. Grignon begs leave to inform the public and his friends in general, that he has engaged the Saloon at the Exchange Hotel, for the purpose of giving lessons in Dancing, teaching waltzing, and all the fashionable dances now in vogue in Europe. . . .

The quilting bee was a favorite form of entertainment. Suppers served the workers were prodigious: Turkey, pork, venison, "Pies, cakes, chickens, eggs, butter, milk, preserves."

The race track was a favorite gathering place. "Splendid and refined amusement" was advertised. General Thomas Green wrote of the race meet of 1839, "Many fine women and horses are in attendance." In the *Telegraph and Texas Register,* on July 31, 1839, was this item:

> There was a 'feast of reason and flow of souls' recently up at Spring Creek, consisting of a horse race, and three stump speeches.

The saloon was to some extent a social institution; especially in German communities was the beer garden a rendezvous. In most of the growing communities men met socially over beer and champagne. But rowdyism in any form was resented. The *Daily Telegraph* (Houston) of September 25, 1872, said:

> Houston is too elegant a city to be afflicted with such places as Smoky Row, Jones' Woods, Hash Row, French Soldier, and Frogtown in Galveston.

As foreign immigrants arrived they brought their customs and social institutions with them (*see Racial Elements*). In some sections developed certain customs having racial significance. And in other sections—Texas is too big to be uniform in anything—the people built up customs peculiar to themselves. Thus in San Antonio, where the past is present in everything, there developed observances associated with the city's early history, with descendants of those who had participated in that history gradually becoming the social leaders. Notable among the observances is the Fiesta de San Jacinto, which is the brilliant climax of the city's social season. Typical social groups in San Antonio are the Pioneers' Association, the San Antonio Conservation Society, the Daughters of the Republic of Texas, and the Old Trail Drivers' Association. The latter organization is the only one of its kind in the world, and its members are men who drove herds up the cattle trails, or their descendants. In their social functions these men keep alive the customs of other days—they serve supper from real chuck wagons, attend dances wearing red bandanna handkerchiefs and boots, and consume black coffee from tin cups.

In west Texas the rodeo and the Fourth of July barbecue are still major social events. There are found such colorful observances as the Cowboys' Christmas Ball at Anson in the Abilene district (*see Tour 10a*), and the Cowboys' Reunion at Stamford (*see Tour 10a*). Elaborate rodeos are held, and are the signal for cattlemen and their families to gather from the most distant points for a few days of intensive social activity.

Also important in modern Texas social life are the various county and State fairs. The State Fair Association sponsors the Boys' and Girls' Encampment at the State Fair in Dallas, where about 800 farm youths annually are provided entertainment and social contacts equaling in importance of the educational benefits received. Every county fair is the occasion of much "neighboring," feasting, friendly rivalry, and general enjoyment. The old pastimes prevail—even, as in the case of the Bandera Annual Frontier Celebration, including spinning and weaving contests (*see Tour 17a*). And invariably at these festivities the barbecue pit sends forth its fragrant message. Old settlers' reunions are held in many communities (*see Calendar of Events*), and other rural social activities include county "sings" or singing conventions, a survival of a frontier institution. Cooperation and neighborliness still motivate many customs, especially in east Texas—including cemetery workings, poundings for the new preacher (when everyone brings a pound of food), and school entertainments held as benefits. In many rural sections the school is the center of social life; the teacher arranges entertainments and programs.

But there have been many changes in social life in Texas, notably the urban tendency to break up into small groups. Formerly the churches were looked to for social as well as moral guidance. While the "ice cream social" and other forms of church functions are still in existence, particularly in rural communities, they are not as popular as in the past. Religious revivals, once week-long gatherings, today bring neighbors together more briefly, since good roads make it possible for farmers to attend "meeting" after supper, and return. Luncheon clubs and service organiza-

tions exist in abundance. The early organized social groups of Texas were
the usual literary societies, musical, recreation and card clubs. In most of
the State these organizations survive. The Idlewild Club of Dallas, one
of the oldest exclusive social groups in Texas, was founded in 1884. One
of the largest organizations with social attributes is the Parent-Teachers'
Association, launched in 1909. Another important factor in the social life
of women of the State, particularly of rural sections, is the State Federation of Women's Clubs. Historical and study clubs dating to the early
part of the century, when women first began to organize generally in the
State for cultural advancement, are found in almost every community. In
Dallas alone there are 400 private clubs.

Social activity with a benevolent purpose is popular. Among the newer
developments are the Dogie Club of Amarillo, an organization for the
welfare of Negro boys, and the Maverick Club, which has for its goal the
rehabilitation of boys. The Maverick Rangers, composed of boys, are
taught respect for laws that affect the welfare of others.

Social events built primarily upon the physical features of various sections, include the Onion Fiesta at Raymondville in the Rio Grande Valley
and the Oleander Fete in Galveston.

Whether the stranger encounters his first taste of social life in the
State among the weather-beaten pioneers, with their warm greetings and
their friendly calloused hands, in the traditional folk festivals of the Mexicans (*see San Antonio and Tour 19f*), or in the more sophisticated circles
of society, he will be likely to find there something of the past, something
which makes the occasion belong peculiarly to Texas.

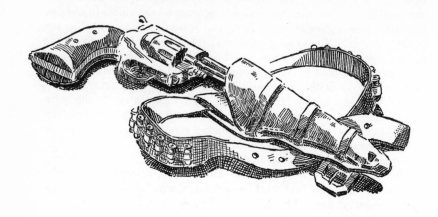

Guardians of the Public Safety

NO POLICE force in the country has the high prestige, right across the continent, of the Texas Rangers. The man in the tan trousers and shirt, wide-brimmed western hat, black tie, leather holster and sidearms not only commands respect, but admiration. His effectiveness was expressed by another Ranger years ago: "No man in the wrong can stand up against a man in the right who keeps on a-comin' ".

The Texas Rangers constitute the enforcement arm of the Department of Public Safety, organized in six companies, with a captain, a sergeant, and one or two Rangers stationed at each of the Regional Headquarters of DPS, at Houston, Dallas, Lubbock, Corpus Christi, Midland and Waco. The rest are roaming the State as trained criminal investigators, traveling on horseback, according to tradition, or, if necessary, by motor car, helicopter, airplane, motorboat, and jeep.

The Rangers date from 1823, when none other than Stephen F. Austin referred to these hard-riding enforcers as ranging all over the country. Austin brought 300 colonists to the Spanish province of Texas, and when both the Mexicans and the Comanche and Apache Indians threatened his settlers, the Rangers rode out to protect them. By 1835 three companies of Rangers were organized and in subsequent years of the fight for Texas independence they engaged in hot and often disastrous fighting with both Indians and Mexicans. Walter Prescott Webb says in his memorable *Story of the Texas Rangers:* "The Ranger captain did not order his men to 'go', but 'come' ". Some of the Ranger captains of this type were Ben McCulloch, Sam Walker, Big Foot Wallace, John McMullen, Adison Gillespie and John Coffee Hayes—known to the Indians as Captain Jack and to the Mexicans as El Diablo (the Devil).

The Rangers tangled with all the disturbers of the peace in Texas history. They fought in the big and little wars, in Indian and Mexican raids, in the Salt War near El Paso, in forays against horse thieves and train robbers. The Rangers were the first to use the Colt six-shooter on the plains. They put an end to the operations of Sam Bass and other bandits.

The Ranger is still able to make his choice of weapons. No special type of gun is prescribed. Some Rangers still carry the old Colt Frontier model single-action .45, while others carry .38 caliber Colt automatic pistols, or .357 Magnums.

Available to the Rangers are other facilities of DPS to combat the rising dangers of attacks on person and property—the Intelligence Section, which conducts surveillances and undercover investigations of organized crime and vice and subversive activities; the Narcotics Section, of an agent-in-charge, three supervisors, and 11 field agents; the Identification and Criminal Records Division, which has on file nearly 1,500,000 sets of fingerprints and exchanges information with police authorities everywhere; the Modus Operandi Bureau (the "M. O." of detective stories) which files reports of criminal offenses and individuals; the Crime Laboratory, which takes latent fingerprints at the scene of a crime and has sections on chemistry, toxology, questioned documents (forgeries), photography, and firearms. All these facilities for fighting crime and protecting the public are coordinated under the direction of the Public Safety Commission, which appoints the director of DPS. The Commission consists of three members appointed to six-year staggered terms by the Governor of Texas.

The problem of holding down the number of fatal accidents on the highways is acute in Texas, where more than 5,000,000 vehicles are rolling over the smooth concrete roads every minute of the day. The number of deaths has been rising above 3,000 in recent years, and the property loss has reached many millions of dollars. But, as the Department says, "the amount of economic loss pales into insignificance when it is realized that a like sum of money cannot return even one of the lives lost."

Every driver in the State is familiar with the Highway Patrol, which enforces the rules of the road. Although the patrolmen are seen everywhere, there are only 829 of them, working out of 12 districts of the six Regional Commands. They give information, investigate accidents, render first aid, including blood tranfusions, and apprehend felons. Each man works nine hours a day for a 54-hour week and some work at night where traffic is heavy.

Traffic supervision also is responsible for the License and Weight

Service, which checks the weight of loads to avoid damage to the highways. Fees and fines assessed against violators are applied to road maintenance. Driver licensing is a major function of the State government, and DPS has 207 trained patrolmen appointed to insure the competence and ability of drivers, to license safe drivers and educate or "unlicense" unsafe ones. There are well over 5,000,000 drivers. In 1964 there were 5,980,-250 registered vehicles, of which 4,200,000 were passenger cars. Since 1951 motor vehicles have to pass annual inspection, and this service is performed by the Motor Vehicle Inspection Service, which has 5,200 inspection stations. There is a mandatory fee of $1. The Department enforces the Safety Responsibility Law, effective 1964, and keeps full records of accidents.

Texas is not remote from the danger of nuclear attack and fallout. The State continues programs to protect its citizens from such possibilities. Even more certain are the disasters that nature frequently bestows in the form of tornadoes. The Department of Public Safety is involved in insurance against both contingencies. On January 16, 1963, the Governor's office transferred the Office of Defense and Disaster Relief to the Department. Because of its excellent system of communications and policing DPS was able to add much to the Texas Operational Survival Plan, which implements the Civil Protection Act of 1951, and assures quick, effective action in an emergency. Coordination of authority to combat disaster is considered vital. Whether the disaster be from hurricane, tornado, fire, flood, explosion, or man-made, there is need for an emergency control agency in every community. More than 1,000 cities and counties in Texas coordinate their activities with DPS.

In February, 1964, a new underground Emergency Operating Center was opened at the headquarters of DPS in Austin. It is 24 feet underground, has its own water well, generators for emergency power, air conditioning, food stocks for 30 days, infirmary, kitchen, dining area, offices, and dormitory for 120 persons. The Center was built on a matching-fund basis with the Federal Government at a total cost of $674,382, and is intended to provide protection against the effects of a 20-megaton blast 3 to 5 miles distant, including air blast, radiation and biological warfare.

Training for emergency service is part of the responsibilities of DPS through its Office of Defense and Disaster Relief. It trains radiological monitor instructors, shelter manager instructors, medical self-help and civil defense personnel. It supports the National Shelter program by locating, licensing and stocking public fallout shelters. Food, water, medical and sanitary supplies for a 14-day period are installed. At the close of 1964 2,528,000 shelter spaces had been licensed.

Communication Services

REVOLUTION against Spain gave Texas its first newspaper, *El Mejicano,* published in Nacogdoches by José Alvarez de Toledo in 1813. The revolutionists had brought to their headquarters "a printing press and a few fonts of type, and the printer himself formed one of the party." From this beginning, the story of Texas journalism was for many years to be one of stormy interludes.

Nacogdoches also saw the second newspaper venture, under the guidance of Dr. James Long, last of the filibusterers. He, too, had come for the purpose of ousting the Spanish, and the *Texas Republican* was issued to enlist sympathy in the United States. Copies were sent to large contemporary newspapers, and the *St. Louis Enquirer* (September 25, 1819) was moved to say:

> These are strange things to be seen in a Spanish town; a newspaper called Republican; the citizens attending to the establishment of a school; mills building. . . . We wish they may go on, that the revolution may triumph.

For a long time after this, news from outside Texas drifted in belatedly and only occasionally, and so eager were the settlers from the United States to learn what had occurred in that country and beyond, that "well-behaved strangers" were welcome visitors everywhere. It was reported upon more than one occasion that the traveler, anxious to hasten about his business after a night's lodging, was courteously but forcibly detained until his host was certain his budget of information had been exhausted.

This general avidity for news caused the establishment of various papers, which usually had short lives. They had no means of getting dispatches from the outside world; Texas news of more than local interest was likely to have a political angle, and Anglo-American printers were obliged under Mexican law to take an oath not to "disturb the peace with seditious papers." Distribution, because of the scarcity of roads, was accomplished principally on horseback. Publications often had to be suspended for lack of paper, and sometimes the editor closed the shop in order that he might help his subscribers chase Indians.

Godwin Brown Cotton appeared in 1829, to establish a weekly publication, the *Gazette,* at San Felipe. Subscriptions were acceptable in "cash or produce." From Cotton's press came several newspapers.

As the revolution started in 1835 the *Telegraph and Texas Register,* most significant of the earlier news journals, was established in San Felipe, and became an invaluable repository for historical documents of the revolution. Inventor Gail Borden, its part owner, realized the importance to the cause of a publication and printing press, and valiantly stood by his task (at Harrisburg after the ad interim government had gone there from San Felipe) until the arrival of a Mexican army. Later, in Columbia and Houston, Borden's paper was the official organ of the Republic's early government. It mirrored frontier life—the flurry caused by the presentation of a play called the *Dumb Belle;* the promise of "splendid and fine amusement" at the horse races; a three-column account of the legal hanging of two murderers. The *Telegraph* continued its useful career until 1877. Copies of the earlier issues are in the University of Texas archives.

Texan prisoners of the Santa Fé expedition issued (1842) in the castle prison of Santiago for six weeks a handwritten sheet, the *True-Blue,* copies of which are in existence in Galveston.

When the *Northern Standard* was established at Clarksville in 1842, its editor, Colonel Charles De Morse, announced his willingness to accept lard, tallow, beeswax, and other commodities in lieu of money for subscriptions. His newspaper became the strongest influence in northeast Texas. Most of the papers of this early period and for many years afterward had outstanding causes, not always political, for which they fought; some demanded more and better schools, some the building of railroads. Among the picturesque pioneer newspaper editors was Colonel John S. (Rip) Ford, Ranger and Indian fighter, who had a tendency to sell out or close his plants, so that he could join current wars or lead his own expeditions.

The first modern Texas newspaper was the *Galveston News,* which according to a memoir in the *Texas Almanac,* saw the light on April 11,

1842, when a roving printer named Samuel Bangs printed its four pages in a one-room shack on Galveston island. In 1844 the paper was acquired by Willard Richardson, a man of considerable enterprise who managed it until 1875. He established the *Texas Almanac* in 1857. In 1885 Richardson, with the aid of Colonel A. H. Belo and Belo's associate, George B. Dealey, established the *Dallas Morning News*. The *News* dates its origin to the original founding in Galveston in 1842 but uses a volume number dating back to the founding of the *Dallas Herald,* 1849, which it absorbed.

By one of those changes of ownership that do not affect the title or continuance of a newspaper, the *Galveston News* in 1963 was sold by the Moody estate; W. P. Hobby, Jr., president of the *Houston Post,* and Mrs. Oveta Culp Hobby, its editor and board chairman, assumed similar posts on the *News* and its affiliate, the *Daily Sun.*

When this *Guide* was first issued in 1940, Texas had 761 newspapers, 110 of which were dailies, 68 with Sunday issues. In 1967 Texas had 112 dailies and 543 weeklies, a total of 655. In some of the intervening years there were more dailies than in 1967, but circulation figures, more than 3,000,000 today, are larger. The influential dailies, chiefly in the large cities, are powerful agents for improvement of economic and cultural life, and their usefulness as advertising media has not been diminished by television, as was the case in larger eastern cities.

Several newspapers are affiliated with chains, and some have connections with radio and television stations. The Harte-Hanks Newspapers are published in Abilene, Big Spring, Corpus Christi, Denison, Greenville, Marshall, Paris, San Angelo, and San Antonio. The Whittenberg Newspapers are published in Amarillo, Lubbock, and Borger. The *San Antonio Light* remains the only Texas newspaper in the Hearst chain. Two dailies, the *El Paso Herald-Post* and the *Fort Worth Press* are Scripps-Howard Newspapers One important addition of recent years is the *Wall Street Journal,* owned by Dow, Jones & Co. of New York, which established one of its transcontinental editions in Dallas. This was recognition of the financial dominance of Texas in the South Central area.

Only two daily newspapers in foreign languages are listed by the *Editor and Publisher Yearbook: El Continental* of El Paso, Spanish, with a circulation of 4,000, and the *Laredo Times,* English and Spanish, with a circulation of around 18,000. There are, however, weeklies in Spanish and other languages, although their number is decreasing. Negro newspapers are the Dallas *Express* and *Post-Tribune;* the Fort Worth *Como Weekly, Mind,* and *La Vida;* the Galena Park *West Texas Voice;* the Houston *Informer,* and *Forward-Times;* the San Antonio *Register* and *Snap News,* and the Waco *Messenger.*

There are 19 schools or departments of journalism in Texas colleges and universities, where all forms of writing for newspapers are taught.

The largest number of graduates is at the University of Texas, which in a typical year grants around 60 degrees. Student newspapers are usually weeklies, but five dailies are publishing, the most widely circulated being the *Daily Texan* of the University of Texas, which has a circulation of 21,000. The others are the *Battalion,* published at Texas A. and M. University, College Station, with 10,500 circulation; *Lass-O* of Texas Western University at Denton, printing 4,000; *University Daily* of Texas Technological University at Lubbock, and the *Baylor Lariat,* Waco, printing 5,500.

William Sidney Porter, O. Henry, began his newspaper career in Texas. His humorous weekly, the *Rolling Stone,* was published in Austin, and he was for a short time a reporter in San Antonio, and for several months a reporter and columnist in Houston. A Texan who made his mark in New York City journalism was Stanley Walker of Lampasas, who was a reporter on the *Austin American* and the *Dallas News,* and wrote *City Editor* about his experiences on the *New York Herald Tribune,* where his methods became famous.

Radio broadcasting has grown from Station WRR, Dallas, in 1920 with a power of 20 watts, to 408 in 1967. The first television program was produced by Station WBAP-TV of Fort Worth on September 27, 1947.

The Texas Quality Network was established in 1934 and included the basic stations of WOAI (San Antonio), WFAA (Dallas), WBAP (Fort Worth), and KPRC (Houston).

The Lone Star Chain and the Texas State Network were established in 1938.

Literature

ALMOST contemporary with the discovery of Texas by Europeans was the beginning of its literature, for the first Spaniard to see the interior of the new land wrote a book about it. Wrecked on the Texas coast and for years a prisoner of Indians, Cabeza de Vaca escaped in 1535 and in 1542 published at Zamora, Spain, a travel narrative of which the title, 48 words in length, may best be condensed into *La Relación de Cabeza de Vaca*. A translation, made by Buckingham Smith in 1851, and edited by F. W. Hodge, is included in *Spanish Explorers in the Southern United States, 1528–1543* (1907). The third edition of De Vaca's book (Madrid, 1749) is known by the word *Navfragios* added to its title. A translation by Fanny Bandelier, *The Journey of Alvar Nuñez Cabeza de Vaca,* was published in 1905.

Following De Vaca came the colorful Coronado (1541) crossing, from the southwest, a part of the present Texas Panhandle in search of Gran Quivira, and three of his letters, with one report to the viceroy whom he served, survive. The story of the expedition was also told by four persons who took part in it, the outstanding account being that of Pedro Castañeda de Nagera. George Parker Winship, in *The Journey of Coranado, 1540–1542* (1904), translated and edited Castañeda's narrative, which, as edited by F. W. Hodge, is also included in *Spanish Explorers in the Southern United States.*

In 1542, after the death of Hernando de Soto, a band of his followers under the command of his successor, Luis Moscoso, moved westward from what is now Arkansas in an attempt to find other Spaniards of whom they had heard from Indians—probably the Coronado expedition—and traversed some 20 present-day north Texas counties before giving up their quest and returning. *Spanish Explorers in the Southern United States* contains a narrative of their experiences by a "Gentleman of Elvas," edited by Theodore H. Lewis.

After Coronado and Moscoso, few things worthy of printed note occurred in the new land for almost a century and a half. Then records were made of the tragic adventures in 1684–87 of the French Sieur de La Salle, notably by Henri Joutel, who wrote a painstaking *Journal of La Salle's Last Voyage, 1684–1687,* a translation of which was published by Joseph McDonough in 1906. La Salle, who following his establishment of Fort St. Louis in 1685 explored an area in southeast Texas roughly equivalent to one-tenth of the present State, had at least a dozen chroniclers, and the stories by seven of his companions are contained in *The Journeys of Robert René Cavelier, Sieur de La Salle* (1905), edited by Isaac Joslin Cox. A notable account of this expedition is Francis Parkman's *La Salle and the Discovery of the Great West* (about 1869).

Historian Herbert Eugene Bolton's *Spanish Exploration in the Southwest, 1542–1706* (1916) and *Spanish Borderlands* (1921) treat of the early visits to Texas of *conquistadores* and adventurers. Hubert Howe Bancroft (1832–1918) spanned the period from 1851 to 1888 in his two-volume *History of Texas and the North Mexican States* (1890), in which work particular emphasis is placed upon the early period of exploration.

Writings of the early mission period were largely confined to accounts by inspectors sent by kings of Spain to review the condition of the country. A notable exception is Fray Juan Agustín Morfi's *History of Texas, 1673–1779.* Fray Morfi was a contemporary of the Texas missionaries, and his account of the times has been translated (1935) by Dr. Carlos E. Castañeda, an authority on the history of the Spanish era. Doctor Castañeda's *Our Catholic Heritage in Texas, 1519–1936* (1936–   ), and John Dawson Gilmary Shea's *History of the Catholic Missions among the Indian Tribes of the United States, 1529–1854* (1855) embody many of the reports, messages, and other writings of the Spaniards in Texas.

In 1819, in Paris, was published a novel by an anonymous author, *L'Heroine du Texas,* the action of which takes place at a Trinity River settlement and in the Galveston of Jean Lafitte. This stilted story of the French colony of Champ d'Asile, having for its heroine a young woman "of rich proportions," is believed to be the first novel ever published with a Texas background. It has been translated by Donald Joseph and edited by Fanny E. Ratchford in *The Story of Champ d'Asile* (1937).

Stephen F. Austin (1793–1836) brought the works of Sir Walter Scott and Sismondi with his first colony in 1821, and many of the men who joined him gave precious space in their wagons to well-treasured volumes, but reading had to be distinctly secondary to plowing and fighting; an early traveler in Texas wrote, "The bookcase may be half full of books and half full of potatoes." And those who read the books did not write new ones. The first volume printed in Texas, *A Translation of Laws, Orders and Contracts on Colonization* (1829), was published by Austin. His cousin, Mary Austin Holley, wrote, in 1833, the first history in English of Texas, much of it descriptive of Austin's venture.

Since Texas biography, quite naturally, has dealt principally with the picturesque and powerful characters who were active in establishing the Republic, it is not surprising that Austin's career inspired the State's outstanding biographical work, *The Life of Stephen F. Austin,* by Eugene C. Barker (1925). In it Doctor Barker, professor of history at the University of Texas and for years editor of the *Quarterly* of the Texas State Historical Association, illuminatingly traces the social background and the social and political influences which shaped the destiny of the Father of Texas and his colony.

Among Austin's contemporaries was General Sam Houston (1793–1863), whose heroic career has produced much biographical and historical literature. Although Houston's writings were confined largely to letters, public messages, reports and speeches, those who have written about him are many. *The Raven* (1929), by Marquis James, well annotated and thoroughly reliable historically—although in the opinion of some critics slightly too favorable to Houston on certain controversial subjects—is the best biography of the General. It restores to life one of the most dramatic figures in American history, and tells the story of the man and his times with understanding and clarity. A work less readable but with greater wealth of source material is the *Life and Select Literary Remains of Sam Houston of Texas,* a 672-page volume written in collaboration with Mrs. Margaret Houston, the General's widow, by William Carey Crane.

Another figure of this period, Mirabeau Buonaparte Lamar (1798–1859), was one of the State's first poets. His volume of *Verse Memorials* (1857) contains several romantic poems of merit, notably "The Daughter of Mendoza." Lamar's personal letters and messages were augmented by a vast amount of documentary and manuscript material during his tenure of office as President of the Republic of Texas; and this collection has been published in six volumes in *The Papers of Mirabeau Buonaparte Lamar* (1922–27). A modern contribution to Texas biography of the early great is Herbert Pickens Gambrell's *Mirabeau Buonaparte Lamar, Troubadour and Crusader* (1934), in which is told the story not only of President Lamar's career but of his times as well. As Lamar and Sam Houston were politically opposed, this work is a story of the "other side" of Texas politics in the 1840's and 1850's.

In 1827, Noah Smithwick, an ambitious, adventure-loving boy of seventeen, listened in Kentucky to the lure of an *empresario* named Robertson who had lands to sell in Texas, and set out with a few dollars, one change of clothing, and a rifle, to seek his fortune in what, as he later wrote, he conceived to be a "lazy man's paradise." Being a good blacksmith and gunsmith, Smithwick made a living from the start, participated in the revolution, and became a solid citizen. He is remembered, however, not because of that, but because he had a knack with his pen. Of his journey into the colony from the coast he wrote: "The beautiful rose color that tinged my vision of Texas through Robertson's long distance lens paled with each succeeding step," and his word pictures of the land and its people, particularly of the 1820's and 1830's, are lucid and comprehensive. His book, *The Evolution of a State* (1900), was arranged and parts of it dictated by him when he was more than 90 years old, but his memory was crystal clear, his vision was still not too rosily tinted, and most serious studies of early-day Anglo-Americans in Texas quote him.

The Texas Revolution and subsequent dramatic episodes produced a wealth of literature, including the autobiography of David Crockett, *Exploits and Adventures in Texas* (1837), only the first part believed to have been written by Crockett; the remainder by an unknown contemporary. Although little meritorious verse was written in early Texas, principally because venturesome pioneers fighting for land or life in a new country are not likely to be poets or lovers of poetry, one sonorous composition, "The Hymn of the Alamo," was penned, soon after the heroic event that it commemorated, by Captain Reuben M. Potter. Historians found in the sweeping epic of a land under changing flags ample dramatic materials to chronicle and interpret. The very competent works of William Kennedy (1841) and Henderson Yoakum (1855) were written when the period of the revolution was still fresh in memory.

Texas adventure fiction in English had its beginning with a story, supposedly by Anthony Ganilh, bearing the unimaginative title, *Mexico versus Texas* (1838). In 1842, General Thomas Jefferson Green was a member of the ill-fated party which invaded Mexico and at the town of Mier was forced to surrender, and following his escape from the prison of Perote he wrote the *Journal of the Texian Expedition Against Mier* (1845).

In 1844 appeared in print a work of real distinction which became a best seller of its day, the *Narrative of the Texan Santa Fe Expedition,* by George Wilkins Kendall (1800–68), excellent journalist and first of the great modern war correspondents (*see Tour 17d*). Another widely circulated book of this period is Josiah Gregg's *Commerce of the Prairies* (1844), which had six editions in English and three in German within 13 years.

In 1843, in Leipzig, was published Captain Frederick Marryat's *Travels and Adventures of Monsieur Violet in California, Sonora, and*

Western Texas, a piece of romantic fiction which, although highly inaccurate, had its place in the field of imaginative writing.

With few exceptions, every book worthy of note by a Texan or dealing with Texas up to this time had been reportorial rather than creative; but now a novelist appeared whose prolific work, although based upon authentic background and personal experience, was sheer fiction.

To New Orleans in 1840 had come Mayne Reid (1818–83), a dashing youth from Ireland who sought and found adventure up the Red River with trappers, buffalo hunters, and Indian warriors. He received a lieutenant's commission in the Mexican War, led a charge and was severely wounded at Chapultepec, and was commended in official dispatches. With peace achieved, he wrote a war romance, *The Rifle Rangers* (1850), which was followed in 1851 by *The Scalp Hunters,* and then by *The Boy Hunters* and many another tale of adventure by land and sea, which made him one of the most widely read and successful writers of the period. Nearly all his books were translated into French, and some into German. Although most of his last 30 years were spent in England, many of his stories dealt with the American Southwest, of which the best is considered to have been *The Headless Horseman* (1867), based on a Texas legend.

The period of early German immigration was highly productive of descriptive literature. Notable is the work of Carl, Prince of Solms-Braunfels, the colonizer, entitled *Texas, a Description of Its Geographical, Social and Other Conditions, with Special Reference to German Colonization.* It was published at Frankfort-on-the-Main in 1846, and presents a sorry picture of the Anglo-Americans and Americanized Germans in Texas. Of the latter he said, "I admonish my immigrating countrymen to be twice as cautious with them." Solms-Braunfels was followed by Viktor Bracht, who wrote *Texas in 1848,* a book of general description, and by Dr. Ferdinand Roemer, another German, who in 1849 published at Bonn his *Texas, with Particular Reference to German Immigration and the Physical Appearance of the Country, Described Through Personal Observation* (translated by Oswald Mueller, 1935). A fine geographical and economic study, Doctor Roemer's work is notable for its vivid description of the times.

In 1857 a volume was published which is considered by many to be the best word picture of ante bellum life in Texas, *A Journey Through Texas, or, A Saddle Trip on the Southwestern Frontier,* by the brilliant New York landscape artist and architect Frederick Law Olmsted (1822–1903). The work of a contemporary of Olmsted's, John C. Duval (1819–97), although his *Early Times in Texas* did not appear in print until 1892 and its half-fictional sequel *The Young Explorers* a little later, also belongs to the ante bellum period. Duval, a Kentuckian, had attended the University of Virginia, was a survivor of the Fannin massacre at Goliad, led subsequently a life of high adventure, and possessed a keen and individual outlook. The quality of his writings, which also included a biography, *The Adventures of Big-Foot Wallace, The Texas Ranger and Hunter* (1885), entitles him, in the opinion of at least one recognized authority, to be called the Father of Texas Literature.

Amelia E. Barr (1831–1919), who became a highly popular novelist with more than 60 published books between 1870 and 1913, lived in Texas from 1854 to 1869, and much about the State is in her romances and in her autobiography, *All the Days of My Life* (1913).

During the era of the cattle trails a poem with a Texas theme was published which reached the ears of multitudes because it long was a standby for elocutionists from coast to coast. It had many stanzas; its heroine was the Mexican girl whose name it bore, "Lasca"; and its climax was a tragic cattle stampede. Its author, Frank Desprez, has no other work listed in anthologies, but this one had fire and rhythm, and typified, although romantically, cowboy life and perilous adventure along the Rio Grande. Its opening:

> I want free life and I want free air
> And I sigh for the canter after the cattle;
> The crack of whips like shots in battle,
> The medley of hoofs and horns and heads
> That wars and wrangles and scatters and spreads;
> The green beneath and the blue above,
> And dash and danger, and life and love,
> And Lasca.

From then until now, cowboys, cattle drives, and the activities of range and ranch have inspired many good books and a host of lesser ones. The classic writers of cowboy life are Charles A. Siringo and Andy Adams. A phenomenal sale greeted Siringo's *A Texas Cowboy, or Fifteen Years on the Hurricane Deck of a Spanish Pony,* when it appeared in paper-back form in 1886, although his best-known work is *Riata and Spurs* (1912). *The Log of a Cowboy* (1903), Adams' first work, has been called the finest piece of fiction about "cows and cow people." In 1883 Alex E. Sweet and J. Armoy Knox, originators of *Texas Siftings,* produced *On a Mexican Mustang, Through Texas from the Gulf to the Rio Grande,* introducing humor and satire into cowboy literature. J. W. Wilbarger's *Indian Depredations in Texas* (1889), illustrated with woodcuts attributed by some authorities to O. Henry, is a reliable description of Indian fights. Among the most colorful factual accounts of Texas pioneer life and of cowboys is *Trail Drivers of Texas* (1923–24), in two volumes, collected and edited by George W. Saunders and J. Marvin Hunter.

In 1882 a young North Carolinian named William Sidney Porter

(1862–1910), who was to become the most widely read short-story writer of his day, drifted into Texas, lived briefly on a ranch, worked as book-keeper, land office draftsman, and bank clerk in Austin, published there a little magazine called *The Rolling Stone,* and served as a newspaper re-porter in San Antonio and Houston. Indicted for a bank embezzlement of several years before, he fled to Honduras, returned, was convicted in 1898, and was sent to a Federal prison. Texas Rangers, sheriffs, cowboys, outlaws, and other direct actionists later appeared in many of the tales written by him under his pseudonym, O. Henry. An outstanding example of his stories with a Texas background is *A Departmental Case.*

Dorothy Scarborough (1877–1935), a native Texan who became as-sociate professor of English at Columbia University, wrote one of the first successful novels with a Texas background, *The Wind* (1925). Its scene west Texas, it attracted wide attention for the realistic manner in which it dealt with ranch life during the drought of 1885. A valuable contribution to Texas literature, published in the same year, was her *On the Trail of Negro Folk Songs.*

By the outbreak of World War II it was clear that the three big reputations thus far in twentieth-century writing by Texans were those of J. Frank Dobie, Walter Prescott Webb and Katherine Anne Porter, all of whom remained dominant figures on down into the 1960s. Miss Por-ter's *The Leaning Tower and Other Stories* was published in 1944; in 1952, *The Days Before;* in 1962, *Ship of Fools.* Her influence, both per-sonal and direct and also through her books, is at once evident in three of the finest young Texan fiction talents to emerge after the War, each be-laureled by the Texas Institute of Letters with "best novel of the year," prizes: William Goyen (*House of Breath, Ghost and Flesh*), William Humphrey (*Home From the Hill, The Ordways*) and Walter Clemons (*The Poison Tree*). Miss Porter, of course, lived away from Texas, in Mexico and in Europe most notably, after 1930.

Four of Dobie's most enduring books came between 1941 and his death in 1964: *The Longhorns* (1941), *A Texan in England* (1945), *The Voice of the Coyote* (1949) and *The Mustangs* (1952). Only a few days after his death (he got his first author's copy the day he died of heart failure) his memorable recall of ranch folk he knew, *Cow People,* was published. An autobiography of his early days, down to about age 30, titled *Some Part of Myself,* was published posthumously in 1967. His book, *The Longhorns,* was illustrated by his younger friend, Tom Lea, who turned from painting to novel-writing for his immensely successful novel of 1949, *The Brave Bulls.* After a brilliant second novel, *The Wonderful Country* (1952), Tom Lea spent five years writing a history of the world's most famous ranch, *The King Ranch* (1957), a two-volume work that continued in non-fiction Tom Lea's absorption in southwestern history. He turned to the novel again for an evocation of Spanish colonial lore in his prize-winning *The Hands of Cantu* (1964), winner of the Texas Institute $1,000 fiction award.

Walter Prescott Webb, most original and enigmatic of American historians, capped his studies of frontier history with his major opus, *The Great Frontier,* in 1953. Tragically killed in an automobile accident ten years later, he is said to have left a half-completed autobiography; it has not been published.

Roy Bedichek, a close friend of Dobie and Webb, was practically coerced by those two into writing his first book at age 70, *Adventures of a Texas Naturalist* (1947), a beautifully written work followed by the equally observant and philosophic *Karankaway Country* (1949), about the lore of the Texas Gulf Coast. Dobie, Webb and Bedichek formed a triumvirate of close friends in Austin who represented a three-man brain trust and idea center. Their influence on younger thinkers—journalists, writers and teachers—is incalculable.

All three also devoted themselves to a very curious and very Texan institution, the Texas Institute of Letters, founded in 1936 as an afterthought in Texas' celebration of the Centennial Year of its liberation from Mexico, after the battles of the Alamo, Goliad and San Jacinto in 1836. The State Government's Centennial Commission decided some organization ought to represent the State's achievement in literature, hence the organization founded (as the cynical have so often derisively observed) on the model of the French Academy. Without vanity, a few leading writers took the organization as a means of intellectual fraternity and developed it into an astonishingly powerful force in the State, resolutely opposing censorship and backwardness.

The Institute early won financial support from Texas "rich"; two $1,000 prizes—for non-fiction and fiction—were endowed by the Carr P. Collins Foundation and the Jesse H. Jones Foundation; smaller awards were created by such newspapers as the *Dallas Morning News* and the *Houston Post;* other awards were offered by libraries and interested individuals. For nearly thirty years, the judges of the Institute have made an extraordinarily fine record in selecting prize awards each year. The Institute has given solidarity and prestige to Texas writers; and it has fostered both writing and reading in the State, without jingoism. Self-perpetuating, it is free from outside pressures.

Thus, the annual Institute awards since 1939, the first year offered, represent a reliable clue to Texas writing of the past thirty years. The Institute itself published its history and a complete record of members and prize awards, in 1967, by long-time secretary and founder William H. Vann, with a foreword by Lon Tinkle, four-time president of the organization in its crucial years. This work, *The Texas Institute of Letters,*

1936–1966 (Encino Press, Austin), is the indispensable reference for Texas writing of the past three decades.

Aside from Dobie (three-time winner), Bedichek and Webb, the non-fiction award of the Institute has gone, among other books, to: *Adventures of a Ballad Hunter,* by John A. Lomax (1947), memoirs of a great folklorist; *Anson Jones: The Last President of Texas,* by Herbert Gambrell (1948); *Gail Borden, Dairyman to a Nation,* by Joe B. Frantz (1951), an illuminating biography of a career launched in Texas before achieving national success; *Great River: The Rio Grande in North American History,* by Paul Horgan (1954), also winner of the Pulitzer Prize in history; *Mighty Stonewall,* by Frank Vandiver (1957); *13 Days to Glory: The Siege of the Alamo,* by Lon Tinkle (1958); *Aristotle and the American Indian,* by Lewis Hanke (1959); *Goodbye to a River,* by John Graves (1960), a masterly combination of history and philosophy and lyricism by a first-rate talent; *Napoleon and Josephine,* by Frances Sanger Mossiker (1964), a second prize-winning work on French history by a distinguished Dallas scholar.

Fiction awards of the Institute reflect the major talents of the past three decades, most notably the following: George Sessions Perry, *Hold Autumn in Your Hand,* about farming difficulty in drought-ridden, blizzard-prone Texas; Edwin Lanham, *Thunder in the Earth,* about oil exploration; Frank Goodwyn, *The Magic of Limping John,* border Mexican folkways; David Westheimer, *Summer on the Water,* an early poignant study of race relations, winner of the fiction award in 1948; Fred Gipson, *Hound-Dog Man,* the book that started Gipson's profitable association with Walt Disney; Dillon Anderson, *I and Claudie,* east Texas vagabond life cunningly and humorously evoked by a famous Houston lawyer-banker; George Williams, *The Blind Bull,* subtle and disturbingly critical of Texas values; Madison Cooper, *Sironia, Texas,* a jumbo-sized novel that won immense national attention in 1952, disillusioned and sardonic treatment of great cotton-rich Brazos Bottoms families; Larry McMurtry, *Horseman, Pass By,* a nostalgic recall of a good cattleman (movie version titled *Hud*); J. Y. Bryan, *Come to the Bower,* a brilliant historical novel about the Texas Revolution. This list does not include earlier-mentioned novels by Katherine Anne Porter, William Humphrey, William Goyen, Tom Lea or Walter Clemons.

William A. Owens has won both the top fiction and non-fiction $1,000 awards. Owens, now a professor at Columbia, won the novel prize in 1954 for *Walking on Borrowed Land,* a story of southwestern farm life; in 1967, he won the non-fiction award for his memoir of his early difficult days in rural Texas, *This Stubborn Soil,* an unflinching memoir of impoverished but courageous existence.

The Institute also makes annual awards in the fields of poetry and of juveniles. The major poetry prizes, however, are given by The Poetry Society of Texas (around $3,000 at the annual awards banquet). Among the major names in Texas poetry: Arthur Sampley, Vassar Miller, William D. Barney, Frederic Will, William Burford, Thomas Whitbread, William Bard.

The most striking thing in imaginative literature in current Texas writing is the continued use of regional material, but used for clear-sighted scrutiny and criticism rather than for home-style flag-waving. Such nationally watched young novelists as William Humphrey, William Brammer, Larry King, Larry McMurtry, Edwin Shrake, all measure various aspects of the life of the State with sophisticated and unprovincial minds. In the novel, more than anywhere else, the critical temper has come to Texas; this genre may well dominate the rest of the century, as history and folklore have dominated the first sixty or so years.

Theater, Music and Dance

THE upswing of the living theater during the years following World War II has been one of the inspiring elements in Texan culture.

From precarious beginnings with performances by dedicated amateurs in halls seating 200 or fewer, the dramatic art has been accepted as one of the best media for individual and group expression. In the universities and colleges a drama department, with opportunities for acting, or at least a course in the dramatic art, have become necessary parts of curricula. The frequent qualification of the theater as civic and communal indicates that play acting has become a social activity. It is not necessary to grade the acting, which obviously runs from adequate to exceptional; what is important is the welcome that is being extended more and more generally to the theater.

Much credit for this development belongs to the individuals who had the toughness to make their dreams come true. There is general recognition that Margo Jones, who organized little theaters in Houston and Dallas, well earned the honor of having a fine new theater at Southern Methodist University named for her. The accomplishments of Mrs. Nina Vance, director of the Alley Theater in Houston, and of Paul Baker, director of the Dallas Theater Center, are part of a noble record. The expansion of the little theater movement into the theater center, with affiliated educational and experimental organizations, is proof of the support sponsors and the public are giving to these undertakings.

The number of study and acting groups in the colleges are almost as numerous as the colleges. Widely known are the Drama Department of the University of Texas, the Arden Club at Southern Methodist University, the Baylor Theater at Waco, the Aggie Players at Texas A. and M. University. Of the training given the statement of the College of Fine Arts of the University of Texas is typical of the best: "Drama students major not only in acting, or directing, but in costume, dance drama, playwriting, technical production, or drama education. Courses in children's theater and creative dramatics are offered. Classroom principles will be applied to practical situations in an annual production schedule of at least seven major productions and hundreds of one-act plays." A drama library follows in due course. Some of the collections are of books of plays and acting; others like the Mary McCord Theater Museum at Southern Methodist University, include memorabilia, playbills, costumes and manuscripts as well.

There are community acting groups in approximately forty cities, including suburbs of central cities. Success in one city inspires efforts at emulation in another.

In 1845, Joseph Jefferson, then seventeen, appearing with his parents, was one of the first of many famous actors to find their way to Texas. When the railroads began to make overland travel relatively simple, the professional theater followed close behind them. Six months after the rails reached Dallas, in 1872, an opera house was built there, and many others were erected in Texas cities to accommodate touring companies for "one night stands." Stars such as Edwin Booth, Edwin Forrest, Helena Modjeska, Sarah Bernhardt, Richard Mansfield, and Lily Langtry regularly included the State in their tours.

In 1909 Stark Young, who was teaching for a few years at the University of Texas, founded a college dramatic association there, the Curtain Club, which was the first organization in Texas to herald modern expression in nonprofessional play production. With the decline and virtual disappearance of road shows, the Little Theater movement became very active, with groups in many towns and cities.

The professional theater, practically eclipsed when "the road" disappeared, also has come back to life. Hit musicals on Broadway have been so widely publicized by television, news magazines and record albums that a new public has been created for them across the continent. Producers discovered that the national, or No. 2 company, could play to crowded houses in major cities without risk of being stranded. The popularity of summer musicals, using Broadway shows with guest stars and local support, is demonstrated in Texas, especially in Dallas. When producers of touring companies exacted a guarantee, it has been readily available.

Relatively few native or resident Texans have been playwrights. George Scarborough, a generation ago, was known on Broadway for plays which included *The Son Daughter*, *The Heart of Wetona*, and *Moon-*

light and Happiness. Stark Young has written one border play, *The Col-onnade.* Ten short plays by John William Rogers of Dallas are published, listed in a dozen anthologies, and widely performed throughout the coun-try, most notable among them being *Judge Lynch,* with which the Dallas Little Theater won its first Belasco cup, and *Bumblepuppy.* Of the plays by J. Frank Davis, of San Antonio, the burlesque 1890 melodrama *Gold in the Hills* has had hundreds of Little Theater productions. Jan Isbel Fortune of Dallas, who had been successful with historical radio dramas, wrote the *Cavalcade of Texas,* produced at the Dallas Centennial Exposi-tion in 1936.

MUSIC

For centuries, the music of Texas has inherited color from Spain and Mexico, from countries of eastern Europe, and from many an American State. The earnest spirituals and melodious work songs of the American Negro have contributed to it. The ballads of the cowboy are indigenous.

The first music schools within the present boundaries of the United States were those of Texas missions, in which Indian neophytes were taught to sing the ritual music of the Franciscans. Fray Juan Agustín Morfi in 1778 wrote, of Mission San José: "These Indians . . . are today well instrumented and civilized. . . . Many play the harp, the vio-lin, and the guitar well, sing well . . ."

Spanish and Mexican folk songs influenced the ballads of the *va-queros,* one of which, "La Paloma" (The Dove), is still frequently heard.

To this day the making of new ballads has flourished among the people of Mexican birth or descent. Each warm, clear evening, on the streets and plazas in the Mexican Quarter of San Antonio, strolling troubadours with guitars offer the songs of their people. It is not rare for a new ballad to come into being, based on some humorous or tragic happening of the day. Its tune may be of the moment and spontaneous, or it may be an old melody. Typical of the Mexican folk songs is "Alla en el Rancho Grande," popularly called "Rancho Grande."

The Mexican is best at singing love songs, and he sings them with pathos, in seemingly interminable verses.

Tunes usually were of the popular or folk variety; music of the classic type could hardly be expected to have penetrated to the frontiers. But as early as 1839 operatic airs were heard in the theaters of Houston.

German settlers in the 1840's, and the French in 1854, brought their native music.

During the cattle drives, Texas cowboy music came into national sig-nificance. Its practical purpose is well known—it was used primarily to keep the herds quiet at night, for often a ballad sung loudly and continuously enough might prevent a stampede. However, the cowboy also sang because he liked to sing, and he was a spontaneous composer, creating ballads as he rode, often about some incident of the day's work. In this music of the range and trail is "the grayness of the prairies, the mournful minor note of a Texas norther, and a rhythm that fits the gait of the cowboy's pony." Of those early ballads there is no authorship record, and there are few of them that probably were not amended and added to by many singers. The men who devised them did not think of themselves as composers, and in addition they were modest. As one cowboy song puts it, "My name is nothing extry, so that I will not tell."

John A. Lomax, collector of cowboy ballads, saved much of this folk music from possible oblivion by his publications and phonograph recordings. Arrangements of some of the melodies have made them nationally popular, notably that by Oscar J. Fox and David Guion of "Home on the Range" which dates from 1872. The "Cowboy's Lament" (Oh, Bury Me Not on the Lone Prairie), which is as old as cowboy music, has been given new life by frequent public singing. Lomax discovered the late Negro folk singer, Lead Belly. His son, Alan Lomax, has continued the collecting of folk ballads.

Companions to the cowboy songs are those dealing with Texas badmen, such as "Sam Bass," and the song about Billy the Kid, in which the retribution that came to that desperado is simply stated:

> But one day he met a man who was a whole lot badder,
> And now he's dead, and we ain't none the sadder.

Indigenous spirituals are an interesting phase of Texas Negro folkways. There are Negro song leaders and verse makers who "call" the words at church, going from one group to another like old time circuit riders. Examples of the songs spread by their "calling" are "Jesus Rides a Milk White Hoss," "I'm New Bawn," and "My Lawd's a Battle Ax." In the last-named the climax exults, "Oh, my Lawd's a battle ax, a shelter in de time of storm." Most of the Negro folk music is religious, but it also includes work songs.

Texas was the home of white spirituals, also, some of which still are occasionally sung at old-fashioned camp meetings in groves or under arbors in a few sections of the State.

Texans of German descent have continued their pioneer musical activities, and hold regular *Saengerfests* which are major social events.

The number of Texas artists who make national reputations grows every year. Among pianists the bestknown are Van Cliburn, Ivan Davis, James Mathis, Alfred Moledour, Lucien Leinfelder, Bomar Cramer and Harold Morris. Dr. Paul van Katwijk and his wife, Viola van Katwijk, pianists and teachers, have had an important influence in the development of pianists and teachers. Dr. van Katwijk was formerly conductor of the

Dallas Symphony Orchestra and dean of the School of Music of Southern Methodist University. Dr. Silvio Scionti, former head of the piano department of North Texas State University, has been an influential teacher.

Texas has contributed many fine singers to grand opera, among them Leonora Corona, Rafael Diaz, Yvonne de Treville, May Peterson Thompson, and Mack Harrell. Mary McCormick, formerly of the Chicago Opera, is teaching singing in Amarillo. A star of the musicals, Mary Martin, came from Weatherford, Texas.

Since the close of World War II there has been a steady increase of support for symphony orchestras, as one community after another organized opportunities for musical appreciation. When the first issue of this *Guide* appeared there were already nine well-endowed symphony orchestras in the large cities—Austin, Amarillo, Dallas, El Paso, Fort Worth, Houston, San Antonio, Tyler and Waco. In 1968 symphony orchestras were giving programs in these cities and in addition were permanently established in Abilene, Beaumont, Corpus Christi, Irving, Richardson, Lubbock, Midland-Odessa, San Angelo and Wichita Falls. Some went on tour. Sir John Barbirolli had become conductor emeritus in Houston, with Andre Previn first conductor, and the orchestra was now using the resplendently new Jesse H. Jones Center for the Performing Arts.

Dallas provides symphonic music not only in the central city but in its environs; its symphony orchestra was formed in 1900 and gives its major programs in McFarlin Auditorium on the campus of Southern Methodist University, and profits from the strong support of the Dallas Symphony Orchestra League. It makes efforts to reach the younger generation by its Dollar Concerts in Memorial Hall, begun in 1962, where young artists who have won the G. B. Dealey Memorial Award are heard. Its conductor, Donald Johanos, was at one time the only native-born American conductor. The San Antonio Symphony Orchestra is conducted by Victor Allesandro.

The University of Texas, the University of Houston, Southern Methodist University and many other universities and colleges either maintain symphony orchestras as part of their curricula or conduct schools of music that offer opportunities for public appearances of young artists. Musical education also is extensively cultivated in the secondary schools, while the uniformed bands of Texas are conspicuous examples of successful musical discipline.

THE DANCE

The present activity and interest in the dance in Texas is largely due to the impact of the National Regional Ballet movement. This began in the 1950s when the Atlanta, Ga., Civic Ballet organized and held the first regional ballet festival. Many semi-professional ballet companies were formed in Texas soon after this event. Most of these companies are members of the Southwest Regional Ballet Festival Association. They are the Austin Civic Ballet, Houston Youth Ballet, Dallas Civic Ballet, Fort Worth Ballet Association, Wichita Falls Ballet Theatre, San Antonio Civic Ballet, Greater Houston Ballet, Amarillo Civic Ballet, Allegro Ballet, of Houston; Houston Metropolitan Ballet, Dallas Metropolitan Ballet, Dallas Ballet Theatre and Houston Ballet Foundation.

Annual ballet festivals have been held since 1963 in Austin, Dallas, Fort Worth, Houston, and Wichita Falls. Dance schools have flourished in many cities and towns and have produced dancers and choreographers of ability. These regional companies are striving to become a part of the local cultural scene, along with painting, music and the theatre. The Dallas, Houston, Fort Worth and Amarillo symphonies have cooperated in concerts with their local dance companies. The Dallas Civic Ballet, the Dallas Symphony Orchestra, and the Dallas Civic Opera, produced eight concerts under a Title I grant in 1967. Both Fort Worth and Dallas musicals and operas offer opportunities for local dancers.

Among leading teachers and choreographers in the regional festival organization are Fernando and Nancy Schaffenburg, Frank and Irina Pal, Denise Brown, Ann Etgen, Jerry Bywaters Cochran, Lorraine Ceanford, Stanley Hall, Ruth Matlack, Edna Herzog, Maxine Asbury, Emma Mae Horn, Camille Long, Judy McCook, and Victor Moreno.

Dance departments in Texas colleges and universities also have had rapid growth. Dr. Ann Duggan and Mary Campbell have pioneered successfully in this category at Texas Women's University.

Among Texas dancers and choreographers on the national scene are Valerie Bettis, Scott Douglas, Sally Wilson, Jonathan Lucas, Cyd Charisse, Ann Miller, Alvin Aily, Yvonne Chouteau, Jeff Duncan, La Meri, and Nana Gollner. Russian luminaries in the dance world who reside in Texas and participate in the State's dance activities include Nathalie Krassovska and Marina Svetlova in Dallas, and Nina Popova, head of the Houston Ballet Foundation.

The Arts

PAINTING his pictures on sheer rock walls, the first Texas artist was a prehistoric man—perhaps a cave dweller. Of the extensive examples of Indian picture writing and the rock carvings known as petroglyphs, many, in semi-arid sections, were probably guides to water sources. Others may have been crude historical records of the chase or of war, and symbols belonging to elemental religious mysteries.

With the Plains Indians—Comanches, Kiowas, and Apaches, nomadic hunters—the distinctive art medium became the buffalo hide. Their shields were emblazoned with the Sun, emblem of the most potent medicine and protector of their lives. They decorated the exterior of their tepees with representations of their heroic deeds in war and hunting, and with family insignia.

East Texas Indians—chiefly the Caddoes who lived in villages and cultivated the soil—were, at the coming of the white man, skilled in pottery making, tanning, weaving, and feather working. They carved on bone with tools made of stone and shells, and used fire to erode their woodwork. Early travelers wrote of their smooth earth floors, covered with vivid figures of birds, beasts, and flowers. Poles hung with painted skins were set up in circles about the fire pits in such a position as to resemble, when illuminated, a brilliantly-hued fire screen. Many of the better domiciles were kalsomined inside with white clay, the walls decorated with shields, weapons, skins, and pottery. The women were highly proficient in the weaving of baskets.

Living in the desert, the Indians of Pueblo stock made of their art an almost invariable prayer for rain. Their women were skilled in the making of baskets and pottery, and before their clay vessels were baked the men decorated them with rain, cloud, and bird symbols, and with charms aimed at securing a sufficiency of water and the fecundity of the earth.

Thus, when the white men appeared, Texas already had sincere indigenous art. The European art which the Spaniards brought was often amended and modified by it.

To the missions, in the early eighteenth century, came good paintings. In Mission San José and in San Fernando Cathedral, for example, dim pictures survive, some of them gifts of the kings of Spain (*see San Antonio*). And classic sculpture was introduced by the Franciscan monks, who carved figures of saints and cherubim principally, the best known example of mission art in Texas being the carved window of the sacristy at Mission San José near San Antonio. This window was done by Pedro Huizar and is considered one of the finest works of its kind in the United States. Stone was the principal medium, but wood attained popularity for carvings of the crucifix, images of the saints, and ornamental doors. Much work was done, too, by Indian neophytes, working under the direction of the mission monks, and this soon began to display native characteristics. Clothing of many types and colors, products of the Indian neophytes' own looms and dye vats, was placed upon the figures.

Frescoes in the missions became a commingling of Spanish and Indian art—with a native Mexican influence which is sometimes called "the Aztec tradition." Authorities believe that the brilliantly hued and symmetrical patterns outlining arches and windows, both exterior and interior, were not only incorporated to attract the natives to the church by satisfying their love for color and perhaps including some of their own religious symbolism, but in many cases were the actual work of the Indians, a combination of Christian and pagan expression.

The architecture of the missions—and of the better residences which developed in the larger communities during the next century—was influenced by Mexican craftsmen who worked in iron and copper and who fashioned door hinges, bolts, decorative flat studs, and window grilles.

Following the arrival of Austin and his Anglo-American colonists in the third decade of the nineteenth century, the characteristics of a part of Texas became those of the western United States of that day rather than of Spain and Mexico. To the immigrants from the North American republic Texas was a far frontier, and on every frontier necessity takes precedence over art. Yet before 1836 there was at least one silversmith in Texas; and from 1836 through the pioneer era, several men were at work in this field. Of these, Samuel Bell of San Antonio was perhaps the outstanding representative. Cabinetmaking flourished; in nearly all the older towns appeared furniture made by local pioneer craftsmen, that of Paul

Maureaux of San Antonio, a Frenchman, being probably the most distinguished in workmanship.

In the 1840's, under the Texas Republic, began a great expansion of population, and the establishment of French and German communities with their traditional crafts and their professionally trained painters. A pioneer artist was Theodore Gentilz, a Frenchman who came in 1844 with Castro's colony. Gentilz walked from Castroville to his studio in San Antonio, a distance of 30 miles, because the city was the nearest market for his work, often pausing on the way to trade a sketch for buffalo meat at an Indian camp. *Comanche Chief* and *Camp of Lipanes* are two of his best known works. Many of his small but accurate paintings can be seen in the Alamo and Witte Museum.

Hermann Lungkwitz and Richard Petri, German gentlemen, came to Fredericksburg as colonists in that same decade. They went to the barnyard armed against surprise attacks by Indians, and their wives, attired in the stiff silks brought from Europe, milked the cows while they painted. *Milk for Breakfast,* by Petri, shows one of these milking scenes.

Eugenie Lavender had shared the grandeur of the French court under the Bourbons, Louis Phillipe, and the third Napoleon, and had won acclaim in Europe, yet because Texas offered a new field for her art, she came here in 1851. Her husband, a professor, was held captive for a time by Indians, and the Lavenders fought prairie fires and killed rattlesnakes. Mrs. Lavender, having exhausted her supply of paints, made colors from herbs, leaves, and flowers. The Lavenders lived for some time in Corpus Christi, where much of her work remains; notable is her *Saint Patrick* in the cathedral there.

A large number of accurate transcriptions of the early pictographs and petroglyphs in West Texas were made to scale by a Dallas artist, Forrest Kirkland, and published in *The Rock Art of Texas Indians* by W. W. Newcomb, Jr.

Modern sculpture in Texas began with Elisabet Ney, the great German individualist, who had won recognition in her native land before emigrating to this country in 1870. Protegée of the master sculptor, Christian Rauch, she was the friend of Cosima, daughter of Liszt, and of such men as Schopenhauer, Baron von Liebig, and members of the Hanoverian royal family, while the kings of Bavaria and Prussia were her patrons. Yet she came with her husband to the wilds of Texas and settled near Hempstead on the plantation Liendo (*see Tour 24a*). Here for several years she was content to mould the lives of her two children, one of whom died here in her arms. Hardship and heartbreak were hers, but finally she was summoned to Austin to make sculptures for the new capitol building. Here she established her studio, now a museum.

One of the ambitions of Elisabet Ney in coming to Texas was that she might establish an academy of liberal arts, and this she did informally in her studio, so that now she is credited with having initiated formal art education in the State. Her statues of Sam Houston and Stephen F. Austin are in the Hall of Statuary at Washington, and duplicates are in the lobby of the State capitol. Washington officials complained because Houston's statue was tall, Austin's short. Elisabet replied, "God Almighty made the men ; I only made the statues."

Another pioneer sculptor was Frank Teich, who settled in San Antonio in 1883. For many years until his death at the age of 83, in January, 1939, he was a resident of Llano and the "grand old man" of sculpture in Texas, with at least 25 major creations to his credit.

As mighty herds of longhorns went up the cattle trails, wealth came in, and there were strivings for culture such as theretofore had not been possible. The socially and politically prominent had their likenesses preserved for posterity, and encouraged the painting of Texas historical scenes and landscapes. William Henry Huddle was a portrayer of statesmen, and his *Surrender of Santa Anna* hangs in the entrance hall of the capitol building at Austin. H. S. McArdle painted historical scenes; his *Dawn at the Alamo* and *Battle of San Jacinto* are in the Senate chamber. Robert J. Onderdonk loved to paint hazy sunset scenes, indolent Mexican women, and missions bathed in soft sunlight; his daughter Elinor Onderdonk became art curator for the Witte Museum.

Texas landscapes first became nationally known through the Onderdonks, father and son. The younger man—Julian—painted the first bluebonnet fields to become popular, although his work was by no means limited to this subject. (Paintings by Julian Onderdonk are in the art museums of Dallas, Houston, San Antonio, and Fort Worth.) He was among the first Texas artists to be influenced by impressionism. Others similarly influenced have been Frank Reaugh, sometimes called the dean of American painters, whose paintings are principally cattle and ranch scenes; José Arpá, Spanish born, who came to San Antonio by way of Mexico and reveled in picturing hot sunshine; E. G. Eisenlohr, whose technique of broad brush strokes or bold palette knife is often expressed in landscapes; Hale Bolton, Olive Travis, Reveau Bassett, and Frank Klepper. Of these and many other artists who have perpetuated Texas scenes it has been said that they have their roots deep in "dusty roads beneath fulsome sunshine . . . the blooming cactus and hillsides of blue lupin." Whether they paint gaunt longhorns, broad landscapes, or soft-eyed *señoritas,* their subjects are usually distinctively native.

S. Seymour Thomas, as a talented youth of 15, painted a number of detailed pictures of Texas subjects, including the San José mission, before leaving for Europe to study and reside there. An excellent survey of art and artists of this period is *Painting in Texas—The Nineteenth Century,* by Pauline A. Pinckney.

Since the development, following the World War, of the American trends in painting which have found principal expression by such men as Benton and Wood in the United States and Rivero and Orosco in Mexico, a number of Texas artists have done work of that type which has won critical praise. Notable among them is Alexandre Hogue of Dallas, an interpreter of the dust bowl area, whose dramatic painting *Drouth Survivors, 1936,* was purchased by the French government and is included in the collections of the Jeu de Paume Museum in Paris.

Most appropriate to a State which once was a part of Mexico and which contains many people of Mexican birth or descent has been the influence in painting of Diego Rivero and his pupils. The Mexican crafts have not needed restoration; they have remained intact in those sections of Texas where Mexicans are numerous, and except for drawnwork and tinwork, in which there is Anglo-American competition, are still a Mexican field. Pottery, glass, tile, hand-made furniture, and some weaving, is done by people of trans-Rio Grande blood, chiefly in the San Antonio district, and there is a considerable production of hand-made lanterns, candle holders, *nichos* (niches for holy pictures), and similar articles.

Internationally known Texas artists include Seymour Thomas, portrait painter, Murray Bewley, best known for his studies of children, and Mary Bonner, famous etcher. Best known of the marine painters are the late Boyer Gonzales and Paul Schumann. Dawson Dawson-Watson of San Antonio specialized in paintings of cactus in bloom. Tom Lea of El Paso has a mural in the Post Office Department Building in Washington, and murals in the El Paso Post Office.

Many native Texas sculptors have been women. Bonnie MacCleary, born in San Antonio, won international recognition, her commissions having included one from the Irish Free State and the Columbus monument in Puerto Rico, and her work is in the Metropolitan Museum of Art, New York, and the Brooklyn Children's Museum. Her bronze statue of Ben Milam is in the park that bears his name in San Antonio. Another distinguished Texas sculptor is Waldine Amanda Tauch, whose first successful piece was a figure of a woman churning, modeled in butter, which was exhibited at a county fair. Her *Gulf Breeze,* in bronze, is notable. Allie Victoria Tennant, winner of many awards for portrait sculptures, made her home in Dallas.

Clyde Chandler's Sidney Smith Memorial Fountain in Dallas fairgrounds is an imposing creation featuring the *Gulf Cloud,* a symbolic figure. Edwin E. Smith, cowboy sculptor, is known for his portrayals of Western life. Joseph Lorkowski Boulton, whose *Devil Dog* is in the Marine Barracks, Washington, was born in Dallas. Decorative sculpture upon the towering commemorative monument at the San Jacinto battlefield (*see Tour 6a*) was done by William M. McVey of Houston, who also has an outstanding monument to James Bowie in Texarkana, a statue of David Crockett in Ozona, and did the bronze doors and exterior sculptures at the Museum of History at the University of Texas.

Among the Texan sculptors by adoption, none has contributed so many pieces to the State as has Pompeo Coppini, who came to this country from Italy in 1896. Coppini created important Texas memorials or monuments, including the elaborate Littlefield Memorial in Austin and a centennial monument in Alamo Plaza, San Antonio, in which city, also, his bronze doors depicting George Washington and Sam Houston as Freemasons are at the main entrance to the Scottish Rite Temple. Gutzon Borglum, spending parts of many winters in San Antonio, made the model for a Trail Drivers' Memorial there. Enrico Filberto Cerracchio, an Italian, has created several important memorials, the best known being his equestrian statue of General Sam Houston, in Houston.

Following the early independent teachers represented by such artist-professors as R. J. Onderdonk, who taught both in San Antonio and Dallas, art activities in classes and exhibitions between 1910 and 1935 gravitated to the museums being established by art "associations" and art "leagues" in the larger towns. At first these organizations, usually composed of only female members, met in libraries, town halls or exposition buildings until funds could be raised or municipal bonds voted for art museum buildings. Despite meager funds and impermanent quarters, these art groups were the first agencies to provide large exhibits, and the examples acquired from such exhibits became the foundations for most of the permanent collections at the public museums.

All the original buildings of the major museums in Texas have required expansion in recent years to accomodate increased activities and growing collections. The Museum of Fine Arts of Houston, built in 1924, received its largest addition in 1958 with the completion of the Cullinan wing, designed by Mies van der Rohe. The 1936 Dallas Museum of Fine Arts doubled its space by erecting a two-story addition in 1965. The Witte Museum in San Antonio has received extensive rebuilding, and the Fort Worth Art Association, which was housed in the Public Library, began a building program in 1955 and completed its structures, designed by Herbert Bayer, in 1966. Nearby, the Amon Carter Museum of Western Art, designed by Philip Johnson, was completed in 1961 and enlarged in 1966. To round out a very unusual complex of three art museums in one location in one city, the Kimbell Art Museum, designed by Louis Kahn, is to be finished in 1971.

Other museums, somewhat smaller but having collections of distinction and active exhibit programs, are the McNay Art Institute and Museum in San Antonio, opened to the public in 1954; the Meadows Museum and the Pollock Galleries at Southern Methodist University in Dallas, and the University Art Museum at the University of Texas in

Austin. Museums and galleries of more specialized interests include Bayou Bend Museum, and Contemporary Arts Museum, both in Houston, and Laguna Gloria Museum, Austin headquarters of the Texas Fine Arts Association. Art galleries and art activities are spread over the entire state in such towns as Longview, Tyler, Paris, Nacogdoches, Beaumont, Corpus Christi, Galveston, San Angelo, Wichita Falls, Midland, Lubbock, Amarillo, Canyon, and El Paso.

At most of the larger museums and some of the smaller galleries competitions in painting, sculpture, printmaking and crafts have encouraged and rewarded the development of Texas artists. Through purchase prizes works by Texas artists have been added to museum collections. Typical of the larger competitive exhibits is the Painting and Sculpture annual, held by the Dallas Museum of Fine Arts, where as many as 900 entries are received, and which also sponsors special exhibits for regional craftsmen and printmakers. An example of similar exhibits on a different basis is the annual invitational exhibit held by the Junior Service League in Longview with generous awards.

By 1940 universities and colleges assumed an increasingly important role in the arts in Texas. Art departments and Schools of Art at these institutions have developed large enrollments, retaining talented Texas artists as teachers as well as attracting established artists from other areas to Texas campuses.

The school of the arts with the largest enrollment and faculty is at the University of Texas, equipped with a new building and museum. Art instruction at Southern Methodist University acquired new quarters in 1968 in part of the Owen Fine Arts Center, one of the largest in the country, which also accomodates activities in music, drama, dance, radio, television and movie production. Other large art schools are at North Texas State and Texas Women's University in Denton; Texas Christian University in Fort Worth; Baylor University in Waco; Sam Houston State College in Huntsville; Trinity University in San Antonio; the University of Houston and Rice University in Houston; Texas University in Arlington; East Texas State University in Commerce; Southwestern University in Georgetown; Texas Technological College in Lubbock; and at other universities and colleges in San Marcos, Nacogdoches, Kingsville, Alpine, El Paso, Brownwood and Canyon.

Extensive adult and junior educational programs are offered at the museums in Dallas, Houston, San Antonio, and Fort Worth. The McNay Art Institute is among the leading private schools of art. These schools also offer additional opportunity for Texas artists who engage in full or part-time teaching.

On the art faculty at the University of Texas the large number of artists includes painters Everett Spruce, William Lester, Don Weismann, Kelly Fearing, John Guerin, Loren Mozley, Michael Frary,

Gibbs Milliken, and sculptor Charles Umlauf. In Dallas at Southern Methodist University are painters DeForrest Judd, Roger Winter, Dan Wingren, Don Bradley, Jerry Bywaters and sculptor Wilbert Verhelst; among those at the University of Dallas are Lyle Novinski, Heri Bert Bartscht and John McElroy; the faculty of the school of the Dallas Museum of Fine Arts includes Otis Dozier and, David McManaway. Other artists in Dallas are Chapman Kelley, Herb Rogalla, Donald Vogel, Ruth Tears, Paul Maxwell, Perry Nichols and sculptor Octavio Medellin.

Houston artists include James Boynton, E. M. Schiwetz, John O'Neil, David Adickes, Lowell Collins, Henri Gadbois, Marc Moldawer, Bill Condon, Pat Colville, Dorothy Hood, Herbert Mears, Richard Stout and Jim Love. In Fort Worth are McKie Trotter, Bror Utter, Cynthia Brants, Dickson Reeder, David Brownlow, Emily Guthrie Smith, James Alley, Ed Blackburn, and John Z. Thomas, and sculptors Evaline Sellors, Charles Williams, and Gene Owens. Among San Antonio painters are Cecil Casebier, Bill Bristow, William Reily, and Jim Stoker, and sculptors Philip John Evett and Richard H. Rogers.

Teaching in other towns over the state are Wilfred Higgins and Henry Whiddon at Denton; Carles McGough at Commerce; Stephen T. Rascoe and Bill Stegall at Arlington; Robert Wade at Waco. Artists working independently include the author-artist Tom Lea in El Paso; painters Wayne Amerine, Forrest Harrisberger, Merrill Cason, Scott Gentling, Forrest Bess, Frank Hursh, and sculptors Elmer P. Petersen, and Bill Wiman. Among those Texas artists who have followed their careers outside the state are: Thomas M. Stell, Jr., Alexandre Hogue, James O. Mahoney, Harry Carnohan, Lloyd Goff, Xavier Gonzales, George Grammer, Robert Preusser, Boyer Gonzales, John Rosenfield, Gray Foy, Joe Glasco, and James Brooks.

Architecture

TEXAS architecture is diverse, due to wide variations in topography and climatic conditions, as well as to the many racial strains that, at different times, came upon the scene.

The effects of two centuries of Spanish colonization have never been erased. In the arid west, the Spanish and Mexican influence is a dominant characteristic; here are the houses of adobe or sunbaked clay bricks, and old missions, of the period when Spain was attempting to perpetuate its power and glory in this outpost of a great colonial empire. In the 1840's Texas became the magnet of a tide of European emigration. These immigrants were largely Germans, although lesser groups of Alsatians and Poles swelled the ranks of the newcomers. In south central Texas, a rare type of village sprang up. After learning to build the log cabin of the Anglo-Americans, the immigrants, in the early 1850's, replaced this primitive type of dwelling with the stone and half-timber (*Fachwerk*) houses of their native land.

From the northeast and east, however, Anglo-American immigration was constantly increasing. The frontier soon receded before the ax and plow. The log cabins of settlers from east of the Sabine were followed by the two-room dog-run house, and, soon thereafter, by the mansion of the Old South. In the 1860's and 1870's the irresistible driving power of the American trek westward opened the high plateaus of the northwest to settlement. Here dugouts and sprawling ranch houses tell how the frontier was pushed across the plains.

No vestiges of the aboriginal habitations of Texas remain, other than the smoke-blackened shelters of the cave dwellers and slab-house ruins along the Canadian River. Texas Indians were principally nomads, and the agricultural tribes, such as the Caddoes, had impermanent, thatched straw, hide or earthen huts that the rainfall has long since obliterated. Because of the scarcity of wood in western Texas, adobe construction was borrowed from the Indians. Walls, sometimes five feet thick, were built of sunbaked mud slabs, and clay was used for mortar. Roofs were flat and made of adobe and leaves, laid on closely placed saplings in herringbone pattern, or wattle. Wall-to-wall supports consisted of cottonwood logs placed about two feet apart. Adobe construction was used extensively in the western arid area, but rainfall was a deterrent to its use in other localities.

Religion was the strongest influence during the era of the rule of Spain (1519–1821). Missions and presidios were built at strategic locations, and the homes of the settlers, usually of palings or stone, clustered near their walls. Beside *El Camino Real* (The King's Highway), the Nacogdoches Road and other dim highways of the wilderness, isolated settlements sprang up. However, the failure of the east Texas missions caused Spanish colonization to center in the area between San Antonio and the Rio Grande, the eastern towns of San Augustine and Nacogdoches soon becoming Anglicized.

Mission architecture reflected the Renaissance grandeur of Spain. Built by the Franciscans—greatest builders of the religious orders—the foreign influence in the design of the buildings was modified only by the limitations imposed by the frontier. Mission establishments usually had the same plan elements; a church with a bell tower or twin towers; sometimes a separate chapel for the neophytes, a granary, a gristmill, schools and living quarters for the Indians, and quarters for the missionaries and soldiers, all within the compound walls. At Mission Espíritu Santo in Goliad, recent excavations have uncovered the foundations of corrals and Indian dwellings built in the *jacal* or vertical paling manner, a characteristic of primitive Latin construction brought from below the Rio Grande. Cedar posts, when available, were sunk into the ground. The spaces between were filled with similar uprights, probably tied with strips of hides and pegged. Usually the top was surmounted with a horizontal member for further stiffening, although sometimes all the vertical members were spiked. It is believed that the east Texas missions, which so soon disintegrated, were built in this fashion.

In the San Antonio area *tufa*—a porous limestone—was available. Mission San José is an outstanding example of the use of this material, which was brought to a smooth finish by the use of lime mortar. Lime and sand for mortar were found in abundance, but the Spaniards and Mexicans often raised their masonry without mortar, filling in crevices with chinks of suitable sizes, depending on the flow of stucco to permeate the remaining voids.

For the student of early Spanish architecture in America, the missions of the San Antonio group offer interesting examples (*see San Antonio*). Mission San José (founded 1720) claims the greatest distinction in architectural design and detail. Pedro Huizar was the sculptor-architect of its carving, which is of the elaborate Churrigueresque style of the late Spanish Renaissance. The best known feature of Mission San José is the baroque carved window of the sacristy. This mission has recently been restored to some semblance of its former grandeur under the direction of Harvey P. Smith, architect.

A notable example of the better type of Spanish residence in colonial Texas is the restored Governors' Palace in San Antonio, date of erection unknown (*see San Antonio*).

Among the primitive Spanish types is the oldest house in east Texas, near Milam in San Augustine County, built about 1790 by Gil Ybarbo. It consists of two rooms, adzed cypress logs being notched into each other at the corners. Probably the chimney and fireplace once were stone, since stone was found on the site, but the present chimney is of mud and bricks, the crevices being chinked with red mud and moss, which was also used to close the cracks between the logs. Packed earth served for a floor. There were no windows. Batten doors, two for each room, front and back, swung inward and could be made fast with wooden beams that fell into slotted keepers. The loopholes have since been cut into windows.

The change from Spanish to Mexican influence was slight. From San Antonio, Mexican culture spread into the surrounding country, penetrating as far east as Bastrop County. In the Aaron Burleson house near Webberville, and other buildings, a style of brickwork is observed that is reminiscent of typically Mexican buildings along the Rio Grande.

Except in west Texas where wood was scarce, primitive building types of the various racial elements that invaded Texas were usually of wood; horizontally laid log cabins with hand-split shingle roofs, or *jacal* vertical paling huts with thatched roofs.

Mexican influence in the area east of San Antonio was impeded by the coming of Anglo-American colonists, who brought with them the frontier types of construction of Tennessee, Mississippi, and Alabama, and the more pretentious types of architecture of the Old South. Because of the limited resources of the frontier, however, the colonists usually confined themselves to the traditional log cabin and the dog-run house that found its way westward from the Atlantic seaboard.

The dog-run house consisted of two rooms with an open space between, covered with a continuous, gabled roof. The dog-run or breeze way, the open hall between the rooms, had many uses. In summer it was a sitting room, where the washing could be hung on rainy days. Actually, the dogs slept there, rain or shine, and so did an overflow of guests. Viktor Bracht, writing in 1848, said, "Saddles, bird cages, and wash basins, guns . . . and rocking chairs, cradles and dressed skins, are sometimes stored in the shade of the porches." These houses were built with batten doors and shutters.

Log and masonry construction was identical with that of the western United States of that period; the logs were hand-hewn; the ends dove-tailed; ashlar stonework with large, flush, quoined corners prevailed, where stone was available. After the sawmills came, log walls were often covered with weather-boarding.

Beginning in the early 1850's Anglo-American settlers in east Texas built their homes of lumber. Pine, cypress, magnolia, and cedar were plentiful then and were used throughout for houses. Sawmills were gradually introduced, and although some of the millwork was unloaded from ships at various points along the coast and transported to destinations in the interior, much of it was made by local craftsmen. Many of the settlers owned slaves and made bricks where clay was available, with which they built large manor houses of the type found in the Old South. Plantation homes, built at least partly of brick, and brick sugar mills sprinkled the fertile bottoms of the Brazos River (*see Tour 22b*). Cedar and cypress were used for making hand-split shingles. The interior trim was often of walnut.

In east Texas, chimneys took a peculiar form. Above the fireplace opening, on the outside, the chimney itself was offset about eight inches and extended up the gable free of the walls. As stick-and-mud chimneys, the type most often used, frequently burned, this was possibly done to reduce the fire hazard.

Excellent examples of the early Anglo-American house are the Gaines residence, near Pendleton's Ferry in Sabine County (1820); the John Gann or Bonner house, in Angelina County near Lufkin (1843); and the Tait plantation home near Columbus (1842).

From 1845 to 1860 the primitive early dwellings were being replaced by more expansive structures using various types of construction, as more immigrants poured in and brought with them inherited architectural standards which they applied often in modified forms.

The use of local materials to suit natural conditions resulted in the development of an architectural form that is typically Texan, the ranch house of the San Antonio vicinity. Many of this type were built by Mexicans. These houses were rectangular, one room deep, two or three rooms long, with a pitched roof extending over a porch or porches. The entire house was raised off the ground, but was never more than one story in height. Stone construction was used almost entirely, often stuccoed or whitewashed; shingle roofs and long porches across the front were further characteristics. There were fireplaces of stone, simple mantels, plastered and whitewashed walls and ceilings of wide boards.

Anglo-American houses of this transitional period were usually variations of the dog-run type, rectangular, with low ceilings and roofs pitched less than 45 degrees, gabled at the ends. Occasionally, the center hall was omitted and the stair was located on the continuous porch across the front. The walls were usually of stone, drop siding or lime concrete.

Often a classical influence was evident in minor details, such as stairs with simple turned balusters terminating in gracefully rounded and turned newels. Interiors were simple, with wide board flooring, lime plaster walls, board and batten ceilings and millwork that was often crude. In the Anson Jones house (1840) at Washington on the Brazos, a good example of this type of dwelling is found, with the porch, square columns and pediment above, becoming only an entrance. Service wings, wherever used, were one story high; sometimes, where the influence of the Old South was strong, they were entirely detached from the house. This classic influence prevailed particularly in the region of the great cotton plantations along the Brazos, the Colorado, and the Trinity Rivers.

In eastern Texas are many fine examples of classical and Greek Revival types of houses and churches. The Baptist parsonage at Carthage is one of the most pleasing examples, a frame one-story building with two facades carrying a four-columned portico with pediment above. The one-story frame Presbyterian manse in Jefferson is an adaptation of the Greek Revival style, in which the classical simplicity has given way to delicately handled ornamentation. Another fine example of this type is the John Vance house in San Antonio designed by John Fries. One of the best known classical types of the later period is the Governor's Mansion in Austin.

In the John Smith or Sledge house at Chappell Hill the Louisiana influence is pronounced. Although cast iron balcony rails and other ornamental features were often imported from New Orleans, the French influence of Louisiana is seen infrequently in east Texas.

Bringing traditional forms of architecture with them in the 1840's the Germans built in stone and mortar, almost invariably creating one-story rectangular houses, two rooms long with a narrow kitchen under a lean-to roof across the rear, and a porch (sometimes against the sidewalk) across the front. Often stairs led to the loft from the outside, but these were added later. Community life was expressed in the erection of such buildings as the quaint Vereins-Kirche in Fredericksburg. The Germans introduced half timber and half masonry construction, or *Fachwerk,* but this was abandoned when they learned that the stone they were using would support itself. The woodcarver's art was more evident among these people than elsewhere; fine transoms, doors, and interior trim are abundant.

Urban houses were of massive baronial type. The best examples of German houses are found in Gillespie County, in or near Fredericksburg, and in New Braunfels.

The Alsatian type of building found in Castroville, and the native peasant forms transplanted by the Poles near Panna Maria, are distinctive foreign contributions to the architecture of the State.

Adaptations of the Gothic style characterized churches of this period, the best urban example being St. Mark's Episcopal Church in San Antonio (1859). The old St. Mary's Roman Catholic Church in Fredericksburg (1861) is an unusual example.

Forts built across the moving line of the frontier consisted of a disconnected group of buildings on four sides of a parade ground. Most of the buildings were of stone. Fort Leaton (1850) and Fort Cibolo (c. 1870), examples of the single unit type, were built of adobe.

Along the Mexican border there was a gradual transition from the early adobe and *jacal* huts to houses built in the manner of the Mexican haciendas—ranch houses on a grand scale. On the ranches of southwest Texas in the 1870's large establishments came into being, such as those at San Ygnacio and San Bortolo near Laredo. Most of these houses were of stone, one room deep, opening into a patio enclosed by walls that often had loopholes. Flat roofs were drained by projecting waterspouts. Interior walls were plastered, and *chipichil* (sand, gravel and lime), tile or dirt floors were used. Often, rooms were added, in an ell.

Although not built by primitive people, but by the first settlers of the Panhandle in the 1870's, the dugout house was of primitive construction. The lack of wood on the plains caused the settlers to seek shelter in the earth. One habitation of this type is thus described:

> His dugout was made in the conventional way. A hole was excavated about four feet deep. The walls were built up about three feet with sod. A ridgepole was placed across the center and smaller poles were laid across these. On the poles was placed brush, a layer of sod and then a layer of earth.

The architecture of the ante bellum period in Texas was superseded in the late 1860's and in the 1870's especially in Galveston, where striking examples still stand, by types characterized by the ostentation and ornamental frills of the Victorian era. In the 1880's and 1890's this vogue in building culminated in the so-called jig-saw style.

Public buildings, like residences, in the period from 1870 to 1900, were generally devoid of architectural merit. The State Capitol at Austin (E. E. Myers of Detroit, architect), a neo-classic red granite structure built in the eighties and using the National Capitol building as its prototype, is the outstanding example. Today it is flanked by State office buildings in the latest flat-surface, many-windowed mode, including the Su-

Education

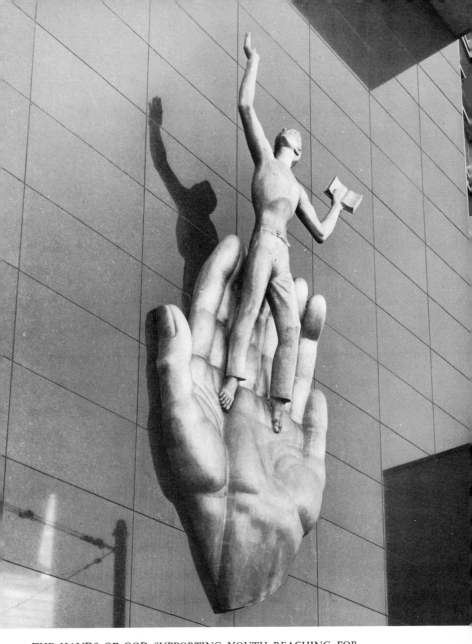

THE HANDS OF GOD SUPPORTING YOUTH REACHING FOR
LEARNING THROUGH BOOKS

Dallas Public Library

LAMAR FLEMING BUILDING, UNIVERSITY OF HOUSTON

Ray Blackstone Photo
University of Houston

UNIVERSITY CENTER, UNIVERSITY OF HOUSTON

Ray Blackstone Photo of Architect's
Drawing, University of Houston

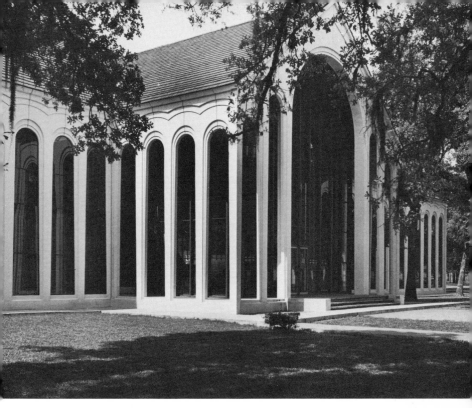

RELIGION CENTER, UNIVERSITY OF HOUSTON

NEW ENGINEERING BUILDING, UNIVERSITY OF HOUSTON

DALLAS HALL, SOUTHERN METHODIST UNIVERSITY
Southern Methodist University

OWEN FINE ARTS CENTER, SOUTHERN METHODIST
UNIVERSITY, DALLAS

Messina Studios, Dallas
Southern Methodist University

ENTRANCE DRAMA BUILDING, UNIVERSITY OF TEXAS

University of Texas

AERIAL VIEW, UNIVERSITY OF TEXAS CAMPUS

University of Texas

DORMITORY-ACADEMIC COMPLEX, UNIVERSITY OF TEXAS

Architects' Drawing
University of Texas

NEW SCIENCE COMPLEX AT EAST TEXAS STATE
UNIVERSITY, COMMERCE

Architect's Sketch, University Information Office

UNDERGRADUATE LIBRARY AND ACADEMIC CENTER,
UNIVERSITY OF TEXAS

Walter Barnes Studio
University of Texas

LYNDON B. JOHNSON LIBRARY AND EAST CAMPUS
RESEARCH BUILDING

Ezra Stoller Photo of Architects' Model.
University of Texas

BUSINESS ADMINISTRATION AND ECONOMICS BUILDING,
UNIVERSITY OF TEXAS

University of Texas

preme Court Bldg., the John H. Reagan State Office Bldg., the Sam Houston State Office Bldg., the Archives & Library Bldg., and especially the rectolinear State Insurance Bldg. The newer structures use the same granite as the old Capitol.

When the foregoing comment on Texas architecture was published in 1940, the writers concluded that the Texas Centennial Exposition in Dallas in 1936 had influenced building in two ways: it had turned attention to pioneer types of houses, and encouraged restoration, and it had shown the utility of plain surfaces, with vertical and horizontal motives and much glass, primarily adaptable to commercial structures. Both tendencies have been greatly augmented since, until today Texas is turning from the Mediterranean style and adopting the most advanced designs for attaining light, air, and usefulness. Many tall office structures are indistinguishable from the huge blocks of glass and steel that have obliterated separate identities along Park Avenue in New York, but the buildings designed for theaters, libraries, lecture halls and student centers in the universities show a wide range of original treatment inside this modern style. Among the best expressions in this style are the Jesse H. Jones Center for the Performing Arts in Houston; the Undergraduate Library and Academic Center, and the Dormitory-Academic complex at the University of Texas in Austin, the Owens Fine Arts Center at Southern Methodist University in Dallas, and the permanent exhibition halls that are the legacy of the HemisFair in San Antonio.

Downtown Houston presents the most impressive "forest of skyscrapers" in Texas, although Dallas and Fort Worth also are preempting air space. The new Shell Oil Building, One Shell Plaza, rises 50 stories and 700 feet. The Humble Oil Building in Houston rises 44 stories and 606 feet, the Tennessee Building is 497 feet tall. The familiar emblem for Gulf Oil stands high above the 37 stories, 428 feet, of that corporation's offices. Dallas is close on the heels of Houston; its First National Bank rises 51 stories, 614 feet. At least four other banks in Dallas have exceeded the 430-foot level. The three tallest buildings in Fort Worth also are owned by banks.

The rush to accommodate conventions—professional, mercantile, political, technological and agricultural—has released much building energy. With exhibition halls go accommodations for spectator sports. In this Houston has led with its Astrodome, an extraordinary structure of the latest design in seating, lighting, ventilation, and parking, able to accommodate over 60,000 persons under one roof, feed and entertain them, and staging prize fights, rodeos, livestock shows, baseball and football contests, and mass meetings. One architectural achievement can be regarded as a memorial of a pioneer—the Kalita Humphreys Theater in the Dallas Theater Center, one of the last designs by Frank Lloyd Wright.

PART II

In Fifteen Texas Cities

Amarillo

Airlines: Braniff International, Central, Continental, Eastern, Trans World Airways. Amarillo Air Terminal, US 66. Also Tradewind Airport, handling traffic using a runway up to 4,000 ft.
Bus Lines: Central Greyhound, Continental Trailways, New Mexico Transportation at Greyhound Terminal, 814 Taylor St.; also Trailways Bus Center, 700 Tyler St.
Highways: Amarillo is served by the main east-west US 66, which is also Interstate 40; by US 87 and 287, north-south roads; by US 60, which joins 66 through the city and runs southwest with US 87 until the latter goes due south alone. State 136 enters the city from the northeast.
Railroads: Panhandle & Santa Fe, S. 4th Ave., near Grant; Rock Island, N. Polk St., near 1st Ave.; Forth Worth & Denver City (Burlington) 1st Ave. and Pierce St.

Climate: Mean annual temperature, 56.6°; summer average, 76°, may drop 30° by nightfall; fall average, 57.7°. Mean annual precipitation, 21½ in. Sunshine 76 per cent.
Recreation: Baseball at Potter County Stadium, April-September. Golf at Ross Rogers Municipal Course, 722 NW 24th St., open daily, weekdays, $1, Saturday, Sunday & holidays, $1.50; Wonderland Amusement Center, Thompson Park, N. Fillmore and 24th St., 18 hole course and miniature course. Swimming, fishing, tennis, softball, also in Thompson Park, which has facilities for camping. Picnic sites also in Ellwood Park, 11th and Jackson Sts., and Memorial Park, 2400 S. Washington St.
Theater and Music: Amarillo Little Theater, 2019 Civic, Amarillo Symphony Orchestra, Municipal Auditorium, 505 Buchanan St., Amarillo Civic Ballet. Consult newspapers for dates.

Information: Amarillo News and *Amarillo Globe Times,* Globe-News Publishing Co., 900 Harrison St. Amarillo Chamber of Commerce, Amarillo Bldg. Parks & Recreation Commission, Auditorium.

Annual Events: Amarillo Fat Stock Show, Tri-State Fairgrounds, January. Mother-in-law Day, Mar. 5. Will Rogers Range Riders Rodeo, July 1-4. Cal Farley's Boys' Ranch Rodeo, off US 385, 36 *m.* NW., Labor Day weekend. Tri-State Fair, September.

AMARILLO (3,676 alt., 137,960 pop., 1960; 167,374 est. 1967), the fastest growing city in the Texas Panhandle, draws into its metropolitan area the industrial and agricultural interests of Potter and Randall Counties. The seat of Potter, it straddles the Potter-Randall line. Gas, oil, agriculture and cattle are the principal sources of its income; the leading crops in its area are wheat, grain sorghums, cotton, sugar beets and vegetables. Important also are the petrochemical industries. Potter County shares with six other counties of the Panhandle the prosperity engendered by petroleum, and much of this helps Amarillo.

Despite the development of minerals and the growth of industry, agriculture continues to play a major part in the Amarillo area. Feed lots complement ranching and cattle are fattened before shipment. The favorable climate, huge supply of grain sorghum, and easy access to highways, have drawn cattle from long distances for feeding. In a recent year 239 feed lots in the area around Amarillo fed 1,000,758 head. As part of this activity has come the growth of the Amarillo Livestock Auction Company, said to be the world's largest feeder-cattle auction. In 1965 393,027 cattle were sold for $43,539,662 through this facility.

Amarillo also is headquarters for the American Quarter Horse Assn., which has 428,398 quarter horses in its registry, 95,465 of them in Texas. It issues the *Quarter Horse Journal,* called "the largest horse breed magazine in the world." Horses are bred throughout the contiguous area.

One of the nation's largest irrigated regions is located north and south of Amarillo, accounting for extensive agriculture of which Amarillo is a major trade and financial outlet. With only 45 per cent of the land north of Amarillo developed drilling for wells is continuous, and irrigation is being extended.

The production of natural gas in the Panhandle is only second in value to gasoline, which leads the mineral products. Another important factor is helium, which is refined in two plants of the U. S. Bureau of Mines near Amarillo. The U. S. Government buys helium and stores it in the CLIFFSIDE GAS FIELD north of the city. Thence the gas is conveyed by a 425-mile pipeline to plants in Texas, Oklahoma and Kansas.

A tremendous development of civic and private construction took place in Amarillo in the 1960–1970 decade. This included the new MUNICIPAL BUILDING, costing $1,625,000; the HIGH PLAINS BAPTIST HOSPITAL at the Medical Center, an investment of $6,255,-000; the ADULT PSYCHIATRIC HOSPITAL, costing more than $2,000,000. Nine new office buildings included the ten-story home of the BANK OF THE SOUTHWEST and the District Headquarters of the SOUTHWESTERN BELL TELEPHONE COMPANY.

The new CIVIC CENTER COMPLEX envisaged a group of facilities under one roof, including a Coliseum seating 5,000; an Auditorium with stage, seating 2,500; an exhibit hall and a banquet area. This called for an expenditure of $5,510,000.

In the meantime the AMARILLO MEDICAL CENTER was growing in usefulness to the whole southwestern area as one building after another rose in a remarkable program of expansion. The buildings stand on 396 acres bordering US 66 between Coulter Road and 9th Street inside the city limits. Of the three major hospitals, the VETERANS ADMINISTRATION HOSPITAL (150 beds) was completed some time ago; the PSYCHIATRIC PAVILION of NORTHWEST TEXAS HOSPITAL (100 beds) was ready by 1968. Largest is the HIGH PLAINS BAPTIST HOSPITAL (241 beds, with plans for a total of 440) erected by a non-profit trust at a cost of $6,255,000 and operated by a board approved by the Baptist General Convention of Texas. Also included in the Medical Center are the KILGORE CHILDREN'S PSYCHIATRIC CENTER AND HOSPITAL, the MARY E. BIVINS NURSING HOME, and a number of other institutions with specialized functions. The Amarillo hospitals annually admit more than 32,000 patients.

Cultural activities include the CIVIC BALLET, which performs twice yearly with local talents; the Amarillo SYMPHONY ORCHESTRA, 4 programs, January-April, in the Municipal Auditorium; the Amarillo LITTLE THEATER, 2019 Civic, and the Amarillo GUILD OF ORGANISTS, whose annual recital enlists state-wide organists.

The State of Texas once thought so little of the Panhandle's future worth that it exchanged 10 Panhandle counties, 3,050,000 acres, to pay for building the State capitol (*see Austin*). There were some, however, who thought differently, for at the close of the Civil War the first settlers were pushing into the Panhandle. The years 1875, 1876, and 1877 saw the establishment of several ranches, including the Goodnight Ranch in Palo Duro Canyon, and the Tom Bugbee Ranch in Hutchinson County. Towns sprang into being where cattle trails and stage lines met or crossed. Buffalo hunters slaughtered uncounted thousands of these animals on the Panhandle plains from 1876 to 1886. Buffalo hides sold at $3.75 each, and with a good hunting outfit, able to kill and skin more than a hundred animals a day, money could be made. Freighters hauling hides to the market came in for their share of the profits, and so did the trading stations.

Railroads pushed their way across the Panhandle in 1887, and it was beside a construction camp of the Fort Worth and Denver City Railway that the first settlement at present Amarillo had its beginning. It was a collection of buffalo-hide huts that served as a supply depot and shipping point for the hunters, then sweeping the last of the great herds from the prairies. It even had a hotel, the walls, partitions, and roof made of buffalo hides.

The buffaloes vanished, but their passing did not affect the little community that sprawled beside the railroad tracks and utilized the name of Ragtown. Some thrifty individual early realized the commercial value of the bones bleaching on the ranges, and bone gathering became an industry. Thousands of tons of buffalo bones were shipped from Ragtown for fertilizer within the next few years.

The first real settlers were cattlemen. The division and sale of the lands of the great XIT Ranch, formed of the acres received for building the State capitol, brought still more ranches and towns into being.

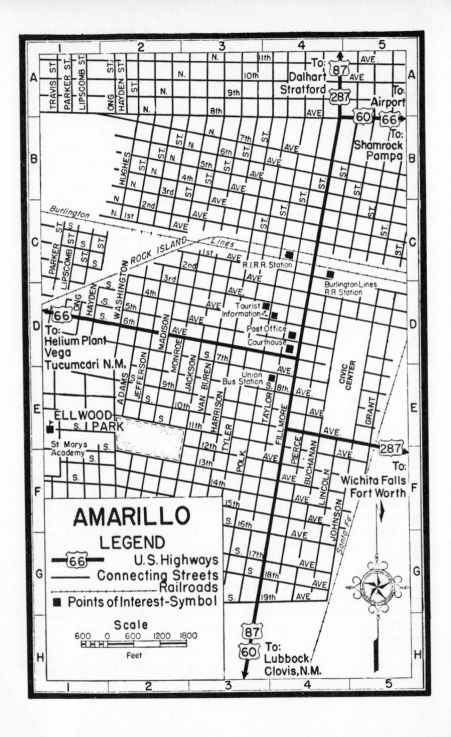

In 1887 a land developer, Henry B. Sanborn, laid out a town site southeast of Ragtown, at a point where the railroad tracks curved around a natural body of water called Amarillo or Wild Horse Lake. With the organization of Potter County there developed a contest for the county seat, and Sanborn, the promoter of what then was known as Oneida, offered the cowboys of the LX Ranch a town lot each if they would vote for his town. Since the LX hands constituted the majority of the legal voting strength, the victory was easy.

The name of the town was changed to Amarillo, and the community soon included the first site of Ragtown. The selection of the name Amarillo (yellow) is said by some to have been due to the nearness of Amarillo Creek, named because of its yellow banks, while others insist that the name resulted from the yellow flowers that blanketed the prairies in spring. At any rate the name so pleased Sanborn, who ran the hotel and several business houses, that he had them all painted a bright yellow.

For years there was no town organization and the affairs and laws of the community were administered by county officials and Texas Rangers, who were stationed in Amarillo to curb cattle rustling. Lines of cowponies stood tied to the hitching racks of the main street, and their riders crowded the hotels, saloons, gambling houses, and cafes. Available food consisted of canned goods, beef, and wild game. A pile of empty cans marked the rear of every eating place as conspicuously as the sign in front.

The early roads of the Panhandle were marked by furrows plowed in the prairie sod, which indicated the lines of communication to other Panhandle towns, while one extended southwestward across the State Line to Roswell, New Mexico. Ranchers blazed the roads from their ranch houses in the same manner, for on the prairies it was easy for a traveler to become lost. So scarce were landmarks, especially timber, that the lone giant cottonwood tree standing in a pasture a few miles north of Amarillo was known to every range rider in the Panhandle, and its branches yearly sheltered the round-up headquarters of the Frying Pan Ranch.

Sanborn and J. F. Glidden fenced their ranch property near Amarillo in 1882 with Glidden's invention, barbed wire, which he had patented in 1874. Before that time, however, barbed wire "drift fences" were built to prevent the stock from straying south in the winter. One such fence extended across the Panhandle strip. A section of the old drift fence of the Frying Pan Ranch was preserved for a long time on Western Avenue at Fourth Street.

The farmers, or nesters, seeking small acreage, further cut up the grazing land of the cattlemen who, despite their disinclination to relinquish free grazing grounds, were fencing their property. Agricultural development resulted from the productivity of the soil. The first farmers raised such immense cabbages on subirrigated land that 100 heads weighed 1,600 pounds. Cotton was cultivated after the accidental discovery that "woolly beans," cottonseeds in which a shipment of eggs had been packed, would grow, and the plow turned thousands of acres of range land into fields.

Today the PANHANDLE NATIONAL GRASSLANDS are administered by a Forest Supervisor, whose headquarters are in the Barfield Bldg., Amarillo. The Grasslands are part of the National Forest System and held by the U. S. Dept. of Agriculture. District Rangers are located in Alvord, Bonham and Texline, Texas.

Blizzards and droughts came to harass farmers and cattlemen, and to retard the growth and development of Amarillo. The howling storms of winter caused severe losses. Thousands of cattle, driven before the storms, piled up at drift fences to die. Drought was the terror of the farmer and dry years meant crop failures and suffering.

In early days Amarillo depended for its water supply on windmills and tanks, but to provide for its increased population, deep wells were drilled. There were 40 in 1927. The city bought a ranch 20 miles southwest in the shallow water belt, drilled wells and piped the water into Amarillo. The supply has a daily capacity of ten million gallons.

Meanwhile, the Panhandle oil field proved itself a major discovery. Oil towns sprang up overnight, but it was Amarillo that profited as a center of supplies and banking. In 1965 the U. S. Bureau of Mines valued mineral production in Potter County at $17,692,040.

Operators, drillers, speculators, flocked into the city. The population tripled in a few months and feverish building activity resulted in hotels, office buildings, and hundreds of new dwellings. Cheap fuel made available by the proximity of gas and oil attracted new industries.

Gradually the city has adopted the oilman, as it did the farmer and the cattleman, blending them all into that conglomeration of citizenry that is neither oil, soil, nor cattle, but is Amarillo.

POINTS OF INTEREST

AMARILLO COLLEGE, junior, was established 1929 by the municipality. It enrolls more than 2,300 students in its regular term.

THOMPSON PARK, N. Fillmore and 24th Sts., is a 640-acre recreation area, with opportunities for baseball, tennis, golf, fishing and swimming, and facilities for picnics and some camping. Plays are given in a summer theater. Inside the park is the Wonderland Amusement Center with rides, miniature golf, and concessions.

ELLWOOD PARK, S. 11th Ave. between Washington and Jackson Sts. is an attractive landscaped area with playgrounds, tennis courts and picnic facilities. Here stands a monument to FRAY JUAN DE PADILLA, a Franciscan who entered the Southwest with Coronado and three years later in 1544 was killed by Indians, presumably near the present town of Higgins.

AMARILLO AIR FORCE BASE is located east of Amarillo on US 60 and 66. It provides military and technical training for the Air Force, the Air Force Reserve, the Air National Guard and other Defense agencies. It was constructed in 1942, closed at the end of the war and turned over to the 3320th Technical Training Wing in 1951. Among other functions it trains missile technicians. It now has 78 Field Training Detachments, 25 Mobile Training Detachments and 54 Mobile Training Units.

More than 200,000 students have trained here. In a typical year nearly $75,000,000 is expended here for all purposes, including military pay of $39,000,000 and civilian pay of more than $10,000,000. The Base population has varied between 13,000 and 16,000. The Hospital has 100 beds, 27 physicians and 290 other professional personnel. The 589th Air Force Band is responsible for all musical matters in the Golden Spread—West Texas and parts of Kansas, New Mexico and Oklahoma.

LAKE MEREDITH, a 27-mile long reservoir and recreation area on the Canadian River, is the latest addition to Amarillo's water supply. It will share this with ten other cities—Borger, Brownfield, Lamese, Lubbock, Levelland, O'Donnell, Pampa, Plainview, Slaton, and Tahoka. It is 10 *m.* from Amarillo to the Canadian River on US 87, and 46 *m.* on State 136 to the SANFORD DAM, 9 *m.* northwest of Borger. This rolled earthfill dam is 6,300 ft. long at the crest, 40 ft. wide at the top and 1,300 ft. at the base, and rises 199 ft. above the stream bed. The reservoir covers 12,800 acres at the top of the conservation pool and 25,500 at the spillway crest and has a storage capacity of 500,000 acre-ft. The National Park Service has provided facilities for recreation. Fishing is supported by stocks of blue gill, black bass, channel cat and walleyed pike.

An act approved by President Johnson August 31, 1965, established 600 acres on the south shore of Lake Meredith as a National Monument for the development of ALIBATES FLINT QUARRIES and the TEXAS PANHANDLE PUEBLO CULTURE CENTER, appropriating $265,000 for this purpose. This historical site is considered of such importance that local authorities expect well over 1,000,000 visitors annually when it is fully accessible.

One of the two facilities in Texas owned by the U. S. Atomic Energy Commission is located about 23 *m.* northeast of Amarillo. This is the Pantex Plant, operated for the AEC by the Mason and Hanger-Silas Mason Co., Inc. It is part of the AEC weapons production complex. The other AEC-owned facility is at Rice University, Houston. There are several nuclear research reactors elsewhere licensed by the Commission.

Austin

Airlines: Braniff International and Trans-Texas Airways, Robert Mueller Municipal Airport, on Airport Blvd., and Interregional Highway (State 35, US 79, 81, 290).

Buses: Continental Trailways, Bus Center, 1001 Congress Ave.; Central Greyhound, Arrow Coach, Kerrville Bus, Greyhound Bus Terminal, 118 E. 10th St.

Highways: Interstate 35, principal north-south artery, combines in Austin with US 79, 81 and 290. US 290 comes from the east, has junction with US 183 northeast of city limits; after traversing the center of Austin it leaves Interstate 35 at Ben White Blvd., proceeds west. State 71 from the Gulf Coast also uses Ben White Blvd., continues northwest. Interstate 35 (with US 81) is the main highway connecting Dallas, Fort Worth, Waco, Austin and San Antonio.

Railroads: Missouri-Kansas-Texas, 301 Congress Ave.; Missouri Pacific, 250 Lamar Blvd.

Information: Austin Chamber of Commerce, 901 West Riverside Dr., Austin, 78767; *Austin American* (morning), *Austin Statesman* (evening), *American-Statesman* (Saturday and Sunday) 308 Guadalupe St.; Information Center, the University of Texas. Austin has 5 radio and television stations with all major networks.

Recreation: Austin provides every form of activity for leisure time, has large convention and hotel facilities and spectacles. It has 7 major parks comprising more than 1,800 acres; 37 playgrounds, 21 swimming pools, 39 tennis courts, 4 community recreation centers, 4 golf courses, 71 athletic fields. There are two public golf courses of 18-holes each, the Municipal Course near Tom Miller Dam and the Morris Williams Course near the Municipal Airport. Barton Springs Pool in Zilker Park is most popular. Lake Austin Metropolitan Park has about 3 *m.* of lake front on Lake Austin, and City Park is at the end of the lake where Tom Miller Dam impounds the Colorado River. Swimming, boating, fishing from pier. Tours of Tom Miller Dam and power station start at the west end of Austin Blvd.

Special Events: Texas Relays, Texas Memorial Stadium, April. Baseball by Austin Senators of the AA-Texas League, Disch Field, spring and summer. University football by Longhorns, and Southwest Conference teams, Texas Memorial Stadium, fall season.

AUSTIN (550 alt., 186,545 pop., 1960; 212,000 1965, est.) is the capital of the State and headquarters of the University of Texas; it also is the seat of Travis County, the 1,051 square miles of which constitute the metropolitan area of Austin, with an estimated population of 240,000. Austin lies on low hills above the Colorado River, which flows west and south of the main part of the city; the Tom Miller Dam impounds its waters in Lake Austin, which has a surface area of 1,830 acres and provides opportunities for boating and yachting. The physical appearance of Austin has been augmented in recent years by the extensive building programs of the State government and the University, the latter developing a new research center around the Lyndon Baines Johnson Library.

Educational and State administrative activities dominate; besides the University, Austin has St. Edward's University, a Roman Catholic institution for men; the Lutheran Concordia College, the Austin Presbyterian Theological Seminary, the Huston-Tillotson College, St. Mary's Academy, and the Texas State School for the Blind and Deaf. Nevertheless Austin is a busy trade mart, an outlet for the products of Travis County and a center of wholesale and retail enterprises. The county produces dairy products, sheep, poultry and some cotton. Petroleum is relatively minor, averaging around 20,000 bbl. a year, but the county ranks fourth in lime production.

Bergstrom Air Force Base is located 7 miles southeast of downtown Austin and is reached by US 183 after its junction with Ben White Blvd. It was formerly Del Valle AFB and is now controlled by the Tactical Air Command and tenanted by the Command Service Unit and the Strategic Air Command.

At first glance Austin seems strung along one main thoroughfare, and although this impression is erroneous, the effect is a concise panorama of the city's character. For six miles this thoroughfare is like a giant show window, with Austin on display. Set deep in commodious grounds, their spires and turrets reaching through the treetops, are various eleemosynary institutions. Signs direct the stranger to museums and historic sites. Along lateral streets are glimpses of fine old homes and wide, cool lawns under trees. Down the broad length of Congress Avenue, the principal business street, rise modern office buildings and hotels. Congress Avenue is used by Branch Route 81, which runs into Guadalupe Ave., and thence into Lamar Blvd. Parallel with Congress runs the Interregional Highway, the major route through Austin from north to south, used by US 79, US 81 and Interstate 35. Another fine connecting highway is Airport Blvd.

Viewed from the ridge overlooking the Colorado from the south, Congress Avenue seems to split the city asunder, a broad street at whose farther end bulks the capitol, with the tall tower of the University of Texas rising beyond and to the left, against the background of hills so tinged at evening by a faintly purplish mist that O. Henry called Austin the "City of a Violet Crown."

At night a system of skylights, in each of its 29 towers 165 feet above the streets, sheds a bluish radiance over the city, like an eerie moonlight, contrasting with the brilliant white and neon lighting of Congress Avenue and the red glow of the statehouse dome.

A huge acreage in parks and playgrounds contributes to Austin's beauty, and the hills on the west, networked with drives, are a source of scenic and recreational attraction. The newer residential additions are spreading into the seclusion of the thickly wooded hills, with houses of brick and stone hidden deeply away from winding drives, while south of the river suburban districts extend far along the highways. Austin's southern heritage is plainly evident in many of its public buildings and in the old residential sections.

Established after Texas became a Republic, Austin shows neither the

Spanish influence nor that of the German-settled adjacent communities. Its racial and social background is predominantly Anglo-American, derived from the plantation South, and aside from its Negro and Mexican inhabitants, the city has no other distinct racial element. Austin's Negro population, centered in the eastern part of the city, has its own business, social, and professional life, and supports numerous churches.

Many persons who have achieved fame have lived here. Major George W. Littlefield, one of Terry's Texas Rangers during the Civil War, moved to Austin in 1883, where he made generous gifts to the University. Elisabet Ney, sculptor, made the city her home. O. Henry (William Sidney Porter) at one time lived in Austin, where he published *The Rolling Stone.* Amelia E. Barr lived here in the 1950's and wrote many novels and poems of the sentimental type then in vogue. Her *Remember the Alamo* was read in nearly every Texas home. Far different was the fame of Ben Thompson, one of the most notoriously desperate man killers in the Southwest, who became city marshal of Austin in 1882, and was shot to death in San Antonio in 1884.

Although explorers, from the earliest days of Spanish occupancy, passed through the Austin region, and Anglo-Americans built forts and settlements in the vicinity, the town did not come into existence until after the passing of Spanish rule. The first settlement on the north bank of the Colorado, where the southern parts of the city proper now lie, was called Waterloo.

In the fall of 1838 before he became President of the Republic of Texas, Mirabeau B. Lamar, then Vice President, camped with a party of buffalo hunters at Jacob Harrell's cabin near the Colorado River ford and was impressed by the location. In January, 1839, when the third commission created to select a permanent capital site prepared to depart, Lamar is said to have told the five commissioners to inspect the spot he remembered. Its elevation and freedom from the fevers of the coast country were in its favor, and while the site was dangerously far out on the frontier, it was finally chosen, and the name changed from Waterloo to its present designation, in honor of Stephen F. Austin.

Austin's early days were difficult. In May, 1839, when construction was begun on the streets and governmental buildings, workmen were protected from Indians by armed guards. The first capitol, a drafty, one-story structure called the Hall of Congress, erected that summer on the site now occupied by the city hall, was surrounded by a stockade eight feet high, with loopholes. Edwin Waller, later the first mayor, directed development of the town. The *Gazette,* Austin's first newspaper, appeared in October. A month later the archives of the Republic arrived by oxcart, President Lamar having preceded them on October 17.

In the 1840's, it was reported that, because of Indians, "you were sure to find a congressman in his boarding house after sundown." Another Austin resident wrote: "The Indians are stalking through the streets at night with impunity. They are as thick as hops about the mountains in this vicinity, and occasionally they knock over a poor fellow and take his hair." The stockade remained around the capitol as late as 1845.

By 1840 Austin was an incorporated town of 856 persons. Many nationalities and creeds were represented, and it was a lively place politically. President Lamar lived in a pretentious two-story building, while his political enemy, Sam Houston, resided in a shanty with a dirt floor on Congress Avenue, where he received men of affairs and hurled derision at the President and his followers. Another newspaper, the *Texas Sentinel,* came into being in that year.

The town's most pressing problem was transportation. Under the most favorable conditions freighting wagons, drawn by oxen, required a month to make the round trip from Houston or Port Lavaca. Mail arrived once a week by pony express. Most of the routes followed the early Indian and old Mexican trails. River transportation was attempted, small flat-bottomed boats floating downstream with the current and returning by sail when the wind was favorable. But this was far from successful. In 1841 a line of accommodation coaches was established between Austin and Houston, carrying mail and passengers.

By 1841 the Republic of Texas had been recognized by France, England, Holland, and the United States, and France sent Count Alphonse de Saligny as Chargé d'Affaires. The house that he built for use as the French Legation still stands in East Austin.

The year 1842 was a critical chapter in the history of Austin. Following the invasion by a Mexican army which occupied San Antonio, and the rumor that a detachment was heading for the capital, many families abandoned Austin and the seat of government was hurriedly removed to Houston. From this situation developed the historic Archives War.

Feeling that Austin was no longer safe from Mexicans or marauding Indians, President Sam Houston dispatched James B. Shaw, comptroller, who rode Captain Buck Pettus' fine blooded mare, to the nearly deserted capital for the Republic's supply of stationery. The citizens, believing that Shaw had come to Austin to remove the archives, and fearing that their removal would mean the final abandonment of the city as the capital, sheared the mane and tail of Shaw's mount and sent him back without the supplies. On December 30, an effort was made to remove the records secretly, but Mrs. Angelina Eberly, a hotel proprietor, saw them being loaded on a wagon in the alley back of the land office and spread the alarm. Citizens followed the wagons to Brushy Creek, about 18 miles north, and the following day succeeded in retrieving the records and returning them to Austin.

The Mexican threat subsided, and after a three-year interval during which the government was conducted at Washington on the Brazos, Austin resumed its life as the capital. Then, in 1845, came the annexation of Texas to the United States. By July of 1850 tri-weekly mail stages made the trip from Austin to San Antonio, 90 miles, in one day. Soon afterward, the dream of navigating the river was revived when the steamer *Colorado Ranger* arrived in Austin, but that dream soon faded.

From 1850 to 1860, the population reached 3,494. The separation between North and South impended, and in Austin were three distinct parties, one advocating remaining with the Union, a second demanding a

Southern confederacy, while a third wished Texas to resume its independence as a Republic. Travis County citizens voted against secession 704 to 450 but the State as a whole voted for the Confederacy. The war came.

A cartridge and percussion cap factory was installed in the Supreme Court Building northwest of the capitol. All the machinery was homemade. A large wooden building was erected as a foundry where cannons, guns, sabers, and other weapons wre produced. The Austin City Light Infantry was organized, and B. F. Terry was commissioned by President Jefferson Davis to raise a regiment of cavalry, which later gained fame as Terry's Texas Rangers. Part of one company was composed of Travis County volunteers.

When Lee surrendered there were 15,000 Confederate soldiers in Texas. They had received no pay for months and some of them began to seize Confederate and State property. Austin was in a critical position because they concentrated their demands on the capital. The city swarmed with desperate veterans and renegades, a party of whom finally broke into the treasury house and made off with part of the State's funds.

With the Reconstruction era came troublous times, but Austin prospered in spite of political strife and bitterness. In 1871 the Houston and Texas Central Railroad reached the city, directly stimulating its growth and business. That line was followed by the International-Great Northern in 1876. The State in 1856 had established a hospital for the insane and an institution for the blind; and in 1857, one for the deaf and dumb. Schools had been established and increased. The Austin Library Association opened a library and reading room in 1873 "to elevate the tone of our society." A municipal railway—horse car service—traveled over two miles of track through the main part of town. The city's social and cultural life was enhanced by an opera house, a theater, and four halls.

In 1883 the University of Texas opened its first term, attracting students from all parts of the State. After graduation, many students whose families in most instances had moved to the capital, elected to remain and begin their careers in either governmental or private positions; the institution proved a boon to the city's economic, as well as cultural development, even though its first years were hard because of limited funds and the general unfriendliness of the citizens.

In 1888, completion of the present capitol was celebrated with a full week of festivities. There followed a slow period of industrial growth, culminating in the building of a million dollar dam and power plant on the Colorado River, which were destroyed in 1900 in one of the disastrous floods that have visited the lower sections of the city. A new power plant was constructed, and in 1912 the dam was rebuilt.

From the turn of the century, what might be termed Austin's modern life made great strides. The University grew rapidly, and with St. Edward's University, founded in 1878, and other institutions, the city became the State's educational center.

In 1909 Austin, with a population close to 30,000, received a charter for a commission form of government. A third railroad, the Missouri-Kansas-Texas, was added, and with the improvement of highway facilities

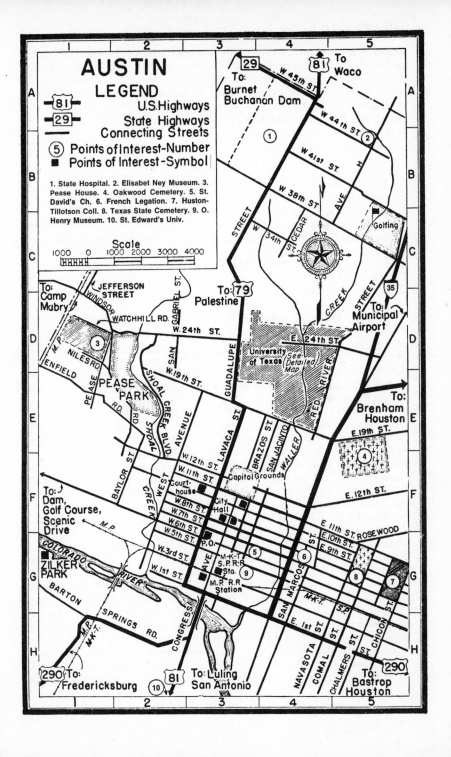

and modern transportation methods, its importance as a commercial center and trading point increased. Industries began to take root. In 1926 Austin adopted the city manager form of government. Work was begun in 1938 on the Tom Miller Dam, final unit of the Lower Colorado River Authority's $40,000,000 program to harness and put to work the Colorado River, which twice has destroyed dams embodying hope of industrial progress for Austin.

POINTS OF INTEREST

ST. MARY'S ACADEMY (*open 8–5 daily*), E. 7th St. between Brazos and San Jacinto Sts., part of St. Mary's Cathedral at Brazos and E. 10th Sts., is a Roman Catholic school for girls. Founded in 1874 by Sisters of the Holy Cross, it is on the site of the residence of the President of the Republic. The stone building was erected in 1885, in the architectural style of the Victorian era.

ST. DAVID'S EPISCOPAL CHURCH (*open 10–12, 2–5 daily*), E. 7th and San Jacinto Sts., is the second oldest Protestant church in Texas. In 1847 the parish was organized and in 1855 Bishop Freeman consecrated the structure which forms the old part of the present Gothic.

The O. HENRY MUSEUM (*open 10–12, 2–5, weekdays except Tues.; 2–5 Sun.*), 409 E. 5th St., is housed in a one-story frame cottage of the "jigsaw" era, since removed from its first location on E. 4th St. W. S. Porter (O. Henry) lived in this house from the summer of 1893 to the autumn of 1895. Several rooms are furnished as they were during the author's occupancy, although many of the present furnishings were not among his possessions.

RELIGIOUS EDUCATION is the basic instruction in several church-related institutions. LUTHERAN CONCORDIA COLLEGE, 3400 East Ave., founded 1926, enrolls approx. 125. PRESBYTERIAN THEOLOGICAL SEMINARY, 100 E. 27th St., under the auspices of the United Presbyterian Church, has about 150 candidates regularly training for the ministry. Austin also is the location of schools for the handicapped: the TEXAS SCHOOL FOR THE BLIND, the TEXAS STATE SCHOOL FOR THE DEAF, and the TEXAS BLIND, DEAF AND ORPHAN SCHOOL.

The FRENCH LEGATION (*open 1–6 P.M. for a fee*), 817 E. 8th St., on Robertson Hill in East Austin, was designed and begun in 1841 by Count Saligny, Chargé d'Affaires to the Republic of Texas from France, and was the most pretentious building in Texas at that time. The house, now the oldest one in Austin, is in the provincial French cottage style of architecture, with double doors, and locks and hinges brought from France. The doors are of barrel design with serpentine hinges.

The Count did not spend much time in the legation. Indians, frequent and unfriendly visitors to Austin, affected the poise of the Old World representative. Further, that ridiculous affair, known in history as the Pig Episode, not only estranged him, but caused France to abandon the idea of lending the financially embarassed Texas Republic seven million dollars.

The trouble began when one of Innkeeper Richard Bullock's pigs broke into the Count's stable and ate his corn. Saligny's servant killed the pig. Bullock thrashed the servant and put the Count out of the Bullock Inn. Saligny appealed to the Secretary of State for an apology and, failing to get it, departed for New Orleans. Recalled as French representative, the Count returned to Austin as Chargé d'Affaires late in 1843 or 1844.

HUSTON-TILLOTSON COLLEGE, 1820 E. 8th St., is a senior college established 1952 by the merger of Samuel Huston College, opened in 1900 by the West Texas conference of the Methodist Church, and Tillotson College, opened 1877 by the American Missionary Assn. Both were pioneering efforts to bring higher education to Negro youth. In 1936 Tillotson was made a member of the American Association of Colleges. The college has a campus of 23 acres. In 1966 it had 619 students of both sexes and a faculty of 44.

The TEXAS STATE CEMETERY, Navasota St. between E. 7th and E. 11th Sts., extending to Comal St., is the burial place of many distinguished Texans. Stephen F. Austin's grave is surmounted by a bronze statue by Pompeo Coppini. It occupies the highest knoll on the grounds. The reclining marble figure of General Albert Sidney Johnston was done by Elisabet Ney. Coppini did the bronze figure of Johanna Troutman, a Georgian, who made a Lone Star flag of white silk with an azure star that was brought to Texas by the Georgia Battalion in December, 1835. The grave of W. A. (Big Foot) Wallace, Indian scout and Texas Ranger, is also in the cemetery.

TEXAS FEDERATION OF WOMEN'S CLUBS (*open 8–5 daily*), SW. corner San Gabriel and W. 24th Sts., was completed in 1935 under the supervision of Paul Knight, architect.

Of red brick with white limestone trim, the building is a reproduction of the Georgian-Williamsburg colonial type of architecture. Within the building are a library, music room, auditorium with stage, the Georgian Tea Room, and dormitory rooms.

The CONFEDERATE WOMAN'S HOME (*open 9–11, 3–5 Tues.-Sat., 3–5 Sun. and Mon.*), 3710 Cedar St., was opened by the Daughters of the Confederacy to a small number of dependent women in 1908. In 1911 the State assumed control and enlarged the activities of the home. The Main Building and the Memorial Hospital, the two principal units, are of concrete blocks and limestone.

The ELISABET NEY MUSEUM (*open 10–12, 3–5 Tues.-Sat., 3–5 Sun. and Mon.*), NW. corner Ave. H and E. 44th St., is reminiscent of a medieval castle, and was the workshop and home of the noted sculptor, Elisabet Ney, who designed it. After her death in 1907, her collection of statuary was given to the University of Texas on condition that it remain in the studio.

The AUSTIN STATE HOSPITAL (*visiting hours 9–11, 2–4 Tues.-Sat. except holidays*), between 38th and 45th Sts., entrance on Guadalupe St., is on 382 acres of land and has 25 fireproof buildings, 10 semi-fireproof, and numerous frame structures, designed by several architects, in various styles. Rentals from 100,000 acres of grazing land in west Texas are used toward support of the institution.

The GOVERNOR ELISHA M. PEASE HOME (*private*), 6 Niles Rd., was purchased by Governor Pease in the 1850's from its builder, James T. Shaw, a native of Ireland. Shaw's intended bride, who had assisted in planning the home, deserted at the eleventh hour. Death destroyed a marriage that took place shortly after the first unhappiness, and Shaw left the house forever. Designed by Abner Cook, and built in 1853, the Pease home is contemporaneous with the Governor's Mansion, and like it, is of the Greek Revival period.

ST. EDWARD'S UNIVERSITY (*open 8–5*), 3 *m.* S. of the Capitol, US 81, is a Roman Catholic institution for men. Its grounds embrace 300 acres. The college buildings are in modified Gothic style, designed by N. J. Clayton. The institution was chartered in 1885 as St. Edward's College by members of the Congregation of the Holy Cross from the University of Notre Dame, Indiana. Its library contains more than 40,000 volumes in addition to public documents, including the Roman Catholic archives of Texas and a special collection of papers and manuscripts on early Texas history. Four murals of the San Antonio missions, painted by the Reverend John J. Bednar, are on the first floor of the main building. The university in 1967 enrolled 865 men.

The CENTRAL LIBRARY of the Austin Public Library System, 401 West 9th St., adjacent to Wooldridge Park, is two blocks from City Hall and the Governor's Mansion. The building was erected in 1933 and makes available 92,000 volumes of the 230,000 in the Library System. Circulation at Central was 381,235 in 1966; the circulation for the system reached 1,348,232. The Catalogue Department processes books for the entire system and added 5,263 new titles and 33,000 volumes in 1966. The east wing of Central houses the Austin-Travis County Collection of historical materials, including the family papers of such distinguished Austin families as Pease, Brackenridge, Collins and Bremond. In its encouragement of art and music the library circulated 45,683 recordings and 2,199 framed prints in one year.

When the present Central Library was erected it replaced the original building, which was removed to East Austin to become the first branch. It is located at 1165 Angelina St., in Kealing Park, an urban renewal project, and is known as the George Washington Carver Branch, serving patrons within a mile and a half radius who are predominantly Negro.

The Library System comprises, in addition to Central, eight branches, three stations, and three bookmobiles. Its extensive activities reach areas as far as 40 miles away. Branches and stations are located in and near shopping centers, in sections of urban renewal and new housing, and in a community recreation center. Librarians tell stories to little children at 10 Day Care Centers and encourage parents to read to their children. The facilities of the system are regularly brought to the attention of public school pupils and business men, and are publicized in the newspapers and on television.

CAPITOL AND GROUNDS

A Tourist Information Center is located in the Rotunda of the Capitol (open 8–5). Maintained by the Texas Highway Dept., it provides information about the Capitol and the State.

The TEXAS STATE CAPITOL stands on an elevation near the center of Austin, in a square area of 25 acres, the main front facing the north end of Congress Avenue.

It is the second capitol built on this spot and the fourth building used for this purpose since the founding of Austin. The first stone capitol built here, and dedicated in 1855, was destroyed by fire in 1881, and some of the early records with it. A temporary statehouse was used from 1883 to 1888, pending the erection of a permanent building.

Owners of Granite Mountain, at Marble Falls, offered to donate stone for the structure, provided that they could be assured of a railroad from Austin to Burnet—the line being necessary to convey the granite to Austin, 60 miles away. Their offer was accepted. The legislature had already set aside 3,050,000 acres of its public domain in the Panhandle, to pay for the construction of the building and for the survey and sale of those lands. As a result the great XIT Ranch came into existence, the contractors taking over the Panhandle acreage piecemeal as their work progressed. The new capitol was completed in 1888.

The building is of classic architecture, with the National Capitol as its prototype. Its red granite walls approximate the Greek cross, with projecting center and flanks, and a rotunda and dome at the intersection of the main corridors. The center section and the wings extending north and south are of four stories, and the east and west wings have three.

The dome and the triumphal arch over the south entrance are distinctive features. The base of the dome is about 130 feet above the basement floor. At 156 feet is the base of the colonnade formed around the rotunda by huge bronze columns enclosing an open-air promenade. On the top of the dome stands a statue of the Goddess of Liberty.

Twin cannons presented to the Republic of Texas in 1836 by Major General T. J. Chambers, and used in the Texas Revolution and the Civil War, stand on each side of the south entrance of the Capitol.

Twelve Texas battles are memorialized on the terrazzo floor of the foyer. Flanking the entrance to the Rotunda are marble statues of Stephen F. Austin and Sam Houston, by Elisabet Ney. A copy of the Texas Declaration of Independence (1836) and of the Ordinance of Secession (1861) are displayed behind glass. Four floors of the building open to the Rotunda, with portraits of the Presidents and Governors of the State on the walls and a bust of Mrs. Miriam A. Ferguson, only woman Governor, on the main floor. On the Rotunda floor are depicted seals of the nations under which Texas served. The seal of the Confederate States bears a statue of George Washington.

The GOVERNOR'S RECEPTION ROOM, on the second floor, is open to the public (*10–12, 2–4, Monday through Friday*). The HOUSE OF

REPRESENTATIVES, 150 members, is in the West Wing. The SENATE is in the East Wing. Visitors may not go on the floor of either chamber without permission, but may use a third floor balcony. The Speaker of the House has an office and living quarters nearby.

The REFERENCE LIBRARY, maintained for the legislators but open to the public, is located in the north wing of the second floor. Besides official reports, it has microfilms of many newspapers.

The GOVERNOR'S MANSION (*open 10–12, Mon.-Fri.*), Colorado St. between W. 10th and W. 11th Sts., has been the home of the State's Governors since 1855. The building was designed by Abner Cook in the Greek Revival style, combined with the stately appearance and classicism of the South. Its tall Ionic columns are backed by a typically southern gallery. Interesting articles include the Sam Houston bed, the Stephen F. Austin desk, and crystal chandeliers; there is a fine collection of paintings.

OFFICIAL BUILDINGS

The official buildings that border the grounds of the Texas Capitol reflect the gradual change from eclectic victorianism to modern streamlining in architecture. Most of the newer structures stand east and north of the Capitol.

The SUPREME COURT BUILDING, northwest of the Capitol, is one of the exceptions. Here meet the State's highest tribunals, the Supreme Court and the Criminal Appeals Court. Here also is the Third Court of Civil Appeals.

North and east of the Capitol stand three huge office buildings that testify to the expansion of official business. The first is the JOHN H. REAGAN STATE OFFICE BUILDING, the second the building of the TEXAS EMPLOYMENT COMMISSION, and the third, to the east, the SAM HOUSTON STATE OFFICE BUILDING. Next along the southeast side of the park—the grounds do not run exactly north-south—comes the STATE ARCHIVES AND LIBRARY BUILDING, the permanent depository of historical documents and archival collections, built of the same granite as the Capitol. South of it stands the STATE INSURANCE BUILDING, almost the whole length of a city block. Facing it is one of the oldest structures on the grounds, the OLD LAND OFFICE MUSEUM BUILDING, built in 1857. This stone pile was styled after formal buildings along the Rhine by its German-born architect. Until 1919 it housed patents, land titles and deeds. In 1919 it became a museum. On the first floor is the TEXAS CONFEDERATE MUSEUM, operated by the Daughters of the Confederacy. On the second floor is the MUSEUM OF THE DAUGHTERS OF THE REPUBLIC OF TEXAS, with exhibits related to the Republic. (*Open 9–12, 1–5, daily except Sunday and Monday*).

Across the street is the building of the TEXAS EDUCATION AGENCY, and in line with that south of the Capitol grounds is the large

9-story headquarters of the TEXAS HIGHWAY DEPARTMENT, completed in 1933 and reflecting the modern style of its decade.

MEMORIALS

Monuments and Memorials on the Capitol grounds direct attention to notable phases of Texas history.

The CONFEDERATE DEAD MONUMENT, center walk, was erected in 1901. Bronze figures on the granite base represent President Jefferson Davis and three Confederate soldiers and one sailor. It was designed by Pompeo Coppini and executed by Frank Teich.

The VOLUNTEER FIREMEN MONUMENT, center walk, created by Frank Teich, is a bronze figure on a granite base, depicting a fireman holding a frightened child in the crook of his left arm, and a lantern in his right hand. The monument was erected in 1896 by the State Firemen's Association of Texas.

The TEXAS COWBOY MONUMENT, SW. of the Capitol on the main lawn, by Constance Whitney Warren, was presented to the State by the sculptor in 1925. This bronze statue is of a typical Texas cowboy riding a rearing pony. Exhibited in a Paris salon, it received honorable mention.

The TERRY'S TEXAS RANGERS MONUMENT, center walk, erected in 1907 in commemoration of the Eighth Texas Cavalry, an independent unit in the Confederate Army, portrays one of Terry's Texas Rangers astride a spirited horse. The sculptor was Pompeo Coppini.

The ALAMO MONUMENT, center walk, by J. S. Clark, was erected in 1891. Of Texas granite, it is surmounted by a bronze statue of a young Texan holding a long-barreled muzzle-loader. On the four granite supports are inscribed the names of men who died in the Battle of the Alamo.

The HOOD'S TEXAS BRIGADE MONUMENT, on the east lawn, is a granite shaft topped by the bronze figure of a Confederate soldier, designed by Pompeo Coppini.

THE UNIVERSITY OF TEXAS

The Main Campus of the University of Texas comprises 232 acres on a hill behind the State Capitol, centering at University Ave., and 21st St., where the heart of the University System enrolls more than 26,000 students annually, and 1,700 faculty members teach in 55 divisions and work in 50 research units. Segments of this main body are the Balcones Research Center northwest of Austin (393 acres), and the Brackenridge Tract near Lake Austin (444 acres), where housing units for married students are located. The University at Austin has six colleges: Arts and Sciences, Business Administration, Education, Engineering, Fine Arts, and Pharmacy, and seven schools: Graduate, Law, Communication, Architecture, Social Work, Library Science, and Business. The University

System also includes the Galveston Medical Branch, Southwestern Medical School, Dallas; South Texas Medical School, San Antonio; Texas Western College, El Paso, and at Houston the Dental Branch, M. D. Anderson Hospital and Tumor Institute, and Graduate School of Biomedical Sciences. The University of Texas at Arlington was Arlington State College up to 1967. Other teaching and research units are the McDonald Observatory near Fort Davis and the Institute of Marine Science at Port Aransas.

With its Tower rising 307 feet above the landscape the university provides, with the Capitol complex, an imposing area of formal buildings second only in architectural distinction to those of Washington, D. C. For a number of decades all buildings except a few early structures were adaptations of Spanish Renaissance patterns, with red-tile roofs, broad eaves, limestone, and buff brick, but the big construction impetus since World War II has brought the best of modern styles to the campus, providing a maximum of light, conditioned temperatures, easy accessibility, and effective use of space.

Because the first campus comprised 40 acres, the University is often referred to as Forty Acres. The original plot has had accretions on all sides. San Jacinto Boulevard was crossed in order to find room for the Texas Memorial Museum, Memorial Stadium, the University Junior High School, the Defense Research Laboratory, Townes Hall of the Law School, the Art Building, the Band Hall, Clark Field, and the University of Texas Press. Several of these already have been located elsewhere.

The newest plans stipulated the erection on 19 acres east of the Main Campus of a new library complex, to include the Lyndon Baines Johnson Library housing the President's papers, and other historical collections, and the East Campus Library and Research Building, to house the Texas Collection, Archives, Latin American Library, and headquarters of the Texas State Historical Assn., Latin American Institute, and the Lyndon Baines Johnson Institute of Public Service. The two buildings are expected to cost $10,750,000. The architects are Skidmore, Owings & Merrill of New York and Brooks, Barr, Graeber and White of Austin. Gordon Bunshaft, partner of the New York firm, is responsible for the design of the project and R. Max Brooks of the Austin firm is responsible for coordination.

Not only have the educational facilities of the University enhanced to an extraordinary extent in recent decades, but the physical plant has been enlarged by modern buildings that will provide for expansion in the future. When a decade of growth was summarized officially in 1966, the value of the plant in Austin had risen from $95,000,000 to $230,000,000; the permanent endowment from $287,000,000 to $478,000,000 (chiefly from oil leases and royalties); the average academic salary from $6,000 to $12,700, and the maximum salary to $30,000, and $82,000,000 had been earmarked for new construction. The operating budget is $39,000,000, more than half for instruction.

The most impressive structure at the University is the TOWER of the Main Building, which rises 27 stories above the campus to a height of 307 feet. That part of the building which houses the General Library was completed in 1933, while the Tower and front portion of the building were finished in 1937. A 17-bell carillon in the Tower chimes the quarter hours from 6:15 A.M. to 8 P.M. The Tower is frequently illuminated in the University colors, orange and white, and various combinations of colors are shown to mark special athletic and other events. A trip to the observation deck of the Tower always has been prized by visitors for its extraordinary view of the campus, the grounds of the Capitol and adjacent parts of Austin. On August 1, 1966 a demented student with a shotgun reached the top of the Tower and shot and killed 14 persons and wounded 32 before he was killed by a policeman. He previously had murdered his wife and mother.

Campus grounds were set aside when Austin was laid out in 1839. A bill to establish a university "of the first class" was enacted by the legislature in 1858, but it was not until 1882 that the plan materialized. When the University opened on September 15, 1883, it had six professors in the academic department and two professors of law.

Although the University was endowed with public lands, funds were rarely available. Legislatures wrangled over budgets and the relative value of cultural and practical education. Still enrollment grew, and overflowed the early buildings; wooden shacks were constructed. By 1924–25, when registration mounted to 5,163, the prevalence of these flimsy structures gave the campus the appearance of a military cantonment.

In 1924 oil was discovered on University land in Reagan County and later in Andrews, Winkler, Crane and other west Texas counties, producing much wealth for the permanent fund from which the institution derives its income. This increase, with gifts and Federal assistance, has aided in meeting needs of expansion. Since 1925 the University has spent millions of dollars for buildings and improvements in Austin and Galveston, and at Mount Locke near Fort Davis, where the McDonald observatory is located.

The Littlefield Memorial Fountain, located at the main entrance at West 21st St. and University Ave., is a large semicircular basin with two smaller superimposed basins at higher levels. From this rises a sculptured group, the work of Pompeo Coppini, depicting three horses, ridden by Tritons, drawing a boat which carries a winged Columbia, the principal figure. A bronze plaque on the wall behind the figures commemorates those of the University who gave their lives in World War I. The fountain is the gift of Major George W. Littlefield.

The approach to the main building is a double walk with statues by Coppini of Robert E. Lee, John H. Reagan, Albert Sidney Johnston, James Stephen Hogg, Jefferson Davis, and Woodrow Wilson, gifts of Major Littlefield.

The components of the LIBRARY OF THE UNIVERSITY OF TEXAS are the GENERAL LIBRARY, the UNDERGRADUATE LIBRARY, the special collections and the fifteen units serving the colleges and departments. The General Library, in the Main Building, con-

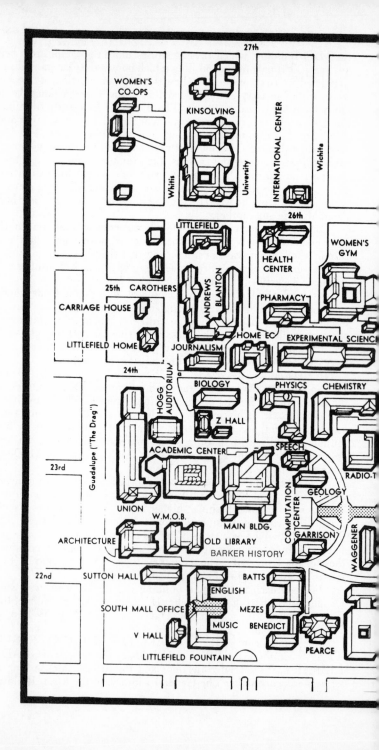

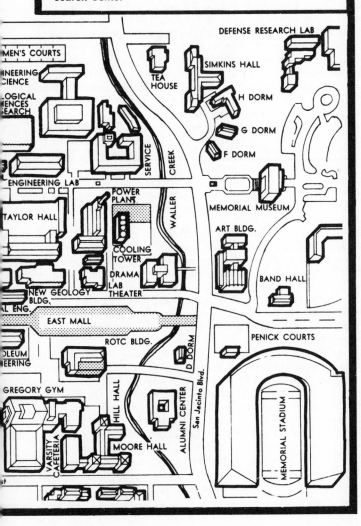

THE UNIVERSITY OF TEXAS

MAIN UNIVERSITY CAMPUS

New section east of Red River Road is site of Lyndon Baines Johnson Library, East Campus Library and Research Center

MEN'S COURTS

NEERING
CIENCE

LOGICAL
ENCES
SEARCH

DEFENSE RESEARCH LAB

TEA HOUSE

SIMKINS HALL

H DORM

G DORM

F DORM

SERVICE CREEK

ENGINEERING LAB

POWER PLANT

WALLER CREEK

MEMORIAL MUSEUM

TAYLOR HALL

COOLING TOWER

ART BLDG.

DRAMA LAB THEATER

BAND HALL

NEW GEOLOGY BLDG.

L ENG.

EAST MALL

ROTC BLDG.

PENICK COURTS

D DORM

OLEUM
EERING

GREGORY GYM

HILL HALL

San Jacinto Blvd.

ALUMNI CENTER

MEMORIAL STADIUM

VARSITY CAFETERIA

MOORE HALL

tains 1,000,000 of the 2,000,000 catalogued volumes and is the focal point for study and research in the social sciences, humanities, and related subjects. Here are available State, Federal and United Nations documents.

One of the show places of the University, the Rare Books Collection on the fourth floor, Main Building, totals thousands of fine volumes including literary manuscripts, and first and early editions, chiefly in English and American literature. The library is of uniform excellence; among many outstanding collections are those for the study of Spencer, Milton, Pope, Dryden, Byron and Keats, the Spencer Collection said to be the best this side of the Atlantic. The British drama volumes comprise a majority of all editions of English plays published before 1800.

The Rare Books Collection is founded on the Wrenn Library, an aggregation of about 6,000 volumes of English literature ranging from Spencer to the middle nineteenth century and confined principally to poetry and drama, presented to the University in 1918 by Major Littlefield; the George A. Aitken Library, which includes early English newspapers; and the Miriam Lutcher Stark Library of over 10,000 manuscripts, first editions and de luxe volumes, housed in a room furnished from the Stark home. The Bieber collection of American poetry, principally of the nineteenth century, is shelved in the general stacks.

Other notable collections bear the names of Hanley, Parsons, Vanderpoehl, Payne, and DeGolyer; the Hoblitzelle Theater Arts Center, the History of Science Collection, books purchased from the Littlefield Fund for Southern History and the University Writings Collection.

The University's LATIN AMERICAN COLLECTION, in the Main Building, has been developed from the purchase of the Genaro Garcia library in 1921 to a library of the first rank on Mexico, Central and South America.

The UNDERGRADUATE LIBRARY fills three floors of the Academic Center and Undergraduate Library Building and serves undergraduates, especially those of the freshman and sophomore level. There is an open shelf collection of 75,000 volumes, a working area for 1,400 students, and an audio library with 144 listening stations. The building was completed in 1963. It is constructed of limestone, shellstone, granite, mosaic tile, and heat-absorbing glass. At the south entrance stands a bronze group by Charles Umlauf, The Torch Bearers, while his Three Graces have a place in a fourth-floor court.

The ACADEMIC CENTER LIBRARY is the repository for recently acquired collections of modern American and English literature, the history of science, western Americana, and Texana. It has the books and manuscripts of more than 100 English and American writers of the twentieth century, including Joseph Conrad, T. S. Eliot, William Faulkner, Ernest Hemingway, James Joyce, W. H. Auden, Christopher Morley, Eugene O'Neill, Bernard Shaw, John Steinbeck, Dylan Thomas, Tennessee Williams and others of contemporary interest. When the Academic Center was dedicated Warren Roberts wrote: "Here is no museum of dead matter, but rather the living spirit of the century, fashioned by the men whose words have so distinguished its first decades."

THE EUGENE C. BARKER TEXAS HISTORY CENTER, housed in the Old Library Building, contains in the Texas Collection and the Archives Collection the most extensive collection of Texana in existence as it relates to the development of the State. The Texas Collection is primarily concerned with printed resources while the Archives Collection stresses documents. Since the Bexar Archives, the Austin papers and the Texana of Sir Swante Palm came to the University about 1900 these collections have been kept current to bring together a complete repository of information on Texas.

THE NEWSPAPER COLLECTION supplements both the Latin American Collection and the Eugene C. Barker Texas History Center with portions of the 30,000 volumes of newspapers housed in the Main Building. By 1970 the overcrowded collections, including the Texas and Latin American newspapers, will share adjoining space in the campus expansion adjacent to the Presidential Library.

THE JOSEPH LINDSEY HENDERSON TEXTBOOK COLLECTION of 30,-000 volumes is a comprehensive collection of 19th and 20th century textbooks. There is a modest endowment for its perpetuity.

The new GEOLOGY BUILDING, completed 1967, located south of Taylor Hall and facing the new East Mall, has five floors and houses an auditorium, laboratories, a library and map room and one floor devoted to the Bureau of Economic Geology. Rainbow granite slabs from Minnesota adorn one wall of the Chairman's conference room; blue pearl granite from Norway is used in a faculty meeting room; Texas pink granite decorates the graduate seminar room and 19 varieties of North American granite make a checkerboard for the graduate students' room. The building cost $2,450,000.

The ART BUILDING AND MUSEUM, completed 1963 at East 23d St. and San Jacinto Blvd., has laboratories for instruction in painting, drawing, sculpture, ceramics and allied arts, facilities for print-making, a kiln room and photography rooms. The two-level museum includes the Archer M. Huntington Gallery, built from funds provided by the late financier, who deeded the income from Galveston oil and gas leases to the University. Winding staircases of black cast-terrazzo slabs, each slab weighing 1,500 lbs., connect the museum floors.

In 1964 the College of Engineering and the Physics Department moved into the new ENGINEERING-SCIENCE BUILDING, near East 23rd St. and San Jacinto Blvd., which cost more than $3,333,000 to build. The north wing contains three particle accelerators (atom-smashers) that together can produce energies up to 17 MEV (million electron volts). Numerous laboratories for electrical engineering, electromagnetics, control systems, biomedicine, acoustics, dynamics and electronics are located in the building.

The DRAMA BUILDING, at the northwest corner of East 23rd St. and San Jacinto Blvd., erected 1962, has the most advanced facilities for teaching drama. The experimental theater is small—60 by 60 feet, with a 20-foot ceiling—but can be adapted to various styles of staging; major productions continue to be shown in Hogg Auditorium.

The one-story sandy-beige brick structure overlooking Waller Creek on San Jacinto Blvd. is the LILA B. ETTER ALUMNI CENTER, opened 1965, and built by a legacy from Mrs. Etter of Sherman and donations from the Ex-Students' Assn.

Two structures connected by a cross-section are the BUSINESS-ECONOMICS CLASSROOM BUILDING and the OFFICE BUILDING. They contain the Business-Economics Library, laboratories of accounting, economics, management, marketing, statistics and secretarial functions, a bureau of business research, and associated studies.

In 1960 the University greatly expanded and modernized the UNION, the student recreation center, which had been erected in 1933 in a modified Spanish Renaissance style. In this building are centered many of the extracurricular activities of the students; here they find rooms for relaxation, reading and games, including the use of a 16-lane bowling alley. A Commons cafeteria is a popular institution. There is also an auditorium that can be adapted for plays. The original building was designed by Robert Leon White, with Paul P. Cret consultant.

The Union faces Guadalupe Avenue at the west side of the campus and has as neighbors the Academic Center, already described, and the HOGG MEMORIAL AUDITORIUM, which seats 1,325 and contains modern theater equipment. It was built of limestone and shell, designed by Robert Leon White.

South of the Union on Guadalupe is the ARCHITECTURE BUILDING. It is modified Spanish Renaissance in style, designed by Greene, LaRoche and Dahl, Paul P. Cret, consulting architect. There is usually a display of paintings in the exhibit room on the first floor. The Architecture Department Library, on the second floor, has a ceiling depicting the development of architecture. Student work hangs on the wall.

The HOME ECONOMICS BUILDING, one of the show places of the campus, is of cream shell stone and limestone in modified Spanish Renaissance style, designed by Greene, LaRoche and Dahl, Paul P. Cret, consulting architect. An iron-grating gate across the front of the building, joining the east and west wings and enclosing the patio between, and several small iron-grating balconies add to the Spanish motif.

GREGORY GYMNASIUM, Speedway between E. 22d and E. 21st Sts., is of face brick, Italian Romanesque of the masculine type inspired by the Church of St. Ambrogio, Milano, Italy. It was designed by Greene, LaRoche and Dahl. The main gymnasium floor is large enough to permit five basketball games to be played simultaneously. Chairs convert the gymnasium into an auditorium.

WAGGENER HALL, of rusticated limestone, brick and terra cotta, with a decorative cornice and frieze and tile roof, is modified Spanish Renaissance style, and was designed by Greene, LaRoche and Dahl, Paul P. Cret, consulting architect. This is the business administration building and houses classrooms, the public-speaking offices, business laboratories, and anthropology offices.

THE SANTA RITA OIL WELL RIG, reassembled at 19th St.

and San Jacinto Blvd. commemorates Santa Rita No. 1, the first oil well to "blow in" on University-owned land in West Texas in 1923.

The JOURNALISM BUILDING, of brick in the conventional institutional style derived from the classic, was designed by Coughlin and Ayres. At the northeast end of the basement floor is the DEPARTMENT OF GEOLOGY MUSEUM containing rocks, minerals, meteorites, fossils and cases of gems.

GARRISON HALL, the Social Science Building, is of limestone and yellow face brick and terra cotta. Designed by Greene, LaRoche and Dahl, it follows the style of Sutton Hall and the Old Library. Noted Texas cattle brands, and names of heroes of the Texas Republic are used in cornice, window and entrance decorations.

MEMORIAL STADIUM occupies 13 acres between San Jacinto Blvd. and Red River St., bounded on the north and south by E. 23d St. and E. 20½ St. Designed by Greene, LaRoche and Dahl, the stadium was completed in 1936. It is of concrete in the shape of a horseshoe, and has a seating capacity of 48,000.

TEXAS MEMORIAL MUSEUM, San Jacinto Blvd. and 24th St., offers an extensive display of objects related to the development of the State, as well as prehistoric fossils and artifacts, Indian relics, and dioramas showing the growth of the oil industry. The fine formal building is approached by a plaza and stone steps divided by a large bronze group of rearing mustangs, donated 1948 by Ralph Ogden.

The WOMEN'S GYMNASIUM, W. side of Speedway between 26th and 24th Sts., is in Spanish Renaissance style in a manner appropriate to the mild climate. Built around a patio used for outdoor exercise, the structure houses five gymnasiums; a dance studio; a swimming pool with spectators' gallery; two large dressing rooms, each with 70 shower stalls, 1,100 lockers and 140 individual dressing rooms; a library; a lounge; offices for instructors and physicians; and kitchenettes for the use of clubs.

The UNIVERSITY OF TEXAS PRESS, 102 West 20th St., founded 1950, publishes more than 40 scholarly and regional studies a year. About 30 per cent of its books are on Texas or Southwestern subjects, and a similar number deal with Latin America. Among the learned journals that it issues are the *Southwestern Social Science Quarterly* and the *Journal of American Folklore*. It also publishes *The Daily Texan,* the first daily college publication in the South.

The COMMUNICATION CENTER was organized in 1967 and occupies a remodelled building within easy reach of the Main Building and the Tower. It comprises the University's radio and television activities—teaching, production and broadcasting—formerly scattered. The Center has facilities for teaching radio and television production on tape for distribution to commercial and educational stations, closed-circuit broadcasting to classrooms, a microwave network linking 11 Texas colleges, and several other radio and television stations. The Center has six videotape machines and can broadcast five television programs at once.

The MUSIC DEPARTMENT of the University in 1967 moved

most of its facilities from temporary quarters to the University Junior High School, south of the Memorial Stadium. The Music Building, erected in 1942, was designed for 200 students; present enrollment exceeds 500. A new Music Building will be erected between the Texas Memorial Museum and the Law School, to house the Symphonic Band, Symphony Orchestra, Longhorn Band and choral organizations.

The operating budget for the University at Austin for 1966–1967 was $39,180,000, more than half of which went to instruction. The University derives its support from State appropriations, interest on the Permanent University Fund, student fees, gifts and grants and other sources. Its government is vested in a nine-member Board of Regents, nominated for six-year terms by the Governor with approval by the Senate.

OTHER POINTS OF INTEREST

CAMP MABRY, headquarters of the Texas National Guard, occupies 375 acres on State Street west of the railroad. It is the main storage, maintenance and administrative headquarters for supply of the Texas Air National Guard. Established 1892, it was named for Brig. General W. H. Mabry. An encampment of the Volunteer Guard was held here as early as 1892. During World War I the post was used by the U. S. Army and the University of Texas conducted training units of the School for Automobile Units and a part of the School of Military Aeronautics. The Federal Government erected an administration building, officers quarters, barracks and other permanent facilities in 1918. When the Texas Army Guard returned from France after the war Camp Mabry was again used as an annual encampment site.

During the 1930's, the grounds were greatly improved by Federal funds through the Reconstruction Finance Corporation and the Work Projects Administration. During World War II, when the National Guard was overseas, the U. S. Air Corps established a school for training Air Corps intelligence officers.

In November, 1940, the Texas National Guard was called to bolster the strength of the U. S. Army. The 112th Infantry Division sailed for New Caledonia in July, 1942. It took part in four campaigns. The 36th Infantry Division sailed for North Africa in April, 1943. The 124th sailed in July, 1944 for the Burma area. After the war they became the Texas Air Guard unit. During the Korean war the 136th Fighter Bomber Wing was the first Air Guard Wing to go into combat as a unit.

In 1962 the Army National Guard went into active air defense for the Dallas-Fort Worth area. The 4th Missile Battalion, 132nd Artillery, had headquarters at Duncanville and units at Denton and Terrell, Nike-Hercules sites, where Texas Guardsmen manned missile defenses. Army National Guardsmen are members of 122 company-battery size units throughout Texas. Air Guardsmen are members of 26 units in seven Texas cities and number 2,750. As of January 1, 1968, there were 17,079 Army Guardsmen.

Under the latest reorganization, January 15, 1968, Austin, Dallas, Houston, San Antonio, Odessa and Fort Worth became major headquarters of the Texas National Guard. The two Guard divisions, the 36th Infantry and the 49th Armored, were replaced by two brigades and other units. Under the new plan, a mechanized infantry brigade with headquarters in Dallas covers the North Texas Area and the Panhandle; an airborne infantry brigade with headquarters in Houston is stationed in an area extending from the Port Arthur-Beaumont area northwestward to Austin and Waco, and a traditional infantry brigade with headquarters in San Antonio covers all of South Texas. West Texas cities have units that are not part of the three brigades.

Guardsmen of Fort Worth-Dallas and Odessa-Midland areas form two new types of command headquarters, which are called Emergency Operations Headquarters or EOH. The EOH is a separate troop unit with command and control capability.

LAGUNA GLORIA, on State St., 0.5 *m.* W. of Camp Mabry, is near MOUNT BONNELL, a 775-ft. tall promontory above the Colorado River. This site, said to have been chosen by Stephen F. Austin for his home, became the estate of Clara Driscoll Sevier, who helped preserve the Alamo as a Texas shrine. Laguna Gloria is now a museum conducted by the Texas Fine Arts Assn. *Open 10–12, 2–5 daily except Sunday and Monday mornings.*

ZILKER PARK (*adm. free*), on the Bee Caves Rd. at the city's southwestern limits, is widely known for its natural beauty and as a recreation center. Barton Creek runs through the south part of the irregular tract of 350 acres, and the curving Colorado River is its northern boundary. Its elevation gives a view of Austin's skyline to the east and glimpses of misty purple hills to the west. The tract has virgin growths of laurel, sycamore, elm and twisted live oak. There are rocky banks along streams, and springs, lily ponds and rock gardens where Texas plants bloom.

The park has swimming and wading pools, a dancing pavilion, two large, well-lighted athletic fields, a skeet field, municipal pistol range, canoe club, riding stable and bridle paths, polo field and picnic sites with tables, benches and fireplaces, large barbecue pits and an amphitheater that will seat 1,000 persons.

The largest unit in Austin's park system, Zilker Park was the gift of A. J. Zilker, on the condition that the city pay to the Austin Public Schools the sum of $200,000 to be used as an endowment fund for industrial education. Zilker Park is the scene of many regular attractions, including various swimming meets, community singing, and pageants.

A ford, during the early days the only means of crossing the Colorado River, was near the mouth of Barton Creek, and before that, the Indians used the place as a camp ground.

BARTON SPRINGS, first road south, is a popular bathing resort. (*Adults, 30¢, students, 20¢, children, 10¢*). There are grassy slopes beneath the great pecan trees, and limestone ledges form the upper, natural part of the pool, which is 900 feet long and 150 feet across at its greatest width. The springs have a maximum flow of 42 million gallons and a minimum flow of 17 million gallons a day.

Long before Austin was founded, the lure of gushing spring water had attracted settlers to Barton Springs. One of three Spanish Franciscan missions that were in this vicinity for a period of about six months in 1730 is believed to have been on the bluff of the south bank. William Barton had a homestead here in 1837. The springs early became a favorite meeting place; grist mills were turned by the swift-running water. The rustic concession stand of today is part of an old mill.

HORNSBY'S BEND, 8 m. E. on the Webberville Rd., covers the Mexican land grant of the first non-Latin settler of present Travis County—Reuben A. Hornsby, a surveyor who came to Texas in 1830. The tract spreads over a high bluff in a bend of the Colorado River, and is owned by Hornsby's descendants. The village, Hornsby Bend, is largely inhabited by kinsmen of the pioneer.

HORNSBY CEMETERY (open), contains the graves of two young men sent from the Texas army to protect the family; they were killed by Indians, as were Daniel Hornsby and William Atkinson, buried here in 1845. Graves of other members of the family are inside the walled-in enclosure.

It is said that Reuben Hornsby's grant (a league and labor of land) in 1832 yielded the first harvest in present-day Travis County, and that the earliest local Baptist church service was held here. When Hornsby arrived from Mississippi with his wife, Sarah, their children, slaves and furniture, his was an isolated settlement on the western frontier.

LAKE AUSTIN METROPOLITAN PARK (adm. free), 10 m. NW. on Bull Creek Rd., covers 1,008 acres. The waters of Lake Austin are available for boating, swimming and fishing.

The tract has nearly three miles of lake front and beach, with tree-lined, rocky Turkey Creek winding through its center; hills climb to 1,070 feet, affording a magnificent view of Austin over the top of Mount Bonnell. Bridle paths, unhampered by thoroughfares and traffic, camp sites, fishing, boating, a wildlife preserve and an organized camp that accommodates large units are available.

Most of the tract has cedar and live oak dotting the slopes with year-round greenness, and mountain laurel, redbud, huisache, catclaw, Indian blanket and sumac giving color to the hills in the spring. Strata of limestone along Turkey Creek's banks are used in constructing stone cabins, boat docks, riding stables, and fireplaces. The lake covers 1,830 acres. At its foot is Tom Miller Dam, which impounds the waters. West of the dam and fronting on the lake is CITY PARK, with usual park facilities. East of the dam and the Colorado River is the MUNICIPAL GOLF COURSE.

LAKE TRAVIS, important water supply 12 m. northwest of Austin, was formed when Mansfield Dam impounded the waters of the Colorado River, which was also responsible for several large reservoirs in adjoining counties. The Lake, named for Col. William B. Travis, hero of the Alamo, covers 29,000 acres and has a capacity of 1,950,000 acre-ft.

Beaumont

Airlines and Airports: Eastern Airlines, Delta Airlines and Trans-Texas Airways, 22 flights daily from Jefferson County Airport, between Beaumont and Port Arthur on US 69; has three runways 5,000 to 5,750 ft. Beaumont Airport, west of Beaumont on US 90.

Bus Lines: Greyhound, 650 Park St.; Transcontinental Trailways, College & Osborn Sts.; Coastal Coaches, Beaumont-Silsbee and Lufkin-Beaumont lines; 70 departures daily.

Highways: Interstate 10, US 69, 90, 96, 287; State 12, 105, 124, 347.

Railroads: Southern Pacific, Missouri Pacific, Kansas City Southern, Gulf Coast & Santa Fe.

Accommodations and Information: Numerous modern hotels and motels, including Beaumont Hotel, Orleans & Fannin Sts.; Crosby Hotel, Orleans & Crockett Sts., historic headquarters of the oil boom operators; King Edward Towers, Pearl & Wall Sts.; Holiday Inn, on US 69. Trailer parks. For information: Beaumont Chamber of Commerce, San Jacinto Bldg.; *Beaumont Enterprise* (morning and Sunday) and *Beaumont Journal,* evening, 380 Walnut St.

Recreation: Beaumont has 23 parks, some, like Magnolia, Wiess Ave. & Gulf St. with swimming pools, picnic areas and many other facilities; others, like Spindeltop Monument Park, with Outdoor Oilfield Museum, a small commemorative plot. Golf at Tyrrell Park on Fannett Road, city's largest. There are 5 baseball diamonds (one for the Texas League); 17 tennis courts and 22 softball courts; 3 theaters with 4,046 seats and 2 drive-in theaters. Cruises along the Gulf Coast and tours to Mobil Oil Co. refinery and other plants can be arranged. Consult hotel porters.

Annual Events: Wild Flower Show, spring; Neches River Festival, with crowning of king and queen, water shows and regatta, April; Babe Zacharias Golf Tournament for women, Tyrrell Park, May; Beaumont Country Club Invitation Golf Tournament, first week in June; Annual Trailride and Rodeo at Fair Grounds, last week in June; South Texas State Fair, Fair Grounds, 10 days in October; Spindletop Charity Horse Show, Junior League, summer.

BEAUMONT (21 alt., 119,175 pop., 1960; 127,800, est., 1967; metropolitan area including highly industrialized cities of Port Arthur and Orange, 332,900 est.) is the seat of Jefferson County and the southeast Texas city "where oil became an industry," and where huge wealth has been taken from the wells since the Spindletop gusher erupted in 1901. At first lumber, then rice, became its major products. It is in the eastern part of the Coastal Plain, where the low prairies made flooding for rice culture easy, where the geological formation has stored great resources of oil, sulphur and salt, and where it became possible to make the city a port of the Gulf of Mexico by dredging the sluggish Neches River and building coastal canals to expedite traffic.

The GOLDEN TRIANGLE is the name applied to the great industrial area that has Beaumont and Orange at the west and east points of the north side and Port Arthur at the southern apex of the triangle. Inside are the resources and plants of some of the country's largest petroleum refining and chemical corporations. Eight refineries employing nearly 14,000, include the fourth, fifth and sixth largest in the world, these being Mobil Oil, near Beaumont (220,000 bbl. daily), Gulf Oil at Port Arthur (279,000 bbl.), and Texas Company (Texaco), at Port Arthur (275,000 bbl.). Expansion at Mobil Oil will further raise the output. The refineries in the Golden Triangle include also those of Atlantic, Great Lakes Carbon, Pure Oil, and Union Texas. Among the chemical organizations, making synthetic rubber, plastics, sulphuric acid, industrial organic chemicals and similar products are E. I. duPont de Nemours, Goodyear, Olin Mathieson, Sinclair-Koppers, Firestone, Allied Chemical, Phillips Petroleum and others of like stature, employing nearly 10,000. There are plants making structural steel and pipe, such as American Bridge Co. at Orange; barges and offshore drilling equipment, such as Bethlehem Steel Corp. at Beaumont; forgings, foundry products and trucks, employing 7,000.

In the Beaumont-Port Arthur metropolitan area—Jefferson and Orange Counties—the Texas Employment Commission counted 115,900 employed in July, 1966, of which 35,400 were in manufacturing, 22,900 in wholesale and retail trade, and only 1,200 in agriculture, the principal occupation before Spindletop changed the face of east Texas. But rice still tops the food products and cattle, dairying and lumber still bring profits.

In a typical year, 1944, analyzed by the Lamar Research Center, Jefferson County produced 9,423,969 bbl. of crude petroleum, 109,668,506 cubic ft. of natural gas, and 1,690,407 bbl. of liquids. The sulphur produced in Jefferson County from the Spindletop and Fannett domes by Texas Gulf Sulphur Co. was one-fourth of the whole Texas output. Sulphur also was recovered by sour crudes and from refinery off-gases by Atlantic Refining, Atreco plant; Gulf Oil, Port Arthur plant, and Olin Mathieson, Beaumont plant. Another major industry is the recovery of salt in brine. There are 20 salt domes within 40 miles of Beaumont. Spindletop is estimated to have 9.5 billion tons of salt above the 5,000 ft. level. Each gallon of brine weighs about 10 lbs. and contains $2\frac{1}{2}$ lbs. of salt.

The PORT OF BEAUMONT became practicable by the dredging of the Neches River, providing a 21-mile ship channel from the Gulf of Mexico via Sabine Pass and Sabine Lake. The Channel is 200 ft. wide and 32 ft. deep. Enlarging the Channel to a width of 400 ft. and a depth of 40 ft. is a current objective. The construction of the Turning Basin has proved most useful to ships of 1,000 ft. length or more. The Port handles up to 30,000,000 tons of shipping annually, which puts it in eighth place among United States ports. But the tonnage that reaches the Gulf through the Sabine Pass is so large that the combined shipping of Beaumont, Port Arthur and Sabine Pass Harbor makes the Neches-Sabine channel compete with Houston for third place after New York Harbor and New Orleans. The bulk of the tonnage is petroleum and petrochemical products, but there also is a sizable grain shipment and both Beaumont and Port Arthur have modern elevators.

French and Spanish explorers and trappers who traded with the Indians were the first white men in the vicinity. About 1825, Noah and Nancy Tevis emigrated to Texas, probably from Tennessee. They built their home on the banks of the Neches River, and the little settlement that grew up about their cabin was known as Tevis Bluff and River Neches Settlement. The proximity of the Gulf salt marshes and numerous rivers and bayous abounding with raccoon, opossum, mink, beaver, and muskrat, made for a lively trapping industry; but aside from being the most important fur center west of Calcasieu Parish, Louisiana, the settlement's history for a decade or more was that of any frontier community in the piney woods.

During 1835, Henry Millard, member of a land-purchasing group known as Thomas B. Huling and Company of Jasper County, purchased 50 acres of land from Noah Tevis, and in October a town was laid out. Of numerous stories regarding its name, one asserts that Millard named it Beaumont for his brother-in-law, Jefferson Beaumont, another, that Beaumont (Fr., beautiful hill), was chosen because of a slight elevation southeast of town.

In 1837, Millard and Pulsifer & Company (the latter including Thomas B. Huling), owners of 100 acres covering the town site, invited Joseph Grigsby, owner of 50 acres between the town and the Tevis estate, and the widowed Nancy Tevis, to enter "into mutual convention for the enlargement and more perfect formation of the town aforesaid." This timely move was rewarded when Beaumont, in 1838, replaced the town of Jefferson as the seat of present Jefferson County.

By 1840, Beaumont was an actuality, busily engaged in the development of a lumber industry. Shingles were made by sawing logs into shingle lengths, splitting these cuts into proper thickness and thinning the edges with a drawing knife. Cotton, sugar cane, and cattle were produced by southern planters who had settled in the vicinity.

There was a 60-foot depth in the river at the end of present Main Street, and nosing through Sabine Pass and up the Neches River, Gulf schooners and side-wheel river boats carried on a busy traffic in cotton, cattle, and shingles, thus early laying the foundation of the town's importance as a port.

Soon after the founding of Beaumont, a number of settlers braved the enmity of cattlemen who disliked fences, and began to plant rice. Their primitive process consisted of plowing the lowlands in the early spring with a walking plow drawn by oxen, sowing the rice broadcast and harrowing it in with a wooden-tooth harrow, leveeing the field with a small embankment—then waiting hopefully for the necessary rainfall to irrigate the crop.

The first yields, though meager, were enough to demonstrate the possibilities of rice culture. Production of "Providence rice," so called because nature provided the moisture, was increased annually. After the October harvesting, accomplished with a reaping hook, these first crops were placed in stacks, and the daily or weekly supply was husked by beating it with a wooden pestle in the chiseled hollow of a gum log. After the

Civil War farmers began to grow rice for market, and irrigation was introduced into local cultivation.

Settlement and rebuilding after the war created a great demand for lumber, which was shipped or floated down the river. Four large sawmills, built in Beaumont in 1876–78, littered the adjacent regions with sawdust and slabs, but when the railroads began hauling out the mills' products, river traffic dwindled, as the river was constantly filling with silt. Lumbering reached its peak in the 1880's and 1890's, when the output of the Beaumont sawmills averaged 200,000 feet daily, with other wood product plants producing in proportion.

Rice farmers made rapid strides in the development of their irrigation systems. Pumping plants were installed, more acreage planted, and more miles of irrigation ditches dug. Beaumont's first large commercial rice mill was opened in 1892. Although lumber was still the region's leading industry in 1900, rice growing was running it a close second, with 5,859 acres of rice or 62 per cent of the State's rice area in the vicinity of Beaumont.

At that same time, out on the prairie south of Beaumont, Anthony F. Lucas was drilling for oil. On January 10, 1901, the drill was down about 1,160 feet when the sand formation gave way to a rock stratum and the crew shut down to change the bit and sink new casing. Neither Lucas nor the experienced members of his crew were unduly optimistic over the oil signs, but suddenly, almost without warning, there was a deafening roar. Tons of pipe were projected through the rig floor, up and out of the hole and high into the air. Spindletop was in!

A geyser of oil spouted 200 feet in a wind-frayed, greasy plume that spread crude oil over the vicinity. No tanks had been built for storage and the oil ran where it willed as the gusher spouted unchecked. At last, after wild days, it was brought under control by a firmly-anchored valve.

Beaumont became a city literally "in bonanza"; as wild as any gold camp of an earlier America. Ham and eggs were a dollar an order and the demand was greater than the supply. Blankets were a luxury, cots almost unobtainable, and weary men flopped in their clothes wherever sleep overtook them.

Roughs, toughs, petty thieves, soldiers of fortune, lease gamblers, spurious stock promoters, and all the riffraff, male and female, that seeks the easy pickings of an oil-mad crowd, swarmed over the town. The chief of police warned people to walk in the middle of the street after nightfall and "to tote guns." "An' tote 'em in your hands," he added, "not on your hips, so everybody can see you're loaded."

Though the unscrupulous found smooth enough going for a time, they ultimately faded from the picture. It was such men as James S. Hogg, former Texas Governor, Jim Swayne, and J. S. Cullinan, who emerged with great fortunes. They lifted Beaumont out of the boom-day madness and stabilized the oil industry.

Business-minded as those men were, it is possible that they and their kind might never have seen the full opportunity offered by the Spindletop pool but for an Englishman, James Roche. A soldier of fortune, shrewd, resourceful, but with a reputation for square dealing, he was the first to

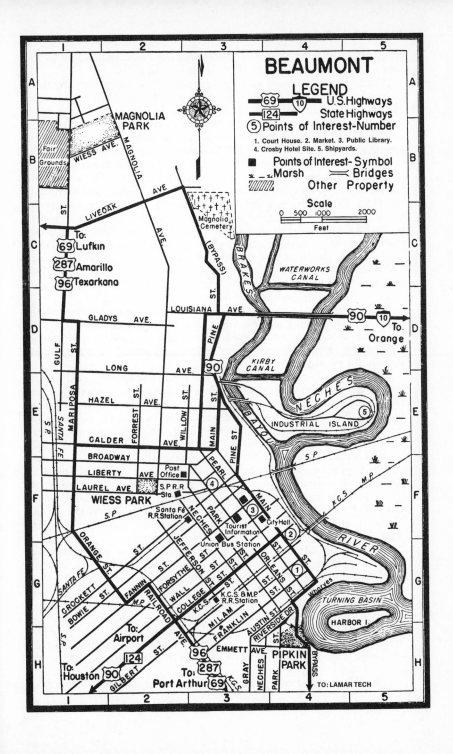

realize that oil must be sold if production were to continue. Up to the time of his appearance men had been selling wells, not oil.

Roche obtained options on oil production at Spindletop, offering three cents a barrel for it. He had no money, but he had genius as a promoter. His next move was to negotiate a 60-day option on a 40-acre site for a refinery, and no money down. He then sold everything covered by these options to the Hogg-Swayne Syndicate, which soon organized a refining company called the Producers' Oil Company. That was the beginning of one of the State's greatest oil corporations, the Texas Company.

The operations of the oil titans—Hogg, John W. (Bet-a-Million) Gates, Cullinan, Swayne, Andrew Mellon, J. M. Guffey, and eventually the elder Rockefeller—caused the fly-by-night, catchpenny boomers to move out, taking their "quick money" with them, and the oil "game" began to acquire solidity. Refineries were built, tank farms were established, and the earth was gashed for the first pipe line in southeast Texas.

By 1903, the boom had sagged from peak production of 17,420,949 barrels in 1902—96 per cent of the State's oil production—to about half that amount. Spindletop became a "pumper" field, but a sound producer, and oil remained the backbone of Beaumont's development.

The lumber industry throve during the boom days by meeting the needs of rush building and the frenzied construction of derricks, but as the boom steadied to normal production, lumbering sank into a decline. On the other hand, Beaumont's rice industry flourished. In 1907, 60,000 acres in the vicinity were planted to rice.

By 1908, transportation needs of the rapidly developing area had revived the old dream of opening the Port of Beaumont. A nine-foot channel, 15 miles long, was completed during the year, its area extending between the Sabine and Neches Rivers and 12 miles from the mouth of the Neches to the head of the Port Arthur Canal, which had been transferred to the Government by its owners.

The Beaumont and the Orange navigation districts secured the passage of a $498,000 bond issue, and work on completion of a channel 25 feet in depth to Beaumont was begun in 1911. Completed in April, 1916, this project gave the city a turning basin, cutting off two bends in the river, and access to the Gulf by way of the Neches River, the Sabine-Neches Canal, the Port Arthur Canal and Sabine Pass, including the jetty channel.

In 1919 the city-manager and commission form of government was adopted, replacing the aldermanic form in use since 1881.

Throughout the next decade, oil maintained its lead. Lumber fell off badly, but the rice yield to the acre increased with improved methods. High prices had led to overproduction, curtailed somewhat when salt water—entering by the way of the ship channel and pumping plants—periodically overflowed certain acreage. Problems of this industry were now in the hands of the Southern Rice Growers Association, which sponsored a campaign that made packaged rice the favorite of consumers of the Nation.

One November evening in 1925 the crowds at the South Texas State

Fair were thrilled as men excitedly relayed the message: "Old Spindle-top's brought in a new gusher." Experienced oil men, drilling to a greater depth than the old production level, had struck a new pool.

Again Beaumont boomed, but not with the rowdy, unorganized, rough-and-ready wildness of its previous demonstration. There was plenty of excitement and new fortunes were made, but the steadying influence of organization and experience made itself felt. The new field proved even more productive than the former. It roared to a new peak and maintained an amazingly high level of production.

By 1935 the new Spindletop pool reached the astounding yield of more than 75,000,000 barrels, with a good promise of substantial production for years to come. Big business controlled the field's operation and the pay-off was on a grand scale. As an outstanding example, Stanolind Oil Company bought the Yount-Lee Company, the discoverers of the new field, in August, 1935, for $41,600,000 cash, the third largest cash transaction in American business history. Today the Spindletop field, with its tank farm and closely-spaced derricks, is a dominating factor in Beaumont.

Meanwhile a 30-foot ship canal was finished in 1927, and in that year a new project was authorized for a 32-foot channel; this was completed in 1930. The present canal is 200 feet wide and 21 miles long to the point where it joins the Sabine-Neches Canal. The port has a turning basin 1,500 feet long and 500 feet wide, with berthing space of 2,900 feet and 449,190 square feet of storage space in covered sheds, also 137,000 square feet of open docks and wharves. Modern loading equipment has been installed and world-ranging freight lines use the port's facilities.

The rice industry, with its 200,000 acres of potential rice lands in the city's vicinity, and approximately 65,000 irrigated acres planted to this crop, furnishes production for the large rice-milling industry.

Although oil is supreme in Beaumont, lumber is still vital, and the pulp and paper industry is being attracted because of the vast supply of raw material. Contributing further to the modern industrial picture of Beaumont are iron and brass works engaged in the manufacture of supplies for oil fields and refineries, and shipyards, turning out tugs, tankers, and various types of oil carrier barges. Within the boundaries of Jefferson County farm income, including returns from livestock, earns about $12,-000,000 a year.

POINTS OF INTEREST

PIPKIN PARK (*open, free*), Riverside Dr. and Emmett St., is a 4.66-acre wooded tract occupying a part of the Noah Tevis league. It contains playground equipment and a wading pool for children. From Riverside Drive, it offers an excellent view of the Turning Basin, which borders its northern boundary.

TEMPLE TO THE BRAVE (*open 8–5 holidays only, free*), SE. corner of Pipkin Park, is a red stone building dedicated as a memorial honoring Texas heroes of all wars. The one-story, one-room structure is Gothic in feeling. Three small stained glass windows on each side wall depict Texas under six flags, a circular window at the back above the little chapel recess shows the flags of the allied nations of World War I and the Great Seal of the United States, while the large Gothic window above the door depicts three divisions of national defense, the Army, the Navy, and the Air Corps. The front part of the room is devoted to a museum, while at the back within the little chapel is the altar, dedicated to world peace.

The CLIFTON WALKING BEAM, on a narrow strip of the park across Riverside Dr., is a relic of the *U. S. S. Clifton* and a memento of the capture of that vessel by Dick Dowling's detachment at Sabine Pass, September 8, 1863 (*see Tour 5c*).

The JEFFERSON COUNTY COURTHOUSE (*open day and night*), between Pearl and Main, Milam and Franklin Sts., is of modern architecture, designed by Fred C. Stone and A. Babin. A 14-story central tower is flanked by two wings of two stories each. The outer construction is of light buff brick and cream-colored Cordova limestone; imported marble was used for the floor and wainscoting. Interior decorations include a bas-relief map in the main corridor, illustrating county activities and industries, and courtroom panels representing tables of Mosaic law and Roman fasces. The structure, dedicated on January 17, 1932, represents an expenditure of one million dollars. In it are housed all the county offices, courts, and the county jail.

The JEFFERSON COUNTY LIBRARY (*open 8–5 workdays except Sat., 8–12, free*), has more than 38,000 volumes. A book wagon, called the Jefferson County Book Directory, is a feature of the library service. Through it several thousand volumes are made available once each week to the school children and adults of rural communities throughout the county.

The NANCY TEVIS MARKET (*open 6–6 workdays*), Main St. between Gilbert and College Sts., was named in honor of Nancy Tevis, wife of one of the city's founders. Here farmers display their produce. The three-story white stucco building is of modified Spanish architecture, designed by Douglas E. Steinman. It has corner buttresses, arched windows, and an outside stairway.

The TYRRELL PUBLIC LIBRARY (*open 9–9 workdays; 2–6 Sun.*), N. corner Pearl and Forsythe Sts., opened July 5, 1926, is a beautiful adaptation of an old Romanesque type stone church transformed to library purposes. It has a high vaulted roof, stained-glass windows and gray ashlar stone walls. A. N. Dawson was the architect. Captain W. C. Tyrrell purchased this building, which then housed the First Baptist Church, for $70,000 on April 22, 1923, and donated it to the city for use as a library. Following exactly the terms of his will, the interior was altered very little. The art room usually has on display one or more collections loaned by individuals or institutions, and has an art library and thousands of mounted pictures. The Library's total stock amounts to more than 100,000 volumes.

LAMAR STATE COLLEGE OF TECHNOLOGY (Lamar Tech) is said to occupy the largest group of modern functional buildings in Texas education. It has a campus of 120 acres in the southeastern part of Beaumont, fronting on the Port Arthur Road (US 69). Opened as a junior college in 1923, it received its present name in 1951 with full senior standing in 32 academic departments and schools of business, education, engineering, liberal arts, fine and applied arts, sciences and graduate work.

Of more than regional importance is its School of Vocations, which has developed departments that train the student for practical work in scientific fields. It confers degrees in electronics, industrial electricity, machine shop, diesel engineering, refrigeration, air-conditioning, and welding. Access to petrochemical plants makes possible observation by the students of practical application of their studies.

Lamar planned to expand its facilities greatly by 1970 with the expenditure of $11,000,000. It already has allocated about $1,000,000 to the enlargement of the Library, which has more than 125,000 volumes. Its circular Administration Building is unique in architectural records. Of the 11 dormitories housing more than 1,000 students, the latest was opened in 1967. Recent typical enrollment was 9,051, with 294 in the faculty. There is a six-week summer session. Costs for 9 mos. in residence are estimated at $671 to $810.

Lamar plays an important part in the city's cultural activities. It supports the Lamar Symphony Orchestra, the Cardinal Theatre, the Cardinal Singers, the Symphonic Band, a jazz ensemble, the A Cappella Choir, the Grand Choir, the Madrigal Singers, and the Opera Workshop.

SPINDLETOP, site of the most spectacular oil strike in history, is marked by a tall spike of granite, 58 ft. tall, on the spot where the Lucas Gusher came in, January 10, 1901. A small park surrounds it inside the extreme southeastern limits of Beaumont, reached by Cardinal Drive (Loop 251) off Interstate 10, and Spindletop Ave., off Port Arthur Road (US 69). The inscription on the monument recites the details of the event and adds: "Petroleum has revolutionized industry and transportation; it has created untold wealth, built cities, furnished employment for hundreds of thousands, and contributed billions of dollars in taxes to support institutions of government. In a brief span of years it has altered man's way of life throughout the world." In the park is the Outdoor Oilfield Museum, maintained by the Monument Association and the Beaumont Rotary Club, and comprising the "authentic 1901" derrick and crown block, drilling platform, drawworks and mud pump, steam engine, boiler and band wheel, and storage tanks. Nearby is the Texas Gulf Sulphur Spindleton plant. The field continues to be a major producer of oil, gas, sulphur and salt.

MAGNOLIA CEMETERY (*open sunrise to sunset*), 2200 Pine St., is the burial ground of many of Beaumont's pioneers. Its 40 acres, bordered on the east by Brake's Bayou, are shaded by pines, magnolias and cypresses. In the original three-acre plot near the bayou old tombstones—"sad rocks," the Negroes call them—bear the names of members of the Tevis, Wiess, McFaddin, Fletcher, O'Brien, Pipkin, Broussard and other prominent first families. In the newer part of the cemetery stands the $100,000 mausoleum of Manitou greenstone which contains the remains of Frank Yount, rediscoverer of the Spindletop oil field in 1925.

The SOUTH TEXAS STATE FAIRGROUNDS (*open day and night*), pedestrian entrance at Gulf St. and Simmons Ave.; entrance for vehicles on Gulf St. between Regent St. and Wiess Ave., are headquarters of the South Texas State Fair. Many other events, including a four-day Fourth of July celebration, a Boy Scout "round-up" and a Negro "Juneteenth" barbecue and picnic are held here. The Agricultural Building, Main Exhibit Building, Auditorium and other structures are of modernized Spanish architecture, designed by F. W. Steinman and Son. The average annual attendance at the Fair is 150,000.

The BEAUMONT LITTLE THEATER (*open by arrangement*), NE. corner of the Fairgrounds, at Gulf St. and Wiess Ave., is headquarters for the Beaumont Community Players. Built in 1930, it is a one-story structure of brick, painted white, with green shutters, and was designed by Douglas E. Steinman. Two broad flights of steps lead to the porticoed entrance on Regent Street. The theater auditorium seats 250.

MAGNOLIA PARK (*adm. free*), on Wiess Ave. between Gulf St. and Magnolia Ave., the city's principal recreation ground, contains swimming pool, zoo, tennis courts, fishpond, playgrounds and picnic tables; free motion pictures are shown at intervals during the summer.

Brownsville

Airport: Rio Grande Valley International Airport, 3 *m.* east of city; Braniff International Airways, Eastern Airlines, Pan-American World Airways. Aeronaves S. A. at Matamoros.
Buses: Brownsville Bus Station, 13th and Adams Sts.; Continental Trailways, Transporte del Norte.
Highways: US 77 direct from north via Dallas and Waco. US 281 direct from north. US 83 from west, joins US 77 at San Benito. State 48 to Port Isabel. State 4 to Boca Chica. Toll bridge to Matamoros. To San Antonio, 271 *m.;* Houston, 352 *m.;* Corpus Christi, 159 *m.* Two toll bridges to Mexico (25¢ per motor car), Gateway and International, the latter for motor cars and railroad only. Monterrey, 200 *m.;* Mexico City, 638 *m.*
Railways: Missouri Pacific, Southern Pacific.

Information: Brownsville Herald, 1235 E. Van Buren St., Brownsville 78521. Phone LI 2–4331. American Automobile Assn., Ramada Inn, 2534 Central Blvd. Brownsville Chamber of Commerce, 1600 Elizabeth St.

Recreation: Fort Brown Memorial Civic Center for municipal golf course, swimming pool (fee), tennis, shuffleboard. Ringgold Park for croquet, darts, shuffleboard, tennis, swimming, picnics. Golf at Brownsville Country Club (greens fee). Weekly games and social affairs by the Winter Visitors Club, sponsored by the Chamber of Commerce.

Fishing, Hunting, Salt-water Bathing: Charter boats leave for Gulf fishing almost daily from Fishing Harbor. Ship Channel has trout, snook, red fish; fresh-water resacas (pools) have bass, catfish. Gulf has red snapper, bonita, crevelle, dolphin, king and spanish mackerel, ling, tuna, trout, redfish, tarpon, sailfish, marlin. Hunting in season for doves, ducks, geese, quail, turkeys, whitewings, deer. Bathing and picnics in environs of Brownsville: Isla Blanca Park, after crossing Queen Isabella Causeway at Port Isabel to South Padre Island. Also at Boca Chica Beach, 22 *m.* from Brownsville on Highway 4.

Fishing license: All over 17 and under 65 must have license for fresh and saltwater fishing, $2.15. Hunting license: Nonresident, $25; resident, $3.15. Special 5-day migratory fowl stamp, nonresident, $5.25.

Special Events: Charro Days, pre-Lent (February) costume festival by people of Brownsville and Matamoros, and tourists, with parades, dances, dining, and Mexican Night. Rio Grande Valley Kennel Club annual show at Memorial Center, March. Annual orchid show, Fort Brown Memorial Center, March 21–24; bull fighting, Sundays, at Matamoros.

BROWNSVILLE (57 alt., 48,040 pop., 1960, with annexation of 3,267; 52,800, 1966, est.; metropolitan area, including Harlingen and San Benito, 151,098, 1960). Seat of Cameron County, it is the largest city of the Lower Rio Grande Valley and an important Texas seaport with access to the Gulf of Mexico through a 17-mile Ship Channel. It is an export center for cotton, citrus fruits and products of the Valley, and port of entry for minerals from Mexico. As the terminus of fine highways it provides an easy route across the border.

It is a flourishing winter resort with numerous motels and a mild temperature. Gulf breezes in summer and warm sunshine in winter make year-round sports possible. Salt water fishing in the Gulf of Mexico and the attractions of beach resorts, duck and goose shooting, wild game hunting in outlying brush country, golf and boating offer a diversity of recreation. Sparkling *resacas*—old beds of the Rio Grande—at the city's doors are bordered by orange, grapefruit, lemon and lime groves; on the streets grow retamas, mimosas, locusts, bananas, pepper and citrus trees, and broad-leafed papayas, all overshadowed by palms, often of great height and age. Residential areas have many beautiful houses of Spanish or Mexican types, set in spacious grounds planted in subtropical shrubs.

A wide variety of industries has located in Brownsville, running all the way from fruit packing, food processing, orange and grapefruit concentrates, petrochemical production to the manufacture of ceramics, glass, garments, mattresses and furniture. It is at the edge of the frost belt, with an equable climate averaging 73.4°, with the average high 82° and the average low 64.8°. The prevailing southeast wind from the Gulf of Mexico averages 9 *m.* per hour.

Brownsville is a center of the shrimp fishing industry. In 1966 Texas led shrimp production with 43,730,000 lbs. landed, valued at $32,144,-000. Brownsville-Port Isabel landed 15,578,000 lbs., valued at $11,437,-000. There are five freezing plants at Brownsville and two at Port Isabel.

The big increase in leisure time and the movement south of retired persons have made Brownsville a prosperous recreation and tourist center. The city administration has supported many recreation, entertainment and convention facilities. Both young people and senior citizens are provided for in outdoor sports and indoor functions. The cities of the Valley make special efforts to acclimate "retirees." Stanley B. Crockett, banker and citrus grower, placed the source of income in the Valley in the following order: agriculture, industry, petroleum, tourism, retirees, fishing and international trade. The towns in the metropolitan area of Brownsville annually welcome 150,000 winter visitors, who spend up to $60,000,000.

Brownsville is on one of the shortest routes to Mexico City. Two toll bridges connect it with Mexico. It is possible to leave the United States border at Brownsville and reach Mexico City by motor car the second day. A twice-daily bus service covers the 638 miles in 22 hours. The 194 miles to Ciudad Victoria, the junction with the Pan American Highway, are filled with spectacular scenery and ancient settlements. The northward highway, US 77, carries the motorist through Waco and Dallas on fine roads all the way to Winnipeg.

HISTORY

Ranches occupied the lower Rio Grande Valley in the 18th century, Rancho Viejo, north of the present Brownsville, dating back to 1771. The area was part of the Mexican state of Tamaulipas until the Republic of Texas claimed it in the Treaty of Velasco in 1836. A small settlement grew up, although the principal town on the River was Matamoros.

In 1846 the United States Army built a fort here and called it Fort Taylor, in honor of the commander of the Army of the Rio Grande, General Zachary Taylor. When a force of Mexicans from Matamoros menaced Taylor's line of supply from Point (now Port) Isabel, Taylor left Major Jacob Brown in command at the fort and moved out to save his supplies. Before Taylor could return the Mexicans attacked Brown, who called for reinforcements. Taylor thereupon moved his army to relieve the fort.

At about noon the next day, May 8, 1846, Taylor found himself confronting a superior Mexican force at Palo Alto, nine miles northeast of his objective. Taylor gave battle in the first major engagement of the war, and drove the Mexicans from the field. Resuming his advance at daybreak, Taylor was again confronted by a Mexican army a little more than three miles north of Fort Taylor, and there was fought the BATTLE OF RESACA DE LA PALMA, where a swiftly executed cavalry charge and an infantry flank movement sent the enemy flying across the river in disorder.

Arriving at the fort, General Taylor found that the detachment had been successful in defense, but that Major Brown had been fatally wounded. On the death of the Major an order from General Taylor changed the name of the post to Fort Brown, in his honor.

The fort brought an influx of merchants and settlers. Charles Stillman, of Wethersfield, Conn., who had joined his father in Matamoros in 1828, and had been a merchant there until 1846, formed the Brownsville Town Company in 1848 and platted lots near Fort Brown. With two steamboat captains, Mifflin Kenedy and Richard King, he bought Army steamboats and started hauling river cargo. Kenedy and King formed the great King Ranch about 1860.

In 1849 and 1850 the straggling village received another boost. Westbound gold seekers landed at Point Isabel in increasing numbers and converged on Brownsville, where they outfitted for the long journey up the Rio Grande and across the mountains of northern Mexico to the gold fields in California. Thousands thronged the town, awaiting transportation on the little river steamers that would take them to the head of navigation. Others, too impatient to await steamer facilities, outfitted and streamed up the military road laid out by General Taylor's engineers. Some, seeing greater possibilities nearer at hand than in California, remained and became pioneer citizens. It was Brownsville's first boom, and the town prospered.

From 1850 to 1861 Brownsville served as the distributing center for a vast area of developing cattle country. Ranches in the region were large and their thousands of cattle roamed the open range. Cattle thieves and other outlaws were numerous, and there were many bloody conflicts between ranchers and the gentry of the brush. Yet trade was brisk, and boats plied the Rio Grande bearing cargoes of supplies to the landing stations maintained by the ranches along the river's winding banks. It was during this period that Charles Stillman laid the foundation of what later became, under his son, James, one of the greatest fortunes and banking houses in America. It was Stillman and his associates who laid out the town site of Brownsville.

This period also gave rise to an unsavory practice of favoritism on the part of various Texas politicians, which resulted in some instances in the loss of property among Mexican landholders north of the Rio Grande. Rebellion burst forth when Juan Nepomuceno Cortinas rallied a Mexican force that swept into Brownsville in a surprise raid, captured the city and held it in September, 1859. After his departure Cortinas figured in numerous dramatic episodes, until a combined force of Texas Rangers and Federal troops drove him back into Mexico (see Tour 9c).

During this period Mexico was in constant turmoil, due to political strife, and Brownsville received, with almost equal frequency, the bullets and the refugees of battles between rival Mexican factions in Matamoros. Deserters from the various factions looted both sides of the river impartially, and so great was the disorder that Lieutenant Colonel Robert E. Lee was sent to investigate the situation, spending several months in Brownsville, during the inquiry.

Following that particular event, Brownsville spent a comparatively quiet interval, but within a year the Civil War began and again the city reverted to what, by that time, seemed its normal state of turmoil. Fort Brown was evacuated by Federal troops and Captain B. H. Hill, post commander, removed his force to Brazos Santiago, from which point it embarked for the north. Before leaving the fort, the force burned military supplies to keep them from falling into the hands of the Confederates, who immediately garrisoned the post.

From the outset Brownsville was one of the principal ports of the Confederacy. For months boats plied the river, taking cotton to ships lying in the Gulf of Mexico, off the mouth of the Rio Grande. The city throve as merchants and army contractors came to take advantage of its war-born commerce. During the dry season the city was powdered white with thick dust that lay ankle deep in the streets; in the rainy season it swam in a sea of liquid mud through which army wagons struggled with their heavy loads. The roads northward were crowded with an almost continuous stream of wagon trains bringing cotton, wool, and hides, and carrying medical and military supplies to the army distribution centers at Shreveport and Marshall.

As the Northern offensive tightened, a Federal force of more than 6,000 men was landed at Brazos Santiago, whence it moved to attack Fort Brown. General H. P. Bee, Confederate commander at the post, believing himself outnumbered, retired without offering resistance, after setting fire to the large stores of cotton and military supplies.

Later, reinforced, the Confederates returned to capture Fort Brown, pushing back the Federal outposts and capturing a subpost detachment at Las Rucias Ranch, after which it advanced on the fort. In his turn, the Federal commander retired, establishing a fortified camp at his seacoast base. Once more in Brownsville the Confederates resumed their commercial activities, but under a new system.

The outgoing cotton and incoming supplies moved across the river and were hauled along the south bank, the neutral Mexican town of Bagdad, at the river's mouth, serving as port of entry and export. Anchored off Bagdad scores of ships loaded and unloaded, disregarding the Federal troops in Clarksville, on the American side of the river. Clashes between Federal and Confederate units were frequent, but no engagement of major proportions occurred, and Brownsville became the back door of the Confederacy—a door which the Federals never closed until the end.

The last battle of the Civil War was fought at Palmito Hill, May 12 and 13, 1865, more than a month after General Lee had surrendered at Appomattox (*see Tour 16d*).

Immediately another conflict threatened Brownsville, in the Maximilian situation in Mexico, where the empire set up by Napoleon III of France was in conflict with the United States Monroe Doctrine. General Joseph O. Shelby, with his Missouri cavalry, and many other Confederates of recognized fighting ability, were known to have crossed into Mexico, and the United States Government anticipated a possible coalition between them and Maximilian's European soldiers.

On May 17, 1865, General U. S. Grant ordered General Philip H. Sheridan to proceed from Washington to Fort Brown. He arrived on June 23, to command a force of approximately 25,000 men. From Sheridan's arrival until November of the following year he maintained an active campaign of threatening demonstrations along that part of the Rio Grande. In addition, he closed the ports of Louisiana and Texas to all persons embarking for Mexico. Gradually Maximilian withdrew his forces from northern Mexico and the crisis ended without open hostilities.

While in Brownsville, Sheridan constructed a railroad from the port at Brazos Santiago to the White Ranch landing, and an entirely new roadbed from Boca Chica to the White Ranch (Palmito Hill). The remains of the roadbed and of the railroad bridge at Boca Chica are still visible.

In the years immediately following the war, trade was stimulated by cattle drives from the area toward northern markets.

The first commercial railroad was built from Brownsville to Point Isabel in 1870, a narrow-gauge road that served to convey what little commerce remained to be shipped by sea. Shallow-draft craft still plied the Rio Grande, and overland traffic moved north and west by wagon train and stagecoach. One of the last stage lines in Texas operated between Brownsville and Alice as late as 1904, when the Gulf Coast Lines Railway reached Brownsville.

In 1877 political strife across the Rio Grande again flared into open rebellion, and Brownsville became a hotbed of plots and counterplots. In a house on 13th Street, Porfirio Diaz planned the initial moves of a campaign that opened with the capture of Matamoros and swept onward in the successful revolution that made him dictator.

In August, 1906, the Army post at Fort Brown became news of national scope when a group of Negro soldiers of the 25th US Infantry

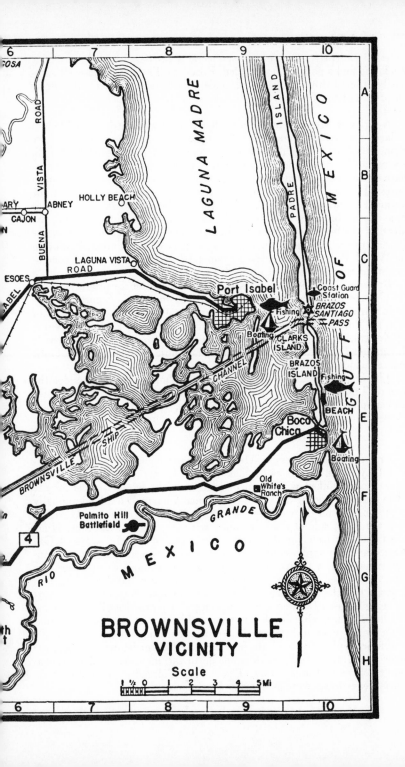

BROWNSVILLE
VICINITY

Scale

½ 0   1   2   3   4   5 Mi

protested violently when refused service at a restricted bar. A bartender was killed and a policeman wounded. President Theodore Roosevelt summarily ordered three companies, 250 men, mustered out. His action drew hot protests from Congress and the press, but only 14 men were ever reinstated.

A series of Mexican revolutions that started when Francisco Madero declared a provisional government in 1910, again set the border country aflame. In 1916 a large part of the National Guard strength of the U.S. was assembled along the international border, and Brownsville drew its share of the visiting contingents, most of them from northern and eastern States. The warm climate and the nearness of the Gulf delighted the National Guardsmen, who thronged the beaches and basked in the sunshine. Returning later to their homes, those thousands of military visitors talked of the beauties of Brownsville, awakening national interest in the city and the country surrounding it. The entry of the United States into the World War in 1917 delayed promoters' plans, but after the conclusion of the war development proceeded rapidly.

Brownsville felt its position was the natural outlet for products of the Rio Grande Valley, and made several attempts to become a port. In 1930 a substantial port plan was undertaken and finally adopted. By midyear of 1936 the Port of Brownsville was opened as the result of a Public Works Administration project costing $5,500,000, sponsored by the Brownsville Navigation District, which built jetties, a 17-mile channel from the Gulf, and a spacious turning basin.

The District is an independent public authority operating under the laws of Texas, with power to develop marine terminal facilities and industrial plant sites. It includes Brownsville, Olmito and Los Fresnos. Three commissioners are elected and operation is by a professional staff.

Brownsville's nearness to Mexico gives it frequent occasions for *fiestas*. Many of the visitors and residents of the Lower Valley, whose towns are so closely linked with rural districts that the whole area is largely urban, gather here for the celebration called Charro Days, held annually in Brownsville on the week end before the beginning of Lent. Mexicans from the south side of the river unite with Texans in this event. Huge entertainments have for their theme the gay and colorful ways of Old Mexico and the border country, including such typical features as an international ball, a Court of the Brush and a costume street dance, the latter advertised as "the world's largest costume ball." Throughout Charro Days the people wear Mexico-Texas border costumes, only tourists being excused from an otherwise compulsory practice. Thus Brownsville helps to keep alive its old heritage, and to cement the friendship that characterizes relations between the people of both sides of the Rio Grande.

On September 20, 1967, the hurricane Beulah hit Brownsville and the lower Rio Grande Valley with winds up to 130 mph. Much damage was done to citrus and other crops. The Arroyo Colorado overflowed farmlands. Heavy losses were incurred at Harlingen.

PORT BROWNSVILLE, 4 *m.* from the city line, is the salt-water harbor with terminal facilities at the end of the 17-mile SHIP CHANNEL to Port Isabel and the Gulf of Mexico. It was opened in 1936 and is administered by the Brownsville Navigation District, an authority separate from the city. It is reached by State 48 and the Missouri Pacific Ry. More than 4,400,000 tons are handled annually by the port, putting it in a category with Galveston, Wilmington, N. C., and Oakland, Calif. The main harbor has a depth of 36 ft. and has 7,500 ft. of dry cargo wharves with deepsea and barge berths, 4 tanker docks and warehousing. It is the southern terminus of the Inland Waterway System. Its location makes possible quick deliveries to the towns of the Lower Rio Grande Valley and northern Mexico. The freighters of more than 50 lines from all foreign ports dock here. In addition 8 barge lines reach all the waterways on the Gulf Coast. Some freighters carry a small number of passengers but passenger and cruise ships do not dock.

Port Brownsville is a major cotton port; also handles produce, citrus fruits, processed products. Northern Mexico uses it as an outlet for cotton, cotton by-products, refined lead and zinc, and concentrates. Other traffic includes crude and refined petroleum, petrochemicals, and a large tonnage of bananas. Fruits and staple products received at Brownsville reach as far as St. Louis, Chicago and Pittsburgh by waterways such as the Gulf Inland Waterway, and the Mississippi-Ohio and Illinois River systems.

The SHIP CHANNEL plays an important part in the Brownsville economy. A fine fishing harbor is located on the channel just east of the turning basin, with 7,600 ft. of dock space, sufficient for 600 vessels. It is equipped with the most modern apparatus, such as icing and fueling docks, freezing and processing plants and marine ways and machine shops. The fleet of fishing trawlers is unusually large and the catch of shrimp extraordinary. The FISHING HARBOR has brought much traffic to Brownsville with the development since 1940 of deepwater shrimp trawling. About 600 trawlers are operating out of Brownsville and Port Isabel and their annual haul of about 30,000,000 lbs. has a value of $20,000,000.

POINTS OF INTEREST

The FORT BROWN RESERVATION, 358.8 acres, at the foot of Elizabeth Street, was for 100 years the site of the southernmost military post of the United States, established 1846 by General Zachary Taylor. When it became surplus Government property it was awarded to the Brownsville School District in 1948 for a college site.

FORT BROWN MEMORIAL CENTER on the Fort Brown Reservation is the headquarters for tourist and community activities and information. It was erected in 1953 and has facilities for conventions, visitors' entertainment and tourist guidance. The JACOB BROWN AUDITORIUM seats 2,500 and has arrangements for stage productions, dances and indoor sports. STILLMAN TOWN HALL is used for smaller gatherings and social functions. The FORT BROWN WOMEN'S CENTER accommodates auxiliaries of conventions and women's interests. The ROBERT E. LEE YOUTH CENTER concentrates on the activities of young people. The facilities of the ZACHARY TAYLOR LIBRARY of Texas Southmost College are open to visitors. Outdoor arrangements include the A. A. U. swimming pool, the children's wading pool, tennis courts and shuffleboard courts. Also located on the Reservation is the RIVERSIDE MUNICIPLE GOLF COURSE.

In 1967 the BROWNSVILLE CHAMBER OF COMMERCE moved to a spacious new building at 1600 Elizabeth St., in the Fort Brown area. Some of the historical relics displayed in its former headquarters may be seen in the lobby.

A dwelling of historic interest in the Fort Brown area is the former WILLIAM NEALE HOUSE, now owned by the Brownsville Art League. It is a Southern Colonial house, built in the 1840s on E. 14th St., near Washington, and removed to this location.

TEXAS SOUTHMOST COLLEGE occupies 45 acres of the Reservation and makes use of some of the reconstructed buildings of the old Fort. It was founded by the County in 1926 as Brownsville Junior College and changed to its present title in 1949. It enrolls about 800 students and has courses in business, agricultural, engineering and Latin American subjects, as well as pre-medical and pre-dental. Its Administration Building is the former Army Post Hospital, built 1868 with Spanish arches and breezeways. Here Dr. William C. Gorgas, later surgeon general of the U. S. Army, began his studies of yellow fever in 1882–1884. Four other buildings of the original compound are the Post Commissary-Guardhouse, the Army Post Morgue, and the Medical Laboratory. The Zachary Taylor Library is administered jointly by the College and the City and has more than 90,000 volumes. The College recently has built the Cleve Tandy Liberal Arts Building and the Camille Lightner Student Center. The Applied Arts Building is being constructed.

The CITY HALL and MARKET PLACE occupy a plaza donated in 1850 by Charles Stillman. It was planned as a two-story structure with archways and a cupola for a bell and a clock. Open stalls were the market, while the second floor was used by the Presbyterians for services. A hurricane destroyed the upper part and it was a one-story structure until 1912. In 1949 a modern building was erected on the foundations, preserving the original arches. The old bell, missing for years, was rehung in 1966.

The CAMERON COUNTY COURTHOUSE, Jefferson and E. 12th St., built 1882 at a cost of $60,000, is now the MASONIC TEMPLE, home of Rio Grande Lodge No. 81, AF and AM. Brownsville became the county seat in 1848. The house had a courtroom two stories tall. It was used until 1912. A hurricane damaged it badly in 1933, when it was rebuilt.

The YTURRIA BANK, 1255 E. Elizabeth St., built 1853, was the first privately-owned bank south of San Antonio and Corpus Christi. Francisco Yturria, the founder, was born in Matamoros, the son of a Spanish Army officer and a woman whose parents were refugees from

Indian attacks. He worked for Charles Stillman and became a land and railroad promoter. The building is owned by Fausto Yturria, and the ancient safe of the bank is at the National Bank of Commerce, of which Fausto's son Frank is a board member. There is a shop on the first floor; the Yturria ranch offices are on the top floor.

The CHARLES STILLMAN HOUSE, 1304 E. Washington St., built 1850 and former home of a founder of Brownsville (and, incidentally, father of James Stillman, one-time New York banker) has been a museum operated by the Brownsville Historical Assn. since 1958. It is filled with period furniture and heirlooms.

The HYNES TOWN HOUSE, 826 E. Levee St., once known as Casa Blanca, was built in 1867 by Lawrence J. Hynes, a Santa Maria ranch owner, and has iron grill work from New Orleans. Adjoining it is the TREVINO HOUSE, 838 E. Levee St., built 1889. It is a Southern colonial brick structure, with long French windows, built by Indalecio Trevino, brother-in-law of Francisco Yturria, and now occupied, unspoiled, by a restaurant and a savings and loan association. Another building with fine original trim retained in a furniture store is the former home of FRANK B. ARMSTRONG, 1328 E. Washington St., naturalist who studied wild game and bird life and 'sent specimens to the Smithsonian Institute and the Field Museum, Chicago.

The CHURCH OF THE IMMACULATE CONCEPTION, E. 12th and Jefferson Sts., a fine Gothic structure started 1855, consecrated 1859, was designated a cathedral in 1965. It was built by members of the Oblate order, who arrived in 1849. A replica of a Madonna and Child by Murillo was placed in the church in 1959.

The CAMILLE PLAYHOUSE in Ringgold Park was dedicated in 1964. The house was donated by the Sams Foundation to carry on the work in repertory begun by the Brownsville Community Players.

GATEWAY BRIDGE, foot of 14th St., SE, connecting Brownsville and Matamoros (*toll, 25¢ per motor car going to Matamoros, 5¢ returning; passengers, 5¢ each; pedestrians, same. Heavy trucks, $2 going, $2 returning.*)

All motor cars going and returning are subject to inspection, by U. S. and Mexican customs officials. No passports or permits are needed, but some identification should be carried. Luggage will be inspected. No firearms or guns may be taken into Mexico, but cameras and films are allowed. U. S. Currency is accepted by Mexican shops. One-way streets are marked on sides of buildings with arrow and "Transito." Ascertain U. S. Customs regulations before trip. Citrus fruits, certain plants, pets such as parrots and parakeets, may not be taken into the U. S. Visitors desiring to make a longer stay farther into Mexico are subject to more detailed regulations; consult the U. S. Customs and other information services.

The Gateway Bridge is owned by Cameron County and in 1966 earned $395,888 net profit.

In the fall, 1967, Cameron County and the Public Works Dept. of Mexico began construction of a new Gateway Bridge. It is a dual span bridge built almost entirely of concrete. The northbound span is 481 ft. long; the southbound 551 ft. long. Each span has a 24.5 ft. road for vehicles and an 8-ft. walk for pedestrians.

The BORDER PATROL ACADEMY of the U. S. Immigration & Naturalization Service was moved from El Paso to 28 *m*. northeast of Brownsville in 1961. It is the only training school of the Service.

RIO GRANDE VALLEY INTERNATIONAL AIRPORT, 3 *m*. east of the city, is a busy facility for commercial and executive planes, with U. S. Government inspection available for quick clearance. It is served by Eastern Airlines and Braniff International Airways. Brownsville is an interchange point for passengers, mail, express and cargo. Aeronaves S. A. of Mexico provides nonstop flights to Mexico City at Matamoros Airport. Charter planes are available; overhaul of private planes is provided.

MATAMOROS, MEXICO

MATAMOROS, Tamaulipas, Mexico (126,000 pop., est., 1967) across the Rio Grande from Brownsville, is a distributing point for cotton, sorghum, fruit, vegetables, and meat production of the province. Some antimony, lead and iron ore also are shipped to the United States. In 1958 cotton raising in the Province reached its peak with 545,000 bales ginned and 700,000 acres planted, but overproduction caused losses and farmers turned to grain sorghum, corn and beans. Large crops of tomatoes are exported to United States markets. Cattle fattening pens are located on the Matamoros-Reynosa highway.

Settlers led by Jose de Escandon and Juan Jose de la Garza founded the city as Congregacion del Refugio in around 1820. Later it was named for Mariano Matamoros, who died in Mexico's struggle for independence. Matamoros has many attractions for the American visitor, in shops, arts and crafts, dining, night clubs, and bull fights. During Charro Days (pre-Lent, February) people pass freely between Brownsville and Matamoros, but the U. S. Immigration Service maintains check points on the highways leading out of Brownsville.

The OLD CITY CEMETERY, Calle Independencia, between Calles (streets) 12 and 14. Until the government prohibited the practice in 1934, the bodies were removed and heaped on a common bone pile when a family failed to pay rent on a grave.

In CASA MATA, Calle B-2 and Camino (road) a los Cemeterios, there were numerous executions during the various revolutions. Openings for rifle barrels are in the second-story walls, and a large dome, probably used as a lookout post, rises above the flat roof. The building is now used as a residence.

The CITY MARKET, Calle Abasolo, between Calles 9 and 10, is a typical Mexican market place, vibrant with colors, and filled with odors and sounds. Articles ranging from foods to jugs, kettles, and mats can be purchased here.

Corpus Christi

Airlines and Airports: Braniff Airlines, Eastern Airlines, Trans-Texas Airways. Corpus Christi International Airport, 4 *m.* from center on US 44. Cuddihy Field, 8 *m.*

Bus Lines: Continental Trailways, Union Bus Center, 523 Schatzel St. Greyhound Bus Lines, Greyhound Station, 819 N. Broadway.

Highways: A direct route from Houston is State 35, the shore line, which joins US 181, from San Antonio, just before entering Corpus Christi. Part of US 181 is also Interstate 37 (incomplete). US 281 from San Antonio has a junction beyond Whitsett with State 9, and with State 44 at Alice, which terminate at Corpus Christi. US 77 from Oklahoma runs in a straight line down Texas and touches Corpus Christi.

Railroads: Missouri Pacific, Southern Pacific. Station, Tancanhua and W. Broadway.

Accommodations and Information: Corpus Christi has 3,500 rooms available in modern hotels and motels, with many of the latter close to the beach; also apartments for seasonal lease and trailer parks. Corpus Christi Chamber of Commerce, 1201 N. Shoreline, (512) TU 2–9453. Tourist Bureau, Box 1147. Newspapers: *Caller* (a.m., cir. 67,000); *Times,* p.m., *Caller-Times,* Sunday; Caller-Times Publishing Co., 820 Lower Broadway. There are 7 weekly newspapers and 7 radio stations.

Recreation: One of the prime seaside resorts, Corpus Christi has extensive facilities for fishing, swimming, sailing, cruising, golf and tennis, and numerous activities for children. Two municipal swimming pools and two beaches are open during spring and summer, with lifeguards from May 1 through Labor Day. The Marina Division supervises rental of 206 boat slips and the Bay area. Four sightseeing cruises leave daily beginning at 10:30 a.m.

The Oso Municipal Golf Course has 145 acres. Basketball, badminton, volley ball, tennis and shuffleboard courts are in all the important parks. There are special classes for youngsters in art, games, ballet and square dancing, even baton twirling, and bridge, chess, and dancing classes for elders. Championship tennis matches are played in the H. E. Butt Tennis Center.

Annual Events: New Year's Day Swim; Corpus Christi Day, second Thursday after Pentecost, observed by Roman Catholic churches; Buccaneer Days, with pagentery, floats, beauty parade and royal ball, 10 days beginning first week in June; Galveston-Corpus Christi yacht contests, June. See newspapers for dates of All-Texas Jazz Festival, Navy Relief Festival.

CORPUS CHRISTI (40 alt., 167,690 pop., 1960; 193,000 est., 1967; Metropolitan Area, Nueces Co., 234,500; San Patricio County, 43,000) on the Gulf of Mexico in southeastern Texas, is an expanding city noted for industries and recreation facilities. Its port ranks fourth in Texas, after Houston, Beaumont and Port Arthur, and 13th in the United States. Its principal manufactured products are refined petroleum and petrochemicals, primary metals, chemical products, stone, clay and glass products. Agriculture provides major handling; fishing is important both commercially and as a sport, large quantities of shrimp being taken.

The city is favorably situated on Corpus Christi Bay, formed by Mustang Island, a sand barrier between the mainland and the Gulf of Mexico. The PORT OF CORPUS CHRISTI, opened 1926, handled 20,282,-869 tons of cargo in 1965. The channel is 400 ft. wide and 40 ft. deep. The inland harbor connects with the Intracoastal Canal. While many of the cargoes are related to the oil industry, shipments to foreign ports include large quantities of grain sorghums, wheat and raw cotton.

The HARBOR BRIDGE, dedicated October 23, 1959, is the newest bridge in the Gulf area. A high-level cantilever truss bridge, it is 5,817 ft. long with approaches, with the main span 620 ft. long. Its height is 235 ft. and clearance under the span is 140 ft. The channel is 400 ft. wide between piers. The Texas State Highway Dept. built it at a cost of $9,000,-000. According to local advices interchanges and rights-of-way raised the whole outlay to $18,000,000.

Industry has expanded greatly in recent decades because of easy access to materials and fuel, water transportation and markets. Nueces County produces around 9,500,000 bbl. of oil annually, valued at over $75,000,-000. Suntide Refinery processes 65,000 bbl. of crude oil per day; Pontiac Refinery, 52,000 bbl.; Southwestern Oil & Refining, 45,000. Among other corporations are the Chemical Division of Pittsburgh Plate Glass Co., Celanese Chemical Co., Hess Oil & Chemical Co., Corn Products Co. About 10,200 persons are employed in manufactures, earning an estimated $53,000,000 annually.

The historical background of Corpus Christi is that of a lusty frontier seaport which, from the time of earliest exploration, knew high adventure. Its name was taken from that given the bay by the Spaniard, Alonso Alvarez de Pineda, who, in 1519, claimed the outer island and the land beyond for his king.

Other explorers, traveling by land and sea, visited the vicinity of the present city during the two centuries following. Although Spanish settlements were attempted in the region of the Bay of Corpus Christi, isolation from Spanish presidios and the constant menace of cannibalistic Karankawa and other tribes of Indians, prevented their development. There were, however, Spanish ranchmen whose great estates and fortified houses were like those of feudal lords.

Legend has it that Jean Lafitte, notorious Gulf pirate, holed up in Corpus Christi sometime between 1817 and 1821, and in the wake of this tale follow stories of buried treasure in the dunes of Mustang and Padre Islands. No treasure, other than a few old coins, has ever been found.

In search of a land and a life that would erase the memory of a broken romance, Colonel Henry L. Kinney, a Pennsylvanian, arrived to found present Corpus Christi in 1839. A dynamic, aggressive man, he established Kinney's Trading Post, well fortified with walls of shell-cement. The landlocked harbor made snug refuge for contraband cargoes.

During this time the region adjacent to Corpus Christi was a noman's land, claimed by Texas and Mexico. Old documents show that in the Corpus Christi area, Mexican laws were in force and Mexican grants operative until the United States won its conclusive victory.

As the Mexican War threatened, General Zachary Taylor came, bringing United States troops in small boats across the bay, on August 1, 1845. It was a great day for Kinney's Trading Post. Colonel E. A. Hitchcock, Taylor's chief of staff, said in his memoirs that "the officers and command of General Taylor's army fraternized with the citizens, social affairs were many, and the town grew rapidly as the flood of army gold brought about the establishment of new enterprises." Another member of the expedition described Kinney's Trading Post as "the most murderous, thieving God-forsaken hole in the Lone Star . . . or out of it."

The troops increased to approximately 5,000, and in March, 1846, Taylor began his historic march to Mexico, leaving Kinney's Trading Post depopulated.

The resourceful Kinney began a real estate promotion in 1848, advertising his sun-baked town of shacks as the Italy of America. Colonizers were importing settlers for the unpeopled lands, and boatloads of immigrants arrived; many of the newcomers remained in the small port town and started building a better community. A little later Kinney and his associates sent a large wagon train to open trade with El Paso and Chihuahua. This started wagon commerce between Corpus Christi and Mexico and with inland points. The armed wagon trains transported everything from onions to gold and silver. Shortly before this time Kinney's Post had been changed to Corpus Christi. The gold seekers of 1849 used Corpus Christi as an assembling point on the southern immigrant route.

In August, 1862, a Federal fleet of two small boats established a land base on the outlying islands. Surrender of the town was demanded and refusal brought a bombardment on August 16, which was repeated on August 18. Tradition relates that some of the shells that fell during the attack were loaded with whisky. Captain Kittredge of the Federal forces missed a barrel of bourbon and it developed that some of his men had emptied the charges from shells and substituted whisky. There was no way to change the shells before the bombardment without revealing the theft.

A Mexican raid in 1875 furnished the basis of a feud between local settlers and Mexicans of the brush country southwest of the town, a situation lasting many months. Corpus Christi, however, was maturing. A railroad was started. Shipping over a shallow canal increased. The resort advantages of Corpus Christi and the coast around it drew attention. Agriculture gained in importance. On the level black lands back of the town, cotton won ascendancy. Between 1875 and 1885 Corpus Christi was one of the largest wool markets in America. The ranchmen, including Captain Richard King, whose holdings lay in the vicinity, turned to sheep for revenue, one ranch having 40,000 head. When the free range disappeared, following the introduction of wire fences, this industry vanished, and was replaced by herds of Hereford cattle.

For half a century Corpus Christi enjoyed a hardy development. Not even a destructive hurricane in 1919 deterred increasing growth. Indeed, it stimulated progress by calling attention to the safety of the high bluff

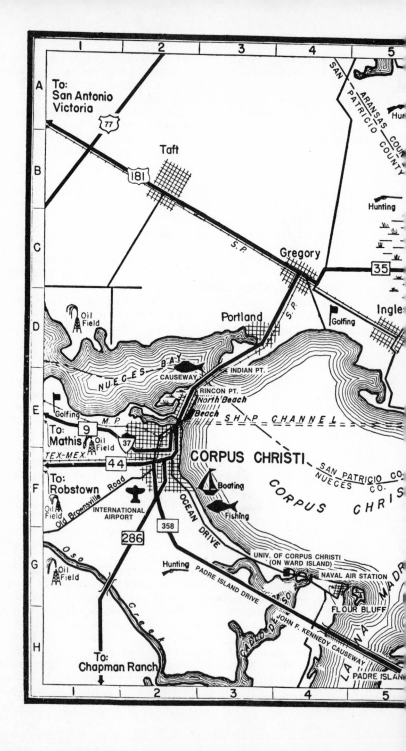

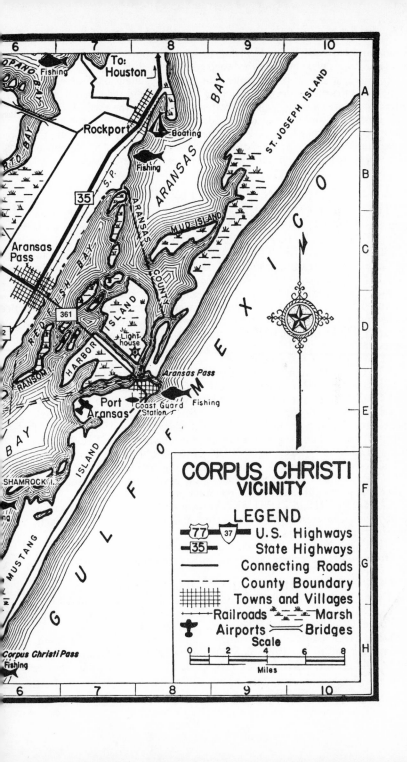

CORPUS CHRISTI
VICINITY

LEGEND

77 37	U.S. Highways
35	State Highways
	Connecting Roads
	County Boundary
	Towns and Villages
Railroads	Marsh
Airports	Bridges

Scale

0 1 2 4 6 8

Miles

section and hastened Federal aid for an adequate port. Tall office structures and hotels were built on the beach and on the bluff.

In 1913, a gas well of tremendous pressure "blew out" at White Point, six miles across the bay. Catching fire, it lighted the area for many miles and before choking itself off created a deep pit in the earth. Explorations continued, and in 1923 the city drilled its first gas well about four miles west of Corpus Christi. Since then Nueces County has become the second ranking producer of natural gas. In 1965 the U. S. Bureau of Mines reported mineral production reached nearly $90,000,000.

POINTS OF INTEREST

The CIVIC CENTER has been developed along the East Shoreline near the YACHT BASIN and MARINA. It comprises the recently built CITY HALL, the new MEMORIAL COLISEUM and the EXPOSITION HALL. The two latter units are well equipped to handle large and small conventions and exhibits. Just beyond, on the West Shoreline are the piers of the Marina, consisting of two T-heads and one L-head. The waterfront has been made secure and attractive by the erection in 1940–1941 of a 15-ft. concrete sea wall, reinforced with creosoted piling and interlocking steel for nearly two miles. Behind it runs the OCEAN DRIVE, which offers motorists a superb view of residential houses, both traditional and modern in design, especially in the Hewitt Drive area, entered at the 3200 block.

The Ocean Drive crosses the Cayo Del Oso to Ward Island, wholly occupied by the UNIVERSITY OF CORPUS CHRISTI, opened 1947 by the Southern Baptist Convention, which enrolls 600 students. It then contniues to the grounds of the U. S. NAVAL AIR STATION, opened 1941, which trained 40,000 naval fliers during World War II and now trains about 500 pilots a year. The AERONAUTICAL DEPOT MAINTENANCE CENTER, U. S. ARMY, over-hauls planes and helicopters. It employs 2,000 civilians and 250 military personnel. The Ocean Drive connects with Lexington Blvd., also State 358, which proceeds in a straight line through the outer part of the city.

CORPUS CHRISTI MUSEUM, opened 1957, shows many exhibits of regional interest, such as shells from Padre Island, Indian artifacts, and live turtles, squirrels, and reptiles.

CENTENNIAL ART MUSEUM, 902 Park St., gives opportunity for exhibits by regional artists as well as contemporary painters from everywhere.

CENTENNIAL HOUSE, 411 N. Broadway, formerly known as the Evans House, is a two-story structure of shell, concrete and brick, erected 1848–49 and used as a hospital during the Civil War. It is considered the city's oldest house and has never been altered.

DEL MAR COLLEGE, junior, occupies a 23-acre campus at Baldwin and Akers Sts. It enrolls more than 2,700 and has a faculty of 145. Its subsidiary, DEL MAR TECHNICAL INSTITUTE has courses in chemistry, electronics and allied scientific subjects, and vocational instruction for industrial services.

LA RETAMA LIBRARY, in the central business district, has an annual circulation of more than 400,000 volumes. It has erected one branch library, and is expanding. Other cultural activities are the Little Theatre group, the Corpus Christi Symphony Orchestra, the Civic Music Association and the Buccaneer Commission, the latter two sponsoring programs by national artists.

The site of GENERAL TAYLOR'S CAMP, Mesquite St., where the drawbridge crosses the ship channel, was the center of Zachary Taylor's tent city, occupied between 1845 and 1846, and near by is the site where the first United States flag was raised on Texas soil south of the Nueces River. The flag was displayed from a point on North Beach about 200 yards from where the Breakers Hotel stands. The army's roster of officers was studded with such notable names as those of Jefferson Davis, U. S. Grant, Franklin T. Pierce, Robert E. Lee, John Bankhead Magruder, Albert Sidney Johnston, George B. Thomas, Joseph Hooker, George G. Meade, Don Carlos Buell, and James Longstreet. In the army were many Texas frontiersmen, among them "Mustang" Gray and "Old Rip" Ford, frontier characters, and the noted Texas Ranger, Jack Hays.

ARTESIAN PARK, 800 Chaparral St., contains a granite shaft marking the site of General Taylor's headquarters, and has a city drinking fountain. A well in the park, drilled by the General's orders, was abandoned when mineral water was struck, but restored later when its sulphur content was found healthful.

LAKE CORPUS CHRISTI, the city's water supply, is formed by Wesley Seale Dam, which impounds 300,000 acre-ft. of Neucas River water. It is on State 9, northwest of city. At MATHIS turn left on State 359 for State Park recreation facilities.

PADRE ISLAND and MUSTANG ISLAND are great barriers of sand separating the Gulf of Mexico from the Texas mainland. At the north Mustang Island creates Corpus Christi Bay. State 35 runs from Aransas Pass to Port Aransas over the Dale Miller Causeway and a ferry. Mustang Island is separated from Padre Island by Corpus Christi Pass. Padre Island is 110 miles long; at its northern end is Nueces County Park and the Bob Hall Pier (for fishing) reached by the John F. Kennedy Causeway from Corpus Christi (*toll, $1*). In 1963 President Kennedy signed an act creating PADRE ISLAND NATIONAL SEASHORE, an 80-m. strip of 237,600 acres, administered by the National Park Service. Motor cars may drive as far south as the Port Mansfield Cut, an 18-ft. channel which admits ships from the Gulf to the Laguna Madre, the intercoastal waterway.

By means of the Cut PORT MANSFIELD became the 13th port of Texas in 1962. Up to that time it had little more than 500 people. It is in Willacy County and reached by State 186 from RAYMONDVILLE, 25 *m.* (10,000 pop. est.) county seat, a junction with US 77, and center for farm products and game hunting. North of Raymondville is La Sal

Vieja, an ancient salt lake. Along the shore is Laguna Atascosa Wildlife Refuge.

South of the Port Mansfield Cut on Padre Island is the site of a village of the Karankawa Indians, who are supposed to have practiced cannibalism. Padre Nicolas Balli, a Spanish missionary came about 1800 to convert the Indians and the island was named for him. South Padre Island has been developed as a recreation resort by Cameron County, which built the Queen Isabella Causeway from Port Isabel.

Dallas

Airlines and Airports: American, Braniff, Continental, Delta, Eastern Frontier, and Trans-Texas airlines at Love Field, 6 *m.* from Downtown on US 77, Interstate 35. Also scheduled air taxi and commuter airlines, Altus, DAL, Central Texas, Hood, Davis, and Southern Aviation.

Non-airline aviation is served at Red Bird Airport, south on Ledbetter Drive. US Air Force and US Naval Air Force use Hensley Field. Besides these three municipal airports there are several private fields.

Bus Lines: Continental Trailways, Bus Center, 1500 Jackson St. Greyhound Bus Lines, Terminal, 205 S. Lamar St. Central Texas Bus Lines, Texas Motor Coaches.

Railroads: Fort Worth & Denver, Missouri-Kansas-Texas, Rock Island, Santa Fe, Texas & Pacific, Frisco, Southern Pacific, Louisiana & Arkansas (KCS), St. Louis Southwestern. Union Station, 400 S. Huron St.

Highways: Dallas is the hub of a network of Interstate, US, State and Farm-to-Market roads connecting with every major artery in Texas. Six Interstate roads are completed. US 67 and Interstate 30 enter from the northeast. US 77 and Interstate 35E come from the northwest. US 75 comes from the north and with Interstate 45 runs southeast. US 175 runs southeast. US 80 and Interstate 20 come from the east. Interstate 635 is a loop road. US 80 runs west to Fort Worth and beyond. State 183 runs to Richland Hills, at Forth Worth. A Toll Road connects Dallas and Forth Worth.

Information and Accommodations: Dallas Chamber of Commerce, Fidelity Union Tower; Industrial Dept., 1501 Pacific Ave. *Dallas News,* morning and Sunday, Communications Center; *Times Herald,* evening and Sunday, 1101 Pacific; *Wall Street Journal,* Southwest Edition, morning except Saturday, 1232 Regal Row. Major radio and television networks. More than 10,000 first-class rooms are available at motels and hotels, which include the new Statler-Hilton and the Sheraton-Dallas.

Recreation: All parts of the city have facilities for outdoor activities. There are 14 lighted and 25 unlighted baseball diamonds; 58 lighted and 168 unlighted softball fields; 132 public tennis courts; 11 roller skating rinks; one ice skating rink; 18 soccer fields. Also 19 bowling centers; 9 riding academies; 21 adult swimming pools (some commercial); 71 junior pools. For golf Dallas County has 10 public or commercially operated courses and 9 driving ranges; a new 19-hole course in Elm Fork Park was opened in 1967. The Tennis Center, where the American Zone Davis Cup competition was held, has 12 lighted courts . . . The Dallas Park System, continually being expanded in 1967 had 144 parks and 14,000 acres. There are 112 supervised playgrounds, 13 recreation centers. About 20 country clubs in Dallas and environs are open to members and their guests. Local golf tournaments include the Dallas Open, Civitan Open (for women), City Junior. National contests frequently come to Dallas.

Skating in the Fair Park Ice Arena, Tues.-Friday, 2–4, 8–10, closed Monday; Saturday and Sunday, 3–5, 8–10.

Observation Decks: First National Bank Bldg., 50th floor, 10–8 daily, (25¢ for charity); Southland Center, 41st floor, 10–8 daily (25¢ for charity); Love Field, all hours.

Spectator Sports: Football in the Cotton Bowl begins in September, with the Mustangs of SMU, Cowboys of the National Football League, outside teams. The

New Year's Day classic is played between the champion team of the Southwest Conference and the champion of another conference. Also the Dallas-Fort Worth Spurs of the Texas League (baseball), the Chaparrals (American Basketball Assn.) the Golden Gloves contests and the NAAA boxing meets.

Special Events: Cotton Bowl Parade, New Year's Day. Six Flags Over Texas park on Turnpike opens in April for weekends until May 28, thereafter daily. Metropolitan Opera season, May. Summer Musicals, Fair Park, begin in June for 12 weeks. State Fair of Texas, October. Giant Balloon Parade, Downtown, Thanksgiving Day, November. Dallas Symphony, Civic Opera, Civic Ballet, Theater Center, open seasons, November. Christmas Cotton Bowl Festival, December.

DALLAS, in North Central Texas (434 alt.) is the second largest city in the State and an industrial, financial, and goods distribution center of primary importance to the Southwest. This closely packed city on the Trinity River covers 295 sq. mi., and in 1960 had 679,684 people, which number had grown to an estimated 840,000 seven years later. In its metropolitan area of four counties—Dallas, Collin, Denton and Ellis—there were more than 1,400,000. Inside Dallas County are a number of independent municipalities contiguous with the city. Developed as a premier wholesale market, with more than 3,000 wholesale firms doing an annual gross of $4 billion, Dallas has built a group of trade marts to accommodate exhibits. Its trade fairs attract more than 100,000 buyers annually. By its enterprise it has become an arbiter of fashions in apparel. Its State Fair, which includes livestock exhibits, has an average attendance in October of more than 2,500,000, largest in this category.

Dallas is the hub of six Interstate highways, nine railroads, and thirteen airlines, one of which, Braniff, is based there. Love Field, a model of airport planning, is the busiest in Texas, with 319,575 flights, 3,541,000 passengers in 1966, double that of Texas's largest city, Houston. These extensive facilities have made Dallas a convention city of the first rank. More than 200 large conventions meet there annually, and on January 1, 1967, 562 organizations had applied for future bookings.

At one time a big cotton market, Dallas has been expanding its heavy and light industries. The three top ones in durable goods in the metropolitan area are electronic and electrical equipment, transportation equipment (including aircraft), and non-electrical machinery. The three largest in nondurables are food processing, wearing apparel, and printing and publishing. In recent years orders from the Federal Government for helicopters and other military aircraft have been a large source of income. Of national importance are such firms as Collins Radio, Dresser Industries, Ling-Temco-Vought, and Texas Instruments. The business district of Dallas has a forest of new office buildings. They include the First National Bank, 51 stories, 615 ft.; the Republic Bank Tower, 53 st., 594 ft.; Southland Life, 42 st., 550 ft.; Republic Bank, 36 st., 452 ft.; Ling-Temco-Vought, 31 st., 434 ft.; Mercantile National Bank, 31 st., 436 ft.; Mobil Bldg., 31 st., 430 ft.; Fidelity Union Tower, 33 st., 400 ft.; Sheraton Hotel, 28 st., 352 ft.; Adolphus Hotel, 25 st., 312 ft., and the new Fairmont Hotel, 24 st., 395 ft. The most ambitious building project is Main Place, bounded by Commerce, Field, Elm, and Lamar Sts. The first unit, One Main Place, completed in 1968, rises 34 stories and cost approx. $40,000,000. It houses the Texas Bank & Trust Co., Equitable Life Assurance Society, General Electric Corp. and other national concerns. Plans include a 45-story office tower, a 500-room hotel, a department store, and 10 acres of passages and garages below street level.

Divided by the Trinity River, and with a vast prairie over which to spread, Dallas could have developed in a sprawling manner, instead of becoming, as it is, the most compact city in Texas. However, where the three forks which give the river its name converge, they met a hard rock obstruction which constricted the valley's width from five miles to one, and on that comparatively narrow foundation Dallas piled itself up. East of the river the downtown area and East Dallas, North Dallas, and South Dallas merged into one, carrying approximately two-thirds of the total population. On the west, Oak Cliff carries the other third. Highland Park and University Park, two self-governed suburbs, and Preston Hollow, lie in close association with the eastern and northern sections. Fruitdale adjoins the southern limits of the city.

Unlike some other Texas cities, Dallas has no tradition of wild days. It came into existence as a serious community with citizens of a peaceable and cultured type. Today it has a large church-going population, 80 per cent of which is Protestant. Baptists make up nearly one-half of the church membership. The principal denominations are Southern Baptist, Methodist, and Southern Presbyterian. The largest congregation is the First Baptist Church, which has 12,000 members and a budget of over $1,000,000.

Commercially, it can be said that even before Dallas existed it was a trade center. At the turn of the eighteenth century French traders from Louisiana penetrated to the Dallas area (1712, 1719, and 1771), to barter with the Anadarkos, a Caddo tribe that lived in conical grass huts along the banks of the Trinity.

John Neely Bryan came to Texas from Van Buren, Arkansas, in 1840, intending to establish a trading post on the upper Trinity. Finding the Indians friendly, he built a hut on the river's east bank in 1841, becoming the first white settler of present-day Dallas. Bryan probably chose his site because the Republic of Texas had already provided for a military highway from Austin to the Red River to cross the Trinity River "at or near its three forks." As this road came into use, Bryan started a town on his 640-acre headright tract.

Texas in the meantime had contracted (February 4, 1841), with William S. Peters and his associates of Louisville, Kentucky, for settlement of a land grant, covering approximately 16,000 square miles in the region of the upper Trinity. This grant became known as Peters Colony, although the name of the company formed to operate it was the Texan Emigration Land Company.

The first actual settlement of Dallas began in 1842, when Bryan persuaded three families to move to his site from Bird's Fort, a Ranger stockade to the northwest. Other settlers took up residence in the village, which was called Dallas as early as 1842. The origin of the town's name is uncertain, one group of historians believing it was named for George Mifflin Dallas, a Pennsylvanian who three years later became Vice President of the United States; another group that the name honored Commander Alexander James Dallas of the United States Navy, brother of George Mifflin Dallas; a third that the town was named for Joseph Dallas, a friend of John Neely Bryan, who came to the region from Washington County, Arkansas, in 1843, and settled at Cedar Springs, now within the Dallas city limits. There is no reasonable doubt, however, that the county of Dallas, which was organized in 1846, was named by the Texas legislature in honor of George Mifflin Dallas, who had been elected Vice President partly on the issue of Texas annexation.

In 1846 the town site was surveyed and platted. Bryan had been appointed postmaster, and used his home both for a post office and store, carrying a stock of powder, lead, whisky, and tobacco.

Judge William Hord, in 1845, started a settlement on the west bank of the Trinity called Hord's Ridge (present Oak Cliff). His original cabin is at the entrance to Marsalis Park. Hord's Ridge was soon contesting with Dallas for the site of the new Dallas County seat, but was defeated at the polls in 1850. Dallas acquired a newspaper in 1849, the printing press and the town's first piano arriving simultaneously by ox-cart. A school, a bowling alley, a wagon and buggy factory, and a tavern were established. Alexander Cockrell, a Kentuckian, engaged in the manufacture of bricks, branched into the lumber business and started a building campaign. He operated a ferry over the Trinity and later built a bridge across it.

Most of the settlers in Peters Colony, after they had filed colonist headrights with a special land commissioner, failed to have their lands surveyed. Consequently the Texan Emigration Land Company could not determine which were the alternate sections allowed them by the State in payment for colonizing the area. The company appealed to the legislature, which in 1852 passed an act compelling all settlers to have their holdings surveyed. Fearing that through this act they might lose their farms, Dallas County citizens, led by Captain John J. Good, marched on the land company's headquarters at Stewartville in Denton County and threatened to lynch the agent. After much agitation, the legislature reversed its stand and gave the settlers deeds to their homesteads.

John Neely Bryan sold his holdings in the town of Dallas in 1852 to Alexander Cockrell for $7,000.

About the same time efforts were made toward establishing water transportation on the Trinity and in 1852 J. W. Smith, pioneer merchant, poled a flatboat out of Dallas, with Galveston as its destination. The boat was unable to get farther than Porter's Bluff, near Corsicana, and the hope of transportation of freight by river boat temporarily subsided.

In the spring of 1854 a dozen men, wearing long smocks and speaking a strange language, arrived in Dallas from France, by way of New Orleans. They formed the advance guard of about 350 Frenchmen, Belgians, and Swiss recruited by Victor Considerant, a disciple of François Charles Marie Fourier, French socialist, to establish a cooperative community in the Texas wilderness. The main body of the immigrants, about 200, arrived with a caravan of oxcarts from Houston, on June 16, 1855.

Among these European immigrants were highly educated professional men, scientists, artists, authors, musicians, naturalists; experts in everything but the practical skill required to wrest a living from a primitive land. After three years of struggle with droughts, grasshoppers, and "blue northers," they disbanded their colony, La Reunion, which had been established four miles west of Dallas. Many of them moved to Dallas, thus adding to the local population a body of trained and talented men, unusual in frontier settlements.

The town was incorporated in 1856. The building campaign, then in progress, attracted a floating population of buffalo hunters, trappers, and unskilled laborers which threatened disorder, but immediate steps were taken to meet the threat. The tin cup and the whisky barrel—free drinks to customers—were banished from the settlement's stores and gambling houses were subdued.

Private schools were available to those who could afford them, and schools for the poor were supported by assessments from community funds. Itinerant preachers attracted crowds to camp meetings as early as 1844, and regular Protestant church services started in 1846.

During the Civil War a concentration camp for Confederate troops, and offices of the quartermaster and commissary departments of the trans-Mississippi armies were established in Dallas. In the war years, the town's population of 2,000 increased rapidly; the growth continued, on a more substantial basis, when Reconstruction brought settlers from other Southern States, ruined by the war. Cotton growers soon discovered that the black lands of Texas were the finest they had ever seen, and were not long in returning to their favorite crop and prospering thereby. Dallas prospered in proportion.

In 1868, a stern-wheel steamboat succeeded in completing the trip from Galveston to Dallas, but it took a year and four days.

The Houston and Texas Central brought the first train to Dallas in July, 1872, while 5,000 shouting, perspiring people milled around in the dust, struggling for a better view of this emblem of progress. It had taken 24 years, a bonus of $5,000 in cash, 115 acres of land, and a free right-of-way to induce the railroad to come to Dallas, but less than a year after its arrival the population rose from 3,000 to 6,000.

A year later the Texas and Pacific arrived.

Then Dallas really began to boom. From the Blacklands and the Grand Prairie long wagon trains brought wheat, wool, cotton, and hides. Sheep and cattle were driven in. Passenger fares, cut to half the stagecoach rate, encouraged travel by rail. The town was swamped. Wagons jammed the streets and sank to the hubs in black, waxy mud.

Dallas was hammering away to obtain a railroad of its own toward

Santa Fé, New Mexico, when the panic of 1873 delayed construction, but a depression could only delay, not stop the frantic building. The road to Santa Fé did not materialize, but by 1866 Dallas had six railroads and a population approaching 35,000. In that year the city's first cotton mill was established. The Trinity River Navigation and Improvement Company, in 1893, succeeded in bringing a 113-foot sternwheeler from Galveston to Dallas in a little over a month.

The city streets (already made dangerous by grade crossings) were too narrow for necessary traffic, and tracks blocked the normal northward expansion of the business district, forcing it to spread to the east along three different streets.

Dallas was a strangled, congested city. Four walls and a roof constituted a building unless it had architectural pretensions of the "gingerbread" era, expressed in turrets, cupolas, and scrolls. The Praetorian Building, built in 1907, C. W. Bulger & Son, architects, was 15 stories above a jumble of roofs and was hailed as "the first skyscraper in Texas." It marked the turning point in construction, although Victorian in style. It, in turn, was modernized in 1960.

The need for something other than rapid growth was emphasized when the Trinity River broke its own record for floods in 1908, driving 2,000 people from their homes and causing damage of two million dollars. For three nights the city was in darkness. The drinking water supply was cut off and an epidemic of malaria followed. It was realized that conditions called for an immediate remedy.

This need was crystallized by the *Dallas News*. By January, 1910, the Dallas Chamber of Commerce, converted to the *News'* proposal, formed the Dallas City Plan and Improvement League and induced the city to employ George E. Kessler, a planning engineer. The Kessler Plan involved such radical changes as straightening the Trinity River and placing the railroad tracks out of town, thereby arousing much opposition. Some of his suggestions were adopted, but the Texas & Pacific Ry. still ran into the heart of Dallas, with fatal accidents. In 1919 the city called on Kessler to return and revise his plan.

The revision, expanded, was basically the same. In addition to straightening the Trinity River channel, it called for flood control and land reclamation; the construction of the belt line railroad to eliminate grade crossings; building inner and outer boulevards; segregating land areas for adaptable uses and to prevent infringement of business upon residential districts and the consequent creation of "blighted districts."

This required immense sums of money, which could not be raised without tremendous effort and constant agitation. The *News* continued its campaign. Other papers co-operated. To complete the street-widening projects property owners were assessed in proportion to the benefit to be derived by them from the improvement. In 1925 the Texas and Pacific's double line of tracks and switches were removed from downtown Pacific Avenue.

The city's growth had by then outstripped its water supply in White Rock Lake reservoir and a dam was constructed in the Elm Fork of the

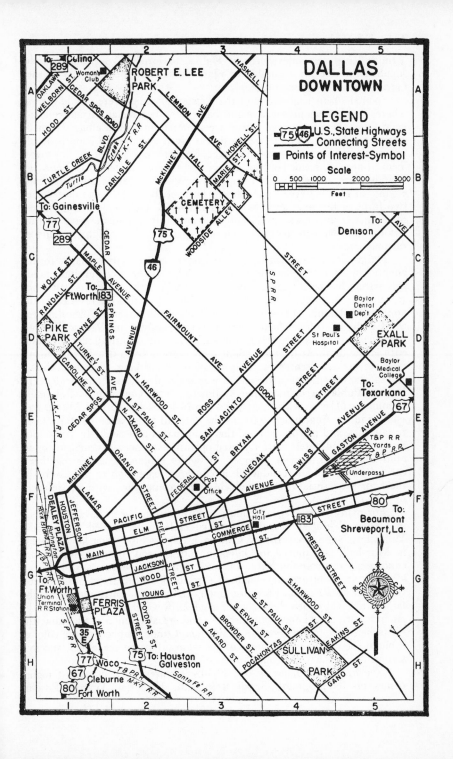

Trinity River, 30 miles north of Dallas, to form Lake Dallas, which supplied the city for a number of years. It has now become part of the Garza-Little Elm group of reservoirs.

Soon the beneficial effects of the Kessler city plan were visible everywhere. Pacific Avenue, freed of railroad tracks, became an attractive boulevard and the city's traffic flowed freely north and south along widened intersecting streets. Public approval was given an omnibus bond issue of $23,900,000 in 1927 to complete the Kessler plan and other improvements. Spots for scenic boulevards and parks were donated by citizens. In 1926 property owners in the Trinity River Valley organized the City and County of Dallas Levee Improvement District. By 1931 it had united the two forks of the river and changed the channel, reclaiming 10,553 acres for industrial purposes. Steel viaducts were built to join the parts of the city east and west of the river, and underpasses to carry highways under railroad tracks.

Dallas city government is operated under council city-manager form, adopted by charter amendments in 1931. One of the accomplishments of this system has been budget control under which the budget is based on reasonable expectancy of tax collection. The new system has resulted in an annual "underrun," or saving, below budget allotments. According to the Census of 1960, which counted 951,527 people in Dallas County, there were 137,974 Negroes in the same area, or slightly under one-seventh of the total. At the same count there were only 14,921 foreign-born. Negroes are represented in the professions, publishing, churches, clubs, and sports. Desegregation of schools was accomplished without incident in Dallas. Public accommodations followed. The Community Relations Committee of seven white men and seven Negroes was formed March 20, 1960, and set August 15, 1961, as the date for integration of stores and restaurants, and in 1963 applied this to all parks and pools. In 1965 280 restaurants and hotels were reported open to everyone. A statement by a municipal authority said "Negro and white leaders, working together, carefully planned and conducted an education campaign to prepare both races for these social changes, which were accomplished without violence or demonstrations."

For many years Negro business and professional men have prospered in Dallas. Wheatley Place, in southern Dallas, was named for Phyllis Wheatley, Negro poet. Bishop College, a Baptist institution long located in Marshall, was moved to Dallas in 1961 to add to opportunities for education already established in Dallas. It enrolls more than 1,000.

The city's cultural development dates back to the arrival of the settlers from La Reunion. Foremost among those early contributors to Dallas' culture was Julien Reverchon, for whom Reverchon Park was named. An internationally known botanist, he came to La Reunion as a youth with his father, Jacques Maximilian Reverchon. Other members of the colony brought the civilizing influences of art salons, dancing academies, and instrumental music to the young town.

The first opera house, called Field's Theater, carried many famous names on its programs. Sarah Bernhardt, Frederick Warde, Edwin

Booth, and Maurice Barrymore found that the theater lacked dressing rooms but offered a clamorous and appreciative audience.

The greatest tragedy in the history of Dallas took place on November 22, 1963, when President John F. Kennedy was fatally wounded by rifle shots while riding in an open car in a motorcade. John B. Connally, Jr., Governor of Texas, was wounded at the same time, but not fatally. The wounded men were rushed to Parkland Hospital, where Kennedy died at 1 P.M. An official commission of inquiry headed by Chief Justice Earl Warren established, to its satisfaction, with the aid of the FBI, that three shots were fired from a six-story window by Lee Harvey Oswald, a man with a communist and pro-Castro record, who soon after shot and killed a policeman who tried to arrest him. Two days later, on November 24, Oswald was fatally shot in the City Jail by Jack Ruby, a night club owner, who was tried and convicted but died from cancer before serving a penalty.

Immediately after President Kennedy's death Vice President Lyndon B. Johnson proceeded to the executive plane, U. S. Air Force Jet No. 1, at Love Field. Here Judge Sarah T. Hughes administered the presidential oath of office to him at 2:47 p.m. The plane then departed for Washington with the body of Kennedy, his wife and staff, and President Johnson aboard.

The site of the attack was DEALEY PLAZA, a landscaped triangle west of Houston Street, where Elm, Main and Commerce Streets converge to a triple underpass, above which run railroad tracks. The streets were stopped there originally by the Trinity River, now moved some distance west. The Plaza has decorative peristyles with fountains and basins on both sides of Main Street, where it enters the Plaza, and peristyles also at the outer edges of Commerce and Elm Streets. The President's motorcade came down Main Street, turned right at the Criminal Courts Building, went one block west past the Dallas County Records Building, then turned left at Elm Street and headed for the underpass on the way to the Trade Mart. The President's car was the second in line. It had moved less than one-third of the way to the underpass when three shots were fired from the east corner window on the sixth floor of the Texas School Book Depository Building at Houston and Elm Streets. According to the official record Kennedy and Connally were hit by the first shot and Kennedy by the second. After the Warren Report was published several authors dissented from its conclusion that Oswald was apparently the sole assassin. In New Orleans an investigation was begun into reports that Oswald had taken part in a local conspiracy.

President Kennedy was shot near the spot where John Neely Bryan built the first cabin on the banks of the Trinity River in 1843. The cabin has been reconstructed on the lawn of the Courthouse at Commerce and Houston Streets. It is 16 ft. square, built of 12-inch hewn cedar logs, chinked with clay. There are two windows with heavy wooden shutters and handwrought iron hinges. There is a floor of cedar logs hewn flat and a limestone chimney. The original cabin served as a postoffice during the Republic of Texas, and as a temporary courthouse from 1848 to 1850.

CULTURAL ACTIVITIES

The DALLAS SYMPHONY, organized in 1900, today leads the city's musical programs. During a 28-week season the orchestra of 92 musicians gives a subscription series of concerts in McFarlin Auditorium, and also fills the 10,000 seats of the Memorial Auditorium with its Dollar Concerts. It gives "pops" concerts in the Great Hall of the Apparel Mart and provides the music for the Civic Opera, the Civic Ballet, and the Summer Musicals. It is estimated that 300,000 attend these events. The Music Director, Donald Johanos, is one of only three directors of major symphony orchestras who are American born and trained.

Opera comes to Dallas through two media: the Dallas Civic Opera and the Metropolitan Opera Company of New York. The Metropolitan made a solitary visit in April, 1905, when it presented *Parsifal,* with Fremstad and Dippel. In January, 1939, it asked $65,000 as a guaranty for four performances; Dallas raised $100,000. Now there is a guaranty of $225,000 by the Dallas Grand Opera Association, but it is never needed. The Chicago Opera Company appeared annually for a number of years, and the Dallas Civic Opera began in 1957. It offers eight performances by famous artists with regional support. The Community Arts Fund is raised annually to aid major organizations in the performing arts.

The DALLAS CIVIC MUSIC ASSOCIATION presents seven subscription concerts a year, bringing great artists and orchestras to the city. The DALLAS CHAMBER MUSIC SOCIETY sponsors important quartets and quintets for five concerts annually in Highland Park Town Hall. Among many other programs, including jazz, folksong and hillbilly music, are the performances of the SPEBSOSA, or Society for the Preservation and Encouragement of Barber Shop Quartet Singing in America, which has three chapters in the area and stages contests.

The DALLAS THEATER CENTER is a repertory organization that provides as extensive a program of classical and modern plays as any professional group. In the course of an 11-month season it accounts for 200 nights of performances, producing nine new plays each year. The Center operates in six groups: the Repertory Artists; the Graduate School, which is affiliated with Trinity University of San Antonio and gives the degree of master of arts; the Academy providing two years of training; the Teen-children's Theater; Drama in the Evening, an educational program, and the Technical Laboratory, for experimentation in light, sound, and film. There is a permanent faculty of fourteen.

The home of the Center is the KALITA HUMPHREYS THEATER, 3636 Turtle Creek, the only theater designed by Frank Lloyd Wright. It was opened in December, 1959, after $1,000,000 had been raised by civic effort and seats 440.

Other dramatic activities include THEATER THREE, an arena stage seating 160, producing modern and avant garde plays. The Dallas Broadway Theater League supports theatrical successes at the Memorial Auditorium Theater. Such groups as the Royal Shakespeare Company and the National Repertory Theater are sponsored in Dallas by the Community Course. Outlets for dramatic expression are the Oak Cliff Civic Theater, Town North Theater, the Barn Theater, and the Junior Players' Guild.

An inspiring leader in the dramatic art whose memory is cherished in Dallas was Margo Jones, who started Theatre 47, a theater-in-the-round, which stimulated interest far beyond its immediate circle. She was born near Houston, was a student at Denton, and died in 1955. The new Margo Jones Theatre at SMU commemorates her work. Also in her honor is the $1,000 award for playwrights offered annually by Jerome Lawrence and Robert Lee, authors of *Inherit the Wind*. Miss Jones produced their first version of this play at her Dallas theater.

POINTS OF INTEREST

DALLAS PUBLIC LIBRARY moved into its new Central Building, 1954 Commerce St., in September, 1955. Designed by the George L. Dahl organization, the style is modern, with simple lines well defined by black Cold Spring opalescent granite, white Georgia marble, and glass. Hanging against the black marble facade is a 20-ft. sculpture cast in aluminum and magnesium alloy which the artist, Marshall Fredericks, says represents the hands of God supporting youth reaching for learning through literature. The Library has greatly expanded its usefulness to the public. In 1967 it had 933,273 books and circulated 3,423,859; it loaned 34,277 films and answered 1,056,546 questions. It has been designated the Major Resource Center for Northeast Texas by the State Library and as such plans library development in 36 counties. A vigorous expansion program since 1958 has resulted in the construction of eight branch libraries; four more have moved into better quarters, and the Capital Improvements Program of 1967 has provided funds for seven additional units to come.

The DALLAS COTTON EXCHANGE, SE. corner St. Paul and San Jacinto Sts., is the hub of the Dallas cotton industry. The exchange is housed in its own 17-story modern building. A substantial part of the Mexican cotton crop is handled by members of the Exchange. The annual volume of business is in excess of $300,000,000.

ROBERT E. LEE PARK, Hall St. and Turtle Creek Blvd., contains a community house which is a reproduction of Arlington, the Virginia home of Robert E. Lee. In the SW. corner of the park is a STATUE OF GENERAL ROBERT E. LEE on his favorite horse, Traveler, with an accompanying orderly, also mounted, sculptured by Phimister Proctor and dedicated in June, 1936, by President Franklin D. Roosevelt.

DALLAS MARKET CENTER, on the outskirts of town, easily reached by major highways, is a concentration of buildings devoted to exhibitions and displays by wholesale houses. The distinction that Dallas has won as the fashion center of the Southwest springs from the enterprise of its apparel houses and the strong support of the municipality. Five major women's and children's apparel markets, and three men's and boy's markets, are held annually, and buyer registration exceeds 50,000, representing leading stores in the United States, Canada, and Latin America.

These activities are concentrated in the Market Center. The newest of the buildings is the APPAREL MART, with over one million square feet of space to devote to displays and fashion shows. Here also are the TRADE MART, an $18,000,000 investment, which has four floors, 920,000 square feet, and 1,500 show rooms for displays by wholesalers. Adjacent is the HOME-FURNISHINGS MART, with 434,000 sq. ft. of space. The DECORATIVE CENTER occupies a quadrangle in the Trinity Industrial District and can exhibit 115 lines of furnishings and fabrics. Its fifth unit has just been completed. Another huge commercial facility is the MERCHANDISE MART, in the downtown district, packed with showrooms for general merchandise.

Many important events take place in the DALLAS MEMORIAL AUDITORIUM, which has an arena seating 10,000, a theater with 1,773 seats, exhibit space of 110,000 square feet, and parking room for 1,100 vehicles.

NEIMAN-MARCUS, a name internationally famous for quality merchandise, has become synonymous with Dallas in the minds of Texans, and possibly also of the couturiers of Paris and the diamond-cutters of Amsterdam. This luxury store is frequently in the news because its president, Stanley Marcus, sponsors such extraordinary offerings as a matched pair of airplanes marked "His" and "Hers" for $176,000, an ermine bathrobe for $6,975, a shoehorn for $25 and, for more modest incomes, five tubes of toothpaste flavored with brandy, martini, rum, curacao, and cherry, for $4.75. The true base of the business, however, is the ability of Neiman-Marcus to anticipate changes in taste and supply all demands. When Marcus instituted his annual fortnight festivities in 1957 with a "Quinzaine Francaise," bringing the representatives of art, music, and craftsmanship from Paris to Texas, official, artistic and business organizations of Dallas joined in making the occasion an international event, and some of the special programs were associated with raising funds for worthy causes. This is the practice also at the annual Spring Awards Luncheon and Fashion Presentation—the 1967 event was staged for Florentine flood relief.

Neiman-Marcus was founded 1907 by Herbert Marcus, his associate, Al Neiman, and his sister, Carrie, who was Neiman's wife. Marcus trained four sons in the business, which remained wholly a family enterprise until 1959, when 133,800 shares out of 598,800 were sold to the public. There are branch stores in North Park, a suburb; Houston and Fort Worth. In December, 1964, at the peak of holiday buying, the Dallas store was heavily damaged by fire, smoke and water between 3:45 A.M. and 7 A.M. At 8 o'clock the management announced that it would fill all orders from its suburban stores; at 10 it set up a bridal salon in a hotel and stocked it with wedding dresses from the Houston store, to accommodate brides whose dresses were not ready. The store reopened 27 days later with temporary decorations and was greeted by an augmented clientele.

SOUTHERN METHODIST UNIVERSITY occupies a 160-acre campus along Hillcrest Avenue in University Park, an incorporated residential district surrounded by Dallas. It was established in 1911 by an educational commission of the Methodist Church. Opened in 1915, SMU is devoted to the ideals of Christianity but nonsectarian. It is coeducational. Of more than 80 buildings, 60 were built after World War II. It enrolls nearly 9,000 in its regular term and more than 3,500 in its summer term. The School of Commerce became the School of Business Administration in 1941. SMU opened its University College in 1964 to provide basic training in the relationship of fields of learning, required of all students. Its endowment is more than $17,000,000.

Down the center of the campus runs the broad tree-lined Bishop Blvd., ending at the original building, DALLAS HALL, a fine Jeffersonian type of architecture. Most of the buildings are modifications of the Georgian style in red brick and stone. FONDREN LIBRARY, opened 1940, heads a system of libraries remarkably rich in historical material. In 1964 there was a total of 798,860 catalogued books, additions coming at a rate of 65,000 a year. The Methodist Historical Library had 15,703 books and 25,000 manuscripts, including much Wesleyana. The Science Library had a map collection of 115,000 items and the E. DeGolyer Foundation Library of Geology. McCord Theatre Museum is a section of Fondren Library; the DeGolyer Trans-Mississippi Library is on loan.

OWEN FINE ARTS CENTER, the newest addition to the physical plant, costing $8,500,000, is the partially completed headquarters for the School of the Arts. Plans include the Mudge Art Bldg., the Bob Hope Theatre, the Margo Jones Memorial Theatre in the Ruth Collins Sharp Drama Bldg., an orchestral hall and a choral hall. Completed are the Pollock Art Galleries, the Virginia Meadows Museum, the Caruth Auditorium, the Forbes Music Bldg. and the Elizabeth Meadows Sculpture Court. The Virginia Meadows Museum, supported by gifts from the Meadows Foundation, headed by Algur H. Meadows, chairman of the General American Oil Company, is specializing in Spanish masters. It has acquired a Velasquez portrait of King Philip IV (c. 1684), five Goyas, three Murillos, and a Juan de Sevilla.

In November, 1967, the University opened a Center of Ibero-American Civilization for the study of Spanish and Portuguese influences on the economics and cultures of the American hemisphere.

The LEGAL CENTER QUADRANGLE has three buildings devoted to the law. The PERKINS SCHOOL OF THEOLOGY QUADRANGLE has eight buildings, including apartments for married ministerial students.

Grants and contracts for research provide SMU with about $1,000,000 annually for projects ranging from archaeology on the Nile River, the Red River and Trinity River, to studies related to the United States space program. Two projects in geophysical research deal with Laser instrumentation in earthquake detection and a special-purpose computer for seismic research. The ANTHROPOLOGY RESEARCH CENTER possesses a large collection of prehistoric African material. The SMU HERBARIUM, a research museum, has about 285,000 specimens of plants. It is housed in the SCIENCE INFORMATION CENTER, which also has the Science Library and the SMU Press. The Center has 120,000 books and other materials

DALLAS
AND VICINITY

1. Southern Methodist University. 2. Site of La Reunion
3. Toll Road to Fort Worth. 4. USAF and Naval Airport.
5. White Rock Lake Park. 6. Fair Park. 7. Marsalis Park.
8. University of Dallas.

Scale

1/2 0   2   3   4
Miles

dealing with engineering, mathematics and the natural sciences. It has been designated a Regional Technical Report Center by the National Science Foundation and the U. S. Department of Commerce. FONDREN SCIENCE BLDG. has the principal laboratories, including the Karcher Spectograph Lab. and an acoustics laboratory with an anechoic chamber in the Physics Dept. as well as a Seismological Observatory. The JORDAN C. OWNBY STADIUM, seating 12,000, is used for track meets and freshman football; Varsity games are played in the Cotton Bowl.

McFARLIN AUDITORIUM on the campus is the home of the Dallas Symphony Orchestra and each season presents stars of the caliber of Van Cliburn and Artur Rubinstein. It seats 2,500.

The A. V. LANE MUSEUM (*open 9–4 workdays*), first floor Kirby Hall, contains Oriental and Graeco-Roman archeological exhibits, and a pre-Aztec and pre-Inca collection from Latin America, clay cylinders and tablets from Babyon, papyri from Egypt, and an Egyptian mummy.

In the southwest corner of the campus a small wooded area, Arden Forest, so named for a Shakespearian play given here by the University Dramatic Society in 1916, is said to have been used as a hideout by Sam Bass, the notorious train and bank robber of the 1870's.

The UNIVERSITY OF TEXAS SOUTHWESTERN MEDICAL SCHOOL came to Dallas in 1949 at the invitation of a group of public-spirited citizens who had formed the Southwestern Medical Foundation to promote medical education and research. At first it was called a branch, but in 1954 the present name was adopted. The first unit, the Basic Science Building, was built in 1955 at a cost of $2,850,000 and had quarters for the six basic science departments, laboratories, lecture rooms and a library. The Clinical Science Building was completed in 1958 at a cost of $3,500,000. Other laboratories and facilities are being added.

DALLAS BAPTIST COLLEGE, of the Southern Baptist Organization, moved to Dallas from Decatur in 1965 and started building five lecture halls on its 100-acre campus at Mountain Creek Lake. Its enrollment has been under 200.

The UNIVERSITY OF DALLAS, in Irving, a Roman Catholic institution that opened in 1956, has an enrollment of about 850. It has lately added a new science lecture hall, and prepared to award doctorate degrees in science and business administration, in addition to the humanities. The university is coeducational.

BISHOP COLLEGE, 3837 Simpson-Stuart Rd., was founded 1880 by a Baptist organization as higher education for Negroes and moved to Dallas from Marshall in 1961. It has a campus of 385 acres. It offers business, liberal arts, science and the humanities and enrolls more than 1,200.

The COLLEGE OF DENTISTRY OF BAYLOR UNIVERSITY, 800 Hall St., and Baylor's SCHOOL OF NURSING, 3513 Junius St., are flourishing branches of Baylor, which also operates the BAYLOR MEMORIAL HOSPITAL at 3500 Gaston St. At one time Baylor had a School of Medicine here, but it has been taken to Waco.

Two privately-supported research centers that have proved their use-

fulness to the community are located in Dallas County. The GRADU-
ATE RESEARCH CENTER OF THE SOUTHWEST was estab-
lished in 1960 on 1,226 acres at Richardson for post-doctoral research in
the earth and planetary sciences. Its first permanent laboratory, the
Founders Building, was opened October 29, 1964. The TEXAS RE-
SEARCH FOUNDATION was established after World War II to
study the development of grasses and oil-bearing vegetation to help restore
exhausted pasture and crop lands.

FAIR PARK, in East Dallas, main entrance on Parry Ave., covers
187 acres of landscaped grounds and is the site of the STATE FAIR OF
TEXAS. The Fair calls forth upwards of 2,500,000 visitors from all
parts of the State and the Southwest. The Fair is not operated by the
State but by a nonprofit corporation that plows back all earning into its
plant, already worth more than $40,000,000. The Pan American Live-
stock Exhibition also is held here, and the Midway, with a Monorail ride
and other entertainment, is open from May through September. Musicals
and ice shows, fashion shows and numberless activities take place during
the Fair. The State Fair Music Hall, which seats 4,000, is used for 12
weeks in the summer by Dallas Summer Musicals, a civic nonprofit organization that presents stage successes with Broadway and Hollywood stars
and a resident chorus and ballet. Starlight Concerts also are given in the
summer.

Grouped here in an impressive setting are a number of the foremost
museums of Dallas: the Dallas Museum of Fine Arts, the Museum of
Natural History, the Dallas Aquarium, the Dallas Health and Science
Museum, including a Planetarium seating 70; and the Texas Hall of
State, a shrine of Texas history. The Dallas Garden Center has on display
seven acres of Southwestern gardens, and a unique Scent Garden, with
markers in braille to identify the flowers for blind persons. It has a 500-
seat auditorium for horticultural programs.

The TEXAS HALL OF STATE (*open 9–5 workdays; 2–6 Sun.*),
facing the State Court of Honor, is a permanent monument in the form of
a historical museum and memorial to the pioneers who won Texas independence. It is built of Texas materials in neoclassic design. The Dallas
Historical Society Museum, containing a large collection of Texiana,
Mexicana, and Indian artifacts, is in this building.

In the entrance is the statue, TEJAS BRONZE INDIAN, by Allie Ten-
nant. Life-size bronze portrait statues of six Texans occupy the Hall of
Heroes: Stephen F. Austin, General Sam Houston, David Crockett,
Mirabeau B. Lamar, Thomas J. Rusk, and Colonel J. W. Fannin, Jr.
The statues were sculptured by Pompeo Coppini. The two front wings of
the building are devoted to the Halls of East Texas, West Texas, North
Texas, and South Texas, and with interior finishing largely of Texas
materials. Murals by Savage adorn the walls.

The MUSEUM OF NATURAL HISTORY (*open 8–5 workdays, 12–6
Sun.*), facing east toward the lagoon, is neoclassic in design, of cream-
colored limestone. It is a two-story building, its wall unbroken by windows
or other openings, except the entrance and the high windows serving the

lobbies. Carved stone plaques relieve the wall expanse while at intervals pilasters rise from the base to the cutstone entablature. The trim used for the entrance and windows is aluminum.

The museum is divided into four great halls, in two of which are shown Texas mammals. Thirty-three bird groups occupy the other two. Native grasses, trees, rocks and shrubs provide for each exhibit its natural environment. There is also an exhibit of mineral resources of Texas, wild flower paintings and fossils and restorations of rare fossils.

The DALLAS MUSEUM OF FINE ARTS, in Fair Park, was built in 1936 with fourteen galleries, and practically doubled by construction of a new wing in 1965 (*open Tues.-Saturday, 10–5; Wednesday to 9 p.m.; Sunday, 2–6, free*). In 1963 the DALLAS MUSEUM FOR CONTEMPORARY ART was merged with the museum. Its large permanent collection of all media and periods, its special exhibitions four times a year, and its collection of American and especially Southwestern paintings and sculpture give it an influential place in education and art appreciation. It lives up to the dictum: "the museum is not a static showcase." The museum has an art library of books, photographs and slides, art classes for children and adults taught by artists of the region; a circulating rental collection, and the Acoustiguide, a taped commentary that follows the order in which pictures are hung. Four major competitions are the Texas annual exhibit of painting and sculpture, the Texas crafts exhibition, the Dallas County exhibit, and the Southwestern print and drawing exhibition. The Dallas Art Association, with 2,600 members, supports the museum with funds for activities, scholarships and purchases. The Art Museum League, the Contemporary Arts Council, the Dallas Print and Drawing Society, and numerous other organizations cooperate with the museum.

The AQUARIUM (*open 8–5 workdays, 12–6 Sun.*), facing H. A. Olmsted Drive, is of neoclassic design, similar to the other buildings of this group, with walls of cream limestone combined with hard shellstone. In the center of one long side is the high-pillared entry. The smooth, severe lines of the two wings are broken by recessed panels, topped by marine carvings in stone. There are 44 plate glass display tanks, containing a fairly representative assortment of fish from Texas and other States. The Southwestern Historical Wax Museum in Fair Park is open Monday through Saturday, 10–9; Sunday, 2–9 (*admission is charged*).

SYDNEY SMITH MEMORIAL FOUNTAIN, commonly called the Gulf Cloud, was executed by Clyde Chandler, Dallas sculptor, and stands in a circular plot of grass and flowers in front of the auditorium. Sydney Smith for 26 years was secretary of the State Fair of Texas.

MARSALIS PARK (*adm. free*), main entrance Thirteenth St. at Crawford St., covers about 50 acres along the wooded course of Cedar Creek. *Cars use Ewing exit of Thornton Freeway.*

The old HORD HOUSE near Opera St. entrance at NE. corner of the park, is a reconstruction of the first house built in Oak Cliff and one of the oldest in Dallas. A story and a half in height, it was built in 1845 of squared logs with a chimney of white limestone blocks by Judge William

H. Hord, for whom the settlement of Hord's Ridge (now Oak Cliff) was named. It was reconstructed by Martin Weiss in 1927 and house and grounds are loaned for parties and picnics.

The MUNICIPAL ZOOLOGICAL GARDEN (*open daylight hours, free*), along both sides of the creek, is the park's chief attraction. It contains about 1,000 animals, birds and reptiles, and is one of the ten largest municipal zoos in the country. The Dallas Municipal Zoo really began in 1904 with 27 Texas animals and snakes acquired from the State Fair of Texas. In 1920 Frank (Bring-Em-Back-Alive) Buck, who spent his youth in the city, under contract with the Dallas Park Board brought back from Asia and the East Indies a collection of beasts, birds and reptiles. Some of the animals are in habitat surroundings. A unique specimen is the onager, or wild ass of Biblical lore. A Children's Zoo is stocked with farm animals.

WHITE ROCK LAKE PARK (*adm. free*), in the extreme northeastern part of the city between the Northwest Highway and US 67, with an area of 2,314 acres, is one of the largest municipal parks in Texas. It extends around the shores of White Rock Lake, covering 1,095 acres, which serves Dallas as a reserve water storage basin. The park offers picnicking, horseback riding, fishing, boating, bathing and aquatic sports, including annual regattas for sailboats and inboard and outboard motor craft. There are several clubhouses, numerous private fishing and boating camps and a municipal bathing beach, fish hatchery and boathouse. The dam, spillway, and emergency filtration plant are at the southern end of the lake; near the northern end an archipelago of small artificial islands is being constructed with silt removed from adjacent marshy inlets. All points along the lake shore are reached from a circular drive.

The site of LA REUNION, north of Fort Worth Cut-off Rd., at Westmoreland Rd., is marked by the crumbling foundations of a single house, all that remains of the ill-fated French Utopian colony established in this area in 1855. The house was built in 1859 for the widow of Alphonse Delord after the cooperative colony had ceased to function as such. The main settlement on a limestone bluff farther north along Eagle Ford Road was obliterated by blasting to make way for a cement plant. Some of the graves of the colonists can be seen in FISHTRAP CEMETERY, W. side of Fishtrap Rd., 0.5 *m*. N. of Eagle Ford Rd.

BACHMAN LAKE, in northwest Dallas, is smaller than White Rock Lake. Two nearby lakes also useful for recreation are MOUNTAIN CREEK LAKE, covering 2,940 acres, 4 *m*. south of Grand Prairie, and NORTH LAKE, 820 acres, 2 *m*. southeast of Coppell.

Of greater importance are the huge reservoirs developed since 1950 as part of a comprehensive plan to supply Dallas and environs with water for decades to come. LAKE GRAPEVINE, on State 114, covers 12,740 acres with 435,000 acre-ft. of water, 80 percent of which is available to Dallas. LAKE LAVON, on the east fork of Trinity River, covers 20,050 acres and holds 423,000 acre-ft. A new reservoir, LAKE TAWAKONI, often called Iron Bridge Reservoir, was completed in 1961. It is on the Sabine River, southeast of Dallas, covers 36,700 acres with more than 1,000,000 acre-ft., and 80 percent of its water is available to Dallas. GARZA-LITTLE ELM, including the former Lake Dallas, also has more than 1,000,000 acre-ft. of water. The newest of the reservoirs is LAKE FORNEY, on the Trinity River, 4 *m.* north of Forney, which covers 21,300 acres and holds 490,000 acre-ft.

El Paso

Airlines: American Airlines, Continental Airlines, Trans-Texas Airways. El Paso International Airport, 7 *m.* NE off US 62. Transfer for flights into Mexico. More than 660 takeoffs and landings daily.

Bus Lines: Carlsbad Cavern Coaches, Greyhound Bus Lines, New Mexico Transportation Co., Parrish Stage Lines, Moore Service, stop at Greyhound Terminal, 212 San Francisco; Continental Trailways and most of the foregoing lines stop at Continental Trailways Station, 300 W. San Antonio St.

Highways: Thirteen U. S. and international routes, including Interstate 10, US 54, 60, 62, 67, 70, 80, 85, 90, 180, 260, 285, 380; also Mexico 45. Paso del Norte Bridge, Santa Fe St., pedestrian traffic to and from Juarez; vehicles entry to United States only; Good Neighbor (Friendship) Bridge, S. Stanton St. one-way south.

Railroads: Southern Pacific Co., Panhandle & Santa Fe R. R., Texas & Pacific Railroad, using Union Station, San Francisco and S. Davis Sts. National Railways of Mexico and Chihuahua Pacific Railroad have terminals in Juarez.

Accommodations: Hilton Inn at Airport; 3 major hotels downtown; 160 motels and trailer courts.

Information: Chamber of Commerce, 310 San Francisco St.; American Automobile Assn., Hotel Paso del Norte; El Paso Industrial Development Corp., Electric Bldg.; Southwestern Sun Carnival Assn., P. O. Box 95. *The El Paso Times* (morning, Sunday) and *The El Paso Herald Post* (evening).

Educational and Cultural Facilities: Texas Western College (U. of Texas); Radford School for Girls; Loretto Academy; Public Library, with 5 branches and bookmobiles; Texas Western College Library (open to public); El Paso Museum of Art; Centennial Museum, at College; Community Concert Assn., College Community Opera Society, El Paso Symphony Assn.

Medical Services: El Paso Medical Center, University Towers Medical Center; Wm. Beaumont Army Hospital; 11 general hospitals, 1,100 beds.

Recreation: There are 45 parks in El Paso County, many of them with public swimming pools. The largest park is Ascarate, off US 80, with a lake, a 27-hole municipal golf course and a sports-car race track. Tennis courts are available in Arroya Park, Washington Park, Memorial Park and others. Golf may be played at El Paso Country Club by visiting members of out-of-town clubs. Outings to McKelligon Canyon Park in the Franklin Mountains are popular. The so-called highest golf club in the country is at Cloudcroft, two hours away. Skiing is available in the mountains. Boating is possible in Elephant Butte Lake, 100 miles away.

Annual Events and Spectator Sports: Southwestern Sun Carnival, starts last week in December, ends New Year's Day. Pageants of floats, coronation of Queen of the Carnival, championship football game Jan. 1 between Texas Western College and winner of Border Conference games in Sun Bowl. Southwestern Live Stock Show and Rodeo last week in March at El Paso County Coliseum, includes range bull sale, quarter-horse and Palomino show, Junior Division livestock show, 4-H exhibits. Pilgrimage to Sierra de Cristo Rey, 4,576 ft. summit, with sandstone statue of Christ 30 ft. tall on 12-ft. base, last Sunday in October. Alpine Aerial Tramway to top of Mt. Franklin, daily. Baseball by El Paso Giants and visiting teams during summer. Horse racing, October-April, at Sunland Park, N. M., US 80.

Ciudad Juarez: Across the bridge to Mexico; horse races, dog races, at Juarez Race Track; bullfights on Sunday afternoons; restaurants, night clubs, shops, fiestas. Consult newspapers and bus lines.

Climate: Winter temperatures from 14° to 70°; summer from 63° to 103° with cool nights. Dry atmosphere with average rainfall 8.5 in. No fogs or tornadoes.

EL PASO (3,762 alt.). In 1960 its population was 276,687, of which 124,155 was in an area annexed after the 1950 census, when the city had 152,532. In 1966 the estimated population was 320,000. About 35,000 were Mexican-born, and many others are of Spanish or Mexican descent. Across the Rio Grande is Cuidad Juarez, which had 40,000 people in 1950 and an estimated 300,000 in 1966. Located at the westernmost tip of Texas, 563 *m.* west of Dallas, El Paso is the largest port of entry to the United States from Mexico, with more than 32,000,000 persons crossing the border northbound in a typical year of the 1960 decade. It is the fifth largest city in Texas, has a Federal Reserve bank and 10 commercial banks, and more than 400 industries of major capitalization, included in the city's slogan of the five C's—Copper, Cotton, Cattle, Clothing and Climate.

El Paso stands at the lowest natural pass where the westernmost tip of Texas touches Mexico and New Mexico. A settlement has stood here since the *Conquistadores* came north four centuries ago. To the north are the Franklin Mountains, bare, craggy peaks reaching up to 7,167 ft.; to the east lie arid plains broken only by flat desert tablelands. South and west the Sierra Madre form a background for Ciudad Juarez. El Paso lies under the crumbling peak of Comanche. Much of its residential area has overcome the bleakness of the gray land by irrigation, which has produced large swaths of green.

The close association of El Paso with Juarez was emphasized through many decades by the intrusion of Cordova Island, a Mexican area, into a busy part of El Paso because of the erratic course of the Rio Grande. In 1851 the river had shifted its course to the advantage of Texas, forming a large wedge of land called El Chamizal. After years of bickering, the area was awarded to Mexico by arbitration in 1911, but the United States rejected the decision and held fast to the territory. Eventually the Americans realized that this situation was poor neighborliness. A review in 1963 awarded Mexico 436.6 acres and the United States 193.2. This meant that Mexico had to be compensated by land long occupied by El Pasoans. More than 3,500 Americans had to be relocated. This was accepted by both nations and on October 28, 1967, President Lyndon B. Johnson and President Gustavo Diaz Ordaz of Mexico met and formally endorsed the settlement.

As a great manufacturing and distributing center El Paso ranks sixth in the number of persons employed in Texas cities. In a typical month in 1967 it had 109,400 employed, with unemployed only 4 per cent of the total. The American Smelting & Refining Co. employs 950 in its customs smelter, largest in the country, and has an annual payroll of nearly $500,-000. The Phelps Dodge Refining Co. plant, devoted in the electrolytic refining of copper, refines 28 per cent of the copper in the country. The oil refineries of Standard Oil Co. of Texas and Texaco, Inc., handle more than 77,000 bbl. a day, receiving oil by pipeline from the Permian basin. Four pipeline operators are located here, which is the national headquarters of El Paso Natural Gas Co. The business district has begun to build skyward. Among buildings of recent construction are the El Paso National Bank Bldg., Mesa and Main Sts., the Southwest Center Bldg., which also houses the Southwest National Bank, at Stanton and Main Sts., and the R. E. Thomason General Hospital, 4815 Alameda Ave.

The clothing industry has taken a surprising jump in recent years and employs between 5,000 and 10,000. Its chief products are blue jeans, slacks, men's wear, children's wear, and western outfits. Income is more than $50,000,000 annually. The food processing plants are of large proportions and there is a profitable industry in leather goods, cement and fabricated metals. The Northrop Corporation works on space parachutes and makes drones for missile target practice.

Many of the products of El Paso county are processed here. Supima cotton produces a crop valued at $100,000,000 annually. In addition more than 62,000,000 lbs. of cotton-seed oil are produced. The Stahmann Farm near El Paso with the world's largest pecan orchard, 96,000 trees, produces 5,000,000 lbs. of pecans annually; also raises 200,000 geese. Cotton was first planted by Charles Davis, one-time mayor, in 1914. In 1916 the U. S. Government built Elephant Butte Dam, 125 *m.* n. of El Paso in New Mexico, and subsequent irrigation produced a cotton boom. Alfalfa, the area's second crop, averages four tons per acre from four cuttings. Feed crops are profitable and many cattle are on feeding lots here. The cattle industry has an annual value of $150,000,000.

Smaller towns in El Paso County and on the highways leading to the city are ANTHONY (1,125 pop.) and CANUTILLO (1,425 pop.) in the upper valley on US 80; NEWMAN, on the State line between El Paso and Alamagordo; SOCORRO (600 pop.), SAN ELIZARIO (1,064 pop.), FABENS (3,300 pop.) and TORNILLO (250 pop.) in the lower valley, on US 80. HORIZON CITY is a new development in the sand hills east of El Paso

When Cabeza de Vaca was in the vicinity of the present-day city of El Paso, in 1536, he visited Indian pueblos along the Rio Grande. Fray Agustin Rodriguez had come into this region in 1581, headed northward; Antonio de Espejo arrived the following year. In 1598 came Juan de Oñate, who alone of the early explorers took formal possession, proclaiming the country the property of King Philip II of Spain. He reached the crossing of the Rio Grande on May 4, 1598, and named it El Paso del Norte, "the Pass of the North."

Missionary efforts to convert the Mansos resulted, by 1659, in the establishment of Mission Nuestra Señora de Guadalupe, in present Ciudad Juarez. Other mission settlements sprang up on both sides of the river, about 1680, when the Pueblos of New Mexico turned on the Spanish colonists, who fled to the Rio Grande. El Paso del Norte became the seat of government for northern Mexico and a base of operations for attempted reconquest of the Pueblos in 1681, but not until 1827 was settlement made in present El Paso, that community growing around the ranch house of Juan Maria Ponce de Leon.

El Paso del Norte knew little of the Texas Revolution, remaining a thoroughly Mexican town long after Texas became a republic.

Prisoners of the Santa Fé Expedition reached the Pass in the fall of 1841. The military commandant of El Paso was furious at the brutal treatment they had received and ordered them fed and clothed, declaring a three-day rest before they resumed the journey to Mexico City. Among the prisoners was George Wilkins Kendall, who wrote of his experiences in his *Narrative of the Texan Santa Fé Expedition*. He spoke well of El Paso's citizens, described the commandant as "a well bred, liberal and gentlemanly officer," and said of the town: "Almost the only place in Mexico I turned my back upon with anything like regret was the lovely town or city of El Paso."

Colonel W. A. Doniphan descended from the mountains of New Mexico in 1846 with his regiment, bringing the first taste of the Mexican War to the isolated station. The town of El Paso del Norte surrendered amiably, and was later split in half by the treaty of Guadalupe Hidalgo (1848), which made the Rio Grande the boundary between Texas and Mexico.

Simeon Hart, of Ulster County, New York, started a mill by the Rio Grande about 1850, establishing a community which became known as Hart's. Benjamin F. Coontz (whose name is also spelled Coons and Kuntz), having established a trading post near the two settlements, succeeded in obtaining a post office in 1852 for the town which he founded and called Franklin. An extra Anglo-American element had been added in 1849, when a detachment of United States Infantry established the military post later to become Fort Bliss.

The California gold rush of '49 brought a surge of west-bound traffic, and soon two important stage lines were sending their great leather-slung coaches through the Pass. Franklin was an important midway station when the Butterfield Stage Line opened the longest overland mail coach line in the world, connecting St. Louis with San Francisco.

Early travelers were surprised to find the valley a rich and flourishing vineyard. Grapes of an Asiatic variety were said to have been introduced by the Franciscans. By the middle of the nineteenth century a traveler referred to El Paso del Norte as ". . . a city of some size . . . many good homes, the vine extensively cultivated," with a great trade in wine, raisins, and dried fruits. "Paso wine" and brandy were shipped into Chihuahua, up through New Mexico and east over the Santa Fé Trail, and for a time constituted the chief source of revenue.

Use of the name of Franklin was officially discontinued after 1859. El Paso was still only a huddle of squat, one-story adobe houses wedged in between the mountain range and the river, without even a mission tower to break its flat sky line. The business district consisted of two stage stations with corrals, a hotel, a few stores, and enough saloons to satisfy everybody. The townspeople found leisure to watch for the incoming stages, played monte, poker, and faro with the traders who rode into town on regular sprees, and bet on straightaway races and cock fights.

A relic of that period, preserved in the basement of the county courthouse, is the stump of an old cottonwood, the "Notice Tree" which stood where El Paso Street enters Pioneer Place. This tree was the bulletin board where notices were posted for violators of the unwritten code of the frontier town to "git." During this period the gunmen aided the campaign by eliminating each other as fast as possible. The people visited, traded, and intermarried across the river, celebrated the same fiestas, venerated the same saints.

The Civil War came to El Paso with the surrender of the Federal garrison at Fort Bliss, March 31, 1861. Texas troops occupied Fort Bliss, July 14, 1861, and on July 23, Colonel John Baylor moved north up the valley against the Federals in New Mexico. By August 1 he had accomplished his mission and returned to the El Paso region to establish headquarters at Mesilla. Brigadier General H. H. Sibley reinforced Baylor in December of 1861 and took over command of the column, which was designated as the Army of New Mexico. Sibley made his headquarters at Fort Bliss. After an ineffectual campaign to conquer New Mexico, he withdrew to San Antonio about the middle of July, 1862. Federal troops occupied Fort Bliss on August 18. From that time until the close of the war the Federals remained in undisputed control of the Middle Valley of the Rio Grande.

El Paso was incorporated in 1873 when the population consisted of 23 Anglo-Americans and 150 Mexicans. Benjamin S. Dowell, who ran a saloon as a side line, was its first mayor. "Don Benito," as he was called, found his hands full when he attempted to make the settlement a city. The first city ordinance made it ". . . a misdemeanor for any person to bathe in any *acequias* in this city . . . or to drive any herds of sheep . . . or other animals into any *acequia* . . ."

The Apaches were making their final raids while prospectors swarmed down from the Rocky Mountains, along with hordes of desperadoes and gunmen who found the river at this point a convenient crossing, all combining to keep the infant city in a state of turmoil.

The habits of the river added to the confusion. This stream, often referred to as "a mile wide and a foot deep, too thin to plow and too thick to drink," was forever changing its course. One might be living in El Paso one day and in El Paso del Norte the next, and the lawless of two nations evaded pursuit by simply wading into another country.

At that time the Indians, Spaniards, and Mexicans obtained water by ditching it to their fields and homes from the river. Water from shallow wells was unpalatable, and those who could afford it bought drinking water from firms which obtained it in Deming, New Mexico. Efforts to pipe water from the Rio Grande failed because silt clogged the mains.

In 1877 El Paso felt certain effects of the Salt War, which centered near San Elizario (*see Tour 19f*). During the height of this controversy over the ownership of salt deposits, the handful of Anglo-American residents of the city sent their families to New Mexico as a precautionary measure. But the only important local incident was the slaying of Don Luis Cardis by Judge Charles Howard in the Schutz store on San Francisco Street.

The coming of the railroads meant even more to isolated El Paso than to other communities. The city was the goal of two transcontinental roads which raced for the strategic crossing near the Rio Grande in the pass above the town. The Southern Pacific built eastward from San Diego, California, the Texas and Pacific westward from Fort Worth. It was a battle of money giants as well as of laboring track crews. The financial manipulations of the Southern Pacific interests so delayed Texas and Pacific construction as to virtually put that road out of the running. The Southern Pacific reached El Paso on May 19, 1881, and pushed on down the Middle Valley of the Rio Grande, the second strategic point. Meantime, the Santa Fé built down the valley of the Rio Grande, arriving at El Paso on June 11. The Texas and Pacific finally reached Sierra Blanca near El Paso on January 1, 1882, to make connection with the Southern Pacific at that point, from where it continued westward over the tracks of the latter road. At about the same time the Mexican Central was completed between Juarez and Mexico City.

Population boomed, and along with the railroad builders and their labor gangs came a rush of Wild West desperadoes and gamblers. El Paso became a resort for gunmen, and gambling halls and saloons blossomed.

The clash between lawless elements and "the law" provided the basis for countless Western stories. Among gunmen who made their headquarters in the city was John Wesley Hardin, reputed to have killed 27 men.

Order was re-established through the efforts of a succession of straight-shooting sheriffs, city marshals, and Texas Rangers. El Paso voted out gambling houses and dance halls, and applauded the informal kind of justice meted out to its undesirables.

Even after 1910, the city was frequently swept into turbulence. Following the example of Benito Juarez, who took refuge in El Paso del Norte in 1865 and from there returned to the Presidency of Mexico when Maximilian was executed, Francisco I. Madero and his supporters, among them Guiseppi Garibaldi, grandson of the Italian patriot, made El Paso headquarters for their revolutionary *juntas;* and soldiers of fortune flocked to the city to take part in the fighting.

With the abdication of Porfirio Diaz, refugees from Chihuahua poured into El Paso to escape the revenge of the rebels, and many remained. While Pancho Villa harried the border, and the mountains beyond Juarez rang with "La Cucaracha," revolutionary song of the Villistas, the city again saw warfare.

In 1917 it was discovered that both El Paso and Juarez were lying above an underground lake, and several deep wells provided an abundance of water. Elephant Butte Dam, 125 miles northward in New Mexico, furnished irrigation for 74,600 acres in El Paso and Hudspeth Counties, which would otherwise have remained a desert. Irrigated fields yield sugar beets for seed purposes, tomatoes, chili peppers and beans for local canning plants, and onions for an extensive market. Pear orchards furnish a profitable yield. An especially fine grade of long staple, strong fiber cotton is raised. Cottonseed oil mills process cotton from a wide area. Some mills are owned by a farmers' cooperative. There are 22 gins in the county.

Mexican craftsmen weave rugs, blankets and *sarapes* on old-fashioned hand looms in their shops along Third Street, and modern factories in the neighborhood of South Stanton and Second Streets make tortillas. Pottery makers work in southern and eastern parts of the city, especially in the vicinity of Washington Park. Another industry is the manufacture of hand-tooled leather goods and furniture.

The Tularosa Basin, in which El Paso County is located, was one of the famous old western cattle areas. In recent years the livestock industry has become largely one of cattle feeding and dairying.

El Paso holds a strategic position as a port of entry, being the largest city on the Texas-Mexico border, and across the river from the largest city in northern Mexico. Crude ores are shipped to its smelters from mines in north Mexico, New Mexico, Colorado and Arizona, and quantities of refined ores are exported. El Paso has canning plants, copper refineries, and oil refineries. The city is headquarters for the El Paso Customs District, which includes New Mexico and Texas west of the Pecos River.

Exports through the Customs District in 1960 had a value of more than $45,000,000, while imports were valued at more than $51,000,000.

The nation's huge investment in military installations here has been estimated at $400,000,000. The payroll at the Fort Bliss post, after taxes and allotments, exceeded $64,000,000 annually a few years ago, $11,000,-000 going to the civilians employed there. The Post buys about $21,000,-000 worth of supplies a year, of which 87 per cent reaches El Paso establishments.

POINTS OF INTEREST

SAN JACINTO PLAZA, bounded by Main, Mills and N. Oregon Sts. and N. Mesa Ave., is said to mark the spot where Juan de Oñate found a cultivated garden in 1598. The alligator pool has been discontinued and the surviving alligator lives at the El Paso Zoo.

The site of the JUAN MARIA PONCE DE LEON HOME, NW. corner N. Oregon and Mills Sts., marked by a bronze plaque, is occupied by the 12-story Anson Mills Building, said to have been the first structure of monolithic reinforced concrete to be erected in the United States.

CARNEGIE SQUARE, bounded by W. Franklin, N. Oregon, N. El Paso and W. Missouri Sts., affords landscaped grounds for the EL PASO PUBLIC LIBRARY (*open workdays, 9 a.m.-9 p.m.*). The two-story yellow brick structure is of classic style, designed by Mauran, Russell and Garden of St. Louis. There are four branch libraries and more than 315,000 volumes. Two bookmobiles help serve the city. Facing North Oregon Street is the MILLS MEMORIAL SHAFT, honoring seven citizens of El Paso killed by Indians at Cook's Spring, New Mexico, in 1861. As employees of the Southern Overland Mail, they were attempting to pre-

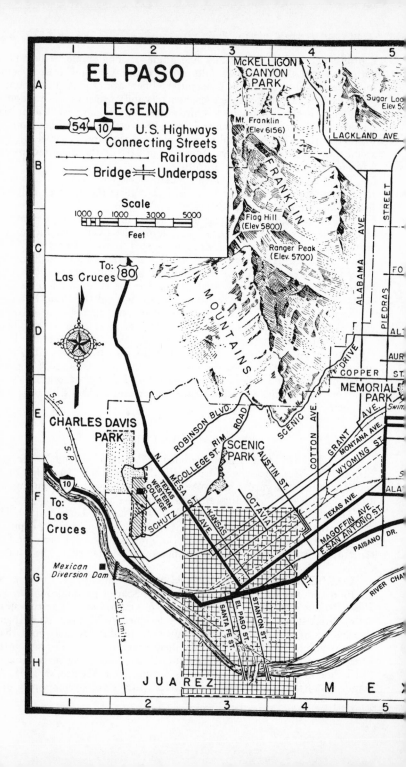

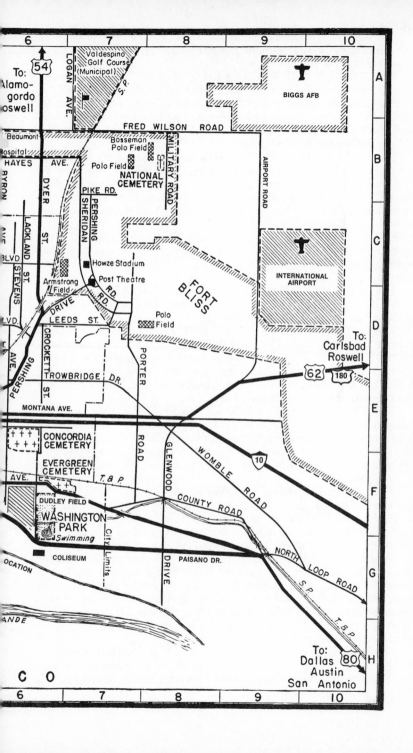

vent company property from falling into the hands of the Confederates at the outbreak of the Civil War.

The GOLDEN AGE RECREATIONAL CENTER (*open daily, 12 m.-8 p.m.*), bounded by Franklin, N. Santa Fé, W. Missouri and N. El Paso Sts., was formerly Cleveland Square. Cards issued by leading hotels admit visitors free to the badminton, ring tennis and quoit courts, the horseshoe and washer pitching lanes, the chess, checker and domino tables and other recreational facilities.

The SCOTTISH RITE CATHEDRAL (*open 8–10 workdays, 8–6 Sun., holidays*), W. Missouri and N. Santa Fé Sts., designed by Herbert M. Greene, is a reproduction in brick and terra-cotta of the Pan-American Building in Washington. Pieces of furniture and other articles are mementos of pioneer Masonic activities dating back to 1854, presented to the lodge by Albert Pike.

ENGINE NO. 1 of the Southwestern & El Paso Railroad, exhibited for years at Franklin St., between N. Kansas and N. Stanton Sts., has been presented to the University of Texas at El Paso and funds have been raised for a new shelter.

The site of the SOUTHERN OVERLAND MAIL STAGE STATION is at Overland and S. El Paso Sts. This block was covered by the station and its stables, in 1857–1861.

The EL PASO CITY-COUNTY BUILDING, occupies the block bounded by San Antonio, Overland, S. Campbell and S. Kansas Sts. Its fine modern facade gives distinction to what was formerly the County Courthouse, a classic-type building that underwent a thorough remodeling in the 1950's. It houses municipal and county offices and Liberty Hall, the city's concert, theater and meeting hall.

The FEDERAL DISTRICT COURTHOUSE, on the block bounded by San Antonio, Myrtle, N. Campbell and N. Kansas Sts., is a three-story white limestone structure in modern classic style, designed by McGhee, Frazier and Lippincott. Erected in 1936, it cost $653,000. In the lobby a mural by Tom Lea, Jr., shows a group of characters typical of El Paso's history.

The 125-foot LOOKOUT TOWER, at the foot of S. El Paso St. on the north bank of the river, highest of nine steel towers set at strategic points along the Rio Grande, stands by Camp Chigas, home of the Border Patrol. The towers are equipped with short wave sending apparatus used effectively to prevent smuggling and illegal entry of aliens.

THREE INTERNATIONAL BRIDGES cross the Rio Grande from El Paso to Juarez. The Paso del Norte Bridge begins at the foot of Santa Fé St. The Good Neighbor Bridge is at the foot of Stanton St. The Bridge of the Americas is at the Avenue of the Americas. A street car runs across the Stanton Ave. Bridge. It costs 10¢ a ride into Mexico and 7¢ for the return trip to El Paso. Automobiles going south pay 15¢, going north 3¢; pedestrians southbound 2¢, northbound 1¢.

Mexican immigration officers halt all cars at the southern end of the bridge; the sign *Alto* (stop) must be obeyed. No passports are required for one-day visitors to Juarez. Customs inspectors usually examine parcels

Cities

THE ASTRODOME AT HOUSTON

Greater Houston Convention & Visitors' Council

THE ASTRODOME: LARGEST ROOFED ARENA

Greater Houston Convention & Visitors' Council

BUSINESS CENTER, DALLAS; MEMORIAL AUDITORIUM
IN FOREGROUND

Dallas Chamber of Commerce

CHANGING SKYLINE OF HOUSTON

Gulf Oil Corporation

JESSE H. JONES HALL FOR THE PERFORMING ARTS, HOUSTON
Greater Houston Convention & Visitors' Council

BAYFRONT OF CORPUS CHRISTI WITH MAN-MADE T-HEADS
FOR MARINAS

Texas Highway Dept., Travel & Information Division

AIR VIEW OF GALVESTON: SEA WALL BLVD. IN FOREGROUND,
CHANNEL AT UPPER RIGHT

Texas Highway Dept., Travel & Information Division

TEXAS STATE CAPITOL COMPLEX, AUSTIN
Texas Highway Dept., Travel & Information Division

TEXAS DEPARTMENT OF PUBLIC SAFETY HEADQUARTERS,
WITH UNDERGROUND STATE EMERGENCY CENTER

Texas Dept. of Public Safety

TEXAS HIGHWAY DEPARTMENT TOURIST BUREAU, EL PASO

Texas Highway Dept., Travel & Information Bureau

HOME OFFICE, EL PASO NATURAL GAS COMPANY, EL PASO
El Paso Industrial Development Corporation

TOWER OF THE AMERICAS, 622 FT. TALL, SAN ANTONIO
Drawn by O'Neil Ford, Architect HemisFair, San Antonio

and baggage for dutiable goods. Foodstuffs and drygoods in small quantities are passed duty free. Return traffic is routed over the Santa Fé St. Bridge (Avenida Juarez).

The UNIVERSITY OF TEXAS AT EL PASO is the title now given to Texas Western College, W. end of College Ave., in the foothills of Mt. Franklin W. of US 80. It was known until 1949 as the Texas College of Mines and Metallurgy. When the University of Texas discontinued its courses in mining in 1911 El Paso bid for its School of Mines. In 1923 it began offering a bachelor of science in mining engineering degree. By 1932 it expanded its facilities to include the degree of bachelor of arts. It is coeducational and in 1965 enrolled 6,632 in its regular courses.

When the first four buildings were erected in 1917, limestone rock was quarried from the mountainside and used as building material. Many of its 43 buildings are of Bhutanese architecture, copied from an ancient Tibetan monastery and fort on the southern slopes of the Himalayan Mountains. The walls are plastered outside in a rich cream stucco, with a frieze of brick and tile in bright colors a few feet below the eaves. The roofs are low-pitched, covered with red crushed brick, and project far out from the walls. The outside walls are battered, sloping inward.

The LIBRARY has more than 105,000 vols., and among its rarities are old Texan newspaper files. The SUN BOWL, costing $1,750,000, seats 30,000 and is the site of major football games. The college sponsors the Texas Western Ballet, the College Community Opera Society, and the Community Concert Association. Plays are produced during the year.

The TEXAS CENTENNIAL MUSEUM (*open Mon.-Fri., 8–5; Saturday, 8–12; Sunday, 2–5, free*), on the south edge of the campus, was completed in 1937, Perry McGhee, architect, and follows the general design of the school buildings. It is two stories high, housing a permanent collection of minerals and ores, paleontological and archeological exhibits.

HART'S MILL is 1.5 m. NW. on the north bank of the Rio Grande, left of the intersection of highways at the viaduct. Broken adobe walls, part of the dam and the great wall and stone arch through which the water entered to turn the wheel are still visible. The mill was built about 1850 by Simeon Hart, who utilized an ancient dam, of unknown origin, estimated to have been built nearly two centuries earlier. The mill, rebuilt in 1856, ground corn and wheat for a large area until the late 1880's, while Hart's homestead (a large adobe brick house still standing at the west end of the viaduct) became known as a center of hospitality.

The MAGOFFIN HOUSE (*private*), Octavia St. between Magoffin Ave. and San Antonio St., designed in 1875 by Joseph Magoffin, is an example of early-day El Paso dwellings. The one-story adobe building surrounds an open patio 60 by 40 feet; the outside walls are four feet thick and 15 feet high, with a frontage of 100 feet.

MILITARY INSTALLATIONS

FORT BLISS was established Nov. 7, 1848, as the Post of El Paso in New Mexico Territory and became a part of Texas when the territory was divided. In 1854 it was named Fort Bliss to honor the son-in-law of President Zachary Taylor. It has occupied its present location northeast of El Paso since 1893. In 1914 60,000 soldiers were assembled here and General John J. Pershing took command and led a punitive expedition against Pancho Villa in 1915. Victoriana Huerto, former president of Mexico, was detained here, 1915, and died in El Paso.

The post became the home of the 1st Cavalry Division. In 1945 German missile scientists led by Werner von Braun came to Fort Bliss. It is now the U. S. Army Air Defense Center, which supervises and coordinates the Air Defense School, Training Center (Air Defense), Combat Support Group, Range Command, Service Group, 6th Artillery Group (Air Defense), Army Dental Detachment, and Army Dispensary. The Air Defense Center trains missilemen in the use of Nike and Hawk missiles. About 5,000 missilemen a month are trained at the Air Defense School and 1st Training Brigade of the Training Center. Approx. 8,000 basic combat trainees fill the remaining units.

On July 1, 1966, BIGGS AIR FORCE BASE, adjacent to the post, was transfered to the Army to provide facilities for the Defense Language Institute. The German Air Force Air Defense School, first foreign military base on U. S. soil, began training here at the same time.

Activities separate from Defense Center are the Army's Air Defense Board, the Combat Developments Command's Air Defense Agency and its Institute of Nuclear Studies, and the Air Defense Human Research Unit. The first three test all guided missiles and the use of atomic energy in the field. In 1966 there were 40,000 military at Fort Bliss and 4,800 civilian employees.

Fort Bliss is the free world's largest guided missile center and the second largest post in the U. S. Army. Its Military Reservation comprises 1,125,510 acres in Texas and New Mexico and 4,500 buildings, and with equipment the post is worth more than $750,000,000. The White Sands Missile Range in New Mexico was opened in 1946.

WILLIAM BEAUMONT GENERAL HOSPITAL of the U. S. Army is located on the slopes of Mount Franklin. Its 174 buildings occupy 272 acres near Dyer St. and US 54. It is a teaching hospital and annually graduates 20 medical and four dental internes. There are 800 military and 750 civilian personnel at the hospital, which has 14,000 patients and more than 400,000 outpatients each year. Approx. 1,800 babies are born annually here. There are 47 resident physicians and 40 civilian physicians are consultants.

IN THE ENVIRONS

The ALPINE AERIAL TRAMWAY moves up the eastern slope of Mount Franklin to Ranger Peak, which is 5,632 ft. above sea level. The view from the top includes parts of three states and two nations.

The EL PASO SMELTING WORKS of the American Smelting & Refining Co. is the largest custom smelter in the country as well as one of its oldest non-ferrous smelters. It was established in 1887 and reportedly has 4 per cent of the nation's copper-smelting capacity. It contributes to the El Paso skyline a smokestack 820 ft. tall, and no one has challenged the statement that it is "the world's tallest."

The STATUE OF CHRIST on the summit of Sierre de Cristo Rey, 4,576 ft. above sea level, is the object of an annual pilgrimage by Roman Catholics on the Feast of Christ the King, the last Sunday in October. The statue, of Texas sandstone, is 33.5 ft. tall on a 9 ft. base. The path leads past the Stations of the Cross and is 4 *m.* long. It is followed by pilgrims on occasions other than the annual observance.

LA MISSION DE CORPUS CHRISTI DE LA ISLETA DEL SUR, founded 1682, is located in the suburb of Ysleta, on US 80, in El Paso. This was founded after the pueblo revolt of 1680. The Mission was built of adobe by the Indians and what had survived was destroyed by fire in 1907. The succeeding church is called the Church of Our Lady of Carmel. Four of its 7 acres have been continuously cultivated since 1682. Also in this area is the site of the Mission and Pueblo of San Antonio de Senecu.

East of Ysleta and about 24 miles from the center of El Paso is SAN ELIZARIO, which started as a settlement around a presidio built after the Indian revolt of 1680. Floods caused the presidio to be moved three times. The fourth chapel, CAPILLA DE SAN ELIZARIO, was erected in 1877 on the site of the earlier ones. With white walls, an arched tower with two bells, and an arched portico, it resembles the California missions.

Another church in the environs of El Paso is the MISSION DE LA PURISIMA CONCEPCION DEL SOCORRO, at Socorro (US 80).

CIUDAD JUAREZ, MEXICO

Juarez, Ciudad Chihuahua, Mexico (3,800 alt.), the ancient El Paso del Norte from which the Texas city derived its name, has an important import and export trade, and is a tourist amusement resort.

Twice Juarez has assumed national importance. In 1865 President Benito Juarez, reformer and national hero, defeated by 30,000 French troops of Maximilian, retired to El Paso del Norte, where he continued to maintain his "capital" in the face of French occupation. In 1888 the town's name was changed to Juarez in his honor.

During the Diaz-Madero struggle, the Battle of Juarez and its fall climaxed the seven-month revolt of Madero. On May 8, 1911, General Navarro and a federal garrison were in possession of Juarez, when a rebel force attacked. By May 10 the federals, who had retreated into their last stronghold, the barracks, were forced by a bombardment of rebel artillery to surrender. During the battle many bullets fell in the streets of El Paso and several residents were killed. A large part of Juarez was destroyed by shells and fire. This battle ended the dictatorship of Diaz and marked the beginning of the Mexico of today.

Urban renewal is the order of the day in Juarez, which has been developing an Art Center, a Convention Hall, and a Museum in a former slum area.

Most of the houses are built on the usual Mexican plan, with flat roofs. In poorer homes mud and thatch or reeds do for covering, but space is always provided for a garden; even crowded quarters have at least a few flowering vines.

The amusement lanes, two streets leading from the international bridges, and the main street, Calle (street) 16 de Septiembre, are marked by brilliant neon signs and the blare of jazz music. Here are found all the border city attractions: cabarets, saloons, night clubs, curio shops, and eating places, while just off these busy thoroughfares are the cockpits where chicken fighting is as much a national pastime as the bullfight is a holiday spectacle. The small section bounded by these three central streets is the city's only foreign district, occupied by hundreds of Chinese.

POINTS OF INTEREST

BRIDGES TO JUAREZ AND RETURN. Automobiles use the Good Neighbor Bridge, foot of Stanton St.; toll, 15¢ going, 3¢ returning. The return is made over the Paso del Norte Bridge, foot of Juarez Ave. Pedestrians use the Paso del Norte Bridge, paying 2¢ going, 1¢ returning. The Juarez street car may be boarded at El Paso St. and San Antonio Ave., and at Stanton St. and Overland Ave. Fare is 10¢ going, 7¢ returning. The Avenue of the Americas Bridge may be used by cars for going to Juarez only. Mexican immigration officials inspect automobile permits and tourist cards. American customs inspectors and immigration officers inspect luggage on return. (*See General Information for customs regulations*).

Juarez has two bullrings: the Alberto Balderas downtown, which seats about 12,000, and the Monumental on the Sixteenth of September Avenue, which seats about 18,000. The music of *La Virgen de la Macarena* as the trumpet soars out above the crowded arena; the entrance parade of the matadors and their *cuadrilla*, the entrance of the bull and the thrilling sight as the matador matches his skill against the bull are unforgettable. *Sundays, 5 p.m. in summer, 3 p.m. winter.*

La ADUANA FRONTERIZA, or Custom House (*open 8:30–12 m., 2:30–5:30 Mon.-Fri., 8:30–2 Sat.*), SE. corner Calle 16 de Septiembre and Ave. Juarez, is one of the older civic buildings. A fort-like appearance is given by towers which rise at each corner and over the main entrance on Calle 16 de Septiembre. Here United States President William Howard Taft and Mexico's President Porfirio Diaz, met when El Paso and Juarez entertained the two in 1909. A state dinner was served on the gold plates of Emperor Maximilian of Mexico. A short while later (1911) in front of the building, the peace treaty between Diaz and Madero was signed.

MISSION NUESTRA SENORA DE GUADALUPE DE EL PASO (*open daily, except from 11–1:30; guides optional*), SW. corner Calle 16 de Septiembre and Calle Nicolas Bravo, was founded on December 8, 1659, for the conversion of the Mansos, and the church completed in 1668. This mission became the nucleus for the settlements at the Pass. The church has undergone little change. A high wall surrounds it on three sides. In front is an ancient cemetery.

All walls are 56 inches thick, made of adobe bricks and plastered inside and out. The single bell tower is of Moorish architecture. The roof is flat, and was at first covered with more than three feet of earth, but now is roofed with modern material.

The ceiling is of hardwood beams and perfectly matched saplings, the beams intricately carved in a deeply cut diagonal design, and supported at the ends by graceful carved brackets. The spaces between the beams are filled with small, round polished saplings, set at a slant, alternating right and left in each succeeding space.

Until about 25 years ago the church had no pews, worshipers bringing in *sarapes,* cushions, or small stools on which to sit during services. Apart from the added pews the interior is the same as it was when all worshipers were Indians, and each missionary had to keep a bodyguard to prevent his charges from carrying him into the mountains.

MERCADO CUAUHTEMOC (*open 7–7 daily*), SE. corner Ave. Vicente Guerrero and Calle Mariscal, official public market, is usually crowded with buyers and sellers of foodstuffs, household necessities, and transportable bric-a-brac. The market is a large stucco building, almost hidden behind shops of many descriptions, its narrow sidewalks cluttered with small stands that make passage difficult. Every inch of the dark interior is utilized, the stalls placed close together on narrow passageways which weave in and out in all directions.

Fort Worth

Airlines and Airports: Greater Southwest International Airport is one of the busiest airports in Texas. Trunk lines are American, Braniff, Continental, Delta, Eastern, and Mexicana. Local service airlines are Central and Trans-Texas. Meacham Field accommodates third-level carriers and private planes. Third level carriers are Aerosmith, Altair, American Flyers, Hood, Longhorn, and Solar.

Bus Lines: Continental Trailways Bus Center, 8th & Commerce, for Continental Lines; Greyhound Bus Terminal, 1005 Commerce, for Greyhound lines, Central Texas. Texas Motor Coaches Station, 1508 Main, half-hourly motor coach service between Fort Worth and Dallas. Freight is handled by 36 regular route carriers and other carriers for special commodities.

Highways: Interstate 35W, 20 and 820, the latter the loop around the city connecting all routes; US 80, 81, 180, 287, 377; State 121, 174, 183, 199 and 356. The Fort Worth-Dallas Turnpike connects the two cities.

Railroads: Texas & Pacific Railroad Station, Texas & Pacific, Fort Worth & Denver; Union Station, C. R. I. & P., Santa Fe. The Fort Worth Belt Railway connects the 9 trunk lines. There are 25 daily passenger schedules and 50 freight schedules. Freight service only is provided by the Missouri-Kansas-Texas, Missouric Pacific, St. Louis-San Francisco, St. Louis Southwestern, and Southern Pacific.

Climate: Yearly normal temperature, 66°; annual rainfall, 33.69 in. Extreme heat and cold occur for short periods. Days with 20° or lower average six times a year; hot periods are usually broken by thunderstorms. Windstorms are rarely destructive.

Information: Fort Worth Chamber of Commerce. *Fort Worth Press,* 507 Jones St., evening and Saturday; *Fort Worth Star-Telegram,* 400 W. 7th St., morning, evening and Sunday. There are 14 radio stations and all major television networks are shown.

Recreation: Large bowling centers have up to 40 lanes and are open 24 hours. Golf, tennis and swimming are available in the parks and horses at commercially operated stable. Easily accessible for picnics, swimming, fishing and camping are the six lakes within motoring distance—Worth, Eagle Mountain, Bridgeport, Possum Kingdom, Benbrook and Arlington.

Events and Spectator Sports: The Southwestern Exposition and Fat Stock Show is a major event in Southwest Texas, late January-February, in Will Rogers Memorial Coliseum. The Original Indoor Rodeo is a part of the Exposition. The Fort Worth-Dallas Spurs of the Texas Baseball League play in Turnpike Stadium, as do the Dallas Cowboys of the National Football League. Southwest Conference football and basketball is brought to the Amon Carter Stadium by TCU, home of the Horned Toads. The National Invitation Golf Tournament and the Colonial National Tennis Tournament are held at the Colonial Country Club. There is weekly wrestling at the Northside Coliseum and regional and State Golden Gloves boxing contests are held in Will Rogers Coliseum. In the fall high school football is played four nights a week at Farrington Field. Consult newspapers for dates.

FORT WORTH (670 alt., 356,268 pop., 1960; 390,500, 1967, est.) seat of Tarrant County and fourth largest city in Texas, is in the center of a thickly populated metropolitan area that had 627,000 people in 1965. Between 1950 and 1960 the city annexed 56,799. It prospered first with the livestock and meatpacking industry, then became the major shipping point for oil and oil well supplies in northwest Texas. The railroads carried forward its commercial impetus and air traffic continues it today. Fort Worth is located in north central Texas, about 250 miles from the Gulf of Mexico. It is near the headwaters of the Trinity River, which lie in the upper part of the coastal plain on the Fort Worth prairie. The rolling hills of the area range from about 600 ft. to 800 ft. in elevation. The area has rich grass and farm lands with wooded sections along many streams.

Fort Worth's banks and savings-and-loan associations have resources of $1½ billion. It is headquarters for 33 insurance organizations, with assets of a similar amount. Industry is diversified, producing fabricated metals, helicopters, airplane parts, oil well drills and other oil field apparatus, plastics and mobile homes. Airplane manufacturing is pursued by General Dynamics, Bell Helicopter Co., Wren Aircraft, Menasco, Wilson Specialty Manufacturing Co., H. & M. Machining, and other makers of airplane equipment. In November, 1967, when Fort Worth had 277,300 employed, unemployment was only 2.1 per cent.

The incessant hum of wholesale and retail business is music to the ears of Fort Worth residents, who see the customary expression of local enterprise in the rise of the new Federal Center, the John Peter Smith hospital, the General Motors plant, and the elaborately planned Tarrant County Convention Center. American Airlines has established its first training school for stewardesses adjacent to the Greater Southwest airport. Central Airlines makes its headquarters in Fort Worth. Acquisition of terrain for a projected Regional Airport has begun east of Grapevine, with the object of meeting air travel needs of the near future for a wide area.

Livestock continues to add to the prosperity of the city and meat packing is highly profitable. The number of ranches and farms that supply Fort Worth has decreased, but values have risen by more than one-half in recent decades. Farm labor also is less in numbers, largely because of mechanization. Fort Worth grain elevators can store 89,184,000 bushels, fourth largest capacity in the country.

Natural gas is the principal source of fuel in Fort Worth and North Texas and the area is criss-crossed by many miles of pipelines used for transmission and distribution.

Fort Worth frequently is the site of large conventions and exhibitions, for which its Will Rogers Memorial Coliseum, Municipal Auditorium, Amon Carter Stadium and similar structures serve admirably. In order to keep pace with the demands on its hospitality it began enlarging these facilities in the 1960s. In 1964 the voters of Tarrant County authorized a bond issue for the COUNTY CONVENTION CENTER and the TURNPIKE STADIUM. The latter, costing $1,500,000, was opened in 1965. It is located on the Fort Worth-Dallas Turnpike and easily accessible to the two-city area. It is the home base of the Fort Worth-Dallas Spurs. A 14-block area in downtown Fort Worth was cleared for the Convention Center and construction began in 1966. Its cost was estimated at $16,000,000. The plans called for a circular arena seating 10,000, an ice rink, a theater with portable stage and seating 3,000, and 25 conference rooms. The main hall was planned for exhibits, public meetings and sports events.

Rather oddly, Fort Worth was never a fort. Originally it was a camp where, in 1849, Brevet Major R. A. Arnold and a troop of dragoons kept a watchful eye on the Indians. The camp was named Fort Worth in honor of General William Jenkins Worth, Mexican War hero. After the Civil War, when the cattle drives trailed up through the little community, it became an important trading and supply center. By 1866 educational facilities were urgently needed, so its citizens bought a wagonload of flour which they traded for lumber, to convert the Masonic Hall into a school building.

In 1870, when it became apparent that a railroad might soon reach the settlement, Fort Worth enjoyed rapid growth. It was incorporated in 1873. That same year, with the railroad as near as Eagle Ford, 26 miles distant, land values boomed and the population was more than 5,000. Then came the "Panic of '73," with the failure of Jay Cooke & Co., which held most of the liens against the new railroad, the Texas and Pacific, and also against much property in Fort Worth.

That blow immediately sifted the weak-hearted from the community. A majority of the new residents headed east and the population fell below 1,000. During the hegira a young lawyer wrote a letter to the *Dallas Herald* asserting that Fort Worth was so dead he had seen a panther lying asleep and unmolested in the main street.

The thousand stalwarts who remained greeted that calumny with hoots of derision. The fire department bought a panther cub for a mascot. Local clubs attached the name "Panther" to their former titles, and the "Panther City" was born.

The Panthers sharpened their claws. They wanted a railroad, and a railroad they would have if, as a local resident declared, "every bank and peanut stand in the entire East failed." They offered to grade the remaining 26 miles of unfinished roadbed in exchange for a lien on the road. The Texas and Pacific agreed and the Panthers set out to help complete the moribund railway before the land grant subsidy given by the legislature should expire. In 1876 the situation developed into a race against time. The road had to be completed before the legislature adjourned—and adjournment day was near.

Meanwhile, Fort Worth scratched gravel. Every business house operated with the barest minimum of workers and sent the bulk of its men to the railroad right-of-way to wield pick and shovel. The women of the city worked in relays, preparing hot coffee and food, and feeding and watering the mules. The legislature remained in session until the road was completed, and on July 19, 1876, the first train into Fort Worth stopped at what is now Boaz Street and Lancaster Avenue, its whistle cord tied down and the editor of the local newspaper frantically shoving fuel into the firebox to keep the steam whistle going.

That was the start of the city's nine trunk line railroads, of which four still compete with air and bus travel.

During the construction of its first rail line, and for some time thereafter, Fort Worth was a typical frontier town. Gamblers, cattlemen, and all types of characters familiar to the Old West thronged the city. A bit of unusual excitement was provided when the Comanche chiefs, Yellow Bear and Quanah Parker, the latter famous for his raids against the whites, visited town and went to bed after blowing out the gas. Yellow Bear never awakened, but Quanah Parker recovered and lived to become a friend of his former enemies.

By 1875 citizens of Fort Worth had sensed the value of capitalizing the city's strategic location as the market place of a great southwestern empire of cattle and cattlemen. They organized a meat packing company and built the first stockyards in Fort Worth. A quarter century later Swift & Company, Armour & Company, and Libby, McNeill & Libby entered the field, and by 1902 those companies had completed a group of packing houses in Niles City, then on the outskirts of Fort Worth. Their presence attracted allied industries, and during the decade that followed, the population jumped from 26,688 to 73,312.

In 1909 fire ravaged 20 blocks. Failure of the artesian water supply was largely responsible for the disaster, and shortly afterward the city conceived the idea of building Lake Worth.

World War I wrote a new chapter in the story of Fort Worth, with the establishment of Camp Bowie within the city and of several flying fields in its immediate vicinity. The site of Camp Bowie is now filled with residences. The principal military establishment in this area is CAS-WELL AIR FORCE BASE, 7 miles west, a heavy bomber base built on what formerly was Tarrant Field. Its main unit is the Strategic Air Command. It is used also by the Continental Air Command, the Air Training Command, and a Command Service Unit.

Oil was discovered in 1912 at Burkburnett, 125 miles northward, and immediately after the World War, the Ranger field, 100 miles westward, was brought in. Oil men of all descriptions flocked to Fort Worth, as the most convenient center of the new oil territory. Oil companies, promotion companies, wildcatters and every form of enterprise identified with oil activities sprang up and flourished.

Fort Worth never has lacked an adequate supply of fresh water for residential and industrial needs. Until recently reservoirs holding the clear waters of the Trinity River have been its main source. In 1916 LAKE WORTH, 5.4 m. northwest of the city, with a surface of 3,267 acres and a capacity of 33,660 acre-ft., was adequate. In 1931 EAGLE MOUN-TAIN LAKE, 14 m. northwest on US 81 was added; it covers 8,500 acres and holds 182,000 acre-ft., and its shoreline of 61 m. provides fishing and recreation. Still farther out is LAKE BRIDGEPORT, in Wise and Jack Counties, 47 m. from Fort Worth and 4 m. from Bridgeport; this covers 10,399 acres, holds 270,900 acre-ft., and has a shore line of 85 m.

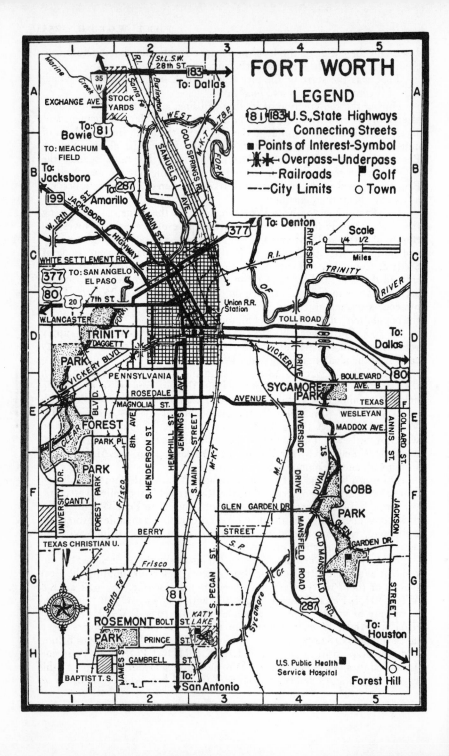

Supplementary reservoirs serving places in the Fort Worth environs include LAKE BENBROOK on the Clear Fork of the Trinity River, which covers 5,820 acres; LAKE ARLINGTON, 7 *m*. west of Arlington, covering 2,275 acres, and AMON CARTER LAKE on Big Sandy Creek, 6 *m*. south of Bowie in Montague County. But the largest enterprise in this region was started in the late 1960s and is a huge reservoir on Cedar Creek, 3 *m*. northeast of Trinidad in Henderson County, generally referred to as Cedar Creek Lake and recently named JOE B. HOGSETT LAKE. Covering 34,000 acres, it will hold 678,900 acre-ft. of water at full capacity.

A project to make possible barge traffic all the way to the Gulf of Mexico is the canalization of Trinity River. The Trinity development passed Congress and was approved by President Johnson in October, 1965, but funds were contingent on studies by the Galveston District of the Corps of Engineers, U. S. Army. Several supplementary projects were begun, however; the building of the Wallisville Dam and Reservoir in Chambers County, near the spot where the river enters the bay waters of the Gulf at Anahuac, included the first modern navigation lock in the Trinity system. Washington also allocated funds for dredging the channel from Houston Ship Canal to Liberty, a segment of the Trinity plan.

POINTS OF INTEREST

A concentration of cultural enterprises in and near Amon Carter Square has provided Fort Worth citizens with many new artistic satisfactions. New impetus was given to the study of art when the AMON CARTER MUSEUM OF WESTERN ART was opened in January, 1961. Located at 3501 Camp Bowie Boulevard, it faces the Fort Worth skyline from across the Trinity River. It is a bequest of Fort Worth's public-spirited newspaper publisher, the late Amon G. Carter, and houses a collection of paintings and sculpture assembled during his lifetime. The Museum is famous for the paintings and bronzes of Frederic Remington and Charles M. Rusell, but it also is strong in 19th century art, and as an institution dedicated to "the visual documentation of the culture of westering North America," it has been acquiring American work of the 20th century. Changing exhibitions of paintings and photographs, and publications in American art, anthropology and history, are basic in its educational program. Traveling exhibits increase its range. The Museum maintains a reference library of Texana and western Americana and a microfilm collection of western newspapers published prior to 1900. The building, designed by Philip Johnson, is constructed of Texas shell-stone with the interior of bronze and teak. An administrative wing was added in 1963. *Open free, daily except Monday, 10–5; Sunday, 1–5:30; open on Monday from June 1 through Labor Day.*

FORT WORTH ART CENTER, 1309 Montgomery St., at Amon Carter Square, offers a large collection of paintings and sculpture, not only of the Southwest but also by old masters. It was established in

1892. It sponsors regular traveling exhibits. *Free, Tuesday through Saturday, 10–5.*

The performing arts have experienced such enthusiastic support in recent years that new avenues for the expression of talent are opened regularly. One of the newest is the WILLIAM EDRINGTON SCOTT THEATRE, adjacent to the Art Center, designed by Donald Oenslager and equipped with all modern technical devices for the presentation of ballet, chamber music, drama, and other arts. It opened in 1966.

Much community interest also centers on CASA MANANA, a theater-in-the-round on Camp Bowie Boulevard at Amon Carter Square. Its repertory has much variety; it offers concerts and plays and in the summer produces musicals with Broadway stars in the leading roles. The Texas Boys' Choir performs here. Every Saturday the theater offers children's classics. The Casa Manana Academy of the Performing Arts offers instruction in acting to young aspirants. The Community Theater is also active.

The Fort Worth Symphony Orchestra gets strong support for its annual series of concerts. The Fort Worth Opera Association annually presents a number of performances of four grand operas with nationally known artists in the principal roles. An event that stirs global interest is the Van Cliburn International Quadrennial Piano Competition. The Texas Boys' Choir adds to its activities in Fort Worth by going on tour.

KIMBELL ART MUSEUM is the newest project to rise at Amon Carter Square. It was authorized by the Kimbell Foundation, which administers the estate of Kay Kimbell, whose fortune was based on trading in groceries, grain, oil and insurance. The Museum, a nonprofit undertaking, will be operated by the Foundation until the end of its corporate existence, when the Museum will be maintained by the City. The collection is rich in examples of the major artists of the Dutch, Flemish, Spanish and Italian schools. Louis I. Kahn, Philadelphia architect, was commissioned to design the building, and Dr. Richard Fargo Brown, former director of the Los Angeles County Museum, was named director.

The FORT WORTH CHILDREN'S MUSEUM, 1501 Montgomery St., is scaled to the interest of children in all forms of human and animal life, historic as well as current. There are live and mounted animals; exhibitions of fossils, Indian artifacts, and period rooms illustrating Texas history. Special activities, such as a pet show and a science fair, enhance the usefulness of the Museum. Guided tours are available to schools. *Open free, Tuesday through Saturday, 9–5; Sunday, 2–5.* Included in the Museum is the CHARLIE M. NOBLE PLANETARIUM, which has a Spitz projector and 100 seats. *Open only on Saturday, 11 a.m., 2:30 p.m., 3:45 p.m., and Sunday, 2:30 p.m., 3:45 p.m. Adults 50¢, children under 12, 25¢; children under 6 not admitted.*

The COOK MEMORIAL HOSPITAL CENTER FOR CHILDREN, 1212 W. Lancaster Ave., W. G. Clarkson and Company, architects, was built and endowed by Mrs. W. I. Cook as a memorial to her husband and daughter. The discovery of oil on a west Texas ranch enabled her to realize her ambition to build a perfectly equipped hospital for the benefit of needy women. It is built in Italian Renaissance style, of Indiana limestone, with a green tile roof. The reception room has Italian travertine walls, with heavy walnut beams across a gold-leaf ceiling; its quiet beauty is the motif of the building.

The FIRST METHODIST CHURCH (*open daily*), 800 W. 5th St., has a million-dollar group of buildings covering most of a city block, and includes, besides the church proper, structures housing a banquet hall, recreation rooms, and the church offices. Of modified Gothic design, all in cream, W. G. Clarkson and Company, architects, the church is topped by twin towers that house a set of 16 cylinder chimes.

The MASONIC TEMPLE (*open 1–4 Tues., Wed., Thurs.*), 1101 S. Henderson St., is of neoclassic design, built of Indiana limestone, with the interior of travertine marble. W. G. Clarkson and Company were the architects. The building is on the crest of a rolling hill, its central unit of seven stories flanked by two-story wings. The central portals of polished steel form a triptych, each panel bearing the etched figure of an ancient Master of Masonry.

The FORT WORTH PUBLIC LIBRARY system has its main building at 9th and Throckmorton Sts., seven branches in other sections of the city, and four bookmobiles that serve both city and county. The main building is a three-story structure completed in 1939, with a base faced with granite and Indiana limestone and Texas Leuders stone on the exterior above. It stands on the site of the first Carnegie library opened in 1902. Five of the seven branch libraries were opened in the spring of 1967. They are of contemporary design, each by a different architect. Ease of access is a dominant characteristic, and all are carpeted throughout. The library system has more than 1,000,000 books, documents and periodicals. Special items include the Mrs. Charles Reimers Collection of Rare Children's Books, an earth science library, and materials for the study of Southwest history and genealogy. Annual circulation is more than 1,000,000. The director is Wyman Jones; the assistant director is Mabel Fischer.

THE LAST SUPPER, 600 Throckmorton St., is a life-size display in wax of Leonardo da Vinci's famous fresco painting in Milan. *Open, with admission fee, 10–8:30, Monday and Friday; other weekdays, 10–6; Sunday, 1–5.*

The UNITED STATES POST OFFICE, SE. corner Jennings and W. Lancaster Aves., designed in the classic Greek manner by Wyatt C. Hedrick, architect, was completed in 1933 at a cost of $1,050,000. The light gray outside walls are of Cordova limestone, with 16 four-foot Corinthian columns capped by Grecian spans of Bedford limestone between the entrances. Steps and foundation trim are of Texas granite, and a seven-foot wall encloses a light-well in front of the building. Emblems of the United States are on bronze medallions at each end of the structure. At each north entrance foyer are four 20-foot columns of green Grecian marble. Floors also are of marble. The corridor is 260 feet by 22 feet, lined on both sides by offices and service windows. The walls are tan, marble-lined to a height of eight feet, and above that is a bronze grille with an American eagle perched between the United States Shield and the Texas Star. The frieze on both sides carries the same motif and the ornamental plaster ceiling is richly decorated with gold leaf and bright colors.

The TEXAS AND PACIFIC PASSENGER STATION, W. Lancaster Ave. from Main to Throckmorton Sts., was designed according to the ideas of J. L. Lancaster, president of the road. The designer was H. P. Koeppe, the architect, Wyatt C. Hedrick. The station, of modern design, is 13 stories high, with a base of brown polished granite, limestone in the first section, and the upper stories of gray rough-textured brick. On each corner are 10-foot towers on the outside faces of which futuristic eagles have been carved.

The STOCKYARDS, N. Main St. and Exchange Ave., covers an area of 253 acres lying between 23d and 28th Sts. At the right as the area is entered, is the Coliseum. Beside it is the Livestock Exchange Building, in which are offices of the Fort Worth Stock Yards Company, cattle commission houses and railroad freight agents. Both buildings are of Spanish architecture.

PIONEERS' REST, Samuels Ave. and Cold Springs Rd., is a cemetery of historic interest, its roster of graves containing the names of those who were most active in the early life of the city. Markers show that burials were made as early as 1850. Here are graves of Major Ripley Arnold, and General Edward H. Tarrant, for whom the county was named.

The FORT WORTH BOTANIC GARDENS are an allurement the year around in Trinity Park, the wooded recreation area along the Clear Fork of the Trinity River. Here in 50 acres of rolling lawns and natural forest are displays of possibly 150,000 plants of 2,500 different species, with terraces of roses for which Texas is famous. The FORT WORTH GARDEN CENTER, 1 m. S. of the entrance, marks the beginning of the Botanic Gardens. The Center occupies the Horticultural Building, a structure of rough-hewn slabs of Palo Pinto stone. It was designed by Hubert H. Hare in early Texas architecture. The combined office, library, and reception room has a flagstone floor and pioneer furnishings. The main objectives of the Center are the encouragement of gardening and to provide a suitable environment for the study of natural sciences. It is under the joint sponsorship of the Fort Worth Garden Club and the Fort Worth Board of Education. The ALBERT RUTH HERBARIUM (*open 10–4 daily*), in Garden Center, of more than 8,500 specimens, many of them rare, is the leading collection of scientifically classified dried plants in the Southwest. That part devoted to Texas contains more than 1,000 native plants. An instructor is available to show and explain the collection. The herbarium is the work of Professor Albert Ruth, who died in 1932. He was the discoverer of six plants, which have been named for him.

TEXAS FRONTIER CENTENNIAL PARK (*open daily*), 3100–3600 W. Lancaster Ave., covers 147 landscaped acres. Near the center rises the 210-foot PIONEER MEMORIAL TOWER, dedicated to

Texas pioneers. West of the tower is the MUNICIPAL AUDITORIUM (*open by arrangement*), which seats 3,000 persons. A 10-foot tile mosaic across the front wall presents the "History of the Settlement and Development of the West." To the east is the WILL ROGERS MEMORIAL COLISEUM (*open by arrangement*), with a maximum seating capacity of 10,000. The tower, auditorium, and coliseum are designed in the neoclassic style, faced with cream, rough-textured brick, and trimmed in ivory limestone, Wyatt C. Hedrick and Elmer G. Withers, architects.

FOREST PARK, an attractively landscaped terrain of 283 acres on Forest Boulevard, contains some of the most eye-filling features of Fort Worth's three major parks. The most popular installation is the FORT WORTH ZOOLOGICAL PARK, a large aggregation of wild animals, birds, and reptiles displayed in spectacular settings, such as the Rain Forest, where tropical birds fly freely; the House of the Great Apes, the Herpetarium, and the Children's Zoo. Here also is the JAMES R. RECORD AQUARIUM, in quarters of recent construction, displaying all forms of marine life, including porpoises, alligators, eels, and snapping turtles. *Open daily, 9:30–5:30; adults 20¢, children under 12, 10¢.* Another attraction of Forest Park is the LOG CABIN VILLAGE, in which original cabins of the early settlement era have been assembled to portray pioneer ways.

EDUCATION

As an educational center Fort Worth is remarkably well-equipped to train men and women for scholarly, technical, vocational and religious careers. This capacity is still expanding, for as late as 1967 it opened Tarrant County Junior College, with the humanities, technical and semi-professional training, on three separate locations, to which adults also have access. This topped a system of 87 elementary and 28 junior and senior high schools. The largest institution is Texas Christian University, church-controlled but secular in its courses; others of like administration are Fort Worth Christian College and Texas Wesleyan College, while Southwestern Baptist Theological Seminary is the largest institution for religious training in the Southwest. Not in Fort Worth but near enough for commuting is Arlington State College, Arlington, ("only 20 minutes from Downtown Fort Worth") part of the University of Texas system, with its two-year program in engineering technology of value to Fort Worth industry. The colleges are closely associated with the Graduate Research Center of the Southwest, established in Richardson in 1961, and in 1965 formed the Association for Graduate Education and Research (TAGER) with emphasis on the sciences and engineering.

TEXAS CHRISTIAN UNIVERSITY occupies a campus of 243 acres in the southwestern residential district. It is a private, coeducational university related to the Disciples of Christ and developed from a small college founded 1873 in Thorp Spring, augmented by Waco Female College in 1895, and acquiring its present name in 1902. Its 40 buildings, many of recent erection, include 14 residence halls. It has five undergraduate schools and colleges, two graduate-level schools and an evening college. In 1967 the University began construction of a Science Research Center, to cost $6,900,000. The University has an endowment of $27,-000,000 and an annual operating budget of $11,500,000. Tuition is $40 per semester and the board and room minimum is $323.

While the University emphasizes religious faith it is nonsectarian in its teaching. BRITE DIVINITY SCHOOL has prepared many students for the ministry and church-related vocations, and as military chaplains. The HARRIS SCHOOL OF NURSING and the Ranch Training Program typify practical aims. Of special interest are the Foreign Language Laboratory and the Computer Center.

The MARY COUTS BURNETT LIBRARY, remodelled and tripled in size in 1958, has more than 575,000 volumes and receives approx. 2,700 periodicals regularly. Its facilities include graduate carrels, microfilm and typing rooms, and stacks accessible to the students. Of striking aspect are the immense louvers that automatically shield the interior from the sunlight.

Athletic installations include the TCU-Amon Carter Stadium, with 45,627 seats, and the Daniel-Meyer Coliseum, with 7,166 armchair seats. In spring, 1967, TCU enrolled 7,040, with a faculty of 308.

SOUTHWESTERN BAPTIST THEOLOGICAL SEMINARY has a campus of 100 acres on Seminary Hill, the highest point in Tarrant County. It was established 1901 as a part of Baylor University at Waco and began as a separate seminary in 1908, moving to Fort Worth in 1910. It is controlled by the Southern Baptist Convention. It has six main buildings and more than 600 family living units. The newest building is the STUDENT CENTER. What is described as the largest theological library in the United States is the FLEMING LIBRARY, with more than 374,000 volumes and 1,200 subscriptions to periodicals. The three schools are those of Theology, Religious Education and Church Music. Study in the last leads to the degrees of bachelor, master and doctor in church music. The Seminary has announced that "the modern-day ministry of music demands the church musician to be a highly technical specialist with Christian dedication and calling." The Experimental Teaching Area uses, among other devices, the videotape recorder, which enables preaching students to study instantaneous replays of their sermons. The School of Religious Education operates the Baptist Marriage and Family Counseling Center, open to nonstudents. With a faculty of 77 it enrolled 2,031 in a recent year.

TEXAS WESLEYAN COLLEGE, occupies 25 acres at the crest of Polytechnic Hill. It is controlled by the Northwest Texas Conference of The Methodist Church. It has a faculty of 76 and enrolls nearly 2,000 students annually. Its predecessor, Polytechnic College, was founded in 1890. The college has a strong music department, and its Library is notable for books on Texas history and folklore.

The newest educational institutions are FORT WORTH CHRIS-
TIAN COLLEGE and TARRANT COUNTY JUNIOR COL-
LEGE. The first was opened in 1957 on a 48-acre campus in north Fort
Worth, as a junior college. The second is an effort by the county to extend
the opportunities for two-year technical and vocational training in order
to meet the demands of industry and business. Tarrant was planned for
three campuses at once in northeast, northwest and south Fort Worth.
Adult courses are part of its curriculum.

Galveston

Airport: Galveston Municipal Airport at Scholes Field. Trans-Texas Airways has 4 flights daily. Flight instruction, charter flights, service and repairs. FAA Communications Station.

Barge Lines: Six, using Intracoastal Canal to major ports.

Bus Lines: Central Texas and Texas lines, with transcontinental connections, 2127 Ball St. bus line covers 52 *m.*

Ferries: Three, from Galveston to Port Bolivar on State 87; free.

Highways: Main route from Houston is US 75 (Interstate 45), which connects Houston with Dallas and Oklahoma; US 59, Laredo to Houston, has a junction 8 *m.* beyond Richmond with State 6, which runs to Galveston. State 6 connects at Alvin with State 35, route to Corpus Christi. State 146 leaves US 59 and US 190 at Livingston, continues to Galveston. State 87 runs south along Louisiana line via Port Arthur to Port Bolivar; ferry to Galveston, *free of tolls.*

Motor Freight Lines: Ten, covering coastal area.

Railroads: Union Station for Missouri Pacific, Missouri-Kansas-Texas, Southern Pacific, Gulf, Colorado & Santa Fe. City is also served by Rock Island and Burlington connections.

Steamships: Piers are numbered according to streets leading to them. Lines represented, 90, chiefly cargo. Regular passenger service to Caribbean ports.

Accommodations: Galveston makes good its title of Port and Playground of the Southwest by providing numerous hotels and motels close to recreation areas along Seawall and Beach Boulevards. Several have large swimming pools and provide baby-sitters; others do not permit pets. Galveston Chamber of Commerce, 315 Tremont St., will furnish recommended list. Consult also *Galveston News, Sun* and *News-Sun.*

Amusement Parks: Fort Crockett Park, 4021 Ave. U; Galveston Playland, 2328 Boulevard; Stewart Beach Park, Beach Blvd.

Aquarium: Sea-Arama, 91st St. and Sewall Blvd., also Oceanarium and Aqua-Amphitheater.

Badminton Court: Kempner Park, 2704 Ave. O, *free.*

Band Concerts: Municipal Band, Sunday during summer, Menard Park and Youth Center, 27th St. and Seawall Blvd., *free.*

Baseball and Softball: Stewart Park, 43rd St. and Ave. P; Adult Softball, 81st and Ave. V½; Little Leagues, same, *free.*

Basketball: Menard Gymnasium, 2119 27th St.; Wright-Cuney Gym., 718 41st St., *free.* Also Volley Ball courts, *free.*

Bowling: Bowl Lanes, 2402 Ave. Q ½; Gulf Bowl, 625 53rd St.; Seahorse Bowl, 3424 Boulevard.

Camping: Permitted on beaches west of city limits; no facilities. Trailer Camps: 6027 Broadway, 4501 Broadway, 1428 Boulevard, 6401 Broadway, East Beach.

Diving: Scuba and Skin: Offats Bayou.

Fishing: Piers, lighted, along Seawall Blvd. at 10th, 17th, 29th, 37th and 61st Sts., *free.* Deep-sea Fishing: Anderson's (parties), 7th and Wharf; Capt. Doc, Yacht Basin; Golden Boat and Gulf Boat, both Pier 18; William Service, Pier 19. Fishing, general: Pelican Park, Pelican Island; Perry Park, 73rd and Bayou; Andy's Camp, 1520 8-mile Rd.; Dorothy's Bait Camp, 7519 Broadway; Dugan's, 61st St. Pier; Martin's, Teichman Rd.; P & W Camp, 9301 Teichman Rd.; Pleasure Island Resort, Highway 75; Ralph's, 8815 Teichman Rd.; Smitty's, 7609 Broadway.

A license is required for both fresh and salt-water fishing for all over 17 and under 65, resident or nonresident, except for deepsea fishing beyond the 10-mile limit. Cost $2.15 and expires August 31, regardless of date purchased. Available at sporting goods stores and county courthouses in Texas.

Golf: Municipal, 6402 Beach; Galveston Country Club, Stewart Rd. Miniature: Stewart Beach; Fort Crockett Amusement Park.

Hunting: License needed for duck and goose hunting, available at courthouses and sporting goods stores.

Picnic Areas: Lindale Park, 4th and Bonita; Kempner Park, 27th and Avenue N; Menard Park, 27th and Seawall Blvd.; Lasker Park, 40th and Ave. P; Wright Cuney Park, 40th and Ave. G; Crockett Park, 53 and S-½; Pelican Park, Pelican Island. Perry Park, 73rd and Heards Lane and Offats Bayou; Ziegler Park, 27th and Ave. R. *All free.*

Plant Tours: Falstaff Brewery, 33rd and Church; University of Texas Medical Branch, by arrangement; Todd Shipyards Corp., by arrangement; Thos. J. Lipton Tea Plant, by arrangement.

Playgrounds: Lindale, 4th and Bonita; Menard Park, 27th and Boulevard; Wright Cuney, 40th and G; Crockett, 53rd and S-½; Lasker, 42nd and Ave. P; Ziegler, 27th and Ave. L. *All free.*

Surfing: Surf boards can be rented along the beachfront for $1.00 to $1.50 per hour. Surfing is restricted. Consult the Chamber of Commerce for limits.

Swimming: Gulf of Mexico beach, 32 *m.* long, *free.* Stewart Beach has lifeguard May through Labor Day, *free.*

Tennis Courts: Menard Park, Lasker Park, Wright Cuney Park, *free.*

Theaters: Broadway, 5121 Broadway; Galveston Little Theater, 2110 Market; Martini, 524 Moody; State, 2021 Postoffice; Rey (Spanish films), 2521 Market.

Annual Events: Mardi Gras, before Lent; Oleander Fete, April; Port Holiday Marina opening, Yacht Basin, usually latter part of May, with sailboat review, festival parade, blessing of the shrimp fleet. Splash Days open the summer tourist season and everybody joins in activities. Lipton Tea Cup race, late May; Galveston County Fair and Rodeo, Arcadia, first week in June; Beachcombers Golf Tournament, Galveston Country Club, early in June; Treasure Isle coin fiesta, Galvaz Hotel, late June; Isle musicals begin in July, close first week in September, with weekly change of bill; Jaycee's sports car races, Scholes Field, July. See newspapers for dates of summer fishing rodeo, auxiliary boat race, tennis tournament.

GALVESTON (6–17 alt., 67,175 pop., 1960; 69,820 est. 1965) occupies the eastern extremity of Galveston Island, which is 30 *m.* long, 2 *m.* wide and 2 *m.* off the mainland. A ship channel, 1,200 ft. wide and 35 ft. deep, leads from the Gulf to the harbor. The city is connected with the mainland by three causeways; the newest, built 1961, is 8,402 ft. long; another was rebuilt and elevated, 1964. These are for vehicles; the third is used by railways. US 75 (Interstate 45) crosses the channel at 61st St. Galveston also has a free ferry service to Port Bolivar on State 87, maintained by the State, which annually carries 900,000 vehicles and 3,355,-000 passengers. The city is served aerially by SCHOLES FIELD, the municipal airport, which has three runways, each 6,000 ft. long, and four flights daily by Trans-Texas Airways.

PELICAN ISLAND, developed from a sand spit, is connected with Galveston by a causeway. Its 4,000 acres are uses by industries, including ship repair facilities.

At TODD SHIPYARD is the original servicing facility for a nuclear merchant vessel. It was built to accommodate the Government's nuclear ship, *Savannah,* which demonstrated its practicability but was laid up because of the cost of operation.

The Port of Galveston handles about 4,000,000 tons of shipping annually, chiefly cotton, grain, sulphur, wheat and fuel oils. It has 37 piers, two grain elevators with a capacity of 7,000,000 bu., an unloader moving 12,000 bu. per hour and a grain dump unloading 14 trucks per hour.

Commercial fishing for shrimp gives a livelihood to many in the Galveston Bay area. The take on the Coast is from 60,000,000 to 80,000,000 lbs. a year and the value may reach $25,000,000. Also found in coastal waters are sea trout, blue crab, drum, red snapper and oysters. The State has been starting new oyster beds along the Coast.

The prosperity of Galveston is reflected in the upsurge of new construction built or building. This included a new Police and Courts building costing more than $1,000,000; a new County Courthouse costing more than $2,500,000; the new Public Safety Building as an annex to the City Hall; the erection of the new San Luis Pass Bridge from the southwest extremity of Galveston Island to Freeport by the County, for which the voters approved a bond issue of $3,595,000 in 1964; the Fisherman's Wharf at Piers 19 to 22, for which the Port appropriated $1,400,000; a $2,000,000 expansion of the Yacht Basin; a new luxury hotel at the base of the Pleasure Pier costing $1,200,000; the Magic Harbor Park, a Disney-type enterprise expected to cost more than $9,000,000. Among the numerous funds allocated to the building of new schools was a bequest of $1,100,000 from the Weiss family to the Galveston School District for the Weiss Junior High School.

Galveston publicizes "the only hotel over the Gulf of Mexico," this being The Flagship, 240 rooms, on a pier, with a fishing pier at the T-head.

Galveston is the county seat of Galveston County (157,000 pop. est.), since 1922 one of the State's major oil regions. About 450 wells produce nearly 28,000 bbl. daily. Pumping rigs tap wells offshore. Most of the petroleum is handled at Texas City, on the mainland, where shipping reaches 18,500,000 tons annually, fifteenth largest in the nation. There is in addition a tremendous amount of natural gas in the area, which is supplied to Galveston industries at special rates. Byproducts of the gas are used in making synthetic rubber and chemicals. The County's farm production reaches nearly $5,000,000 in value yearly, about $1,500,-000 of that in rice, the other crops being grain, sorghum, hay, and vegetables. Livestock has an annual value of more than $3,000,000.

In the streets nearest the harbor are many narrow business buildings, often with ornate fronts, that date from the days when all the activities of the city were those of a seaport. Here and along the water front surges a cosmopolitan company. Lascars from tramp steamships, Cornishmen from blunt British freighters, sailors of every nationality—the city contains 27 foreign consulates—mingle with those home folk whose business takes them to the harbor side and with vacationists from every section of the country.

Charming houses of classic beauty are in the older residential sections, but more striking are unusual examples of self expression by builders in the periods of maritime affluence before and after the Civil War—men who had been in many parts of the world before they settled down to establish homes on the island, and who in designing their mansions borrowed from and combined, to suit their tastes, almost every conceivable type of architecture.

On the Gulf side is the beach and recreation center which, with the facilities for fishing and boating, and the mild and equable climate, has made Galveston a playground for tourists. Upon and just back of the sea wall are dance pavilions, restaurants, cafes, night clubs, a huge skating rink, a Ferris wheel, roller coaster and other amusement devices for speed and excitement, curio shops, wheels of fortune, games, and an almost continuous spirit of carnival.

A peculiar characteristic of much of the Galveston residence construction is the raised first floor; what ordinarily would be the ground floor is a semi-basement, and the lower living floor of the house is six to ten feet above the ground and reached by an outside stairway. This is principally a survival of custom from the days when storms flooded parts of Galveston, before the sea wall was built and the grade of the island changed. Before the great storm of 1900, in no place did the altitude reach nine feet. Since then the sea wall has been constructed, 17 feet high, and back from it a great part of the city has been raised to slope gently to the bay.

No visitor in the downtown area is likely to remain unaware of Galveston's three principal exports. On every hand are evidences of cotton; second today among United States ports in cotton shipments, the city has fireproof space for millions of bales and operates high density compresses. Seen from the bay, a section of the water front has a distinctly yellowish cast; the bulk of the state's 2,000,000-ton annual output of sulphur is shipped here. On the skyline loom grain elevators; one of them has room for the storage of 6,000,000 bushels.

Negroes—some of them, from Louisiana and West Indian islands, speaking French patois—constitute about 20 per cent of the population, and Galveston's many and varied industrial plants, together with a large and steady demand for longshoremen, create an industrial situation that makes living conditions among them better than in many cities. For this, as well as for the rareness of friction between the races and the unusually large proportion of Negroes in the professional classes, credit is commonly given to Norris Wright Cuney, Galveston leader of the Negro race in Texas in the late nineteenth century, whose passion was the advancement of Negro education. In 1883 a strike of white longshoremen had almost closed the port and appeals were made to him to supply Negro workmen. He did so, on the condition that when the trouble was settled Negroes should work on the docks on a wage equality with whites. He organized the Negro Longshoremen's Association, which today supplies a large part of the water front labor, and so wisely directed it as to establish standards of equity and tolerance in labor relations. They have been maintained.

The present island of Galveston, when white men first landed on it 400 years ago, was two islands, and remained so until a storm in the early nineteenth century closed the narrow pass between them. It was almost certainly here or on the next bit of land to the westward—now called San Luis Island—that Cabeza de Vaca, the first European to see the interior of present-day Texas, was wrecked in 1528. He and his companions called it *Malhado* (Misfortune), but after their escape from the Indians and his publication in Spain of the narrative of his journeyings, it was given the name *Isla de las Culebras* (Island of the Snakes), and later it was called San Luis. The bay between the island and the mainland was surveyed in 1785 or 1786 and named in honor of Count Bernardo de Galvez, Viceroy of Mexico.

A Mexican revolution against Spain was in progress in 1816, when Don Luis Aury arrived from New Orleans with a fleet of 15 vessels, claimed the island in the name of Mexico, established a settlement and fortifications, and set up a government. Using the harbor as a base of operations, Aury's ships preyed on Spanish merchant vessels. He was joined by another soldier of fortune, Francisco Xavier Mina, who brought 200 men. Together they planned an expedition against the Mexican coast, but quarreled on the way, and Aury turned back.

Meantime Jean Lafitte, notorious Barataria buccaneer who had been driven from the Louisiana coast, sailed his little fleet into Galveston Bay in May, 1817, and hoisted the Mexican flag over the almost deserted settlement. When Aury returned to the island, he took one good look at Lafitte's ships in the harbor, and sailed away.

Lafitte renamed the settlement Campeachy, and pirates, European soldiers of fortune, privateers, a riffraff crowd of adventurers, Indian squaws and loose women flocked there. Surrounded by more than a thousand lawless followers, Lafitte constructed a combination home, warehouse and fortress which he called *Maison Rouge* (Fr., Red House), at the corners of which and from the upper story protruded the muzzles of cannon.

A village sprang up around the fortified house, consisting largely of slave marts, saloons, gambling halls, and kindred dens. Swashbuckling rovers from all points of the compass came to the island principality. The peak of its prosperity was reached in 1818, when raiding and pirate expeditions brought great stores of spoils to be heaped on the shore and sold, and several shiploads of slaves—for whom Lafitte's standard price was a dollar a pound. In that year two French generals, L'Allemand and Rigaud, ex-officers of Napoleon's Imperial Guard, arrived with 400 dashing adventurers and a touch of elegance. They established a settlement nearby, and a semblance of court life sprang up, centering at the Red House in carousals less coarse than the drinking bouts of the rougher buccaneers.

Many Spanish ships had been seized—before Lafitte's departure they were to number more than 100—and Spain was powerless to prevent it, yet protested any action by the United States that might become a precedent for authority in Texas, and Lafitte was careful not to commit depredations against United States vessels. But one of his captains in 1819 disobediently fired on a United States cutter, and although Lafitte, as soon as the offender returned to Campeachy, hanged him—"for piracy," he blandly assured the cutter's commander—this was the beginning of the end. When another similar incident occurred, United States authorities caught the perpetrators, and hanged two of them, and public sentiment in the States demanded that the pirates' nest be cleaned out.

A fierce hurricane the next summer sank most of the vessels in the harbor, drowning many men, and left the settlement in ruins. Even the Red House partly collapsed, the heavy cannon in the upper story crashing down on women who had been crowded into the building for safety. Food stores had been ruined, famine threatened, and Lafitte's problem was to reduce the number to be fed and provide funds for the survival of the community. He did it by seizing a schooner that came in from New Orleans, and ordering all Negroes in Campeachy to be carried aboard. Not only the slaves, but free men and women, if they were of African blood, were taken to New Orleans and sold.

Early in 1821 came trouble with Indians. The ferocious cannibalistic Karankawas had often visited the western part of the island, but left the pirates alone until four men of the settlement, out on a hunting expedition, stole a squaw. The Indians retaliated by killing and eating four of Lafitte's men, and the result was the Battle of Three Trees, in what is now the site of Lafitte's Grove. The fight lasted three days, the Karankawas being finally routed when the buccaneers brought up several small cannon.

Soon afterward a United States cutter arrived with an ultimatum to Lafitte that he must depart, and in May he and his remaining followers set sail southward into legend, leaving Campeachy in flames. When the fire had burned itself out, there remained only the Red House and buildings in the French village.

Although the legislature of Coahuila and Texas made Galveston a port in 1825, it was not until after 1830 that the new settlement began to gain importance. In 1834 Michel B. Menard, with nine associates, most of them Anglo-American, acquired title to one league and labor of land (about 4,600 acres) and formed the first Galveston City Company.

When the Texas revolt against Mexico impended, in the following year, the provisional government of Texas authorized a navy of four ships and the granting of letters of marque to privateers, and designated Galveston as the naval base. During the Revolution these ships operated against the Mexican navy and prevented a blockade of the Texas coast. Briefly, just before and until the successful outcome of the Battle of San Jacinto on April 21, 1836, the village became the temporary capital of the Republic through the arrival of President ad interim David Burnet and his cabinet, who, with Santa Anna's army at their heels, had fled from Harrisburg.

With the Republic firmly established, a tide of immigration from the United States and Europe poured through the port, many of the arrivals remaining to establish homes. By 1839, when the city was incorporated, it had more than 250 houses, and within three years the customs duties were going far toward the support of the Republic, Port Collector Gail Borden reporting receipts for one quarter of a year to be more than $40,000. Notwithstanding serious storms, epidemics of yellow fever, and a fire that destroyed much of the business district, the city had gained great commercial importance and a population of more than 10,000 before the Civil War began.

After a long blockade by United States naval vessels, Commander William B. Renshaw took command of the fleet on October 1, 1862, and a few days later demanded the surrender of the city, but gave four days, if his demand should be refused, for the evacuation of noncombatants. His occupation of the harbor on October 9 was not resisted, and the force of marines that landed to raise the Union flag over the customhouse and be given formal possession of the city by the mayor was received at the city hall by the Galveston fire department in full parade uniform. On January 1, 1863, after a stirring battle on land and water—in which boats piled high with cotton bales, called "cotton-clads," attacked the Union ships—General John Bankhead Magruder retook the city for the Confederacy. Galveston remained under the Stars and Bars until the close of the war.

On June 19, 1865, Major General Gordon Granger unwittingly established an annual holiday that has endured ever since, when he took over the city and proclaimed that all slaves in the state were free. "Juneteenth," as it is commonly called, is Emancipation Day in Texas, the greatest Negro day of celebration.

After the Civil War, trade channels opened quickly, and cotton shipments became heavy. The epidemics of yellow fever that had afflicted the island were conquered. In 1889 Congress decided to make Galveston a deep-water port, and the channel and harbor improvements, made at a Federal cost of $6,200,000 and completed in 1896, included two jetties of great granite blocks, one jetty five and the other seven miles long. The last year of the century found the city with a population of 38,000, with foreign commerce increasing, and with the general outlook exceedingly bright. Since its first settlement it had suffered from severe hurricanes, but the year 1900 was destined to be that from which most later Galveston history has been dated—the year of The Storm.

The island's highest elevation, then, was eight and a fraction feet, and there was nothing to break the force of the gale from the Gulf which reached hurricane proportions on September 8. As water inundated the lower parts of the city and the wind increased, people sought refuge on higher ground and many left for the mainland, but by night those who remained were unable to leave, or even to venture out of doors safely because of flying debris. The wind attained a velocity of at least 110 miles an hour, and at the hurricane's height the water rose four feet in as many seconds and washed over the island.

Survivors emerged from the wreckage of their homes the next morning to contemplate indescribable scenes of horror. Some sections along the Gulf were entirely bare, while others were covered with great hills of splintered timbers, twisted roofs and battered human bodies. Fifteen hundred acres of houses were totally destroyed. Nobody knows precisely how many lives were lost, but conservative estimates place the number at 6,000. Eight thousand people were homeless, many of them destitute. The property loss was $20,000,000. Most extreme example of what had happened to vessels in the harbor is that of a 4,000-ton British steamship which had been torn from its moorings, carried over Pelican Spit and Pelican Island, and ultimately stranded on a 30-foot bank in Chambers County, 22 miles from deep water.

As soon as the city leaders could get together, the day after the storm, they organized a relief committee, and a department of safety which functioned until martial law could be established. All able-bodied survivors were impressed for the task of finding and caring for the injured, and cleaning up the city. Burial of the dead was impossible, and bodies, many of them crushed beyond all possibility of identification, were piled on barges, towed far out into the Gulf and committed to the sea. The tides of the following day brought most of them back, strewing them along the beach, whereupon huge pyres were built and the corpses were burned.

For a few days Galveston had to be sufficient to itself. Famine and a water shortage threatened. Efficiently the city lived up to its motto, *Yo Solo* (I Alone) which it took from the escutcheon of the Count of Galvez. Then aid came—money, supplies, the Red Cross with Clara Barton herself in charge, 30,000 laborers supplied by the State, credit. Rehabilitation began.

It soon became evident that the city's problems could not be solved under its charter, or under the existing charter of any other American municipality. Out of numerous conferences grew a new form of city government, which, with greater or less modification, has since been adopted by many other American cities as the Galveston plan, more recently called the commission plan.

That there might never be a recurrence of such a disaster, two vast engineering projects were undertaken—the sea wall and grade-raising. The bulwark that has been reared against waves is 53,100 feet or 10 miles long, 16 feet wide at its base and five at its top, which is 17 feet above mean low tide. It is built of reinforced concrete, and as a further protection a 27-foot-wide breakwater was constructed of huge granite blocks. The level of the city was raised as high as the sea wall on the Gulf side, sloping from there to the natural level at the bay. Thousands of acres were elevated at least eight feet, and in large sections 12 to 15 feet. Canals and ditches were laid out, all structures that could be raised in the areas progressively filled in were placed on stilts, and dredges drew soggy sand from the floor of Bolivar Roads, to be pumped beneath the houses as a new foundation. For years, while the channel was being deepened and its bed transferred to the city, large sections of "roost" houses stood high in the air, connected by sidewalks raised on trestles.

The efficiency of the sea wall's protection—although its length was then much less than now—was put to a severe test on August 15, 1915, when another hurricane struck the island. Great waves beat upon that part of the wall which had been finished and sent spray flying 50 feet into the air. So fierce was the storm that the three-masted schooner *Allison Doura,* loaded with sisal, was swept shoreward from a hundred miles out in the Gulf and thrown over the sea wall and into Fort Crockett, where soldiers rescued the crew. But the barrier held. Only eight lives were lost

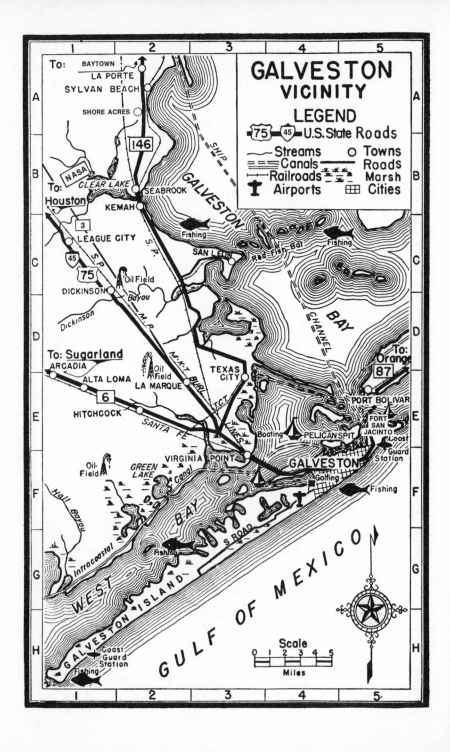

in the city, although on the mainland coast the mortality was close to a hundred. The greatest property damage resulted from partial destruction of the causeway. Two interurban cars, loaded with passengers from Houston, were stranded in the middle of the causeway when power lines were blown down. Marooned a few feet above the frothing water for hours, the passengers emerged when the storm subsided, to find that they had occupied the only part of the structure not washed away.

Educational facilities in Galveston have been greatly expanded since World War II. The Medical Center of the University of Texas is described elsewhere. TEXAS A. AND M. UNIVERSITY dedicated its oceanographic research vessel, the *Alaminos,* which had cost $3,500,000, and made Galveston its permanent anchorage in connection with the University's Marine Laboratory. The TEXAS MARITIME ACADEMY began its courses for the merchant marine at Fort Crockett. The Texas State Board of Education approved establishment of the GALVESTON JUNIOR COLLEGE. New academy and chapel buildings have been constructed by URSULINE ACADEMY at a cost of $900,000. The city invested millions in new high schools.

Galveston has four auditoriums with a seating capacity of 6,000. Its facilities were increased when the Moody Foundation gave $3,500,000 for the MOODY CIVIC CENTER, which has an auditorium with 3,500 seats, conference rooms and an exhibit hall.

Much attention has been given in recent years to provisions for recreation. The SEA-ARAMA on the West Beach presents an oceanarium, an aquarium and an amphitheater for marine exhibitions. Fishing and boating are popular activities and a number of fishing piers are lighted evenings. Large crowds of sportsmen come to Galveston Island for fishing at camps and resorts, and for deepsea fishing. It is reported that 51 varieties of edible fish can be found in these waters, including speckled trout, flounder, red fish, sheephead, drum, mackerel, tarpon, king, bonito, amber jack and red snapper.

POINTS OF INTEREST

The MOSQUITO FLEET, Pier 20, foot of 20th St., is made up of about 150 boats, some motored, others sailboats with auxiliary power, whose owners shrimp or fish around the island and far south. They leave the harbor between midnight and dawn and return toward sunset, accompanied by flocks of sea gulls, eager for shrimpheads. When shrimp are scarce the men of the fleet, numbering about a thousand, engage in commercial fishing, and in the trading of farm produce. The name Mosquito Fleet dates from early years, and is supposed to have come from a fancied resemblance, as the little sailboats of those days went out, the craft being small and swarming together.

The former Galveston *News-Tribune* plant, located at 2108 Mechanic St. from 1884 to 1965, has been superseded by the new PUBLISHING CENTER in West Galveston, a modernistic million-dollar structure erected in 1965 by the Galveston County Publishing Co. It houses the *Galveston News,* which is issued daily, afternoon and Sunday, and the *Daily Sun.* The *News* was established in 1842 and had a number of enterprising owners before it was bought by W. L. Moody, Jr., in 1923. It was the first Texan newspaper to have a regular telegraphic news service and it was a charter member of the Associated Press. In 1926 Moody combined it with the *Galveston Tribune.* In March, 1963, several years after Moody's death, the two papers were sold to a new corporate body, the Galveston County Publishing Co., of which W. P. Hobby, Jr., president of the *Houston Post,* is president and Mrs. Oveta Culp Hobby, editor of the *Houston Post,* is chairman of the board. In 1963 the *Texas City Sun* became the *Daily Sun,* serving Texas City, La Marque, Hitchcock (5,216 pop.) and the mainland of Galveston County. In March, 1965, the *Tribune* was absorbed by the *News.* In 1966 a third daily, *News-Sun TODAY,* was launched to serve the northern tip of the County, including League City (2,622 pop.) Dickinson (4,715 pop.) and other Bay communities. All three newspapers are produced at the Publishing Center.

ST. MARY'S CATHEDRAL, SE. corner of Church and Center Sts., is of early Gothic design. Two octagonal towers with pointed roofs rise high above the main structure. The stone walls are surfaced with plaster, marked off in blocks. Behind the crossing of the main nave and the transept rises the belfry tower, surmounted by a statue of "Mary, Star of the Sea," placed there after a hurricane of 1875. During the storm of 1900 residents looked anxiously toward the swaying tower, for it had become legendary that as long as the "Star of the Sea" remained aloft the island would not be destroyed. Although the two-ton bell was torn from beneath it, the marble statue weathered the storm.

Erected in 1848 as the cathedral for the Roman Catholic Diocese of Texas, St. Mary's is the oldest church building in Galveston. The Right Reverend John Murray Odin, first Bishop of Texas, directed its construction. A marble obelisk in front of the building bears the names of priests who died of yellow fever while ministering to victims during the epidemic of 1853.

TRINITY EPISCOPAL CHURCH (*open 8–8:30 daily*), SW. corner 22d and Winnie Sts., of medieval Gothic type, is a structure of unusual dignity and architectural grace. The ivy-covered, red brick walls create an atmosphere of age. A square tower with a crenelated parapet and octagonal buttresses on each corner forms the main entrance. Large stained glass windows of Gothic type are set between the buttresses. A cloister extends from the main building across the landscaped lawn to the parish house. The ten-bell bronze chimes, a memorial to John Sealy, can be played in three keys. Stowe and Stowe designed the building, which was completed in 1857.

The ROSENBERG LIBRARY (*Open 9–9, Monday through Thursday; 9–6 Friday and Saturday; closed Sundays*), 828 Tremont St., was opened in 1904. Henry Rosenberg, Galveston merchant and banker, bequeathed a fund of $620,529 for a Galveston free public library. Of this, $200,000 was spent for the site and building, leaving an ample endowment. The two-story structure, of late Italian Renaissance design, is faced in buff-colored brick, with terra cotta trim. The hip roof of green tile has a flat deck, around which is a copper cresting.

The Library contains about 129,000 volumes and approx. 198,400 manuscript items dating from 1655 on, including some bearing the signatures of Washington, Lafayette, Lincoln, Austin, Houston, Andrew Jackson, Grant, Jefferson Davis, Lafitte, Napoleon and Santa Anna. During a typical year, 1966, Rosenberg and its branches, the Dickinson, Friendswood and La Marque Public Libraries and the bookmobile serving Galveston County, loaned 284,479 books. It has a large collection of periodicals, films, records and microfilms.

The BISHOP'S PALACE of the Roman Catholic Church, nw. corner of Broadway and 14th St., an architectural landmark, has been owned by the Church since 1923 and is occupied by the Coadjutor Bishop when in Galveston.

The house was built in 1885–1892 by Col. Walter Gresham, prominent Galveston lawyer, Congressman and Civil War veteran. Nicholas J. Clayton was the architect. An ornate pile of stone designed along Romanesque lines, but with many Victorian details, the structure of three stories and a basement has a steep-pitched tile roof, above which rise high ornamental chimneys and minarets. Wings project to the east and west and the roof has dormers on all sides. In front of the main entrance and around the circular corner bay is a very delicate wrought iron grille. Ornamental wrought iron balconies project from the third story. The main walls are of rough limestone with pink and gray-blue granite introduced in panels and bands. The basement has been remodeled to serve as headquarters of the Newman Club of the University of Texas Medical Branch.

The tapestries, paintings and rich furnishings of the Gresham regime are gone, but remaining are the fine woodwork of hand-carved white mahogany from the Caroline Islands, red mahogany from Mexico, oak from Texas, satinwood from the West Indies, pine from Louisiana, cherry and walnut from northern States, the columns, fireplaces, and mantels of African and Italian marble and Mexican onyx, and the great, curving stairway. (*Adults, $1; children, 50¢*).

The SACRED HEART CHURCH, NE. corner 14th St. and Broadway, designed by Brother Otten, member of the Jesuit Order, and completed in 1904, is a two-story building of white monolithic concrete, with Moorish and Byzantine influences predominating. On the two front corners of the church proper are three-story octagonal towers, with a fleur-de-lis cresting of stone. Round columns support the Moorish arches of the porch. An ornamental Byzantine dome is surmounted by a stone statue of Christ.

EL MINA SHRINE TEMPLE (*open 9–5 except Sun., 9–3*), 2328 Broadway, was constructed in 1859 by Captain J. M. Brown, and is also called the Brown Home and Ashton Villa. It is occupied by El Mina Temple. Order of the Mystic Shrine. The main structure is a Louisiana-French Renaissance mansion of ante bellum days, three stories in height and faced in red brick, with white stone lintels and sills. The front facade has a two-story, ornamental iron porch reminiscent of the old French Quarter in New Orleans. All windows have full-length shutters. Brick for the house was brought by schooner from Philadelphia.

Left of the entrance hall is the gold room, or old parlor, scene during Captain Brown's ownership of many brilliant social gatherings. The walls and ceiling, decorated in white and gold, with cornices of an ornamental leaf beautifully carved in plaster, are exactly as when first completed by a Parisian artificer. The graceful old staircase has a mahogany newel post and handrails and a white painted banister.

The house was used as a hospital through yellow fever epidemics and during the Battle of Galveston. Here Major General Gordon Granger accepted the surrender of Galveston in 1865.

The TEXAS HEROES MONUMENT, Broadway and Rosenberg Ave., a memorial to heroes of the Texas Revolution, was the gift of Henry Rosenberg, Galveston citizen and philanthropist. An impressive bronze figure of Victory, sword in left hand and olive wreath in right, towers high on a marble pedestal. At the base sculptured bronze figures and bas-relief bronze entablatures depict outstanding events of the Revolution. The statue was unveiled on April 21, 1900, the sixty-fourth anniversary of the Battle of San Jacinto. The sculptor was Louis Amateis.

URSULINE CONVENT (*open 3–5 schooldays*), Ave. N between Rosenberg Ave. and 27th St., has served as school, hospital and refuge for nearly a century. The first building, now the convent proper, was erected in 1854, and the east wing was added in 1861. The central unit, completed in 1892, was designed by Nicholas J. Clayton. It presents a blending of Gothic, Romanesque, and Moorish lines and color treatment. The walls are faced in red brick with white and gray limestone trim, varied with bands of alternating red and white. Two flat-topped, octagonal towers rise a story higher than the main body of the structure. The walls of the three-story east wing are smooth, cream-colored plaster on masonry, pierced by numerous green-shuttered windows. Between this wing and the main building is wedged a small chapel built in 1871, with plain Gothic lines that contrast with the ornate main unit. The main entrance, on the west, rises three stories in a series of arched openings and tall Gothic windows.

The convent was established in 1847 by Bishop J. M. Odin, aided by six nuns from New Orleans. Within a decade after its founding it housed a flourishing day and boarding school, and later at times served as a hospital through yellow fever epidemics. During the Battle of Galveston the Ursulines refused General Magruder's offer of transportation to a safety zone and maintained in the convent a hospital for the wounded of both armies. Young Lieutenant Sidney A. Sherman, son of General Sidney Sherman, died here.

Federal forces, mistaking the convent for a Confederate stronghold, concentrated their fire on it. General Magruder sent word to the Sisters to hoist a yellow flag, the signal for quarantine. Shells fell closer as the gunners on the ships improved their range, while the Sisters hunted frantically for yellow cloth. Local tradition says that one of them found a wide yellow skirt in a student's trunk, that a soldier climbed to the belfry and waved it aloft, and the bombardment stopped immediately. For years afterward the Sisters picked up spent bombs on the grounds and used them for flatiron stands, until one exploded and shattered a wall of the laundry.

For years delegates representing Confederate veterans and the Grand Army of the Republic assembled here to decorate the grave of Mother St. Pierre Harrington, superior of the convent during the Civil War. Her name and those of five Sisters of the Galveston Ursulines are inscribed upon the Nuns of the Battlefield Monument in Washington, D. C.

The MENARD HOUSE (*private*), is on the sw. corner of Ave. N½ and 33d St. Michel B. Menard, of French descent, came to Texas as a fur trader, prospered in land deals, and organized the Galveston City Company. In 1838 he had white pine and four fluted Ionic columns shipped to him from Maine in sailing vessels, built a two-story house of Greek Revival design, and named it The Oaks. The mortised walls and joists set in white lead have withstood the weathering of more than a century. The ells and the two rooms at the back were added at a later date, and the interior has been remodeled. Civic groups bought the house in 1937, to preserve it as a memorial to the city's founder.

MENARD PARK, Seawall Blvd. at 27th St., has a well equipped Youth Center as well as rooms for games, dancing, reading. A Sightseeing Train with places for 64 departs four times daily on a 15-mile tour, May 1 through Labor Day, and twice daily Labor Day to May 1, except for December 15 to January 15, when it rests.

The WILLIAMS-TUCKER HOUSE, at southwest corner 36th St. and Ave. P, was built about 1838. It is a one-story structure of northern white pine, with hand-hewn pine sills. The brick kitchen remains almost unchanged since the days when the crane and the pothooks in the large fireplace were in use, and bread was baked in the built-in bricken oven by slaves. Maintained by Galveston Historical Foundation.

Samuel May Williams came to Texas in 1824, and soon after was appointed secretary of the Austin colony. In partnership with Thomas F. McKinney he became a successful merchant in Quintana, and he and McKinney were members of the first Galveston City Company. He established here the first chartered bank in Texas, in 1835; and in 1839 he arranged for the sending of a ship from Liverpool to receive the first direct European export shipment to leave Galveston.

FORT CROCKETT (*not open*), adjoins Seawall Blvd., between 39th and 53d Sts., a Coast Artillery post occupying 125 acres, was completed in 1899 and named for David Crockett. The buildings are of modified Spanish type, most of them yellow, with red roofs. Parades can be seen from the sea wall, and directly opposite the parade grounds are seacoast batteries with modern heavy artillery.

During the Mexican border troubles of 1912 this fort was used as a mobilization center, and General Frederick Funston's 5th Brigade was stationed here until it sailed to Vera Cruz.

Fort Crockett in 1962 became the temporary home of the TEXAS

MARITIME ACADEMY, pending development of a permanent campus. The Moody Foundation gave the Academy $1,000,000.

MEDICAL CENTER of the University of Texas Medical Branch, has doubled its facilities in the last decade. Established 1890–1891, the older buildings of stucco and brick follow a Spanish Renaissance design, with red tile roofs. The University here enrolls nearly 600 students and has 2,900 employees. Its hospital cares for 18,500 patients and 117,000 outpatients annually. It has a Nurses' School. The Moody Foundation gave $1,000,000 for a new MOODY MEMORIAL LIBRARY to replace the Branch library, which has 60,000 volumes. A $30,000,000 building program is under way, including a Basic Sciences Bldg., a Clinical Bldg., a 150-bed hospital and an animal facility. In the Medical center are the SEALY HOSPITAL, first unit built 1890; the Sealy & Smith Foundation financed a 10-story MEDICAL-PROFESSIONAL building in 1964. Here also are ST. MARY'S INFIRMARY, with a Nurses School; the CHILDRENS' BURN HOSPITAL of the Shrine of North America; the TEXAS STATE HOSPITAL FOR CRIPPLED AND DEFORMED CHILDREN; the U. S. PUBLIC HEALTH SERVICE HOSPITAL and a number of other medical facilities.

OFFATT'S BAYOU, paralleling Broadway, and reached by 61st St., a deep indentation of Galveston Bay, is a popular camp site, fishing resort, and motorboat racing course.

FORT SAN JACINTO (*not open*), E. end of Galveston Island, occupies a Government reservation of 419 acres adjoining the sea wall. Armaments are under the command of the Coast Defense.

Houston

Airlines: Air France, American Airlines, Braniff Airways, Continental Air Lines, Delta Air Lines, Eastern Air Lines, KLM, National Airlines, Pan American World Airways, Trans-Texas Airways. Also Slick Airways, freight. Houston International Airport; take the Gulf Freeway to junction with State 35. The airport is able to provide helicopter, rent-a-plane, rent-a-car and taxicab services. Beeling Airport is a small field in northwest Harris County across Green Road from the site of the new 7,000-acre Jetero, Houston Intercontinental Airport, which is designed to accommodate supersonic as well as conventional aircraft.
Bus Lines: Continental Trailways Bus Center, 1114 McKinney St., Bayshore Lines, Continental Trailways, Midwest Trailways, Texas Bus Lines. Greyhound Bus Terminal, Texas & LaBranche Sts., Bayshore Lines, Central Greyhound, Kerryville Bus, Midwest Trailways, Texas Bus Lines. Hourly service to all Texas points and beyond. Buses run once daily from the larger hotels to the Astrodome. Schedule information, CA 3-7171.
Highways: Houston is the radial center of numerous State and US roads covering all parts of East Texas. The direct route from Dallas and Fort Worth is US 75 and Interstate 45; from San Antonio Interstate 10; from Austin US 290; from Corpus Christi, State 35 or US 77 plus US 59. In describing current construction of a vast freeway system of 245.5 miles, costing $500,000,000, the Houston Chamber of Commerce says the completed system will form an inner and outer loop of freeways from the heart of the city to all parts of Harris County and beyond. Two of these highways, US 75 (Interstate 45) and US 90 (Interstate 10) plus the north, south, east and west loops (Interstate 610) have been designated parts of the US Interstate and Defense Highway System. Other freeways included in the master plan: US 59 (north) to Northeast Texas; US 290 to Northwest Texas; US 59 (south) to Southwest Texas; State 288 to the Gulf Coast, and State 225 to the Galveston Bay area.
Railroads: Missouri-Kansas-Texas Depot, 1811 Ruiz St. Southern Pacific Depot, 431 Franklin St. Union Station, 501 Crawford St., for Burlington, Fort Worth & Denver, Missouri Pacific, Rock Island and Santa Fe. Sixteen passenger trains daily.

Information and Communications: Houston Chamber of Commerce (Chartered 1840 by the Republic of Texas) C. of C. Bldg. *Houston Chronicle,* evening and Sunday, 512-20 Travis St. *Houston Post,* morning and Sunday, 2410 Polk Ave. Greater Houston Convention & Visitors Council, 1006 Main St. Also 14 radio stations, 4 television stations, major networks and independents. Houston has many hotels and motels of the first rank, including the nationally known Shamrock Hilton, S. Main St. at Holcombe Blvd.; Sheraton-Lincoln, 777 Polk St., between Milam and Louisiana; Rice, Main St. and Texas Ave.; Lamar, Lamar at Main and Travis Sts., Ben Milam, at Texas and Crawford Sts.; The Towers, S. Main St. and Holcombe Blvd.; Hotel America, South St. at Jefferson.

Parks and Recreational Areas: Houston has 169 municipal parks and playgrounds that serve all sections of the city; 4 municipal golf courses, 41 municipally operated swimming pools; 145 softball and boys' baseball fields; 15 regulation baseball diamonds; 87 tennis courts; 43 community recreation buildings. Principal areas for golf, tennis, baseball, riding and picnics are in Hermann Park, Fannin St.; Memorial Park on Memorial Drive; Alexander Deussen Park at Lake Houston; San Jacinto State Park, off LaPorte Road (State 225) 3 *m.*

east of Pasadena; Sylvan Beach Park off State 146 at La Porte on Galveston
Bay; Clear Lake Park, at Clear Lake.

Sightseeing Tours: Port of Houston. The Port is open for motor car drives Sundays, 8–6. Cruise along Ship Channel on the inspection yacht, Sam Houston, two
2-hour trips daily except Monday, at 10 a.m. and 2 p.m. Make reservations by
calling CA 5–0671. NASA Manned Spacecraft Center. 2 a.m. on Gulf Freeway
and NASA road; open every Sunday, 1–5, free. Special arrangements required
for weekday visits; call HU 3–3366. A list of industrial tours may be obtained
through the Greater Houston Convention & Visitors Council, 1006 main, CA
4–5201.

Annual Events: Livestock Exposition, Fat Stock Show & Rodeo, February.
Azalea Trail and Pilgrimage, River Oaks, usually early April. River Oaks
Tennis Tournament, April. Houston Classic Invitational Golf Tournament,
April; Baseball season opens, Astrodome, April; Bluebonnet Trail, April;
Frontier Fiesta, University of Houston, April; International Flower & Garden
Show, April; Pin Oaks Stables Horse Show, June; International Trade & Travel
Fair, September; American Football League season opens, September; Texas
Prison Rodeo, Huntsville, October; Hunting season opens, deer, October-Decem-
ber; geese, October-January. Major college football by teams playing Rice and
Houston at Rice Stadium, Saturdays, during fall. A list of events and exhibitions
is published monthly by the Greater Houston Convention & Visitors Council.

HOUSTON (41–53 alt.) is the largest city in Texas, a tidewater port
50 *m.* inland, connected with the Gulf of Mexico by the Houston Ship
Channel, and handling the third largest ocean tonnage in the United
States. It is the hub of the vast aggregation of oil and natural gas refineries and petrochemical plants located along the Gulf Coast, a distributing
center for oilfield equipment and farm products, and closely associated
with the Manned Spacecraft Center which plans the voyage to the moon.
So continuous is its expansion in all fields of manufacturing, trade and
investment, that statistics are merely milestones that have been passed.
Thus Houston, which had 506,163 people according to the U. S. Census
of 1950, raced to 938,319 by 1960. The relation of births to deaths is
more than 3 to 1. In common with other industrial cities Houston has had
an influx of Negroes displaced by mechanization on farms; they constitute
about 19.6 per cent of the population. A number of incorporated cities are
practically surrounded by Houston; thus BELLAIRE, on Interstate 610
and crossed by Bissonet Road, calling itself the "Biggest City in Houston," incorporated in 1918, has approximately 21,000 people, while
WEST UNIVERSITY PLACE, adjoining Bellaire, and only a few
blocks from Rice University, has more than 14,000 residents. Almost an
enclave inside West University Place is South Side Place, with about
1,400. These and other Harris County towns, such as Piney Point Village
(2,000 pop.), South Houston (7,000 pop.) and Bunker Hill (2,500
pop.), contribute to the population of the metropolitan area of Houston,
including Harris, Brazoria, Fort Bend, Liberty and Montgomery Counties, which the Census Bureau in July, 1965, said contained approximately
1,695,000. This indicated that Houston, covering 359.7 sq. mi., was well
over the 1,000,000 mark.

Practically all of the United States accepts the report that Houston has the highest wealth per capita in the world, and one observer has expressed the conviction that Houston is the one place where a man possessing only $4 or $5 million is not considered wealthy. In 1965 the 79 Harris County banks had resources of $4 billion; more than 600,000 persons were employed in the County and the total of wages and salaries reached $3.3 billion. Out of 751,509 motor cars registered, 588,311 were passenger cars, and in a typical year 2,000,000 air travelers used the International Airport, a fair proportion in executive planes. Only the weather did not follow the Houston trend of upward and onward; it remained fairly neutral with a normal daily maximum-minimum of 64°–46° in winter, 91°–75° in summer; 80°–60° in spring and fall, with precipitation around 36 inches, and "Polar air" providing what the U. S. Weather Bureau calls "stimulating variability" on occasion.

Rising above the flat terrain is the towering skyline that symbolizes the energy and enterprise of this financial and business capital. Tall office structures of glass and steel multiply in Houston's downtown area. Many are headquarters for oil companies that dominate Gulf Coast industries. Several have annual incomes of more than $1 billion—Gulf Oil Co., Texaco, Inc., and Shell Oil Co. Shell in 1968 was constructing the city's tallest office building, One Shell Plaza, rising 50 stories and 700 ft. Other tall structures are the Humble Oil Bldg. 44 stories, 606 ft., which houses a veritable millionaires' club, the Petroleum Club, in its top story; Tennessee Bldg. 497 ft., home of Tenneco, Inc., gas transmission corporation and of Anderson, Clayton & Co., cotton brokers; Gulf Bldg., 428 ft.; First City National Bank, 410 ft.; Bank of the Southwest, 369 ft.; Sheraton-Lincoln Hotel, 352 ft.; Southwest Tower, 310 ft., home of Pennzoil and Zapata Off Shore Co., and numerous other buildings in the 300-ft. range.

But when the men and women who occupy desks in these buildings go home, they head for detached, one-story cottages on miles of suburban streets that only a few years ago were grassbound prairie.

The industrial frontage along the Houston Ship Channel occupies 23.6 sq. m. and is 2,500 ft. deep. The Turning Basin at the head of the Channel is churned up continuously by steamships and tugs. Property on both sides of the Buffalo Bayou pays state, county and school taxes, but is exempt from any city tax.

Office buildings and refineries can be seen in many other parts of Texas, but Houston alone has the ASTRODOME, an innovation in the architecture of sports arenas. It is as exceptional in its own way as are the Taj Mahal and the Washington Monument in theirs. This is the central structure of the Harris County Sports Stadium complex. Located between Kirby and Fannin Drives north of the South Loop Freeway, it has a diameter of 710 ft., a roof with a clear span of 642 ft., is 25 ft. below normal ground level and 208 ft. tall above the playing field. It seats 45,000 for baseball, 52,000 for football, 60,000 for conventions, and is completely airconditioned. The steel skeleton supports a roof containing 4,596 skylights made of transparent plastic. An extraordinary feature of the stadium is the scoreboard, which is adaptable to all spectator sports. It is 474 ft. long, four stories high and gives a great amount of detailed information. Other facilities in the Stadium area are planned to provide accommodations for conventions, conferences, exhibits and dining, together with an extensive parking area for 30,000 cars.

The Astrodome was opened April 1, 1965. It was built with the support of Houston citizens, a County bond issue for $31,000,000, and $6,000,000 raised by the Houston Sports Assn. The driving force was Roy Hofheinz, one-time mayor of Houston and former judge of the Harris County Court. Hofheinz controls the Houston Sports Assn., which controls the Astrodome and the Houston Baseball Team of the National League. Many innovations reflect the enthusiastic showmanship of Hofheinz who, a few years ago, realized a boyish ambition by acquiring a one-third interest in Ringling Bros.-Barnum & Bailey Circus. (For example, luxurious boxes, with equipment for partying, occupy the upper tier, six stories above the playing field, and rent for $15,000 a year.) The Astrodome stands in the center of 406 acres, 116 of which hold the Astroworld, a Disney-type amusement area opened by Hofheinz in June, 1968; 12 acres are used by the Astrohall, an exhibition center. The Colt Stadium, seating 32,000, is at present unused. Motor hotels, built or building at a cost of $16,000,000, account for 1,500 rooms. In 1967 1,333,762 spectators attended baseball at the Astrodome. Its gross income is around $15,000,000. The football clubs return 16 percent of the gross to the Sports Assn. Among those appearing here are the University of Houston Football Team, the Houston Oilers of the American Football League, the annual Livestock Show and Rodeo, the Indoor Motorcycle and Polo Championship contests, the Ringling Circus, and numerous basketball, soccer and similar sports.

The distinction Houston has achieved in its industry, banking, and civic projects applies also to its public schools. The Independent School District, which extends its control to some of the incorporated suburbs, administers 224 schools, 35 of them junior high, and 21 senior high, and with an enrollment of 240,797 in 1967 operated on a budget of $150,-958,638. Its Board of Education of seven members, elected by popular vote for four-year terms, has been constructing new facilities as part of a $53,000,000 program. Since Houston has no sub-standard schools the interference of outsiders has had little effect, and although the Board has placed a number of white teachers in Negro schools and Negro teachers in white schools, it has so far (1968) had no occasion to institute busing pupils from one area to another.

HISTORY

No visitor can fully appreciate Houston without a knowledge of its early days. Its story is a drama of handicaps overcome; of opportunities accepted. Its skyline becomes doubly impressive when superimposed upon a mental picture of the city's earliest years. A flamboyant real estate promotion of 1836 has become the Texas metropolis.

The promoters were the Allen brothers, John K. and Augustus C., who came to Texas from New York. Thirteen years before the Allens' venture took form, the town of Harrisburg, now within the southeastern corporate limits of Houston, was founded as a trading post by John Richardson Harris, a native of the State of New York, who arrived in Texas in 1823 as one of Stephen F. Austin's colonists.

Harris sought a location on a waterway readily accessible to both land and ocean traffic, and in July, 1824, obtained title to a tract at the confluence of Buffalo and Bray's Bayous, then the head of navigation.

Within two years the settlement became a lively maritime trading post. When John Harris' three brothers joined him, the combined Harris interests built up a small fleet, and Buffalo Bayou for the first time saw regular navigation. Harrisburg became a timber town, shipping its lumber to New Orleans and Mexican ports. In 1829, John Harris sailed for New Orleans to purchase supplies and machinery for his sawmill, and while there died of yellow fever. His heirs became involved in litigation over his estate.

Augustus C. and John K. Allen reached Nacogdoches from New York in 1832 and speculated in real estate. Augustus, who was not robust, sought a milder climate and invested heavily in land at Galveston and elsewhere along the coast. During a long legal contest over the Harris estate he and his brother banked their pirogue (a hollowed log boat) at Harrisburg and made the Harris heirs a proposal to purchase their town. The price, however, was too high, and there was little indication that the Mexican government would settle the legal dispute over the property at any time in the near future.

In March, 1836, President ad interim Burnet and his cabinet hastily transferred the seat of government from Washington on the Brazos to Harrisburg, considered at that time the safest refuge from Santa Anna's approaching Mexican forces. The executives were received in the Harris home, where they conducted the business of the newborn republic, keeping an eye on the advancing Santa Anna. Gail Borden's newspaper, the *Telegraph and Texas Register,* official government organ, followed the officials to Harrisburg and there resumed publication.

The Mexican dictator, hoping to capture the provisional officers, arrived on the night of April 14, 1836. His entry was lighted by the glare of burning buildings as the town was evacuated by the citizens, some of them putting the torch to their own homes to deprive the Mexicans of that pleasure. The Mexicans, enraged at finding their quarry gone, completed the destruction. They found only three men, printers, in the Borden shop. These they arrested but released the next day. The newspaper plant was completely destroyed.

Only 22 miles beyond, at the junction of Buffalo Bayou and the San Jacinto River, General Sam Houston defeated the Mexicans on April 21, 1836, and freed Texas from further depredations. The Allens decided to find a new site for a town. A. C. Allen paddled up the bayou in his pirogue, sounding the depth frequently, until he arrived at what seemed to be the highest point of navigation for medium-draft boats. This spot was near a rich farming area, already in the process of settlement. Disembarking, he sat on a grass-covered bank, and, tradition says, using his hat for a table, sketched a plan of his proposed city on a scrap of paper. This he sent to his brother, a member of the Texas Congress at Columbia, who displayed it in the capitol.

The land, granted first to John Austin, was acquired after much legal maneuvering, and on August 24, 1836, the Allens bought the upper league from William T. Austin, son of John Austin, for $1 an acre, one-half in cash and the balance secured by a promissory note. Two days later, at the Brazoria home of Dr. T. F. L. Parrott, who had married the widow of John Austin, they purchased the south half of the lower league for $5,000. The lower league was the site of the early town. The modern city completely covers both leagues.

This wild and desolate stretch of prairie might have caused less experienced promoters than the Allens some hesitation. There were two perennial problems, mud and mosquitoes. Indians roamed the woods; alligators infested the bayous; yellow fever was an ever-impending menace. But the Allens platted a town, named it after Sam Houston, and on August 30, 1836, placed the town site on the market. In May, 1966, nearly 130 years later, the Allens were commemorated at the spot at Buffalo Bayou, where they had landed, which became Allen's Landing Park.

A pretentious map, made by Gail and Thomas H. Borden, was displayed in the Senate Chamber at Columbia, showing a square set aside for a capitol and congressional building.

The mapped town site embraced 62 blocks, and to put settlers on them the Allens turned to high-pressure publicity. Advertisements lauding Houston to the skies appeared in newspapers throughout the United States. As a result, frontiersmen, ever pressing west, came overland by horseback or oxcart from the Blue Ridge and Great Smokies and from the rolling hills of the Ozarks; others came from down the Mississippi, and from the big cities of the North and East. Families trekked in from Brazoria, Columbia, and other settlements in Texas. Land speculators, banking on the acumen of the Allens, hastened to the valiant little upstart metropolis, paddling up the root-tangled bayou in flatboats.

Despite the publicity campaign and the steady immigration of pioneers, the "Town of Houston" was still so insignificant in January, 1837, that the skipper of the stern-wheel steamboat *Laura M.* went three miles past the stakes marking the trail from river to town, and had to back up. It had taken him three days to navigate the 16 miles between Harrisburg and Houston, hacking his way through overhanging vegetation, yet the only mishap on the journey was the loss of the ship's cook, who went overboard at a sudden lurch.

The *Laura M.* cleared Buffalo Bayou, between Harrisburg and Houston, of all impediments save shoals, and now larger vessels ventured to navigate the waterway. The schooner *Rolla* arrived with a cargo for the Allen brothers in April, and presently two sister sidewheelers, the *Diana* and the *T. M. Bagby,* went into regular service. They were described as palatial, with a 32-foot beam and a length of 170 feet each, and were luxuriously furnished.

A month before the government moved into its new capitol, in May,

1837, the Allens completed the capitol, a one-story pine structure extending from Prairie Avenue nearly to Texas Avenue on the west side of Main Street. In one wing was the Senate Chamber, in the other, Congressional Hall. The administrative offices occupied the center. Later Thomas W. Ward was awarded a contract by the Allens for the construction of a two-story structure, built of Maine lumber, to occupy two and one-half lots on the northwest corner of Main Street and Texas Avenue. This building was leased by the Allens to the Republic of Texas at an annual rental of $5,000. Chairs for the lawmakers were not ordered until after sessions had begun.

In 1837 Houston, then the seat of county and national government, boasted a population of about 1,200 people, with political officials and their families in the majority. On June 5 of that year it was incorporated.

Gail Borden and his brother had followed the government to Houston, and set up the equipment for the town's first newspaper on May 2. It was sold in a short time to Jacob Cruger and Dr. Francis Moore. On April 8, 1839, the *Morning Star* came into existence. Quite early in its life this newspaper made the first suggestion for the systematic improvement of the ship channel. Complaining of the shoals of Clopper's Bar (now off Morgan's Point), the *Star* advised: "If boats will keep buoys along the lines of the channel over this bar, boats always passing will rub the channel deep enough."

With its fast-growing importance as the capital of the young Republic, Houston felt that its new dignity warranted a municipal government, and a gesture in that direction was undertaken. A volunteer group, called the Protection Fire Company No. 1, functioned on the "bring-your-own-bucket" system until the city acquired its first fire apparatus. This object of civic pride was a whisky barrel mounted on a gig, and it is said that a mild epidemic of pyromania resulted from curiosity to see the fire "engine" operate. The town was a yearling before any semblance of a court of justice was set up. Disputed land titles caused most of the trials of those days, with homicide cases running a close second.

A tale which paints a striking picture of the place and period deals with the first theatrical performance, in June, 1838, when a traveling company presented Sheridan Knowles' *The Hunchback,* resulting in a threatened battle between armed gamblers and infantry. A play of light nature, *The Dumb Belle, or I'm Perfection,* accompanied *The Hunchback.* Local tradition says that President Houston and party, who had been attending a dinner, were late in reaching the theater, and that meantime the town's gamblers had occupied the seats reserved for the guests and ignored an appeal from the stage to vacate them, whereupon the sheriff came with some soldiers whom he lined up against a wall. The gamblers promptly lined up opposite them. Sam Houston, arriving before the showdown, issued an executive order for the soldiers to stack their arms. The gamblers passed out of the door, stopping long enough to get their money back, and the actors performed to a quiet house.

In 1839 President Lamar caused the effects of the Republic of Texas to be transferred to the new capitol at Austin. Public indignation flared over

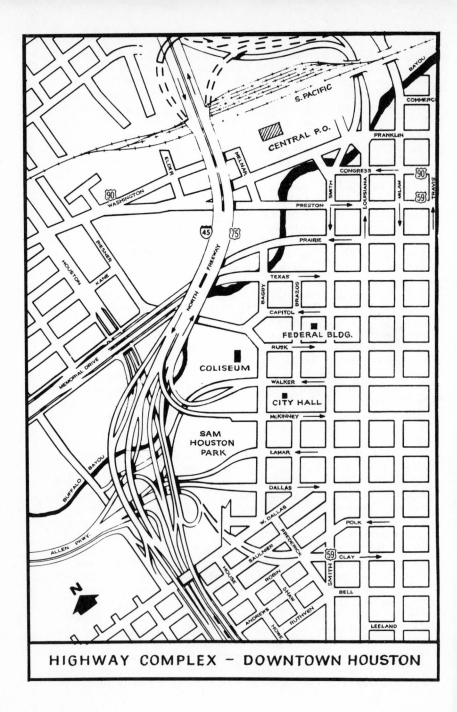

HIGHWAY COMPLEX – DOWNTOWN HOUSTON

the loss of the capital, except with the group most interested in the town's commercial development. Houston had known three years of turbulent government administration, exercised on a highly personal basis when statesmen brawled with each other outrageously, often without cause, and partisanship flamed high. The removal of the capital thus permitted the town's promoters to center attention upon business.

Farmers, cultivating their rich acres in the prairie area flanking the town, looked to Houston for an outlet for their cotton, and that commodity began to come down the bayou on barges and flatboats, the loads picked up at deep water by seagoing vessels. The first local dock was constructed in 1840. A city ordinance in 1841 established the Port of Houston.

In July, 1840, the *Telegraph and Texas Register* reported that "appropriate ceremonies . . . commemorated the commencement" of the first projected railroad in Texas, which was to have been the Harrisburg and Brazos, an unchartered road promoted by Andrew Briscoe, of Harrisburg. After completing two miles of roadbed, Briscoe encountered financial difficulty and was forced to abandon the project. The Fifth Congress of the Republic of Texas granted a charter to the Harrisburg Railroad and Trading Company, but again the project was abandoned by its promoters.

Rich trade and agricultural production were developing in the back country along the bottom lands of the Brazos. Many hundreds of wagons, each requiring an average of 14 oxen, were engaged in transporting raw products to Houston and hauling merchandise back to the interior.

A survey was made of Buffalo Bayou as far as Harrisburg, in 1846, and Houstonians, unwilling for improvement of the channel to stop 16 miles below their shallow-water port, began to besiege the legislature, then sitting in Austin.

In 1847 General Sidney Sherman bought the properties of the abandoned Harrisburg Railroad and Trading Company. By 1850 he had a charter for the Buffalo Bayou, Brazos and Colorado Railroad—its tidewater terminal to be Harrisburg, not Houston—and had northern capital backing the project. In 1853 the road was completed from Harrisburg to Stafford's Point, 20 miles southwestward, and great was the exultation when the *General Sherman,* a 12-ton locomotive, finished its initial run. The passenger coaches, second-hand streetcars from the East, had only four wheels, and the *General Sherman* could not always round curves without leaving the tracks, because both engine and tender were on the same frame, but the completion of the railroad was a decided victory for transportation—and for Harrisburg.

In 1850 Houston merchants formed the Houston Plank Road Company to grade a thoroughfare to some point on the Brazos River, thus making an all-weather route over which freighters and independent farmers could haul to Houston at all seasons. This idea was discarded when the Houston and Texas Central began grading at Houston in 1853. Official recognition of the importance of a deep water channel came in the same year, with an appropriation by the legislature of $4,000 for preliminary work on the Houston ship channel.

To connect Houston with the West, the Houston Tap and Brazoria Railroad was begun in 1856, joining the Buffalo Bayou, Brazos and Colorado at Pierce's Junction. With the establishment of the Houston Tap, the ambitious city's battle with Harrisburg was won, for the Tap diverted to Houston the commerce in sugar and cotton that previously had followed the Brazos line into Harrisburg. In 1858 the Houston and Texas Central reached Hempstead, and by then a line had been built by the Galveston, Houston and Henderson Railway which linked Houston with Galveston, 50 miles away.

Houston's natural handicaps, however, slowed its development for years. Drainage was poor and rainfall heavy. The city suffered floods and disastrous fires. In 1859 the downtown business district, bordered by Main, Travis, Congress, and Preston Streets, was wiped out by a conflagration originating in a carpenter shop. Two disastrous fires occurred in 1860, one destroying $350,000 worth of property. There were also serious recurrent epidemics.

The Civil War was almost ruinous to Texas railroads, but an exception was the Houston and Texas Central, which was preserved for military use. By 1868 the road had laid new rails, purchased new rolling stock, and discharged all obligations.

Impetus for port improvement and channel deepening and widening was under way. In 1869 the Buffalo Bayou Ship Channel Company was organized, pledged to widen the bayou and make it navigable for ships, a project for which citizens subscribed $100,000. Commodore Charles Morgan, founder of the Morgan Lines, and sometimes called "the father of the ship channel," in 1873 undertook private dredging at Redfish Reef, and deepened the channel off Morgan's Point. Other foresighted citizens saw the need of a deep water channel large enough to accommodate modern steamships, although it involved serious financial and engineering problems.

In 1900 civic leaders went to Congress and after determined efforts obtained approval for deepening the waterway to 18½ feet and for construction of a harbor within the city limits. This work was carried on from 1902 to 1905, but proved inadequate.

General cargo vessels found the new channel hazardous. Houston asked the Government to increase the depth to 25 ft. and to get going offered to pay half the cost. The Government agreed and the improvement was completed in 1914.

The Harris County Ship Channel Navigation District and the city completed the first public wharf in 1915, and regular Houston-New York service was established. Thereafter shipping zoomed. The Port of Houston became the greatest of the Gulf outlets. The Ship Channel became 300 ft. wide, 36 ft. deep. In the 1960 decade work began to make it 400 ft. wide and 40 ft. deep. By that time Houston had become the third largest U. S. post, moving 59,162,653 tons in 1964 alone. In that year the United States Government collected $29,300,000 in customs revenue, thus repaying the Federal investment every two years. More than 4,194 ships visit the Port annually. The Port has 25 public docks, 65 private docks, and 47 terminal docks for barges. The prosperity of the Port has led to the erection of the WORLD TRADE CENTER BUILDING, where many of the 35 foreign consuls in Houston have their offices.

In addition to oceanic cargoes, Houston profits from barge transportation on waterways linking Houston with inland waterways moving more than 22,000,000 net tons annually.

From the turning basin the Channel extends down Buffalo Bayou through Galveston Bay to Bolivar Road and the Gulf of Mexico. Lining the turning basin and the Channel is an extensive industrial area of oil refineries, cotton compresses and other industrial plants. A radial pipe line system brings crude oil from as far as the Wyoming field near Casper. There are numerous producing oil fields within miles of Houston, and every phase of the oil industry is represented in the city. Petroleum products comprise the largest proportion of exports from the port, cotton ranks second, and scrap iron, sulphur, lumber, rice, and other natural products play prominent parts.

A large part of the petrochemical industry of the United States is located in the Houston area. Over half of the country's synthetic rubber is produced here. Abundance of hydrocarbons, salt, sulphur, oyster shell for lime, are principal factors in the growth of the Gulf Coast chemical industry. A 1,000-mile network of pipelines carrying chemicals connects 65 major plants and six underground salt domes in southeast Texas. *See also articles on Beaumont and Port Arthur.*

POINTS OF INTEREST

The CIVIC CENTER of Houston is an area of about 150 acres in the busy downtown section where a number of spectacular buildings for cultural and exhibition purposes are rising amid the tall skyscrapers of the business community. The newest complex begins with the JESSE H. JONES HALL FOR THE PERFORMING ARTS at Louisiana St. and extends along Capitol St. to include the CONVENTION AND EXHIBITION CENTER, the SAM HOUSTON COLISEUM, and the MUSIC HALL, all connected by an underground concourse with an underground parking space for 2,000 vehicles.

The Jesse H. Jones Hall for the Performing Arts was opened for the Houston Arts Festival, Oct. 1–31, 1966, and became the home of the Houston Symphony and the Grand Opera Assn. During the season five operas are presented under the direction of Walter Herbert. The Hall stands on the site of the Houston Auditorium, where the great performing stars, from Caruso to Pavlova, appeared from 1913 on. It was built with funds given by Houston Endowment, Inc., the creation of Jesse H. Jones and his wife, Mary Gibbs Jones, and cost $7,500,000. It commemorates the career of Jones, (1874–1956) who led in cultural and business activities during his lifetime. A man 6 ft., 6 in. tall, he served the nation as director of Military Relief under President Wilson, of Reconstruction Finance Corp. under Hoover and as chairman of the RFC under Roosevelt. At the same time he was Federal Loan Administrator. A farm boy, he did manual labor until he found his place in lumber and construction. He "could peer out from his penthouse atop the Lamar Building and count 35 buildings he had added to the city's skyline."

The Hall seats from 1,800 to 3,000, is 120 ft. wide and 55 ft. deep, has an adjustable ceiling and a soundproof rehearsal hall. An attempt has been made by the sculptor Richard Lippold to catch the spirit of the Space Age by a composition, Gemini II, consisting of 2,300 hexagonal rods of stainless steel connected by "miles and miles" of goldplated wire.

The Convention and Exhibit Center, on Capitol St., has 300,000 sq. ft. of space divided into exhibit areas, meeting rooms, committee rooms, executive quarters and kitchens that can accomodate 3,000 diners.

In the same area, fronting on Bagby St., is the Sam Houston Coliseum, structurally connected with the Music Hall. There are 50,000 sq. ft. in the Coliseum and 158,000 sq. ft. in the Upper and Lower Annex, which can accomodate 500 motor cars when not used for exhibits. The Coliseum has 13,000 seats, 9,000 of them permanent. The arena is 91 by 217 ft., and there are conference and committee rooms. Professional Portuguese bullfights (not fatal to the bull) are held at intervals in the Coliseum.

The Music Hall seats 3,036. Before Jones Hall it sheltered the Houston Symphony Society, with an orchestra of 90 conducted by Sir John Barbirolli. The Symphony was founded more than 50 years ago and now has an annual budget of $700,000.

Houston has many other attractions for the musically-minded. Every summer Music Under the Stars is given in Hermann Park, with the aid of the Houston Chorale and the Houston Youth Symphony. Also active are the Bach Society, the All-City Symphony Orchestra, the Gilbert and Sullivan Society (presenting operas in July); the University of Houston Symphony Orchestra, the Texas Southern University Symphony Orchestra, and the Houston Baptist College Orchestra.

The ALLEY THEATRE, 709 Barry Ave., has become nationally famous for its plays, both traditional and experimental. It represented American dramatic arts at the Brussels World's Fair, and has been the beneficiary of aid from the Ford Foundation. It was founded by Nina Vance, who was discovered by Margo Jones, who for seven years directed the Community Players. The Alley Theatre will have a new house, costing $3,500,000, opposite Jones Hall. The original Little Theatre at 707 Chelsea, the first theater-in-the-round, is now the home of Theatre, Inc. Also active are the Houston Theatre Center on Main St., directed by Marietta Marich, the Civic Theatre for Children, the Theatre Suburbia, the Country Playhouse, the 2,800-seat Houston Music Theatre in Sharpstown, and companies in Pasadena, Baytown, and Bellaire. The Houston Foundation for Ballet supports companies for children and adults. Also active are the Greater Houston Ballet Company, the Allegro Ballet, and the Youth Ballet.

The site of the CAPITOL of the Republic of Texas (1837–1839) 518 Main St., is marked by a plate near the Main Street entrance of the Rice Hotel. The two-story frame building used by the Texas Congress was remodeled after the seat of government was moved to Austin in 1839, and became the Capitol Hotel. In 1858, Anson Jones, last President of the Republic of Texas, despondent over disappointments attending the close of his political career, committed suicide in the building. In the late 1870's the hotel was taken over by J. L. Barnes. It was demolished in 1882 and replaced by the New Capitol Hotel by A. Groesbeck. William Marsh Rice acquired it and named it the Rice Hotel. The present Rice Hotel was erected in 1912.

The site of the WHITE HOUSE of the Republic of Texas is marked by a plate at the Main St. corner of the Scanlan Building. It was a story-and-a-half frame dwelling with dormer windows, built by Francis R. Lubbock in 1837. He sold it to the Republic of Texas that same year for $6,000, for which promissory notes of the Republic were given in lieu of cash. Presidents Sam Houston and Mirabeau B. Lamar lived there during their administrations.

CHRIST CHURCH CATHEDRAL, Episcopal, 1101 Texas Ave., is an example of medieval Gothic architecture. The church, parish house, and educational building form a U-shaped group covering a block frontage, with an open lawn in the center. The church proper is overgrown with ivy, brought to Houston from Westminster Abbey some time between 1874 and 1884. The site was donated by the Allen brothers and the church built in 1893 of bricks salvaged from a church erected in 1860.

The CHURCH OF THE ANNUNCIATION, Roman Catholic, 601 Crawford St., is Romanesque in style, of limestone and cement plaster with brown marble trim. The cornerstone was laid in April, 1869, and the building completed in 1871. The architect was Nicholas J. Clayton. Marble altars, statues, stained glass windows, and a fresco painting on the dome of the sanctuary combine to make the building one of the architectural attractions of the city. The remainder of the block is occupied by the Incarnate Word Academy, established in 1873.

The HOUSTON PUBLIC LIBRARY, originally occupying only the fine Spanish Renaissance building at 500 McKinney Ave., since 1954 has expanded into a metropolitan system, with its central administration in the Julia Ideson Building at that address, 13 branches, 3 "traveling branches" (bookmobiles) and 4 new branches in the planning stage. By taking advantage of the Amendments of 1966 to the U. S. Library Services and Construction Act, the League of Women Voters and the Regional Library Council increased their efforts to make the library services keep pace with "the continuing explosion of knowledge." The support of the Texas State Library and the impetus created by the First Texas Governor's Conference on Libraries prepared the Houston Public Library to become the major resource center for library work in seven counties.

By January, 1967, the Library had 859,836 volumes, a net gain of 70,812 during the year. It circulates more than 2,500,000 books annually and has a staff of 233.

The JULIA IDESON BUILDING occupies an entire block. The main entrance, a projecting pavilion faced in limestone, is three stories, with inset marble columns. A circle-headed window is over the doorway, above this

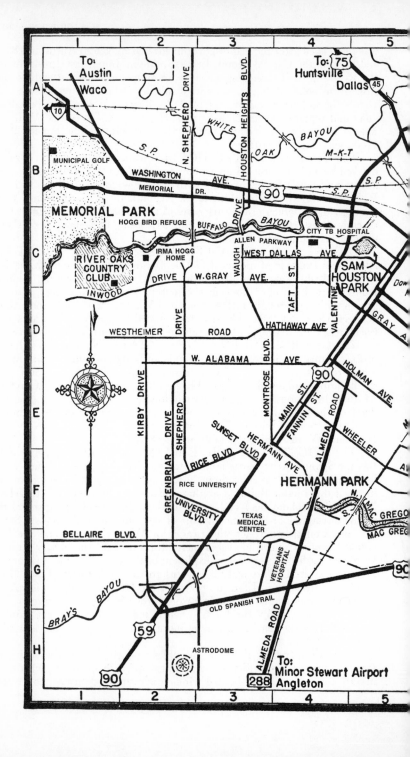

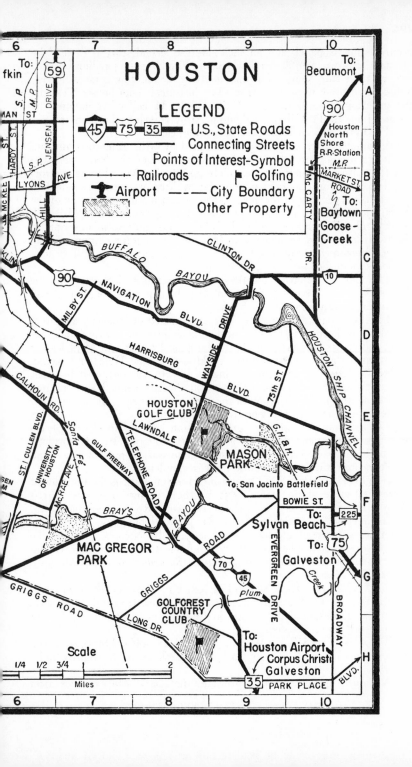

occurs a lunette panel, and on each side the second story is divided by pilasters into ornamental window panels. Flanking the pavilion on each side are three-story wings. The main body of the building is faced in dark buff-colored brick with stone trim. The historical room houses Texiana, the genealogical collections, and the Circle M collection donated by Major John E. T. Milsaps, Salvation Army traveler who gathered unusual and rare books and curios, chiefly Americana.

A valuable asset is a collection donated by Miss Annette Finnigan, consisting of 65 items showing the development of the book from the twelfth century to modern times. Collected during Miss Finnigan's foreign travels, the gift contains manuscripts written on vellum by monks of the Middle Ages. One of the most costly is a Latin Vulgate Edition of the Bible, once owned by William of Orange. Others are a beautiful Flemish *Book of Hours* with many colored illuminations and two manuscripts of the twelfth century. Incunabula include the first Aldine edition of Caesar's *Commentaries* printed in Venice in 1513, and an edition of Terence's *Comedies* published in Strasbourg in 1499.

The Library received a collection of great historical value in the Texas Well Log Records, which comprise the papers of 500,000 oil and gas drilling, 1920–1965.

The Philosophical Society of Texas, composed of pioneers, including Mirabeau B. Lamar, wanted to awaken an interest in science and literature; and as first president of the Philosophical Society, in 1838 Lamar inaugurated the library movement in Houston. The Houston Lyceum, granted a charter in 1848, maintained a library, supporting it by dues, subscriptions and donations, and in 1899 the city council appropriated $200 a month for the library with the condition that $150 of this be spent for books and that the library be free to the public.

The group became known as the Houston Lyceum and Carnegie Library Association, and through a gift of $50,000 by Andrew Carnegie, a new building was erected. The present name was adopted in 1921, and five years later, the $500,000 building was completed.

HISTORIC HOUSTON in Sam Houston Park is a collection of houses and stores dating from 1837 to 1868, preserved by the Harris County Heritage Society. Tours start at Long Row, 1100 Bagby St., and include the San Felipe cottage (1837), the Noble house (1847), the Rice-Cherry house, built by Gen. Ebenezer B. Nichols (1850), the Pilot house (1868). The Long Row includes a store, barber shop, saloon, library-book store. *Monday–Friday, 10–4; Saturday 10–2, Sunday, 1–5. Adults, $1; children 35¢.*

TEXAS SOUTHERN UNIVERSITY, 3201 Wheeler St., was opened 1947 by the State on a campus of 58 acres. It enrolls more than 4,000 and gives special instruction in English and Mathematics for the academically disadvantaged.

The UNIVERSITY OF ST. THOMAS, 3812 Montrose Blvd., was opened 1947 by the Roman Catholic Church. It enrolls slightly under 1,000.

A unified medical research program that came into existence after

World War II is the TEXAS MEDICAL CENTER, which occupies 164 acres at Hermann Park provided by the M. D. Anderson Foundation in 1946. The Center is intended to coordinate health education, medical research and patient care; in 1967 16 institutions and 14 medical organizations were furthering its aims and the Center was still in process of expansion. Some of the major units are Baylor University College of Medicine, University of Texas Dental Branch, Postgraduate School of the Biomedical Sciences and M. D. Anderson Hospital & Tumor Institute; Texas Women's University College of Nursing, Houston Academy of Medicine, Jewish Medical Research & Training Institute, Houston State Psychiatric Institute; also hospitals conducted by religious and secular organizations. More than 4,000 persons are employed at the Center, which needs an annual budget of more than $35,000,000.

The MUSEUM OF FINE ARTS, 1001 Bissonnet, was the earliest art museum in Texas when opened in 1924 (*free; open weekdays except Mondays, 9–5; Sundays, noon-6; Wednesdays to 10, Oct.-June*). Additional units and collections were given by representative Houston families, including the Joseph F. Cullinans, the John H. Blaffers, the Jesse H. Joneses, Mrs. Harris Masterson, Mrs. Harry C. Weiss, and the George Hermann Estate, Mrs. Nina Cullinan's gift of 1958 is encompassed in Cullinan Hall, designed by Mies van de Rohe. Bayou Bend, the former home of Miss Ima Hogg, was presented in 1966 and houses American decorative arts, with period rooms, American silver and pewter, and paintings by Greenwood, Copley, C. W. Peale, Badger, Hicks and Gilbert Stuart. James Johnson Sweeney became director in 1961.

The permanent collections include the Annette Finnegan Collection of ancient art from Egypt, Greece and Rome; the Edith A. and Percy S. Straus Collection of Renaissance paintings and bronzes; the Robert Lee Blaffer Memorial Collection of 15th- to 20th-century European paintings; the Samuel H. Kress Collection of Spanish and Italian paintings of the High Renaissance; the Hogg Brothers Collection of paintings by Frederic Remington; the Bayou Bend Collection of Indian Art of the Southwest; the Bayou Bend Collection of Prints, Drawings and Watercolors; the Hanzen Collection of Pre-Columbian Art; the McDannald Collection of Spiro Mound Artifacts; Native arts from Africa, Australia and the South Pacific Islands; Contemporary American and European paintings and sculpture, including works by Alechinsky, Soulages, Mondrian, Brancusi, Calder, Chillida, Tinguely, Fontana and Oldenburg.

Six exhibitions are installed annually in the Junior Gallery, with lectures, storytelling, puppet shows, etc., which nearly 30,000 young people attend. Another 35,000 school children enjoy group tours. Visitors exceed 250,000 each year. The Art School has both junior and adult divisions and adults may earn the degree of bachelor of fine arts by supplementary studies at a college. The Museum of Fine Arts is maintained by contributions, endowment funds and an annual appropriation from the City.

The CONTEMPORARY ART MUSEUM, 6945 Fannin St., has collections of all forms of modern and avant-garde art.

The UNIVERSITY OF HOUSTON, 3801 Cullen Blvd., is located on 330 acres south of the Gulf Freeway (Interstate 45) three miles from Houston's business center. It was formed as a junior college in 1927 and became a four-year university in 1934. In 1939 it began constructing on its present campus a $40,000,000 investment in modern, well-lighted classroom and laboratory buildings for its ten colleges and schools, which enrolled 19,588 students in its 1965–1966 year, three-fourths of them from Harris County. A building program costing $22,000,000 has been adding greatly to the University's facilities in the 1960's. This includes the UNIVERSITY CENTER, which provides for all the social wants of students, such as bowling and billiards, television, music rooms and ballroom; an expansion of the M. D. ANDERSON MEMORIAL LIBRARY to eight stories accommodating more than 700,000 volumes, with its rare book room on the top floor parreled in pecan and a carillon on the roof. The seven-story GENERAL CLASSROOM BUILDING is in an ornamental sunken garden and has elevator and escalator facilities. Unusual architectural design distinguishes the new RELIGION CENTER, with rooms for major denominations and a chapel with clear glass panels on all sides. A twin-tower dormitory complex, rising 17 stories and housing 1,250, has been financed by Moody Foundation. The University also conducts a DOWNTOWN SCHOOL and other off-campus programs. The football team is known as Cougars. The school colors are red and white.

RICE UNIVERSITY, 6000 S. Main St., on a 300-acre landscaped campus, is a hedge-enclosed area of red-roofed buildings and courts surrounded by groves of live oak and cypress. It is coeducational and nonsectarian. The program emphasizes science study and offers degrees in civil, electrical, chemical, mechanical, and architectural engineering. Annual enrollment is limited to outstanding students whose selection is determined by scholastic ability and record of application. Enrollment in the 1960's has reached 2,474, with 285 in the faculty.

William Marsh Rice, the founder, was born in Springfield, Massachusetts, in 1816, and came to Houston in the late 1830's. He died in 1900, having endowed Rice Institute, which was formally opened in 1912. The name was changed in recent years. The school uses thirty well-equipped buildings.

The buildings were designed by Cram, Goodhue and Ferguson, of New York, and erected under the direction of William Ward Watkin, who remained in Houston as head of the school of architecture. The style is a blending of Byzantine, Moorish, Italian and Spanish forms, to which is added an almost indefinable touch of Gothic.

The approach to the Administration Building is through one of four entrances facing South Main Street. The architectural design of this building reflects the influence of early Mediterranean countries in the employment of Dalmatian brickwork with Spanish and Italian details of design. Texas granite, local pink brick and delicately tinted marble from the Ozarks give the building a warm gray tone, relieved by variations of tile and foreign marble. Other buildings follow this defined style. The vaulted opening of the Administration Building frames a vista of campus more than a mile long. The LIBRARY (*open 8–5 Mon.-Fri., 8–1 Sat.*), in the north wing, contains many volumes on scientific research.

The Physics Laboratories adjoin the Administration Building on the north side of the court. Beyond is another court, where stands the STATUE OF WILLIAM MARSH RICE, whose ashes are entombed in the base. Across the lawns and to the right are the Chemistry Laboratories, and just beyond, the Mechanical Laboratory, whose lofty campanile commands the immediate horizon, and the Machine Shop and Power House, all belonging to the Engineering group.

HERMANN PARK, S. Main St. between Hermann Ave. and Marlborough Drive, is a 545-acre natural park named for George H. Hermann, donor of part of its site. The park has miles of winding scenic driveways. At the main entrance is a bronze equestrian STATUE OF GENERAL SAM HOUSTON, the work of Enrico Filberto Cerracchio. Sam Houston's son, Colonel Andrew Jackson Houston, sought to prevent unveiling ceremonies on the ground that the statue in no way resembled his father. The statue was unveiled, however, with appropriate ceremonies, in 1924. Beyond is the MILLER MEMORIAL THEATER, used by educational societies and clubs for the presentation of plays and pageants. It was erected at a cost of $50,000 from the $75,000 bequest of Jesse Wright Miller to the City of Houston.

HOUSTON ZOOLOGICAL GARDENS (*open 9–7 daily*), contain thousands of specimens, ranging from a Texas albino flying squirrel to lions, tigers, and elephants. Board walks, bordered by palms and evergreen camphor trees, traverse the 30-acre oval.

The HOUSTON MUSEUM OF NATURAL SCIENCE in Hermann Park has been expanding into new quarters for which $2,500,000 has been appropriated. The first unit, costing $750,000, included the Space Age Museum and the BURKE BAKER PLANETARIUM and was opened in 1964. Important exhibits are the Milsaps collection of coins; the Fisher botanical collection; the Westheimer group of minerals, and the Meigs display of handicrafts from Ecuador. The Planetarium stages performances daily. Admission, adults $1; children 12 and under, 50¢; children under 5 not admitted.

The MANNED SPACECRAFT CENTER of the National Aeronautics & Space Administration, originally at Houston, has been located since September, 1963, on 1,620 acres at Clear Lake, 22 miles southeast of downtown Houston. By June, 1964, all the personnel had been shifted from Houton offices to the new headquarters at Clear Lake, which is located on Farm Road 528, or Seabrook Loop, which connects with State 3 and Interstate 45. Some of the personnel has been assigned to ELLINGTON AIR FORCE BASE nearby. The Center has the responsibility for the design, development, and testing of manned spacecraft and associated systems, for the selection and training of flight crews (astronauts), and for the operation of manned space flights. The scientists and engineers at the Center were responsible for placing the free world's first man in space. For flight testing of spacecraft the Center has facilities at Cape Kennedy, Fla., and White Sands Missile Range, N. Mex.

The erection of buildings at Clear Lake has been proceeding swiftly and what in 1962 was a cow pasture is now full of huge steel and glass structures for scientific and administrative work. The Auditorium Building has offices and a lecture room with 800 seats. It costs $1,133,934. The Project Management Building cost $4,666,509. Among others are the Laboratory for Flight Crew Training ($2,296,690); the Life Systems Laboratory ($988,666); the Technical Service Office Building ($1,314,-548) the Technical Services Shop ($1,764,775) and the Electronics Systems Laboratory ($1,463,161) MSC Building 30 houses the Mission Control Center, which provides centralized control of manned space flight missions.

The location of the MSC Center has brought about a development of nearby land for settlement. Clear Lake Shores, Glen Cove, Lakeside, El Lago, and Taylor Lake Village are emerging communities. Shore Acres and Seabrook are located on State 148 which connects Baytown with Texas City along the shore of Galveston Bay. Seabrook connects with Webster on State 3. Ellington AFB is located along the State 3, the Galveston Road. Houston suburbs are increasing between Galveston Road and the Gulf Freeway (Interstate 45) because of the excellent highway facilities.

Laredo

Airports: Laredo International Airport, north of the city near US 81, for private planes. Laredo Air Force Base permits commercial and larger plane operation. Commercial service into Laredo and Nuevo Laredo area is handled by Trans-Texas Airways. The Mexican segment, with airport south of Nuevo Laredo, is served by C. M. A., and Compania Mexicana de Avacion.

Buses: Central Greyhound, Winter Garden Lines, Transporte Del Norte, Continental Trailways. Intercity bus service to Nuevo Laredo, where Mexican bus lines have terminal.

Highways: Laredo is southmost terminal of Interstate 35, US 81, and US 59. It also is served by US 83 and State 359. International Bridge, foot of Convent St.; vehicle and driver, 20¢; each passenger, 5¢; pedestrian, 5¢.

Railroads: Missouri Pacific, 2115 Farragut St. Connections with Trans-Mexican Railway and National Railways of Mexico.

Information and Accommodations: Laredo has many first-rate hotels and motels, including the Hamilton and Plaza downtown and Holiday Inn and many other motels on San Bernardo Ave., or near US 81 and US 83. Laredo Chamber of Commerce, Tourist Dept., Bruni Plaza. American Automobile Assn., near City Hall. *The Laredo Times,* daily, 1404 Matamoros St.; *The South Texas Citizen,* weekly, 1202 Victoria St. There are two radio stations and one for television.

Recreation: Boating, fishing, swimming, at Lake Casa Blanca. Public golf at Country Club at Lake; $1 weekdays, $1.25 Saturdays, Sundays and holidays. Fishing also on Lake Falcon, 75 *m.* downstream on US 83. Deer and wildfowl hunting during the fall on privately-owned lands; inquire at tourist bureaus. Laredo Civic Music Assn. sponsors concerts; the Little Theatre group presents plays; exhibits of Mexican arts and crafts are sent periodically by Mexican Foreign Ministry.

Special Events: Washington's Birthday celebration, week of Feb. 22, in which the people of Nuevo Laredo join. Border Olympics, outdoor track and field meet, high school and college competitions, also golf, Shirley Stadium, first week in March. Christmas festivities are observed nightly beginning Dec. 16. There are frequent fiestas in Nuevo Laredo, especially that of Cinco de Mayo, May 5.

LAREDO (438 alt., 60,678 pop., 1960; 71,875, 1967, est.) the Gateway to Mexico, is one of the busiest ports of entry in Texas, with more than 2,500,000 vehicles and 8,000,000 persons annually crossing the International Bridge that spans the Rio Grande between Laredo and Nuevo Laredo, a Mexican city of 120,000 (est.). A manufacturing, livestock and agricultural center and military base, Laredo also is a major tourist objective. In a typical year, 1966, 214,743 tourists and 77,479 touring cars crossed the Bridge to the Pan American Highway. Laredo is a terminal of Interstate 35, 150 *m.* south of San Antonio, and of US 59, which crosses Texas in a direct line from Texarkana; it also is served by US 81 and US 83 from the north, the latter continuing into the Lower Rio Grande Valley, and by State 359, which connects with highways to Corpus Christi. Commercial traffic accounts for U. S. Customs receipts of nearly $12,000,000 annually.

Laredo authorities report a "spring season" of nine months, from September to May, an average temperature of 74°, and 350 days of sunshine a year. Whereas six flags have flown over Texas, Laredo counts seven, because its people proclaimed a Republic of the Rio Grande in 1840, when Mexican administration was ineffective, yielding to the Republic of Texas in 1844.

Grapefruit and orange trees grow along the public highways and in the yards of residences, although citrus fruits are not raised commercially. Oranges ripen on grounds surrounding the City Hall in the heart of the city, and on Jarvis Plaza in front of the Federal Bldg. Palmettos and date palms are common, as are the huisache, mesquite, mulberry and pomegranate. Predominant in the flower gardens are roses, geraniums and, in springtime, bluebonnets. Daisies grow wild amid the bluebonnets. Ligustrums and oleanders are poplar shrubs, and bougainvillaea flourishes.

The international tone of the city is manifest everywhere. Display signs, placards and window posters printed in Spanish are seen more often than those in English. School children recite in English but their playtime is marked by vociferous staccato exchanges as they lapse into the "border lingo," an English-Spanish hybrid which seems to come naturally to those whose diction is acquired partly from the parents and partly from the school teacher. During the annual Washington's Birthday celebration, Nuevo Laredo, across the border, participates, and both cities are crowded with visitors. Side by side march the Spanish-Mexican, the Indian-Mexican, the Latin- and Anglo-American in parades. About 85 per cent of the people of Laredo are of Mexican descent. Nuevo Laredo supplies no small part of the entertainment, the feature of which is the bullfights.

Laredo was one of the first settlements in Texas not established as a presidio or a mission. It was the sixth to be founded along the lower Rio Grande, and the second community on the north bank of the river. Don José de Escandón, Count of Sierra Gorda, and colonizer of the region, reported the site suitable for settlement in 1755, designating it as "ten leagues northwest of Dolores, at Paso de Jacinto."

Tómas Sánchez, Spanish ranchman, offered to found a settlement at his own expense, and to maintain a ferry for "the convenience of traffic and the royal service." For this he asked a grant of 15 *sitios* of land. Escandón approved the plan and appointed Sánchez captain of the settlement, granting him 15 *sitios de ganado mayor* (15 square leagues of range land), for the use of himself and the settlers.

On May 15, 1755, with three or four families, Tómas Sánchez formally founded the Villa de Laredo. The settlement prospered and by 1757 included 11 families, numbering 85 persons. One thing, however, marred the satisfaction and comfort of the people. The only religious solace and administration they had consisted of an annual visit of Father Miguel de Santa Maria of Revilla. Although overworked in his own parish, the priest once a year made the 44-league round trip to minister to the people of Villa de Laredo. For this he received the equivalent of 30 *pesos* (dollars) "in kind"—produce of some sort.

Unable to support a priest of their own, the people of Laredo asked the king to supply this need, but nothing was done. The settlement continued to thrive; recognition of its importance is found in the report of López de la Cámara Alta in 1758. He said, "This town is important and should be increased in size as a means of communication between the interior provinces and Texas." From it roads led to Monclova, Dolores, La Bahia, San Antonio de Bexar, and Revilla.

The lack of religious administration was remedied by the Bishop of Guadalajara in 1759. On his way back to Mexico from La Bahia the bishop spent three days in Laredo and administered baptism and confirmation to many. He was so deeply impressed by "deplorable spiritual conditions" that his report described the people as "living like heathens, neither hearing Mass nor the Word of God." A secular priest was at once ordered to Laredo.

The settlement grew in population and importance, until at the turn of the eighteenth century the residents numbered about 1,000.

Laredo saw Santa Anna's army in 1835–36, while it was on its way to attack the Alamo, and, later, the retreat of the defeated Mexican forces in the weeks following the Battle of San Jacinto. Disagreement over the southern boundary of the Republic of Texas placed Laredo in a no man's land. In 1837 Captain Erastus (Deaf) Smith marched there with 20 men, "with the intention of raising the flag of independence on the spire of the church at Laredo." A force of Mexican cavalry met him and Smith considered himself too outnumbered to proceed. Laredo took advantage of this to form the Republic of the Rio Grande and elected Jesus Cardenas president. Laredo identifies a building in the old quarter (Seccion Original) as the capitol.

General Alexander Somervell reached Laredo in pursuit of General Woll following the latter's raid on San Antonio. Somervell met no resistance but his troops pillaged the town, an act for which he wrote a letter of apology to the alcalde of Laredo on December 9, 1842. The Republic of Texas moved in during 1844.

The Mexican War brought troops to Laredo in 1846, when the town was occupied by Captain R. A. Gillespie's company of Texas Rangers, who were on their way to join General Zachary Taylor at Brownsville. The following year, General Mirabeau Buonaparte Lamar with his small army was stationed in Laredo; during the two years that Lamar occupied the town, Webb County was organized. A declaration was made by the Texas general that an election would be held on July 13, 1847, in which "all free citizens of this place, and twenty-one years of age, will be entitled to vote." This was the first election held in Laredo under the laws of Texas.

In 1849 the United States Government established Camp Crawford (later Fort McIntosh) beside an old ford which was being used by smugglers. That year Laredo watched thousands of gold-hungry immigrants pass along the Rio Grande route to the California gold fields. They stopped to rest and replenish their supplies, and for a time the community felt the impetus of its first boom.

Laredo was chartered as a Texas city in 1852, and progressed normally and uneventfully until the outbreak of the Civil War. Confederate forces occupied the vacated Fort McIntosh under General Santos Benavides and held it until the close of the conflict; General Benavides was a grandson of Don Tómas Sánchez.

The advent of two railroads, one from Corpus Christi in 1880 and the other from Mexico in 1881, put an end to Laredo's isolation and opened a large part of the Mexican markets to Texas. Ten years later, with irrigation, farmers placed the arid river valley under cultivation. By 1890, Laredo was described as a "very plain city" whose prevailing style of architecture utilized stone or sun-dried brick walls and thatched roofs. The city nevertheless had a police department composed, in equal numbers, of "Mexicans and Americans" and the customs house was reporting great volumes of merchandise.

The beginning of Laredo's onion industry is credited to Thomas C. Nye who, in 1898, bought land four miles north of the city, along the railroad tracks, and began irrigating from the Rio Grande. By 1906, 500 carloads of Bermuda onions were shipped. Later the Laredo Truck Growers Association was formed. The discovery of natural gas in 1908, and of large oil pools in 1921, led to stimulation of industry.

Among Laredo's principal imports from across the border are grain, cottonseed, vegetables and other raw products; also quail, which are trapped in Mexico and shipped to the United States for restocking game preserves. The principal exports are mining and agricultural machinery, electrical appliances, and large quantities of shoes and clothing. Laredo has an important antimony smelter, getting the ore from Mexico.

The two most important industries are oil refining and shipping. Laredo makes saddles, mattresses, transistors and diodes, insecticides, brick and tile and strawhats. There is a labor force of 25,000. Retail sales are high and many people from northwest Mexico buy in Laredo. Many tourists come for the gay fiestas and for hunting and fishing.

POINTS OF INTEREST

SECCION ORIGINAL is the site of the beginnings of Laredo in the Villa de San Augustin de Laredo (1755). It takes in San Augustin Plaza and overlooks the Rio Grande. Opposite the Plaza on Zaragoza Street is a small building identified as the capitol of the Republic of the Rio Grande (1840–1844), now a museum conducted by the Laredo Historical Society. East of the Plaza is the Church of San Augustin, erected 1872 on the site of the original of 1767. Its genealogical records go back to 1789.

The LAREDO CIVIC CENTER, completed 1965 at a cost of $1,200,000, was specially designed to accommodate conventions. It is a complex of four buildings and a public swimming pool on 24 acres in the City Park area. It is bordered on the east by San Bernardo Avenue, which parallels US 81, US 83 and Interstate 35, and near which are located most of the city's motels. Also in the area are the Shirley Stadium, the

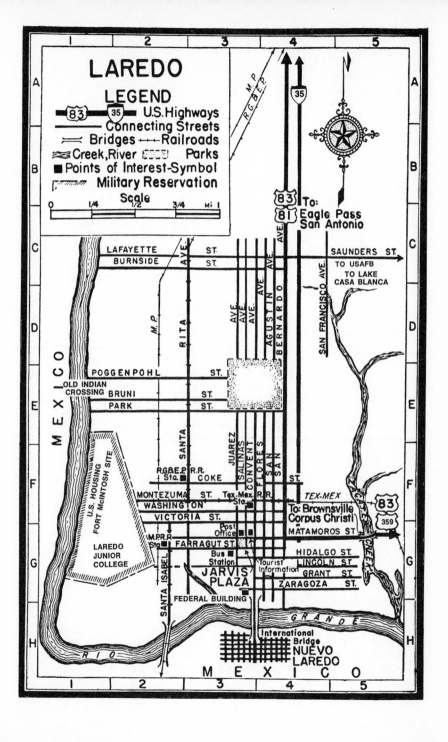

Martin High School, and the Leyendecker Elementary School. The impressive AUDITORIUM has seven large arches decorated with flag staffs on which fly the "Seven Flags over Laredo." The Auditorium seats 1,979 and has a stage equipped for plays and concerts. The BANQUET AND EXHIBITION HALL seats 1,500, has 24,470 sq. ft. of exhibition space and four large conference rooms.

The INDIAN CROSSING, north of the river end of Bruni Street is a ledge of limestone used as a ford for centuries by the Indians. They often crossed it taking into Mexico cattle and horses they had stolen in raids on settlers. When Texas entered the Union the United States Army built a military post on the bluff overlooking the Crossing. Originally Camp Crawford, it later became Fort McIntosh.

FORT McINTOSH, an area of approx. 208 acres west of the business district on the Rio Grande, was an army post from 1849 to 1945. It is now the site of LAREDO JUNIOR COLLEGE, and a U. S. GOVERNMENT HOUSING PROJECT, maintained for the personnel of Laredo Air Force Base. The latter has 31 sets of quarters. In 1849 the earthwork called Camp Crawford was begun as part of border defense; in 1850 it was named Fort McIntosh. Union troops evacuated it in 1861 and Texas State troops and several companies of Confederates occupied it. The Federals failed to recapture it in 1863. A new fort was erected nearby in 1868–1877. The post was continuously occupied until 1945, when it was closed. Laredo Junior College, founded 1943, supported by the city and the State offers a two-year college curriculum as well as courses in continuing education for Laredo citizens. It uses 147 acres of the area and has about 600 students.

The LAREDO CACTUS GARDENS, 3201 San Bernardo Ave., have won national acclaim for the comprehensiveness of the plantings, some cacti being as tall as 35 ft., others minute specimens. There also are exhibits of pre-Columbian pottery, shells and artifacts. (*Open 6 a.m. to 6 p.m., free*).

The INTERNATIONAL BRIDGE at the foot of Convent Ave. is one of the great highway links of the continent. It is a 4-lane structure, completed in 1957, which replaced a bridge badly damaged by floods in 1954. A railroad bridge crossed the Rio Grande in the 1880's. The first traffic bridge was opened in 1879 and destroyed by a storm in 1903. Rebuilt, it was burned by Mexican revolutionists in 1920. A new bridge was opened in 1922 and lasted until 1954. (*The one-way rate over the bridge is 20¢ for vehicle and driver, 5¢ for each passenger, and 5¢ for a pedestrian*).

LAREDO AIR FORCE BASE of the USAF is one of the country's major training bases for jet pilots. It comprises 1,782 acres and has been an Air Force installation since 1952. It began as an auxiliary landing field maintained by Kelly Field (San Antonio) after World War I. During World War II it became the Laredo Army Air Field Flexible Gunnery School, with a peak population of 15,000. Bombers of the B–25, B–24 and B–39 types were employed. In 1945 the field was transfered to the War

Assets Administration. When air fields were reactivated in 1952 Laredo was considered preeminent for its facilities and favorable climate.

Today Laredo AFB trains only USAF officers and students from Allied countries. All-jet training was begun in 1958. In 1961 this was one of 8 Undergraduate Pilot Training Bases of the Air Training Command, where students received the three phases of pilot instruction—preflight, primary and basic, during 55 weeks. The first T–38 superior jet trainer arrived in December, 1964. There are 8 classes in training, averaging 62 students per class. They get 30 hours in the 7–41 light plane, 90 hours in the T–37 jet trainer, and 120 hours in the T–38.

Operations at the base are not limited to flight training. Here also are (1) a detachment of Central Aerospace Rescue & Recovery Center, which uses two helicopters for rescue and fire suppression; (2) a district unit of the Office of Special Investigation, dealing in counter-intelligence; (3) a Communcation Squadron; (4) a unit of the Weather Squadron; (5) a unit of the USAF Auditor General Group; (6) a Field-Mobile Training Detachment, and (7) a detachment of ATC Management Engineering.

The base provides for every need and desire of its personnel, their wives and children. There are not only the usual commissary, BX, medical and hospital services, but clubs, delicatessen, snack bars, a movie theater, a Gymnasium with 800 seats, a Youth Center, a library with 14,000 volumes, bowling, swimming, a skeet range, a Child Care Center, legal aid, bank, credit union, clothing store, and units of Cub Scouts, Boy Scouts, Air Explorers, Junior Girl Scouts, and clubs for wives and quarters for bachelors. The supply store even stocks food for cats and dogs. Personnel may send a radio message free to any place in the world via the Military Affiliated Radio System.

LAKE CASA BLANCA, 2 *m.* east of Laredo on US 59, is the principal recreation spot, with boating, fishing, swimming, skiing and picnic facilities. The lake covers 1,500 acres and is owned by Webb County. On its banks is the Country Club Golf Course, 18 holes (*weekdays, $1; Sundays and holidays, $1.25*).

NUEVO LAREDO

NUEVO LAREDO, Tamaulipas, Mexico, founded 1847, is located across the Rio Grande from Laredo, Texas. Like many Mexican cities Nuevo Laredo has had a large increase in population in recent years. It had 92,000 in 1960 and an estimated 120,000 in 1967. The commercial and tourist traffic across the International Bridge is heavy and benefits both cities. Nuevo Laredo has five radio stations and one television station. It has many attractions for American visitors, such as curio shops, basketry and pottery, the Mexican cuisine, entertainment in night spots, and finally, bullfighting, about which many Americans express curiosity despite ingrained disapproval.

Bullfights are held usually on the first Sunday of the month between

May and October, and on Sundays near American and Mexican holidays. Schedules may be consulted at the Laredo Chamber of Commerce, Bruni Plaza. The Nuevo Laredo International Fair & Exposition is held the second week in September. It has livestock and agricultural exhibits, and a gay fiesta, with brilliant costumes and dancing.

Advice for tourists visiting Mexico. Citizens of the United States need no permits, passports or tourist cards when visiting Nuevo Laredo for a period not exceeding 24 hours. Military and government personnel and their families with identification cards may enter Mexico for 29 days without charge, provided they do not wear uniforms except on official business.

Tourists making a limited visit are advised that traffic delays can be avoided by parking a motor car in Laredo and walking across the Bridge. On a short visit tourists are advised not to carry luggage, fruits, plants and packages, as they will be subject to inspection by customs officials on both sides. When returning inspection is enforced by both nations. A special permit from Mexican customs is required for taking firearms into Mexico. Americans may bring back $100 worth of merchandise duty free every 29 days if for personal use. This may include one quart of alcoholic beverages. There are special regulations governing perfumes, also fruits, plants and pets from Mexico; consult the U. S. Customs. Two packs of cigarettes are duty free.

U. S. currency is accepted in Mexico. Banks and tourist agencies exchange money at 12.50 pesos for $1. Every tourist, regardless of age, may carry one camera and one portable motion picture camera with 12 rolls of film for each. Expensive cameras should be registered with the U. S. Customs. Mexican automobile insurance is recommended. It can be bought inexpensively on a daily, weekly or monthly basis at tourist agencies.

Port Arthur

Airlines: Delta Airlines and Trans-Texas Airways, daily flights from Jefferson County Airport, west of Nederland and of the combined highways US 69, 96 and 287, between Beaumont and Port Arthur.
Bus Lines: Central Greyhound and other Greyhound lines, Greyhound Terminal, Waco Ave., and 5th St.
Highways: US 69, 96 and 287 are combined from Beaumont to Port Arthur; connect there with Interstate 10. State 87 from Galveston (63 *m.*) leaves coast at Port Arthur, moves north parallel with Louisiana boundary. State 347 from Beaumont passes through Nederland. State 73 to Houston, 120 *m.* State 82 to Louisiana via causeway over Channel (toll).
Railroads: Kansas City Southern, Proctor & Houston Sts.; Southern Pacific.

Information: Port Arthur Chamber of Commerce; Port Director, Port of Port Arthur; *Port Arthur News,* evening and Sunday, 549 4th St.

Recreation: Fishing and sailing are primary attractions, both freshwater fishing in Lake Sabine and deepwater fishing in the Gulf. Boats can be chartered. Water skiing is practiced on Lake Sabine and in the Ship Channel. Crabbing in Lake Sabine, shell and driftwood collecting on the sandy beach of the Gulf. Duck and geese are plentiful in the marshlands during the hunting season. Activities of all kinds are provided on Pleasure Island, the city's 2,000 acres outside the front yard, with the Ship Channel on the north and Lake Sabine on the south. Here are an 18-hole golf course, swimming pools, tables for picnics, barbecue pits, baseball diamonds. Golf also is available at the 18-hole course at Port Groves, Port Arthur Country Club and the Bayou Din Country Club.

Special Events: Camellias in bloom, January. Azaleas on exhibit, March. Cav-oil-cade, salute to the oil industry, October. Consult newspapers for dates.

PORT ARTHUR (18 alt., 66,670 pop. 1960 after annexation of 9,544; 69,000, 1966, est.), one of the nation's great centers for oil refining and the production of petrochemicals, is located on Lake Sabine of the Neches-Sabine River System and connected by a 7-mile canal with the Gulf of Mexico. It is the city nearest the Gulf of the three in the Golden Triangle, the others being Beaumont and Orange. The annual tonnage, 27,573,000 tons, is slightly less than that of Beaumont, which has 29,637,000 tons. Port Arthur and Beaumont benefit by each other's commercial and transportation facilities and share in a metropolitan area with full employment and an annual payroll of about $220,000,000.

Port Arthur is the Gulf terminal of two railroads, the Southern Pacific and the Kansas City Southern. The latter owns a grain elevator that has a capacity of 3,500,000 bu. and is so well mechanized that it absorbs the grain of 10 loaded cars per hour and pumps 50,000 bu. per hour from elevator to ship. Besides the dock of the Kansas City Southern, large docks at the Port are owned by Gulf Oil Corporation, Texaco, Inc., and Atlantic Refining Co. These have the largest refineries in Port Arthur. Pure

Oil is located at Nederland and the Neches Butane Products Co. is at Port Neches, northeast. Three shipyards build barges, towboats and do other marine work.

The Port Authority for the District of Jefferson County was created by the Texas legislature and ratified by referendum in 1964. It covers 58 sq. mi. and includes Port Arthur, Griffing Park, Lakeview, Pear Ridge and part of Groves. It is administered by a 5-man elected Board of Port Commissioners. The same channel serves both shipways up to a point a few miles south of Orange, where the Intracoastal Canal turns sharply into Louisiana. The channel is open 24 hours daily to navigation. Located only 19 miles from sea, the new $9,500,000 Public Ocean Terminal of the Port is designed to meet the requirements of shipping methods of the next halfcentury. The Terminal is squarely on the 1,200-mile long Intracoastal Waterway, 285.4 m. west of New Orleans, 1116 m. from Mile Post, 100 m. below St. Louis, and 398 m. east of Brownsville, Texas.

This waterway is invisible at a short distance and, as buildings are constructed near the water front, the slow-moving freighters seem to be slipping silently through city streets as their stacks and masts are seen above the trees and houses. At Austin Avenue a $300,000 bascule-type bridge is raised to permit the passage of ships, and gives access to Pleasure Island, one of the city's park developments.

Over a period of years Port Arthur has steadily covered itself with exotic plants, shrubs, and trees, until its present appearance is in many respects tropical. Along the streets are palms, American holly, southern magnolia, live oak, Chinese tallow, camphor and eucalyptus trees. These are many landscaped esplanades, and everywhere are blossoms—especially, oleanders, crep myrtles, asters, camellias, azaleas and poinsettias. Roses are extensively cultivated, particularly in the city's park areas.

Port Arthur has a city manager, mayor and council government. Like all busy seaports, Port Arthur has a cosmopolitan flavor. On its sidewalks are sailors from many a foreign port, rivermen clad in boots and khaki, sun-tanned cattlemen, refinery workers, fishermen, longshoremen, and well-dressed businessmen. The Mexican population is small. Other foreign groups include Italians, Germans, English, Canadians, Irish, French, Syrians and Dutch. Consulates are maintained by Argentina, Brazil, the Dominican Republic, Uruguay, Haiti, Norway, Honduras and Holland. About 20 per cent of the population is Negro.

History in the region of Port Arthur dates back to the sixteenth century, when a storm swept the expedition of Hernando de Soto ashore on July 25, 1543, in the vicinity of Lake Sabine. French traders and trappers frequented these lands from about the time that New Orleans was founded. From Mexico, Spanish officials heard frequently of these French incursions and sent various expeditions to expel them. The English made at least one attempt to penetrate the Sabine area. An English merchantman ran aground near the mouth of the Neches River in Lake Sabine (1777) and was abandoned, to be found later by the apprehensive Spaniards. Trappers from St. Louis appeared during the early 1800's, and Jean Lafitte, who operated from Galveston Island between 1817 and

1821, frequently sent his buccaneers to the lower Sabine region to trade Spanish doubloons for food.

Who the earliest settlers were along Lake Sabine has never been chronicled. Soon after Mexico won independence from Spain (1821), its leaders, fearing Anglo-American designs on the vast Texas area, enacted laws prohibiting foreigners from settling near the coast without official permission. But when *empresarios* obtained colonization grants, many settlers arrived in the Sabine area under the contract of Lorenzo de Zavala, whose grant was issued in March, 1829. Other colonizers of the region were Joseph Vehlein and David Burnet. A young English immigrant, Thomas Courts, in 1829, established his home southwest of modern Port Arthur, on De Zavala's grant. Others followed Courts and settlements were established. One, called Aurora, on Lake Sabine, failed to survive, and the other, City of the Pass, later became Sabine City.

John Sparks, a native of Tennessee, in 1836 began a long overland journey by ox team with his wife and two small children. Reaching Pavell's Island in 1838, Sparks soon inaugurated ferry service on Taylor's Bayou, and built a house on a site now occupied by the Gulf Oil Corporation Refinery. He prospered and by 1853 had saved the money to buy two parcels of land fronting on Lake Sabine. Here he built his home.

The Sparks settlement for a time was called Aurora in memory of the older colony which had failed to take root. After an epidemic in 1885, a hurricane ravaged the region and virtually all families moved nearer to Beaumont. By 1895, Aurora and the shores of Lake Sabine were deserted save for the alligators, the curlew and the plover. Yet before that year had ended the modern city of Port Arthur was born.

Its development became the dream of a promoter who had unlimited resources and who, on a hunch, resolved to establish a rail and shipping terminus here. This man was Arthur Edward Stilwell, scion of a wealthy pioneer New York family. He had been an insurance salesman, was the builder of the Kansas City, Pittsburg & Gulf Railroad (now the Kansas City Southern), and had become head of a million-dollar organization at the age of 28.

Arthur Stilwell believed in hunches and supernatural creatures which he whimsically called "Brownies," and maintained that his "Brownies" had urged him to choose the Port Arthur site when he was looking around for a Gulf terminus for his railroad. He claimed that he was able, in his dreams, to envision Port Arthur, exact in all detail, as it was subsequently developed. Later he wrote that this city was the only one "ever located and built under directions from the spirit world . . . so recognized and acknowledged."

Having fixed upon the Lake Sabine shores as the site of his dream city, in 1895 Stilwell caused a town site to be surveyed which he named Port Arthur in his honor. The Port Arthur Townsite and Land Company and the Port Arthur Canal and Dock Company immediately began construction of a ship canal, docks and streets and business houses. Stilwell's interests built a railway whose only traffic was in freighting supplies from Beaumont to the booming new town.

A widespread advertising campaign throughout the country attracted many homeseekers, businessmen and financial interests. Among the newcomers were two publishers who simultaneously began preparations to give the town its first newspaper. The publisher of the *Port Arthur Herald* arrived two weeks earlier than the man who was launching the *News*. On March 17, 1897, local residents saw the first *Herald,* and on the same day the *News* was printed in the baggage car of a train nearing the town. Thus prospective residents saw the *Port Arthur News* first while the established settlers got the *Herald*. In September of that year, while Stilwell was in the North, a hurricane ravaged Port Arthur and Stilwell at once dispatched a trainload of workers and supplies and sent $15,000 to hasten rehabilitation and reconstruction.

By the end of 1897 the town had 1,100 residents, and in March, 1898, it voted to incorporate. After many delays due to opposition from Sabine Pass promoters—the Kountze interests—the canal was opened on March 25, 1899. Five months later the British ship, *St. Oswald,* drawing 17 feet of water, docked at the grain elevator, the first steamship to reach Port Arthur. By this time Stilwell, his money spread over his labyrinthine enterprises, found himself in need of financial aid. Into the breach stepped the second of Port Arthur's colorful promoters, John Warne Gates, better remembered as Wall Street's "Bet-a-Million" Gates.

Gates and Stilwell had met before they joined interests at Port Arthur and, although he operated chiefly in the financial circles of The Loop and Wall Street, Gates was no stranger to Texas. In 1876, as a cocky young drummer, he sold barbed wire to the ranchers of Texas. When he arrived in San Antonio the cattlemen laughed at him. In response to their jibes, Gates fenced in a city plaza and called for the "worst fence busters" of the herds. Prepared to scoff at his experiment, the cattlemen readily accommodated him and gathered to watch the spectacle. The cattle charged the wire as was expected but, their hides pierced by the small barbs, they soon retired. Gates crammed his salesbooks with orders.

The stories of how Gates got his nickname are legion. The most plausible is that which tells how he and his partner, Isaac L. Ellwood, the barbed wire manufacturer, were riding a train from Chicago to Pittsburgh. Gates was morosely staring out at a rainstorm and idly watching the raindrops gather on the windowpane and trickle down to the sill. Suddenly the bored Gates spoke: "Ellwood, I'll pick a drop and you pick a drop and I'll bet you a million mine gets down first." Ellwood reduced the wager to a thousand, and they bet on many drops running down the windowpane. Before they reached Pittsburgh, Gates had won $22,000.

Gates bought stock in Stilwell's companies, and soon brought them under his control by shrewd manipulation. The embittered Stilwell retreated to Europe, convinced that he had been frozen out.

In 1901 the first Spindletop gusher was discovered 15 miles north of Beaumont, and the overflow of humanity from the oil fields came to Port Arthur. Out of Spindletop came the three major oil companies that started to dominate the Texas industry, the Gulf, the Texas and the Magnolia. Capitalists seized the opportunity to invest in Port Arthur.

While other men were drilling for new wells, they were making this the refining and shipping point for the tremendous output of petroleum wealth. Transportation was improved, streets were built, pipe lines laid from the oil fields to the docks. When the boom subsided the city retained much of its large population because it was then recognized as a mature industrial center. Pipe lines have since been extended, through which oil flows into the refineries from distant fields.

Designation as a port of entry came only after a hard fight, including the efforts of local Congressmen. On June 4, 1906, the Brooks Bill, passed in the House of Representatives, gave Port Arthur its desired designation. The city was made a full port of entry in 1908. Its shipping has steadily increased; Port Arthur in 1965 was third among the seaports in Texas in export and coastwise shipments.

But commerce is not the city's sole attraction. Sportsmen find this an ideal region. The outlying salt marshes, bayous and rice fields are frequented by great numbers of ducks and geese that make this section their winter feeding ground. Salt water fishing is available within the city limits in Lake Sabine where trout, redfish and perch abound. Fresh water varieties of fish are caught in streams west of the city, while deep sea fishermen take tarpon, amberjack and Spanish mackerel from the Gulf of Mexico, 11 miles south. Cattle early were a leading source of wealth for Port Arthur, and in its general vicinity the livestock industry is still important. Rice and cotton are the leading crops. Many acres are covered with refineries, storage tank farms, byproducts plants and the shipping facilities of the petroleum industry; oil and shipping still dominate the modern city that Stilwell dreamed into existence with the aid of the "Brownies" of his other world.

POINTS OF INTEREST

The CITY HALL, Lake Shore Drive at Dallas Ave., a three-story brick structure of Spanish mission architecture designed by Charles A. Logan, architect, was formerly the Mary A. Gates Hospital. In 1967 it was scheduled to be replaced by a modern structure in the governmental complex of Port Arthur.

The GATES MEMORIAL LIBRARY, 317 Stilwell Blvd., is a gift of Dellora R. Gates to the people of Port Arthur in memory of her husband, John Warne Gates, and their son Charles. The classic beauty of Renaissance style architecture of the original building was carefully preserved when an addition in 1955 more than doubled the floor space. The original is a one-story structure, oblong in shape, of reinforced concrete faced with Bedford limestone. The loggia has six large columns of carved limestone in classic Renaissance style. Marble wainscoting and walls and floors of plastered imitation limestone create a rich interior finish. Warren and Wetmore, architects of New York City, designed the original building. The addition has provided additional shelving and seating area, a music room, an all-purpose room that doubles as an art gallery, a larger work area, a staff lounge and additional office space. Staub and Rather of

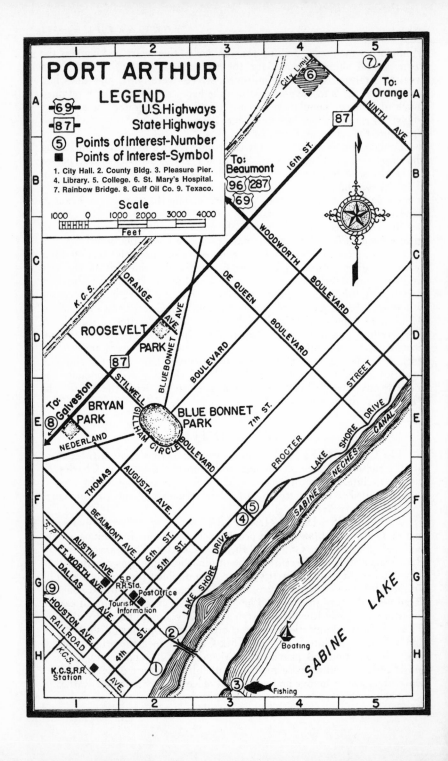

Houston designed the addition. In 1966 the Library had a stock of 65,121 volumes, having added 4,646 during the year, and a circulation of 260,-799. It had a collection of thousands of photographs and prints, stereoscopic views, periodicals and films. Among its books are the Gates family Bible and the *Book of Psalms* published in 1858 by the American Bible Society. The Library operates one branch.

The Library is open 9 a.m.-9 p.m., Monday through Friday; 9 a.m.-6 p.m. on Saturday. From September through May hours are 2–5 p.m. on Sunday.

PORT ARTHUR RADIO AND BUSINESS COLLEGE, 1500 Procter St., was presented to the city in 1909 by its founder, John W. Gates. It is a coeducational and nonsectarian commercial college. The four buildings, of cream-colored brick, costing approximately $500,000, occupy a 15-acre campus. This is the only commercial and radio college in the United States not privately owned, or operated for a profit. The governors are a self-perpetuating board of trustees, selected from the city's leading citizens, who serve without remuneration. Students may enroll any Monday, as the college is in session throughout the year. Radio Station KPAC is operated by the school and used to train students.

ST. MARY'S HOSPITAL, GATES MEMORIAL, 1931 9th Ave., was opened in 1930 as the successor to the hospital that John W. Gates endowed in the name of his mother, Mary A. Gates. It is controlled by the Sisters of Charity of the Incarnate Word, maintains schools of medical and x-ray technology and cooperates with Lamar State College in vocational nurse training. The 5 buildings of rose-colored brick with white stone trim are the hospital, chapel, convent, nurse's home and utility structure. The chapel has glazed windows of 13th century type and an altar of Italian marble. A modern wing was added in 1954. The hospital has bought 6.25 acres of adjacent land for expansion.

The SHRINE OF THE ARCHANGEL and the SHRINE OF OUR BLESSED MOTHER are near a hedge that separates the hospital grounds from a parking lot. PIONEER PARK, a landscaped plot of 20 acres, adjoins the hospital grounds on the left.

The PORT ARTHUR-ORANGE RAINBOW BRIDGE, 5 *m.* E. of the Port Arthur city limits on State 87, towers high above the Neches River, which it spans. A 7,700-foot-long structure that rises to a tiptop height of 230 feet, this was, in 1940, the tallest highway bridge in the South. Its vertical clearance for ocean-going vessels is 176 feet. Construction was completed on April 13, 1938, representing a cost of $2,750,-000. For 20 years Port Arthur interests had attempted to obtain an overland connection with points east; this was made financially possible through a grant of $1,141,742 by the Public Works Administration on August 24, 1935. Eleven thousand tons of steel, 31,700 cubic yards of concrete and 19,000 gallons of paint were used.

The GULF OIL CORPORATION REFINERY is adjacent to the city limits on State 87. This is one of the largest oil refineries in the world, its plant covering 4,000 acres. More than 276,000 barrels of crude oil, conveyed through pipe lines and by barges and tank steamers, are processed daily. Products include gasoline, kerosene, fuel and lubricating oils and greases, paraffin wax, and other specialties having a petroleum base, such as insecticides, cleaning fluids, automobile wax and polish and household lubricants. The refinery operates plants for the manufacture of coke, sulphur, sulphuric acid, and many petrochemicals. The 2,200 storage tanks have a capacity of 16,000,000 barrels. A six-tanker dock projects into an arm of the Sabine-Neches Canal where ocean-going ships load their cargoes.

The refinery was launched by James Guffey and John Galey, backers of the Spindletop discovery well; its pioneer stockholders included Andrew W. Mellon. The Gulf Refining Company was chartered in November, 1901, and assumed control of two refineries then under construction in Port Arthur. The refinery employs 3,800 at 300 different job classifications and the monthly payroll is more than $2,500,000. A freshwater reservoir covers 1,060 acres of its property. The plant uses as much fresh water as Pittsburgh and can supply enough electricity for a city as large as New Orleans. Out of 100 gallons of crude oil the refinery produces 42 gallons of gasoline, 23 of distillate fuel (heating oil, diesel oil), 20 of residual fuel, 5 of lubricating oils and 10 of various other products.

Visitors enter the refinery on West 7th St. and are taken on a tour in a bus, with guides. The bus starts at 9 a.m. and 12:30 p.m. for two-hour tours. Reservation is necessary: write Gulf Oil Corp., Box 702, Port Arthur, or phone YU 3–3301.

The TEXACO, INC., REFINERY, N. end of Houston Ave. (*guided tours by arrangement*) is the largest of this company's refineries in the Southwest and one of the largest in the country. The refinery location includes approximately 5,000 acres, half of which is occupied by plant equipment. Its primary distillation facilities can handle nearly 330,000 bbl. of crude oil each day; close to 500,000 bbl. of additional refining capacity is provided for subsequent operations, such as cracking, reforming, solvent refining and other highly technical methods. Enormous quantities of cooling water are needed—over 600,000 gallons pass through refinery equipment each minute. Lubricating oil is produced at a rate in excess of 19,000 bbl. a day and the grease plant is the world's largest. Tanks provide more than 25,000,000 bbl. of storage capacity. The company operates tankers, motor ships, tugs and barges, and is served by pipelines from fields in a number of contiguous states.

ATLANTIC REFINING COMPANY is another of the Big Three refineries that operate on Port Arthur's doorstep. It opened in 1923, covers 1,350 acres and has a refining capacity of approximately 84,000 bbl. a day Its 2,400 ft. of berth accommodates two supertankers and 9 barges.

A number of other large plants use the facilities of the Port of Port Arthur. The JEFFERSON CHEMICAL COMPANY began operations in 1948. It owns 1,100 acres and produces 42 organic chemicals, two inorganic, and nine chemical by-products. The firm is owned jointly by Texaco, Inc., and American Cyanamid Co.

GOODRICH-GULF CHEMICALS, Inc., opened in 1943 by the Gulf Oil Co. and the B. F. Goodrich Co., has an annual capacity of

160,000 tons of synthetic rubber. It also produces organic chemicals and chemical byproducts.

TEXAS-U. S. CHEMICAL CO., opened in 1955 by Texaco, Inc., and the U. S. Rubber Co., has an annual capacity of 156,000 tons of synthetic rubber. It occupies 74 acres.

Extremely useful to the economy of Port Arthur is the big grain elevator of CARGILL, Inc., operating the facilities under lease from the Kansas City Southern Railroad. There is storage capacity of 3,500,000 bushels; 553 ft. of berthing space for ships and loading capacity of 50,000 bushels per hour. More than 60,000,000 bushels of grain are exported annually.

Shipbuilding also profits by use of the Port Arthur Ship Channel. The GULFPORT SHIPBUILDING CORPORATION has four floating drydocks among its facilities. BURTON SHIPYARDS, established in 1946, is another large construction and overhauling operation.

Among the numerous corporations that profit from the communication facilities of Port Arthur are the Great Lakes Carbon Corp., Jones & Laughlin Steel Corp., Sinclair-Koppers Co., Allied Chemical Corp., U. S. Steel Corp., and Warren Petroleum Corp.

San Antonio

TRANSPORTATION

Airport and Airlines: San Antonio International Airport, US 281, Interstate 37; American Airlines, Braniff International Airways, Compania Mexicana de Aviacion, Continental Air Lines, Eastern Air Lines, Trans-Texas Airways. All-American Airlines (non-schedule) has office at Airport.

Buses: Continental Trailways, Broadway at 3rd; also Randolph Field Bus Co., regular trips to Randolph Field, one way 50¢; round trip, 90¢. Central Greyhound Lines, 500 N. St. Mary's, also Kerrville Bus Line (El Paso, Amarillo, Denver); Painter Bus Line (Uvalde, Del Rio, Eagle Pass). Gray Line Tours, Alamo Plaza.

Highways: US 81, Interstate 35, connects Fort Worth, Waco, Austin, Laredo; Branch Road 81 passes Fort Sam Houston, joins Broadway. Interstate 10 comes into the city parallel with US 90 from Houston, then moves northwest through Balcones Heights and US 87 to San Angelo and beyond; US 90 moves southwest to Del Rio. US 281, main north-south route from Wichita Falls to the Lower Rio Grande Valley, enters city near International Airport, will parallel Interstate 37. US 181 connects San Antonio and Corpus Christi, is route to the Missions and USAF Aerospace Medical Center. Interstate 410 is a loop highway connecting with the principal roads. State 16 is a major north-south road through the ranch country. Distances from San Antonio (miles): Brownsville, 278; Corpus Christi, 144; Dallas-Fort Worth, 275; El Paso, 570; Houston, 199; Laredo, 152.

Railroads: Missouri-Kansas-Texas, 415 S. Flores St.; Missouri Pacific, 123 N. Medina St.; Southern Pacific, 654 E. Commerce St.

INFORMATION

Information and Accommodations: San Antonio Chamber of Commerce, 202 E. Commerce; Municipal Information Bureau, 153 Navarro St.; American Automobile Assn., 606 Broadway . . . ; *San Antonio Express* (morning); *San Antonio News* (evening); *Express & News* (Saturday and Sunday), Avenue E and Third St.; *San Antonio Light* (evening, Saturday and Sunday morning), 420 Broadway. Dept. of Tourism, Republic of Mexico, St. Mary's at Travis Ave.

San Antonio has many large and commodious hotels and motor hotels; the historic Menger Hotel, 225 rooms, has added a 4-story motel of 111 rooms; the 9-story El Tropicano Motor Hotel has 350 units; the Blue Bonnet, Crockett, Gunter, St. Anthony and Travis-Plaza are well known. Some of the newest are the Palacio del Rio, a Hilton Hotel; La Posada del Rio, 2 La Quinta motor inns, 3 Holiday inns.

RECREATION

Parks: San Antonio has more than 3,000 acres devoted to parks offering every form of outdoor activity and all easily accessible. Brackenridge Park, Broadway at Pershing Ave., has an 18-hole golf course, baseball diamonds, softball courts, tennis courts, horses for riding, picnic areas, a sky ride and a miniature train. In 9 other metropolitan parks there are similar facilities, including swimming pools, sail boating, fishing, and all have concessions to serve the appetite. A supervised recreational program is provided in 16 year-round and 46 summer recreation centers, with 13 municipal swimming pools and 5 junior pools, 33 tennis courts and 47 ball diamonds. Swimming fees range from 35¢ to 50¢ for adults and 15¢ to 25¢ for children.

Baseball: The San Antonio Missions Team is a farm club of the Chicago Cubs, with frequent games with other city clubs. Admission, adults, $1.25, children 50¢. *Softball* is played nightly on many diamonds, no admission charge.

Basketball: Trinity University is in the Southland Conference; St. Mary's University is in the Big State Conference, and San Antonio College is in the Texas Junior College Conference, all with regular schedules.

Boating: Woodlawn Lake, inside the city limits; Lake McQueeney, near Seguin, 25 *m.*, has speed boating, water skiing, etc. Lakes with many facilities in the outskirts are Medina Lake, 30 *m.*, and the chain of Highland Lakes, about 80 *m.*, including Lake Austin, Lake Lyndon B. Johnson, Lake Marble Falls, Inks Lake, and Lake Buchanan. Also Canyon Lake, 25 *m.*

Dude Ranches: Some excellent dude ranches have been developed in the hill country north and west of San Antonio, usually a 30-minute drive away. Facilities include all forms of outing and families are accommodated. Consult Chamber of Commerce or your hotel.

Football: Trinity University plays teams of the Southern Conference during the season. For other Conference games the nearest are at the University of Texas in Austin. High schools are members of the Texas Interscholastic League and play regularly. San Antonio Toros is a team in the Texas League.

Golf: There are 4 municipal golf courses, of which Olmos Basin Course, opened 1963, has become most popular. Of these courses three have 18 holes and one has 20 holes. Green fees are $1 on week days and $1.50 on Saturdays, Sundays and holidays. Six country clubs have golf courses, and a pitch and putt course open to the public has a 50¢ green fee. There are 4 miniature golf courses and 4 driving ranges. The Texas Open Golf Tournament is held the first two weeks in February.

Hunting: Deer and other wild game are either close to San Antonio or easily accessible by motor car; these include wild turkey, dove, quail, bobcat and javelina. Resident licenses, $3.15 per person; nonresident, $25.

Fishing: Freshwater fishing is available in the Guadalupe River at New Braunfels,·25 *m.*, Lake Seguin, 30 *m.*, and the Highland Lakes, 80 *m.* Fishing licenses are $2.15 per person, without residential restriction.

CULTURAL EVENTS AND ENTERTAINMENT

Music: San Antonio Symphony Society sponsors the San Antonio Symphony, 90 musicians, in weekly concerts from October to March, with leading soloists. Grand Opera Festival, 4 operas first two weeks in March, with stars of Metropolitan Opera of New York. San Antonio Chamber Music Society, 4 concerts a year. Tuesday Musical Club, 4 concerts. Touring ballet companies, symphony orchestras, plays and musicals appear each season, many in the Municipal Auditorium and Civic Center.

Fiesta de San Antonio: 8 days of festivities including San Jacinto Day, April 21, and a pilgrimage to the Alamo, processions, coronation of the Queen in the Municipal Auditorium and dancing.

Fiesta Noche del Rio, Tuesday, Thursday, Friday and Saturday evenings in June, July, August, with gondola rides on the San Antonio River and musical programs, including Mexican singing and dancing, at Arneson River Theater. Fun-tier Nights, Wednesday evenings in Juarez Plaza of La Villita, with the Chordsman Chorus, Dixieland jazz, barbershop quartet harmony.

San Jose de Aguayo Mission Theater: Los Pastores, a Spanish miracle play, at Christmas; Drama Festival, two or more weeks, in midsummer.

Shows and Fairs: Bexar County Junior Live Stock Show, January; Senior Live Stock Show and Rodeo, February. Health Fair, Brooke Army Medical Center, October.

SAN ANTONIO (650–800 alt., 587,718 pop., 1960; 699,768, 1966, est.) is the third largest city in Texas, with more citizens of Spanish and Mexican descent than any other in the State. In 1960 white persons with Spanish surnames numbered 245,627; out of the half million population only 43,221 were nonwhite. In the projection for 1966, 647,985 were white and 51,783 nonwhite, and 289,704 were whites with Spanish surnames.

Incorporated cities inside San Antonio are Alamo Heights (7,000 pop. est.); Balcones Heights (1,000 pop. approx.); Castle Hills (3,400 pop. est.); Olmos Park (3,000 pop. approx.); and Terrell Hills (5,500 pop.).

San Antonio is an industrial, trade, cultural and recreational center in a state of dynamic expansion. Its major activities include manufacturing of durable goods and food processing that enlist the activities of more than 25,000 workers. It is headquarters for technical, medical and surgical research of major proportions. In its environs are a number of the most important military pilot training and airplane maintenance bases in the country, with a personnel of 54,000, in addition to which the Federal Government employs 39,000 in this metropolitan area. Blessed with a climate in which the normal mean temperature ranges from 52° in January to 84° in midsummer, San Antonio has become the ideal objective of thousands seeking leisure and recreation, many of whom take up permanent residence.

There were human habitations on this site in the 17th century, and San Antonio was already a Spanish outpost when the proseltyzing Franciscan padres began building their Mission churches in 1720. In the battle for Texan independence from Mexico it became the scene of the immortal heroism of the Alamo. Its Latin American relations did not diminish after Texas broke with Mexico; on the contrary the Mexicans settled in such large numbers west of Downtown that one-third of San Antonio's residents are of Mexican or Spanish derivation. The soft syllables of their speech are heard everywhere and their food preparations are relished by tourists. San Antonio is favored by visitors from Mexico, who come to buy American products. The city's appreciation of this relationship was expressed when for its 250th anniversary in 1968 it mounted the Hemis-Fair and dedicated it to continuing Latin American friendship.

While the Anglo-American stock is dominant, a large segment of the remainder derives from the German immigrations of the 19th century. German was taught in the schools and some solidly-built German dwellings still stand, although the bigger German communities were settled farther north, toward New Braunfels. Negroes constitute less than 10 per cent of the population. The French and Belgian strains are represented, and there are Chinese who speak their own version of Mexican.

As a balance for the large numbers engaged in trade and industry is the emphasis placed on education and military service. The public school system enrolls approximately 150,000; the Roman Catholic parochial schools serve between 28,000 and 30,000. Higher education is provided by two universities, four colleges, and several military and private institutions, and medical education has superior facilities.

San Antonio has a large church-going population. The Baptists constitute the largest Protestant denomination, with 130 churches. The Roman Catholics have 55 churches and among their communicants are practically all citizens of Mexican background. Other large denominations and their churches are: Methodist, 51; Lutheran, 40; Church of Christ, 29; Presbyterian, 28; Pentecostal, 16, and Episcopalian, 13. Many other sects are represented, including the two Mormon groups; Adventists, Nazarene, Jehovah's Witnesses, and Foursquare Gospel.

San Antonio is at the heart of a huge military establishment, having within its limits and environs four major bases devoted to air pilot training and aircraft maintenance, and one military center for medical research. They are Fort Sam Houston, headquarters of the Fourth U. S. Army, in northeast San Antonio, which has on its grounds the Brooke Army Medical Center, with the General Hospital; Brooks Air Force Base, home of the USAF School of Aviation Medicine and the Aerospace Medical Division of the Air Force Systems Command, 6 *m.* southeast of downtown San Antonio on US 181; Kelly Air Force Base, headquarters of the San Antonio Air Materiel Area and a great repair and maintenance organization; Lackland Air Force Base, adjoining Kelly AFB, the major recruit training center of the Southwest, and Randolph Air Force Base, 17 *m.* northeast on US 81. With three other installations, Camp Bullis, Camp Stanley, and Medina Base these account for the 54,000 military personnel.

Throughout the city lingers the influence of the *conquistadores,* the *padres,* and the early Spanish settlers. Its skyscrapers appear alien beside historic buildings. Its many important industries and commercial institutions serve a large part of the Southwest, yet close beside them, queer, musty old establishments near Main and Military Plazas still specialize in serving the ranch and chuck wagon. Traffic rolls over streets that follow trails beaten by mustangs and cattle drives. In the apt expression of an earlier day, a map of the downtown section still shows considerable resemblance to a "skillet of snakes."

Not the least of the city's charms is the river, so winding near its source in San Antonio that an oft-repeated legend most adequately describes it. Back in the days when the Indians learned much from the Spaniards besides the doctrines piously expounded by the padres, they characterized the river by an Indian word which meant "drunken-old-man-going-home-at-night." Spanned by bridges in the business and residential districts, this unhurried stream travels 15 miles to cross six miles of city blocks. In 1939 a $300,000 river beautification project, financed by means of a city bond issue and a Work Projects Administration grant, was inaugurated. Conversion of the river into a thoroughfare by means of walks leading from all principal downtown streets, and deepening of the stream to make it navigable for small river craft, was part of the program, which included the construction of river-edge walks, landscaping, building of electrical fountains, and the creation of an outdoor theater equipped with water curtains. (*See the Paseo del Rio San Antonio*).

Indians inhabited the site of the city unnumbered centuries before the white man set foot on the Western Hemisphere, as indicated by archeological remains. It is believed that Cabeza de Vaca visited the neighborhood in 1536 and discovered a village of friendly natives.

On June 13, 1691, Don Domingo Terán de los Rios, accompanied by Father Damian Massanet and an escort of 50 soldiers, found a large *rancheria* of Payayas at the headwaters of a pleasantly shaded river. The Indians called the village "Yanaguana," but Father Massanet, having set up a cross and erected an arbor of cottonwood boughs under which to say mass, rechristened the place San Antonio, in honor of St. Anthony of Padua. In 1714 the French explorer, Louis Juchereau de St. Denis, reported the advantages of the location for settlement.

Don Martin de Alarcón, Captain General and Governor of the Province of Texas, and Fray Antonio de San Buenaventura Olivares, with 72 settlers, monks, and soldiers, pushed laboriously across 600 miles of wilderness from Mexico, and reached the "site called San Antonio," in May of 1718, driving before them 200 cows, 548 horses, 1,000 sheep, and 200 oxen. The soldier Alarcón and the missionary Olivares quarreled mightily, and the expedition split before its destination was reached.

On May 1 Father Olivares founded the Mission San Antonio de Valero (the present Alamo), named for St. Anthony and the viceroy, and built a hut as a temporary mission structure. Governor Alarcón, four days later, founded the Villa de Bejar (later spelled Bexar, and pronounced Bay-ar), and left a guard of soldiers.

Within the next 13 years four more missions raised their stone walls along the green-banked river for a distance of seven miles.

Fifteen families from the Canary Islands limped into the Villa de Bejar, March 9, 1731, after a year's journey, and established the Villa de San Fernando, across the stream from the Mission San Antonio de Valero. They built flat-roofed stone and adobe houses around two plazas, and, like the padres at the missions, dug *acequias* (irrigation ditches) to water their fields. They quarreled with the missionaries, the soldiers, and among themselves. Their church was built by public contributions, generously increased by the King of Spain, and a school was established in 1746 (*see Education*).

In 1786 Francisco Guadalupe Calaorra was awarded a grant of land in recognition of his ownership of a boat, with which he established a ferry across the San Antonio River. Thus, although San Antonio is 150 miles from the sea, and near no navigable stream, its first public transportation was by water.

The missions prospered, declined, and in 1793–94 ceased to function. The fort, villa, and the settlement about the secularized Mission San Antonio de Valero, were consolidated into San Antonio de Bexar, the capital of the Province of Texas.

A motley crew of Anglo-American filibusterers and Mexican and Indian revolutionists held the town when Mexico attempted to free itself from Spanish rule, but retaliation came swiftly with the Spaniard, Don Joaquin Arredondo, who exterminated the rebel army, and imprisoned 300 citizens (August 20, 1813) in an airless building where 18 smothered before the remainder were taken out and shot. He forced the women to convert 24 bushels of corn into *tortillas,* daily, for the Spanish army, and so mistreated many of them that the street which passed the place of imprisonment is to this day *Dolorosa*—the Street of Sorrow. When Arredondo finished, the town was well-nigh deserted, its prosperity drowned in blood.

After Moses Austin arrived in San Antonio one December day of 1820 and opened Texas to Anglo-American settlement, the city's history became, in large part, the history of the State, although it remained a typically Mexican town. Not until after the Texas Revolution in 1836 did Anglo-American influence begin to make itself really felt. In the 1840's another racial element arrived to help mold the community—a heavy influx of German immigrants. Beer gardens began to dot the river banks, and *Saengerfests* made San Antonio a music center.

As early as 1834, however, the desire for self-government was manifest in San Antonio. A number of local Mexicans joined the cause of independence from the harsh rule of Santa Anna, dictator-President of Mexico. The Battle of San Antonio began on December 5, 1835, when Texas revolutionists under Ben Milam stormed the town, and resulted, five days later, in the formal surrender of General Martin Perfecto de Cos. But the military success of the Texans was temporary. Santa Anna, with an army of more than 5,000, reached San Antonio in February, 1836, and on March 6 took the Alamo fortress after every defender had died. After this tragedy San Antonio was almost deserted until the rout of the Mexicans at San Jacinto in April, 1836, after which San Antonio became an outpost of the new Republic of Texas.

In 1861 General David E. Twiggs, commander of the Department of Texas, surrendered the Department to volunteers of Major Ben McCulloch's Confederate forces who had seized the army post and the town. On the afternoon of that day, February 16, Lieutenant Colonel Robert E. Lee arrived in San Antonio from Fort Mason, under orders to report in Washington. Those in charge of military offices informed him that unless he joined the Confederacy transportation of his baggage would be denied; he refused, on the grounds that he owned allegiance to Virginia and to the Union, but not to "any revolutionary government of Texas," and, technically a prisoner, on departure was forced to leave his baggage, which he never recovered. John Baylor began recruiting his Partisan Rangers in San Antonio in 1862, a year marked by a riot on Christmas Eve by some members of a Confederate company of Taylor's Battalion. The rioters destroyed chili stands on the plazas, and clashed with a company of local Mexican volunteers. By 1863 San Antonio had contributed 40 companies to the Confederacy. As the war ended, soldiers of the lost cause, on their way to join the army of Emperor Maximilian in Mexico, passed through the city.

The beginning of the cattle drives, immediately after the Civil War, and the coming of the first railroad (1877), when the Southern Pacific built westward, brought great changes. Other railroads soon followed. Immigrants poured in. The lusty business of the open range boomed in the late 1870's and early 1880's, and San Antonio became a concentration point for the livestock industry and developed meat packing, flour mills, cement plants and breweries.

When the 250th anniversary of the founding of San Antonio came in 1968, the city marked the event and its eminence as a center of Latin-American culture and trade by presenting the HEMISFAIR, the first international exposition in this part of the Southwest. The theme, "The Confluence of Civilizations in the Americas," was proclaimed to the world in the President's message of November 11, 1966. The city had taken over an underdeveloped area of 92.6 acres east of South Alamo Street, south of Commerce and Market Streets, and north of Durango Boulevard, and with the help of the Federal Urban Renewal program had cleared it of run-down dwellings and stores and relocated its residents in better quarters. Here was placed the HemisFair, at an estimated cost of upwards of $156,000,000 for buildings and landscaping, covered by municipal bonds and State and Federal appropriations.

In order to get permanent use out of the principal buildings the City erected the CONVENTION CENTER, to continue as the CIVIC CENTER. It includes the Exhibition Hall of 200,000 sq. ft., and banquet facilities for 3,100; the Center for the Performing Arts, seating 2,800, and the Arena, seating 10,500 and especially suited for conventions, sports events and spectaculars. The San Antonio River was tapped for an extension into the Fair grounds at this point. The architects of the Center were Noonan & Krocker.

To dominate the grounds the City built the TOWER OF THE AMERICAS, a huge concrete and steel observation structure rising 622 ft., 22 ft. taller than the Seattle Space Needle and 67 ft. taller than the Washington Monument. It surpasses in height San Antonio's tallest office structure, the Tower-Life Building, 550 ft. Glass-enclosed elevators are used to carry visitors to the top. The first level, 550 ft. up, has a restaurant and can make a complete revolution in an hour. Two other levels are provided for observation of the city and a vast panorama of fields and towns. The tower was designed by O'Neil Ford.

Designed for permanent use also was the United States Pavilion, for which the Federal Government appropriated $6,750,000. It includes the Confluence Theater, a circular structure 70 ft. tall, which has innovations such as disappearing interior walls and screens for motion picture purposes. The architects were Donald Deskey Associates of New York and Marmon & Mok of San Antonio. The Texas Pavilion, or Institute of Texan Cultures, is a colonnaded building of limestone, granite and glass, 368 ft. long and 242 ft. wide, which exhibited the progress of life on Texas soil since prehistoric times. Caudill, Rowlett & Scott of Houston were the architects. This also was built for permanent use.

The Woman's Pavilion was designed to show the numerous interests of the women of Texas. To provide unusual means of transportation inside the grounds the Fair provided the Mini-Monorail, moving over 1½ miles, built of fiberglas and aluminum; the Skyride, one-fourth of a mile long, 82 ft. above the surface; also boats and gondolas. Aware that most of Texas moves by motor car the Fair authorities cleared more than 44 acres east of the grounds for parking.

Industry in San Antonio is diversified and there are slightly under 1,000 manufacturing plants. Aircraft and aircraft components, road building machinery and oil equipment, are representative durable goods; pharmaceutical and electronics establishments have been increasing in recent years; there are 80 apparel makers and there is substantial employment in meat packing, frozen food processing, furniture and millwork. The wide range of manufacturing is indicated by San Antonio's production of prison cell blocks, stained glass windows, and bowling balls.

POINTS OF INTEREST

The ALAMO (*open 9–5:30 workdays, 10–5 Sun. and holidays*), E. side of Alamo Plaza, stands in the shadow of a modern skyscraper. This little low gray chapel and the crumbling ivy-covered walls about the courtyard northwest of the chapel are all that remain of the mission-fort in which at last 187 Anglo-Americans laid down their lives that Texas might be free.

Many believe that in its original form the chapel—built about 1756 and the third one to be erected on this spot—resembled Mission Concepcion with its twin towers. The mission of which the chapel was a part ceased to function as a church institution in 1793. Though used irregularly as a fort thereafter, it fell progressively into decay, and at the time of the siege (February 23-March 6, 1836), it was a roofless ruin almost filled with debris; but a high rock wall about three feet thick, combined with buildings that had been cloisters and later were barracks, formed an enclosed parallelogram, slightly enlarged at the north, which covered much of what is now Alamo Plaza. Within that enclosure the battle was fought, with a last stand in the chapel.

In 1849, Major E. B. Babbitt, U. S. A., repaired the building for use as a quartermaster depot. He restored the chapel walls to support a new roof, and the arched top of the present front was his design, although the carved entrance remains as it was originally.

The chapel was purchased by the State in 1883, and other property about the courtyard in September, 1905. The wall along the sidewalk from Houston Street toward the chapel is a part of the original ruins.

In 1936, as a Texas Centennial project, $250,000 was appropriated by the State to complete the purchase of the block, and work was begun to convert the area into a park.

Except for repairs, including a new roof and new stone flagging, the chapel remains as it was built, its walls in the form of a cross, with small rooms on each side of the large central part of the church.

On the right is the baptistry. Opposite it on the left is the confessional. The second door to the left leads to a chamber called the monks' burial

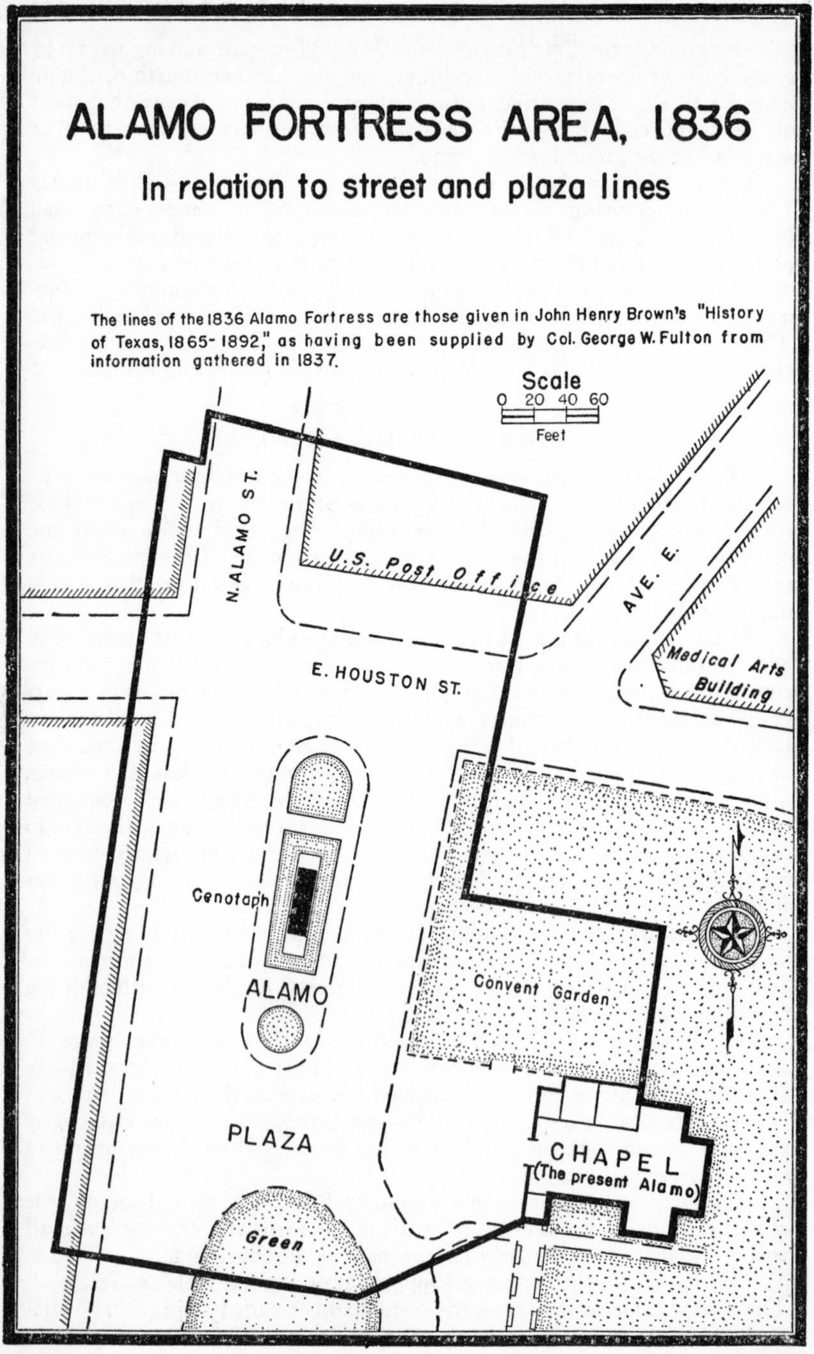

ALAMO FORTRESS AREA, 1836

In relation to street and plaza lines

The lines of the 1836 Alamo Fortress are those given in John Henry Brown's "History of Texas, 1865-1892," as having been supplied by Col. George W. Fulton from information gathered in 1837.

Scale
0 20 40 60
Feet

N. ALAMO ST.

U.S. Post Office

E. HOUSTON ST.

AVE. E.

Medical Arts Building

Cenotaph

ALAMO

Convent Garden

PLAZA

CHAPEL
(The present Alamo)

Green

room, which opens into the sacristy. Left of the chapel is the ALAMO MUSEUM (*open 9–5 workdays, 10–1 Sun.*), erected by the State in 1937. The building is of Spanish Colonial architecture, designed by Henry T. Phelps. Relics of the Alamo and of the era of the Republic of Texas are housed here.

The HEROES OF THE ALAMO CENOTAPH, in Alamo Plaza, occupies the approximate center of the former Alamo fortress area. The blunt shaft rising from a sarcophagus bears on the south face a heroic male figure, the Spirit of Sacrifice rising from the funeral pyre of the Texans, while a female figure on the north face represents the Spirit of Texas, bearing under her arms reversed shields symbolizing Texas and the United States. Travis, Bonham, Crockett and Bowie are central figures in groups of soldiers on the other sides. Names of the Alamo defenders are carved around the rim of the sarcophagus. Of Georgia marble, the Cenotaph was erected in 1939 as a project of the Centennial Division of the State Board of Control. Adams and Adams were the architects; Pompeo Coppini, the sculptor.

The MENGER HOTEL, northeast corner of Alamo Plaza and Blum St. dates from 1859 and has been enlarged recently. In its years it sheltered Robert E. Lee, Theodore Roosevelt, Benjamin Harrison, William Howard Taft and William Jennings Bryan. Opposite is JOSKE'S, a huge department store that masks St. Joseph's Catholic Church on three sides. Another well known hostelry, the CROCKETT HOTEL, occu- .pies the southeast corner of E. Crockett and Bonham Sts. Among the new hotels and motels built in time for the Fair is the PALACIO DEL RIO, a Hilton hotel that rises 21 stories above the river at the very gates of the HemisFair area. La Posada del Rio hotel was built in the shell of St. Mary's Law School on College St. The historic facade was retained.

The GERMAN-ENGLISH SCHOOL BUILDINGS, 421 South Alamo St., were restored in 1964 for use as general offices of the Hemis-Fair Exposition. They date from 1859, when two stone buildings were erected by citizens of German background. The school, with several additions, operated until 1897. Subsequently the buildings were used by the George W. Brackenridge Grammar School (1903–1923), the Thomas Nelson Page High School (1923–1925), the San Antonio Junior College (1926–1961), and finally by the Civil Defense and County Welfare organizations.

LA VILLITA (Sp. Little Village) is an approximation, amid the tall buildings of downtown San Antonio, of a Spanish-Mexican village located here 200 years ago. In a square block bounded by S. Presa, Villita, Alamo and Nuevo Sts., is an oasis of small shops and houses where products of arts and crafts are displayed. Early traders and workers are said to have lived here with their families. Womble Alley is now King Phillip V St. The open square is Juarez Plaza, honoring Benito Juarez. The Cos House is reportedly the restored house of the Mexican general who surrendered here to General Austin in 1835. The village was built with the help of the National Youth Administration. In May, 1959, the circular ASSEMBLY BUILDING was dedicated for community use. It has massive rock walls, heavy oaken doors and iron gates. It can seat 1,900 and accommodate 1,350 at banquets.

PASEO DEL RIO SAN ANTONIO, 21 blocks long, is the result of beautification of the river begun in 1939. It has 31 stairways, each of an individual design. Decorative shops line the banks. At one bend the ARNESON RIVER THEATRE provides an air of old-world enchantment. On the bank opposite are tiers of grass-covered seats accommodating 1,000 spectators. Beside the stage a Spanish house contains dressing rooms. Here the Fiesta Noche del Rio annually brings songs and dances of old Mexico to the city, while river taxis glide under the bridges and colored lights illuminate the scene.

The SAN ANTONIO PUBLIC LIBRARY occupies new headquarters at Market St. and St. Mary's. It is the hub of an expanding library system. It has seven branch libraries, four book trailers, and two bookmobiles, more than 450,000 books and 250,000 Government reports. All the services of a modern library, including microfilm, microcards, 16mm. sound films, records and photo-duplication are fully supplied.

Special libraries throughout the city—educational, scientific, statistical —substantially raise the reading and research facilities. The BEXAR COUNTY MEDICAL LIBRARY of the Bexar County Medical Society and the International Medical Assembly of the Southwest, occupies a new building that cost $310,000. The library of the Southwest Research Institute has more than 14,000 volumes and receives 1,000 periodicals. Other medical research libraries are the Stimson Library and the Brooke General Hospital Library, at Brooke Army Medical Center; the Aerospace Medical Library at Brooks Air Force Base and the Wilford Hall USAF Hospital Library. The Mexican Government has installed 5,000 volumes about Mexico in the Mexican Consulate. Besides the libraries in the colleges and universities, separate law libraries are located in the School of Law of St. Mary's University and the Bexar County Courthouse.

The HERZBERG CIRCUS COLLECTION for a number of years has been located on the third floor of the former building of the San Antonio Public Library. The Library has moved but the collection was still housed at 210 West Market St. in 1968. It has more than 20,000 items, including posters, wagons, Gen. Tom Thumb's carriage, and memorabilia of special value as Americana.

The BEXAR COUNTY COURTHOUSE, between W. Nueva St. and Main Plaza, Dwyer and S. Main Aves., is built of red Pecos sandstone and red granite from Marble Falls in a Romanesque style. The front section was erected in 1892, the rear 1928. The FEDERAL RESERVE BANK BUILDING occupies the next block south, and the new COUNTY JAIL is two blocks west.

The site of the COUNCIL HOUSE FIGHT, 114 Main Plaza, is indicated by a marker on the Citizens' Industrial Bank building. In 1840, 12 Comanche chiefs who had brought a party of 65 Indians to San Antonio, bargained with citizens for the freedom of 13 white captives. The Indians brought only one captive, and a fight started when settlers proposed that the chiefs be held as hostages against the delivery of the remaining white prisoners. Of the Indians 33 were killed and 32 captured, with 7 whites killed and 8 or 10 wounded. At this spot in 1842, General Woll, with a Mexican army, captured Bexar's judges and jury and took them prisoners to Mexico.

The site of the MUSQUIZ HOUSE, 336 W. Commerce St., is indicated by a marker on the Main Plaza side of this corner building that replaces the Ramon Musquiz house in which the Mexican general, Santa Anna, received the women and children survivors of the Battle of the Alamo.

At the FATAL CORNER, 401 W. Commerce St., occurred six major homicides in the days of the "bad men." On this site stood the Jack Harris Vaudeville Theater, in which, one night in 1884, took place the killing of Ben Thompson and King Fisher, both gunmen of great repute, and the fatal wounding of Joe Foster, one of the theater's proprietors. Jack Harris, a partner of Foster's, had been killed by Thompson in 1882. A blood feud had developed between the proprietors of the theater and Thompson, because of a gambling debt.

The site of SANTA ANNA'S HEADQUARTERS, 409 W. Commerce St., has a marker on the division wall between the building at this number and the one on the corner.

SAN FERNANDO CATHEDRAL (*open 6–8:30 daily*), on Main Plaza between Trevino and Galan Sts., has the oldest parish church building in the State. The iron cross mounted on the Moorish dome of the earliest part of this Catholic cathedral once marked the geographical center of the city. In the Villa of San Fernando a parochial church stood here; its cornerstone was laid in 1738. Colonel Francis W. Johnson raised the flag of victory from its towers in 1835 following the Battle of San Antonio; Santa Anna used the church during the Alamo siege, and from its top flew the blood red flag of no quarter. The building as it now appears was completed in 1873 (the rear of the building being original), and the parish church became a cathedral in 1874. In 1936 fragments of bone were disinterred from beneath the floor, believed by some authorities to be remains of Alamo heroes, buried there after their charred bones had been recovered from the site of the funeral pyres.

In the rear of the main building is the CATHEDRAL MUSEUM (*open 9–5:30 workdays*), which contains church relics and objects of historic interest, including a door of the former parish church, equipped with 10 locks.

MILITARY PLAZA, between S. Flores, Camaron, W. Commerce and Dolorosa Sts., established by the Canary Islanders in 1731 as the Plaza de las Armas, or "place of arms," was the center of protection for the settlers. Here the buildings were built low, of adobe, with flat roofs and few outside openings, so that in case of Indian attack they could be used as forts. At night, rawhides were stretched across the narrow openings between houses, to repel arrows. Here the soldiers of the garrison resided, ready to respond should the sentinel in the church tower give an alarm. CITY HALL, in the center of Military Plaza, is an Italian Renaissance building of limestone, designed by Otto Kramer. It was erected in 1888 and partly reconstructed in 1927. On the NW. corner of the grounds is a bronze STATUE OF MOSES AUSTIN, executed by Waldine Tauch, sculptor.

San Antonio, rich in memorials of its Spanish-Mexican periods, has taken care in recent years to restore houses associated with its 19th-century affluence. With the help of the San Antonio Conservation Society, the King William Street Area Association, and other civic leaders, buildings were rescued from neglect and refurbished for public edification. One is the NAVARRO HOMESTEAD, a group of three at Nueva and S. Laredo Sts., inhabited by Jose Antonio Navarro, who signed the Texas Declaration of Independence in 1836 and died here in 1877. Its two-story house, at one time an inn, is now a museum of antiques. Similarly furnished is the fine Victorian EDUARD STEVES HOMESTEAD, 509 King St., erected by a German merchant in 1876. It has two-story porches across its street front. The ornate two-story SCHULZE STORE was restored in time for the HemisFair and became the Humble Pavilion. The Beethoven Maennerchor (male chorus) in 1895 built its BEETHOVEN HALL, 418 S. Alamo St. It was destroyed by fire in 1913 and rebuilt. Eventually it was put to commercial uses. It has now been restored as a theater.

The FRANCISCO RUIZ HOUSE, formerly at 420 Dolores St., has been moved to Brackenridge Park. It was the home of Francisco Ruiz, signer of the Texas Declaration of Independence. His son, who was *alcalde* (mayor) of San Antonio at the time of the Alamo battle, was assigned by Santa Anna to the task of burying the dead Mexicans and burning the bodies of the Texans.

The TWOHIG PLACE, formerly behind 201 N. St. Mary's St., has been removed to Brackenridge Park. It is part of a house erected by John Twohig about 1840. One of the city's first merchants, Twohig was called "the breadline banker of St. Mary's Street," because he distributed bread to the poor. The two-story limestone structure stood on the bank of the San Antonio River.

The SPANISH GOVERNORS' PALACE (*open 9–5 Mon.-Sat., 10–5 Sunday; adm. 15¢; children up to 14, 5¢*), 105 Military Plaza, contains Spanish Colonial furniture and wrought iron. The arms of the Hapsburgs are on the keystone over the main entrance.

Carved in the keystone is the date 1749. The exact date of erection of the building, however, and its actual use except as the *comandancia* (residence of the captain of the presidio), is not definitely known, but according to tradition Spanish governors or vice governors of the province of Texas made it their home, and here gave gala receptions and balls, performed administrative duties and held judicial tribunals.

In 1804, however, it was the property of Ygnazio Perez, whose heirs held it for 125 years. It became a second-hand clothing store, a restaurant, and a barroom called "The Hole in the Wall." In 1929, when the City of San Antonio purchased it for the purpose of restoration, it was a junk-cluttered eyesore, with only parts of the old structure remaining.

The long, low building is white, plastered inside and out. There are ten rooms and a loft, *la dispensa,* where food supplies were stored. At the right of the entrance hall is the Room of the Blessed Virgin, for family worship. At the left is the Sala de Justicia, where the affairs of government are supposed to have been conducted, also used as a ballroom. Other rooms are the "governor's office," several bedrooms, and the dining room, which has a fireplace and a stone *lavabo,* for washing the hands before eating. An open brazier of stone is in the kitchen.

In the patio are a "wishing well," a central fountain, winding paths and grounds landscaped with native flowers and shrubs.

The palace is a challenge to laymen and experts alike to detect the old part from the new. It was restored under the direction of Harvey P. Smith, architect, and is administered by the City of San Antonio.

The SAN ANTONIO SYMPHONY SOCIETY is the principal musical organization in the city. It sponsors the San Antonio Symphony Orchestra of 90 musicians under the direction of Victor Allesandro, which gives weekly concerts from October to March. It also sponsors the Grand Opera Festival, one of the leading social events, which takes place the first two weeks in March at the Municipal Auditorium, when four operas are sung with artists from the Metropolitan Opera in New York as soloists. The city supports many other musical and dramatic programs. Its Civic Ballet is a member of the Southwest Regional Ballet Assn. The Chamber Music Society sponsors four concerts by important groups, and the Tuesday Musical Club supports four concerts by famous artists. National touring companies bring musicals and plays to San Antonio.

SAN ANTONIO LITTLE THEATRE presents six plays and a musical each season in the SAN PEDRO PLAYHOUSE, which stands in San Pedro Park, San Pedro Ave. and Ashby. The building is owned by the City and the Little Theatre has been performing there since 1958. There are 500 seats. BILLBOARD THEATRE, 231 S. Broadway on the River, is a nonprofit theater in the round, presenting plays, musicals, and children's programs.

The former MEXICAN QUARTER, which began west of San Pedro Creek, has lost much of its picturesqueness by the spread of its population to the west and south. There are, however, plenty of Mexican neighborhoods that enable the visitor to feel he has crossed the Rio Grande. Here are odd shops, distinctive foreign odors, women wrapped in black *rebozos* huddling over baskets of freshly made *tortillas,* venders of candy, *pan dulce* (sweet bread), balloons, and brilliant paper flowers. Street singers wander over this district, often improvising folk songs as they go. Among them are many Mexican singers whose songs have been recorded.

The picturesqueness of the Mexican neighborhoods does not obscure the big problem of rehabilitation. San Antonio probably had more business and professional men of Mexican extraction than any other Texas city, but it also had a big stratum of day laborers who lived in congested areas in badly constructed dwellings, often doing piece-work, such as shelling pecans in the home. This was prohibited in 1936. That year San Antonio tackled slum clearance seriously and in 1938 organized the San Antonio Housing Authority, which began to raze dwellings and erect low-cost one-family units with Federal financial help. But that this was slow and insufficient to clear the city of substandard housing was indicated in a report of the Housing Authority as late as 1967. The Authority agitated for a substantial increase in the low and moderate income housing supply, with special attention to the needs of families that were not even able to pay a modest rent. The Census of 1960 listed 13,849 families with incomes under $3,000 a year and 3,343 families, or 15 per cent, with incomes under $1,000.

San Antonio has moved slowly but deliberately to the goal that "a decent, safe, and sanitary dwelling and suitable living environment should be available to every family and individual in San Antonio." It has cleared slum areas and developed a number of projects for providing apartments at low rentals. This has included provision for the elderly. The Housing Authority works closely with the City Planning Department and the Urban Renewal Agency.

Though a large proportion of the Mexican population is native-born, perhaps for generations, no other national group clings so closely to the traditions and customs of its homeland (*see Folklore*).

Los Pastores, nativity play, is presented during the Christmas season. The popular *Dia de Inocentes* is celebrated by local Mexicans on December 28. The *Blessing of the Animals* is observed in most of the churches of the Mexican quarter, but especially at the Church of Our Lady of Guadalupe, 1321 El Paso Street, on January 17. The local *Matachines* dances can usually be seen at Guadalupe Church on December 12. Mexicans of all ages take part in the solemn festival of the *Dia de Animas,* All Souls' Day, November 2, the largest observance being at San Fernando Cemetery No. 1, between S. San Marcos, Colorado, Tampico, and Vera Cruz.

Chinese grocery stores are numerous throughout the Mexican district, though San Antonio had few Chinese residents until 1917, when Brigadier General John J. Pershing brought back from his expedition into Mexico 452 Chinese whose lives were in danger because of aid rendered Americans. They were admitted as refugees, and in 1922 a special act of Congress legalized their residence.

Mexican shops are to be found along Produce Row and in the area of the busy Produce Market, which takes the place of the former Hay Market.

These shops specialize in earthenware, bristling assortments of brushes and mats, baskets, hand-woven chairs and hampers, rock *metates* used to grind corn, *molcajetes,* used to grind spices, and wooden *molinillos* with which to froth chocolate, a favorite drink. Other shops have bins of jerked meats, and strange herbs which minister to a host of ills and have fanciful names such as "the Dancer," the "Bad Woman," "Christ," "the Mule." Charcoal, used as a dental powder, is sold in cakes. Tallow candles, hand-made, hang from ropes in bunches. Men parade the streets balancing on their heads baskets of candies made of cactus, sweet potatoes, pumpkin, or of pecans and unrefined loaf sugar. Street corner peddlers sell wrapped bundles of dry corn shucks, with which the Mexican housewife makes tamale wrappers and rolls her cigarettes.

MILAM SQUARE is between W. Commerce, W. Houston and N. San Saba Sts., and N. Santa Rosa Ave. Here, on Sundays especially, ragged preachers of strange doctrines and nattily dressed and fiery *politicos* harangue their audiences, while many a penniless Mexican enjoys his *siesta* on the grass. The GRAVE OF BEN MILAM, near the center of the square, is marked by a granite monument on its approximate location. Milam was killed during the siege of Bexar, December, 1835. Facing the grave, but on the west edge of the square, is a heroic-size bronze STATUE OF BEN MILAM, the work of Bonnie MacLeary, sculptor.

The BUCKHORN HALL OF HORNS and the old Buckhorn Bar are two of the historic items exhibited on the grounds of the Lone Star Brewing Company, on Roosevelt Ave. The horns of wild game and other hunting trophies were collected in the Buckhorn Saloon, opened about 1881. In 1957 the Lone Star Brewing Company made it a part of its museum, which also has North American and African Halls. The little house in which W. S. Porter, (O. Henry) once lived has been moved to the grounds. (*Open daily including Sundays and holidays, admission free.*)

ST. MARY'S ROMAN CATHOLIC CHURCH, SE. corner N. St. Mary's and College Sts., a modern edifice of modified Romanesque style, was designed by Fred B. Gaenslen, on the site of an earlier structure built in 1855. At the rear is the former ST. MARY'S COLLEGE, founded in 1852, and used as the night school of St. Mary's University.

The MUNICIPAL AUDITORIUM, in the center of Auditorium Circle, was built as a memorial to World War dead, at a cost of $1,500,-000. This limestone building of Mediterranean design has seats for 6,065. The stage is 75 ft. wide and has an asbestos curtain with a painting by Hugo Pohl depicting the arrival of the early Spaniards in San Antonio. Architects were Atlee B. and Robert M. Ayres, with George Willis and Emmett Jackson.

ST. MARK'S EPISCOPAL CHURCH, NW. corner of Jefferson and Pecan Sts., cornerstone laid in 1859, is built of stone in a manner suggesting the English Gothic style, with its ivy-covered walls and shaded, informal garden. Its bell was made from a cannon buried by revolutionists in San Antonio in 1813, and the ground on which it stands once belonged to the Alamo property. An early member of the congregation was Lieutenant Colonel Robert E. Lee, who was made a life member of the first missionary society in 1860. The PARISH HOUSE adjoining the church is of more recent construction, but carries out the modified English Gothic style. The Lyndon B. Johnsons were married here.

TRAVIS PARK, between Pecan, Travis, Navarro, and Jefferson Sts., was named for William Barret Travis, Alamo hero. The St. Anthony Hotel is opposite the Park in Travis St. West of Navarro are the Travis Park Methodist Church and the Gunter Hotel; in the area are also the Blue Bonnet Hotel, the Travis-Plaza Hotel, and the B. P. O. E. Club (Elks).

The U. S. POST OFFICE AND FEDERAL BLDG., between E.

Houston, E. Travis and N. Alamo Sts. and Ave. E, is a five-story building of cream-colored limestone in modern Spanish Colonial style, designed by Ralph Cameron, architect, and erected in 1935–37 at a cost of approximately $1,864,000. Murals in the lobby were painted by Howard Cook of Taos, New Mexico, and include, on the southwest and north walls, subjects of Texas history, while on the east wall are scenes illustrating the State's industries and resources. The spot on which the building stands was a part of the Alamo battlefield, and, years before that, the burial ground of Mission San Antonio de Valero.

The SCOTTISH RITE TEMPLE (*open 8–5 workdays; guides*), SE. corner Ave. E. and Fourth St., has the design of a Greek temple with a pyramidal roof, the material being light gray limestone trimmed with terra cotta. Ralph Cameron was the architect. Heavy entrance doors were sculptured by Pompeo Coppini. The right door portrays Sam Houston as he presided over the convention that organized the first Masonic Grand Lodge of Texas; the left door portrays George Washington as he presided over Alexandria Lodge of Virginia as Master. The cornerstone was laid in 1922 by the Grand Lodge of Texas, A.F. & A.M., and the cost of the building was $1,500,000.

JOE FREEMAN COLISEUM, located 3 *m*. east of the business center, is a huge exhibition hall where the San Antonio Livestock Exhibition and Rodeo is held annually in February. Auctions of livestock are held frequently in another building. The whole enterprise stands on a tract of 170 acres.

FORT SAM HOUSTON starts at Grayson St. and N. New Braunfels Ave. covers 3,330 acres and houses up to 10,000 military and civilian personnel. Part of the site was given by the city in 1870 and during 1876–1879 a Quartermaster depot was built of gray limestone with loopholes like a fort. This is the QUADRANGLE, once the post of Theodore Roosevelt (while training the Rough Riders); John J. Pershing, Frederick Funston, Courtney Hodges, Jonathan Wainwright, and Dwight D. Eisenhower. Dominating the site is a stone clocktower, 88 ft. tall, which originally supported two water tanks. Since 1882 it has held a 600-lb. bell cast in Cincinnati, which is struck every half hour by a Seth Thomas clock mechanism.

Most of the active Army affairs in Texas, Arkansas, Louisiana, Oklahoma and New Mexico are controlled by Fourth US Army Headquarters in the Quadrangle at Fort Sam Houston. This hq also supervises and supports the activities of the Army Reserve, ROTC and National Guard, the Army's civilian components. Often called the A-Plus Army, it supervises Artillery, Armor, Air Defense and Aviation as well as Infantry and Medical. Fort Sam Houston also is the site of a field office of the USA Map Service, Alamo Area Support Center, Army & Air Force Exchange Service, and the National Cemetery. Parts of the Fort's command are the USA Medical Training Center and the 67th Medical Group. The Center conducts basic training of enlisted aid men and hospital corpsmen, and all enlisted Reserve Forces Act medical training.

Fort Sam's subpost for troop training is Camp Bullis, 18 *m*. northwest of San Antonio, with 28,500 acres and approx. 108 buildings. Much of the training simulates Vietnam operations.

An important historical event occurred in 1910, when Lieutenant Benjamin D. Foulois, a student of the Wright brothers, arrived and uncrated a collection of bamboo poles constructed around a gas engine. The United States Congress had bought him an old Wright plane that had been wrecked once, and appropriated $150 for its upkeep. Foulois spent $300 of his own money repairing the plane. He made his first flight March 2, 1910, getting the ship off the ground by having it hurled from a catapult. That was the beginning of the Army Air Corps.

The SOUTH TEXAS MEDICAL CENTER in northwest San Antonio was initiated by the San Antonio Medical Foundation, formed 1948 to promote facilities for medical, dental, and nursing education, hospitalization and research. It began on a site of 200 acres and made provision to expand on 300 more. In 1961 the citizens voted $5,000,000 in bonds to establish the Bexar County Teaching Hospital. In that year also the University of Texas moved to erect its South Texas Medical School on 100 acres of the Center, along the lines of its Southwestern Medical School in Dallas, developed since 1949. The first to begin construction was the Southwest Texas Methodist Hospital, on 67 acres of the San Antonio Center, completing the first unit of 175 beds of a 1,000-bed project at a cost of $5,100,000. A five-story building, it has two floors of reinforced concrete below the surface for a "survival complex," equipped to sustain a nuclear attack. Also operating at the Center are the United Cerebral Palsy Treatment Center and the Community Guidance Center. Here also provision was made for including the new hospital of the Veterans Administration.

SOUTHWEST RESEARCH CENTER is the largest of five exceptionally equipped research laboratory facilities in San Antonio. It is located on 1,500-acre campus 8 m. west of downtown and comprises three independent organizations. The largest is SOUTHWEST RESEARCH INSTITUTE, a nonprofit organization with a staff of more than 600 scientists, engineers and aids, working in 17 laboratories and cooperating with industry, government and individuals to apply the advantages of science and technology to the benefit of society. Among its numerous programs is one devoted to naval research, which conceived and developed the Aluminaut, the world's first deep-diving submarine. The Institute also is engaged in studies of submarine and surface ship structure, the dynamics and power-plant requirements of hydrofoil boats, and direction finder programs for the U. S. Navy. The Institute's effective studies of fuels and lubricants for automotive and aerospace uses led the U. S. Army Ordnance Corps to place its Fuels and Lubricants Research Laboratory here. For studies of blast effects and industrial pressures the Institute has available pressure chambers of high power. An arc imaging furnace can generate temperatures up to 10,000° F.

Another organization in the Research Center is the SOUTHWEST FOUNDATION FOR RESEARCH AND EDUCATION, dealing with basic research in bio-medicine. Here more than 200 baboons are used

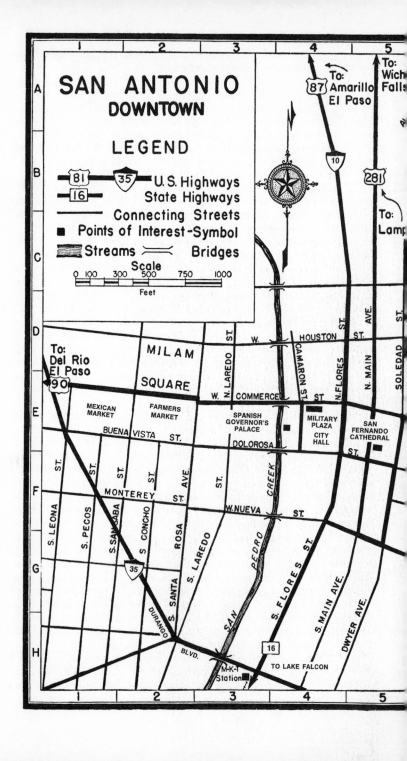

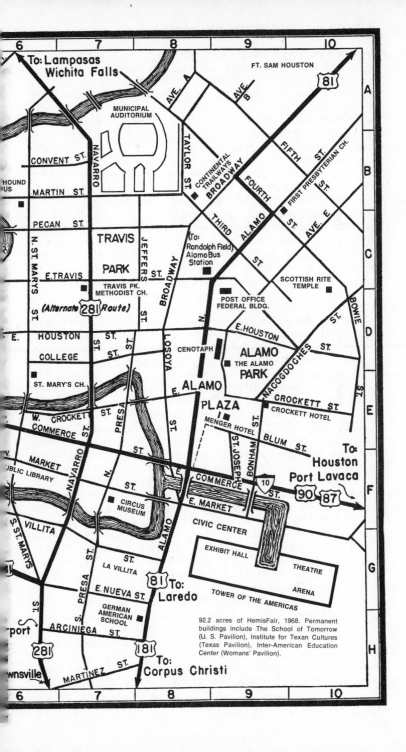

92.2 acres of HemisFair, 1968. Permanent buildings include The School of Tomorrow (U. S. Pavilion), Institute for Texan Cultures (Texas Pavilion), Inter-American Education Center (Womans' Pavilion).

for study of endocrinology, atherosclerosis, virology, and organ transplantation. The staff numbers 100 and the budget is $1,300,000 a year. A third unit is the SOUTHWEST AGRICULTURAL INSTITUTE, which deals with the problems of dry land ranching. It owns the Essar Angus breeding herd.

The AEROSPACE MEDICAL DIVISION of the U. S. Air Force Systems Command at Brooks Air Force Base is the nation's most comprehensive military research organization devoted to medicine, education and consultation. Formed in 1961 it brings together under its direction the USAF School of Aerospace Medicine, at Brooks; the USAF Epidemiological Laboratory, the Wilford Hall USAF Hospital (1,000 beds) and the Personnel Research Laboratory, at Lackland AFB; a base unit at Kelly AFB, and several laboratories outside the state. Six of the buildings at the Brooks headquarters were dedicated November 21, 1963, by President John F. Kennedy, one day before his death. AMD started as $14,000,000 complex employing 2,200 military and civilian personnel and has been expanding ever since. It conducts studies in a wide range of medical problems associated with flying. It cooperates with the space projects of the National Aeronautics & Space Administration. It provides medical care and diagnostic services.

The School of Aerospace Medicine was functioning for a number of years before AMD was formed. It has about 300 specialists in the various phases of medicine and introduced space medicine into its curriculum in 1951. In 1957 it established the electrocardiographic library, which contains electrocardiograms of every man flying in the USAF, and of astronauts. The School provides training for physicians and nurses of the Army, Navy and Air Force, and of Allied Nations.

The fifth major research facility in San Antonio is the USA SURGICAL RESEARCH UNIT at Brooke Army Medical Center, founded 1947 to study military trauma and the management of surgical infections, which has made important contributions in the treatment of burns and acute kidney failure. Patients suffering from burns are flown in by Military Air Transport Service from wherever the military is engaged; in special instances a team headed by a burn specialist flies to the site of the disaster and supervises treatment on the flight back to Brooke.

BRACKENRIDGE PARK is part of an area of 363 acres between Broadway, Hillebrand Ave., and N. St. Mary's St. which includes also the SAN ANTONIO ZOOLOGICAL GARDENS AND AQUARIUM, the ALAMO STADIUM AND GYMNASIUM, and the Park's Public Golf Course. Adjoining are Trinity University and Incarnate Word College. The Park is the largest metropolitan tract operated by the Dept. of Parks & Recreation, which recalls that more than 200 years ago a grant from the King of Spain established a park of 46 acres around San Pedro Springs. Brackenridge Park was donated in 1899. The San Antonio River winds through it. It has two touring facilities for visitors: the BRACKENRIDGE EAGLE, a miniature railroad of 3 miles, with a small-scale replica of a steam locomotive and coaches of 1865, and a one-fifth scale model of a modern diesel-drawn train of the Missouri Pacific, built by General Motors. The other device is an aerial Skyride, 100 ft. above the grounds, permitting a panoramic view of the Park and Fort Sam Houston, located to the east.

The WITTE MEMORIAL MUSEUM, near the main Park entrance on Broadway is built in Mediterranean style. A large art gallery occupies the upper floor. The TRANSPORTATION EXHIBIT includes a stage coach, a mule-drawn car, a street car, and old carriages and automobiles. A collection of early Texas houses has been established here. It includes the CELSO NAVARRO HOUSE of 1835, which has a doll collection; the FRANCISCO RUIZ HOUSE, 1765, in which lived a signer of the Texas Declaration of Independence, and the TWOHIG HOUSE, 1841. There also is a pioneer log cabin. The largest Canary diamond, 49.40 carats, on display here, was purloined in 1968. (*Open weekdays, 8:30–6; Sundays, 3:30–7; adults, 25¢, children, 9¢*).

The PIONEER MEMORIAL BUILDING (*open weekdays, 10–12; Sundays 1–5, free*) near the Witte Museum, is dedicated to the Old Trail Drivers Assn., Texas Pioneers, and Texas Rangers. In front is the TRAIL DRIVER MEMORIAL, by Gutzom Borglum. The limestone building of Italian design was erected with funds allocated by the United States-Texas Centennial Commission.

The SAN ANTONIO ZOOLOGICAL GARDENS AND AQUARIUM, 3903 N. St. Mary's St., at Brackenridge Park, is operated by a nonprofit organization and has a collection of approx. 4,500 specimens of beasts, birds, reptiles and fishes. The exhibits are housed in numerous buildings and in the open bear pits that make use of the stone configurations of a former stone quarry. Brown and polar bears, giraffes, zebras, lions, tigers, antelope and rhinoceros live in comfort. Penguins have their special place and there is a large collection of water fowl and shore birds. The Monkey Island is equipped with trapezes and other apparatus. Elephants and seals give daily performances and children may ride an elephant with proper supervision. The RICHARD FRIEDRICH AQUARIUM has thousands of tropical and cold water fish (*Zoo open daily, 8–5 in winter, 8–6 in summer; adults, 50¢; children, 10¢*).

The CHINESE SUNKEN GARDEN is located in a depression, formerly a rock quarry, on the northwest edge of Brackenridge Park. Here winding walks lead the visitor over stone bridges amid pools of water lilies and decorative plantings of a wide variety of flowers. The SUNKEN GARDEN THEATER adjoins the Sunken Garden. Here plays are sometimes presented during summer. A stage of classic Grecian design with a mechanical compression screen that rises from the stage floor dominates the scene. The seating capacity is 3,100.

The ALAMO STADIUM, entrances on Alpine Drive at the Sunken Garden, Hildebrand Ave. near Devine Road, W. side of Dial Ave. between Hildebrand and Bushnell Aves., and Hildebrand Ave. at W. limits of Brackenridge Park, was constructed in 1940–1941, and designed to seat more than 23,000 persons. The stadium was sponsored by the San Antonio Independent School District for school and college football and other athletics and for outdoor civic events. The west side of the huge bowl was constructed on the sides of an abandoned rock quarry. Cost was $477,000. The GYMNASIUM is auxiliary to the Stadium. A 30-acre tract is used for parking.

The MARION KOOGLER McNAY ART INSTITUTE, 6000 New Braunfels Ave., at the intersection of Austin Highway, occupies a decorative Spanish-type house on a hilltop, built 1927 and willed to the City and State in 1950. Mrs. McNay filled her home with a remarkable collection of works by Cezanne, El Greco, Gauguin, Van Gogh and many French artists; American water colors, Mexican paintings, Indian arts and crafts, and sculptures. There are exotic gardens (*Open weekdays except Monday, 9–5; Sunday, 2–5 free*).

The NATIONAL SHRINE OF THE LITTLE FLOWER, SW. corner N. Zarzamora St. and Kentucky Ave., a Roman Catholic church, was erected in 1931 in Spanish Renaissance design at a cost of $500,000; C. L. Monnot, architect. The Little Flower group and the statue of the Blessed Mother were imported from Spain, stations of the cross from Germany. Three altars are of Carrara marble. The walls bear tablets of white marble on which are inscribed the names of those who, from all over the globe, contributed to the erection of the building. Services are conducted by the Discalced Carmelite Order.

At the SAN ANTONIO HORSE AND MULE MARKET, SE. corner S. San Marcos and S. Laredo Sts., a weekly auction is held on Thursdays. Horses and mules are brought from all parts of the Southwest, with hundreds of other animals sold simply from description. Often representatives of foreign governments are bidders.

The UNION STOCKYARDS (*open day and night*), 1715 S. San Marcos St., cover 34 acres surrounded by eight packing plants. From this district cattle are shipped. These stockyards provide a glimpse of the West, for here ten-gallon hats and high-heeled boots are numerous, and speech is in the phraseology of the open range.

HIGHER EDUCATION

TRINITY UNIVERSITY, 715 Stadium Drive, has become San Antonio's largest institution of higher learning since it moved to its new campus of 107 acres on Trinity Hill in 1952. It had a modest beginning in 1869 when the Texas Synod of the Presbyterian Church located it at Tehuacana. In 1902 it was moved to Waxahachi, and in 1942 San Antonio was chosen as its site. It has courses in engineering science, the humanities, the arts and pre-medical, and in 1964 dedicated Chapman Graduate Center, the city's first university center for graduate education. A well-supported building program has resulted in a modern, highly efficient physical plant, to which recent additions have been the University Chapel, the Moody Engineering Science Building for a four-year curriculum in engineering, the 166-ft. Murchison Memorial Bell Tower and the gymnasium-social center. The RUTH TAYLOR THEATER was formally opened in October, 1966. Its innovations in design include a 412-seat hall called Theater One, which has a three-sided stage forming half of the hexagonally shaped room: a 108-seat hall and stage called Attic Two, and a space in front of the house called Cafe Theater, for informal entertainment. The architects were O'Neil Ford and Associates. In a recent year this co-educational university enrolled 2,350 and had a faculty of 170. Trinity is a member of Southland Conference in football.

SAN ANTONIO COLLEGE is a tax-supported, two-year junior college, controlled by the Board of Trustees of the Union Junior College District, who are elected. It occupies 37 acres at 1300 San Pedro Avenue, and in a typical year enrolled 9,730, in day and evening classes, about 24 percent of whom was military-connected personnel. The building program has included the McAllister Fine Arts Center, the new Chemistry-Geology Building, with a Planetarium, (1961), a vocational-technical center and a new building for the Library, which has more than 50,000 volumes. The curriculum includes specialties such as business administration, dentistry, journalism, librarianship, mortuary science, speaking, electronics, refrigeration, air-conditioning, psychiatric nursing and secretarial training.

(*The Planetarium, Myrtle & Maverick Sts.; lectures Thursdays at 7:30 p.m., Sundays at 6:30 p.m. Adm. 50¢; children, 5 to 17, 20¢; none under 5 admitted*)

A second institution of the Union Junior College District is ST. PHILIP'S COLLEGE, 2111 Nevada St., which offers, besides most of the specialties named above, courses in aeronautic technology, auto mechanics, clothing, plumbing, radio servicing, food preparation, tailoring, upholstery and vocational nursing. Founded 1898 as a Negro college, it became fully integrated in 1955.

The Roman Catholic Parochial Schools in Bexar County enroll from 26,000 to 30,000 pupils in five high schools, 55 elementary schools, and eight combined elementary-high school units. Higher education sponsored by the church is provided by St. Mary's University, Incarnate Word College (for women) and Our Lady of the Lake College.

St. MARY'S UNIVERSITY, 2700 Cincinnati Ave., founded 1852, is the oldest institution in San Antonio and one of the oldest in the State. In addition to its major campus of 130 acres it operates a school downtown and conducts evening classes. The curriculum includes such subjects as government, international relations, accounting, finance, marketing, physical education, and Spanish. The Graduate School gives masters' degrees in chemistry, economics, government, sacred doctrine, student personnel service and other subjects, and the School of Law has a well-deserved reputation for excellence. The total enrollment is more than 3,000.

INCARNATE WORD COLLEGE, 4301 Broadway, founded 1881, is a nationally accredited Catholic college for women, with a typical attendance of 1,200. It has a campus of 200 acres and a library of more than 60,000 volumes. Besides courses in the humanities and arts, and some vocational subjects such as teaching, nursing, radiology, dietetics, and medical record, it gives degrees of bachelor of music in piano, violin, voice and music education.

OUR LADY OF THE LAKE COLLEGE, 411 SW. 24th St. has a campus of 115 acres and a curriculum that includes the humanities and the arts and such special courses as business administration, medical technology, theology, home economics, and speech pathology. It conducts the Harry Jersig Speech and Hearing Center and the Worden School of Social Service. The majority of its 1,370 students are women, men being enrolled chiefly in the graduate schools.

TOUR OF THE MISSIONS

From the ALAMO, 0 *m.*, the route of this 18.9 *m.* tour is south on Alamo Plaza; continue on S. Alamo St. to S. St. Mary's St.; L. on S. St. Mary's St. (at the railroad underpass S. St. Mary's becomes Roosevelt Ave.); R. from Roosevelt Ave. on Mitchell St. to Mission Road; L. on Mission Road.

Tour tickets may be obtained from the Chamber of Commerce, 202 E. Commerce St., or the Missions, $1 for adults.

MISSION CONCEPCION (*Nuestra Señora de la Purisima Concepcion de Acuna;* Our Lady of the Immaculate Conception of Acuna), 2.9 *m.*, is the best preserved of the Texas missions, (*open 8–6 workdays, 9–6 Sun., adm. 35¢; students, 20¢; children, 10¢*).

Danger from the French in Louisiana caused the reestablishment in the San Antonio area in 1731, of Mission Concepcion and two other east Texas missions which had been founded in 1716. Mission Concepcion is owned by the Roman Catholic Church, which conducts services in the chapel on special occasions.

The original frescoes in its rooms are very rare; vegetable and mineral dyes, red, blue, and ochre, were used. The front of the church retains some of its frescoed color. In the baptistry, the first room at the right, above a carved font set into the wall, a fine fresco of *Our Lady of Seven Sorrows* is partly visible, and above that, a fresco of the crucifixion. Opposite on the left, in the belfry room, elaborate frescoed designs adorn the corners and doorways. These paintings were done by the monks.

Concepcion is built of adobe and a porous gray rock called tufa, quarried near the mission. The tufa, similar to the stone in the catacombs of Rome, was carried piece by piece on the backs of Indian converts, the priests doing most of the construction and all of the engineering. The church follows the usual cruciform floor pattern, with two small offsets for the identical twin towers and a slightly pointed cupola surmounting the dome and the crossing of nave and transept. Hand-hewn stones were used for cornices and door frames. The north and east walls are heavily buttressed and have no openings, a precaution against attacks. All walls are 45 inches thick.

The acoustics of the chapel under the dome have been compared to those of the Mormon Tabernacle in Salt Lake City, Utah.

Above the arch over the central front door is an inscription dedicating the mission to the Immaculate Conception of the Blessed Virgin.

Buildings Old and New

ONE SHELL PLAZA, 714 FT. TALL, HOUSTON

Architect's Projection, Shell Oil Company

AUDITORIUM BUILDING, MANNED SPACECRAFT CENTER,
CLEAR LAKE

National Aeronautics & Space Admin.

PROJECT MANAGEMENT BLDG.,
MANNED SPACECRAFT CENTER,
CLEAR LAKE

National Aeronautics & Space Admin.

KALITA HUMPHREYS THEATRE, DALLAS; FRANK LLOYD
WRIGHT ARCHITECT

Dallas Chamber of Commerce

ART BUILDING AND MUSEUM, UNIVERSITY OF TEXAS, AUSTIN

University of Texas

MISSION CONCEPCION NEAR SAN ANTONIO

Southern Pacific Railway

SAN JOSE MISSION, MAIN FACADE, NEAR SAN ANTONIO

National Park Service

SAN JOSE MISSION, UNRESTORED SOUTH ELEVATION

National Park Service

SAN JOSE MISSION, GRINDING APPARATUS

National Park Service

SACRISTY WINDOW, OFTEN CALLED ROSE WINDOW, MISSION SAN JOSE

MAIN ENTRANCE, STATE NATIONAL BANK OF EL PASO

Samuel Fant, El Paso

Strongly reminiscent of the ancient Roman aqueduct in Segovia, Spain, is the simple arcade which runs south from the front entrance to the church. Three doorways open from this cloister. The first door opens into the former storeroom, with the old timbers from which hung curing meat. The second chamber was the living room of the padres, and the roof has two vents, one for light and one for smoke. The third room is the library, with bookshelves of stone. The former infirmary, above the sacristy, is reached by climbing worn stone stairs.

To the R. of the road at this mission is the SITE OF THE BATTLE OF CONCEPCION (*see History*), extending into Concepcion Park. Entrance to the park is from Theo Avenue.

Continue on Mission Road.

At the old Fairgrounds near ROOSEVELT PARK, 3.4 *m.* (L), Theodore Roosevelt organized and trained the Rough Riders.

MISSION SAN JOSE (*San José y San Miguel de Aguayo,* St. Joseph and St. Michael of Aguayo), (*open 9–6 daily, 10–6 Sunday; adm. 50¢; groups of 10, 35¢; children, 15¢*), 5.1 *m.*

Mission San José is known as the Queen of the Missions. Among its features are a carved window, circular stairs to the belfry, fine cloisters, the granary, the mill, and a new outdoor theater, where a drama festival is given in midsummer.

In 1719 Fray Antonio Margil de Jesus, who had been driven from east Texas by the French, obtained permission from the governor of Texas to found a mission in the valley of the San Antonio River. San José, established on February 23, 1720, became the most beautiful, most prosperous and best fortified of all Texas missions, and held supreme position in New Spain. After its secularization the Roman Catholic Church retained possession of only the chapel and 15 acres.

The San Antonio Conservation Society purchased the old granary and completed its restoration in 1933. Civil Works Administration funds in 1934 made possible the beginning of a complete restoration program, carried out after research at the mother house of the Franciscans in Mexico. It is now a National Shrine.

The Indian pueblo of 84 compartments, the soldiers quarters, granary, and civilian officers' quarters, all form part of the immense quadrangle wall. The restored OLD MILL is north of the acequia, which runs a few feet outside the north wall. North of the old mill is the HUISACHE BOWL, an outdoor theater having a rustic stage, used for historical plays and pageants.

Mission San José is built of brown sandstone and tufa, and its rich sculptural ornamentation has made it one of the most photographed buildings in America. Complete restoration has made possible here the picture of an ancient mission establishment, even including an outdoor oven and a water system conducted through hand-made tiles. The most modern note is found toward the top of the beautiful Gothic arches of rooms in the convent wing, where red bricks were placed by Benedictine monks in 1859. Padre Morfi (1778) related that ducks and other wild game could be shot from the cloister roof.

The building problem of the Franciscans was colossal. When the walls grew too high to be reached from the ground, tradition says, earth was packed in the enclosure, the walls raised, more earth packed in, and the process repeated. When the spring line of the roof was reached, with earth molded beneath, the arched roof was built. The flying buttresses of the granary were constructed of great rocks, yet one of the missionaries complained that the Indians "are by nature inclined to idleness and they work very slowly." Tobacco was rationed to them as one means of persuasion.

The carving of the church of Mission San José is considered its most notable feature. The upper part of the front facade, with its simple wreath of curving acanthus leaves and conchoids framing the small windows above the archway, is as skillfully done as the rich carving of the doorway below. The carving of pillars, niches, and sculptured saints in a background of profuse ornamentation was condemned by Padre Morfi with the words, "The main entrance is very costly, on account of the statues and trifling mouldings." While the building itself is of simple Moorish and Spanish origin, the stone carvings reflect rich Renaissance influence of the Churrigueresque school of Spanish Baroque.

The church has only one tower, with a pyramid top and an open belfry which is reached through a round turret housing an ingeniously designed stairway. Each of the 23 steps is hewn from a single live oak log, set with each step fanwise over the preceding one, in such a way that the pivot end resembles a pillar cutting through the center of the spiral. Above the heavily buttressed walls of the church a hemispherical dome rises 60 feet in height, almost as tall as the 75-foot tower. The chapel at the right of the church has three small flat Moorish domes.

The carved south window of the sacristy, incorrectly designated as the "rose window" by many writers, has been painted by great artists. Legends concerning Pedro Huizar, the sculptor, who for five years toiled on this small area, are too numerous for a correct version; but the substance of the stories is that the window was the result of an unhappy romance, which caused Huizar to pour his heart into this work. Huizar's son, Juan Antonio, inherited title to the granary and his family retained the title for 116 years. Ancestors of the sculptor helped create the beauty of the Alhambra at Granada.

In the chapel are three old paintings said to have been gifts from the King of Spain.

On leaving Mission San José drive out the SE. entrance; L. is the modern monastery of the Franciscans, just outside the mission wall.

Continue on Mission Road.

STINSON FIELD, 7 m. (R), was founded in 1915 as a municipal airport and air mail station. There are several flying fields in the vicinity.

At 7.5 m. is the junction with Ashley Road; L. on Ashley Road.

At 7.8 m. is the junction with the Espada Road; R. on Espada Road.

The quaint highway leading to Mission Espada winds through one of the oldest settlements in the State. Small farms of the area date from the period following the secularization of the missions (1793–94), when the converts were given church lands. Many of these families possess old statues and ornaments of the mission, which is the hub of their settlement, but will not restore them because of their reputed miraculous powers. Note the line of trees (L) which marks the main acequia of Mission Espada.

An ancient MISSION AQUEDUCT is indicated at 7.8 *m.* (L) by a marker near the spot where the acequia, by means of a graceful masonry arch, spans Piedra Creek. Thus, water from the San Antonio River, half a league distant, is conveyed to the small fields of this section—an engineering feat considered to be remarkable.

The Espada Road leads directly into another mission quadrangle.

MISSION SAN FRANCISCO DE LA ESPADA (Mission St. Francis of the Sword), (*open 9 a.m. to 6 p.m., adults 35¢; children 15¢*), 9.3 *m.*, was established at the same time as Mission Concepcion. The Roman Catholic Church, which owns the mission, conducts services regularly in the chapel. Barracks of the old fort (restored), in the southeast part of the quadrangle wall, are used to house a school for children of nearby families. Espada has retained its Spanish atmosphere. The original church crumbled in 1758. The present building dates from 1898.

The *baluarte* or fortified tower, claimed to be the only complete mission fort extant, has a round bastion with vaulted roof, three-foot-thick stone walls, strongly buttressed, and portholes for rifles and cannon. The rough stone chapel has no tower, but an extension of the fort wall rising into an open bell gable or *campanario* is surmounted by a wrought iron piece said to have been fashioned by the padres. The main Moorish doorway (upper part) copies the design of the carved window of Mission San José.

The plain wooden cross standing beside the chapel door was placed there as a reminder of a saving deluge which, according to tradition, fell in response to the congregation's prayers after a long drought. Statues at Espada are hand-carved of wood, probably of native trees, and glass eyes, separately cut teeth, and flexible joints give them realism. Walls and buildings of this mission have been seriously damaged by treasure hunters. Old silver church vessels are kept in the school.

Retrace Espada Road; R. on Mission Road; after crossing river, R. on San Juan Mission Road.

MISSION SAN JUAN CAPISTRANO (Mission St. John Capistrano), (*open daily, adults 35¢, children 15¢*), 11.6 *m.*, was also reestablished here in 1731. Services are held Sundays by the Roman Catholic Church, which owns the mission, reputed to have converted many Indians to Christianity. No attempt was made at sculptured decoration, but the walls are thick, the rooms commodious, and the use of frescoes created a cheerful atmosphere.

Most of the original square remains within the walls, offering an authentic picture of the mission plan. The convent, chapel, workrooms, and living quarters of the establishment are in varying degrees of repair. The chapel was rebuilt in 1907. In this mission, flat arches prevail rather than round ones; and pointed gables are a departure from other Franciscan architecture. Another unusual feature is the pierced *campanario,* which rises above the entrance in lieu of a steeple.

Retrace to Mission Road; R. on Mission Road, L. on US 181; straight ahead on US 181 (S. Presa St. inside the city limits); R. on S. Alamo St.; continue on S. Alamo to Alamo Plaza.

Waco

Air Transportation: Trans-Texas Airways, Waco Municipal Airport.
Bus Lines: Arrow, Central Greyhound, Central Texas, 116 trips daily; Greyhound Terminal, 700 Columbus Ave. Texas Electric Station, 1002 Austin Ave. Also 14 motor freight lines with 81 daily stops.
Highways: US 77 from Dallas and US 81 from Fort Worth (Interstate 35) join at Hillsboro and separate at Waco for the routes south. US 84 passes through Waco east-west. State 6, State 31, State 164 enter Waco. Interstate 35 is the direct route to San Antonio.
Railroads: Missouri-Kansas-Texas, depot at 801 Jackson Ave.; Missouri Pacific, Southern Pacific, St. Louis Southwestern, Union Station. Four passenger, 20 freight trains daily.

Accommodations and Information: Eight hotels, 625 rooms; 35 motels, 1,300 rooms. Waco Chamber of Commerce, 414 Franklin St. *Waco News-Tribune* and *Waco Times-Herald* (daily), 900 Franklin St.; *Waco Citizen,* semi-weekly, *Farm & Labor Journal,* weekly. Waco Public Library, 1717 Austin Ave. Baylor University Library (by permission). Armstrong Browning Library, Baylor University.

Churches and Hospitals: Waco has more than 130 churches representing 2 religions and 21 denominations. Four hospitals led by the huge U. S. Veterans Administration complex with 2,214 beds; also Hillcrest Memorial of the Baptist General Convention and Providence of the Roman Catholic Church.

SPORTS, RECREATION AND OTHER ACTIVITIES

Auto Races: Heart o' Texas Speedway.
Baseball: There are 18 Little Leagues, 130 teams, 3 high school stadiums.
Boating and Fishing: Lake Waco.
Camping and picnicking: Cameron Park, Herring Ave. and N. Fifth St.
Children's activities: Cameron Park playgrounds; Candy Cane Park (fee); Central Texas Zoo, Municipal Airport; Westview Playground, with roller skating, West Waco Drive.
Football: Baylor University Stadium, in season; seats 50,000.
Golf: Lake Waco course, 36 holes, public; Ridgewood Country Club, for members and guests.
Riding: Bridle paths in Cameron Park.
Swimming: Lake Waco, 4 municipal pools, Kiwanis, Lions, YMCA and YWCA pools.
Tennis: Tournaments at the Sul Ross Tennis Center, Jefferson Ave. and 12th St. Waco has 27 public courses.

Theaters and Orchestras: Civic Theater, Baylor (University) Theater, Children's Theater, Waco Symphony Orchestra, Baylor A Capella Choir and Symphony Orchestra; Children's Orchestra; Waco Civic Music Assn. See newspapers for dates.

Special Events: Heart o' Texas Fair and Rodeo, agricultural exhibits, horse show, rodeo competitions, Coliseum at Fair Grounds, usually first week in October.

WACO (427 alt.; 97,808 pop., 1960; 110,500 1967, est.), pronounced Way-co, lying in the wide valley of the Brazos River—a big green bowl rimmed about by the low hills of the Balcones Escarpment—is a thoroughly modern city, the cultural and educational center of east central Texas. Through Baylor University, it annually sends forth hundreds of teachers and professional men and women whose activities extend to all parts of the State and to many sections of the Soupthwest. The muddy *Rio de los Brazos de Dios* bisects Waco, and its rich black bottom lands have given McLennan County the basis for its cotton-seed industry.

Waco, like many central cities with easy access to the open country, lost people in the 1950–1960 decade, actually only 2,030, but it gained 15,132 by annexing settlements in its periphery. Its metropolitan area, identical with McLennan County, had an estimated 160,000 in 1968. This is the largest marketing area halfway between Dallas and Austin. Although famous as an educational center Waco has become a prosperous manufacturing city, where millwork, glass, automobile tires and containers supplement the income from processing cottonseed, livestock, and dairying. But the city remains a prime distributing center for cotton and livestock, which funnel into its market from a wide area in east central Texas.

The climate of Waco is a combination of the humid climate of East Texas and the continental climate of the north. In the spring warm, moist air moves over the area from the Gulf, bringing maximum precipitation. The greatest 24-hour amount, 7.18 inches, was recorded on May 11, 1953. Normal monthly temperatures vary from 47.3° in January to 85.5° in August, with a yearly normal of 67.3°, but the summers frequently have weeks above 90°. Temperature falls below 32° about 26 days a year. Severe storms are rare in this part of Texas and although about 37 thunderstorms are recorded annually, Waco was unfamiliar with tornadoes until May 11, 1953, when a severe blast struck the central business section, causing 114 deaths and $41,000,000 worth of damage.

Waco is believed to have been the name of a tribe of Tehuacana Indians, called Hueco by the early Spanish explorers. There was an Indian village on the banks of the river that the Spaniards named Los Brazos de Dios,—The Arms of God. The site was an easy crossing for soldiers and traders moving into Texas. In 1829 a band of Cherokees raided the area, drove out the Huecas and destroyed their settlement. They also made the route unsafe for early settlers and in 1837 Texas Rangers were sent there to keep them back.

But the region was not cleared of Indians. Their dangerous activities prevented settlement of whites until the Scotsman, Neil McLennan, and Captain George B. Erath, surveyors, pushed into the vicinity in 1840.

Intrigued by the natural attractions of the site of the present city, they brought their families and built log cabins in the wilderness beside the Bosque, a tributary of the Brazos, which enters the larger stream at Cameron Park. They were followed in 1848 by Captain Thomas H. Barron, who built a log house, parts of which are incased in the two-story residence standing at North Seventh Street and Jefferson Avenue.

In 1848 a General Chambers, who had been given title to the land surrounding Waco by the Mexican Government, sold his rights. Jacob de Cordova, a general land agent and a customer of Erath, was authorized to dispose of the land at $1 per acre. De Cordova was given one-third of the land for his services—over 1,000,000 acres which stretched from Waco into South Texas. He laid out the village of Waco in 1849 and offered lots for sale at low prices. He is considered the founder of Waco.

The town site was laid out in 1849. The first town lot, sold to Shapley P. Ross, was a riverside tract at the foot of present Washington Avenue. At this point on the Brazos he operated a ferry boat, on which he collected tolls ranging from 10¢ for foot passengers to $1.50 for four horses and a wagon. This ferry brought traders, freighters, hunters, and travelers in such numbers that Ross built a hotel, the first in the city.

A Methodist missionary, Joseph P. Sneed, came to the region in 1849 and preached the first sermon in a log cabin. He spent the night under a tree, sleeping on his saddle blankets, and was awakened by the howling of wolves. He began the organization of his church, and in 1850 a building was erected by the Methodists on Second Street and Franklin Avenue.

Forces of law and order were rapidly organized. The first district court began its sittings on April 14, 1851. The next day, Richard Coke, later Governor of Texas, was licensed by this court to practice law. The country commissioners issued land scrip for a school fund.

The following November, Dr. Alexander Montgomery Barnett with his family arrived in a wagon. They traded two bedquilts and a rag carpet, brought from Kentucky, for ten acres of land, and Doctor Barnett announced his readiness to perform the services of a country physician.

Settlers from the Southern States brought educational ideals and traditions, and Waco Female College was established by the Methodists in 1859. The Baptists founded Waco University in 1861. Baylor University absorbed Waco University in 1885.

The community's growth was interrupted by the Civil War. Waco furnished six high ranking officers to the Confederate cause: Lawrence Sullivan Ross, J. E. Harrison, Hiram Granbury, W. H. Parsons, J. W. Speight, and Thomas Harrison. The citizens, almost to a man, rushed to the Confederate standard, and many families were left without support. By 1862 taxes were levied at 5¢ per $100 for food and medical attention for the indigent. In 1864 the county bought 2,000 bushels of wheat, 20,-000 pounds of bacon, 5,000 pounds of wool, and 10,000 pounds of cotton for 254 destitute families.

During the war Bayliss Earle ran the blockade with machinery for a cotton mill, which blazed the way for Waco's economic development.

During the Reconstruction period, settlers came from the ruined Southern States, seeking new livelihoods. Cattle moved up the trails toward northern markets, and on January 6, 1870, a suspension bridge replaced the ferry on the Brazos. There was no other bridge across this stream, and travelers journeying westward swarmed through Waco, which began to grow and to lose the decorum that had graced its earlier years. From a dignified, live-oak shaded village, steeped in the traditions of the South, Waco became a rip-roaring frontier town of false-fronted hotels and notorious gambling halls. Great herds of cattle, wagons loaded with hides, cotton, and wheat, and long freighting trains lumbered across the bridge. Rampaging cowboys and lawless buffalo hunters shattered the ancient calm. The Star Variety Theater, ever noted for its rough clientele, found itself but one among many other amusement resorts.

Judge John W. Oliver, an appointee of Governor Davis' carpetbag regime, sought to impose unwelcome ideas upon the community, but was blocked by the county court which, representing the citizenship, refusd to vote funds necessary to support an increased sheriff's force. Thereupon, Judge Oliver ordered the entire county court into jail.

The members of the court were prominent men and a movement was started to lynch the judge. On the suggestion of a local physician that Judge Oliver was mentally unbalanced, a declaration of his insanity was drawn. A writ was issued by the imprisoned county court, and a constable who was not in jail arrested the judge and placed him behind bars on a charge of lunacy. This unusual situation, where both courts were in jail simultaneously, resolved itself harmlessly by the release of each court by the other.

With the advent of the railroads in 1881, Waco was quickly converted into a progressive city. The population had increased to 20,000 by 1890, and with the surrounding country developing rapidly as a rich agricultural region, it became evident that a larger supply of fresh water was needed. This was obtained in 1929 when the first Lake Waco was formed. This has now been expanded to the new Lake Waco (*see below*).

The gracious living of other days is reflected in houses now being preserved. These include EAST TERRACE, Brazos River at Mill St., built 1867 of pink brick made on the premises, now museum and headquarters of Heritage Society of Waco; FORT HOUSE, erected 1868 by Col. Wm. Aldridge Fort, has two tall Ionic pillars with balcony; WACO GARDEN CENTER, 1705 N. Fifth St., built 1879, uses walnut panelling; McCULLOCH HOUSE, 407 Columbus Ave., 1867 and KENNARD HOUSE, 814 S. Fourth St., 1866, erected by a former Confederate captain from Alabama.

Waco supports the Waco Symphony Orchestra, which has a long fall and winter season of concerts, the Waco Theater of Baylor University, and the Waco Civic Theater.

Waco was the home of three Governors—Richard Coke, Sul Ross, and Pat Neff. The late Dr. Dorothy Scarborough, novelist and essayist, and her brother, George Moore Scarborough, playwright, passed their youth here and were educated at Baylor University. The Negro singer, Jules Bledsoe, who became nationally known for his singing of "Old Man River" in *Show Boat,* was born in Waco.

POINTS OF INTEREST

BAYLOR UNIVERSITY, the largest Baptist university in the world, occupies a campus of 45 acres at Dutton and Speight, S. 5th and

7th Sts. It annually enrolls more than 7,000 students and has a faculty of 800. Baylor was opened May 18, 1846, at Independence, Texas, by the Education Society of the Union Baptist Assn. and received a charter from the last congress of the Republic of Texas. It was named for Judge R. E. B. Baylor, organizer of the Union Assn. In 1886 it was removed to Waco and Waco University was merged with it. As the university grew it acquired three professional schools in Dallas, the COLLEGE OF MEDICINE and the SCHOOL OF NURSING, the COLLEGE OF DENTISTRY, and the SCHOOL OF PHARMACY, the last discontinued in 1931. In 1920 it added the BAYLOR MEMORIAL HOSPITAL in Dallas, which was a part of the School of Medicine until the latter was moved to Houston in 1943.

In recent decades Baylor has added numerous new buildings and facilities. CARROL LIBRARY and CARROL SCIENCE HALL were built early in this century and thus became ready for replacement. WACO HALL, the college auditorium, came later, as did McLEAN GYMNASIUM and the STUDIO THEATER. Since the 1950's Baylor has acquired the BAYLOR STADIUM, seating 49,000. In the 1960's new efforts to improve campus facilities bore fruit. The university set a goal of $5,000,000 for new buildings by 1968. It modernized Waco Hall and gave it a new wing for the SCHOOL OF MUSIC. It completed the MARRS McLEAN SCIENCE BUILDING in 1963. A new Science building to complement McLean was also prepared. Finally came the construction of the new LIBRARY, at a cost of $2,800,000. There are more than 300,000 volumes in the library system.

Of remarkable value to the study of English literature, is the ARMSTRONG BROWNING LIBRARY, which occupies a building erected at a cost of $1,500,000 and dedicated December 3, 1951. It contains the collections of manuscripts and books by and about Robert and Elizabeth Barrett Browning, built up through 40 years by Dr. A. Joseph Armstrong, head of the English department from 1912 to his death in 1952. Construction was designed by Otto R. Eggers of Eggers & Higgins, architects of New York; the George L. Payne Studios of Paterson, N. J., which provided stained glass windows, and Robert Weinman, who modeled the massive bronze doors that carry themes from Browning's poems. Ten pictorial windows in the Research Hall were made by the Jacoby Art Glass Co., St. Louis. The Renaissance-Byzantine architectural note runs through the interior. The sumptuous decoration of the Foyer of Meditation contains a dome covered with 23-karat gold; three cathedral windows in stained glass, eight red Levanto marble columns, and walls paneled in black walnut. The Cloister of the Clasped Hands contains the hands of the two poets in bronze. The Hankamer Treasure Room has a Renaissance ceiling, a formal Italian fireplace, eleven stained glass windows by Charles J. Connick. The third floor is devoted to the Elizabeth Barrett Browning collection.

There are first editions of hundreds of publications and volumes associated with Browning; 5,000 titles in English, and more than 1,000 in 34 other languages, with approximately 500 titles in Japanese. Among the most treasured objects are Browning's private copy of Homer's *Iliad,* the volume of *Aeschylus* from which he translated *Agamemnon,* and the

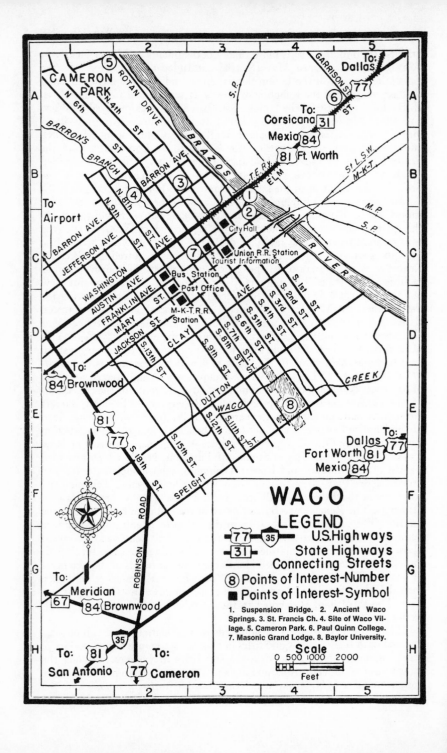

bronze "Clasped Hands," taken from a cast of the clasped hands of Elizabeth and Robert Browning by Harriet Hosmer. Several hundred drawings by the Brownings are included, as are hundreds of letters, among them the Isa Blagden series and Browning's love letters. There is a portrait of Robert Browning by his son, and a bust of Robert Barrett Browning by Munro.

The HANKAMER SCHOOL OF BUSINESS is housed in a new building of Bedford limestone at 5th and Speight Sts. Students majoring in the various business courses must also enroll in liberal arts and sciences and may quality for a law degree.

The university estimates that "a student who is careful in his expenditures" may need about $1,200 to $1,400 for nine months. Any student who marries secretly is indefinitely suspended. Baylor is a member of the Southwest Conference; its football team is called the Bears and its colors are green and gold.

The various collection of the Baylor museums include specimens of minerals, idols from many lands, mounted birds of Texas and the United States, and artifacts and skeletal remains of American Indians.

The old SUSPENSION BRIDGE OVER THE BRAZOS crosses the river at S. First St. and Austin Ave. When the bridge was opened it was the longest single span suspension bridge in the United States, and the second longest in the world. Its single span of 475 feet is supported by four great towers containing 2,700,000 bricks made in Waco. The bridge was designed by Thomas Griffing. August Roebling, of New York, manufactured the wire cables, which were shipped by sea to Galveston and hauled by ox team to Waco.

WACO SPRINGS, just below the suspension bridge on the west side of the Brazos, at one time provided sufficient water to supply a Waco Indian village. As the Wacos were being removed to a reservation, they took a last drink from their revered spring. It is protected by a concrete rim, and a small public park has been created around it.

The Roman Catholic CHURCH OF ST. FRANCIS ON THE BRAZOS (*open 6–7:40 daily*), NW. corner N. 3d St. and Jefferson Ave., a reproduction of Mission San José in San Antonio, was built in 1931, after months of painstaking study of the old mission by the archiect, Roy E. Lane. The facade is ornamented with six life-size statues of saints, and the entire arch of the entrance is carved in a flower and fruit design, its stone carving done by Frank T. Johnson. The famous sacristy window of San José has been faithfully reproduced. All services are in Spanish.

The SITE OF A WACO VILLAGE, NW. corner Barron Ave. and N. 6th St., is occupied by a Negro church. Rangers scouting through the region before the coming of white settlers came upon the remains of the Waco village. When the Waco Theater was built near by, on 6th Street, Indian skeletons were unearthed.

CAMERON PARK on Rotan Drive has an entrance marked by large stone columns with bronze tablets. This 680-acre park has large springs, clear streams, and thickly wooded hills. Great banks of flowers and a terraced rose garden add to its beauty. Recreational facilities include a municipal clubhouse, tennis courts, wading pools, playgrounds, picnic units, and shaded drives.

Connected with the romance and legend of the region is the high white crag overlooking the Bosque, Lover's Leap. From this point, there is a view of the surrounding country.

PAUL QUINN COLLEGE, 1020 Elm St., was established in 1881 by a small group of African Methodist ministers and maintained by the African Methodist Church. It was an accredited four-year college until 1937, when it became a standardized three-year college under the State Department of Education. On the 22-acre campus are the principal buildings and a farm which includes an eight-acre garden. In 1965 it enrolled 364 in the regular term and 383 in the summer session.

MEMORIAL TEMPLE of the GRAND LODGE OF TEXAS, A. F. and A. M., dedicated 1949, opened 1953, faces Columbus Ave., between North 7th and North 8th Sts. This monumental building is practically a square, 249 ft. wide, 226 ft. deep, 88 ft. tall. The main doorway is flanked by two stone towers, 77 ft. above the level of the porch, at the base of which two sculptured friezes portray the building of King Solomon's Temple. Two stone pillars 39½ ft. tall, stand free on the porch at the main doorway, topped by monolithic terrestrial and celestial globes. The Grand Lodge Auditorium has 3,750 seats, with chairs and carpets in deep blue. The Memorial Room contains a book with the names of Freemasons of Texas who served in the U. S. Armed Forces. The Library and Museum contains many rare volumes on Masonry and related subjects, and memorabilia of Stephen F. Austin, Sam Houston and other Texas Masons, including a gavel from Jerusalem used by Houston at the first Grand Lodge meeting in the Republic of Texas.

VETERANS ADMINISTRATION FACILITY, on Dutton St. 2.5 m. SW. of city limits, covers a landscaped area of 345 acres. There are scores of three-story red brick buildings in the plant, which was constructed at a cost of $25,000,000. The hospitals can accommodate 2,000.

HOME FOR NEGLECTED AND DEPENDENT CHILDREN, at N. 19th St. and Park Lane Drive is maintained by the State. On a tract of 94½ acres, the home was established by an act of the legislature in 1919 and opened in 1922. In addition to the dormitories there are a modern hospital, a school for grades one to twelve, and a baby cottage.

LAKE WACO, 5 m., is a reservoir covering 19,440 acres of waters from the North Bosque and Middle Bosque Rivers behind a dam completed 1965 by the Corps of Engineers, USA. The rolled earth dam is 24,618 ft. long, 20 ft. wide at the top, 990 ft. at the base, rising 140 ft. above the river bed, with a spillway 560 ft. long. With a conservation pool covering 7,260 acres total storage capacity is 732,300 acre-feet of water (one acre-foot equals 326,000 gallons). The new dam, replacing an old one, became necessary because of costly floods. The recreation area is reached by State 6. The MUNICIPAL AIRPORT adjoins the Lake and is served by Trans-Texas Airlines. CENTRAL TEXAS ZOO is located in Airport Park (*admission 10¢; reptile house, 25¢*).

JAMES CONNALLY TECHNICAL INSTITUTE, 7 m. NE.

of Waco, was organized to use the buildings of the former James Connally Air Force Base, deactivated 1966. The technical and vocational institute is operated by Texas A. & M. University. Connally, a native of Waco, was killed in a bombing raid over Japan, 1945.

TWELFTH AIR FORCE COMMAND HEADQUARTERS, N. 25th & Windsor Ave., is part of the supersonic air force and in part trained with the Starfighter, F104C, 1500 mph aircraft.

HEART O' TEXAS COLISEUM & FAIR GROUNDS, N. 46th St. & Bosque Blvd., (1953) can seat 11,000 as auditorium and 7,650 as coliseum. Besides the annual agricultural fair in October it has ice shows, rodeos, motor car exhibits and conventions.

Wichita Falls

Air Transportation: Braniff International Airways and Continental Airlines, Wichita Falls Municipal Air Terminal; Kickapoo Airport and Wichita Valley Airport, for private planes.

Bus Lines: Continental Trailways, Continental Dixie Trailways, Jordan, Mid-Continent, Oklahoma Transportation Co., Southwest Coaches. Union Bus Station, Lamar and 7th Sts.

Highways: Red River Valley Expressway System, US 277, US 281; also US 82, 287; State 79.

Railroads: Fort Worth & Denver City Ry.; Missouri, Kansas & Texas. Union Station.

Accommodations and Information: Two major hotels, 40 motels and motor lodges. Chamber of Commerce, Hamilton Bldg., 8th and Lamar Sts. *Wichita Falls Record-News* and *Wichita Falls Times,* 701 Scott Ave.

Churches and Hospitals: 151 churches, 27 denominations. Wichita General Hospital, municipal; Bethania Hospital, Roman Catholic; Wichita Falls State Hospital, 2,550 patients; North Texas Rehabilitation Center; Southwestern Regional Hospital, Sheppard Air Force Base.

Recreation: Fishing, boating, swimming and water skiing at Lakes Wichita, Kemp, Diversion, Kickapoo. Nine neighborhood parks with playground facilities. Five bowling alleys, two 18-hole golf courses, one 9-hole course. Tennis courts and bridle paths. Hunting in season for dove, quail, deer and water fowl.

Events and activities: Wichita Falls Symphony Orchestra; Civic Music Assn.; Civic Playhouse; Art Assn., Broadway Theatre League, Wichita Falls Ballet Theatre, Midwestern University Choir and String Ensemble. *Halls:* Memorial Auditorium, seats 2,716; Midwestern University, seats 700; Woman's Forum, seats 900; Midwestern Student Center, seats 1,500; Museum and Art Center, seats 300. Spectator events, outside of college games are Brazos Valley Fair and Annual Roundup Rodeo, Scudder Park, both in fall.

WICHITA FALLS (946 alt., 101,724 pop., 1960; 113,000, 1967, est. Average temp. varies from 31° F. in winter to 97° in summer; annual rainfall, 26.20 in.) is the seat of Wichita County (123,528 pop., 1960) on the Red River Valley Expressway from Oklahoma City, 16 *m.* from the Texas-Oklahoma line. It is a center for beef cattle and oil, the headquarters of about 225 oil production and service firms in an area grossing $200,000,000 a year, and where agricultural products are grossing $170,-000,000 annually. The discovery of natural gas about 60 years ago started an industrial boom and the development of reservoirs made available a large supply of water for irrigation.

The city is headquarters for the North Texas Oil & Gas Assn., which controls thousands of producing leases in the area. The Wichita Oil Co. in 1904 found oil near Petrolia in Clay County, (State 79 and 148), where gas in quantity also was found in 1907. The first gusher in North Texas was brought in at Petrolia in 1910, when it produced 700 bbl. a day at 1,600 ft. Important wells were dug in 1911 at Electra, on US 287 west of

Wichita Falls, and at Burkburnett, 12 *m.* north of Wichita Falls, in 1918. As late as 1937 important strikes were made at Kamay, in Wichita County.

From the Scott Avenue Overpass, an imposing viaduct over the Fort Worth and Denver City Railway, at its northern edge, Wichita Falls can be seen to best advantage. Beyond the Big Wichita River, which traverses the northern area, are the oil refineries, factories, and machine shops. On the south, beyond the older section, which includes the business district, the city rises to high bluffs where new dwellings overlook the river.

Office buildings and commercial houses, massive and clean in design and construction, blocked off by wide, paved streets, have little in common with the pre-oil wooden structures and rough wagon roads, still within the range of memory. For the casual observer, no evidence remains of the tumult of oil speculation that shook Wichita Falls for two years. Only the map shows clearly the swift changes in its physical characteristics. Its checkerboard design tells of city additions piled hurriedly on city additions with little regard for what had gone before; new residential sections, parks, and curving drives reflect wealth from oil. The highways and two important bridges that span the Big Wichita are recent improvements.

There are several legends regarding the name Wichita, but according to the Smithsonian Institution the name is "of uncertain meaning and origin." John Gould, columnist of the *Wichita Daily Times,* after a visit to a tribe of Wichitas in Oklahoma, said that he was convinced the name means "men from the north." The "Falls" was used in the town's name because of a five-foot waterfall which in early years existed in the river.

Into the vicinity of present-day Wichita Falls, in 1542, came a tragic little company of Spaniards, hungry and ragged, lost in a trackless wilderness. Don Hernando de Soto, great explorer of the Mississippi, while dying on the banks of the mighty stream, made Luis de Moscoso his successor; and, in search of New Spain, the survivors of the expedition marched across the uncharted northern expanse of a region now in Texas, skirting the plains below the Red River. They traveled through an Indian province called Soacatino, believed by the historian, Carlos E. Castañeda, to have been "slightly to the west and not far from present Wichita Falls." Hearing of countrymen "towards the south . . . moving about," as the Gentleman of Elvas—chronicler of the expedition—wrote, the forlorn little band marched on, traveling through a "very thinly peopled country, where great privation and toil were endured." Disappointment awaited them and they retraced their march, returning at last to the Mississippi. Thus the Gentleman of Elvas was the first man known to have described the region of this Texas city.

A map of the area, bearing the date 1767, shows the vicinity of Wichita Falls as uninhabited. Spanish explorers wrote of a Rio del Fierro (River of Iron), now believed to have been the Wichita. Athanase de Mezieres in 1772 told of the veneration Indians of this region gave a "mass of metal," possibly part of a meteorite discovered by Major R. S. Neighbors in the 1850s. Major Neighbors wrote that the Comanches believed the twisted iron to be "possessed of extraordinary curative powers

. . . and it was the custom of all who passed it to deposit upon it beads, arrow-heads, tobacco and other articles."

On the banks of the Wichita lived the Indians of that name, also other tribes, some of them in villages whose conical buffalo hide wigwams were built neatly in rows upon well defined streets. Corn and pumpkins, beans and squash grew in the fields. Early in the eighteenth century French traders were here, exchanging muskets and beads for pelts.

Buffalo hunters, soldiers, cattlemen, and adventurers passed up and down the valley of the Wichita but none tarried until 1861, when Captain Mabel Gilbert, a native Mississippian, who was a member of the expedition that had established Bird's Fort in Tarrant County in 1841, appeared with his family in the northwest part of Wichita County.

Gilbert and his family are believed to have lived along the Texas side of the Red River for at least a year, or until the beginning of the Civil War. Early settlers agree that he cultivated the soil and traded with Indians across the river, but otherwise the accounts vary. Some claim he died and was buried on the land he tilled—the first white man buried in the later confines of Wichita County.

Pioneer settlers in present-day Wichita Falls were W. T. Buntin and his family, who established themselves in a dugout at the point where Tenth Street intersects Kemp Boulevard. A few years later Buntin built a log cabin about a mile north of the bluffs, in what is now the Indian Heights addition. He filed the first claim to land in that section, and the first patent in Wichita County was issued to him.

Buntin raised horses, drove them to Fort Sill in the then Indian Territory, and traded them for supplies. He was a big man, of simple manners, usually found attending to his own affairs. The Indians did not bother him. The numerous Butin children, as wild as mesquite brush and buffalo grass and as fearless as their father, contributed much to the pioneer lore of Wichita Falls. J. B. Marlow, one-time mayor of the city and one of its first residents, who, as a lad, played with the Buntin boys, recalled:

They went barefooted summer and winter, and wore crude, homemade garments fashioned by their mother from tarpaulins which their father brought back from Fort Sill. . . . I remember going hunting with one of the boys. . . . He insisted that we go barehanded. We climbed into a mesquite tree and down in the brush below us was a big bobcat. The Buntin boy cut a branch from the tree and poked down into the brush to rout the bobcat. Then he jumped on top of the 'cat and subdued him with his bare hands.

The Buntins were prospering when their first neighbors, the Craig family, came in 1878. The Craigs remained until 1889, when they sold their property to J. H. Barwise, who had arrived in 1879. Barwise often is called the Father of Wichita Falls, because of his deep conviction that the place was properly situated for future development and his tireless work toward making a city of the settlement he found there.

A crude plat of the town was made in 1876 by the heirs of John A. Scott, a Mississippi planter. The story of how the Scott heirs came into possession of the land dates back to the time when Texas, finding money raised by taxation in the sparsely settled country inadequate for government support, was obliged to sell land scrip to make up the deficiency. In 1837, in New Orleans, 19 certificates of 640 acres each were sold, and finally came into Scott's possession. The tradition that he won the certificates in a poker game and considered them of little value seems plausible, for he put them away at the bottom of a trunk and apparently forgot them. It was not until after his death in 1854 that the scrip, discovered by his heirs, was found to cover land in what is now a part of Wichita County. When a railroad (Dallas & Wichita) was proposed in Dallas in 1876, heirs of Scott sent a representative to Wichita Falls to map a town site that would accommodate itself to the position of the railroad. The plan fell through, however, and this railroad was never built.

The attempt of the Scott heirs to appropriate land already occupied by settlers resulted in lawsuits. In the meantime, since no railroad made its appearance, what was locally called the T. B. & W. (Two Bulls and a Wagon) continued to bring into Wichita Falls everything that could not be tied behind the cantle of a saddle. In 1880 the first census showed a population of 433.

A railroad, the Forth Worth and Denver City, agreed to build through Wichita Falls for 55 per cent of the proceeds from the sale of town lots. Claimants to the land entered into the agreement, and the railroad arrived on September 27, 1882. Lots marked for sale were largely on the north side of the river, but before the first trainload of buyers arrived a big rain put the north side under water. It became necessary to shift the location, and it is due to this accident that the greater part of the city is now on the south side of the Wichita.

Cattle raising was the chief industry, with dry-land farming fighting for success until 1884, when J. B. Marlow began experiments with irrigation. In 1886–87 came the "great drought" when for 18 months not a drop of rain fell. But the community grew steadily, and was incorporated in 1889.

J. A. Kemp, a pioneer in Wichita Falls, impressed by the success of Marlow's experiments, urged the organization of an irrigation project. In 1896 he began a campaign to interest sufficient capital to build a dam across the Wichita. He was unable to finance the project from private sources, and the State constitution of 1879 was construed to prohibit the issuance of bonds to cover the cost of irrigation systems. Kemp and a few associates immediately submitted an amendment to the constitution, which was defeated. It was submitted again in 1899, with the same result.

To demonstrate irrigation was practicable for the Wichita Valley, Kemp and his associates organized the Lake Wichita Irrigation and Water Company, and in 1900 built a dam across Holliday Creek, forming Lake Wichita, which became the water supply for the city and for the irrigation of neighboring lands. In 1904 an amendment to permit the voting of bonds for irrigation projects was adopted, but the amount of the bond issue was limited to 25 per cent of the taxable values of a proposed irrigation district. At once two irrigation districts called Number 1 and Number 2, were created in the vicinity of Wichita Falls, but for several years the plans were carried no further.

By 1907 the town was still basing its prosperity on cattle and, more recently, on wheat, with a grain elevator and the railroads to speed up distribution.

Oil first was found in Wichita County in 1900, when it appeared in shallow wells dug by W. T. Waggoner, who was seeking water for cattle on his ranch near Electra. However, oil was not produced in commercial quantities until April, 1911, when the Clayco No. 1 Putnam near Electra roared in. Not until 1918 did full development bring the rush of boom days. Wichita Falls awoke to the amazing fact of oil, became headquarters for supplies and offices, and suddenly discovered the town was over-crowded. Hotels were inadequate and rooming houses forced their guests to sleep in relays. The problem was to get foot space, let alone office space, in which to hawk shares in leases and oil companies. Sidewalks became stock exchanges, fronts of buildings were knocked out and spaces roped off in which hundreds of oil companies were promoted.

Despite the boom, the city was building substantially. It clung to the belief that its future was based on agriculture, but not until the drought of 1917–18 seriously threatened the water supply from Lake Wichita did it awake to the need of increased water resources. In the meantime Texas authorized bonds for irrigation facilities and in 1920 the town voted two bond issues totaling more than $6,000,000. These bond issues resulted in the construction of two important dams, one forming LAKE KEMP in Baylor County, 6 miles north of Maybelle, with 20,820 acres and a capacity of 461,800 acre-ft., and the other LAKE DIVERSION, on the Archer-Baylor line, 14 miles west of Holliday, covering 3,419 acres and holding 40,000 acre-ft. The principal water supply of the city is LAKE KICKAPOO, on the north fork of the Little Wichita, 10 miles north of Archer City, covering 6,200 acres and holding 106,000 acre-ft. of water. The newest addition to the water and irrigation facilities is LAKE AR-ROWHEAD, 13,500 acres, which when fully filled holds 228,000 acre-ft.

At the same time the press of traffic caused by the oil boom necessitated improved highways between Wichita Falls and the oil fields. The Burnett Street Bridge, a concrete structure over the Wichita River, was completed in 1920. The more important Scott Avenue Bridge, of three-span concrete construction, built in 1927, became part of a plan for centralizing all highways entering the city. Scott Avenue was widened to accommodate the traffic, leading it through the city and out over the Holliday Creek Bridge at the foot of the avenue. The Scott Avenue Overpass, over the Fort Worth and Denver City Railway, was completed in 1937 at a cost of $110,000.

Wichita Falls is the business and supply center for the vast North Texas Oil Field, which includes the counties of Wichita, Wilbarger, Baylor, Archer, Young, Clay, Montague, Cooke, Wise, Foard, Jack and Throckmorton. The Wichita Oil Company was organized in 1904 and

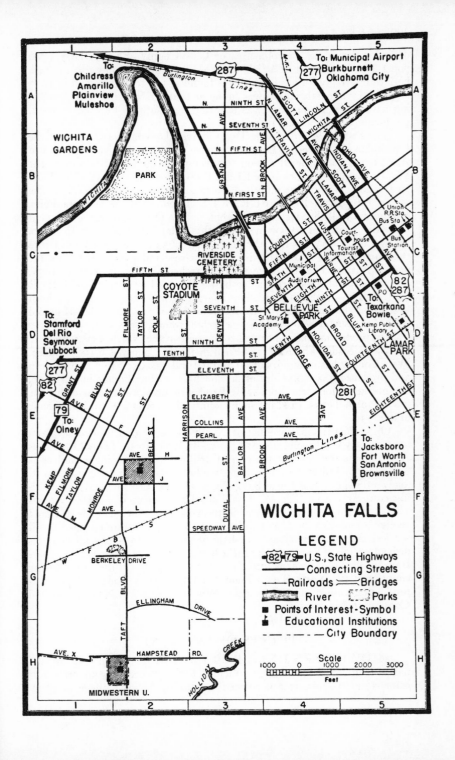

drilled wells in the Petrolia area of Clay County. PETROLIA (700 pop.) 15 *m*. northeast of Wichita Falls, is reached by State 79 and 148, both connecting with US 82. Oil was found at 150 to 350 ft., and in 1907 at 448 ft., while natural gas was found at 1,500 ft. The first well producing natural gas in quantity was opened 1 *m*. south of Petrolia in 1907, producing 10,000,000 cu. ft. daily.

The first gusher of North Texas arrived December 17, 1910, at the Dorthukia Dunn well at Petrolia. It gave 700 bbl. a day at 1,600 ft. On April 1, 1911, a gusher threw oil 100 ft. into the air from 1,600 ft. on the W. T. Waggoner ranch near ELECTRA, 27 *m*. west of Wichita Falls on US 287. Within five months Electra grew from 500 to 5,000 people.

In July, 1912, BURKBURNETT, 15 *m*. north of Wichita Falls, produced a well that yielded 7,500 bbl. a day. The result was a rush that made this a town of 20,000 in six months; today it is credited with 8,750. During the four years that the boom lasted 65,000 people crowded into this northern area and half a dozen towns rose and disappeared from the postal register. The first deep well in Archer County, in March, 1931, brought 750 bbl. a day from a depth of 2,212 ft., 4 *m*. north of ARCHER CITY. This is the county seat, approx. 2,000 pop., 25 *m*. south of Wichita Falls on State 79. Drills went deeper; in 1937 the Mangold well of the KMA field produced 2,000 bbl. from a depth of 3,750 ft.

Oil production has continued to increase in the North Texas Field in the 1960 decade. The Rasberry Field in Foard County is 6,160 ft. deep. Wise County has reservoirs of oil and natural gas 4,500 to 7,500 ft. deep and produced 3,000,000 bbl. of oil and hydrocarbon liquids in one year; one gas field alone, the Bonnsville Bend, produces 70 per cent of all the gas in North Texas. In Hardeman County discoveries are still being made at 8,000 ft.

Oil is the principal product of North Texas. Production comes from approx. 33,500 oil wells and 953 gas wells. The North Texas Oil & Gas Association estimates that the cost of drilling and producing a well costs $12 a foot or $38,400 for an average well of 3,200 ft., but one at 6,000 ft. may cost $84,000 and one at 8,000 ft., $128,000. The rotary rig for drilling costs $150,000. The Wichita Falls Chamber of Commerce reports 16,000 are employed by oil firms in the area, 8,500 owners of leased land receive a monthly check as royalty, and about 32,000 are engaged in oil services and supplies. About one-half of these North Texas oil counties depend on oil and natural gas for a living, while the other half prospers from the flow of oil money into the channels of trade. Of the 12 producing counties in the North Texas Field Wichita County leads with mineral production valued at $36,000,000; Wise is next with $33,000,000 and Cooke with $31,000,000.

POINTS OF INTEREST

MIDWESTERN UNIVERSITY on Taft Boulevard is the principal institution of learning in Wichita Falls. It occupies an attractive campus of 80 acres. It was formed as Hardin Junior College in 1922, became a four-year senior college in 1946 and a state-supported college in 1961. It gives degrees in the principal arts and sciences, as well as in business administration, education, music and medical technology. Coeducational, it enrolls approximately 3,000 students annually with a faculty of 101. The Library contains more than 150,000 volumes. The University has been adding new buildings to its facilities, including the Library, costing $800,000, the Science Bldg., at $2,300,000, and a dormitory. A Coliseum is in the plans.

SHEPPARD AIR FORCE BASE, 5 miles north of Wichita Falls, is the site of the Sheppard Training Center, the home of the 494th Bombardment Wing of the Strategic Air Command and of the 900th Air Refueling Squadron. The mission of the Training Center is carried by the departments of aircraft maintenance, comptroller, communications, intelligence, intercontinental missile, transportation and utilities. The budget of the Base for a typical year is approximately $147,000,000, and about 21,500 military and civilian personnel are located there, contributing mightily to the income of the municipality. Training also is provided by the Medical Service School and the Base Hospital has extensive facilities. The Base was named for Sen. Morris E. Sheppard (d.1941).

The U. S. Naval and Marine Corps Reserve Training Center is located at 1823 Fifth St., Wichita Falls.

WICHITA FALLS MUSEUM AND ART CENTER is the newest addition to the cultural facilities of the city. Completed in 1967, it has 15,000 square feet for exhibitions, administration, class rooms and an auditorium seating 300. A planetarium is included in the plans.

WICHITA FALLS DAY NURSERY (*open daily except noon hour; free*), 403 Lamar St., provides daily meals and supervision for about 100 children of employed mothers. It ranks first among institutions of its kind in the Southwest. The idea of the nursery had its inception in 1918 when student flyers at an aviation camp near the city made a practice of giving food and delicacies, sent them by friends, to children living in shacks along the river. In 1919 local women launched a movement to provide permanent care for under-privileged children. They now have a modified Spanish type building of fireproof brick, concrete and tile construction, surrounded by a large yard, with numerous items of playground equipment.

PART III

Along the State's Highways

KEY TO
TEXAS TOURS
LEGEND

– · – · –	State Boundary
———	Tour Routes–Main and Independent
———	Side Tours – Unnumbered
7a	Section Numbers – Main Tours
23A	Section Numbers–Independent Side
★	Section Ends–Main Tours
⊛	Tour Section End–Principal Cities
✪	Tour Section End– Small Cities
◎	Principal Cities
○	Small Cities and Towns

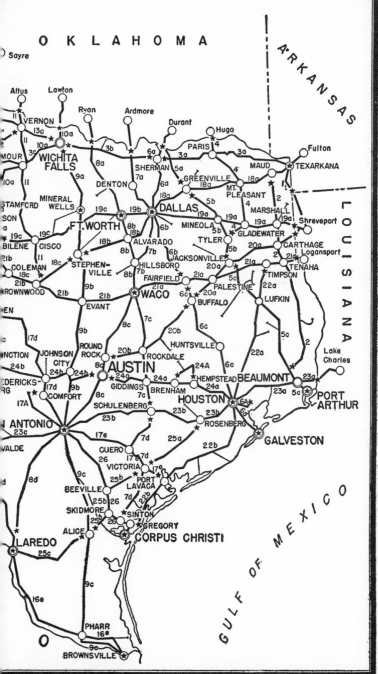

Tour 1

(Texarkana, Ark.)—Texarkana—Atlanta—(Shreveport, La.); US 59 and State 77.
Arkansas Line to Louisiana Line, 38 *m.*

This is the northeastern gateway to Texas, where major state and national highways come from Oklahoma, Arkansas and Louisiana to converge at Texarkana, the city that straddles the Texas-Arkansas border. US 71, having merged with US 59 in Arkansas, touches Texas briefly, then continues alone into Louisiana, while US 59 resumes an independent route that coincides with State 77 until Atlanta. Beyond this point State 77 crosses the line to become a Louisiana state road. US 67 and US 82 come from Arkansas and proceed west; US 82 is the main highway along northern Texas to Wichita Falls, and US 67 joins Interstate 30.

Here the highway traverses a rolling, forested region where shortleaf pine clothes the uplands, with white, red, and burr oak, sweet gum, and wild magnolia trees along the streams. Sawmills dot timbered areas. Dogwood blooms profusely in the spring, and the wild rose, shame vine, Virginia creeper, and swamp pink are among the plants that ornament the roadside. Ponds have white and yellow lilies. In dense woods along creeks, small animals are hunted and trapped for their fur; mink and muskrat pelts are most valued.

Since the time of settlement in the 1840's, cotton has been the leading money crop, and cotton picking and chopping are the only seasonal activities. The white population is largely of Anglo-American stock, and most of the rural estates have passed, from the plowing of their first furrows, from father to son.

The route starts at the State Line, at W. 7th St. and State Line Ave., in TEXARKANA, 0 *m.* (295 alt.). The U. S. Census counted 30,218 in Texarkana, Texas, in 1960, a rise from 21,435 in 1950 partly attributed to annexation of 8,783. In Texarkana, Arkansas, it counted 21,652, a rise from 15,875 in 1950. The area of the city is 8.7 sq. mi. in Texas and 6 sq. mi. in Arkansas. It is a railroad and industrial center, which lies on the Texas-Arkansas line, 30 miles southeast of the Oklahoma border. It is served by the Texas & Pacific Ry., the Missouri Pacific and the Kansas City Southern. A network of rails sharply divides the industrial section on the south, in a sandy valley, from the business and residential areas, where broad streets are lined with pin oaks, sycamores, box elders, and a few pines. Thoroughfares running at 45-degree angles form small grassy triangles on which are modern public and commercial buildings. The city carries three identifications: Texarkana, Texas, Texarkana, Arkansas, and Texarkana, Arkansas-Texas, the last being the official designation of the United States Post Office. A single, urban community, two civic identities make it a Siamese twin among cities. Each twin has a head of its own (a mayor and a city administration), but the two necessarily co-operate rather closely.

Texarkana was founded in 1873. Early settlers had built up with the Indians of present-day Oklahoma, then Indiana Territory, a trade that until the Civil War continued to be the chief activity. A Caddo village originally occupied the site of the city, and at least 70 Indian mounds are in the neighborhood.

Texarkana grew rapidly and today its industrial products include lumber, galvanized iron, baskets, caskets, cedar chests, and boxes, brick, tile and pottery, textiles, refined sulphur, cottonseed products, oil and fertilizers. Processing, canning, and shipment of vegetables and fruits add to the town's industries. Some iron has been mined.

The center of State Line Avenue, which runs through the heart of the Texarkana business district, is the boundary between Texas and Arkansas. On the Arkansas side liquor is sold, but the Texas' half is "dry." At the northern end of this thoroughfare is the FEDERAL BUILDING, which houses the post office of Texarkana, Arkansas-Texas, and the judiciary and administrative offices of the Eastern District of Texas and the Western District of Arkansas.

Besides the Union Station, used by the railroads, Texarkana has the Continental Trailways Bus Center and the Greyhound Bus Terminal. Its MUNICIPAL AIRPORT has regular flights by Braniff and Trans-Texas lines.

The Four States Fair and Rodeo is held annually in September.

RED RIVER ARMY DEPOT uses Texarkana as its post office but actually is located 17 *m.* west on US 59. It occupies a 50 sq. mi. area with approximately 3,000 buildings and structures. The primary mission of the depot is to store, recondition and issue supplies and ammunition for the Armed Forces. It carries in stock about 85,000 different supply items and more than 7,000 types of ammunition. The depot has 3,000,000 sq. ft. of warehouse space, more than 700 underground ammunition caches and above-ground magazines. There are a limited number of military personnel and 5,500 civil service employees.

LONE STAR ARMY AMMUNITION PLANT is located adjoining the Depot. It is a government-owned contractor-operated ammunition loading plant and its lands are considered part of the greater Red River reservation.

TEXARKANA COLLEGE, a municipal junior college founded 1927, enrolls more than 1,900 annually.

At 9 *m.* US 59 reaches LAKE TEXARKANA, a huge reservoir fed by the Sulphur River, covering 119,700 acres and with a capacity of 2,654,300 acre-feet. It extends from Bowie County into Cass County. Built for conservation of water and flood control, it offers recreation facilities, with fishing for bass, crappie and catfish and small game hunting. On the southern bank are the 1,475 acres of ATLANTA STATE PARK.

QUEEN CITY, 20 *m.,* a farm products center, has 1,081 pop.

ATLANTA, 27 *m.* (264 alt., 4,076 pop.), has modern buildings housing wholesale stores, a brick factory, and a canning plant which processes the tomatoes, beans, and other vegetables grown in the surrounding truck-farming area. A nearby oil field, and lumbering activity based upon forests of pine and hardwoods, add to the prosperity of this clean, animated community.

The Texas, Louisiana, and Arkansas borders come together at 38 *m.* as the route crosses the LOUISIANA LINE, 4.6 miles northwest of Rodessa, Louisiana (*see Louisiana Guide*).

ᛞᛞᛞᛞᛞᛞᛞᛞᛞᛞᛞᛞᛞᛞᛞᛞᛞᛞᛞᛞᛞᛞᛞᛞᛞᛞ

Tour 2

Maud—Linden—Jefferson—Marshall—San Augustine—Jasper—Junction with US 69; 248 *m.,* US 59 and US 96.

US 67 comes out of Texarkana and moves west. At Maud it meets State 8, which comes south from Arkansas. Since the filling of Lake Texarkana US 59 runs along the eastern shore. State 8 crosses the Lake and joins US 59 at Linden.

This route roughly parallels the eastern boundary of the State, of which the meanderings of the Sabine River form a little more than the southern half. Through virgin forests of pine, past stump-dotted clearings and areas of sparse second growth; over low, red, sandy hills and across reeking, stagnant swamplands, US 59 and US 96 lead southward, traversing an area that knew the first northward sweep of settlement following the Texas Revolution. In the northern part lumbering is the leading industry, seconded by agriculture, which becomes more important toward the south; cotton is the largest crop. Lignite and iron ore, both undeveloped, underlie much of the route. Oil developments have added materially to the economic welfare of the region. Small towns are strung close together like beads along the ribbon of the highway, each one much like the other—a huddle of brick or stone business structures along the single main street or around a tiny square, a scattered residential section of small frame houses dominated by two or three more substantial homes of leading citizens, a cotton gin or a lumber mill, or both—only minor details of arrangement marking a difference. Pioneer customs prevail in the "back country," where, in houses with wide, open halls called windways or dog-runs, Saturday night gatherings locally called play parties are given; they may be candy pullings, "sings," or game parties. Square dances and all-day quilting parties are popular. Each farm house has its hounds for hunting raccoons and opossums; young people have hunts that result in " 'possum" dinners for their friends.

Along this way, through the homeland of the Caddoes, came French and Spanish explorers, and later, some of the first Anglo-American immigrants. South of Carthage, almost midway between the Sabine and Neches Rivers, was the Neutral Ground, an area once without law or government, set up as a buffer between Spanish holdings and the territory of the United States. Here were hatched many schemes of conquest, and hither fled many men "wanted" in the United States and in Texas.

South of MAUD, 0 *m.* (284 alt., 900 pop.) (*see Tour 18a*), at the junction with US 67 (*see Tour 18*), State 8 passes between dark walls of towering pines. Ben Milam, a hero of the Texas Revolution (*see History*), surveyed this region.

The highway crosses Lake Texarkana.

In DOUGLASSVILLE, 10.3 *m.* (328 pop.), founded in 1853, the log cabin erected in 1854 by John Douglass still stands, somewhat modernized. In this village of houses made of pine lumber, large stockyards serve a wide area; livestock auctions are held twice weekly.

The population between Douglassville and the junction with US 59 is from a quarter to a half Negro. During the era of settlement, plantation owners had large numbers of slaves; their descendants still farm the cotton fields, remaining as sharecroppers or renters. A few Negroes work in sawmills. Old customs and superstitions remain; in this area a deserted church was considered haunted and mammies used to frighten children with tales of Old Coffinhead, a giant rattlesnake.

LINDEN, 25.1 *m.* (410 alt., 1900 pop.) where State 80 joins US 59, is a busy shipping point for livestock and dairy products. Surrounded by forests of pine and hardwoods, its frame residences—many of them aged—circle a small business district around a stucco courthouse. Here, in the plant of the *Cass County Sun,* a George Washington press made in 1853 had a remarkable history. Used first to print a newspaper in Shreveport, Louisiana, it was sunk in the Red River, with a barrel of type and three imposing stones, to keep it from falling into the hands of Federal forces under General Banks when they captured the town in 1864. After the war the press was recovered and brought in 1875 to Linden.

A great change has come over the topography of the lowlands where formerly Cypress Creek flooded the Big Bayou Swamp. With the construction of Ferrill's Bridge Dam the LAKE O' THE PINES was formed 9 m. west of Jefferson, covering 38,200 acres in 5 counties and holding 842,200 acre-ft. of water. Cypress Creek also enlarged CADDO LAKE, east of US 59, when a dam was built at Mooringsport, La. The lake now covers 32,700 acres, 11,000 of them in Texas.

West of Linden 14 m. to HUGHES SPRINGS (2,000 pop. est.) said to rest on a huge iron ore deposit. Six m. west is DAINGERFIELD (3,133 pop.), out of which 2 m. on State 49 is DAINGERFIELD STATE PARK, 580 acres, with camp facilities.

JEFFERSON, 42 m. (191 alt., 3,062 pop.), formerly a stagnant port, in 1939 found new life in the development of a near-by oil field. Weathered buildings dating from the period of the Republic of Texas, and on through the architectural eras of gables and gingerbread ornamentation, line quiet streets shaded by pecans, locusts and box elders. Some of the houses—The Manse (1838), The Magnolias (1868), Colonel Epperson's, are the objects of tours led by the Garden Club in May.

As early as 1832 a handful of Anglo-Americans had settled seven miles east on Big Cypress Bayou, about a ferry landing belonging to S. P. Smith. There was a Caddo village nearby, but as immigrants came in, the Indians moved away. Big Cypress and Caddo Lake, into which the Bayou flowed, were then navigable waters, connected through the Red River with the Mississippi. Early-day shipping prospered but defective land titles obstructed development at Smith's Landing.

Jefferson was established in 1836 on land donated by Allen Urquart. It was on Trammel's Trace, over which Sam Houston and, later, David Crockett entered Texas. Large sawmills were erected here in the forests, and the town soon became the principal river port of Texas, to which came side-wheelers from St. Louis and New Orleans. Oxcarts and wagons brought the produce of northeast Texas to Jefferson's wharves. The years of the Republic saw an immigrant rush from the Southern States.

In the early fifties an iron foundry was set up by Lockett and Stewart, its young foreman being George Addison Kelly. Within a few years Kelly assumed direction of the plant, which he moved five miles west, establishing the town of Kellyville. In the new town he began to manufacture Kelly plows.

Jefferson reached full development in the decade following a destructive fire in 1866. The water front was rebuilt, and new mercantile enterprises were launched. In 1867 artificial gas was made here by subjecting pine knots to intense heat in iron drums or conical retorts. The gas issuing from the top of the cone was carried into mains laid under the principal streets, along which ornamental gaslight fixtures were installed. Another pioneer enterprise was the manufacture of artificial ice. In 1868 a man named Doyle devised a method of freezing water in thin, flat pans. Built up by layers and congealed into blocks, the ice was sold for 10 cents a pound, but the undertaking was not a success.

The EXCELSIOR HOUSE, Austin and Vale Sts., built before the Civil War, has a long porch across its front with iron grillwork on the roof. It retains its period furniture and stages costume fetes. The HOUSE OF THE SEASONS, with a four-sided cupola, and the Greek Revival MANSE are well-preserved historic houses.

South of Jefferson US 59 passes through wooded hills, and at 43 *m.* crosses Big Cypress Bayou.

MARSHALL, 58 *m.* (375 alt., 25,000 pop. est.) is at the junction with US 80 and State 43 (*see Tour 19*).

In this region Sacred Harp singers hold frequent well-attended gatherings. Brought to Texas by emigrants from Alabama and Tennessee more than a century ago, this type of community singing is distinctive because, used in Elizabethan England, its system of calling the scale consists of only three notes, repeated twice, adding the dominant seventh to introduce the new position. Thus it reads fa-sol-la-fa-sol-la-mi-fa, instead of the familiar do-re-mi-fa-sol-la-si-do. In the printed music, notes are recognized by their individual shapes rather than their position on the staff, a system devised about 100 years ago.

The simplicity of Sacred Harp music is largely responsible for its general appeal and acceptance. New tunes are learned by singing them first in melody, calling the notes instead of the words. No instrumental accompaniment is used. Singers are divided into four groups: bass, alto, tenor, and treble or soprano. A pitch pipe or tuning fork gives the key.

Themes of the songs indicate a close relation to ancient English ballads, although today they are all of a sacred nature, the most popular bearing such titles as "Vale of Sorrow," "Farewell Vain World," "Rest in Heaven," and "Show Pity, Lord."

A typical Sacred Harp gathering is an all-day affair; folk from far and near arrive early and bring picnic lunches. The first half hour or so is spent in visiting, the women discussing domestic affairs, the men talking of crops and weather. Then the meeting is called to order, and after a brief business session the crowd is divided into its singing parts; the leader takes his position before them, the pitch is given, and singing starts. Thin and wavering a trifle at first, the voices gather strength and inspiration until they flow forth powerful, melodious. A pause occurs at noon while lunch baskets are lightened, and then comes the afternoon session which lasts until almost dark. Sometimes there is an evening session but more often, especially in the deep rural regions, people start home at dusk, many having long miles to go.

A State convention of Sacred Harp singers, several district conventions, and innumerable local gatherings are held annually in east Texas.

CARTHAGE, 89 *m.* (292 alt., 5,262 pop.), is at the junction with US 79 (*see Tour 20*).

A large roadside park at 98.6 *m.* offers picnicking facilities.

TENAHA, 106 *m.* (351 alt., 1,097 pop.), has reminders of its past in store buildings with false fronts, and in the presence of an old-fashioned hitching rail along an entire block in the business district. It is at the junction with US 84 (*see Tour 21*), and US 96. South of Tenaha the route is US 96, through an area where truck gardens are passed in cut-over areas.

CENTER, 117 *m.* (345 alt., 4,400 pop. est.), notable for its fine homes of the period of the Republic of Texas, featuring vine-covered lattices, large porches and many gables, is an active trade center with lumber mills, broom, mattress, and handle factories, cotton gins and yards. State 7 and 87 cross here.

The town came into being in 1866 as the result of a law requiring that the county seat be in the approximate center of the county. Quick to take advantage of this, Jesse Amason donated 50 acres for a town site that was quickly surveyed and named Center. Shelbyville, then the county seat, refused to give up the county records and placed armed guards around the courthouse. After a few days, when the guards had been removed, the county clerk quietly removed the records by night and deposited them in the new log courthouse here.

SHELBYVILLE, 124 *m.* (250 pop.), is built on a high hill 7 *m.* SE of Center on State 87 and as if to tell its story, has an old cemetery on the northeast side of the highway, while oil derricks rise on the west side. The town was founded about 1817, and has been variously called Tenaha, Nashville, and Shelbyville, the last in honor of General Isaac Shelby. Here the first sawmills, operated by horsepower, cut one log a day on an average.

The surrounding region was the scene of internecine warfare that at its climax in 1844 neared revolutionary proportions. The Neutral Ground contained a motley crowd of men, many of whom were fugitives from the States—gamblers with slippery fingers, "land pirates" who dealt in forged land certificates, counterfeiters of paper and silver money, horse thieves, highwaymen, and slave stealers. Numbers of them banded together and became a part of the Clan of the Mystic Confederacy, outlaw and slave-stealing organization of John M. Murrell, known as "the Man in the Bolivar Coat," who had operated along the Natchez Trace and on the Mississippi and Red Rivers in the 1830's. The desperadoes terrorized law-abiding citizens and a group formed a body called the Regulators, who were supposed to combat the outlaws but were later accused of being in league with some of them. Another group, the Moderators, was then organized to regulate the Regulators. In a foray the Moderators killed the leader of the opposing faction. The latter retaliated by capturing those implicated in the killing and hanging three of them after a farcical trial. Feudal warfare then raged openly.

The Regulators took the town of Shelbyville, and it was dangerous for a Moderator even to be seen on the streets. Courts were openly defied. When the Regulators placed 25 leading citizens under the ban of exile or death, 65 men banded together to drive the Regulators from the region.

Both sides enrolled recruits until the armed forces of each numbered almost a hundred.

Two indecisive battles were fought. Finally, on August 15, 1844, President Houston issued a proclamation commanding all parties to lay down their arms and return to their homes, and ordered out the militia under General Travis G. Broocks. When the General arrived at Shelbyville, the Moderator leaders at once surrendered, as did the leading Regulators soon afterward. At their arraignment President Houston appeared and scolded them much as a father might scold quarreling boys. Resolutions were drawn up and signed by both parties, disbanding the party organizations and agreeing that they call themselves neither Moderators nor Regulators, but Texans.

Shelbyville and Shelby County sent two companies to the Mexican War, one made up of old-time Regulators, the other of old-time Moderators. They marched with Taylor's army and fought shoulder to shoulder during the Monterrey campaign.

US 96 continues south parallel to the eastern edge of SABINE NATIONAL FOREST, one of the great southern pine timber lands; later it has ANGELINA NATIONAL FOREST on the west. This is a region of making fiber board and laminated wood beams.

SAN AUGUSTINE, 141 *m.* (304 alt., 2,500 pop.), is built on small red hills. Its houses, many of them old and of weathered pine, are set deep in yards smothered in oleanders, gardenias and mimosas. Vacant lots are a tangle of Cherokee roses. Around the wide, tranquil courthouse square, farmers and Negro farm hands gather to discuss the crops. Sidewalks, and many of the houses, are tinged with the red earth. A few large white frame residences of Southern Colonial architecture crown the hilltops. The town developed from a settlement that grew around the Mission Nuestra Señora de los Dolores de los Ais (Mission of Our Lady of Sorrows of the Ais), which was re-established on Ayish Bayou by the Marquis de San Miguel de Aguayo in 1721. Four years previously the mission had been founded somewhere within half a league west of the bayou, but, because of French colonial expansion, had been abandoned in 1719. The second mission remained active until 1773. In 1756, still uneasy about French intentions, the Spanish established the Presidio de San Agustin de Ahumada (Fort of St. Augustine of Ahumada), here. The presidio was abandoned in 1771, the mission in 1773. The first Anglo-Americans came into the territory in 1818.

Though in 1890 a fire destroyed a large part of the town, some old buildings remain, sturdy and mellowed by the years. San Augustine has 33 historical "medallion" homes, more than any city in East Texas. The Garrett House, oldest in the county, is said to date from around 1830. Of special interest today is the Ezekiel Cullen House, which was restored by Hugh Roy Cullen, grandson of Ezekiel Cullen and presented to the Ezekiel Cullen Chapter of the Daughters of the Republic of Texas in 1953. It houses a collection of paintings by S. Seymour Thomas, a native of San Augustine. It is open daily except Mondays in June, July and August.

Three blocks east of the courthouse square is the CARTWRIGHT

HOUSE (*open by arrangement*), a dignified two-story frame structure, also built in 1839, when it stood directly across the street from the University of San Augustine, a pioneer institution of learning incorporated June 5, 1837, and active until the outbreak of the Civil War.

PINELAND, 165 *m.* (267 alt., 1,236 pop.), is a lumber-mill town in the piney woods, where the homes stand "back yonder quite a piece" in little clearings of stump-dotted land. Usually the houses are isolated, but here and there a byroad leads past a cluster of frame houses around a store, a post office, a blacksmith shop, and perhaps a church. These people, who are highly individualistic, are largely of old English stock and speak a dialect that contains odd idioms. They "pitch" a crop when they plant it, refer to a funeral as a "buryin'," call a hound a "potlicker," have a "cuss fight" when they quarrel without violence, describe a religious conversation as a "perfessin'," and—most recent word, probably, in their peculiar vocabulary—speak of a radio as a "radiator."

BROOKELAND, 171 *m.* (179 alt., 813 pop.), in a hilly sawmill section, is the nearest town to the huge SAM RAYBURN RESERVOIR, flooded by the Angelina River and located at the borders of Jasper, Sabine and San Augustine Counties. It is planned to cover 150,730 acres and contain 4,478,800 acre-feet for irrigation, flood control, power and recreation.

Lumber overshadows all other interests at JASPER, 187 *m.* (221 alt., 6,889 pop.), though the town is a trade center for a large area producing livestock and agricultural commodities.

The building of John Bevil's log cabin in 1824 marked the beginning of this settlement, which was named in honor of Sergeant William Jasper, South Carolina hero of the American Revolution. During the days of Reconstruction, when Federal troops occupied Texas, the tall uniformed figure of General George A. Custer, his long yellow hair falling about his shoulders, was a familiar sight on the streets.

1. Right from Jasper on State 63, to OLD ZAVALLA, 14 *m.*, a hamlet in the Angelina section of the Texas National Forests, on the site of the administrative settlement of the colony of Don Lorenzo de Zavala. Texas herds once passed near here over the old Beef Trail, on their way to Louisiana. State 63 continues northwestward to ZAVALLA, 37 *m.* (900 pop.), at a junction with US 69 (*see Tour 5*).

2. Left from Jasper on US 190 to NEWTON, 17 *m.* (172 alt., 1,000 pop.), in the midst of virgin forests of tall pines, with a scattering of oak, gum and cypress. Alligators inhabit many of the streams of this region and the woods are filled with small animals. Fox hunting with hounds is a favorite sport. Founded in 1846, Newton is peopled by descendants of the first settlers, who cling to old customs and are supported by lumbering and farming. Hunting and fishing along dark winding creeks and bayous are popular pastimes.

Left from Newton 14 *m.* on State 87 to BURKEVILLE (350 pop.), founded in 1844 by Colonel John R. Burke, who had built his cabin on the spot about 1821. The forests tend to segregate it from the outer world. Present-day citizens still farm a few acres around the old homesteads, using a one-horse plow, planting their crops by hand, picking their cotton into corn or oat sacks and hauling it to the mill and gin in one-horse wagons. The combined mill and gin, built in 1865, is still a one-man enterprise. A chair shop makes old-fashioned chairs by hand from well-seasoned magnolia wood and covers them with un-dressed rawhides, hair side out.

Northeast of Burkeville 14 *m.* on Farm Road 692 to TOLEDO BEND RESERVOIR on the Sabine River in Newton and Sabine Counties and the state of Louisiana. One of the State's largest, it is planned to cover 181,600 acres, 80,000 in Texas, and have a capacity of 4,661,000 acre-ft., half alloted to Texas for irrigation, power and recreation, as developed.

South of Jasper US 96 cuts through a well-forested area, locally called Scrapping Valley because of a blood feud carried on by two rival families in the 1870's. There were several killings, and the members of one family were placed in jail, from which two prisoners managed to escape. These two rallied relatives and continued the feud until Texas Rangers ended it in a gun battle that cost 11 lives. Southwest of Jasper on US 190 is DAM B RESERVOIR, also called Town Bluff Reservoir, covering 16,830 acres on the Neches River. Also on this route is the new (1965) MARTIN DIES, JR., STATE PARK, 705 acres, with camping, fishing and boating facilities.

A fire-control tower, 202.1 *m.,* rises high above the towering pines. The bayous, creeks, and rivers of this section sometimes contain huge alligators; at times the mud-covered brutes are seen sunning themselves.

Established in 1894, KIRBYVILLE, 208 *m.* (101 alt., 1,660 pop.), was named for John Kirby, sawmill operator. A large lumber mill is still in operation, and dominates the small business section. The town serves mainly as a supply center for corn and cotton farmers of the surrounding cut-over lands. Many of these farmers live in log cabins, plastered with mud. Negroes comprise 25 per cent of the population, and are largely farm tenants. Most of the white farmers own their land.

At 224 *m.* is the junction with State 62.

Left on this road to BUNA, 0.6 *m.* (76 alt., 900 pop.), a sawmill community in an area where tung orchards have been planted and are now producing the nuts from which oil is extracted for use in paints. Wildlife is abundant here on the eastern edge of the Big Thicket (*see Tour 5c*).

Named for a railway official, SILSBEE, 239 *m.* (79 alt., 9,000 pop., est.) was founded in 1892 at a logging camp of John H. Kirby. It is now the market center of farmers and lumbermen. Situated between two parts of the Big Thicket, it offers excellent hunting and fishing. Its unpretentious business buildings, strung along the east side of US 96, have low-hanging wooden awnings. Saddle horses and teams are hitched on the unpaved streets.

The route continues southward through orchards and tilled fields and at 244 *m.* crosses Village Creek. A group of three German families, political refugees, settled in this vicinity in 1854, and after four generations their descendants have the distinguishing racial characteristics and speech of their ancestors. The great oaks along the highway are said to have grown from acorns brought from the Fatherland.

At 248 *m.* is the junction with the combined US 69 and US 287 (*see Woodville, Tour 5*), at a point north of Beaumont.

I⟨◊I⟨◊I⟨◊I⟨◊I⟨◊I⟨◊I⟨◊I⟨◊I⟨◊I⟨◊I⟨◊I⟨◊I⟨◊I⟨◊I⟨◊I⟨◊I⟨◊I⟨◊I⟨◊I⟨◊I⟨◊I⟨◊

Tour 3

(Texarkana, Ark.)—Texarkana—Sherman—Wichita Falls—Lubbock;
US 82.
Arkansas Line to Lubbock, 487 *m.*

US 82 runs westward, parallel to the Red River, across the extreme
northern part of the State for slightly more than half the route, then
pierces rolling, treeless plains. It begins in the piney woods of the northeastern corner of Texas, where the soil is red, the sawmills large, and the
population more than half rural. From the deep forests the route emerges
onto the Blacklands, a fertile prairie belt notable for its long-staple cotton,
the many white steeples of churches, and modern schools. Entering the
North Central Plains, US 82 climbs the escarpment and levels off across
the High Plains, where hundreds of windmills turn unceasingly. Between
Wichita Falls and Lubbock, some of the State's most picturesque cattle
domains occupy vast acreages; ranches with such names as the *Pitchfork,
Spur,* and *6666,* are known throughout the West. The tour follows a
route used by French and Spanish explorers; later, immigrants were often
turned back by Comanches. On the plains, buffalo hunters and soldiers
cleared the way for settlers, who dared not venture this far beyond civilization until after the Civil War. The people were occupied chiefly with
ranching until 1900, when the first farmers broke the dusty sod in defiance of drought (*see Agriculture and Livestock*). Cotton, wheat, and
small grains are grown on fields terraced to prevent soil erosion, a menace
in this land of sparse vegetation. Oil development has brought new industries to scattered areas along the way.

Section a.   TEXARKANA to SHERMAN; 161 m.   US 82

This section of US 82 follows closely the southern edge of the broad
Red River Valley, through a region explored by Moscoso in 1542. In the
deep pine forests where the tour begins, the people till inherited patches, or
fell pines—as their fathers did—in dark, fragrant woodlands that contain
Florida flying squirrels, red foxes, and timber wolves; log-rollings, fiddlers' contests, and community sings are popular. "Camp Meeting," a
song inspired by customs in this part of east Texas, illustrates another
phase of community life:

> I felt the old shoes on my feet, the glory in my soul,
> The old-time fire upon my lips; the billows ceased to roll . . .
> We all got happy over there, and shouted all around.

About one-third of the population is Negro, and spirituals echo over the fields in a wealth of spontaneous composition. On cold winter evenings, great pine logs burn in stick-and-mud chimneys of log cabins—a favored type of habitation in the backwoods. In larger communities, where settlement often dates from the 1820's, a growing consciousness of historical tradition has caused the organization of societies which have meetings that are often the basis of section-wide celebrations.

In the Blacklands Belt between Paris and Sherman cotton is the money crop, and farms average from 50 to 100 acres, although a few are 1,000 acres or more. The normal prosperity of this region is shown in large, comfortable farmhouses, in animated towns with factories that process the rich harvests of the area, and in cultural progress centering around numerous schools, public libraries, art galleries, and similar institutions. Yet here, too, the inheritance of the rural folk is that of time-honored custom: box and pie suppers, singing schools, and conventions, and work-out-a-crop parties are popular. The latter are held when neighbors decide they should help a farmer. Medicine show fakirs are welcomed, their patent cure-alls finding ready sale.

US 82 crosses the Texas Line at Seventh St. and State Line Ave., Texarkana (*see Arkansas Guide*).

TEXARKANA, 0 *m.* (295 alt., 21,652 Texas pop., 30,218 total pop.), is at junctions with US 67 (*see Tour 18*) and State 11 (*see Tour 1*).

Westward the route is through a cultivated area where towns lie close together. There are vast undeveloped lignite deposits in this region.

HOOKS, 15 *m.* (375 alt., 680 pop.), was established as a supply center in 1836, and still serves a large trade area.

Right from Hooks on a graveled road to the site of the old community of Myrtle Springs, 2.8 *m.,* where the two-story frame HOME OF WARREN HOOKS (*private*), still stands. It was built in 1858 by slave labor and was a social and civic center of the then sparsely settled region.

NEW BOSTON, 22 *m.* (352 alt., 3,750 pop.), built along the double S of the highway, is one of three towns of similar names within a radius of four miles, the others being Boston and Old Boston. Boston, seat of Bowie County, adjoins New Boston and has only about 100 people. Both are offspring of the pioneer town of Old Boston.

North of New Boston is the SITE OF PECAN POINT (*inaccessible*), one of Texas' earliest Anglo-American settlements. In the early nineteenth century this area was part of the then Arkansas Territory and a boundary dispute raged until after Texas became a State, in 1845. A ferry at Pecan Point transported many of the earliest colonists across the Red River.

In the region are numerous BURNED ROCK MOUNDS, the kitchen middens (refuse dumps) of the Caddoes, Wichitas, Tonkawas, and Coahuiltecans. On the old Richard Ellis plantation, between New Boston and the Red River, is a mound 150 feet long, 50 feet wide, and 14 feet high.

The lower levels of this and other mounds in the vicinity indicate a very ancient culture.

Westward, through cultivated lands, US 82 enters a region where the population is about 75 per cent native white, with Negroes constituting the remaining 25 per cent. A majority of farmers own their land, but some of the Negroes are employed as farm hands, or are tenants.

DE KALB, 34 *m.* (407 alt., 2,042 pop.), founded about a half mile north of its present location, was named in honor of Baron de Kalb, a German general in the American Revolutionary Army. It covers a hilltop, and commands a broad view of surrounding farms and woodlands. In this vicinity cotton is the leading crop, but truck farming is developing rapidly.

AVERY, 45 *m.* (476 alt., 400 pop.), is the center of a fruit and truck growing region, and has numerous sheds for tomato packing. A festival is held here annually during the early part of July in honor of the tomato.

Right from Avery on a paved road to ENGLISH, 6 *m.* (213 pop.), grouped about its one general store, on an elevation overlooking—toward the west—a vast, open, black land prairie. English was once prosperous, but a new highway passed it by. It was founded in 1840 by Judge Oliver English. The old HOME OF JUDGE ENGLISH (*private*), reconstructed, and typical of the architecture of its period, is near the highway (R), set in spacious grounds, with an entrance through an archway supporting a large bronze eagle.

Lumber, cotton, and livestock contribute to the prosperity of CLARKSVILLE, 61 *m.* (442 alt., 3,851 pop.). This dignified old town spreads out from a small circular park adorned with a profusion of shrubs and wild roses; north of the public square is a weathered stone court-house. Clarksville was founded in 1835 as a remote frontier settlement. Its story has largely been that of the black waxy soil that sweeps up to its doors, although development in recent years has also been based on nearby oil discoveries. One block northeast of the square is the DE MORSE HOME (*private*), built in 1834. The structure is of hand-hewn logs, now covered with clapboards. It contains many relics of pioneer days.

1. Left from Clarksville on the old McCoy Road to the RUINS OF McKENZIE INSTITUTE, 4 *m.,* which was organized by James Witherspoon Pettigrew McKenzie, and was one of the best known early schools of the State. Only one of the dormitories remains, used as a barn. The old McKENZIE HOME (*visited by arrangement*), is occupied by descendants of the educator. It contains furnishings of the period, an extensive library of old books, records of students who attended the institute, family portraits, and an autographed picture of General Robert E. Lee.

2. Right from Clarksville on the Madras Road to SHILO CUMBERLAND PRESBY-TERIAN CHURCH (*open*), 6 *m.,* established about 1833 by seven pioneer families from Tennessee. Richard Ellis, R. H. Hamilton, and Albert Latimer, charter members, were also signers of the Texas Declaration of Independence. Albert Latimer was elected to the Texas Congress in 1840, at the time that his father, James Latimer, living under the same roof, was named to the Arkansas legis-lature—a circumstance made possible because of the boundary dispute between Texas and Arkansas.

DETROIT, 76 *m.* (482 alt., 850 pop.), shows its age in weathered brick business buildings, and in numerous old residences half hidden under great oak trees. This was the boyhood home of John Nance Garner, who was born on a farm nearby, and after a notable political career became Vice President of the United States. The old GARNER HOME (*private*), a two-story frame plantation type building, stands two blocks south of US 82, near the center of the town.

Five-sixths of the population of this vicinity live on farms, and rural habitations are largely "shotgun" houses one room wide, extending back one or two rooms to a lean-to. Cotton is produced on the black lands, corn on the red sand, and sawmills dot clearings in areas of shortleaf pine.

PARIS, 95 *m.* (592 alt., 20,977 pop., 1960; 23,500 est. 1965) seat of Lamar County, has a modern architectural look that is a result of two great fires which destroyed virtually all old buildings. The streets are very wide, and parks are large and numerous. Gifts of art—paintings and sculpture—from public-spirited citizens have adorned Paris with such notable pieces as the CULBERTSON FOUNTAIN, center the public plaza, bounded by Bonham, Main and 20th Sts. and Grand Ave., a three-tiered fountain topped by a marble Triton; and the PERISTYLE in Bywaters Park, S. Main and 21st Sts.

In Paris is a junction with US 271. The airport, Cox Field, on this route, is served by Central Airlines. Continental Trailways Bus Center is at 245 S. Main St.

Paris participates in an ancient dispute concerning the origin, route, and real name of the so-called Old Chisholm Trail, claiming it was blazed by Claiborne Chisum's son, John, who was born in Red River County in 1824, and lived in Paris until 1855.

PARIS JUNIOR COLLEGE (municipal) enrolls more than 500 annually.

The Red River Valley Exposition & Fair is held annually the last week in August.

The Woman's Christian Temperance Union in Texas was organized in Paris by Miss Frances Willard in 1882. When no local minister would offer his church for the meeting, Miss Willard secured the opera house.

National attention was centered here in the 1890's when a Federal court, with jurisdiction over much of the then Indian Territory and Kansas, sat here for the Hay Meadow Massacre trial. Twenty men were charged with murdering a group of officers who had opposed them in a county-seat war in a part of Kansas, close to Indian Territory, known as No Man's Land. Eight were convicted and sentenced to be hanged.

Just west of the plaza in Paris was the route of the Central National Road of the Republic of Texas, surveyed in 1844. The road ran from San Antonio northward, through Paris, to cross the Red River at the mouth of the Kiamichi River.

On the eastern edge of the town is CROCKETT CIRCLE, so named because near-by stands an old oak tree under which Davy Crockett slept one night in 1835, on his way to death in the Alamo.

A long-fibered cotton is known as Paris cotton. Beef cattle are increasing. Agriculture adds about $18,000,000 to the county economy annually. Corn, sorghum, soybeans, and peanuts are profitable. LAKE CROOK (1,226 acres) and LAKE GIBBON are recreation areas. The latter is the site of the Canada Geese Refuge originated by John C. Gambill in Paris many years ago.

HONEY GROVE, 119 *m*. (668 alt., 2,071 pop.), has its post office in the center of the public square, around which are brick and hewn stone buildings. Dairying is the leading industry of the vicinity. In recent years Honey Grove has constructed a Civic Center, which includes a new library, museum, and auditorium.

Northwest of Honey Grove 11 *m*. on a farm road to LAKE DAVY CROCKETT, 4,500 acre-ft. of water; 12 *m*. to COFFEE MILL LAKE, 704 acres, 8,000 acre-ft. This is a recreational area. Deer, bears, wild turkeys, and other native wildlife, are protected in this area.

West of Honey Grove US 82 traverses a section where experimentation with soy beans is rapidly developing a new cash crop. In this agricultural region "donation parties" are given when misfortune overtakes a neighbor; a house may be rebuilt, crops worked out, or the larder restocked. Singing conventions are outdoor all-day picnic events, attended by the people of several communities.

Elms, willows, box elders, and pecans line the highway leading into BONHAM, 135 *m*. (568 alt., 7,357 pop. 1960), a city of many dignified old buildings, broad streets and dense shrubbery. The courthouse lawn has a bronze statue of James Butler Bonham, heroic messenger of the Alamo.

Bonham, seat of Fannin County, engages in processing agricultural products and diversified industries. It has the SAM RAYBURN LIBRARY, maintained by the Sam Rayburn Foundation, formed 1949, which preserves the records of Speaker Rayburn, who was a farm boy in Fannin County. A White House chandelier and marble mantel, and a fireplace from the U. S. Capitol are among the memorabilia.

During the Civil War, Bonham was headquarters of the Northern Military Sub-District of Texas, Brigadier General Henry E. McCulloch commanding. Here, Jayhawkers and Indians, deserters and conscript dodgers, were a continual menace. In November of 1863 Quantrell passed through Bonham after having reported to Lieutenant General E. Kirby Smith at Shreveport. When McCulloch complained to General Smith about the deserters he was told to send Quantrell after them. There is a tradition that Quantrell rode in to report to McCulloch, who, after receiving him, hurried off to his dinner. Irked by such casual treatment, Quantrell stalked from the commandant's office, and led his men back across the Red River.

In the northeastern city limits, adjacent to the Bailey Inglish Cemetery, E. 6th and Linn Sts., is a REPRODUCTION OF FORT INGLISH (*open; key obtained from first residence east*). The structure is of logs, two stories high, the lower floor 16 by 16 feet, with the upper story, which is 24 by 24 feet, overhanging.

LAKE FANNIN, 15 *m*. NE of Bonham, is a government reservoir under the National Forestry Service and center of LAKE FANNIN PARK, a recreational area.

Left from Bonham on State 78 to Gober Road, 2 *m.;* left here to BONHAM STATE PARK (*bathing facilities, rest rooms, camp sites*), 4 *m.,* a recreational area containing 532 acres, with a 60-acre lake.

US 82 continues through miles of cultivated lands, the heart of the rich Blacklands section of north Texas. Back-country communities of this part of the State sometimes have queer names, supposedly given them by Wallace Partain, an early settler. One such town is Seed Tick. Bug Tussle, another, is said to commemorate a fight between two pugnacious bugs. The community of Greasy Neck owes its name, according to tradition, to the fact that Partain's mare skidded in the slippery mud on the banks of a little "neck" of the creek near the town.

A cluster of small frame houses, with no sidewalks or curbs, surrounds the block-long business district of BELLS, 149 *m.* (674 alt., 700 pop.). The clang of the anvil in a blacksmith shop adjacent to the modern school building was a musical reminder of horse-and-buggy days.

In Bells is the junction with US 69 (*see Tour 5*).

Right from Bells, on a graveled road to DUGAN'S CHAPEL, 5 *m.,* where Daniel Dugan settled in 1840. He was killed by Indians, and over his grave in the family burial ground his family swore vengeance. The sons waged relentless war on the Indians, hunting them down and killing many in the years that followed. The conflict came to a dramatic climax when Emily Dugan, daughter of Daniel, while knitting in the sturdy log cabin home, heard a turkey call from the brush behind the house. Suspecting that an Indian was attempting to lure someone from the house, she thrust a rifle through a loophole and waited. Presently one stole from the brush into the open and crept toward the house, and she killed him. When no other Indians appeared the girl went out, dragged the body to the woodshed and decapitated it with an axe. Placing the head on a pole, she nailed it to the front gate, where the grisly trophy remained for a long time—a warning that was not disregarded. The skull of this last hostile marauder has been passed down in the family as an heirloom, and is today in the home of William Dugan.

Westward the route is through a comparatively level area of black sandy loam. Cotton, corn, oats, and wheat are the leading crops. The homes of the region are old and worn, sagging as if tired of the struggle to provide shelter for generations that have neglected them. Sometimes there is a little white country church, always with a weed-grown graveyard near by.

SHERMAN, 161 *m.* (720 alt., 26,000 pop.) (*see Tour 6a*), is at the junction with US 75.

Section b.   SHERMAN to WICHITA FALLS; 117 m.   US 82

This part of the route traverses a region where black lands yield enormous cotton and wheat production, with oil development an important economic factor. At the beginning of the section and near its end, irrigation and power projects inaugurated in the 1930's have begun to change the agricultural picture, with crop diversification possible in areas once given over almost solely to dry-land cotton farming. Farm tenancy, ranging from 25 to 50 per cent of the rural population, has decreased with the introduction of truck, dairy, and stock farming. Soil erosion prevention and flood control work were started under the Work Projects Administration and Texas A. & M. University. Reservoirs, lakes, and irrigation ditches afford good hunting and fishing; there are many varieties of ducks, and fish include bass, crappie, sunfish, and channel catfish. Great herds of buffalo once grazed on waist-high sage grass in this rolling, fertile area. The westward surge of forty-niners opened the region to settlement, but frequent Indian depredations discouraged extensive development until after the Civil War.

West of SHERMAN, 0 *m.,* the WOODMEN CIRCLE HOME (*open*), is at 2.1 *m.* (R). It was founded by the women's auxiliary of the Woodmen of the World for aged women and the children of members of the organization.

The highway broadens to form a rectangle at WHITESBORO, 18 *m.* (783 alt., 2,485 pop.), which replaces the familiar town square. The community presents an industrial aspect with its cotton gins and cottonseed, feed, and flour mills.

GAINESVILLE, 33 *m.* (730 alt., 14,500 pop.) (*see Tour 7a*), is at the junction with US 77.

MUENSTER, 48 *m.* (970 alt., 1,190 pop.), is a modern, neat town in the center of a pioneer German colonization project, and has retained its racial integrity. It is an active market and supply center for the farmers of the region and the workers of adjacent oil fields. Its industries include a flour mill, an oil refinery, and a community-owned and operated cheese factory. Founded in 1889 by two brothers, Muenster was named for a city in their fatherland. First settlers were all Roman Catholics, and few of other faiths reside here today. Dominating Muenster is the SACRED HEART ROMAN CATHOLIC CHURCH (*open*), near the center of the town. The 70-foot steeple is visible from some distance, and on quiet days the bells of the carillon are audible for five miles. This church, said to be one of the purest examples of Gothic architecture in Texas, was built in 1896–97. It is in the shape of a cross, surmounted by a high-pitched roof. The stained-glass windows are set in pointed arches of true Gothic type.

Westward, as the terrain becomes more hilly, livestock and dairy cattle are raised.

SAINT JO, 57 *m.* (1,146 alt., 960 pop.), is surrounded by hills covered with woodland and pastures. The Old California Trail of 1849 passed through this valley, as did the cattle trails of the 1870's. Saint Jo's rodeos, held every Saturday night during the summer, bring together some of the finest riders of the range.

NOCONA, 70 *m.* (930 alt., 3,127 pop.), named for Peta Nocona, an Indian chief, is a leading leather-goods center of the Southwest, producing cowboy boots worn throughout the cattle country, and footballs used all over the United States. The town's three leather-goods plants are the outgrowth of a single pioneer saddle shop. An adjacent oil field also has contributed materially to Nocona's progress.

Right from Nocona on a dirt road to the *Site of Old Spanish Fort*, 17 *m.*, scene of one of the decisive battles of early Texas history. As early as 1700 the French were active along the Red River, and in 1719 Bernard de la Harpe established on the south bank of the river, on the site of the principal village of the Caddoes, an outpost which he called Fort St. Louis de Carlorette. It served as a traders' and trappers' supply station but was abandoned after a few years. In 1759 Colonel Diego Ortiz Parrilla, advancing from San Antonio and San Saba, came upon Indians entrenched behind a stout stockade, over which flew the French flag. His report described the fort as consisting of high oval-shaped structures, surrounded by a ditch and a log stockade. Armed by the French, the Indians soundly defeated Parrilla and sent him back in hasty retreat. Under the treaty of Fontainebleau in 1762 the French ceded Louisiana Territory to Spain, and abandoned their western outpost. Spanish exploration parties and patrols visited the site from time to time until as late as 1800. Then all reports of the old post ceased until its ruins were found in 1859. The description of the ruins of that date correspond remarkably with the data of Parrilla 100 years before. Today, hardly discernible mounds are all that remain.

BELCHERVILLE, 74 *m.* (887 alt., 85 pop.), a faded village, was once an important cattle and cotton shipping point of northwest Texas and a large part of the then Indian Territory. Then the railroad pressed on, creating other shipping points, and Belcherville declined.

RINGGOLD, 83 *m.* (890 alt., 415 pop.) (*see Tour 8a*), is at the junction with US 81 (*see Tour 8*).

The HOME OF CAPTAIN WILL JOHNSON (*private*), 96.5 *m.* (L), a two-and-a-half-story rock house built in 1878, was constructed entirely by one man. It is of stone and has five gables.

HENRIETTA, 98 *m.* (886 alt., 3,575 pop.), seat of Clay County, was named for the wife of Henry Clay. In Indian days it was a supply center for Fort Sill.) Here US 287 joins US 82. The town is a shipping point for Hereford and Durham cattle, and for cotton, corn, and dairy products. Its stores cater to ranchmen, some of whom have large homes here, houses with many porches, gables, spires, and pillars. Founded in 1857, Henrietta was abandoned in 1861 because of continued Indian depredations and lack of military protection. It remained a settlement of empty houses until General R. S. Mackenzie's campaign of 1873 removed the Indian menace.

In the HOME OF B. B. SCHWEND (*open*), one block north of the square, is an unusual private collection of weapons. There are pistols once owned by Buffalo Bill, Pat Garrett, Captain Bill McDonald, Sam Bass, Frank James, Dan and Bud Campbell, Bat Masterson, Cole Younger, and Billy Dixon, and rifles carried by Joshua Parker, one of the original Austin colonists, by "Wild Bill" Hickok, Pat Garrett, Sam Bass, and others. Also Chief Quanah Parker's bow.

The TEX RICKARD STADIUM, 6,500 seats, is site of the annual Pioneer Reunion and Rodeo. Rickard once was city marshal here.

WICHITA FALLS, 117 *m.* (946 alt., 109,500 pop. est.) (*see article*), is at junctions with US 287 (*see Tour 13*), US 281 (*see Tour 9*), and US 277 (*see Tour 10*), which unites southwestward with US 82.

Left from Wichita Falls on State 79 to WICHITA FALLS STATE HOSPITAL (L), 6 *m.*, a plant consisting of 32 three-story red brick buildings and 12 frame structures housing the administration, hospitalization, and living quarters. The hospital has a capacity of 2,230 patients. Landscaped grounds cover 940 acres overlooking Lake Wichita.

LAKE WICHITA (R), 6.7 m., the source of Wichita Falls' water supply, was created at the beginning of the present century following more than a decade of planning and development. The lake, covering 2,900 acres, was formed by building a dam one mile and three-quarters long, across Holliday Creek. Here is LAKESIDE PARK (*dancing, swimming, boating, fishing, picnic facilities*). An annual event at Lake Wichita is the regatta of the Wichita Sailing Club, which features sailboat races between club members.

Section c. WICHITA FALLS to LUBBOCK; 209 m. US 82–277

This part of US 82 begins in the rolling, fertile Wichita and Brazos River Valleys. West of Wichita Falls it enters an eroded region of ranches so great that wagon crews leave headquarters to remain on the range for half the year; and finally, after ascending the wall of the escarpment, it traverses the level, far-flung High Plains. West of the river valleys vision is unobstructed by trees. Scrubby mesquites and cedars, less than two feet high, dot hillsides that reach to the escarpment; and in this open land they resemble the tufts of a candlewick bedspread. On the plains even these low growths are rare, destroyed under the plows of cotton and wheat farmers.

Farm and range lands alike are overwhelmingly peopled by racial stock descended from English-speaking countries, although, back from the highway, there are a few small communities of Swedes, Germans, and Bohemians, and in the agricultural areas, a handful of Negroes. Ranch hands prove true to cowboy traditions on the rare occasions when they are able to reach a "wet" town on Saturday night; but the farmers are abstemious—their communities are mostly "dry," and amusements center about Protestant church activities and the social events of their co-operatives.

Buffalo hunters were the first to penetrate this region, close on the heels of the army's campaigns to drive the Indians back to their reservations. Cattlemen followed the buffalo hunters, and fought for their holdings against bands of Indian raiders who from time to time escaped from their soldier-keepers.

On the western outskirts of WICHITA FALLS, 0 m., is a group of white houses (R) in the valley of the Big Wichita River, the WICHITA GARDENS HOMESTEAD COLONY, erected in 1935 (*see Wichita Falls*). Beyond, scattered along the highway, are country estates owned by citizens of Wichita Falls.

A minnow farm (L), 6 m., supplies the needs of fishermen bound for Lake Diversion and Lake Kemp.

HOLLIDAY, 14 m. (1,055 alt., 1,100 pop.), with modern buildings and facilities, has a prosperous air. With the discovery of oil in 1920 Holliday boomed for a time; after the excitement passed, the town continued to thrive on steady oil production, and because of increased farm income from sandy acres watered by Wichita Valley Irrigation System.

The route is southwestward into prairie, farm, and ranch country.

Fossil remains found in this vicinity have attracted scientific expeditions. Vertebrae of ancient amphibians, and evidences of reptiles and mastodons have been found. Fossil records of giant insects, chiefly Meganevra, a dragonfly with a wingspread of two feet, are among the most interesting. Paleontologists from many parts of the United States have studied the local fossil fauna and flora, and amateurs can see specimens by making inquiries of residents as to their location.

The history of this region is associated closely with days of the open range. Early farmers met with stubborn opposition from cattlemen, and their attempts to fence their small holdings brought on the Fence-cutting War (see History). Natural forces in the form of droughts and the ravages of prairie dogs and wolves also were against them. They persisted, however, until today the cattle range is broken up into tilled fields.

At 23.5 m. is the junction with a graveled road.

Left here to a KARAKUL SHEEP RANCH (open), 2.5 m., which owns one of the largest flocks of registered karakul (Bokharan fur-bearing) sheep in America. It numbers approximately 1,000 head and is valued at $100,000. The development of this breed became possible in the United States only after Theodore Roosevelt, then President of the United States, requested the aid of Czar Nicholas II of Russia, who had soldiers bring a consignment of sheep across the Bokhara frontier to St. Petersburg, whence they were sent to this country. Because of Bokharan native superstitions, the kind and quality of sheep desired could not have been obtained without this assistance. The pelts of newly born karakuls, called Persian lamb, are of great value.

DUNDEE, 27 m. (1,143 alt., 132 pop.), was founded in 1891 on the holdings of the T-Fork Ranch. Farms and ranches surround the quiet little town.

Right from Dundee on a graveled road to DIVERSION RESERVOIR 8 m., extending for 25 miles along the valley of the Big Wichita River. Fishing is excellent. Ducks, geese, quail, and plover are found here. Clubhouses and cottages line the shores. Left of the lake is DIVERSION FISH HATCHERY where 58 ponds are in use. At 37 m. is LAKE KEMP a reservoir covering 20,820 acres.

MABELLE, 43 m. (1,265 alt.), a trading center for farmers and ranchers, is at the junction with US 283, which unites westward with US 82 and US 277.

SEYMOUR, 52 m. (1,290 alt., 4,000 pop. est.), on Salt Fork of the Brazos, draws its chief income from cotton, as its cotton oil mill, compress, and three gins indicate; wheat is also an important crop. The general prosperity of the farmers is evidenced in the fact that three-fourths of all farms have tractors and other modern machinery. About one-fourth of the population is Bohemian. Seymour was settled in 1878 by a group from Oregon. A feud between the settlers and the hands of an adjacent ranch who objected to nesters on their range developed serious proportions. Herds were stampeded across fields of growing crops. Discouraged, most of the early settlers left, but others came and finally crowded out the ranchers.

At Seymour US 82 and US 277 part company, the latter turning southwest. US 183 and US 283 from Oklahoma pass through Seymour on the way south; they separate 37 *m.* farther down. State 199 from Fort Worth terminates at Seymour.

At 79 *m.* US 82 follows a high tableland called THE NARROWS. It is the crest of a narrow ridge which separates the breaks or rough watersheds of the Brazos and Wichita Rivers. To the south the wide expanse of the Brazos Valley falls away in eroded ridges, and north are the cedar-clad canyons and ravines which wind toward the Wichita. Here the highway follows an old trail of unknown origin. The first white men in the region found it well defined and to all appearances often traveled. Along its course have been found numerous arrowheads and other artifacts. South of the Narrows is Wild Horse Prairie, so named because of the great numbers of mustangs it once held.

The newest, most dominating thing about BENJAMIN, 84 *m.* (1,456 alt., 485 pop.), is its modern, streamlined, two-story white stone courthouse. One of the earliest mercantile establishments was the Barton General Store, which in the course of its much-traveled existence was in two States and three towns. "Uncle" Bob Barton, originally of Arkansas, tore down his store building there, loaded it on wagons, and rebuilt it in Jacksboro, Texas. After a few years the wanderlust again seized him, and again the building was torn down, loaded in wagons, and hauled westward to Benjamin.

Tradition places some lost lead mines in Croton Breaks, 97 *m.* The bald, rounded dome of BUZZARD'S PEAK (L) was so named because of its bare crest, and beyond looms the more pointed summit of KIOWA PEAK (2,000 alt.), once a lookout point for the war parties of the Kiowas. Houses are few along this stretch of hills, canyons, and plains. For miles vast pastures roll away in every direction. Close at hand the hills are green and red with the tints of cedar and the soil; in the middle distance they are blue-green as earthy shades blend with the cedars.

At 115 *m.* is the junction with US 83 (*see Tour 16*), which unites northward with US 82.

GUTHRIE, 116 *m.* (1,754 alt., 318 pop.), is in the heart of one of the largest ranches in the State. This ranch, the great 6666 (Four Sixes) covers 206,000 acres. Guthrie is one of the three post offices in King County, which has no newspaper within its borders. The town is also said to be 40 miles from a barber, a beauty shop, or a preacher. Guthrie is a collection of cafes featuring bottled goods, a big stone jail, a courthouse, a large dance hall, and a few small frame residences. The sole supply store is at headquarters of the 6666 Ranch, a short distance west, on the highway. This is the only "wet" community in a wide area, and is the rendezvous of cow hands seeking to break the monotony of chuck wagon food and range life. Friday night is the "big time" for local cowboys, and consequently the calaboose is called the "Friday night jail." Notable are the wide-brimmed straw hats worn by Guthrie's cowboys. There is a story that a thief looted the 6666 Ranch store, removing all the expensive ten-gallon hats and that this headgear was never restocked.

In Guthrie is the northern junction with US 83 (*see Tour 16*).

The headquarters buildings of the PITCHFORK RANCH, 131 *m.,* can be seen from the highway (L). This is a small village within itself, with a large ranch house surrounded by smaller buildings, in carefully landscaped grounds. There is a school building for the children of the ranch, also a powerhouse, a laundry, and a canning house. The mess hall is equipped like a city restaurant, with electrical appliances and a steam table. The bunkhouse shelters from 20 to 25 cowboys. The ranch consists of 120,000 acres, on which are 75 windmills.

Old-timers contrast the modern luxury of the Pitchfork's bunkhouse and mess hall with the facilities of pioneer ranches of the region. Then rough wooden bunks lined crowded, dingy, sod or log buildings, a pail and tin basin were on a bench outside the door, and on rough wooden tables were tin cups and plates. These were home ranch comforts. Most of a cowboy's days then were spent on the range.

Here also are the Matador and SMS ranches.

Westward the highway skirts the north bank of the dry course of the South Fork of the Wichita River, which flows only in times of heavy rains. The country is a high tableland, broken by wide shallow valleys, sloping away to join the higher hills on the horizon. The road dips suddenly into a narrow canyon where cedars cling precariously to the steep, rock-studded walls. This region is described by Zane Grey in *The Thundering Herd,* in which he tells of the destruction of the buffalo. Numerous game preserves are in this area.

DICKENS, 147 *m.* (2,464, alt., 500 pop.), a typical western town about eight miles below the frowning rampart of the Cap Rock has been modernized in part by the stark newness of its white stone, blockhouse-like courthouse.

Left from Dickens on State 70 to SPUR, 10 *m.* (2,274 alt., 2,300 pop.), founded in 1909, and named for the famous Spur Ranch. At various times such well-known writers as Emerson Hough, B. M. Bowers, George Patullo, and John A. Lomax have stopped at Spur, gathering data for their western writings. The Mackenzie Trail, route of numerous United States Army forays against the Comanches and Kiowas, passed through or near the site of the town.

Right from Spur 5 *m.* on a county road to SOLDIER'S MOUND, where in 1874-5 an army supply camp called Anderson's Fort was maintained as the base of operations for the infantry units of the command of General Mackenzie, in his expeditions against marauding tribes. Temporary fortifications were erected here to protect the camp from attack.

West of Dickens the route traverses a rolling terrain. The hill that lifts above all others on the northern skyline (R) is MACKENZIE PEAK. This land was once part of the Spur Ranch.

CROSBYTON, 172 *m.* (3,300 alt., 2,650 pop.), differs from most other west Texas county seats in that a bandstand occupies the center of the town square, usually filled by a courthouse, while the courthouse is on the northwest corner. Crosbyton was founded in 1908 on the lands of the old Two Buckle Ranch.

Crosbyton ships grain, cattle, and cotton products. It is located near the edge of CAP ROCK, with the fertile High Plains to the west. Crosbyton gets its water from WHITE RIVER RESERVOIR, 16 m. SE off Ranch Road 651. It covers 1,808 acres and contains 38,200 acre-ft. of water. This also supplies Post, Spur and Ralls. The rolled-earth dam is 3,230 ft. long and 84 feet tall. The county has about 200,000 acres in irrigation.

Right from Crosbyton on a dirt road to HACIENDA GLORIETA (*open*), 10 m., the first home in the plains country west of Fort Griffin, built of stone in 1876. The CROSBY COUNTY PIONEER MEMORIAL BUILDING has a hall and stage conference room and kitchen facilities. Adjacent to the house is UNCLE HANK SMITH MEMORIAL PARK, an area of 24 acres, where each year the members of the West Texas Old Settlers Association meet in reunion. A barbecue, fiddlers' contest, "speakings," a rodeo and sometimes a parade in old-time costumes constitute the festivities of each day of the event, while in the evenings old-time dances are held.

In the vicinity of Crosbyton, especially to the north, are prairie dog "towns" of unusual size. The animals can be seen beside the mounds marking the entrances to their homes, or gathered like village gossips in little groups. They are in reality barking ground squirrels and exist nowhere except in the western part of the United States. Their destruction of grass and vegetation is enormous and they are exterminated as fast as ranchmen can accomplish it. (*Watch for rattlesnakes in "dog towns."*)

Behind its masking screen of gins and cotton sheds the false-fronted, one-story brick business section of RALLS, 180 m. (3,108 alt., 2,229 pop.), sits well back from the highway, quiet except at cotton picking time. Cotton and wheat are shipped from Ralls. US 62 joins US 82 at Ralls.

The TEXAS AGRICULTURAL EXPERIMENTAL SUB-STATION No. 8 (*open*), at 206.7 m., is constantly experimenting with new crops and improved methods of farming.

MACKENZIE STATE PARK, 207.4 m., is a recreational area (L) along the east side of YELLOW HOUSE CANYON, which includes one of the old camp sites of the many Mackenzie expeditions into this section. Here also was an ancient Indian encampment. About 600 acres in extent, the park is operated by the city of Lubbock.

LUBBOCK, 209 m. (3,241 alt., 182,240 pop.), is at junctions with US 87 (*see Tour 17*), and US 84 (*see Tour 21*).

Tour 4

(Hugo, Okla.)—Paris—Mount Pleasant—Gladewater—Tyler; US 271.
Oklahoma Line to Tyler, 137 *m.*

US 271 forms a rough arc through the fertile Blacklands Belt and the upper east Texas timber region. It traverses a section where the population is from 50 to 80 per cent rural, and where the number of Negroes is often only slightly under that of native-born whites. In this predominantly agricultural region, cotton has been the leading crop since the first settlers —including many planters from the South—broke the fertile sod. Industries in the larger towns are based upon processing produce or natural commodities: plants manufacture cottonseed products, make fertilizer, saw lumber, cure sweet potatoes, or, at the end of the tour, refine oil. Near Tyler, a large industry has been built upon the production of roses. Black gum, hickory, ash, oak, chinquapin, bois d'arc, cedar, and pine trees are abundant, and magnolias bloom profusely in the spring. The mayhaw, resembling a small red apple, is a favorite fruit for jelly. The rural folk cling to old customs, have Sacred Harp singing conventions, religious revival meetings, and in some areas, hold wakes.

Bass, perch, crappie, catfish, and other fresh water fish abound in the streams along the route. Tackle can be purchased at most of the towns. Quail hunting is especially good; geese and ducks are plentiful in season.

US 271 crosses the OKLAHOMA LINE and the Red River, 0 *m.,* 11 miles south of Hugo, Okla. (*see Oklahoma Guide*).

ARTHUR CITY, 0.3 *m.* (426 alt., 250 pop.), an old town with few modern facilities, is at or near the site of one of the French trading posts known to have been established on the Red River. According to tradition Francôis Herve, an agent of the Louisiana colony, was in this vicinity in 1750.

Southward the route is through flat prairie country, heavily wooded with post oak and pecan. At 10 *m.* is a junction with a paved road.

Right on this road to LAKE CROOK PARK (*free camping, fishing; boats for rent*), 10 *m.,* a heavily timbered tract on the 1,226-acre lake created by Pine Creek, and which is the water supply of Paris.

PARIS, 15 *m.* (592 alt., 23,000 pop.) is at the junction with US 82.

Through this region ran the Central National Road of the Republic of Texas.

Eastward, many folk customs remain from the period of the pioneers.

Home-made farm tools and implements are still in use, and furniture is often hand-hewn from native hickory and white oak. Tobacco is grown and cured for home use, and hand-made walnut shingles are on many of the farmhouses. Leather is tanned at home by a process that involves the use of hickory bark. This section was once claimed by Arkansas, and local families relate many stories of the confusion resulting from boundary uncertainties. Members of one family sometimes held official positions in two States.

TALCO, 49 m. (358 alt., 1,024 pop.), has the appearance of a community that is resting after a hectic oil boom—its many small frame shacks mushroom out from an older business area. In 1935 the discovery of oil zoomed the population from 140 to more than 5,000. Business was so rushing that the cashier of the little bank handled deposits by tying a string around each roll of bills, marking it with the name of the depositor, and tossing it in a corner, to be credited later. Today Talco is a quiet town almost exclusively engaged in business hinging upon the near-by oil field.

Lignite beds and iron ore underlie this region.

GREEN HILL, 59 m. (80 pop.), has grown around GREEN HILL PRESBYTERIAN CHURCH, whose congregation was organized in 1860. The main room of the present building was erected in 1868 from lumber shipped up Big Cypress Bayou by boat to Jefferson (*see Tour 2*), and hauled to Green Hill in oxcarts. This old room, made of hand-planed heart pine, is in good condition. The church, visible from the highway, claims one of the largest memberships of any rural Presbyterian church west of the Mississippi River.

MOUNT PLEASANT, 67 m., (416 alt., 11,270 pop. est.) is at a junction with US 67.

In this general vicinity, in areas remote from cities, rural sports and recreations reflect the daily tenor of the lives of the people. "Riding the ring," a survival of the classical tournaments of old England, is a popular diversion. Riders on horseback, armed with wooden lances, charge a series of suspended rings, and he who secures the most rings wins the "joust." Community 'possum hunts are held by the young folk, and fox hunting is a regular sport. Annual hunts call people from several counties for three or four days. Because of their scarcity, no foxes are destroyed. When they are hunted down the hounds are called off. At the conclusions of public gatherings, it is the custom for those in attendance to concoct huge "pot stews"—a type of "mulligan" made with chicken and vegetables, cooked in wash boilers over open fires.

PITTSBURG, 78 m. (392 alt., 3,796 pop.), is the seat of Camp County, which produces oil, beef cattle, farm products, fruit. It sprawls in neighborly fashion, the newer homes and buildings blending with those of more ancient vintage. Few people hurry in Pittsburg. Its most outstanding feature is the odd elbow effect of the main street. According to local tradition, when the town's one street was being laid out, a huge, beautiful tree blocked the way, and rather than cut it down the citizens chose to walk and drive around it.

Southward, the route passes through a heavily timbered area where gum lumber is sold.

The VAN PITTS HOME (*open*), 80 *m.*, was constructed (L) several years prior to the Civil War by a slave for whom the owner paid $3,000 in gold. A two-story portico and wide hallway are indicative of its ante bellum construction.

This region was once inhabited by Cherokees and Caddoes, and from the vicinity the Department of Anthropology and Archeology of the University of Texas has removed quantities of artifacts and skeletal remains, which are preserved in the Anthropology Museum, Waggener Hall (*see Austin*).

GILMER, 97 *m.* (370 alt., 4,312 pop.), is a rapidly growing oil and farming center, built around a smart cream-colored courthouse that is surrounded by drab weathered brick buildings.

Tradition says that San Jacinto corn came from this vicinity and was given to Houston by the Cherokees. While Houston lay wounded under an oak tree after the Battle of San Jacinto, the story goes, he was shelling the corn on which he had subsisted almost solely for days, when some of his soldiers gathered and began to talk about the future. "Take this corn home and plant it," Houston is said to have told them. Someone suggested that they call it "Houston corn." "No, call it San Jacinto corn," Houston said. And according to the story, every grain of this corn was planted, in widely scattered communities.

Gilmer's annual celebration is the Yamboree, a gay festival during the early part of October, in celebration of the harvesting and curing of yams.

Right from Gilmer on a graveled road to KELSEY, 8 *m.* (200 pop.), a colony established by the Church of Jesus Christ of Latter Day Saints in 1902. Kelsey Academy, a school conducted by the church, with 150 students, places emphasis on poultry and stock raising and dairying.

At UNION GROVE, 107 *m.,* in the neglected remains of a rock garden at the former home of John O'Byrne, Jr., can be found some of the shamrock plants grown from seed brought from Ireland by John O'Byrne, Sr., in the early nineties. Despite lack of care the symbol of Old Erin continues to come up each March and thrives throughout April, May, and June, in contradiction to the often heard statement that this particular plant grows nowhere outside of Ireland. There are also a few plants at the new home of John O'Byrne, near by.

GLADEWATER, 112 *m.* (333 alt., 6,000 pop.) is at the junction with US 80 (*see Tour 19*).

Pine forests line both sides of the highway, then timber becomes sparse and farms and pasture lands increase. The SITE OF CAMP FORD (L) is at 132.9 *m.* This Confederate prison camp was established in 1863 and named for Colonel John S. (Rip) Ford. Here several hundred Federal soldiers and sailors were imprisoned, their shelter consisting of caves dug in the hillside and huts constructed of sticks, mud, and sheet tin.

TYLER, 137 *m.* (558 alt., 55,104) is at the junction with US 69 (*see Tour 5*).

I◄+IC◄IC◄IC◄IC◄IC◄IC◄IC◄IC◄IC◄IC◄IC◄IC◄IC◄IC◄IC◄IC◄IC◄IC◄IC◄IC◄IC◄IC◄IC◄IC◄IC◄

Tour 5

(Durant, Okla.)—Denison—Tyler—Lufkin—Beaumont—Port Arthur; US 69.
Oklahoma Line to Port Arthur, 357 *m.*

This route runs between the Red River and the Gulf of Mexico, passing in a southeasterly direction through a region that saw the first sweep of the Republic's tide of home seekers. Cotton, supreme in the black lands of the first miles of US 69 south of Denison, is replaced in economic importance by roses near Tyler, then by lumber, then by rice and oil. Iron ore underlies much of the area traversed. Except near the coast the population is more than half rural, with many tenant farmers. A small percentage of the farmers are Negroes, among whom illiteracy is rapidly decreasing because of the number of schools in the area. Singing conventions are held by the country folk, and logrollings are among old customs still in vogue. Fishing is excellent in the many streams, with bass, perch, crappie, bream, and drum in the waters. Small animals, geese, ducks, quail and doves are abundant.

Section a. OKLAHOMA LINE *to* GREENVILLE; 61 *m.* US 69

This part of US 69 penetrates the fertile Blacklands Belt. Here was the hunting ground of the peaceful Caddo tribe. Luis Moscoso passed this way, and into the timbered fastness came French trappers and traders from Louisiana colonies. This land was finally claimed and held by sturdy settlers—of English, Irish, French, and Dutch stock—who became cotton farmers. Today cotton is the source of most of the region's income. On this uppermost division of the Gulf Coastal Plain, where good roads afford facilities for quick marketing, truck farming is on the increase, but the predominantly rural population clings to the one-crop idea; cotton represents their heritage. Farm tenants—of whom there are a great number—live in small houses, but with a degree of comfort. The relationship between landlord and tenant is generally friendly; successive generations of sharecroppers frequently remain on one farm. Amusements for all classes are close to the soil: outdoor singing meets, hunting and fishing parties, church picnics, revival "preachings." Fully three-fourths of all rural folk own automobiles. The towns have industrial plants that process the produce of the area.

US 69, united with US 75 (*see Tour 6*), crosses the OKLAHOMA LINE, 0 *m.,* over the Red River at the Denison Bridge, 15 miles southwest of Durant, Okla.

DENISON, 5 *m.* (767 alt., 25,946 pop.) (*see Tour 6*), is at the junction with US 75 (*see Tour 6*).

BELLS, 18 *m.* (674 alt., 428 pop.) (*see Tour 3*), is at the junction with US 82 (*see Tour 3*).

WHITEWRIGHT, 25 *m.* (1,315 pop.); TRENTON, 31 *m.* (712 pop.) are farming centers.

The modern appearance of LEONARD, 41 *m.* (704 alt., 1,131 pop.), with its paved streets and smart business houses, belies the rough-and-ready story of its early days. A tale that illustrates this past is of the town's first post office, which was in a saloon; the cash and stamps were kept in an old cigar box under the bar. Displeased because a post office inspector asked too many questions, the postmaster slammed the cigar box on the bar and told the inspector to take his post office and get out.

In the south part of the town is LEONARD PARK (*fishing; picnicking facilities*), a wooded area. Here, since 1880, a community four-day festival has been held annually.

CELESTE, 48 *m.* is a farm village of 600 pop.

GREENVILLE, 61 *m.* (554 alt., 19,087 pop.) (*see Tour 18*), is at the junction with US 67 (*see Tour 18*).

Section b.   GREENVILLE to JACKSONVILLE; 111 m.   US 69

This section of US 69 begins in the Blacklands area, and enters a more rolling, timbered region where lumber and cotton are important.

In some spots along the way, farm tenants outnumber resident farm owners. The population—more than half rural—fosters folk music: singing conventions and festivals are held regularly, and public schools emphasize musical training. The social customs of rural folk are those of their pioneer ancestors, who developed a co-operative system in order that all might survive: new houses and barns are erected at "raisings," there are shucking and quilting bees, and graveyard workings. Square dances are popular; in the Gingham and Overall Dance, everyone wears work clothes. Hay rides and moonlight picnics are held. Signs govern many of the actions of farmers: cotton is planted when the whippoorwill cries; the worm or bottom rail of a log fence is laid when the moon is waning, so that it will not sink or rot; and it is believed by many that there will be a frost four weeks from the time of the first cricket-chirp overheard by a farmer in the fall.

Although the population is predominantly agricultural, near Tyler oil development has brought new industries. In 1940 efforts were again being made to find a suitable available fuel for use in developing vast iron ore resources, long neglected.

Southeast of GREENVILLE, 0 *m.*, US 69 passes through farms broken by the heavily timbered bottom lands of the Trinity River.

Large deposits of lignite underlie the region, at 39 *m.*, and several mines using the strip method are in operation in the vicinity.

At 50 *m.* is the junction with US 80 (*see Tour 19*), which unites with US 69 to MINEOLA, 54 *m.* (414 alt., 3,810 pop.), which is at the junction with US 80 (*see Tour 19*).

The route continues through red hills covered with heavy timber. A lake (R), 63.6 *m.* offers excellent fishing and numerous camping and picnicking locations. Southeast, US 69 runs through the heart of a vast rose garden.

TYLER, 81 *m.* (558 alt., 51,230 pop., 1960; 55,104 est., 1964) is the nation's largest center of rose culture. Although the East Texas Oil Field dominates the business activity of Tyler, flowers come second. Its 360 nurseries supply half the field-grown rose bushes of the United States, shipping $7,500,000 worth annually. The city also has 75 azalea gardens, and the Azalea Trails.

Tyler is the seat of Smith County and half way between Dallas and Shreveport, La. The County had 91,800 est. population in 1966, 22.3 per cent nonwhite. The city, incorporated 1846, was named for John Tyler, tenth president of the United States, who signed the joint resolution under which Texas was admitted to the Union. The city remains a large shipping center for farm products, including peaches, tomatoes, and vegetables. More than 334 oil corporations have headquarters in Tyler.

Tyler is served by the Missouri Pacific Lines, Central Greyhound Bus Line and Continental Trailways. Trans-Texas Airways uses the Municipal Airport and provides commutation to Dallas in 35 min. The city is well supplied with hotels and motels that can accommodate the large crowds that come for Tyler's special events. Foremost of these is the Rose Festival in October, with its Rose Show, Field Tours, and Coronation Pageant, a blaze of colors. The East Texas Agricultural Fair is held in September.

The MUNICIPAL ROSE GARDEN on West Front. St. displays many acres of formal planting with bushes multiplying and new varieties being added annually.

The GOODMAN-LEGRANDE HOUSE, 624 North Broadway, built 1859 by Gallatin Smith, is a well-preserved example of a mansion of Civil War times, now a city museum. It contains period furniture and clothing and historical objects collected by the Historical Society. *Open daily 9–5.*

TEXAS COLLEGE, 2404 N. Grand St., founded 1894 by the African Methodist Episcopal Church, has been a 4-yr. senior college since 1932. Coeducational, it enrolls more than 400 students. TYLER JUNIOR COLLEGE, on Henderson Highway, founded 1926, enrolls more than 2,300. Its Wise Auditorium is the home of the East Texas Symphony Orchestra. Hudnall Planetarium is open to the public Sunday afternoons and Thursday evenings during the school year (*adults 50¢; children 25¢*).

The EAST TEXAS TUBERCULOSIS HOSPITAL, 825 beds, is an important Tyler institution.

LAKE TYLER, the city's 2,450-acre reservoir impounded by Prairie Creek, is 12 *m.* southeast of the city on State 64. MUD CREEK RESERVOIR, 13 *m.* southeast, covers 2,580 acres.

Site of CAMP FORD, in which 6,000 Union soldiers were held prisoner during the Civil War, is indicated by a granite marker on US 271, 2 *m.* northeast of Tyler. It was a stockade of poles 16 ft. tall surrounding huts built by the prisoners. The descriptive marker was placed in 1959 by the Texas Tourist Marker Committee.

TYLER STATE PARK, 994 acres, is a wooded recreation area with facilities for camping and boating, 10 *m.* north of Tyler on Farm Road 14.

Right from Tyler on State 31 to a STATE FISH HATCHERY, 6 *m.*, where 30 ponds covering 100 acres produce much of the game fish supply used to stock Texas streams. Near-by GREENBRIAR LAKE supplies water for the hatchery.

A 100-foot FOREST SERVICE LOOKOUT TOWER (*visitors permitted to ascend at their own risk*), 105.4 *m.*, overlooks Love's Lookout Park (L) and affords a wide view of the countryside.

The entrance (L) to LOVE'S LOOKOUT PARK is at 105.6 *m.* Here a recreational area of 63 acres contains a swimming pool, a natural rock amphitheater, and picnic facilities. Quail, doves, squirrels and deer are abundant in the vicinity.

JACKSONVILLE, 111 *m.* (516 alt., 9,590 pop.) is at the junction with US 79 (*see Tour 20*).

Section c. JACKSONVILLE to PORT ARTHUR; 185 m. US 69

US 69 continues through a heavily timbered area—the center of the lumbering industry in Texas—thence onto the fertile Coastal Plain. In dense forests of pines and hardwoods, trees and shrubs rare to the Southwest are found: maples, chinquapins, beeches, and holly. Myrtles, yaupons, and dogwoods bloom beneath the big timber, in perpetual twilight. Flowering woodbine, yellow jasmine, and Virginia creeper twine around tree trunks, and elderberries bloom along the highway. Each little farmhouse has its orchard. Windmills are rare; water wells often have the proverbial old oaken bucket. Logs are used for houses, barns, fences, furniture—in every possible way. Trucks loaded with logs crowd the roads.

As the coast is neared the terrain flattens. At Port Arthur, an inland port on the Sabine-Neches Canal, sea-going ships load oil, cotton, and other products of the rich outlying prairies. The atmosphere changes to one of brisk commercial and shipping activity, the buildings to modern, tall structures.

South of JACKSONVILLE, 0 *m.*, US 69 traverses an area of farms, orchards and woodlands.

The RUSK STATE HOSPITAL, 12 *m.*, on a tract (R) of 2,100 acres, is one of the State institutions for the mentally ill.

RUSK, 13 *m.* (489 alt., 5,000 pop.) seat of Cherokee County, was named for Gen. Thos. J. Rusk, lawyer here 1829–1856, who helped expell the Cherokees in 1839. Rusk was active during the Civil War as a supply center for salt, iron ore, and lumber. An iron foundry opened in 1884 was modernized during World War I, but was again abandoned because of lack of suitable fuel. Oil production began in 1914. Fruit, vegetables, dairy products are handled here. A condensed milk plant operates in Rusk. The Rusk Memorial Hospital was opened in 1947.

In Rusk is the junction with US 84 (*see Tour 21*).

Southeastward a heavily timbered area is broken by pastures and tilled fields. Turpentine is extracted from the longleaf pines, just as maple syrup is extracted from maples; after it is refined, the residue of rosin—commercially known as naval stores—is also sold. Many of the pine logs are creosoted and sold for use as telephone or telegraph poles, or for railroad cross ties.

Fuller's earth is mined in this area, which also produces cotton, corn, and cane. At cross roads stand little general stores, pungent with the smell of fresh-ground coffee, spices, harness oil, and gasoline. Patent medicines and dress goods line the shelves, and usually, at a table in the rear, visiting farmers can consume cove oysters, salmon, crackers, and cheese.

ALTO, 25 *m.* (433 alt., 1,500 pop.), is active in tomato canning and cotton ginning. In 1839 the order of Mirabeau B. Lamar, then President of the Republic of Texas, to expel the Cherokees who had emigrated to this region in 1822 and obtained land through treaties with Mexico and later with Texas, was carried out in this vicinity by General Thomas J. Rusk and Colonel Edward Burleson. The Cherokee chiefs, Big Mush and The Bowl, resisted the order, and after several pitched battles the Indians were routed, Chief Bowl being among those killed.

1. Right from Alto on State 21 to INDIAN MOUNDS, 7 *m.* These mounds are visible from the highway (R) and are south of the site of the reestablishment of Mission San Francisco de los Tejas (Mission St. Francis of the Tejas). The mission was maintained on this, its second site, from 1716 to 1719. In 1721 the Spanish again established a mission here, calling it Mission San Francisco de los Neches.

The site of an old Neches Indian village (L) is at 7.4 *m.*

The Neches River is crossed at 8 *m.* In this vicinity, at an inaccessible spot R. of the highway, is the approximate site of the Mission Santisimo Nombre de Maria (Mission of the Most Holy Name of Mary), the second mission to be established in east Texas (1691).

WECHES, 12.4 *m.* (261 pop.), is notable chiefly because somewhere in the vicinity, southwest, L. of State 21, is the site of a large village of the Tejas tribe, from which Texas derived its name.

At 15 *m.* is the junction with a graveled road.

Right on this road 1 *m.* to the FIRST SITE OF THE MISSION SAN FRANCISCO DE LOS TEJAS, the earliest east Texas mission, established in 1690, burned and abandoned in 1693 because of hostile Indian and French activities. This site is within the boundaries of the Davy Crockett Division of the Texas National Forests. A modern structure reproduces the earlier mission building.

State 21 continues to the old STAGE COACH INN, 31 *m.,* built (R) about 1830, and used today as a barn.

CROCKETT, 33 *m.* (350 alt., 5,356 pop.), seat of Houston County, which produces timber, cotton and natural gas, is a center for farm products and woodworking. More than 10,000 pecan trees yield a valuable crop while beautifying the streets. Here is the ranger headquarters of the Davy Crockett Division of the Texas National Forests. The town was founded in the 1830's beside the Old San Antonio Road, whose route here follows closely that of State 21. It was named for Davy Crockett, who is said to have camped, while on his way to the Alamo, under a large oak near a spring about 500 feet from Crockett Circle. Fox hunting is a popular sport in the vicinity. Old Fiddlers championship contest takes place in June.

In cleared places of the fragrant, dim interior of Davy Crockett National Forest, bayous and ponds offer excellent fishing for perch and catfish. Occasional signs warn the motorist to *Watch Out for Hogs.* The reference is to razorbacks that roam the east Texas woods—angular, vicious descendants of hogs brought more than two centuries ago by the Spaniards—and known in this area as "piney rooters." Anyone can claim an unmarked wild hog by putting his mark on the animal's ear, but to appropriate an already marked hog is a serious offense, and on occasion has caused bloodshed.

Right from Crockett 35 *m.* on US 287 northward to PALESTINE, at the junction with US 79 (*see Tour 20*) and US 84 (*see Tour 21*).

Southwest of Crockett, State 21 continues to MADISONVILLE, 39 *m.,* at the junction with US 75 (*see Tour 6*).

2. Left from Alto on State 21 to DOUGLASS, 13 *m.* (225 pop.), active in the events of and following the Texas Revolution.

Right from Douglass 5.5 *m.* on Legg's Store Road to the SITE OF PRESIDIO DE NUESTRA SEÑORA DE LOS DOLORES DE LOS TEJAS (Fort of Our Lady of Sorrows of the Tejas), founded 1716, rebuilt in 118-acre STATE PARK.

Southwestward, Legg's Store Road leads to Goodman Crossing of the Angelina River, turning sharply L. without crossing the river, and following the east bank to ascend a hill to the SITE OF MOUNT STERLING, 8.4 *m.* Mount Sterling was founded in the 1830's by Colonel John Durst, who made the town an important port, shipping cotton to New Orleans and receiving merchandise. He built a handsome home overlooking the Angelina, and excavated an underground dining room from solid rock. Here he and his neighbors placed their women and children during raids by hostile Cherokees. The Cordova rebellion of 1838 blasted Durst's hopes of making Mount Sterling the metropolis of east Texas.

Left of the site of Mount Sterling, on the old San Antonio-Nacogdoches Road, is the SITE OF MISSION NUESTRA SEÑORA DE LA PURISIMA CONCEPCION (Mission of Our Lady of the Immaculate Conception), 9.5 *m.,* established in 1716 and abandoned in 1730.

East of the site of Mount Sterling, the Pleasant Hill-Nacogdoches Road runs to NACOGDOCHES, 14 *m.* (*see Tour 22a*), and the junction with US 59 (*see Tour 22*).

2A. Left from Douglass 12 *m.* on a dirt road to CUSHING (420 alt., 800 pop.), a lumbering and agricultural center; thence straight ahead on the Cushing-Laneville Road to the junction with a rambling dirt road, 14.2 *m.;* thence R. to a hill overlooking Bill Creek, to the SITE OF MISSION SAN JOSÉ DE LOS NAZONIS (Mission St. Joseph of the Nazonis), 15.1 *m.,* founded in 1716 and abandoned in 1730. (*Bad road; be careful.*) About a mile east is the site of an old Indian cemetery. A few miles north is the site of the Indian village of Anadarko, and a few miles west, at an inaccessible spot on Indian Creek, are the remains of the village of the Nasenitos, where the French trader Bernard de la Harpe made his headquarters in 1719 and defied the Spanish governor, Alarcón, who had ordered him to leave the territory.

Left from Cushing on State 204 10 *m.* to a junction with US 84 (*see Tour 21*).

LUFKIN, 56 *m.* (326 alt., 19,000 pop. est.) is in the heart of a forest area covering 12,285,000 acres. Seat of Angelina County, which produces 1,233,900,000 board ft. of saw timber and 54,294 cords of pulpwood annually. Timber production includes short and longleaf pine, cypress, hickory, oak and magnolia. Angelina County has manufacturing sales of $95,000,000 and a payroll of $31,000,0000 annually.

In 1965 Lufkin voted a $4,400,000 bond issue for capital improvements that included an all-purpose CIVIC AND CONVENTION CENTER building.

Nearby are ANGELINA NATIONAL FOREST (153,000 acres), DAVY CROCKETT NATIONAL FOREST (161,000 acres) and LAKE RATCLIFF (80 acres).

The U. S. Forest Service protects over 1 billion acres of virgin pine forests. The headquarters of the Angelina Division of the Texas National Forests is in Lufkin. Here paper mills produce wood pulp suitable for newsprint from longleaf pine.

The County Airport is 7 *m.* south of Lufkin and served by Trans-Texas Airlines. Continental Trailways, Greyhound, and Lufkin-Beaumont Motor Coaches also serve the area: also Southern Pacific and St. Louis Southwestern.

LUFKIN STATE SCHOOL helps the mentally retarded.

HERTY (1,400 pop.) a suburb of Lufkin, is named for Dr. Charles H. Herty, inventor of converting yellow pine into wood pulp for newsprint. KELTYS (1,056 pop.) also near Lufkin, is a lumber center. DIBOLL (3,004 pop.) 10 *m.* south of Lufkin on US 59, has a huge lumber mill. HUNTINGTON, (1,009 pop.) 10 *m.* east of Lufkin near Sam Rayburn Lake has a weekly livestock market.

In Lufkin is the junction with US 59 (*see Tour 22*).

The route continues through a stretch of the heaviest timber in east Texas. Extensive stands of pine line both sides of the highway. A lookout tower of the State Forestry Service is L. at 67.5 *m.*

ZAVALLA, 80 *m.* (228 alt., 900 pop.), is named for an old settlement near Jasper that was the seat of government for the De Zavala colony in 1829. For some reason the modern name has two l's. Left from Zavalla on State 63 to OLD ZAVALA, 18 *m.* (*see Tour 2*).

ROCKLAND, 92 *m.* (128 alt., 216 pop.), on the south bank of the Neches River, has the appearance of a town grown old before its time; lumbering and quarrying activities ended, and its commercial impetus dwindled. Today a little fuller's earth is mined in this otherwise agricultural district.

Southeast of Rockland on the Tyler-Jasper County boundary is Dam B on the Neches River and TOWN BLUFF RESERVOIR, 16,830 acres, capacity 124,700 acre-ft. The purpose is flood control, irrigation of the rice lands down stream, and water for Beaumont, Port Arthur, and neighboring communities. On the south bank of the Neches at an inaccessible point 2.5 miles upstream, is the SITE OF OLD FORT TERAN.

WOODVILLE, 108 *m.* (232 alt., 1,920 pop.), seat of Tyler County, is at the junction of US 69, 287 and 190. Here US 287 joins US

69 south to Beaumont. Woodville spreads over red, sandy hills; the high-pitched whine of sawmills, the odor of raw pine, and talk of lumber, dominate the town. Woodville folk specialize in country dinners, served boardinghouse style (*watch for signs*). Tyler County Dogwood Festival, held when the dogwoods bloom in March or April, includes ceremonies in the Woodville amphitheater and a Queen's Coronation Ball.

Shivers Library and Museum in the former home of Governor Allan Shivers has Texas memorabilia.

1. Right from Woodville on US 287 to a junction with a dirt road, 13 *m.*
Right on this road 1 *m.* to the SITE OF THE FENCED INDIAN VILLAGE. Here, prior to 1835, the Tejas Indians had a large fenced enclosure to protect the tribe and its livestock.

US 287 continues to CHESTER, 15 *m.* (237 alt., 319 pop.).
Right from Chester 2 *m.* on a dirt road to the SITE OF PEACH TREE VILLAGE. Here, long before the coming of the Anglo-American settlers, was a large community, first occupied by local Indians and later by the Alabamas. According to tradition, the Alabamas brought with them the pits of wild peaches, from which orchards grew. With the removal of the Alabamas to a reservation white settlers came, and continued the name until the removal of the town's businesses to Chester. A cotton plantation occupies the spot.

US 287 continues northwestward 15 *m.* to a junction with US 59 (*see Tour 22*).

2. Right from Woodville on US 190 to the ALABAMA-COOSHATTI RESERVATION, 17 *m.* (*see Tour 22*).

South of Woodville the route is through a part of the Texas National Forests. In this vicinity are sites of many Indian villages.

VILLAGE CREEK is crossed at 129.9 *m.* On its banks have been found an old Indian burial ground and numerous artifacts.

The little sawmill town of KOUNTZE, 140 *m.* (85 alt., 1,768 pop.), strings its small business houses along the highway, leaving the three-story courthouse forlorn and alone within its iron fence, two blocks to the right.

Kountze is adjacent to the BIG THICKET, a well-named forest area that once covered a million acres and in places is so thick with undergrowth as to form an almost impenetrable jungle. The paths of Indian hunters and wild beasts were long the only roads through this wilderness, and even the Indians avoided straying far from these beaten trails. The first white man to come here found scattered droves of wild cattle and goats that are presumed to have strayed from the mission herds of the Spaniards. The thicket was said in early times to have been 113 miles long, and in some places, 42 miles wide. Unlike similar areas in other parts of the country, it is neither swamp nor marshland, but dry and rich of soil, except in a few places where widening bayous have formed small muskegs.

Nearly every variety of hardwood and of pine native to this latitude is found here. Of late, lumber and oil companies have greatly depleted the timber growth, but large areas remain in a natural state. Vines, creepers, and shrubs abound, their blossoms running the scale of the spectrum. There are rare ferns, some six feet tall, and botanists have discovered seven varieties of orchids. The streams, lakes, and pot holes are bordered with wild flags and iris, white and red lilies, hyacinths, and cat-tails. Some of the palmettos grow to the height of eight to ten feet before the fronds begin, the more common variety forming a knee-high mass of green.

Nearly every stream, lake, and pond in the thicket offers excellent fishing. Bears and panthers—once numerous—are still found, chiefly in the more inaccessible parts. Deer bound unexpectedly from cover, and small game is plentiful. The eastern part of the thicket has a Lost Creek, which drops suddenly into a hole at the foot of a large tree between Bragg and Honey Island, to reappear just as suddenly from under a bank of ferns northeast of Saratoga, more than five miles to the south.

William O. Douglas, Associated Justice of the U. S. Supreme Court, and ardent conservationist, says the Big Thicket covers only 300,000 acres and is losing 50 acres a day to cultivators and lumbermen. *In Farewell to Texas, A Vanishing Wilderness,* he cited a 500-year old white oak with a spread of 135 ft., and a huge holly tree known 130 years ago. In 1966 Senator Ralph W. Yarborough introduced a bill in Congress to make Big Thicket a National Park.

During the Civil War the area became a refuge for service-dodging Texans, and gangs of bushwhackers, as they were called, hid in its fastnesses. Conscript details of the Confederate Army hunted the fugitives and occasional skirmishes resulted. Down through the years have come many tales of lost travelers, of sudden disappearances, of murder, and other crimes committed here.

Southeast of Kountze the route is through prairie lands dotted here and there with clumps of low timber.

At 153 *m.* is a junction with US 96 (*see Tour 2*).

The leading industry of this region, lumbering, now gives way to areas devoted to the cultivation of rice. On the south bank of Pine Island Bayou a large irrigation system for rice culture has a pumping plant.

This area is one of the most important rice-growing districts in the United States. About 40,000 acres are devoted to the rice industry in Jefferson County alone, of which this vicinity is the center. One of the first large rice plantations in Texas was established here in 1895 by Willard Lovell. Rice fields meant barbed wire fences, a menace to the free open range of the cattlemen, and opposition almost as bitter as that found by the nesters and sheep raisers in western Texas developed, but the pioneer rice growers persisted. By 1910 there were 75,983 acres of the county in rice. Overproduction caused a decrease in acreage, but modern farming methods have increased the yield to the acre. The average value of the yearly rice crop in this vicinity is $2,200,000.

BEAUMONT, 166 *m.* (21 alt., est. pop. 1966, 127,800) (*see Beaumont*), is at the junction with US 90 (*see Tour 23*).

At 169.2 *m.* is a junction with a paved road.

Left on this road to NEDERLAND, 5 *m.* 25 alt., 3,805 pop., 1950; 12,036, 1960), a rural community founded in 1896 by colonists from Holland. Distinctive Dutch dishes still prevail in many homes, but the residents are in other respects fully Americanized. Although most of the townspeople are oil-refinery workers, there is much truck-farming and dairying in the vicinity.

PORT ARTHUR, 185 *m.* (4 alt., est. pop. 69,000, 1966) (*see article on Port Arthur*).

1. Right from Port Arthur on State 87 to the INTRACOASTAL CANAL, 2.8 *m.* This inland waterway extends along the Gulf coast from St. Marks, Florida, to Brownsville, Texas. The Texas section enters the Laguna Madre after passing Corpus Christi Bay and moves between the Coast and Padre Island to Port Isabel.

SABINE PASS, 14 *m.* (8 alt., 800 pop.), is scattered over a treeless expanse of tall salt grass. Its cafes feature sea food dinners. The highway, its main street, divides around a granite slab erected to the memory of Dick Dowling, Civil War hero. The town throve in the days when pirates roamed the Gulf, and tales of buried treasure abound in the vicinity. Sabine Pass is at the head of the SABINE-NECHES WATERWAYS, a system of canals that make inland towns accessible to merchant craft. The entrance of the Pass, which connects the Sabine and Neches Rivers with the Gulf of Mexico, was formerly obstructed by a bar. Dredging and the construction of the Sabine jetties, each three and a half miles long, removed this obstacle. (*Duck hunting and salt water fishing especially good in this locality.*)

Left from Sabine Pass 1.6 *m.* on a shell road to SABINE, (17 alt., 364 pop.), a fishing village on the low bluff overlooking the waters of Sabine Pass. Weather-beaten, false-fronted, unpainted store buildings face the highway, from which sandy streets lead out. Here L. of the highway, in a park area, stands a heroic size bronze STATUE OF LIEUTENANT DICK DOWLING, C.S.A., commander of the battery actively engaged in the Battle of Sabine Pass, September 8, 1863, which resulted in the defeat of a large Federal force attempting to effect a landing. A small Confederate garrison at Fort Griffin, a mud fortress guarding the Pass, captured two gunboats during a 45-minute engagement, and prevented the landing of approximately 4,000 Federal soldiers on transports waiting outside the bar. Thus, a contemplated invasion of Texas was prevented and a concerted campaign planned by the Federal department commander to break the line of communications and supplies between Texas and Louisiana, was forestalled. The park covers the site of the old battery emplacement.

South of the Neches River is GROVES, a Port Arthur suburb, with 17,304 pop. in 1960 and 21,000 est. in 1967.

2. Left from Port Arthur on State 87 to the PORT ARTHUR-ORANGE BRIDGE, 5 *m.* This $2,750,000, mile-and-a-half long structure towers 230 feet above the surface of the river. It was officially opened with elaborate ceremonies in September 1938.

BRIDGE CITY, an unincorporated community, has grown up here; it had 4,611 pop. in 1960. State 62 joins State 87 2 *m.* north.

Farm and Range

INSPECTING BRUSH CONTROL ON ZAVISCH FARM,
McMULLEN COUNTY

CONTOUR FARMING: OATS AT SIXTY BUSHELS PER ACRE,
VALLEY VIEW

USDA Soil Conservation Service

CONTOUR FARMING: GRAIN SORGHUM AND FALLOW STRIPS,
FLOYD COUNTY

USDA Soil Conservation Service

CONTOUR FARMING: REDUCING WATER RUNOFF AND SILT,
BELL COUNTY

USDA Soil Conservation Service

CONTOUR FARMING: DIVERSIFIED CROPS ON A HILL,
BELL COUNTY

USDA Soil Conservation Service

BRAHMA BULLS GRAZING, DAVENPORT RANCH, DIMMIT COUNTY
USDA Soil Conservation Service

SPRINKLER IRRIGATED PASTURE, JENNINGS FARM, CROSBY COUNTY
USDA Soil Conservation Service

COTTON AND SIPHON IRRIGATION NEAR BROWNSVILLE
USDA Soil Conservation Service

COTTON GROWING ON TURNED-OVER GUAR, WILBARGER COUNTY
USDA Soil Conservation Service

HEREFORD COWS GRAZING IN CLAY COUNTY

USDA Soil Conservation Service

LONGHORNS CROSSING RED RIVER AT DOAN'S

USDA Soil Conservation Service

ENDURANCE CONTEST; RIDING STEER AT RODEO

HYBRID CORN BESIDE IRRIGATION SYSTEM, FRIO COUNTY

USDA Soil Conservation Service

Tour 6

(Durant, Okla.)—Denison—Dallas—Corsicana—Huntsville—Houston
—Galveston; US 75; Interstate 45.
Oklahoma Line to Galveston, 374 *m.*

US 75 drops southward between north central Texas and the timbered area of the eastern part of the State, thence over the coastal prairies
to the shore line of the Gulf of Mexico. Beginning in the Blacklands Belt,
it traverses the richest, most productive agricultural and industrial section
of Texas—a region where cotton is a mighty economic factor, with corn
second and wheat, small grains, truck crops, and fruits important; where
high-grade livestock, especially horses and mules and newly-introduced
sheep, boost rural incomes. Along the first third of the route seven-eighths
of a land is tillable. Most small towns are not more than eight or ten miles
from a shipping point. In this area is Dallas, the State's second largest city.
The fine highway of Interstate 45 now follows US 75 to Galveston.

As the piney woods appear, cotton and lumber, oil and, nearer the
coast, rice, are important. Other crops are onions, black-eyed peas, carrots,
and tomatoes.

Section a.   *OKLAHOMA LINE to DALLAS; 79 m.   US 75*

This section of US 75 passes through the broad, fertile valley of the
Red River, crosses a low divide, and pushes out into the northeast part of
the Great Plains. It has highly developed agriculture and industry.

US 75, united with US 69, crosses the State line 15 miles south of
Durant, Okla.

DENISON BRIDGE (*free*), 0 *m.,* across the Red River, is where
the Colbert Toll Bridge was built about 1874, and within sight of the
location of the still older Colbert's Ferry, at Colbert's Crossing, 1.5 miles
upstream. Colbert, a trader, in 1858 obtained authorization from the
Chickasaw nation to establish a ferry, paying a yearly fee.

The present bridge was the cause and site of the bridge war of 1933,
in which Governor William H. (Alfalfa Bill) Murray of Oklahoma,
with vocal pyrotechnics and a display of armed force, obtained for Texas,
as well as his own State, the free use of the structure.

LAKE TEXOMA, largest man-made reservoir serving Texas, is impounded by DENISON DAM on the Red River and is partly in Cooke
and Grayson Counties; the major part in Oklahoma. With 5,530,300 acre-
ft., it is one of ten largest man-made lakes in the country. Surface area is
144,100 acres. Washita River also contributes to it. The dam is 190 ft.

tall, 15,350 ft. long. The shore line is 1,224 miles. The Corps of Engineers, U. S. Army, supervises the area, which attracts about 6,000,000 vacationists annually. The Hagerman National Wildlife Refuge, 11,300 acres, borders Lake Texoma.

DENISON, 5 *m.* (22,748 pop., 1960; 25,946, 1965, est.) shipping point on the M-K-T and gateway to the Lake Texoma recreation area, which begins 4 *m.* north on State 75A at Denison Dam. The EISENHOWER BIRTHPLACE, a two-story white frame cottage where the President was born Oct. 14, 1890, when it stood at 208 E. Day St., now stands in a two-acre State Park. The father worked in the M-K-T Railway shops and moved his family to Abilene, Kansas, when the infant was one year old. Seven *m.* ne of Denison, off US 75A, is the EISENHOWER STATE PARK, 450 acres, estab. 1954.

In its early days buffalo hunters, traders, cattlemen, freighters, and the laxity of law enforcement earned Denison the reputation of a "tough" town. Following the Civil War ex-Confederate soldiers put an end to rowdyism. The subsequent establishment here of a railroad division point with its shops, roundhouses, and staff of permanent workers, and the influx of citizens, proved a balancing influence.

The JUSTIN RAYNAL MONUMENT, Woodward St., facing the Denison High School, is a granite shaft erected to the memory of Justin Raynal, gambler and saloonkeeper, who, dying in 1879, left his estate of $15,-000 to the Denison schools.

GRAYSON COUNTY JUNIOR COLLEGE was opened in 1965 west of Denison on State 691. The new MEMORIAL HOSPITAL opened in 1965. The PUBLIC LIBRARY has more than 35,000 vols.

In Denison is a junction with US 69 (*see Tour 5*).

For information about recreational areas consult Lake Texoma Assn., 609 W. Chestnut, and Denison Chamber of Commerce, 313 W. Woodward. The latter also supplies a list of historical markers for tourists.

Right from Denison on State 91 is OLD PRESTON, 15 *m.* submerged since 1945 under Lake Texoma's waters. Here in the 1830's, Colonel Holland Coffee founded a trading post that was the rendezvous of white trappers. The Texas Republic in 1840 established Fort Preston here. Jim Bridger, Kit Carson, John Colter, "Old Misery" Beck, and others of the so-called mountain men visited the outpost during their wanderings. Colonel Coffee's friendship with the Indians was such that he was able to redeem many white captives taken in raids. In 1845 Colonel Coffee erected a large, two-story log house, GLEN EDEN, which, its logs covered with clapboards, became an attraction for history-minded tourists.

At 9 *m.* beyond Denison is PERRIN AIR FORCE BASE of the Air Defense Command, devoted to fighter-interceptor training.

SHERMAN, 15.4 *m.* (720 alt., 26,000 pop. est.), industrial and marketing center, retains its beauty through native foliage, wide streets, and many flower gardens. Its growth was assured when, in 1857, John Butterfield was persuaded to route the St. Louis to San Francisco stage line through the town. Transcontinental transportation, responsible for Sherman's birth and early growth, still plays an important part in its prosperity and progress. The stage line has given place to railroads, passenger bus lines, motor freight lines, and air services.

Sherman has factories turning out gin machinery, cotton garments, cotton piece goods, cottonseed oil products, flour, and numerous other items. It also is the supply center for a large productive agricultural area from which its industries draw their raw materials.

The first courthouse here was a log structure, which was torn down in 1857 to settle a bet as to whether or not an old gray duck had her nest under the building. History does not relate whether she did, but does recount that when the sheriff came the next morning with a legal notice to be posted on the courthouse door, he dug the door from the debris, propped it up, and affixed the notice.

AUSTIN COLLEGE, Presbyterian, has a plant consisting of buildings of classical and modern design around a formal quadrangle. The campus covers 40 acres, with a large athletic field adjoining. Austin College was founded in 1849 at Huntsville, with Sam Houston and Anson Jones, both former Presidents of the Texas Republic, among the first trustees. It was moved to Sherman in 1876. Enrollment is more than 1,000 students and 103 faculty.

In Sherman is the junction with US 82 (*see Tour 3*).

Onion production has become important in the region southward. Small centers are 21 *m.*, HOWE (680 pop.) ; 28 *m.*, VAN ALSTYNE (1,608 pop.) both in Grayson County; 38 *m.*, ANNA, (639 pop.) ; 35 *m.*, MELISSA (405 pop.) in Collin County. Collin McKinney, Texas founder, is commemorated in the names of county and city.

Church spires rising above treetops indicate McKinney, 47 *m.*, (612 alt., 14,750 pop., 1965), at a junction of State 24 and 121. It has a cotton textile plant employing 650, three meat packers, cotton gins and garment makers. There is a monument to James W. Throckmorton, eleventh governor of Texas. In Fisk Park is the COLLIN MCKINNEY HOUSE and at 49.8 *m.* a monument to McKinney stands in a roadside park off US 75.

Collin County is in the black land belt where growers raise cotton, corn, wheat, sorghum, oats, dairy and beef cattle, some sheep, poultry, garden truck and honey.

ALLEN, 54 *m.* (1,300 pop.) is on State 5, as US 75 takes a new road west of it. PLANO, 60 *m.* (655 alt., 11,500 pop. est. 1966) is a growing residential and industrial center. A small institution with a large name is the University of Plano, a private coeducational school opened in 1964, which in 1966 had 46 students and 6 teachers.

RICHARDSON, 65 *m.* (630 alt., 35,598 pop. 1966, est., up from 16,800 in 1960) a rapidly growing city in Dallas County near the Collin County line. Here in 1961 was established the *Graduate Research Center of the Southwest*, with which all the principal colleges in the Dallas-Fort Worth area are affiliated (*see Fort Worth*).

DALLAS, 79 *m.* (*see Dallas*).

Left from Dallas on US 175 to the junction with Simonds Rd., 16.7 *m.*
Right here 0.6 *m.* to the FEDERAL REFORMATORY FOR WOMEN (L). This insti-

tution consists of 18 buildings of modernized Virginia Colonial architecture. Efforts have been made to avoid the appearance of a prison by the use of ornamental grilles for the windows, and electrically controlled doors. On a 780-acre tract, the reformatory can house 550 prisoners.

Section b.   DALLAS to FAIRFIELD; 89 m.   US 75; Interstate 45

This part of US 75, Interstate 45, pass through the cultivated lands of the Trinity River bottoms, following the general direction of that stream past the first rise of foothills.

HUTCHINS (1,400 pop.) is in an area of rich bottom and prairie lands that have produced bumper crops of cotton and corn.

FERRIS, 20.1 *m.* (468 alt., 1,807 pop.), built along narrow, brick-paved streets, is an industrial community.

PALMER, 27 *m.* (468 alt., 613 pop.) founded in 1845, was named for Martin Palmer, a participant in the Battle of San Jacinto.

ENNIS, 35 *m.* (548 alt., 9,347 pop.), although essentially a railroad town, is also an important commercial and industrial center. Here each autumn is held the Ellis County Fair.

Between Ennis and BARDWELL, 7 *m.* southwest on State 34 is the huge BARDWELL RESERVOIR, 7,240 acres, fed by Waxahachie Creek, Mustang Creek and other water in the Trinity River Basin. The rolled earth-fill dam is 15,900 ft. long, 82 ft. high; storage capacity is 140,000 acre-feet. The project was built by the Corps of Engineers, USA.

CORSICANA, 55 *m.* (448 alt., 20,344 pop. 1960; 22,000 est., 1965) county seat of Navarro County had the first oil well in the Southwest. It is a distributing center for cotton, grain, dairy products and oil. Navarro County produces more than 2,000,000 bbl. of oil annually. The Lone Star Petrochemical Co., a $25,000,000 investment near Trinity River, began producing fertilizer in 1964. The city, drilling for water, struck oil June 9, 1894, to the dismay of the officials. In October, 1895, an oil well brought in 2½ bbl. a day. J. S. Cullinan, a Standard Oil operator, built a pipeline to a shipping point, started a refinery, and in 1900 developed first use of crude as fuel for locomotives. The rotary drill was first applied to oil drilling in the Corsicana field. Cullinan founded the Texas Company and the Magnolia Petroleum Company.

In 1966 Corsicana gained access to 15,000,000 gallons of water daily from the new Bardwell Reservoir. The city financed a $2,750,000 filtration plant and a 16-mile closed conduit. The reservoir covers 5,071 acres and impounds 212,000 acre-feet.

LAKE HALBERT, 56.8 *m.,* stores 7,500 acre-feet of water from Chambers Creek, for Corsicana use.

A 6.8 *m.* Interstate 45 bypass around Corsicana was completed in 1964. Also completed was a 4-lane, 8-mile section on State 31 from Corsicana to POWELL. A new oil boom started at Powell in March, 1923. The first well caught fire, burned for 13 days and took 13 lives. Soon 1,200 wells were producing 400,000 bbl. a day at a depth of 2,900 ft. Many are still producing.

STREETMAN, 74 *m.* (300 pop.) is on the line between Navarro and Freestone Counties.

FAIRFIELD, 89 *m.* (461 alt., 1,781 pop.) (*see Tour 21a*), is at the junction with US 84 (*see Tour 21*).

Section c. FAIRFIELD to HOUSTON; 156 m. US 75; Interstate 45

This section of US 75 crosses the western part of the great pine timber belt of east Texas. There are cut-over areas and huge lumber mills; yet agriculture remains the leading means of livelihood.

BUFFALO, 19.3 *m.* (1,108 pop.) is at the junction with US 79 (*see Tour 20*).

Beneath its oaks and sycamores, CENTERVILLE, 35 *m.* (353 alt., 836 pop.), huddles around an old brick courthouse, on the grounds of which there is a reproduction of Fort Boggy, Texas Ranger post of the 1840's. Also on the courthouse lawn is the Tree of Justice, where several men were hanged in early days.

At 48 *m.* is a junction with a highway marked *OSR.* This is a State highway which follows, for a distance of nearly 50 miles, the route of the OLD SAN ANTONIO ROAD—for two centuries the main artery of travel between San Antonio and Nacogdoches.

MADISONVILLE, 56.8 *m.* (278 alt., 2,324 pop.). Here US 190 joins US 75 to Huntsville.

HUNTSVILLE, 85 *m.* (401 alt., 11,999 pop., 1960; 14,210 est. 1965) county seat of Walker County, which is 76 percent pine forest. It is a Sam Houston shrine and has the main unit of the Texas Department of Correction.

Walker County originally was named for Robert J. Walker, Secretary of the Treasury under President James K. Polk. In 1863 the charge was made that he had "leagued with Lincoln." The legislature then voted that the county was named for Samuel H. Walker, a Texas Ranger who died in the Mexican War.

Huntsville is at the entrance to the SAM HOUSTON NATIONAL FOREST, and is served by US 75, US 190, State 19, State 30 and Interstate 45. In addition to the Main Prison, where Union prisoners were confined during the Civil War, there are Wynne Prison Farm, 2 miles north, and Goree Prison Farm, 4 miles south, a woman's penal institution.

SAM HOUSTON STATE COLLEGE, 1 *m.* S. of the courthouse on US 75, founded in 1879, was one of the pioneer training centers for Texas teachers. It enrolls more than 5,500 annually. Part of the former campus is now the SAM HOUSTON MEMORIAL PARK. The STEAMBOAT HOUSE in the park, in which Sam Houston died July 26, 1863, was his home after he was removed in 1861 as governor of Texas because he refused to support the Confederacy.

The builder's inspiration was a Mississippi River steamboat. Long deck-like galleries run the length of the two-story structure, above and below, and in front wide steps lead from the ground level to the second floor. In 1936 the house was moved to its present location.

The HOUSTON RESIDENCE (*open 9–12:30 workdays, 11–5 Sun., free*), also in Memorial Park, is reached by a flower-bordered road. The white dog-run house stands beside a pond, and is a typical early Texas home, showing development from a single-room log cabin to a larger cabin with a roofed-over runway. Then came the addition of shed-like ells; clapboards completed the transformation. The result is an attractive six-room, story-and-a-half house with a set-in porch. In the yard are the restored LOG KITCHEN and one-room LOG LAW OFFICE (*each open 9–12:30 workdays, 11–5 Sun., free*).

Also in the park is the SAM HOUSTON MEMORIAL MUSEUM (*open*), a brick structure surmounted by a copper dome.

The shortest designated highway in Texas, State 219 leads to SAM HOUSTON'S GRAVE. It begins two blocks east of the courthouse, on 11th St., and extends 972 feet northwest to the cemetery. The monument is of gray granite with an equestrian bas-relief figure of Houston, and bears the tribute of Andrew Jackson: "The world will take care of Houston's fame."

HUNTSVILLE STATE PARK, on US 75, 6 *m.* south of Huntsville, covers 2,100 acres in the piney woods, with facilities for fishing, boating, camping, water skiing. Its LAKE RAVEN is named for the title given Sam Houston by the chief of the western Cherokees. (*Camp shelters, $2.50 a day per car; trailer space, $1 per car; fishing 50¢ per day.*)

An annual event is the Prison Rodeo, held each Sunday in October, in which prisoners perform.

NEW WAVERLY, 99 *m.* (362 alt., 650 pop.), is an old plantation center, settled 1830–40. Polish settlers arrived in 1870.

WILLIS, 107 *m.* (381 alt., 975 pop.) W. on Farm Road 1097 to MONTGOMERY, (286 alt., 975 pop.). Interest in pioneer customs is stimulated by the TEXAS TREK, an annual observance on the third Sunday in April sponsored by the historical societies of Montgomery and Grimes Counties. About 150 homes, many of them a century old, are opened to visitors and residents attired in period costumes play host at country-style dinners and sell homemade delicacies.

CONROE, 115 *m.* (213 alt., 9,912 pop., 1960, 12,000 est., 1966) seat of Montgomery County, processes oil and timber. CAMP STRAKE of the Boy Scouts of America is located here.

HOUSTON, 156 *m. See Houston.*

Section d.   HOUSTON to GALVESTON; 50 m.   US 75 (Interstate 45), State 3. Also Livingston to Galveston, State 146

Here the highways cross an almost level sweep of coastal plain, where the tang of salt is always in the air. The region includes Harris County, where Houston is absorbing what formerly were small unincorporated villages, and Galveston County, where oil is being drilled, refined and shipped. The main highway, US 75, is also Interstate 45. Running parallel with it a few miles to the north State 3 connects several communities.

An industrial district extends to SOUTH HOUSTON, 11.5 *m.* (44 alt., 9,000 pop. est.).

Since 1922 the contiguous area has become one of the major oil fields of Texas, with more than 450 wells in the Dickinson, Franks and Gulf Coast oil fields farther southeast. State 3 serves WEBSTER, LEAGUE CITY, (2,622 pop.) and DICKINSON (4,715 pop.)

East of State 3 between South Houston and Webster is Ellington Air Force Base.

Crowding Dickinson is sprawling TEXAS CITY, the major oil refining and shipping port on Galveston Bay. In 1950 it had 16,620 population; by 1960 this had risen to 32,065, and the 1967 estimate was more than 38,000. The majority of its inhabitants is associated with the oil industry. The port accommodates 18,000,000 tons of shipping a year and is the nation's 15th largest. It has a 23 ft. seawall and a dike stretching 5 miles into the Bay. One of its major plants is the Longhorn Tin Smelter. Union Carbide employs 2,400.

On April 16, 1947, Texas City waterfront experienced one of the greatest ship explosions in history. A vessel loaded with nitrates exploded and set off adjacent cargoes, with a reported total of 561 dead and many others injured.

Texas City also is entered by State 146, which divides it from LA MARQUE, 37 *m.* from Houston, so named in 1882 and the outlet for a fruit raising area. Its expansion to an estimated 13,000 population is attributed to the increase in oil and refinery employees. With HITCHCOCK, on State 6 farther south, (5,216 pop.) it is part of the Galveston-Texas City metropolitan area. As the highways from Houston converge on Galveston, US 75 emerges at 42.3 *m.* On a causeway that crosses Galveston Bay. This structure was completed in 1939 at a cost of more than $2,000,000.

State 146 runs parallel to these roads to Galveston along the shore of the Bay. It traverses the Coastal Plain from LIVINGSTON in Polk County (194 ft. alt., 3,398 pop.) where it leaves the north-south highway, US 59, and the east-west road, US 190. At 22 *m.* RYE is a junction with State 105. Right on 105 23 *m.* to CLEVELAND, (6,100 pop.) a lumber and oil supply center. Back on State 146 to 42 *m.* HARDIN, and 50 *m.* LIBERTY, (30 ft. alt., 6,127 pop.) seat of Liberty County, which in 1837 succeeded a Mexican settlement called Trinita de la Libertad. It is said that Alonso de Leon may have crossed the Trinity River here in 1690. The site of old Spanish Atascosita, 1757, lies 3 *m.* northeast. In this area Spaniards attempted to checkmate French settlers.

Then State 146 follows US 90 for 8 *m.,* to 58 *m.,* DAYTON (3,367 pop.), where the route truns south. 72 *m.,* MONT BELVIEU (1,206 pop.) in Chambers County, notable for a large salt dome, which produces brine. Two miles beyond the State road crosses Interstate 10, which runs from Beaumont to Houston.

82 *m.* BAYTOWN, (15 ft. alt., 28,159 pop., 1960; 38,000 est.

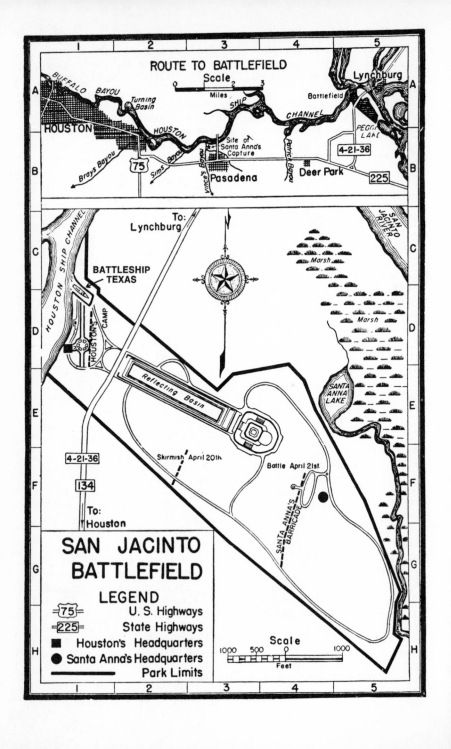

ROUTE TO BATTLEFIELD

Scale

Miles

BUFFALO BAYOU

Turning Basin

HOUSTON

HOUSTON SHIP CHANNEL

Lynchburg

Battlefield

PEGGY LAKE

Brays Bayou

Sims Bayou

Vince's Bayou

Site of Santa Anna's Capture

Patrick Bayou

4-21-36

Pasadena

Deer Park

225

To: Lynchburg

HOUSTON SHIP CHANNEL

BATTLESHIP TEXAS

HOUSTON'S CAMP

SAN JACINTO RIVER

Marsh

Marsh

Reflecting Basin

Skirmish April 20th.

Battle April 21st.

SANTA ANNA LAKE

4-21-36

134

To: Houston

Santa Anna's Barricade

SAN JACINTO BATTLEFIELD

LEGEND

75   U. S. Highways

225   State Highways

■   Houston's Headquarters

●   Santa Anna's Headquarters

─── Park Limits

Scale

1000   500   0   1000

Feet

1967) part of the Harris County industrial complex. In 1965 it was merged with Pelly and Goose Creek. Its Sterling Municipal Library is distinctive for its modern design and facilities. Lee College (Junior) enrolls up to 2,000 students.

State 146 now moves down the Bay shore where a number of small towns cluster around refineries and shipping points. The largest is LA PORTE (4,512 pop.), followed by SHORE ACRES, SEABROOK, KEMAH in Galveston County, and BACLIFF (1,707 pop.) State 146 becomes the dividing line between Texas City and La Marque and joins US 75 into Galveston.

<hr />

Tour 6A

Houston—San Jacinto Battleground Park, 22 *m.;* State 225 and State 134.

This route runs to the site of the Battle of San Jacinto. An industrial area on the fringe of the city reaches almost to the bayou region where General Sam Houston and his Texans defeated the Mexican army in 1836. Residents along the route almost exclusively are factory or refinery workers. The San Jacinto Battleground Park contains the Monument commemorating the battle and nearby is the Battleship *Texas.*

HOUSTON, 0 *m.*

Near a point (L) at 9.5 *m.,* Houston's army crossed Buffalo Bayou. The Texans got their ammunition across the stream on a raft made of lumber from Isaac Batterson's house, and began the march that ended on the field of San Jacinto.

PASADENA, 10.2 *m.* (34 alt., 58,737 pop., 1960; 73,000 est. 1967) is largely residential, with its people employed in Houston and in oil refineries. Vince's Bayou in 1836 was crossed by a bridge that was destroyed by Deaf Smith at General Houston's command to delay the Mexicans. In Pasadena is the site of the capture of the Mexican General Santa Anna after the Battle of San Jacinto.

SAN JACINTO COLLEGE (Junior) opened in 1961, has a campus of 142 acres on Spencer Highway and enrolls up to 3,000 students.

Adjoining Pasadena on the east is DEER PARK, (4,865 pop.) At 18.2 *m.* the road meets State 134, which becomes the Memorial Highway bordering San Jacinto State Park. State 225 continues to LA PORTE, (4,512 pop.), on Galveston Bay. Sylvan Beach Park is opened annually in May with a bathing beauty pageant. Sylvan Beach Amusement Park is a popular resort.

SAN JACINTO STATE PARK (*cafes, public rest rooms, picnicking facilities*), 22 *m.*, has had extensive developments since the centennial year 1936, at a cost of several millions. The SAN JACINTO MEMORIAL MONUMENT (*elevator, adults 50¢, children 15¢; 10–7 daily, spring and summer; 10–6 in autumn and winter*), is surmounted by a great Lone Star of Texas. It is 570 feet, 4¼ inches tall, and its base, which is 124 feet square, holds the SAN JACINTO MUSEUM OF HISTORY, opened in April, 1939. The museum has collections depicting the development of Texas from its discovery in 1519 to the period of the opening of the Civil War in 1861. Visitors can take the elevator to the observation level near the top. In front of the museum is a long reflecting pool that mirrors the lofty memorial. In the center of the great circle is the MEMORIAL SUNDIAL, designed by Julian Muench, Houston sculptor, in memory of General Houston's soldiers killed in the battle. The sundial is 12 feet high, on a base of Texas granite. Roads and paths give access to markers that designate the position of the commands before and during the battle. Live oaks shade part of the area, and rose gardens and flower beds add beauty to the grounds near the keeper's cottage. At the north and west runs Buffalo Bayou; on the east the San Jacinto River.

Within the 402 acres of the park lies the SAN JACINTO BATTLEFIELD, where, on April 21, 1836, 783 Texans under command of General Sam Houston defeated a Mexican army numbering at least 1,150, and according to some historians 1,400 or more, under General Santa Anna. This battle terminated the Texas Revolution and made possible the firm establishment of the Republic of Texas. It came at the conclusion of a strategic retreat, during which General Houston refused battle until the enemy's armies became separated and far from their base of supplies (*see History*). After a forced march Houston's weary army reached Harrisburg, to find that Santa Anna had destroyed the town and pressed on to the coast in an attempt to capture the officials of the provisional government, who were fleeing to Galveston. Learning from prisoners the size of the Mexican force and that Santa Anna was in personal command, Houston set forth as pursuer instead of pursued. Receiving reports that Santa Anna was moving leisurely toward the junction of Buffalo Bayou and the San Jacinto River, Houston reached the spot some hours ahead of him, and made camp in the curve of the bayou at a wooded point now in the western part of the park area. This was on the morning of April 20.

The arriving Mexican forces, when their scouts discovered the Texans, advanced a fieldpiece to within range and fired a shot that was at once answered by the "Twin Sisters," two small cannons donated to the Texas cause by citizens of Cincinnati, Ohio. These cannons had been received only a few days before and there had been no opportunity for practice, but it chanced that the first discharge of one of them so damaged the Mexican fieldpiece that thereafter it could not be fired accurately. A desultory artillery duel followed, and in the afternoon a Texas cavalry reconnaissance became a skirmish that engaged parts of both armies. During that days' fighting three Texans were wounded, one mortally. The Texans withdrew to the shelter of the trees and the Mexicans retired nearly a mile and made a camp before which, during the night, a barricade of saddles, impedimenta, and brush, was set up.

On the following morning, Santa Anna received reinforcements numbering some 400, who arrived, however, so exhausted as not to be ready for immediate fighting. The more impetuous of the officers in Houston's camp demanded that he give battle, but at a council of war which he called, a majority opposed it. Houston refused to give any indication of his intentions. He sent Deaf Smith and a detachment with axes to destroy Vince's Bayou bridge, telling Smith, "and return like eagles, or you will be too late for the day."

The complete inactivity in the Texans' camp, as the afternoon advanced, lulled Santa Anna into the belief that Houston would not attack. The Mexican forces were therefore engaged in routine camp duties or sleeping, Santa Anna and his officers enjoying their siesta, when Houston suddenly formed the Texans and attacked. The actual battle was over in less than 30 minutes—some said 18. The pursuit of fleeing Mexican soldiers to the cry of "Remember the Alamo! Remember Goliad!" continued until dark. Two Texans were killed and six mortally wounded. The other Texas wounded were given in General Houston's report as 17 (some later historians have increased this number to as many as 32). The Mexican loss, according to Houston's report, was 630 killed, 208 wounded and 730 (including the wounded) prisoners. Santa Anna was captured the next day and agreed to withdraw all Mexican armies.

The Battleship *Texas* lies moored in an inlet at the Park. On April 21, 1948, the ship was decommissioned by the United States Navy and presented to the State of Texas. It was dedicated as a State shrine by Governor Beauford Jester. On April 21, 1958, Governor Price Daniel on deck read his order activating the Texas Navy, with the *Texas* as its flagship. The battleship was built in 1914, is 573 ft. long, has a beam of 106 ft., a speed of 21 knots and 21-inch guns. The first launching of a plane from a ship took place on its deck in 1919. It served in both World Wars. The *Texas* may be visited from May 1 to September 17, noon to 6 p.m. and September 18 to April 30, 11 a.m. to 5 p.m.

❧❧❧❧❧❧❧❧❧❧❧❧❧❧❧❧❧❧❧❧❧❧❧❧❧❧

Tour 7

(Ardmore, Okla.)—Gainesville—Dallas—Waco—La Grange—Sinton —Kingsville—Sarita—Brownsville, US 77, Interstate 35. Oklahoma Line to Brownsville, 616 *m.*

US 77 takes a winding course a little east of the geographic center of Texas, between the Red River and Copano Bay. The route begins on the eastern fringe of the rich Blacklands Belt of the north central section, and proceeds across the deep black acres of the cotton plantations of the Brazos and Colorado Rivers. Thence it swings slightly west through old towns of Irish and German flavor to ghost ports on the placid bay that washes the shores of St. Joseph's Island, whose long protecting sandy bulk lies between the mainland here and the Gulf of Mexico.

The prosperity and progressiveness of the northern half of the route is based upon enormous wheat, grain, dairy, livestock, cotton and oil production. Southward cotton remains supreme, although the tendency is toward diversification. As the terrain flattens onto the coastal prairies, vast ranches whose one modern note is an occasional oil derrick remain the undivided estates of families whose titles reach back to Spanish and Texas Republic grants. Cowboys sometimes patrol these great domains in automobiles, but round-ups retain the same aspects, and neither wealth nor change in style can remove the big hats, boots and spurs from the everyday attire of the ranchmen.

In average warm, rainy spring seasons the coastal prairies along US 77 have several carpets of wild flowers, beginning with bluebonnets, changing then to white and finally to yellow daisies. In years of normally abundant rainfall, high grass ripples in waves over the flat or gently rolling pastures, where often not a tree or bush appears for miles. Great oaks and pecans line the banks of streams, and at intervals are thickets of mesquite and huisache—the latter golden with blossoms in March.

Section a. OKLAHOMA LINE to DALLAS; 79 m. US 77

This section of US 77 is through the Blacklands Belt, a region of rolling prairies given over to farming, livestock raising, dairying, and oil development. Along this way came Moscoso, successor of De Soto. A few miles upstream, on the Red River, has been determined the site of an early French trading post. The lumbering wagons of the forty-niners creaked along a trail laid out by Army explorers, and the Butterfield Stage Line later followed the same route. With the railroads came steady growth and development.

This part of the State was once the stamping ground of Sam Bass, the outlaw, who bought a horse—later known in song and story—from a trader in Denton:

> Sam used to deal in race stock, one called the Denton mare,
> He matched her in scrub races, and took her to the Fair.
> Sam used to coin the money and spent it just as free,
> He always drank good whiskey, wherever he might be.

Near the end of the section, numerous fossil beds (*on private property; permission from owners necessary*), occur in sands and alluvial deposits. Fossils found since 1887 include the skulls and other bones of 13 elephants, remains of a sea lizard 37 feet long, bones of a sabre-toothed tiger, Pleistocene horses, and other creatures of antiquity.

US 77 crosses the OKLAHOMA LINE, 0 *m.*, on a steel bridge across the Red River, 33 miles south of Ardmore, Okla. (*see Oklahoma Guide*).

GAINESVILLE, 8 *m.* (730 alt., 14,500 pop.), in a broad valley of the Elm Fork of the Trinity, has a shady residential area notable for its many flower gardens. Business houses are largely of brick. Established as a frontier settlement along the route of the gold seekers of 1849, California Street follows the course of their old trail through the heart of the town. In 1858 the Butterfield Stage Line made Gainesville one of its stops. Later the town became a base of supply for cowboys driving herds of Texas longhorns up the Dodge City cattle trail.

During the Civil War the community suffered from Indian raids and depredations by organized bands of Jayhawkers. The citizens took matters into their own hands, hunted down 200 supposed Jayhawkers, tried them summarily and hanged 40 of them, 19 in one batch.

Gainesville, seat of Cooke County, is a center for cotton, grain, live-stock, poultry and oil. It has a natural gas refining industry. In recent years oil production in the County has helped its economy. The city has a lively business area, is served by the Santa Fe Railway and Continental Trailways, and has a Municipal Airport.

A distinctive feature of Gainesville's civic life is its community circus, established in 1930. Members of the cast are residents who work without pay and outfit themselves. Equipment is designed and built by volunteer workers. Judges, lawyers, bankers, school teachers, druggists, doctors, merchants, clerks, oil field workers, and school children, their ages ranging from 6 to 60 years, take part as trapezists, tumblers, acrobats, clowns, and in every other circus capacity. Two shows are given annually, usually during the summer.

GAINESVILLE JUNIOR COLLEGE, established 1924 by the city, enrolls about 350 annually. GAINESVILLE STATE SCHOOL FOR GIRLS is at the northeastern edge of town. The Southwestern Diabetic Foundation operates Camp Sweeney.

In Gainesville is a junction with US 82 (*see Tour 3*).

DENTON, 39 *m.* (620 alt., 26,844 pop., 1960; 30,117, est. 1966) is located at the junction of Interstate 35E (to Dallas) and 35W (to Fort Worth). It is the southern terminal of State 99 and served east-west by State 24, and to the west by US 380. It is an agricultural, livestock and educational center.

Denton has the first UNDERGROUND CONTROL CENTER of the Office of Emergency Planning and Office of Civil Defense, Dept. of Defense, regional headquarters for five states.

The Chamber of Commerce announces: "More than 300 Denton residents have earned Ph. D. degrees." NORTH TEXAS STATE UNIVERSITY, opened 1890 as Denton Normal School, enrolls more than 10,000 students annually and has a building program that will cost $10,000,000 in ten years. Its library has more than 400,000 volumes. In athletics the Eagles compete in the Missouri Valley Conference and use a 20,000-seat stadium. It is a member of the Interuniversity Council of five, which includes the Texas Woman's University of Denton and institutions in Dallas and Fort Worth. NTSU is especially strong in scientific research.

TEXAS WOMAN'S UNIVERSITY, formerly the State College for Women, enrolls up to 4,000 annually and offers training for a wide variety of careers. It has a 220-acre campus and more than 60 buildings. All offices are held by students and the Cooperative Dormitory System for inexpensive living calls for each occupant to devote one hour a day to household duties. The Little Chapel in the Woods is popular for weddings and much visited by tourists. It maintains a College of Nursing at Houston.

TEXAS AGRICULTURAL EXPERIMENT STATION, 4 miles northwest of Denton, is part of Texas A. & M. University System. Denton County raises cotton, corn, wheat, oats, grain, sorghum, peanuts and hay. Dairy products are worth $3,500,000 and agricultural and livestock bring in $18,000,000 annually.

Since 1959 Denton citizens have developed a new campus with installations costing $9,000,000 for DENTON STATE SCHOOL, 1,750 students, an institution for the mentally retarded. The SELWYN SCHOOL, a nondenominational kindergarten-through-high school private institution, occupies a 100-acre campus.

LAKE DALLAS, 48 m. (581 alt.), a cluster of oak-shaded stores and homes, is a recreational community on the western shore of Lake Garza-Little Elm.

LAKE GARZA-LITTLE ELM, also known as LAKE LEWISVILLE, and formerly called Lake Dallas, part of the Dallas water supply, is impounded by Lewisville Dam on the Elm Fork of the Trinity River, covers 38,900 acres and has a top storage capacity of more than 1,000,000 acre-ft. The dam is 11,000 ft. long and 30 ft wide at top.

The main street of LEWISVILLE, 54 m. (484 alt., 6,000 pop.), cuts across US 77, with most of the brick business section at the left. Its industries make building materials. It is popular as a residence for Dallas commuters. South of town 2 m. State 121 leads to GRAPEVINE (650 alt., 3,750 pop.) and LAKE GRAPEVINE, 2 m. north, covering 12,750 acres and holding 435,500 acre-ft. of water.

In this area in 1843 Sam Houston, President of the Republic of Texas, camped while attempting to negotiate with north Texas Indian chiefs for a treaty designed to keep the Indians from joining with Mexico in a war on the young Republic. The chiefs failed to appear, but the treaty was later signed at Bird's Fort, 15 miles westward.

Southward US 77 parallels the lush bottom lands of the Trinity River, heavily wooded except where fruits, berries, vegetables, cotton and corn are grown. Roadside stands sell fruit and cider, and there are many tourist lodges and stores catering to the fisherman's needs.

The site of the headquarters office of PETERS COLONY is at 66.5 m. Here in the 1840s the Texan Emigration Land Company, of Louisville,

Kentucky, settled about 1,000 people. Nothing remains except the old graveyard at Webb's Chapel.

DALLAS, 79 *m*. See article on Dallas.

IRVING, (470 alt.) on State 183 and 356, adjoining Dallas on the west, is a suburb that has had a phenomenal rise in population. The 1950 census found 2,621 living along the Rock Island Railroad, in a town platted in 1902. Ten years later the census counted 45,985. In 1967 the Texas Almanac estimated a population of 86,100. There are numerous industries, but many of the residents commute to Dallas.

Section b. *DALLAS to WACO; 99.7 m. US 77–81*

US 77 continues through the fertile Blacklands region where the chief business is farming and the chief crops are cotton, corn, and small grains. Settled largely by Southern planters, this area was early established as a cotton-producing empire reaching far across the Brazos, east and west. Close-knit, self-sufficient villages developed. Goods roads have served as a common denominator in changing each community to resemble its neighbor; larger towns have become the center of social and commercial activity. White tenantry decreased in the 1930's with reduced cotton acreage, and many Negroes moved away because mechanization lost them their jobs.

Southwest of DALLAS, 0 *m.*, the UNITED STATES VETERANS HOSPITAL has a plot of 244 acres at 6.3 *m*.

Covering a valley, WAXAHACHIE, 30 *m*. (530 alt., 12,749 pop., 1960; 15,000 1965 est.) seat of Ellis County, is part of the Dallas metropolitan area and has many commuters who work in Dallas. It is one of the largest primary cotton markets in Texas, in the heart of an agricultural region noted for its heavy production of this crop.

. A textile mill utilizes the lower grades of locally produced cotton in the manufacture of duck and other heavy materials. The town's industries also include cottonseed oil mills, a cotton compress, a fiberglas plant and poultry processors.

During the Civil War a powder mill was operated by the Confederate government in Waxahachie, but a terrific explosion ended the enterprise early in 1863. The site is marked.

TRINITY UNIVERSITY, Presbyterian, co-educational, founded in 1869, was located here for more than eighty years until 1952, when it was reestablished in San Antonio. The TEXAS BAPTIST HOME FOR CHILDREN is now located here.

In the vicinity of Chambers Creek, 41.2 *m.*, small game hunting is excellent.

ITALY, 45 *m*. (576 alt., 1,183 pop.), is a thriving market center. During the Civil War a hat factory was operated for the Confederate government at a point one mile north of where the town was later established.

Several lakes in this vicinity afford excellent fishing.

Southwestward the terrain roughens somewhat as the watershed of the Trinity and Brazos Rivers is approached. Farms in this area are usually as large as the owner and his family can cultivate; help is hired only in harvesting season. Cotton and corn cover the tilled acres, with enough small grain or hay crops to feed the stock; a tiny garden, a few hogs and a cow or two are usually included. Electrification of farm homes has added greatly to the comforts and living standards of rural life.

HILLSBORO, 64 m. (634 alt., 7,823 pop.), is in the center of a large cotton growing area. There is about the town an air of dignified old age and church-going respectability. Its industrial aspect is created by a textile mill, cotton gins, asbestos-cement plant, furniture factory. The streets surrounding the courthouse are used as a farm market, the first Monday in each month being Trades Day, when the rural population swarms to town. Much of the trading is horse swapping.

The limestone courthouse in the center of the square is a far cry from Hill County's first edifice of justice—an elm pole structure with a dirt floor and no desks or chairs. The first case was tried with the litigants, judge, jury, and spectators seated on the floor or standing against the walls. The present building stirs controversy.

At the southwest corner of Line and Harris Sts. stands the HARRIS HOUSE, the oldest structure in the community, occupied in 1940 by descendants of the builder. Tradition says that a Comanche chief was killed beneath a tree that still stands in front of this house; he bore the mouth-filling name of Hollow-Hole-in-the-Air.

At the northern edge of Hillsboro is HILLSBORO LAKE PARK, with swimming, fishing and cabin facilities.

In Hillsboro is a junction with US 81 (see Tour 8).

Right from Hillsboro on State 22 to WHITNEY, 12 m. (585 alt., 1,050 pop.). Seven miles SW of Whitney is the huge LAKE WHITNEY, covering 49,710 acres in Hill and Bosque Counties, holding 2,017,500 acre-ft. of water. LAKE WHITNEY STATE PARK is a most popular fishing, swimming, camping and general recreation area.

The dirt road continues northward to old FORT GRAHAM, 23 m. This frontier post was established in 1849 on the site of the Indian village of José Maria, and was abandoned in 1853. Crumbled ruins and foundation outlines are all that remain.

At 94.7 m. is the junction (L) with a bypass route.

Right (straight ahead) on the main routes of US 77 and 81, Interstate 35, is WACO, 2.3 m. (427 alt., 107,500 pop., est.) (see Waco).

At 95.5 m. is the junction with US 84 (see Tour 21).

At 99.7 m., is the southern junction of the bypass route with the main tour routes of US 77, 81, and 84 through Waco. Here US 81 (see Tour 8) diverges to the southwest, US 84 (see Tour 21) branches sharply west (R), while US 77 leads almost due south.

Section c. *WACO to SCHULENBURG; 141 m.* US 77

US 77 emerges from the level black land prairies into a rolling area of sandy soil broken by many small watercourses whose banks are usually well-timbered.

Along the first part of this section the fields are white with cotton in August, and trucks piled high with singing workers and with hard-packed bales crowd the highways. These hands have many superstitions focusing on two subjects important to them: cotton and snakes. According to their deep-rooted beliefs, the following things are true: If a young man sits on a bale of cotton with his legs crossed, he will be blessed with many children. . . . Good luck comes to those who make love while they are picking cotton. . . . Wherever a whirlwind drops a cotton boll, there you will find money. . . . Always pick the first boll of cotton that opens in the field, carry it home, put it over the front door, pick out the seeds of the boll and plant them under the back doorstep. You will get good prices if you do this, but woe if you do not.

Snake stories include many that tell of a victim having been charmed by a rattlesnake, and of "friendly" rattlers that persist in becoming the companions of certain people or animals.

Near the end of the section, in rural communities south of La Grange, is the oldest center of Czech settlement and culture in Texas. These people have largely become Americanized.

South of WACO US 77 proceeds to CHILTON, 18 m. (425 alt., 884 pop.), an agricultural supply center and shipping point. While drilling for oil, in 1924, a Swede named Myrin struck hot artesian water at a depth of 2,709 feet. Flowing at a natural 75-pound pressure, the water is piped and distributed throughout the town.

Left from Chilton on State 7 to MARLIN, 11 m. (383 alt., 6,918 pop. in 1960; 9,394 1964 est.). About 1891, when one of the major problems facing Marlin was an inadequate supply of soft water, a drill at 3,350 feet struck a great pool of hot water that shot 75 feet over the derrick. The well continued to flow 380,000 gallons daily, supposedly unfit for anything, and a ditch was dug to carry the flow to Big Creek. According to local tradition a tramp, suffering from eczema, each night bathed his arms and legs in the hot water of the ditch. His recovery was so prompt and complete that he told his story to local people and a two-room bathhouse was built. Later a larger bathhouse was erected, and thus began the now famous baths, sanatoria, hospitals, and clinics of Marlin. Two other wells were drilled in 1909; their output is used largely in the manufacture of mineral crystals. Marlin's institutions of healing are many.

At the Bluebonnet Photo Festival, usually held annually the last week in April, prizes are given for pictures of bluebonnets in bloom taken that week.

At the northern edge of LOTT, 24 m. (522 alt., 921 pop.), is a small lake (*fishing 50¢ a day*).

Left from Lott on the Lott-Marlin Road to the FALLS OF THE BRAZOS (*camp sites, fishing, picknicking*), 6 m. Here is the SITE OF SARAHVILLE DE VIESCA, founded by Sterling C. Robertson before the Texas Revolution, and named in honor of his mother and the governor of Coahuila and Texas. Indian troubles doomed the settlement to a short life.

The highway widens to become the main street of ROSEBUD, 35 *m.* (392 alt., 1,644 pop.), its narrow sidewalks flanked by brick business houses. Long, wide porches and broad lawns distinguish the residential area.

Rosebud lives up to its name, claiming at least one rose bush in every yard in the community. Its citizens are chiefly of Czecho-Slovakian and German extraction, and are engaged in large-scale farming and ranching in the vicinity.

CAMERON, 52 *m.* (402 alt., 5,640 pop.) seat of Milam County, which in 1836 took in one-sixth of Texas. Captain Ewen Cameron was a pioneer cowboy. Statue of Benjamin R. Milam at Court House honors patriot who died 1835 fighting Mexicans. Center for farm products, cattle, peanuts.

ROCKDALE, 69 *m.* (462 alt., 4,481 pop.), is a community of wide, tree-lined streets and weathered buildings; the town has a general air of indolent contentment. The chief industries are oil refining and cottonseed processing; Rockdale is also one of the largest lignite-shipping points in Texas. Strip mining is used to obtain lignite. Industries include an aluminum plant.

LEXINGTON, 87 *m.* (456 ft., 711 pop.) is a farm village.

GIDDINGS, 103 *m.* (520 alt., 2,821 pop.) is at the junction with US 290 (*see Tour 24*).

LA GRANGE, 124 *m.* (272 alt., 3,623 pop.) is the seat of Fayette County, named for Marquis de la Fayette. It has some old houses built by planters who developed cottonfields. Moore's Fort was a blockhouse owned in 1828 by Col. John H. Moore, whose house, 9 miles north of La Grange, dates from 1838. Indian depredations harassed the settlers, and Moore led several expeditions against them.

During the Texas Revolution fighting men from the La Grange vicinity performed gallantly on nearly every field of the war. They had been at Velasco in 1832, and it was Moore who in 1835 defied the Mexican commander at Gonzales, and is said to have inspired the challenge, "Come and take it," in reference to the cannon that the Mexicans demanded. Men from La Grange also fought with Sam Houston at San Jacinto, and Joel W. Robinson, who lived within a few miles of La Grange, was one of the captors of Santa Anna.

Captain Nicholas Dawson organized a company of 53 men under a great live oak which still stands in La Grange, and marched away to annihilation at the hands of General Woll's invading army at the Battle of Salado. Captain William M. Eastland was among the men of La Grange and Fayette County in the ill-fated Mier Expedition, and was one of 17 Texan prisoners who drew the fatal black beans at Salado, Mexico.

Beneath the same oak, flag presentation exercises took place with the organization in La Grange of a Confederate company. The old tree also saw the gathering of those enlisting for the Spanish-American War in

1898, and from under its branches marched the La Grange contingent on its way to Camp Bowie in 1917.

At 127 *m.* is a junction with State 167.

Right here to MONUMENT HILL, 1 *m.,* where, on a bluff overlooking a great bend of the Colorado River, a tomb of gray Texas granite shelters the remains of those who died with Dawson near San Antonio, and of 16 of the 17 men who drew black beans at Salado. The remains of the last-named were recovered in Mexico by General Walter P. Lane of the Texas Rangers, escorted to La Grange by Captain Quisenbery, and interred. The present tomb was dedicated September 18, 1933, on the eighty-first anniversary of their burial at Monument Hill. A tall memorial shaft overlooks the tomb.

South of La Grange is the house N. W. Faison, survivor of the Dawson massacre, built in 1866. Over rolling open country, the highway winds across a landscape of groomed neatness; out-buildings are sturdy, the barns sometimes finer than the big, roomy white frame homes. This is a region of German and Czech farmers who often join in dancing the polka and the *Beseda.* Sometimes there are plodding oxen in the fields; the next farm may have a tractor. The love of these people for their land is reflected in spick-and-span premises.

SCHULENBURG, 141 *m.* (344 alt., 2,207 pop.) is at the junction with US 90 (*see Tour 23*).

Section d. SCHULENBURG to SINTON; 146 m.; SINTON to BROWNSVILLE; US 77

The section of US 77 is through the highly productive Coastal Plain, a region of broad sweeping prairies, well-watered and fertile.

Along much of this section the people are of German descent, and have neat, prosperous farms and big dairy, poultry and other similar businesses. South of Victoria, cattle and oil have created one of the richest small areas of Texas. Irish immigrants, of Roman Catholic faith, many of them political exiles, came to these prairies in 1828–29. Their cabins were burned by Indians, their crops were destroyed by droughts, and, finally, many of their men were killed by the Mexican army of 1836. But these sturdy folk endured, and founded a clannish, devout society based upon the ownership of land. Cattle made them rich, then oil was found, and many of them disliked this upset in their system of landed aristocracy. Today their children attend exclusive schools, and they have big automobiles and trips to Europe—but the most important thing still is the tradition handed down by their religious, hard-playing and hard-fighting forefathers who never forgot Old Erin.

South of SCHULENBURG, 0 *m.,* Mixon Creek is crossed at 11.2 *m.* Here, according to tradition, a family of German settlers was murdered by three Negro employees. The murderers were hunted down by a posse, returned to the scene of their crime, hanged, and their bodies riddled with bullets. It is told that when the corpses had been reduced to well-bleached skeletons a resident cut one of them down and from the bones fashioned himself a set of keys and a tailboard for his violin. According to the legend the instrument ever afterwards possessed a wonderful tone of weird, haunting quality.

In HALLETTSVILLE, 17 m. (232 alt., 2,800 pop.), descendants of German and Polish immigrants comprise a large part of the population. The town has a distinctive atmosphere of rural isolation and benign antiquity. Drab buildings of brick and gray stone, with outmoded exteriors and old-fashioned high-ceiling interiors, face the courthouse square. Automobiles are plentiful, but until recently farm wagons and buggies were still often seen and the clatter of horses hoofs is still heard. Even an ox team is common enough not to attract more than a passing glance.

Around Hallettsville persists one of the legends of the Lost Dutchman's Lead Mine. According to the tale, a Dutchman who lived on the Lavaca River sold lead to the settlers for making bullets. The source of his supply he kept to himself. He was found dead, and although circumstances indicated suicide the rumor was that he had been murdered because he refused to tell the location of the lead mine.

At 33 m. is a junction with a concrete-paved road.

Left here to YOAKUM, 1 m. (322 alt., 5,656 pop.), an urban community in the midst of rolling prairies. It has a marked industrial aspect, due to a large leather tannery, railroad shops, and several factories. The town is on the line between Lavaca and DeWitt Counties, a fact which has created several peculiar situations, such as that of a school in which the teacher sits in one county while her pupils sit in another.

Yoakum was founded in 1887 on a league of land granted to John May, of Ireland, in 1835. The area became a concentration point for great herds of cattle about to be driven up the long trails.

At an annual harvest celebration, the Tomato Tom-Tom, Yoakum becomes gay with carnival attractions. The date varies slightly with the opening of the tomato season, but is usually around the first of June. In April three tours with guides follow the Wild Flower Trail during two weeks.

CUERO, 51 m. (177 alt., 7,250 pop. est.) seat of DeWitt County, processes cotton, turkeys, meats, other poultry. The Texas longhorns were bred in this area and moved to New Orleans as early as 1842. The Chisholm Trail reputedly started here.

The town received its name from the creek on which it is located. This creek, called *Arroyo del Cuero* (Creek of the Rawhide), was so named because of its exceedingly boggy banks in which wild cattle and buffaloes, seeking water, became mired and unable to extricate themselves. Mexicans and Indians killed the helpless beasts chiefly for their hides, which were a medium of exchange.

In the vicinity of Cuero occurred the numerous bloody incidents of the Taylor-Sutton feud. Beginning in 1869, with the killing of Buck Taylor, member of a prominent ranching family, and one of his kinsmen, this incident embroiled the county in factional warfare until 1876. Men were killed in their fields, on the roads, and in their homes. There were shootings and hangings in all sections of the county, and many citizens were aligned with one faction or the other.

Among the few neutrals was Judge H. Clay Pleasants, who tried to bring peace to his community. At first he argued; then, alone, he faced large armed parties of both factions with a shotgun and ordered them to go home. He bluffed them that time, but they soon broke out again and the feud went on. Even after there was no Taylor or Sutton as leader of the respective parties, it continued.

Cuero used to be famous for its Turkey Trot. This was a spectacle of thousands of turkeys marching down the main street, headed by a trumpet corps and a band, and followed by the gaily decorated floats of the "Sultana" of the festival and her attendants. It was the turkeys' big day, and for most of them their last, as the majority of the birds were taken immediately to the pens of the large packing plants to be killed, dressed, and shipped to all parts of the country. But turkeys are bred for weight and when the parade harmed them, the event was called off.

Although Cuero is one of the largest turkey-shipping centers in the State, that industry is secondary to the handling and shipping of the huge cotton crops of this fertile lowlands region.

In Cuero is a junction with US 87 (*see Tour 17*).

VICTORIA, 79 *m*. (93 alt., 33,047 pop., 1960; 36,700, 1965, est.) known for its attractive public square, and the profusion of roses in its gardens and parks, is rich in romantic history. In 1685 the doomed La Salle crossed the region, and in 1721 the Spanish established a fort and mission in the locality. Later (1824) a group of Spanish settlers under Don Martin de Leon established the colony that was to develop into the Victoria of today.

Victoria is a busy commercial center, shipping cotton, cattle, starch and petroleum products. Its intersecting highways are US 77, 87, and 59, and State 185. Victoria County Airport on US 59 is served by Trans-Texas Airways. Ball Airport served local planes. Victoria reaches the Gulf Intracoastal Waterway by the Matagorda Ship Channel and the new Victoria Barge Canal. Major industries include Du Pont, Alcoa, Union Carbide, and National Starch. A Youth Rodeo takes place late in August.

During its early years Indian raids were frequent. Despite Mexican laws barring them, Anglo-American settlers entered the region and took an active part in local events of the Texas Revolution. General Urrea made headquarters at Victoria after Fannin's surrender (*see History*).

With the influx of German immigrants in the 1840's, much of the aspect of the town changed from Spanish to Colonial German. Settlers from earlier Anglo-American communities had drifted to Victoria, and the village population became a medley of several races. In 1846 the town experienced a terrible cholera epidemic, during which victims died so rapidly that they could not be buried properly, and were hurriedly dumped into shallow excavations in a common burying ground, the present Memorial Square.

Victoria preserves a number of buildings of historical and architectural interest. The McNamara-O'Connor Historical and Fine Arts Museum, in a white southern colonial building of 1869, has antique furniture

and documents. The Robert H. Clark House was washed off its founda-
tions at Indianola in a great storm of 1875, then rebuilt in Victoria.
Handhewn pine and oak timbers were brought from New York for the
Callender House. The Denver Hotel is notable for its long veranda. In
Memorial Park stands the Dutch Grist Windmill, erected in Goliad with
grinding stones brought from Germany before 1860; moved to Colletto
Creek near Raisin; rebuilt in 1870 at Spring Creek. In 1935 it was moved
to its present site as an exhibit.

Victoria citizens have approved a bond issue of $800,000 for the con-
struction of a new County Building. The Courthouse of 1892, with architecture of the period, is to be preserved.

The site of La Salle's Fort St. Louis is said to have been discovered on
the Keeran Ranch, 19 miles southeast of Victoria. Remains of the Spanish
presidio and church, the PRESIDIO NUESTRA SEÑORA DE LORETO DE LA
BAHIA (Fort of Our Lady of Loretto of the Bay) and the MISSION
NUESTRA SEÑORA DEL ESPIRITU SANTO DE ZUNIGA (Mission of Our
Lady of the Holy Spirit of Zuniga) are 13 miles north of town. The
mission and the fort were established here in 1726 on their second location
(see Goliad, Tour 25). Both sites are on private property and almost
inaccessible, but directions can be obtained at the Chamber of Commerce
in Victoria.

Cattle, grazing on the wide salt meadows around the town, are still
Victoria's main source of revenue. Cotton is the leading crop. Recent oil
developments have been extensive, although the antipathy of some of the
wealthy ranchers of the region to having their fields and pastures "messed
up with smelly oil," with resultant refusals to lease to oil companies, has
amazed promoters.

Several large Indian mounds are in the vicinity.

VICTORIA COLLEGE, Junior, founded 1925, enrolls more than 1,500
students annually in its regular and summer courses.

Southwest of Victoria the highway crosses the mile-wide valley of the
GUADALUPE RIVER, a well-forested area with a virgin growth of
giant oaks, pecans, and cypresses, many of which are canopied with wild
grapevines and somberly festooned with Spanish moss.

At 82 m. is a junction with US 59 (see Tour 25).

Oil wells and pumping stations are visible from the road at 120 m. as
the route traverses the Refugio oil field.

REFUGIO, 122 m. (50 alt., 4,944 pop.), dignified and old, enjoys
the stimulus of recent oil developments. It is the seat of Refugio County,
which prospers from oil, beef cattle, grain and cotton production. Pipe
lines carry oil from the Refugio area to deep-water port facilities at Aransas Pass.

Despite its modernized appearance and atmosphere, Refugio was
founded in 1790 when Franciscan monks built MISSION NUESTRA SE-
ÑORA DEL REFUGIO (Mission of Our Lady of Refuge), which was first
destroyed in wars between Karankawas and Comanches, and later bom-
barded by the Mexican army in 1836. A chapel was fitted up in the ruins
in 1840, but this and the debris of the mission were removed in 1860. The

mission first served Karankawas and Copanoes. Later it housed a garrison for the protection of the port of El Copano from pirates and smugglers.

In 1829 Irish colonists, under a grant issued to James Power and James Hewetson the preceding year, began coming to Refugio. The municipality was established in 1834, and in August of that year the Pueblo of Refugio was founded.

During the colonization era the ruins of the mission housed the land offices, and at that time a small chapel was restored. General Cos made his headquarters in the mission while on his way to Bexar in 1835. In January, 1836, General Sam Houston maintained headquarters here while he argued the assembled Texas soldiers out of starting on the so-called Matamoros Expedition. Colonel James W. Fannin, Jr., established headquarters here a month later on his way to Goliad, and on the mission grounds his regiment was formed and officers elected.

Following the fall of the Alamo, settlers at Refugio were exposed to the wrath of the victorious Mexicans, and Colonel Fannin sent Captain Amon B. King with 20 men to their relief. On March 12, 1836, King was confronted by a large Mexican force and took refuge in the mission. He sent to Fannin for reinforcements, and on March 13, Lieutenant Colonel William Ward and his Georgia Battalion arrived. Then next morning, when King marched down the river to burn certain ranch houses, the entire command of General Urrea surrounded the mission, where Ward barricaded himself. He successfully withstood four furious attacks, and at midnight cut his way through the cordon of Mexican troops and made his escape. Later he was overtaken at Dimmit's landing on the Lavaca River and his entire command captured, to be shot soon afterward in the Fannin tragedy at Goliad (*see Tour 25b*). King and his command were also captured and returned to Refugio, where they were sentenced to death, and about 31 men, including a few stragglers from Ward's command, were shot. The site of their execution is about one mile north of the mission, in Sunshine Addition. The Mexican army occupied the mission as a hospital until after San Jacinto. In 1841–42 the mission walls were again used as a refuge by local citizens during Mexican invasions, when all men of the village who offered resistance were hanged, and others were taken to Mexico and held prisoners for months.

A charter issued in 1842 by the Republic of Texas is still in force.

South of Refugio on US 77 is the WELDER WILDLIFE REFUGE. More than 400 species of birds have been observed here.

In KING'S STATE PARK, formerly the *Plaza de la Constitution,* opposite the courthouse, is the KING MONUMENT, erected in honor of Captain King and his men.

At the southwestern edge of town, on the north bank of the Mission River, is the SITE OF THE MISSION, now occupied by a Roman Catholic church. In the churchyard hang two bells, dated 1751, said to have been taken from the mission during the days of the Texas Revolution and later returned.

WOODSBORO, 127 *m.* (48 alt., 2,081 pop.), is surrounded by large ranches.

Left from Woodsboro on a paved road to BAYSIDE, 12 *m.* (308 pop.), a resort community on Copano Bay and within a mile of the old town of SAINT MARY'S, once an active port of entry situated northeast along the bay shore. Only half a dozen houses and the old cemetery remain. Saint Mary's, founded in 1840 by Joseph Smith, served as a port for nearly half a century, and through it passed many of the settlers who entered Texas in the early days of statehood; here were unloaded quantities of lumber for the building of new settlements. Here also were shipped thousands of head of cattle. In 1862 Federal gunboats landed troops who sacked the town and then sailed away.

Ten miles farther along the bay shore are the ruins of EL COPANO, which can best be reached by boat from Bayside. Shortly after the re-location of the mission and presidio of La Bahia in 1749, the port and customhouse of El Copano came into being. Half a century later it was of sufficient importance and wealth to attract the attention of pirates and smugglers of the Gulf, and a garrison at the mission at Refugio was established for its protection. In 1829 it served as the port of entry for Irish colonists who settled Refugio and San Patricio. Cholera swept the little port and many of the seekers after new land found it in sandy graves along the beach. General Cos landed his army there in 1835, but shortly thereafter the town was seized by Texans and used as a port of entry for volunteers who flocked in from the United States. With General Urrea's advance and his success at Refugio and Goliad, the Mexicans again occupied the port and established a garrison. Knowing nothing of the change, Major William P. Miller landed his company of Nashville Volunteers, who were promptly captured and marched to Goliad, but having been taken without arms they did not suffer the fate of Fannin's men. A town grew up at Copano in 1840, but was abandoned in 1880. Only ruins, old concrete cisterns, and the sea-battered piling of wrecked wharves remain.

SINTON, 146 *m.* (49 alt., 6,000 pop.) has a junction with US 181, which terminates at Corpus Christi (*see Tour 26*). US 77 proceeds south about 25 *m.* inland from the Coast, through the great ranching counties of Nueces, Kleberg, Kenedy, and Willacy.

ROBSTOWN, 168 *m.* (85 alt., 12,500 pop., est.) is a center for truck farming and oil supplies. Named for Robert Driscoll, as was DRISCOLL, 178 *m.* (650 pop.) Six *m.* south Ranch Road 70 runs east to the Chapman Ranch.

BISHOP, 175 *m.* (59 alt., 4,000 pop. est.) is a center for petrochemical plants.

KINGSVILLE, 181 *m.* (66 alt., 26,905 pop. est.) junction with State 141, which connects west with US 281. Seat of the great King Ranch. Captain Richard King and Captain Mifflin Kenedy developed two great ranches in Kleberg and Kenedy Counties.

RIVIERA, 192 *m.* (40 alt., 1,000 pop. est.) Gulf waters enter Baffin Bay, a few miles east of Riviera.

SARITA, 198 *m.* (34 alt., 200 pop.) seat of Kenedy County and ranch trade center. Named for the granddaughter of Mifflin Kenedy. Mifflin Pens, in vicinity, is approx. center of Kenedy Ranch, of which more than 500,000 acres are said to be fenced in. Kenedy financed 700 miles of the San Antonio & Aransas Pass Railroad. Other ranch headquarters are Armstrong, Morias and Rudulph. There are only 13 ranches in the 7,878 sq. m. of Kenedy County, which has gained 471 sq. m. by the Tidelands act of 1953, extending its authority 10.35 *m.* into Laguna Madre.

RAYMONDVILLE, 249 *m.* (40 alt., 10,200 pop. est.) is the seat of Willacy County and has connections with Port Mansfield, 23 *m.* east on Laguna Madre, via State 186, which runs west and connects with US 281.

HARLINGEN, 270 *m.* is at the junction with US 83, which joins US 77.

BROWNSVILLE, 296 *m.* Terminus of US 77.

Ic+Ic+Ic+Ic+Ic+Ic+Ic+Ic+Ic+Ic+Ic+Ic+Ic+Ic+Ic+Ic+Ic+Ic+Ic+Ic+Ic+Ic+Ic+Ic+Ic+Ic+

Tour 8

(Ryan, Okla.)—Fort Worth—Waco—Austin—San Antonio—Junction with US 83—(Laredo) ; US 81.
Oklahoma Line to Junction with US 83, 498 *m.*

Three of the major cities of Texas are along the route—Fort Worth, important grain and cattle market; Waco, wholesaling, jobbing and educational center; and San Antonio, romantic, historic, tourist city.

Near its end, US 81 traverses the Winter Garden area, where thousands of acres of irrigated lands produce winter vegetables. Many a northern and eastern schoolboy has reason to know Winter Garden spinach.

Section a.   *OKLAHOMA LINE to FORT WORTH; 90 m.*
US 81

This section of US 81 is through a region that was traversed by two important pioneer routes, the California Emigrant Trail, and the Butterfield Stage Line course. Here was the northern end of the first line of defense, established by the United States Government following the annexation of Texas, against the Indians of the West. The first settlers were ranchmen, and cattle was all they had; today, prosperous farms and ranches combine cotton, grain and truck crops with diversified livestock production.

US 81 crosses the OKLAHOMA LINE, 0 *m.*, in the middle of the bridge across the Red River, 11 miles south of Ryan, Oklahoma.

RINGGOLD, 4 *m.* (890 alt., 415 pop.), has a junction with US 82. Southward the way is through rolling, hilly pasture lands. Coffer dams, built to impound water for livestock, are visible at intervals.

BOWIE, 23 *m.* (1,135 alt., 5,738 pop. est.) has been changing from farm products to metal and clothing industries and natural gas plants. US 287 joins US 1 at Bowie, leaves it at Fort Worth. Bowie in early days was known as the "chicken and bread town," because when trains wheezed in, the passengers could purchase delicious fried chicken sandwiches.

A white leghorn poultry farm, reputedly one of the largest in the world, is L. at 24 *m.* (*open; apply at office*). The plant consists of 350 acres and 150 buildings.

FRUITLAND, SUNSET and ALVORD are farm villages on US 81 between Bowie and Decatur.

CARTER LAKE, 1,540 acres, 6 *m.* south of Bowie, on Big Sandy Creek, is the town's water supply.

DECATUR, 51 *m.* (1,097 alt., 3,563 pop.), spreads over a hill and is the seat of Wise County. The town is the leading shopping and shipping center for the surrounding agricultural and dairy region. Here is DECATUR BAPTIST COLLEGE, coeducational, founded 1892, enrollment approximately 124 during two terms. The Waggoner Mansion, built 1870, is a castle-like stone structure. The WISE COUNTY MUSEUM is the newest attraction here.

Right from Decatur on State 24 to BRIDGEPORT, 11 *m.* (754 alt., 3,218 pop.). The closing of nearby coal mines has somewhat slowed the tempo of Bridgeport's normally animated existence. Brickyards and rock-crusher plants are among its industries.

Left from Bridgeport 4 *m.* to LAKE BRIDGEPORT (*fishing, swimming, camp sites*), a large body of water impounded by the Bridgeport Dam and the Berkshire Levee. The dam is 1,850 feet long, and together with the 3,500-foot levee, will hold 285 billion gallons. Bridgeport sponsors an annual free tournament at the opening of the fishing season, with prizes for the largest bass and crappie taken each day.

RHOME, 66 *m.* (934 alt., 450 pop.) a farm town.

MEACHAM FIELD (R), 87.8 *m.*, is one of Fort Worth's airports, handling air mail, passengers, and express.

FORT WORTH, 90 *m.* (670 alt., 390,500 est. 1967) (*see Fort Worth*), is at the junction with US 80 (*see Tour 19*).

Right from Fort Worth on State 199 to LAKE WORTH, 9 *m.* This lake, created by impounding the waters of the West Fork of the Trinity, was completed in 1916 at a cost of $1,000,000. The maximum lake area of 3,267 acres has a potential storage capacity of 33,660 acre-feet, drained from a 200-mile watershed. Adjacent to the lake is a 2,779-acre park controlled by the city park department. A $2,500,000 irrigation system was designed by the Tarrant County Water Control and Irrigation District No. 1, to serve 28,000 acres below the lake, extending toward Dallas.

EAGLE MOUNTAIN LAKE, 14.5 *m.*, 10 miles long by approximately a mile and a half wide, is the second of three lakes created by dams on the West Fork of the Trinity River, a part of the irrigation and navigation system designed to assure Fort Worth an adequate water supply, control flood waters, and provide water for irrigation. The lake is unusual in that the retaining system consists of a main dam and a levee entirely separate and some distance apart. The project was completed at a cost of $3,250,000. Eagle Mountain Lake is stocked annually by the State Game, Fish and Oyster Commission with various fresh-water fish native to the State. The Fort Worth Boat Club has its home on the east side of the lake and regattas are held at intervals from late spring until late October (*free*).

Section b.   FORT WORTH to WACO; 92.7 m.   US 81; Interstate 35

This section of the route is over parts of the Blackland and Grand Prairie belts, across level to gently rolling prairies. Cotton, corn, truck and fruits are the largest crops; livestock is increasing. Interstate 35 W joins Interstate 35, from Dallas, a few miles north of Hillsboro.

Throughout this region are many Negroes, chiefly concentrated in Waco. In the Brazos River Valley, in this vicinity, many customs are primitive. To cure rheumatism, a string dipped in turpentine is tied around an ankle. Since the last one in a graveyard is believed to be the next one fated to die, funerals often end in a mad scramble. To ward off disaster following a funeral, the chief mourner picks up seven little stones from the dirt that came from the grave; these stones are tied in a handkerchief, the parcel is wet with tears, slept on nightly, and one stone a day is discarded; this is guaranteed to console the bereaved and to speed the deceased along his way.

South of FORT WORTH, 0 *m.*, Deer Creek (*camping and fishing 25¢ a day*), is crossed at 12 *m.* In this section a high-crowned pavement necessitates caution in wet or icy weather.

ALVARADO, 27 *m.* (693 alt., 1,907 pop.), drowses six days a week, but comes to sudden life on Saturdays. Its town square, lined with brick business buildings, is a circular park usually abloom with old-fashioned flowers. The early-day home of William Balch here was called the Sprawler Hotel, because his many guests sometimes had to sleep on pallets in the front yard. The first school in Alvarado had a stout, eight-foot log fence around it to keep the pupils at play from being trampled under the hoofs of passing north- and west-bound herds of cattle.

In Alvarado is the junction with US 67 (*see Tour 18*).

Passing through small fields, US 81 penetrates a region where mechanized farming has been slow in application. Farm work often enlists the help of the farmers' wife and children.

ITASCA, 45 *m.* (704 alt., 1,439 pop.), is a neat attractive community whose present-day industrial activity centers around a textile mill.

HILLSBORO, 56 *m.* (621 alt., 7,823 pop.) Hill County, is at the junction with US 77 (*see Tour 7*), which unites with US 81 for 36.7 miles (*see Tour 7b*) to Waco (*see Waco*).

At WACO, 92.7 *m.*, are junctions with US 84, US 77, and State 6, 31 and 164.

Section c.   WACO to SAN ANTONIO; 178 m.   US 81; Interstate 35

This section of US 81 trends southward through a prairie farming belt to the eastern edge of the Texas hill country. Here, where the Balcones Fault and the Edwards Plateau divide the countryside partially into hills and deep, rich, black land valleys, goats and sheep graze the uplands and cotton, grains, fruits and truck crops are produced on lower levels. Through south central Texas the route penetrates oak-studded pastures, touching Austin, State capital and educational center, and the historic German settlement of New Braunfels, passing San Antonio, circled by Franciscan missions. Interstate 35, which parallels US 81, follows the old Chisholm Trail in part of the route.

TEMPLE, 32 *m.* (630 alt., 30,419 pop., 1960; 34,000 1965, est.) on the main lines of the Santa Fe and the M-K-T railroads, is an industrial and distributing center with a climate considered especially beneficial for respiratory ailments. It was founded in 1880 by the Gulf, Colorado & Santa Fe Railroad and named for its chief construction engineer. In 1882 the M-K-T arrived and railroad shops were located here. In 1891 the GULF, COLORADO & SANTA FE RAILROAD HOSPITAL was erected and has served the system ever since. Other large facilities are the KING'S DAUGHTERS' HOSPITAL, and the large SCOTT-WHITE MEMORIAL HOSPITAL AND CLINIC, founded in 1904. The McCLOSKEY VETERANS ADMINISTRATION CENTER, with 800 beds, treats military veterans for respiratory diseases.

The temperature averages 67° and 32.95 inches of rainfall annually. July and August have registered some extremely hot days.

Here are State hq for the U. S. Conservation Service and the State Soil Board. The home of two Texas governors, Jim and Miriam Ferguson ("Pa and Ma"), is preserved here. TEMPLE JUNIOR COLLEGE enrolls about 1,000 students annually. TEMPLE LAKE PARK, 172 acres on Lake Belton, is a recreation area 10 *m.* from the city. Northwest of Temple on State 36 is the site of the Bird Creek Battle, May 26, 1839, in which the Rangers routed Chief Buffalo Hump. South of Temple on State 436 is the site of FORT GRIFFIN.

BELTON DAM AND RESERVOIR, on the Leon River 9 *m.* west of Temple, impound 210,000 acre-feet of water normally and can hold 887,000 acre-feet during floodtime. In 1934 Frank W. Mayborn, Temple editor, began an energetic campaign to get fresh water. In 1948, when the dam was begun and in 1954 when it was completed the speaker was Senator Lyndon B. Johnson. It cost $13,000,000, and supplies 13 parks with recreational facilities. A residential project with marina is developing at Morgan's Point on Lake Belton.

Southward are stretches of woodland, pasture land, and cultivated fields. Somewhere in this vicinity Captain S. P. Ross killed a famous Indian Chief, Big Foot, in a hand-to-hand encounter. One of the several stories as to why the famous frontiersman William Alexander Wallace was called Big Foot credits the nickname to his desire to kill this Indian.

In BELTON, 41 *m.* (511 alt., 9,300 pop.), dignified old homes and weathered stone business buildings blend with the natural growth fringing the valleys of the Leon River and Nolan Creek; the latter flows through the town.

The old jail building on N. Pearl St., witnessed a tragic event in

1874, when nine men, eight charged with horse stealing and one with wife murder, were seized by a mob and shot to death. The building now houses a beauty shop.

MARY HARDIN-BAYLOR COLLEGE, a Baptist institution for women, has a 375-acre campus. Baylor-Belton, as the college is called locally, is one of the oldest institutions in the State, having been founded as the Primary and Female Department of Baylor University in 1845 at Independence. It was removed to Belton in 1886. Average enrollment is 900 students.

South of Belton marched the Aguayo expedition of 1721. Other Spaniards searched this area for gold and silver, and in inaccessible spots the mine shafts are still visible.

West from Belton on US 190: 9 m. NOLANVILLE; 17 m. KILLEEN (830 alt., 30,000 pop. est. 1966). Killeen was a small farm village until 1942 when the U. S. established FORT HOOD adjoining it on the west. It had 1,263 pop. in 1940; 23,377 in 1960, 29,500, 1966, est. It is served by the Gulf, Colorado & Santa Fe Ry., and Southwestern and Arrow Bus Lines. On its eastern limits is HARKER HEIGHTS (2,600 pop. est.) incor. 1960. Killeen is the birthplace of Mrs. Oveta Culp Hobby.

FORT HOOD covers 322 square miles in Bell and Coryell Counties (207,000 acres). It is hq for the III U. S. Army Corps, now Strategic Army Corps; also of the 1st Armored Division (Old Ironsides) and 2nd Armored Division (Hell on Wheels); the 1st Logistical Command and the 4th Army Language Training Facility. Normally 36,000 troops and 4,000 civilian employees are active, while 8,800 Army families live in the area. The Government spends about $108,000,000 and collects about $3,000,000 in taxes from the troops annually (1965). Darnell Army Hospital, a $6,000,000 center, was opened in 1965.

KILLEEN BASE, 6 m. west of Killeen on US 190, is a Defense Atomic Support Agency covering 8,894 acres, under Army control. ROBERT GRAY ARMY AIRFIELD is 8 m. west. Capt. Gray was one of the Tokyo air raiders and died later in a plane accident.

At 26 m. on US 190 a farm road leads 1 m. to COPPERAS COVE (4,567 pop.); 29 m. KEMPNER; 41 m. LAMPASAS.

Along the banks of the LAMPASAS RIVER, 45 m., are prehistoric dwellings, Indian burial grounds and kitchen middens.

STILLHOUSE HOLLOW RESERVOIR on the Lampasas River, 5 m. southwest of Belton, was built by the U. S. Corps of Engineers and the Brazos River Authority (Waco), began filling September, 1967. The earthfill dam is 15,350 ft. long, rising 200 ft. The reservoir covers 204,900 acre-feet normally and 390,600 acre-feet for flood control, total 630,400, and will cover 11,830 acres. Cost $21,000,000 (est.)

SALADO, 50 m. (350 pop.) was founded 1859 by General Sterling C. Robertson. The STAGECOACH INN includes the restored Shady Villa Inn, built 1860. Opposite is the CENTRAL TEXAS AREA MUSEUM (*open Monday through Saturday, 10–6; Sunday 1–6*). The burned ruins of Salado College, estab. 1860, are on a hill. Opposite is the Robertson House, built 1856.

Salado in November plays host to the Scottish Clans of Texas and has the Tartan Banner Parade.

JARRELL, 59 *m.* (547 alt., 1,000 pop.), is a community of Czechs who have preserved many of their racial customs. Neighbors gather to prepare goose feathers for bedding to be given newly-married couples; when the feathers have been stripped from their stems, the hostess serves a feast. On Christmas Eve, one youth will dress as St. Nicholas, another as an angel, a third as the devil, and as they question the children, St. Nicholas rewards the obedient ones, while Satan administers a few light blows to the less worthy. In rural sections of this region young boys dip all the girls in water on the Saturday night before Easter. Czech national dances, including the *Beseda,* are performed, especially on festival days.

GEORGETOWN, 73 *m.* (750 alt., 5,218 pop.), is dominated by buildings mellow with age; stone and weathered pine houses are shaded by oaks, hackberries and cedars. An industrial trend is manifest in cotton gins, cottonseed oil and grain mills. There is a junction with State 29.

Its status as an educational center is maintained through SOUTHWESTERN UNIVERSITY, a co-educational Methodist school, occupying a large campus with buildings chiefly Georgian in design. The predominant university units are of white limestone, reinforced concrete and brick, and are three stories high. Southwestern was established in 1873 by the Methodist Episcopal Church, South, when the students of four earlier schools were taken over. These were Rutersville (1840), McKenzie (1841), and Wesleyan (1844) Colleges, and Soule University (1856), the latter a direct forerunner of the present institution, which for two years was called Texas University. Enrollment is approximately 800.

SAN GABRIEL PARK, on San Gabriel Lake, formed by damming the San Gabriel River, affords recreational facilities (*fishing, picnic grounds*). This area—on the Balcones Fault—has an unusual water supply that bursts through limestone formations in clear, gushing springs to feed San Gabriel Lake. Under Interstate 35 is COBB CAVERN.

The quiet, shady town of ROUND ROCK, 82 *m.* (709 alt., 1,878 pop.), seems much like an old person sitting quietly beside the highway, ready to tell a story. And it has one to tell.

In 1878 Round Rock took its place in the list of famous Texas towns because of an incident that terminated the career of Sam Bass, notorious outlaw celebrated in song and story. For years Bass and a gang of bandits, varying in numbers, rode the brush trails of Texas, robbing banks, holding up trains, stealing horses, and raiding isolated ranches and settlements. A captured member of the gang was prevailed upon by Texas Rangers to turn traitor, and was released in order that he might rejoin the gang and aid in trapping them. When Bass planned to rob the bank at Round Rock, the informer got word to the Rangers.

On the day appointed Bass, with three men, entered Round Rock. They tied their horses and walked down the street past the bank building. Bass was about to make a purchase in the general store when a deputy sheriff and another peace officer entered and questioned him. Sensing a trap, the outlaw chief drew and fired. The deputy fell. Bass, continuing to fire, moved toward the door, while the outlaws with him also went into action. The other officer was shot. Reaching the street, the bandits were met by the pistol fire of Texas Rangers and citizens, and one of them fell; but Bass and his remaining companion backed down the street, shooting as they went. Return fire blazed from the store windows and doors.

Just as the outlaws reached their horses, Bass slumped to the ground. His companion dragged him upright, lifted him into the saddle, untied the horses and led the wounded leader through a heavy fire out of town into the brush. The next day Bass was found lying mortally wounded beneath a tree.

In Round Rock is the junction with US 79 (*see Tour 20*).

AUSTIN, 101 *m.* is at the junction with US 290 (*see Tour 24*).

St. Edwards University is L. at 104 *m.* (*see Austin*).

SAN MARCOS, 131 *m.* (581 alt., 14,445 pop. est., 1965) is a center for industry and recreation, making cotton-seed oil, furniture, meat processing and wool scouring.

The seat of Hays County, it was settled about 1846, the town site being laid out on a league of land purchased by William Lindsey and General Edward Burleson. The town took its name from the earlier settlement of San Marcos de Neve, established at the Camino Real Crossing of the San Marcos in 1808 and abandoned in 1812.

On a stony hillside a few hundred feet above the headwaters of the San Marcos River, one mile northwest of town, are the remains of the old log cabin HOME OF GENERAL EDWARD BURLESON (*open; free*), which he occupied from 1847 until 1851. Here also has been erected a monument in honor of the general.

About 1858 a criminal case was transferred from Travis to Hays County, and the defendant, failing to appear for trial, forfeited a $2,000 bond. With this money the first Hays County courthouse was erected.

The community is a popular pleasure resort, with cabins along the river and several moderately priced hotels. The San Marcos River emerges about a mile northwest of the city from a fault line where huge springs pour a subterranean stream from the foot of a cliff into the river bed. A steady flow of clear, cold water is unfailing, and the capacity of the largest spring is estimated at 98,000,000 gallons every 24 hours. Along the river are many caves and several parks. The vicinity is also rich in plant life, specimens of which are sought by botanists. San Marcos Springs is an important industry.

Here is the AQUARENA, a tourist attraction near the Aquarena Springs Motor Hotel, a feature of which is the Submarine Theatre, which, with 150 spectators, is lowered in a lake for underwater entertainment. Also available are a sky ride and Texana Village, reproduction of a pioneer town.

A descent into the WONDER CAVE enables visitors to inspect the Balcones Fault, 150 ft. below the surface.

SOUTHWEST TEXAS STATE COLLEGE, located on a 28-acre tract on

Austin St., has its major buildings of brick or reinforced concrete, of modern mixed architecture. A demonstration farm adjoins the campus, making available extensive facilities for dairying and poultry raising. The college has an annual enrollment of about 4,500, with 2,000 in the summer.

Here also are the SAN MARCOS BAPTIST ACADEMY and the BROWN SCHOOL for exceptional children.

NEW BRAUNFELS, 148 *m.* (644 alt., 15,631 pop., 1960; 17,000 est., 1965) seat of Comal County, retains many picturesque houses erected by Germans who settled here after 1845. It calls itself the Beauty Spot of Texas, but also has been publicized as the Sausage Capital of the World, and Wurst Week, the first week in November, commemorates its distinctive product. The Smoke House is one of its industries. Textile, hosiery and flour and feed mills flourish. The Chamber of Commerce says New Braunfels has the "largest per capita payroll in Texas," meaning practically everybody works profitably, as did their German forebears.

New Braunfels added a colorful chapter to the history of Texas. A spick-and-span neatness and a wealth of quaint old houses create a distinct and faintly Old World atmosphere. Here the quixotic Prince Carl Zu Solms-Braunfels, for whom the city is named, established a German settlement in 1845 and, surrounding himself with a retinue of velvet-clad courtiers and soldiers who wore brilliant plumes in their cocked hats, amazed the matter-of-fact Texas pioneers with his magnificence. The Prince was commissioner-general for the Society for the Protection of German Immigrants in Texas, an association of noblemen which undertook to place a great number of colonists. Before the enterprise was well under way the officers of the company discovered that the land they had accepted for colonization was no longer available, as the contract had been canceled. The Prince met a group of immigrants at Carlshafen, later to be called Indianola, headed inland and finally located on the Comal River. He purchased the site of the town, two leagues of land, from Rafael and Maria Veramendi Garza, of San Antonio, for the sum of $1,111. About 200 immigrants founded the town on Good Friday, March 21, 1845.

On a high hilltop where he could command a view of the country for miles around, the Prince built his fort. Lacking a German flag, he raised the flag of Austria above the building and called it Sophienburg, in honor of his "ladye." The Texas flag was also raised. Here he lived for a short time in great style. When he received Indians he appeared in the full dress uniform of the Austrian Army, of which he was an officer.

The followers of the Prince could not adapt themselves to the wilderness, and lack of training resulted in great privations and hardships. There was much suffering during the first years of the settlement. Prince Carl resigned his post and returned to Germany following the annexation of Texas in 1845, leaving New Braunfels even before John O. (Baron von) Meusebach, his successor, arrived.

Approximately 5,000 Germans were landed at Indianola within the next seven months, but no means of transportation from the port to the colony was available. A contract made with teamsters was broken because the outbreak of the war with Mexico led to higher-paying army contracts. The colonists were poorly housed at Indianola and soon exposure and hunger brought on an epidemic of a disease that has not been clearly identified. Scores died and in desperation hundreds of others attempted to walk from Indianola to New Braunfels. Weakened, and without sufficient supplies, a great many more died on the way. "The trail from the coast town to the colony was lined with German graves." Those who survived to reach New Braunfels brought the pestilent fever with them, and it spread rapidly through the community. "Two or three died in New Braunfels each day." The total number of deaths from the epidemic, as reported by various authorities, differs greatly, but it was certainly more than 800 and may have been 3,000. Because of suffering and privation many of the settlers, disheartened and broken in spirit, left the town. Meusebach resigned his post in July, 1847. The company continued to administer the affairs of the community until 1853, when an assignment of rights and properties was made to Texas creditors.

One peculiar celebration held annually, on or about April 25, is the Children's Masquerade. This event, introduced in 1864, has been preserved with all its picturesque features. School children dressed in fanciful costumes dance on the public square and in the downtown streets, then parade to the Comal County Fair Grounds, where a children's masked ball is held.

New Braunfels contains what is said to be the shortest river carrying a large volume of water in the United States, the Comal, which rises at Comal Springs and empties into the Guadalupe. With its source and mouth both within the city limits, the Comal's winding course is only about four miles, yet it is deep, clear and full-running. A striking feature of the river is the luxuriant growth along its banks of giant caladiums, whose broad, shield-like leaves add a tropical note to the scenery. The abundant water supply adjacent to New Braunfels is utilized by means of several dams. A $5,000,000 plant supplies electric current to San Antonio and other cities, and to numerous industries. The town's recreational facilities and tourist accommodations are excellent and the surrounding area affords many scenic drives.

On the site of the Sophienburg stands the SOPHIENBURG MEMORIAL MUSEUM.

LANDA PARK, a recreation center now inside the city, contains the springs of the Comal River.

NATURAL BRIDGE CAVERNS, filled with impressive rock formations, halls and pools and a canyon 250 ft. below the surface. State 46 to Farm Road 1863 and 12 m. southwest. (*Open 9 a.m. to 5 p.m. daily; adults, $2, children, $1.50.*)

CANYON LAKE, formed by Canyon Dam on the Guadelupe River, 18 m. northwest of New Braunfels, is 15 m. long, covers 12,890 acres and has a capacity of 740,900 acre-ft. Canyon City is a settlement at the foot of the dam, which is 4,410 ft. long, 224 ft. tall.

162.5 m. (US 81) SELMA, a small German town. At 164 m. is a junction with State 218.

Left on this road to RANDOLPH FIELD, 3.5 m., termed the West Point of the Air, one of the largest military airdromes in the world. Here are the primary and basic flying schools of the Air Corps, U. S. Army, in which all aviators received training until 1938, when more bases were established.

The site was donated by citizens of San Antonio through the San Antonio Airport Corporation when the legality of the city's purchase of it was questioned. This corporation raised $60,000 to obtain options on the land, the city pledging back-tax money to the banks, which advanced $600,000 to the corporation for the purchase. Construction began in October, 1928, and the field was dedicated June 30, 1930, and named in honor of Captain William Randolph, former post adjutant of Kelly Field, who was killed in an airplane crash in 1928.

Randolph Field is a complete city within itself, with its own utilities, post exchange, shops, stores, and recreational facilities. It has a resident population of more than 3,000, of whom about 1,700 are army personnel. The reservation, improved at a cost of $10,400,000, is approximately two miles square and so planned that the building area, which now includes 475 acres, may be expanded symmetrically as needed.

The grounds have been artistically landscaped, with tree-lined boulevards and drives separated by strips of green lawn and attractive beds of flowers. The colorful effect is further enhanced by the bright, red-tiled roofs of the one- and two-story officers homes in the circular residential section, where a Spanish type of architecture has been consistently employed.

The ADMINISTRATION BUILDING, of Spanish treatment with panels of Moorish design, and with a tower 175 feet high, is directly south of the main entrance, the key structure of the field and an excellent base for orientation by visitors. The powerful beacon of this tower can be seen by pilots for a distance of 50 miles. South of the administration building is the officers club, a well-appointed recreation center, from which radiate streets as from a hub, with parallel circular drives around it. To the left of the main entrance boulevard is the post chapel where services of all denominations are held. This also follows the Spanish motif. The post exchange, consisting of three wings with a patio in the center, is an octagonal building across the boulevard from the chapel. The field hospital housed the first School of Aviation Medicine, which formulated the original procedures to train medical officers of the Regular Army, National Guard, and Organized Reserves in the practice and duties of flight surgeons. By studying large numbers of students in close contact with the exacting requirements of the service, they gradually built up standards that reduced the number of student failures and overcame handicaps. Randolph AFB today is headquarters of the Air Training Command and of the 4th Reserve Region, Continental Air Command, and specializes in pilot instructor training, and map training.

Surrounding the circular area, auxiliary buildings are grouped in a larger square, including shops, hangars, barracks, and lesser structures. The latest facilities for military flying are embodied in the fields adjacent to the central grouping, enabling hundreds of airplanes to take off or land almost simultaneously. The force is housed in officers homes, two forty-apartment bachelors quarters, non-commissioned officers quarters, and modern barracks for enlisted men and flying cadets. The academic building, near the cadet barracks, has classrooms where ground instruction is given, and is equipped with a radio laboratory and a technical library.

In 1942 Lackland Air Force Base, 9 m. southwest of San Antonio, was designated San Antonio Aviation Cadet Center and basic training of all recruits in the area was transferred there. Besides courses in flying there is instruction in allied subjects useful to airmen. Therefore Lackland is now known as the Gateway to the Air Force.

ALAMO HEIGHTS, 174.5 m. (7,000 pop.) (see San Antonio).

SAN ANTONIO, 178 m. (656 alt., 699,768 pop., est.) (see San Antonio), is at junctions with US 281 (see Tour 9), US 90 (see Tour 23), US 87 (see Tour 17), US 181 (see Tour 26), and State 16 (see Tour 17A).

Section d. SAN ANTONIO to JUNCTION WITH US 83; 137 m. US 81

US 81 continues across gently undulating plains covered with thorny growths, the famous brush country of south Texas. This is still a region of vast uninhabited reaches, where cattle raising is the main industry and agricultural efforts are principally confined to small sections where artesian irrigation is possible.

Here prickly pear is often so abundant as to form an impenetrable undergrowth in the chaparral. Until the pear burner was invented it was a menace to the pasture lands of the area, crowding out the succulent range grass. During winters and extended droughts, cattle fed on the leaves and beans of the huajillo, the soft brittle stems of the white brush; they nibbled at the hard pulpy leaves and stems of the Spanish dagger and, best of all, the thorny, but juicy, leaves of the prickly pear, for which they had a great fondness. The pear burner, which operates on the principle of a large blow-torch, enables the ranchers to burn off the thorns so the cattle can feed freely. The searing flame causes the thorns to disappear as if by magic, and wise old cattle "come a-runnin' " when they hear the familiar roar of the burner.

Hidden in mesquite and huisache thickets near the end of the route are small *jacales* occupied by Mexicans who cherish old customs. These humble people also "live at home"; small patches of beans and corn, a few chickens and goats, furnish their simple needs. On All Souls Day these isolated folk come out of the brush in antiquated conveyances, or go afoot to the nearest cemetery, there to join in all-day "visiting with the dead." Graves are cleaned, and are often adorned with cherished articles, such as a string of dime-store beads or a gay platter; the work finished, *tortillas* are heated on an open fire at the graveside, and while the children play, old friends gossip and young men pay court to their sweethearts.

South of SAN ANTONIO, 0 *m.,* is a junction with the Quintana Road, 4.5 *m.*

KELLY AIR FORCE BASE, the great repair and supply center for military aircraft, is located about 5 *m.* south of San Antonio. It is headquarters of the San Antonio Air Materiel Area and although a Federal installation is called the largest industry in San Antonio. It employs 18,-000 to 20,000 civilians in its massive aircraft repair and maintenance shops, and the impact on the local economy is formidable. Activities include the complete overhaul, maintenance, and modification of piston-driven and jet planes, rehabilitation of engines, and repair of intricate electronic equipment and accessories such as radar, radios, and electronic firing. Kelly also has a complete machine and sheet metal shop capable of manufacturing aircraft parts not readily available from private sources.

Of the thousands employed here, the largest number, 7,580, is in administrative clerical, and technical white collar work. Of craftsmen, 1,527 are engaged in electronic equipment installation and maintenance, and 1,159 in electrical installation.

Before Kelly Field was designated as the chief maintenance center, Duncan Field was the repair depot. Its excellent shops were made a part of Kelly AFB in 1943. Kelly has several facilities not connected with repair work, such as the USAF Security Service, but these are minor beside its big task of rehabilitation. Of special interest is the nation's largest airplane hangar, covering 24 acres.

Kelly Field was established in April, 1917, after the United States had entered the war against Germany. It was named for Lieutenant George E. M. Kelly, who died in a plane crash at Fort Sam Houston in 1911. Although only four planes were available when Kelly Field was opened, by December, 1917, there were 1,100 officers and 31,000 men training there. After World War I Kelly Field was an air service mechanics school, later called Air Corps Flying School. Up to the second

World War cadets and student officers who had finished primary instruction at Randolph Field were sent to Kelly for four months of final training and specialization.

LACKLAND AIR FORCE BASE adjoins Kelly Field on the west, 9 *m*. southwest of downtown San Antonio. It has been so named since July, 1947, to honor the late Brigadier General Frank D. Lackland, one-time commander of Kelly AFB. All basic training of recruits in this area has been transfered to Lackland AFB, so that it has become known as the Gateway to the Air Force. In 1942 it was designated the San Antonio Aviation Cadet Center and a great number of the aviators of World War II here received their first training.

Lackland AFB has available an area of 2,818 acres and its usual population is from 28,800 to 30,000. Its training facilities include a Technical School, with a curriculum that covers much more than flying. There are also courses in languages, secret communications, and security arrangements. In one section dogs are trained for sentry duty. The Personnel Research Laboratory is a part of the Aerospace Medical Division.

Visitors may obtain passes for admittance at the main gate. Of special interest is the museum of aircraft equipment ranging from the earliest types used in World War I to the latest designs in engines. A Spad VII is one of the relics (*open weekdays, 10–5*).

NATALIA, 29 *m*. (686 alt., 1,154 pop.), has made no effort to crowd within a small civic area. A fringe of business houses borders the highway, from which roads wind out to widely scattered dwellings hidden in the mesquite. Natalia is the headquarters of Medina Irrigated Farms, Inc. The surrounding region is known for its large production of vegetables. Truck farms are irrigated from the waters impounded by Medina Dam (*see Tour 17A*), and canning is the leading industry.

Right from Natalia on a dirt road to CHICON LAKE, 3.5 *m.;* L. here 0.5 *m.* to a recreational area (*obtain fishing permit at Improvement District offices in Natalia*).

Southward, the route traverses slightly rolling country covered with thick growths of mesquite, huajillo, and huisache. That the route is nearing an area of much Mexican population is shown by the highway signs in both English and Spanish.

PEARSALL, 55 *m*. (641 alt., 4,957 pop.), crowds its one-story business area close to the highway. Red sandy streets lead to frame residences, and in many yards are orange trees. This is the northernmost town of the Winter Garden district and the home of the annual Winter Garden Fair. There are 600 producing oil and gas wells on proration in Frio County. The town markets livestock, peanuts, watermelons, pecans, grains, vegetables and honey.

DERBY, 63 *m*. is a farm center of nominal population.

The brush country around Pearsall provides excellent deer hunting in season, and javelinas, or wild hogs, are plentiful. Turkeys, quail, doves, and squirrels abound. Bobcats and pumas which prey on livestock can be hunted at any time.

FRIO STATE PARK (*fishing for catfish, perch, and drum*), 65.9 *m.*, a 51-acre recreational area, is at the confluence on the Frio and Leona Rivers. Here occurred a battle between settlers and Indians on July 4, 1865. Members of the Martin settlement were attacked while enjoying a picnic. Rallied by Captain Levi English, they repulsed the Indians, but the battle so discouraged the settlers that they abandoned their town.

Southward the highway passes through typical brush country. In this region was born the State's great cattle industry; early ranchmen developed the methods by which the Texas cowboy evolved as a distinct type. It was a rough school, and riding the brush in search of wild longhorn cattle was a tough job. Here the prickly pear grows higher than the head of a mounted man, and here also grows every type of thorny vegetation known to the Southwest; the catclaw, huajillo, agarita, *vara dulce,* amargosa, rat tail cactus, Spanish dagger, and the shunned *junco,* which Mexicans of the region believe was woven into Christ's crown of thorns. Riders of the brush country wear heavy leather "chaps," duck jackets, and a wide *sombrero* with a strap under the chin.

DILLEY, 70 *m.* (586 alt., 2,118 pop.) a farm marketing center, is at a junction with State 85. Watermelons contributed so greatly to its prosperity that it raised a monument to the watermelon.

MILLETT, 76 *m.,* is a small farm center.

At COTULLA, 88 *m.* (442 alt., 3,960 pop.), wide streets and new business houses fail to alter an atmosphere of the old West; here are cattlemen in big hats and boots, and cow ponies are tied to hitching posts at the railroad parkway. It is the seat of LaSalle County.

Cotulla in the early days was a community where gunplay was frequent and killings more or less commonplace. The town was so tough that railroad conductors announced it something after this fashion: "Cotulla! Everybody get your guns ready." The recorded death toll was three sheriffs and 19 citizens. Elections usually called forth a display of arms, one faction holding the polls with drawn guns and sending word to the opposition to "Come and vote right or fight."

In the vicinity of Cotulla was staged what is said to have been the largest round-up of wild mustangs ever conducted in Texas. More than a thousand were driven out of the brush and into the opening of two wide-flung wings which narrowed to the entrance of a 50-acre pole corral. The animals so captured went to fill a contract with the Argentine government.

Indian raids were frequent in this section in the early days, and from them arises the story of the capture of two children, a boy and a girl, in 1871, the escape of the little girl the same day, and then their reunion years later in San Antonio. The girl, grown to womanhood, met her brother, then one of the Indian contingent of Buffalo Bill's Wild West Show and known only as Two Braids.

W. S. Porter (O. Henry) lived for a time on a ranch near Cotulla and was a frequent visitor to the town. Old-timers still remember him as a boy who wanted to be a top hand, and who rode a clay-bank pony into town to get his mail.

Welhausen Elementary School, a plain two-story red brick building, is now historical because here Lyndon B. Johnson taught his first class.

South of Cotulla the highway crosses the NUECES RIVER (*free camp sites, L*).

ARTESIA WELLS, 99 *m*. (440 alt., 150 pop.), is named for the source of water supply from deep-flowing wells which irrigate a large district specializing in the cultivation of Bermuda onions. This town is a cluster of small houses around a filling station. The railroad still calls it by a former name, Bart.

Right from Artesia Wells on a dirt road to EL RANCHO LUIZ (*deer, duck, dove, and quail hunting in season; pumas, bobcats, and wolves can be hunted at any time*), 10 *m*., a dude ranch where, on a 90,000-acre range, guests can ride with the hands who care for thousands of head of cattle.

ENCINAL, 116 *m*. (575 alt., 925 pop.) has a junction with State 44 (east to Corpus Christi) and in 1967 was reached by Interstate 35 moving north from Laredo.

At 137 *m*. is the junction with US 83 (*see Tour 16*), 18.5 miles north of Laredo (*see Laredo*).

❧❧❧❧❧❧❧❧❧❧❧❧❧❧❧❧❧❧❧❧❧❧❧❧❧❧❧❧❧

Tour 9

Wichita Falls—Mineral Wells—San Antonio—Alice—Brownsville; 631 *m.*, US 281.

Bisecting Texas almost equally, US 281 runs between the State's northern and southern boundary streams—the Red River and the Rio Grande. It traverses several large natural divisions including, in turn, the north part of the Central Plains, the Grand Prairie, the Balcones Escarpment and the Coastal Plain. Level to rolling regions of the northern area rise sharply in the wooded Edwards Plateau section between Mineral Wells and San Antonio. Then the terrain flattens again to become fertile prairies that slope toward the Gulf of Mexico—grassy plains dotted with acres of citrus groves and miles of planted palm trees, but devoted largely to pastures of vast proportions, where there is nothing taller than an occasional oil derrick or mesquite tree.

Through varying types of soils and climate, cotton is the big cash crop along this section; beef cattle constitute a time-honored basis of wealth; other sources of income are as diversified as petrified wood, pecans, granite and butter. Several counties of the region traversed rank high in Texas in the raising of corn, small grains, livestock and dairy products. Toward the south, where the large ranches are swept by the breezes of the Gulf, the glossy green foliage of citrus trees and the orange and yellow of their fruits annually make a bright winter picture, and provide an extensive industry.

People of the north central area are traditionally agricultural; those of the hills and Coastal Plain engage principally in ranching. An interesting social study is presented by the Mexicans, including a tenant farmer group in the central section, and the much discussed, little known *vaqueros* of the southern region.

Section a. *WICHITA FALLS to MINERAL WELLS; 89 m.* US 281

This section of US 281 traverses one of the State's most productive agricultural regions. Here soldiers and Texas Rangers once fought bitterly to protect the settlements that were encroaching on the hunting grounds of Indians.

Oil has enriched much of the first part of this section; but wheat and cotton—both of which are often produced in fields irrigated by means of canals from storage projects, or from home-made earthen tanks—have created the larger proportion of common wealth. Since the 1840's ranching has flourished, and today more than half the land is devoted to diversified livestock production. But pioneer farmers who struggled against drought and the ravages of prairie dogs and rabbits have won a rich reward, and as a result of general prosperity have built many pleasant little towns.

Sturdy descendants of immigrants—of Norwegian, Polish, German, Austrian and other European stock—till many of the fertile acres. There are roomy farm houses, big barns, fat dairy herds, a few goats and sheep and much poultry. Constant warfare is waged by these people against the greedy mesquite trees that constantly encroach upon their cleared lands.

As the route approaches Mineral Wells, stock farming increases; much of the livestock is pure-bred. An abundant growth of several kinds of prairie grass is augmented by the production of small grains. More than half this land is tilled by means of tractors.

A quickly changing panorama of prairies, hills, woodlands, clear lakes and streams, and miniature cities with large school buildings and many churches, characterizes this part of Texas.

WICHITA FALLS, 0 *m.* (946 alt., est. pop. 1964, 109,500) (*see Wichita Falls*), is at junctions with US 82 (*see Tour 3*), US 287 (*see Tour 13*), and US 277 (*see Tour 10*).

Broad hills and wide valleys encircle WINDTHORST, 24 *m.* (500 pop.), a spotless little town of rock houses perched around a hill. From the hilltop a Roman Catholic church building lifts a tall clock tower, visible for miles. This community is composed of descendants of German immigrants who founded a town here in 1891.

Southward US 281 passes through lands once owned by the great Circle Ranch. Hereford cattle graze here, on smaller pastures.

GAP MOUNTAIN is R., 34.5 m. Here thick growths of mesquite and oak have encroached on the highway.

In ANTELOPE, 36 m. (1,205 alt., 166 pop.), many houses are of rough lumber, have adobe chimneys, and are enclosed by split rail fences; smoke houses and barns are of logs. In contrast is a modern school building. Antelope was once a supply point on the cattle trail leading north from this area; the cowboys watered their herds at Antelope Springs, just east of the town.

Southward are low, steep hills, and the valleys—narrow and fertile— are dotted with truck gardens and fields of small grains.

Downstream from the highway crossing of CAMBERON CREEK, 44 m., the Cambren and Mason families were attacked by Indians in 1859, only two of the Masons escaping. The creek's modern name is a corruption of Cambren.

At 45 m. the highway enters LOST VALLEY, scene of an Indian-Ranger encounter in 1875. Here a brave and a squaw, separated from the main band, were surrounded by Rangers, and the warrior—though mortally wounded—fought to the last, even rising to his knees to swing with clubbed rifle as the white men closed in. The squaw had blue eyes and brown hair, and was believed to have been a white girl captured by Indians when a child; but she could speak no English and remembered nothing of previous associations.

Throughout this region, goat ranching and turkey production are leading industries.

Lacy mesquite trees shade the green lawns of JACKSBORO, 58 m. (1,074 alt., 3,960 pop.), where weathered yellow stone buildings predominate, some of them dating back to 1867 and the establishment of near-by Fort Richardson. Jacksboro has a variety of business enterprises, including a flour mill, a rock crushing plant, and an oil refinery.

In the center of town is the Jack County courthouse, erected in 1939 on the site of an old courthouse in which occurred the murder trial of two Kiowa chiefs in 1871. Satanta, Big Tree, and Satank had led a band of Kiowas in a particularly brutal attack on an army wagon train, and had overwhelmed the 12 teamsters, killing six and capturing one who had been wounded.

Five teamsters escaped and carried news of the attack to Fort Richardson. Satanta had boasted of being the leader. On the way to Jacksboro for trial he rushed his guards and was shot and killed. The other two Indians were tried and sentenced to be hanged; this sentence was later commuted to life imprisonment, and still later both chiefs were paroled. Satanta broke parole, returned to raiding and killing, was again captured, and leaped to his death from the upper window of a prison. Big Tree devoted his later years to missionary work among the Indians.

At the southern edge of Jacksboro is the site of a Butterfield stage station. At 59.3 m. is a junction with a dirt road.

Right here to FORT RICHARDSON, 0.4 *m.* The mile-square area of the former reservation contains many of the old limestone buildings. Some have been repaired and are in use; one, used once as the hospital building, houses a library and a museum of historical lore. The fort consisted of about 40 buildings, and was one of the more elaborate frontier army posts. It was abandoned by the Government in 1878. A 40-acre park surrounds it.

SW of Jacksboro on State 24, 27 *m.* to GRAHAM (9,500 pop., est. 1965) seat of Young County. Graham markets farm, ranch and oil products and is the gateway to a lake recreation area. Graham Lake, 2 *m.* nw of Graham, fed by Flint and Salt Creeks, covers 2,550 acres and connects by a canal with Eddleman Lake, 6,100 acres.

OLD FORT BELKNAP, estab. 1851, abandoned 1867, partly restored, is 10 *m.* nw of Graham on Farm Road 61. It has a museum and a recreational park, open daily except Fridays, 9 a.m. to 5 p.m.

OLNEY (4,300 pop.) is in the northeast corner of Young County.

South of Jacksboro the highway crosses a sparsely settled, hilly section, and emerges on a high, level stretch of prairie land which produces grains and native prairie hay for forage.

On the banks of KEECHIE CREEK, 72 *m.,* occurred another Indian depredation—the killing of two boys who were hauling water, and the capture of two others who were held for ransom.

Southward US 281 crosses what is locally called DILLINGHAM PRAIRIE, which in 1847 was the pasture of the Dillingham Plantation. The Dillinghams had come to this frontier territory from the Deep South. Their numerous slaves built a manor house of the plantation type, with slave quarters and many outbuildings. The venture was unfortunate. Indians drove off the stock, enticed the slaves away or killed them as they worked in the fields, and at last raided the plantation house. Although the attack was repulsed the owners were disheartened and pulled up stakes.

US 281 descends into valleys between beautiful PALO PINTO HILLS, sliding down from high, flat prairies to wind through the so-called breaks that form these elevations.

MINERAL WELLS, 89 *m.* (925 alt., 11,011 pop. 1966, est.), in a setting of wooded hills, welcomes thousands of visitors who come annually for recreation.

Mineral Wells is primarily a health resort, although livestock shipments, brick and ceramic tile are profitable. The Crazy Woman Well, dug 1878, was found to have medicinal qualities and hundreds of wells have been opened since. Medicinal crystals are produced commercially. Hexagon House, 701 N. Oak Ave., was built as a hotel in 1897. Baker Hotel, 200 E. Hubbard Ave., 450 rooms, is the principal hostelry, but there are numerous motels and up to 150,000 visitors come annually in pursuit of health. The city has the Texas & Pacific Ry., two bus depots, and a municipal airport.

FORT WOLTERS, established 1941 as an infantry replacement training center, and later an Air Force Base, was designated in March, 1966, as U. S. Army Primary Helicopter Center. The Helicopter School has been teaching two courses since 1956: a 16-week course for officers without previous flying experience, and a 4-week preflight indoctrination course before the 16-week course for enlisted men who volunteer. Southern Airways of Texas, Inc., teaches the first half, flight division instructors the second. Trainees go to Fort Rucker, Ala., for additional study. Fort Wolters was named for Brig. General Jacob F. Wolters, Texas National Guard. It covers 8,306 acres. In addition to two heliports there are seven permanent and seven tactical stage fields in operation. More fields are being constructed. The post also has Beach Army Hospital, 84th Military Police, 311 U. S. Security Agency Battalion, and Battery D, 4th Missile Battalion.

LAKE MINERAL WELLS, 4 *m.* northeast near US 281, 646 acres, supplies water and recreation facilities. Right on US 180, 4.8 *m.* is the Brazos River. PALO PINTO, 12 *m.* (1,000 alt., 500 pop.) founded 1858, was so named (Sp. for painted post) because of varicolored petrified wood used as building material. The white limestone courthouse dominates the business area. LAKE PALO PINTO, 14 *m.* south on F-M 4, covers 2,275 acres and holds 32,350 acre-ft. of water.

From Palo Pinto on US 180 west 14 *m.* to State 16. North on State 16, 14 *m.* to LAKE POSSUM KINGDOM, one of the most popular recreation areas in central Texas. The water of the Brazos River, impounded by the Morris Sheppard Dam, 1,450 ft. long, since 1941, covers 19,800 acres and holds 724,700 acre-ft. of water. It has a serpentine shoreline of 310 miles, and is located in Palo Pinto, Young, Stephens and Jack Counties. It offers year-around fishing for black bass, cat, bream, bluegill and crappie; scuba diving, deer and duck hunting, with 2,500 acres set aside for archers during the deer season.

There is still a great quantity of unmined coal in this general area. Mining was active decades ago but the discovery of gas and oil and the development of hydroelectric power curtailed it.

Section b.   MINERAL WELLS to SAN ANTONIO; 248 m.
US 281

This section of the route is south across part of the Grand Prairie, and through the hill regions of the Edwards Plateau. The large-scale farming practiced in the northern area is impossible in the hills, where only narrow valleys have sufficient soil for cultivation. Southward towns become fewer, older in appearance and more solid of construction—for these hill folk since the days of the pioneers have preferred stone in building. Throughout the section the population is from half to three-quarters rural; a mixture of native-born whites, descendants of Italian, German and Polish immigrants, and Negro and Mexican farm hands. Toward San Antonio the influence of German immigration of the 1840's is still evident in the thrift and energy with which the inhabitants wrest livelihoods from the rocky soil. In the matter of produce the change is largely from cotton and grains to wool and mohair. Land holdings increase somewhat in size and to a great extent are estates passed from father to son.

Mexicans along the route present the most vivid ethnic picture. They are almost all tenant farmers. Their houses are of the lowest order to be found in the area; those of non-Latin and Negro tenants usually have a few modern touches, such as running water in the kitchen or a radio in the front room. Since living standards of Mexicans in this region are low, landlords prefer them as laborers. Although far from their usual haunts in the State, they differ not at all in customs and habits from their *compadres* along the Rio Grande. Here, as in Mexico, the women endlessly make *tortillas,* and here the chili pepper is considered to be a necessity of diet. The religious shrine, consisting usually of a highly colored picture of a saint, is found more commonly than beds and chairs. Usually there are flowers blooming beside the doorways, and in season, patches of corn and peppers in the tiny yards.

South of MINERAL WELLS, 0 *m.,* US 80 crosses the Brazos River at 12 *m.*

STEPHENVILLE, 42 *m.* (1,283 alt., 7,800 pop.) is at junctions with US 67 (*see Tour 18*) and US 281.

The route is southward on US 281 through a region timbered with post oaks and elms, to HAMILTON, 83 *m.* (1,150 alt., 3,106 pop.), a quiet, prosperous wholesale and industrial center whose many new homes and business structures give it a distinctly modern aspect. In the old cemetery is the grave of Captain F. B. Gentry, a participant in the Battle of San Jacinto. It is the seat of Hamilton County.

EVANT, 99 *m.* (350 pop.), is a little crossroads town of one-story frame buildings. In Evant is the junction with US 84 (*see Tour 21*).

Southward the fields grow milo maize, kaffir-corn and cotton. Farm houses are mostly of stone, neat and well kept, and the fields are bounded by stone fences, very old but still sturdy, their gray rocks neatly piled and covered here and there with thick growths of wild vines. Creek beds and river bottoms have many pecan trees that provide a money crop.

The spaciousness of Texas is reflected in the unusually broad streets of LAMPASAS, 128 *m.* (1,025 alt., 5,670 pop.), and in its large public square, where an old two-story stone courthouse dominates the surrounding business district. Most of the store buildings are of stone, aged and worn by years. During the 1870's this town had its wild era when cowboys on the long cattle trails rode here to "blow off a little steam." Today Lampasas is an important shipping point for livestock, pecans, wool, mohair and furs.

In early days this region was open range, running thousands of wild Texas longhorns. Pioneer cattlemen fought Indians, for the Comanches harassed settlers until 1875, when a combined campaign of soldiers and Texas Rangers drove them farther west.

In a Lampasas saloon facing the town square the Horrels shot and killed an officer and three members of the State police (not Rangers) in 1873. The affair was the result of an attempt on the part of the radical Governor, E. J. Davis, to tame the then wild cow town. The Horrels fled the State, but returned in 1877 to again precipitate bloody action in the Horrel-Higgins family feud, which wound up in a blaze of gunfire when the two factions fought it out in the public square. More than 50 men took part in the battle. The arrival of a company of Texas Rangers put an end to hostilities.

Opposite the Santa Fe Station is the KEYSTONE HOTEL, still in use, which served passengers of stage lines. It was built in 1856, of limestone. Today, although modernized, it retains to some extent the picturesque atmosphere of the old days.

HANCOCK SPRINGS, half a mile from the courthouse, is a medicinal spa to which the Indians once brought their aged and injured. It is the center of HANCOCK PARK, 164 acres, prized for its fine pecan and elm shade trees. Swimming and picnic facilities are available.

BURNET, 150 m. (1,294 alt., 2,216 pop.), seat of Burnet County, is a center for crushed stone, graphite, and farm products. It grew up near FORT CROGHAN, established 1849 at the foot of Post Mountain, half a mile southwest. There is a Pioneer Museum on US 281. Halfway between Burnet and LLANO (1,029 alt., 2,660 pop.) on State 29 is LAKE BUCHANAN, largest of the Highland Lakes, covering 23,200 acres and holding nearly a million acre-ft. of water. It is impounded on the Colorado River by a huge multiple-arch dam, 150 ft. tall and 11,200 ft. long. Its shoreline is 192 m. long. Burnet County Park and Black Rock Park are popular with fishermen, for black bass, white bass, crappie and catfish abound. Below Lake Buchanan and 10 m. from Burnet is LAKE INKS, only 830 acres but no less known for good fishing on its 3 m. shoreline.

South of Burnet sheep and goat ranches produce large amounts of wool and mohair.

At 155 m. is a junction with Park Road No. 4.

Right here to LONGHORN STATE PARK and LONGHORN CAVERN (*three trips daily, with guides, through the well-lighted part of the cavern, at 10:30 a.m., 2:30 p.m., and 4 p.m.; Sun. and holidays at 9 a.m., 1 p.m., and 4 p.m. Night trips and parties guided by special arrangement with officials at the administration building. Fees, $1.20 for adults, 50¢ for students, 25¢ for children 7 to 12, under 7 free*).

Although the cavern is only partly explored, its known length is more than 11 miles. It contains numerous winding tunnels and large rooms along and within which are weird formations in limestone and crystal. In the cavern are the Dome Room, the five Crystal Rooms (presenting a huge deposit of Iceland spar), the Main Room, Cathedral Room, the Fountain of Youth, the Queen's Throne, the Silent Watcher, the Pink Elephants, the Suspended Boulder, and many other chambers and formations. The cavern was a hiding place for Indians and outlaws, and powder was manufactured in it during the Civil War. The gang of the notorious Texas outlaw, Sam Bass, took refuge here following several robberies, and the cavern's main opening is called the Sam Bass entrance.

US 281 continues through the hills. In a valley difficult of access east of the highway, a huge cypress post set upright in the ground, a grass-grown cemetery, and the moss- and vine-covered remains of a mill race are all that is left of the once thriving settlement of Mormon Mill. To this hidden valley, with its lake and waterfall, Lyman Wight in 1851 led a party composed of members of the Church of Jesus Christ of Latter Day Saints whose views differed from those of Brigham Young.

Wight, an apostle of the church, had been a disciple of Joseph Smith, and after Smith was slain by a mob at Carthage, Illinois, in 1844, he declined to accept Young's authority. Young believed the promised Zion for the church was to be found in the Rocky Mountains; Wight, basing his belief on his last conversation with Smith, was convinced it was in Texas. Wight and his followers crossed the Red River at Preston on October 3, 1845, remained for a short time in Grayson County, moved southward to a point near Austin, then to a place on the Pedernales River, near Fredericksburg. There they established a communistic settlement, with a grist mill, the millstones of which had come from France. They called the settlement Zodiac, and to representatives of Brigham Young who arrived to threaten Wight with excommunication if he did not come to Salt Lake, he replied, "Nobody under the light of heaven except Joseph Smith could call me from Texas."

In 1850 a flood destroyed their mill, their crops, and took a number of lives. When another disastrous flood came in the succeeding year, Wight rode with some of his followers in search of a new Zion, looked down upon the blue lake in this green valley, and moved the colony here. They built log dwellings and a schoolhouse, made shingles and furniture, and tilled the soil, but they greatly missed their mill, the grinding stones of which had disappeared in the Pedernales flood. Wight fasted in his cabin for three days and prayed that a way might be shown him to recover the stones, following which he journeyed with a group to the site of the Zodiac settlement, studied the terrain, and then commanded his companions to dig at a spot where the receding water had left a pile of sand. The stones were found at a depth of four feet. They were taken to the new settlement, where, following a feast of thanksgiving for what they regarded as a miracle, the colonists built a mill race to the 28-foot waterfall, and a mill with an overshot wheel. From distances up to a two-days' journey, settlers brought their grist to be ground. The colony prospered, but in 1853 Wight felt a call to move to another area, and sold his rights at this place. The mill was still standing in 1881.

MARBLE FALLS, 164 m. (764 alt., 3,000 pop.), is surrounded by cedar-covered hills. At its southern outskirts the Colorado River widens and tumbles over great rock formations, into a lake. In the old, weathered business district some buildings are of granite, the source of the town's chief industry—quarrying. Turkeys, cedar posts, pecans, wool, mohair, and polo ponies are shipped from here.

Right from Marble Falls on a graveled road to GRANITE MOUNTAIN, 2 m., a dome of igeneous rock composed of quartz, feldspar, and mica, covering 180 acres. The stone for the State Capitol was quarried here by convict labor during the 1880's. Granite is shipped from this area to all parts of the United States for building construction.

South of Marble Falls US 281 crosses the Colorado River. The falls are a quarter of a mile upstream. The Max Starke Dam impounds LAKE MARBLE FALLS, covering 780 acres.

LAKE LYNDON B. JOHNSON, popularly called Lake LBJ, is

the newest name on the map but not the newest lake. The former Granite Shoals Lake on the Colorado River, 4 *m.* southwest of Marble Falls, was renamed to honor the President. It is a 45-minute drive from the LBJ Ranch. The lake is impounded by the Alan Wirtz Dam, covers 6,200 acres and holds 138,500 acre-ft. of water when full. It is one of the chain of Highland Lakes that are exceedingly popular with fishermen, whether flycasters, dabblers, cane pole or trot line operators. Lake LBJ is known for lunker bass, often weighing 6 lbs., black bass and catfish. Its popularity has brought a large increase in dwellings for permanent or weekend residence.

JOHNSON CITY, 186 *m.* (1,197 alt. 660 pop.) seat of Blanco County is at the junction with US 290, 50 miles west of Austin. The County takes its name from the Blanco (Sp. white) River. It is a sparsely populated (c. 3,500) area of large ranches specializing in sheep (100,000 hd.) turkeys, goats and cattle. Johnson City has become a dateline of national import because of the nearby ranch of President Lyndon B. Johnson, who frequently transacted business of state here and in his office in Austin. It has become a tourist objective and visitors often outnumber the permanent residents. It is described more fully under Tour 24b, on U.S. 290, page 615.

BLANCO, 200 *m.* (1,350 alt., 789 pop.) is a former county seat. On the night before Christmas men and boys stage a sham battle at the town square with roman candles.

At the southern edge of the town, along the banks of the BLANCO RIVER, is BLANCO STATE PARK (*free swimming and picnicking, small fee for fishing*), a 110-acre recreational area. In this vicinity, 94,347 acres of land are in game preserves (*hunting leases obtainable from ranchmen, subject to State game laws*).

TWIN SISTERS, 206.8 *m.* (100 pop.), on the south bank of the LITTLE BLANCO RIVER, grew around a general store and post office housed in a stone building that served as a stage station. Its name was derived from twin conic peaks that rise near the town (R). Many of the residents are of German descent, and each February a colorful masked ball, featuring folk-costumes of the Fatherland—with an old-time German band furnishing the music—is held here.

SAN ANTONIO, 248 *m.* (656 alt., 699,768 pop., est.) (*see San Antonio*), is at junctions with US 81 (*see Tour 8*), US 90 (*see Tour 23*), US 87 (*see Tour 17*), US 181 (*see Tour 26*), and State 16 (*see Tour 17a*).

Section c.   SAN ANTONIO to BROWNSVILLE; 294 m.
US 281

This section of US 281 gradually descends almost to sea level. It passes the King Ranch, largest and best known of Texas cattle ranches, and in terminating follows the lower reaches of the Rio Grande through a land that seems to have defied progress, remaining today much the same as it was at the time of settlement 300 years ago.

Mexicans live in stark simplicity in this region of great ranches. Mexican *vaqueros* are replacing non-Latins in a role as old as history along the Rio Grande. Spanish *rancheros* held royal grants in this flat, sparsely populated region, and here the *vaqueros* of colonial Spain rolled cornshuck cigarettes and rode the range—as they do today. The system of living has changed but little; the *vaquero* is still virtually a vassal on domains feudal in their extent and isolation—a vassal by choice, for he gives unquestioning loyalty to the ranch owners, and regards their wishes as law, the only law he knows. In a survey of this area J. Frank Dobie found that the Mexican cow hand still weaves his cinches from horse manes, makes *reatas* of rawhide, and tans buckskin. He brews a tea made of cenizo leaves, to cure a cough. "He can trail a cow or any wild animal as unerringly as Comanche warrior ever trailed," Dobie wrote.

Most of these Mexicans speak Spanish only; they make music around campfires to the accompaniment of coyote calls, and their songs have a note of sadness, "of something far away." They tell tales of buried treasure, of ghosts and witches. Their favored doctors are *curanderos,* whose remedy for a fever may be a pair of javelina fangs worn on a string around the neck. The *vaquero* knows every bush and tree, its properties and character; he is hospitable, generous, loyal to the point of dying for a friend.

These isolated Mexicans dance often and long. Rough benches are set around a hard-packed earth floor, and from these stern mothers watch the behavior of their daughters; no respectable girl is expected to talk to her partner while dancing. Saint's days and religious occasions are observed with festivities, usually all-night dances; and although there is little conversation between the young men and women, these events are usually followed by weddings. Mexican wives are expected to do all the domestic work, and fade early; but they and their large families usually live happily —though in primitive fashion—to ripe old ages.

South of SAN ANTONIO, 0 *m.,* the route is through a section of irrigated lands devoted to the growing of winter vegetables. The reconstructed Mission San José is at 4.7 *m.* MITCHELL LAKE, 9.9 *m.,* is a private duck-hunting preserve. The MEDINA RIVER is crossed at 12 *m.,* its banks lined with groves of giant pecan trees. At 13.2 *m.* is a junction with a graveled road.

Left here to the junction with the South Flores Road, 2 *m.* In this vicinity in 1813 occurred the Battle of the Medina. The Spanish general, Joaquin Arredondo, led an army of 4,000 to conquer a revolutionary force under General José Alvares de Toledo. The revolutionists were lured into a trap, and of their army of 1,700 men (many of whom were adventurers from the United States), only 90 escaped in the engagement that followed (August 18, 1813). Many of the prisoners taken by the royalists, it is claimed, were made to dig their own graves in the form of a long trench, were lined up along its side and shot. The bones of the vanquished bleached on the battlefield between the Medina and Atascosa Rivers for nine years, until, after Mexico had gained its independence, Governor Trespalacios had the remains buried with military honors, placing on an oak tree a tablet with the inscription: "Here lie the braves who, imitating the immortal example of Leonidas, sacrificed their fortunes and their lives, contending against tyrants."

South of the Medina River US 281 follows closely for a short distance the route of the old Lower Laredo Road, one of the main thoroughfares of early-day travel. It knew the marching feet of Spanish, Mexican, Texan, and later, American armies, and the rumble of stagecoaches. At 22 *m.* LEMING is a small settlement.

PLEASANTON, 33 *m.* (365 alt., 3,467 pop.), settled in the 1850's, was one of the cattle concentration points on the old Western Trail to Dodge City, Kansas. The town, strung out along the highway, is shaded by giant live oaks. Local tradition says a tavern keeper built a room in one of the oak trees for gambling trail drivers. One, trying to climb up while intoxicated, fell and broke his neck.

Right from Pleasanton 5 *m.* on State 97 to JOURDANTON (490 alt., 2,000 pop.), seat of Atascosa County, junction with State 16 and 163. After Pleasanton come CAMPBELLTON (271 pop.), and WHITSETT (280 pop.). At 69 *m.* is a junction with State 9.

Left here to OAKVILLE, 7.5 *m.* (150 pop.), a quiet little town which, during and after the Civil War, was frequented by the outlaw knights of the brush following raids and hold-ups. The region was a hotbed of lawlessness until Ranger Captain L. H. McNelly and his company, after considerable effort, cleaned it up in 1876. Old-timers still tell tall tales of days when rustlers and highwaymen gathered in the town's saloons, shot it out on the streets and even hanged intruding sheriffs to the limbs of oaks that shade the roadway.

State 9 runs direct to Corpus Christi, 74 *m.,* also passing through DINERO, EDROY (250 pop.) and one mile north of MATHIS (6,000 pop.). West of the highway extends LAKE CORPUS CHRISTI, 15,500 acres, 185,900 acre-ft. capacity, impounded by the Wesley E. Seale Dam on the Nueces River. There also is a State Park.

THREE RIVERS, 74 *m.* (155 alt., 1,932 pop.) is at the confluence of the Frio, Atascosa and Nueces Rivers. State 72 proceeds west through the town. The rivers proved a liability in September, 1967, when torrential rains accompanying hurricane Beulah inundated the town, which became part of a disaster area of 29 counties.

GEORGE WEST, 84 *m.* (162 alt., 1,878 pop.) was named for the ranchman who gave the town its public buildings and bridges. At the northwest corner of Courthouse Square is a mounted longhorn steer, representing the vanished breed once raised here.

ALICE, 124 *m.* (205 alt., 20,861 pop., 1960; 23,000, 1965, est.) seat of Jim Wells County, cattle shipping point since 1888, was incor. 1910 and named for a daughter of a founder of the King Ranch. Purebred cattle are sold at the County Fair, October. Many high schools compete in the Hub City Track Relays. Rattlesnake hunting is popular in the area. At the edge of the city is AUDUBON WILDLIFE REFUGE. Here is a junction with State 44.

BEN BOLT, 131 *m.* (138 pop.) has not caught up with Alice.

At 138 *m.* US 281 meets State 141. East to US 77 and KINGSVILLE, 14 *m.* (66 alt., 25, 297 pop., 1960; 26,905 1964), center for large ranches raising Herefords, Shorthorns and Brahmas. It is headquarters for the great KING RANCH, and site of the TEXAS COLLEGE OF

ARTS AND INDUSTRIES, which enrolls about 4,400. It has a museum of frontier Americana and a Citrus and Vegetable Training Center at Weslaco. PRESBYTERIAN PAN AMERICAN SCHOOL, 3 *m.* south of Kingsville on US 77 occupies 700 acres donated by Mrs. Henrietta King.

The King Ranch permits a 15-mile drive around part of the premises, called the Loop Tour, but furnishes no guides. The holdings of nearly 1,000,000 acres in several counties are part of the vast properties acquired by the onetime Rio Grande steamboat captain Richard King. *Santa Gertrudis,* as the first unit of the ranch was named, was established in 1854. In 1860 Captain King entered into a ranching partnership with Captain Mifflin Kenedy, a business associate of river boat days, and together they expanded the property until the partnership was dissolved and the ranch divided in 1868. Captain King continued to buy property until he owned 1,270,000 acres, almost 2,000 square miles. Although now slightly smaller, this is still one of the largest cattle ranches in the world; it has 120,000 head of cattle and 12,000 horses. Many descendants of families brought from Mexico by Captain King work and live on the property. Fully 700 *vaqueros* ride the ranges of the three units of the ranch—the Santa Gertrudis, Laureles and Norias Ranches. Two great round-ups, one in February and one in August, engage the *vaqueros,* whose task it is to place the Running W brand on thousands of calves. The cattle, which received their first infusion of Brahma blood in 1915 with the importation of that strain from India, are dipped and branded in a process that requires only about one minute for each animal.

In September, 1967, torrential rains that accompanied the hurricane Beulah flooded the King Ranch as far north as the Norias division in Kleberg County, where cowhands had to make repairs from floating marsh wagons.

U. S. Naval Auxiliary Air Station, 3 *m.* S on US 77 trains jet fighter aviators.

Humble King Ranch Gas Plant, 13 *m.* SW of Kingsville on State 141, draws on Humble production in the 12-county area.

At 144 *m.* is PREMONT, (3,049 pop.) a marketing center.

FALFURRIAS, 161 *m.* (119 alt., 6,515 pop.), with cotton processing plants, gypsum plant, two citrus fruit packing plants, and a large creamery, is best known for its production of an annual average of one million pounds of butter. The late Ed. C. Lasater gave the dairying industry impetus when in 1908 he imported Jersey cows. Here is a junction with State 285 (28 *m.* east to US 77).

South of Falfurrias the land becomes more rolling, and mesquite and cactus give way to a dense growth of oak that crowds close to the highway. In this area salt cedars grow very large, and are planted close together in rows, for windbreaks. Here vast pastures contain Hereford cattle; the native grasses are luxuriant in normal seasons.

At 181 *m.* ENCINO, (1,300 pop.) ; 184 *m.,* RACHAL.

A U. S. QUARANTINE STATION, 192 *m.,* is operated during the fruit-harvesting season to inspect shipments from the Lower Rio Grande Valley. This is to prevent the spread of insect pests.

SAN MANUEL, 207 *m.,* is little more than a filling station stop. A short distance (L) is LA SAL DEL REY (The Salt of the King), a surface deposit connected with the Laguna Madre by a road laid out in early days of settlement of the Rio Grande Valley. Across this wilderness thoroughfare in the last quarter of the eighteenth century, oxcarts loaded with salt rumbled eastward, to cross the shallow waters of Laguna Madre over an oyster-reef ford. Thence they wound between the sand dunes of Padre Island to where ships waited in the Gulf to convey the salt to Spanish and Mexican ports.

South of San Maunel 1 *m.* State 186 runs east 24 *m.* to RAY-MONDVILLE on US 77. (40 alt., 10,200 pop. 1965, est.) seat of Willacy County and market for cotton, vegetable products. The highway runs east to PORT MANSFIELD on the Laguna Madre (125 pop.) where pier and boat fishing are available, duck hunting in season. The Port Mansfield Fishing Tournament is held on July 4. Opposite the PORT MANSFIELD CHANNEL cuts through Padre Island to the Gulf since 1962.

On the Laguna Madre about 15 *m.* south of Port Mansfield is the LAGUNA ATASCOSA WILDLIFE REFUGE.

EDINBURG, 226 *m.* (91 alt., 18,706 pop., 1960; c. 20,000, 1966) seat of Hidalgo County, is major market for cotton, citrus fruit and vegetables of County. Some oil processing. Originally called Chapin, it was moved from the Rio Grande banks in 1908 and renamed 1911. Reached by Continental Trailways, has a Municipal Airport and another, Edinburg Airport.

PAN-AMERICAN COLLEGE, estab. 1927 by State and County as Edinburg Junior College, changed its name in 1952 and qualified as a State senior college in 1965. It enrolls 2,300 in the regular term and more than 1,000 in summer. The Observatory may be visited free, on application.

PHARR, 234 *m.* (107 alt., 14,106 pop.) (*see Tour 16*), is at the junction with US 83. At 243 *m.* is the junction with a paved road.

Right here to HIDALGO, 3 *m.* (1,222 pop.), a town that has often been swept by floods, raided by bandits, and—in the years before irrigation—scourged by droughts when the brown flow of the Rio Grande dwindled to a thin trickle meandering down the middle of its sandy bed. The years of prohibition brought to Hidalgo thirsty thousands seeking relief in the saloons of the Mexican town of Reynosa, across the river, and also the smuggler, whose illicit trade in contraband liquor from Mexico caused Texas Ranger camps, U. S. customs offices, and other headquarters for special officers, to be located here.

The route is almost due east, bearing closely to the windings of the Rio Grande and following the course of the Old Military Road laid out by U. S. engineers during the Mexican War. Along this road marched General Taylor's troops on their way to attack Monterey, and along it Texas Rangers and U. S. Army detachments have fought raiding Mexican bandits. The atmosphere is one of primitive antiquity, little changed, the very houses seeming to have sprung from the soil in the tinge of unpainted adobe. PROGRESO, 260 *m.,* is now a land development and at one end of a private toll bridge, with Nuevo Progreso, a tourists' town, on the Mexican side. SANTA MARIA, 266 *m.* (281 pop.) has an early 19th century Chapel. LA PALOMA, 280 *m.* is an old river town.

Oil lamps and flickering tallow wicks gleam in the windows of homes and store buildings, and much of the family cooking is done over charcoal braziers in the yards. Many of the houses are mere *jacales* of mud and sticks, but few are so humble that a flowering potted plant or two does not rest on a little bench beside the doorstep.

SANTA RITA, 290 *m.,* is hardly recognizable as a town. Census officials seem to have overlooked it completely, and the two or three adobes, old and weather-worn, that stand beside the highway appear to have always been there. There is nothing to indicate that in 1859 this was the ranch home of Juan Nepomuceno Cortinas, Mexican Robin Hood, also called Cheno and the Red Robber of the Rio Grande—a picturesque red-bearded character who for a time was a thorn in the side of certain Texans and a hero in the eyes of many of his fellow countrymen. To Texas peace officers he was a bandit; to certain peons and Mexican landholders he was a daring champion of liberty and legal rights.

A colorful border episode started July 13, 1859, when Cortinas rode into Brownsville for his morning coffee. The town marshal, in arresting a drunken peon, who had formerly been Cortinas' servant, became more abusive than Cortinas thought proper. The young Mexican remonstrated with the officer, who cursed him, and Cortinas shot the marshal in the shoulder. While the officer helplessly clutched his wound, Cortinas dragged the peon up behind him on his horse, and galloped out of town. That incident changed Cortinas from a suspected cattle thief—although a member of the wealthy class of Mexican ranchers—into a militant champion of his people.

Some of the non-Latin Texans of the period, through processes of law and otherwise, were confiscating desirable lands held by Mexicans on the north bank of the river. The latter, holding their property under old Spanish grants, were given little consideration, and lost either in court or to the lawyers they were forced to hire to defend their ownership. Cortinas declared against these practices, and maintained that if necessary he would resist such methods by force. And he did.

On September 28, 1859, while Brownsville was sleeping off the effects of a grand ball held the evening before at Matamoros, the red-bearded one with about a hundred followers swept into town, shooting and yelling. They raced through the streets, terrorized the inhabitants, killed five men who offered resistance, sacked stores, turned prisoners out of the jail, and threatened to burn the town. Cortinas especially sought to locate the marshal, but was unsuccessful. While he held the town, he kept the frightened citizens indoors; his men caroused on the streets and in the public square. Finally, through the influence of some Mexican officials, Cortinas was persuaded to ride back to Santa Rita.

From the ranch he issued the first of two proclamations announcing his stand for legal rights for the persecuted Mexican landholders, and declaring open war on all their enemies. Mexicans flocked to his standard and Brownsville, recovered from its fright, quickly took steps to eradicate the menace at its gates. A local military organization called the Brownsville Tigers essayed an expedition against the Cortinas stronghold. Heavily armed, and with two small pieces of brass artillery, they advanced on Santa Rita. It took them a week to reach their destination, although the ranch was a scant seven miles up the river. With great deliberation and with a display of uniforms and banners they finally drew up in battle array, only to withdraw at almost the first volley from Cortinas' men who were hidden in the chaparral. So rapid was the departure of the Tigers that they left their cannon and were in Brownsville in one of the quickest local retreats on record.

From his Santa Rita headquarters Cortinas held up the mail stage and kept the driver captive ten days, so that all the letters might be read to him. After listening carefully, the bandit had the letters resealed and re-placed in the mail sack, which he hung on a mesquite tree beside the old military road. Then he notified the authorities at Brownsville where it could be found.

A force of Texas Rangers under Captain W. G. Tobin next tried to oust Cortinas from Santa Rita, but they too were soundly defeated and chased back to Brownsville. The Rangers did, however, save the cannon they had brought with them.

Cortinas' second proclamation followed this attack, and in it he called on all Mexicans of the Valley to rally to his banner. He declared confidence in his friend, Governor-elect Sam Houston, and maintained that he fought only to resist illegal attempts to oust him from his property, and to obtain legal rights for his people.

In December, 1859, United States troops were sent against Cortinas. This time his resistance amounted to hardly more than a rear guard action covering his retreat into Mexico. From that time on Cortinas played tag with soldiers and Texas Rangers who sought to capture him. He sacked and burned the ranches of non-Latin Texans, raided their towns and then vanished into the brush. He attacked Rio Grande steamboats and invaded Texas territory again and again, after circling the forces that sought him.

The scope of Cortinas' activities was such that Lieutenant Colonel Robert E. Lee, then department commander, made a personal tour of investigation of conditions in the Lower Rio Grande Valley. Lee's reports to the War Department, State authorities, and the Mexican government resulted in co-operative action that ended the difficulty. At last Cortinas withdrew into the interior of Mexico and joined the Mexican Army, becoming a brigadier general and later governor of the Mexican State of Tamaulipas.

Between Santa Rita and Brownsville US 281 hugs the river.

BROWNSVILLE, 294 *m.* (33 alt., 48,040 pop., 1960) is at the junction with US 83 and US 77 (*see Brownsville*).

C+C+C+C+C+C+C+C+C+C+C+C+C+C+C+C+C+C+C+C+C+C+C+C+C+C+C+C+C+

Tour 10

(Lawton, Okla.)—Wichita Falls—Seymour—Abilene—San Angelo
—Junction with US 90; US 277.
Oklahoma Line to Junction with US 90, 414 *m.*

US 277 and US 281 enter Texas together from Oklahoma and proceed as
far as Wichita Falls. Here US 277 proceeds southwest, whereas US 281 continues south through San Antonio to the Rio Grande. For a short distance US 82,
which reaches Wichita Falls from the east, follows the route of US 277 through
Archer and Baylor Counties, turning directly west at Seymour and proceeding
to Lubbock.

The heart of one of the State's greatest unchanged cattle regions is
pierced by US 277, which zigzags in a general southwesterly direction
through central west Texas between the Red River and the vicinity of the
Rio Grande, near Del Rio.

Along its beginning on the northern part of the Central Plains, the
route leads through a fertile area where agriculture, oil and gas furnish
growing industries for prosperous towns. But the rolling prairies of most
of the remainder of the way are primarily adapted to ranching. Here the
first few settlers fought Indians in order to claim lands covered with
buffalo and mesquite grass—rich lands normally too dry for dependable
harvests. Water has always been a determining factor on this eastern
fringe of the Great Plains. When it was discovered that artesian water
underlay a large part of the area, farming began; and today cotton, corn,
wheat, truck crops and fruits are produced where once cattle sometimes
died of thirst.

But along the sparsely populated miles of US 277 south of Abilene the
ranchman—usually of native white stock, fairly well educated, as modern
in his methods as finances will permit, yet of a type true to traditions of
the range—predominates. Near San Angelo a great sheep and goat ranching region begins. Throughout this part of Texas the atmosphere of the
West prevails, modified only by such inevitable modern notes as motion
picture houses and automobiles.

Section a.   OKLAHOMA LINE *to* SAN ANGELO; *259 m.*
US 277

This part of US 277 extends southwesterly, then south through a
region of diversified farms and cattle ranches. Along its general line were
the frontier forts of the 1870's, and the fringe of civilization from which

buffalo hunters and the first of the cattlemen pushed out into the Indian's domain.

Oil, Herefords, cotton and wheat create the wealth of this prosperous section of Texas. Modern towns with industrial plants that process the yield of the soil are spaced along the way to Abilene. Southward the rural influence is stronger: in some of the small communities play parties are still in vogue. These gatherings were favored by stern parents of early days, who frowned upon dancing. No instrumental music is permitted at the play party; ring games—variations of square dance movements—are accompanied by songs, the players executing some simple steps in time to their own vocal accompaniment. Verses are improvised during the games, but there are a few old favorites, including *Four Handed Josie,* performed to such words as these:

> Hold my mule while I jump Josie . . .
> Josie this and Josie that
> Josie killed a yellow cat.
> Josie do and Josie do (dough)
> Swing her around a time or so.

Another favorite game is called *Sandy Land.* The couples move toward the center of a circle and bow and dance back, as they sing:

> Great big 'taters in sandy land,
> Slices of middling's big as your hand—
> Mighty good living in sandy land.

There are many other verses of the same type. Square dances are popular in other sections along the route, and are usually featured at annual events commemorating early days.

A region rich in traditions is traversed by this section of US 277. There are the new, fabulous tales of sudden oil gushers, those of the less spectacular but equally as surprising development of vast wheat, cotton and grain fields, and, as a background for all this, the lore of the cattle industry—greatest in the past, and most generally favored still.

The route crosses the OKLAHOMA LINE and the Red River, 0 *m.,* 43 miles south of Lawton, Oklahoma (*see Oklahoma Guide*).

BURKBURNETT, 2 *m.* (1,054 alt., 8,750 pop. est.), shipping center for livestock and farm produce, has modern buildings and fine residences, an oil refinery, and casinghead gasoline plants. In 1911 oil development began, and in 1918 the Fowler well came in, shooting oil over the crown block. Gusher after gusher followed, and from a little town of about a thousand people Burkburnett blossomed into an oil-mad community of 30,000. Speculators and promoters, drillers, roughnecks and roustabouts, merchants and saloon keepers, adventurers and gamblers flocked in. Land prices ranged from $1,500 to $40,000 an acre.

There was no wilder oil town than Burkburnett in the heyday of its boom, but the production of flowing wells lessened, and conditions are almost back to normal—although there still are producing wells, even in the downtown section.

WICHITA FALLS, 15 *m.* (946 alt., 109,500 pop., 1964, est.) (*see Wichita Falls*), is at junctions with US 287 (*see Tour 13*), US 281 (*see Tour 9*), and US 82 with which US 277 unites for 52 miles (*Tour 3*).

SEYMOUR, 67 *m.* (1,290 alt., 4,000 pop.) (*see page 395*), is at junctions with US 82 (*see Tour 3*) and US 283 (*see Tour 11*).

Southward US 277 passes through a region called Wild Horse Prairie —here once roamed thousands of mustangs. Here, too, are to be found interesting fossil remains.

HASKELL, 112 *m.* (1,553 alt., 4,016 pop.), seat of Haskell County, which raises grain and beef cattle. It has many residents of Swedish and German descent.

The first house in Haskell was erected in 1882, and the first store, a grocery and whisky establishment, in 1884. The first post office was in the home of Mrs. R. A. Standefer, postmistress, who kept the mail in her old-fashioned bureau. One of the town's early-day saloons had a sign over the door that read, "The Road to Ruin Saloon." Oddly, the place was also used for church services.

The springs at Haskell were long the camping grounds of Comanches, Kiowas, and Kickapoos. Marcy's trail of 1849 passed in this vicinity, and later west-bound gold seekers followed his route. RICE SPRINGS PARK is a local recreation area.

South of Haskell many Indian fights occurred in the days when troops from Fort Griffin and adjacent posts sought to protect settlers. Paint Creek, Double Mountain, California Creek and Lipan Point were scenes of frontier battles.

"Mustangers," men who captured or killed wild horses, found this section an excellent hunting ground. Many great herds were rounded up and driven overland to northern markets. Varied were the methods employed in catching these animals. They were snared, creased, run down in relays, penned in box canyons, starved away from water, and, finally, when they became a menace to the domestic stock of settlers, slaughtered as ruthlessly as were the buffalo. Names of mustang stallions and herd leaders are remembered—the Pacing White Stallion, Black Devil, Star Face, and perhaps best known of all, Midnight, whose almost uncanny understanding of men and their wiles long protected his herd and himself from human traps.

The mustangs went the way of the buffalo, but they are perpetuated in such place names as Wild Horse Mesa, Wild Horse Knob, Mustang Spring, Mustang Crossing, Mustang Hollow and Wild Horse Tree.

At 126 *m.* is the junction with US 380 (*see Tour 27*).

In STAMFORD, 128 *m.* (1,603 alt., 5,400 pop.), sturdy red brick and stone houses have been built by a population predominantly of German and Swedish descent. Primarily an agricultural center to which has been added an industrial aspect, the town still has a distinct air of the cow country, largely because of the headquarters of the SMS Ranch (*open*), which occupies a recently erected concrete building on the northeast corner of the town square. The facade of the building bears the old ranch brand, made with both S's backwards. Inside is a large collection of pictures of cowboy life, pioneer ranch activities, brands of early-day ranches, and other items of interest.

Stamford is the scene of the Texas Cowboy Reunion, held annually in July. This is a three-day event, one day of which is always July 4. Rodeos, bunkhouse dances, chuck wagon meals, and a big parade are among the features. LAKE STAMFORD, on Paint Creek, equidistant from Haskell and Stamford, covers 5,125 acres and holds 60,000 acre-ft. It makes LAKE STAMFORD PARK a recreation area.

At 142 *m.* is the junction with US 83 (*see Tour 16*), which is united with US 277 for 81 miles southward.

ANSON, 143 *m.* (1,716 alt., 2,980 pop.), is a cotton shipping center which in cotton picking time booms with activity, as the pickers flock to town on Saturdays and trade days, giving the place a carnival air. Booths appear on the streets, offering hamburgers and soda water; peddlers of coffee and food cry their wares; pitchmen hawk lotions and razor blades. Medicine shows thrive, and countless bottles of questionable elixirs are sold. Anson is the seat of Jones County, named for Anson Jones, last president of the Republic of Texas.

The town's outstanding social event is the Cowboys' Christmas Ball, described in the famous verses of that name by Larry Chittenden, cowboy poet, whose home was in the vicinity of Anson. The affair, always well attended, is held on Christmas Eve in the Anson High School Auditorium, admission "four bits" (50 cents).

ABILENE, 167 *m.* (1,719 alt., 60,368 pop., 1960; 100,000, 1965, est.) is the seat of Taylor County and the metropolis of Taylor and Jones Counties, with more than 150,000 pop. (est.) in its statistical area. Located at the gateway to the rich lands of the Panhandle, it is served by Interstate 20, US 80, 83, 84, 277, and State 36 and 351. It is a shipping point for cattle, sheep, cotton and petroleum, and an expanding educational center, and profits from the mineral production of Taylor County —petroleum, natural gas, natural gas liquids, stone and gravel—which has a value of around $18,000,000 annually. The first settlers were buffalo hunters, followed by cattle men. Abilene is served by the Texas & Pacific Ry. and the Burlington; a dozen bus lines come in at the Continental Trailways and Greyhound terminals. Abilene Municipal Airport, southeast of the city, has two runways, one 6,000 ft. long, and regular flights by Continental Airlines.

The city's outstanding cultural development has been in music, particularly band music. The Cowboy Band of Hardin-Simmons University, arrayed in all the paraphernalia of the cowboy, is not only striking in appearance, but has an international musical reputation.

All the schools and colleges have bands, orchestras and choral societies which participate in Abilene's numerous music events, held annually to determine eligibility to compete in the Tri-State Music Festivals. Abilene Christian College holds a spring festival for students in voice, piano and violin. Hardin-Simmons University sponsors an A Capella choir and a piano tournament. The High School Eagle Band has been a winner of state tournaments.

Abilene is unusual for the manner and costume in which it plays polo. The game is popular, but the natty uniforms, scant saddlery, and thoroughbred horseflesh so closely associated with it elsewhere, are lacking. The spirit of the cattle range prevails, with the players arrayed in denim trousers, cowboy boots, and big hats. They sit regulation range stock saddles, horn and all, and their mounts are cow ponies. Yet their game lacks nothing in speed, horsemanship, and skill with the mallet.

Abilene has reservoirs for water supply and recreation on all sides, including LAKE KIRBY, 5 m. south, which covers 740 acres.

HARDIN-SIMMONS UNIVERSITY, whose tree-shaded campus is bounded by Vogel, Ambler, and Simmons Aves. and Cedar St., is a co-educational institution, founded in 1890 by the Sweetwater Baptist Association, and opened in 1892. It was raised to university rating in 1935. The buildings, varying in architecture, include several older ones of the plantation type, while others follow simple collegiate designs. The university has an annual enrollment of about 1,800 students, and confers bachelor's and master's degrees. It is heavily endowed.

ABILENE CHRISTIAN COLLEGE occupies a 34-acre campus, bounded by College Dr. (continuation of 13th St.), Aves. D and E, and N. 15th St., on a high hill that overlooks the city. Extensive green lawns, broken occasionally by flower-bordered walks and large cottonwood, pecan, and mesquite trees, surround the seven college buildings, which adhere to a uniform modern classic style in cream-colored brick construction. The college was organized as a co-educational and denominational school in 1906 by Texas members of the Church of Christ. Its average enrollment is nearly 3,000 students.

McMURRY COLLEGE, between Sayles Blvd., Hunt St., Ave. A, and S. 14th St., was opened in 1923. The 51-acre campus is well equipped with recently augmented buildings. The institution is controlled by the Northwest Texas Conference of the Methodist Church, and has an average annual enrollment of more than 1,700 students.

Near Abilene are prehistoric sites having artifacts of the Sand Hill culture (see Tour 21c).

DYESS AIR FORCE BASE, in Taylor County, is a base of the US Strategic Air Command, comprising headquarters of the 819th Strategic Aerospace Div., the 96th Bomb Wing, the 516th Troop Carrier Wing, the 91st Aerial Refueling Squadron and the USA 5th Missile Battalion (not generally open to the public).

1. Right from Abilene on the Buffalo Gap Road to BUFFALO GAP, 15 m. (1,979 alt., 325 pop.), where ruins of an old courthouse and jail stand as gaunt reminders of the past. Here, in the narrow confines of a pass through the mountains, returning forty-niners are believed to have buried a considerable quantity of gold when they were ambushed by hostile Indians. Here too, in 1874, soldiers battled with Indian raiders.

At 22 m. is ABILENE STATE PARK (swimming, fishing, camp sites), a 508-acre playground on the shores of Lake Abilene, which was created in 1922 by the city of Abilene for its municipal water supply. The lake has a storage capacity of 9,200 acre-feet.

2. Left from Abilene, on US 80A to a junction with a dirt road, 2 m.; left

here to the RUINS OF FORT PHANTOM HILL, 18 *m.*, a United States Army post established in 1851 on the then extreme western frontier. It served as an important link in the chain of protective forts across Texas. Abandoned by the Government in 1854, it was taken over by the Butterfield Stage Line, and served as a rest and relay station. Its final abandonment came in 1880.

LAKE FORT PHANTOM HILL, part of the Abilene water supply, covers 4,246 acres.

South of Abilene US 277 moves independently southwest to San Angelo. At 57 *m.* south of Abilene it is joined by State 70. N. is Oak Creek Reservoir, 2,375 acres. NW 5 *m.* on State 70 to BLACKWELL, (2,100 alt., 300 pop.) in Nolan County.

US 83 and US 84 run concurrently for 18 *m.* out of Abilene. Then US 83 turns southwest to BALLINGER (1,630 alt., 5,000 pop.), seat of Runnels County. It has an annual singing festival on the 4th Sunday in April. San Clemente Mission was located south of town. Here US 67 joins US 83 and they run concurrently for 36 *m.* to San Angelo.

BRONTE, 215 *m.* on US 277 (1,893 alt., 1,000 pop. est.) is a commercial center in Coke County.

SAN ANGELO, 259 *m.* (1,847 alt., 58,815 pop. 1960; 60,000, 1965, est.), is one of the largest primary wool markets in America. In the area are about 100 wool and mohair warehouses. It is also a big market for sheep and lambs. The industrial plants produce cottonseed, dairy and petroleum products. Modern business structures house the offices of oil companies, and of cotton, wool, mohair and cattle buyers. From the extensive business district, on all sides extend residential areas of wide tree-bordered streets. A plentiful water supply keeps fresh the greenery of parkways, lawns and gardens.

San Angelo owes its birth to the army, for it was the establishment of Camp Concho, on the height of ground between the North and Middle Concho Rivers, that led to the building of a settlement across the North Concho. First known only as Over-the-River, and not to be compared with the already established town of Ben Ficklin, approximately three miles downstream and then an important stage station, the village subsisted on the patronage of soldiers. In 1882 a flood wiped out Ben Ficklin and, instead of rebuilding, survivors of the wrecked town moved upstream—and Over-the-River became Santa Angela, named by one of its founders, Bartholomew De Witt, for his sister-in-law, a nun of the Ursuline Convent at San Antonio. Later the name was changed to the masculine form of San Angelo.

The Goodnight-Loving Cattle Trail, the Chidester Stage Line, and the California Trail passed through the present site of San Angelo. The city's history is rife with stories of the wild behavior of cowboys, soldiers, trail drivers, and freighters. Famous pioneer characters were Smoky Joe, Jake Golden, Monte Bill, Mystic Maud, and, most picturesque of all, the Fighting Parson. He nightly, with Bible in one hand and revolver in the other, entered one or another of the gambling establishments, walked to the nearest faro table—his usual choice for an impromptu pulpit—and announced that he had come to preach. Only once did anyone object to the procedure. The Parson rapped the objector over the head with the barrel of his gun and laid him in the sawdust before the bar.

SAN ANGELO STATE COLLEGE, founded 1928, became a 4-year college called Angelo State College in 1965. It enrolls 2,000.

Since 1950 the San Angelo Water Project has coordinated Lake Nasworthy, original water supply, with San Angelo Dam and Reservoir, and the huge TWIN BUTTES DAM AND RESERVOIR, between US 277 and 87, adjoining Nasworthy. San Angelo Dam and Reservoir is on the North Concho River, 128 ft. tall, 37,325 ft. long, stores 277,200 acre-ft. for flood control. (In 1936 a 30-in. rain in 84 hrs. flooded the town). Twin Buttes, also called Three Rivers for Middle and South Concho and Spring Creek, has the 8th largest rolled earth-fill dam, 1,991 ft. crest elevation, 8.1 *m*. crest length, capacity 600,000 acre-ft., with shore line 56 *m*. at conservation level, 65 *m*. at flood control level.

The WEST TEXAS MUSEUM (*open*), is housed in the former officers' headquarters at Fort Concho. The sundial of the fort is near the museum. Exhibits include pioneer relics and artifacts.

San Angelo City Auditorium seats 1,860; its Coliseum (1958) at Fair Grounds, seats 5,432; the Stadium seats 12,000. The Tom Green County Library has 50,000 vols.

GOODFELLOW AIR FORCE BASE, 3 *m*. from City Hall, since 1958 has been used by Security Service.

The San Angelo Fat Stock Show is held during March. The city also stages the national Miss Wool of America Pageant in June, and the Steer Roping and Branding Contest.

There is good hunting for deer and small game, and fishing for bass, perch and catfish, in this vicinity.

In San Angelo are junctions with US 67 (*see Tour 18*) and US 87 (*see Tour 17*).

Section b. SAN ANGELO to JUNCTION with US 90;
155 m. US 277

US 277 continues through vast cattle, sheep, and goat ranges, over broken hills and grassy slopes. In spring and early summer the country is a riot of color in reds, yellows, and blues of wild flowers. Recreational facilities are excellent, with fine hunting and fishing and many excellent camping and picnicking sites available.

The first cattlemen in this region had to drive buffaloes from the range. When the Texas & Pacific Railway built south from Abilene in the 1880's, settlement became permanent.

Irrigation has made farming fairly extensive near the end of the section; this semi-arid region today has bumper crops of alfalfa, vegetables, and corn. But ranching is the largest industry in this area near the Rio Grande. Here the Mexican *vaquero*, half Indian and half Spanish in origin, has a folklore rich in religious symbolism and pagan superstition. He tells how the *paisano*, once a proud and haughty bird, was punished by the eagle—monarch of all feathered creatures—for his vanity, being condemned to walk instead of fly; thus was the lowly "road-runner" created. There are countless other tales, all with the same subject: nature. Living far from cities, these *vaqueros* are suspicious of new things; they regard the introduction of barbed wire upon the free range as the beginning of a time of hunger for their people.

South of SAN ANGELO, 0 *m.,* US 277 and US 87 (*see Tour 17*) run concurrently for a distance of about three miles.

At 3.3 *m.* is the junction with US 87 (*see Tour 17*).

At 6 *m.* is the junction with a dirt road.

Right here 4.2 *m.* to BEN FICKLIN (*swimming, free camping, fishing*), once an important supply station on the California Trail. This old town on the bank of the South Concho River was completely destroyed by a flood in 1882. Many lives were lost, and the survivors moved to present San Angelo. Today the site of old Ben Ficklin is the playground for a large area.

Southward the route traverses rocky hill country. Large timber becomes scarce, and is found mostly along the course of the South Concho River, which through this section parallels the highway at frequent intervals.

CHRISTOVAL, 20 *m.* (2,000 alt., 600 pop.) (*swimming, fishing, tourist accommodations*), is a health resort whose mineral wells are widely known for their curative qualities. Great groves of pecans and live oaks along the river offer delightful spots for outdoor relaxation. An Old Settlers Reunion is held annually in Christoval on the last Friday in July.

A ROADSIDE PARK (*ovens, fireplaces, and tables for picnicking*), 20.9 *m.,* consists of three acres enclosed within a rock wall and shaded by large trees.

The route now follows somewhat the winding course of the South Concho River, often visible. Grass-covered hills dotted with clumps of cedar and mesquite, rise on both sides of the highway.

A large roadside sign reading, "High—Healthy—Hospitable," marks the entrance to a place of old-fashioned, weathered houses, the ranchers' headquarters, ELDORADO, 45 *m.* (2,410 alt., 2,790 pop.). First a stage station known as Verand, it was located in Vermont Pasture. The town was moved on top of the divide in 1895 and took the name *El Dorado* (the gilded one). It is the seat and only town of Schleicher County, has a refinery and a woolen mill.

Southward US 277 passes through some of the finest ranch lands in the State. Abundant wildlife includes deer, wild turkeys and foxes. Along the many draws in this vicinity, especially west of the highway, are beds of petrified reptiles and ancient aquatic animals, some of whose bodies measure a foot or more in diameter. In the ranch homes these petrified remains are often used as door stops.

SONORA, 67 *m.* (2,120 alt., 2,800 pop.), is the seat of Sutton County and a center for the wool and mohair trade. It has the National Wool and Mohair Show in June, the Quarter Horse Futurity in late April, the National Quarter Horse Show in September. Sonora was settled in 1889 on the Dry Fork of the Devil's River. Saloons were outlawed in deeds to property, but finally the clause was accidentally omitted from a deed to a city lot. The saloon then opened was called the Maud S, for the famous trotting mare. Two years after Sonora was founded it was learned that the site was owned by a New York firm and the residents had to buy back their own holdings.

The CAVERNS OF SONORA, 8 m. west of Sonora on US 290 and 6 m. south on Ranch Road 1989, are considered the most fantastically beautiful caves in the country. When opened to the public in 1960 they were provided with an attractive entrance building, protected walks and staircases, and illuminated to disclose 5 miles of gleaming, translucent crystals, stalactites coral and calcite formations. Five more miles remain to be mapped. Available are the Hall of Ivory, Corinthian Room, the Butterfly, the War Club Room, the Auditorium, and numerous passages (*open from mid-July to December, adults, $1.50; children, 75¢*).

VINEGARONE, 116 m. (1,800 alt., 50 pop.), was named for the area it is in, known to cowboys as Vinegarone Hollow because of the great number of large whip scorpions—of the variety called vinegaroons—found there. The insects emit a vinegar-like odor when alarmed.

LOMA ALTA (high hill), 118.6 m., marks the crest of the southern divide. It is a filling station stop with an adjacent roadside park offering picnic facilities.

South of Loma Alta the hills gradually lessen in altitude. Cedar and oak give way to mesquite, chaparral, shin-oak, sotol, Spanish dagger, yucca, and other varieties of cactus and semi-desert growths. This is an arid region where only the deep-rooted bunch grass offers grazing for scattered herds of cattle.

At 155 m. is the junction with US 90 (*see Tour 23*).

Tour 11

(Altus and Hobart, Okla.)—Vernon—Seymour—Cisco—Junction with US 67; US 283 and US 183.
Oklahoma Line to Junction with US 67, 209 m.

US 283 and US 183, which jointly traverse a section of the northern plains south of the Red River after reaching Vernon, enter Texas some miles apart.

US 283 crosses the Texas line from Oklahoma over the Red River 14 m. south of Altus, Okla. At 6.8 m. it meets farm road 21 from ODELL, a Wilbarger County farm village with a nominal population.

Left on this road to DOAN'S CROSSING, 3 m., and an adobe house, built about 1879, once the home of C. F. Doan, who also had a store here. At the time when trail traffic was at its height, a little community of houses and saloons was grouped about the old building. In the trail-drive days thousands of head of cattle poured over the high south bank of the river, splashed through the shallow waters of the ford or breasted the flood tide of a swollen stream in a melee of tossing heads and horns. Once on the far bank they were headed northward through 250 miles of wilderness to the next point of supply, and then on to the railhead at Dodge City. Herds using Doan's Crossing followed what was known as the Western or Dodge City Trail.

At 10 *m.* FARGO, a small farm village.

At 20 *m.* VERNON, where it is joined by US 183.

US 183, coming from Davidson and Hobart, Okla., is joined by US 70 in Oklahoma before crossing the Red River several miles east of US 283. It then proceeds south 10 *m.* to OKLAUNION, (150 pop.) a farm village, and joins US 287 for 9 *m.* west to VERNON. Here it joins US 283 and the two highways proceed south as indicated below.

This area is on the eastern edge of the northern part of the Central Plains, between the Red River and the rolling prairies of central Texas. The soil is reddish and sandy except around streams, where pecans trees thrive in black land. The light loam and the general use of tractors enables each farmer to cultivate extensive acreage, and lessens tenantry and its problems. Cotton is the chief commercial crop, since most of the small grains produced are consumed at home. Peanuts and fruits are cash crops, and truck farming is on the increase. Many ranchmen specialize in the production of fine Herefords. Rabbit drives are conducted in the spring in many localities, and combine the aspects of sport, recreation and social events. A gallery looks on and applauds while ranchmen on horseback round up the rabbits. Fox and wolf hunts are also popular.

VERNON, 20 *m.* (1,205 alt., 12,141 pop., 1960; 13,000, 1966, est.) originally called Eagle Flats on account of eagles and later named after Washington's home, is the seat of Wilbarger County and engaged in meat processing, cottonseed milling, seed breeding, and cattle marketing. Here the huge W. T. Waggoner Ranch, which sprawls over six counties, transacts much of its business. In the 1880's Vernon was the supply base for the big herds of cattle that moved over the Western Trail to Doan's Crossing on the Red River a few miles north. There was nothing available between this and Camp Supply on the Canadian River, about 16 to 18 days away for the average herd, which needed a crew of 15. Consequently Vernon provided bars for the overnight halt, but today it is dry territory.

Vernon is served by the Fort Worth & Denver Ry., by half a dozen bus lines, including Continental Trailways, Jordan and Mid-Continent. The Wilbarger County Airport is 5 *m.* north. It has junctions of US 70 and US 287, while US 183 and 283 join routes here on the way south.

The SANTA ROSA ROUNDUP, rodeo and quarter-horse show, is held here the third week in June and draws about 50,000 spectators. The Wilbarger County Memorial Auditorium seats 2,000.

About 15 *m.* south of Vernon and west of US 283 is ZACAQUI-ESTA, the headquarters of the W. T. Waggoner Ranch, which breeds

Hereford cattle and horses. (*Not open to visitors*). The original ranch was bought by Daniel Waggoner in the 1850's and enlarged by the family until today parts of it are in Wilbarger, Wichita, Baylor, Archer, Foard and Knox Counties. On the land of the Waggoner Ranch, to the west of US 283 15 *m.* south of Vernon is LAKE SANTA ROSA, a water supply formed by a dam on Beaver Creek. It covers 1,500 acres and holds 11,570 acre-ft. of water.

LAKE KEMP, 49 *m.* to the right of the highway, was impounded by the dam of the Wichita Valley Irrigation Project on the Wichita River. The latter, only 90 *m.* long is formed by a group of tributaries in the northwest corner of Baylor County. Lake Kemp covers 20,620 acres and holds 461,800 acre-ft. of water. It has a shoreline of 100 *m.* and facilities for camping, boating, hunting and fishing. The lake is stocked with speckled trout, bass, crappie, catfish, bream, and buffalo. The Wichita River, after filling Lake Diversion, flows into the Red River. A drive along the top of the dam at Lake Kemp is recommended for its scenic beauty.

Southward the highway climbs a tall hill, its top offering a broad view of miles of rolling grasslands, dotted with clumps of mesquite.

MABELLE, 55 *m.* (1,265 alt., 58 pop.) (*see page 395*), is at the junction with US 82, which units with US 283 for 9 miles, and with US 277.

SEYMOUR, 64 *m.* (1,290 alt., 4,000 pop.) (*see Tour 3*) is at the junction with US 82 and US 277.

THROCKMORTON, 94 *m.* (1,700 alt., 1,299 pop.), is the seat of Throckmorton County, and a junction with State 24 and State 79.

After Throckmorton, 101 *m.* US 283 and US 183 separate. US 283 proceeds south through Callahan County and US 183 moves southeast through Eastland County. US 283 continues, crossing the Clear Fork of the Brazos.

FORT GRIFFIN, 112 *m.* (1,275 alt., 100 pop.) is one of the most famous of Texas frontier towns. Here in 1867 a military post was established, around which a town sprang up that served for many years as an important supply depot and shipping point. Northwest, the plains sweep unbroken for 150 miles to where the up-flung ramparts of the escarpment mark the beginning of the High Plains, which in their turn roll away another 200 miles to the north and west. In 1867 this vast area was unpeopled except for wandering bands of hostile Comanches, Kiowas, and Apaches, who made the passage of their domain hazardous to settlers. Great herds of buffalo roamed the rolling grasslands.

Determined to open that vast region to settlement, the State of Texas demanded protection from Indian raiders, and a military post was established on the old Maxwell Ranch near the Clear Fork of the Brazos. From here sortie after sortie was made against warring tribes, until the country in the immediate vicinity was freed of hostiles. Then the soldiers assumed the duty of conducting and protecting parties sent out by the State to survey land grants being issued in the South Plains and Panhandle areas. In small groups those men went about their jobs, which necessitated fighting more often than working. Surveyors trudged with transit or chain in one hand and rifle in the other.

This era saw the advent of the buffalo hunters, and Fort Griffin became the supply center for those working the South Plains. Hunting outfits bought supplies in the town that sprawled along the bank of the river and around the foot of the hill on top of which the post was located, and headed westward, ascending the escarpment through the crumbling passes of Tule, Yellow House, or Palo Duro Canyons. When their supplies were exhausted and their wagons loaded, they returned to Fort Griffin, then the leading market south of Dodge City for buffalo hides.

Many notable figures walked the town's dusty streets in those days: Pat Garrett, later to win fame by killing Billy the Kid; Billy Dixon, army scout and plainsman; John Poe, first of the range detectives; Bat Masterson, later Dodge City's famous gun-fighting sheriff; and Charlie Brent, pioneer trader. Generals Mackenzie, Miles and Shafter, and other prominent officers were stationed at the post at various times. Goodnight, Loving, Potter, Bacon, Chisholm, Slaughter, and Adams, all famous frontier cattlemen, pushed their holdings northwestward in the wake of the troops and buffalo hunters.

Saloons, gambling halls, dance halls, stores, hide warehouses and stock corrals, formed the business part of this bustling frontier community. There were two ramshackle hotels for transients; the motley array of citizens housed themselves in shacks and hide huts. Fights were frequent, and the town was without law other than that of the six shooter. After the Indians were subdued the troops were withdrawn.

Fort Griffin State Park covers 503 acres along the Clear Fork of the Brazos River. Its appeal is historical and recreational. Camping sites are available. The Old Johnson Ranch House, restored, is hq for the Park Administration. A number of stone buildings, the bakery, powder magazine and sutler's store, have survived; others have been restored. A 16-ft. monument commemorates the frontier days. A notable attraction is the Longhorn Herd of Cattle protected by the State. Although the Longhorn is a symbol of Texas the breed is no longer developed commercially.

ALBANY, 128 m. (1,429 alt., 2,180 pop.), is located on the north fork of Hubbard Creek. On the courthouse lawn, mounted on a sandstone pedestal, is a great iron kettle used in the Ledbetter Salt Works, a pioneer industry. Albany has an athletic field built in hills that form a natural amphitheater. The town is a shipping point for fine Herefords and petroleum. Albany annually in June has the Fort Griffin Fandangle, a pageant of history. Here US 380 moves southeast to Cisco, 33 m. from Albany and joins US 183.

US 183, after leaving US 283 south of Throckmorton, reaches, 9 m., WOODSON, (1,280 pop.). After crossing the Clear Fork of the Brazos, it continues east of HUBBARD CREEK RESERVOIR, which covers 15,250 acres and holds 320,000 acre-ft. At 37 m., BRECKENRIDGE (1,220 alt., 6,273 pop.) seat of Stephens County. The oil strike of 1916–1917 boomed the population to 30,000; after 1921 it shrank. It markets livestock and has petroleum-based industries. Here US 180, east-west highway, forms a 24-mile connection between US 183 at Breckenridge and US 283 at Albany. US 183 passes LAKE DANIEL, part of the Breckenridge water supply, where Gonzales Creek Dam impounds 10,000 acre-ft.

At 55 *m.* LAKE CISCO is formed by Williamson Dam impounding Sandy Creek. It covers 1,059 acres.

CISCO, (1,608 alt., 4,500 pop. est.) is a manufacturing town in a farming county. CISCO JUNIOR COLLEGE, opened 1940, enrolls about 450. Ten miles east of Cisco on US 80 is EASTLAND, (3,500 pop.) seat of Eastland County (*see Tour 19c*).

After Cisco US 183 passes through RISING STAR (916 pop. est.), junction with State 36, the southwest highway from Abilene to Freeport on the Gulf of Mexico. About 10 *m.* farther on US 183 meets a farm road.

Right on this road to BROWNWOOD STATE PARK (*fishing for crappie, bream and bass; swimming, boating, picnicking*), 8.8 *m.,* of 529 acres, embraced by two arms of Lake Brownwood, a 7,300-acre body of water. Drives, trails, and paths lead to inviting spots. An annual regatta is held here on dates fixed by the National Outboard Motor Association.

US 183 proceeds south in Brown County to Brownwood (*Tour 18c*).

Tour 12

Vernon—Paducah—Plainview—Muleshoe—Farwell—(Clovis,   N. Mex.); US 70.
Vernon to New Mexico Line, 238 *m.*

US 70 leads through a region peopled almost exclusively by non-Latin white Americans whose lives are centered around their churches and the price of wheat, cotton, or cattle. Wrested from the Indians after bloody years, the land finally fell into the possession of ranchmen whose domains were vast. When homesteaders and nesters arrived war again flared, as cattlemen fought to retain the free range.

Today ranches and farms—both on a grand scale—operate without rancor. Only the pleasanter side of pioneer life crops out: nearly every community has an Old Settlers Day when men and women in frontier costume dance merry Virginia reels to the rhythm of cowboy bands. The bass viol has won social acceptance, but for the most part the fiddle, the scraping of a hoe, and the pounding on horse shoes or an anvil complete the orchestra.

In sections of the route the world seems to be one great wheat field, only to give way to breaks and canyons suitable solely for ranching. There are wide vistas of sage brush and bear grass, all with a scant over-coating of mesquite.

Larger ranch and farm houses bear marks of luxury, but the unpainted—though seldom dilapidated—dwellings of sharecroppers, or the bunkhouses of cow hands, are much more numerous.

The towns—most of them established in the early 1900's—are much alike, built around the courthouse plaza or public square. From a distance many are given a metropolitan appearance by grain elevators, and a few by tall hotels.

In summer hot winds blow, and clouds of dust often ride them. Mirages are common in this season and rivers and lakes appear, where actually only dust and sage exist.

VERNON, 0 m. (1,205 alt., 12,141 pop.) is at junctions with US 283 (see Tour 11) and US 287 (see Tour 13).

As US 70 winds southwestward it crosses an area of extensive cultivation, where cotton, grain, and garden truck are the principal products. The summer traveler is almost certain to see a mirage. An oil field has added to the region's prosperity.

In CROWELL, 31 m. (1,463 alt., 1,946 pop.), a cupola clock tower on the top of the three-story yellow brick courthouse dominates the small business section. The population includes a few Bohemians, who though largely Americanized, still use their mother tongue.

Right from Crowell on State 283 to a junction with a dirt road, 5.5 m.; R. here past MARGARET, 10.5 m. (200 pop.), a farming community with a few stores, to the SITE OF THE RECAPTURE OF CYNTHIA ANN PARKER, 12.5 m. Here on December 18, 1860, took place a skirmish between Rangers under command of Captain L. S. Ross and a band of Comanches under Peta Nocona, which resulted in the death of the war chief and the rescue of his wife, Cynthia Ann Parker, who had been captured by Indians in 1836.
A daughter, Prairie Flower, was captured with her. One of her sons, Quanah, became a war chief and was later active against the whites.

PADUCAH, 67 m. (1,886 alt., 2,492 pop.), seat of Cottle County raises cotton, grain and livestock. Cotton gins and a farm equipment plant are industries in this quiet little prairie town.

At Paducah is the junction with US 83, which comes from the north combined with US 62. Here US 62 joins US 70 and turns west. They separate at Floydada.

The SOUTH PEASE RIVER, crossed at 81 m., is locally called the Tongue River, and the general vicinity the Land of Tongues, because Indian tribes, Mexicans, and English-speaking settlers once gathered here for conferences.

In an inaccessible spot in this vicinity is TEE PEE CITY, settled by Anglo-Americans in 1879 on a site that had long been a favorite camping ground of the Comanches. It derived is name from the large number of teepee circles found by the first settlers. Tee Pee City was a frontier supply station for freighters and cattlemen. In 1900 there were so few people left that the post office was abolished. Today it is a ghost town and Tee Pee is a creek.

MATADOR, 99 m. (2,347 alt., 1,384 pop.), seat of Motley County, is a town where cowboys still ride in to cash their pay checks. Boot and saddle shops are by far the most popular places of business. Matador's paint-peeled stores straggle around three sides of the courthouse square; the residential district wanders out into the surrounding ranch lands along dusty, unpaved streets. Cowboys come here largely to attend the movies, and they jeer with gusto some of the Hollywood versions of range life. The community's atmosphere of the Old West is due largely to the proximity of the great ranch from which it takes its name.

Matador is on a school section that had not been patented when it was selected as the town site and future county seat. Under the law the patent could not be issued until an affidavit had been filed in the General Land Office, showing that the site was occupied by a town with at least 20 business establishments. To meet this requirement, cowboys of the Matador Ranch opened the required number of places of business, although most of them were literally in the "wide open spaces," without even a roof. A few cans of food, borrowed from the ranch storehouse, constituted a grocery store. A few yards of cloth, displayed on a box, was a drygoods store. A lumberyard came into being with a stock of several fence posts and a spool of barbed wire, and a sack of shelled corn and a bucket of speckled peas became a feed store. But by far the most substantial and prosperous place of business was a saloon. Matador "made the grade," and the patent was granted.

Left from Matador on US 62 to the former headquarters of the huge MATADOR RANCH, which was sold in 1950 and has been broken up. The Matador, with hundreds of thousands of acres under fence, was one of the largest ranches in Texas. It was established in 1879 with headquarters on the present location at Ballard Springs. A dugout near the springs was the first home of the manager, but when his wife arrived lumber was hauled from Fort Griffin to build a two-room shack later called the "White House"—and the manager's house still bears that title—because from it so large a domain was governed. The ranch holdings in 1940 constituted 466,000 acres in Texas, and acreage in Montana. The headquarters was a small village in itself. A dam across a canyon nearby forms a lake stocked with bass and trout. Wolf Creek, Mott, Dutchman Creek, Tee Pee, Turtle Hole, and Roaring Springs line camps are maintained.

Southward on US 62 is ROARING SPRINGS, 8 m. (2,520 alt., 405 pop.), a rural community that is named for springs three miles farther southward in a canyon on the north bank of the Tongue River (swimming, picnicking, camp sites). Roaring Springs was once an Indian camp.

Westward US 70 traverses a region of rugged breaks that is Matador range. Tunnels beneath the roadway permit cattle to pass between pastures.

FLOYDADA, 130 m. (3,137 alt., 4,435 pop. est., 1966) is a center for a large agricultural area. The business district, largely composed of one-story, light face brick structures, surrounds the inevitable courthouse square. Floyd County was named for a defender of the Alamo. Tall grain elevators store and load most of the wheat produced in this vicinity. The town's first business concern (1890) was a saloon—five barrels of whisky displayed on the open prairie—and its first water supply a public well. A contrivance known as a rolling water keg was a familiar sight in early-day Floydada.

Left from Floydada on State 207 and a dirt road to BLANCO CANYON and COCHRAN'S PEAK, 7.5 *m.,* a beauty spot and recreation ground. Through the canyon flows White River. General Mackenzie's expedition against the Comanches camped in the canyon in 1874. The first settlers into the country built there in 1877; they chose this spot because water was available.

PLAINVIEW, 157 *m.* (3,366 alt., 18,753 pop., 1960; 22,525 est., 1966) is the seat of Hale County, which ranks first in grain production in Texas and in the nation. It ranks third in cotton and second in farm income, which has been more than $60,000,000 annually since 1960. Petroleum and natural gas are also county products and Plainview profits as a shipping center by its location on US 87 and 70, principal Texas highways, its Santa Fe and Fort Worth & Denver railroads and numerous motor freight lines.

WAYLAND BAPTIST COLLEGE enrolls more than 700 students.

Shallow water irrigation from 4,300 county wells is responsible for the big crops of the High Plains area.

In OLTON, 183 *m.* (3,615 alt., 1,917 pop.), all except a few brick buildings plainly show the prevailing direction of the wind: the little frame structures lean frankly toward the north, as though tired of the struggle to remain erect before the predominating southerly gale. A belt of sand hills stretches for miles south of the town, and when the wind blows, a fine film of sand descends. Cowboys and old-timers return here for the annual rodeo and reunion held early in August.

In this section's agricultural areas, auction sales assume important proportions. On Saturday afternoons the street corners of small towns are often occupied by strange merchandise, for anyone can hire an auctioneer to sell anything. The rural folk have great social events when some farmer decides to "pull up stakes," and puts his possessions up for auction. These sales are not necessarily the result of misfortune, but are often held when a family wishes to move. Church organizations sell cakes, pies, and candy on the grounds; housewives band together and serve chicken and turkey dinners, or, if the sale is large, the farmer often provides free lunch of hot dogs, cookies, and coffee. Livestock is usually sold first, then the fowls— "rounded up" according to age and type—and finally, household goods and tools. The auctioneer is also a jokester, and is depended upon to add to the crowd's enjoyment.

EARTH, 201.4 *m.* (1,104 pop.), was named during a sandstorm for obvious reasons. A short row of one-story stucco store buildings lines the highway. The July rodeo is popular. The development of a shallow-water belt makes this part of Lamb County a region of irrigated farms.

At 205.2 *m.* is a junction with a private road.

Left on this road to the MASHED O RANCH (*closed to hunters*), 0.6 *m.,* with its headquarters hidden in a grove of cottonwoods and locusts. The owners have set out more than 10,000 trees. The range consists of 120,000 acres and grazes between 7,000 and 8,000 head of fine Herefords. Some acreage is under cultivation for the production of feedstuffs. Bobwhites and Mexican blue quail, prairie chickens, and a small herd of antelopes are found here, and large flocks of wild geese frequent adjacent lakes.

MULESHOE, 217 *m.* (3,789 alt., 3,871 pop., 1960), is the site of the former Muleshoe Ranch from which it took its name. A colonization movement early in the century proved a failure, but the discovery of shallow water resulted in an irrigated district that yields abundant crops. Muleshoe is the seat of Bailey County, a big producer of cotton, grain sorghum and alfalfa. Cowboy music amounts to more than a hobby; almost every house is said to have a guitar, violin or "bull fiddle." Cowboy races are the most popular form of sport. A statue of a mule was unveiled in 1965.

In Muleshoe is the junction with US 84. Besides Muleshoe Ranch, XIT Ranch was partly located in Bailey County. In 1882 the State of Texas gave 300,000 acres of land to a syndicate backed by British investors to insure building of the capitol in Austin, and 50,000 acres for surveying. Large herds of cattle were raised on these huge ranches. By 1917 XIT Ranch had been broken up.

South from Muleshoe on State 214 to NEEDMORE, 14 *m.* (210 pop.). Between this town and ENOCHS, 25 *m.* (275 pop.) is the large MULESHOE NATIONAL WILDLIFE REFUGE (5,809 acres), where huge flocks of ducks, geese and other fowl rest on the Great Western Flyway, from Canada to southern climes.

US 70, now joined by US 84, proceeds to FARWELL, 238 *m.* (4,375 alt., 1,009 pop.) where it is joined by US 60 from Amarillo. John V. Farwell and Charles B. Farwell, brothers, were members of the syndicate that profited from the land appropriated for building the Capitol of Texas. The town is on the State Line, and is the market center of an agricultural region. It has a Highway Commission Information Station.

US 70 crosses the State Line 9 miles east of Clovis, New Mexico (*see New Mexico Guide*).

❧❧❧❧❧❧❧❧❧❧❧❧❧❧❧❧❧❧❧❧❧❧❧❧❧❧❧

Tour 13

Wichita Falls—Quanah—Childress—Amarillo, 225 *m.*; US 287.

Running parallel to the Red River, then northwestward into the heart of the Texas Panhandle, this route is over rolling prairies, flat, grassy plains, and past rough, eroded regions called breaks. It penetrates a rich wheat and cotton belt south of the Red River, then enters one of the State's most picturesque cattle domains—scene of earliest settlement in the Panhandle, a section where lonely dugouts, or houses built of pickets and mud or of buffalo hides, sheltered the pioneers of the High Plains.

Although it is modernized today, this region of great farm and ranch estates retains the flavor of earlier times—a spirit evidenced in numerous barbecues and reunions, in the return of square dances to popularity, in the interest shown by groups and individuals in the preservation of frontier relics and history. Western hospitality prevails; it is reminiscent of the kind displayed earlier here by a host who said to an unexpected guest, "Stranger, you take the wolf skin and the chaw o' sowbelly—I'll rough it."

Economically the people of this northern fringe of Texas have made enormous strides: where once ranching alone was possible large-scale farming has developed, aided by irrigation, and the towns and cities have factories that convert the products of the region into foodstuffs, feed, cloth, building materials and other goods.

The population is predominantly native-born white; Negroes are scarce, and Mexicans are seldom seen except during harvesting seasons, when they migrate from more southerly climates. Part of the first section was settled by Germans and Scandinavians, and in the Panhandle area are many people of English, Scotch or Irish descent.

Section a. WICHITA FALLS to CHILDRESS; 108 m. US 287

This part of US 287 traverses a region of rich agricultural lands and mineral deposits. Diversified farming, livestock raising, oil production, mining of gypsum, and the manufacture of gypsum products are all in evidence. Early settlers battled with Indians for possession of this part of the Great Plains; soldiers, buffalo hunters, and trail drivers forced the pathway for permanent settlement.

Federal irrigation and soil conservation projects have materially aided farmers in this region. Even cotton is grown best on irrigated lands, and truck farming, fruit and small grain production have doubled since the introduction of modern agricultural practices and the conservation of water by means of storage projects and artesian wells.

WICHITA FALLS, 0 m. (946 alt., 109,500 pop. est. 1965) (see Wichita Falls), is at junctions with US 82 (see Tour 3), US 281 (see Tour 9) and US 277 (see Tour 10).

West of Wichita Falls the route is over a wide, four-lane highway, past irrigated fields.

At 16 m. the rambling, old-fashioned white TRIANGLE RANCH HOUSE (R), is headquarters for a large cattle ranch.

ELECTRA, 27 m. (1,229 alt., 4,759 pop., 1960) a busy town of modern appearance, was named for his daughter by W. T. Waggoner, who, while drilling for water on his 600,000-acre ranch in 1911, struck oil. Deep, long-producing wells have maintained Electra's wealth and have given rise to factories that manufacture drilling tools and oil well machinery.

OKLAUNION, 41 *m.* (1,227 alt., 254 pop.), is in a farming community.

Right from Oklaunion on US 183 to the Red River, 6 *m.*, and the State Line, two miles south of Davidson, Okla. (*see Oklahoma Guide*).

VERNON, 50 *m.* (1,205 alt., 13,000 pop.) (*see page 477*), is at junctions with US 283 (*see Tour 11*) and US 70 (*see Tour 12*).

In CHILLICOTHE, 66 *m.* (1,400 alt., 1,610 pop.), the elm-shaded streets are overshadowed by towering grain elevators, flour and cottonseed oil mills. Some of the richest wheat and cotton lands of the Red and Pease Rivers lie around this town, which teems with migratory laborers during harvest seasons.

The near-by State Experiment Farm has developed a drought-resistant grain sorghum called Chiltex. Local farmers have also experimented successfully in rice culture by irrigation.

At 74 *m.* is a junction with an improved road.

Left on this road to LAKE PAULINE (*boats and cabins for rent*), 1 *m.*, an artificial body of water covering 600 acres and impounding three billion gallons. East of the lake are four natural elevations called MEDICINE MOUNDS. The largest and northernmost mound is 250 feet higher than the surrounding terrain, while the smallest and most southern of the group is 200 feet. Around these landmarks are woven many tales of the Comanches. The first settlers found remains of Indian camp sites at the bases of the mounds, and artifacts are still unearthed there. From the Indians, the whites learned that the mounds bore a Comanche name which meant "Making Medicine."

QUANAH, 79 *m.* (1,568 alt., 4,584 pop.), seat of Hardeman County, which raises cotton, wheat and cattle. Since the opening of the Conley oil field in 1959 Quanah has profitable oil refining. The county produces 1,500,000 bbl. annually.

The town was named for Quanah Parker, one-time war chief of the Comanches, son of a white mother, Cynthia Ann Parker. Quanah means Bed of Flowers, but it is hardly symbolic of the life of this chief, who for years fought stubbornly to prevent the advance of white settlement. Time and again he flung his warriors relentlessly at soldiers, Rangers, and settlers, until at last, realizing that further resistance was useless, he returned to the reservation, where he lived as a farmer and tribal leader until 1911. Upon being informed that the town had been named for him he bestowed the following blessing: "May the Great Spirit smile on you, town. May the rains fall in due season; and in the warmth of the sunshine after the rain, may the earth yield bountifully. May peace and contentment dwell with you and your children, forever."

Quanah was founded in the 1880's and became the county seat in 1890 following a hotly contested election. A ruling which established a man's voting place as the place where he had his laundry done for six consecutive weeks qualified the railroad workers, and the county seat was literally washed to its present location.

Quanah has in its vicinity numerous plaster plants, which utilize large deposits of gypsum found nearby.

Left from Quanah on State 283 to the junction with a ranch road, 9 *m.*

Right on this road 1 *m.* to the C. T. Watkins Ranch, the SITE OF THE TEXAS-OKLAHOMA WOLF HUNT (*last week in September*), a distinctive annual sporting event held over the 20,000 acres of hilly lands stretching along the breaks of the Pease River. Here a tent town called Wolf City springs into being; it has a bureau of information, a restaurant tent, a supply tent, and carnival concessions of many kinds. In addition to the hunt, which is called a field trail, there are the bench show, a horn-blowing contest, a hog-calling contest, and an old fiddlers' contest.

For the hunt the dogs are taken to the edge of the breaks, where they are lined up, with the field—afoot, horseback, and in cars—gathered behind them. The master of the hounds gives the final instructions to the dog owners and warns the spectators not to override the dogs. The start is at 4 a.m. Judging in the field trials is somewhat complicated, but the sheer thrill of the chase offers sufficient excitement.

Southward, State 283 dips into the Pease River Valley. The miniature peaks standing side by side in the desert valley to the right are the TEA CUP MOUNTAINS.

At 16 *m.* is a junction with a dirt road.

Left on this road 6 *m.* to the SITE OF THE RECAPTURE OF CYNTHIA ANN PARKER (*see Tour 12*).

ACME, 84 *m.* (1,517 alt., 250 pop.), derives importance from the large gypsum deposits in the vicinity. Since 1891 Acme plants have manufactured wallboard, roofing, plaster of paris, stucco, gypsite, and similar products. Frame cottages of company employees are set in gardens of flowers and vegetables and appear neat in spite of the pall of smoke that always envelops the town.

CHILDRESS, 108 *m.* (1,877 alt., 6,399 pop.), is a railroad division point in an important cattle and agricultural region. Vast wheat fields roll almost to its doors. There is a cooperative cotton compress, a grain elevator and feed factory. Childress has grown around its public square. Home owners have beautified their grounds, so that the houses are set in a profusion of flowers.

Childress occupies land that was once a part of the great OX Ranch. In early days the town had its wild era, and numbered among its outlaw visitors Jesse James. The SCHULTZ HOTEL still stands at the corner of Ave. A and Commerce St., while near the railroad station on Main St. is an old rock building that once housed the OCEAN WAVE SALOON.

Childress is the seat of Childress County and for annual events has its Home Show in April, Greenbelt Golf Tournament, Memorial Day, Greenbelt Quarter Horse Show, May; Greenbelt Bowl Game of prize-winning high school athletes, August.

Section b.   CHILDRESS to AMARILLO; 117 m.   US 287

US 287 proceeds northwestward into the center of the Texas Panhandle. It traverses vast cattle ranches and regions of extensive cultivation, and scales that distinctive geological barrier, the Plains Escarpment, to reach the level of the High Plains.

Northwest of CHILDRESS, 0 *m.*, the route is through broad ranch lands. At 7.5 *m.* is a junction with a dirt road.

Left on this road to LAKE CHILDRESS (BAYLOR LAKE) 610 acres, formed by a dam on a creek flowing into Prairie Dog Town Ford of the Red River.

ESTELLINE, 17 *m.* (1,759 alt., 950 pop.), was once one of the greatest cattle shipping points in the State. Ranchers for hundreds of miles trail-herded to Estelline. Adjacent to the town were established several of the best known large ranches of the State, including the 62 Wells, the Mill Iron, the Diamond Tail, and the Shoe Nail.

Northwestward the route traverses a rich agricultural region; this fertile valley was once the bed of the Red River. Here land terracing is practiced extensively.

MEMPHIS, 31 *m.* (2,067 alt., 3,332 pop.), has a big-city appearance, largely the result of the high cost of lots in early days: business men erected structures of several stories instead of the usual one-story buildings. Memphis is the center of a highly productive and diversified agricultural region where scientific, modern farming methods produce bumper crops of cotton, feedstuffs, vegetables, and fruit.

A business district built largely of red brick surrounds an old courthouse that looks like a private mansion, at CLARENDON, 58 *m.* (2,727 alt., 2,152 pop.). This town is the offspring of one of the first settlements in the Panhandle. Old Clarendon was founded in 1878 by a Methodist minister. Gentlefolk who helped establish the town were joined by other cultured people—graduates of Harvard, Yale, Princeton, and the University of Virginia. Lots were sold with the proviso that the buyer must never sell liquor nor operate a gambling house. Cowboys and buffalo hunters checked their "hardware" at the general store, and so peaceful was the community that it was dubbed Saints Roost. A stage line to Dodge City was started, and a hotel—its walls made of buffalo hides—served travelers. Huge ranches surrounded the little town; round-ups were festive events, marked by a dance each night. Titled Englishmen were ranchmen in this area. In 1887 the railroad missed Old Clarendon, and the town site was moved to the rails.

CLARENDON COLLEGE, stresses courses in agronomy, business and education, enrolls about 186 annually.

GOODNIGHT, 77 *m.* (3,145 alt., 180 pop.), has a few business houses in a bend of the highway, and some frame residences around the old HOME OF COLONEL CHARLES GOODNIGHT (*open*). Behind the house is a pasture enclosing the Goodnight Buffalo Herd of approximately 200 head (*adm. free on request at the Goodnight house*).

Colonel Goodnight was the first cattleman and the first settler in the Panhandle (*see Tour 17b*). From his former home here the view to the northwest reveals the sharply defined outline of the Plains Escarpment, the rugged, twisting shelf that marks the step up to the High Plains.

Most of this region was once part of one of the greatest ranches in the world—the JA Ranch, owned jointly by Colonel Goodnight, the trail blazer, and John Adair, Irish nobleman and financier. The ranch totaled more than a million acres. Today the JA, smaller, is operated by descendants of the Adairs.

From Goodnight the route is northwestward over a roughened terrain, due to the proximity of Palo Duro Canyon to the south.

CLAUDE, 88 *m.* (3,405 alt., 1,041 pop.), is a sprawling, sun-drenched town. Here stands the old ARMSTRONG COUNTY JAIL, erected in the early nineties, which was so unnecessary to the law-abiding community that it was used as a parsonage by the local Methodist minister.

AMARILLO, 117 *m.* (3,676 alt., 167,374 pop. 1965, est.) (*see Amarillo*), is at junctions with US 60 (*see Tour 15*), US 66 (*see Tour 14*), and US 87 (*see Tour 17*).

❧❧❧❧❧❧❧❧❧❧❧❧❧❧❧❧❧❧❧❧❧❧❧❧❧❧❧❧❧❧

Tour 14

(Sayre,   Okla.)—Shamrock—Amarillo—Glenrio—(Tucumcari,   N. Mex.) ; US 66; Interstate 40.
Oklahoma Line to New Mexico Line, 178 *m.*

US 66 slices through the center of the Texas Panhandle, east to west, crossing the High Plains through a region once occupied by great herds of buffalo and bands of Kiowas and Comanches. Here the Indians made their last concerted resistance to white settlers in Texas. Here too, at an unknown date, came the *pastores* (shepherds) of New Mexico to herd their sheep in the rich pasture lands along the Canadian River. There was abundant water, grass and shelter for their flocks. Somehow they remained at peace with the Indians of the region and their little villages throve long before the coming of the Anglo-Americans. Some authorities place the date of the establishment of the earliest of these communities as in the latter part of the eighteenth century. All that is definitely known is that some of them were found in 1875.

These villages were small, probably of never more than 100 population, their houses of adobe and rock huddled together in some sheltered break close to a running stream. Small irrigated fields grew the few crops they needed and their flocks ranged the broad plains, following the best grass. Cattlemen drove most of the sheep herders back into New Mexico, and forced the few who remained to turn to cattle raising.

Today there are only the scattered ruins of buildings and corrals. In Oldham County alone there are nearly a dozen such sites in isolated spots inaccessible except afoot or horseback. On private property, they can be visited only by permission of the ranch owners.

Today this level expanse is rich, producing oil, gas, wheat, small grain crops, and fine Herefords. At intervals the countryside is covered with a pall of smoke from factories and refineries. The land, once believed to be suitable only for ranching, is generally fertile, and tractors have furrowed it mile upon mile. Arid areas contain gypsum and caliche. Approximately 2,000 feet below the surface, an underground extension of the Wichita Mountains of Oklahoma contains enormous oil reserves. Much of the world's supply of helium comes from this section and its natural gas is piped to distant States.

On this treeless plain, days may begin in warmth and end with snow. Dust swirls before northers, sometimes darkening the sun. As the prairie sod was tilled, erosion increased because the protecting cover of grass was gone; and in 1940 the most concerted single program was that of the United States Soil Conservation Service. Strip crops are planted to prevent erosion by wind. Panhandle folk relish their own jokes about the weather; the stranger is likely to hear that in a certain dust storm, "There was a prairie dog 200 feet in the air, trying to dig out."

The population of the region is predominantly native-born white. Since settlement is comparatively new, any 25-year resident is considered an old-timer. Reunions of early settlers and their descendants are popular, and almost every family has a member of the Panhandle Old-timers' Association, which preserves folklore.

Jackrabbits and prairie dogs scurry from the roadside, and quail rise from grain fields. Almost every large ranch is a game preserve. Canada geese and many varieties of ducks stop at watering places on seasonal migrations.

US 66 crosses the OKLAHOMA LINE, 0 *m.,* 24 miles west of Sayre, Okla. (*see Oklahoma Guide*).

SHAMROCK, 14 *m.* (2,281 alt., 3,113 pop.), is in the eastern part of the Panhandle gas field, one of the largest known gas reservoirs in the world. It maintains a neat appearance despite the heavy clouds of black smoke that rise from the stacks of nearby carbon black plants. Shamrock also has several gasoline extraction plants. Wells flowing as much as 100 million cubic feet of gas daily have been discovered in the surrounding field, and the use of the product in the manufacture of gasoline formerly caused wide protest because of waste.

Here, each fourth week in February is held the Eastern Panhandle Live Stock Show. In Shamrock is a junction with US 83.

In the 93 miles between Shamrock and Amarillo are a number of farm towns, some of which have lost population in recent decades. They include LELA, McLEAN, ALANREED, GROOM, LEEK and CONWAY, largest of which, Alanreed, has less than 500. LAKE McCLELLAN is west of Alanreed in Gray County. It holds 5,105 acre-ft. of water.

In AMARILLO, 107 *m.* are junctions with US 87 and US 287.

More than half the world's supply of helium has been recovered and processed in the UNITED STATES HELIUM PLANT (*visited only by special arrangements made in advance*), 116 *m*. (L).

BUSHLAND and WILDORADO are farm towns in the 36 miles between Amarillo and Vega.

VEGA (meadow), 142 *m*. (4,030 alt., 658 pop.), is the seat of Oldham County. A grain elevator and cattle shipping pens indicate its chief activities.

Right from Vega on a dirt road to OLD TASCOSA, 22 *m.*, queen of Texas ghost towns. Here, on the north bank of the Canadian River, where once four blocks of business establishments served a motley frontier population, nothing remains but the rock courthouse and a few crumbling adobe structures. Giant cottonwoods shade the silent, sandy streets, and wind-driven sand drifts deeply where once patient cowponies stood tied to the hitching rack of the Equity Bar.

Tascosa developed from the sheep camp called Plaza Atascosa. In 1876, Harry Kimble opened a blacksmith shop and general merchandise store, and a saloon soon followed. A north-bound cattle and freight trail crossed the Canadian at the old Tascosa ford. The second town in the Panhandle, Tascosa soon won the title of "The Cowboy Capital of the Plains," and no community of the old West ever had a more hectic existence. Wild Riders of the High Plains, in from the ranches or stopping over on the trail, indulged in carousals. Food, liquor, and women—Tascosa offered them all; and the cowboys, buffalo hunters, freighters, and plainsmen flocked to the feast. Saloonkeepers, gamblers, and legitimate tradespeople welcomed them with open arms. Any night in the colorful era of Tascosa's heyday, crowds filled the saloons and gambling halls, and clattered along the board walks. Wild yells, discordant songs, jangling music, and pistol shots were familiar sounds, and not infrequently alcoholically-quickened tempers flared into tragic gunplay.

It was more than 150 miles to Springer, New Mexico, the first town west; more than 100 to Mobeetie, nearest settlement to the east; and 200 barren miles to Dodge City, Kansas, the closest town to the north. Before the opening of the mail route, Old Dad Barnes gathered up mail, and for 50 cents a letter carried it to the railhead at Dodge City.

Isolated from the restraints of civilization, without law other than that of the six-shooter, Tascosa was indeed a "tough town to tame." Men whose names have appeared frequently in the pages of history and story were familiar figures in this wildest of Wild West communities—Pat Garrett, John W. Poe, Bat Masterson, Charlie Siringo, and George Sutton, all famous later as gunfighters on the side of the law; Billy the Kid, Tom O'Halliard, Charlie Bowdre, Dave Rudabaugh, Bob Campbell, and Frank James, of the outlaw tribe. Tascosa grew and so did its BOOT HILL, the little mound where were buried those who died with their boots on. The exact number of graves on Boot Hill is unknown, but 28 are visible. The largest consignment to this doubtful honor was the indirect result of that unusual labor dispute, the cowboy strike of the 1880's. About 200 cowboys saved their wages for months prior to the date set for their demonstration, and when the strike went into effect they had a plentiful supply of food and cash. A group of about 50 of the strikers rode to the ranch of one of the cattlemen who opposed their demands for higher wages, but he had been warned and met them with several shots. This was virtually the end of the strike, but rustling and "sleepering" (the unlawful branding of unmarked calves) became increasingly worse, and when the ranchers imported hired gunmen to stop it, a fight ensued in the streets of Tascosa. Four were killed and several wounded. The dead, wrapped in their saddle blankets, were buried the next day in Boot Hill.

Tascosa never became a really peaceful community. Like the citizens on Boot Hill, it literally died with its boots on when the railroads passed to the west and south. The county seat was moved to Vega, and only "Frenchy" McCormick remained of the many colorful figures Tascosa had known. She was the belle of the gay days when the town boomed with the trade of a cattle empire. When Tascosa faded and its citizens moved away, "Frenchy" refused to leave. "Her man," gambler Mickey McCormick of the old days, lies buried in the little cemetery, and her one wish in life was to stay close to him until the time when she would occupy the grave by his side. From 1915 to the spring of 1939 she lived alone here, and it was not until infirmities overtook her that she consented to move.

"Frenchy's" departure did not leave Tascosa untenanted for long. The Maverick Club of Amarillo had peen planning the establishment of a boys ranch patterned after the famous Boy's Town of Omaha, Nebraska, and on June 1, 1939, MAVERICK BOYS' RANCH was opened. Ranch headquarters were established in the old courthouse building, a rock structure that had weathered the years. In the ancient halls of justice that once rang to the sonorous tones of Temple Houston and other frontier lawyers, youthful voices sound in the boys' dormitory. The courthouse vault now serves as a library. This building and another, together with 140 acres of land, were the donation of Julian Bivins, son of a pioneer cattleman.

The institution is non-sectarian. Maverick Boys' Ranch is open to any youngster whose circumstances are such that he would otherwise have little chance of becoming a good citizen. In 1940, 16 boys were enrolled, ranging in age from 6 to 15 years. The project is financed by private donations.

Younger boys attend school in an adobe building which served as a church in the old town. The others attend high school in Channing. The boys are taught handicrafts, and they work about the place, caring for the ranch milk cows and tending the garden. They have marked the foundations of buildings of the vanished community, indicating their former uses. This pleases the tourists who come to visit the old town and its lonely Boot Hill.

Only ADRIAN, with less than 300 people, breaks the monotony of the plains in the 36 miles between Vega and Glenrio. Here begins State 214, proceeding straight south parallel with the New Mexican border until it ends at Seminole.

GLENRIO, 178 m. (3,812 alt., 150 pop.), sits astride the Texas-New Mexico Line, in Deaf Smith County, its small stores and dwellings in the grassy hollow of a little creek.

US 66 crosses the State Line 41 miles east of Tucumcari, New Mexico (see New Mexico Guide).

I◆◆I◆◆I◆◆I◆◆I◆◆I◆◆I◆◆I◆◆I◆◆I◆◆I◆◆I◆◆I◆◆I◆◆I◆◆I◆◆I◆◆I◆◆I◆◆I◆◆I◆◆I◆◆I◆◆I◆◆

Tour 15

(Arnett, Okla.)—Higgins—Pampa—Amarillo—Farwell—(Clovis, N. Mex.) ; US 60.
Oklahoma Line to New Mexico Line, 224 m.

Running diagonally and in a southwesterly direction, this route traverses the almost treeless undulations of the High Plains across the Texas Panhandle. Here granite mountains—now deeply buried—once stood, and the oceans of past ages deposited immense strata of marine limestone. Evidences of ancient human habitation have been found, including one culture indicating that man existed here in the Stone Age. Certain of these early inhabitants lived in houses built underground, their walls made of limestone slabs set in adobe. Along the Canadian River archeologists have found traces of a civilization resembling that of the Pueblos. Certain historians believe that in the present northeast corner of the Panhandle of Texas, Coronado found his Gran Quivira among Indian towns clustered along the Canadian and its tributaries. Coronado's expedition, it is believed, supplied the name *Llano Estacado* (Staked Plains) as applied to the High Plains, because his men found it necessary to stake their trail with piles of bones and buffalo skulls so that the rear guard would not go astray, as the vast open region had no landmarks.

Ranching was attempted here only after buffalo hunters and United States soldiers had helped subdue the Indians. Railroads building through in the 1880's gave rise to most of the towns. English and Scotch syndicates owned huge ranches in the vicinity of the route, retarding settlement until their holdings were reduced. Farming began at the turn of the century, and constantly increasing agricultural operations have converted thousands of acres into wheat and cotton fields. Oil and gas development has more recently increased general prosperity.

Less than two per cent of the population is foreign-born. Largely because the people are predominantly rural, they think and behave usually as a section. Educational standards are high, and both urban and rural schools have benefited from petroleum wealth. Musical organizations perpetuate cowboy songs and other indigenous expressions. The lore of the plains is cherished, and old-time outdoor gatherings feature the costumes, dances and music of the past.

Wildlife, except for jackrabbits and prairie dogs, is relatively scarce. Duck hunting is available in season on numerous ponds and small artificial lakes.

With an altitude in some places as great as 4,500 feet, these unbroken plains are subject to sudden extreme changes of temperature, especially in the late autumn and early spring. In the summer severe dust storms sometimes sweep the area.

US 60 crosses the OKLAHOMA LINE, 0 *m.,* 15 miles west of Arnett, Okla., into Lipscomb, farthest NE county.

HIGGINS, 1.5 *m.* (2,569 alt., 812 pop.), is a small but important marketing and shipping center. At some unknown spot, believed to be about 15 miles northwest of Higgins, is the unmarked grave of Fray Juan de Padilla, the Franciscan who accompanied Coronado to Gran Quivira, and who one year later returned to preach and minister to the Indians. For two years he labored, and it was upon a trip to extend the influence of his ministry that he encountered a band of strange Indians and was killed, in November, 1544. His companions escaped and returned to tell the tale of his martyrdom—the first missionary killed within the present boundaries of Texas.

Southwest of Higgins lies an unbroken sweep of grasslands.

GLAZIER, 16.8 *m.* (2,601 alt., 125 pop.), old and weathered, is a supply point for the far-flung ranches of the region. A careful check of the movements of Coronado's expedition from the time it left the accepted landmark of Palo Duro Canyon, places part of the location of the long-sought Gran Quivira in the immediate vicinity of Glazier, on the divide between Wolf Creek and the Canadian River.

Southwest of Glazier the highway crosses more range land. (*Dry creek beds are dangerous during heavy rains.*) The terrain roughens into the breaks of the Canadian River. North of Glazier on State 305 to LIPSCOMB, seat of Lipscomb County.

At 25.2 *m.* is the junction with US 83 (*see Tour 16*), which is concurrent with US 60 for a distance of 9.7 miles.

The CANADIAN RIVER, 25.5 *m.,* is crossed on a narrow bridge. Cottonwoods and willows along its banks are the only trees for miles.

CANADIAN, 27.1 *m.* (2,340 alt., 2,068 pop.), lying in a curve of the Canadian River, was known first as Hogtown, then as Desperado City. The first citizens were railroad construction men, buffalo hunters, and soldiers. It is the seat of Hemphill County. Its Rodeo and Old Timers Reunion on July 4 is a big regional event.

Near Canadian, at a point about 18 miles southeast of town, inaccessible except by little-used roads, is the SITE OF THE BUFFALO WALLOW FIGHT. Here on September 12, 1874, Amos Chapman, Billy Dixon, and four companions fought an all-day battle against a large force of Indians. Caught on the open prairie, the frontiersmen took refuge in the shallow depression of a buffalo wallow and, plentifully supplied with ammunition, held their ground against repeated attacks. Every man of the group was wounded. With darkness came a terrific storm that drove the Indians to shelter and provided water for the parched defenders. Unable to move because three were seriously wounded, they awaited the renewal of the attack at dawn, but were unexpectedly relieved by a column of cavalry from Camp Supply.

East of Canadian 11 *m.* on Ranch Road 2266 is LAKE MARVIN on Boggy Creek, a small reservoir.

MIAMI, 51 *m.* (2,802 alt., 953 pop.), is strung along a shelf between a steep hill and the banks of Red Deer Creek; every street runs uphill. The weathered houses, with their abundance of lightning rods, are like dignified old pincushions. Here is the only post office in Roberts County, an area of 900 square miles. The surrounding territory is rich in prehistoric ruins and fossil beds. Coronado described the habitations of the Indians of this locality as "rude huts of straw and hides." In the office of the county judge, in the courthouse, is a COLLECTION OF ARTIFACTS AND FOSSILS (*open workdays, free*).

A veritable forest of oil derricks surrounds PAMPA, 73 *m.* (3,230 alt., 24,664 pop.), so named because of the resemblance of the encircling prairies to the Argentine pampas. Its Industrial Foundation, a non-profit civic enterprise, draws factories; the community backed the new Coronado Inn and the Youth and Community Center. The cattle feeding pens can serve 12,000 head at one time. The Top o' Texas stock show in

March and the Rodeo in August draw crowds. Pampa is the seat of Gray County. LAKE McCLELLAN, 25 *m*. south, is a recreation area.

In PANHANDLE, 101 *m*. (3,451 alt., 2,500 pop.), grain elevators lift their great bulks over the flat prairies. In this vicinity the great 6666 Ranch, 160 sections of land, still presents a saga of the cattle industry.

Due north from Panhandle on State 15, 41 *m.*, to BORGER (20,911 pop., 1960) metropolis of Hutchinson County and hub of a vast reservoir of natural gas. It is a base for Phillips Petroleum Co. and has petro-chemical industries. A huge dome serves as a civic center. It is reached by Central Airlines. FRANK PHILLIPS COLLEGE, junior, opened 1948, enrolls more than 600. LAKE MEREDITH FESTIVAL, with beauty contest, is held first week in June. Hutchinson County produces nearly 10,000,000 bbl. of oil annually. STINNETT (2,695 pop.) county seat, 15 *m*. farther north on State 15, is grain center.

Across the Canadian River in northeast part of county is the site of THE BATTLE OF ADOBE WALLS, 60 *m*. Here in 1874, 28 white men and one woman battled for nearly three days against an attacking force estimated variously as between 500 and 1,500 warriors, from the Kiowa, Comanche, and Cheyenne tribes. The Indians were under the leadership of Quanah Parker, half-breed son of Cynthia Ann Parker, who had been captured when a child in 1836 (*see Tour 12*). Lone Wolf led the Kiowa contingent, while the Cheyennes fought under the leadership of a chieftain named White Shield.

The plan, as devised by Parker was a surprise raid that would sweep across northern Texas, through Oklahoma, and up into Kansas, wiping out all the buffalo hunting outfits that dotted the unpeopled plains. This place, the most important gathering point of the buffalo hunters, was chosen for the opening attack. Adobe Walls disposed of, the raiders could then proceed, "keeping the news behind them," and annihilating camp after camp throughout the territory which the Indians believed rightfully theirs under the treaty of Medicine Lodge (1867). The time of attack was set for the morning of June 27, just before dawn, when the hunters would probably be asleep.

On the night of June 26, occupants of the buildings at Adobe Walls got into their blankets early, as several of the outfits planned to leave at daylight on a hunt. They slept without sentries, there having been no Indian trouble for a long time. About 2 a.m. the ridge pole of one of the buildings broke and awakened the sleepers. Billy Dixon decided not to turn in again, but to prepare his kit for the day's hunting. While so engaged he discovered the approaching Indians. His shouted alarm aroused his companions just as the Indians arrived in so swift a charge that two freighters sleeping in a wagon were killed in their blankets.

With their heavy caliber buffalo guns and six-shooters the hunters blasted the opening attack into a retreat, but, re-forming, the Indians charged again and again, throughout the day. Riding up to the buildings, some tried to force their horses through the barricaded doors, while others dismounted and tried to climb in through the windows. So narrow were these openings that only one defender at a time could take position at them, but the others hurriedly reloaded the rifles and pistols, so that an almost constant stream of lead poured upon the attackers.

Other buffalo hunters, on their way to Adobe Walls, saw the fight from a distance and rode to sound an alarm. A small rescue party was quickly assembled, but before they arrived the Indians, discouraged and weakened in leadership by the wounding of Quanah Parker, had given up the fight and retired.

Ten years earlier, in 1864, Colonel Kit Carson, famed scout and frontiersman, with a force of 396 Federal soldiers and Indian scouts, fought an all-day battle with 1,000 Indians near Adobe Walls. The fight ended in a draw, but the following day Carson retreated to Taos, New Mexico.

At 124 *m*. is the junction with US 66 (*see Tour 14*).

AMARILLO, 129 *m*. (3,676 alt., 167,374 est. 1967) (*see Amarillo*), is at junctions with US 66, US 287, and US 87.

Southwestward the highway traverses level prairie lands. Far to the left a ribbon of green marks the winding course of Tierra Blanca Creek, one of the few streams of running water in the region.

HEREFORD, 176 *m.* (3,806 alt., 7,652 pop., 1960; 10,000 est., 1965) is the seat of Deaf Smith County, so named for Erasmus (Deaf) Smith, commander of scouts at the battle of San Jacinto. It is a center for white-faced Hereford cattle, marketing about 22,000 head valued at $7,000,000 annually. Principal crops are grain sorghum (8,000,000 bu.) and wheat (3,000,000 bu.). Since World War II Hereford has become the center for a huge vegetable industry, including potatoes, onions, carrots and lettuce, profiting by extensive irrigation. The Holly Sugar Co. in 1964 located a large refinery in Hereford with a capacity of 50,000 tons or more, giving importance to the sugar beet crop. There are 365,000 acres of irrigated land in Deaf Smith County. An average farm, land and buildings, is valued at $200,000.

Hereford won national attention when a dental expert reported fewer cavities than usual among the teeth of school children. The water was believed to contain beneficial qualities.

Here in 1881 one of the first barbed wire fences to be built in Texas was erected, to keep the cattle of the T Anchor Ranch from drifting southward. Many pioneers of this region lived in dugouts, some of which remain in varying stages of ruin. In the vicinity are found ruins of slab houses erected by prehistoric people (*see First Americans*).

Westward US 60 traverses a region where grain is king. Only occasionally is there a section of unplowed range land.

FARWELL, 224 *m.* (4,375 alt., 1,009 pop.), is at the junction with US 70 (*see Tour 12*).

US 60 crosses the State Line in Farwell, nine miles east of Clovis, New Mexico (*see New Mexico Guide*).

Tour 16

(Gray, Okla.)—Perryton—Childress—Abilene—Junction—Laredo—Brownsville; US 83.
Oklahoma Line to Brownsville, 923 *m.*

The slightly less than a thousand miles of contrasts lying between Texas' northernmost boundary and southernmost point are traversed by this route, which begins in the eastern half of the Panhandle and extends in almost a straight line down the State's full length to Port Isabel. No other Texas route offers such differences in topography, produce, climate and people. Starting on the high, rolling plains of the Llano Estacado, where snow flies in winter, it skirts the rugged outline of the Cap Rock, the geological barrier that separates the High Plains and the Central Plains, crosses the wooded, hilly Edwards Plateau and the Balcones Escarpment, descends to the rolling, open, semitropical Coastal Plain, and ends in warm sunshine at the Gulf of Mexico.

Wheat lands and cotton fields, alternating with vast grassy flat pastures, lie between the State Line and Abilene; goats, sheep and Herefords, honey, small grains and the great pecan bottoms of many running streams furnish livelihoods in the next large geographical section, to Uvalde. Beyond, on the broad prairies that hug the north bank of the Rio Grande, citrus fruits, onions, spinach and carrots create wealth in the Winter Garden. Southward, the citrus orchards of the palm-studded Lower Rio Grande Valley yield subtropical harvests.

Sociologically the contrasts are fully as great. The predominantly Anglo-Saxon Panhandle section, with its traditions of huge cattle ranches owned by English noblemen, is related to the cosmopolitan Lower Rio Grande Valley population only by the bonds of statehood. A Swedish colony on the plains and the folk of the grass or stick-and-mud *jacales* of the Texas-Mexican border have but one thing in common—both are Texans.

Section a.   OKLAHOMA LINE to CHILDRESS; 159 m.
US 83–60

Running across almost treeless plains, this part of the route pierces vast grain and cotton lands through a region once occupied solely by enormous ranches. The weather is erratic in winter, when northers sometimes bring a swift change from sunshine to howling blizzards. Livestock thrive on nutritious prairie grasses in summer, and are sheltered in the rugged breaks of streams during the cold months.

This area was one of the last in the State to be settled. An interval of about 300 years elapsed between the expedition of Coronado in 1541 and the arrival of the earliest non-Latin explorers. Following the Civil War, the plains Indians made a stubborn stand against white settlement, thus delaying general development until the 1880's.

US 83 crosses the OKLAHOMA LINE, 0 m., six miles south of Gray, Oklahoma (*see Oklahoma Guide*).

PERRYTON, 7 m. (2,942 alt., 9,000 pop. est.), is most northern county seat in Texas. The town is of recent origin (1919) and was formed largely by citizens of Ochiltree, Texas, and Gray, Oklahoma, who moved to the new town site hauling their homes intact, hitched to tractors.

Surrounded by great wheat fields, Perryton in June teems with harvest hands—men from all parts of the State, who are forced to sleep in box cars or in the fields, for accommodations are limited. Perryton has many harvester supply houses.

Right from Perryton on State 15 to a junction with a graded road, 37 *m.;* L. here to a junction with a dirt road, 44 *m.;* R. here to the SITE OF THE BATTLE OF ADOBE WALLS, 50 *m.*

South of Perryton one great grainfield succeeds another, except where pasture lands intervene.

Nothing remains at the SITE OF OCHILTREE, 15 *m.,* to indicate that here was once a thriving community that became a ghost town with the removal of the county seat.

Southward across Wolf Creek the way is through what was once buffalo country. A legend tells of the existence of a white bull buffalo that roamed this section. Indians feared the ghostly creature and hunters tried to kill him. When the great herds were scattered it was said the big bull led a last mad stampede southward.

At 51 *m.* is the junction with US 60, which is concurrent with US 83 for a distance of 9.7 miles (*see Tour 15*). At 61 *m.* US 60 turns west, US 83 proceeds south. BRISCOE, (210 pop.) is a few miles east of US 83 in Wheeler County. After crossing the Sweetwater River it meets State 152 at WHEELER (1,150 pop. est.) county seat.

SHAMROCK, 104 *m.* (2,281 alt., 3,113 pop.) is at the junction with US 66 (*see Tour 14*).

The route now enters a range of hills called the Rocking Chair Mountains. In this section were the lands of one of the most unusual ranching ventures of early days in the Panhandle. Here, in 1883, a group of British noblemen, headed by the Baron of Tweedmouth and the Earl of Aberdeen, purchased 235 sections of land, stocked it with approximately 15,000 cattle, and through it scattered the estates of members of the organization. The domain was called the Rocking Chair Ranch, from its brand; but Texas cowboys dubbed it the Nobility Ranch. As a refuge for British younger sons it also came to be called The Kingdom of Remittance Men. The scions of nobility, however, proved to be poor cattlemen. Systematic stealing quickly depleted their herds and the venture soon was a financial failure. Disgusted, they returned to England, leaving the town names of Tweedy, Shamrock, Wellington, Clarendon, and Aberdeen.

WELLINGTON, 129 *m.* (1,980 alt., 3,190 pop. est.) was part of the Rocking Chair lands. It is a cotton center and seat of Collingsworth County. Beyond Wellington US 62 from Oklahoma joins US 83 for nearly 50 *m.*

CHILDRESS, 159 *m.* (1,877 alt., 6,399 pop.) is at the junction with US 287 (*see Tour 13*).

Section b. CHILDRESS to ABILENE; 154 m. US 83-277

This region—through the High Plains—is about equally divided between stock raising and agriculture. The semi-arid lands produce abundant grass and many mesquite trees. Cotton is a leading crop; it is picked by migratory Mexicans who swarm into the region in automobiles of all ages and descriptions, large families and their friends squeezed inside, and the washtub, lantern and bedrolls tied outside, with sometimes a chicken coop dangling from the rear bumper.

This part of west-central Texas is pitted with canyons and breaks, and its hills are gray-green with cedars.

South of CHILDRESS, 0 *m.,* the road is through the breaks of the Pease River. Eroded hills roll away on every hand, their gullied slopes showing flashes of dull red soil streaked with blue-white gypsum.

DUNLAP, 21 *m.* is a hamlet in Cottle County.

PADUCAH, 31 *m.* (1,886 alt., 2,492 pop.) (*see Tour 12*), is at the junction with US 70 (*see Tour 12*).

The route now enters cattle country. Among the large ranches of King County are Matador and Four Sixes.

GUTHRIE, 59 *m.* (1,754 alt., 300 pop.) county seat, is at the junction with US 82.

Low hills sparsely covered with clumps of cedars are crossed, and at intervals signs give notice that the land is a game preserve. Wolves, wildcats, and coyotes inhabit this region. Wolf hunts are held regularly by ranchmen.

The road climbs to the top of a steep bank, 77 *m.,* and skirts the winding course of the SALT FORK OF THE BRAZOS RIVER, crossed at 79.5 *m.*

At 91 *m.* is a junction with US 380 (*see Tour 27*).

ASPERMONT, 94 *m.* (1,773 alt., 1,286 pop.), retail and shipping center, is on the rise of land between the Salt Fork and the Double Mountain Fork of the Brazos. A few miles northeast, on a ridge above the breaks of the Double Mountain Fork there lived a man reputed to have spent a fortune searching for treasure. According to an old map, the land around his place was the site of a forgotten Spanish mission, within the walls of which was buried a huge amount of Aztec gold. Aspermont is the seat of Stonewall County, named for Stonewall Jackson. (Jackson County was named for Andrew).

Also in the vicinity of Aspermont, in an almost inaccessible spot, is the SITE OF THE GHOST TOWN OF ORIENT. Here a promoter with a "salted" silver mine sold claims to hundreds, at from $50 to $1,000 a claim, and absconded with the proceeds. At the height of the boom Orient was a tent and shack city of several thousand persons. Today only the partly caved-in shaft of the mine is left.

Southeast of Aspermont, on the banks of the Double Mountain Fork, once stood Rath City, a thriving dugout town, one of the most widely known of the buffalo hunters supply depots, from which were shipped thousands of hides. Not a trace remains of its dugouts, one of which—the supply store and saloon—was 25 feet wide and 50 feet long.

In Aspermont is the junction with US 380 (*see Tour 27*).

Southward US 83 winds through rugged hills and twisted ravines. Southwest lie the twin peaks of DOUBLE MOUNTAIN (2,500 alt.), a landmark for early-day travelers. In the region overlooked by the two summits ran the trails blazed by Marcy, Pope, Johnston, and Mackenzie. Southeast stands FLAT TOP MOUNTAIN, another landmark.

HAMLIN, 113 *m.* (1,750 alt., 3,500 pop.) has most of its residents in Fisher County, others in Jones. It is a railroad division point. Gypsum, sand, and gravel deposits furnish local industries.

Right from Hamlin on a dirt road is the site of SWEDONA, 7 *m.,* once an immigration objective. It was founded in 1877 by a colony of Swedes, and it and the farming section around it retain many old-country customs. Men, women, and children shoulder their implements and march off to work in the fields. At noon the *matmoder* (food mother) serves a meal of hard-baked rye bread, potatoes, bacon, sausage, home-made cheese with hot boiled milk, and home-brewed ale. Sometimes there are cheese dumplings, puddings, cobblers, and home-made mincemeat. Saturday night socials are popular, and on these occasions old-timers gather about the fiddlers. An aged grandfather produces his *nyckelharpa* (harmonica) and plays the old familiar *folkviser* (folk songs) while others join hands in a rollicking, boisterous dance. These and other farmers of the vicinity conduct rabbit drives regularly to protect their crops.

At 129 *m.* is the junction with US 277 (*see Tour 10*), which runs concurrent with US 83 for a distance of 81 miles (*see Tour 10*).

ABILENE, 154 *m.* (1,719 alt., 103,076 pop.) (*see Tour 10*), is at junctions with US 80 (*see Tour 19*) and US 84 (*see Tour 21*). Here US 83 leaves US 277, and joins US 84 for a short distance south; US 277 moves southwest. The main east-west highway, US 80, is the route of Interstate 20.

Section c.   ABILENE to JUNCTION; 152 m.
US 83–84–277–290

Crossing the southeastern expanse of the High Plains, this part of the route climbs into the Edwards Plateau, traversing a rugged region where fishing for black bass, perch and crappie, and wild turkey and deer hunting, are excellent. Cotton and small grains are grown on the plains area, but goat and sheep ranching are major industries in the plateau's hills.

In rural communities of this section life is much as it was in early days: church socials, box and pie suppers, quilting bees and cemetery beautifications are held. Singing schools and community Sunday night "sings" are popular.

Between ABILENE, 0 *m.,* and Ballinger the route runs parallel and a few miles east of US 277 (*see Tour 10*).

BALLINGER, 56 *m.* (1,630 alt., 5,000 pop.), is at junctions with US 67 (*see Tour 18*) and State 158, which connects with US 277 farther west.

At 71.3 *m.* is a junction with a dirt road.

Right here through a gate to PAINT ROCK PICTOGRAPHS (*adm. by permission obtained at cottage just inside gate*), 0.9 *m.,* an area where hundreds of rock pictures cover sheltered spots on a bluff along the Concho River. Most of the paintings are in red, but others are in black and white or orange and white. Some of the pictographs are prehistoric, while others were made by later tribes. Among the more modern subjects are a mission and a devil with barbed tail and pitchfork.

The CONCHO RIVER (*fishing, camping, boating, and swimming facilities*), is crossed at 71.5 *m.*

PAINT ROCK, 72 *m.* (1,640 alt., 893 pop.), is the seat of Concho County. The town is a shipping center for wool, and a railroad terminal. Its name is derived from the numerous rock paintings along the Concho River in this vicinity.

EDEN, 93 *m.* (2,046 alt., 1,486 pop.), built on hills and shaded by oaks, is a shopping center for cotton farmers and sheep ranchers.

In Eden is the junction with US 87 (*see Tour 17*).

The route now winds through the hilly country of the Edwards Plateau, grazing grounds for thousands of sheep and goats. The hills are rocky, brush- and cedar-covered.

Wool and mohair are shipped from MENARD, 114 *m.* (1,870 alt., 1,969 pop.), which is scattered along the banks of the San Saba River in a beautiful green valley. In Legion Park, in front of the courthouse, remains part of an irrigation ditch that was in a system laid out by Franciscan monks. State 29 is an east-west highway.

1. Right from Menard on an unimproved dirt road to PRESIDIO DE SAN LUIS DE LAS AMARILLAS (Fort St. Louis of the Amarillas), 3 *m.*, established in 1757 by Colonel Diego Ortiz Parrilla to protect a nearby mission establishment. It was also a halfway station between San Antonio and Santa Fe, and was to safeguard the opening of the reputedly rich silver deposits of the vicinity. The purpose of the presidio failed, ten settlers and soldiers and two padres being killed in an Indian attack one year later. Further hostilities led to the campaign of 1759 in which a force under Parrilla marched to the Red River (*see Tour 3b*). The wooden buildings of the presidio were replaced in 1761 by a fort of stone and mortar. In the river here, ruins of the dam built by the mission Indians are visible; and until a few years ago, farmers used the old irrigation ditches to water their crops.

Recent restorations have re-created a part of the presidio establishment, including the chapel and adjacent rooms, and a bastion at the northwest corner, rebuilt on old foundations disclosed by excavation. The chapel is used as a museum.

Westward the road leads to the town of FORT McKAVETT (110 pop.), 23 *m.*, housed in the former buildings of Fort McKavett, established by the Federal government in 1852.

2. Left from Menard on a dirt road to MISSION SANTA CRUZ (Holy Cross), known as the San Saba Mission, 0.8 *m.* Here, on the south bank of the San Saba River were the mission buildings erected in 1757. The settlement was abandoned by the Spanish in 1758, after an Indian attack. The site is now a park and some of the Spanish buildings have been restored.

South of Menard the route is through rolling hill country.

CLEO, 140 *m.* (36 pop.), caters to hunters and fishermen who, in season, flock to this section of Texas (*obtain permission to hunt or fish from property owners*). Armadillos are abundant in this vicinity.

In the rugged hill region now traversed, towering limestone cliffs frown down on the highway, and the surrounding hills are covered with thick growths of cedar (*camp sites plentiful along streams*).

At 147.6 *m.* is the western junction with US 290 (*see Tour 24*).

JUNCTION, 152 *m.* (2,180 alt., 2,500 pop., est.), wedged between high hills and on the wooded banks of the clear Llano River, has modern buildings, but its wide streets are frequented by big-hatted ranchmen.

Junction is the seat of Kimble County and the market center of a large area in which sheep and goat raising, and the livestock industry, are paramount. Fishermen and hunters find good sport in the vicinity.

In 1877 Major John B. Jones of the Frontier Battalion ordered a "round-up" of Kimble County. The Rangers combed each draw and arroyo and literally herded every man in the county, good and bad, into a mesquite flat between the river forks just outside of Junction. The round-up completed, the Rangers "cut the herd," exactly as though they were cattle. The robbers, outlaws, cattle- and horse-thieves, hold-up men and murderers were escorted to old Kimbleville and held there, chained to trees—there being no courthouse nor jail—until court could be called. That was the last of organized outlawry in this area.

In the City Park, on the southern edge of Junction, a cliff towers above a pool of clear water. Junction has ranch motels with swimming facilities and the V Bar H Dude Ranch on the Llano River. Hunting for deer in season.

In Junction is the eastern junction with US 290 and US 377.

Section d. JUNCTION *to* LAREDO; *256 m.* US 83, US 377; State 55

This part of the route leads through canyons and over divides of the southern section of the Texas hill country into the rolling reaches of the upper Coastal Plain, which sweeps away toward the Rio Grande.

Between Junction and Montell, ranchmen who occupy houses built by their forefathers shape their own destinies and those of towns upon the price of wool and mohair. Black bass, perch, and trout are in the streams; deer and small game are abundant.

Southward, where Mexican laborers have for decades chopped chaparral from fertile acres, intensive agriculture made possible by irrigation has created a winter vegetable belt. From a sheep and goat range this area since 1920 has become truly a Winter Garden, as it is nationally known. In the transplanting season from October to January, and in the Bermuda onion harvesting season from March to May, thousands of Mexicans toil in the fields here; men, women and children work incredibly fast in transplanting onion sets.

Between Catarina and Laredo, Herefords with a trace of Brahma blood graze on the flat, brushy acres.

Southwest of JUNCTION, US 377 moves up the canyon of the South Llano River. This section lays claim to one of the largest native pecan orchards in the world. In this vicinity are several guest ranches catering to vacationists, offering swimming, fishing, horseback riding, and boating.

LEWIS CROSSING, 13.1 *m.,* is a concrete slab ford across the South Llano, the first of eight crossings of this river as the road makes its way along the rock-walled canyon. The road goes up the middle of the rock river bed for a short distance. These fords are not deep except during heavy rains, but they should be entered and crossed slowly to avoid flooding the engine. Fishing is excellent in rapids where small creeks enter the stream, or in the deep pools.

At 14.1 *m.* is the junction with a dirt road.

Left here to FLEMING'S CAVE, 1.5 *m.,* a series of tunnels extending some distance down and into the side of a rock hill. The formation is mainly limestone, water-carved into grotesque shapes and figures.

Heading over a divide, the road descends again into the bed of the river. This is ideal vacationing country. Camp sites are numerous, and at nearly every ranch permission can be obtained to camp, fish, hunt, and explore. (*Rates vary from a cheerful "help yourself," to $5 a day during hunting season.*)

SEVEN HUNDRED SPRINGS, 20.5 *m.,* are visible across the river. About halfway down the face of a 100-foot bluff is a thick outcropping of rock, and from a fissure under this the springs flow forth almost in a solid sheet more than 100 yards wide, cascading down to the stream. Most of the water comes from a main spring, but its hundreds of rivulets pouring down the face of the rock give the illusion of multitudinous outpourings, which blend, separate and blend again, creating a brilliant pattern of crystal liquid lace.

The river bed is dangerous here, as ferns and moss make it slippery.

In less than three miles it is necessary to ford the river on concrete slabs five times, the last at PAINT ROCK CROSSING, 24 *m.* The route then climbs out of the Llano canyon onto a region of upland pastures covered with rocky outcroppings and growths of cedar and oak.

ROCKSPRINGS, 49 *m.* (2,450 alt., 1,182 pop.) is the seat of Edwards County and center of Angora goat and sheep raising. Wool and mohair are shipped; pecans are produced. In 1927 a tornado destroyed the town and 67 lives were lost. From here US 377 continues south to Del Rio and the Mexican border, while State 55 turns southeast. Following this route, the visitor passes through the narrow canyon of Little Hackberry Creek.

INDIAN CAVES (R), 66.4 *m.,* are visible across the canyon. High up on the cliffs their openings show black against the gray of the rock walls. These caves have recently been excavated by scientists from the University of Texas.

CRAIG CROSSING, 68.7 *m.,* fords Pulliam Creek, just below its beginning at the junction of Little Hackberry Creek with Polecat Creek.

BARKSDALE, 79.3 *m.* (1,500 alt., 100 pop.), built on a wooded plain, is surrounded by rugged hills. Its old, well preserved houses give it an appearance of unspoiled rustic simplicity. In its vicinity are many points of scenic beauty—narrow, winding canyons, caves, pictographs, Indian mounds and camp sites. The streams afford excellent fishing for bass, perch and crappie.

BARKSDALE CROSSING, 79.6 *m.,* across the NUECES RIVER, is over a caliche-topped fill.

At 83.2 *m.* is a reconstruction of the old Spanish mission of SAN LORENZO DE LA SANTA CRUZ (St. Lawrence of the Holy Cross) on the foundations of 1762. This was an outpost among the Lipan Indians, whose presence in this area went back to prehistoric times.

CAMP WOOD, 83.6 *m.* (1,449 alt., 800 pop.), received its name from the old United States military post established here in 1857. The town was established in 1921, but settlement of the site goes back to the date of the founding of Mission San Lorenzo.

In the vicinity of Camp Wood are many recreational features—camp sites, excellent hunting, fine fishing streams and caves. A remarkable collection of Indian artifacts is at the Hibbitt's Magnolia Service Station in Camp Wood. Visible for many miles are Meridian Mountain, (2,250 alt.), crossed by the 100th meridian, and Military Mountain, (2,018 alt). South of Camp Wood, 3 *m.* is LAKE NUESCES.

Left here to FERN LAKE RANCH, 0.8 *m.,* where a huge wistaria vine, planted in 1884, has more than 10,000 feet of tendrils which furnish a dense shade for a two-story ranch home and spread out to cover two large arbors, one 6 by 80 feet, the other 16 by 40 feet. Near its base the main stem of the vine is 49 inches in circumference.

East from Camp Wood on State 337 to junction with US 83 at LEAKEY (1,609 alt., 700 pop. est.) seat of Real County. The tiny hamlet of RIO·FRIO, 7 *m.* south on US 83 is notable for the "largest live oak in Texas," 52 ft. tall, 22 ft. circumference, 102 ft. spread. A few miles south is GARNER STATE PARK.

The RANGER LOG HOUSE (L), 89.6 *m.,* stands in the shade of five giant oaks. Built in the 1840's it is the site of an Indian fight in which Captain Jack Hays and a party of Texas Rangers participated in 1844. An old bee tree mentioned in the Ranger captain's official report still stands beside the house and shows scars made by a Ranger who was cutting into the tree for honey when he sighted the Indians.

MONTELL, 93.2 *m.* (1,292 alt., 250 pop.), is the SITE OF MISSION NUESTRA SENORA DE LA CANDELARIA DEL CANON (Our Lady of Candlemas of the Canyon), one block north of the post office. Here once stood the fairly extensive rock buildings of the mission, founded in 1762. Raids by hostile tribes from the north caused its abandonment. The remains consist only of low mounds and the nearly vanished lines of irrigation ditches dug by the Christianized Indians.

The route now follows the winding rock-walled valley of the Nueces River. Excellent hunting, fishing, and camping are available all along the way. Then the valley widens, hills lessen in height, and the highway emerges from the hill country to enter the gently rolling prairies of the Gulf Coastal Plain below the Balcones Escarpment, the second step-like shelf from the High Plains to the sea.

UVALDE, 122 *m.* (913 alt., 10,293 pop., 1960; 11,500, 1967 est.) is the seat of Uvalde County, where the principal products are vegetables raised by irrigation, honey, pecans and asphalt. It is publicized as the

Honey Capital of the World. The name is a variant of Ugalde, a Spanish commander who fought Indians in 1790.

Uvalde was settled in 1853 under the protection of nearby Fort Inge, its first citizens being cattlemen. Following the Civil War the region to the southwest, along the Nueces River, was infested with bands of cattle thieves and outlaws, but the worst menace to the settlers was that of Indians, whose raids continued until the 1880's.

Uvalde became nationally famous as the home of John Nance Garner, Speaker of the House and Vice President of the United States during Franklin D. Roosevelt's first term. He turned over his home at 333 N. Park St. and it became the ETTIE GARNER MEMORIAL BUILDING, housing the city Library and a. museum of Garner memorabilia, including numerous gavels. Garner thereupon moved to a smaller house nearby and enjoyed greeting visitors until his death on November 7, 1967. He would have been 99 years old on November 22.

SOUTHEAST TEXAS JUNIOR COLLEGE, estab. 1946, enrolls about 400 students annually.

In Uvalde is the junction with US 90 (*see Tour 23*).

Southward the route is US 83.

Pecans are a commercial crop in this section, the owners threshing the natural groves in the late autumn. As the fields begin (L), irrigated patches of spinach appear in season.

LA PRYOR, 143 *m.* (761 alt., 1,000 pop.), occupies part of the vast Pryor Ranch. Spinach is the money crop. BATESVILLE is a community of 750, 15 *m.* east on State 76.

Truck gardening increases near CRYSTAL CITY, 161 *m.* (580 alt., 9,000 pop.) seat of Zavalla County, a farming country. This is the self-styled "spinach capital of the world," and vast quantities of the vegetable are shipped every year. A STATUE OF POPEYE, erected in 1937 on the town square, honors the belligerent spinach-eating sailor of newspaper and motion picture cartoons. Spreading out from this vicinity is the Winter Garden area of Texas, where extensive irrigation has made agriculture possible on a large scale.

Southward the land is low and flat, a checkerboard of irrigated fields and occasional groves of citrus trees. In the brushy back country of this region, panthers, wild hogs, coyotes, and wildcats are found. Deer, quail, and dove hunting is excellent in season. (*Take warning that rattlesnakes are plentiful.*)

The TEXAS EXPERIMENTAL FARM (R), 163 *m.*, is constantly conducting tests to increase the crops grown successfully in this region.

A roadside park is L., 164 *m.* Through the trees is visible ESPANTOSA (ghostly) LAKE, long a stopping place on the Upper Presidio Road, highway between the Spanish settlements of Texas and Coahuila. Grim tales are told of dreadful deeds and horrifying incidents on the lake shores. Here camped supply trains north-bound for the far-flung Spanish mission system; Texas Rangers stopped on its banks, outlaws haunted the brush lands around it; raiding Indians knew it well; and Santa Anna, marching on the Alamo, camped his army here.

One story tells of a wagon train loaded with silver, gold and other valuables, which camped one night beside the lake. Suddenly, while all were asleep, the ground on which they camped sank, and every member of the party was drowned. None of the treasure was ever recovered, legend says, and Mexican residents in the vicinity still tell of a phantom wagon which, during the dark of the moon, can be heard rumbling southward.

It is believed that beside this lake the so-called lost colonists of Dolores met their fate. These were the survivors of 59 immigrants, mostly English, who came with Dr. John Charles Beales to found a colony between the Nueces and the Rio Grande. In March, 1834, they reached their destination, which they named Dolores, about 25 miles above the present city of Eagle Pass. The colonists suffered from the beginning. Their crops failed. They became desperate. Many finally sought homes in other places. In March, 1836, a few days after the fall of the Alamo, the last of the colony—eleven men, two women, and three children set out for San Patricio or some other coast point in the hope of returning to England. Thereupon they vanished, and it was not until many years afterward that Texans learned their fate.

There was no road to the coast and their wagons made slow progress. Late in March they remained in concealment for several days to avoid Santa Anna's invading army, whose supply trains they heard, and whose soldiers they dreaded no less than the Indians. On April 2 they resumed their march and early in the afternoon camped at a large lake, which is believed to have been Espantosa. There, a few hours later, they were surprised by Comanches; all the men were killed and the women and children captured. Long afterward, when three women were ransomed from separate Indian bands by a Santa Fe citizen, two of the Dolores tragedy were among them, and the mystery of the party's disappearance was cleared.

CARRIZO SPRINGS, 174 m. (600 alt., 6,065 pop.) is the seat of Dimmit County. Artesian irrigation and colonization were promoted and today the community terms itself "The Hub of the Winter Garden." Date palms in this section bear heavily. Only one of the early residences remains; the old MCLAUGHLIN HOUSE, east of the courthouse, built in 1870 and often used as a fort against the Indians.

Right from Carrizo Springs on US 277 to EAGLE PASS, 44 m. (735 alt., 13,000 pop.), a tourist resort of narrow streets and Mexican border atmosphere, which during the days of the war with Mexico, was the site of a U. S. military encampment at the crossing of the Rio Grande. It was named Camp Eagle Pass from the daily flight of an eagle back and forth across the river to its nest in a huge cottonwood tree on the Mexican bank. In 1849, one of the favorite southern routes to California came over northwestern Texas to cross the Rio Grande at this point and proceed through the mountains of Mexico to the coast. This trail of the forty-niners was about four miles upstream from an old Indian ford beside which the army encampment had been. At that upstream point another tent town called Camp California sprang up on the American bank where the westbound gold seekers stopped to rest and replenish their supplies from the stores established there to serve them. At about the same time, the Federal government established a military post called Fort Duncan on the river halfway between Old Camp Eagle Pass and Camp California. As the stream of California-bound emigrants lessened, the tent city turned to the personnel of the army post for its trade, and in time moved near the fort. A little town was laid out in 1850, called El Paso del Aguila (Eagle Pass).

The years that followed saw much activity in repeated expeditions against the Indians. In 1855, Captain James Callahan was authorized by the Governor of Texas to organize a troop to quell Indian disorders. Callahan's command pursued a raiding party of Lipans, who crossed the Rio Grande into Mexico at a point a few miles upstream from Eagle Pass. Captain Callahan rode down to obtain permission from Mexican authorities in the town of Piedras Negras (Black Rock), to follow them into that country. His account of the incident states that permission was granted. At any rate, he crossed into Mexico and continued the pursuit. He was met by a large force of Indians and Mexicans drawn up in battle array. Firing commenced immediately and in the ensuing engagement, Callahan's Texans defeated the motley army and put it to flight. The Texans then continued on the trail of the Lipans, but word soon reached them that Captain Menchaca of the Mexican Army was advancing with a large force of infantry and dragoons. Callahan retreated to Piedras Negras, burned the town and crossed to the American side of the Rio Grande. International complications resulted, the Mexican authorities claiming that the Texans' leader did not have permission to enter Mexico and that the invasion thus constituted a breach of neutrality.

During the Civil War, Fort Duncan for a time was garrisoned by Confederate troops. The port of Eagle Pass was active during those years in the shipment of vast quantities of cotton, which was taken across the river and hauled overland down the wet bank to the Gulf, for shipment to Europe. At the close of the war, General Joseph O. Shelby crossed the Rio Grande at Eagle Pass with his unsurrendered division of Missouri Cavalry. On the morning of July 4, 1865, the general's 500 veterans silently gathered around their battle flag, and four colonels at last lowered it, weighted, into the muddy waters of the Rio Grande. General Shelby tore the plume from his hat, and cast it into the river. Theirs was the last flag to fly over an unsurrendered Confederate force, and the spot where it was buried has been called the grave of the Confederacy.

Fort Duncan was regarrisoned with Federal troops in 1868 and again became an active post on the western frontier. One unusual military organization which served at Fort Duncan during this period was a force of Seminole Indian-Negro scouts. Originating from a commingling of Indians with runaway slaves, these people had fled from the reservation years before, at the close of the Seminole War, and found refuge in Mexico. Their knowledge of the country and their excellence as trackers made them valuable guides.

Beginning in 1890, only a caretaking detachment was stationed at Fort Duncan, until the mobilization of the National Guard along the border in 1916 resulted in troops again being assigned there. Eagle Pass has developed in recent years as a prosperous commercial and recreation area profiting from the extensive irrigation results and oil production of Maverick County. It is opposite Piedras Negras and has an important U. S. Immigration and Customs Station. It is served by the Southern Pacific and Continental Trailways. Municipal installations include an airport, a swimming pool, golf course and tennis courts; accommodations for tourists have been increasing. FORT DUNCAN PARK, a place of historic interest, contains the Robert E. Lee museum in the one-room dwelling he occupied there. The park has recreational facilities.

South of Carrizo Springs US 83 continues through a section of irrigated farms. ASHERTON, 182 m. (1,760 pop.) is a farm market center.

CATARINA, 194 m. (370 alt., 200 pop.), has wide, palm-bordered streets with esplanades bright with flowers. At vegetable-shipping time it hums with unusual noise and activity.

Southward the route runs through a very thinly settled area. The Winter Garden is left behind, and brush-covered rangelands appear.

At 238.5 *m.* is the junction with US 81, from San Antonio, along which runs Interstate 35.

LAREDO, 256 *m.* (438 alt., pop. 64,600, 1967 est.), is at the junction with US 59 and State 359 (*see article on Laredo*).

Section e.   LAREDO to BROWNSVILLE; 202 m.   US 83

US 83 continues along the approximate course of the Military Road cut through chaparral and across desert hills by General Taylor's army in 1846. The route runs from the barren, semi-arid plains of the Laredo region across the rolling, sage-covered hills of the Zapata-Roma section, and then into the flat, highly cultivated citrus fruit belt of the Lower Rio Grande Valley between Mission and the Gulf.

Mexicans here cling to customs of their homeland across the river. One- and two-room *jacales* made of willow branches, daubed with mud or thatch, make homes for the humbler folk; milk goats, dogs and cats, chickens and children swarm over these *casitas*. The more prosperous enjoy formal dances; printed invitations are usually sent, but lacking these, a committee calls upon those to be invited—telephones are not used. Sometimes whole families attend; the girls are chaperoned. All classes of Mexicans observe the old forms of salutation: men embrace, using a perfunctory cheek kiss. Handshaking is reserved for strangers.

Recreational and scenic features make this section enjoyable at all times of the year. Along the course of this valley Spanish colonists found a foothold before the middle of the eighteenth century. An interesting feature of this region is the wide variation in acreage of old Spanish land grants, *porciones,* which were theoretically of the same size. The grants were measured with rawhide chains and some of the Spanish settlers arranged to have their lands measured on wet days, when the chains would stretch far beyond their usual length.

South of LAREDO, 0 *m.,* the route follows that used in 1747 by Captain Miguel de la Garza Falcon, explorer for Don José de Escandón, who, in 1749, began a large-scale settlement of the region between the lower Rio Grande and the Nueces River.

SAN YGNACIO, 34 *m.* (324 alt., 800 pop. 1965 est.), was settled in the eighteenth century and, after the fashion of the times, named for a patron saint of the founder. Nearby was the ranch settlement of Nuestra Señora de los Dolores (Our Lady of Sorrows), founded in 1750 by José Vásquez Borrego, cattle baron of Coahuila.

At 34.3 *m.* a dirt road leads to the old STONE FORT, built 1835. It has a double-faced sun dial.

The most spectacular and economically useful engineering development in the Rio Grande Valley is LAKE FALCON, a reservoir created by a dam near Falcon Heights, which impounds the waters of the Rio Grande for a distance of 40 miles, with a shoreline of more than 375 miles. The dam is 311 ft. above bedrock. The lake begins near San Ygnacio, 34 *m.* south of Laredo on US 83 and extends beyond Falcon Heights, where a bridge crosses the river to Nuevo Guerrero, a free crossing. The lake, which was dedicated by President Dwight D. Eisenhower, covers 98,960 acres and has a capacity of 3,280,700 acre-ft., of which 1,923,500 is alloted to Texas, the rest to Mexico. The use of the waters for irrigation is expected to extend acreage and be reflected in the commercial prosperity of the farmers on both sides of the boundary. A big extension of recreation facilities also is under way in both Starr and Zapata Counties.

The International Boundary and Water Commission has supervision of the area. Fishing licenses may be obtained at Zapata.

ZAPATA, 47 *m.* (311 alt., 2,000 pop.) seat of Zapata County, was formed on this site when the original Zapata was abandoned to the Falcon Reservoir. That town, founded by Spanish ranchmen on land granted by Jose de Escandon in 1750 was the site of Camp Drum, established by the U. S. Army in 1852. State 16 from San Antonio ends at Zapata. State 83 continues south through Lopena and Falcon, 71 *m.,* last village in Zapata County.

EL TIGRE ISLAND, 16 *m.* south of Zapata on US 83, is a recreation area with facilities for camping, picnics, boats, and fishing supplies. There is a launching ramp on the lake and a 24-unit trailer park.

About 28 *m.* south of Zapata near Roma is FALCON STATE PARK, 572.6 acres, with complete recreation facilities, including electricity, rest rooms with showers, food supplies and a 3,500-ft. landing strip for private planes. Also reached by FM 2098.

The road now follows the banks of the lake. The country becames more hilly, and the slopes are covered with purple sage, which, when it blooms in the spring, covers the landscape with a mauve haze.

ROMA, 88 *m.* incorporated with LA SAENZ (243 alt., 1,500 pop.) and administered separately, was settled by Indians occupying the *visita* (civil village) of Escandón's colony at Mier. Ranchers took up holdings on the north bank of the river, where gradually a settlement developed. Until 1886 steamboats plied the Rio Grande to Roma, and during the Civil War much cotton was shipped. A mission chapel built more than a hundred years ago still stands, retaining, as do the cobblestone streets, an atmosphere of Old Mexico. Adajcent to the chapel is a large collection of petrified wood, oyster shells and other geological specimens gathered in the vicinity. Directly across the river is Mier, Tamaulipas, Mexico, site of the battle fought by the Mier Expedition in 1842 (*see History*).

The SITE OF CARNESTOLENDAS (L), 100.3 *m.,* a village of Mission San Agustin de Laredo (St. Augustine of Laredo) in Mexico just across the river, is the place at which, in 1753, one of the first settlements on the Rio Grande's north bank in the Lower Valley was established. The colony extended to RIO GRANDE CITY, 101 *m.* (238 alt., 6,000 pop.), occupied by Spanish settlers of Escandón in 1753, and founded as a town in 1847 by Henry Clay Davis, soldier of fortune, who came into the region during the Mexican War. It was long known locally as Rancho Davis, and was for years an important stop for the river steamers plying

The Land and Conservation

╠╬

RANCHHAND USES CHEMICAL SPRAY ON WEEDS

USDA Soil Conservation Service

SMOOTHING SOIL WITH LAND PLANE NEAR TRINIDAD,
HENDERSON COUNTY

USDA Soil Conservation Service

SMALL POND FOR WATERING STOCK, ERATH COUNTY

USDA Soil Conservation Service

MAN-MADE LAKE RECREATION AREA

RIO GRANDE NEAR EL PASO

IRRIGATION SIPHONS IN WHEAT FIELD, ARMSTRONG COUNTY
USDA Soil Conservation Service

RANGE SEEDED FOR BRUSH CONTROL, COTTLE COUNTY
USDA Soil Conservation Service

ERADICATING PRICKLY PEAR BY CHEMICAL VIA HELICOPTER,
McMULLEN COUNTY

USDA Soil Conservation Service

IMPLEMENT CHOPS WEEDS, PLANTS GRASS, FORT STOCKTON
USDA Soil Conservation Service

BLUESTEM GRASS ON STONY SITE NOLAN COUNTY
USDA Soil Conservation Service

IMPROVING SANDY SOIL FOR CULTIVATION, LIVE OAK COUNTY
USDA Soil Conservation Service

WASTELAND ALONG THE GULF COAST

National Park Service

BATTLE OF WIND AND SAND, PADRE ISLAND

National Park Service

CONSERVATION EXPERT TAKING SOIL SAMPLE

USDA Soil Conservation Service

the Rio Grande. It is the seat of Starr County, which raises truck and cotton and produces oil. It has many historic adobe houses.

FORT RINGGOLD, 102.4 *m.,* once a station of a squadron of cavalry and other service detachments. It was established as Camp Ringgold in 1848 and named for Brevet Major David Ringgold, killed at the Battle of Palo Alto. The post was occupied by United States troops in 1859 to stop the bandit Cortinas. It was bought by the Rio Grande School District for use as a school.

This vicinity saw much activity in 1875 in the Las Cuevas War, a series of raids and skirmishes between Texas Rangers under Captain Mc-Nelly and a band of Mexican outlaws under Juan Flores.

Southeast of Fort Ringgold the rolling hills are left behind and the terrain gradually flattens into level, cultivated fields.

SAMFORDYCE. 122 *m.,* was the center of a new oil development in the 1930's.

East of this point the route enters one of the nation's great citrus fruit producing districts. Starting virtually as a wilderness at the turn of the century, this region has experienced an almost phenomenal development. Along this fertile plain, at intervals averaging about seven miles, are thoroughly modern towns whose populations range from 3,000 to 12,000. Between them vast citrus groves crowd close to the highway. Along the main roads the glossy fronds of date palms, frequently so luxuriant that they serve as windbreaks for citrus groves, contrast with the lighter green of the orchards, the dusty emerald of salt cedars and the duller tones of unusually tall, slender *Washingtonia robusta* palms; the latter are strung out in long lines across the landscape, often marking the boundaries of property or the windings of irrigation canals. Added to the many tones of green are the brilliant hues of two varieties of the bougainvillaea—almost every house, no matter how humble, has masses of purple or red flowers of this subtropical vine. During winter months the crimson of poinsettias flames in almost every yard, and even along the highway's edge. Graceful papaya trees, their big leaves making an umbrella-like top, are plentiful, sometimes standing alone and again in groves. Bamboo and wild cane grow tall along the irrigation canals.

Irrigation plays a vital part in citrus culture and other agricultural operations in this district, and huge pumping plants draw water from the Rio Grande for use in orchards and fields.

The Valley has become what is probably the most cosmopolitan district in Texas, its residents representing virtually every State in the Union and various foreign countries. Nearly all are busy with the development of citrus groves that range in size from a few acres around a farm home, to estates of thousands of acres.

Despite the progress made by man in transforming the Lower Rio Grande Valley into a garden, the forces of nature remain uncontrolled. In five days beginning before dawn on September 20, 1967, the hurricane Beulah swept into the Valley from the West Indies with winds that reached 136 to 140 miles an hour, drenched the area from Brownsville to Corpus Christi with tons of water that reached as high as 36 inches in

Harlingen and Mission, and broke up into as many as 80 tornadoes in 29 counties, which were declared a disaster area.

The damage was worst in the towns along US 281 and US 83, the area of the fine citrus groves and new dwellings. By September 25 Mission, McAllen, Harlingen, and Brownsville not only had rivers in their streets but tons of mud had poured into dwellings and left thick deposits on furnishings. The tempest ruined garden-truck farms, irrigation systems, fruit groves, roads, and houses. Damage to a twin-span expressway bridge at Harlingen was estimated at $650,000. Eight other bridges sustained damages of more than $1,000,000.

The towns of the Lower Valley, strung along the gray ribbon of the highway, are, for the most part, as alike as peas in a pod—a litter of small cities born in the throes of early citrus development, differing in appearance only as one offspring might differ from its brother. So close together are these communities that residents call the highway between Mission and Harlingen the "longest Main Street in the world." Along that 39 miles only a line of business houses, hotels, fruit packing and canning plants and long loading platforms indicates a town. The intervals are filled with far-flung residential sections, uncrowded and beautiful. Set in deep, green grounds are houses chiefly of the Monterey or other types of Mexican architecture, adapted to local influences of climate and materials; most of the buildings are painted white, and are dazzling in the sunlight. Flower gardens and palms adorn the yards, and citrus groves separate the houses.

MISSION, 136 m. (134 alt., 14,081 pop.), was laid out on La Lomita Rancho, the property of the Oblate Fathers, who, carrying on work started by the Franciscan Order nearly a hundred years before, in 1824 founded a chapel on the north bank of the Rio Grande and nurtured a pioneer citrus grove. In January the city holds the Texas Citrus Fiesta.

At eastern city limits leave US 83 for Bryan Road; 2 m. HOME OF WILLIAM JENNINGS BRYAN, 3-time Democratic nominee for President; U. S. Secretary of State. S. from Mission on Farm Road 1016, 6 m. to ANZALDUAS DAM AND BRIDGE, $8,000,000 project for flood control and Mexican irrigation.

Right here to CAPILLA DE LA LOMITA (Chapel of the Little Hill), 4.4 m., of the Oblate Fathers (1824). The chapel retains the hand-hewn window- and door-sills of mesquite wood and much of its old adobe construction. It stands on a low hill overlooking the muddy Rio Grande and the old Military Road.

McALLEN, 142 m. (122 alt., 32,728 pop., 1960; 38,000 1966, est.) 3 m. west of US 281 calls itself the City of Palms. It is a convention center and official port of entry to Mexico, via bridge at Hidalgo to Reynosa, 8 m. south. A center for citrus fruits, cotton and petroleum products, it stresses recreation in the Lower Rio Grande Valley with tours, fishing, rodeos; a spring fiesta in March and the South Texas Oil Show in November. The McALLEN MEMORIAL LIBRARY, circulation about 100,000 annually, has modern quarters. Trans-Texas Airways serves Miller International Airport, 1½ m. south. McAllen ships 47 varieties of vegetables grown in Hidalgo County, where cotton averages 150,000 bales a year. The city receives oil and gas royalties of $98,000 a year from fields under its streets and parks.

PHARR, 145 *m.* (107 alt., 14,106 pop. 1960; 15,432, 1965 est.) ships produce from farms and citrus groves. The Valley Vegetable Show is held in December. Southeast of Pharr 11 *m.* on US 281 to SANTA ANA NATIONAL WILDLIFE REFUGE, 1,980 acres. *Open daily 8 a.m. to 4:30 p.m.*

SAN JUAN, 147 *m.,* (102 alt., 4,550 pop.) laid out in 1909, stages a Sport Shirt Festival on February 22. Its Shrine of Our Lady of San Juan of the Valley was erected 1954 by many donors to fullfil a priest's vow.

DONNA, 153 *m.* (88 alt., 7,522 pop.), ships great quantities of citrus fruits, winter vegetables, and canned goods.

WESLACO, 157 *m.* (75 alt., 15,649 pop., 1960; 17,009, 1965), estab. 1919; its buildings conform to Spanish architecture by law.

MERCEDES, 162 *m.* (61 alt., 10,943 pop.) estab. 1906 by St. Louis financiers, was named for the wife of Mexican President Diaz. It has the Valley's largest irrigation district. The Rio Grande Valley Livestock Show is held in March.

North 7 *m.* on Farm Road 506 to SANTA ROSA, 1,542 pop., at intersection of State 107.

LA FERIA, 168 *m.* (60 alt., 3,047 pop.) a citrus shipping center, and a debt-free municipality.

Right from Mercedes on a graveled road to the CHAPEL OF SANTA MARIA, 10.1 *m.,* one of the missionary institutions established by the Oblate Fathers in the Lower Valley in 1824. The building is in a good state of preservation. Many interesting old houses are in this vicinity, which in actual settlement dates back to the colonization of this region by Escandón in the 1750's.

HARLINGEN, 176 *m.* (36 alt., 41,207 pop., 1960). US 77 meets US 83 here. It is the center of one of the most extensive of the irrigation projects. Its founder's house, built 1905, is located in the Lon C. Hill Park. In 1963 the MARINE MILITARY ACADEMY was formed and took over the 30 buildings of the Air Force Navigation School, 320 Iwo Jima Blvd. Training is patterned after the USMC. The Memorial Chapel seats 350. Estimated annual fees are $2,050; uniforms, $275.

In early days Harlingen was the home station of a company of Texas Rangers, and the presence of armed Rangers and United States customs and immigration inspectors on the streets and at the railroad station earned the town the name of Six-shooter Junction. Harlingen's annual winter event is the Fiesta Turista, in February. It also has the Life Begins at Forty golf contest, and a Cotton Festival in summer.

SAN BENITO, 183 *m.* (35 alt., 16,422 pop.), is both an agricultural and recreational center. Stately palms border its wide streets and edge the banks of a *resaca,* whose waters sparkle in the sunshine.

The U. S. Fish & Wildlife Bureau, Post Office Bldg., San Benito, furnishes maps and directions for reaching the LAGUNA ATASCOSA NATIONAL WILDLIFE REFUGE, 25 *m.* northeast.

BROWNSVILLE, 202 *m.* (33 alt., 48,040 pop. 1960) (*see Brownsville*) is at the junction with US 281.

1. Left from Brownsville on State 4 to the SITE OF THE BATTLE OF PALMITO HILL (R), 15 *m.*, the last engagement of the Civil War, fought May 12 and 13, 1865, more than a month after the surrender of General Robert E. Lee at Appomattox. There are several versions of the story of this battle. Lieutenant Colonel David Branson, who commanded the Federal troops actually engaged, stated on numerous occasions that the battle was already impending when he received news that the war had ended. As there was a regiment of Negro troops in the brigade, and the Confederates refused to recognize a flag of truce from any military organization containing a Negro unit, he was unable to send word of the situation to the Confederate force, and consequently was obliged to retreat slowly, maintaining a rear guard action, until he could find a Texan and send him to the Confederate commander with news that peace had been declared. According to another version, both sides were fully informed that the war had ended, and the Confederate force in Brownsville was even being disbanded, when the Federals conceived a plan to seize Brownsville and capture several hundred bales of cotton in storage there. Learning of the plan, Colonel John S. ("Rip") Ford rallied all available Confederate troops, following which came the engagement. Whichever version contains the more truth, it is a fact that a few days after the battle Colonels Branson and Ford posed together in Brownsville for a tintype photograph.

State 4 continues to a recreational area along the Gulf shore called BOCA CHICA, 24 *m.* (*surf bathing, fishing*), with a beach drive extending on the right to the MOUTH OF THE RIO GRANDE, 0.5 *m.;* and on the left to the resort of DEL MAR, 0.4 *m.*, reached by a toll bridge (*25¢ a car*). In this region of sand dunes and marshes, the Gulf of Mexico washes seven miles of accessible shore line. Here in early days the well-to-do Spanish ranchers of Matamoros came for recreation, making the spot one of the oldest beach resorts in the United States. It was slightly south of Boca Chica, at the mouth of the Rio Grande, that Alonso Alvarez de Pineda, with the first Europeans known to have reached the Texas coast, overhauled his fleet in 1519 (*see History*). The Spaniards explored the country for 40 days while their ships were being repaired. Thus this region was probably the second place to be visited by Europeans in the present United States. Here, later, pirates and freebooters sought port in times of storm or battle.

At Del Mar, which consists of a handful of restaurants, fishermen's supply houses and tourist lodges, on a sandy point that is part of the Boca Chica playground, is BRAZOS SANTIAGO PASS, connecting the Laguna Madre with the Gulf and separating Brazos Island, on which Del Mar stands, from Padre Island. Surf fishing is excellent where jetties flank the Pass (*redfish, trout, tarpon*). Here was a base of General Taylor's army during the Mexican War, and here in 1866 General Sheridan established a large supply depot in preparation for a possible campaign against Maximilian of Mexico. The campaign was not necessary, but today relics of Sheridan's occupation are found, and remains of old railways, foundations of buildings, and the like, are visible.

2. Left from Brownsville on State 4 to a junction with South Point Road, 1.8 *m.;* R. here to a dirt road, 7.8 *m.;* R. again to a NATURAL PALM GROVE, 9 *m.* Here a prolific growth of native palms offers an interesting botannical study.

3. North from Brownsville on the Paredes Line Road to the SITE OF THE BATTLE OF RESACA DE LA PALMA (R), 3 *m.*, the second engagement of the Mexican War, fought May 9, 1846. From here the Mexican army fled southward across the Rio Grande.

The Paredes Line Road continues northward to the SITE OF THE BATTLE OF

PALO ALTO (R), 8.8 *m.*, the first engagement of the Mexican War, fought May 8, 1846.

LOS FRESNOS, 12 *m.* (1,289 pop.), a small farming community, annually holds a Charity Horse Show in June.

Right 30 *m.* on State 100 to PORT ISABEL (8 alt., 3,575 pop.), located at the eastern end of the 17-mile Brownsville Ship Channel, has become a cargo port handling more than 320,000 tons a year, especially deepsea shrimp. Here is an old brick lighthouse, erected in 1853 and discontinued in 1905, which has been restored and is now in a state park. Port Isabel is separated from PADRE ISLAND by 3 *m.* of shallow water, the Laguna Madre, over which Cameron County has built the Queen Isabella Causeway, costing $2,750,000. It has developed South Padre Island as a recreation resort. At the southern end is Isla Blanca Park, with a pavilion, shelters and beach facilities. A 722-ft. pier provides deepsea fishing. North 5 *m.* is Andy Bowie Park. Port Isabel celebrates an international fishing tournament and a shrimp fiesta, usually in August.

On September 20, 1967, the hurricane Beulah hit Port Isabel with winds at 130 miles per hour, doing excessive damage to houses and bringing rains that flooded the streets. About one-half of the town needed major repairs.

ᛣᛒ

Tour 17

(Clayton, N. Mex.)—Amarillo—Lubbock—Big Spring—San Angelo —Fredericksburg—San Antonio—Victoria—Port Lavaca; US 87. New Mexico Line to Port Lavaca, 798 *m.*

Spanning Texas between the Panhandle and the Gulf of Mexico, US 87 traverses the High Plains and the stony hill country, and emerges upon the lush Coastal Plain, to end at tidewater on a storied bay. Central areas of the State's western and south-southeastern parts are crossed.

In the north and west the highway leads through an empire of wheat and cattle. Here live many people who have never seen a steamboat, but have complete familiarity with the mechanism of huge combination harvesting machines. While settlement along this section of the route is comparatively new, the towns appear much as the first settlers built them. Civic pride is almost invariably expressed through the construction of large, elaborate and expensive courthouses.

Southeastward, as the hill country is approached, cattle give way to goats and sheep; and wheat to fodder and truck crops. The land becomes stony and for long stretches it is rugged, sometimes even wild. Scrub oaks and stones cover the countryside. Deep in these hills, almost always hidden from the highway, there are colorful ranch houses—many made of stones picked up and mortared together by the pioneers who braved Apaches to claim this land.

As San Antonio is approached the hills melt into a sweeping, rolling region. This is an in-between area, dividing the hills from the Coastal Plain. There are many small farms upon which are raised cotton, small grains, corn, peanuts and garden truck.

Southeastward from San Antonio another cattle empire is entered, one of the oldest in Texas. Here the people take profit from their herds and cotton crops as a matter of course, many of them seemingly indifferent to the wealth of oil that lies beneath their ranges.

From end to end this route is dotted with oil fields, and the new industry has quickened the pulse of the people. It has built new factories, modern school plants and other improvements.

Section a. NEW MEXICO LINE to AMARILLO; 124 m. US 87

Taking a southeasterly course, US 87 traverses the center of the Panhandle, through a region that was once part of the vast rangelands of the XIT Ranch. Much of this section today is like one great, undivided wheatfield. Grain elevators create metropolitan skylines that are visible for many miles across the prairies, yet the towns are usually small and dusty, and the houses are reminiscent of the early cattle era. Ranching still is important on these treeless, short-grass North Plains.

The region is sparsely settled except at harvest times. Then men who follow the crops come to the Panhandle. Life changes. Business houses remain open all night. Hotels, rooming houses and tourist lodges are filled to overflowing, and men sleep in the fields when accommodations are unavailable. With the crops in, the towns return to their brisk, but quiet, peaceful routine.

A stone lodge is beside the highway (R) where US 87 crosses the NEW MEXICO LINE, 0 *m.,* 11 miles southeast of Clayton, New Mexico. It houses an INFORMATION STATION of the State Highway Department.

TEXLINE, 1 *m.* (4,694 alt., 500 pop.), is in a shallow well irrigation area, and ships wheat, small grains and cattle.

DALHART, 37 *m.* (3,985 alt., 6,100 pop.) is the county seat of Dallam County and on the line of Dallam and Hartley Counties. It is at the intersection of US 54, 87 and 385. Once a tough cow town, it was often filled with cowboys, land speculators and railroad construction men.

Gaining the county seat in 1903, Dalhart assumed a more permanent aspect. Frame buildings became common although the lumber had to be shipped in from long distances. The blizzard of 1912 cut off the town for days while ten-foot snowdrifts blocked roads and the railway. Thousands of cattle died on the unprotected plains.

The clang of railroad shops, the scream of locomotive whistles and the hum of a large feed mill sound almost incessantly. Grain elevators and shipping pens for cattle complete the industrial scene.

During the 1920's the plow turned many thousands of acres of rangeland into grainfields. Until droughts caused dust storms during recent years, bumper crops were raised. In this vicinity extensive soil reclamation work is being done by the Federal government.

Irrigation of wheat and maise has helped the area. Dalhart has enlarged the Coon Memorial Hospital and added a new packing plant and motels, RITA BLANCA LAKE, southeast, is a recreation spot.

1. Left from Dalhart on US 54 to STRATFORD, 31 m. (3,690 alt., 873 pop.), where business and residential districts seem worlds apart. The flimsy frame store buildings appear sun-baked, but the residential sections are neat, and the brick and stucco houses have retained their color.

Winning the county seat election from Coldwater in 1901, Stratford sprang into great activity. Men of Coldwater sought an injunction against the change, but an armed group from Stratford visited the contending community, took the county records and held them under guard in a tent.

Through a region rich in wheat, US 54 proceeds to TEXHOMA, 51 m. (2,605 alt., 300 pop.), a town that straddles the Texas-Oklahoma State Line, 22 miles southwest of Guymon, Oklahoma. Latest population estimate is 1,750, with less than 400 in Texas, but its line of great grain elevators is in Texas.

2. Right from Dalhart on US 54, through a region of unspoiled cattle country, and a strip of rocky, weather-worn breaks, a region of winding gullies and bare, rock-crowned hills, to ROMERO, 33 m. (4,101 alt., 100 pop.). This tiny settlement dates back to an era long before the coming of the non-Latin ranchers. New Mexicans from Taos and Santa Fe came into this section in the early 1800's on large, organized buffalo hunts. These hunters, known as *ciboleros,* rode the High Plains on friendly terms with the Comanches. They killed with the lance, Indian fashion, although the *fusil* (bell-mouthed musket) was sometimes used. They hunted for meat as well as for hides, "jerking" the buffalo meat into *carne seca* (dried meat).

With these hunters sometimes came *comancheros,* who traded with the Plains Indians, first for buffalo hides and later for stolen horses and cattle. This illegal trade flourished during the Civil War, and some authorities maintain that over half a million head of Texas cattle were lost to outlaw traders.

After the *comancheros* came the New Mexican *pastores* (shepherds). They established permanent supply stations and ranged their woolly charges in the vicinity of their camp ground plazas. Remains of these semi-settlements are still visible, and their names linger.

The non-Latin ranchmen's ruthless demands for land and yet more land drove away the *pastores.* The few that survived did so only by entering the cattle business. Romero was named for Casimero Romero, one of the early shepherds.

Southwestward a ridge of low hills parallels the highway (L). Their slopes are covered with the dusty green bunch grass, but their summits gleam yellow with crests of bare sand, which when the wind is high are whipped away in long misty banners.

US 87 dips into a creek bottom at 41 m. On the far side of the stream is the Texas-New Mexico Line, seven miles northeast of Nara Vista, New Mexico (*see New Mexico Guide*).

Southeast of Dalhart the route is through a wind-swept region of seemingly endless prairies to DUMAS, 76 m. (3,638 alt., 10,547 pop. 1966 est.), seat of Moore County, where farm income has been outdistanced by oil, natural gas and petrochemicals with a county value of more than $54,000,000 annually. Crude helium is produced here and at EXCELL, west of MASTERSON, 16 m. south of Dumas on US 287 by Phillips Petroleum Co. and sold to the U. S. Bureau of Mines for storage at Cliffside. Dumas has junctions with US 287 and State 152.

US 87 now winds into a stretch of country broken by ravines and gulches, some dry, others with little creeks twisting toward the Canadian River. JOHN RAY BUTTE, the flat-topped mound (L) at 95 *m.* looms above the surrounding prairie.

The highway climbs to the top of a low divide from which (L) are visible the buildings of the DIAMOND RANCH, one of the famous early-day Panhandle domains. From the tall bridge over the CANADIAN RIVER, 104 *m.*, the course of the river is visible for miles in each direction. During the dry season its bed is a floor of gleaming sand, along which winds a narrow ribbon of running water. In times of flood the river surges high in a mad, debris-strewn torrent. The quicksands of the Canadian are notoriously dangerous and in early days made fording a risky business.

AMARILLO, 124 *m.* (3,676 alt., 167,374 pop. est. 1967) (*see article*), is at junctions with US 60 (*see Tour 15*), US 66 (*see Tour 14*) and US 287 (*see Tour 13*).

Section b.   AMARILLO to LUBBOCK; 120 m.   US 87

US 87 continues almost due south along the edge of the High Plains. Coronado passed this way nearly 400 years ago. Spanish and American explorers followed him. But history did not really begin here until the comparatively late era of American pioneering, when settlers came to the plains seeking health, fortune or homes. Their worldly goods, from skillet to parlor organ, were piled high in covered wagons.

The men battled Indians, then settled into a cattle business based on the survival of the fittest. The women founded a culture based on courage. A Virginia school teacher fought against opposition until she had collected sufficient funds to build the first church in Lubbock.

The region was isolated and life was that of pioneers. Herds and families were protected from Indians and thieves only by "six-gun" and rifle. A quieter battle was waged against the tick, for this parasite at first afflicted the cattle.

Other women followed the example of the Virginia school teacher, and gradually more churches and schools were built. The gaiety centered in three-day festivities held after cattle round-ups. Today wheat, corn and small grains have been added as sources of revenue, but religion and work are predominant. The three-day celebrations have been supplanted by old settlers' reunions. There are colleges now on the plains, and life is no longer a struggle for survival, but a normal American pattern of usefulness and civic improvement.

Between AMARILLO, 0 *m.*, and Canyon, US 60 (*see Tour 15*) and US 87 are one route, which leads through miles of broad wheatfields.

At 10 *m.* is the junction with an improved dirt road.

Left on this road to the HARDING RANCH (*moderate rates*), 10 *m.*, a 10,000-acre range that embraces the upper reaches of the rugged Palo Duro Canyon.

This remains a typical western ranch with pole corrals, bunk houses and all the other buildings of the old days, plus ample facilities for paying guests. The Palo Duro Canyon area offers trails, waterfalls, and Indian writings. Visitors can participate in herd riding, round-ups, bronco busting and branding.

Southward the country roughens into breaks that lead to the T-ANCHOR RANCH, 15 *m.* At the foot of a hill (L) is the headquarters building, one of the oldest in the Panhandle. The house was built in 1887 of logs cut in Palo Duro Canyon; shingles and finished lumber were freighted in by oxcart from Trinidad, Colorado.

At 17 *m.* is the junction with US 60 (*see Tour 15*), at the northern edge of CANYON, 17.5 *m.* (3,566 alt., 5,864 pop., 1960; 7,000 1965, est.) seat of Randall County and a cowtown that has achieved the dignity of a seat of learning.

WEST TEXAS STATE UNIVERSITY was a college until 1963. Its buildings occupy former lands of the T-Anchor Ranch. In 1965 the regular session enrolled 4,571, the summer, 1,705. In addition to arts and science degrees, it gives degrees in musical education and business administration.

The PANHANDLE-PLAINS HISTORICAL SOCIETY MUSEUM, PIONEER HALL, is on the campus (*open Tues., Thurs., Sat., and Sun.; 2–6 p.m.*).

Engraved on the facade of the building are the brands of the Panhandle cattle barons, past and present. Indian artifacts and relics of the early days of west Texas ranching share space with priceless records in the society's archives in the west wing of the museum. Old Charlie, huge bull buffalo, long mascot of the college and once a member of the Goodnight buffalo herd, stands mounted just within the entrance. The collection also includes the widespread horns that once graced the head of Old Blue, Colonel Goodnight's lead steer.

Left from Canyon on State 217, the old Goodnight-Loving Cattle Trail of half a century ago, to PALO DURO CANYON STATE PARK (*adm. 50¢ for car and driver; 30¢ each additional adult, children 15¢. Just within the area is El Coronado Lodge, park administration and refreshment building, where full information regarding the park is given. Camp grounds; tourist lodges and saddle horses for rent*), 12.2 *m.* Directly across the gulf of the canyon is visible the rock slide down which Colonel Charles Goodnight brought his first wagon train from the plains in 1876. Colonel Goodnight had come to Texas from Illinois when nine years old, and was reared on the frontier in the vicinity of Palo Pinto County. At the close of the Civil War he took the first herd of cattle through on the northwest trail from Texas to Colorado. Here at Palo Duro Canyon, in partnership with John Adair, Irish-American capitalist, he founded the old JA Ranch, the first ranch in the Panhandle, and later blazed a cattle trail from this point to Dodge City, Kansas. For more than a half century he was an active leader in the Panhandle region. He retired in 1927 at the age of 91, and died in Arizona two years later.

Many others before Goodnight had seen this great gash in the Llano Estacado escarpment. The followers of Coronado came to the western wall in 1541. For days they had pushed eastward "without sight of a mountain range, a hill, nor a hillock which was three times as high as a man . . . all so flat that, on seeing a herd of buffalo in the distance the sky was visible between their legs."

"Who would believe," wrote Pedro de Castañeda in his journal of the expedition, "that a thousand horses and five hundred of our cows, and more than five thousand rams and ewes, and more than fifteen hundred friendly Indians and servants, in traveling over these plains, would leave no more trace where they had passed than if nothing had been there—nothing—so that it was necessary to make piles of bones and cow dung now and then, so that the rear guard could follow the army. The grass never failed to come erect after it had been trodden down. . . . The country is like a bowl, so that when a man sits down, the horizon surrounds him all around at the distance of a musket shot."

Speaking of the Indians met on the plains, either Comanches or Apaches, Castañeda wrote: "They go about with the buffalo, and eat the meat raw and drink the blood of the cows they kill. They tan the skins with which all of the people clothe themselves." It was while exploring Palo Duro Canyon that Coronado met members of the Tejas tribe, whom Castañeda described as "very intelligent; the women are well made and modest. . . . They wear shoes and buskins made of tanned skin. The women wear cloaks over their small under-petticoats, with sleeves gathered up at the shoulders, all of skin."

On questioning the Indians he found here, Coronado made his dramatic decision to send his army back to Mexico while he, with 30 horsemen, sought the mythical wealth of Quivira for the King of Spain. Here the army turned westward, while the commander and his escort started north.

PALO DURO CANYON, carved by a branch of the Red River and the erosion of years, discloses the strata of successive geological formations from the basic red Permian of possibly 300 million years ago through the Triassic of the reptiles, the Pliocene of the dinosaurs, and the Pleistocene of the ice age. The sun brings out brilliant colors in the hills and valleys.

The PIONEER AMPHITHEATRE has seats for 1,300 and a 600-ft. wall for the back of its stage, where the pageant *Texas,* written by Paul Green, is presented nightly except Tuesday from the second week in June to the first week in September. *Adults, $1; children, 50¢.* The Park provides opportunities for hikes, rides, picnics and nature study. From the foot of Sad Monkey Peak the little Palo Duro, Burlington & West Texas Railroad makes a 2-mile tour with explanations by the engineer. Charles Goodnight's dugout is preserved. The Park cautions visitors to wear protective clothing on hikes and rides, to carry a canteen for drinking water, and to watch for rattlesnakes. El Coronado Lodge supplies lunch and supplies and accepts reservations for cabins. Camping facilities are available. No firearms are permitted.

Buffalo Lake and Park is about 12 *m.* SW of Canyon on US 60.

Modern houses characterize TULIA, 49 *m.* (3,501 alt., 4,410 pop), a town that began in 1890 when W. G. Connor started a post office on the prairie. Tulia handles grain and dairy products, the town's dominating structure being a 35,000-bushel elevator.

TULE CREEK, 50 *m.,* winds eastward to emerge from the confines of Tule Canyon, 12 miles distant. Around this spot are woven some of the most picturesque stories of the Panhandle. During his campaign of 1874, General Mackenzie ordered the killing of 1,450 horses captured from the Indians near here, necessary to keep the Indians from recapturing the herd.

PLAINVIEW, 74 *m.* (3,366 alt., 18,735 pop.), is at the junction with US 70.

HALE CENTER, 86 *m.* (3,423 alt., 2,100 pop.) transacts business for a large area of irrigated farms. It holds the Texas records for snowfall. The greatest single snowstorm, February 2-5, 1956, dropped 33 in.; the greatest monthly snowfall, also 1956, was 36 in.

ABERNATHY, 101 *m.* (3,359 alt., 4,491 pop.) ships farm prod-

ucts. NEW DEAL, 108 *m.* (600 pop.). Six *m.* east of US 87 is
PETERSBURG, (3,270 alt., 1,400 pop.).

LUBBOCK, 120 *m.* (3,241 alt., 71,747 pop., 1950; 128,691, 1960
with annexations; 155,200, 1965, est.) county seat of Lubbock Co. (182,-
240 pop., 1965). Mean temp., winter, 38.8° F., summer, 75.8° F., humidity, 63.5%, annual rainfall, 17.6 in. Market center of the South
Plains, shipping cotton, grain and livestock. In 1891 two small towns
moved to form Lubbock, Incor. 1909, when the Santa Fe arrived; in
1928 came the Fort Worth & Denver. In 1900 first cotton was planted
in the South Plains; today they produce nearly half of the Texas crop
and 12.5% of U. S. total; also one-third of the nation's grain sorghum.
The area is irrigated by wells, has oil fields and refineries. Industries in
the city include cotton spinning, cotton oil and cotton gin manufacturing
and electronics.

TEXAS TECHNOLOGICAL COLLEGE, estab. 1925, is the
third largest state-owned college in Texas. It specializes in textile engineering and management, agricultural and petroleum engineering, and
has a well-rounded curriculum including home economics and business
administration. It enrolled 15,790 in 1966, with a faculty of 760. Its 19
dormitories accommodate 7,147. It is a member of the Southwest Football
Conference and its JONES STADIUM holds 47,000. Nearby on the campus
are the LUBBOCK MUNICIPAL AUDITORIUM (seats 3,000) and connecting COLISEUM (seats 10,000) The WEST TEXAS MUSEUM is on campus, which covers 1,844 acres.

LUBBOCK CHRISTIAN COLLEGE (Junior) was opened 1956
by the Churches of Christ and enrolls 600–700. In 1964 the city obtained
authorization for a new State School for Retarded Children to accommodate 2,000.

Lubbock is a member of the Canadian River Municipal Water Authority and although nearly 200 miles from Lake Meredith on the Canadian River obtains part of its water supply from that source through the
new Acqueduct System completed in 1967, which cost $52,000,000 and
extends 322 miles.

REESE AIR FORCE BASE for jet training, covers 2,862 acres
and has a personnel of 2,766. The MUNICIPAL AIRPORT on Amarillo Road (US 87) has daily flights by Braniff, Continental and Trans-
Texas lines.

MACKENZIE STATE PARK, 549 acres, is famous for its
PRAIRIE DOG TOWN, the last resort of animals once plentiful on the
Plains. BUFFALO SPRINGS LAKE is a boating area east on State
835.

In Lubbock City Park is the SITE OF SINGER'S STORE, 1879–1886, a
supply house that catered to buffalo hunters. Here was the first post office
in Lubbock County, and here two of the military trails crossed, one from
Fort Concho to Fort Sumner, New Mexico, the other from Fort Stockton
to Fort Elliot. For years this was one of the only two stores on the South
Plains.

In Lubbock are junctions with US 84 (*see Tour 21*) and US 82 combined with US 62.

Section c.   LUBBOCK to SAN ANGELO; 193 m.   US 87

This part of US 87 follows the rim of the Cap Rock until, at Lamesa, it turns southeastward and descends into a draw leaving the South Plains.

Cattle and farm lands and areas of recent oil development are traversed and toward the end of the section an extensive goat and sheep ranching region is reached, one of the centers of Texas' vast mohair and wool industry.

Development of the plains area began after the coming of the railroads. Most of the people along this section of the route are ranchers and farmers, living much in the manner of their forefathers, except that modern transportation takes them into the towns more often.

South of LUBBOCK, 0 *m.*, there is a large cultivated area.

At 19.5 *m.* is a junction with an improved dirt road.

Left here to TAHOKA LAKE, 6 *m.*, where, at the headquarters of the old Tahoka Lake Ranch (once the C. C. Slaughter ranch house, built in 1899), coyote hunts can be arranged. Those eager to explore will find ruins of ancient dugouts and rock corrals, the habitations of early-day sheepherders, Indian camp sites and graves, and evidences of the prehistoric Sand Hill culture. The bed of Tahoka Lake, when dry, yields sodium sulphate.

A detachment of Coronado's men is believed to have reached this lake. The military expeditions of Generals Shafter and Mackenzie often camped at Tahoka while hunting down Comanches and Kiowas. Later cattle drives, stage lines and freight outfits made it a stopping place, and deep wheel ruts on the old trail are still visible on the west and south shores. Springs pour their waters into the alkali bed of the lake.

Cotton, cattle and grain are shipped from TAHOKA, 30 *m.* (3,090 alt., 3,012 pop.). When the itinerant labor arrives at cotton-picking time, the town becomes exceedingly active. Grocery stores remain open all night. The fast tempo of Mexican folk music, lured from guitars by speeding fingers, blends into the sweet, melancholy strains of the American Negro's spirituals as work-weary field hands play in the cool night hours.

Local Negro farm laborers in 1939 celebrated "Juneteenth" (Texas emancipation day, June 19) with the first all-Negro rodeo ever held here.

In Tahoka is the junction with US 380 (*see Tour 27*).

As the route continues southward the pastures to the right are those of the T-Bar Ranch, whose holdings total 80,000 acres. GUTHRIE LAKE, another of the dry alkali lakes of the region is passed (R) at 33 *m.* This lake is sometimes visited by scientists interested in the Cretaceous invertebrate fossil deposits found on the west shore.

Another small lake is passed (R) at 37.3 *m.*, its distant shore showing the white scars of recent excavations, which mark rich deposits of silica, or volcanic ash.

The highway swerves to skirt the edge of O'DONNELL, 45 *m.*

(3,000 alt., 1,356 pop.), which sprawls behind the gray, inverted funnels of its cotton gins.

Cotton, cattle and the oil production of Dawson County are mainstays of LAMESA, 62 *m.* (2,975 alt., 12,438 pop.). Its position on the plains at the edge of the Cap Rock gave Lamesa its name, which makes one word of the Spanish *la mesa* (the table.)

Southeast of Lamesa US 87 dips over the edge of the Cap Rock, crossing a region that in times of normal rainfall raises an abundance of cotton and corn. Vast fields sweep away to the distant skyline. In dry years this area becomes a land of desolation, only to spring back into fertility with the return of the rains.

BIG SPRING, 106 *m.* (2,397 alt., 34,800 pop.) (*see Tour 19d*), is at the junction with US 80 (Interstate 20). The route is southeastward through a brief section of small farms.

At 108.2 *m.* is the entrance (R) to BIG SPRING STATE PARK (*picnic facilities*), 363 acres, where an excellent Alpine drive leads to the top of SCENIC MOUNTAIN (2,811 alt.). WEBB AIR FORCE BASE for training jet pilots is 2½ *m.* west. HOWARD COUNTY JUNIOR COLLEGE, founded 1946, enrolls more than 800.

The route now enters the shallow upper valley of the North Concho River and the HOWARD-GLASSCOCK OIL FIELD, 119.7 *m.* Derricks dot the landscape and the air is heavy with the smell of sulphur, this field producing what is technically known as sour oil.

Sheep ranches are traversed as pastures begin to show wolf-proof fences. In this section some sheep ranches utilize the latest in equipment, one having an unusually modern barn with the newest type of facilities for housing and shearing sheep. The barn is of reinforced concrete, two stories high, with an elevator for carrying the wool to the upper floor for storage. The stalls are so constructed that they can be folded to the ceiling out of the way of the crews during the shearing season.

STERLING CITY, 150 *m.* (2,295 alt., 2,294 pop.), is seat of Sterling County, which raises cattle, sheep, goats; ships wool, mohair. Here the *Sterling City News-Record,* became one of the notable country newspapers of the State. It appeared every Friday after October 15, 1889, and gained its reputation through the philosophy of its editor-owner, W. F. (Uncle Bill) Kellis, who helped clear brush from the town site.

US 87 now winds through rugged hill country. Wildlife abounds, with deer, turkeys, blue quail and bobwhites to tempt the hunter.

The high peak overlooking the valley from the west at 158 *m.* is TOWER HILL, on top of which the crumbled outlines of an old fort are visible. The ruins are clearly those of an ancient fortress; the walls, with loopholes to permit rifle fire, are in fairly good condition. The barrels of muzzle-loading rifles were found in the enclosure, and bullet marks on rocks and trees of the west slope indicated that at some time it was the scene of a battle, but its origin and history are unknown. Its walls were a landmark to the first settlers of the region in 1864.

Near the fortification an arrow, carved on a rock, led to the discovery of a small cavern in which was found a skeleton wrapped in a beaded mantle. Strings of beads, a silver ornament beaten from a Spanish dollar, brass finger and ankle rings, a gold nose ring, and a silver goblet were found. The goblet was engraved: "For the best Carlisle Colt, 1830."

In this vicinity on private property is James Hollow, reputed to be the site of a horse ranch run by the notorious James brothers, Frank and Jesse, in the 1870's, and used by them as a hideout. Today this region is given over to the raising of blooded cattle and sheep.

Along the North Concho River in this area are heavy growths of giant oaks and pecans.

The TEXAS STATE TUBERCULOSIS SANATORIUM (L), 176 m., has its plant backed against the swell of the foothills of the Carlsbad Mountains. This is a health center, a small city composed of 37 buildings. It has a post office, power plant, library, farm and dairy. The hospital has a capacity of 800 patients.

At 178.5 m. the highway passes the point where US 87 crosses the route of the California Trail, later followed by the Butterfield Stage Line. Abundant water in this region decided the course of these pioneer transportation routes, and drew early settlers to this locality.

SAN ANGELO, 193 m. (1,847 alt., 60,000 pop. est.) is at junctions with US 277 (see Tour 10) and 67 (see Tour 18).

Section d.   SAN ANGELO to SAN ANTONIO; 218 m.
US 87

US 87 now leads through the picturesque hill country of Texas, predominantly a rough, rolling region of sheep and goat ranches. This area, settled by the German immigrants of the 1840's, was to a large degree isolated from contact with other parts of the State until the era of modern highways and automotive transportation. As a result the people are largely of German descent, speak the German language, and cling closely to many of the customs and habits of their Teutonic forefathers. Thrifty, intelligent, and hard working, they have struggled to develop their rugged acres, early introducing sheep and goats, and they till the vailleys. Their crops are principally grains and forage.

Deer, wild turkeys, quail, doves and other game abound in the cedar- and oak-clad hills. Stop-over accommodations are excellent, ranging from single camp units to modern hotels.

South of SAN ANGELO, 0 m., fields of red sandy loam border the highway.

At 3.3 m. is the junction with US 277 (see Tour 9), and (R) at 5.8 m. is the San Angelo Municipal Airport.

EDEN, 44 m. (2,048 alt., 1,486 pop.) (see Tour 16c), is at the junction with US 83 (see Tour 16).

The route is eastward following the windings of the little valley of the North Fork of Brady Creek, so named after Peter Brady, a member of the Giddings survey of 1847.

BRADY, 76 m. (1,670 alt., 6,000 pop.) is protected by a retaining wall from the flood waters of Brady Creek. It is the seat of McCulloch

County, named for Confederate Gen. Ben McCulloch, who fought at San Jacinto. Its principal industries are the scouring and combing of wool and mohair, and the production of sand for glass and oil industries. The Heart of Texas Band Festival is held by high school bands in February.

The city's water comes from LAKE BRADY, (2,020 acres) 3 *m.* west. At CALF CREEK, 14 *m.* south, Indians halted James Bowie's party for 8 days and forced it to return to San Antonio.

MERCURY, 26 *m.* north of Brady on US 377 is at the geographical center of Texas.

US 87 turns south at Brady, proceeding through a terrain of low, rolling wooded hills past sheep, goat and turkey ranches. Ahead, higher hills loom against the skyline—the highlands of the Edwards Plateau. The SAN SABA RIVER (*good fishing*), is crossed at 86 *m.* At 88.4 *m.* is a side road.

Left here to CAMP SAN SABA, 2 *m.,* a pioneer settlement of McCulloch County, which marks the site of an old Ranger fort where settlers bought peace from the Comanche Indians in 1847.

Rugged ridges of red granite jut through the soil of the hillsides and stones litter the fields along the valleys as US 87 proceeds southward. These are outcroppings of a soft, flaky, non-polishable granite quarried only for highway and roadbed construction. In this section mile-long rock fences line the highway.

Weathered stone buildings stand on rocky, uneven levels at MASON, 106 *m.* (1,450 alt., 1,910 pop.). Much of the stone used in construction was taken from the barracks of old Fort Mason. The Dodge cattle trail started around Mason.

Mason is active in the shipping of wool and mohair. It is near the Llano River and at the northern edge of the hill country, and deer, wild turkeys, quail, doves and squirrels abound in the vicinity (*hunting permit rates range from $5 a day to $500 a season*). Fishing for bass, perch and crappie is good in the Llano and James Rivers.

In 1875 this vicinity was the scene of the Mason County War, a disagreement between German and American settlers, which reached such proportions that it was necessary for a detachment of Texas Rangers to intervene. Threats had been made in the hill country to "burn out the Dutch," and in the report of his investigation Major John B. Jones of the Rangers stated: "I find the houses closed, a deathlike stillness . . . and an evident suspense if not dread in the minds of the inhabitants." A German settler was shot on the street in Mason, and the hotel fired. Major Jones restored peace within a few weeks.

POST HILL (L), 107.1 *m.,* is the site of old Fort Mason. The post's roster contains the names of many noted military personages, among them Thomas, Longstreet, Johnston, Van Dorn, Kirby Smith, and Lee. The post, which was abandoned in 1869, at one time had more than one hundred stone buildings. A few ruined walls and foundations are all that remain.

The little group of old-time buildings that comprise the German village of LOYAL VALLEY, 125 *m.*, is in the center of a popular hunting area (*hunting rights leased by agents at Mason or by owners, by the day, week or season; rates from $5 a day upwards*).

Throughout this area the farmhouses, built of stone, are excellent examples of German Colonial architecture.

FREDERICKSBURG, 149 *m.* (1,742 alt., 5,000 pop.) (*see Tour 24b*), is at the junction with US 290 (*see Tour 24*).

The route now pierces the heart of the hill country. The highway climbs a hill, only to dip down into the green depths of a valley beyond. Autumn finds the hillsides ablaze with the reds and yellows of frost-tinted oaks, pecans, cottonwoods, and sumacs, while the evergreen of the cedars, shin-oaks, and cypresses offers a verdant scene even in winter. Rugged granite outcroppings show on the bare crests of hills, or gleam dull red or gray in the faces of cliffs above the timber growth of the valley floors. Rivers wind through narrow passes with the roar and rush of white-foamed rapids, or idle along the valleys in deep streams.

Spanning the valley of the Pedernales River, an excellent fishing stream, the highway climbs to the top of a ridge called Big Hill, from which is visible a wide panorama of wooded hills and deep narrow valleys. Stone farmhouses in this region sometimes show their age in the loopholes built to permit rifle fire against Indians.

Founded by German immigrants in 1854, COMFORT, 172 *m.* (1,429 alt., 1,600 pop.), is a prosperous retail and recreational center on the edge of the Guadalupe River Valley. Many of its houses are old, but all are well preserved and most of them are painted white. Many boys and girls camps are nearby. The adjacent hills and streams offer sport to hunters and fishermen.

Five blocks north of the post office, on the main street, is a monument in honor of a group of German settlers who, rather than serve forced enlistments in the Confederate Army, fled toward Mexico. Overtaken by a Confederate force at a crossing on the upper Nueces River, 19 out of 65 were killed and 9 badly wounded. After the Civil War the survivors and friends of the slain gathered the remains and returned them to Comfort, where they lie beneath the monument.

In Comfort is the junction with State 27 (*see Tour 17A*).

US 87 descends a hill to enter the green valley of Cibolo Creek, where BOERNE, 188 *m.* (1,405 alt., 2,169 pop.), health and recreation resort ringed around by wooded hillsides, spreads its winding streets past old stone houses. Narrow windows, outside stairways, steep gables, and prim little front-yard gardens show its Old World influence.

Members of the German colony of Bettina founded Boerne in 1849. Five men who settled east of the present town were of an idealistic group that had founded "Latin settlements," composed of students of the classics, at other points in Texas. Their farm was called Tusculum, for Cicero's country home. After two years they moved to the site of the present town, which was named for Ludwig Boerne, one of the founders. There is an old STAGE STATION BUILDING northeast of the intersection of US 87 with the old San Antonio Road. The town became the home of George Wilkins Kendall, first war correspondent of the modern type, and Colonel Robert E. Lee once maintained quarters in a little stone building that still stands on the main street.

Kendall, of New Hampshire birth, had been a printer in Washington and with Horace Greeley in New York, and became one of the founders in 1837 of the *New Orleans Picayune*. Four years later, as a journalist, he joined the ill-fated Santa Fé Expedition (*see History*), was captured and imprisoned for a year in Mexico. His book, *Narrative of the Texan Santa Fe Expedition,* had a large sale.

When the Mexican War broke out in 1846, he developed the first modern system of war correspondence. On muleback from Algiers, Louisiana, he set out for the Rio Grande, where he joined General Zachary Taylor. On the way, he organized a chain of pony express riders by whom —and also by ships—he sent back news stories which so "scooped" the other American papers that the latest war news in even the largest New York journals was frequently preceded by: "The *New Orleans Picayune* says." He participated in battles, personally captured a Mexican cavalry flag, was wounded in the fighting which preceded the capture of Mexico City, and entered the city with General Winfield Scott. The climax of his successful exploits was that news of the American victory reached Washington by pony express from the *Picayune* ahead of official dispatches, and the Treaty of Guadalupe was published in that paper before the U. S. Government had received its text. Following the war he went to France, whence he sent letters on European affairs. On his return, although he retained his financial interest in the *Picayune* and made further short visits to Europe, he made his home for the remainder of his life at Boerne. Much of present Kendall County was his ranch.

At 192.5 *m.* is the junction with a dirt road.

Left here to CASCADE CAVERNS (*guides*), 3 *m.* Here amid cave formations are to be seen Pleistocene fossils, mammoth molars, and a mammoth tusk.

US 87 now winds through hills which rapidly lessen in height and ruggedness. The valleys broaden but are less fertile, and are used largely as pasture lands. The heavy timber almost vanishes, the slopes of the hills showing growths of mesquite and scrub oak.

On past a limestone quarry which has scarred deeply the face of a low hill, and past an old STAGE STATION (R), 210.1 *m.,* the highway climbs a hill from which is visible the sweeping valley of the San Antonio River, topped by the skyscrapers of the San Antonio business district.

SAN ANTONIO, 218 *m.* (656 alt., 699,768 pop., 1966 est.) (*see San Antonio*), is at junctions with US 81 (*see Tour 8*), US 90 (*see Tour 23*), US 181 (*see Tour 26*), US 281 (*see Tour 9*), and State 16 (*see Tour 17A*).

Section e. SAN ANTONIO to PORT LAVACA; 143 m.
US 87

The route continues southeast across the Coastal Plain to tidewater midway of the arc of the Texas Gulf Coast. The elevation gradually lessens from 600 feet near San Antonio to little more than sea-level at Port Lavaca. It is a well timbered region throughout, with fine groves of cottonwoods, live oaks, cypresses, pecans and willows along the water courses. Broad pasture lands are dotted with clumps of mesquites and oaks. The clay and sandy loam soil produces large crops of cotton, corn and small grains. In the spring and summer a profusion of wild flowers covers the fields and brightens the roadsides.

Oil, cotton and beef cattle are the largest sources of wealth in this region. Livestock includes dairy cattle. Fishing and recreational resorts abound in the coastal region.

Predominantly a rural area of small towns, its population is largely of Anglo-American and Irish stock, although in some localities the people are descendants of German immigrants. Industrious and thrifty, many are owners of vast estates. Farm laborers and tenant farmers are mostly Mexicans.

Southeast of SAN ANTONIO, 0 *m.,* is SUTHERLAND SPRINGS, 32 *m.* (423 alt., 400 pop.), an extension of the old town, half a mile to the left. With the building of the new highway, filling stations and a huddle of stores sprang up.

Left from Sutherland Springs on a dirt road to SUTHERLAND SPRINGS PARK, 0.5 *m.* This former health center, now a ghost town, embraces hundreds of springs which include 27 varieties of hot and cold mineral waters. The gaunt old hotel building was a week-end rendezvous for San Antonians in horse-and-buggy days. The resort declined when automobiles gave access to other more widely advertised places. The POLLEY MANSION (*private*), 4.2 *m.,* was erected in 1854 by Colonel Joseph H. Polley. This two-story cut stone house, showing semiclassical influence, was built by slave labor. Robert E. Lee was often entertained here.

Southward US 87 traverses the Texas watermelon belt. Here, in season, the sides of the highway resemble a watermelon bazaar, for they are lined with stands from which melons are sold, either whole, or in huge, iced slices, fresh from the fields.

Storage tanks and several processing plants are in NIXON, 51 *m.* (396 alt., 1,751 pop.). A peanut grading plant handles the local crop; the town also has a poultry dressing and packing plant, and others. Nearby, large flocks of chickens and turkeys are usually visible from the highway.

At the GUADALUPE RIVER, 83 *m.,* a pecan and live oak grove presents a fine camping spot.

CUERO, 88 *m.* (177 alt., 7,338 pop.) DeWitt County, is at the junction with US 77 (*see Tour 7*), which runs concurrent with US 87 to Victoria, a distance of 28 miles.

VICTORIA, 116 *m.* (93 alt., 37,000 pop.), is at junctions with US 77 (*see Tour 7*) and US 59 (*see Tour 25*).

The route continues across level farm and pasture lands. Drainage canals are frequent, for this is a region of abundant rainfall.

The business houses of PORT LAVACA, 143 *m.* (22 alt., 11,000 pop. est.) perch on a low bluff on the shore of Lavaca Bay.

The waterfront is lined with fish houses and packing sheds that jut out into the shallow waters. Fishing for sport, however, is provided by the longest pier on the Coast, 3,202 ft., on the west side of Lavaca Bay.

Founded by the Spanish in 1815, the early town was called La Vaca (the cow), the Lavaca River having been thus named by La Salle.

The present town is on the approximate site of Linnville, which was wiped out by enraged Comanches on August 8, 1840. Angered by the slaughter of their leaders in the Council House fight in San Antonio (*see San Antonio*), an army of 500 Indians stormed Victoria and marched on Linnville. Residents took no precautions until too late. When first sighted the Comanches were believed to be Mexican traders, and Linnville was nearly surrounded before residents realized their peril. Then they could only flee to the bay, where they took refuge on a lighter beyond arrow shot. The Indians pillaged the town, burned everything they did not want or could not transport, and departed after loading their loot on 1,500 captured horses. They were overtaken at Plum Creek (*see Tour 23b*).

Port Lavaca was a busy port of entry, with regular services to New York by the Morgan Line until the tides of Matagorda Bay choked the channel. Activity was limited to handling fish and shrimp until oil increased business. The new MATAGORDA SHIP CHANNEL has restored the sea route and connects with the Intracoastal Canal. The fine fishing and sailing help make Port Lavaca a resort. The annual Regatta takes place on Labor Day weekend. State 35 passes through Port Lavaca.

Across the causeway north on Highway 35, over Lavaca Bay is the plant of Aluminum Company of America, where radial diesel engines convert primary aluminum ore into ingots (*open to visitors, Monday through Friday, 8–5*).

Right from Port Lavaca on a graveled road to MAGNOLIA BEACH (*limited tourist facilities*), 12.3 *m.* (91 pop.), a summer resort overlooking the waters of Lavaca and Matagorda Bays. From Magnolia Beach a sandy road along the shore leads southward to the SITE OF INDIANOLA, once the most active and important of Texas seaports. Founded in 1844 by Prince Carl Zu Solms-Braunfels as Carlshafen, a port of entry for German immigrants, Indianola (or Indian Point) developed rapidly, and through it passed most of the commerce and immigration of Texas during that half-century when thousands of French, German, Polish and Irish settlers were brought in by colonization companies. Swept by cholera in 1846, when the dead lay unburied in the streets, the town survived until 1875, when it was wrecked by a Gulf storm. An attempt was made to rebuild it, but another storm in 1886 completed its destruction.

A most unusual cargo was landed at Indianola in 1856, when 32 camels were imported for military service in the Southwest on the recommendation of Jefferson Davis, Secretary of War under President Pierce. Camp Verde, south of Junction, was the eastern terminus of a camel caravan to California. The experiment was so successful that in 1857 40 more camels were imported. Davis' successor recommended an additional 1,000 camels, but the outbreak of the Civil War stopped the experiments.

❧❧❧❧❧❧❧❧❧❧❧❧❧❧❧❧❧❧❧❧❧❧❧❧❧❧❧❧❧❧❧❧❧❧❧❧

Tour 17A

Comfort—Bandera—San Antonio; State 27, 16, and Bandera Road; 91 *m.*

This scenic route twists and climbs through the southwestern fringe of the rugged, wooded hill country of Texas, into a region of strong sectional and racial trends, where old rock fences enclose little fields of grain —tilled for generations by the same family—and where stone houses built in the 1840's by German, English or Polish immigrants lift steep roofs. Delaine Merino sheep graze rocky pastures in deep valleys, and Angora goats browse on perilous perches above gorges, or on steep hilltops. Wild turkeys often fly from the roadside, deer flash across the highway, quail decorously shepherd their broods, undisturbed by human passage—for here they are protected by game laws—and in the tangled woodlands along numerous small streams, an occasional mountain lion hides. Although ranch lands are posted, arrangements can be made with owners for hunting and fishing (*rates vary from $2 to $5 a day*). Caves, rapids, waterfalls, dinosaur tracks, fossils, artifacts left by the Apaches, historic sites, are found deep in the rock-ribbed hills. Particularly in the vicinity of Bandera, pioneer customs prevail, including the splitting of shingles by hand, spinning, carding, weaving and other frontier crafts. Rural folk of the whole tour area subsist independently on their small holdings, produce all except a few items of food, raise feed crops sufficient for their stock, and even grow enough tobacco for their own use.

COMFORT, 0 *m.* (1,429 alt., 1,600 pop.) is at the junction with US 87. West of Comfort the route is State 27.

West of Comfort the route is State 27.

An ARMADILLO FARM (*open*) and curio shop is (R) at 2 *m.* Here, armor-plated armadillos, small harmless animals (*see Resources and Their Conservation*), are raised for their shells, which are processed, made into baskets and sold to curio dealers throughout the United States and abroad.

Northwestward, State 27 passes through a region devoted to sheep and goat ranching. Cedar-clad hills crowd close to the highway.

At 15.9 *m.* is the junction with State 264.

Right on State 264 to a U. S. VETERANS ADMINISTRATION FACILITY (*open 3–5 daily*), 1 *m.*, a hospital with accommodations for 1,300 patients.

At 16 *m.* is the junction with the Bandera Road, on which the route continues southward. This is an alternate to State 16 between Bandera and Kerrville.

Right (straight ahead) on State 27 to (R) the SCHREINER INSTITUTE, 0.2 *m.,* a military school and junior college for boys, founded in 1922 and endowed by Captain Charles Schreiner. The institute is housed in modern buildings on a well-landscaped 140-acre campus. It is supported by the United Presbyterian Church.

KERRVILLE, 2 *m.* (1,645 alt., 8,901 pop.) (*facilities ample, from camp sites and tourist lodges to modern hotels, with varying rates; hunting and fishing information available at Chamber of Commerce*). Because of its altitude and its clear, cedar-scented air, Kerrville is a popular recreation and health resort. Modern facilities for housing and entertaining vacationists and health seekers have given the town a smart appearance. The compact, modern business district is neat, and residential sections are roomy. The town is in an area locally called the Heart of the Hills, on the banks of the Guadalupe River. In the surrounding hills are numerous privately owned camps and hunting lodges, summer camps for boys and girls, and for religious groups. Kerrville is a major wool and mohair market. Deer and turkey hunting is popular. The Texas Lions Camp for Crippled Children is here. West of the town is the SCHREINER GAME PRESERVE (*private*).

South of the junction with State 27 the route offers much scenic beauty and numerous points of interest.

The GUADALUPE RIVER is crossed at 16.1 *m.* on a low-water bridge. (*Observe depth gauge before crossing.*)

The Bandera Road traverses sparsely settled country deep in the hills, crossing numerous little creeks. MEDINA (470 pop.) is a farm village.

CAMP VERDE, 29 *m.,* a cluster of houses on a private ranch, is the site of a United States military post established in 1856, famed as a home of Jefferson Davis' camel corps. Seeking a dependable means for transportation of army supplies to posts in the semiarid regions of the Great Plains, Jefferson Davis, then Secretary of War, imported a camel herd and native herders. The animals were landed at Indianola in 1856 and marched overland to the post here.

The corps was made up of men from cavalry units, who were taught by the foreign herders the art of handling and packing camels. Cavalrymen thus detailed—derisively called "cameleers"—quickly developed an antipathy for their new mounts. A mixed column of cavalry and camels usually resulted in a stampede, the range-bred cavalry horses bolting and bucking so that formation or steady progress was impossible.

During the Civil War, Camp Verde was surrendered to the Confederates, and the camels were left without special supervision. Many wandered away into the hills, and survivors of them were found at intervals for many years. The camp was regained by the Federal Army and abandoned 1869.

BANDERA PASS, entered at 31.3 *m.,* is a deep narrow gorge 0.3 miles long and 125 feet wide. This is the site of several engagements between Indians and white men. In the middle eighteenth century the Apaches were defeated here in a fierce encounter with Spanish soldiers, reputedly under General Bandera, and here, during the early 1840's, a force of Texas Rangers under Captain Jack Hays was ambushed by Comanches, who were repulsed.

Visible at 37 *m.* is POLLY'S PEAK (L), so named in memory of Policarpo Rodriquez, pioneer, scout, preacher, and Indian fighter. At the foot of the peak, inaccessible, are the remains of the rock chapel where he preached, and near by is his grave.

BANDERA, 44 *m.* (1,258 alt., 1,000 pop. est.), in a bend of Medina River, is hemmed in by high, barren hills; its old rock houses, built of materials taken from those hillsides, line winding country roads. This is one of the few Texas towns retaining a frontier appearance and atmosphere; its people enjoy square dances, have hog-calling and fiddlers contests, wear sunbonnets and homespun. Bandera was founded in the 1850's, as a shingle camp, later enlarged by a temporary Mormon settlement, and still later it became a Polish colony.

Among the guest ranches is Lost Valley Resort Ranch and its Frontier Town, where life in the old West is reenacted.

One block north of the courthouse is FRONTIER TIMES MUSEUM (*open 8–6 daily*), containing a collection of early-day relics, pioneer pictures, and Texas literature. Each July 4 Bandera holds a barbecue, and has demonstrations in shingle-making and other frontier crafts; there is also old-time dancing and cowboy singing.

Southeastward, the route is State 16.

At 63.1 *m.* is a junction with a graveled toll road.

Right on this road (*50¢ a car*) to MEDINA LAKE, 11 *m.* (*fishing for bass, perch, catfish*), a large lake whose shores are lined with camps that offer accommodations and fishing facilities. There are also numerous privately owned lodges and camps.

Medina Lake is formed by a dam impounding the waters of the Medina River. The main dam is 1,580 feet long and 160 feet high. Supplementing this is a smaller diversion dam, 500 feet long and 48 feet high. The impounded 250,000 acre-feet of water forms a lake with 96 miles of shore line, and is estimated to be capable of irrigating 60,000 acres of land. The village of MICO (450 pop.) has grown up at the lake.

At 63.6 *m.* is a junction with a graveled road.

Right on this road to GALLAGHER RANCH (*riding, hiking, swimming*), 3.6 *m.*, an old cattle range converted into a dude ranch.

As State 16 winds its way out of the hill country and crosses the first belt of the Balcones Escarpment, at 79.8 *m.* is the old HUEBNER HOME (*private*), built (L) in 1862 by Joseph Huebner.

At 87 *m.* is the junction with Cincinnati Avenue. At 2700 Cincinnati Ave. ST. MARY'S UNIVERSITY, founded 1852, occupies a campus of 103 acres. Long restricted to men, but more recently opened to women, it still has only about 200 woman students out of 1,900 enrolled. Its first dormitory for women is one of its new structures. The Graduate School is on the campus; the School of Law at 112 College St., San Antonio. The library has more than 100,000 volumes.

SAN ANTONIO, 91 *m.* (656 alt., 699,768 pop. est.).

Tour 18

(Texarkana, Ark.) — Texarkana — Greenville — Dallas —Cleburne — Stephenville — Brownwood — San Angelo — Fort Stockton — Alpine—Presidio. US 67; Interstate 30.
Arkansas Line to Presidio, 774 *m*.

Spanning the breadth of Texas, US 67 begins in the pine forests of the northeast part of the State, traverses the fertile Blacklands Belt prairies, winds through a tangle of low hills along the upper area of the Edwards Plateau, and crosses arid plains to end in a mountain wilderness at the muddy Rio Grande. Four commercial activities mark the course of this route, and tell the story of its development: lumbering in the eastern region, agriculture in the central area, and ranching and mining in the western reaches.

In the moist, deep forests where the route begins, a man's coon dog is one of his most valued possessions; the highly rural population clings to simple, old-fashioned things. Throughout the next section, where cotton is all-important, there are more sharply defined social divisions, with white and Negro tenants farming about half of the land. Next is the urban belt surrounding Dallas, where houses, roads, people and customs are wholly modern. Beyond Dallas, stock farming, cotton, and livestock are the general means of livelihood, with at least one town almost hidden by oil derricks, and other scattered fields pumping up from the depths the evil-odored treasure of petroleum. Between San Angelo and Presidio a great, rugged slice of Texas offers a glimpse of little-changed Western conditions: here droughts, the price of beef cattle, goats and sheep, black coffee and whole-hearted human associations retain an old importance in a sparsely inhabited land where the miles separating ranch houses and towns are long and lonely.

As US 67 moves southwest from Dallas it runs parallel to US 377 until it reaches Stephenville, where the two highways are united to Brownwood, where US 67 turns west and US 377 continues south. On US 377 out of Fort Worth are:

BENBROOK, 3 *m*. (658 alt., 3,254 pop.) ; to the east the Clear Fork of Trinity River supplies LAKE BENBROOK, a Fort Worth Reservoir of 5,820 acres and 164,800 acre-ft. capacity.

CRESSON, 26 *m*. (260 pop.) has a junction with State 171 (Weatherford to Mexia).

GRANBURY, 39 *m*. (725 alt., 2,500 pop.) seat of Hood County on the Brazos River. Here State 144 is a link between US 377 and US 67.

TOLAR, 48 *m*. (280 pop.) BLUFF DALE, 55 *m*. (300 pop.) is in Erath County. Both are farm villages.

Section a. *ARKANSAS LINE to DALLAS; 187 m.   US 67*

This part of US 67 is along the southern watershed of the great Red River Valley, through the pine forests, the Blacklands Belt and the small hills of east Texas, on to the eastern edge of the Central Plains. Beyond the lumbering area it is a region of extensive cultivation with cotton and truck crops leading. French traders, pushing up the Red River from Louisiana colonies, early penetrated this section and established trading posts. Trappers, the Mountain Men of Kit Carson's and Jim Bridger's day, explored the rivers at about the opening of the nineteenth century. Actual settlement began during the era of the Texas Republic.

US 67 crosses the ARKANSAS LINE, 0 *m.,* at W. Seventh St. and State Line Ave., TEXARKANA (295 alt., 30,218 pop., 1960) across the street from Texarkana, Arkansas (21,652 pop., 1960).

In Texarkana are junctions with US 82, US 59, US 71, Interstate 30.

Beside a pool in a little hollow in the pine forest, REDWATER, 15 *m.* (286 alt., 319 pop.), a railroad town, was renamed when a religious revival in 1886 converted so many of the residents that they felt their town's title—then Ingersoll—should not honor that renowned agnostic. The birth of four daughters to the local Page family in 1890 gave America its first quadruplets of record.

Westward US 67 passes a checkerboard of second-growth pine and dwarfed oak woodlands, orchards, and fields devoted to the growing of tomatoes, cabbages, potatoes and other garden vegetables.

MAUD, 20 *m.* (284 alt., 950 pop.), built along the L of the highway, supports a sawmill, and ships fruits and vegetables produced on the red sandy soil of the surrounding region.

In Maud is the junction with US 59 (*see Tour 2*).

Through a forest where stately oaks and hickories predominate, US 67 winds westward past a string of tiny settlements that seem to crowd each other in an effort to find a place along the highway.

The SULPHUR RIVER (*camp sites, fishing for bass, perch, crappie*), is crossed at 41 *m.*

MOUNT PLEASANT, 67 *m.* (416 alt., 8,027 pop., 1960; 11,270 est. 1964) is at the junction with US 67. Seat of Titus County, it is served by the St. Louis Southwestern Ry. Many weathered houses here are made of cypress joined together with wooden pegs, and have wide porches and rambling wings. Poultry processing, meat packing, and oil refining are chief industries.

In Mount Pleasant is the junction with US 271 (*see Tour 4*).

Many a stately old house enclosed by a picket fence stands in MOUNT VERNON, 80 *m.* (476 alt., 1,338 pop.), where a profusion of honeysuckles, hydrangeas, roses, and tiger lilies colors the elm-shaded square and the deep grounds of residences. Cotton gins and a sawmill are the largest industrial plants.

Customs of other days prevail in Mount Vernon. Church socials, basket parties, community "sings," fiddlers conventions, quilting bees and cemetery beautifications are all social events.

S. on State 37 to WINNSBORO (533 alt., 2,690 pop.), which extends from Franklin County into Wood and Hopkins, famous for its autumn Trails Festival, lasting 8 weeks and bringing 20,000 visitors. (*Write Autumn Trails Assn., Box 151, Winnsboro.*)

At SULPHUR SPRINGS, 103 *m*. (494 alt., 9,160 pop.), a milk processing plant and cheese factory provide prosperity. The first Monday of each month is Trades Day, when farmers crowd a vacant space in the business section to swap livestock, hay, and produce of all kinds for something they can use. Farm housewives make this a social event, while the merchants and restaurants profit by the influx of people.

Surrounded by great cotton fields of black, waxy soil, GREENVILLE, 134 *m*. (554 alt., 19,087 pop.) seat of Hunt County and once a cotton capital, now has diversified industry making aircraft and oil well equipment, electrical products, and foods, including a nationally known fruit cake. It developed a huge cotton compress before production declined. Livestock and grain crops now supplement cotton as an agricultural base. Shippers are served by the M. K. & T., Cotton Belt and Kansas City Southern Railways. Major's Field (airport) accommodates executive planes on an 8,000-ft. runway. Greenville is served by US 67 (Interstate 30) and State 23, 34, 66.

The town's first session of court was held under a large oak, standing at St. John and Bourland Sts., and the first post office was a box in the rear of a saloon. Mail was brought on muleback from Jefferson, more than 120 miles to the east. The first railroad was a narrow-gauge line from Jefferson, built in 1876.

LAKE TAWAKONI, 16 *m*. south on US 69, a 37,000-acre reservoir fed by the Sabine River, offers fishing, boating and duck hunting. Bass, crappie, perch and catfish abound.

Right from Greenville on State 24 to a junction with a dirt road 6.8 *m.;* R. here 0.5 *m*. to NEYLANDVILLE (70 pop.), a town whose unpainted houses stand on winding country lanes. It was founded by a former slave and is inhabited solely by Negroes. "Uncle" Jim Brigham was able, before the Civil War, to purchase his own freedom, that of his wife and one of his ten children. He pioneered as a farmer on the rich black land of this section. After the war, other freed slaves joined him. A railroad arrived in 1886 and the town was named by "Uncle Jim" in honor of the son of his former owner. The pioneer families initiated customs insuring the independence of the little community; for example, all orphans are adopted by residents of the town. St. Paul's School is an outgrowth of this custom.

State 24 continues to COMMERCE, 15 *m*. (548 alt., 5,780 pop.) a shipping center and site of EAST TEXAS STATE UNIVERSITY, which enrolled 5,330 in the regular 1965 term, 2,589 in summer term. It has a main campus of 140 acres between State highways 22, 11 and 513; with adjoining farm, 1,052 acres. Estab. 1889 as Teachers College, the university title was adopted 1965. It has 87 main buildings, many of modern architecture, including 32 dormitories of recent construction. The STUDENT CENTER of aluminum and glass, can seat 1,000 in its big room.

US 67 now crosses the Blacklands Belt of Texas, where normal yields in cotton are enormous. A U. S. COTTON CONTROL FIELD STATION, 136.3 *m.,* was established to aid cotton quality.

On a hill covered by hackberry and locust trees, ROCKWALL, 161 *m.* (552 alt., 2,166 pop.) seat of Rockwall County, smallest in Texas, was named because of a subterranean geological formation, which in conformation resembles a rock wall of artificial construction. The wall is vertical, of thickness varying from one-half inch to 18 inches, and has the appearance of being constructed of jointed blocks. Definite fossil remains were found against its sides.

GARLAND, 172 *m.* (541 alt.) a residential and industrial city, has had a phenomenal growth in 20 years. In 1940 it had 2,233 pop.; in 1960, 38,501; in 1965 local authorities claimed 60,000. Many commute to Dallas, 15 *m.* away. Garland's industries employ 11,126 and have an annual payroll of $56,000,000. It has a large recreation area at LAKE LAVON, 2 *m.* west of Lavon, which covers 20,050 acres.

MESQUITE (491 alt., 43,900 pop., est.) directly south of Garland and on State 352 and Interstate 20, was settled in 1872, incor. 1882. It has a Saturday eve. rodeo, April-Sept. Site of a train holdup by Sam Bass on the Texas & Pacific, 1872.

DALLAS, 187 *m.* (*see Dallas*).

Section b.   DALLAS to STEPHENVILLE; 111 m.   US 67

US 67 proceeds in a southwesterly direction across one of the most fertile areas in the State. Cotton and corn are the principal crops, with fruits and vegetables important in some communities.

The broad Brazos Valley drew settlers early in the years of the Republic. Most of the people today are descendants of those settlers, largely of Anglo-Saxon stock. The land here is generally level to gently rolling, with most of the farms tenant-operated. The practice of canning fruits and vegetables, and curing meat, permits even the poorer tenant families to live in comparative affluence.

Toward the end of the section, spring-fed streams in hills contain perch, bass and channel catfish.

Southwest of DALLAS, 0 *m.,* prosperous farms and tiny rural communities serve the needs of their immediate neighbors. The terrain is one of low rolling hills covered with cedars and small oaks. In this thickly populated region fields are often enclosed by bois d'arc hedges, some of which are 100 years old. Black land farms surround ALVARADO, 42 *m.* (693 alt., 1,775 pop.) (*see Tour 8b*), at the junction with US 81 (*see Tour 8*). At 49 *m.* is the junction with an unpaved road.

Left here to KEENE, 0.5 *m.* (1,700 pop.), neat and trim under a grove of oaks. Its present name honors a leader of the Seventh Day Adventist Church, whose members comprise the population. Tea, coffee, tobacco and alcoholic liquors are barred here, and no meat is eaten. The women use no rouge, lipstick or powder, and wear no jewelry or other items of personal adornment. The church frowns upon fiction, jazz music and competitive games. Gatherings of young people are chaperoned.

Two stores sell coffee, but only in catering to non-church members living outside the town limits. Wedding rings and wrist watches are permitted, these not being considered as indicative of personal vanity. Keene is the seat of the

Adventist SOUTHWESTERN JUNIOR COLLEGE, which offers general and business courses and others in music, pre-nursing, and pre-medicine. The college operates a planing mill, broom factory, printing plant, and dairy farm, which furnish work for students wishing to earn their school expenses. The library contains 6,000 non-fiction books.

The town has no mayor, no judge, no court, no police, no jail, and no motion picture house. Crime is almost unknown. The post office here is the only one in Texas that is closed on Saturday and open on Sunday.

Southwestward US 67 winds around and over a stretch of hills to CLEBURNE, 54 *m.* (764 alt., 16,000 pop.), where West Buffalo Creek, winding through the streets, enhances the wooded beauty of the town with the charm of its parked banks.

Cleburne is the shipping and trading center for a productive agricultural area surrounding it, where cotton is the money crop. Livestock raising and dairying are profitable. Industry has prospered and the city makes air conditioners, aircraft parts, electrical and other mechanical products. The Santa Fe Railroad has large shops here.

Southwest of Cleburne US 67 climbs a hill from which is visible the valley of the Nolan River, named for Philip Nolan, filibuster who, local tradition says, was killed by Spanish soldiers upstream. LAKE CLEBURNE, formed by the Nolan River, covers 1,545 acres.

At 59 *m.* is the junction with State 174.

Left here to the junction with a graveled road, 1 *m.;* R. here to CLEBURNE STATE PARK (*boating, bathing, fishing, 18-hole golf course*), 3 *m.*, a recreational center of 508 acres including a 110-acre lake. Graveled drives, bridle paths, foot trails, and 25 picnic units are in this area. The park is in the rolling lands at the edge of the Brazos breaks in a region of superb woodlands, offering 110 varieties of trees and shrubs. Wildlife is protected. An exposed strata of Fredericksburg limestone, interspersed with fossil deposits, is of geological interest.

The highway climbs slowly to the top of a hill where a parking space called LOOKOUT POINT, 64.5 *m.*, affords a broad, sweeping panorama of the Brazos Valley. In the foreground cedars stand out against white rock hillsides; below, the cultivated valley floor shows squares of green when crops are growing. Along the winding river, white bluffs rise over red sand bars. The green of the hills across the valley fades into a bluish haze, above which rises the bulk of mile-long SUGARLOAF MOUNTAIN (1,000 alt.).

Descending into a valley, US 67 crosses the BRAZOS RIVER, 74 *m.* (*camping 25¢, cabins 50¢*).

GLEN ROSE, 78 *m.* (600 alt., 1,495 pop.) seat of Somervell County is often referred to as the Petrified City, because of its extensive use of petrified wood as a building material.

In the vicinity of Glen Rose are more than 300 flowing springs and mineral wells, said to be of medicinal value. There are four sanatoriums. Along the Paluxy River, which skirts the town, are numerous tourist accommodations and recreational facilities.

Three sets of dinosaur tracks, embedded in deposits of limestone, are within a short distance of Glen Rose. One large track is in the bandstand at the southwest corner of the courthouse square.

Interesting in Glen Rose's history is the tradition that has grown up around one of its citizens of the 1870's. John St. Helen, as he was locally called, seriously ill and believing himself to be dying, told his lawyer that he was in reality John Wilkes Booth, the slayer of President Lincoln. St. Helen recovered, only to commit suicide later at Enid, Okla. Marks on his body were said to have been identified as identical with those on the person of Booth. Years later his shrunken corpse was exhibited in side-shows at carnivals.

The highway winds over a divide and drops down into the valley of the Bosque River. This is a section of the Cross Timbers, where postoaks, elms and sumacs predominate in the uplands, with pecans and cotton-woods bordering the waterways. Here, ranches outnumber fields. Farther on, prairie country rolls away from the highway; then, beyond a divide, the scene again changes. Fields here grow cotton, corn, small grains, mel-ons, berries, and fruit.

Long before the coming of the white man a Caddo village stood where STEPHENVILLE, 111 m. (1,283 alt., 7,800 pop.), now is. Built on a slight elevation, the town overlooks a region of truck farms and orchards. Cowboy boots are displayed, suggesting customers from ranches. This is the seat of Erath County, which raises cattle, turkeys, pecans and has some oil.

In Stephenville is TARLETON STATE COLLEGE, which was founded in 1899 and became a State college in 1917. For many years it was known as the John Tarleton Agricultural College. The present name was adopted in 1949. It enrolls approximately 1,500 in its regular term and 450 in the summer.

In Stephenville is the junction with US 281 (*see Tour 9*).

Section c. STEPHENVILLE *to* SAN ANGELO; 161 m.
US 67, US 377

The route continues in a general southwesterly direction, traversing a high tableland broken by a jumble of hills and fertile valleys. Throughout this section early settlers found their advance west and north protested every step of the way; Indians prevented settlement until the military had cleared the area and established a protective line of forts.

Cattlemen founded the civilization of this region, and handed down traditions of chivalry, courage and hospitality that remain as patterns for their descendants. Cowboy songs and dances, the rodeo, the barbecue, con-tinue in popularity. Of this general area Larry Chittenden wrote:

> Where the cattle are a-browsin'
> An' the Spanish ponies grow . . .
> Where lonesome, tawny prairies melt into airy streams,
> While double mountains slumber, in heavenly kinds of dreams . . .

Southwest of STEPHENVILLE, 0 *m.,* US 67 runs between two rows of tall sycamores. Here US 67 is joined by US 377 out of Fort Worth and the two highways keep together until Brownwood.

The name of DUBLIN, 13 *m.* (1,450 alt., 2,490 pop.), despite its Celtic sound, has a purely local origin. It was derived from a huge double log cabin erected by early-day citizens as a protection against Indians. "Doublin' in" was a term for a retreat to the cabin, and the town became known as Doublin, later contracted to Dublin. An Irish railroad man added to the impression that the town had an Irish origin by giving many of the streets Celtic names. Dublin's business buildings are largely of square-cut limestone.

Trades Day is held on the first Monday of each month. Merchandise of all kinds, farm produce and livestock are offered for sale at Elm and Camden Streets.

Peanuts, one of the paying crops of Erath County, are processed here, as also are dairy products. Here is a junction with State 6. West 12 *m.* on State 6 is De Leon, (2,000 pop.), a junction with State 16, which runs through Comanche.

PROCTOR, 22 *m.* a village of nominal population, has given its name to one of the biggest reservoirs in Texas, LAKE PROCTOR, on the Leon River, 9 *m.* NE of Comanche. It covers 14,010 acres and has a capacity of 374,200 acre-ft.

COMANCHE, 34 *m.* (1,358 alt., 4,000 pop.) is the seat of Comanche County. Its prosperous commerce is based on production in the County of peanuts, pecans, fruits, grains, cattle, cotton, and dairy products. It is said to have the largest peanut crop in the country.

Comanche was a cowman's town in its early days, a supply point for the hardy ranchers who dared to push their herds out into Indian country. The local newspapers carried advertisements of cattle brands and ear marks, with one statement that "anyone is welcome to kill my cattle for food, but anyone killing them for their hides will be prosecuted by law." Gangs of outlaws raided isolated ranch houses and even the town itself.

In May, 1874, Ranger Sergeant J. B. Armstrong tangled with John Wesley Hardin, then only about 23 years old, but a killer with more than a score of dead men to his credit. Hardin had killed a deputy sheriff of Comanche, and Armstrong was sent out with orders to bring him in. The chase led through half a dozen States, ending at last in Florida, where the Ranger sergeant arrested his man, and after tiring of waiting for official papers to arrive, brought him back to Texas with only the authority of his six-shooter. Following the era of the buffalo hunters and the trail drivers, Comanche grew as a ranching center.

The low pass through the hills southwest of Comanche is Logan's Gap, where (L) is a ROCK GARDEN, 43 *m.,* containing specimens of stones and fossils. These include imprints of fossilized giant ferns and other prehistoric vegetation, obtained in this vicinity where many unusual geological formations and fossil remains are to be found.

The agricultural region beyond the Gap produces grain, fruits, vegetables and pecans, to which has been added the wealth of recent oil and gas developments.

At 57 *m.* is the junction with US 84 (*see Tour 21*), which runs concurrent with US 67 for a distance of 32 miles.

At 58 *m.* is the junction with US 283 (*see Tour 11*).

BROWNWOOD, 59 *m.* (1,342 alt., 18,204 pop., 1964) county seat of Brown County, ships cotton, farm products and oil. During World War II Camp Bowie, military training base, raised the civilian population from 13,964 to 23,479. After 1856 the county was on the cattle frontier and settlers lost their lives and livestock in Indian raids. The Santa Fe Ry. came in 1885 when it received a free right of way and a bonus of $25,000; the Fort Worth & Rio Grande came in 1892 after similar inducement. The area produces stone, natural gas, petroleum and clays, valued at $2,356,382 in 1963.

The town's Industrial Foundation bought 536 acres of the former Camp Bowie for an industrial park.

A shaft of Texas granite in Coggin Park bears the names of 172 Brown County men who died in World War II. BROWNWOOD COLISEUM, (1963) is circular, 200 ft. in diameter, with a lift slab done.

HOWARD PAYNE COLLEGE, 900–1114 Center Ave., was opened 1890 by the Baptist General Convention of Texas. In 1965–66 it enrolled 1,096. It offers a four-year liberal arts program, with emphasis on Christian principles. Since 1962 the DOUGLAS MACARTHUR ACADEMY OF FREEDOM, a unit of the Division of Social Sciences, trains students for diplomatic and social service careers. The Fountain of Freedom was donated in part by the Freedoms Foundation of Valley Forge.

DANIEL BAKER COLLEGE, was founded as a private religious institution in 1889, but in 1903, control was transferred to the Southern Presbyterian Church. In 1953 it was merged with Howard Payne College.

Principal recreation area of Brown County is LAKE BROWNWOOD STATE PARK, northwest of Brownwood on State 279, which crosses the lake on Jim Ned Bridge. The irregular coastline of 93 miles provides many coves and bays.

The Texas Ranger Association holds an annual meeting at RANGER MEMORIAL PARK, 79.2 *m.*, which extends along the lower slopes of SANTA ANNA MOUNTAIN (2,000 alt.).

The business center of SANTA ANNA, 80 *m.* (1,743 alt., 1,320 pop.), lies in a curve facing the slopes of Santa Anna Mountain. A nearby deposit of high-grade silica is used in glass industry.

COLEMAN, 88 *m.* (1,710 alt., 6,700 pop.), is near the geographic center of Texas. Its unusually wide streets are said to have been made to permit the turning of an ox team without backing. It is the seat of Coleman County, which produces 3,000,000 bbl. of oil annually. A new water conservation project is LAKE COLEMAN, 510 acres. HORD'S CREEK RESERVOIR, 8 *m.* from Coleman on State 53 provides a large recreation area.

In COLEMAN CITY PARK a reproduction of OLD CAMP COLORADO (*open*), serves as a pioneer museum. Camp Colorado was a U. S. military post nine miles northeast of Coleman on Jim Ned Creek, and was abandoned at the outbreak of the Civil War.

In Coleman is the junction with US 84 (*see Tour 21*).

BALLINGER, 125 *m.* (1,637 alt., 5,043 pop.) (*see Tour 10a*), is at junctions with US 83 (*see Tour 16*) and US 277 (*see Tour 10*), which latter unites with US 67 southwestward for a distance of 36 miles (*see Tour 10a*).

SAN ANGELO, 161 *m.* (1,847 alt., 60,000 pop. est. 1965), is at junctions with US 87 (*see Tour 17*) and US 277 (*see Tour 10*).

Section d. SAN ANGELO to PRESIDIO; 315 m. US 67

This part of the route first traverses a region of high, rolling prairie lands, devoted chiefly to stock raising. Crossing rugged hills to the valley of the Pecos River, the road climbs steadily into the rock-crested ranges of the trans-Pecos region. Thence, bearing southward, it enters the vast mountain maze of the western edge of the Big Bend wilderness, winding and twisting through canyons and over high passes where lofty ranges criss-cross in a labyrinth of stark, lonely ridges—a country of early settlement, yet still thinly populated.

Great natural wealth lies undisturbed in the mountains of the Rio Grande area—rich ores of lead, copper, silver, gold, mercury, uranium and tin. The isolation of the region has retarded its development, and although silver mining has long existed near Shafter, the largest industry continues to be ranching.

High mountain areas, deserts and plains insure a wide variety of plant and animal life. Grama grass is most important to the ranchmen; for the hunter there are deer, antelopes, wolves, mountain lions, and bobcats.

The culture of this area reflects the ruggedness and vigor of all its other attributes. Along the Rio Grande are peons who make remarkable houses of the thorny stems of ocotillo, daubing the crevices with adobe. In April the desert blooms, and to these humble folk it is the Creator releasing the only living beauty they have ever seen. The Mexicans of Presidio still burn candles and decorate crosses on Holy Cross Day in thanksgiving for deliverance from the devil, who once, they believe, ruled this land from a cave in the mountains across the river. A priest, so the story says, in early days marched with cross in hand against the Evil One, and subdued him with his holy powers. But the priest instructed his children to remember what had happened, and to prevent the devil's re-appearance by holding an annual observance honoring the cross. This they do, while their *compadres* across the Rio Grande burn brush in front of the devil's cave to keep that unwelcome one from escaping his cramped quarters.

Southwest of SAN ANGELO, 0 *m.,* US 67 winds through wooded hills, the slopes of which are covered with thick growths of cedar, oak, mesquite, and agrita. In this section the chaparral cock is frequently seen.

Against the skyline (L), 10.5 *m.,* are TWIN BUTTES. An Indian legend says that the twin daughters of an Indian chief had vowed never to leave each other, but their father was vanquished by a neighboring chief who demanded one of the beautiful twins as a prize. The maidens went to a lonely spot and prayed that they would not be separated, and in answer the Great Spirit turned their kneeling forms into the buttes which now rise in similarity of outline.

US 67 now runs for miles through ranching country monotonously unchanging. At long intervals a ranch house is tucked away in a sheltered place between hills. The MIDDLE CONCHO RIVER (*fishing, swimming, boating facilities*), is crossed at 12.1 *m.*, and the road winds out of the valley into another stretch of hilly ranch lands.

The few houses of TANKERSLY, 16.1 *m.* (2,003 alt., 48 pop.), huddle around the general store and the village church.

Right from Tankersly on a good dirt road to FOSTER PARK (*free fishing and swimming; picnicking facilities*), 1.5 *m.*, a well-wooded, well-watered recreational area of 12 acres shaded by pecan, oak, hackberry, and mesquite trees.

The marketing and shipping town of MERTZON, 28 *m.* (2,184 alt., 684 pop.), is shaded by the great oaks that grow in the valley of Spring Creek.

The road follows the windings of Spring Creek as it flows southwestward. Here are small truck farms and groves of giant pecan trees. The country grows more rugged, the hills higher, and KETCHUM MOUNTAIN looms on the north. To the southeast is INDIAN PEAK, on top of which is the SITE OF THE DOVE CREEK INDIAN FIGHT of January 8, 1865, in which a detachment of citizen-soldiers attacked a band of Kickapoos and killed a large number. The Indians were on their way to Mexico, traveling under a permit from the Governor of Texas—a fact of which their attackers were unaware. The battle, fought in deep snow, lasted all day. Hampered by their women, children and baggage, the Kickapoo warriors nevertheless fought desperately. The whites were forced to fall back, but later rallied and drove the Indians from the field. This attack sent the Kickapoos on the warpath in a long series of retaliatory raids during which they even joined their old enemies, the Comanches. At 30 *m.* is a junction with a dirt road.

Left here to a LARGE LIVE OAK TREE, 2 *m.*, its trunk having a circumference of 23 feet, its branches a spread of 90 feet.

Cattle, sheep and goats are raised in the region southeastward. The hills break into a lower, rolling terrain covered with buffalo grass, prickly pear, and devil's pincushion.

BIG LAKE, 71 *m.* (2,678 alt., 3,000 pop. 1966, est.), was so named because the natural sink nearby fills during heavy rains. The University of Texas reaps a large income from the production of deep oil wells in this vicinity. On the courthouse square is CAMP GRIERSON MEMORIAL, in the form of a huge stone taken from the ruins of a frontier army post ten miles southeast of Big Lake. The stone bears the simple inscription, "Co. E, Tenth Cav., USA. November, 1879."

Southwestward US 67 follows closely the route of the old Chidester

Stage Line, on which Camp Grierson was a station, through thinly wooded rocky hills. Well back from the highway at 78.5 *m.*, are scattered (L) the great squat tanks of an oil company. Oil was discovered in 1923 at SANTA RITA.

The town sprawled under derricks L. of the highway is TEXON, 88 *m.* (2,710 alt., 1,200 pop.), in the heart of one of the world's deepest oil fields. For miles in every direction oil derricks lift their skeleton frames in a dark lacy pattern. The dull noise of pumping engines is constant, the reek of crude oil is in the air, and the earth is crisscrossed with pipe line furrows and stained by slush-pit overflows. These wells average a depth of almost a mile and three-quarters and between 1923 and 1966 yielded more than 210,000,000 bbl. of high-grade crude oil and many million cubic feet of gas.

RANKIN, 100 *m.* (2,495 alt., 935 pop.), a livestock market, is the seat of Upton County, a farming center.

Oil and cattle are the leading interests in the region now traversed. The county is rough, with but little vegetation other than those drab, colorless, stunted growths which exist in this arid, alkaline country.

McCAMEY, 118 *m.* (2,241 alt., 3,446 pop.). At McCamey US 67 is joined by US 385 coming south from Odessa. The highways are joined until they meet US 290 14 *m.* east of Fort Stockton.

When the No. 1 Baker well blew in on November 16, 1925, Mc-Camey came into almost instant being. Dawn of the next day found a grader cutting streets through the mesquite and greasewood flats, following the lines of the hurrying surveyors just ahead, who were laying out the town site. On November 18 the first lot was sold with the stipulation that a building was to be started within one hour. The buyer had carpenters at work within 30 minutes on a filling station and cafe.

Other buildings were erected in mad haste. People poured in, and above the roads hung an ever-present cloud of choking white alkali dust. Trucks lumbered in with drilling supplies, foodstuffs and furnishings. The town overflowed itself; tents bloomed white wherever on untenanted land their owners chose to set them up. The population reached 10,000 within a short time, and still they came. Prices went sky-high. Water sold at a dollar a barrel and was hard to get at that.

On the fringe of the town, in tents and shacks, the hangers-on of every new oil field plied their outlaw trades. One Ranger represented the law in McCamey. Troublemakers found themselves introduced to a new form of confinement. There was no jail, so the Ranger chained his prisoners to a stout post. The story is told that several husky roughnecks, chained to the picket line, as it was called, pulled up the post and dragged it after them to the nearest saloon.

In April, 1936, McCamey was the scene of the world's first recorded Rattlesnake Derby, with a huge crowd in attendance. It was held in correct racing form with a starter, a timekeeper, an official physician (for the handlers, not for the rattlesnakes), an announcer and a staff of judges. Thousands came to see Slicker, Esmeralda, Drain Pipe, Wonder Boy, Air Flow, and May Westian Rosie compete for the $200 purse.

The gallery watched wide-eyed as the handlers drew the reptiles from their containers, tagged them and placed them in the starting box. A forty-five roared, and the starting box fell apart, revealing a mass of squirming, rattling reptiles, which seethed and heaved for a moment. Then out of the mass slithered thick bodies with ugly flat heads, and, while cameras clicked, snakes moved toward the finish line. Slicker won.

Right from McCamey on State 51 to a junction with a sandy road, 10.3 m.; R. here to CASTLE GAP, 12.3 m., one of the mountain gateways of west Texas. Through the narrow canyon ran the route of the gold seekers of 1849; later the towering walls echoed to the rumble of Butterfield stagecoaches, pulling in to the Castle Gap station. Pack trains clattered through behind their patient bell mares, and freighters' wagon trains wore deep ruts in the canyon floor, visible to this day. Many tales of fights with outlaws and Indians center around Castle Gap. The Indians watched for approaching wagon trains or stagecoaches from the tall, windowed rock that gives the pass its name. Outlaws lurked in hiding to catch travelers within its narrow confines. Legends tell of buried outlaw gold, and of a treasure in gold and jewels hidden in the canyon by servants of the Emperor Maximilian. Today treasure seekers still come here to dig, principally in the vicinity of the ruined rock building that was the stage station.

Westward the route is through a rolling, sun-baked land. Red oil tanks are visible at first, then there is nothing except a vast sweep of sage and mesquite, dotted with dozens of kinds of cactus.

The PECOS RIVER, 126 m., long marked the boundary between the law and the lawless. West of it the only authority was that of the gun. Beyond the Pecos Valley the way is across a high semi-barren plateau that stretches away to the dim, blue bulk of distant mountain ranges.

At 150 m. is the junction with US 290, which unites with US 67 and US 385 for 14 miles to the westward.

The stark outline of SEVEN MILE MESA, 158 m., is visible (R), and farther on is a similar uplift, THREE MILE MESA (L), 162 m.

FORT STOCKTON, 164 m. (3,052 alt., 7,500 pop.) is at the western junction with US 290 (see Tour 24).

US 67 now runs over rolling cattle ranges that sweep away to distant mountains. Along the highway appear signs warning the motorist to look out for cattle. The high green mass to the south is that of the Glass Mountains, a range of rounded peaks, grass-covered except on outcroppings of red and yellow rock. BEATTY'S PEAK (6,523 alt.) dominates the southern end of the range, flanked by OLD BLUE MOUNTAIN (6,286 alt.) on the east and CATHEDRAL MOUNTAIN (6,125 alt.) on the west. Northwest rise the lofty peaks of the forest-crowned Davis Mountains far on the distant horizon.

At 217 m. is the junction with US 90 (see Tour 23) which unites with US 67 for a distance of 35 miles through ALPINE (see Tour 23d).

MARFA, 252 m. (4,688 alt., 3,400 pop.) is at the western junction with US 90 (see Tour 23).

US 67 turns south at Marfa, and climbs gradually toward the mountain rampart visible across the southern horizon. Range after range piles higher and higher. Valleys, canyons and ravines cross and crisscross, often ending in a blind canyon against the frowning face of a cliff. The road is ever upward, winding, twisting, descending a short way as if to gain momentum for the climb to a higher ridge just beyond.

Through Rancheria Hills (5,000 alt.) the road makes its way into the confines of a narrow canyon-like valley, the grade increasing as it winds crookedly between the steep slopes. Crossing a low saddle in the western projection of a ridge called Frenchmen Hills (5,250 alt.), it slides down into the upper valley of Ciénega Creek.

Back against a low bluff (R), 270 m., a crumbled mound is all that remains of an old stage station. Across the valley tower the heights of the Cuesta del Burro (foothills of the burro) (5,750 alt.).

Southward the road climbs on. The Black Hills (5,550 alt.) are R. as the road drops into the narrow valley of Cibolo Creek. Southwest rise the Chinati Mountains topped by CHINATI PEAK (7,730 alt.).

Mesquite, creosote, sagebrush, and bunch grass grow on the floor of the little valley now traversed. Higher up the slopes show the eternal green of the piñon and juniper, blended into the soft haze of thickets of oaks.

Three silver mines made SHAFTER, 294 m. (3,900 alt.) a mining center for some years. The mines were closed in 1942, then reactivated in 1952, but the results were inadequate and the effort failed. The little adobe houses are now roofless and their walls are crumbling. Tunnels are said to extend for long distances under the mountain, but most of them have become waterlogged. When the mines were being worked the operators often staged barbecues to break their lonely lives, but the slogan was B. Y. O. B.—Bring your own beer.

Near Shafter is an old building once used as a fort. Built by ranchers and called FORT CIBOLO, it was often occupied by detachments of U. S. troops on their way from Fort Davis to Fort Leaton.

South of Shafter US 67 skirts the foothills of the Chinati Mountains to drop over the cap rock, 302 m. There is an abrupt change in the country; on the tableland are grass and timbered slopes, then suddenly the heights slide away in a rubble of debris to the edge of a stark desert, hundreds of feet below. In this dead expanse the sun beats down with a scorching, dazzling heat, reflected blindingly from the gleaming sands. The road streaks straight across the rock-strewn desert; there is no shade and no vegetation other than cactus, sage, and the ghostly, snake-like arms of the ocotillo.

PRESIDIO, 315 m. (2,400 alt., 1,062 pop.), is an old town of sun-baked adobe houses, squatting like an aged *hombre* in the shade of giant cottonwoods. To it came Spaniards in the latter part of the sixteenth century to explore the region they called La Junta de los Rios (junction of the rivers). Three priests and nine soldiers with 19 Indian servants, 600 head of cattle and 90 horses journeyed north, down the valley of the Rio Conchos to its junction with the Rio Grande. The object of the expedition was "to serve God our Lord and His Majesty by establishing the Holy Gospel wherever we might find a suitable place and wherever the Divine Majesty might guide us."

They found numerous Indian *rancherías* in this vicinity and placed crosses in several. "The men are very handsome and the women beauti-ful," wrote Hernán Gallegos, the narrator of the expedition, speaking of the tribe found there. "They wore stripes on their faces and appeared to be happy and carefree; they lived in houses made of logs and brush plas-tered with mud and although they raised little corn, they had an abun-dance of pumpkins and beans."

Later emissaries from these Indians traveled to the nearest Franciscan mission in Mexico urging that priests be sent to their people. So insistent were the chiefs that they measured the chapel at the El Paso Spanish settlement and sent runners back with instructions to have their tribesmen build a similar church. Missionaries were sent, and when they arrived were astonished to find not one, but six or seven chapels already con-structed. On June 12, 1684, on the banks of Alamito Creek in the vicinity of Presidio, formal establishment of the missions at La Junta de los Rios was completed. Some time after 1830 the name of the settlement was changed to Presidio del Norte (Fort of the North), and later shortened to Presidio.

It was here that the Chihuahua Trail, one of the main freight routes into Mexico, crossed the Rio Grande. Non-Latin settlers arrived in about 1848, and in 1849 built Fort Leaton to serve as a protection against Indi-ans. With the removal of the Indian menace the fort fell into decay, but it has been restored. The house of Ben Leaton, 4 m. east of Presidio, also has been restored.

Presidio is a port of entry into Mexico, via a privately-owned toll bridge to Ojinaga, which has a picturesque cathedral and shops interesting to tourists. The Santa Fe Ry. connects with the National Railways of Mexico. From Ojinaga the Chihuahua to Pacific Ry. offers a spectacular ride through the Sierra Madre, using 73 tunnels and 27 bridges in 572 miles, with stops at the huge Copper Canyon (Barrancas del Cobre) and other scenic sites.

From Presidio FM 170, El Camino del Rio or River Road, runs northwest to ADOBES, but not as far as CANDELARIA. Between the latter and Marfa are Capote Creek and, on a private ranch, the spectac-ular CAPOTE FALLS, 170 ft. tall (*visits by permission*).

Justice William O. Douglas of the U. S. Supreme Court has agitated for public protection of the Falls area. Candelaria Peak is 6,560 ft. tall.

Ϧ⟐

Tour 19

(Shreveport, La.) — Marshall — Dallas — Fort Worth — Abilene — Big Spring — Pecos — El Paso — (Las Cruces, N. Mex.) ; US 80. Louisiana Line to New Mexico Line, 822 *m.*

Along the Texas-Louisiana boundary, where the pines grow tall and the soil is red, and small farms are many, neighbors exchange labor, farm tenants and owners fraternize in true rural democracy, and the preaching service at one of many small country churches is the week's biggest event. The important annual occasions are county fairs and religious revival meetings held after harvests are in. Houses are never too far from school buildings, for education is one of the great common goals. Cooperative associations for farmers have aided materially in such matters as marketing, financing and legislation.

In the middle region urban and industrial influences have molded a progressive, energetic type of Texan. This is in the Blacklands Belt; farms are larger, more productive, and are operated along scientific methods. Local factories process much of the produce, and oil has further enriched the owners of the soil.

Section a. LOUISIANA LINE to DALLAS; 168 m. US 80

This section of US 80 traverses the northern fringe of the Coastal Plain. Running parallel with it a few miles south is Interstate 20. Westward farming is increasingly important, and when the Blacklands area is entered the country becomes almost wholly agricultural. This is an area rich in natural resources, two of which—oil and salt—have brought much wealth to their respective communities. Lignite and iron ore underlie the soil; longleaf and shortleaf pines, productive fields of cotton and corn, truck crops and other harvests present a changeable parade of products.

Negroes comprise a large part of the population of this region. An important cultural and educational center of the race is in Marshall, where leaders have long exerted a wide influence over Texas Negro youth. Largely descendants of former slaves, these people congregate in cities, or till farms in the area. Many of the properties in the residential areas have landscaped lawns; but the greater number live in small houses of one or two rooms, where families lounge on summer days on porches, laughing, singing songs that end on minor chords, or listening to radios. The old superstitions still exist; the people nail horseshoes in the fireplace to keep hawks from catching their chickens; the men turn their pockets inside-out at night to ward off ghosts and witches; and to cure warts, they steal someone's dish rag and never tell where it is hidden.

US 80 crosses the LOUISIANA LINE, 0 *m.*, 17 miles west of Shreveport, Louisiana (*see Louisiana Guide*), and passes through an area of extensive oil and gas activities.

At 12 *m.* is a junction with a dirt road.

Right here to SCOTTSVILLE, 1.1 *m.* (390 alt., 113 pop.). Founded in 1834, this quiet, shady town is one of the oldest camp meeting sites in the State. The meetings, held since 1840, are non-denominational and attract thousands. The vine-covered YOUREE MEMORIAL CHURCH and the old cemetery are surrounded by the meeting grounds. Nearby is the old SCOTT HOMESTEAD (*private*), with its slave cabins.

Westward the route is through a truck farming and dairying area.

MARSHALL, 20 *m.* (375 alt., 25,000 pop. est.) seat of Harrison County, has many reminders of the leisurely southern ante-bellum life, although the manufacture of rocket engines has given it a place in the Space Age.

An industrial and educational center, Marshall enjoys the peculiar distinction, although it has always been in Texas, of having been for a time, so far as the operations of the Confederacy were concerned, the active administrative capital of Missouri.

This circumstance came about following the death of Governor Claiborne F. Jackson in Little Rock, Arkansas, in December, 1862, Missouri being physically in the possession of the Union and its Southern-sympathizing officials having left the State but holding themselves still to be legally in office. Lieutenant Governor Thomas C. Reynolds, succeeding Jackson as governor, moved to Marshall when a Federal advance threatened. He rented two houses, one at 402 S. Bolivar St., which served as the CAPITOL OF THE STATE OF MISSOURI, and another at 109, E. Crockett St., which became the GOVERNOR'S MANSION. From this temporary capital State orders were issued, vouchers drawn, bills paid, and other official business transacted until the break-up of the Trans-Mississippi Department of the Confederacy.

Because of its location Marshall assumed a place of importance in the administration of Confederate affairs. The Trans-Mississippi Agency of the Post Office Department occupied the home of Lucy Holcomb Pickens, which was used for years by the former Bishop College. The Ordnance Department was housed on W. Fannin St., and the Edmund Key home, at 109 W. Grand Ave., served as a Confederate hat factory. The Quartermaster and Commissary Departments were in Marshall, and the basement of the First Methodist Church (a building constructed in 1851 by slaves) was used for the storage of military supplies, as was the Odd Fellows Hall. Generals E. Kirby Smith, commander of the Trans-Mississippi Department, Buckner, Magruder and Shelby rode frequently into Marshall on military business.

Marshall, named for U. S. Chief Justice John Marshall, was established in 1841. It was built on land donated by Peter Whetstone, pioneer settler, whose site was said to have been selected by commissioners when they found a jug of whisky he had "planted" in a spring for the purpose of enhancing the charm of the location.

WILEY COLLEGE, one mile south on State 43, is one of a series of pioneer institutions established by the Freedmen's Aid Society of the Methodist Church; it is the oldest Negro college in Texas (1873), and has an annual enrollment of 600 students. BISHOP COLLEGE of the Northern Baptist Convention was located here from 1881 to 1961, when it was moved to Dallas, where its attendance reaches more than 1,200 students.

EAST TEXAS BAPTIST COLLEGE was founded by Baptists in 1912 as The College of Marshall; the present name was adopted in 1944. It is coeducational and has about 600 students enrolled annually. ST. MARY'S ACADEMY on Railroad Ave., between E. Burleson and E. Grand Aves., is a Roman Catholic coeducational institution.

Near KARNACK (2,795 pop. est.) 13 m. northeast of Marshall on State 43, is the BIRTHPLACE OF MRS. L. B. (LADYBIRD) JOHNSON, a plantation house of 1854. Near the crossroads is a State marker noting her birth there Dec. 22, 1912. In Karnack an old two-story brick store has the sign: "T. J. Taylor, Dealer in Everything." Taylor, her father, died in 1960. A brochure about the birthplace and Caddo Lake may be obtained from the Chamber of Commerce, Marshall. East of Karnack in the Caddo Lake area is UNCERTAIN, (240 pop.) incorporated since 1960.

In Marshall is the junction with US 59 (*see Tour 2*).

North from the Harrison County Courthouse in Marshall, on Bolivar St. to E. Grand Ave.; R. on E. Grand Ave. 12 blocks, across the railroad tracks; L. here to a junction with State 43; R. here to CADDO STATE PARK (*lodges, guides, boats, fishing tackle and hunting equipment*), 16 m. Here is an area of 600 acres on the south shores of Big Cypress Bayou, where that stream flows into CADDO LAKE, once the South's largest natural lake, today a huge reservoir covering 32,700 acres, 11,000 of which are in Texas. A dam was built at Mooringsport, La., and when the waters were impounded much of the former wild beauty of Broad Lake, Caddo's main body, was obliterated, but the new lake is a major facility for recreation, with fishing, hunting, boating and swimming calling visitors from Texas and Louisiana.

There is a legend of the Caddoes who once had a populous village in this vicinity, of a chief who was warned by the Great Spirit to take his tribe to high ground, or see his people destroyed by earthquake and flood. The chief paid no heed to the warning, and one day a party of warriors returning from a hunting expedition found the village gone and a lake covering the place. They referred to the region as the "trembling ground," and maintained that it was the predicted earthquake that had formed the lake. The more prosaic explanation of the lake's origin is that it formed behind a log jam in the Red River.

This is a fisherman's paradise, offering large- and small-mouthed bass, barfish, bream, several varieties of perch, pickerel, buffalo, drum, gar, channel and mud catfish, and the rarer Opelousas catfish which grows here to weigh as much as 800 pounds. In season there is excellent duck and goose shooting.

None but the old-timers here ever venture far into the lake's awesome wilderness of hidden arms and bayous without that picturesque character, the Caddo Negro guide. These local Negroes have an uncanny knowledge of the lake; not only can they find their way along the water roads on the darkest night, but they seem to instinctively know where and when certain kinds of fish are biting.

LONGVIEW, 42 m. (339 alt., 40,050 pop. 1960, after annexation of 12,236: 45,100 1966, est.) had only 5,036 people in 1930 when the

East Texas oil boom started its industrial expansion. Seat of Gregg County, which produces more than 26,000,000 bbl. of oil annually, valued at more than $97,000,000. It is served by the Missouri Pacific, Texas & Pacific and Santa Fe, by Trans-Texas Airlines and Continental Trailways. It has numerous hotels and motels. It is a terminal of Longview Barge Canal on the Sabine River, for transporation to the Gulf.

LE TOURNEAU COLLEGE, founded 1946, has a campus of 161 acres. It offers the humanities and technical courses, and enrolls more than 585.

US 80 meets US 259 10 *m.* west of Longview. S. on US 259 8 *m.* to KILGORE (371 alt., 10,092 pop. 1960, 11,200 1965 est.) a city famous for more than 1,000 steel derricks rising above the business streets, illuminated at night. Has offices of the oil industry and is a major oil center; also has oil field supplies, clothing, bathroom fixtures industries. KILGORE JUNIOR COLLEGE (estab. 1935) enrolls 1,849.

LAKE CHEROKEE, 12 *m.* southeast of Longview, covers 3,987 acres and holds 46,700 acre-ft. of water.

At 47.6 *m.* is the first view of the great EAST TEXAS OIL FIELD, which produces more than 100,000,000 bbl. annually.

The oil-inspired expansion of GLADEWATER, 54 *m.* (333 alt., 6,000 pop.), is evident. It is chiefly in Gregg County, partly in Upshur. There are more than 500 producing wells in the town.

In Gladewater is a junction with US 271 (*see Tour 4*).

The route is over timbered hills, where windmills—so common in most of Texas—are seldom seen, since shallow water permits the use of old-fashioned wells. Near HAWKINS, 67 *m.* (868 pop.) the buildings of JARVIS CHRISTIAN COLLEGE are grouped on a 456-acre, oak-studded campus. A coeducational college for Negroes, controlled by the Disciples of Christ Church, it has an average annual enrollment of 400 students. LAKE HAWKINS is a recently completed reservoir on the Little Sandy.

Cleanliness is a civic trait in MINEOLA, 88 *m.* (414 alt., 3,810 pop.), where railroad shops, sawmills and factories supply a brisk atmosphere. In Mineola is the junction with US 69.

The center of the salt industry in Texas, GRAND SALINE, 101 *m.* (407 alt., 2,006 pop.), has its homes on a hill, surrounded by salt flats. South and east are shafts going down into deposits of hard rock salt; it is dug and blasted out, pulverized and refined for use. West are other flats where wells are sunk to the salt strata; hot water is pumped to the rock salt. The resulting brine is raised to the surface to be crystallized. Evaporation in a vacuum produces cube crystals for table use, while evaporation in the open air results in snowflake crystals used in manufacturing. The salt is kiln-dried.

Rich salt deposits of this vicinity are found over an area of more than 30 square miles. Almost pure rock salt has been mined to a depth of more than 700 feet, while test borings show the depth of some deposits to be 1,500 feet.

In the west-central part of the town is the MORTON SALT

COMPANY'S MINE (*open 7:30–11:30 a.m., 1:30–4 p.m., guides*), where mining and processing operations are to be seen.

Westward US 80 winds over low, rolling hills.

The HOME OF WILLIAM WILLS (*open*), 118 *m.*, was built in 1847 of great oak logs. On the old Jefferson Trail, this double log house was a haven for travelers. It was restored in 1936.

WILLS POINT, 120 *m.* (532 alt., 2,500 pop.), a marketing and shipping center, has a profusion of wild roses, elms and pecan trees. Dove and quail shooting is excellent in season in this vicinity. NE from Wills Point 9 *m.* on State 47 to LAKE TAWAKONI, formed by Iron Bridge Dam on the Sabine River, 36,700 acres and 936,200 acre-ft. capacity. It has a 225 *m.* shoreline, and numerous marinas, cabins, fishing clubs; see *Tawakoni News* of Quinlan, on State 35, (600 pop.).

Flowered lawns flank the business district of TERRELL, 136 *m.* (530 alt., 14,000 pop.), industrial city whose factories process cottonseed, lumber, wheat, dairy products, and feed crops.

In Terrell are the TERRELL STATE HOSPITAL and TEXAS MILITARY COLLEGE. On its campus is the HOME OF ROBERT TERRELL (*open*), a log structure built in 1860. It has been modernized.

Left from Terrell on State 34 to KAUFMAN, 12 *m.* (439 alt., 3,087 pop.), seat of Kaufman County, which has produced oil since 1948. Has meat packing and cotton processing. KEMP, (800 pop.) 10 *m.* southeast on US 175 is near JOE B. HOGSETT LAKE (formerly Cedar Creek Lake), 24,000 acres, partly in Henderson County. KAUFMAN LAKE, 1 *m.* northeast of Kaufman, retains floodwater and supplies city.

DALLAS, 168 *m.* (512 alt., est. pop. 679,684, 1960) (*see Dallas*).

Section b.   DALLAS to FORT WORTH; 32 m.   US 80

GRAND PRAIRIE was a farming region with a small village west of Dallas on US 80 until World War II, when the village of 1,595 acquired one war industry and numerous war plant workers. By 1950 it had 14,594 people and in 1960 30,386. Development of the Great Southwest Industrial District increased its population annually and Grand Prairie developed recreation centers, an auditorium seating 2,055, a city hall and library, and municipal and private golf courses. State highway 360 crosses the Dallas-Fort Worth Turnpike and US 80 in Grand Prairie.

IRVING (470 alt.) an industrial suburb of Dallas north of Grand Prairie on Texas 183 and 366, exemplifies the growth of the area; in 1950 it had 2,621 pop.; in 1960, 45,985; in 1967, over 70,000, est.)

HENSLEY FIELD, U. S. Army Airport is passed (L) at 12.1 *m.*, and at 15.1 *m.* (R) are the grandstands, barns and playing field of EL RANCHITO POLO CLUB.

EL PORVENIR (the future), 16.5 *m.*, is the late W. T. Waggoner's breeding farm (R) for thoroughbred horses. Adjacent is the partially dismantled racing plant of Arlington Downs, which before the repeal of pari-mutuel betting in Texas, was one of the largest establishments of its kind in the Southwest.

ARLINGTON, 19 *m*. (616 alt., 7,692 pop., 1950; 44,775, by annexation of 35,401, 1960; 60,600 est. 1967). Its industries, originally medicinal crystals and roses, have expanded greatly into machinery, rubber products and chemicals. ARLINGTON STATE COLLEGE, founded 1895 and long known as North Texas Agricultural College, is now Arlington University. It is part of the University of Texas System and enrolls 11,000 in its regular term and about 6,000 in the summer. An elaborate amusement park, SIX FLAGS OVER TEXAS, opened 1961 by Angus G. Wynne, Jr., with shows and a zoo, draws huge crowds.

The city's water supply, LAKE ARLINGTON, 7 *m*. north, covers 2,275 acres and has 45,710 acre-ft. of water.

FORT WORTH, 32 *m.,* is at the junction with US 81 (*see Tour 8*).

Section c. FORT WORTH to ABILENE; 154 m. US 80;
Interstate 20

Beginning in the Grand Prairie region of rolling, open lands, this section of the route soon leads into the hills and plains of western Texas. Its oldest industry is ranching, but its most spectacular development is that of oil.

West of FORT WORTH, 0 *m.,* herds of white-faced cattle graze within sight of the city's skyscrapers. Sudan, Bermuda and Johnson grass cover lush prairies where these cattle fatten; they bring fancy prices at the Fort Worth stockyards.

At 6 *m*. is the junction with US 377.

Left on US 377 to ACTON STATE PARK and ELIZABETH CROCKETT MEMORIAL, 23 *m.,* honoring the wife of Davy Crockett.

At 24.1 *m*. is a junction with a graveled road.

Left here 3 *m*. to ACTON (325 pop.), once the home of Elizabeth Crockett, who died in 1860.

CRESSON, 26 *m*. on US 377, 260 pop., is a State 171 junction.

US 377 continues to GRANBURY, 30 *m*. (725 alt., 2,227 pop.). Ashley W. Crockett, grandson of Davy Crockett, in 1939 was publisher of the *Hood County Tablet* in Granbury. This is an active shipping point for the agricultural produce of the surrounding region, and a county seat.

Right from Granbury 3 *m*. on a graveled road to THORP SPRING (308 pop.), a tiny village, shady and colorful. Here, on top of a hill, stand the remains of ADD-RAN CHRISTIAN COLLEGE, the forerunner of Texas Christian University.

US 377 continues southwestward. Many of the buildings in TOLAR, 39 *m*. (1,013 alt., 318 pop.), are constructed of petrified wood, and the collecting and shipping of this unusual building material is a local industry.

Southwest the highway follows the valley of the South Paluxy Creek, crossing and recrossing it many times. In this vicinity Canada geese, ducks, and many other kinds of waterfowl are found in season.

Leaving the valley, US 377 ascends a wooded divide; the soil becomes red and yellow clay with outcroppings of rock, and the country is more barren.

At 59.9 *m*. is the junction with US 281.

US 377 continues to STEPHENVILLE, 61 *m*. (1,283 alt., 7,359 pop.), at junctions with US 67 (*see Tour 18*) and US 281 (*see Tour 9*).

US 80 proceeds past the PYTHIAN ORPHANS HOME, 27.5 *m.*, maintained by the Knights of Pythias.

One of the State's most diversified farming areas surrounds WEATHERFORD, 29 *m.* (864 alt., 9,759 pop., 1960; 13,000 1966; est.) Its best known product is watermelons. Parker County melons are sold widely, and the seeds are exported. Market Square in Weatherford during the spring, summer and fall is a riot of earthy colors, as great baskets of sweet potatoes, string beans, radishes, tomatoes, Japanese persimmons and Spanish peanuts are offered for sale. Pecans are a fall crop.

WEATHERFORD JUNIOR COLLEGE has been a municipal institution since 1949. It was opened by the Methodists in 1869 as a branch of Southwestern University, and was a denominational junior college from 1921 to 1949. It enrolls more than 700 students.

The Texas Railroad Museum is located at Weatherford. Seven miles east is LAKE WEATHERFORD, covering 1,280 acres, the city's water supply.

At 51 *m.* is the junction with US 281 (*see Tour 9*).

RANGER, 86 *m.* (1,429 alt., 3,313 pop.), modern, quiet and substantial, is one of the State's best known oil towns. It was founded in 1881 and named for a camp of Texas Rangers, near which the tent village of the first citizens took shape. Until 1917 it was just another cattle and cotton shipping point of the Central Plains, but in that year the McCleskey well came in with a roar that announced the birth of another great oil field. Ranger went mad. Crowds poured in by train, car, wagon and even afoot along the dusty roads.

Again Ranger became a tent city, with the newcomers finding shelter where they could and paying fabulous prices for beds and food. No oil boom since the Spindletop field came in at Beaumont (*see Beaumont*) had been more spectacular. The population of Ranger quickly grew to between 40,000 and 50,000, all frantic to share in the money that flowed from oil. Men of national note came to join the throng—Tex Rickard, Jess Willard, Rex Beach, Lew Wentz, Jake Hamon, Harry Sinclair and T. B. Slick.

In 1919, at the peak of production, the Ranger field's output was 22,380,000 barrels. By 1928 production had dropped to 2,227,000 barrels and the population had decreased accordingly. In 1963 the value of minerals produced in Eastland County was $4,907,711, including petroleum, liquids, natural gas, clays and stone.

South of US 80 is LAKE LEON, created by a 1,500 ft. dam and covering 28,000 acre-ft. It is stocked with bass. A smaller reservoir in Eastland County is LAKE CISCO. At 87 *m.* is junction with a farm road.

Left here 1 *m.* to the MERRIMAN CEMETERY, burial ground of Eastland County pioneers, and known as the "cemetery that was not for sale." During the Ranger oil boom days prodigious prices were offered for this land, but the people refused to disturb their dead and the area remained undrilled. All around its fences are derricks and pumping wells.

The prosperous, unhurried town of EASTLAND, 96 *m.* (1,421 alt., 3,350 pop.), boomed with the discovery of oil, 1917 to 1922. In the courthouse is the CASKET OF OLD RIP, which contains the embalmed remains of a horned toad, placed in the corner stone of the old court house in 1897 and recovered in 1928. It revived and lived 11 months longer, during which it was exhibited and shown to President Coolidge. The PEANUT BOWL publicizes a major Eastland County crop.

CISCO, 106 *m.* (1,608 alt., 5,000 pop.) a junction with US 283.

PUTNAM, 116 *m.* (1,692 alt., 200 pop.).

BAIRD, 132 *m.* (1,708 alt., 2,000 pop.) seat of Callahan County, has oil refinery and cooperative feed mill. The county has the CALLAHAN DIVIDE down the center between the Colorado and Brazos watersheds.

CLYDE, 139 *m.* (1,980 alt., 1,116 pop.).

ABILENE, 154 *m.* (1,738 alt., 100,000 pop. est.). *See Tour 10.*

Section d.   ABILENE to BIG SPRING; 108 m.   US 80;
Interstate 20

On level to gently rolling terrain largely devoted to ranching, with some cotton and grain fields, US 80 continues slightly south of west.

Sectional customs include huge rabbit drives, in which as many as 800 men and boys have participated. One-third of the hunters form a straight line; others, in a line facing the first formation, flush the rabbits. As the lines converge, rabbits burst from cover in every direction and the shooting begins. At noon, a feast is served by women of the community. Prairie dogs, considered as the Number Two pest in this area, are frequently decimated by sportsmen who make a game of this difficult form of target shooting. Without wholesale drives on the rabbits, crops would suffer.

Play parties are popular among the rural folk of this section, and many a Saturday night gathering makes merry to the words of "Kill the Old Red Rooster" and "Shoot the Buffalo."

West of ABILENE, 0 *m.,* US 80 runs concurrent with US 84 (*see Tour 21*) to Roscoe, a distance of 49 miles.

Far on the southern horizon bulk the mountains through which are Buffalo Gap and Mountain Pass. The region is largely gently rolling range land.

At 36 *m.* is a junction with a paved road.

Left here to LAKE SWEETWATER, 4.5 *m.,* where a dam across Bitter Creek forms a 760-acre lake. It serves Sweetwater, as also do Lakes Trammel and Oak Creek, the latter 5 *m.* southeast of Blackwell (Coke County).

Primarily a cattle shipping center, SWEETWATER, 41 *m.* (2,164 alt., 13,914 pop.) now has gypsum, cement, cotton-oil and other industries. Sheep and Hereford cattle are produced in Nolan County in large numbers and stock shows and the Allgirl Rodeo are held in the County Coliseum. The annual Rattlesnake Roundup is famous throughout Texas. The 683rd Aircraft Control and Warning Squadron operates a control center as part of the defense of the 29th Air Division. State 70 runs N-S through Sweetwater.

Sweetwater's beginning was in 1877 when a trader, Billy Knight, following the buffalo hunters and Government surveyors, opened a store in a dugout on the banks of Sweetwater Creek. The first house constructed of lumber was used for a saloon. Later two saloon keepers acted as bankers for the stockmen. The blizzard of 1885 and the great drought of 1886–87 were serious handicaps to the town's development. Dorothy Scarborough's novel, *The Wind,* laid in Sweetwater, deals with that devastating drought.

Grain elevators and railroad shops create an industrial aspect in ROSCOE, 49 *m.* (2,391 alt., 1,250 pop.).

In Roscoe is the junction with US 84 (*see Tour 21*).

Over open ranges US 80 continues to COLORADO CITY, 69 *m.* (2,067 alt., 6,457 pop.), an industrial and agricultural center, with plants processing petroleum and cotton products. One of the largest livestock shipping points in this part of Texas, Colorado City is the county seat of Mitchell County. Fishing, water skiing and shore camping have become popular since the Texas Electric Service Co. built dams for LAKE COLORADO CITY (1,665 acres, 46 *m.* shoreline) and CHAMPION CREEK LAKE (1,560 acres). The lakes provide power and the city's water supply.

At 90.5 *m.* is RATTLESNAKE GAP, through which passed the exploration trail of Captain Marcy, U. S. Army explorer of 1849. IATAN LAKE (R), a small body of brackish water—one of many in this region—is at 93.6 *m.*

Cotton fields now replace range lands. Far to the south appears a mountain range of which the highest point, an almost perfect cone with the top squared off, is SIGNAL PEAK, from which Indians once watched for immigrant trains.

Surrounded by the hills of the Cap Rock, BIG SPRING, 108 *m.* (2,397 alt., 31,230 pop.), named for a large spring, now dry, was formerly a frontier watering place where buffalo hunters and bone gatherers erected their hide and wood huts. Still earlier it marked a stopping point on the Comanche war trail, which swept down from the High Plains and curved southwest to follow a line of watering places to the Comanche Crossing deep in the Big Bend (*see Tour 23a*).

A railroad reached this point in 1881. Saloons outnumbered other business establishments. Cowboys shot up the town regularly and were in continual conflict with railroad construction workers until the line moved west.

In Big Spring's youth numerous titled Englishmen bought ranches in the neighborhood. The long drought of 1894 ruined most of them, but one, the Earl of Aylesford, remained and bought the Cosmopolitan Hotel, in which he died. He also bought a meat market in order to secure the grade and cuts of meat he desired.

Time worked against the original cattlemen, and the plow of the farmer yearly turned under more and more square miles of range land; cotton and grains grew well except in periods of drought. Agriculture could not be ruled out. The final step in development here came with the discovery of oil in 1928. The soil of a yellow bluff northeast of the town assays some placer gold. A scenic drive south up Ranch Road 700 leads to the mesa on Big Spring Mountain where BIG SPRING STATE PARK occupies 349 acres. Also off Road 700 is WEBB AIR FORCE BASE.

HOWARD COUNTY JUNIOR COLLEGE, Birdwell Lane, was opened in 1945 and enrolls about 850 annually.

Big Spring, where planted trees are yet small, refines oil, gins cotton, stores and distributes natural gas, and ships cattle. It has two outstanding annual events, the Cowboy's Reunion and the Old Settlers' Reunion. The former is held annually on Labor Day. The Howard County Livestock Show is held in March and the County Rodeo in June.

The Old Settlers' Reunion is held on the last Friday of each July, at Cottonwood Park. After an outdoor feast, the older folk perform the dances of yesteryear, the schottische, polka, mazurka, and two-step.

In Big Spring is the junction with US 87 (*see Tour 17*). MOSS CREEK RESERVOIR provides both a water supply and a recreation area.

Section e.   *BIG SPRING to VAN HORN; 221 m.   US 80; Interstate 20*

US 80 continues across the southern edge of the High Plains, traverses the trans-Pecos region, and climbs into mountainous country. Across rolling hills, rough breaks or flat, gray plains, the chief theme is ranching, the greatest interest, cattle. In this semi-arid land small grains are raised where water can be dug, or where streams afford irrigation; oil has been found, and potash, silica, lime, clay, salt and sulphur underlie the area. In the mountains, silver, lead, copper, coal, mica, gold, turquoise, marble and building stone are found in varying quantities.

Life is very simple and sincere in this sparsely peopled region. Pie suppers on Friday nights, school plays, rabbit drives, and all-night dances where the tempo is more hearty than modern, are among the amusements. Larry Chittenden's poem still describes some of the cowboys' festivities:

> The boys were tolerable skittish, the ladies powerful neat,
> That old bass viol's music just got there with both feet . . .
> The dust riz fast an' furious, we all just galloped 'round.
> Till the scenery was so giddy that Z Bar Dick was downed.

West of BIG SPRING, 0 *m.*, the route continues to SULPHUR DRAW, 7.5 *m.*, which has dry reaches extending far to the northwest. This is the longest dry draw in Texas, coming down from New Mexico to cut its arid furrow across four counties. Indians and frontiersmen used its bed as a highway long before roads were built.

The shallow salt lakes on both sides of the highway, 13.4 *m.*, are favorite duck hunting spots.

STANTON, 21 *m.* (2,664 alt., 2,228 pop.), is a cattle and cotton shipping town of sprawling, sandy streets. Founded by monks who established first a small Roman Catholic colony of German immigrants, it was once called Mariensfeld (Ger., Mary's Field). The first Monday of each month is Trades Day, and a horse show held in the afternoon usually ends with a street parade.

At 35.7 *m.,* tank farms of three major oil companies (L) extend for three miles.

MIDLAND, 40 *m.,* (2,779 alt., 62,625 pop., 1960, after annexation of 31,981; 68,000 1966, est.) seat of Midland County on the Texas & Pacific Ry. rises like a mirage of tall buildings in the sandswept ranch country. It has become the headquarters for more than 700 oil corporations interested in the Permian Basin. A 22-story building, erected before the boom, was quickly filled in the 1930's; other big structures followed and Midland became the Tall City. County ranches are valued at $30,500,000 and 530 acres are classified as grazing lands. There are a community theater and a symphony orchestra. Midland Air Terminal has 35 flights daily.

ODESSA, 60 *m.* (2,890 alt.) oil shipping and refining center of the Permian Basin, had 29,495 people in 1950 and lost 328 in that area by 1960, but annexation in the meantime of 57,171 made the 1960 total 80,338. In the ensuing years the population of the metropolitan area was racing toward the 100,000 mark. Seat of Ector County, Odessa originally was a cow town located by the Texas & Pacific Ry. in 1881. The Methodist influence outlawed saloons until the county sheriff opened one in 1898. Ector County produces up to 60,000,000 bbl. of oil a year. Odessa has refineries and black carbon plants, makes machinery, plastics and rubber.

The SANDHILLS HEREFORD AND QUARTER HORSE SHOW AND RODEO is held in the County Coliseum in January.

ODESSA COLLEGE, founded 1946 by the County, has a two-year course and enrolls more than 1,300. Its replica of Shakespeare's Globe Theater is used for classic plays.

To provide better railroad connections for the huge oil production of Ector, Andrews and Gaines Counties in the South Plains the Permian Basin Railroad in 1967 obtained the approval of the Interstate Commerce Commission for a new freight line. It will connect the Texas & Pacific at Odessa with the Santa Fe at Seagraves, 78 *m.* distant, parallel with US highway 385. Seagraves (2,250 pop. est.) also serves south Yoakum County as a shipping point. The towns between are SEMINOLE (6,252 pop. est.) seat of Gaines County, and ANDREWS (3,190 alt., 11,740 pop.) seat of Andrews County, oil processing center, both also on US 385.

At 67.4 *m.* is the junction with a dirt road.

Left here to METEOR CRATER, 2 *m.,* the third largest meteoric depression in the United States. When this meteor fell is unknown, but today large mesquite trees grow in the depth of the ten-acre depression. The Odessa Meteorite Museum has displays of minerals found here.

DEAD MAN'S CUT, 71.2 *m.*, is so named because of deaths caused by a delayed dynamite explosion during the construction of the railroad in the 1880's. Graves of the victims can be seen on the hillside.

Through a newly developed oil area and on into cattle country, again the highway rolls westward. Off to the north and south sweeps MONA- HANS SANDHILLS STATE PARK, 75 *m.* long, 5 *m.* wide. It has a museum, an art gallery, and shelters. An Easter Sunrise Service is held.

MONAHANS, 95 *m.* (2,613 alt., 8,567 pop. 1960; 10,500, 1965 est.). Nearby oil development has had its effect in new business buildings and residences. For years it existed solely as a supply center for ranches, but with the development of the Winkler Oil Field, to the north, the town's shipping facilities have brought prosperity.

In the heart of Monahans a pioneer building houses the HAYES MU- SEUM (*free*). Here is a collection of fossil remains, artifacts, and relics from the ruins of a large wagon train that at some time in the 1880's was destroyed by Indians near Willow Springs.

Monahans, is the seat of Ward County, which annually draws more than 20,000,000 bbl. of oil out of the sandy soil, worth more than $70,-000,000.

BARSTOW, 126 *m.* (2,557 alt., 600 pop.), is like an oasis, with its irrigated gardens. The canals of the Red Bluff Irrigation Project bring life-giving water, which transforms the dusty sagebrush lands into fertile fields. Here are raised excellent crops of cantaloupes, grapes, alfalfa, cotton and honey.

Along the PECOS RIVER, 130.2 *m.*, traveled exploring Spaniards, and for years there was "no law west of the Pecos." Toward its fords converged the trails of Indians, pioneers, and cattle drivers.

PECOS, 132 *m.* (2,580 alt., 14,000 pop., est. 1965), marketing center for long-staple cotton, cantaloupes, grain feeds, livestock and oil, was a pioneer cow town. In its early days Pecos was a metropolis of the desert cow country. Hitching rails lined the streets and the clatter of boot heels on the board walks mingled with the musical jingle of spurs. Not only was homicide frequent but the tough *hombres* of the town added a distinctive touch in their manner of disposing of the body and were responsible for the creation of a new verb, to "Pecos." "Pecosin' a feller," meant killing him, filling the body with rocks and dropping it into the waters of the river.

The story is told of one Pecos bad man who, when a dentist inadvertently pulled the wrong tooth, drew his gun, marched the dentist to the town's blacksmith shop, and there, with the smith's shoeing forceps, pulled every one of the unfortunate man's teeth. "Thar," the bad man is reported to have declared: "Reckon that'll l'arn yuh not to make any more mistakes."

One of the country's earliest versions of the rodeo is credited to Pecos. Here in 1884, the foreman of several ranches conducted a Fourth of July celebration that included roping, racing, and riding contests. The annual West of the Pecos Rodeo commemorates this event. The old Orient Hotel is now a museum, and there is a replica of Judge Roy Bean's Langtry bar.

A huge automobile tire testing track here makes a 9-mile circle. Pecos is located over an underground water basin that irrigates nearly 185,000 acres. Annual rainfall is only 12.68 inches and the plain of Reeves County is classified as semi-desert.

Pecos still supplies the needs of ranchers, but recent developments in oil and irrigation have added materially to its prosperity. To the north is the Red Bluff Irrigation Project (*see Tour 28*), which waters 60,000 acres. Cactus is plentiful in this region, and abundant wildlife includes the mountain lion and the wolf. Prairie dog colonies are frequent, and quail and doves abound. In the vicinity are deposits of gypsum, sulphur, silver and copper.

In Pecos is the junction with US 285 (*see Tour 28*).

At 174 *m.* is the junction with US 290 (*see Tour 24*).

The route is upgrade toward the mountains on the western horizon. To the north rise the rugged crests of the Apache Mountains (5,696 alt.), and to the south is the high forest-crowned mass of the Davis Mountains. Sagebrush and yucca-covered range land climbs to distant foothills. Vagrant gusts of wind kick up a dried weed that whirls in a brief mad dance.

The route descends somewhat into the little valley between the Wylie Mountains (5,031 alt.) to the south and the Baylor Range (5,560 alt.) on the north.

VAN HORN, 221 *m.* (4,010 alt., 2,000 pop.), has modern buildings that contrast sharply with its old adobes. It was named for Van Horn Wells, a frontier watering place a short distance to the south. Adjacent mountains to the northwest are rich in mineral resources, especially silver. It is the seat of Culberson County.

In Van Horn is the junction with US 90 and State 54.

Section f. VAN HORN to EL PASO; 119 m. US 80;
Interstate 10 parallels the highway

This section traverses the narrowing western apex of the State through a region of rugged mountains, and then passes up the verdant length of the Middle Valley of the Rio Grande. The rugged trans-Pecos peaks, hung with misty purple haze, hedge arid plains until suddenly, almost incredibly, the gardens and farms of the irrigated Valley region appear—fields of alfalfa, orchards, patches of melons, gardens of roses, dahlias and chrysanthemums, and vineyards.

West of VAN HORN, 0 *m.*, the road skirts the foothills of BEACH MOUNTAIN (5,935 alt.), and ascends a gradual grade past THREE MILE MOUNTAIN (4,845 alt.), and HACKETT PEAK (5,280 alt.), thence runs over the crumbling backbone of the Carrizo Range, whose eroded peaks average about 5,000 feet. To the south are the barren ridges of the Eagle Range, culminating in EAGLE PEAK (7,510 alt.). Between Van Horn and Allamoore, 11 *m.*, 200 pop., Central Time changes to Mountain Time.

Mountain breezes cool sun-baked plains in the vicinity of SIERRA

BLANCA, 33 *m.* (4,509 alt., 915 pop.). At 60 *m.* Interstate 10 follows a new route parallel with US 80.

Westward the route climbs to the top of a low pass between two ranges of barren mountains. The Quitman Mountains (6,600 alt.) reach southward to the Rio Grande (L), and the Finlay Range (5,650 alt.) is R. Just beyond the Quitmans are the Malone Mountains (5,200 alt.). Here very ancient rocks are found.

Entering the lower end of the Middle Valley of the Rio Grande, US 80 passes through an area of extensive cultivation. Here waters of the river and of the Elephant Butte Irrigation Project are conveyed in canals.

Along US 80 farm towns in the irrigated valley with less than 500 population include McNARY, FORT HANCOCK, ACALA, TORNILLO. The largest is FABENS, (3,300 pop., est.).

CLINT, 98 *m.* (3,630 alt., 600 pop.), is a town of adobe houses.

Left from Clint on a paved road to the sleepy little town of SAN ELIZARIO (formerly spelled Elzeario), 3 *m.* (3,628 alt., 1,064 pop.). Once a Spanish stronghold, it was later the seat of and the most important town in El Paso County. A few squat adobes and the Capilla de San Elizario, the graceful, simple chapel of the ancient fortress, are grouped about the old plaza.

Established following the Pueblo revolt in New Mexico (1680) by Indian refugees and Spanish soldiers, it was a presidio town with a chapel, rather than a mission settlement. The thick adobe walls of the fort surrounded an enclosure into which two gates gave entrance. Round watchtowers built outside the walls guarded these gateways. Almost nothing remains of the first settlement, which has been repeatedly swept by floods. One old building is pointed out as the governor's palace.

On the plaza in 1877 Charles H. Howard, John McBride, and John Atkinson were shot to death before an adobe wall in the final tragedy of the Salt War. Howard filed claim to some salt lakes 90 miles northeast of San Elizario, from which the residents of the village had for years hauled salt free. With the granting of his claim Howard placed a fee on the salt, which greatly enraged the people, who maintained that Howard had no right to claim that which had always been theirs, and threatened to take salt without payment. These threats caused the arrest of two Mexicans, and at once a mob formed which seized Howard and others, including the sheriff. In danger of death, Howard gave a $12,000 bond pledging the release of his claim to the salt lakes and his departure from the country.

He left, but appeared in El Paso within ten days. There he shot and killed Don Luis Cardis, Italian politician of the area and instigator of his seizure. With Cardis' death violence again threatened in San Elizario, and Major John B. Jones of the Frontier Battalion of Texas Rangers stationed a detachment in the little town. While peace prevailed on the surface, there was an undercover movement toward retaliation. Secret plans to draw Howard and his associates into a trap were successful when he and McBride hurried to San Elizario upon hearing that a train of carts had gone to get salt from the lakes.

Immediately following Howard's arrival an armed mob formed on the plaza. Howard sought the protection of the Rangers, whose commander refused to give him to the mob. A fight resulted and after a siege of several days the Ranger force surrendered. Howard, McBride and Atkinson were executed. The Rangers were given their horses and allowed to depart.

The CAPILLA DE SAN ELIZARIO (Chapel of St. Elzear) (*open, free*), is the largest and richest of the El Paso group. The present building, which strongly resembles the early California missions, with white walls, arched tower with two bells, and long arched portico, was the fourth to be erected and was started in the year of the Salt War (1877). It occupies the third site of the presidio which, when founded on the Mexican side of the Rio Grande in 1683, was called Presidio de Nuestra Señora del Pilar y Glorioso Señor San José (Fort of Our Lady of Pilar and the Glorious St. Joseph).

A flood destroyed the statuary and paintings of the first chapel, but one of the two bells is believed to be from that structure.

In 1850 a garrison of U. S. troops was stationed at San Elizario, and the California Volunteers made their headquarters there in 1862.

At 102.5 m. is a junction with a paved road.

Left here to SOCORRO, 5.5 m. (3,650 alt., 600 pop.), and the MISSION DE LA PURISIMA CONCEPCION DEL SOCORRO (Mission of the Most Pure Conception of the Socorro). Before 1766 the establishment bore the name of Nuestra Señora de la Concepcion de Socorro. This building occupies the third site of the mission. The first one, probably erected in 1683, was abandoned because of trouble with Indians; the second building was destroyed by flood. The present church structure was built from the ruins of a previous one, erected early in the nineteenth century, and contains the same timbers and carved beams.

Socorro Mission is famed for its old statue of St. Michael. Legend says that this statue was intended for a New Mexico mission, but that while it was being freighted overland the cart stuck in Socorro and three yoke of oxen were unable to move it, so the people of Socorro bought it and made the saint their secondary patron. The statue is excellently carved from wood and beautifully painted.

Four old paintings, one of St. Peter, adorn the mission walls. Another relic is a hand-carved ivory crucifix, which is kept in the sacristy. The wooden statue of the patron saint of the mission is partially covered with etched gold leaf. In the graveyard in the rear of the rectory the Indian neophytes buried their dead in layers, one above the other, only one grave being allowed to a family. The people of the little town retain many of the manners and customs of their forebears.

A modern building, 106.5 m., is on the SITE OF MISSION DE CORPUS CHRISTI DE LA ISLETA DEL SUR (Mission of Corpus Christi of the Little Isle in the South) (open, free), founded in 1681.

The first building stood on a small island in the Rio Grande, but the river changed its course and the site is now on the Texas side of the international boundary.

This mission was a part of a network of 14 pueblos populated by New Mexican Indians. Each pueblo had a civil and a spiritual head, and Isleta, like the others, had the protection of a centrally-located presidio of 50 Spanish soldiers. The Tiguas built the mission buildings of adobe. The oldest part of the structure of today is that where the altar stands. In 1907 a fire destroyed the old building, even its five-foot-thick walls. All the statues save one of Christ, and the gold and silver vessels, were lost.

The present building, locally called the Church of Our Lady of Mount Carmel, is a reproduction of the first one. Four of the mission's seven acres of land have been in constant cultivation since 1682. The monks built the irrigation ditch that surrounds the town.

The mission yard is still the scene of ceremonial Indian dances dating back to the time of the Tigua village. They are held on the feast days of saints, especially on the anniversary of Our Lady of Mount Carmel, July 16. St. Anthony's Day, June 13, is also usually thus observed. Descendants of the Tiguas perform these pagan dances in the weird costumes of their forefathers.

YSLETA, 107 *m.*, founded 1682, after the Indian revolt, is called the oldest town in Texas. It is now the southeastern suburb of El Paso. Squat, flat-roofed, whitewashed old adobe buildings stand between more modern structures. Age-old superstition is manifest in the blue door and window frames which are so painted to insure happiness and good luck, and to repel evil spirits.

West of Ysleta the highway follows the route of El Camino Real toward the mountain portals of El Paso del Norte (The Pass of the North), along the gateway from Old Mexico to the upper valley of the Rio Grande.

The approximate SITE OF THE MISSION AND PUEBLO OF SAN ANTONIO DE SENECU (St. Anthony of Senecu), another of the string of missions and towns established in the Rio Grande Valley in the early 1680's, is L. at 109 *m.*

The tree-lined highway continues up the valley past orchards and truck gardens. Irrigation ditches often parallel the road, their waters reflecting the patchwork shade of overhanging trees.

EL PASO, 119 *m.* (3,762 alt., 320,000 pop. 1966 est.) (*see El Paso*), is at the junction with US 62.

The major highway is Interstate 10, which is joined by US 180 to the New Mexico line. US 80, which runs closer to the river, continues independently to the border and beyond.

North of EL PASO, 0 *m.*, the PLANT OF THE AMERICAN SMELTING AND REFINING COMPANY is visible (L) about three-quarters of a mile away. A tawny cloud of smoke and jets of snow-white steam hover about the brick and sheet metal buildings by day, while at night the regular dumping of white-hot slag weirdly illumines the scene. Beyond, on top of the 4,576-foot crest of SIERRA DE CRISTO REY, is a large white sandstone cross and figure of Christ the King. This statue, officially dedicated October 29, 1939, when a host of more than 10,000 persons made the pilgrimage afoot up the long winding road to the summit, is the realization of an idea which first formed in the mind of Father Lourdes F. Costa, priest of a little smelter parish on the outskirts of El Paso. The work was begun by members of this parish; they first erected a wooden cross and later a metal one on the mountain peak. Donations for a stone statue poured in from a wide area, and those unable to give money gave of their time and labor in the construction of a road and parkway. The figure of the Christ is the work of Señor Urbici Soler, who worked for many months on the wind-swept peak. The figure represents the Christ Triumphant standing before the cross, the arms outstretched in eternal benediction on those humble ones whose labors and sacrifices made possible the completion of this symbol. Frequent pilgrimages are made to the summit by Roman Catholics of adjacent parishes, the most outstanding being on the day of the Feast of Christ the King. These occasions are attended by thousands who toil up the road past the Stations of the Cross, to bow in reverence at the foot of the statue.

Northward the route leads through a rich irrigated area of the Rio

Grande Valley. Green, well-watered fields are always in various stages of cultivation.

LA TUNA DETENTION FARM (*visitors Tues. and Fri., 9–11, 1–3*), 19 *m.,* is a short-term Federal prison for the districts of New Mexico, Arizona and West Texas. The prison reservation contains 635 acres. Buildings are of modern Spanish design.

Straggling across the State Line is the village of LA TUNA, 19.8 *m.* (4,000 alt., 200 pop.).

At 20 *m.* US 80 crosses the NEW MEXICO LINE, 24 miles south of Las Cruces, New Mexico.

Tour 20

(Shreveport, La.) — Jacksonville — Palestine — Taylor — Round Rock; US 79.
Louisiana Line to Round Rock, 270 *m.*

Beginning in the east Texas timbered region, this route runs from the Louisiana Boundary in a southwesterly direction across an area of early settlement, where first the Caddoes and then settlers from the Old South claimed rich acres watered by many streams. The scent of pines often mingles with that of oil, yet the cotton fields that flank the length of the route present scenes little changed since the 1830's. Multicolored rural landscapes unfold, as the white fleece of cotton and the yellows of grains alternate with the hues of acres of tomatoes, peaches, melons, and other vegetables and fruits. Fingers of timber reach between the tilled regions and pastures have sleek dairy cattle, horses and mules.

Colonists of predominantly Anglo-Saxon stock settled the agricultural areas, and their descendants remain. There were later infiltrations of Czechs, Germans, Swedes, and Italians, who today retain some of their Old World customs. Negroes, mostly descended from former slaves, till the deep black lands of the Brazos and other rivers, living much as their forefathers did, in tiny, unsightly shanties, spending their days chopping or picking cotton, and seldom leaving the plantation where their parents were born. Their faded jeans and bright sunbonnets are part of the Southern tradition of this region of long cotton rows and dank bottom lands where 'possums abound.

A virile note in this old plantation culture is the progressive influence of the Agricultural and Mechanical College of Texas, near Bryan, where yearly hundreds of young men are graduated as engineers or as scientific farmers.

Section a. LOUISIANA LINE *to* BUFFALO; 144 *m.* US 79

This part of US 79 traverses the piney woods of the east central section of Texas, where lumbering is still one of the leading industries—although much land has been cut over, cleared, and is now under extensive cultivation. The region is rich in deposits of iron ore, lignite and brick clay. Cotton is the largest money crop, with truck farming second. The streams have perch, bass, bream, and catfish, and the timbered areas afford small game hunting.

US 79 crosses the LOUISIANA LINE, 0 *m.*, 23 miles southwest of Shreveport, Louisiana. The village of PANOLA, Texas, is just across the line.

CARTHAGE, 24 *m.* (302 alt., 5,672 pop.), was founded in 1848 as a town of log houses. School and religious worship were held in the Masonic Hall, and the town's favorite gathering place was the ginger cake and beer shop of Sam Sprauls. It is the seat of Panola County and profits from the huge natural gas and lumber industries. It also has meat and food processing and manufactures trailers.

PANOLA COUNTY JUNIOR COLLEGE, established 1948, enrolls up to 350.

LAKE PANOLA, or Murmaul Reservoir, is 10 *m.* SW near Clayton, a village on State 315. It covers 3,820 acres and holds 45,840 acre-ft. of water.

HENDERSON, 52 *m.* (505 alt., 10,000 pop.), has gorgeous splashes of magenta-hued blossoms in the spring, as its many redbud trees bloom; and above these tower large magnolias. This is a relatively old community, founded in 1844. First lumber, then agriculture, was its supporting industry, but since 1930 oil and gas have brought big profits. It is the seat of Rusk County. A statue of Thomas J. Rusk, Texas leader and senator, stands in the city square.

At the southern edge of Henderson is the SITE OF OLD SHAWNEE TOWN, a village once inhabited by Indians of that tribe. Artifacts are plentiful.

Right from Henderson on State 323, the Henderson-Overton Highway to NEW LONDON, 10 *m.*, scene of a school disaster on March 18, 1937, that cost the lives of 279 pupils, 12 teachers, and two visitors. Probably the worst of its kind in history, this tragedy was caused by a gas explosion in the high school. On the grounds is a MEMORIAL SUNDIAL erected by the Texas Retail Jewelers Association to the memory of those who lost their lives in the explosion. The dial is set with semi-precious stones, one in memory of each of the victims.

JACKSONVILLE, 85 *m.* (516 alt., 11,346 pop.), thrives as the trading and shipping center of a tomato-producing area. During tomato season it is full of activity. Jacksonville Baptist College enrolls around 160.

In Jacksonville is the junction with US 69, US 175 and State 135. Northwest on US 175 12 *m.* the highway crosses the Neches River. One *m.* up from the bridge is Blackburn Crossing and the dam that impounds

Neches River water in LAKE PALESTINE. The dam is 4,000 ft. long and the lake has a shoreline of 30 miles and covers 6,000 acres. It can supply 40,000,000 gals. daily and is stocked with black bass, crappie, bream and catfish. Boats and tackle are available. LAKE JACKSON-VILLE on the Gum River, 5 *m*. southwest, covers 1,320 acres.

After crossing the Neches River US 175 continues over the hills of red sandstone to FRANKSTON, 16 *m*. (389 alt., 1,109 pop.), a sawmill town which, from the crest of a hill, looks down upon a landscape spread in a checkerboard of cultivated fields, pasture lands and wooded tracts.

Right from Frankston 1 *m*. on a dirt road to SCARBOROUGH SPRINGS, where each Thanksgiving Eve is held a widely known 'Possum Fete. This event, an outdoor feast, had its beginning with four people, and has grown in popularity. Opossum, beef, pork, mutton, chicken, turkey, guinea hen, deer, crackling bread and buffalo meat are often served. Public speaking and athletic events in the 'Possum Bowl are program features.

Left from Frankston 2.5 *m*. on a dirt road to the SITE OF THE KICKAPOO BATTLEFIELD, where General Thomas J. Rusk and 200 Texans were victorious over a band of hostile Indians and their Mexican allies on October 16, 1838.

US 175 continues to ATHENS, 39 *m*. (490 alt., 10,000 pop. 1965 est.) seat of Henderson County. A fruit center it also has oil and gas, clothing, furniture and face brick industries. Henderson County Junior College enrolls approx. 700. The new JOE B. HOGSTETT LAKE (formerly Cedar Creek Lake) is 5 *m*. from Athens and 3 *m*. from TRINIDAD (pop. 1,300, est.). It covers 34,000 acres with a capacity of 678,900 acre-ft. Old Fiddlers Reunion, last Friday in May, is a famous folk festival.

Cynthia Ann Parker, captured in childhood by the Indians, lived in Athens following her recapture. Lonely, yearning for the wild life of her years on the plains, mourning for her Indian husband and sons, she lived on until the death of the one child who was with her. With the passing of Prairie Flower, Cynthia Ann failed rapidly, died and was buried in the old Fosterville Cemetery. Later her son, Quanah Parker, war chief of the Comanches, removed the remains of his white mother, reinterred them in Oklahoma, and erected a monument over her grave.

PALESTINE, 111 *m*. (510 alt., 13,974 pop.), is charmingly old-fashioned, although oil developments have added to its wealth. The main business street slopes down from the public square; throughout the residential section are fine old houses of the era of gables, cupolas and ornamental copings. Several pioneer residences date from c. 1849. Palestine is the seat of Anderson County (28,162 pop.). The SCIENTIFIC BALLOON FLIGHT STATION, built 1962, covers 183 acres.

The PALESTINE SALT DOME, one of the largest domes in the interior United States, covering an area 30,000 feet in diameter, provided salt when its brine was evaporated. Coal has been mined in the vicinity, lignite and fuller's earth are abundant, and Orangeburg clay (deteriorated iron ore) has been used successfully to pave local roads. Oil was discovered in Anderson County in 1929.

In Palestine is the junction with US 84 (*see Tour 21*), which unites with US 79 for 13 miles; also US 287, State 155 and State 19.

At 112 *m*. is the junction with a dirt road.

Left on this road across a railroad, then L. again to the old JOHN H. REAGAN HOME (*private*), 0.3 *m.*, which is still occupied by the Reagan family. The house is of frame construction, two-story, painted white, and of English colonial design. Almost 100 years old, it is in a good state of preservation, and contains the furniture of Postmaster General Reagan of the Confederacy. Within 200 yards, southwest, is the SITE OF FORT HOUSTON, a military post of the Republic of Texas, established in 1836.

From Palestine US 287 proceeds southeast, passing through GRAPELAND, in Houston County (1,100 pop.) to Crockett (*see Tour 5*), the county seat. US 287 runs along the DAVY CROCKETT NATIONAL FOREST to GROVETON, (1,100 pop.) seat of Trinity County and a market center for farm products and lumbering. From Groveton it is 17 *m.* on State 94 to TRINITY (1,190 pop. est.). From Groveton 18 *m.* southeast on US 287 to CORRIGAN (1,050 pop.), junction with US 59 coming south from Lufkin (*see Tour 5*).

BUFFALO, 144 *m.* (397 alt., 1,108 pop.), on US 79, is a farming center. Here is a junction with US 75 (*see Tour 6*).

Section b.   BUFFALO to ROUND ROCK; 126 m.   US 79

US 79 continues through a region where agricultural developments vie with more recent oil activity.

In the spring, the blooming stalks of flaming standing cypress, wild cannas, Indian paint brush, bluebonnets and other Texas wild flowers color the roadsides and pastures. Cotton bales piled along railroad tracks indicate the importance of this crop, which early caused the founding of a landed culture. When thrifty immigrants descended upon this region, many of them profited by the decline of cotton markets and bought much of the plantation land. Because they often did not want luxurious houses expensive to maintain, these newcomers allowed many of the fine old frame manor houses to decay, and replaced them with compact brick structures.

Women work in the field alongside their menfolk in the Czech colony near Taylor, and at other points where European immigrants have settled. A *Sokol,* athletic organization, is the largest social influence among Czechs of this region; it teaches the creed of sound bodies and clean morals. Italian farmers invaded the Brazos bottoms in the 1880's, and through the hard labor of their entire families, have become prosperous.

Great plantations remain intact in the vicinity of Bryan, and here Negroes are still called to and from their fields by means of bells that were in use when their forefathers were slaves.

South of BUFFALO, 0 *m.,* the route is through a region of level prairie land, mostly under cultivation, with cotton and corn the leading crops.

There is a hardwood sawmill in NEW BADEN, 36.5 *m.* (427 alt., 185 pop.), a town established in 1880 by J. G. Meyer, colonizer who worked with a land company that brought in cultured German colonists, principally from Baden. These immigrants had little experience in farming, and only about 100 of them remained. Until lands could be allotted them and their homes built, the colonists were quartered in the IMMI-GRANT HOUSE, partly intact today.

A roadside park (*picnic tables, benches and fireplaces*), 37.7 *m.*, has a flowing spring (R). This is the site of the ghost town of Inglewood, of which only a few brick wells and cisterns remain.

In FRANKLIN, 40 *m.* (443 alt., 1,065 pop.), buildings are red from the color of the dust on unpaved streets. The fourth side of its public square was never developed, and is today a pasture. It is the shipping point of a large agricultural area but its population remains static.

HEARNE, 53 *m.* (305 alt., 5,072 pop.), neat and quiet, is a rail junction and has railroad shops. Many buildings of the 1890's with modernized facades line the wide streets. Cotton contributes to its prosperity. RCA World Championship Rodeo is held in June.

Left from Hearne on US 190 to BRYAN, 20 *m.* (367 alt., 27,542 pop. 1960; 32,500, 1965 est.), seat of Brazos County. It is the home of Allen Academy, founded in 1886, enrollment about 600 students. Many of its large homes are owned by Italian and Bohemian residents. Its air of well-being is based upon the marketing of truck crops, fruits, livestock, dairy and poultry products.

In this vicinity, south and west, lie great plantations whose prosperity reached a peak following the Civil War, when railroad facilities became available. Former slaves were retained as sharecroppers or tenants, and overseers, through the handling of commissary accounts, were said to have kept the Negroes firmly bound to the soil of their late masters. During these years, vagrants were taken from trains, fined, and made to work out sentences on the plantations. The Federal government at last intervened. With the passing of old-time overseers, day laborers were substituted for tenants.

With the retirement of much cotton acreage and the planting of alfalfa, another era of prosperity has come to the plantations.

COLLEGE STATION, 4 *m.* SE. of Bryan on State 6 (11,396 pop.), is the home of TEXAS AGRICULTURAL & MECHANICAL UNIVERSITY, which since 1871 has had a big part in the improvement of Texan agronomy. With a central core of just under 100 buildings, many of recent erection, it boasts of a "campus" of 5,200 acres and enrolls more than 8,000 students for the regular term and 4,400 for the summer courses. It operated on a budget of $25,287,718 in 1965, has available $963,561 for scholarships and fellowships, and figures average annual expenses of a student at $394, including board and room. The University combines teaching and research. More than 150 laboratories and centers of specialized research are on the campus; others are scattered over the State. The Texas Agricultural Extension Service cooperated with 17,000 local leaders in 1964, a typical year. The College of Engineering has a Department of Nuclear Engineering, with a reactor that cost $2,500,000, and a cyclotron in process of building at a cost of $6,000,000. There are Departments of Aerospace and of Agricultural Engineering. The School of Architecture occupies a new building of ultra-modern design. Research engineers have led in activation analysis, an automatic process for determining the chemical composition of materials through the use of nondestructive nuclear radiation of samples. The College of Geosciences has, among others, a Department of Oceanography, which operates a marine laboratory at Galveston, another in Florida, and sends its research vessel, the *Alaminos,* as far as the Antarctic to investigate biological productivity. Its far-flung agricultural research touches every product developed by Texas; its development of new varieties of grain sorghum hybrids alone is estimated to have increased agricultural income by $110,000,000 annually.

The Texas A. & M. University System also embraces Tarleton State College,

Stephenville, Prairie View A. & M. College, Prairie View, and the James Connally Technical Institute. The University's Graduate College gives about 100 degrees of doctor of philosophy annually for work in 50 fields. The Graduate Institute of Statistics was established in 1963.

The University's RESEARCH ANNEX was established 1963 on the former Bryan Air Force Base, 8 m. west of Bryan. It has 1,991 acres and 112 buildings built by the U. S. Government. Here is located the LUNAR PROBE PROJECT, sponsored by the Atomic Energy Commission and the Aeronautics & Space Admin. An electronics training school for non-college students was established here in 1963.

Southwest of Hearne the route is through rich bottom lands where there are many cotton fields. The region is highly productive, cotton sometimes growing to the height of more than five feet.

Just south of the highway, on the west bank of the BRAZOS RIVER, 59.2 m., a cemetery marks the SITE OF NASHVILLE, a frontier outpost during the colonial period.

ROCKDALE, 83 m. (462 alt., 4,481 pop.) (see Tour 7c), is at the junction with US 77 (see Tour 7).

In this vicinity lignite is mined and mineral water is abundant.

THORNDALE, 96.1 m. (460 alt., 1,002 pop.), has plants processing cotton and mineral water crystals. Many tales of buried treasure are told of this vicinity. One is of a man who lived alone in an oak grove and was murdered for his hoard of gold, after which his ghost haunted the spot in the form of a dog—visible to only one person in a party—that would disappear should anyone try to touch it, and was impervious to bullets.

At inaccessible points in the vicinity of Thorndale were three Spanish missions: San Francisco Xavier de Horcasitas (St. Francis Xavier of Horcasitas), established in 1748; San Ildefonso (St. Alphonsus), established in 1749, and Nuestra Señora de la Candelaria (Our Lady of Candlemas), built in 1749. They were abandoned in 1755. Indian hostilities caused the establishment of a presidio to protect the missions, but the soldiers led such vicious lives that many neophytes deserted. This brought about trouble between the soldiers and the missionaries, which culminated in the murder of one of the padres at the instigation of the soldiers. Legend describes a visitation of divine retribution in the form of elemental phenomena. A terrifying ball of fire appeared in the sky and exploded; the river ceased to run and its waters became intolerably foul; many died; and the accursed plain was converted into a thicket with horrible crevices, forcing the survivors to move away to escape extermination.

THRALL, 101 m. (569 alt., 600 pop.), has, during two periods of its history, been the scene of oil booms. In 1925 the first wells were discovered and the town became prosperous almost overnight. Scarcely had it settled to normal when the second boom came in 1930. The field proved to be shallow, most of the wells failing; the few that remain work on pumps. The slump that followed the second boom is evidenced in many vacant residences and business buildings.

TAYLOR, 108.2 m. (583 alt., 9,434 pop.), is a trading center for an area of extensive cotton cultivation, and has one of the largest mattress factories in the South. A cheese factory, thriving dairying and poultry-

raising industries, cotton mills and two oil refineries create a brisk atmosphere on the broad business streets. Many Czech names are on the store
fronts; nearly half the population is of this nationality. The third largest
group is German. The inherent neatness of these residents has made the
many miles of Taylor's streets clean and attractive. In big houses of plantation type live the older families, many of them deriving wealth from
cotton and oil.

Westward, the highway passes through one of the most productive
cotton areas in the United States.

At 124.2 *m.* is a junction with a graveled road.

Left here to the SITE OF KENNEY'S FORT, 0.3 *m.,* built in 1839. It consisted of
four log cabins within a picket stockade of logs about eight feet high, on the
bluff of Brushy Creek. Here rendezvoused the ill-fated Santa Fé Expedition
(*see History*). Only the foundations of the cabins and a few cedar posts remain.

ROUND ROCK, 126 *m.* (750 alt., 1,878 pop.) (*see Tour 8c*), is at
the junction with US 81 (*see Tour 8*).

I✧I✧I✧I✧I✧I✧I✧I✧I✧I✧I✧I✧I✧I✧I✧I✧I✧I✧I✧I✧I✧I✧I✧I✧I✧I✧I✧

Tour 21

(Logansport, La.) — Palestine — Waco — Brownwood — Abilene —
Lubbock — Muleshoe; US 84.
Louisiana Line to Muleshoe, 643 *m.*

Running between the Louisiana and New Mexico State Lines, US 84
spans Texas through its central area, beginning in the approximate middle
of its eastern pine belt and ending on the western reaches of the Panhandle, upon the High Plains. The route crosses the Blacklands Belt, the
Grand Prairie and the rugged region of the Cap Rock.

The hills and rolling, red, timbered lands of the pine forest section
ravel out into a broad, rich prairie of black soil, much furrowed; then US
84 winds across hills where farms are smaller and diversified, to flatten
out on the vast semi-arid ranges of western Texas.

Traditions and history differ widely in the three general divisions of
the route. In the eastern part acreages are fairly evenly distributed and
customs democratic; the central area was settled by Southern planters
who built a culture founded upon the castes of cotton; and in the western
section, sturdy pioneers battled adverse weather, Indians and outlaws
with a firmness based partly upon the challenge of adventure, but chiefly
upon the desire to claim the land—cheap in a day when prices elsewhere
were soaring. Sawmills provided the earliest prosperity in the first section,

slave labor and cotton in the second, and ranching in the third. Oil and mechanized agriculture have somewhat changed the old aspects of these regions, but their customs and attitudes savor of the past. In two respects they have something in common: the population is predominantly native-born white, and highly rural.

Section a.   *LOUISIANA LINE to WACO; 207 m.   US 84*

This section of US 84 crosses the pine and Blacklands belts of east and central Texas, a region of lumbering, oil and gas production, diversified farming, and livestock raising.

About three-fourths of the population is white, with approximately two per cent Mexican and the remainder Negro. The first settlers here were largely of Anglo-Saxon stock, and most of the land is owned by their descendants. The pioneers were primarily home-builders and founded moral, religious-minded communities where once a year brush arbors sheltered camp meetings. Today numerous little white frame churches dot the clearings, and, in the cities, imposing structures house large Christian congregations. Schools also are many in number, and during recent years the illiteracy rate has decreased rapidly, even among the Negroes, who are largely farm tenants or sharecroppers.

US 84 crosses the LOUISIANA LINE, 0 *m.,* over the Sabine River, 1 mile west of Logansport, Louisiana. (*see Louisiana Guide*).

TENAHA, 15 *m.* (351 alt., 1,097 pop.) is at the junction with US 59 (*see Tour 2*).

TIMPSON, 25 *m.* (394 alt., 1,150 pop.) is at the junction with State 35 (*see Tour 22*).

MOUNT ENTERPRISE, 43 *m.* (479 alt., 625 pop.), moved most of its business houses to the recently built highway at the edge of the old town, as its new buildings indicate.

Right from Mount Enterprise on State 26 to HUDMAN WELL, 3 *m.* This well was dug before 1850, is curbed with rock, and still serves the public who come to picnic here.

RUSK, 73 *m.* (489 alt., 5,000 pop.) is at the junction with US 69 (*see Tour 5*).

This region is rife with tales of pioneer adventure. Into it came the Spanish as early as 1690, when missions were established a few miles to the south and east. Settlers who arrived after the Texas Revolution had trouble with the Indians, and Fort Houston and Fort Duty were established for their protection.

In this vicinity the highway crosses the crest of the KEECHI SALT DOME, which appears to be rising at the rate of about an inch a year, causing transverse cracks in the concrete roadway.

PALESTINE, 103 *m.* (510 alt., 13,974 pop.) is at the junction with US 79 (*see Tour 20*), which unites with US 84 for 13 miles (*see Tour 20a*).

At 114 *m.,* is a junction with US 79 (*see Tour 20*).

FAIRFIELD, 138 *m.* (461 alt., 1,900 pop.), has grown about a graveled public square, along streets shaded by oaks and hackberries. It is a retail and market center and seat of Freestone County.

In Fairfield is the junction with US 75 (*see Tour 6*).

Southwest of Fairfield the terrain is one of long sweeping hills, heavily timbered with sand jack and post oak. Fishing for bass, perch and catfish is good in several small lakes in this region.

TEAGUE, 148 *m.* (497 alt., 2,728 pop.), a modern town in the center of a cotton and grain belt, has a cottonseed oil mill, railroad shops, cotton gins, and ships freestone and limestone.

MEXIA, 161 *m.* (534 alt., 6,579 pop.), was named for the owner of a local Spanish grant, Colonel José Antonio Mejia, whose son, H. A. Mexia, changed the spelling of the name (pronounced May-he′ ah). It is an agricultural center to which has been added the prosperity of oil development, following a spectacular boom in 1920.

Oil tanks and derricks still circle the town, and some of the flimsy shacks of boom days remain. But Mexia's smart business district and substantial homes have been created by the wealth produced from cotton, which forms the basis for its largest industrial plants.

LAKE MEXIA, 7 *m.* southwest of the town, is impounded by Bistone Dam on the Navasota River. It covers 1,200 acres and holds 10,000 acre-ft. of water, the town's supply.

Left from Mexia on State 14 to FORT PARKER STATE PARK, 8 *m.* Here, within an area of 1,700 acres, stands a reproduction of old Fort Parker, where, in 1836, Cynthia Ann Parker was captured by a band of Comanches and Kiowas (*see Tour 12*).

A veritable forest of oil derricks is encountered northwest of Mexia, the field where the highway crosses it being more than a half-mile wide. Numerous wells are still producing on pumps.

TEHUACANA, 165 *m.* (412 pop.), was founded about 1844 and named for an Indian tribe that had a village in the vicinity. Here, in 1869, was established Trinity University, which was later moved to San Antonio. The presence of a small preparatory educational institution still lends the atmosphere of a college town to Tehuacana, which sits on top of a hill, tranquil within its stout houses of stone.

WESTMINSTER JUNIOR COLLEGE AND BIBLE INSTITUTE, 165 *m.,* stands on the former site of Trinity. It is a branch of Southwestern University and has a small enrollment. Adjacent are the beautiful Tehuacana Hills, scene of many Indian fights. From the road are visible the openings of many caves said to have been used as hiding places by Indians and, later, by white outlaws.

WACO, 207 *m.* (427 alt., est. pop. 1940, 58,000) (*see Waco*), is at junctions with US 77 (*see Tour 7*) and US 81 (*see Tour 8*).

Section b.   WACO to ROSCOE; 254 m.   US 84

US 84 continues between the western fringe of the agricultural region of the Grand Prairie and a section where ranching predominates.

Beginning in central Texas, the route turns sharply northwestward toward the southern fringe of the High Plains. Since earliest settlement the land has been all-important to these people, who produce and preserve a large part of their food and other necessities. Sparsely settled, the region is one of inherent hospitality, and its life revolves around small towns churches and schools. Hereford cattle are the mainstay of the rural folk, but sheep and goats thrive on uplands and rough, eroded regions. Cotton is the greatest crop. Oil and gas, gypsum, clays, salt and potash, fuller's earth and manganese are found in varying quantities.

From this section westward evidences of ancient human occupation are many, particularly along the courses of streams, where mounds, camp sites and rock shelters are found.

West of WACO, 0 *m.*, the route is through a farming region.

At 9.6 *m.* is a junction with a graveled road.

Right here to TONKAWA STATE PARK (*swimming 25¢; picnic facilities*), 10 *m.*, a 100-acre area of rock cliffs, springs, waterfalls, a small lake, dense underbrush and huge pecan trees.

At 19 *m.* is a junction with a graveled road.

Left here to McGREGOR, 0.3 *m.* (713 alt., 4,825 pop.), center of a large livestock and agricultural area. Its predominantly brick business area is flanked by a flour mill, grain elevator, and cotton gins. Large cotton plantations are numerous in this region.

Left from McGregor 8 *m.* on an improved road to MOTHER NEFF STATE PARK, a 256-acre tract presented to the State by former Governor Pat M. Neff and his mother, and named in her honor. In summer it is the scene of protracted meetings and community gatherings.

Westward the route is parallel to that of a Comanche trail that ran from Comanche Springs (*private*), just north of the highway at 19.9 *m.*, to Waco. The terrain is rough and the highway winds with many twists and turns through a heavily wooded section.

GATESVILLE, 39 *m.* (795 alt., 7,500 pop.), seat of Coryell County, is a prosperous industrial town with cotton processing, plastics and livestock feed mills. It was named for Fort Gates, a frontier post established in 1849 as a unit of the earliest U. S. Government defenses. The site of the fort is six miles southeast, on the Leon River. Fort Hood is four miles south of Gatesville.

Right from Gatesville on State 36 to the STATE TRAINING SCHOOL FOR BOYS, 3 *m.* Here, on a tract of 887 acres, this corrective institution has 23 buildings, including dormitories, a mess hall, shops, school and administrative buildings to care for about 1,000 inmates. Most of the clothing for the boys is made at the school and the bulk of the foodstuff used is grown on its farms.

Near the LEON RIVER (*fishing for perch, catfish, bass; dove and squirrel hunting*), 39.8 *m.*, fossils are found.

The highway winds through the narrow valley of Cow House Creek, so named from the fact that caves along its banks shelter cattle from northers.

EVANT, 63 m. (350 pop.) (see Tour 9b), is at the junction with US 281 (see Tour 9).

The route now climbs from Cow House Valley and slips over the divide to the slopes of the Lampasas watershed. From the crest of the divide is visible a broad panorama of rolling, wooded hills and cultivated lowlands.

The LAMPASAS RIVER, 72.1 m., has a dangerous low-water crossing (be careful if water is over the slab).

CENTER CITY, 82 m. (35 pop.), gained its name from the fact that at one time it was thought to be the geographic center of the State—a point later officially established at a spot 20 miles northeast of Brady. CENTER OAK, which the pioneers believed marked the exact center of Texas, still stands, protected by a concrete wall.

Hills circle GOLDTHWAITE, 88 m. (1,580 alt., 1,324 pop.), where old stone buildings face a quiet, restful public square. Wool, mohair, turkeys, peanuts, are products handled here. Dinner is a noon meal in Goldthwaite; the storekeepers and clerks walk home for it, and following it a little nap is in order for many of them. Fishing for carp, perch and catfish is good in the vicinity, and squirrels and doves are plentiful.

At 121 m. is the eastern junction with US 67 (see Tour 18), which, passing through BROWNWOOD, 122 m. (1,342 alt., 16,974 pop.), unites with US 84 for a distance of 32 miles (see Tour 18).

COLEMAN, 151 m. (1,710 alt., 6,371 pop.) (see Tour 18c), is at the junction with US 67 (see Tour 18).

At 189 m. are junctions with US 83 (see Tour 16) and US 277 (see Tour 10), both of which unite with US 84 for a distance of 18 miles (see Tour 10a).

ABILENE, 205 m. (1,738 alt., 90,368 pop.) (see Tour 10a), is at junctions with US 83 (see Tour 16), US 277 (see Tour 10), and US 80 (see Tour 19), which last unites with US 84 for a distance of 49 miles, passing through SWEETWATER, 246 m. (2,164 alt., 13,918 pop.) as does Interstate 20.

ROSCOE, 254 m. (2,380 alt., 1,490 pop.) (see Tour 19d), is at the junction with US 80 (see Tour 19).

Section c. ROSCOE to MULESHOE; 182 m. US 84

Across the High Plains, where Spanish explorers and buffalo hunters blazed the earliest trails, US 84 traverses the free range empire of the last decades of the nineteenth century, where great cattle domains stretched over seemingly endless miles. Barbed wire and the sale of school lands to farmers broke up those vast acreages. Tractors, and the development of shallow water wells in the early 1900's, have converted many thousands of acres into wheat and cotton fields, and oil has added its changes. But today many of the people and some of the towns remain truly Western, sun-browned, interested in "cow critters" and county fairs. A wealth of cowboy lore survives here where once trail herds were driven north by a rough-and-ready band whose songs resembled this one:

> Whoopee, ti yi yo, git along little dogies,
> It's your misfortune and none of my own . . .

Today the tendency toward practical jokes, so dear to the cowboy, remains; occasionally the tail of the parson's cow is curled or otherwise decorated. Horse racing and barbecues on the Fourth of July are still popular.

Traces of mastodons and tools of an ancient type of man are found near lake beds and in canyons. Remains of prehistoric horses, elephants, bison, camels, phytosaurs, turtles, sharks and other forms of age-old life are in fossil beds and gravel; and certain archeologists ascribe to artifacts of the Plains region a similarity to those of men of the Folsom epoch.

Northwest of ROSCOE, 0 *m.,* the route is across the rolling prairies, with a view so broad that the effect is that of being in a vast shallow bowl.

HERMLEIGH, 19 *m.* (2,392 alt., 544 pop.), retail center, has an unusually fine school building, which, by means of busses, serves the children of a large area.

Right from Hermleigh on a dirt road 6 *m.* to SAND STONE CANYON, where, on the walls, are Indian picture writings and with them the engraved names of hundreds of buffalo hunters, cowboys, and other pioneers. Many of the cattle brands of the region are also entered on the red stone face of this enduring ledger. Along the canyon floor are found thousands of small, perfectly round stones, locally called "buckshot rocks."

SNYDER, 31 *m.* (2,316 alt., 13,850 pop.), built on the slope of a hill, is modern and clean; it gins and refines cotton and cottonseed and ships cattle. When Pete Snyder established a trading post here in 1876, the lumber and merchandise were hauled overland from Dallas with seven-yoke ox teams. Around the little building sprang up a huddle of buffalo-hide huts, sheltering so many lawless men that it was called Robbers Roost. Early in the 1880's cattlemen began to establish ranches in the vicinity. Later, fence cutting warfare flared between homesteaders and ranchers. Life in Snyder became tense and partisan, an era which culminated when the sheriff was imprisoned in his own jail by cowhands. A new sheriff restored order.

Snyder is also served by US 180, State 208 and State 350. It is the seat of Scurry County, which produces 28,000 bales of cotton annually and has 49 oil fields producing 33,000,000 bbl. Southwest of Snyder 17 *m.,* via IRA, (13 *m.* on State 350) to LAKE J. B. THOMAS, (1955) Colorado River water supply for Snyder, Odessa and Big Spring, 3½ by 12 *m.,* capacity 204,000 acre-ft.

The American Heritage Museum is located in Snyder.

Left from Snyder on State 15 to GAIL, 36 *m.* (100 pop.), one of the few remaining unchanged range towns of Texas. It is the county seat of Borden

County, both the town and county having been named for Gail Borden, Texas pioneer and inventor of the process for condensing milk. Gail lies within the shelter of a protruding arm of the great plains escarpment, the Cap Rock, which here juts out into the lower prairie. It has the one street of an old-time cowtown, lined with buildings having false fronts, and with board sidewalks flanked by hitching racks.

Within the courthouse the walls of the hallways still show bullet holes from shots fired by jubilant cowboys in celebration of frontier legal victories. Cowponies stand hitched along the unpaved street, and there are more buckboard and freight wagon tracks in the powdery dust than those of automobile tires. Only when court meets are any number of automobiles to be seen here.

Gail was the scene of much activity during the school land rushes in 1902, when efforts of claim filers to maintain a position at the door of the county clerk's office until the day designated for the sale of school lands resulted in shirt pullings, as they were called. The cattlemen of the county resisted the efforts of farmers or nesters to file claims by having their cowboys forcibly eject the farmers from their places in line. This resulted in fights, some serious; however, the ranchers won and Borden County remained "cow country."

Northwest of Snyder low, rugged hills appear in the distance. Along this part of the route Indian and pioneer trails crossed and re-crossed. In the narrow, sheltered canyons Indians often made their winter camps. The way is through rough broken rangelands scarred by gullies and draws. What appears to be a low mountain range (L) are the sheer cliffs of the plains escarpment, the distinctive geological line of demarcation that winds for hundreds of miles to outline the High Plains. The gap in the rock wall is the mouth of Double Mountain Canyon.

POST, 75.1 m. (2,590 alt., 4,663 pop.) (see Tour 27), is at the junction with US 380 (see Tour 27).

The highway sweeps up a gradual grade at 78.3 m. to the top of the escarpment barrier, 400 feet above the level of the lower plains, from where a far-reaching panorama extends to the east and south.

Corrugated iron structures housing cotton gins, compresses, and warehouses fringe SLATON, 99 m. (3,040 alt., 6,750 pop.), where home gardens have great planted beds of bluebonnets. Slaton is a railroad division point.

At 105 m. is the junction with a dirt road (bad in wet weather).

Right here 4.5 m. to BUFFALO SPRINGS and YELLOW HOUSE CANYON (fishing, swimming, camp sites; fee 25¢ a day). The color of the canyon's steep cliffs in part explains its name. Fossil beds, and Indian battle grounds and camp sites are abundant. Spanish explorers came this way because of the water at Buffalo Springs. In 1877, Z. T. Williams established a sheep ranch here, and in 1884 the Western Land and Livestock Company of Iowa bought Williams' holdings and established the great IOA Ranch, whose brand became widely known. Its headquarters are three miles from Buffalo Springs. At one time the ranch measured about 13 by 40 miles. Several caved-in dugouts near the springs are said to have been the homes of early trappers and hunters.

LUBBOCK, 116 m. (see page 521) is at junctions with US 82 (Tour 3), US 87 (Tour 17) and State 116. Directly west on 116 about 30 m. is LEVELLAND, (3,523 alt., 10,000 pop.) seat of Hockley County. Settled in 1921, it is a station on the Panhandle & Santa Fe, and is as level as its name. SOUTH PLAINS COLLEGE, junior, founded 1957, enrolls 1,000 annually.

Westward US 84 enters a section that was formerly part of the great Spade Ranch owned by Isaac L. Ellwood, who with J. F. Glidden, was the first manufacturer of barbed wire; Ellwood introduced the new fence into Texas. The ranch today has 80,000 acres, stocked with Herefords. The Spade Ranch has long been known for its old-time dances, formerly attended by cowboys from several counties, who danced all night. In this region also was the vast Yellow House Ranch, part of the XIT holdings (*see Austin, and Tour 17a*).

LITTLEFIELD, 152 *m.* (3,556 alt., 8,000 pop.), is an example of the rapid growth of the comparatively new towns of the Panhandle. It was grazing ground until 1912. In 1924 a land boom increased the population rapidly. Intensive cotton production in the vicinity supports cottonseed oil mills, compress and gins. The seat of Lamb County, which has more than 360,000 acres in irrigation, it is also the shipping center for beef cattle. A number of lakes in the vicinity afford goose and duck hunting, and fishing.

The highway leads through a region where fertile land and a plentiful supply of shallow water usually result in bumper crops, to AMHERST, 160 *m.* (3,701 alt., 964 pop.), a town which came into being with the arrival of a railroad in 1923. It occupies lands once part of the Mashed O Ranch, and is near the former holdings of the XIT Ranch syndicate.

Right from Amherst on a graveled road 6 *m.* to SOD HOUSE SPRING MONUMENT, which commemorates the establishment of the first cow camp in this section of the Panhandle, at a spring 100 yards distant.

SUDAN, 168 *m.* (3,752 alt., 1,395 pop.), named for the grass that is one of the principal crops of the region, is a group of sun-stripped frame houses clustering about the main street, which is lined mostly with red brick stores. Ranches of the surrounding yucca-covered prairies support it. A general practice of this and other towns of the region is that of community sales of farms and farm produce. Tenant farmers often dispose of their household and farm goods in this manner, particularly if they are forced to find a new location for the coming year. The sales, advertised, attract buyers from long distances and are made the occasion of social, church, and neighborhood reunions, which last all day and end with the homeward-bound successful bidders driving livestock before them or hauling furniture or food in trucks.

Vast prairies sweep away on each side of the roadway, and in the distance (R), a yellowish-brown ridge marks the SAND HILLS of this part of the High Plains. This big belt of sand dunes runs east and west, dividing the county and the people. The vote in county elections, policy in school matters, and the general attitude toward life and affairs are all largely determined by whether the person lives north or south of this barrier of sand. For no apparent reason, it makes a social as well as a natural line of demarcation.

The sand hills serve as a recreational area for the people of the vicinity, particularly for hunters, and as a region of study and excavation for archeologists. Camp sites of prehistoric people are constantly being uncovered by the winds. Dove and quail hunting is excellent in the sage grass on the dunes.

MULESHOE, 182 *m.* (3,789 alt., 3,871 pop.), is at the junction with US 70 (*see Tour 12*).

Tour 22

Timpson—Nacogdoches—Lufkin—Houston—Bay City—Port Lavaca—Gregory, 382 *m.;* US 59, State 35.

Between avenues of pines, magnolias and hyacinths this route winds through the forested central and southern areas of east Texas, turning southeast to skirt the shores of the Gulf and cross the broad, treeless expanses of the Coastal Plain.

Nearness to the Sabine, across which river many adventurers and settlers entered Texas in the early nineteenth century, and to the pioneer ports of the Gulf of Mexico, made most of this region the scene of very early settlement. Spaniards and Frenchmen preceded people of other nationalities in the east Texas areas by more than a century. Southeast of Houston Stephen Austin, carrying out his father's dream of colonization west of the Sabine, directed the destinies of the first Anglo-American colony in Texas, and finally laid down his life in the cause of his new Nation.

The red, sandy hills of the pine belt and the flat coastal prairies are covered with lush vegetation caused by abundant rainfall. People largely of Anglo-Saxon stock work at lumbering, oil, shipping and other industries between Timpson and Houston; southward, cotton farming, oil and sulphur production, and livestock are the leading industries for a population largely descended from Texas' early settlers; and along the Gulf shores an Irish strain imported by colonizers of the 1820's is dominant among ranchmen, farmers and businessmen who reside in old port towns. Fishermen are largely non-Latin Americans, although a few are Italian or Scandinavian.

Section a. TIMPSON *to* HOUSTON; *167 m.* US *59*

The Red Lands, where this section of the route begins, are known in Texas history as the provincial center of settlement on the eastern Spanish colonial frontier in the seventeenth century; and later as the home of men like Sam Houston, who here recruited soldiers for the Battle of San Jacinto. Early seat of culture and scene of many a battle and rebellion, these hills of red soil long were stormy ground. Today they whine with sawmills, yield bumper crops of cotton, fruits and vegetables, and are white in May with gardenias, grown in almost every yard. Frame houses, many of the plantation type, often have chimneys made of hand-shaped bricks—the work of slaves.

Farmers in this area can buy undeveloped land at from $10 to $15 an acre, hence tenants are few; moderate prosperity is general, since crops are easily made because of abundant rains. Most of the Mexicans of the region are large land owners, descended from early-day *rancheros*.

Near Houston the industrial activity centers around oil.

TIMPSON, 0 *m.* (394 alt., 1,150 pop.), is a tomato-shipping point. In Timpson is the junction with US 84 (*see Tour 21*).

At 24 *m.* is the junction with a dirt road.

Left here to the OLD NORTH CHURCH (*open*), 0.3 *m.,* one of the very early meeting-houses of east Texas. The first church, in which several denominations held services, was erected in 1838. The present structure is a reproduction, erected in 1852 and repaired in 1936. It is a weatherbeaten wooden building, unpainted and unadorned. The furnishings are home-made benches, an altar and an old organ. The adjoining cemetery contains the graves of some of the earliest settlers.

NACOGDOCHES, 27 *m.* (283 alt., 12,674, pop. 1960; 15,450, 1965 est.) seat of Nacogdoches County, is at a junction of US 59 (lately joined by 259) and State 7 and 21. Nacogdoches is the outgrowth of the Mission Nuestra Señora de Guadalupe, established in 1716. The Nacogdoches tribe had a permanent village on the site, and beside an Indian trail the Spaniards built their mission.

One of the great tragedies of Texas history was to have a happy ending in Nacogdoches, the tragedy of the removal of settlers from Los Adaes, Spanish capital near the Sabine. On June 6, 1773, the inhabitants were suddenly given five days in which to abandon their homes, the order having been issued by the governor of the province in obedience to a command of the King of Spain. A scene similar to that described in *Evangeline* occurred as a mournful cavalcade started toward San Antonio. Graves of children marked the route. The exiles soon petitioned for permission to return. Captain Antonio Gil Ybarbo, Spanish rancher, at last succeeded in obtaining authority to remove them to the Trinity, where the town of Bucareli was founded. But the people, threatened by hostile Indians, grieved for their old homes among the friendly Tejas; and in 1779 Ybarbo took matters into his own hands and returned his people to east Texas. The site of Nacogdoches was deserted, but the buildings of the Mission Guadalupe still stood. The return of the Los Adaes exiles to this spot was the actual beginning of Nacogdoches as a civil town.

Following the Louisiana Purchase, a heavy Spanish garrison was maintained in Nacogdoches to guard the western border of the Neutral Ground. During this era the infiltration of non-Latin Americans was slow but steady, and the Magee Expedition of 1812 (*see History*) found many supporters in the town. In 1819 Dr. James Long with an army of American filibusterers took Nacogdoches. A Spanish army quickly drove them out.

The activities of Hayden and Benjamin W. Edwards (1825–26) caused friction with Mexican citizens of the vicinity. Hayden Edwards, an *empresario,* threatened to seize the lands of the old settlers unless good titles could be shown. His colonization contract was canceled, and he decided to defend the region that had been granted him. On December 16, 1826, he declared Texas independent of Mexico and named it the Republic of Fredonia. Cherokees near Nacogdoches agreed to help Edwards in return for lands. The Austin colonists, realizing that Mexico would crush the revolt, refused to aid the so-called Fredonian Rebellion; settlers of Nacogdoches also remained loyal to the Mexican government. The rebellion ended in 1827 when the Edwards brothers fled to the United States.

The petty tyranny of Colonel José de las Piedras brought about an uprising of Anglo-American settlers in 1832 and caused the Battle of Nacogdoches, which resulted in the expulsion of all Mexican troops.

Sam Houston reached Nacogdoches in 1833, Thomas J. Rusk in 1835. Nacogdoches is often credited with having financed the Texas Revolution; it fed and armed many of the volunteers who came from the United States to join Houston's army.

In 1838 Vicente Cordova, Mexican agent, promoted a rebellion among east Texas Indians and Mexicans, but it was soon crushed.

One of the earliest Texas schools was located here. Mainly because of the destruction of the plantation system the Civil War ruined the town, and it slumped into insignificance until the coming of the railroad in 1882, after which it grew steadily. In 1923 the establishment of the Stephen F. Austin State Teachers College stimulated civic progress. Nacogdoches is on the main line of the Southern Pacific, and has many dairy, poultry and lumber industries.

On Mound St. at the Nacogdoches High School is the SITE OF NACOGDOCHES UNIVERSITY (*open*), established in 1845. The brick building that housed the male department still stands. Both Confederate and Union troops used it as a hospital.

The Liberty Hotel, southwest corner of the public square, stands on the SITE OF SAM HOUSTON'S HOME.

On the left side of Main St., on Orton Hill, stands the old ORTON HOME (*open*), built in 1836 of hand-hewn planks. The timbers are held together by wooden pegs. It was on the second floor that Orton, chief justice of Nacogdoches County, kept prisoners in the "strong room," there being no jail.

On North St. is the first SITE OF MISSION NUESTRA SEÑORA DE GUADALUPE (Our Lady of Guadalupe).

There are many other interesting sites and old buildings in and around Nacogdoches, all easily accessible.

STEPHEN F. AUSTIN STATE COLLEGE, formerly Teachers, occupies a forest-like campus of 40 acres, facing North St. The main buildings occupy a slight elevation overlooking a dense forest of tall trees, formerly part of the Thomas J. Rusk estate. New modern structures have been added. The college was founded in 1923, and enrolled 4,290 students in its 1965 regular term, and 1,917 in the 1964 summer term.

On the campus of the College is a reproduction of the OLD STONE FORT. The original was rebuilt in 1907 and 1936 and is a State monument. It was first erected by Gil Ybarbo in 1779, and at various times was held by Spain, the Magee-Gutierrez Expedition, filibusters of the so-called Long Republic and the Fredonian Republic, and by Mexico, Texas, the Confederacy, and the United States.

LUFKIN, 47 m. (326 alt., 17,641 pop.), is at the junction with US 69 (see Tour 5).

At 48 m. (L) is a house made of the petrified wood found in this section.

US 59 winds now through miles of well-wooded rolling countryside. The timber is largely pine, with some oak and gum. Lumber and farming towns south of Lufkin are BURKE (300 pop.), DIBOLI, (2,500 pop.) and CORRIGAN (1,025 pop.). Five m. south of Corrigan is MOSCOW (200 pop.) site of Moscow Male & Female Academy. A narrow-gauge railway, the Moscow, Camden & St. Augustine, runs Monday through Friday to CAMDEN, 6 m. east (1,131 pop.) (Adults 50¢, children 30¢).

LIVINGSTON, 94 m. (194 alt., 3,950 pop.), is a county seat town where sawmills, oil, livestock and farm products provide industrial activity. Livingston is at one end of the Big Thicket, Woodville being at the other end on US 190.

Left from Livingston on US 190 to the ALABAMA-COOSHATTI INDIAN RESERVATION, 18 m., located in the center of the Big Thicket. It is not a village but a number of small houses scattered throughout the wooded reservation. The community center is on the old council grounds of the tribe. Here are the church, school buildings, hospital, agent's home, and cemetery. Of all the hundreds of thousands of Indians who roamed the great area of Texas, there were in 1940 within the boundaries of the State only the 290 Alabamas and Cooshattis on this reservation. The Alabamas, a tribal unit of the Creek Confederacy, came into Texas early in the nineteenth century; their early home was in an area now in the State of Alabama. They located above the junction of the Angelina and Neches Rivers, their chief settlement being at a spot now called Peach Tree Village. At that time the Cooshattis, who had entered Texas in 1807, lived in two villages on the east bank of the Trinity River.

In 1840 the Congress of the Republic of Texas appointed an agent for these tribes and voted to give each two leagues of land, including the villages in which they lived. But white men claimed the land and drove the Indians out. In 1854 the State legislature gave the Alabamas about 1,250 acres of the land they occupied, in response to a petition sent in by the Indians at the suggestion of Sam Houston. The land was purchased from the whites who claimed it, and the Alabamas moved in, but it was not until 1881 that the tract was formally deeded to the tribe.

The Cooshattis presented a similar petition to the State legislature, and although it was granted in 1856, the land was never actually located; and in 1858 the tribe was moved to share the holdings of the Alabamas. For a time, under the watchful eye of the agent, the tribes prospered. But the agency was abolished soon after the Civil War, and, left to themselves, the Indians were helpless against the actions of ruthless white men who robbed them, taking their crops and driving away their livestock.

They had only one friend, Barnet Hardin, who labored mightily in their behalf, often recovering and returning the stolen property. Their poverty became intensified with the years. It was not until 1918 that the Federal government intervened on their behalf. The first Federal allotment of $7,000 was for educational purposes, $5,000 of which was used for a school building. The years 1921 and 1924 saw additional appropriations; in 1928 the State appointed an agent, and a large appropriation was obtained from the Federal government. Tracts and grants were increased progressively.

The Indian Village on the Reservation is open daily except Sunday mornings during June, July and August. From March through May and from September through October it is open only on Saturday and on Sunday afternoon. There are available Indian foods, and handicrafts in leather, pottery, and jewelry. Indian dances are performed and tours into the Big Thicket arranged. This is a great, untouched primeval forest, filled with many varieties of flora and fauna.

The conversion to white civilization has been so complete that in dress, speech and habits the members of the reservation can hardly be distinguished as Indians. A Presbyterian minister, Rev. Dr. C. W. Chambers, who began his work on the reservation in May, 1899, succeeded in obtaining from the Presbyterians of Texas funds for a school, two churches, and a hospital.

After Livingston GOODRICH, 102 m. (300 pop.) and SHEP-ARD, 110 m. (500 pop.) are lumber towns, the latter at the edge of SAM HOUSTON NATIONAL FOREST. This huge domain of 158,204 acres, opened 1936, also entered at Cleveland and Huntsville, has excellent camping, hunting and fishing at Stubblefield Lake and Double Lake. CLEVELAND, 122 m. (6,100 pop.), junction with State 105 and 321, center for lumber and oil field supplies, is gate for the BIG THICKET section of the Forest.

HUMBLE, 148 m. (92 alt., 2,500 pop.), is a prairie town in the midst of oil wells, small truck farms and ranches. The discovery of oil in 1904 boomed Humble to unanticipated wealth that has since declined. The oil industry is supplemented by that of lumber.

HOUSTON, 167 m. (53 alt., 1,095,000 pop. est.). See article on Houston. After passing through Houston US 59 moves through the rich prairielands of Fort Bend, Wharton, Victoria, Goliad, Bee, Live Oak, Duval and Webb Counties to Laredo.

Section b. HOUSTON to GREGORY; 215 m. State 35

This section of the road is locally called the Hug the Coast Highway; it traverses the broad sweep of the Coastal Plain. (The highway becomes dangerous along the coast line during tropical storms.)

The area crossed is of historical interest to Texans; many of the towns were scenes of the Austin colony drama of the 1820's–30's. Plantation districts, with their tangled gardens, great oaks and ruins, retain some of the romance of their golden age through stories told of them. Many Negroes descended from the slaves of the early colonists till the black land fields of the section, picking huge crops of cotton in normal years; other Negroes are a big segment of the labor force in the ports.

Ranching is a time-honored occupation; cattle blending Hereford and Brahma blood graze the broad flat prairies. Most of the cattlemen are large land owners, and live in big houses in the towns. Some have oil on their lands, but this seldom causes them to forsake old haunts or old friends.

Islands of oaks on the prairies and great groves of trees along streams indicate the encroaching growth; in times of early settlement only the river bottoms were wooded. In the spring wild flowers are abundant, particularly bluebonnets and white daisies.

South of HOUSTON, 0 m., the route is through extensive oil developments.

HOUSTON INTERNATIONAL AIRPORT, 10 m., is the municipal airport for Houston and offers full facilities for the handling and refueling of all kinds of planes.

In ALVIN, 26 m. (51 alt., 7,643 pop., est.), are many gardens on shady streets. The discovery of oil in 1933 added to its prosperity. ALVIN JUNIOR COLLEGE, founded 1949, enrolls nearly 1,000.

Southward the highway is paralleled at intervals by deep drainage ditches with intersecting laterals, important in this region of more than abundant rainfall. Flat prairies sweep away on each side. Timber clings close to the many winding bayous, which are of varied size and overgrown with water plants.

CHOCOLATE BAYOU, 32.7 m., is said to have been named by Stephen F. Austin when he surveyed his first grant. It was long a route for shipping to inland points.

ANGLETON, 48 m. (31 alt., 9,300 pop. est.), is the seat of Brazoria County in the old plantation area of Texas. General Albert Sidney Johnston was one of the early planters of this section. A number of the old plantation homes remain, and the sites of others are easily located. Descendants of the Bryan and Perry families, relatives of Stephen F. Austin, reside in Angleton, as do many whose forefathers were of the so-called "original 300" of the Austin colony.

On OYSTER CREEK, 50.2 m., many of the Austin colonists chose home sites, and lavish plantations were established.

Broad fields which, according to the season, are fallow or planted with cotton or corn, line the highway. Spreading live oaks fringe the shoulders of the road and from their gnarled, widespread branches trail long streamers of Spanish moss.

At 57 m. (L) is BAILEY'S PRAIRIE, local name for this broad sweep of the Gulf Coastal Plain. Here settled J. Brit Bailey, who, according to reports, was an eccentric character. He died of cholera in 1832 and is said to have been buried, at his own request, in a standing position, facing the west, his rifle on his shoulder and a jug of whisky at his feet. The site of his grave is lost in a jungle of live oak trees, but even today Negroes of the vicinity tell of a ghostly light that sometimes flickers and dances around the prairie; they believe it to be the spirit of old Brit, guarding his own.

EAST COLUMBIA, 60 m. (34 alt., 525 pop.), on the banks of the

Brazos River, is a cluster of old residences remaining from the river town of early days of settlement. It was founded as Bell's Landing, about 1824. WEST COLUMBIA, 62 m. (34 alt., 3,525 pop.), has the contrast of antiquity in stores and residences, and newer construction as a result of oil development. Great live oaks draped with Spanish moss shade many fine houses.

In 1826, after he had laid out a town site on the Brazos, Josiah Bell cleared an avenue two miles long out into the prairie, and at its farthest end started this town, which he called Columbia. It became the capital of the Republic of Texas when Congress met there on October 3, 1836, and Sam Houston was inaugurated president. Stephen F. Austin died December 26, 1836, in the house of George B. McKinstry.

The pillared plantation house built 1836 by Martin Varner, who received this grant from the Stephen F. Austin Colony in 1824, was the country home of James S. Hogg, first native-born governor of Texas. It is the center of the VARNER-HOGG STATE PARK of 53 acres.

In the vicinity of West Columbia are the sites of homes of people prominent in the affairs of Texas before and during the Revolution and the plantation period. The sites of many are marked by old cisterns, built of bricks that sometimes show the finger marks of the slaves who made them. Such a cistern is on the site of the Josiah H. Bell residence in the southeast part of town. Orozimbo is the name of the home of Dr. James A. E. Phelps; here Santa Anna was held prisoner for six months, following his capture at San Jacinto.

Left from West Columbia on State 36 to a junction with a dirt road, 8.5 m. Left here 0.2 m. to MASONIC OAK. This huge live oak is so named because beneath its branches, in March, 1835, Dr. (later President) Anson Jones, John A. Wharton, and four other Freemasons met to petition the Grand Lodge of Louisiana for a dispensation to organize a lodge at Brazoria. The lodge, with Jones as its first Worshipful Master, was called Holland No. 36, in honor of the Louisiana Grand Master, and was the beginning of organized Masonry in Texas. Today, spikes supporting a panel fence have been driven into the ancient oak and some of its massive roots are exposed by roadway ditches.

South on State 36 is BRAZORIA, 9 m. (32 alt., 1,100 pop.), consisting of a few business houses that moved to the railroad from near-by Old Brazoria.

Left from Brazoria on a shell road 0.5 m. to OLD BRAZORIA, once an important port of the Austin colony and chosen as a town site about 1826. It was named for the Brazos River. Before the Texas Revolution, many leaders in the movement for independence lived here, including William H. and John A. Wharton. Citizens of Brazoria went by boat to participate in the Battle of Velasco (see below). The main street along the river bank was the business center. Its buildings stand empty and neglected. Ruins of the courthouse and the wagon bridge remain. Here, too, are residences built before the Civil War: frame houses with fireplaces of plantation-made bricks, and with live oak foundations.

South of Brazoria the route continues on State 36 to a junction with a graveled road, 10 m.

Right on this road, across the San Bernard River, to the SITE OF THE PLANTATION HOME OF COLONEL JAMES W. FANNIN, JR. (L.), (see History).

Southeastward State 36 is lined with live oaks. The CLEMENS STATE CONVICT FARM of 8,116 acres, 12.7 m., is on both sides of the road. At 15.9 m. is the junction with a graveled road.

Right here 3 m. to the HUNTINGTON PLANTATION, founded by J. Greenville

McNeel. It was considered one of the show places of the State until the manor house burned early in the 1890's. The overseer's house is included in the domicile of the present residents. In the yard is the old plantation bell, once used to summon slaves. Near the house are some of the old brick slave quarters. Nearby are the crumbling brick walls of the old plantation office and the great sugar house.

State 36 continues to PEACH POINT PLANTATION, 18.2 *m.*, the home of Mrs. Emily M. Perry, only sister of Stephen F. Austin. It was built in 1833 and at the request of Austin a room was erected solely for his use. Only two rooms of the Perry house remain, one the room set aside for Austin. Here is the bookcase that once held Austin's papers and his favorite books. The logs and beams of the rooms, though worm-eaten and warped, are intact, and except that the logs of the walls have been enclosed, the rooms are much as the Perrys left them.

When Austin died in 1836 his body was brought to the plantation burial ground at the Presbyterian Church in Peach Point. Here he was buried in a sarcophagus of slave-made bricks. On it there is a large coverstone bearing an inscription that tells Austin's life history. In 1910 Austin's remains were re-interred in Austin, and a statue was erected over the spot.

FREEPORT, 25 *m.* on State 36 (15 alt., 13,000 pop. 1967 est.) is a major Texas port handling more than 5,000,000 tons a year, chiefly sulphur and petro-chemicals. Its principal shipping facilities have been at Brazos Harbor since 1954. The industrialized area around Freeport is known as Brazosport and comprises Lake Jackson (11,850 pop.), Clute (5,800), Gulf Park-Jones Creek (2,000), Surfside (1,908), Oyster Creek (700) and Lake Barbara (500). Despite the dominance of sulphur Freeport calls itself the world's shrimp capital. The shrimp fleet has around 300 vessels. In May the "Fishin' Fiesta" is celebrated with a regatta and on Memorial Day weekend the Sun Fest opens the season. Deepsea fishing is popular and swimming and outings are available at Surfside and Bryan Beaches.

Freeport has one of the original Government plants for desalination of water. The Dow Chemical Co. obtains magnesium metal and magnesium compounds from sea water plants at Freeport, also lime and salt in brine, the latter used in chlorine and sodium compounds. The Ethyl-Dow Chemical Co. uses bromine, recovered from sea water, in ethylene dibromide.

Sulphur production started in 1913 at Bryan Mound, four miles southwest of Freeport, and for a while development here was rapid, as the industry flourished. When the discovery site was abandoned for another, 17 miles north-east of town, Freeport suffered a temporary decline. Extensive port improvements were completed in 1932. The Bryan and Perry families of Freeport are descendants of Emily Perry, Austin's sister (*see Peach Point, above*). About May 1 an annual regatta (outboard motor races) is held, attracting large crowds.

Left from Freeport 1 *m.*, just across the Brazos River, to VELASCO (11 alt., 755 pop.), an old town of weathered houses annexed by Freeport in 1957. Settled in the 1830's, it served as a port of entry. In 1939 the shoreline was designated VELASCO STATE SCENIC PARK.

Here the Mexican colonel, Domingo Ugartechea, refused to permit the Texans on the Brazos free passage through Velasco for a small amount of artillery needed at Anahuac, where a disturbance had already occurred between the Mexican garrison and the Texans (*see Tour 23a*). Farmers of the Velasco neighborhood, resentful because of the attitude of the Mexican officials, decided on June 25, 1832, to attack Fort Velasco. A schooner lying aground above the fort was dislodged and set afloat, and about 40 Texans were placed aboard, with ammunition and some artillery. The boat was floated down the river and moored close to the fort. About 72 Texans, meantime, marched to Velasco by land. The fort was attacked by the land forces and subjected to fire from the schooner, and after 11 hours the Mexican garrison surrendered.

The treaty that concluded the Texas Revolution was signed in Velasco between President ad interim Burnet and General Santa Anna, on May 14, 1836. In this vicinity were fine plantations established in early days of colonization.

One was Eagle Island, owned by William H. Wharton, revolutionary leader and first Texas minister to the United States.

Southwest of West Columbia State 35 continues through farms and marshland well wooded with white oak, pine, and cypress. At 66.3 *m.* is a junction. Left to SWEENY, 5 *m.,* (38 alt., 3,195 pop.) once the plantation of John Sweeny (1832), now site of the largest refinery of Phillips Petroleum Co. (95,000 bbl. a day), and the gasoline plant of the Pan American Petroleum Corp. Adjoining Sweeney is OLD OCEAN (1,100 pop.), also a refining center.

BAY CITY, 85 *m.* (55 alt., 11,656 pop. 1960, 14,000 est. 1967) is the seat of Matagorda County, a rich oil and natural gas area, where minerals have an annual value of more than $60,000,000. It ships rice, cattle, cotton, sulphur and petrochemicals. In 1964 the Port of Bay City was established with a barge channel up the Colorado River 15 *m.* from its junction with the Gulf Intracoastal Waterway. The development of the city as a deepwater port continues. The city is on the main line of the Missouri Pacific and is served also by the Southern Pacific and the Santa Fe. The new Matagorda County Courthouse was erected in 1966 at a cost of $1,600,000 and the Municipal Airport began operations in 1964. A new Public Library also has been opened. Agriculture is second in value in Matagorda County, rice being the principal crop. About 100,000 head of beef cattle, chiefly Brahma, graze on the coastal prairie.

Left from Bay City on State 60 to MATAGORDA, 21 *m.* CHRIST CHURCH, built in 1839 by a "foreign missionary" from the United States, has in use its original furnishings although the building was greatly damaged by four hurricanes.

Another of the old harbors of the Austin colony, Matagorda was officially designated as a port of entry by the Mexican government at Austin's request in 1831, and was important in colonial affairs. The town was settled in 1825. A report of Almonte, Mexican government inspector in 1834, gave Matagorda a population of 1,400 at that time. Near here, at Decro's Point, lived Samuel A. Maverick, one of the State's best known pioneers, whose name, because an employee failed to brand a herd of stock, has lived in Texas as a synonym for unbranded cattle.

Southwest of Bay City, State 35 crosses the Colorado River on a mile-long bridge and enters a prosperous ranching section.

At 97.1 *m.* is a junction with a graveled road.

Right here 1 *m.* to HAWLEY's CEMETERY, on the banks of Tres Palacios Creek. It contains the burial place of Abel Head (Shanghai) Pierce, Texas cattle king. Pierce is credited with having been among the first to plan the importation of Brahma cattle from India into Texas, to develop a hardier breed. His vast ranch, in the days before fences, was that part of the Gulf coast where his herds chanced to roam. It was said that the Gulf was "Shanghai's" only drift fence. Later the ranch included thousands of acres in central Jackson County. A statue of Pierce stands on his grave.

The grazing lands in this section were once part of the great Pierce Ranch. Today they are still cattle ranges, the broad sweep dotted here and there by windmills and water tanks.

The blue expanse of Tres Palacios Bay is visible (L) at 105.5 *m*.

PALACIOS, 114 *m*. (17 alt., 3,676 pop.) (*boats for rent; mackerel, redfish, tarpon, trout; wild ducks and geese*), center of a large fishing industry, is said to have been founded as part of Austin's colony. The schooner *Only Son* is reported to have landed supplies here at the mouth of the Colorado River as early as 1822.

The origin of the name Palacios is in dispute. Some authorities assert that it was given in honor of Felix Trespalacios, an early Mexican governor of Texas. Other sources present the far more romantic story of storm-driven Spanish sailors, their compass lost, finding safety by steering toward a mirage of three palaces that led them to the shelter of a bay which they named Tres Palacios, for the three mystic castles that had saved their lives. The town took its name from the bay.

Weatherbeaten houses of Palacios are scattered along sandy streets. Some of the buildings show scars from the batterings they have received from Gulf storms.

Palacios annually handles about 4,000,000 pounds of shrimp, 150,000 gallons of oysters and quantities of fish, the revenue from the industry totaling $400,000. Canned and dried shrimp are shipped as far as Japan, Australia, and Hawaii.

The PIER AND PLEASURE PAVILION at the bay shore, two blocks south of the business district, offer facilities for fishing, boat mooring, dancing, bathing, and cafe service.

The TEXAS BAPTIST ENCAMPMENT GROUNDS, overlooking the bay, are used by that denomination during July. At other times the cottages are available to tourists.

CAMP HULEN, 115.8 *m.*, is a Texas National Guard camp, where the 36th Division frequently holds its annual training period.

The route skirts the deep indentation of KARANKAWA BAY (the name is variously spelled on available maps), named for the cannibalistic Indians who inhabited a large part of the Texas coast line. Hostile to Spanish and American settlers, they are said to have spent their days in the leafy tops of trees where their enemies could not find them, raiding at night along the coast and the river courses. They were mainly a fish-eating people, although the bones of birds, bison, deer and human beings have been found in their kitchen-middens.

Karankawa Bay is crossed on a causeway at 128.7 *m*. This region of small bayous, channels and other indentations presents an abundance of bird life and excellent hunting for ducks and geese in season.

LAVACA BAY is crossed on a long causeway at 139.4 *m*. Along this coast, in 1685, sailed the ships of René Robert Cavelier, Sieur de La Salle. One of them ran aground in attempting passage of the bar at the shallow entrance to Matagorda Bay and was destroyed. The *Belle* sailed deeper into the bay, past Sand Point and on up to discover the mouth of a stream that La Salle named *Les Vaches* (Fr., the cows), because of buffalo grazing on the banks. Here La Salle lost two men to the Karankawas during their first night on Texas soil. He built a fortification on the bank of a stream believed to be Garcitas Creek and called it Fort St.

Louis, and in this vicinity is said to have found evidence that Spaniards had visited and stayed in the region at a much earlier date, probably about 1598. It was from Fort St. Louis that La Salle set forth on his three attempts to find the Mississippi, on the last of which he was murdered.

PORT LAVACA, 144 *m.* (22 alt., 10,000 pop. est.) (*see Tour 17e*), is at the junction with US 87.

State 35 continues across broad coastal prairies, with some areas under cultivation. On wooden bridges the highway crosses Goff's Bayou, Shallow Bayou, Frenchman's Bayou, Hog Bayou, and Schwing's Bayou. The marshes are breeding grounds for waterfowl.

The 5,420-acre body of water called GREEN LAKE is R. at 158.8 *m.* It was on its shores that Federal troops surrendered by General Twiggs at the outbreak of the Civil War gathered to await transportation north.

The GUADALUPE RIVER is crossed at 162 *m.*, only a short distance above its mouth. Woodlands close in on the road at 173.4 *m.*, presenting a wall of giant live oaks and thick underbrush. Salt cedars and oleanders have been planted to beautify the highway.

At 186 *m.* is a junction with a shell road.

Left here, past a fishing wharf and along the bay shore, to a monastery, VILLA STELLA MARIS, 1.8 *m.*, where Missionaries of the Holy Family conduct a training school and home for students and missionaries. Scattered along this road are the ruins of old Lamar, once a thriving settlement, established by Irish colonists about 1835 and burned during the Civil War. Several of the buildings, of shell-cement construction, remain. Farther along the bay shore are the picnic facilities and shelter buildings of GOOSE ISLAND, 3 *m.*, a State Park and bird sanctuary. (*Picnic and parking, $1 per car; camping, $2*).

Eastward the Federal government in 1939 purchased approximately 46,800 acres, consisting primarily of St. Joseph Island and Mud Island, for the ARANSAS NATIONAL WILDLIFE REFUGE, for migratory waterfowl. This is one of the few places in the United States where the whooping crane is known to winter. Platforms equipped with telescopes are available for bird watchers. Cranes, egrets and herons show no fear of visitors. Fishing is not allowed (*free, 8–5 daily*).

On a causeway, State 35 crosses the narrow strip of water between Aransas and Copano Bays. This is a region of excellent fishing and hunting, popular as a vacation area, especially during the summer months. During the Texas Revolution Major Isaac W. Burton, with a company of mounted Rangers, surprised and captured in the Bay of Copano a vessel that was laden with provisions for the Mexican army. While they were prevented by contrary winds from proceeding to Velasco with their prize, two other merchantmen, similarly laden, anchored nearby. Using the captured captain as a decoy, the Rangers lured the commanders of the other two ships aboard and captured them and their craft also, proceeding with all three vessels to Velasco. For this achievement Major Burton and his men became known as the Horse Marines. Tradition names Copano Bay as having for a time been the hide-out of two of Jean Lafitte's ships, following his evacuation of Galveston Island.

ROCKPORT, 195 *m.* (6 alt., 3,200 pop. 1966, est.) seat of Aransas

County, has fine fishing and swimming and thrives on the fish, shrimp and oyster industry, boat building, and its tourist trade. Some truck garden vegetables are shipped. It is a weatherbeaten town behind wind-twisted oaks and salt cedars. The Morgan Steamship Company of New York built Rockport in 1868 upon the guarantee of the King-Kenedy and Coleman-Fulton cattle companies that they would ship $1,000 worth of hides, tallow, bones and hoofs every ten days. With the development of the cattle industry it soon became a leading Texas seaport. Here were slaughter houses that handled thousands of cattle, taking the hides and rendering the tallow for shipment, and a bone mill for making fertilizer. The meat was thrown into the bay, until a packing plant was built at FULTON, 4 m. northeast (450 pop.), where the house of George W. Fulton, built 1872, is a tourist attraction. To Rockport came steamships as well as numerous sailing vessels.

General Zachary Taylor's army camped for a time at Rockport, and in commemoration of the event a large live oak near the center of the town, under which he is said to have pitched his tent, is called the TAYLOR OAK.

The MARINE LABORATORY AND AQUARIUM at the Yacht Basin (*open 8 a.m.-5 p.m.*) has tanks of live fish, mounted specimens and collections of sea shells. A field boat is maintained for scouting purposes. Established in 1935 by the State Game, Fish and Oyster Commission, the laboratory is maintained to study coastal fisheries resources, and for research into other phases of the fishing industry, including oyster farms. Supplied with constantly flowing sea water, the aquaria contain specimens of interest to researchers.

In the vicinity of Rockport are camp sites attributed to the Karankawa or Coahuiltecan culture, with sometimes an overlapping of Attacapan. Hacked and grooved human bones have been found in kitchen-middens, with fragments of other food.

Southwest of Rockport the route is along the bay shore. Yards where cement ships were built for the Federal government during World War I are at 197.7 m.

ARANSAS PASS, 205 m. (20 alt., 6,956 pop.) is in the region settled by the Irish colonists in the 1820's–30's.

It has an 18-foot sea wall, and the bay front completely surrounds the town between the north and the south limits. In addition to its thriving fish, shrimp, and oyster industry, the port is the tidewater terminus of oil companies and has petrochemical plants. In July a festival called Shrimporee, with fishing derby and queen, publicizes its principal product.

The INSTITUTE OF MARINE SCIENCE, founded 1941 as a division of the Graduate School of the University of Texas, is located at Aransas Pass. Included are a pier laboratory over the Pass, a boat house, a class-room-office building and dormitories. It maintains a trawler, or cruiser, small boats, experimental ponds, isotope facilities and a library.

Left from Aransas Pass over a long causeway and a ferry (*$1.50 round trip, 50¢ for house trailers*), to PORT ARANSAS, 5 m. (950 pop.) (*boats and tackle*

for rent; ample tourist facilities), at the Gulf entrance to the Aransas Pass opening of the ship channel. This is a fishing resort on sandy, treeless Mustang Island,
its few residences lost among the tourist lodges. Here are the United States Coast
Guard Station and the Federal Weather Bureau Office, the latter stationed at this
point to warn of hurricanes. A tarpon rodeo is held here annually.

These waters have been navigated since the beginning of Texas settlement.
In 1910 the first jetty projects were completed and in 1913 the channel had a
depth of about 20 feet. Inside the pass lies a natural landlocked harbor, four
miles long and three-quarters of a mile wide, protected by Mustang, St. Joseph,
and Harbor Islands. The white sand beach of Mustang Island, south of Port
Aransas, offers a drive along the Gulf shore; on one side are the greenish-blue
waters of the Gulf of Mexico, on the other, the dunes of this desert island. It is
possible to continue along this beach on a hard-surface road to the southern tip
of Padre Island. Here is the new PADRE ISLAND NATIONAL SHORE, 80 *m.*
long, with a good road.

West of Aransas Pass the route traverses a section of vineyards and
truck farms. Early Texas strawberries come from here. The grapes are
for making wine, which is sold at nearly all the vineyards. This is in the
vicinity of McGloin's Bluff, scene of an Irish settlement on Nueces Bay in
1832.

GREGORY, 215 *m.* (32 alt., 1,970 pop.), is a cotton shipping center
and retail market, its buildings widely scattered and set among chinaberry
trees, salt cedars and palms.

In Gregory is the junction with US 181 (*see Tour 26*).

❧❧❧❧❧❧❧❧❧❧❧❧❧❧❧❧❧❧❧❧❧❧❧❧❧❧❧❧❧❧❧❧❧❧

Tour 23

(Lake Charles, La.)—Beaumont—Houston—San Antonio—Del Rio
—Van Horn—Junction with US 62; US 90.
Louisiana Line to Junction with US 62, 831 *m.*

This route traverses the State from east to west—running between a
humid, subtropical region of deep pine forests and a land of arid hills and
limestone mountains. In the eastern part lumbering was once the chief
industry, and sawmills still whine where the longleaf pines are tallest.
Between the vicinity of Beaumont, where the Spindletop gusher of 1901
changed American economic history, and beyond Houston, oil has transformed a normally tranquil agricultural region into one of factories, many
millionaires and mansions. East of San Antonio, US 90 follows the northern edge of the rich Coastal Plain, where cotton, sugarcane, corn and
truck crops yield large harvests. West of San Antonio the highway enters
the foothills of the Edwards Plateau, thence penetrates semidesert plains
dotted with mesas and low hills where sagebrush, chaparral and cacti

grow. In the western area, vast cattle, sheep and goat ranches prevail. West of the Pecos the rugged Davis Mountains and other ranges near the Big Bend section afford ideal vacation areas. The people vary as greatly as the topography. In the inland port cities of Houston, Beaumont and Orange, are longshoremen and fishermen, as well as factory workers, planters, oil field "roughnecks," rice farmers and lumberjacks; past San Antonio, ranchmen predominate. Seafood is a chief item of diet along the eastern section of the route, to Houston; Mexican dishes are a tourist attraction in San Antonio—because of the large concentration of Latin-Americans there—and westward, barbecued beef and *cabrito* are representative delicacies.

Section a. LOUISIANA LINE *to* HOUSTON; *112 m.* ### US 90; *Interstate 10*

This section of US 90, between the Sabine River and the Trinity at Liberty, is through the Neutral Ground of the early 1800's. In this area occurred many of the important events of the Texas Revolution and the era of the Republic. Its economic development has been influenced most by enormous oil production, which has resulted in the creation of inland ports. Rice fields dot marshy lowlands, and Herefords graze on prairie pastures. The population is largely Anglo-American, with a marked French influence along the eastern part; in the central section, an occasional German community appears. Houston and Beaumont are two of the State's most important industrial centers, flanked by thriving towns and rural areas producing cotton, sugarcane, rice, corn, livestock, and varied truck and fruit crops that are processed in the near-by cities and shipped by rail and water to distant markets.

US 90 crosses the LOUISIANA LINE, 0 *m.*, 36 miles west of Lake Charles, Louisiana, parallel with Interstate 10.

ORANGE, 0.6 *m.* (10 alt., 7,472 pop. 1940; 25,605, 1960; 1966 est. with environs, 40,000) is at head of navigation of the Sabine and at its junction with the Intercoastal Waterway. A center of rice production it became a ship-building port during World War II; today steel plants build ships and offshore oil-drilling rigs; the city has about 10,000 employed. It has berthing facilities for 200 Naval vessels and is headquarters of Texas Group, Atlantic Reserve Fleet.

It is the easternmost city of Texas. A Tourist Bureau of the Texas Highway Department is stationed at the Texas-Louisiana line off Interstate 10 about 3 *m.* northeast of downtown Orange. It is open the year around.

After shipping lumber and cattle Orange prospered with rice. One of the biggest rice mills in the country was established. But subsequent deep water developments flooded irrigation canals with salt water, and the rice farmers had to turn to other crops. With the recent construction of the Orange County Irrigation Canal, this industry has been revived.

Today six of the country's major industries are represented with big plants along the mile that has been called Petrochemical Row. They include the DuPont Sabine River Works, Firestone Tire & Rubber, and Spencer Chemical Co.

From Orange westward the highway traverses an embankment, often high above the swampy marshlands. Long files of somber pines line the highway, and tall cypresses ring swamps choked with hyacinths.

VIDOR, 18 *m.* (26 alt., had 4,938 in 1960 and nearly 10,000 est.) in 1966. It profits by petrochemical industries. Its annual festival exemplifies the Good Old Days of Vidor.

Right from Vidor on a graded road to WILLIAMSON'S MORMON SET-TLEMENT, 8 *m.* This colony of Mormons is distinctive in that poverty is un-known. Each of the 30 families owns a home and pays a tithe. An annual pageant held on July 24 depicts the Mormon migration to Utah.

The NECHES RIVER is crossed at 25 *m.* Wild magnolia trees, cypresses, and swamp flowers are abundant.

BEAUMONT, 26 *m.* (21 alt., 127,800 pop. 1966, est.) (*see Beau-mont*), is at the junction with US 96.

From Beaumont US 90 proceeds west, while Interstate 10 moves south into Jefferson County, then west, touching, by means of access roads (about 2 *m.*) WINNIE (1,114 pop.), HANKAMER (200 pop.) and MONT BELVIEU (500 pop.), then Houston.

DEVERS, 57 *m.* (58 alt., 213 pop.), is a roadside group of houses, stores, and filling stations.

Left from Devers on State 61 to the old community of ANAHUAC, 21 *m.* (23 alt., 2,000 pop. est.). This town, whose interests is in oil, cattle and rice, is sometimes referred to as the scene of "The Boston Tea Party of Texas." In 1832 Anahuac was an important port of entry. To discourage Anglo-American immi-gration, the Mexican government placed a heavy duty on imports and established a customhouse. A tyrannical Kentuckian, Colonel John Davis Bradburn, was in command. At last several Texans were arrested. Fearing the escape of the pris-oners, one of whom was William Barret Travis, Bradburn had a jail built espe-cially to hold them. An armed force of colonists demanded their release. Brad-burn refused, and after some skirmishing, the colonists finally succeeded in securing Bradburn's promise that he would exchange the Texans for Mexican prisoners. They then retired to Turtle Bayou, where, on learning that Bradburn had repudiated his promise, they passed the Turtle Bayou Resolutions, which recited their complaints and declared for the revolutionary cause of Antonio Lopez de Santa Anna, who was trying to establish himself at the head of the Mexican government. Colonel José de las Piedras came upon the Texans and authorized an agreement that resulted in the colonists dispersing, the release of the prisoners and the removal of Bradburn.

No further attempt was made to collect taxes at the Port of Anahuac until 1835. Then the colonists resorted to smuggling. A merchant was arrested, and during the resulting controversy Mexican soldiers shot a bystander—a young Texan. Again the colonists rose in armed protest. This time their leader was Travis. They agreed to meet at Lynch's Ferry and march against the custom-house. Mounting a six-pounder on wheels, they boarded a sloop, the *Ohio,* and sailed for Anahuac. The commander surrendered and the garrison was allowed to depart.

Outlines of the fort are still visible on a bluff just south of the town.

Spanish missionaries erected a mission and presidio in the vicinity, seven or eight miles up the Trinity from its mouth. The mission was called Nuestra

Señora de la Luz del Orcoquisac (Our Lady of Light of the Orcoquisac), and the fort for its protection, Presidio San Agustín de Ahumada (Fort of Saint Augustine of Ahumada). They were occupied from 1756 to 1771. In 1818 a short-lived French settlement was established near the ruins of Fort Anahuac.

One of the first settlers was James Taylor White, who brought in some cattle, increased his herds with Spanish stock, and became the first Anglo-American rancher of the modern type in Texas. He drove his herds to market in Louisiana. The White home stands beside Turtle Bayou, four miles north.

The CHAMBERS HOUSE, at the southeast corner of Cummings St. and Miller Ave., a pre-Civil War building, was the home of General Thomas Jefferson Chambers, once surveyor-general of Texas and one of its first judges. According to tradition, General Chambers had the house so constructed that enemies would be forced to enter from doors on the verandas; the stairway, rising from a veranda, was circular and only one person at a time could ascend to the second floor. General Chambers was killed in the east room downstairs, by a shot fired through a window.

At 68.4 *m.* is the site of the municipality of Villa de la Santisima Trinidad de la Libertad, established on May 5, 1831.

LIBERTY, 69 *m.* (30 alt., 6,970 pop.), serves the oil, farming and ranching interests of Liberty County. Liberty sent a delegation to the San Felipe de Austin Convention of 1832, and in 1836 a company fron Liberty joined Sam Houston at the Battle of San Jacinto. It has horse shows in May and June and a Fair and Rodeo in October.

State 146 comes from Livingston to Liberty, follows US 90 to DAYTON, (3,367 pop.) for 6 *m.*, proceeds south to Mont Belvieu, crosses Interstate 10 to BAYTOWN (38,000 pop., 1965, est.). This city merged in 1947 with Goose Creek and Pelly. Its largest industry is the refinery of Humble Oil & Refining Co. (*guided tour*). LEE COLLEGE, municipal, estab. 1934, enrolls 1,800 in winter, 1,000 in summer courses.

State 146 moves by tunnel to towns on the east shore of Galveston Bay: MORGAN'S POINT (650 pop.), LA PORTE (5,200 pop.) known for its Sylvan Beach Park; SEABROOK (3,100 pop.); and LEAGUE CITY in Galveston County (2,622 pop.) to Texas City.

BARRETT, 90 *m.* (2,360 pop.) and SHELDON, 94 *m.,* both in Harris County, are about 4 *m.* south of LAKE HOUSTON, on the San Jacinto River, a part of Houston's water supply, 12,500 acres, 158,200 acre-ft.

HOUSTON, 112 *m. See Houston.*

Section b. HOUSTON to SAN ANTONIO; 204 m. US 90;
Interstate 10

This section of US 90 traverses one of the most extensively cultivated areas of the State. Farming is diversified, although cotton is the largest crop. Beef cattle are raised, and dairy farms are frequent. Well-wooded sections are found along the river bottoms, and in the early spring, when rainfall is abundant, bluebonnets cover the prairies.

With the construction of Interstate 10 between Houston and San Antonio changes have been made in the highways. The towns that follow, from Sugarland to Eagle Lake, are now on US Alt. 90. The towns from Columbus west are on US 90. Interstate runs parallel to US 90.

West of HOUSTON, 0 *m.,* the countryside is typical of the Gulf plains: flat, open prairies unbroken except for the outline of timber on the horizon, and occasional clumps of live oaks which make small green islands called mottes in Texas.

SUGARLAND, 21 *m.* (82 alt., 3,900 pop.), centers its utilitarian buildings around the tall Refinery of the IMPERIAL SUGAR COMPANY, which has a large daily capacity.

CAMP NO. 1, CENTRAL STATE PRISON FARM (L), a 5,203-acre tract farmed by prison labor, is at 21.8 *m.*

The buildings of Camp No. 4, State Farm Industries, are visible (R) at 22.3 *m.*

SARTARTIA PLANTATION (*open workdays, free*), 22.6 *m.,* covers a 2,000-acre tract devoted to the production of dairy stock and high grade milk. The dairy building, facing the highway, has large plate glass windows through which the operation of milking machines and the primary stages of milk handling can be seen. The cattle barn, of sanitary modern construction, is cooled in summer and heated in winter. Part of the plantation has been in continuous operation since the days of slave labor.

At the HARLEM STATE PRISON FARM (R), 27 *m.,* prisoners work 5,657 acres and operate a large brick plant.

RICHMOND, 29 *m.* (104 alt., 4,300 pop.), is the seat of Fort Bend County and shares with Rosenberg the industrial and marketing activities of the area, which include cotton, rice, sugar and petroleum processing, food canning, feeds. Settled in 1822 by Austin's colonists, this is among the oldest Anglo-American towns in the State. A log blockhouse was erected here at the foot of the great bend in the Brazos River.

During the Texas Revolution a detachment of Houston's retreating army, sent to guard the crossing on the Brazos, encamped at this point. Santa Anna came downstream and managed to force a crossing.

Racial and factional hatred, born of the Civil War, precipitated a state of armed politics in Richmond and Fort Bend County in 1888, as two political parties, the "Jaybirds" and the "Woodpeckers," fought with shotguns for votes and county domination. The Jaybirds were local whites, while the leading element of the Woodpeckers consisted of Northerners, who, backed by the Negro vote, controlled the county offices. For a year or more the opposing forces potshot at each other whenever opportunity was presented. The crisis came in August, 1889, when the politician-gunmen clashed in a pitched battle on the courthouse square; four persons were killed. State militia brought the war to a close, but from that time the only active political machine in Fort Bend County has been the Jaybird Democratic Association. The Jaybird Monument, at the southeast corner of City Park, commemorates the memory of the Jaybird victims of the feud.

In Richmond are three marked graves of Texas patriots. Erastus (Deaf) Smith, scout for General Sam Houston and leader of the detachment that destroyed Vince's Bridge before the Battle of San Jacinto, is buried near the Episcopal Church; and Mirabeau B. Lamar, commander of Houston's cavalry at San Jacinto and second popularly elected President of the Republic of Texas, is buried in the cemetery near the grave of Mrs. Jane Long, who is called the Mother of Texas. In the cemetery, four blocks southeast of the highway, is the Deaf Smith Memorial Monument, erected by the State.

ROSENBURG, 32 *m.* (106 alt., 10,775 pop. est.), extremely modern in appearance, has many eating places along the broad main street, where open-air markets display the produce of the region. The population is largely of German, Bohemian and Polish birth or descent. The town was founded in 1883 with the construction of the railroad.

At Rosenburg is the junction with US 59 (*see Tour 25*).

Right from Rosenburg on State 36 for 29 *m.* to State 73; R. here to SAN FELIPE, 32 *m.* (313 pop.). This shabby, weed-grown community, established in 1823 as headquarters of the Austin colony, is the birthplace of Anglo-American settlement in Texas. Today almost a deserted village of dusty, narrow thoroughfares bearing names given them in the 1820's, San Felipe was for years the unofficial capital of the first tiny settlements of colonists from the United States, who had come to this Mexican province under the leadership of Stephen F. Austin. In the neglected cemetery are the remains of many of those who dared to pioneer here. Huisache trees that are golden with bloom in the spring crowd upon old Constitutional Plaza, where SAN FELIPE CHURCH still summons the faithful by means of a mellow-toned bell, and where oil lamps and a small pump organ tell of other years.

Austin administered the affairs of his wilderness empire in a log cabin in this town, then called San Felipe de Austin. Here was voiced the colonists' first organized opposition to Mexican rule, at a meeting held in 1832. A similar gathering took place here in 1833, and in 1835 came the convention that led to an open break with Mexico. Here one of the first English-speaking schools in Texas was founded in 1829, and Godwin Brown Cotton's weekly newspaper, the *Gazette,* was launched. In 1835 the *Telegraph and Texas Register* appeared with Gail Borden as editor. San Felipe was burned in 1836 by Captain Mosely Baker, in command of a detachment of Houston's army. With 120 men, Baker resisted Santa Anna's attempts to cross the Brazos at this point, forcing him to march downstream to Richmond, thus delaying his pursuit of the retreating Houston.

San Felipe was rebuilt following the revolution. But in 1848 the county government was moved to Bellville, and the old town faded in importance. The STEPHEN F. AUSTIN MEMORIAL PARK holds many things of historical interest, including AUSTIN's LOG CABIN, a reproduction of the colonizer's home.

Near the cabin is (L) the approximate site of San Felipe Town Hall, built about 1830, where were held the revolutionary conventions. At the entrance to the park area (R) is the STEPHEN F. AUSTIN MEMORIAL MONUMENT, a heroic-size figure in bronze representing Austin seated, facing the site of the old town. The statue is the work of John Angel of New York and was dedicated on November 3, 1938. The JOHN BRICKER MONUMENT honors the one Texan killed in the revolutionary skirmish here. On the bank of the Brazos River, at the foot of former Commercio Plaza, boats that brought supplies to Austin's colonists were once berthed. A ferry similar to the kind used by the settlers still is in operation here.

The Memorial Park also contains AUSTIN's WELL, dug by the colonists in the 1820's. A 640-acre tract donated in 1937 for a State park, may ultimately contain a complete reproduction of the pioneer town of San Felipe.

West of Rosenburg the flat prairie soil is covered with farms where cotton is the largest crop. Poultry raising and dairy products are also important. Commercial gravel is excavated in this region; gaping pits mar the landscape, some deserted, others active.

EAGLE LAKE, 64 *m.* (170 alt., 3,565 pop.), is a prairie town spread around a grassy public square. Many of its brick business buildings have ornate fronts suggestive of the 1890's. It calls itself the "Goose Hunting Capital of the World" and attracts sportsmen. Eagle Lake was founded by the Austin colonists on the site of an old Indian encampment. For more than half a century it has been a rice milling center and shipping point. The adjacent lake of the same name attracts large numbers of wild ducks, and other game birds are plentiful in season.

As US Alt. 90 moves southwesterly, Farm Road 102 moves north 13 *m.* to Alleyton and US 90. From here on the towns are on US 90 (Interstate 10). ALLEYTON, 79 *m.* (188 alt., 200 pop.), was founded in 1824. Here is an Indian Burial Ground, where artifacts indicate a race that anteceded the Karankawas. Animal and human bones had been cracked to secure the marrow, suggesting that these people were cannibalistic. Southeast of Alleyton is the old Atascosita Crossing of the Colorado River, where Santa Anna and his army crossed that stream in pursuit of the Texans in 1836.

The COLORADO RIVER is crossed at 81 *m.,* a short distance above the site of Beason's Crossing, where Houston's army camped on March 19–26, 1836, while on the other side of the river, not far distant, was camped a unit of Santa Anna's army under General Ramirez y Sesma.

Along the highway, huge oaks are covered with grapevines so large that children use the branches for swings. Herefords graze in pastures where grass, in years of normal rainfall, is from one to three feet high.

COLUMBUS, 81 *m.* (201 alt., 3,656 pop.), is on the crest of a small hill amid rolling farm lands. Its graceful, timeworn residences of the plantation type of architecture are shaded by enormous oak trees, moss-draped. A massive stone courthouse is surrounded by tall magnolia trees. Flower beds line the highway; nearly every house has its garden. Columbus was founded in 1823 by members of Austin's colony, assisted by Baron de Bastrop. In 1835 a local company was sent to join Houston's army at Gonzales.

In the center of the street that runs along the east side of the courthouse square stands the COUNTY COURT LIVE OAK, a giant tree under the spreading branches of which the first civil court of Colorado County was held. On the southwest corner of the courthouse square is an old brick water tower, built in 1883 and long the town's only water supply. It became a meeting place of the local chapter of the United Daughters of the Confederacy. On the courthouse lawn is the rusting anchor of the *Moccasin Belle,* an old river steamboat that once carried cotton from Columbus to Galveston.

BORDEN, 90.5 *m.* (293 alt., 25 pop.), is the weatherbeaten, sleepy remnant of a once thriving community that grew up around the meat processing plant established by Gail Borden, surveyor, publisher, and scientist. The plant manufactured a meat biscuit, made by boiling beef juices and whole wheat flour, which was said to have a food value of ten times its weight in fresh beef ration. This product met with strenuous opposition from the meat packers, and was a financial failure. England, however, awarded Borden a medal for it in 1851.

SCHULENBURG, 104 *m.* (344 alt., 1,207 pop.), has high sidewalks and neat, comfortable buildings in the tradition of its founders, German and Bohemian colonists, whose descendants still own the farm lands that encroach on the wide, busy streets around the prim public square. Flour made from cottonseed, used in the treatment of pellagra and diabetes, is milled here.

At Schulenburg is the junction with US 77.

WAELDER, 127 *m.* (367 alt., 1,270 pop.), whose white church steeples dominate the town, is surrounded by red barns, tall silos and patches of fields. At dusk the men of the town drive cows homeward along the quiet shady streets.

At 145 *m.* is the junction with State 97.

Left on this road to PALMETTO STATE PARK (*picnicking facilities, supplies*), 5.6 *m.* This area of about 500 acres, which derives its name from its abundance of palmetto palms, has been described as a bit of subtropical jungle set down in the temperate zone. Mud geysers, white and yellow sulphur springs running cold, warm and hot, floating islands, bogs, swamps, Indian artifacts, fossils, rare and beautiful flowers, ferns, mosses, shrubs, pines and other trees are abundant, as are numerous kinds of insects, birds, and reptiles. An old Spanish trail is said to have run along the edge of the swamp and across it at one place, and there is a tradition of a band of fleeing Indians who sank to their deaths in the quagmire. The park is open for picnics and nature study, some swimming, but without special facilities.

GONZALES, 14 *m.* (300 alt., 5,829 pop.), an oak-shaded town sprawled in the valley of the Guadalupe River, spreads out from two public squares which adjoin diagonally. Magnolias bloom in spacious grounds. On Saturdays, Mexican and Negro farm laborers throng to town, crowding the general merchandise stores. Gonzales was settled in 1825 by James Kerr, who, with a party of six men, was seeking a site for the capital of the colony of Green DeWitt. It was named for Don Rafael Gonzales, then provisional governor of the Mexican province of Coahuila and Texas. In 1826 Indians almost destroyed the settlement. Between Gonzales and the coast lay the lands of the DeLeon colony, peopled with Mexicans, and boundary disputes between the two groups caused much trouble. Mexican authorities favored DeLeon's people, thus causing bitterness that smoldered for years and finally burst into flame in 1835.

The Mexican government had given a small brass cannon to Gonzales to be used against the Indians. When a Mexican corporal and five men were sent from San Antonio de Bexar to remove the gun, the *alcalde,* Andrew Ponton, sent a message begging "to be excused from delivering up said cannon," and at the same time dispatched messengers to the nearest settlements, calling for help. Four days later scouts from Gonzales reported the advance of a Mexican cavalry force of about 100 men.

The Mexicans advanced to the west bank of the river (September 20, 1835), and demanded delivery of the cannon. Lieutenant Castañeda of the Mexican forces was told that the *alcalde* was absent, an excuse that delayed action. The Mexicans were unable to cross over, as all available boats had been hidden. There were then only 18 men in Gonzales, but recruits from other communities soon began to arrive. A Mexican soldier swam the river to demand the cannon and was rebuffed. A monument on the river bank commemorates the famous 18.

The Texans decided to attack; their blacksmiths hammered out a few crude round shot from bar iron, and cut trace chains into short lengths to serve as loads for the cannon, which was dug from its hiding place in a peach orchard and mounted on the wheels of an oxcart. A flag was made of white cotton cloth, bearing a crude drawing of the cannon and the words, "Come and Take It." That night the Texans with a force of about 150 men crossed the river and, hidden by a heavy fog, advanced upon the Mexican camp. At daylight (October 2, 1835), a messenger appeared, to say that the Mexican force had no orders to fight. The Texans replied that it must fight or surrender. A fruitless parley between the leaders followed; as it broke up, the fog lifted, disclosing the Mexican cavalry drawn up in battle array on the brow of a low hill. Then the colonists opened fire—the first shots of the Texas Revolution. The little brass cannon roared again and again, while behind it stood a tall bearded man waving the flag with its taunting challenge. Only one Mexican was killed, but the remainder started for Bexar. The Gonzales Historical Museum, St. Louis and Smith Sts., has a replica of the famous cannon.

At Gonzales, following this battle, the first Texan revolutionary army, which later captured San Antonio, was organized. In March, 1836, Gonzales made the only reply to the appeal of Travis from the Alamo for reinforcements, when its "Thirty-two Immortals" marched to join the doomed garrison. They are honored by a monument erected 1936 at the Gonzales Memorial Bldg. After the Alamo Houston in Gonzales ordered evacuation, burning the town in retreating.

Opposite the courthouse the Heroes of Texas Independence Monument, created by Pompeo Coppini, honors Gonzales' fighting sons of the Revolution.

Another monument at Confederate Square honors the Confederate dead. The affair of October 2, 1835, is celebrated annually with Come and Take It Day, which winds up with naming the Queen of the Lexington of Texas, as Gonzales is called.

LULING, 150 m. (418 alt., 5,000 pop. est.), noted for its broad main street, is the active center of a large oil producing area, with several fields in its vicinity. Oil well supply houses and loading and storage tanks along the railroad—which bisects the town—and piles of pipes, contrast strangely with the time-mellowed brick business houses.

Luling was founded in 1874, and for about two years was the terminus of the railroad. As a wild town in early days, it had its boot hill and knew such notorious gun fighters as John Wesley Hardin, Ben Thompson, and "Texas Jack." It also had its purely local celebrities of the same ilk with such picturesque sobriquets as Rowdy Joe and Monte Joe. Luling throve for a time as a cattle center, and a cattle trail passed just east of the town. During early days it also had the railroad end of a freight road to Chihuahua City, Mexico.

Following its lively youth, the community lapsed into quietude until the discovery of oil in 1922. In 1926, Edgar B. Davis, a former Massachusetts man who had discovered and developed the field and become a citizen of Luling, sold his oil interests in this vicinity for $12,100,000 and immediately gave bonuses to his employees. Among management officials he divided approximately $1,250,000, and to all other employees he gave graded amounts for the same total. He established the Luling Foundation Farm with a $1,000,000 endowment, and gave the town two clubhouses with grounds.

Luling is at a junction with US 183 (Oklahoma to the Gulf via Austin). N. 13 m. on US 183 to LOCKHART, (6,084 pop.) seat of Caldwell County and 4 m. from Lockhart State Park.

Between Luling and Lockhart is the SITE OF THE BATTLE OF PLUM CREEK, 8.3 m., a battle that broke the power of the warring Comanches in this section.

In August 1840, returning from a successful raid on Linnville and their attempt to sack Victoria, the Indians, impeded by loot, including captives and horses, were proceeding slowly. At Plum Creek they were overtaken by the combined commands of Colonel "Old Paint" Caldwell, Colonel Ed. Burleson and others, all under the supreme command of General Felix Huston. The unit was a detachment of the Texas Rangers, and its roster included many names afterward famous in Texas history, such as Ben McCulloch, Henry McCulloch, Monroe Hardeman, Captain Jack Hays, and Alsey Miller. In the fight that followed the Indians were decisively beaten. Many warriors were killed, and captives and stolen horses recaptured. The whites had but seven wounded.

At 150.6 *m.* on US 90 is a junction with an unpaved road.

Left on this road along the western outskirts of Luling to the LULING FOUNDATION FARM (*open, free*), 0.3 *m.*, a demonstration farm that has been of incalculable value to Texas farmers and students of up-to-date farming methods and economics, not only by its classes and demonstrations but by its operations to increase inexpensively the quality of stock on private farms.

The purposes of the foundation are stated in the charter drafted by Edgar B. Davis, the doner, in 1927, which says that, "said Foundation is created as an Institution of free public learning and of purely public charity and the property herein conveyed shall never be used or operated with a view of profit to any person, but the net income derived from such property and money shall be used, operated and expended only and solely for free educational and purely charitable purposes; all without distinction of race, party, sex, creed, or poverty or riches of the recipient." The farm of 1,223 acres has departments devoted to dairying, poultry, sheep, beef cattle, swine, pecans, general farm practice, terracing, silos, farm extension work, exhibits at county fairs, balanced farming programs, new crops, distribution of farm products, and investments. A registered dairy herd and the most advanced dairying methods have given the foundation very high ratings for certified, pasteurized milk. Fine bulls are kept, and through 35 "bull circles," operated in the foundation's early days, the quality of dairy herds in this part of Texas has been greatly improved. This department sells dairy stock for breeding purposes at a minimum cost.

Turkeys of breeding stock number 2,000 or more, and by a system that produces earlier hatching the baby turkeys acquire greater growth before the dangerous hot weather, with the result that an exceedingly low death rate is maintained and healthier, larger turkeys are produced. Approximately 2,000 laying English White Leghorn hens are maintained during the hatching season, and baby chicks and eggs sold to producers at market prices. Thus, farmers may sell their own poultry and eggs, and with the proceeds buy the foundation's registered stock. Trap-nested hens lay 200 eggs or more a year.

About 1,700 bearing pecan trees have been developed. The foundation has handled the selling of the pecan crop for many growers of the section, securing higher prices than individual farmers would have obtained for themselves.

The foundation has demonstrated the worth of terracing, proper fencing, rotation of crops, check dams, contour plowing, and other means of improving the land. Trench silos have been built at a cost of $15 each, and one accomplishment has been the successful ensilage of alfalfa. These and other features are demonstrated on field days, held regularly and open to any person interested.

In 1934 a program for schooling and training young men, ranging in ages from 17 to 22 years, was inaugurated. In a year's course, the youths, whose average number is 20, spend three months each on the dairy farm and poultry farm, and six months doing general farm and livestock work. Night schools cover a course of kindred subjects. In addition to tuition they are given a small salary.

Some of the projects conducted in the late 1960's were: Beef cattle gain evaluation tests; small grain variety tests, cooperating with Texas A. & M.

University; cross-breeding program using purebred Charolais, Charbray, Angus, Santa Gertrudis and Hereford sires on commercial cows to determine the most profitable cross at weaning time; grain sorghum variety tests; fertilizer tests on different pastures and crops to determine the most profitable rate of application, and application of herbicides for control of brush and weeds in the improvement of pastures. This data is recorded and passed on to the farmers and ranchers of the area by Field Days.

Westward US 90 crosses the narrow valley of the San Marcos River, 153.5 *m.*, to proceed through an agricultural region where the farm houses often bear the stamp of old age, even the smallest boasting a stone or brick chimney, denoting an old-fashioned fireplace within. Log barns and other log outbuildings are frequent.

SEGUIN (pronounced Seg-een'), 171 *m.* (553 alt., 15,000 pop.), is brisk with prosperity induced by rich farm lands and local processing industries, including flour, foods, aircraft supplies, fiberglass cloth, structural steel. It is the seat of Guadalupe County, major producer of hogs; also dairy products, cotton and oil. Yards in summer are fragrant with roses and spicy pinks. Pecan trees, native and planted, are abundant. Seguin is attractively situated beside the Guadalupe River, which affords excellent fishing, swimming, boating, and other recreational features that attract large numbers of visitors.

The town was named for Colonel Juan N. Seguin, who commanded the only detachment of Texas-born Mexicans in the Battle of San Jacinto. The first permanent settlement was founded here in 1838 by Southern planters and named Walnut Springs, the name being changed later to honor the Texas patriot, whose home, adjoining the site of the town, was sacked and burned by the advancing army of Santa Anna in 1836. A portrait of Colonel Seguin hangs in the courthouse. In the 1840's and again in the 1870's German immigrants came. Many descendants of early settlers occupy the homes built by their ancestors. The MAGNOLIA HOTEL, corner of Crockett and Center Sts., long a stopover point on the stage line, was constructed in 1840 and added to in 1850. Here Ranger Captain Jack Hays married a Miss Calvert, a descendant of Lord Baltimore.

Through local enterprise Seguin has been expanding its facilities. The new Seguin-Guadalupe County Public Library on E. College St. was donated by local families. The county entered on a $20,000,000 highway development, which included a bridge over the Guadalupe River and improvements to the County Airport. Seguin is on the main line of the Southern Pacific. It holds the Oil Scouts Golf Tournament in June and Bankers Golf in October, and is the home of Texas' Lefthanded Golfers.

TEXAS LUTHERAN COLLEGE of the American Lutheran Church is implementing a $13,000,000 building program, starting with its new Students' Union. A $500,000 grant from the Moody Foundation of Galveston is the base for the Moody Science Hall. It enrolls more than 800 students a year.

LAKE McQUEENEY, 3 *m.* west on Farm Road 98, covers 396

acres and is impounded by Abbott Dam on the Guadalupe River. It is publicized as the Water-Ski Capital of Texas.

SAN ANTONIO, 204 *m. See San Antonio.*

Section c.   SAN ANTONIO to DEL RIO; 154 m.   US 90

This section of the route leads almost due west, entering the hills of the Edwards Plateau, where numerous communities had their beginning in frontier fortifications erected to protect the settlers from Comanches and Apaches. Past these wooded hills, US 90 pierces part of the brush country of Texas, thence passes over alkaline plains dotted with chaparral, or serrated with rock-ribbed hills or mesas. Between the Medina and Frio Rivers are the pioneer settlements of Count Henry Castro, French colonizer of the 1840's. Throughout the area, tiny *jacales* with accompanying patches of chili peppers and beans bespeak the presence of Latin-Americans. Mexican labor predominates. The remainder of the population, west of Hondo, is largely Anglo-American. Only a small proportion of the people live in towns or cities; far-flung ranches claim the majority. By 1930 the sub-humid Edwards Plateau, together with the trans-Pecos area beyond Del Rio, had 83 per cent of the sheep and 90 per cent of the goats in Texas. Farming is limited to irrigated regions or to alluvial land near streams.

West of SAN ANTONIO, 0 *m.*, the country rolls away on each side of the highway in low mesquite-covered hills. Oaks, pecans, and cottonwoods line the water courses.

The MEDINA RIVER (*boats for fishing; camp sites; swimming*) is crossed at 24.5 *m.*

CASTROVILLE, 25 *m.* (787 alt., 1,700 pop.), is a bit of old Alsace, transplanted to the Medina River. It preserves the charm of an Old World setting in a progressive community, where many who work in San Antonio dwell in "rural tranquility." Despite the four-lane highway and the airport where private planes land daily, Castroville cherishes the thick-walled, high-roofed houses with their tall dormers and long, arcaded galleries, which crowd close to the street, weatherbeaten and mellowed by time, unchanged since the days when their builders hewed their stones and timbers from available rocks and trees and erected homes like those in the Alsatian province.

Although more than one hundred years have come and gone, the people of Castroville are little removed from their ancestors, the mixed group of Alsatians, French, Swiss, Germans, Austrians, Belgians, Hollanders, and Scandinavians who founded and developed the community. The Alsatians, however, predominated and, since they arrived first, determined the character of the town. The national traits, habits, and customs of the founders still prevail. There is a modern touch in the filling stations along the highway and the gleam of electric lights, but in many respects the resemblance to an Alsatian village is remarkable.

Castroville is not a suburb. Like Hondo it transacts business for the farming interests of Medina County, where more than 100,000 acres are producing vegetables, alfalfa, corn, grain sorghums, oats, tons of cabbage, potatoes, lettuce. This is beef country too, for more than 50,000 head of cattle and nearly 20,000 head of sheep and lambs graze on the pastures. Some of the farmers still follow the European custom of living in the town and going to the country to tend their fields and herds. There are frequent dances, picnics, barbecues. On church feast days, these celebrations are usually open to the countryside. A forthcoming marriage is occasion for quilting bees for the prospective bride, and at these and other social functions old-fashioned feasts are served, notable for French and German cooking.

Castroville was founded in 1844 by a group of colonists under Count Henri de Castro (who, however, signed all papers Henry Castro), and was named in his honor. Castro, a French Jew, first visited Texas in 1842. He found the young Republic eager to give away large tracts to anyone who could bring settlers, and the dream of a vast colonization plan came to him. Through the French Legation he met President Sam Houston and other government dignitaries, and secured a colonization contract.

He obtained his first recruits in Alsace, and in November, 1842, a party of 114 men, women, and children sailed for Texas. Their arrival was followed by many disappointments. Castro remained in Europe, and it was not until July of 1844 that he at last joined his colonists at San Antonio. Their number had dwindled sadly. Many, discouraged and disheartened, had abandoned the party and of the original group there remained but 27 who, in September, 1844, loaded their plows, pots, pans, and bedding on oxcarts and headed westward into the uncharted wilderness. They toiled through the entangled growths of scrub oak and mesquite until they reached the Medina River. This stream they forded at a spot where the highway bridge now crosses, and camp was made in the grove of pecan trees on the west bank. Many of the stately trees of this grove still stand. The promised land was reached, but the newcomers found themselves confronted by the stupendous task of converting virgin wilderness into farms and homes.

All the vicissitudes of pioneering were suffered by the first colonists and their successors. The drought and subsequent famine of 1848 nearly wiped out the colony. Mothers beat the thickets for birds' eggs to feed their children and the parish priest even dined on rattlesnake. One year clouds of insects came down from the sky and ate up all crops. Then an epidemic of cholera prevailed for six weeks, with many fatalities. There were also threats of Indian attacks. One townsman was felled in his own yard by Indian arrows. One old tombstone bears the legend: "Gross killed by Indians."

Grateful for their deliverance, the survivors gave thanks to God by building a new church. The priest went to New Orleans for funds and returned with the money needed. The church was built of sawed stone and hewn timbers and measured 65 by 40 feet. It was dedicated to King Louis Philippe of France.

A canal that moves south through Castroville comes from Lake Medina, 30 *m.* north (5,575 acres, 254,000 acre-ft. capacity). The Lake controls the flood water of the Medina River. Two farm villages between Castroville and the Lake are Riomedina and Mico. A smaller rock dam at Castroville, which provides swimming and fishing, is a relic of the days when the old GRIST MILL, still standing, served the community. The river has bass, catfish and perch. The adjacent fields offer hunting for deer, dove and turkey.

When the Southern Pacific Railroad was surveying for its right of way in 1880 it asked Castroville for a subsidy of $100,000. The town refused and the roadbed was moved aside 5½ miles, the legal distance required. The railroad then passed through Hondo. In 1892 Castroville, the county seat for 44 years, lost the seat to Hondo after a bitter fight. In 1897 the town voted to give up its corporate structure. In 1948 it renewed its incorporation. It cherished its quiet isolation until surveyors for the great highway ran their lines across some of the ancient houses. Four pioneer structures have been demolished for the highway, among them the Laurent Quintle house on Alamo Street, built in 1850.

The former VANCE HOTEL was renamed the Landmark Inn in 1945. It was built in 1846 as a store and dwelling for Caesar Monod, who in 1854 sold it to John Vance, who added the second floor. The walls are 22 inches thick. The house served as postoffice and hotel until the late 1870s. There are accommodations for tourists. A fee is charged for a tour of the inn. The SIMON HOUSE, in the yard, was the bath house of the Vance family. There was a water reservoir on the second floor and tradition says its lead lining was melted down to make bullets for the Confederates.

ZION LUTHERAN CHURCH, was erected in 1854 at Florrela and London Streets. It was the first public school and often children slept in the balcony when there was fear of Indian attacks. This building was demolished to make room for a new church. The original pews, constructed with wooden pegs, were removed to the present LUTHERAN YOUTH BUILDING across the street, a pioneer house of Alsatian type.

One of the largest buildings in Castroville dominates the highway between Angelo and Amelia Streets. This is the MOYE ASPIRANCY, a two-story rock structure, now a private boarding school for girls of high school age who aspire to enter the religious life. Here in 1869 two Sisters of the Order of Divine Providence opened the first Roman Catholic parochial school west of San Antonio. The parish priest gave his rectory to the nuns for their convent dwelling. In 1873 the present Moye building was erected. The Order moved to San Antonio in 1896 and established Our Lady of the Lake College there. From 1938 to 1959 the Moye Military School for Boys used the quarters.

The CHURCH OF ST. LOUIS (*open daily*), Angelo St. between Paris and Madrid Sts., was completed in 1868. It is an imposing structure in modified Gothic design, of stone and buttressed walls, narrow, mullioned windows, and a corner-buttressed stone tower with a high spire. Over the altar stands a statue of the patron, Louis of France, clad in ermine and velvet trimmed with embroidered fleurs-de-lis. The First Church, built in 1847, was restored by the Castro Colony Historical Association in 1933. It now stands on the grounds of the Moye Aspiracy.

The JOSEPH CARLE RESIDENCE AND STORE (*visited by arrangement*), N. corner Angelo and Madrid Sts., built in 1850, is of French provincial design, with a narrow balcony across the front at the second story. It is one of the largest structures in the community. The former TARDE HOTEL (*visited by arrangement*), S. corner Florrela and Madrid Sts., now a private residence, was noted for its excellent French cuisine. Erected in 1859, it is another example of Alsatian design. The P. F. PINGENOT HOUSE (*visited by arrangement*), W. corner Lorenza and Petersburg Sts., is of whitewashed plaster over rock, having a roof steep in front and gently sloping in the rear. This house was built in 1850. The L. L. WHITE HOUSE, Washington St. between Naples and Mexico Sts., is the ruin of a two- and one-half-story dwelling of French provincial design. White, who had suffered because of his northern sympathy during the Civil War, established a settlement of former slaves on his land near Hondo. In the cement tomb, near the house, White and his favorite horse are buried.

The XAVIER WAGNER HOUSE, built 1855, contains many authentic pieces of furniture, china and glass used by the pioneers.

The Castroville Garden Club makes biennial pilgrimages to historic homes, the most recent in 1968.

CROSS HILL, also called Mount Gentilz, on the continuation of Lafayette St., SW. of Castroville, is sometimes used for commemorative saint-day ceremonies. For some years on Rogation Days, three days before Easter, a solemn pilgrimage would be made from the Church of St. Louis to a large wooden cross, bearing a life-size figure of Christ. Some residents make the pilgrimage to Cross Hill at intervals, alone or in small groups. It is steep-sided and 125 feet high. Ruth Curry Lawler, author of *The Story of Castroville,* writes: "To anyone it is an inspiration to climb to the crest of the hill, and to look away to the farmlands, laid off like patterns in a pieced quilt, and then to look below at the quiet, peaceful village. One feels that perhaps Castroville still possesses something that the busy world outside has lost."

West of Castroville US 90 climbs out of the Medina River Valley and skirts the edge of the great south Texas brush country, a gently rolling plain where thorny trees and bushes are often so thick that penetration is impossible until a path has been hacked out. Many of the people of this area are descendants of colonists imported from Central Europe by Count Castro; their language is a mixture of French and German. Among old customs that have survived is that of the *Niüe Yar Granz* (New Year Ring). On the eve of the holiday women bake a pastry wreath made of lightbread dough, decorated with sugar and spices, and present it to parents or god parents. Another New Year custom is that of thoroughly cleaning the houses, to—as one venerable housewife expressed it—"get out all the old year's dirt to make ready for the new." Black-eyed peas are served on New Year's Day, for to do this, according to an old belief, is to be assured sufficient money in the twelvemonth ahead.

HONDO, (deep), 41 *m.* (887 alt., 4,992 pop.), is notable for its weathered stone and brick buildings, shaded by large hackberries and live oaks. It was named for the Hondo River. Hondo City was incorporated in the 1890's, but the incorporation was dissolved because of expense to the taxpayers. Commercial establishments, by popular subscription, finance the paving of certain streets, and provide for street lighting. Hondo, the County seat, has prospered as a trade center for farm and ranch products; it processes pecan seeds, foods, makes brick and tile. A new postoffice and hospital are recent constructions. So well administered have been the town's affairs that never has it been necessary to ask for large contributions. The population is predominantly of German descent.

At 48.8 *m.* is a junction with a graveled road.

Left on this road to OLD D'HANIS, 0.3 *m.*, a drowsy village of weathered houses. It was founded in 1847 as the second settlement of the Castro colonists (*see above*)—then on the extreme edge of civilization, with no settlements between it and the Rio Grande. In 1849 the Government established Fort Lincoln two miles north of town to protect it from the Indians. The coming of the railroad caused the town to be moved, most of the citizens rebuilding beside the railroad at the present town of D'Hanis. Descendants of those who stayed here still occupy the fine old Alsatian type houses built by their ancestors. The people are clannish but neighborly; they gather in beer gardens, and frequently have dances. They are contented; they like their old houses, old wash pots and homemade lye soap, blood sausage and curd cheese. Their homes usually have billowy feather beds, rag rugs, wax tapers, and stiff family portraits.

SABINAL, 62 *m.* (956 alt., 1,747 pop.), has many old stone stores that lend character to an otherwise colorless business district. The town was founded in the 1850's when a little group of buildings was erected around Camp Sabinal, a temporary army post. The name was taken from that of the Sabinal (cypress) River, which skirts the community's western edge. Giant cypresses grow along the banks of the stream. In 1881 Angora goats were introduced into the region. The industry thrived, and today the area surrounding Sabinal produces a large part of the Texas mohair crop. There are several dude ranches in the vicinity. Fishing for perch, bass and catfish, and hunting for deer, turkeys, quail and doves, are available.

Right from Sabinal on State 127 to a junction with US 83, 21 *m.*; R. here to GARNER STATE PARK, 29 *m.*, named in honor of John Nance Garner, Vice President of the United States, 1933–1941. Here is a recreation area of 478 acres, on the west bank of the Frio (cold) River. Tourist lodges, riding stables, bridle paths, hiking trails, and facilities for fishing and swimming are being developed. In the park is a natural cave 75 feet deep. Deer, wild turkeys, quail, doves and chachalacas (Mexican pheasants) are plentiful.
North from Sabinal on State 187, 10 *m.* to the scenic SABINAL CANYON, 30 *m.* long, and UTOPIA, recreation center. Garner State Park is 20 *m.* west; to the east is the "Dude Ranch Capital of the World."

The SABINAL RIVER (*fishing for bass, perch, catfish*), 63 *m.*, is a turbulent little stream which rises in the hills to the north. Here (L) stand PETERS' STORE, an old stone building built in the 1870's. On the R.

is a house erected at about the same period by Peter Rheiner, father-in-law of Vice President Garner.

The Frio River is crossed at 73.3 *m.*, just below where it emerges from FRIO CANYON, an ideal vacation area. Swimming, fishing, riding, and camping facilities abound, the last ranging from camp sites to modern tourist lodges and guest ranches.

UVALDE, 84 *m.* (913 alt., 11,500 pop. est.) is at the junction with US 83 and State 55.

The route now winds around and over brush- and timber-covered hills. Cenizo, greasewood, huajillo, catclaw, and Spanish dagger are abundant. The ash-colored cenizo is covered in the spring with blossoms ranging in color from lavender to deep purple. Bees thrive on the blooms of these semidesert plants; the honey industry is large. This is chiefly goat ranching country.

The NUECES (*pecans*) RIVER (*camp sites, fishing for bass, perch, catfish*), is crossed at 91.1 *m.*

At 96.1 *m.* is the junction with a graveled road.

Left on this road to BLEWETT, 3.6 *m.* (500 pop.), site of the Uvalde Rock Asphalt Company's No. 2 Mine. Deposits of asphalt in the vicinity cover an area of 50,000 to 60,000 acres. The formation is in scattered pools similar to oil deposits, with occasional outcroppings which were worked to some extent as early as 1888. The annual production of high grade commercial asphalt from these beds has ranged from 1,250,000 tons at peak production, to 125,000 tons in recent years.

BRACKETTVILLE, 123 *m.* (1,100 alt., 1,822 pop.), seat of Kinney County, a center for ranch and farm products, owes its origin to the establishment of an Army post nearby in 1852, first called Fort Riley, and later Fort Clark, honoring Major J. B. Clark, who was killed during the Mexican War.

The fort for many years was an infantry and cavalry post. It dominates the town, its oak-studded reservation extending along the highway. The first permanent buildings were erected in 1857. Fort Clark was abandoned by United States troops in 1861, and except for a short period of Confederate occupancy was without a garrison until 1866. Indians had taken full advantage of the interval of the Civil War, and the soldiers of Fort Clark had great difficulty in restoring peace. Officers once stationed here included Robert E. Lee, George S. Patton, Jr., and J. M. Wainwright. Fort Clark was in military use during World War II and later became a guest ranch.

The reservation covers 3,693.2 acres. Buildings are for the most part of stone. In the old post cemetery (no longer in use), 102 of the 146 graves are marked "Unknown" and are those of freighters, immigrants, and settlers found dead on the surrounding plains.

About 75 per cent of the civilian population of Brackettville is of Mexican or Negro origin, many of the latter descendants of Seminole-Negro Indians who formed a scout detachment attached to Fort Clark in the days of its Indian troubles. The Seminoles came from Mexico after exile from Florida. As long as the Seminole detachment remained in army service they were quartered on the Fort Clark reservation, but with their disbandment moved to the outskirts.

The ALAMO VILLAGE, 6 *m.* north of Brackettville on Ranch Road 674 is a solid reconstruction of San Antonio's historic fort and a Mexican village, built 1959 for John Wayne's film, *The Alamo.* The owner of the ranch has developed a tourist attraction here with food and souvenir shops, and attacks by desperadoes.

DEL RIO, 154 *m.* (948 alt., 18,612 pop.), a blend of modern hotels and aged adobe *jacales,* of *Americano* ranchmen and copper-colored peons, of sleek automobiles and plodding burros—a city on the Rio Grande— was founded by "ditch-digging" farmers in the valley of the San Felipe River, which flows from San Felipe Springs (named by Spanish missionaries for King Philip VIII), a short distance above where the town was later located. For a time the settlement was San Felipe del Rio (Saint Philip of the River).

It was discovered that sheep and goats would thrive on the brushy vegetation of the surrounding hills, and today about ten million pounds of wool and mohair are shipped from here annually. The cultivation of wine grapes, grown on irrigated lands near the Rio Grande and along San Felipe Creek, is another important industry.

WHITEHEAD MEMORIAL MUSEUM occupies the original trading post (1870). LAUGHLIN AIR FORCE BASE is 6 *m.* E. of Del Rio.

Across the International Bridge is CIUDAD ANCUNA, Mexican town where President Mateos of Mexico greeted President Eisenhower on Oct. 24, 1960. On this date the towns unite in the Fiesta de Amistad. Acuna has souvenir shops, restaurants, bullfights. (*Four killer bulls; children free*). No passports required.

On the eastern outskirts of the city, one block right of Avenue O, are SAN FELIPE SPRINGS, which supply farmers with water for irrigation. The presence of these seven springs, which gush forth in the desert country through craters as large as dug wells and flow at the rate of nearly fifty million gallons daily, has never been satisfactorily explained by geologists. It is thought that they flow from some great subterranean river. Near San Felipe Springs is the U. S. CAMEL CORPS WATER HOLE, where camels drank in 1857. They had been introduced by Secretary of War Jefferson Davis.

The GRAVE OF ROY BEAN, "Law West of the Pecos," noted justice of the peace of Langtry (*see below*), is in Woodlawn Cemetery on the western edge of Del Rio. Bean's grave is a block west and a block south of the main entrance.

Section d. DEL RIO *to* JUNCTION WITH US 62;
361 m. US 90

This section of US 90 climbs and twists across a barren region that ascends until the Davis Mountains, wreathed in purple haze, appear; and beyond these, near the New Mexico Line, the peaks become higher and more rugged, the terrain wilder and lonelier. On each side of the highway, the semi-desert acres of sheep and goat ranches roll away in vast estates of greasewood-dotted plains and mesas. At intervals, ranges of distant mountains form dim blue barriers across the skyline, or encroach close upon the roadside. The area is replete with tales of the hardships of early settlers, who wrested this lonely land from the Apaches only after long bloody years. In these western solitudes, the ranchman who drives 50 miles for his mail or a loaf of bread is the rule rather than the exception. The people meet annually at numerous county fairs, frequently traveling many miles across counties.

West of DEL RIO, 0 *m.,* US 90 winds up into barren hills. At 5 *m.* is the junction with US 277 (*see Tour 10*).

The highway passes through a rock cut at 11.7 *m.,* and slides down into the DEVIL'S RIVER CANYON. Left, at the eastern end of the bridge which spans the stream, a stairway has been cut into the side of the rocky hill, the summit of which, 75 feet above the river, is an excellent observation point. Here the river has cut a path through the gray and white rock to varying depths of several hundred feet.

AMISTAD LAKE, one of the largest reservoirs in the Southwest, has been filling up for several years behind Amistad (Mex. friendship) Dam, 12 *m.* upriver from Del Rio, at the confluence of the Rio Grande and the Devil's River. When full the lake will cover 87,400 acres and hold 5,325,000 acre-ft. of water for irrigation and flood control. This is an international project and Texas' share will be 43,200 acres and 2,992,-600 acre-ft. The lake will back up 85 *m.* and cover 135 sq. m., and at some points it will reach to the horizon. The dam is 235 ft. tall and 6 *m.* long. The waters of the lake will reach a smaller Devil's Lake formed by the dam of the Central Power & Light Co. Along that lake was Lake Walk, a section named for the company's district manager, Sam H. Walk. The fine fishing there is expected to be continued a few miles farther north. Here bass, crappie, perch and catfish are readily available.

CASTLE CANYON, 13.8 *m.,* gained its name from the fluted, cylindric columns of gray and white stone that stand out from the canyon walls, in some places towering above its rim like the crumbling towers of a castle. This marks the eastern edge of the sotol region. Sotol, a low-growing plant with stiff leaves having sawtooth edges, was once roasted by the Apaches and the trunks used for food. Mexicans make a fiery liquor from its roots, and soap from the same source.

COMSTOCK, 30 *m.* (1,550 alt., 319 pop.), sun-baked, compact town, was long known as Sotol City. Its patrons are mostly sheep and goat ranchers. The community is unusual in its chosen form of outdoor recreation, which consists of running mountain lions with dogs. The big cats are numerous, preying on herds of sheep and goats. One puma has been known to kill as many as 25 sheep or goats in one night.

This region was once the habitation of cave dwellers. Today archeologists excavate the shallow caves of the canyon walls, where those ancient people made their homes. Fiber baskets, bones, implements, weapons, beads, and other articles have been unearthed.

SEMINOLE CANYON is crossed at 38.5 *m.*, a rocky cleft running north and south. The walls of the canyon have cave shelters that have yielded evidences of extensive occupation by the West Texas Cave Dwellers. Close to the canyon is a series of caves along the Pecos River, with rock shelters in the canyon walls. The entrances to most of these are characterized by the presence of deep mortar holes, indicative of long use, and by stones worn smooth by the tread of countless feet. Seminole Canyon and Pecos River caves are on private property, inaccessible without guides, and can be visited only after permission has been obtained from owners.

The highway suddenly dips over the rim rock in a steep grade at 42.9 *m.* Descending to an iron bridge, it crosses the Pecos River deep down between the rocky walls of the PECOS RIVER CANYON. The gray and yellow stratification of the towering narrow ramparts is broken here and there by shallow caves and irregular, perpendicular cliffs. The Pecos was discovered by Fray Agustín Rodríguez in 1581. During the middle years of the nineteenth century it marked the boundary between law enforcement and outlawry, the territory west of it being peopled with reckless white men and maurauding Apaches.

Climbing out of the canyon of the Pecos, US 90 heads again westward through a maze of barren hills.

At 48.4 *m.* is a junction with a graveled road.

Left on this road to a little HILLTOP PARK, 0.3 *m.* The roadway winds steeply to the crest of the hill, where an improved parkway presents a superb view of the surrounding country. East, about two miles away, is visible the widely known PECOS HIGH BRIDGE, on which the tracks of the Southern Pacific Lines cross the Pecos Canyon, 321 feet above the river, on one of the highest railroad bridges in the world. North and west sweep vistas of rugged hills, while to the south rocky crests hide the canyon of the Rio Grande and the International Boundary Line.

SHUMLA, 49.7 *m.* (1,412 alt.), is a huddle of small frame buildings beside the highway. The Pecos River and the Rio Grande are within a mile of the hamlet, and their waters offer excellent fishing.

About a mile south, straight across a pasture but inaccessible except when accompanied by guides, are the SHUMLA CAVE SHELTERS, which line the steep walls of the canyon of the Rio Grande, where men once lived beneath overhanging rock ledges and cliffs and in caves made by erosion. These ancient inhabitants of a semi-desert area left layer after layer of debris in their cave houses. Some of the sites are now inaccessible except by rope ladders, as the canyons are from 300 to 500 feet deep, and often the shelters are halfway up these rugged limestone walls.

Here in 1933 an expedition of the Witte Memorial Museum of San

Antonio excavated caves, the contents of which revealed the culture of a sedentary people who had left behind caches of seeds, including squash. That the West Texas Cave Dweller held this territory continuously for centuries is indicated.

Burials taken from this area include an infant mummy, and remains of an adult fisherman whose broken net was made of twisted sotol fibers. His woven fur-cloth robes enclosed a fiber pouch containing 49 articles of daily use. A distinguishing relic of these people is the rabbit stick, a grooved wooden club manipulated on the principle of the Australian boomerang. Infant burials have been found beneath crudely made cradles intentionally broken, presumably by mothers, 2,000 to 8,000 years ago.

LANGTRY, 61 *m.* (1,315 alt.) with less than 100 people, was a construction site when the Texas & New Orleans Ry. was built in 1881.

Left from Langtry on a graded road to OLD LANGTRY, 0.5 *m.,* a venerable hamlet now in the far stages of decay, about which volumes have been written. Here still stands the frame building, restored, which housed the SALOON OF JUDGE ROY BEAN, one of the Southwest's best known characters. Above the steps leading to the front porch, a weather-beaten sign, its letters still legible, proclaims that here once ruled "Judge Roy Bean, Law West of the Pecos."

Out of the maze of tradition surrounding Roy Bean a few facts emerge. He led an adventurous life, including a few years as a pony express rider and others as a freighter on the old Chihuahua Trail. Finally he followed the railroad construction camps as a saloon keeper, as the Southern Pacific pushed across Texas. At the construction camp of Vinegaroon he had at first a tent saloon, then, as a more permanent community developed, this building. He was duly elected to the office of Justice of the Peace, but to this title he added "the law west of the Pecos." The latter position he filled with one law book and a six-shooter, rendering witty, unorthodox, prejudiced, but sometimes wise decisions, defying higher courts and scandalizing jurisprudence. Between "trials," and not infrequently in the midst of one, Roy would take his place behind the bar to serve the thirsty. He frequently fined culprits a round of drinks for the crowd. Numerous stories are told of Judge Bean, but probably the most typical of the man is his famous ruling that he could find no Texas law which prohibited killing a Chinaman. In addition he fined the dead Chinese, for carrying a weapon, the $40 which, in addition to a pistol, had been found on the person of the corpse. Tradition says that he renamed the community for Lily Langtry, the famous actress, and the name "Jersey Lily," inscribed in her honor, is still visible over the doorway of the saloon. Tradition says that Bean wrote to Miss Langtry, asking her to visit the town. The actress did visit it, holding the train that bore her special car until she had seen the barroom-courtroom named in her honor, although this was after the judge had died and had been buried at Del Rio.

In 1939, $8,000 was appropriated by the State for the restoration of the saloon, and for the creation of a park around it.

West of Langtry the route continues through rough, barren terrain. Loysier Canyon is crossed at 78.1 *m.* The highway climbs slowly to the level of a high plateau, across which it passes in a straight line. A blue bulk far to the south is a haze-shrouded range of high peaks in Mexico. Without warning the highway rounds a little knoll and skirts the brink of SANDERSON CANYON.

SANDERSON, 121 *m.* (2,775 alt., 2,300 pop.), in a deep canyon, one wall of which rises over the main street, is sun-burned and Stetsonhatted. In early days it was a wild frontier town. Outlaws roamed the mountains and canyons of the Big Bend country to the southwest, and trafficked in "wet" herds, stolen in Mexico and driven across the Rio Grande, often at the old Comanche Crossing deep in the Big Bend.

With the arrival of the railroad came more citizens, more saloons, and more trouble. For a time Roy Bean owned a saloon here. Other characters of the day were "Uncle" Charlie Wilson, the town's founder in the 1880's, and the Reagan brothers, principals in the story of the Lost Nigger Mine. A Negro who had been sent to round up some stray horses, returned not with the horses, but with his pockets full of rocks. The brothers cuffed him for disobedience and drove him from camp, not realizing then that the rocks he had found were rich gold ore. The Reagans are said to have spent a fortune trying unsuccessfully to find the missing Negro.

Sanderson is a repair and crew change point on the Southern Pacific, with large railroad shops and yards. The town ships sheep, cattle, wool and mohair.

At 122 *m.* is the junction with US 285 (*see Tour 28*).

Westward, mountains loom closer on the southern horizon—the peaks of the Bullis Gap Range (3,100 alt.). Far ahead other ranges appear. Those to the left are the far-flung ramparts of the Big Bend wilderness, those directly ahead, the first of the ranges that form the mountain barrier of the trans-Pecos area. The highway winds from a shallow canyon, climbs an eroded, rock-littered ridge, traverses the top of an almost level mesa and dips into San Antonio Creek Canyon. The Haymond Mountains (4,200 alt.), run obliquely southwestward, toward the higher peaks of the Peña Blanca Range (4,520 alt.). A wide, shallow valley extends between the Peña Blancas and the still loftier ridges of Woods Hollow Mountains (4,661 alt.). Northward, on the horizon is the jagged mass of the Glass Mountains (6,311 alt.) ; to the left is Cathedral Mountain (6,521 alt.).

MARATHON, 175 *m.* (4,039 alt., 500 pop.) on the direct route to Big Bend National Park, for many years was the supply center for the vast ranching country extending almost across the 5,935 square miles of Brewster County, covering the Texas Big Bend.

The guayule (Mexican rubber plant) once supplied an industry here, but tariff conditions lowered the price.

In Marathon is the junction with US 385. About 50 *m.* south of Marathon on US 385 is Black Gap Wildlife Management Area of 100,000 acres. Fishing in the Rio Grande, but no hunting.

Mountains crowd still closer to the highway as the way leads westward. On the right the steep face of Cathedral Mountain lifts in lofty spires, while to the left a ripple of lesser ranges rolls away to the Santiago Mountains (6,521 alt.). The Del Norte Mountains (6,151 alt.) sweep down from the south in a long, almost unbroken range, before which the lesser triangular mass of Dugout Mountain (5,195 alt.) stands sentinel-like in advance of the frowning ramparts of the greater range.

At 197 *m.* is the junction with US 67 (*see Tour 18*), which merges with US 90 for 34 miles.

ALPINE, 206 *m.* (4,481 alt., 4,740 pop.), cradled in a valley between towering mountains, is dominated by the hilltop campus and buildings of its college. Shade trees line its paved streets, at the end of which the desert begins. Its business district is modern. Alpine was founded in 1882 with the coming of the railroad. North and south lie large State parks, and the nearby canyons and ranges afford good hunting. Dude ranches are numerous. Gold, silver, copper, lead, quicksilver, marble, zinc, coal, and potash are found in the region.

Alpine retains its western tang, a quality stamped there by the high-heeled boots of cattlemen thronging the streets. The region is called "Cow Heaven," and Highland Herefords raised in the vicinity are in great demand. Cattle barons of the fiction type actually reside in Alpine, operating their huge ranches by making occasional trips of inspection. Sheep and goats as well as beef cattle graze the vast ranges.

SUL ROSS STATE COLLEGE crowns the heights that rise east of town. Its older buildings are of red brick in classical design, while those of more recent construction are of rock in modified Spanish architecture. They are placed in a semicircle on the terraced campus.

Sul Ross was opened by the State in 1920 as Sul Ross Normal College, named for Lawrence Sullivan Ross, noted Indian fighter and Governor of Texas from 1887 to 1891. Until 1923 it operated as a junior college. In that year the names of the normal schools were changed by the legislature to State teachers colleges, and Sul Ross inaugurated courses leading to the bachelor degree. The college is coeducational and has a regular term enrollment of more than 1,360 students, with a summer enrollment of more than 1,474 and a faculty of 240. Its graduate school has courses leading to the master's degree.

On the campus is the BIG BEND HISTORICAL MEMORIAL (*open*), home of the West Texas Historical and Scientific Society. This museum has many thousands of specimens, including fossils, relics of pioneer times and historical importance, and flora and fauna of the Big Bend area. Of special interest is the exhibit of West Texas Cave Dweller material.

Near the college campus on the northeast is Kokernot State Park, an area of 38 acres enclosing the Burgess Water Hole, a spring long the watering place of Indians, explorers, soldiers, immigrants, freighters, and stagecoach passengers.

At Alpine is the junction with State 118, which leads to Big Bend National Park at Maverick.

Right from Alpine on State 118 to the town of FORT DAVIS (4,927 alt., 850 pop.) the "Mile-high City." North of town is FORT DAVIS NATIONAL HISTORIC SITE, 447 acres, under the National Park System since 1963. Built 1854 and abandoned 1891, the Fort was occupied by Confederates in 1862 and by U. S. Negro cavalry after 1867. It helped oppose Comanche and Apache raids. In 1861 a lieutenant and 13 men were ambushed and killed. The Apache were finally routed in 1880. Fort Davis had 50 buildings, some of which have been restored.

Left from Fort Davis 5 *m.* on State 118 to DAVIS MOUNTAINS STATE PARK. Here a recreational area of 2,130 acres presents the rugged beauty of upper LIMPIA CANYON. The park area recently has been improved to offer numerous tourists features, including stopover facilities, hiking, swimming, and horseback riding. Archeological remains in the Davis Mountain region include pictographs on rock walls or in cave shelters.

The main peaks of the Davis Mountains include MOUNT LIVERMORE (Baldy Peak) (8,382 alt.), SAWTOOTH MOUNTAIN (7,748 alt.), PINE MOUNTAIN (7,700 alt.), BLACK MOUNTAIN (7,500 alt.), BLUE MOUNTAIN (7,330 alt.), and EL MUERTO (dead man) PEAK (6,749 alt.).

In seasons of sufficient rainfall wild flowers are abundant. From orchids on Mount Livermore to maguey and sotol on the plains, the flora is as startling as the terrain. Cacti present a great variety. Animals native to the region include white- and blacktail deer, bears, pronghorned antelopes and panthers.

State 118 continues to MOUNT LOCKE (6,791 alt.) on top of which is the WILLIAM J. McDONALD ASTRONOMICAL OBSERVATORY of the University of Texas, named for its donor. It owns 400 acres. When dedicated May 5, 1939, its 82-in. reflector telescope, with a mirror weighing 3 tons, was the world's second largest; in the next decade it became the seventh largest. In 1967 the Observatory completed a new 105-in. reflector, the world's third largest, after Palomar and Lick. There is a 36-in. reflector for stellar photometry. The Observatory has a close working arrangement with the University of Chicago. Visitors are admitted on Saturdays at 1:30 p.m. and on Sundays at 2:30 and 3 p.m. Visitors may peer through the big telescope on the last Wednesday of the month from 8:30 to 10 p.m., after applying by mail to the Observatory, Fort Davis, Texas, and enclosing self-addressed, stamped reply envelope. Groups are limited to 200.

West of Alpine US 90 winds through Paisano Pass (5,070 alt.), highest point on the highway between Del Rio and El Paso. Left looms the cone-shaped summit of PAISANO PEAK (5,750 alt.), and to the right is TORONTO MOUNTAIN (5,350 alt.).

Beyond the pass the route leads across hills almost barren of vegetation. Cactus splays its grotesque, angular shapes against the red, yellow, and white of earth, rocks and sand. Sage fills the hollows with a purple haze.

Far to the right rise the sharp peaks called TWIN MOUNTAINS (6,500 alt., and 6,700 alt.), and beyond to the west is the irregular, twisted mass of the Puertacitas (little doors) Mountains (6,000 alt.).

The high plateau over which the route passes spreads southward from the Davis Mountains and is a remnant of great lava flows.

MARVA, 232 *m.* (4,688 alt., 3,400 pop.), a treeless, jacal-fringed town with a green park around its railroad station, was founded in 1884, and is active in the shipment of cattle and mohair. Among historic sites is old Fort D. A. Russell. Here also is the highest golf course in Texas.

Glider plane amateurs and builders since 1963 have come to the Marfa Soaring Camp to launch sailplanes. The Junior Rodeo, first weekend in June, and the Old-Timers Team Roping, in May recently have won popularity.

Hunting for deer, bears and mountain lions is available, with permits from ranchowners.

US 67 leaves US 90, turns south to Presidio.

Westward the route traverses a wide, high valley. On the left the skyline ridge is called Cuesta del Burro, the scattered rocky crests of which approximate 6,000 feet. To the right is the huge bulk of Mount Livermore, while left of it, and more distant, is El Muerto Peak. The Van Horn Mountains (5,786 alt.), cut obliquely northward to converge (L) on the highway. On the north the mountains recede before the opening of another wide valley from the northeast.

VAN HORN, 306 *m.* (4,010 alt., 2,000 pop.) (*see Tour 19e*), is at the junction with US 80 and Interstate 10, which provide a major highway to El Paso. US 90 now yields to State 54, which heads north up the broad arid valley that lies between the frowning rampart of the Sierra Diablo (6,513 alt.) on the west and the Delaware Mountains (5,870 alt.) on the east, traversing one of the most desolate yet weirdly beautiful stretches of country to be found in Texas. The view sweeps almost level reaches, gray-green with sage and greasewood, dotted here and there with prickly pear, yucca and ocotillo. Beyond the middle distance a streak of blazing white gleams (R) like a hazy silver ribbon. It is the crystal-encrusted shoreline of a salt lake. On the horizon the ragged crest of the Delawares looms stark against the sky. Closer at hand, the sheer wall of the Sierra Diablo rises (L). Somewhere in the tangle of ridges and deep narrow canyons of this range are mines, lost and active. Gleaming white salt lakes appear. Far ahead lifts the blunt nose of the Guadalupe Range where it shoves its triangle of lofty peaks across the State Line from New Mexico. Higher and bolder loom the broad cliffs.

At 361 *m.* is the junction with the combined US 62 and US 180, west to El Paso, thence northeast to Carlsbad Caverns National Park in New Mexico.

❧❧❧❧❧❧❧❧❧❧❧❧❧❧❧❧❧❧❧❧❧❧❧❧❧❧❧❧❧❧❧❧❧❧❧

Tour 23A

Marathon—Persimmon Gap—Big Bend National Park; US 385.

This is a tour that leads straight into Big Bend National Park and then follows the Park roads through the mountain ranges and across the original grasslands and deserts to the Rio Grande with its huge, awesome canyons. Established June 12, 1944, this amazing Park of unspoiled natural phenomena covers 708,221 acres, the larger part of Brewster County, itself so sparsely settled that it was once said to have only one inhabitant to a square mile. Into constantly deepening solitude and ruggedness the Park road leads into a region unequaled in the United States for opportunities to experience days and nights in the wilderness, which has been practically unchanged through the centuries of man's history.

US 385 is one of the major highways of Texas. It proceeds in a straight line from Oklahoma through the Panhandle west of Amarillo, Lubbock, Midland, Odessa and Marathon to the north entrance of the Park at Persimmon Gap. The west entrance of the Park is at Maverick, reached on State 118 from Alpine, 81 *m.* away, which is accessible by US 90 and US 67. Alpine and Marathon are served from east and west by Continental Trailways and from the north by Trans-Pecos buses. From San Antonio it is 410 *m.* to Park headquarters via US 90 to Marathon and then US 385. From El Paso it is 323 *m.* to Park headquarters via Interstate 10 to Van Horn, thence US 90 to Alpine. For the west entrance motorists also may travel to Marfa on US 90, thence south to Presidio on US 67, thence 70 *m.* to a road connecting with State 118.

Although it is customary to speak of the Big Bend area as isolated and practically untenanted, there have been attempts at ranching and village life since the Apache and Comanche Indians stopped their damaging raids. Several large ranches were staked out for raising Herefords, and adobe houses were put up along the short sandy beach of the Rio Grande at San Vicente. The intrepid driver who moved over the dirt roads before the Park came was able to get hospitality at the ranches and gasoline at rural stores such as one at Castolon on the river. The Mexicans who lived on the American side of the Rio Grande were as dependent on the bare natural resources as the pioneers. There are still immense ranches in Brewster County, notably the Stillwell Ranch east of US 385 and the Santiago Mountains, and there are Mexican habitations as primitively furnished as those once on the terrain of the Park. Only the hardiest of men and women braved the loneliness of desert ranches. Virtually all native houses were made of adobe bricks. The Mexicans made what they needed from the materials at hand. Cottonwoods grow along the river; pinons, ash and oaks are found in the mountains. The Mexicans transported timbers on burros, and whittled out their own crude beds, tables and chairs. Food was raised in little cultivated patches, with beans and corn the principal staples; grain was threshed by running burros over the hardpacked earth. Goats were essential; they furnished milk, meat, and hair from which blankets and rugs could be woven, hide for shoes and water bags; even playthings for children, carved from their bones.

MARATHON (4,039 alt., 500 pop., est.) is at the junction of US 385 and US 90, 57 *m.* south of Fort Stockton (*Tour 24c*). This is the last place for outside motel accommodations for those driving to Big Bend National Park. It lies in what is geologically called the Marathon Basin, an ancient sedimentary deposit at the foot of the Glass Mountains. This is the heart of Brewster County. Brewster was named for Sam Houston's secretary when it was sliced from the adjoining Presidio County. The highway follows the trail used by Spanish explorers as early as 1583.

Using a separate route from midtown in Marathon the visitor proceeds to a cattle gate of the Combs Ranch, 3 *m.*; R. through the gate, to old CAMP PENA COLORADO (red rock) (sometimes called Fort Peña Colorado), 3.7 *m.*, near Peña Colorado Springs and Rainbow Cliffs. Established in 1879 as a subpost of

Fort Davis (*see Tour 23d*), it remained in use until 1892. It was built to hold in check the Mescalero Apaches who harassed the Chihuahua Trail. Later the old post housed the headquarters of the Circle Dot Ranch, and the ruins were still being used by G. C. Combs, ranch owner, in 1940. Remaining are the old officers quarters, the corral, and a cemetery.

US 385 leads toward the dim blue bulks of distant mountains. Far to the south, at 6.5 *m.,* looms SANTIAGO PEAK (6,521 alt.), loftiest summit of the Santiago Range. Indians used this eminence as a lookout, and artifacts are found in the old Apache camp site on the flat top of the peak. There is a tale that a Mexican settler of El Paso del Norte in early days pursued a party of raiding Apaches to the peak which now bears his name, and was killed. According to the story, the Indians buried him at the foot of the mountain as a token of respect to a brave man.

At 10.3 *m.* CABALLO (horse) MOUNTAIN is visible. The grove of cottonwoods about GARDEN SPRING, 12.8 *m.,* was planted in 1881.

The honey industry, a growing one in the County, is represented by an apiary at 14.1 *m.* Bees in this area are more traveled than those of other sections; their owners transport hives from one area to another, in search of the desert blossoms productive of honey. Whole apiaries are placed on trucks and "herded," as the bee owning ranchmen express it, sometimes for long distances.

At 23.6 *m.* (R) is the Santiago Chain (average alt., 4,500), a part of the broken backbone of the Rockies, which enter Texas from New Mexico on the 32d parallel and extend south into Mexico. Their eastern range divides Brewster County, through which the tour passes, into equal parts. Across the Rio Grande, the Santiago Range is called the Del Carmen Mountains. The area to the right is Toboso Flats, so named because of the prevalence of buffalo or toboso grass. From a distance, and at certain times of the day, these flats appear to be an expanse of water.

The bare reddish patches on the sides of a lava peak (L), 25.6 *m.,* are iron-stained igneous flows. On the skyline, looming above the ramparts of the Santiagos (R), is the flat-topped summit of Y E MESA (4,740 alt.), named for the old cattle brand of the Buttrill Ranch.

MARAVILLAS CREEK is crossed at 36 *m.*

Far in front is visible SENTINEL PEAK, 60 miles across the Rio Grande, but a landmark in the Big Bend. This was another, Indian lookout, and is one of the Fronterizas (frontier) Mountains. To the left of Sentinel is NEEDLE PEAK, one of the Picotera (pointed) Mountains. The famed Lost Nigger Mine (*see Tour 23d*), is thought by some to be in the Picoteras. In this vicinity, desert willows grow in creek beds. Their blossoms are lavender and bell-shaped, and appear after every rain, regardless of the season.

The twin black peaks of DOVE MOUNTAIN (3,790 alt.), appear (L). South of Dove Mountain is CUPOLA PEAK (3,925 alt.), while at the north is YELLOW HOUSE PEAK (3,363 alt.).

ENTRANCE TO BIG BEND NATIONAL PARK

PERSIMMON GAP, 41.5 m. (2,971 alt.), is a pass in the Santiago Range and the northernmost gate to Big Bend National Park. Here US 385 becomes the fine primary road of the Park, patrolled by Park Rangers.

Through this gap came the Comanche Trail, blazed by raiding Indians from the South Plains on their way to Mexico. It extended south from Horsehead Crossing on the Pecos River, past Comanche Springs (Fort Stockton), to the Comanche Crossing of the Rio Grande. Pieces of petrified trees, said by geologists to be two hundred million years old, have been used in landspacing this spot. This area is a natural botanical garden, containing many plants of the Big Bend region: lecheguilla, sotol, creosote, cenizo, huisache, all-thorn, guayule, black-brush, cacti of many varieties, and wild persimmon.

From this vantage point is obtained the first good view of the distant Chisos Mountains (average alt. 7,000). High, many-colored, and hazy, they bulk in a serrated mass on the horizon to the southwest. Their misty appearance, due to an atmospheric haze, is given as one interpretation of their name—that it is derived from an Apache word meaning ghostly. Another possible derivation is from the Comanche word for echo. The Chisos are part of the Rocky Mountain system; they cover approximately 40 square miles and are noted for their vivid coloring—blue, red, purple, and yellow—and for their ruggedness. In long-past geologic ages they were thrust up through sedimentary limestone beds, and today present a cluster of major and minor peaks which dominate the tip of the Big Bend. Erosion from this uplift has covered the adjacent desert with rubble; the limestone is not again exposed until it outcrops in the walls of three great canyons which the Rio Grande has carved for itself through intervening rock ranges.

In 1933 the Texas Legislature established Texas Canyons State Park. It was intended to make accessible and preserve for public use the three immense canyons of the Rio Grande—Santa Elena, 3,661 ft. above sea level at the rim, with the river bed 2,145 ft.; Mariscal, 3,775 ft. at the rim, and at the river bed 1,925 ft.; Bouquillas, 3,500 ft. at the rim, and at the river bed 1,850 ft. Such wonders were not to be seen anywhere in the world. The U. S. Congress acted in 1935 to authorize a national park, but when no progress was made Texas in 1941 appropriated $1,500,000 for the area. In a little more than a year all but 25 sections had been purchased. In 1944 the Federal Government was ready to develop a national park and Texas voted to transfer its holdings. On June 12, 1944, Big Bend National Park became a part of the National Park Service, Dept. of the Interior.

The Park Service established headquarters at PANTHER JUNCTION, 29 m. from Persimmon Gap, and erected an Administration Building there. It built good roads, improved old trails and added bridges and tunnels where needed. It eliminated grazing and moved out the ranchers and the crumbling settlements. The old village of San Vicente on the American side of the river faded from the map. Instead, near Boquillas, the Park Service erected Rio Grande Village, a modern, fully equipped area for tourist camping.

ADVICE FOR VISITORS

Information: At Park Administration Building, Panther Junction. Post Office in the building, mail deliveries Monday through Friday. A descriptive pamphlet, *Big Bend National Park,* may be had from the Supt. of Documents, Government Printing Office, Washington 25, D. C. (15¢).

Fees: No charge for entrance, but for campground use. The annual permit is the Golden Passport, valid at all Federal recreation areas, April 1 through March 31, $7. Admits individual holder and those who accompany him in a private vehicle. Day use permit, $1 for group, 50¢ for individual. Fees apply to persons age 16 or older.

Transportation: Highways are named at opening of chapter, Tour 23A. Airline, Continental Airlines to Midland-Odessa. Car rental service.

Accommodations: Motels, cottages and trailer sites are operated by National Park Concessions, Inc., at prices approved by the National Park Service. Reservations are advised. Address it at Big Bend National Park, 79834, or phone GR 7-2291, area code 915. Chisos Mountain Lodge, central building opened 1966, accommodates more than 100, all year. Also lodge and stone cottages. Service station, supplies, minor repairs. Panther Junction has service station with sundries and groceries. Castolon has a frontier store with gas, oil, groceries. Rio Grande Village has service station, camp store. There are 7 trailer sites at Panther Junction and 24 at Rio Grande Village, with utilities.

Activities: Evening illustrated programs by Park naturalists or Rangers; see bulletin boards. Interdenominational religious service in the Chisos Basin, fall and winter; also at Rio Grande Village campground. First aid and ambulance at Park Headquarters.

Camping: Groups must make reservations, but individuals are first come, first served. Chisos Basin has camp stoves, tables, water; 14-day limit, June 1–September 10, other months, 30-day privilege. Rio Grande Village has similar accommodations and a 14-day limit. January-April, other months 30 days. Bring own wood or buy charcoal.

Fishing: Rio Grande only, all year from Park side. Ponds and springs are reserved for rare species. Fishermen may use pole and line, rod and line, trot and throw line; minnow seine must not exceed 20 ft. in length. Limit, 25 per person per day or in possession, minnows for bait not counted. Permit is needed before using boat. No fishing license needed.

Horseback trips: Regular all-day trips to South Rim, $15 for one, less for more riders. Trips to Window, half day, $6 for one, less for more riders. Hourly riding, $2.50 per person. Pack trips by arrangement. For information, write Chisos Remuda, Big Bend National Park, 79834, Texas, or phone GR 7-2374, area code 915.

Precautions and Regulations: No firearms or hunting permitted. No collecting of rocks, plants or animals. Swimming in Rio Grande is dangerous because of undercurrents, holes, quicksand. Rock climbing is unstable and generally treacherous. The public is advised to carry drinking water on trails and in the desert, to carry first-aid supplies, including tweezers for extracting cactus

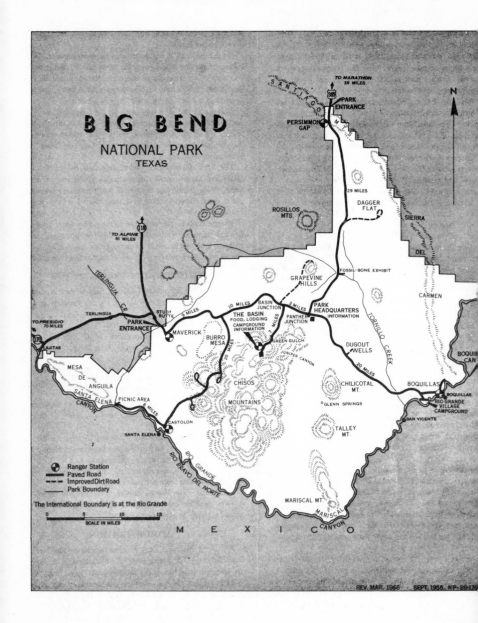

spines, and to stay on trails with flashlight after dark to avoid rattlesnakes (the Bend has four varieties). Pets must be kept on leash.

The main Park road is a continuation of US 385 and of what was State 227 before the change. Some of the former trails are gone, but the natural phenomena noted by the geographers for the original edition of this *Guide* can be seen from the Park roads.

Southeastward the road crosses Bone Spring Flats, and (R) at 43.3 *m.,* is BONE SPRINGS, once a marsh or seep in which cattle in great numbers bogged down and died. Their bones named the spot.

The series of white markings winding up the side of the mountains, visible (R) at 45.6 *m.,* were caused by lightning and cloudbursts.

DOG CREEK, 45.9 *m.,* and DOG CANYON, a 300-foot gash through the Dead Horse Mountains, were so named because of a pack of wild dogs found in the caves of the canyon, presumedly left by Indians.

Narrow bridges span a fork of Dog Creek, at 46.1 *m.,* and Santiago Creek, 47.6 *m.*

Southward the Rosillos (dew) Mountains (5,420 alt.) are on the right, a group of peaks due north of the Chisos mass. Above the Rosillos, in the dim distance rise the Christmas Mountains (5,735 alt.) and the CORAZONES (hearts) PEAKS (5,306 alt.). To the northwest, up Santiago Draw, lies NINE POINT MESA (5,551 alt.), separated from the Santiago Range on the west by the breadth of Chalk Draw.

BORACHES (corruption of *huaraches,* sandals) SPRING, 50.3 *m.,* is distant about three miles, at the foot of the Rosillos Range (R). It is the site of a large Indian camp, where many artifacts have been found. Legend says its name came from a pair of rawhide sandals found in a cave nearby.

At 56 *m.,* there is an excellent view of the Chisos Range. On the left end of the range is POMMEL PEAK (6,630 alt.); R. is LOST MINE PEAK (7,550 alt.). MOUNT EMORY (7,835 alt.) is in the center of the range. The sheer, high escarpment to the north is PULLIAM BLUFF (6,921 alt.). Pommel Peak is supposed to resemble the pommel of a saddle.

Southward the way is across Tornillo Flat, with draws formerly dangerous to cross in running water. Small clay hills colored by iron oxide dot the badlands of this eroded area.

At 59.7 *m.* is a well (L), about 20 feet from the road. On the horizon to the southeast (L), SHOT TOWER PEAK (approx. 8,000 alt.) dominates the skyline. This peak, visible here for the first time, and one of the landmarks of the region, is across the Rio Grande in Mexico. It was named because of its resemblance to a tower such as was once used in making lead shot.

TORNILLO (screwbean) CREEK is crossed at 60.5 *m.* On the south side of the bridge are peculiar cap rock outcroppings—low knolls with fantastic similarity to houses, animals, and other familiar objects.

North of the bridge is the Fossil Bone Exhibit.

At 66 *m.* is PANTHER JUNCTION. Turn right for CHISOS MOUNTAIN LODGE and left for RIO GRANDE VILLAGE.

Left on this road the mountain masses pile ever higher. The Carmen Mountains of Mexico are visible (L), at 3.8 *m.* From near Boquillas, on the Rio Grande, this mighty range sweeps away to the southeast for approximately 40 miles at heights ranging from 8,000 to 9,500 feet. The coloring changes with the atmosphere, but is usually a deep, velvet red, which, as the sunlight fades, becomes a peculiar purplish maroon. Artists regard the Carmens as possessing the most beautiful color combinations of the Big Bend. This range was named for Nuestra Señora del Carmen (Our Lady of Carmen).

At 12 *m.* is a junction with a dirt road.

Left here 2 *m.* to HANNOLD'S, formerly a place for gasoline and food supplies. This was an adobe store and filling station, known chiefly as the home of the Boquillas rugs. A former college professor wove rugs of the Mexican saddle blanket type from native mohair, adapting a primitive art of the Mexicans of this region to his own patented loom, which stood under a brush arbor.

The main side route continues to a junction with a dirt road, 17.3 *m.* (*Signs read "Hot Springs" and "Boquillas."*)

Left here across Tornillo Creek, on the road to the right, 1 *m.* to a junction with another paved road.

1. Right from this junction 0.5 *m.* to HOT SPRINGS. A health resort with primitive facilities originally was built here beside the Rio Grande, where a hot spring gushes forth, possessed, it is claimed, of medicinal qualities.

2. Left from the junction on a dirt road 2 *m.* to BOQUILLAS PASS, where the route follows an ancient Indian and smugglers trail. Directly above the road at this point is visible a stone barricade, built in some fierce and now forgotten border war. At 2.1 *m.* is a new tunnel through this small limestone hill, which the road once skirted and was called Dead Man's Turn. At this high point Boquillas, Mexico, and the Carmen Range, are visible. The road leads directly into BOQUILLAS, Texas, 5.1 *m.*

Nearby is the new RIO GRANDE VILLAGE, developed by the Park and providing visitors with a highly scenic base for viewing the phenomena of the river. There are a service station, camp store with groceries and supplies (including films), and trailer sites with utility connections. The village is administered by National Park Concessions, Inc.

The name Boquillas (little mouths) was applied because of the narrowness of BOQUILLAS CANYON, a great opening here in the rock of the mountain wall through which flows the Rio Grande. The river bed is at an elevation of 1,850 feet, above which the rim is at 3,500 feet, the depth of the canyon thus averaging 1,600 feet. The gorge cut by the waters of the river is 25 miles long. Arrangements can be made daily for a visit to Boquillas, Mexico, once a prosperous mining community. Boys lead visitors across the river on burros. Boquillas, Texas, was raided in 1916 by Mexican revolutionists and has survived many border troubles.

South of the road to Boquillas the River Road formerly led to the tiny village of San Vicente, where a small number of Mexican families, with rarely more than fifty individuals, cultivated small acreage along the Rio Grande and made use in primitive fashion of the resources of nature. The settlement dated from the days of the old Presidio and Mission San Vicente, ruins of which still stand on an eminence on the Mexican side two miles up the river. The Presidio was established by the Spanish government in 1789. Many of the soldiers lived with their families on small plots where they raised vegetables and corn and kept goats. When an alarm was sounded they rushed to the Presidio and became defenders behind its high walls. Most of the danger came from the Comanches, who crossed the Rio Grande a short distance below the Presidio. They burned the grasslands on both sides of the river in order to flush game. Often they raided as far south as Durango in Mexico.

The visitor to these sections of Big Bend National Park has an opportunity to observe the wide variety of desert flora. More than 1,000 different plants have been identified by the park naturalists, who are at hand to explain the natural phenomena. Most species are native to the Park. The desert has blooms the year around, although the spring and fall months make the best showing. In March and April come the lupine (bluebonnet), desert baileya, ocotillo, giant dagger yucca, torrey yucca and feather dalea. Justice William O. Douglas, conservationist, has declared (in *Farewell to Texas, Vanishing Wilderness*) that the *lupinus havardii* of the Big Bend country is "the showiest, the largest, the most spectacular" of the bluebonnets, more impressive than the popular *lupinus subcarnososus,* which has been the state flower since 1901.

The yuccas have white, bell-like blossoms and the octillos, or coach whips, have bright-red blossoms in the spring and often repeat in the fall. In April and May come the blooms of the desert willow, yellow trumpet, lechuguilla, verbena, hechtia and soaptree yucca. May and June have the candelilla (wax euphorbia), longspur columbine, and various cacti. June and July have the havard agave, sotol, and golden-eye. From July to October the silverleaf and the desert baileya are flowering.

Of the shrubs, mesquite displays many yellowish blossoms in the spring. The creosote bush, an evergreen with waxy leaves, has small yellow blossoms. The guayacan, with dense, small leaves, has violet-colored flowers. The strawberry cactus makes a brilliant splash in the landscape with its pink and red blooms. Prickly pears are not friendly to man but their golden-yellow spring flowers, followed in summer by deep purple and maroon fruits, seem to call for admiration. Many of the flowers and shrubs are well armored. The spiny allthorn should be viewed from a distance; the catclaw, no friend of man, has short, curved thorns.

GLENN SPRINGS DRAW is at 22.3 *m.* Somewhere between this point and the waters of Rio Grande one of the most noted tales of the frontier had its setting in the days when Bajo El Sol (under the sun) rode the Comanche Trail as the greatest chief of them all. The State of Chihuahua finally made a treaty with the Comanches, whereby that tribe was to make war on the Mescalero Apaches and was to refrain from ravaging Chihuahua, being left free, however, to raid other Mexican states. While this agreement was in force, Bajo El Sol, with his wife and her young brother, came upon a band of Apaches who had in their possession a captive Mexican boy named Domingo Parras. The chief's wife entreated him to leave the Apaches alone, as they numbered about 30. Bajo El Sol refused, declaring that he would not have it said that he was afraid to enforce the treaty. Sending his wife and her brother on, he prepared for battle. He "tightened the cinch of his skin saddle, examined the rawhide bits in the mouth of his horse. Then he looked to see that his arrows were good and in place, strung his bois d'arc bow, and placed his chimal buffalo hide shield in readiness." Bajo El Sol demanded the surrender of the boy, which was refused and the battle started, lasting several hours. At last a bullet killed the chief, but not until he had taken such a toll that the name of Bajo El Sol was from that day a mighty word on the Comanche Trail.

Close to the left at 22.8 *m.* rise the San Vicente Mountains of Mexico. The long hogback northwest of them is Mariscal Range, in Texas. To the right are the southern peaks of the Chisos.

At 23.6 *m.*, about two and a half miles distant (L), across the river, are visible in plain relief the ruins of the Presidio of San Vicente, occupying the flat-topped mesa below the line of hills.

Across the San Vicente Mountains, at 24.1 *m.*, the winding course of the old Smugglers Trail is visible in the big canyon at their western end. Here silver, gold, and contraband were smuggled past Spain's customs officers, and, in more recent years, drugs, liquor, and ammunition have crossed the international border in dangerous midnight excursions by pack train.

Westward, at 24.9 *m.*, the old road led toward the southern face of the Chisos. Ahead at 25.8 *m.* is ELEPHANT TUSK or INDIANOLA PEAK (5,240 alt.). Close on the left is TALLEY MOUNTAIN (3,800 alt.), locally called Cow Heaven. The range on Talley Mountain was excellent, and grassy valleys were heavily stocked with a good grade of Herefords. A cluster of adobe and frame buildings around a ranch house was GLENN SPRINGS.

Glenn Springs served as a subpost of Camp Marfa during the Mexican border troubles from 1910 to 1918. On May 5, 1916, the store was raided and looted by about 200 Mexicans under Lieutenant-Colonel Natividad Alvarez. The buildings which figured in this episode were just beyond the ranch house, to the rear. Three U. S. soldiers and one boy, a lad named Compton, were killed. W. K. Ellis, then the ranch owner, who had an artificial leg, fled with his wife to the rugged shelter of CHILICOTAL MOUNTAIN (4,104 alt.), which overlooks Glenn Springs on the north.

The main route continues westward on the Park road past LONE MOUNTAIN (4,132 alt.) (L), at 67.6 *m.* To the right is GRAPE-VINE MOUNTAIN (3,238 alt.), and beyond, on the northern sky-line, are the crests of the Rosillos.

PANTHER SPRINGS DRAW is crossed at 68.4 *m.*, with PAN-THER PEAK (6,405 alt.) on the left.

An excellent view of the Chisos Range is ahead at 69.3 *m.*, and the rounded, knobbed crest of MOUNT EMORY (7,825 alt.) will soon be visible.

At 72.1 *m.* is a junction with the Park Road leading to The Basin. This is 20 *m.* from the west Park entrance at Maverick.

Left on this road into the CHISOS MOUNTAINS. Heading due south, the road makes its way straight to the tourist recreation area. To the right is the frowning face of Pulliam Bluff, and on the left looms lofty Casa Grande. The mountain panorama at the rear is impressive. A large piñon tree is R. at 4.2 *m.*, and a quarter of a mile beyond, the road passes through a group of young madrona trees. The slopes and valleys are wooded with piñon, juniper, and oak; sotol and century plants are abundant. A sign at 5.5 *m.* warns of a steep, winding road. The view ahead is through a gap termed The Window, looking almost due west and down upon the lesser peaks and ridges of the Terlingua area. Dim and blue on the distant horizon rise the San Carlos Mountains and other ranges of Mexico. In this vicinity are columns of tufa.

At 6 *m.* is a botanical rarity, a weeping juniper (L). The Chisos Mountains are said to be the only place on the North American Continent where this particular variety is known to grow. There are piñon groves on each side of the road at 7.2 *m.*, as it drops down into the valley of GREEN GULCH and farther on to THE BASIN, a huge bowl at the foot of Casa Grande mountain, the principal tourist center. Here are modern accommodations, dining room, coffee shop, service station, supplies, films, groceries; also lectures, horseback trips, hikes, camping.

The great Chisos Range is a region of rare scenic beauty, especially attractive to archeologists, geologists, entomologists, botanists, students of other natural sciences, and lovers of wildlife. There is a splendid cross section of flora, including 600 species ranging from plants of the Lower Sonoran life zone to and including the Canadian life zone. Birds, both migratory and resident, include 330 varieties, from the tropical birds to those of the East. Surrounding peaks command sweeping views of a vast terrain superb in rugged grandeur.

Southward State 118 crosses PAINT CREEK at 74.3 m. It passes through Paint Gap where the Paint Gap Hills (4,258 alt.) are visible to the north (R), while on the left tower the cliffs of Pulliam Bluff.

Before reaching COTTONWOOD CREEK, a road turns left from State 118, moves east of Burro Mesa and south to CASTOLON on the Rio Grande. This was formerly a small trading post with about 60 people. It now has a store and a gas station for Park visitors. Its name derives from the Spanish *castellan,* or warden of a castle. It is at the foot of Cerro Castolon (Warden Peak, 3,283 ft.).

From here a new high grade road goes to the Santa Elena Canyon. Back to State 118, which crosses Cottonwood Creek, 81 m., and proceeds west along the north side of Burro Mesa. At 86.1 m. (R) is DOGIE MOUNTAIN (3,700 alt.), and beyond, to the northwest, is WILLOW MOUNTAIN (3,820 alt.).

At 90 m. is the junction with old State 118, which has come from Alpine.

Right, 3 m., to STUDY BUTTE, a ghost mining town named for Dr. Bill Study, a pioneer physician. Mercury was mined in the rugged butte until 1946. TERLINGUA CREEK is crossed at 4.2 m. TERLINGUA, 9 m., was a mining community, located near one of the largest quicksilver deposits in the world. It was named for Terlingua Creek; the area was popularly supposed to have been the home grounds of three Indian tribes, hence the adaptation of the Spanish *Tres Lenguas* (three languages). The Chisos Mine, opened in 1891, was closed in 1946. The mine shaft sinks into the underlying limestone flagstones of the region, at the south edge of town. Mexicans, living in the primitive fashion of their forbears, inhabited patchwork houses of adobe and tin. After the discovery of the old Chisos Mine, 14 other mines opened in the neighborhood. This industry furnished several generations of Mexicans with constant employment, and many of the miners for years did not move 10 miles from this spot. North of Terlingua is SAWMILL MOUNTAIN (3,795 alt.) and to the northeast rises CIGAR MOUNTAIN (3,290 alt.).

At 92.5 m., (R) are the Rattlesnake Mountains (3,000 alt.), and L. is TULE MOUNTAIN (3,838 alt.).

Before the National Park was established Elmo Johnson's ranch was one of the best-known spots along the Rio Grande. He conducted a large irrigation project across the river in Mexico and lived in a house of adobe, with cottonwood beams. The house has not been preserved.

The Mexican outpost of Santa Heleña once occupied this spot. Paso de los Chisos (Pass of the Chisos) is a mile and a half from this locality; here the foundations of the old fort are visible. As the crossing of the river at Johnson's was shallow, it was the scene of cattle smuggling on a large scale; in pre-Park years, bandits attempting to steal cattle from the Johnsons were fought off by the rancher and his wife. Johnson's Ranch was headquarters for Texas Rangers and U. S. Customs and Immigration inspectors.

From here expeditions have been made into the mountains by pack train to the dry cave shelters of the West Texas Cave Dwellers, a mysterious race who lived in this arid region and left basketry behind. These people used the atl-atl, which preceded the bow and arrow as a weapon. The atl-atl was a notched stick with a hand grip, used for throwing a short spear with a heavy shaft and head. The increased arc of the thrower's swing gave great driving force. These people also made basketry, rope, twine and woven cloth from the tough fiber of the yucca plant. The fiber was chewed and pounded to make the materials for weaving.

Expeditions conducted by the Smithsonian Institution, the Witte Memorial Museum of San Antonio, and other scientific institutions have here found many evidences of the culture of this probably prehistoric race. Burials were made in basketry wrappings, and from one adult burial alone 56 items of daily use were recovered. The area of the Big Bend National Park is protected, and no material of this sort may be removed.

Due north of Johnson's rise the PINNACLES (4,605 alt.), the southern escarpment of the Chisos range. To the northwest are MULE EAR PEAKS (3,880 alt.), landmarks in the Big Bend country—easily identified by their distinctive shape, which justifies their name. They are still one of the natural signposts by which travel in this area is directed.

At a point inaccessible except by pack train, approximately 18 miles downstream from Johnson's Ranch, the Rio Grande turns northeast around the apex of the Big Bend. Here is the forbidding MARISCAL CANYON, a deep, rugged gash with frowning rock walls that tower 1,950 feet above the bed of the river. This is the most inaccessible of the canyons of the Big Bend.

The new Park road mentioned above continues to the entrance of the GRAND CANYON OF SANTA ELENA, 103 *m*. This fearsome gorge through the Mesa de Anguila (Plateau of the Eel) (3,661 alt.), is 15 miles long and from 1,500 to 1,800 feet in depth. A one-mile trail now leads into the Canyon from the end of this road. The southern entrance is impressive, with great rock walls rising abruptly on each side of the river bed in barren and forbidding grandeur.

❧❧❧❧❧❧❧❧❧❧❧❧❧❧❧❧❧❧❧❧❧❧❧❧❧❧❧❧❧

Tour 24

Houston—Brenham—Austin—Lyndon B. Johnson Birthplace, Ranch and State Park—Fredericksburg—Junction—Fort Stockton—Junction with US 80, 596 *m.;* US 290.

This route runs west across the lower central section of Texas, spanning a widely divergent region between the lush green coastal prairies and a semi-arid trans-Pecos expanse of bald hills and cactus-dotted plains. US 290 leads through the heart of the old German settlements of the State, where the *Kaffeeklatsch*—an informal party, with coffee—is traditional, and prim little spicy gardens guard sturdy stone houses built in the 1840's.

There are the neat, prosperous farms of Czechs and, at Serbin, a settlement of Wends whose children still fear the Moon Lady because she might turn them into imps. And far out on the western plains the highway passes huts of adobe bricks and straw thatch, where youths painstakingly prepare eggshells filled with scented confetti—love tokens that are broken upon the heads of the young women selected to be their sweethearts.

Section a. HOUSTON to AUSTIN; 166 m. US 290

This section of US 290 passes through a rich agricultural region between the State's fastest growing industrial area in the vicinity of Houston, and the capital of Texas. Across level, far-flung pastures, through rich bottom lands of the Brazos River, beneath enormous oaks, moss-draped, and past herds of Hereford or hump-backed Brahma cattle grazing against a background of oil wells and gas flares, US 290 climbs until it reaches the rocky uplands near Austin. It traverses part of the Stephen Austin colony grant of the 1820's, where log barns, shallow wells with wooden buckets, split rail fences, and mule-turned sugar cane presses give evidence of little change in the lives and customs of the people through generations. Other sections, imbued with German flavor, present landscapes of manicured appearance—black, fertile farm land, substantial brick houses with large barns, fat, sleek cattle. Near Austin the Colorado flows gently over sandbars except in times of flood.

Beginning on the soft pastel tones of the coastal plains, where roadside ditches are tinted with water hyacinths and pastures are often covered with bluebonnets and white daisies, the section ends on a stronger, deeper color note in the dark greens of hill cedar, yellow daisies, and the rich leaf reds of autumn.

HOUSTON, 0 m. (53 alt., est. pop. 1940, 385,000) (see Houston), is at junctions with US 90 (see Tour 23), US 75 (see Tour 6), State 225 (see Tour 6A), and US 59 (see Tour 22).

US 290 runs west of Houston, through an industrial area and into a region of dairies, truck gardens, and poultry farms, which in turn give way to a sparsely settled expanse of flat prairies.

In an inaccessible pasture three miles to the north, at 27 m., is the site of New Kentucky, settled in the 1820's by Austin's colonists. By 1831 it was a flourishing settlement, but with the founding of Houston it dwindled, until, in 1840, it was abandoned.

WALLER, 40 m. (250 alt., 900 pop.), with a drab business section and smart new residences, is on fertile plains, opulent in their rich greenness. High grass ripples in waves over the surrounding prairies, a green sea dotted with darker green islands—the oak-shaded homes of landowners. In the center of Waller is GOD'S MERCY STORE, a most unusual general merchandising establishment. All goods in the store are plainly marked with the cost price, which the customers pay, with whatever excess amount they consider proper as a freewill offering. The store has been operated in this manner, at a substantial profit, for years.

At 44 m. is a junction with a dirt road.

Right to the PRAIRIE VIEW AGRICULTURAL AND MECHANICAL COLLEGE, a segment of the Texas A. & M. University System. It was founded 1876 and until 1947 was called the Prairie View State Normal and Industrial College for Negroes. Owned and operated by the State, it was the largest Negro land grant college in the country. Since 1947 there has been integration with white students. The College has a full academic and vocational curriculum, with emphasis on agriculture, business administration, home economics, industrial arts. It has 1,434 acres and numerous buildings and cottages. Besides the academic degrees the College gives teachers' certificates and graduate nurses' diplomas. It enrolled 2,986 in the 1966–67 school year and had a faculty of 202.

At 48.5 m. is a junction with a dirt road.

Right here over a road lined with oaks, yaupons and dogwoods to LIENDO PLANTATION (open by arrangement), 0.9 m. The 15-room house was erected in 1851 by Leonard Groce, and was one of the finest plantation homes in the State. In 1874 it was purchased by Elisabet Ney, noted sculptor, and her husband, Dr. Edmund Montgomery. Their graves are on the plantation.

US 290 proceeds westward through farms and woodlands.

HEMPSTEAD, 50 m. (251 alt., 1,505 pop.), serves the Raccoon oil field near by. In the center of a cotton, truck farming and ranching area, it is a shipping center that has modernized its main street by renovating the fronts of old brick buildings.

In Hempstead is the junction with State 6 and State 159.

CHAPPELL HILL, 63 m. (317 alt., 600 pop.), founded in 1849, is a village of fine old homes set in large grounds, in an atmosphere reminiscent of its heyday before the Civil War. Here lived many rich planters who came from Alabama, Louisiana, and Mississippi. Overseers handled the great Brazos black land plantations and armies of slaves, and the planters resided in town. Chappell Hill was the seat of two early institutions of learning. One, the Chappell Hill Female College, was organized in 1852, and continued in operation until 1912. The other, Soule University, was chartered in 1856; the Civil War caused decreased attendance, and in 1867–69 yellow fever epidemics resulted in its abandonment.

Just north of the business section, where the highway turns west, is the old STAGECOACH HOUSE (private), a two-story, 14-room structure of stone with framework and floors of cypress. An ornamental Greek frieze is worked into the cornice, and the heads of the waterspouts bear the Texas star and the date of construction, 1852.

One of the fine old houses of the Chappell Hill vicinity is the BROWNING HOME (visited by permission), built in 1856 by Colonel Browning of Mississippi. It is of cedar construction throughout. The SLEDGE HOME (visited by permission), built in 1850, is of brick, stuccoed and plastered inside, with ornamental woodwork. A still older building is the ROUTT HOUSE (visited by permission), a structure of cedar and pine logs, c. 1846.

BRENHAM, 72 m. (350 alt., 7,740 pop.), seat of Washington County, founded 1844, ships hogs, beef cattle, dairy products. It throve as one of the rich Brazos Valley towns until the Civil War. During Reconstruction, Brenham experienced trouble between its citizens and Union troops stationed there. The town was partly burned and a number of persons, both citizens and soldiers, killed. Many American settlers sold their holdings to German immigrants, and it was largely on German thrift and industry that present-day Brenham was built. It is the trading and shipping center of a rich agricultural area, and its industries include a cotton mill, cottonseed oil plant, mop and broom factory, dairy products plants and a large hatchery. It is the seat of BLINN COLLEGE, W. 4th St., founded in 1883 as a coeducational Methodist institution, now a non-sectarian junior college. The average enrollment is nearly 1,000. Brenham is in the oil field of that name and is a supply point for fields in adjoining counties.

In Brenham is the junction with State 90. North on this route, 18 *m.,* to Washington-on-the-Brazos State Park.

GIDDINGS, 108 *m.* (520 alt., 2,821 pop.), a neat town, sturdily built, has churches of Gothic design, squat, box-like houses, and weathered public buildings. It was established in 1872 by Wendish immigrants from the older nearby settlement of Serbin. One of the town's newspapers, the *Giddings Deutsches Volksblatt,* owns the only Wendish type in America, but publishes in German and English. Local industrial plants process the rich harvests of this argicultural area of German and Wendish farmers.

In Giddings is a junction with US 77 (*see Tour 7*).

Left from Giddings on a dirt road to SERBIN, 6 *m.* This is the oldest Wendish settlement in Texas. These people pass for Germans, since the parent stock has lived in Prussia and Saxony for 1,500 years. In reality, the Wends—or Serby, as they call themselves—are Slavs, constituting the smallest group of a strain that includes Russians, Poles, and Czechs. Their ancient country of Lusatia is divided between two German provinces.

There are in the world perhaps 80,000 of this ancient group, of whom approximately 7,000 live in Texas. In 1854, 500 Wendish colonists, seeking civil and religious freedom, sailed for Texas from Hamburg. A league of land was bought on Rabb's Creek. Early in 1855 they began building the log settlement they called Serbin in commemoration of their racial origin; this community became the cultural center of the Wends in America.

Only St. Paul's Lutheran Church, with its towering steeple and commodious interior, recalls Serbin's past; within a few years the town will have lost its Wendish individuality. The citizens of today consider themselves of German descent, and the Wendish language is seldom spoken. A few of the ancient folk customs survive—for example, in some of the homes domestic animals are still notified orally when a member of the family dies. Wendish periodicals published in Germany are read, though in dwindling numbers.

PAIGE, 119 *m.* (220 pop.) is near a junction with State 21. This leads, 12 *m.,* to LAKE BASTROP, completed 1964, which covers 906 acres and holds 16,590 acre-ft. of water.

BASTROP, 3 *m.* southwest on State 21 (and State 71) (2,900 pop., est. 1966) is on the Colorado River, the seat of Bastrop County. Bastrop ships cotton, pecans, turkeys, lumber and lignite. Incorporated 1837, it was subject to Indian depredations. Its name honors Baron de Bastrop, Dutch friend of Moses Austin.

During the Civil War B. F. Terry obtained recruits for Terry's Texas Rangers, a Confederate force, in Bastrop. The site of the Confederate Arms factory is marked at 600 Main St., and the Historical Museum, 700 Main has war memorabilia. The Courthouse also has Confederate markers. Bastrop asserts it had the "oldest drug store," 1847.

Bastrop claims one of the first Protestant churches in Texas. In 1833 the Reverend Daniel Parker sought permission from Stephen Austin to organize a congregation on the plea that the laws of Mexico contained nothing prohibiting an already organized Protestant church body from moving into the domain. Parker returned to Illinois, there organized the Pilgrim Church of Predestinarian Regular Baptists, and in 1834 brought it to Texas "bag and baggage." For a time it existed without a church building.

The two-story J. R. WILBARGER HOUSE (*private*), on Main St., was built in 1850 of pine from the nearby forests, hand-hewn, and has a chimney at each end and halls on both floors.

Left from Bastrop on State 71 to the entrance of BUESCHER STATE PARK, 1 *m.*, also reached from Smithville. Here 4,000 acres, thickly wooded with pines, offer a delightful recreation area. A golf course, swimming pool, and large lake afford varied amusements.

BASTROP STATE PARK, 2,100 acres, had 285,948 visitors in the year ended August, 1966. Lake Bastrop, 906 acres, was opened in 1964.

AUSTIN, 166 *m.* (650 alt., 239,500 pop. 1966, est.) (*see Austin*), is at the junction with US 81 (*see Tour 8*).

Section b.   AUSTIN to JUNCTION; 143 m.   US 290

This section of US 290 rolls into the northern part of the hill country. West of Austin, the highway begins its climb from an altitude of less than 700 feet to one of more than 2,000, leaving behind rich farm lands near Austin for the rocky uplands of the Balcones Fault and the Edwards Plateau. Green valleys lie between forested, high hills whose owners wage unceasing warfare with drought and isolation for the rough acres cut through by running streams. Wild game abounds, especially deer and wild turkeys, and fishing for bass and perch is excellent in many of the clear, cold rivers and creeks. Small farms and ranches cover the rugged miles, where goats and sheep have destroyed most of the wild flowers.

In the "back country" of the first miles, people of hardy Anglo-Saxon stock still sing Elizabethan ballads, have play-parties, and flock to brush arbors for revival meetings. Beyond, deep in the hills, live descendants of German pioneers. Their houses, built by early settlers, have rare architectural beauty. Near the end of the section ranchmen typical of west Texas own large holdings.

West of AUSTIN, 0 *m.*, US 290 skirts rugged hills, and climbs steadily toward the higher reaches of the Edwards Plateau.

An unnamed waterfall (R), at 34.6 *m.*, spills the waters of Miller's Creek over its rim in an arching leap to a pool of 20 feet below.

At 43.8 *m.* is the junction with US 281 (*see Tour 9*).

JOHNSON CITY, 50 *m.* (1,197 alt., 660 pop.), seat of Blanco County, was named for the pioneer forebears of Lyndon B. Johnson, President of the United States, 1963–1968. Johnson, who was born on a farm near Stonewall August 27, 1908, came here to live in the Johnson homestead in 1913 and was graduated from the high school in 1924. The house has now been made into a museum. It was built in Civil War times and sheltered wounded from the Deer Creek Indian fight. President Johnson cast his vote at the Blanco County Courthouse and often attended the First Christian Church with Mrs. Johnson.

Near the outskirts is a cluster of stone barns built by Lyndon B. Johnson's father, Sam Ealey Johnson, and his uncle, Thomas.

At 60.9 the highway crosses the Pedernales River.

At 64 *m.* enter Park Road 49 to LYNDON B. JOHNSON STATE HISTORIC PARK, 269 acres, adjoining the Pedernales River. The Park was conveyed to the State by private donations in 1967.

STONEWALL, 76 *m.* (1,512 alt., 200 pop.) was named for Stonewall Jackson in 1870. Ranch Road 1 leaves US 290 here and makes a loop past LBJ Ranch, home of Lyndon B. Johnson. Many visitors have taken this road to view the white, two-story farmhouse that was often the site of important conferences during the Johnson presidency. The farm has accommodations for guests and a landing strip for the Johnson plane.

The President's birthplace has been reconstructed east of the Ranch House at the end of Park Road 49 (*open*). The parents of the President are buried in the family cemetery nearby.

At 77 *m.* a dirt road leads to an old MORMON GRAVEYARD, remains of a Mormon settlement of 1847, called Zodiac. These colonists—experienced farmers —were helpful to the German settlers of the region. Relations between the two groups were harmonious until politics caused a rift. The Mormon leader, Elder Lyman Wight, resigned as chief justice in Fredericksburg because the Germans insisted on keeping the polls open for a week.

The colony moved in 1851, after a flood had destroyed its mill on the Pedernales. The little graveyard is visited annually by a delegation from the Mormon Church at Salt Lake City, Utah.

At 78.5 *m.* a road leads to the site of OLD FORT MARTIN SCOTT. Established in December, 1848, this outpost served as a unit of United States forts on the frontier of Texas. The westward advance of settlement caused its abandonment in 1853. Subsequently it served as a Confederate post and Texas Ranger station.

FREDERICKSBURG, 81 *m.* (1,742 alt., 5,000 pop. est.), in a green valley rimmed about by evergreen hills, is a trim, clannish, thoroughly German town. Its antecedents were conspicuously Teutonic. A State highway through the mile-long main street has shattered its isolation, but the town retains an Old World flavor in architecture and in the tenacious devotion of the inhabitants to the German culture and folkways of the founders.

Its location precisely fits Fredericksburg's temperament and mood. The granite and limestone outcroppings in the encircling hills suggest a permanence reflected in thick-walled limestone houses, mellowed to amber by the sun. The peace of the valley seems crystallized in the uplifting church spires and voiced by the deep-toned peals of their bells.

Because the valley was not wide and because the founders remembered the one-street villages folded away in hills beside the Rhine, they laid their town out beside one wide, long street. Replacing their first crude homes, they built solidly of stone quarried from the hillsides. These thick-walled dwellings crowd close to the street. Many are one story and a half, others are a single story; all have spacious attics and steep, sloping roofs high in front, slanting gradually toward the rear to cover shed rooms. Precipitous outside stairways lead to openings in the attic walls. This type is the German *Fachhaus*. Newer houses, though larger, follow the same general pattern. Between them are trim gardens with clean-swept walks and brick-bordered flower beds.

Though modern buildings are scattered about, Fredericksburg's best known business houses are venerable country stores where townfolk make a complacent living by trading with countryfolk from the surrounding valleys, which were also settled by German immigrants.

Those settlers came in 1846, and theirs was a forlorn undertaking. They had been brought from Germany by the *Adelsverein,* the Society for the Protection of German Immigrants in Texas, but funds for the enterprise had failed (*see New Braunfels, Tour 8c*). John O. Meusebach, secretary of the Adelsverein, made possible for them the establishment of a new German town in an almost inaccessible region claimed by the Comanches. Climaxing bitter hardships, an epidemic took 156 of the 600 settlers in 1847. Undaunted, they named their lonely little village for Frederick the Great of Prussia.

Several moonlight raids by Indians resulted in massacres and loss of stock. To make survival of the settlement possible, Meusebach negotiated a peace treaty with the Comanches in 1847.

When Fort Martin Scott was established on Baron's Creek, it furnished not only needed protection against the still hostile Indians, but a ready cash market for produce. The first private store was opened in Fredericksburg, and the colonists began to prosper. They had chosen well when they selected the town site. The surrounding country was rich in fish and game, with turkey and deer predominating. Fertile valleys were watered by abundant streams, and the heavily wooded hills provided building stone. Thriftily the settlers laid the foundation for the present prosperous region of sheep, goat, and cattle raising, with small plots, intensively farmed, in the narrow valleys.

During the Civil War Fredericksburg fell on evil days. Disapproving of slavery, many of the men refused to enlist in the Confederate army. Some hid in the hills or left for Mexico to evade conscription. A party of Germans from the hill country, on their way to Mexico, were attacked by a force of Confederates and nearly all slain. These disastrous events led to further troubles between the Germans and other Texans during the Reconstruction period. When these disturbances were over, Fredericksburg returned to isolation.

Roads through the hills were tortuous and rocky. Though a railroad for the region had been attempted in 1888, it had failed and in 1912 the citizens of Fredericksburg built their own railroad connection with the San Antonio and Aransas Pass, now the property of the Southern Pacific. Automobile roads soon pushed into the region. In 1936 the broad cement ribbon of US 87 reduced distances and ended the town's isolation.

But through that isolation Fredericksburg became to an unusual extent self-sustaining. Most of the necessities and some luxuries are produced in the community. The largest commerce is in shipment of wool, cattle, and mohair.

Social life, based on community interests, centers about definite traditional events. The *Ball der Verheiraten,* or dance for married couples, is held a number of times each year, and the children have their *Kindermaskenball* annually on the night before the beginning of Lent. The men have their *Schuetzenbund* and shooting contests and an annual *Skattournier,* or elimination tournament, in their favorite card game of *Skat,* in which teams are selected for State tournaments.

During the month of May, when the surrounding hills are bright with flowers, Fredericksburg holds its most important celebration, the county *Saengerfest,* when singing clubs of the district gather for a county-wide contest. German songs and traditional dances are the principal attraction. Toward the end of the singing contest there is usually a massed chorus of all the clubs, followed by a dance.

Another observance is that of the "Easter fires" on the surrounding hills. For years beacons of blazing brush, lighted by local high school students, have thrown their flames skyward every Easter Eve. The children of the town view the conflagrations as "rabbit fires," their legend being that the rabbits use them to cook and color the eggs which are found in the Easter nests the next morning.

Scattered throughout the town are numerous small houses, closed and dark during the week, but bustling with activity on Saturdays and Sundays. These so-called "Sunday houses" are reminiscent of the not long distant past when roads were bad, transportation slow, and the frugal farm families from the adjacent valleys had to spend a night in town to shop Saturday and to attend church on Sunday. The "Sunday houses" are still maintained as a convenient and economical way of spending the week end in town.

The *Abendglocken,* or evening bells, are rung at 6 o'clock on Saturday evenings, when the people are supposed to stop working. One of the characteristics of Fredericksburg is its great number of church bells, rung on many occasions.

Though English and German are spoken interchangeably, German has remained the language of social contact, spoken in many homes.

The KIEHNE HOUSE, which was erected in 1851 at E. Main St. between S. Washington and S. Elk Sts., was considered the first two-story house built in Fredericksburg. All woodwork was hand-hewn, of native timber. Windows with circular heads, and double doors were recessed deeply into the thick walls of stone and timber construction. The NIMITZ

HOTEL, N. corner N. Washington and E. Main Sts., occupies the site of a historic hotel erected in 1853. Here Charles H. Nimitz, grandfather of Fleet Admiral Chester W. Nimitz, built a house in form of a ship. The establishment was widely known for its excellent meals; and among its many notable guests were Robert E. Lee, Kirby Smith, and James Longstreet. When the new Nimitz Hotel was built, relics, documents, and some of the furnishings of the old hotel were preserved, including a spool bed in which General Lee slept. The museum now honors Fleet Admiral Nimitz.

On Main St. opposite the courthouse is the VEREINS KIRCHE (*open 1–5 daily, except Wed.*), an exact reproduction of the town's earliest church, built in 1847 and sometimes called the *Kaffeemuehle,* because it resembles an old-fashioned coffee mill. It is octagonal in floor plan, each side 18 feet long, its walls filled in with stone between upright supporting logs, then plastered inside and out. The roof, an octagonal pyramid, is surmounted by a cupola which also follows the angles of the walls. There are two doors, opposite one another, through which it was customary in early days for men and women to enter separately.

The early Vereins Kirche, which stood squarely in the middle of Main Street, was used not only for religious services but also as a town hall, a fort, and a school; in fact, as the center of community life. Gradually falling into disuse, it was torn down in 1897. In 1934 the present structure was erected near the old site. It is also used as a museum for historical relics.

The OLD COURTHOUSE AND POST OFFICE, S. corner S. Crockett and W. Main Sts., a graceful two-story building of stucco on stone, is now a community center, museum and library. OLD ST. MARY'S ROMAN CATHOLIC CHURCH, N. corner W. San Antonio and S. Orange Sts., erected in 1861 and designed in early German Gothic style, is a rare bit of Nuremberg transplanted to Texas. Although square-headed windows have been substituted for the original Gothic openings, the building retains its Old World elegance in the tall convex-sided stone spire which towers above it. Beside the old church stands a new structure, embodying some of the Gothic features of the earlier building.

The HEINRICH KAMMLAH HOUSE now the Pioneer Museum, W. Main St. between S. Orange and S. Milam Sts., actually two buildings joined, was a store and residence. Designed in early indigenous style, the house has many European features, including several deep, stone cellars, an outdoor oven, and an enclosed courtyard. The STAUDT SUNDAY HOUSE (*private*), W. Creek St., between S. Edison and S. Bowie Sts., built in 1847, is a typical example of the week end houses of the community. It is a small, low stone building with deeply sloping roof and twin chimneys. The TATSCH HOUSE (*visited by arrangement*), corner N. Bowie and W. Schubert St., *c.* 1852, is remarkable for its great Dutch chimney. Inside, an open fireplace, nine feet wide, retains the old iron hooks and chains formerly used for holding kettles and other utensils.

CROSS MOUNTAIN, N. Milam St., on the northern edge of Fredericksburg, was marked with a large wooden cross, already dark with age, when the first settlers came. Who placed it there is not known, but it remained an object of reverence until it rotted and fell. It was replaced by a concrete cross, electrically lighted and visible for many miles at night. In Fredericksburg is the junction with US 87 (*see Tour 17*).

Right from Fredericksburg, out N. Milam St. and Upper Crabapple Road 4 *m* to BEAR MOUNTAIN (1,850 alt). This rugged outcropping of eroded red granite, a mass of scattered boulders and steep slopes, received its name from the fact that in the days of the first settlers, bears frequented its shallow caves. Today its chief attraction is to the amateur mountain climber, and hundreds annually ascend its rugged sides for the excellent view from the summit, and to see a huge boulder called Balanced Rock poised on two small points of granite.
Northeastward the Upper Crabapple Road leads to ENCHANTED ROCK (1,815 alt.), 19 *m.*, said to be the second largest outcropping of granite in the United States. Its smooth, weather-polished dome rises 500 feet or more from the bed of Sand Creek, at its base. Around the foot of the rock lies a tangled mass of granite boulders and fragments, some larger than a two-story house. To the rock are attached many tales of the days of Ranger and Indian warfare. From the top of the rock a broad vista discloses smaller outcroppings of granite in many formations—domes, towers, turrets, battlements and sheer walls. There is a park along the banks of Sand Creek (*tourist cabins, camping facilities*).

Westward the route ascends a high plateau, across which it rolls in gentle undulations.
JUNCTION, 143 *m.* (2,180 alt., 2,500 pop., est.), is at the junction with US 83 and US 377.

Section c. JUNCTION to Junction with US 80;
287 m. US 290

US 290 quits the western part of the hill country to plunge into the barren, rolling lands of the west Texas ranching area, then climbs again toward mountains. On the semiarid range lands vegetation is scant, and some use has been found for most of the prickly plants that grow. The needle-pointed yucca leaves, for example, are used by ranch folk to open wounds caused by rattlesnake bites; a syrup is made of boiled screw beans; and mesquite beans and prickly pear fruits are eaten by the poorer class of Mexicans. The fiber of sotol is used for twine, and its long pointed leaves for roof thatch.
Cattle and sheep, with oil, constitute the largest source of income. In certain irrigated areas fruits, truck crops, alfalfa and small grains are grown. Many ranchmen have begun to raise feed crops to fatten their stock, the animals thus bringing higher prices.
Beyond JUNCTION, 0 *m.*, pecan trees along the streams produce a large revenue.
At 2 *m.* is the junction with US 83 (*see Tour 16*).
ROOSEVELT, 19 *m.* (62 pop.), is a tiny ranch supply point. One of the ranches of the vicinity has something unusual in the use of "sheep shirts" and "goat coats" at shearing time. These garments, made of heavy duck cloth in various sizes to fit animals of all ages, are placed on newly

shorn sheep and goats to forestall losses from sudden unseasonable north-ers. The coats are left on until warm weather is assured or the animals' hair has grown sufficiently to afford natural protection. At 31.5 *m.* is a junction with a dirt road.

Right here to the RUINS OF FORT TERRETT, 4.5 *m.,* established in 1852 and named for Lieutenant John C. Terrett, who was killed in the Battle of Monterey in the Mexican War. The post was abandoned January 16, 1854. Today only four buildings remain, one of them a reproduction of the old headquarters building, rebuilt with the stones of the old structure. It is the headquarters of a modern ranch.

SONORA, 62 *m.* (2,180 alt., 2,800 pop.), is at the junction with US 277 (*see Tour 10*).

West of Sonora the country is rougher, the hills becoming higher with each passing mile.

The sink at 75.4 *m.* is called DAGO'S WATER HOLE because two Ital-ians, traveling west with several thousand dollars in their possession, were held up here. One was killed but the other escaped with the money.

The road climbs to the top of a divide where vegetation is scant, with only a little greasewood, sage, and dwarf mesquite.

OZONA, 98 *m.* (2,348 alt., 3,500 pop.), is the only town in Crock-ett County, an area larger than the State of Delaware. It grew up around the only water hole for many miles in this semidesert range land. Built around a shady courthouse square, Ozona has many fine homes of cattle-men. State 137 from Brownfield, Terry County, joins State 163, 3 *m.* north of Ozona. Westward the highway winds over hilly ranges, climb-ing steadily. At 130.1 *m.* is a junction with a pasture road.

Right here to the RUINS OF OLD FORT LANCASTER, 0.7 *m.,* established in 1854 as Camp Lancaster, and officially designated as Fort Lancaster in 1856. It was abandoned in 1861, at the outbreak of the Civil War. Chimneys stand above the mounds of crumbled stone and earth that once were buildings. The grave-stones in the cemetery bear the names of soldiers, members of their families and Texas Rangers. Beyond the ruins the pasture road leads on to the route of the California Trail, 1.3 *m.* Here the frontier highway descends from a steep hill, and deep ruts made by wagons are still visible.

Along this road ran the San Antonio-San Diego Stage Line and much of the east-west traffic before the days of railroads.

US 290 crosses the Pecos River to SHEFFIELD (350 pop.) Thence 18 *m.* north on State 340 to IRAAN in Pecos County, (2,590 alt., 1,200 pop.) Here Well A No. 1 came in with a gusher in 1928, so powerful its spray reached 4 miles away. It is called "the largest producing oil well on the American continent." Town was named for original owners of site, Ira and Ann Yates. FANTASYLAND is an amusement and recreation park.

TUNIS SPRINGS, 193 *m.,* is the site of a way station of the But-terfield Overland Mail and later of the Texas Rangers, the ruins of which were moved to a Texas Highway Dept. Roadside Park 7 *m.* east of Fort Stockton. This is a region of large sheep ranches and on the gate of one, left of the road, a sign indicating that even sheep are at times entitled to privacy reads: *Please Stay Out While Sheep Are Lambing.*

FORT STOCKTON, 210 *m.* (3,052 alt., 7,500 pop.) is the seat of Pecos County, a ranch and oil area. Adobe houses fringe the town, which spreads out from its limestone and red stucco courthouse. Fort Stockton is a retail center and livestock shipping point. It grew up around a military post established in 1859 near Comanche Springs, known to explorers as early as 1534. Past the spring ran the Camino Real, the California Trail of 1849–50, and the San Antonio-San Diego Stage Line route. Today the water from this great spring, which flows more than 30 million gallons daily, irrigates 6,500 acres north of the town.

The city has natural gas and petrochemical industries, as well as meat packers. Riggs Hotel, Main and Callaghan Sts., built 1898, is a museum of the Fort Stockton Historical Society. The Grey Mule Saloon, restored, is a survivor of free and easy days.

This region offers fine hunting in season, with deer, mountain lions, coyotes, bears, raccoons, opossums and civet cats plentiful.

At Fort Stockton is JAMES ROONEY PARK, in the area surrounding Comanche and Government Springs. Here are the RUINS OF OLD FORT STOCKTON, including the stone guard-house and three units of officers' quarters; the latter, just outside the park area, are used as private residences. These buildings were constructed of adobe bricks and huge blocks of hewn limestone.

In Fort Stockton are junctions with US 285, US 385, US 67 and State 18, which moves north into New Mexico beyond Kermit. On Ranch road 1053, 31 *m.* north, is IMPERIAL (600 pop.) and the IMPERIAL RESERVOIR on the Pecos River, holding 17,000 acre-ft. of water.

Westward the highway traverses mile after mile of rolling range land, a monotonous sweeping vista of yellow and white sand.

At 217.4 *m.* is one of the major irrigation projects of west Texas, Leon Valley Farms, covering 3,500 acres. This area produces fine crops of alfalfa and cotton, and is irrigated by LEON SPRINGS, (L), 219.6 *m.,* which gush from the earth with a flow almost equal to that of Comanche Springs at Fort Stockton. This is another of the important early-day watering places known to Indians, explorers, immigrants and freighters. The springs issue from a series of large holes, 50 to 60 feet in diameter.

US 290 now passes beyond the irrigated section, and again the landscape is semibarren cattle range. Low hills sprawl across the northern horizon, and far to the south is the purple mass of the Glass Mountains (6,286 alt.). The lower hills in the middle distance close in on both sides, and the higher ranges beyond creep nearer, their rugged crests lifting higher and higher into the sky. The northward jutting ridge is known as the Barrilla Mountains (5,560 alt.).

BALMORHEA, 262 *m.* (3,205 alt., 604 pop.), once a cowtown, is now the market center for a 10,000-acre irrigated tract watered from nearby San Solomon Springs, which flow an average of more than 24 million gallons daily. Spring water irrigates fine old trees along Balmorhea's main street board walk in front of a block-long row of stores and dwelling houses. The town has a large swimming pool.

Southwest the route heads straight for the towering Davis Mountains (average alt. 7,000). LAKE BALMORHEA, 3 *m.* southeast, covers 573 acres and holds 6,350 acre-ft.

TOYAHVALE, 267 *m.*, is a tiny crossroads settlement at the edge of BALMORHEA STATE PARK (*boating, fishing, swimming*), a 950-acre recreation area centered about San Solomon Springs. In Toyahvale is the junction with State 17. Left on State 17 to FORT DAVIS, 33 *m.* (*see Tour 23d*). At 271.5 is a junction with a graveled road.

Left here to PHANTOM LAKE, 10 *m.*, in the foothills of the Davis Mountains, another of the Indian and pioneer waterholes of the region. Today it is the water supply for an irrigated section around Toyahvale.

At 272.5 *m.* is a junction with a graveled road.

Left here to MADERA SPRINGS, 9 *m.*, a mountain resort (*cottage and hotel facilities, horseback riding, swimming and hiking*).

Westward US 290 skirts the north fringe of the Davis Mountains. Ahead and to the north rise rocky ranges, distant, blue, and often hazy in the rising heat waves. They are the Apache Mountains, the Delaware Mountains and the Sierra Diablo Range. In the clear, cool air of morning it is possible to discern the lofty, massive bulk of the Guadalupe Range far to the northwest.

At 287 *m.* is the junction with US 80 (*see Tour 19*). Interstate 20 runs parallel to large sections of US 80 and Interstate 10 follows US 80 from the mountains to El Paso.

❧❧❧❧❧❧❧❧❧❧❧❧❧❧❧❧❧❧❧❧❧❧❧❧❧❧❧❧

Tour 24A

Hempstead—Navasota—Washington—Brenham, 46 *m.;* State 6 and 90.

This route is through a rolling region of grassy prairies, rich alluvial bottom lands along many streams, and wooded slopes. Cotton is the money crop, and has influenced the population trend: in the Navasota area, for example, 40 per cent of the people are Negroes, chiefly farm hands or tenants. Between Navasota and Brenham, many land titles date back to Mexican grants; settlers were largely planters from the South, who built in this new land many beautiful manor homes, cultivated cotton and had

Big Bend National Park

RIO GRANDE CANYON AT BASE OF MESA DE AQUILA

National Park Service

SOUTHWEST TEXAS LANDSCAPE, BIG BEND

National Park Service

ERODED CLIFFS ALONG THE RIO GRANDE

National Park Service

SANTA ELENA CANYON WALLS, 1,500 FEET HIGH, BIG BEND

National Park Service

MOUTH OF SANTA ELENA CANYON

National Park Service

LOOKING TOWARD MEXICO FROM THE SOUTH RIM, BIG BEND
National Park Service

BOQUILLAS VILLAGE, MEXICO, FROM BIG BEND NATIONAL PARK
Photo by Jack E. Boucher National Park Service

HERMIT'S HUT, BIG BEND NATIONAL PARK

Photo by Jack E. Boucher
National Park Service

VISITORS PLAY UNDER THE CLIFFS OF THE RIO GRANDE, BIG BEND

National Park Service

PEAKS IN THE CHISOS MOUNTAINS, BIG BEND

Southern Pacific Railway

EARTH HISTORY DISCLOSED BY EROSION, BIG BEND

National Park Service

CENTURY PLANT AND LIGHTNING, BIG BEND

National Park Service

ADMINISTRATION BUILDING, BIG BEND NATIONAL PARK

National Park Service

numerous slaves. Old customs and old houses remain in the plantation areas, although German and Polish farmers have absorbed much of the land, particularly near Brenham. Folklore includes many tales of buried treasure; as late as 1923 a child who, it was believed, could "smell out" buried gold, was carted around Grimes County, sought after for his "gold comprehension." A marathon race is run by Negroes, from Hempstead to Navasota, as an annual feature of the "Juneteenth" celebration. Midway of the route, in old Washington, the Texas Declaration of Independence was signed in 1836; here a State park contains mementos of early days.

HEMPSTEAD, 0 *m.* (251 alt., 1,505 pop.), is at the junction with US 290 (*see Tour 24a*).

North of Hempstead the route is State 6 through an area settled during the early days of Austin's colony. Descendants of some of the Anglo-American pioneers live here.

NAVASOTA, 21 *m.* (215 alt., 4,950 pop.), on an open, rolling prairie, profits commercially from the junction of State 6, 90 and 105. A banking center, it has large white plantation type homes, those on the outskirts set well back from the streets at the end of live oak-shaded drives. The site was settled at the intersection of the La Bahia-San Antonio and Nacagdoches Roads and the Indian trail from Waco. When James Nolan built a double log cabin to serve as a stage stop, the place was called Nolansville. It was officially established as Navasota in 1858. In 1865 the town was partly destroyed by a fire set by a mob of unpaid Confederate soldiers. It was rebuilt in 1866, but a year later a yellow fever epidemic swept it, with a death rate of almost 50 per cent.

Opposite the grammar school on Washington Ave., stood until recently the FREEMAN INN, a stage stop built in 1852. On the esplanade of Washington Ave., facing the business district, stands the LA SALLE STATUE, honoring René Robert Cavelier, Sieur de La Salle, the French explorer who was killed by his own men, probably somewhere in the vicinity of Navasota (1687). The statue is in bronze, by Frank Teich.

In Navasota the route turns sharply southwest on State 90, crossing the Navasota River at the western edge of town. The terrain flattens into choice farm land, devoted largely to cotton production.

WASHINGTON, 28 *m.* (260 alt., 300 pop.), sprawling over a reddish bluff above the yellow, muddy waters of the Brazos River, was the first settlement in Stephen F. Austin's land grant of 1821. A ferry operated just below the mouth of the Navasota River in 1822. Despite its place in Texas history, it has never attracted more than a few hundred residents. Founded in 1835, the town was first called Washington on the Brazos. Here, March 2, 1836, delegates of the people assembled and drew up the Texas Declaration of Independence, wrote a national constitution and adopted an ad interim government. The delegates met in a one-story wooden structure, then unfinished, and cotton cloth was draped over the open windows to keep out the cold wind. The new government and most of the inhabitants fled before the invading Mexican army (March, 1836). Following the Mexican invasion of 1842, the seat of government of the Republic of Texas was again temporarily moved to Washington.

For years Washington remained an important inland town, but when missed by the railroad in 1858 it fast dwindled to the village it is today.

Left from Washington on State Park Road No. 12 to WASHINGTON STATE PARK (*free*), 0.1 *m.*, which contains a REPRODUCTION OF AN EARLY CAPITOL OF THE REPUBLIC OF TEXAS and the TEXAS DECLARATION OF INDEPENDENCE MONUMENT, a granite shaft. The reproduction of the capitol is a one-story frame building, painted white. Near the park entrance is the HOME OF ANSON JONES (*open, no regular hours*), a story-and-a-half clapboarded house with hand-hewn timbers and a wide center hall. This building was moved from its site in Washington, where the last President of the Republic of Texas lived; it is called the last White House of the Republic. Left of the driveway is an amphitheater and a stage of stone and concrete, and near the center of the park, topping a bluff over the river, is a large rock auditorium.

Southwest of Washington, weathered frame houses of the plantation type and modern farm homes afford a marked contrast.

At 44 *m.* is a junction with a dirt road (*impassable in wet weather*).

Right here to INDEPENDENCE, 8.7 *m.* (319 pop.), a village sleeping amid reminders of past importance—dignified, splendid old homes, crumbling walls of former business houses, and the ruins of a once thriving school. Founded in 1836, its name commemorates the signing of the Texas Declaration of Independence at nearby Washington. In the small INDEPENDENCE STATE PARK is marked the site of Baylor College, 1845–1888. In town is the old rock INDEPENDENCE BAPTIST CHURCH, erected in 1839 and still in use. Here General Sam Houston joined the church on November 19, 1854, being baptized in the waters of Rocky Creek south of the town. In the churchyard is a tower surmounted by a bell cast from the family silverware of Mrs. Nancy Lea, mother-in-law of General Houston. Across the road from the church is the HOUSTON FAMILY BURIAL PLOT (R), containing the graves of Mrs. Sam Houston, her mother, Mrs. Nancy Lea, and two Negro servants.

1. Left at the Baptist Church on an intersecting road 0.2 *m.* to the RUINS OF THE LEA HOUSE, which was a typical plantation dwelling. It was here that Mrs. Houston died. The J. M. BLUE HOUSE (R), 0.5 *m.*, a fine example of early Texas architecture, was built by a member of the Austin colony. Exterior walls are of stone; woodwork is of cedar.

2. In the center of town are several old buildings. First is the old MASONIC HALL, where pioneers of Texas Masonry gathered. One block down is the C. J. TOALSON HOUSE (*private*), a one-story adobe structure built in 1835 by the Mexican government for use as a jail.

3. Left from Independence on a side road 0.7 *m.* to the SEWARD HOUSE (*open*), built in 1835. This two-story building is a good example of the homes of its period. It is built of hand-sawed cedar, with stone steps and large porches, and was brought to its present site by slaves, who used logs for rollers.

Proceeding southwestward, State 90 winds through fertile bottom lands of a small valley, and climbs to cross a low range of rolling hills.

BRENHAM, 46 *m.* (350 alt., 7,740 pop.) is at the junction with US 290 (*see Tour 24*).

Tour 25

Rosenberg—Victoria—Alice—Laredo; 311 *m.* US 59.

US 59 takes a southwesterly course across the Coastal Plain, running between the lush, moist, rice and cotton lands south of Houston and the semi-arid, chaparral-covered ranch and oil field region that covers the southern tip of Texas, to the Rio Grande. The first miles parallel the Gulf, through an area made rich by fertile soil and abundant rainfall—a land of prosperous farms, tilled by descendants of German, Polish, Bohemian and Danish immigrants. Irish colonists settled the cotton and ranch lands along the middle of the route; southward, where Spanish ranchmen were followed by cattle barons of non-Latin blood, the Mexicans believe black butterflies to be a sign of disaster, fear Tuesday as an unlucky day, and brew a tea of orange blossoms to cure nervous disorders.

Section a. *ROSENBERG to VICTORIA; 92 m.* US 59

This part of the route crosses the southeastern section of the Coastal Plain, traversing a region of extensive agriculture and ranching. A curious mixture of cultures lingers here: traces of the plantation era with its tangible evidences—rambling white houses set in groves of moss-draped oaks, old-time Negroes, and cotton; some of the glamour of the days of the cattle kings, who erected mansions; and combined with this, the thrift and customs of descendants of European immigrants. In this region of canebrakes, oil wells, rice, pecans and humpbacked Brahmas, the land is black, rolling and open except along streams and where small groves of oaks make islands of darker green in a usually verdant picture.

ROSENBERG, 0 *m.* (106 alt., 10,775 pop.), is at the junction with US 90 (*see Tour 23*).

Southwest of Rosenberg rich grazing lands support numerous herds of Brahma cattle.

KENDLETON, 12 *m.* (102 alt., 200 pop.), a few weathered houses around a general store, is almost exclusively a Negro community. An early land grant was sold to freed Negroes on long-time credit. Nearly all the families are now full owners of the farms they occupy.

Southwest of Kendleton clumps of woodland become more frequent.

The SAN BERNARD RIVER, 15.1 *m.,* has lowlands that are subject to seasonal overflow. Rich and fertile, they have many farms, and attractive farmhouses are visible. To the southwest a rice-growing region is entered.

WHARTON, 27 *m.* (111 alt., 5,700 pop.), was named for William and John Wharton, patriots. John was adjutant general at the Battle of San Jacinto. It is the seat of Wharton County and has rice milling and sulphur processing. WHARTON COUNTY JUNIOR COLLEGE (1946) enrolls about 1,300.

PIERCE, 34 m. (109 alt., 125 pop.), a supply center for adjacent oil fields, was named for Colonel Abel H. (Shanghai) Pierce, pioneer cattle baron (see Tour 22b).

US 59 leads past more pasture lands and low-lying rice fields, with occasionally some oil derricks.

EL CAMPO (the camp), 40 m. (110 alt., 8,000 pop.), was the camping place for the cowboys of four large ranches during early-day round-ups. Today it is a milling, shipping, and trading center for the rice farmers and stockmen of the area. Near-by oil developments have given it many new buildings.

Left from El Campo on State 71 to DANEVANG (Dan., Danish meadow), 12 m. (300 pop.), center of an area of prosperous cotton farms. It was founded in 1894 by Danes, whose descendants today comprise 90 per cent of the population. In 1904 a plague of leaf worms destroyed a large part of the crops, and the people pooled their resources to halt the infestation. The Danevang Farmers Cooperative Society in a few years was able to pay high dividends.

GANADO (cattle), 58 m. (71 alt., 1,600 pop.), a livestock shipping point, was so named because of the numbers of longhorns that roamed surrounding prairies at the founding of the settlement, in 1883. State 172 connects Ganado with the Gulf.

The NAVIDAD RIVER is crossed at 61 m., its banks lined with large trees heavily draped with mustang grapevines.

EDNA, 67 m. (72 alt., 5,038 pop.), has many fine homes and smart, modern shops, the result of oil development near by.

The site of TEXANA, in 1835 the capital of the Municipality of Jackson, is at the junction of the Navidad and Lavaca Rivers, on State 616, south of Edna and 2.5 m. west of Lolita. A number of antebellum houses have been moved from Texana to Edna, including the Wharton, Billups, Horton and Kaape homes. Four m. northeast of Edna on State 111, is the site of Millican Gin, where the first document demanding Texas independence was drafted. Jackson County, of which Edna is the seat, has 30,000 acres devoted to rice.

TELFERNER, 84 m. (96 alt., 200 pop.), was named for the Italian Count Telferner, who conceived the idea of building a railroad from New York to Mexico City. The first division, called the New York, Texas & Mexico, was constructed by the Count from Houston to Victoria, and dubbed the Macaroni Route because it was built with Italian capital. It is today part of the Southern Pacific Lines.

VICTORIA, 92 m. (93 alt., 36,700 pop., est.), is at junctions with US 77, US 87 and State 185. BLOOMINGTON, (1,850 pop.) is 14 m. south.

Section b.   VICTORIA to LAREDO; 189 m.   US 59

Beginning in live oak-studded prairies where cattle kings have acquired greater wealth through oil, the route continues across brushy, rolling ranch country split by the Nueces River, the *Rio de Oro* (river of gold) of the Spaniards, where tales of buried treasure along the vanished courses of old roads still tempt prospectors. Following the Texas Revolution Mexico insisted that the Nueces, not the Rio Grande, marked the Texas-Mexico boundary, a claim not settled until after the Mexican War.

At the southwestern edge of VICTORIA, 0 *m.*, US 59 merges with US 77 (*see Tour 7*), and proceeds jointly with it for a distance of about two and a half miles.

The GUADALUPE RIVER is crossed at 0.5 *m.*, and the way proceeds through pasture lands studded with large oaks, elms and pecans.

At 2.6 *m.* is the junction where US 77 (*see Tour 7*) diverges southward.

FANNIN, 16 *m.* (143 alt., 150 pop.), a quiet, shady one-street town, was named for Colonel James W. Fannin, Jr., Texas Revolutionary hero.

Left from Fannin on State 162 to the FANNIN BATTLEFIELD STATE PARK, 1 *m.,* where Colonel Fannin and his little army (all but a few of them recently arrived volunteers from the United States), were overtaken in their retreat from Goliad to Victoria. Having failed, for reasons which he believed good, to obey an order from General Sam Houston to retreat to Victoria, Fannin fought skirmishes on March 18, 1836, with an advance detachment of General José Urrea's army and began his retreat on the following morning under cover of a heavy fog. His supplies and baggage were in slow-moving oxcarts, and when the fog lifted a few hours later he discovered that he had been overtaken by a Mexican force about equal to his own. He attempted to reach the cover afforded by a strip of woods about half a mile distant, but the breaking of a wheel on the cart carrying his ammunition delayed him to such an extent that he was soon surrounded.

On the open prairie not far from Coleto Creek, Fannin hurriedly erected a fortification of carts and baggage placed in the form of a square, posted his artillery at the four corners, and prepared to meet the impending assault. It came without delay in a combined infantry and cavalry charge, led by General Urrea. The heavy fire of the Texans blasted this attempt quickly, but the Mexicans re-formed their lines and came on again and again. During intervals between the assaults the Texans strengthened their barricades and loaded extra rifles. Every attack had been repulsed when darkness fell, but 60 of Fannin's men were wounded and suffering from lack of water. Fresh Mexican troops reinforced Urrea before dawn, and at daylight Fannin, with 275 men, faced a force of about 1,000. The impossibility of either victory or escape was obvious, and most of Fannin's officers advised surrender, believing that terms could be made under which they would be treated as prisoners of war. Fannin, himself wounded, recalled to them Santa Anna's order that all foreigners taken bearing arms were to be regarded as pirates and executed at once. However, the position of the Texans seemed hopeless, as they were without food, water, or medical supplies, and they raised a white flag just as the opening volley of a Mexican attack was fired.

A misunderstanding existed as to the terms of the surrender, survivors maintaining that General Urrea pledged humane treatment, while the document, in Mexican archives, says that the capitulation was made "subject to the disposition of the supreme government," which was equivalent, technically, to a surrender at discretion. The wounded Fannin and his men were returned to the presidio at Goliad, whence, on Palm Sunday, all except a few were led out and executed (*see below*).

GOLIAD, 25 *m.* (167 alt., 1,750 pop.), has grown old gracefully. The serenity of its oak-shaded streets and the dignity of many of its houses are in contrast to its hectic past. It grew around a mission and presidio established here by the Spaniards in 1749. Since that early date it has passed through eras of development and decay. Once an important link in the colonization system of the Spaniards, Goliad fell into disuse when the soldiers were withdrawn following Mexico's revolt against Spain.

Its bloody history began with the capture of the old Spanish presidio by Magee and his volunteers from the United States, fighting for Mexico in 1812. In 1817 Perry, another Anglo-American adventurer, and his 50 followers were killed at the Presidio La Bahia. Long's Mississippians captured the fort in 1821.

In 1835, with the Texas Revolution seven days old, Ben Milam and George M. Collinsworth drove a Mexican garrison from the presidio and captured it. In December of 1835, a band of revolutionists issued Texas' first declaration of independence at Goliad. Here in March, 1836, Fannin and his men battled Mexican troops surrounding the fort, and on Palm Sunday he and about 330 other Texas soldiers were massacred in the immediate vicinity of the town.

After the Texas Revolution, Goliad's soldiers and adventurers were replaced by merchants, farmers and cattlemen.

Goliad was the scene of the Cart War of 1857, a labor conflict between non-Latin and Mexican freighters. When the Mexicans cut prices, their competitors killed some of them and burned their carts and loads. Texas Rangers ended the conflict. In 1861, Goliad's Aranama College became suddenly defunct when its entire student body marched out of the classrooms to enlist in the Confederate army.

Left from Goliad on Texas Revolution Memorial Highway 29 to GOLIAD STATE PARK, 2 *m.* Within the park area are the restored MISSION NUESTRA SEÑORA DEL ESPIRITU SANTO DE ZUÑIGA (Our Lady of the Holy Spirit of Zuñiga) (R), the well-preserved remains of the PRESIDIO NUESTRA SEÑORA DE LORETO DE LA BAHIA (Fort of Our Lady of Loreto of the Bay) (L), and the SITE OF ARANAMA COLLEGE. (*Mission and presidio open daylight hours, free.*) The Mexican village is the FIRST SITE OF GOLIAD. The mission and presidio were founded at the site of La Salle's Fort St. Louis in 1722. They were moved in 1726 to the Guadalupe, near Victoria, and by the autumn of 1749 were on their present locations. They served the Karankawa Indians. The MISSION MUSEUM (*open daily; free*), was established in 1934 and contains many relics of the mission and colonization eras. The chapel of the presidio has the SHRINE OF NUESTRA SEÑORA DE LORETO DE LA BAHIA, unchanged since it was first constructed nearly 200 years ago.

It was from this presidio that Fannin set forth upon receipt of Travis' appeal for aid for the Alamo, to return when a wagon broke down; and from here were sent out the expeditions of King to the relief of the people of Refugio, and Ward to the relief of King, both of which ended in disaster. Because these expeditions had not returned, Fannin failed, until too late, to obey Houston's order to retreat to Victoria.

After their surrender to Urrea, Fannin and his men were returned to the presidio, and there joined 85 members of Ward's command and 80 volunteers from Nashville, Tennessee, who had been captured when they landed at Copano. On March 27, those able to walk—except the doctors, needed to care for the Mexican wounded, and a few selected for hospital duty or who for other reasons had been spared—were marched from the presidio in three columns, some believing they were going out for labor duty, others having been given to understand that they were being moved to the coast for embarkation to the United States. About a mile from the presidio the rifles of the guards were suddenly turned upon them and they were shot down. A few escaped in the confusion, and a few, badly wounded, were spared on the plea of a Mexican woman, Señora Alvarez, called the Angel of Goliad, who also hid others until the executions were over. At least 330 men, including the command of Major Ward, who had surrendered at Victoria, died that day. Fannin, too badly wounded to march, was taken into the yard of the presidio and there killed with a bullet through the back of his head. The dead were stripped of their clothing, the bodies thrown into heaps and partly burned. More than two months later the charred and mutilated remains were gathered and buried at the spot where now stands the GOLIAD MEMORIAL SHAFT. The order for this slaying of helpless prisoners came from Santa Anna in a message to Colonel Portilla, Mexican commander at Goliad. News of the event, reaching Houston's army, inspiried one of the two battle cries of San Jacinto, "Remember Goliad!"

Southwest of Goliad in a roadside park, 26.1 *m.,* is an elevated observation point. By sighting along an arrow the Presidio of La Bahia is visible. Opposite the Presidio on US 183 is the birthplace of General Ignacio Zaragosa, Mexican minister of war under Juarez, whose defeat of the French at Pueblo averted an invasion of Texas.

At 29.1 *m.* are the ruins (L) of the MISSION NUESTRA SEÑORA DEL ROSARIO DE LOS CUJANES. (Our Lady of the Rosary of the Cujanes), founded in 1754 to serve several of the Karankawa tribes.

BEEVILLE, 55 *m.* 214 alt., 13,811 pop.) is at a junction with US 181, which proceeds to Corpus Christi, and also with State 202, which proceeds east to a junction with US 77 near Refugio, whence another road leads to Aransas National Wildlife Refuge.

GEORGE WEST, 79 *m.* (162 alt., 1,878 pop.) is a farm town at the junction with US 281. Farther southwest on US 59 are the huge ranchlands of Live Oak, Duval and Webb Counties. At 100 *m.* US 59 crosses Ranch Road 624, leading to Corpus Christi.

FREER, 124 *m.* (510 alt., 2,724 pop.) is a commercial center for agricultural and oil interests. Beef and dairy cattle are profitable in Duval County.

LAREDO, 189 *m.* (438 alt., 64,000 pop. est.) is served by US 81 and US 83 combines, Interstate 35, State 359.

Section c.   BEEVILLE-SKIDMORE to LAREDO; State 359

This is a diversionary route that enables the tourist to get into the heart of Bee, Jim Wells, Duval and Webb Counties between the big north-south highways, US 59, US 281, and US 77. From Beeville on US 59 southeast to Skidmore on US 181 is 11 miles. At this point State 359 begins.

South on this road to TYNAN, 8 *m.*, a hamlet in Bee County, and MATHIS, 14 *m.* in San Patricio County (161 alt., 6,000 pop.) business center for agricultural and oil production. Two miles beyond Mathis on the Nueces River Irish immigrant families founded the village of SAN PATRICIO. In 1828 Jim McGloin obtained a charter from the Mexican government. So many immigrants came from Ireland that Gaelic was spoken on the streets. Today only a church, a school, and a store remain. San Patricio County had 45,021 people in 1960. The rainfall is 30 in. a year and the area is wooded.

The highway passes the eastern end of LAKE CORPUS CHRISTI STATE PARK, 4 *m.* southwest of Mathis. The Lake on the lower Nueces River, impounded by the Wesley E. Seale Dam, covers 15,500 acres and is the principal fresh water supply for Corpus Christi.

Then comes chaparral country, where thorny bushes were responsible for the chaps—leather breeches—worn by cowboys. Later, as cattle were trailed northward, these protective "second pants" were made of woolly hides, in the cold country; but here, at the place of their origin, they are always made of plain, well-tanned leather, their only decorative features being silver *conchos* (shell-like fasteners), and tasseled tie strings. Thousands of head of wild cattle roamed this region in the days following the Texas Revolution. Nature created in this area that breed of cattle found nowhere else on earth—the long-legged, lean-flanked, hard-headed, wild-eyed Texas longhorn. Without the stamina, the endurance and hardihood of this breed, the long trail drives over mountains, deserts, and prairies would have been impossible. They throve where the softer, heavier breeds of the East would have starved.

ALICE, 44 *m.* (205 alt., 23,000 pop. is at a junction with US 281 and State 44. South of Alice State 359 runs across undulating prairies, past endless grazing grounds colored with purple sage, blue-green cactus and emerald mesquite, to SAN DIEGO, 54 *m.* (312 alt., 4,795 pop.), once an important cattle shipping point which required Ranger detachments to cope with its gun-toting citizens and cowboys, and with the bands of rustlers that infested the back country. Today its old houses of stone and adobe bask in a quiet atmosphere.

San Diego flared suddenly in 1914, when a fantastic scheme providing for the conquest of Texas, New Mexico, Arizona, and California, and their reannexation to Mexico, was hatched here. From the San Diego headquarters attempts were made to organize Texas Mexicans for a general uprising, scheduled for February 20, 1915.

This plot was bared through the arrest of a Mexican in Brownsville, in whose possession were found copies of the plan. Several Carranzista generals were mentioned as favorable to the scheme, and hints were made of assistance from friends in Europe. Recruits for the revolutionary army were to be selected only from people of Latin, Indian, or Negro blood, and it was stipulated that no Germans were to be killed. The scheme collapsed with its discovery. The Plan of San Diego was closely followed by the famous Zimmerman note to President Carranza of Mexico, which indicated a wish that the United States be embroiled in war with Mexico and thus prevented from participating in the World War.

Other farm outlets on this highway are BENAVIDES, 70 m. (2,250 pop.) and REALITES, 84 m. (240 pop.).

HEBBRONVILLE, 98 m. (550 alt., 4,500 pop.), was a supply center for the far-flung ranches, but oil developments have given it new industrial activity. It is the seat of Jim Hogg County.

OILTON, 120 m. (500 pop.), was once called Torrecillas (little towers), because of some small stone towers of unknown origin that stood on the brow of a little hill at the edge of town. The name was changed with the development of a small oil field in 1922. Weatherbeaten houses on sandy streets indicate the brevity of the boom.

AGUILARES (eagle's nest), 128 m. (617 alt., 50 pop.), is in the vicinity of the SHIPP RANCH, site of one of the best authenticated tales of buried treasure. The story tells how a cowboy—one of the Shipp hands— who was riding the range late one afternoon, lurched as his horse stepped into a hole and, being unable to extricate its foot, nearly fell. The cowboy dismounted, to discover that the horse's hoof had broken through the rotted wooden lid of a good-sized box or trunk filled with Spanish doubloons. Excitedly he filled his saddle bags, his pockets, and even his hat, and yet a large quantity of the coins remained. The cowboy rode rapidly to the ranch house and showed his find to the other hands. A mad dash to the corral followed. The entire outfit rode at a run to recover the remainder of the treasure. They did not, however, for although they searched all night and for many days thereafter, neither they nor the cowboy whose horse had stumbled into it could locate that box of golden coins. For years other people have searched; but while the coins brought in by the cowboy were real enough, the box and its remaining contents have never been found, unless by someone able to keep his discovery a secret.

LAREDO, 154 m. (438 alt., 64,000 pop., 1964, est.) is at the junction with US 83.

Tour 26

San Antonio—Kenedy—Beeville—Skidmore—Sinton—Taft—Gregory —Corpus Christi; 149 m. US 181.

This route runs southeast between the rolling hill country near San Antonio, and tidewater at Corpus Christi Bay, crossing the broad sweep of the Gulf Coastal Plain. Timber lessens as the coast is approached, but along the streams are many large pecan trees. In summer the countryside is bright with wild flowers, bluebonnets, and white and yellow daisies predominating. This was once almost exclusively ranching country, but agriculture now holds an important place. Cotton is the leading crop. Many small farms are tilled by thrifty descendants of the Germans, Poles, and Irish who came into the region nearly a century ago. Rent farmers and sharecroppers are largely Mexicans, as are the majority of seasonal farm laborers. Towns along the route show plainly the economic influence of extensive oil and gas developments. But the people still live for and with their neighbors in the old-fashioned way.

SAN ANTONIO, 0 *m.* (656 alt.) (*see San Antonio*).

The SAN ANTONIO STATE HOSPITAL (L), 4.8 *m.*, has facilities for 2,811 mentally-ill persons. The grounds cover 665 acres.

At 5.2 *m.* is a junction with a paved road that leads to Brooks Air Force Base, described under San Antonio.

BERG'S MILL, 6.9 *m.* (542 alt., 113 pop.), is a sleepy old village. Southward the route enters an area called the "blackjack country," the hideout of many moonshine stills during the days of prohibition.

At 28 *m.* is a junction with a dirt road.

Right on this road to the JUAN N. SEGUIN HOUSE (*open; free*), 0.5 *m.* Built in 1855 by Seguin, a Texas patriot, this structure is of sandstone and has the long narrow lines and large rooms of its period.

FLORESVILLE, 30 *m.* (389 alt., 2,950 pop.), is an old community of tree-shaded streets, its buildings half hidden by flowers and shrubs. The seat of Wilson County, it has a Peanut Festival in October, celebrating one of the principal crops, which grow on 18,000 acres. Sorghums, cattle, swine and watermelons are paying products.

With the coming of the railroad, Floresville was built on land donated by Juana Montez Flores, member of one of the old Spanish families who owned ranches in this vicinity. Many houses of the Spanish and Texas colonial type remain in or near Floresville.

1. Right from Floresville on the old San Antonio Road to LABATT, 6.2 *m.*, a one-store farm community center.

Left from Labatt 0.9 *m.* on a side road to the FRANCISCO FLORES HACIENDA (*adm. 10¢*), once the home of a grandee of Spain. White bricks and adobe blocks (the latter used over the bricks) have been utilized in the one-story colonial dwelling. The main part of the building was erected in 1844; the remainder, at an unknown earlier date.

POTH, 36 *m.* (1,059 pop.); FALLS CITY, 43 *m.* (462 pop.), and HOBSON, 46 *m.* (125 pop.), are farm communities in Wilson and Karnes Counties.

KARNES CITY, 54 *m.* (404 alt., 2,795 pop., est.), is a marketing and shipping community with a wide main street. It is the seat of Karnes County, which has 60,000 acres devoted to flax, also raises beef and dairy cattle, cotton, corn, sorghums and uranium processing.

Left from Karnes City on State 80 to HELENA, 7 *m.* (120 pop.), where the old courthouse still stands. It has existed as Helena since 1852, but for a long time earlier a Mexican settlement called Alamita occupied the site. It was on the old Chihuahua Trail, and long trains of solid-wheeled oxcarts lumbered down the dusty streets, laden with merchandise.

Later the road from San Antonio to Indianola made an intersection here, and the mule-drawn freight wagons of teamsters rumbled through the town. It knew the excitement and strife of the Cart War, when non-Latin teamsters sought to drive Mexican oxcart drivers from the highway.

With the inauguration of a stagecoach line from San Antonio to the coast, Helena became the only stop between San Antonio and Goliad. For 30 years the community prospered, although during part of that period outlaws infested the region, preying on freighters, stagecoach passengers, and lone travelers, and stealing horses and cattle. The "gentry of the brush" came frequently to Helena, which acquired a reputation as a tough town, until the Karnes County vigilance committee and Texas Rangers ousted the undesirables. It was in this vicinity that John Wesley Hardin began building the reputation that later earned him national notoriety as a gunman and killer.

Among the outlaws of this area is said to have originated that sanguinary form of personal encounter called the Helena Duel. It consisted of tying the left hands of the duelists securely together with rawhide, giving each a knife with a three-inch blade, whirling them around rapidly a few times and turning them loose. The shortness of the knife blades prohibited the likelihood of a fatal single stroke, and the fight progressed as a gruesome, gory slashing match while the contestants hacked away furiously. No quarter was given or expected.

But Helena had many industrious citizens, and the town continued to thrive until, in the 1880's, when the railroad passed it by.

East of Karnes City, 1 *m.*, is a junction with State 123; 5 *m.* north is PANNA MARIA (275 pop.) oldest Polish settlement in Texas (1854).

Southward US 181 climbs a hill which affords a view of farms and woodlands. From a distance, twin water tanks indicate KENEDY, 60 *m.* (271 alt., 4,301 pop.), an L-shaped town. There is an uncertain middle-aged appearance about Kenedy, its business houses and residences for the most part indicating the era of its founding (1882). Its hot mineral wells have made it a health resort. It has several large cotton and food processing plants.

PETTUS, 76 *m.* (299 alt., 350 pop.), in Bee County, is a farm village, as are the hamlets of TULETTA and NORMANNA, both with only nominal populations. Some oil supplies pass through Pettus.

BEEVILLE, 92 *m.* (214 alt., 13,811 pop.), is an old community modernized by oil wealth. For years cattle and cotton were its vital interests, but petroleum production nearby has added starkly new business and residential areas, and has created an animated main street.

Irish immigrants settled Beeville in the 1830's. Early-day life in the community was sometimes turbulent. In the surrounding cattle country horse thieves and cattle rustlers were rampant, and many counties of the area found themselves without effective law enforcement. Sheriffs were frequently found shot in the back.

In 1876, Sheriff D. A. F. Walton arrested Ed Singleton, notorious outlaw, who was tried and sentenced to be hanged. Singleton bequeathed his skin to the district attorney, directing that it be stretched over a drum head and that the drum be beaten to the tune of "Old Molly Hare" in front of the courthouse on each anniversary of his hanging, as a warning to evildoers. The remainder of his anatomy he bequeathed to doctors "in the cause of science."

In Beeville is the junction with US 59.

SKIDMORE, 103 *m.* (159 alt., 650 pop.) is a shipping center, scattered along the S curve of the highway. Here State 359 turns south to Laredo.

SINTON, 122 *m.* (49 alt., 6,008 pop.), a flat sun-steeped town with modern public buildings set back from the long main street formed by the highway, is at the junction with US 77 (*see Tour 7*).

Southward the route traverses part of the former lands of Charles P. Taft of Cincinnati, and one of the best cotton areas of the State, producing nearly one bale to an acre. Sinton was laid out in 1893 and named for David Sinton, a Cincinnati investor and father-in-law of Taft. Its location at the junction of two railways and near the center of San Patricio County caused it to be made the county seat.

The ROB AND BESSIE WELDER WILDLIFE REFUGE, off US 77 at Sinton, occupies 8,000 acres along the Aransas River and is the largest privately endowed wildlife refuge. It has buildings for administration, student dormitories and social events. For permission to visit see Chamber of Commerce.

Cotton gins are busy 24 hours a day, during the picking season. Huge trucks heavily loaded with cotton bales crowd the highways in an almost constant stream, and create a traffic hazard, especially at night.

TAFT, 130 *m.* (54 alt., 3,463 pop.), scatters its business section along the highway. Its well-weathered homes stand in the shade of chinaberry trees and wind-whipped palms. Storms of hurricane force sometimes sweep in from the Gulf to batter this region. Taft was named for Charles P. Taft, half-brother of President William Howard Taft. The great Taft Ranch contained more than a million acres before it was subdivided and opened for settlement. President Taft while in office spent four days here as a guest of La Quinta, the ranch headquarters. An oil and gas field is adjacent to the town.

The PRESBYTERIAN MEXICAN GIRLS' BOARDING SCHOOL (L), 132 *m.,* is located here.

GREGORY, 138 *m.* (32 alt., 2,350 pop.) (*see Tour 22*), is at the junction with State 35. Here US 181 turns sharply right and proceeds to the edge of a bluff that overlooks Nueces and Corpus Christi Bays, their gray-blue waters sweeping out to where on clear days, are visible the sand hills of Mustang Island, lying on the horizon like tawny clouds. The coastline curves in a finely arched crescent, at first almost unpopulated, then gradually dotted with cottages, hotels, and tourist lodges, which collectively become Corpus Christi's North Beach—beyond which the two-tiered effect of that city's business district seems to pile office buildings on top of each other, for the reason that buildings on the bay level reach to the top of a bluff, where other structures have their base.

US 181 crosses Nueces Bay on a two-and-a-half-mile causeway, the western end of which is reached at 146.6 *m.* Tourist quarters crowd close together. Here thousands of Texans come to play.

CORPUS CHRISTI, 149 *m.* (40 alt., 193,000 pop. est.) (*see Corpus Christi*).

I(❖I(❖I(❖I(❖I(❖I(❖I(❖I(❖I(❖I(❖I(❖I(❖I(❖I(❖I(❖I(❖I(❖I(❖I(❖I(❖I(❖I(❖I(❖I(❖I(❖I(❖

Tour 27

Junction with US 277—Aspermont—Post—Tahoka—Bronco—(Roswell, N. Mex.) ; US 380.
Junction with US 277 to New Mexico Line, 211 *m.*

Running across the center of the South Plains, US 380 penetrates one of the State's predominantly rural sections, where cotton, corn, wheat and small grains and Herefords, Durhams and other cattle are the chief sources of income on broad, rolling acres. Towns are often little changed from those of early-day west Texas; and between communities, habitations are few.

Into this almost treeless expanse, where in spring the blossoms of prairie flax, wild onions, hollyhocks, prairie lace and other wild flowers make pools of color, buffalo hunters came first, to be followed by cattlemen, who, seeking free ranges, drove gaunt longhorns into the former hunting grounds of Kiowas and Comanches. It was not until 1874, when General Mackenzie literally rounded up the Indians and conducted them to reservations, that actual settlement began.

Wolves and sandstorms, droughts and occasional Indian raids failed to daunt the hardy few who, largely of Anglo-Saxon stock, ventured into this frontier. Longhorns were driven to railheads in Dodge City and Caldwell, Kansas, and points in New Mexico. In the 1880's farmers began to arrive, some to remain and conquer the enmity of cattlemen and the ravages of dry winds and sleet, others to return in defeat to less hostile lands.

Today the great ranches of other years are largely intact in many sections, but where agriculture has proved profitable, ranges are being broken up into broad fields in which tractors are turning more and more of the prairie sod to productivity each year. While urban growth in the 1920's was depopulating rural areas in many parts of the United States, here it merely caused ranchmen and farmers to build houses in the towns nearest their holdings. From these houses today a number of the land barons of the Plains rule their domains.

With no large urban centers along the route, recreation and social life are largely unchanged since the days of the pioneers. Wolves and coyotes abound, and, often, parties hunt these predatory animals with pedigreed hounds. Sometimes the hunts assume large proportions, and become social events. Old-time dances are popular. With increasing wealth, classes of society have become more pronounced, but in general the democratic social attitude of the old West remains.

Natural resources, almost entirely undeveloped, underlie much of the route. Deposits include sand, clay, sulphur, salt, copper, building stone and gypsum, and large oil reservoirs.

The route starts at the junction with US 277, 0 *m.* (*see Tour 10*), 2 miles north of STAMFORD (*see Tour 10a*).

In this part of the State, over 350,000 acres stretch the holdings of the SMS RANCH, established by S. M. Swenson, a Swedish immigrant. Today this great estate is one of the few ranches in Texas that has a mail order business. Feeder cattle are shipped to the Corn Belt, in most cases to buyers who simply place a mail order for the animals.

The junction with State 283, at 8 *m.*, forms the apex of a three-acre triangle utilized as a roadside park (*table, benches, outdoor fireplaces*).

The DOUBLE MOUNTAIN FORK OF THE BRAZOS RIVER, 15.7 *m.*, winds through a region where once great herds of buffalo roamed. Although in this Plains area mesquite trees are most often seen, along the forks of the Brazos are groves of cottonwoods, poplars, salt cedars, live oaks, mulberries, pecans and weeping willows.

The old STONEWALL COUNTY COURTHOUSE (*private*), is visible (R) at 20.7 *m.* It is a two-story stone structure that once stood in the center of the thriving little town of Rayner. The county seat was moved, and Rayner vanished except for this building, used today as a residence.

ASPERMONT, 30 *m.* (1,773 alt., 1,286 pop. est.) County seat, is at the junction with US 83 (*see Tour 16*), which is united with US 380 for a distance of three miles.

At 33 *m.* is the junction with US 83 (*see Tour 16*).

SWENSON, 37 *m.* (1,750 alt., 94 pop.), until recently used its town square, which was surrounded by a stout, five-strand barbed wire fence, as a corral where cattle were held for shipment. In the vicinity of Swenson's winding sandy streets are 40,000 acres of farms, where cotton and corn are grown.

West of Swenson coal and copper have been found, and there are large deposits of gypsum. The land is covered with sagebrush, soapweeds, nettles, and stunted mesquites.

Ranchers in this section wage constant warfare on coyotes. It is customary to hang the carcasses on fence posts along the roads.

At the SALT FORK OF THE BRAZOS RIVER, 44.2 *m.*, the red walls of a deep gash show stratifications of white gypsum. Southward lift the twin peaks of DOUBLE MOUNTAIN (2,550 alt.), which long served as a landmark to early-day travelers.

JAYTON, 54 *m.* (2,016 alt., 750 pop. est.) is the seat of Kent County. In the knife-scarred chairs of the hotel's front porch, the few travelers can sit and view the serenity of the mesquite-dotted public square. Jayton retains the aspect of a cowtown, which it once was to the exclusion of other interests. In the vicinity is the headquarters building of the old O Bar O Ranch.

Cattlemen of this region obtain salt for their stock from surface deposits, where the salt is broken with plows and loaded into wagons.

CLAIREMONT, 70 *m.* (2,127 alt., 150 pop.), established in 1888, has several stores and a post office sprawled around the town square. In the center of the square is a stone courthouse surrounded by a plank fence, which until recently was scaled by means of old-fashioned stiles; but today there is a gap where part of the fence is down. The only church building here is owned by Methodists, but is used by other denominations, the ministers making regular visits after the manner of circuit riders.

Southeast of Clairemont, in farming areas, are some of Texas' Swedish folk. In their communities, many Old Country customs prevail. The mother tongue is used freely, particularly in church services. Eating forms the basis of much social life; food is the feature of nearly every gathering. Huge Sunday dinners are a custom; the friends and relatives invited must, as a matter of accepted etiquette, refuse to be seated at the table until the host or hostess, or both, scolds or virtually drags them to their chairs. For the host to relinquish his insistence would be an insult to the guest, who in all cases must be prevailed upon to partake of the food, and the greater the resistance of the guest, the greater his display of good manners. Noon-day dinner is the principal meal, but it is considered extremely rude not to invite guests to remain for supper. And to accept an invitation to dinner without remaining for supper would be considered an affront to the host and hostess.

The elevation at 95 *m.* presents a broad panorama. Far to the right is Blanco Canyon, through which flows the White River, and in the middle distance is the valley of the Salt Fork of the Brazos, into which the White River empties. The Double Mountain Fork of the Brazos is visible (L) a few miles distant. Along the horizon to the north, northwest, west, and southwest sweeps the ragged, crescent-shaped wall of the plains escarpment, rising 400 feet in places, and resembling a low mountain range. Somewhere in this vicinity ran the route of the Mackenzie Trail, followed by General Mackenzie in some of his forays against raiding Comanches.

Westward the highway follows the crest of a ridge between the Salt and Double Mountain Forks of the Brazos, passing through fine ranching country. Lands of the SMS Ranch and those of the Jaybird are right of US 380, while to the left lies the Connell Ranch.

POST, 109 *m.* (2,590 alt., 4,662 pop. est. 1966), was founded in 1907 by C. W. Post, Battle Creek, Michigan, philanthropist, who dreamed of having here a model town where agriculture and industry were to round out its civic existence. Post died too soon to realize his ambition. He did, however, establish a cotton textile mill that today employs between 100 and 400 workers, depending upon demand. Farmers haul their cotton to the mill's gin, where the lint is sucked up by machinery, and the cotton emerges at the other side of the plant as finished cloth, ready for the market. Sandstone in varying shades of brown and tan was used for many of the business buildings, most of which were erected by Post in a design permitting more comfort and many more windows than usual. Post is seat of Garza County, which produces cotton, cattle and oil.

In Post is the junction with US 84 (*see Tour 21*).

1. Right from Post on a dirt road to TWO DRAW LAKE (*swimming, fishing, boating, camping, picnic facilities and playgrounds*), 3.1 *m.*

2. Left from Post on a dirt road to the CURRYCOMB RANCH HEADQUARTERS (*open*), 2 *m.* The ranch house and 400 acres are used for a camp by the South Plains Area Council of the Boy Scouts of America. The old house, one of the earliest in this part of Texas, is being carefully preserved by the Scouts.

At 5 *m.* is the junction with a dirt road. Left here to the gate of the U LAZY S (Slaughter) RANCH. From here a private road leads to the ranch headquarters, six miles farther on. This was at first called the Square and Compass Ranch. It was founded in 1881 by J. B. Slaughter, one of the area's pioneer cattlemen. Near here is the site of an Indian camp, occupied by Quanah Parker and 300 Comanches in the 1870's. The U Lazy S has other points of interest, including a formation called the Devil's Breakfast Table, an interesting example of erosion. Buffalo Point, nearby, is a ledge over which hunters once drove a herd of buffaloes, killing hundreds. Guides can be obtained at the ranch headquarters for trips to these places, also for a drive along the Canyon Rim Road, which circles Double Mountain Canyon. The U Lazy S contains a game preserve sheltering deer, antelopes, and cataloes; the latter are hybrids resulting from the cross-breeding of cattle and buffaloes.

West of Post US 380 climbs the plains escarpment and enters a gently rolling area of the South Plains. Here modern mechanized agriculture has turned many of the former cattle ranges into cultivated fields, and dairy cattle in some localities have largely replaced beef steers.

TAHOKA, 133 *m.* (3,090 alt., 3,000 pop. est. 1966) is at the junction with US 87.

West of Tahoka there is cattle range. On both sides of the highway lie the lands of the T Bar Ranch.

At 139.5 *m.* is the junction with a dirt road.

Right here to DOUBLE LAKES, 2 *m.,* sometimes called Twin Lakes. On the north shore of the upper lakes is the headquarters of the T Bar Ranch, established in 1883. The lakes are unusually rich in potash content. Hunters whose headquarters were here claimed that more buffaloes were killed in this vicinity between 1877 and 1879 than at any other point in Texas. Survivors of the so-called Lost Negro Expedition, composed of a company of Negro soldiers of the 10th U. S. Cavalry and some buffalo hunters, who lost their way while trailing a band of Indians and wandered for 96 hours without water, found it at these lakes after five of the party had died of thirst.

BROWNFIELD, 161 *m.* (3,312 alt., 11,000 pop. est. 1966) is the seat of Terry County, named for the commander of Terry's Rangers. It has the Bibricora feeding pens, which are large enough to hold 10,000 head of feeder stock. This number is shipped in regularly from Mexico and fattened here for market. Brownfield also has cotton gins, feed mills and chick hatcheries.

SULPHUR DRAW, 193.4 *m.,* so named because of near-by deposits, long served as a highway for frontier travelers. An Indian trail followed it, and wandering bands of Comanches and Mescalero Apaches frequently used it. Later New Mexican traders and sheepherders drove their flocks down the old path toward the South Plains. Soldiers and buffalo hunters also used the route.

PLAINS, 194 *m.* (3,400 alt., 1,325 pop. est. 1966) is the seat of Yoakum County, a cotton and oil producer, prospering from irrigation.

Left from Plains on a dirt road to INK BASIN, 10 *m.,* a depression approximately 1,000 acres in extent containing about 20 shallow water wells dug by Indians—supposedly Mescalero Apaches. There are indications of extensive Indian occupation. The wells are now dry for the most part, having been filled with wind-driven sand.

A SOD HOUSE (L), 197 *m.,* is the type of habitation utilized by early settlers in this treeless region. They simply dug a room or rooms underground, and supported the sod roof with cottonwood poles.

US 380 crosses Sulphur Springs Creek at 204 *m.*

BRONCO, 211 *m.* (12 pop.), is said to have been named by local cowboys in 1904 following a demonstration in bronco-riding for the benefit of a visiting shoe salesman. It has not lost its western aspect, or its cowboys.

The little town is astride the State Line, which US 380 crosses 92 miles east of Roswell, New Mexico (*see New Mexico Guide*).

ー＜◆ー＜◆ー＜◆ー＜◆ー＜◆ー＜◆ー＜◆ー＜◆ー＜◆ー＜◆ー＜◆ー＜◆ー＜◆ー＜◆ー＜◆ー＜◆ー＜◆ー＜◆ー＜◆

Tour 28

(Carlsbad, N. Mex.)—Pecos—Fort Stockton—Junction with US 90, US 285.
New Mexico Line to Junction with US 90, 171 *m.*

US 285, running south from the direction of Roswell, N. M., makes a junction at Carlsbad, N. M., with the combined route of US 62 and US 180, which 20 *m.* farther south reaches White City, entrance to Carlsbad Caverns National Park.
Filling stations far apart; check gas, oil and water frequently.
Guard against rattlesnakes.
Accommodations are limited except at Pecos and Fort Stockton.

South of the New Mexico Line, US 285 in general runs southeastward across a plateau with an elevation of from 2,500 to 3,000 feet. The country is semi-arid, though irrigation has made cultivation possible in limited areas. Along the western horizon looms the blue bulk of mountains; eastward the land rolls away in gently sweeping hills. Salt cedar lends its dusty gray-green tinge to the somewhat brighter green of mesquite and cactus. Greasewood and sage blend neutral tones, and only the outcroppings of white, red and yellow rock strata give perpetual color to the landscape. Following spring rains the country is brilliant for a time with the yellow, red, orange and purple of cactus blooms, but this blanket of color fades rapidly in the almost eternal sunshine. The chief interest of the thinly populated region is the landscape; it is truly a land of great open spaces.

US 285 crosses the STATE LINE, 0 *m.*, 33 miles south of Carlsbad, New Mexico (*see New Mexico Guide*).

RED BLUFF, 6.9 *m.* (12 pop.), now chiefly a filling station, was a construction town during the building of Red Bluff Dam.

At 12.4 *m.* is the junction with a graveled road.

Left on this road to RED BLUFF DAM, 2 *m.*, one of the power and irrigation projects scattered along the Pecos River. Here are a hotel, tourist cottages, and many camp sites. Waters of LAKE RED BLUFF formed by the dam cover the site of Camp Pope and Pope's Crossing, a stage stop and ford of the Pecos in the immigrant and stagecoach eras. The lake covers 11,700 acres and has a capacity of 310,000 acre-ft.

Far westward are the Guadalupe Mountains, topped by GUADA-LUPE PEAK (8,751 alt.). The sheer cliff of EL CAPITAN (8,078 alt.), standing in sharp profile at the 50-mile-distant southern termination of the range, is clearly visible from the highway. El Capitan was a landmark of west-bound travelers, immigrants, trail-herders and stagecoach drivers.

In ORLA, 14 *m.* (2,855 alt., 22 pop.), is a mill reducing the crude sulphur of mines 20 miles southwest.

South of Orla the roadway somewhat follows the Pecos River, traversing the approximate course of the old Butterfield Stage route, which forded the river at Horsehead Crossing, turned sharply up the west bank toward Pope's Camp, then westward again to penetrate the mountains through a gap between towering El Capitan and the lesser heights of the Delaware Mountains. This route was blazed by Captain Marcy in 1849. The Goodnight-Loving Cattle Trail of the 1870's used the river ford.

At 35 *m.* is a junction with a graveled road.

Left on this road to ARNO, 2 *m.* (2,663 alt.), a railroad stop by a bridge that spans the Pecos at what was Rocky Ford, sometimes called Horsethief Crossing. At this point the north-bound cattle drives forded the river on their way to Fort Sumner, New Mexico. That other travelers used the crossing is indicated by the name.

Southeastward the highway runs through typical desert country, the adjacent hills covered with sparse bunches of bear grass, and dotted with devil's pincushion, ocotillo, sotol, and various varieties of cactus. Looming vaguely on the western skyline are the Delaware Mountains. The lesser ridges in the middle distance are Rustler's Hills, the one time hideout of cattle thieves.

PECOS, 52 m. (2,580 alt., 14,000 pop. est. 1966) (see page 561), is at the junction with US 80 (see Tour 19).

South of Pecos US 285 crosses a rolling, almost barren cattle country that extends westward to the Apache Range and the Davis Mountains, whose peaks stand against the sky. Between the ranges is the gap through which the California Trail, now US 80, ran westward (see Tour 19).

At 54.4 m. is a junction with a Ranch Road. Left, 4 m. to TOYAH LAKE, and to the GRANDFALLS irrigation system. The town of GRANDFALLS (1,000 pop.) is on State 18, 19 m. south of Monahans.

Southeastward the road dips at intervals to cross the dry draws of Toyah, Coyanosa, and Comanche Creeks (dangerous after heavy rains, watch depth markers at roadside). This is the land of the purple sage, which in bloom spreads its mauve haze over every hillside. The Glass Mountains are dimly visible on the southwestern horizon.

At 107 m. is the junction with US 67 (see Tour 18) and US 290 (see Tour 24).

FORT STOCKTON, 108 m. (3,052 alt., 7,500 pop.).

Southeast of Fort Stockton the route runs for more than 60 miles through ranches, largely unfenced; signs warn the motorist to "watch out for cattle." Here again is the hazard of flood waters in the draws and arroyos. The low mountain ranges visible far on the southwestern horizon are the Peña Blanca Range, the Horse Mountains, and the cluster of rocky, crumbling hills called Hell's Half Acre.

At 171 m. is the junction with US 90 (see Tour 23), at the northern edge of SANDERSON (see Tour 23d).

***

Tour 29

(Carlsbad, N. Mex.)—New Mexico Line—Guadalupe Mountains National Park—El Paso; US 62 and US 180, combined.
New Mexico Line to El Paso, 130 m.

This is a direct route between El Paso and the Carlsbad Caverns. The combined highway of US 62 and US 180, joined at Seminole in Gaines County, Texas, cuts off a corner of New Mexico, turns south at Carlsbad and reaches the entrance to Carlsbad Caverns National Park at White City, 20 m. farther south.

From the New Mexico State Line the highway runs southwestward for approximately one-fifth of its total distance, then turns almost due west, paralleling the northern edge of the westernmost part of Texas. It traverses a terrain of wild, desolate grandeur. Rugged mountains tower skyward, and white salt flats extend for miles. Trees and plants range from the pines and oaks of the high areas, to sagebrush, bear grass, and cacti in the lower levels. Wide vistas abound, and the clear, thin air seems to bring within walking distance a mountain peak 25 miles away. At midday, weird, heat-created mirages appear and disappear in the distance; heat-devils dance, and the dust-laden weed called Texas Tommy whirls across the highway and beats itself to pieces. Cactus growths and rock formations may tempt the traveler to explore afoot, but care should be taken, as rattlesnakes are plentiful. During July, August, and September frequent rains in the mountains often cause high water hazards at low places in the road.

Ranching is the chief occupation of the few inhabitants. Angora goats and sheep graze on the rocky slopes, and cattle in the high mountain valleys. Natural resources, largely undeveloped, include copper, tin, zinc, gold, mica, gypsum, salt and oil.

In the Guadalupe Mountains are a few black bears, gray jaguars, plateau wildcats, lobo wolves, and many coyotes and wild peccaries. Deer are numerous. Most of the animals, with the exception of those classed as pests by ranchmen, are protected for the purpose of preservation. Bighorns, elks and antelopes are being re-introduced into the region. A total of 150 varieties of yucca, agaves, shrubs, wild flowers and trees are found in the area. The blossoms of cacti are brilliant in the spring, following rains.

US 62 crosses the NEW MEXICO LINE, 0 *m.*, 43 miles southwest of Carlsbad, New Mexico (*see New Mexico Guide*), and heads toward the pass at the southern termination of the Guadalupe Mountains, the rugged slopes of which are visible ahead. Rock and shale, with a scant growth of piñon and stunted oaks, cover the slopes to the 7,000-foot level, where begin the pine forests that clothe the crest of this lofty range. Straight ahead looms the perpendicular face of El Capitan, its 1,500-foot cliff starkly outlined against the sky—a signpost for past generations of travelers. Directly north of El Capitan, which early-day army trail blazers called Signal Peak, rises the rounded, pine-clad crest of Guadalupe Peak.

At 17.8 *m.* is the junction with an unimproved dirt road.

Right here to FRIJOLE, 1 *m.* (5,550 alt.) called the loftiest town in Texas, resting in the shadow of frowning FRIJOLE PEAK (8,245 alt.). Close to Frijole is Manzaneta Spring, and a few hundred yards up nearby Smith Canyon is Smith Spring, both named for a postmaster at Frijole. Above Smith Spring lift the heights of SOLDIER LOOKOUT POINT (5,750 alt.), from where, in the days of the stagecoach era, sentries kept watch for Butterfield stages, which were often beset at this spot by Indians. In the ranch house at Frijole a post office is maintained in an old-fashioned desk in the front room. In the rear of the house is a large fruit orchard of cherry, apple, and peach trees, irrigated by the waters of Manzaneta Spring.

Here begins the rugged wildness of the new GUADALUPE MOUNTAINS NATIONAL PARK, which extends for 77,000 acres in the northwest corner of Culbertson County and partly in northeast Hudspeth County. Sen. Ralph Yarborough presented the Park bill to Congress and it was approved April 15, 1966. The Texas Legislature authorized use of the terrain in 1967. It takes in the Guadalupe Mountains, McKittrick, Pine Springs, West Dog, and Cherry Canyons, and the following peaks: Guadalupe, 8,751 ft.; Pine Top, 8,676 ft.; Bartlett, 8,513 ft.; El Capitan, 8,070 ft., and others slightly lower. US 62 and US 180 touch the southeastern corner of the Park and pass the steep eastern wall of Guadalupe Peak.

Here is the old stage stop of PINE SPRINGS, 14 *m.*, (5,634 alt.), which, when the Park was announced, had a population of 10, mostly serving a filling station. As the Park develops Pine Springs is expected to grow. At 14.2 is a junction with a dirt road.

Right here to the RUINS OF THE PINERY, 1 *m.,* once an important way-station of the Butterfield Stage Line of 1858–60. Pine Springs, from which the stage station took its name, are located about a mile distant at the mouth of Pine Springs Canyon, which cuts a shallow, steep-walled niche into the rocky rampart of the Guadalupes just behind Guadalupe Peak. At the right Shumard summit soars abruptly in an almost perpendicular wall to the height of 8,362 feet. In the Pinery there was stationed a small military detachment which, when the Indians were hostile, rode as an escort with the stages through this particularly dangerous region.

SIGNAL PEAK ROADSIDE PARK (*benches, open-air fireplace*), 22.8 *m.,* is an observation point where the highway has been blasted from the rock near El Capitan, whose steep bulk towers majestically close at hand. Abruptly from here the highway dips into the steep decline of Guadalupe Pass. At 29.8 *m.* the terrain drops suddenly away to the south and west, presenting a one hundred mile panorama. In the foreground to the south the barren Delaware Mountains sweep away in a general southeasterly direction, their rock-ribbed summits crowned by RIM PEAK (5,632 alt.). On top of the Delawares is an airway beacon. Far to the south, across the whitened expanse of great salt flats, rise the Sierra Diablo Mountains (5,000 alt.). Beyond, a dim, blue, low-lying mass on the southern horizon, is the Baylor Range. West of the Sierra Diablo, the Sierra Blanca and the Sierra Prieta Mountains blend. Still farther westward the ragged peaks of the Finlay Range march northwestward to meet the bulk of the Hueco Mountains (5,700 alt.). At sunset the changes of light, color, and shadow on this gigantic landscape are remarkable.

US 62 continues through Guadalupe Canyon and the pass westward, in a series of winding curves (*watch the road; sharp turns are dangerous*). Jutting across the State Line from New Mexico is a wedge-shaped mountain mass which contains the highest peaks in Texas. Approximately 55 square miles in extent, and lifting abruptly from the low salt flats on the west, this part of the Guadalupe Range has 36 summits of more than 8,000 feet elevation. In addition to Guadalupe Peak, with the State's highest altitude, the mass includes the rugged profile of BLUE RIDGE, along which are five peaks more than 8,400 feet in height—BUSH MOUNTAIN (8,606 alt.), and GOAT MOUNTAIN (8,600 alt.), are two of these. Deep canyons, towering cliffs, high park-like valleys and superb mountain vistas make this almost inaccessible region a scenic wonderland.

From the western end of Guadalupe Pass, the highway descends into a desolate area locally called Salt Flats, a desert of salt-impregnated sand, ghastly white in the moonlight, blindingly glaring under the noonday sun. In the middle distance southward the bleak whiteness is broken by vivid blue-green splashes of color, made by shallow lakes, each ringed with low dunes of almost pure salt. Heat waves shimmering and weaving above the intervening expanse often give these lakes the weird, unreal appearance of floating low in the superheated atmosphere, their brilliantly colored waters seeming to flicker in flame-like animation.

Long before the coming of white men, this area was frequented by Indians seeking salt. The broad semidesert, its miles devoid of non-alkaline water, caused great hardship to early-day travelers. It was this region that caused the bloody Salt War of 1877.

At 29 m. is the junction with State 54, which connects with US 90 at Van Horn.

At Salt Flat, Ranch Road 1576 runs north 17 m. past the Salt Basin and then 3 m. west to DELL CITY (1,000 pop. est.) in Hudspeth County settled about 1950. In 1948 a rancher drilling a well in this dry prairie land struck a huge supply of water, so abundant that in less than 20 years wells produced an estimated 750,000,000 gallons of water daily for large-scale irrigation. More than 45,000 acres of former grazing land is now green with truck. The water table is 90 ft. below the surface.

CORNUDAS, 67 m. (4,250 alt.), has a post office, filling station and cafe. Northward rise the rocky heights of the SIERRA TINAJA PINTA (5,600 alt.), and the CERRO DIABLO (5,750 alt.).

CAVERNS WAY SERVICE STATION, 77 m. (4,500 alt.), is another place of supply for automobiles.

At an inaccessible point 15 miles or more to the right, amid the Cornudas Mountains of New Mexico, are the ruins of the old Butterfield stage station of Cornudas del Alamo, third station east of El Paso on the famous Southern Overland Mail route, and long important to this section. Wild grapevines cover the crumbling walls about the spring. Graves of soldiers are in a tiny cemetery near by, one of the headstones bearing the date 1859.

Westward the highway climbs toward the foothills of the Hueco Mountains. The HUECO FILLING STATION, 98 m. (5,250 alt.), is just north of Buckhorn Draw. Ahead looms the wall of the Hueco Mountains (5,700 alt.), and to the left is the conical peak of CERRO ALTO (6,767 alt.), a landmark that in the old days marked the eastern entrance to Hueco Pass, through which ran the Butterfield Stage Line.

An airline beacon is visible (L) on top of a high peak at 104 m.

At 109 m. is a junction with a dirt road.

Right here to HUECO TANKS (*camping and picnicking 50¢ a car*), 6 m., an area rich in historical and archeological interest. Here a great clutter of giant rocks lies scattered in wild confusion over a region nearly a mile long and half a mile wide. Within this rock-bound enclosure which makes a natural fortress, various tribes, from prehistoric men up to the era of the occupation of this section by the Apaches, had villages secure from hostile bands. Wind and rain erosion cut numerous water holes in the soft granite, in which rain-water is retained. Large mortar holes, worn by Indians in grinding their maize or other foods, are among the rocks. Shallow caves and narrow, overhung can-yons offered protection from the elements. Many pictographs adorn the sheltered rock walls. Early Spanish and Anglo-American explorers availed themselves of the plentiful water supply, as did the immigrants of a later date, and passen-gers of the stage line. Ruins of the Butterfield stage station here have disap-peared. It is possible to climb the rock formations, explore twisting canyons and caves, and reach the largest so-called tank, far back among the roughest and highest of the rocks, where there is always a pool of crystal-clear water.

At 124 *m.* are the buildings of the EL PASO MUNICIPAL AIRPORT (R), used by American and Continental Airlines.

EL PASO, 130 *m.* (3,711 alt., 314,000 pop. est.), is at the junction with US 80 (*see Tour 19*).

PART IV

Appendices

Glossary

Acequia: Irrigation ditch.

Adobe: Clay-bearing soil which, baked in the sun in blocks or bricks, makes building material.

Alamo: Poplar or cottonwood.

Anglo-American: In Texas usage, anyone of white non-Spanish or non-Mexican blood who, before and during the days of the Texas Republic, entered from the United States; also, to distinguish between Latins and non-Latins.

Arroyo: A draw, ravine, dry creek, or gully.

Bayou: A sluggish inlet connecting with a lake or bay. (Choctaw *bayuk,* river or creek.)

Brake: A thicket; a dense growth of scrub timber, as cedar brake.

Breaks: In north Texas, west Texas, and the Panhandle, rugged, uneven, eroded terrain in the neighborhood of rivers and streams.

Boot Hill: A cemetery where rest those who died with their boots on.

Bunkhouse: Ranch living quarters for cowboys.

Cap Rock: The escarpment of the High Plains.

Chaparral: Brush, thicket.

Chaps: Full-length leggings of leather worn by cowboys to protect their legs in brushy or thorny country.

Chili Con Carne: A peppery meat dish.

Chuck Wagon: The cook wagon with a ranch outfit.

Cibola (Seven Cities of): Mythical cities of fabulous riches, sought by Coronado.

Cowboy: A ranch hand hired to tend cattle.

Cowman (or Cattleman): A cattle ranch owner.

Dogie: A motherless calf.

Draw: A natural drain or gully; a ravine.

Dugout: An excavation with a sod roof, commonly used by early settlers for dwellings in treeless sections.

Empresario: A person given a contract by the Spanish or Mexican government to bring in colonists.

Enchiladas: A spicy concoction made with tortillas, cheese, and onions, covered with chili sauce.

Fiesta: Festival, celebration.

Gallery (as applied to exterior of a building): Veranda.

Gran Quivira: A reputedly rich region, tales of which lured Coronado into present-day Texas.

Jacal: Hut or shack.

Labor: A Spanish land measure equivalent to approximately 177 acres.

League: A Spanish land measure equivalent to approximately 4,428 acres

649

Mesa: Tableland.

Mescal: A colorless intoxicating drink made from the maguey or century plant.

Nester: Ranchman's term for a farmer who homesteaded one-time cattle range and, consequently, was unwelcome.

Panhandle: That northern part of Texas lying between New Mexico and Oklahoma which, as related to the remainder of the State, resembles the handle of a frying pan.

Pilon: A trifling gift presented by a merchant to a customer.

Pueblo: Town, village.

Quien Sabe: Perhaps; who knows.

Round-up: The gathering of cattle into a herd for branding, shipping, and the like.

Sarape: A shawl or blanket.

Stray: An animal—or, in the language of some sections, a person—not one of the herd or group.

Tacos: Toasted tortillas with meat fillings.

Tamale: Corn dough rolled around a meat filling, the whole encased in a corn shuck and steamed.

Tortilla: A pancake made of mashed corn.

Vaquero: A Mexican herdsman, cowboy.

Vara: Linear measure approximating 33⅜ inches.

Chronology

1519 Alonso Alvarez de Pineda explores and maps the coast of Texas, occupying the mouth of the Rio Grande for 40 days (the first known European visit).

1528 Nov. 6. Alvar Nuñez Cabeza de Vaca and others of the Narvaez expedition are shipwrecked on the Texas coast.

1541 Francisco Vazquez de Coronado, after searching for the Seven Cities of Cibola, marches across the Llano Estacado to locate Gran Quivira.

1542 Luis de Moscoso leads survivors of De Soto's expedition to the High Plains of Texas.

1659 Dec. 8. Mission Nuestra Señora de Guadalupe de El Paso is founded on present site of the City of Juarez, Mex. (Beginning of settlement in the vicinity of El Paso.)

1680–82 Refugees from revolt of Pueblos in New Mexico establish settlements on the Rio Grande at Senecu, Isleta, San Lorenzo, and Socorro.

1681 Mission Corpus Christi de la Isleta del Sur is founded.

1685 Feb. 15. Robert Cavelier, Sieur de la Salle, lands on the shore of Matagorda Bay and establishes Fort St. Louis on Garcitas Creek. (La Salle later is murdered by his own men, spelling failure of the French colony.)

1690 May 25. First mission establishment in east Texas is founded, Mission San Francisco de los Tejas.

1691 Texas officially becomes a Spanish province.

1713–14 Louis Juchereau de St. Denis, French trader, crosses Texas, reviving Spanish interest.

1716 East Texas is settled through the establishment of six missions.

1718 May 1. Mission San Antonio de Valero (later the Alamo) is founded on the San Antonio River.
May 5. Presidio and Villa of San Antonio de Bexar are established.

1731 March 9. Canary Islanders reach San Antonio de Bexar to establish first civil municipality.

1744 Estimated population (exclusive of Indians), 1,500.

1749 Goliad is founded.

1779 Nacogdoches is founded.

1801 Philip Nolan, adventurer, is killed in Texas by the Spanish, his expedition captured.

1803 Louisiana is purchased by the United States, increasing threat of Anglo-American invasion.

1812–13   Gutierrez-Magee expedition invades Texas, is defeated on the Medina River by Arredondo.

1813   May.   First Texas newspaper, *El Mejicano,* is published in Nacogdoches.

1817–21   Jean Lafitte, pirate, operates on Galveston Island.

1819–21   Dr. James Long, filibusterer, leads expeditions into Texas.

1820   Moses Austin secures permission to colonize 300 Anglo-American families.

1821   The Austin colony, first Anglo-American settlement in Texas, is founded by Stephen F. Austin.

Mexico gains freedom from Spain, and Texas becomes a Mexican state.

1824–32   Mexico grants colonization contracts to *empresarios.* Towns of Victoria, Gonzales, are founded.

1826   Hayden Edwards, *empresario,* proclaims "the Republic of Fredonia," but is ousted by Mexicans.

1827   Juan Maria Ponce de Leon builds first home on site of El Paso.

1828   Estimated Anglo-American population, 2,020.

1830   April 6.   Mexico passes law checking further immigration of Anglo-Americans into Texas.

1831   Estimated population (exclusive of Indians), 20,000.

1832   Texans and Mexicans clash at Anahuac and Velasco.

Convention at San Felipe petitions for separation of Texas, politically, from Coahuila.

1834   Stephen F. Austin is imprisoned in Mexico.

1835   June 30.   Mexican troops are driven from Anahuac.

Oct. 2.   Settlers win Battle of Gonzales, first battle of Texas Revolution.

Oct. 9.   Texans capture Goliad.

Oct. 12.   Volunteer Texas army under Stephen F. Austin marches on San Antonio, Mexican stronghold.

Oct. 28.   Battle of Concepcion is won by Texans.

Nov. 3.   Provisional government is created.

Dec. 5.   Concluding siege of San Antonio, Ben Milam leads attack on city.

Dec. 9.   San Antonio is captured.

Dec. 10.   The Mexican general, Cos, surrenders.

Dec. 14.   General Cos and 1,100 men depart; by this evacuation, Texas is freed of Mexican soldiery.

1836   Feb. 23.   Vanguard of General Santa Anna's Mexican army arrives in San Antonio to lay siege to the Alamo.

Feb. 27.   Colonel Frank W. Johnson's command is captured in San Patricio.

March 2.   Declaration of Independence is issued at Washington, on the Brazos; Dr. Grant's command is annihilated at Agua Dulce.

March 6.   The Alamo falls.

March 13.   General Sam Houston, commanding Texas army, begins retreat eastward.   Gonzales is burned.

1836 March 17. Texas Constitution is adopted at Washington on the Brazos, and ad interim national officials are selected.

March 20. Battle of the Coleto ends in surrender of Colonel James W. Fannin and his command.

March 27. Fannin and his men are massacred at Goliad.

April 21. General Houston defeats Mexican army under Santa Anna at San Jacinto, thus winning Texas Revolution and ending Latin domination.

May 14. Treaty of Velasco is signed by Texas officials and Santa Anna.

Sept. 1. Houston is elected President of the Republic of Texas.

Oct. 3. Texas Congress meets at Columbia.

Dec. 27. Stephen F. Austin dies.

1837 The United States recognizes independence of Texas.

General Land Office is established.

1838 Vicente Cordova, inciting Indians and Mexicans, threatens revolt against Texas.

1839 Homestead Law and first educational act are passed.

Cherokees are expelled from east Texas.

Austin is founded as capital of the Republic of Texas.

1841 The Santa Fe expedition, bent on conquest of New Mexico, fails.

John Neely Bryan builds first trading post on site of present-day Dallas.

1842 Invading Mexican troops capture Goliad, Refugio, San Antonio, and Victoria.

Battle of the Salado results in withdrawal of Woll, Mexican general, and annihilation of Dawson's command.

Mier expedition invades Mexico; is captured, and the Texans are forced to draw beans in lottery of death.

Austin citizens fire on troops sent to remove archives.

1843 Hostilities between Texas and Mexico are suspended.

1844 Henry Castro establishes Alsatian colony at Castroville.

1845 Annexation to the United States is voted by U. S. Congress and by Texas convention.

March 21. New Braunfels is founded by German colonists.

Dec. 29. Texas is admitted as twenty-eighth State of the Union.

1846 Feb. 16. Annexation is completed; first State legislature convenes in Austin; J. P. Henderson is inaugurated Governor.

May 8. First battle of Mexican War is won by General Zachary Taylor at Palo Alto.

1848 Feb. 2. Rio Grande is accepted by Mexico as Texas State boundary, in Treaty of Guadalupe Hidalgo.

March. Texas legislature creates Santa Fe County, laying claim to 100,000 square miles outside of present State.

1849 Brevet Major Ripley Arnold establishes Camp Worth (Fort Worth).

1850 Texas accepts $10,000,000 from the Federal government for disputed territory; western State boundary is fixed on present lines. Population, 212,592.

1851 Construction is started on first railroad.

1854 Victor Considerant's French colony begins settlement near Dallas.

1856 Shipload of camels, to be used by U. S. Army, lands at Indianola.

1857 San Antonio and San Diego Overland Mail, and Southern Overland Mail are in operation.

1859 Juan Cortinas, bandit, terrorizes region of the lower Rio Grande.

1860 Population, 604,215.

1861 Feb. 1. Ordinance of Secession is passed.

March 16. Sam Houston is deposed as Governor for refusal to take oath of allegiance to Confederacy.

1862 Oct. 9. Galveston is captured by Federals.

1863 Jan. 1. Galveston is recaptured by Confederates.

July 26. Sam Houston dies at Huntsville.

Sept. 8. Lieutenant Dick Dowling repulses Federal attack on Sabine Pass.

1865 May 12–13. Last battle of Civil War is fought at Palmito Hill.

June 19. All slaves in Texas are declared free.

1866 Constitutional convention is held.

Texas cattle are driven north to market.

1869 Reconstruction convention frames new constitution.

1870 March 30. Texas readmitted to the Union.

Population, 818,579.

1874 March 17. Radical rule is overthrown. Reconstruction ends.

June 27. Battle at Adobe Walls is fought.

1876 Present State constitution is adopted.

Agricultural and Mechanical College is opened.

Barbed wire is adopted by cattlemen.

Sam Houston Normal and Prairie View Normal and Industrial College for Negroes are established.

1877 Stock Raisers' Association is organized.

1878 Sam Bass, outlaw, is killed.

1880 Population, 1,591,749.

1881 May 19. Southern Pacific Railroad reaches El Paso.

Nov. 9. State capitol is destroyed by fire.

1883 Sept 15. University of Texas is opened in Austin.

1886 Indianola is destroyed by storm.

Dallas Fair is inaugurated.

1888 New State capitol is dedicated.

1890 Population, 2,235,527.

1891 State Railroad Commission is created.

1896 Greer County case is settled by Supreme Court, awarding to Oklahoma land claimed by Texas.

1898 During Spanish-American War, Theodore Roosevelt trains the "Rough Riders" in San Antonio.

1900 Sept. 8. Galveston storm takes 6,000 lives.

Population, 3,048,710.

1901   Spindletop oil field is discovered.

Commission form of city government is developed at Galveston and construction of sea wall begins.

1905   Terrell Election Law is passed.

1906   Port Arthur becomes port of entry.

Negro soldiers of 25th Infantry mutiny and riot in Brownsville.

1909   March 3. President Theodore Roosevelt signs bill authorizing completion of Sabine-Neches Canal.

Fire destroys 20 blocks in Fort Worth.

1910   March 2. First official airplane flight of the U. S. Army takes place (Fort Sam Houston).

Population, 3,896,542.

1911   Texas border is occupied by United States troops as result of Mexican revolutions.

1915   Compulsory education law is passed.

Houston ship channel is opened.

1916   National Guard is stationed on Texas-Mexican border as Brigadier General John J. Pershing leads punitive expedition into Mexico.

Port of Beaumont is opened.

1917   Gov. James E. Ferguson is impeached and removed from office.

State Highway Commission is established.

1917–18   Ranger and Burkburnett oil fields are discovered.

Texas becomes training center for recruits in World War.

1918   Law is passed providing free school books.

1919   Dallas city charter is amended to provide for city plan commission, pursuant to remodeling city.

1920   Population, 4,663,228.

1921   Sept. 9. San Antonio River flood takes 50 lives.

1924   Mrs. Miriam A. Ferguson, wife of impeached Governor, is elected Governor of Texas (second woman Governor in the United States).

1926   Ship channel and deep water port are completed at Corpus Christi.

1928   Construction of Randolph Field, "West Point of the Air," is begun.

1930   East Texas oil field is discovered.

Population, 5,824,715.

1931   Governor Ross S. Sterling, attempting to enforce proration of east Texas oil, calls out National Guard.

1933   Treaty is signed between United States and Mexico, empowering International Boundary Commission to direct and inspect construction of the Rio Grande Rectification Project.

State votes $20,000,000 in bonds for relief.

1934   April 30. Longshoremen's strike in Houston is called "waterfront reign of terror."

August. Intracoastal Canal from Sabine River to Galveston Bay is opened.

1935   August. Yount-Lee oil company is sold to Stanolind Company for $41,600,000 cash, third largest cash transaction in history of American business.

Big Bend National Park is projected.

1936   Texas celebrates its centennial of independence.

1937   March 18.   New London school disaster kills 290.

1938   April 13.   The $2,750,000 Port Arthur-Orange Bridge opened.
New Galveston causeway, 8,194 feet long, cost $2,500,000, in use.

1939   May 5.   McDonald Observatory, Mount Locke, dedicated.

1940   U. S. Census gives Texas 6,414,824.
World War II begins; 750,000 Texans in uniform by 1945; 15,764
Army, AF, dead; Marine Corps and Coast Guard, 3,023.

1944   June 12.   Big Bend National Park established.

1945   Werner von Braun and German missile scientists at Fort Bliss.

1947   April 16.   Chemicals explode on French freighter *Grandcamp;* 461
dead, 4,000 injured, est.

1948   Rep. Lyndon B. Johnson won second primary for senator over Coke R.
Stevenson, former governor, by 87 votes.

1949   July 11.   Gov. Beauford H. Jester (elected 1946, 1948) died in office.
Succeeded by Allan Shivers, 3 terms.

1950   U. S. Supreme Court orders Texas to admit Negro student to Uni-
versity Law School. . . . Supreme Court decides Texas lost title to
Tidelands by entering Union. A U.S. quitclaim was voted by Con-
gress, vetoed by Truman. In 1953 a similar quitclaim was voted by
Congress, approved by Eisenhower, May 22, 1953. U. S. Census gives
Texas 7,711,194.

1953   May 11.   Tornado at Waco kills 114, at San Angelo, 11. In year 32
tornadoes killed 146. . . . Mrs. Oveta Culp Hobby first secretary of
Health, Education & Welfare.

1954   June 26, 28.   Hurricane Alice devastated Lower Rio Grande Valley.
27.10 in. rain at Pandale. River rose 30 ft. above flood stage at Eagle
Pass and Laredo. International Bridge, Laredo, damaged; Pecos River
bridge 50 ft. above water level washed out.

1960   Texas gives John F. Kennedy for President and Lyndon B. Johnson
for Vice President 1,167,934, vs. 1,121,699.
U. S. Census gives Texas 9,579,677.

1961   Sept. 8–14.   Hurricane Carla kills 34 in Coast cities; winds 175 mph
in Port Lavaca, 145 mph at Matagorda.

1963   Sam Houston National Forest dedicated.

1963   Nov. 22.   President Kennedy assassinated in Dallas; Lyndon B. Johnson becomes President.

1964   Sept. 25.   President Johnson meets President Mateos of Mexico at
El Paso-Juarez boundary to mark settlement of Chamizal land dispute.

1964   Nov. 3.   President Johnson elected, gets 1,663,185 votes in Texas,
Goldwater, 958,566.

1968   April 6–Oct. 6.   HemisFair, 250th anniversary of San Antonio.

1968   November 5.   In the National Election Texas gives Humphrey, D.,
1,267,317; Nixon, R., 1,227,199; Wallace, Ind., 581,747. Preston
Smith, D., elected governor with 1,659,478, over Paul Eggers, R.,
with 1,252,952. Electoral vote goes to Humphrey. (Electoral total,
Nixon, 302, Humphrey, 191, Wallace, 45.)

A Selected Reading List of Texas Books

Abbott, John S. C. *David Crockett: His Life and Adventures.* New York, 1874 (rep. 1916).

Adams, Andy. *The Log of a Cowboy.* Boston, 1903 (rep. 1931).

Allen, Jules Verne. *Cowboy Lore.* San Antonio, 1933.

Bancroft, Hubert Howe. *History of Texas and the North Mexican States.* 2 vols.. XV and XVI, *Works.* San Francisco, 1890.

Barker, Eugene C. *Mexico and Texas, 1821–1835.* Dallas, 1928. University of Texas research lectures on the causes of the Texas Revolution.

—— *The Life of Stephen F. Austin, Founder of Texas, 1793–1836.* Nashville, 1925. A chapter in the westward movement of the Anglo-American people.

Barr, Amelia Edith (Huddleston). *All the Days of My Life; An Autobiography.* New York, 1913. Includes description of life in Austin and Galveston in 1850's and 1860's.

Bechdolt, Frederick R. *Tales of the Old-Timers.* New York, 1924.

Benedict, H. Y. *A Source Book Relative to the History of the University of Texas.* Austin, 1917.

Benedict, H. Y., and John Avery Lomax. *The Book of Texas.* Garden City, N. Y., 1916.

Biesele, Rudolph L. *The History of the German Settlements in Texas, 1831–1861.* Austin, 1930.

Binkley, William Campbell. *The Expansionist Movement in Texas, 1836–1850.* Berkeley, Calif., 1925.

Bizzell, William B. *Rural Texas.* New York, 1924. An analysis of agricultural and rural conditions.

Bolton, Herbert Eugene. *Spanish Borderlands.* New Haven, Conn., 1921.

—— ed. *Spanish Explorations in the Southwest, 1542–1706.* New York, 1916.

—— *Texas in the Middle Eighteenth Century.* Berkeley, Calif., 1915.

Bracht, Viktor. *Texas in 1848.* Trans. from the German (*Texas Im Jahre 1848*) by Charles F. Schmidt. San Antonio, 1931.

Brown, John Henry. *History of Texas, 1685–1892.* 2 vols. St. Louis, 1892–93.

—— *Indian Wars and Pioneers of Texas.* Austin, c. 1896.

Carl, Prince of Solms-Braunfels. *Texas, 1844–45.* Houston, 1936. A translation of *Texas, a Description of the Geographical, Social and Other Conditions, with Special Reference to German Colonization, etc.,* pub. at Frankfort-on-Main, 1846.

Castañeda, Carlos E. *Our Catholic Heritage in Texas, 1519-1936.* 7 vols.; 4 completed, 1939. Paul J. Foik, C. S. C., Ph.D., ed. Prepared under the auspices of the Knights of Columbus Historical Commission of Texas. Austin, 1936–

────── ed.. *The Mexican Side of the Texan Revolution.* Dallas, 1928. Accounts by the chief Mexican participants.

Chabot, Frederick C., ed. *The Perote Prisoners.* San Antonio, 1934. James L. Trueheart's journal of the Mier Expedition of Texans into Mexico.

Cox, Isaac Joslin. *The Louisiana-Texas Frontier.* Austin, 1906.

Crane, William Carey. *Life and Select Literary Remains of Sam Houston of Texas.* Philadelphia, 1884.

Cross, Ruth. *The Big Road.* New York, 1931. A tale of cotton farmers in Texas.

Cunningham, Eugene. *Triggernometry, a Gallery of Gunfighters.* New York, 1934.

Davis, J. Frank. *The Road to San Jacinto.* Indianapolis, 1936. Romance of the Texas Revolution.

Davis, Mollie E. Moore. *Under the Man-Fig.* Boston, 1895. Novel of character and manners, 1857 to 1875.

De Zavala, Adina. *History and Legends of the Alamo and Other Missions in and Around San Antonio.* San Antonio, 1917.

Dixon, Sam Houston. *The Men Who Made Texas Free.* Houston, 1924. Sketches of the signers of the Declaration of Independence.

Dixon, Sam Houston, and Louis Wiltz Kemp. *The Heroes of San Jacinto.* Houston, 1932.

Dobie, J. Frank. *A Vaquero of the Brush Country.* Dallas, 1929. Partly from the reminiscences of John Young.

────── *Coronado's Children.* Dallas, 1930. The never-ending search for buried treasure.

────── ed. *Legends of Texas.* Austin, 1916.

────── *The Flavor of Texas.* Dallas, 1936.

Duval, John C. *Early Times in Texas.* Austin, 1892.

────── *The Adventures of Big-Foot Wallace, The Texas Ranger and Hunter.* Macon, Ga., 1885 (rep. Austin, 1921; Austin, 1935).

Eby, Frederick. *The Development of Education in Texas.* New York, 1925.

Emmett, Chris. *Texas Camel Tales.* San Antonio, 1932. The U. S. Army's transportation experiment.

Emory, Major William H. *Report on the United States and Mexican Boundary Survey.* 2 vols., 3 parts. Washington, D. C., 1857-59.

Foote, Henry Stuart. *Texas and the Texans, or Advance of the Anglo-Americans to the South-west.* 2 vols. Philadelphia, 1841.

Gambrell, Herbert Pickens. *Mirabeau Buonaparte Lamar, Troubadour and Crusader.* Dallas, 1934. Life of a Texas President and versifier.

Garrison, George P. *Texas; a Contest of Civilizations.* Boston, 1903.

Graham, Philip. *The Life and Poems of Mirabeau B. Lamar.* Chapel Hill, N. C., 1938.

Green, General Thomas Jefferson. *Journal of the Texian Expedition Against Mier*. New York, 1845. The author was among those imprisoned at the Castle of Perote.

Greer, Hilton Ross, comp. *Voices of the Southwest* (verse). New York, 1923.

Greer, Hilton Ross, with Florence E. Barns, comps. *New Voices of the Southwest*. Dallas, 1934.

Gregg, Josiah. *Commerce of the Prairies*. 2 vols. New York, 1844. The journal of a Santa Fe trader.

Haley, J. Evetts. *Charles Goodnight, Cowman and Plainsman*. Boston, 1936.

—— *The XIT Ranch of Texas, and the Early Days of the Llano Estacado*. Chicago, 1929.

Hatcher, Mattie Austin. *The Opening of Texas to Foreign Settlement, 1801–1821*. Austin, 1927.

Hellenbeck, Cleve. *Spanish Missions of the Old Southwest*. Garden City, N. Y., 1926.

Holden, William C. *Alkali Trails, or Social and Economic Movements of the Texas Frontier, 1846–1900*. Dallas, 1930.

Holley, Mary Austin. *Texas*. Baltimore, 1833. Observations, in a series of letters written during a visit to Austin's colony in 1831.

Houston, Margaret Bell. *Magic Valley*. New York, 1934. A Texas ranch tale.

Hunter, J. Marvin, comp. *Trail Drivers of Texas*. 2 vols. Nashville, 1923–24.

James, Marquis. *The Raven, A Biography of Sam Houston*. Indianapolis, 1929.

Johnson, Frank W. *A History of Texas and Texans* (ed. by Dr. Eugene C. Barker). 5 vols. Chicago, 1916.

Joseph, Donald. *October's Child*. New York, 1929. Novel of college life in a Texas village.

Joutel, Henri. *Journal of La Salle's Last Voyage, 1684–1687*. English trans. London, 1714 (rep. Albany, N. Y., 1906).

Kendall, George Wilkins. *Narrative of the Texan Santa Fe Expedition*. 2 vols. New York, 1844 (facsimile ed., Austin, 1935).

Kennedy, William. *Texas; The Rise, Progress and Prospects of the Republic of Texas*. 2 vols. London, 1841 (later ed., 1 vol. Fort Worth, 1925).

—— *Texas; Its Geography, Natural History and Topography*. New York, 1844.

Krey, Laura. *And Tell of Time*. Boston, 1938. A novel of Texas (1775–88).

Lamar, The Papers of Mirabeau Buonaparte. 6 vols. Austin, 1922–27.

Lanham, Edwin. *The Wind Blew West*. New York, 1935. A story of the moving frontier in the 1870's.

Lomax, John A., comp. *Cowboy Songs and Other Frontier Ballads*. New York, 1910 (rev. eds., 1916; 1938).

Lomax, John A., with Alan Lomax, comps. *American Ballads and Folk Songs.* New York, 1934 (rev. ed., 1938).

Lowrie, Samuel Harman. *Culture Conflict in Texas, 1821–1835.* New York, 1932.

Maverick, Mary A. *Memoirs.* San Antonio, 1921.

Maverick, Maury. *A Maverick American.* New York, 1937. Autobiography.

McCampbell, Coleman. *Saga of a Frontier Seaport.* Dallas, 1934. About Corpus Christi.

Morfi, Fray Juan Agustín. *History of Texas, 1673–1779.* Trans. and annotated by Carlos E. Castañeda. 2 vols. Albuquerque, 1935.

Newton, Lewis W., and Herbert P. Gambrell. *A Social and Political History of Texas.* Dallas, c. 1932.

Olmsted, Frederick Law. *A Journey Through Texas, or, A Saddle Trip on the Southwestern Frontier.* New York, 1857.

O'Brien, Esse (Forrester). *Art and Artists of Texas.* Dallas, 1935.

Parkman, Francis. *La Salle and the Discovery of the Great West.* Boston, c. 1869 (later eds., 1879; 1897; 1927).

Pearce, J. E. *Tales That Dead Men Tell.* Austin, 1935. Archaeology and paleontology.

Polley, J. B. *Hood's Texas Brigade.* New York, 1910. Its marches, battles, and achievements.

Porter, William Sidney (pseud. O. Henry). *Rolling Stones.* Garden City, N. Y., 1918 (biog. ed., 1931).

Potts, Charles S. *Railroad Transportation in Texas.* Austin, 1909.

Raht, Carlysle Graham. *The Romance of Davis Mountains and Big Bend Country.* El Paso, 1919.

Ramsdell, Charles W. *Reconstruction in Texas.* New York, 1910.

Red, William Stuart. *The Texas Colonists and Religion, 1821–1836.* Austin, 1924.

Richardson, Rupert Norval. *The Comanche Barrier to South Plains Settlement.* Glendale, Calif., 1933.

Roberts, Oran M. *A Description of Texas, its Advantages and Resources.* St. Louis, 1881. By an early Governor of Texas.

Roemer, Dr. Ferdinand. *Texas, with Particular Reference to German Immigration and the Physical Appearance of the Country. Described Through Personal Observation.* Bonn, 1849. Trans. from the German by Oswald Mueller. San Antonio, 1935.

Santleben, August. *A Texas Pioneer; Early Staging and Overland Freighting.* New York, 1910.

Sayles, E. B. *An Archaeological Survey of Texas.* Globe, Ariz., 1935.

Scarborough, Dorothy. *The Wind.* New York, 1925. Novel with a west Texas background.

Schmitz, Joseph William. *Thus They Lived.* San Antonio, 1935. Social life in the Republic.

Shea, John Dawson Gilmary. *History of the Catholic Missions Among the Indian Tribes of the United States, 1529–1854.* New York, 1855 (later ed., 1881).

Simonds, Frederic William. *The Geography of Texas, Physical and Political.* Boston, 1905.

Siringo, Charles A. *Riata and Spurs.* Boston, 1912 (reps. 1919, 1927). Story of a lifetime spent in the saddle as cowboy and Texas Ranger.

Smith, Goldie Capers. *The Creative Arts in Texas, a Handbook of Biography.* Nashville, 1926.

Sowell, A. J. *Early Settlers and Indian Fighters of Southwest Texas.* Austin, 1900.

Spanish Explorers in the Southern United States, 1528–1543. 3 parts. *The Narrative of Alvar Nuñez Cabeza de Vaca,* ed. by Frederick W. Hodge; *The Narrative of the Expedition of Hernando de Soto,* by the Gentleman of Elvas, ed. by Theodore H. Lewis; *The Narrative of the Expedition of Coronado,* by Pedro Castañeda, ed. by Frederick W. Hodge. New York, 1907.

Sweet, Alex E., and J. Armoy Knox. *On a Mexican Mustang. Through Texas from the Gulf to the Rio Grande.* London, 1883 (later ed., Hartford, Conn., 1887).

Texas State Department of Education. *Negro Education in Texas.* Austin, 1931.

Thompson, Holland, ed. *The Book of Texas.* Dallas, 1929.

Thrall, Homer S. *A Pictorial History of Texas.* St. Louis, 1879.

Venable, Clark. *All the Brave Rifles.* Chicago, 1929.

Warner, C. A. *Texas Oil and Gas Since 1543.* Houston, 1939.

Waugh, Julia Nott. *Castro-ville and Henry Castro, Empresario.* San Antonio, 1934.

Webb, Walter Prescott. *The Great Plains.* New York, 1931.

—— *The Texas Rangers.* Boston, 1935. A century of frontier defense.

Wharton, Clarence R. *Texas Under Many Flags.* 5 vols. Chicago, 1930.

White, Owen P. *Out of the Desert; The Historical Romance of El Paso.* El Paso, 1923.

RECENT PUBLICATIONS

Allen, Henry. *The Texas Rangers.* Random House, 1957.

Bainbridge, John. *The Super-Americans.* Doubleday, 1961.

Beals, Carleton. *Stephen F. Austin, Father of Texas.* McGraw-Hill, 1953.

Carter, Hodding, and Betty D. *Doomed Road of Empire.* McGraw-Hill, 1963.

Casey, Robert J. *The Texas Border and Some Borderliners.* Bobbs-Merrill, 1950.

Day, Donald. *Big Country Texas.* Duell, Sloan & Pearce, 1947.

Dobie, James F. *Guide to Life and Literature of Texas.* Intro. by J. Frank Dobie, 1943.

Douglas, William O. *Farewell to Texas: A Vanishing Wilderness.* McGraw-Hill, 1967.

Flynn, Robert. *North to Yesterday.* Knopf, 1963.

Garst, Doris Shannon. *Big Foot Wallace of the Texas Rangers.* Messner, 1951.

Gambrell, Hubert P. *Anson Jones, the Last President of Texas.* Doubleday, 1948.

Goetzmann, William. *Exploration and Empire.* Knopf, 1966.

Greer, James K. *Colonel Jack Hayes.* Dutton, 1952.

Hogan, William R. *The Texas Republic.* Univ. of Oklahoma Press, 1946.

Hopkins, Kenneth. *A Trip to Texas.* Macdonald, 1962.

Horgan, Paul. *Great River; the Rio Grande in North American History,* 1963; *Mountain Standard Time,* 1962; *The Conquistadores in North American History,* 1963.

James, Marquis. *The Texaco Story, 1902–1952.*

Kilman, Edward H. *Cannibal Coast.* Naylor, 1959.

Kirkland, F. and Newcomb, W. W. *Rock Art of the Indians.* Univ. of Texas, 1966.

Kooch, Mary Francis. *The Texas Cookbook.* Little, Brown, 1965.

Lea, Tom. *The King Ranch.* Little, Brown, 1957.

Leslie, Werner. *Dallas Past and Present.* Grossman.

Morris, Willi. *North to Home.* Houghton, Mifflin, 1967.

Nordyke, Lewis. *The Truth About Texas.* Crowell, 1957.

Owens, William A. *Stubborn Soil.* Scribner, 1966.

Pendleton, Tom. *The Iron Orchard.* McGraw-Hill, 1966.

Perry, George Sessions. *Texas, a World in Itself.* McGraw-Hill, 1942.

Peyton, Green. *The Face of Texas.* Crowell, 1961.

Pinckney, Pauline A. *Painting in Texas: the 19th Century.* Univ. of Texas, 1966.

Preece, Harold. *Lone Star Men.* Hastings House, 1960.

Priestley, John B., and Jacquetta Hawkes. *Journey Down a Rainbow.* Harper, 1955.

Ramsdell, Charles. *San Antonio: A Historical and Pictorial Guide.* HemisFair Edition, 1968. University of Texas Press.

Richardson, Rupert N. *Texas, the Lone Star State.* Prentice-Hall, 1943.

Rister, Carl Coke. *Robert E. Lee in Texas.* Univ. of Oklahoma Press, 1946.

Rogers, John William. *The Lusty Texans of Dallas.* Cokesbury, 1965.

Siringo, Chas. A. *A Texas Cowboy.* Intro. by J. Frank Dobie. Sloane, 1950.

Tinkle, Lon. *Thirteen Days to Glory.* McGraw-Hill, 1958. New edition retitled *The Alamo,* New American Library.

Tolbert, Frank V. *Dick Dowling at Sabine Pass.* McGraw-Hill, 1962.

Walker, Stanley. *Home to Texas.* Harper, 1956.

MAP OF
TEXAS
IN TEN SECTIONS

Index to State Map Sections

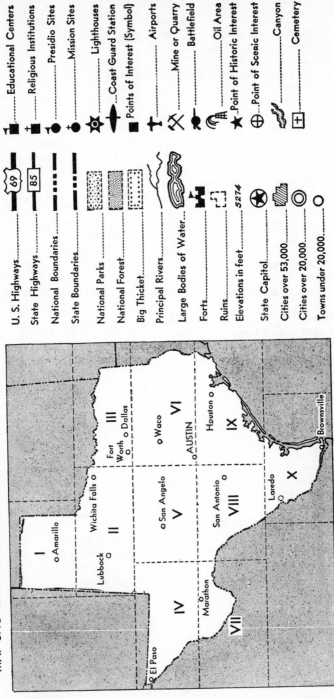

LEGEND FOR STATE MAP

U.S. Highways
State Highways
National Boundaries
State Boundaries
National Parks
National Forest
Big Thicket
Principal Rivers
Large Bodies of Water
Forts
Ruins
Elevations in feet................5274
State Capitol
Cities over 53,000
Cities over 20,000
Towns under 20,000

Educational Centers
Religious Institutions
Presidio Sites
Mission Sites
Lighthouses
Coast Guard Station
Points of Interest (Symbol)
Airports
Mine or Quarry
Battlefield
Oil Area
Point of Historic Interest
Point of Scenic Interest
Canyon
Cemetery

MAP SHOWING SECTIONAL DIVISION OF STATE MAP

El Paso
Amarillo
Lubbock
Wichita Falls
Fort Worth
Dallas
Marathon
San Angelo
Waco
AUSTIN
Houston
San Antonio
Laredo
Brownsville

I
II
III
IV
V
VI
VII
VIII
IX
X

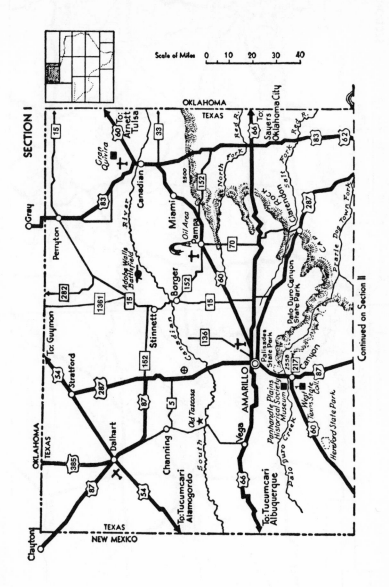

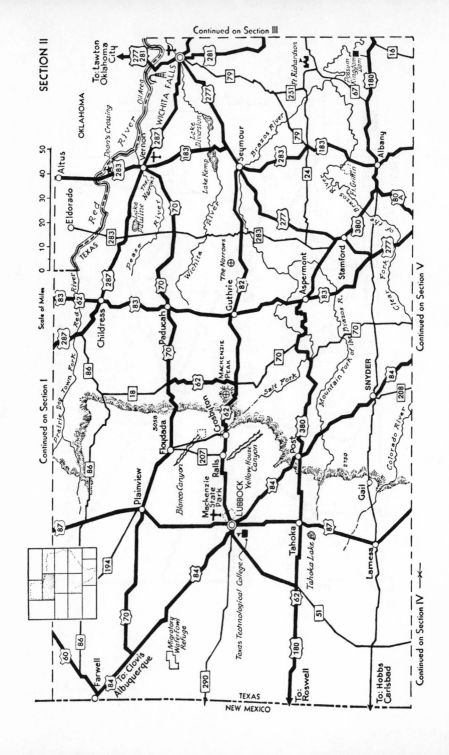

Continued on Section III

SECTION II

Continued on Section I

Continued on Section IV

Continued on Section V

OKLAHOMA

TEXAS

To: Lawton
Oklahoma
City

277
281

281

Altus

283

Eldorado

283

TEXAS

Red River

Doan's Crossing

Red River

Vernon

287

WICHITA FALLS

Lake Diversion

Lake Kemp

183

Seymour

79

277

Ft. Richardson

251

79

183

16

180

67

Possum Kingdom Dam

Albany

283

24

277

283

380

80 A

Clear Fork

277

Brazos River

Ft. Griffin

Brazos River

Scale of Miles

0 10 20 30 40 50

83

62 Red River Fork

287

86

Childress

83

Paducah

70

70

Matador Pauline Trail

Pease River

Wichita River

Guthrie

The Narrows

82

Aspermont

83

Stamford

Mountain Fork of the Brazos R.

70

Salt Fork

70

380

Colorado River

84

208

SNYDER

Prairie Dog Town Fork

86

18

62

MACKENZIE PEAK

62

Crosbyton

3058

Floydada

207

Mackenzie State Park

Ralls

Blanco Canyon

Yellow House Canyon

Post

380

84

87

LUBBOCK

Texas Technological College

Migratory Waterfowl Refuge

Plainview

87

194

84

70

86

60

Farwell

84

To: Clovis
Albuquerque

290

TEXAS
NEW MEXICO

Tahoka

Tahoka Lake

62

51

180

To: Roswell

87

Lamesa

Gail

2750

To: Hobbs
Carlsbad

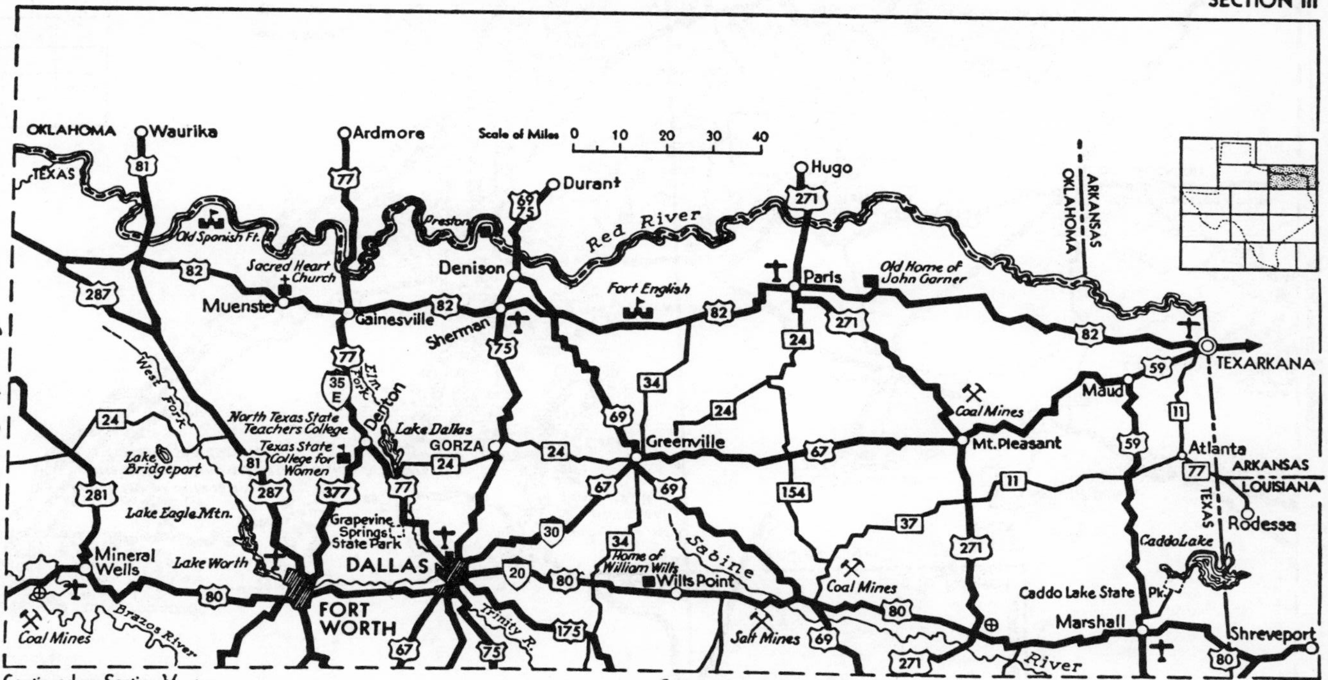

Continued on Section II
Continued on Section V
Continued on Section VI

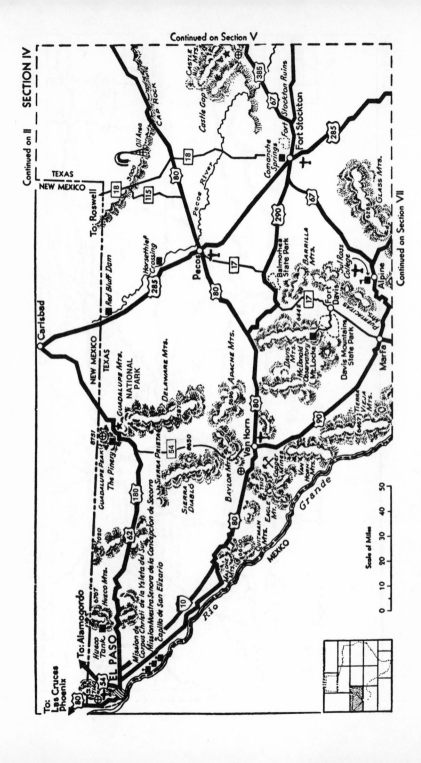

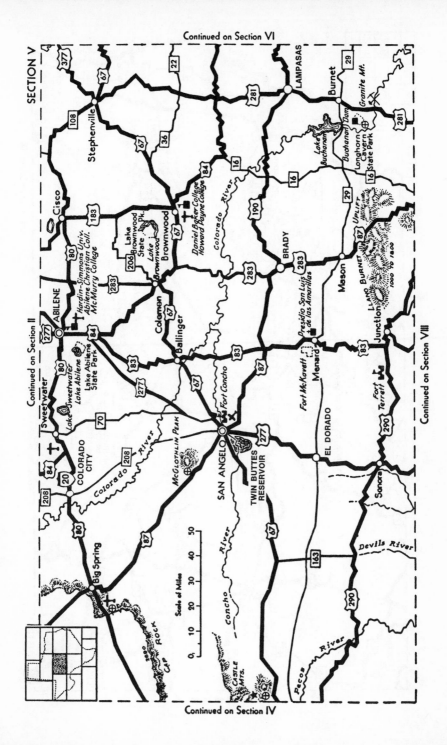

Continued on Section VI

Continued on Section II

Continued on Section VIII

Continued on Section IV

LAMPASAS

Burnet

Granite Mt.

Stephenville

Cisco

Lake Buchanan

Buchanan Dam

Longhorn Cavern

16 State Park

Colorado River

BRADY

Daniel Baker College

Howard Payne College

Brownwood

Lake Brownwood State Pk.

Lake Brownwood

Mason

LLANO BURNET UPLIFT

1000 TO 1800

ABILENE

Hardin-Simmons Univ.

Abilene Christian Coll.

McMurry College

Coleman

Ballinger

Presidio San Luis

de las Amarillas

Junction

Lake Abilene

State Park

Sweetwater

Lake Abilene

Lake Sweetwater

Fort Concho

Fort McKavett

Menard

Fort Terrett

COLORADO CITY

Colorado River

McGlothlin Peak

SAN ANGELO

EL DORADO

Sonora

Big Spring

TWIN BUTTES RESERVOIR

Devils River

CAP ROCK

2600

Concho River

Pecos River

CASTLE MTS.

Scale of Miles

0 10 20 30 40 50

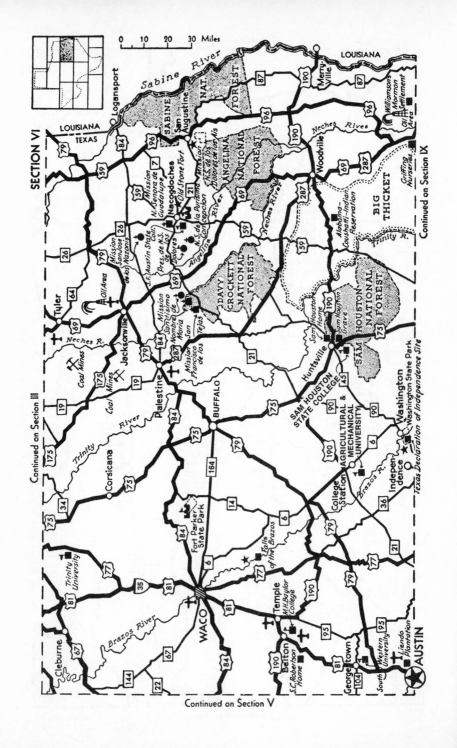

0 10 20 30 Miles

LOUISIANA

Sabine River

Logansport

LOUISIANA
TEXAS

79

84

59

SABINE NAT. FOREST

San Augustine

87

190

Merryville

87

96

Williamsons
Mormon
Settlement
Oil
Area

96

Mission N. Senora de Guadalupe

7

Nacogdoches

Mission N.S. del Pilar
Old Stone Fort

21

N.S. de la Purisima Concepcion

Neches River

ANGELINA NATIONAL FOREST

Mission N.S. de los Dolores
Mission N.S. dolo Ais

190

Neches River

96

Woodville

69

287

Griffing Nurseries

69

287

Mission San Jose de los AZonis

26

Mission San Jose

79

J.F. Austin State Coll.
Pres. de N.S. de los Dolores

69

Neches River

59

BIG THICKET

Tyler

64

Oil Area

Alabama-Coushatti-Indian Reservation

Trinity R.

26

175

Neches R.

Jacksonville

73

84

Mission San Francisco de los Tejas
Mission San
Nombre de
Maria
San
Juan

287

21

DAVY CROCKETT NATIONAL FOREST

59

59

Sam Houston

190

Sam Houston Grave

75

SAM HOUSTON NATIONAL FOREST

Coal Mines

175

19

Palestine

73

Huntsville

45

Coal Mines

River

BUFFALO

21

SAM HOUSTON STATE COLLEGE

Corsicana

75

75

73

90

190

6

90

Washington

Washington State Park
Washington State Park

34

75

Trinity

164

79

AGRICULTURAL & MECHANICAL UNIVERSITY

College Station

Brazos R.

Independence

Texas Declaration of Independence Site

175

19

84

73

14

6

36

Fort Parker State Park

6

81

35

Falls of the Brazos

77

81

Trinity University

77

79

21

Brazos River

WACO

81

Temple

M.H. Baylor College

190

190

77

Cleburne

67

67

84

81

Belton

S.C. Robertson Home

190

95

Southwestern University

95

Liendo Plantation

AUSTIN

67

144

22

81

Georgetown

104

Continued on Section III

Continued on Section IX

Continued on Section V

SECTION VII

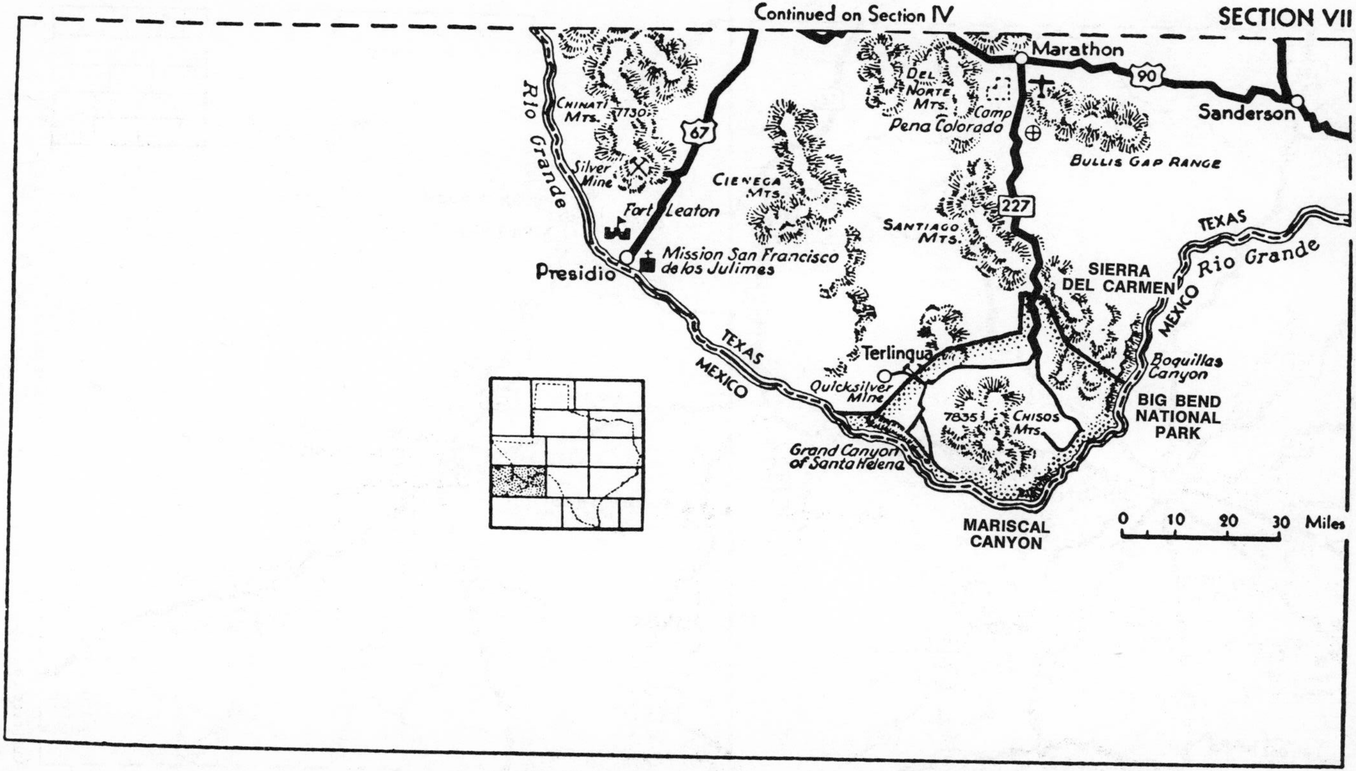

Continued on Section IV
Continued on Section VIII
Marathon
90
Sanderson
Del Norte Mts.
Camp Pena Colorado
Bullis Gap Range
Chinati Mts.
7730
67
Rio Grande
Silver Mine
Cienega Mts.
Fort Leaton
227
Santiago Mts.
Presidio
Mission San Francisco de los Julimes
Sierra del Carmen
Texas
Mexico
Terlingua
Quicksilver Mine
Boquillas Canyon
Big Bend National Park
7835
Chisos Mts.
Grand Canyon of Santa Helena
Mariscal Canyon
0 10 20 30 Miles

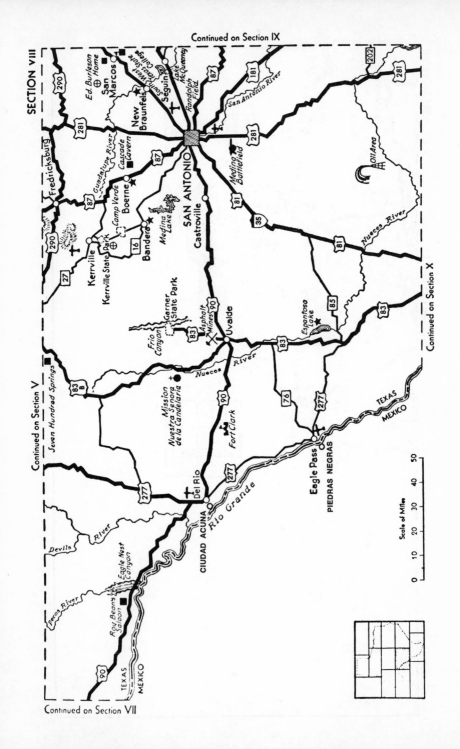

SECTION VIII

Continued on Section V

Continued on Section X

Scale of Miles

0   10   20   30   40   50

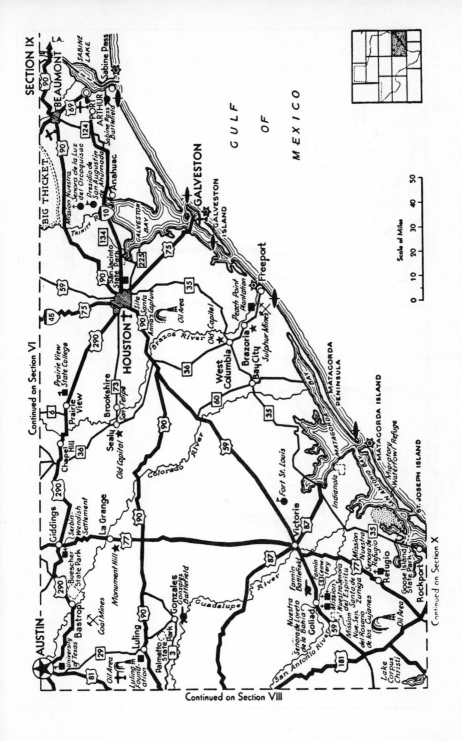

Continued on Section VI

Continued on Section VIII

Continued on Section X

SECTION IX

GULF

OF

MEXICO

Scale of Miles

AUSTIN

HOUSTON

GALVESTON

BEAUMONT

PORT ARTHUR

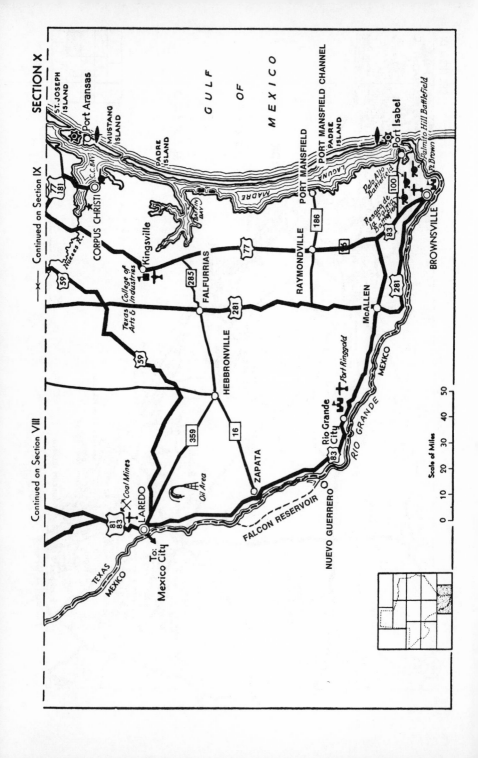

Continued on Section IX

Continued on Section VIII

ST. JOSEPH ISLAND

Port Aransas

MUSTANG ISLAND

C.C. BAY

77

181

CORPUS CHRISTI

Nueces R.

Kingsville

College of Arts & Industries

Texas College of Arts & Industries

59

FALFURRIAS

285

77

281

HEBBRONVILLE

359

16

ZAPATA

Oil Area

Coal Mines

LAREDO

81
83

To: Mexico City

TEXAS

MEXICO

NUEVO GUERRERO

FALCON RESERVOIR

RIO GRANDE

Rio Grande City

83

Fort Ringgold

McALLEN

281

MEXICO

RAYMONDVILLE

PADRE ISLAND

PADRE ISLAND

LAGUNA

MADRE

GULF

OF

MEXICO

PORT MANSFIELD

PORT MANSFIELD CHANNEL

Port Mansfield

186

Port Isabel

Palmito Hill Battlefield

Palo Alto Battlefield

Resaca de la Palma Battlefield

Ft. Brown

100

83

281

BROWNSVILLE

Scale of Miles

0   10   20   30   40   50

Index

ation (Houston), 291; Immaculate Conception (Brownsville), 207; National Shrine of the Little Flower (San Antonio), 338; Old St. Mary's (Fredericksburg), 152, 618; Our Lady of Guadalupe (San Antonio), 330; Sacred Heart (Galveston), 275; Sacred Heart (Muenster), 383; St. Francis on the Brazos (Waco), 351; St. Louis (Castroville), 587, 588, 589; St. Mary's (San Antonio), 331; St. Mary's Cathedral (Galveston), 274; San Fernando Cathedral (San Antonio), 140, 327; San Augustine (Laredo), 302

Seventh Day Adventist, 109, 319, 522-23

Unitarian, 109

Ciboleros, 503

Circus, community (Gainsville), 415

Cisco, 467, 540

Civil Rights legislation, 102-03

Civil War, 47-48, 82, 101, 288, 565

battles, 48, 201, 270, 402, 500

incidents, 168, 200-01, 211, 241, 270, 321, 417, 426, 494, 573, 616

Texan northern sympathizers, 48, 167-68, 589

See also Confederacy, Confederate army

Clairemont, 637

Clarendon, 475, 485

Clark, J. S., 175

Clarksville, 120, 201, 379

Claude, 476

Clear Lake, 297

Cleburne, 523

Clemons, Walter, 129, 131

Cleo, 488

Cleveland, 409, 567

Cleveland, Grover, 56

Cliburn, Van, 136

Clifton, 89

Climate, 10-11, 198, 484

See also Weather

Clint, 546

Clute, 570

Clyde, 540

Coal deposits, 13, 21, 444

Coast Guard station (Port Aransas), 575

Coastal Plain region, 8, 12, 440, 533

Coastal Prairie region, 9

Cochran, Jerry Bywaters, 138

Cody, William F. (Buffalo Bill), 78, 384, 440

Coffee, Holland, 404

Coke, Richard, 48, 347, 348

Colbert's Ferry, 403

Coleman, 526-27, 559

College Station, 122, 553

Colleges and Universities

Abilene Christian, 458, 459

Agriculural and Mechanical University (College Station), 80, 102, 122, 273, 353, 416, 553, 554, 612

Amarillo Junior, 162

Angelo State (San Angelo), 461

Arlington University, 145, 176, 538

Austin (Sherman), 109, 405

Baylor University (Waco), 34, 100, 122, 145, 346, 347, 348-50, 624

Baylor University College of Dentistry (Dallas), 232, 349

Baylor University College of Medicine (Dallas), 349

Baylor University College of Medicine (Houston), 295

Bishop (Dallas), 90, 103, 109, 224, 232, 535

Blinn (Brenham), 613

Butler (Tyler), 90, 103

Dallas Baptist, 232

Del Mar Junior (Corpus Christi), 214

East Texas Baptist (Marshall), 535

East Texas State University (Commerce), 103, 145, 521

Fort Worth Christian, 261, 262

Galveston Junior, 273

Grayson County Junior (Denison), 404

Hardin-Simmons (Abilene), 459

Houston Academy of Medicine, 295

Houston Baptist, 109, 290

Houston State Psychiatric Institute, 295

Howard Payne (Brownwood), 109, 526

Huston-Tillotson (Austin), 90, 171

Incarnate Word (San Antonio), 339

Institute of Marine Science (Aransas Pass), 176, 574

Jacksonville Baptist, 109, 550

James Connally Technical Institute (Waco), 80, 352, 554

Jarvis Christian (Hawkins), 90, 536

Jewish Medical Research and Training Institute (Houston), 295

Kilgore Junior, 536

Lamar State College of Technology (Beaumont), 102, 194-95

Laredo Junior, 304

Le Tourneau (Longview), 536

Lubbock Christian, 109, 507

Lutheran Concordia (Austin), 109, 170

Mary Allen (Crockett), 90, 103, 109

Mary Hardin-Baylor (Belton), 431

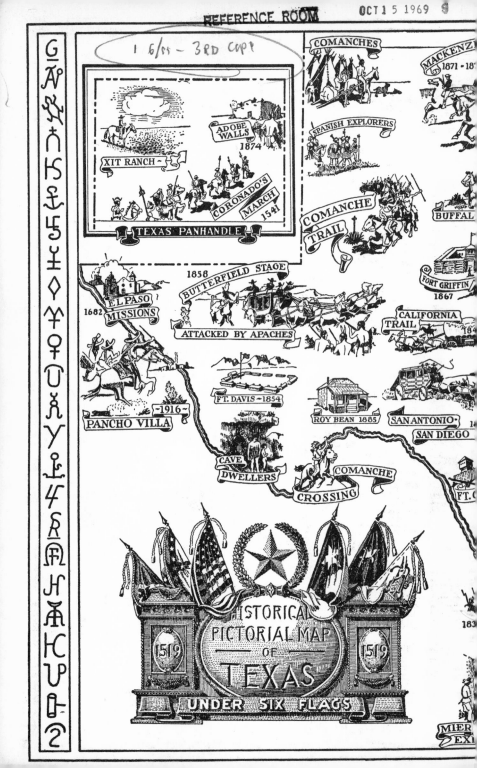

1 6/55 - 3RD COPY

COMANCHES

MACKENZIE
1871 - 18??

ADOBE
WALLS
1874

XIT RANCH ~

SPANISH EXPLORERS

CORONADO'S MARCH 1541

BUFFALO

COMANCHE TRAIL

TEXAS PANHANDLE

FORT GRIFFIN
1867

EL PASO
1682 MISSIONS

1858 BUTTERFIELD STAGE

ATTACKED BY APACHES

CALIFORNIA
TRAIL
184?

~1916~

FT. DAVIS ~1854

ROY BEAN 1885

SAN ANTONIO ·
SAN DIEGO

PANCHO VILLA

CAVE
DWELLERS

FT. C?

COMANCHE
CROSSING

1519

HISTORICAL
PICTORIAL MAP
OF
TEXAS
UNDER SIX FLAGS

1519

183?

MIER
EX?